UNIVERSITY CASEBOOK SERIES®

THE LAW OF CLASS ACTIONS AND OTHER AGGREGATE LITIGATION

SECOND EDITION

by

RICHARD A. NAGAREDA
Late Professor of Law
Vanderbilt University Law School

ROBERT G. BONE
G. Rollie White Excellence in Teaching Professor of Law
The University of Texas School of Law

ELIZABETH CHAMBLEE BURCH
Associate Professor
University of Georgia School of Law

CHARLES SILVER
Roy W. and Eugenia C. McDonald Endowed Chair in Civil Procedure
The University of Texas School of Law

PATRICK WOOLLEY
Beck, Redden & Secrest Professor in Law
The University of Texas School of Law

FOUNDATION PRESS

© 2009 by THOMSON REUTERS/FOUNDATION PRESS
© 2013 by LEG, Inc. d/b/a West Academic Publishing

    610 Opperman Drive
    St. Paul, MN 55123
    1-800-313-9378

Printed in the United States of America

ISBN: 978–1–60930–270–2

Mat #41381184

PREFACE FOR SECOND EDITION

When Richard Nagareda died in the summer of 2010, the world lost a terrific scholar of aggregate litigation. The U.S. Supreme Court's dueling opinions in *Wal-Mart Stores, Inc. v. Dukes* provide ample evidence. Both Justice Scalia and Justice Ginsburg quote Richard's writings on crucial points and claim his mantle. The unanimous opinion in *Smith v. Bayer Corp.* also pays Richard homage. It relies on portions of the American Law Institute's *Principles of the Law of Aggregate Litigation* which Richard primarily drafted.

Naturally, Richard's death left his many friends and fellow academics bereft. To honor his memory and keep alive his effort to make aggregate litigation a distinctive field of inquiry, four of us decided to update his casebook. We produced an Interim Update in 2011 and are now pleased to offer this Second Edition of Richard's masterful and challenging work. The choice of materials and the content of discussions reflect both Richard's judgments and our own. We preserved many of the cases and materials that appeared in the First Edition, but we also added much that is new and revised many of Richard's notes and discussions. Undoubtedly, Richard would have made some of these changes himself, had he lived. Several of the class action decisions handed down by the U.S. Supreme Court would have figured prominently in any revision. But many editorial choices reflect our judgments and interests, which unavoidably differ from his.

Like the First Edition, the Second Edition is designed to enable students to learn about all major forms of aggregate litigation. However, the Second Edition marks the beginning of an evolution in which materials on class actions will receive less emphasis while those on other forms of aggregate litigation are bolstered. The change in weightings reflects our collective judgment that the class action is in decline while other aggregative procedures are prospering. We expect to carry this process farther in the next edition.

We received invaluable help with the preparation of the manuscript from Vicky Killgore and Sylvia Ramirez. We also owe a debt of gratitude to Graham Cotton, Patrick Courtney, Jason Danowsky, Michael Gretchen, Lennon Haas, Anne Horn, Tyson Lies, Joel Thomason, and Collin White for research assistance.

ROBERT G. BONE

ELIZABETH CHAMBLEE BURCH

CHARLES SILVER

PATRICK WOOLLEY

May, 2013

PREFACE FOR FIRST EDITION

This casebook simply would not have been written but for the superbly talented and intellectually engaged students of Vanderbilt University Law School, who used successive draft versions of these materials during the process of refinement. Two dynamic deans with an abiding commitment to innovative legal education—Kent Syverud and, now, Edward Rubin—nurtured the faculty environment that made my work on this casebook possible. I also benefited from the presence, literally in the back row of my classroom in successive years, of three exceptional faculty colleagues whom am fortunate also to count as friends: Brian Fitzpatrick, Tracey George, and Suzanna Sherry. What a privilege it is to be at a place where those who have so much to teach everyone else share a passion to learn new things from others.

I am especially grateful, in addition, to several scholars and teachers at other institutions who took a chance to try a new, untested, and unpublished set of teaching materials in their own counterpart courses. Samuel Issacharoff and Arthur Miller, in particular, enabled me to draw upon their vast experience in both classroom teaching and the real world of complex litigation in order to improve the final product. I gained many additional insights from three scholars and teachers whose emergence in the academy makes me confident of the vitality that this field of study will enjoy in the future: Elizabeth Chamblee Burch, Alexandra Lahav, and David Marcus.

I also owe a considerable debt of gratitude to my co-reporters on the American Law Institute's project *Principles of the Law of Aggregate Litigation*: Robert Klonoff (author of an impressive casebook of his own on the subject) and Charles Silver, as well as the previously-mentioned Samuel Issacharoff. Our multi-year collaboration on the *Aggregate Litigation* project illuminates the legal issues addressed in this casebook in more ways than I can count.

Finally, and certainly not least, an outstanding Vanderbilt law student, Matthew Blumenstein, provided exemplary research assistance, both with my requests for material to be included and with the many important technical details associated with the production process.

RICHARD NAGAREDA

October, 2008

ACKNOWLEDGMENTS

We acknowledge with thanks the copyright owners who have graciously granted permission to reprint excerpts from the following works:

ABA *Formal Ethics Opinion* 06–438 2006 Edition. Copyright © 2006 by the American Bar Association. Reprinted with permission. Copies of ABA, *ABA Formal Ethics Opinions*, 2006 Edition are available from Service Center, American Bar Association, 321 North Clark Street, Chicago, IL60654, 1–800–285–2221.

American Law Institute, *Principles of the Law of Aggregate Litigation* (Prelim. Draft No. 3, Aug. 25, 2005), copyright © 2005, by the American Law Institute. Reprinted with permission. All rights reserved. NOTE: Preliminary Drafts are the work-product solely of the project's Reporter(s) and have not been considered by the Council of the American Law Institute or by its membership. Neither this draft as a whole nor any of its parts should be assumed to reflect or represent a position of the Institute. This is a very preliminary expression even of the drafters, and was produced for the consideration and advice of the project's Advisers and Members Consultative Group; this draft has now been subject to substantial revision, and the section quoted here has been abrogated.

American Law Institute, *Principles of the Law of Aggregate Litigation* (Prelim. Draft No. 5, Sept. 12, 2008), copyright © 2008, by the American Law Institute. Reprinted with permission. All rights reserved. NOTE: Preliminary Drafts are the work-product solely of the project's Reporter(s) and have not been considered by the Council of the American Law Institute or by its membership. Neither this draft as a whole nor any of its parts should be assumed to reflect or represent a position of the Institute. This is a very preliminary expression even of the drafters, and was produced for the consideration and advice of the project's Advisers and Members Consultative Group.

American law Institute, *Principles of the Law of Aggregate Litigation* (2010), copyright © 2010, by the American Law Institute. Reprinted with permission. All rights reserved.

American Law Institute, *Restatement (Second) of Judgments* (1982), copyright © 1982, by the American Law Institute. Reprinted with permission. All rights reserved.

Stephen R. Bough & Andrea G. Bough, *Conflict of Laws and Multi–State Class Actions: How Variations in State Law Affect the Predominance Requirement of Rule 23(b)(3)*, 68 UMKC L. Rev. 1 (1999), copyright © 1999, by the Curators of the University of Missouri.

Aaron-Andrew P. Bruhl, *The Unconscionability Game: Strategic Judging and the Evolution of Federal Arbitration Law*, 83 N.Y.U. L. Rev. 1420 (2008).

Elizabeth Chamblee Burch, Introduction: Dukes v. Wal-Mart Stores, Inc., 63 Vand. L. Rev. en banc (2010).

John C. Coffee, Jr., *Class Action Accountability: Reconciling Exit, Voice, and Loyalty in Representative Litigation*, 100 Colum. L. Rev. 370 (2000), copyright © 2000, by the Directors of the Columbia Law Review Association, Inc.

James D. Cox & Randall S. Thomas, with the assistance of Dana Kiku, *Does the Plaintiff Matter? An Empirical Analysis of Lead Plaintiffs in Securities Class Actions*, 106 Colum. L. Rev. 1587 (2006), copyright © 2006, by the Directors of the Columbia Law Review Association, Inc.

Hanoch Dagan & James J. White, *Governments, Citizens, and Injurious Industries*, 75 N.Y.U. L. Rev. 354 (2000).

Allan Erbsen, *From "Predominance" to "Resolvability": A New Approach to Regulating Class Actions*, originally published in 58 Vand. L. Rev. 995 (2005).

Howard M. Erichson, *Informal Aggregation: Procedural and Ethical Implications of Coordination Among Counsel in Related Lawsuits*, 50 Duke L. J. 381 (2000), copyright © 2000, by the Duke Law Journal.

Eldon E. Fallon, Jeremy T. Grabill & Robert Pitard Wynne, *Bellwether Trials in Multidistrict Litigation*, originally published in 82 Tul. L. Rev. 2323 (2008).

Brian T. Fitzpatrick, *The End of Objector Blackmail?*, originally published in 62 Vand. L. Rev. 1623 (2009).

Myriam Gilles, *Opting Out of Liability: The Forthcoming, Near–Total Demise of the Modern Class Action*, 104 Mich. L. Rev. 373 (2005).

Myriam Gilles & Gary Friedman, *After Class: Aggregate Litigation in the wake of* AT&T Mobility v. Concepcion, 79 U.Chi.L.Rev. 623 (2012), copyright © 2012, by the University of Chicago Law Review.

John C.P. Goldberg & Benjamin C. Zipursky, *Unrealized Torts*, 88 Va. L.Rev. 1625 (2002), copyright © 2002, by the Virginia Law Review Association.

Samuel Issacharoff, *Governance and Legitimacy in the Law of Class Actions*, 1999 S. Ct. Rev. 337, copyright © 2000, by the University of Chicago. All rights reserved. Published 2000.

Samuel Issacharoff & Richard A. Nagareda, *Class Settlements under Attack*, 156 U. Pa. L. Rev. 1649 (2008), copyright © 2008, by the University of Pennsylvania Law Review.

Alexandra D. Lahav, *Bellwether Trials*, 76 Geo. Wash. L. Rev. 576 (2008).

Geoffrey P. Miller, *Competing Bids in Class Action Settlements*, 31 Hofstra L. Rev. 633 (2003), copyright © 2003, by the Hofstra Law Review Association.

Robert L. Rabin, *The Tobacco Litigation: A Tentative Assessment*, 51 DePaul L. Rev. 331 (2001), copyright © 2001, by DePaul University.

William B. Rubenstein, *The Fairness Hearing: Adversarial and Regulatory Approaches*, originally published in 53 UCLA L. Rev. 1435 (2006).

Michael Selmi, *The Price of Discrimination: The Nature of Class Action Employment Discrimination Litigation and Its Effects*, 81 Tex. L. Rev. 1249 (2003), copyright © 2003, by the Texas Law Review Association.

David L. Shapiro, *Class Actions: The Class as Party and Client*, 73 Notre Dame L. Rev. 913 (1998), copyright © 1998, by the Notre Dame Law Review, University of Notre Dame. The casebook publisher bears responsibility for any errors which have occurred in reprinting or editing.

Charles Silver, *A Restitutionary Theory of Attorneys' Fees in Class Actions*, 76 Cornell L. Rev. 656 (1991), copyright © 1991, by Cornell University.

Jean R. Sternlight, *Creeping Mandatory Arbitration: Is It Just?*, 57 Stan. L. Rev. 1631 (2005), copyright © 2005, by the Board of Trustees of the Leland Stanford Junior University.

SUMMARY OF CONTENTS

TABLE OF CONTENTS

TABLE OF CASES

The principal cases are in bold type.

TABLE OF AUTHORITIES

UNIVERSITY CASEBOOK SERIES®

THE LAW OF CLASS ACTIONS AND OTHER AGGREGATE LITIGATION

SECOND EDITION

CHAPTER 1

AN INTRODUCTION TO AGGREGATE LITIGATION

The modern world is increasingly interconnected. Modern corporations conduct their business operations across a national (and, often, international) marketplace. The products developed and sold by modern corporations are increasingly uniform in nature. And modern business activity itself is now financed, in significant part, through the sale of equity interests in the firm—in common parlance, shares of stock—on national (and, often, international) securities markets. Along similar lines, the reach of government itself at all levels has come to touch the lives of private citizens more pervasively than in centuries past. American law, moreover, has witnessed a significant expansion of substantive legal obligations—not only the elaboration of the common law but also the enactment of an array of statutes that regulate the relationships between government and private individuals and amongst those individuals themselves. Civil rights law, antitrust law, securities law, and product liability law—to name just a few examples—are the products of these developments.

The result of this interconnected world is that wrongdoing has the potential to give rise to injury on a mass scale. A defectively designed consumer product has the capacity to injure millions of persons. A fraudulent misstatement concerning the finances of a corporation has the potential to affect the price at which shares of that corporation trade, to the detriment of investors. A government program carried out in an unconstitutional manner has the potential to affect adversely millions of citizens.

The early phases of legal education tend, quite understandably, to focus students' attention on civil claims as isolated events that give rise to one-on-one, single-plaintiff-versus-single-defendant litigation. This book is about the challenges posed for the civil justice system when claims arise not as isolated events but, instead, as part of a larger aggregate—in particular, when wrongdoing on a mass scale gives rise to the potential for large numbers of civil claims that exhibit varying degrees of similarity.

A. MULTIPLE CIVIL CLAIMS WITH SIMILAR FEATURES

Consider three scenarios, among many that one might imagine, in which a given course of conduct might give rise to multiple civil claims with common overlapping features:

Scenario 1: The major airlines currently structure their business operations around one or more "hub" airports. Although direct service is available between major-market cities (say, Los Angeles to New York), passengers often must fly through a hub airport when their travel plans involve a non-major-market city (say, to travel from St. Louis to Corpus Christi by connecting through the hub airport in Dallas). If only for logistical reasons, the hubs used by the various airlines generally do not overlap. American Airlines uses Dallas as its hub; United Airlines, Chicago; Delta Airlines, Atlanta; etc.

Now, suppose that the major airlines agree not to compete on the price of their air service in and out of each other's hubs. Thus, American still would operate flights in and out of United's hub, Chicago; but American would not undercut United's prices for the same routes. United, in turn, would not undercut American's prices for routes in and out of the latter's hub, Dallas; and so forth amongst the major airlines. The result is that airline ticket prices for some routes involving airline hubs are higher than they otherwise would be. In an (ultimately unsuccessful) effort to avoid the detection of their clandestine agreement, the airlines raise the prices of the relevant tickets by only $20 apiece—a per-ticket mark-up that amounts to hundreds of millions of dollars across all tickets sold to passengers for travel on the relevant routes during the period in which the agreement is in force.

Scenario 2: In the aftermath of the controversy surrounding the 2000 presidential election, the state of Florida enacts legislation forbidding all subdivisions of the state from using "butterfly" ballots in any future election. As a result, many counties within the state must select and purchase new forms of voting equipment—e.g., computerized touch-screen voting machines. A longstanding provision of the state constitution, however, prohibits counties from raising property taxes absent authorization from the state legislature. The counties accordingly announce that, as of four months from today, they will charge a $30 "processing fee" for citizens to register to vote, with the fee set so as to cover the cost of the new voting equipment.

Scenario 3: Beta Corporation, a major pharmaceutical manufacturer, develops and markets nationwide, with approval from the Food and Drug Administration, a new prescription drug designed to control cholesterol levels in the human body. The drug is effective for its intended purpose and quickly becomes a huge commercial success for Beta Corporation. After the product is marketed on a widespread basis, however, physicians across the country start to report instances in which a small number of patients among the hundreds of thousands who were prescribed the drug unexpectedly suffer cerebral hemorrhage—a severe, life-threatening condition from which some such patients die. The relationship between cerebral hemorrhage and consumption of the drug remains unclear, however. The patients who were prescribed the drug, after all, had elevated cholesterol levels in their bodies, a condition well known to increase the risk of stroke. Some medical experts nonetheless suspect that everyone who consumed the drug stands at an elevated risk of cerebral hemorrhage—specifically, that such a reaction might occur in some patients long after they consumed the drug.

For each scenario, consider the following questions:

What are the various legal institutions—including, but not limited to, the court system—that one might use to address the conduct described? What objective(s) should those institutions seek to achieve with regard to that conduct? What are the constraints under which each such institution operates? For each, who is the initiator of action? What serves, in practical terms, as the motivation for any such action? Are certain kinds of claims more personal to their holders than others?

How likely is it that the conduct described in each scenario will be challenged by way of a conventional civil lawsuit—one that takes the form of an individual plaintiff suing a single defendant? To what extent, if at all, should the law of civil procedure seek consciously to alter that probability? What likely will serve as the funding mechanism for any civil litigation?

By providing procedural devices to facilitate litigation on an aggregate basis, would the law introduce new problems? Should the use of those devices be simply a matter of contractual consent amongst the various claimants? When, if ever, should the use of those devices be made the presumptive course—perhaps even the required course—of litigation for such claimants?

What underlying body of substantive law is most likely to apply to civil claims arising from the conduct in each scenario? To what extent, if any, should the source of that body of substantive law—i.e., who makes it— affect the desirability or authority of procedural law that facilitates litigation on an aggregate basis?

What would constitute fair and just terms for the resolution of the civil actions spawned by the conduct described in each scenario? Who, in institutional terms, should decide what those terms are? To what extent, if at all, should a court review those determinations? Note that, in general, there is no judicial review of settlements in ordinary civil litigation.

B. PRECLUSION AND ITS LIMITS

A significant objective of any regime of civil procedure is to provide mechanisms for the resolution of claims according to the substantive law. Some refer to this as "closure" or "finality" but as the sociologists and anthropologists remind us, closure and finality are relative concepts: disputing frequently continues after adjudication, although in a different form. Nevertheless, incentives to use a given procedural device for litigation at the front end turn crucially on the degree of closure that the procedural device provides at the back end. This notion is particularly important when one adds the further observation that the dominant endgame of civil litigation today—whether of a conventional, one-on-one sort or in some aggregate form—consists not of full-scale trials but, rather, of settlements, insofar as claims are not otherwise resolved by way of a dispositive pre-trial motion (such as summary judgment). Settlements, not trials, dominate the landscape of civil litigation today, just as plea bargains, rather than trials, dominate the criminal justice system. In fact, the available empirical evidence indicates that only about 2% of cases filed in federal court are disposed of through trial. Most of the remaining cases end in settlement and the rest are dismissed early, disposed of through summary judgment, or concluded before trial in some other way. See Marc Galanter, *The Vanishing Trial: An Examination of Trials and Related Matters in Federal and State Courts*, 1 J. Empirical Leg. Stud. 459, 461 (2004) (reporting data showing that in 2002 about 2% of federal civil cases were resolved by trial).

How does the law achieve closure or finality? Suppose that a lawsuit ends in dismissal, judgment, or settlement. What stops an unhappy party from suing again in hopes of obtaining a better outcome? To be sure, she might be deterred by a rational calculation, based on the negative result in the first suit, that litigating again is just not worth the cost, especially in light of stare decisis effects. But stare decisis is limited: it applies mainly to the resolution of legal, not factual, issues and does not absolutely require that the second judge come out the same way. So what's to stop a party from filing again if she is sufficiently optimistic about success? The answer lies in the law of preclusion. Depending on the coverage in your first-year

Civil Procedure course, the basics of preclusion law may be familiar to you. If not, then there is no need to worry, for the discussion in this Part is designed to introduce (or to refresh your recollection of) basic preclusion principles as they pertain to aggregate litigation.

1. Claim Preclusion

In modern doctrine, preclusion comes in two basic forms: "claim preclusion" (what earlier case law dubbed "res judicata") and "issue preclusion" (what was previously dubbed "collateral estoppel"). The basics of claim preclusion are set forth in the following sections from the Restatement (Second) of Judgments (1982), on which some state and federal courts draw for their own preclusion law:

§ 17.   Effects of Former Adjudication—General Rules

A valid and final personal judgment is conclusive between the parties, except on appeal or other direct review, to the following extent:

(1) If the judgment is in favor of the plaintiff, the claim is extinguished and merged in the judgment and a new claim may arise on the judgment;

(2) If the judgment is in favor of the defendant, the claim is extinguished and the judgment bars a subsequent action on that claim; . . .

§ 24. Dimensions of "Claim" for Purposes of Merger or Bar—General Rule Concerning "Splitting"

(1) When a valid and final judgment rendered in an action extinguishes the plaintiff's claim pursuant to the rules of merger or bar, the claim extinguished includes all rights of the plaintiff to remedies against the defendant with respect to all or any part of the transaction, or series of connected transactions, out of which the action arose.

(2) What factual grouping constitutes a "transaction," and what groupings constitute a "series," are to be determined pragmatically, giving weight to such considerations as whether the facts are related in time, space, origin, or motivation, whether they form a convenient trial unit, and whether their treatment as a unit conforms to the parties' expectations or business understanding or usage.

Section 17 of the Restatement speaks of a judgment extinguishing "the claim," and section 24(1) then indicates that "the claim extinguished includes all rights of the plaintiff to remedies against the defendant with respect to all or any part of the transaction, or series of connected transactions, out of which the action arose." Obviously, the Restatement uses "claim" to mean more than simply an individual legal claim or cause of action. Claim preclusion prevents the splitting up of a single dispute into separate lawsuits by extinguishing "*all* rights . . . to remedies." For example, without claim preclusion, a plaintiff complaining about a doctor's malpractice might bring a negligence claim in one suit, and, if he loses, bring a breach-of-contract claim in a second suit. Claim preclusion prevents this splitting strategy. It forces the plaintiff to join his contract claim with his negligence claim in the first suit, or lose the chance to litigate the contract claim. This is thought to promote judicial economy, avoid inconsistent decisions, and further values of repose.

Notice also that section 24(2) defines "transaction" or "series" pragmatically with an eye to the policies claim preclusion is meant to serve. For example, 24(2)'s reference to "a convenient trial unit" is relevant to judicial economy. The reference to "parties' expectations or business understanding or usage" is relevant to repose. And the relatedness of facts "in time, space, origin, or motivation" is relevant to judicial economy, repose, and decisional consistency.

Consider the claim-preclusion consequences of the following simplified set of variations from the world of one-on-one litigation:

> Defendant's automobile collides with Plaintiff's automobile. Plaintiff sues Defendant. Judgment for Defendant. (Note: claim preclusion only applies when the first suit ends in a final judgment on the merits, which can include a settlement as well as a dismissal on the merits or a trial judgment.)
>
> ■ What if Plaintiff thereafter brings a second lawsuit against Defendant alleging violation of an applicable statute, whereas Plaintiff's first lawsuit had alleged only common-law negligence?
>
> ■ What if the second lawsuit seeks punitive damages based on the alleged extreme misconduct of Defendant, whereas the first lawsuit sought only compensatory damages?
>
> ■ What if the second lawsuit takes place at a time when additional evidence has emerged—say, a witness neither known nor reasonably identifiable at the time of the first litigation—that now makes it quite clear that Defendant was, in fact, at fault for the collision? (See Federal Rule of Civil Procedure 60(b).)

What is the major limitation on the capacity of claim preclusion to serve as a procedural vehicle by which to achieve closure as among the claims of multiple persons arising from the kinds of events described in Part A of this Chapter? To pose the question differently, what would have to happen as a matter of procedural doctrine—what idea or concept would have to be developed—in order for the principles stated in section 17 to function meaningfully as a vehicle for comprehensive (or, at least, broadly encompassing) closure in such situations?

2. ISSUE PRECLUSION

One might say in colloquial terms that claim preclusion operates on the intuition "You already had your chance," whereas issue preclusion operates on the notion "Been there, done that." Stated less colloquially, claim preclusion prevents a party from splitting up a single dispute into more than one lawsuit, whereas issue preclusion prevents a party from relitigating an issue that has already been litigated and determined. Thus, claim preclusion can bar new legal causes of action and remedies that were never raised as long as they *could* have and *should* have been raised in the first suit ("should have" because of their close factual connection to the matters that were in fact raised in the first suit). Issue preclusion, by contrast, bars litigation of only those issues that were actually raised, litigated, and determined in a previous suit.

Specifically, the Second Restatement provides:

§ 27.   Issue Preclusion—General Rule

When an issue of fact or law is actually litigated and determined by a valid and final judgment, and the determination is essential to the judgment, the determination is conclusive in a subsequent action between the parties, whether on the same or a different claim.

As the following Supreme Court decision from 1979 observes, issue preclusion principles long adhered to a requirement of "mutuality"—the notion that A could use issue preclusion against B only if B could have used issue preclusion against A had the issue come out the other way. In effect, the mutuality doctrine required symmetry of preclusion risk—both parties to the second suit had to have been at risk of preclusion depending on the result in the first suit. Given the very narrow scope for preclusion of non-parties (discussed in the following section), the practical result of mutuality was to limit issue preclusion mostly to persons who were parties to the first suit. But, as the *Parklane* Court explains, mutuality is no longer required for issue preclusion.

Parklane Hosiery Co. v. Shore

439 U.S. 322 (1979)

■ MR. JUSTICE STEWART delivered the opinion of the Court.

This case presents the question whether a party who has had issues of fact adjudicated adversely to it in an equitable action may be collaterally estopped from relitigating the same issues before a jury in a subsequent legal action brought against it by a new party.

The respondent brought this stockholder's class action against the petitioners in a Federal District Court. The complaint alleged that the petitioners, Parklane Hosiery Co., Inc. (Parklane), and 13 of its officers, directors, and stockholders, had issued a materially false and misleading proxy statement in connection with a merger. The proxy statement, according to the complaint, had violated [several sections] of the Securities Exchange Act of 1934, as well as various rules and regulations promulgated by the Securities and Exchange Commission (SEC). The complaint sought damages, rescission of the merger, and recovery of costs.

Before this action came to trial, the SEC filed suit against the same defendants in the Federal District Court, alleging that the proxy statement that had been issued by Parklane was materially false and misleading in essentially the same respects as those that had been alleged in the respondent's complaint. Injunctive relief was requested. After a 4–day trial, the District Court found that the proxy statement was materially false and misleading in the respects alleged, and entered a declaratory judgment to that effect. The Court of Appeals for the Second Circuit affirmed this judgment.

The respondent in the present case then moved for partial summary judgment against the petitioners, asserting that the petitioners were collaterally estopped from relitigating the issues that had been resolved against them in the action brought by the SEC.[2] The District Court denied

---

[2] A private plaintiff in an action under the proxy rules is not entitled to relief simply by demonstrating that the proxy solicitation was materially false and misleading. The plaintiff

the motion on the ground that such an application of collateral estoppel would deny the petitioners their Seventh Amendment right to a jury trial. The Court of Appeals for the Second Circuit reversed, holding that a party who has had issues of fact determined against him after a full and fair opportunity to litigate in a nonjury trial is collaterally estopped from obtaining a subsequent jury trial of these same issues of fact. The appellate court concluded that "the Seventh Amendment preserves the right to jury trial only with respect to issues of fact, [and] once those issues have been fully and fairly adjudicated in a prior proceeding, nothing remains for trial, either with or without a jury." Because of an inter-circuit conflict, we granted certiorari.

I

The threshold question to be considered is whether, quite apart from the right to a jury trial under the Seventh Amendment, the petitioners can be precluded from relitigating facts resolved adversely to them in a prior equitable proceeding with another party under the general law of collateral estoppel. Specifically, we must determine whether a litigant who was not a party to a prior judgment may nevertheless use that judgment "offensively" to prevent a defendant from relitigating issues resolved in the earlier proceeding.[4]

A

Collateral estoppel, like the related doctrine of res judicata, has the dual purpose of protecting litigants from the burden of relitigating an identical issue with the same party or his privy and of promoting judicial economy by preventing needless litigation. *Blonder–Tongue Laboratories, Inc. v. University of Illinois Foundation*, 402 U.S. 313, 328–329. Until relatively recently, however, the scope of collateral estoppel was limited by the doctrine of mutuality of parties. Under this mutuality doctrine, neither party could use a prior judgment as an estoppel against the other unless both parties were bound by the judgment. Based on the premise that it is somehow unfair to allow a party to use a prior judgment when he himself would not be so bound,[7] the mutuality requirement provided a party who had litigated and lost in a previous action an opportunity to relitigate identical issues with new parties.

By failing to recognize the obvious difference in position between a party who has never litigated an issue and one who has fully litigated and lost, the mutuality requirement was criticized almost from its inception. Recognizing the validity of this criticism, the Court in *Blonder–Tongue Laboratories, Inc. v. University of Illinois Foundation, supra*, abandoned the

---

must also show that he was injured and prove damages. *Mills v. Electric Auto–Lite Co.*, 396 U.S. 375, 386–390. Since the SEC action was limited to a determination of whether the proxy statement contained materially false and misleading information, the respondent conceded that he would still have to prove these other elements of his prima facie case in the private action. The petitioners' right to a jury trial on those remaining issues is not contested.

[4] In this context, offensive use of collateral estoppel occurs when the plaintiff seeks to foreclose the defendant from litigating an issue the defendant has previously litigated unsuccessfully in an action with another party. Defensive use occurs when a defendant seeks to prevent a plaintiff from asserting a claim the plaintiff has previously litigated and lost against another defendant.

[7] It is a violation of due process for a judgment to be binding on a litigant who was not a party or a privy and therefore has never had an opportunity to be heard. *Blonder–Tongue Laboratories, Inc. v. University of Illinois Foundation*, 402 U.S. 313, 329; *Hansberry v. Lee*, 311 U. S. 32, 40.

mutuality requirement, at least in cases where a patentee seeks to relitigate the validity of a patent after a federal court in a previous lawsuit has
already declared it invalid. The "broader question" before the Court, however, was "whether it is any longer tenable to afford a litigant more than
one full and fair opportunity for judicial resolution of the same issue." 402
U.S., at 328. The Court strongly suggested a negative answer to that question:

> "In any lawsuit where a defendant, because of the mutuality
> principle, is forced to present a complete defense on the merits to
> a claim which the plaintiff has fully litigated and lost in a prior
> action, there is an arguable misallocation of resources. To the ex-
> tent the defendant in the second suit may not win by asserting,
> without contradiction, that the plaintiff had fully and fairly, but
> unsuccessfully, litigated the same claim in the prior suit, the de-
> fendant's time and money are diverted from alternative uses-
> productive or otherwise-to relitigation of a decided issue. And, still
> assuming that the issue was resolved correctly in the first suit,
> there is reason to be concerned about the plaintiff's allocation of
> resources. Permitting repeated litigation of the same issue as long
> as the supply of unrelated defendants holds out reflects either the
> aura of the gaming table or 'a lack of discipline and of disinterest-
> edness on the part of the lower courts, hardly a worthy or wise ba-
> sis for fashioning rules of procedure.' *Kerotest Mfg. Co. v. C–O–
> Two Co.*, 342 U.S. 180, 185 (1952). Although neither judges, the
> parties, nor the adversary system performs perfectly in all cases,
> the requirement of determining whether the party against whom
> an estoppel is asserted had a full and fair opportunity to litigate is
> a most significant safeguard." *Id.*, at 329.

B

The *Blonder–Tongue* case involved defensive use of collateral estoppel—a plaintiff was estopped from asserting a claim that the plaintiff had
previously litigated and lost against another defendant. The present case,
by contrast, involves offensive use of collateral estoppel—a plaintiff is seeking to estop a defendant from relitigating the issues which the defendant
previously litigated and lost against another plaintiff. In both the offensive
and defensive use situations, the party against whom estoppel is asserted
has litigated and lost in an earlier action. Nevertheless, several reasons
have been advanced why the two situations should be treated differently.

First, offensive use of collateral estoppel does not promote judicial
economy in the same manner as defensive use does. Defensive use of collateral estoppel precludes a plaintiff from relitigating identical issues by
merely "switching adversaries."[12] Thus defensive collateral estoppel gives a
plaintiff a strong incentive to join all potential defendants in the first action
if possible. Offensive use of collateral estoppel, on the other hand, creates
precisely the opposite incentive. Since a plaintiff will be able to rely on a
previous judgment against a defendant but will not be bound by that judgment if the defendant wins, the plaintiff has every incentive to adopt a
"wait and see" attitude, in the hope that the first action by another plaintiff
will result in a favorable judgment. Thus offensive use of collateral estoppel
will likely increase rather than decrease the total amount of litigation,

---

[12] Under the mutuality requirement, a plaintiff could accomplish this result since he
would not have been bound by the judgment had the original defendant won.

since potential plaintiffs will have everything to gain and nothing to lose by not intervening in the first action.

A second argument against offensive use of collateral estoppel is that it may be unfair to a defendant. If a defendant in the first action is sued for small or nominal damages, he may have little incentive to defend vigorously, particularly if future suits are not foreseeable. Allowing offensive collateral estoppel may also be unfair to a defendant if the judgment relied upon as a basis for the estoppel is itself inconsistent with one or more previous judgments in favor of the defendant.[14] Still another situation where it might be unfair to apply offensive estoppel is where the second action affords the defendant procedural opportunities unavailable in the first action that could readily cause a different result.[15]

C

We have concluded that the preferable approach for dealing with these problems in the federal courts is not to preclude the use of offensive collateral estoppel, but to grant trial courts broad discretion to determine when it should be applied. The general rule should be that in cases where a plaintiff could easily have joined in the earlier action or where, either for the reasons discussed above or for other reasons, the application of offensive estoppel would be unfair to a defendant, a trial judge should not allow the use of offensive collateral estoppel.

In the present case, however, none of the circumstances that might justify reluctance to allow the offensive use of collateral estoppel is present. The application of offensive collateral estoppel will not here reward a private plaintiff who could have joined in the previous action, since the respondent probably could not have joined in the injunctive action brought by the SEC even had he so desired. Similarly, there is no unfairness to the petitioners in applying offensive collateral estoppel in this case. First, in light of the serious allegations made in the SEC's complaint against the petitioners, as well as the foreseeability of subsequent private suits that typically follow a successful Government judgment, the petitioners had every incentive to litigate the SEC lawsuit fully and vigorously. Second, the judgment in the SEC action was not inconsistent with any previous decision. Finally, there will in the respondent's action be no procedural opportunities available to the petitioners that were unavailable in the first action of a kind that might be likely to cause a different result.

We conclude, therefore, that none of the considerations that would justify a refusal to allow the use of offensive collateral estoppel is present in this case. Since the petitioners received a "full and fair" opportunity to litigate their claims in the SEC action, the contemporary law of collateral estoppel leads inescapably to the conclusion that the petitioners are collater-

---

[14] In Professor Currie's familiar example, a railroad collision injures 50 passengers all of whom bring separate actions against the railroad. After the railroad wins the first 25 suits, a plaintiff wins in suit 26. Professor Currie argues that offensive use of collateral estoppel should not be applied so as to allow plaintiffs 27 through 50 automatically to recover. [Currie, *Mutuality of Estoppel: Limits of the* Bernhard *Doctrine*, 9 Stan. L. Rev. 281 (1957).]

[15] If, for example, the defendant in the first action was forced to defend in an inconvenient forum and therefore was unable to engage in full scale discovery or call witnesses, application of offensive collateral estoppel may be unwarranted. Indeed, differences in available procedures may sometimes justify not allowing a prior judgment to have estoppel effect in a subsequent action even between the same parties, or where defensive estoppel is asserted against a plaintiff who has litigated and lost. The problem of unfairness is particularly acute in cases of offensive estoppel, however, because the defendant against whom estoppel is asserted typically will not have chosen the forum in the first action.

ally estopped from relitigating the question of whether the proxy statement was materially false and misleading.

[In Part II, the Court concludes that the use of offensive collateral estoppel in the case at hand would not violate the petitioners' Seventh Amendment right to jury trial. The dissenting opinion of Justice Rehnquist is omitted.]

NOTES AND QUESTIONS

1.   *Mixed Public and Private Enforcement Schemes.* The basis for issue preclusion against the *Parklane* defendants consisted of the determination, as part of an earlier SEC-initiated lawsuit against the same defendants, that they had violated the securities laws. Why does the basis for preclusion here sound in notions of issue preclusion rather than claim preclusion?

Parallel public and private enforcement schemes—the notion that the same underlying command of substantive law can be enforced by both a government agency via a public enforcement action and the private victims of the wrong via a civil lawsuit—are quite common. Antitrust and employment discrimination law, among others, exhibit this feature, in addition to securities law.

2.   *The Strategic Implications of* Parklane–*Style Issue Preclusion.* Consider the application of the principles in *Parklane* to the situations described in Part A of this Chapter. To what extent does *Parklane* empower issue preclusion to serve as a meaningful vehicle for litigation closure across related civil claims? Does *Parklane* give rise to the potential for strategic gamesmanship in such situations? On this last question, consider the following sequence:

> Plaintiff #1 sues Beta Corporation (in scenario 3 from Part A), alleging that its cholesterol-reducing prescription drug caused Plaintiff #1's cerebral hemorrhage. The general causal relationship, if any, between the drug and cerebral hemorrhages in humans is actually litigated and determined in Plaintiff #1's lawsuit against Beta Corporation.

> What would you expect to happen, under the principles set forth in *Parklane*, if the general causation issue is determined in Plaintiff #1's favor? What if that issue is determined in Beta Corporation's favor? (You should return to the second question after reading *Taylor v. Sturgell* in the following section.) Consider these questions, in particular, from the standpoint of prospective counsel for Plaintiffs #2 through #1000. What strategy should prospective counsel employ if Beta Corporation lost the first suit?

To what extent does *Parklane* guard against undesirable gamesmanship? For a thoughtful treatment of these issues, see Jack Ratliff, *Offensive Collateral Estoppel and the Option Effect*, 67 Tex. L. Rev. 63 (1988).

3.   *Benefits of the Mutuality Doctrine.* After reading the *Parklane* opinion and the passage from *Blonder Tongue* included in it, one could easily conclude that the mutuality principle is thoroughly misguided, a formalistic rule without any sound policy support. The mutuality principle serves a purpose, however, and some states still require it. Requiring mutuality helps to equalize litigation investment incentives across the party line, which in turn helps to avoid systematically biased outcomes.

To see how this works, consider a train crash that injures 100 people (P-1 through P-100). In the first suit, P–1 sues D alleging a negligence claim. Suppose that nonmutual issue preclusion applies, so if P–1 proves negligence in the first suit, P–2 through P–100 will be able to bind D to this negligence determination. Under these circumstances, D has much more at stake in winning the first suit than just P–1's claim, and because of this, D should be willing to invest more in defending the first suit than it would if it just had to worry about liability to P–1. P–1, on the other hand, has nothing to gain or lose from litigation by P–2 through P–100. So P–1 will invest only at the level appropriate for his own case (unless, of course, P–1's lawyer also represents P–2 through P–100). As a result, D, who is concerned about future suits, will invest more than P–1, who is concerned only about his own suit. If the party that invests more is more likely to win—as is commonly supposed—then D is more likely to win the first suit, and this result obtains regardless of the actual merits of the case.

Thus, nonmutual issue preclusion can bias outcomes in favor of defendants. The mutuality rule avoids this particular source of bias by removing the risk of issue preclusion in future suits. The rule, however, doesn't eliminate all sources of outcome bias. The defendant might still invest more in the first suit because it worries about the operation of stare decisis in future suits, and it might still want to send a message to P–2 through P–100 with a resounding victory over P–1.

Of course, the fact that there is a social benefit doesn't mean that the *Blonder–Tongue* and *Parklane* courts were wrong to abolish the mutuality doctrine. Just because mutuality creates a benefit doesn't mean that the benefit is large enough to outweigh the cost of relitigation. Indeed, there are many reasons to think that the cost-benefit balance favors nonmutual issue preclusion when the number of related suits is very large. See Robert G. Bone, *Rethinking the "Day in Court" Ideal and Nonparty Preclusion*, 67 N.Y.U. L. Rev.193, 251– 56 (1993) (analyzing the effect of asymmetric stakes in mass litigation).

    4. Preclusion and Settlement. Parklane assumes, implicitly, that factual issues will actually be litigated and decided. But this is an unrealistic assumption when most cases settle. How does preclusion fit a world in which settlement is the dominant endgame? Can preclusion rules affect settlement even when those rules are rarely invoked? Should the prevalence of settlement affect the design of preclusion rules? These are difficult questions and this is not the place to probe them deeply. For a review of the literature, see Robert G. Bone, *Preclusion, in* Procedural Law and Economics 350 (C.W. Sanchirico ed., 2012).

One point, however, deserves special mention. When settlement is an option for parties, it can be difficult to justify formal claim preclusion rules on the conventional grounds of judicial economy, repose, and decisional consistency. The reason is that when parties settle, the settlement is likely to include an agreement not to file future suits arising out of the same transaction or occurrence. Such an agreement, in effect, creates claim preclusion through private contract. One might still need formal claim preclusion rules to enforce the agreement with finality if a party nevertheless insists on filing another suit, but there are also private devices, such as bonding, that can accomplish the same result. Assuming that the agreement can be enforced privately, the parties will have achieved judicial economy, repose, and decisional consistency through their settlement—without the need for formal claim preclusion rules at all.

Even so, there is still an important reason for claim preclusion. Claim preclusion rules prevent systematically biased settlements. To illustrate, suppose P sues D. Both P and D know that in a world without claim preclusion rules, the losing party—whether it is P or D—could file the same lawsuit again and again indefinitely (assuming that in a world without claim preclusion, D can relitigate by filing a declaratory judgment or other action against P if it lost the first suit). Repeated litigation like this is costly, so P and D have a mutual interest in settling the first suit and agreeing not to file future suits. But there is a problem, and it has to do with outcome quality. In the absence of formal claim preclusion rules, the more powerful and well-financed party—the one with a greater ability to withstand multiple rounds of litigation—can credibly threaten to outlast his opponent. As a result, he can insist on a favorable settlement, which the other side has very good reason to accept. Thus, the more powerful party can obtain a settlement greatly skewed in its favor (again assuming that D can sue P if D loses the first suit, just as P can sue D if P loses). For a discussion, see Bruce Hay, *Some Settlement Effects of Preclusion*, 1993 U. Ill. L. Rev. 21 (1993) (also noting that claim preclusion rules can act as transaction-cost-saving defaults when they match what the parties would have agreed to anyway).

3.   PRECLUSION OF NON–PARTIES

In *Parklane*, the Court recites the general proposition that "[i]t is a violation of due process for a judgment to be binding on a litigant who was not a party or a privy and therefore has never had an opportunity to be heard." The form of issue preclusion recognized in *Parklane*, after all, operated against Parklane Hosiery and its officers, all of whom clearly had "an opportunity to be heard" in the earlier SEC enforcement action now said to be preclusive against them. Like most propositions in the law, the principle that only parties and their privies can be bound by a judgment is subject to various exceptions. Consider the comprehensive treatment of those exceptions in the following decision, in which the Supreme Court rejects the efforts of several federal appellate courts to formulate a coherent, general notion of "virtual representation," whereby preclusion of a non-party would be permissible:

Taylor v. Sturgell
553 U.S. 880 (2008)

■ JUSTICE GINSBURG delivered the opinion of the Court.

"It is a principle of general application in Anglo–American jurisprudence that one is not bound by a judgment *in personam* in a litigation in which he is not designated as a party or to which he has not been made a party by service of process." *Hansberry v. Lee*, 311 U.S. 32, 40 (1940). Several exceptions, recognized in this Court's decisions, temper this basic rule. In a class action, for example, a person not named as a party may be bound by a judgment on the merits of the action, if she was adequately represented by a party who actively participated in the litigation. In this case, we consider for the first time whether there is a "virtual representation" exception to the general rule against precluding nonparties. Adopted by a number of courts, including the courts below in the case now before us, the exception so styled is broader than any we have so far approved.

The virtual representation question we examine in this opinion arises in the following context. Petitioner Brent Taylor filed a lawsuit under the Freedom of Information Act seeking certain documents from the Federal Aviation Administration. Greg Herrick, Taylor's friend, had previously brought an unsuccessful suit seeking the same records. The two men have no legal relationship, and there is no evidence that Taylor controlled, financed, participated in, or even had notice of Herrick's earlier suit. Nevertheless, the D.C. Circuit held Taylor's suit precluded by the judgment against Herrick because, in that court's assessment, Herrick qualified as Taylor's "virtual representative."

We disapprove the doctrine of preclusion by "virtual representation," and hold, based on the record as it now stands, that the judgment against Herrick does not bar Taylor from maintaining this suit.

I

The Freedom of Information Act (FOIA) accords "any person" a right to request any records held by a federal agency. 5 U.S.C. § 552(a)(3)(A) (2006 ed.). No reason need be given for a FOIA request, and unless the requested materials fall within one of the Act's enumerated exemptions, the agency must "make the records promptly available" to the requester. § 552(a)(3)(A). If an agency refuses to furnish the requested records, the requester may file suit in federal court and obtain an injunction "order[ing] the production of any agency records improperly withheld." § 552(a)(4)(B).

The courts below held the instant FOIA suit barred by the judgment in earlier litigation seeking the same records. Because the lower courts' decisions turned on the connection between the two lawsuits, we begin with a full account of each action.

A

The first suit was filed by Greg Herrick, an antique aircraft enthusiast and the owner of an F–45 airplane, a vintage model manufactured by the Fairchild Engine and Airplane Corporation (FEAC) in the 1930's. In 1997, seeking information that would help him restore his plane to its original condition, Herrick filed a FOIA request asking the Federal Aviation Administration (FAA) for copies of any technical documents about the F–45 contained in the agency's records.

To gain a certificate authorizing the manufacture and sale of the F–45, FEAC had submitted to the FAA's predecessor, the Civil Aeronautics Authority, detailed specifications and other technical data about the plane. Hundreds of pages of documents produced by FEAC in the certification process remain in the FAA's records. The FAA denied Herrick's request, however, upon finding that the documents he sought are subject to FOIA's exemption for "trade secrets and commercial or financial information obtained from a person and privileged or confidential," 5 U.S.C. § 552(b)(4) (2006 ed.). . . .

Herrick then filed suit in the U.S. District Court for the District of Wyoming. Challenging the FAA's invocation of the trade-secret exemption, Herrick placed heavy weight on a 1955 letter from FEAC to the Civil Aeronautics Authority. The letter authorized the agency to lend any documents in its files to the public "for use in making repairs or replacement parts for aircraft produced by Fairchild." *Herrick v. Garvey*, 298 F.3d 1184, 1193

(10th Cir. 2002) (internal quotation marks omitted). This broad authorization, Herrick maintained, showed that the F–45 certification records held by the FAA could not be regarded as "secre[t]" or "confidential" within the meaning of § 552(b)(4).

Rejecting Herrick's argument, the District Court granted summary judgment to the FAA. The 1955 letter, the court reasoned, did not deprive the F–45 certification documents of trade-secret status, for those documents were never in fact released pursuant to the letter's blanket authorization. The court also stated that even if the 1955 letter had waived trade-secret protection, Fairchild had successfully "reversed" the waiver by objecting to the FAA's release of the records to Herrick.

On appeal, the Tenth Circuit agreed with Herrick that the 1955 letter had stripped the requested documents of trade-secret protection. But the Court of Appeals upheld the District Court's alternative determination—i.e., that Fairchild had restored trade-secret status by objecting to Herrick's FOIA request. On that ground, the appeals court affirmed the entry of summary judgment for the FAA.

In so ruling, the Tenth Circuit noted that Herrick had failed to challenge two suppositions underlying the District Court's decision. First, the District Court assumed trade-secret status could be "restored" to documents that had lost protection. Second, the District Court also assumed that Fairchild had regained trade-secret status for the documents even though the company claimed that status only "*after* Herrick had initiated his request" for the F–45 records. The Court of Appeals expressed no opinion on the validity of these suppositions.

B

The Tenth Circuit's decision issued on July 24, 2002. Less than a month later, on August 22, petitioner Brent Taylor—a friend of Herrick's and an antique aircraft enthusiast in his own right—submitted a FOIA request seeking the same documents Herrick had unsuccessfully sued to obtain. When the FAA failed to respond, Taylor filed a complaint in the U.S. District Court for the District of Columbia. Like Herrick, Taylor argued that FEAC's 1955 letter had stripped the records of their trade-secret status. But Taylor also sought to litigate the two issues concerning recapture of protected status that Herrick had failed to raise in his appeal to the Tenth Circuit.

After Fairchild intervened as a defendant, the District Court in D.C. concluded that Taylor's suit was barred by claim preclusion; accordingly, it granted summary judgment to Fairchild and the FAA. The court acknowledged that Taylor was not a party to Herrick's suit. Relying on the Eighth Circuit's decision in *Tyus v. Schoemehl*, 93 F.3d 449 (1996), however, it held that a nonparty may be bound by a judgment if she was "virtually represented" by a party. . . .

The D.C. Circuit affirmed [announcing a five-factor test for virtual representation]. The first two factors—"identity of interests" and "adequate representation"—are necessary but not sufficient for virtual representation. In addition, at least one of three other factors must be established: "a close relationship between the present party and his putative representative," "substantial participation by the present party in the first case," or "tactical maneuvering on the part of the present party to avoid preclusion by the prior judgment."

Applying this test to the record in Taylor's case, the D.C. Circuit found both of the necessary conditions for virtual representation well met. As to identity of interests, the court emphasized that Taylor and Herrick sought the same result—release of the F–45 documents. Moreover, the D.C. Circuit observed, Herrick owned an F–45 airplane, and therefore had "if anything, a stronger incentive to litigate" than Taylor, who had only a "general interest in public disclosure and the preservation of antique aircraft heritage."

Turning to adequacy of representation, the D.C. Circuit acknowledged that some other Circuits regard notice of a prior suit as essential to a determination that a nonparty was adequately represented in that suit. Disagreeing with these courts, the D.C. Circuit deemed notice an "important" but not an indispensable element in the adequacy inquiry. The court then concluded that Herrick had adequately represented Taylor even though Taylor had received no notice of Herrick's suit. For this conclusion, the appeals court relied on Herrick's "strong incentive to litigate" and Taylor's later engagement of the same attorney, which indicated to the court Taylor's satisfaction with that attorney's performance in Herrick's case.

The D.C. Circuit also found its "close relationship" criterion met, for Herrick had "asked Taylor to assist him in restoring his F–45" and "provided information to Taylor that Herrick had obtained through discovery"; furthermore, Taylor "did not oppose Fairchild's characterization of Herrick as his 'close associate.'" Because the three above-described factors sufficed to establish virtual representation under the D.C. Circuit's five-factor test, the appeals court left open the question whether Taylor had engaged in "tactical maneuvering."

We granted certiorari to resolve the disagreement among the Circuits over the permissibility and scope of preclusion based on "virtual representation."

II

The preclusive effect of a federal-court judgment is determined by federal common law. See *Semtek Int'l Inc. v. Lockheed Martin Corp.*, 531 U.S. 497, 507–508 (2001). For judgments in federal-question cases—for example, Herrick's FOIA suit—federal courts participate in developing "uniform federal rule[s]" of res judicata, which this Court has ultimate authority to determine and declare. *Id.*, at 508.[4] The federal common law of preclusion is, of course, subject to due process limitations. See *Richards v. Jefferson County*, 517 U.S. 793, 797 (1996).

Taylor's case presents an issue of first impression in this sense: Until now, we have never addressed the doctrine of "virtual representation" adopted (in varying forms) by several Circuits and relied upon by the courts below. Our inquiry, however, is guided by well-established precedent regarding the propriety of nonparty preclusion. We review that precedent before taking up directly the issue of virtual representation.

A

The preclusive effect of a judgment is defined by claim preclusion and issue preclusion, which are collectively referred to as "res judicata."[5] Under

---

[4] For judgments in diversity cases, federal law incorporates the rules of preclusion applied by the State in which the rendering court sits. See *Semtek Int'l Inc. v. Lockheed Martin Corp.*, 531 U.S. 497, 508 (2001).

[5] These terms have replaced a more confusing lexicon. Claim preclusion describes the rules formerly known as "merger" and "bar," while issue preclusion encompasses the doctrines once known as "collateral estoppel" and "direct estoppel."

the doctrine of claim preclusion, a final judgment forecloses "successive litigation of the very same claim, whether or not relitigation of the claim raises the same issues as the earlier suit." Issue preclusion, in contrast, bars "successive litigation of an issue of fact or law actually litigated and resolved in a valid court determination essential to the prior judgment," even if the issue recurs in the context of a different claim. By "preclud[ing] parties from contesting matters that they have had a full and fair opportunity to litigate," these two doctrines protect against "the expense and vexation attending multiple lawsuits, conserv[e] judicial resources, and foste[r] reliance on judicial action by minimizing the possibility of inconsistent decisions." *Montana v. United States*, 440 U.S. 147, 153–154 (1979).

A person who was not a party to a suit generally has not had a "full and fair opportunity to litigate" the claims and issues settled in that suit. The application of claim and issue preclusion to nonparties thus runs up against the "deep-rooted historic tradition that everyone should have his own day in court." *Richards*, 517 U.S., at 798 (internal quotation marks omitted). Indicating the strength of that tradition, we have often repeated the general rule that "one is not bound by a judgment *in personam* in a litigation in which he is not designated as a party or to which he has not been made a party by service of process." *Hansberry*, 311 U.S. at 40.

B

Though hardly in doubt, the rule against nonparty preclusion is subject to exceptions. For present purposes, the recognized exceptions can be grouped into six categories.

First, "[a] person who agrees to be bound by the determination of issues in an action between others is bound in accordance with the terms of his agreement." 1 RESTATEMENT (SECOND) OF JUDGMENTS § 40, p. 390 (1980) (hereinafter RESTATEMENT). For example, "if separate actions involving the same transaction are brought by different plaintiffs against the same defendant, all the parties to all the actions may agree that the question of the defendant's liability will be definitely determined, one way or the other, in a 'test case.'" D. Shapiro, CIVIL PROCEDURE: PRECLUSION IN CIVIL ACTIONS 77–78 (2001) (hereinafter Shapiro). . . .

Second, nonparty preclusion may be justified based on a variety of pre-existing "substantive legal relationship[s]" between the person to be bound and a party to the judgment. Shapiro 78. Qualifying relationships include, but are not limited to, preceding and succeeding owners of property, bailee and bailor, and assignee and assignor. These exceptions originated "as much from the needs of property law as from the values of preclusion by judgment." 18A C. Wright, A. Miller, & E. Cooper, FEDERAL PRACTICE AND PROCEDURE § 4448, p. 329 (2d ed. 2002) (hereinafter Wright & Miller).[8]

Third, we have confirmed that, "in certain limited circumstances," a nonparty may be bound by a judgment because she was "adequately represented by someone with the same interests who [wa]s a party" to the suit. *Richards*, 517 U.S., at 798. Representative suits with preclusive effect on nonparties include properly conducted class actions, see *Martin* [v. *Wilks*], 490 U.S. [755,] 762, n. 2 [(1989)] (citing Fed. Rule Civ. Proc. 23), and suits

---

[8] The substantive legal relationships justifying preclusion are sometimes collectively referred to as "privity." The term "privity," however, has also come to be used more broadly, as a way to express the conclusion that nonparty preclusion is appropriate on any ground. To ward off confusion, we avoid using the term "privity" in this opinion.

brought by trustees, guardians, and other fiduciaries, see *Sea–Land Services, Inc. v. Gaudet*, 414 U.S. 573, 593 (1974).

Fourth, a nonparty is bound by a judgment if she "assume[d] control" over the litigation in which that judgment was rendered. Because such a person has had "the opportunity to present proofs and argument," he has already "had his day in court" even though he was not a formal party to the litigation.

Fifth, a party bound by a judgment may not avoid its preclusive force by relitigating through a proxy. Preclusion is thus in order when a person who did not participate in a litigation later brings suit as the designated representative of a person who was a party to the prior adjudication. And although our decisions have not addressed the issue directly, it also seems clear that preclusion is appropriate when a nonparty later brings suit as an agent for a party who is bound by a judgment.

Sixth, in certain circumstances a special statutory scheme may "expressly foreclos[e] successive litigation by nonlitigants . . . if the scheme is otherwise consistent with due process." *Martin*, 490 U.S., at 762, n. 2. Examples of such schemes include bankruptcy and probate proceedings, and *quo warranto* actions or other suits that, "under [the governing] law, [may] be brought only on behalf of the public at large," *Richards*, 517 U.S., at 804.

III

Reaching beyond these six established categories, some lower courts have recognized a "virtual representation" exception to the rule against nonparty preclusion. Decisions of these courts, however, have been far from consistent. Some Circuits use the label, but define "virtual representation" so that it is no broader than the recognized exception for adequate representation. But other courts, including the Eighth, Ninth, and D.C. Circuits, apply multifactor tests for virtual representation that permit nonparty preclusion in cases that do not fit within any of the established exceptions.

The D.C. Circuit, the FAA, and Fairchild have presented three arguments in support of an expansive doctrine of virtual representation. We find none of them persuasive.

A

The D.C. Circuit purported to ground its virtual representation doctrine in this Court's decisions stating that, in some circumstances, a person may be bound by a judgment if she was adequately represented by a party to the proceeding yielding that judgment. But the D.C. Circuit's definition of "adequate representation" strayed from the meaning our decisions have attributed to that term.

In *Richards*, we reviewed a decision by the Alabama Supreme Court holding that a challenge to a tax was barred by a judgment upholding the same tax in a suit filed by different taxpayers. The plaintiffs in the first suit "did not sue on behalf of a class," their complaint "did not purport to assert any claim against or on behalf of any nonparties," and the judgment "did not purport to bind" nonparties There was no indication, we emphasized, that the court in the first suit "took care to protect the interests" of absent parties, or that the parties to that litigation "understood their suit to be on behalf of absent [parties]." In these circumstances, we held, the application of claim preclusion was inconsistent with "the due process of law guaranteed by the Fourteenth Amendment."

The D.C. Circuit stated, without elaboration, that it did not "read *Richards* to hold a nonparty . . . adequately represented only if special procedures were followed [to protect the nonparty] or the party to the prior suit understood it was representing the nonparty." As the D.C. Circuit saw this case, Herrick adequately represented Taylor for two principal reasons: Herrick had a strong incentive to litigate; and Taylor later hired Herrick's lawyer, suggesting Taylor's "satisfaction with the attorney's performance in the prior case."

The D.C. Circuit misapprehended *Richards*. As just recounted, our holding that the Alabama Supreme Court's application of res judicata to nonparties violated due process turned on the lack of either special procedures to protect the nonparties' interests or an understanding by the concerned parties that the first suit was brought in a representative capacity. *Richards* thus established that representation is "adequate" for purposes of nonparty preclusion only if (at a minimum) one of these two circumstances is present.

We restated *Richards'* core holding in *South Central Bell Telephone Co. v. Alabama*, 526 U.S. 160 (1999). In that case, as in *Richards*, the Alabama courts had held that a judgment rejecting a challenge to a tax by one group of taxpayers barred a subsequent suit by a different taxpayer. In *South Central Bell*, however, the nonparty had notice of the original suit and engaged one of the lawyers earlier employed by the original plaintiffs. Under the D.C. Circuit's decision in Taylor's case, these factors apparently would have sufficed to establish adequate representation. Yet *South Central Bell* held that the application of res judicata in that case violated due process. Our inquiry came to an end when we determined that the original plaintiffs had not understood themselves to be acting in a representative capacity and that there had been no special procedures to safeguard the interests of absentees.

Our decisions recognizing that a nonparty may be bound by a judgment if she was adequately represented by a party to the earlier suit thus provide no support for the D.C. Circuit's broad theory of virtual representation.

B

Fairchild and the FAA do not argue that the D.C. Circuit's virtual representation doctrine fits within any of the recognized grounds for nonparty preclusion. Rather, they ask us to abandon the attempt to delineate discrete grounds and clear rules altogether. Preclusion is in order, they contend, whenever "the relationship between a party and a non-party is 'close enough' to bring the second litigant within the judgment." Courts should make the "close enough" determination, they urge, through a "heavily fact-driven" and "equitable" inquiry. Only this sort of diffuse balancing, Fairchild and the FAA argue, can account for all of the situations in which nonparty preclusion is appropriate.

We reject this argument for three reasons. First, our decisions emphasize the fundamental nature of the general rule that a litigant is not bound by a judgment to which she was not a party. See, e.g., *Richards*, 517 U.S., at 798–799; *Martin*, 490 U.S., at 761–762. Accordingly, we have endeavored to delineate discrete exceptions that apply in "limited circumstances." Respondents' amorphous balancing test is at odds with the constrained approach to nonparty preclusion our decisions advance. . . .

Our second reason for rejecting a broad doctrine of virtual representation rests on the limitations attending nonparty preclusion based on adequate representation. A party's representation of a nonparty is "adequate" for preclusion purposes only if, at a minimum: (1) the interests of the nonparty and her representative are aligned, see *Hansberry*, 311 U.S., at 43; and (2) either the party understood herself to be acting in a representative capacity or the original court took care to protect the interests of the nonparty, see *Richards*, 517 U.S., at 801–802. In addition, adequate representation sometimes requires (3) notice of the original suit to the persons alleged to have been represented, see *Richards*, 517 U.S., at 801. In the class-action context, these limitations are implemented by the procedural safeguards contained in Federal Rule of Civil Procedure 23.

An expansive doctrine of virtual representation, however, would "recogniz[e], in effect, a common-law kind of class action." That is, virtual representation would authorize preclusion based on identity of interests and some kind of relationship between parties and nonparties, shorn of the procedural protections prescribed in *Hansberry*, *Richards*, and Rule 23. These protections, grounded in due process, could be circumvented were we to approve a virtual representation doctrine that allowed courts to "create *de facto* class actions at will."

Third, a diffuse balancing approach to nonparty preclusion would likely create more headaches than it relieves. Most obviously, it could significantly complicate the task of district courts faced in the first instance with preclusion questions. An all-things-considered balancing approach might spark wide-ranging, time-consuming, and expensive discovery tracking factors potentially relevant under seven- or five-prong tests. And after the relevant facts are established, district judges would be called upon to evaluate them under a standard that provides no firm guidance. Preclusion doctrine, it should be recalled, is intended to reduce the burden of litigation on courts and parties. "In this area of the law," we agree, " 'crisp rules with sharp corners' are preferable to a round-about doctrine of opaque standards." *Bittinger* v. *Tecumseh Products Co.*, 123 F.3d 877, 881 (6th Cir. 1997).

C

Finally, relying on the Eighth Circuit's decision in *Tyus*, 93 F.3d, at 456, the FAA maintains that nonparty preclusion should apply more broadly in "public-law" litigation than in "private-law" controversies. To support this position, the FAA offers two arguments. First, the FAA urges, our decision in *Richards* acknowledges that, in certain cases, the plaintiff has a reduced interest in controlling the litigation "because of the public nature of the right at issue." When a taxpayer challenges "an alleged misuse of public funds" or "other public action," we observed in *Richards*, the suit "has only an indirect impact on [the plaintiff's] interests." In actions of this character, the Court said, "we may assume that the States have wide latitude to establish procedures . . . to limit the number of judicial proceedings that may be entertained."

Taylor's FOIA action falls within the category described in *Richards*, the FAA contends, because "the duty to disclose under FOIA is owed to the public generally." The opening sentence of FOIA, it is true, states that agencies "shall make [information] available to the public." 5 U.S.C. § 552(a) (2006 ed.). Equally true, we have several times said that FOIA vindicates a "public" interest. E.g., *National Archives and Records Admin. v. Favish*, 541 U.S. 157, 172 (2004). The Act, however, instructs agencies receiving FOIA requests to make the information available not to the public at large, but rather to the "person" making the request. § 552(a)(3)(A). See also § 552(a)(3)(B) ("In making any record available *to a person* under this paragraph, an agency shall provide the record in any [readily reproducible] form or format requested *by the person.* . . ." (emphasis added)). <u>Thus, in contrast to the public-law litigation contemplated in *Richards*, a successful FOIA action results in a grant of relief to the individual plaintiff, not a decree benefiting the public at large.</u>

Furthermore, we said in *Richards* only that, for the type of public-law claims there envisioned, States are free to adopt procedures limiting repetitive litigation. In this regard, we referred to instances in which the first judgment foreclosed successive litigation by other plaintiffs because, "under state law, [the suit] could be brought only on behalf of the public at large." *Richards* spoke of state legislation, but it appears equally evident that *Congress*, in providing for actions vindicating a public interest, may "limit the number of judicial proceedings that may be entertained." It hardly follows, however, that *this Court* should proscribe or confine successive FOIA suits by different requesters. Indeed, Congress' provision for FOIA suits with no statutory constraint on successive actions counsels against judicial imposition of constraints through extraordinary application of the common law of preclusion.

The FAA next argues that "the threat of vexatious litigation is heightened" in public-law cases because "the number of plaintiffs with standing is potentially limitless." FOIA does allow "any person" whose request is denied to resort to federal court for review of the agency's determination. 5 U.S.C. § 552(a)(3)(A), (4)(B) (2006 ed.). Thus it is theoretically possible that several persons could coordinate to mount a series of repetitive lawsuits.

But we are not convinced that this risk justifies departure from the usual rules governing nonparty preclusion. First, *stare decisis* will allow courts swiftly to dispose of repetitive suits brought in the same circuit. Second, even when *stare decisis* is not dispositive, "the human tendency not to waste money will deter the bringing of suits based on claims or issues that have already been adversely determined against others." This intuition seems to be borne out by experience: The FAA has not called our attention to any instances of abusive FOIA suits in the Circuits that reject the virtual-representation theory respondents advocate here.

IV

For the foregoing reasons, we disapprove the theory of virtual representation on which the decision below rested. The preclusive effects of a judgment in a federal-question case decided by a federal court should instead be determined according to the established grounds for nonparty preclusion described in this opinion. See Part II–B, *supra*.

Although references to "virtual representation" have proliferated in the lower courts, our decision is unlikely to occasion any great shift in actual practice. Many opinions use the term "virtual representation" in reaching results at least arguably defensible on established grounds. In these cases, dropping the "virtual representation" label would lead to clearer analysis with little, if any, change in outcomes.

In some cases, however, lower courts have relied on virtual representation to extend nonparty preclusion beyond the latter doctrine's proper bounds. We now turn back to Taylor's action to determine whether his suit is such a case, or whether the result reached by the courts below can be justified on one of the recognized grounds for nonparty preclusion.

A

It is uncontested that four of the six grounds for nonparty preclusion have no application here: There is no indication that Taylor agreed to be bound by Herrick's litigation, that Taylor and Herrick have any legal relationship, that Taylor exercised any control over Herrick's suit, or that this suit implicates any special statutory scheme limiting relitigation. Neither the FAA nor Fairchild contends otherwise.

It is equally clear that preclusion cannot be justified on the theory that Taylor was adequately represented in Herrick's suit. Nothing in the record indicates that Herrick understood himself to be suing on Taylor's behalf, that Taylor even knew of Herrick's suit, or that the Wyoming District Court took special care to protect Taylor's interests. Under our pathmarking precedent, therefore, Herrick's representation was not "adequate." See *Richards*, 517 U.S., at 801–802.

That leaves only the fifth category: preclusion because a nonparty to an earlier litigation has brought suit as a representative or agent of a party who is bound by the prior adjudication. Taylor is not Herrick's legal representative and he has not purported to sue in a representative capacity. He concedes, however, that preclusion would be appropriate if respondents could demonstrate that he is acting as Herrick's "undisclosed agen[t]."

Respondents argue here, as they did below, that Taylor's suit is a collusive attempt to relitigate Herrick's action. The D.C. Circuit considered a similar question in addressing the "tactical maneuvering" prong of its virtual representation test. The Court of Appeals did not, however, treat the issue as one of agency, and it expressly declined to reach any definitive conclusions due to "the ambiguity of the facts." We therefore remand to give the courts below an opportunity to determine whether Taylor, in pursuing the instant FOIA suit, is acting as Herrick's agent. Taylor concedes that such a remand is appropriate.

. . . A mere whiff of "tactical maneuvering" will not suffice; instead, principles of agency law are suggestive. They indicate that preclusion is appropriate only if the putative agent's conduct of the suit is subject to the control of the party who is bound by the prior adjudication. See 1 RESTATEMENT (SECOND) OF AGENCY § 14, p. 60 (1957) ("A principal has the right to control the conduct of the agent with respect to matters entrusted to him.").

B

On remand, Fairchild suggests, Taylor should bear the burden of proving he is not acting as Herrick's agent. When a defendant points to evidence establishing a close relationship between successive litigants, Fairchild maintains, "the burden [should] shif[t] to the second litigant to submit evidence refuting the charge" of agency. Fairchild justifies this proposed burden-shift on the ground that "it is unlikely an opposing party will have access to direct evidence of collusion."

We reject Fairchild's suggestion. Claim preclusion, like issue preclusion, is an affirmative defense. Ordinarily, it is incumbent on the defendant to plead and prove such a defense, and we have never recognized claim preclusion as an exception to that general rule. We acknowledge that direct evidence justifying nonparty preclusion is often in the hands of plaintiffs rather than defendants. But "[v]ery often one must plead and prove matters as to which his adversary has superior access to the proof." 2 K. Broun, MCCORMICK ON EVIDENCE § 337, p. 475 (6th ed. 2006). In these situations, targeted interrogatories or deposition questions can reduce the information disparity. We see no greater cause here than in other matters of affirmative defense to disturb the traditional allocation of the proof burden.

* * *

For the reasons stated, the judgment of the United States Court of Appeals for the District of Columbia Circuit is vacated, and the case is remanded for further proceedings consistent with this opinion.

It is so ordered.

NOTES AND QUESTIONS

1.   *Why Preclusion of Similar Claimants?* What type of preclusion did the D.C. Circuit in *Taylor* consider applicable in Taylor's lawsuit? Why wasn't the case governed by the holding in *Parklane*?

The Supreme Court holds that Taylor is not precluded from suing to challenge the denial of his FOIA request based on the judgment in the earlier litigation that upheld the denial as to Herrick's request for the same information. But now consider the situation in a different light: Why might a desirable civil procedure regime *want* to generate preclusive effect across multiple, similar claimants—not just those who have chosen to sue in court but also, conceivably, those who have similar claims but who have not decided to sue (indeed, who might never sue individually)? On this question, consider the strategic insight offered by Judge Diane Wood for the Seventh Circuit in *Tice v. American Airlines, Inc.*, 162 F.3d 966, 968 (7th Cir. 1998):

> The vigor with which the defense bar has often opposed class certifications might cause one to think that defendants prefer to take their cases one at a time, but that would be too simplistic a view. In fact, the existence and incidence of another exception to the general rule, the doctrine of virtual representation, suggests that defendants sometimes like the benefits of a group result—because it is usually defendants who argue that a new group of plaintiffs is barred from bringing an action since the plaintiff in an earlier suit was its "virtual representative."

In contrast to the line of lower-court decisions rejected by the Supreme Court in *Taylor*, the Seventh Circuit's decision in *Tice*—a case involving successive lawsuits against American Airlines by different pilots, each seeking to challenge the same company policy as unlawful under the Age Discrimination in Employment Act—expressed what turns out to be a prescient skepticism about the concept of virtual representation. The *Tice* court noted:

> [T]he doctrine of virtual representation is amorphous. Indeed, in our view the term itself illustrates the harm that can be done when a catchy phrase is coined to describe a perfectly sensible result. The phrase takes on a life of its own, and before too long, it starts being applied to situations far removed from its intended and proper context. In the case of "virtual representation," the concept had its origin in the field of probate proceedings, in which "it is often necessary to establish a procedure that will bind persons unknown, unascertained, or not yet born." 18 Charles Alan Wright *et al.*, FEDERAL PRACTICE AND PROCEDURE § 4457 at 494 (1981). In that narrow setting, courts would find an identity of interests between the representatives who participated in the litigation and other individuals whose interests

were clearly aligned with those of the actual litigants. In the argot of *res judicata* law, the technical nonparties were treated as parties to the first suit for purposes of assessing its preclusive force.

Branching out from those roots, the term "virtual representation" began to be referred to as a doctrine. . . .

We think the term "virtual representation" has cast more shadows than light on the problem to be decided. As a matter of fact, a finding that nonparties were virtually represented in earlier litigation has rarely been used actually to bar litigation. . . . The Wright treatise observes that "[a]ll of the cases that in fact preclude relitigation by a nonparty have involved several factors in addition to apparently adequate litigation by a party holding parallel interests." Wright, § 4457 (1998 Supp.) at 420. . . .

These factors are all merely heuristics, however, shortcuts that courts use to determine the answer to the real (fact-specific) question—whether there was (or should be implied at law) the kind of link between the earlier and later plaintiffs that justifies binding the second group to the result reached against the first. This is, of course, the same question we and other courts have already identified as the crux of the privity inquiry. A proper functional analysis of privity, focusing on the general question whether the earlier parties were in some sense proper agents for the later parties, would therefore support preclusion in the cases that have used the lingo of virtual representation. Conversely, if a relationship between a nonparty and an earlier litigant does not satisfy this analysis, serious due process problems would arise if the earlier nonparty were barred from her own day in court.

Id. at 970–71.

The *Tice* court describes the doctrine of virtual representation as "amorphous," and suggests that "a proper functional analysis of privity focusing on whether the earlier parties were in some sense proper agents for the later parties" is superior. But is the privity formulation any less amorphous? What does it mean for a party to be "in some sense" an "agent"? What "sense" is that? Does the Court mean that preclusion can only apply when there is in fact a formal agency relationship as a matter of law? The *Tice* court also refers to "the kind of link between the earlier and later plaintiffs that justifies binding the second group to the result reached against the first." But is that any more helpful? Doesn't it just beg the question of what kind of link qualifies? The Supreme Court in *Taylor* appears to limit nonparty preclusion to six established categories, but what happens when a case arises that does not neatly fit one of these categories? For example, many states allow preclusion of later citizen suits based on an earlier parens patriae suit brought by the state. Does this exception fit one of *Taylor*'s six categories? See *Sierra Club v. Two Elk Generation Partners*, 646 F.3d 1258, 1267–68 (10th Cir. 2011) (questioning whether preclusion of citizen suits is consistent with *Taylor*, but in the end relying on Wyoming preclusion rules rather than *Taylor*). Is the third category, adequate representation, clearly defined? The Court mentions class actions and "suits brought by trustees, guardians, and other fiduciaries." Are these just examples, or are they meant to exhaust the category? If they are only examples, how is one supposed to tell whether a different situation fits the third category as well?

2. *Nonparty Preclusion Policies.* Why not preclude Taylor's suit? What social value is there in allowing Taylor to litigate the same FOIA claim as Herrick did? One is tempted to answer that "due process" requires it, but this answer just begs the question. Why *should* due process require it? Do we get a better outcome by allowing the second suit? Is there social value in giving Taylor an opportunity to control his own suit even if there's no reason to believe that it will improve the outcome from a social point of view? If there is value in participation for its own sake, does that value vary with the type of claim? In this connection, note what the Court says about "public-law claims" in III.C of its opinion, and think about this question again after you read note 5 below. For an analysis of virtual representation and nonparty preclusion from a policy perspective, see Bone, *Rethinking the "Day in Court" Ideal and Nonparty Preclusion*, 67 N.Y.U. L. Rev. 193 (1992) (advocating broader nonparty preclusion).

Note that Herrick failed to raise two important issues relating to the recapture of protected status and that Taylor plans to litigate those issues in his suit. Does that provide a special reason to allow Taylor's lawsuit? Bear in mind that Herrick almost certainly would be precluded from filing a second suit himself even if he argued that he inadvertently left out the issues and should be allowed to litigate them. If there is a special reason to allow Taylor to sue, must we allow him to relitigate all the issues that Herrick actually litigated and lost, as well as the two issues he left out? What about denying claim preclusion but allowing issue preclusion?

3. *Preclusion versus Stare Decisis.* In *Taylor*, the Supreme Court notes that, in the absence of preclusion, principles of stare decisis still operate and can effectively discourage relitigation. Is stare decisis an adequate response to the practical concerns of, say, Fairchild Engine and Airplane Corporation about the prospect of repeated disputes over disclosure of the specifications for the F–45 airplane? In practical terms, how does the assertion of stare decisis differ from the assertion of preclusion as a defense against a second lawsuit?

4. *Preclusion and the Structure of the Judicial System.* Taylor chose to challenge the denial of his FOIA request in a different court (the U.S. District Court for the District of Columbia) from the one in which Herrick had litigated (the U.S. District Court for the District of Wyoming). Why? What does the structure of the judicial system in this country—a system comprised of a federal court system and fifty largely autonomous systems of state courts—suggest about the question raised in note 1 concerning the desirability of preclusion on a mass basis? About the question raised in note 3 concerning the differences between preclusion and stare decisis?

5. *Preclusion and Undifferentiated Public Rights.* At the outset of its opinion, the Court emphasizes that FOIA confers a right on "any person" to request the disclosure of government-held information for any reason. Nothing more than simple curiosity is needed, as Justice Scalia observed at oral argument in *Taylor*. Note how the right conferred by FOIA differs from the usual kind of rights asserted by way of civil litigation: rights confined in one way or another—whether by underlying substantive law or related notions of standing—to particular persons among all those in the general public. Does the undifferentiated nature of the disclosure right in FOIA shed light on why the lower federal courts might have thought it worthwhile to struggle mightily in an

effort to develop a coherent notion of "virtual representation"? Are you persuaded by the Court's response to Fairchild's public-litigation argument in III.C. of its opinion? The Supreme Court recognizes that particular statutory regimes can provide for preclusion beyond the traditional categories listed in the *Taylor* opinion. Should Congress so provide by way of amendments to FOIA specifically?

6.   Taylor v. Sturgell *on Remand*. After the Supreme Court decision vacating and remanding, the case returned to the district court. In 2011, the district court granted summary judgment for Taylor, holding that the F–45 materials he requested were not trade secrets and therefore not exempt from FOIA. *Taylor v. Babbit,* 760 F. Supp. 2d 80 (D.D.C. 2011).

7.   *Virtual Representation After* Taylor v. Sturgell. Lower federal courts have given a broad reading to *Taylor v. Sturgell* and rejected virtual representation in a number of different settings. See, e.g., *Briscoe v. City of New Haven*, 654 F.3d 200, 203–04 (2d Cir. 2011) (applied to a Title VII claim); *In Re Montgomery Ward*, 634 F.3d 732, 737–39 (3d Cir. 2011) (applied to bankruptcy); *National Spiritual Assembly of Bahai's*, 628 F.3d 837, 856–57 (7th Cir. 2010) (applied to a contempt motion). Moreover, they have extended *Taylor*'s holding to issue preclusion as well as claim preclusion. See, e.g., *Palma v. Safe Hurricane Shutters, Inc.*, 615 F. Supp. 2d 1339, 1345–46 (S.D. Fla. 2009); *Lincoln–Dodge, Inc. v. Sullivan*, 588 F. Supp. 2d 224, 234–37 (D.R.I. 2008). Some state courts, however, have read *Taylor* to address only federal preclusion law, leaving room for broader state rules (subject, of course, to due process constraints). See, e.g., *City of Chicago v. St. John's United Church of Christ*, 404 Ill.App.3d 505, 513–15 (2010); see also *Sierra Club v. Two Elk Generation Partners*, 646 F.3d 1258, 1267–68 (10th Cir. 2011) (noting that "some state courts . . . have not altered their preclusion standards after *Taylor*").

C. MAJOR TECHNIQUES OF AGGREGATION

As the previous Parts have suggested, the need for aggregate litigation procedures arises from the mass nature of wrongs in modern society and the limited capacity of conventional preclusion principles, developed in one-on-one litigation, to yield closure on a commensurately mass basis. The term "aggregate litigation" has come to encompass the various procedural techniques used to litigate civil claims on a mass or collective basis in such a way as to yield preclusion. The following discussion surveys the general characteristics of different types of aggregation devices. Before doing so, however, it is important to have a general understanding of the policies relevant to evaluating these devices.

Aggregation produces social benefits. One of the most commonly cited is judicial economy; that is, litigation costs savings from avoiding duplicative discovery and litigation of common issues. To be sure, aggregation also adds litigation costs of its own since a complex case is usually more difficult to manage and litigate than an individual one. Even so, the net savings are likely to be positive when there are lots of individual suits and many common questions. In *Taylor*, for example, a class action aggregating the FOIA claims of Herrick, Taylor, and other potential plaintiffs would have avoided the costly duplicative litigation of common issues, and the resulting aggregation would probably not have been difficult to manage. Of course, the class action achieves the benefits of judicial economy only because all class members are precluded. Note that *Taylor v. Sturgell* explicitly references adequate representation in class actions as a "recognized exception" to the rule against nonparty preclusion.

Judicial economy is not the only benefit of aggregation. Sometimes individual suits create harmful effects for other litigants and when those effects are serious enough, fairness can support aggregation. For example, suppose the defendant's assets and insurance are limited so that the total amount available to satisfy all the claims is less than the total expected recovery. If each plaintiff were to litigate individually, those who sued too late would end up reaching final judgment only after all the funds were exhausted. Aggregating the individual suits into one proceeding facilitates the equitable distribution of the limited fund. You might recall that this is one of the grounds supporting compulsory joinder, see Fed. R. Civ. P. 19(a)(1)(B)(i), and we will see that it is one of the grounds for a class action as well.

There are other potential benefits of aggregation. For example, it can help equalize the plaintiff's and the defendant's relative litigating power. The defendant enjoys economies of scale when the litigation involves a mass accident or mass tort. This is because the defendant can spread the cost of investigating and preparing the common questions across all the lawsuits. By contrast, plaintiffs must investigate and prepare each case separately and thus end up duplicating the investment in developing common questions—unless they share the same lawyer or their separate lawyers cooperate informally. Formal aggregation helps to solve this problem on the plaintiff's side by eliminating the need for duplication. In effect, aggregation gives plaintiffs economies of scale that the defendant already enjoys and thus helps to equalize power across the party line.

Finally, aggregation can enable private litigation to enforce the substantive law when claims are too small to support individual suits. For example, securities fraud typically generates small losses for thousands, even millions, of individual investors. Each loss is too small to support an individual suit, but aggregation makes suit attractive for an attorney who takes a fraction of the total award or settlement as her fee.

Aggregation does not just create benefits. It also generates costs that can outweigh the benefits and problems that can complicate its implementation. For example, attorneys sometimes sell out the plaintiffs in an aggregation in order to settle for a larger fee. Moreover, centralizing claims can distort the meaning and dilute the effectiveness of a state's laws, thereby raising federalism concerns. Furthermore, aggregation can have a negative effect on party control and thus raise due process concerns insofar as individuals in large aggregations have diminished ability to make decisions concerning the conduct of the litigation. In fact, in a mandatory class action, class members may not even receive notice that they are in a lawsuit affecting their rights. In addition, centralizing parties and lawsuits in a single jurisdiction often prevents the public in each of the affected communities from being able to participate through jury trials. This is troubling to the extent that trials in the original fora would further democratic participation values. Finally, some types of aggregation create an attractive environment for frivolous and weak lawsuits.

The benefits, costs, and problems vary with the method of aggregation. Aggregation can take place by contract—specifically, contracts between individual clients and their common lawyer—if more than one party retains the same attorney and agrees to joint representation. It can also take place by non-contractual means. Under certain circumstances, such as with a class action or multidistrict litigation, procedural law itself brings into being the aggregate unit for litigation. Some manner of judicial order, such as an order certifying a class or transferring claims with similar facts to a single judge, serves as the vehicle for constructing the aggregation. In fact, as this Chapter shall explain momentarily, it is even possible for a kind of aggregation to take place by means that are not exactly contractual but still have contractual elements.

This book devotes much of its attention to the most controversial of the non-contractual techniques for aggregation: the modern class action. The premise for this editorial choice is that careful analysis of aggregation in its most controversial form has the capacity to shed light—by analogy or, perhaps, by contrast—on other techniques. In fact, most of the salient characteristics of aggregation in general—its potential as well as its problems—have been explored most carefully in the class action jurisprudence. Thus, we can learn a great deal about all aggregation devices by studying the class action closely.

Nevertheless, other methods of aggregation have become increasingly significant over the past twenty years, and the class action's importance has declined. Starting with two decisions in the late 1990s restricting the availability of settlement class actions, the Supreme Court has cut back significantly on class actions in federal court, as have many federal courts of appeals. As we shall see, Congress, too, has gotten into the act. Lawyers and parties have responded to these developments by focusing on other aggregation techniques, chief among them being multidistrict litigation (MDL). These aggregation techniques are not necessarily exclusive of the class action. An MDL proceeding, for example, can sometimes include class actions as well as individual suits, as we shall see, and MDL judges sometimes transform the MDL proceeding into a class action through class certification. But MDL is a different kind of aggregation device than the class action, and it is an increasingly important one. Accordingly, this book also devotes attention to MDL aggregation, as well as other non-class aggregation devices, in Chapter 3.

In general, we hope the student comes away with a deeper understanding of the policies and principles affecting case aggregations of all types, whether they take the form of class actions, MDL consolidations, or other procedural variations.

1.　CONTRACTUAL AGGREGATION

Perhaps the most straightforward aggregation technique is the joint representation of persons with related claims by a single lawyer or law firm. The clients who collectively constitute the lawyer's "inventory" might be purchasers of airline tickets (in scenario 1 from Part A), prospective voters (in scenario 2), or drug consumers (in scenario 3). Regardless, the distinguishing characteristic of contractual aggregation is that each claimant is individually represented by the same attorney or law firm, usually (but not necessarily) pursuant to the same contractual terms as everyone else. In most instances, the claimants know that the lawyer represents many clients who are situated similarly. Sometimes, the retainer contract states this explicitly. In a smaller fraction of the cases, the contract also sets out terms for collective action. It may provide for the selection of a steering committee to supervise the day-to-day conduct of the litigation, for a formula to govern the allocation of settlement proceeds, or for the manner of distributing common costs.

Of course, when it comes to client-lawyer relationships, contracts are not the only sources of rights and obligations. Agency law also imposes many duties, including the fiduciary duty that requires lawyers to act only in ways expected to make clients better off. The law of professional responsibility, also known as the law governing lawyers, also supplements contracts in many ways. Of particular importance in contractual aggregations is that this body of law contains the so-called "aggregate settlement rule," which establishes conditions that lawyers must meet when settling claims in groups. As set forth in Rule 1.8(g) of the Model Rules of Professional Conduct, the aggregate settlement rule provides that:

> A lawyer who represents two or more clients shall not participate in making an aggregate settlement of the claims of or against the clients. . . unless each client consents after consultation, including disclosure of the existence and nature of all the claims . . . involved and of the participation of each person in the settlement.

Two commentators explain the practical implications of this rule:

> On its face and as interpreted in the few pertinent decisions to date, the [aggregate settlement rule] imposes three requirements on lawyers seeking to settle lawsuits in which they represent multiple clients: (1) disclosure of all settlement terms to all clients, including disclosure to each of what other plaintiffs are to receive or other defendants are to pay; (2) unanimous consent by all clients to all settlement terms; and (3) a prohibition on agreements to waive requirements (1) or (2) even with the clients' unanimous consent.

Charles Silver & Lynn A. Baker, *Mass Lawsuits and the Aggregate Settlement Rule*, 32 Wake Forest L. Rev. 733 (1997). The identified prohibition arises because, unlike other rules governing conflicts of interests, the aggregate settlement rule contains no provision allowing clients to waive its requirements, even with informed consent.

Whether the aggregate settlement rule is desirable as a policy matter is a subject of considerable debate. The rule's opponents contend that claimants should have more freedom to structure their relationships with lawyers and other claimants than the aggregate settlement rule allows. The rule's defenders argue that it imposes much needed constraints; without these constraints, clients would likely be exploited by lawyers interested in collecting the substantial fees mass-tort settlements often afford. Chapter 5 will discuss these matters in more detail.

Contractual aggregation can also occur by other means, and often does. Referrals are an especially common method. They occur when lawyers who are retained by clients forward cases to other attorneys, typically mass-tort specialists, who receive clients from many sources and share fees with referring attorneys. Referrals are contractual because formal agreements, disclosed to and approved by clients, normally govern their terms. Referrals usually help clients by improving the quality of the legal services they receive at no additional cost. The referring lawyer brokers the case to a high-quality specialist and may monitor the specialist's performance, which the client is often unable to do. The referring lawyer has an incentive to choose a first-rate specialist and to monitor with care because the referral share is normally a percentage of the contingent fee. The larger the recovery, therefore, the more money the referring lawyer receives. On the economics of referral practices, see Stephen J. Spurr, *Referral Practices among Lawyers: A Theoretical and Empirical Analysis*, 13 L. & Social Inquiry 87 (1988); Stephen J. Spurr, *The Impact of Advertising and Other Factors on Referral Practices, with Special Reference to Lawyers*, 21 RAND J. Econ. 235 (1990). On plaintiffs' attorneys' use of referrals to encourage specialization and expand the bar's capacity to handle cases, see Stephen C. Yeazell, *Re–Financing Civil Litigation*, 51 DePaul L. Rev. 183 (2001).

Contractual aggregation also occurs when lawyers agree to joint-venture cases, that is, to develop them cooperatively but without formally becoming co-counsel for clients represented by other attorneys. For example, in the mass-tort litigation concerning Vioxx, a prescription medicine used to treat arthritis, lawyers who separately represented thousands of clients created a consortium. By sharing litigation costs and cooperating, the lawyers took advantage of economies of scale and gained bargaining leverage vis-à-vis Merck, the defendant, which could have credibly threatened to outspend them. The Vioxx Litigation Consortium is described in Charles Silver and Geoffrey P. Miller, *The Quasi–Class Action Method of Managing Multi–District Litigations: Problems and a Proposal*, 63 Vand. L. Rev. 107 (2010).

For discussions of contractual and non-contractual aggregation techniques, see Howard M. Erichson, *Informal Aggregation: Procedural and Ethical Implications of Coordination Among Counsel in Related Lawsuits*, 50 Duke L.J. 381 (2000); Howard M. Erichson, *Beyond the Class Action: Lawyer Loyalty and Client Autonomy in Non–Class Collective Representations*, 2003 U. Chi. Legal F. 519 (2003); Charles Silver & Lynn Baker, *I Cut, You Choose: The Role of Plaintiffs' Counsel in Allocating Settlement Proceeds*, 84 Va. L. Rev. 1465 (1998).

2. Non–Contractual Aggregation

In addition to contractual forms of aggregation, several non-contractual forms have emerged in modern procedural law. The focus here is on the major non-contractual devices that facilitate litigation by private persons, as distinct from the government itself. These consist principally of consolidations (governed in the federal courts by Rule 42(a) of the Federal Rules of Civil Procedure) and class actions (governed by Rule 23).* Moreo-

---

* The law of civil procedure also provides for the joinder of parties. See Fed. R. Civ. P. 19–20. As one commentator explains, however, joinder has proven to be only a very limited technique for aggregation:

Joinder of parties is generally permitted when claims arise out of the same transaction, occurrence, or series of transactions or occurrences. The test is easy to satisfy, and there is no numerical ceiling, so it is possible to use joinder to aggregate massive litigation. The shortcoming of permissive joinder is that it is just that—permissive. Plaintiffs themselves control the use of permissive joinder as an aggregation mechanism. Moreover, joinder may not be feasible in some cases, especially where plaintiffs' lawyers practice in different states. In litigation against geographically dispersed defendants, the requirements of personal jurisdiction and venue further complicate joinder and often doom it to incompleteness.

ver, consolidation can be combined with transfer devices, especially the MDL device, to create very large case aggregations. An additional form of non-contractual aggregation not discussed here consists of litigation brought by the government—say, the Attorney General of a particular state—on behalf of its citizens. Chapter 5 illustrates that approach by reference to government litigation to protect the citizenry against a "public nuisance."

a.   CONSOLIDATION

FEDERAL RULES OF CIVIL PROCEDURE
RULE 42.   CONSOLIDATION . . .

(a) Consolidation. If actions before the court involve a common question of law or fact, the court may:

> (1) join for hearing or trial any or all matters at issue in the actions;

> (2) consolidate the actions; or

> (3) issue any other orders to avoid unnecessary cost or delay.

b.   CLASS ACTION

A second and more dramatic form of non-contractual aggregation takes place by way of class actions under Rule 23 of the Federal Rules of Civil Procedure and state class action rules, some of which are modeled on Rule 23. Much of the crucial wording in Rule 23 has remained as originally adopted in 1966. Other portions, however, reflect more recent changes, including amendments in 1998 and 2003 and a small change in 2009. As of December 2007, moreover, the text of the rule was restyled simply to make it easier to read, without any intended change in content. The 2007 restyling of Rule 23 was part of a larger, comprehensive restyling of the Federal Rules as a whole. In several instances, wording has been restructured; in some instances, subsections within the rule have been renumbered. The consequence is that much of the case law on Rule 23 discusses that provision in its original 1966 form, not in its current form, as reproduced here. Do not be surprised, in other words, if the cases and other materials you encounter reflect the pre–2007, un-restyled rule text.

FEDERAL RULES OF CIVIL PROCEDURE
RULE 23.   CLASS ACTIONS

(a) Prerequisites. One or more members of a class may sue or be sued as representative parties on behalf of all members only if:

> (1) the class is so numerous that joinder of all members is impracticable;

Compulsory joinder of parties takes control over aggregation away from the plaintiffs and offers it to defendants and to the court. Compulsory joinder, however, is exceedingly limited. It requires joinder, where feasible, of such inextricably linked claims as those involving ownership of jointly held property. It does not apply to joint tortfeasors, nor does it apply in general to multiple plaintiffs harmed by a single occurrence. Despite some calls for greater use of compulsory joinder, its use remains the exception. For the vast majority of claims on which lawyers coordinate, none of the parties are "necessary parties" within the meaning of the compulsory joinder rule.

Erichson, *Informal Aggregation*, 50 Duke L.J. at 409–10.

(2) there are questions of law or fact common to the class;

(3) the claims or defenses of the representative parties are typical of the claims or defenses of the class; and

(4) the representative parties will fairly and adequately protect the interests of the class.

(b) Types of Class Actions. A class action may be maintained if Rule 23(a) is satisfied and if:

(1) prosecuting separate actions by or against individual class members would create a risk of:

(A) inconsistent or varying adjudications with respect to individual class members that would establish incompatible standards of conduct for the party opposing the class; or

(B) adjudications with respect to individual class members that, as a practical matter, would be dispositive of the interests of the other members not parties to the individual adjudications or would substantially impair or impede their ability to protect their interests;

(2) the party opposing the class has acted or refused to act on grounds that apply generally to the class, so that final injunctive relief or corresponding declaratory relief is appropriate respecting the class as a whole; or

(3) the court finds that the questions of law or fact common to class members predominate over any questions affecting only individual members, and that a class action is superior to other available methods for fairly and efficiently adjudicating the controversy. The matters pertinent to these findings include:

(A) the class members' interests in individually controlling the prosecution or defense of separate actions;

(B) the extent and nature of any litigation concerning the controversy already begun by or against class members;

(C) the desirability or undesirability of concentrating the litigation of the claims in the particular forum; and

(D) the likely difficulties in managing a class action.

(c) Certification Order; Notice to Class Members; Judgment; Issues Classes; Subclasses.

(1) *Certification Order.*

(A) *Time to Issue.* At an early practicable time after a person sues or is sued as a class representative, the court must determine by order whether to certify the action as a class action.

(B) *Defining the Class; Appointing Class Counsel.* An order that certifies a class action must define the class and the class claims, issues, or defenses, and must appoint class counsel under Rule 23(g).

(C) *Altering or Amending the Order.* An order that grants or denies class certification may be altered or amended before final judgment.

[As originally enacted in 1966, Rule 23(c)(1) provided that: "As soon as practicable after the commencement of an action brought as a class action, the court shall determine by order whether it is to be so maintained. An order under this subdivision may be conditional, and may be altered or amended before the decision on the merits."]

(2) *Notice.*

(A) *For (b)(1) or (b)(2) Classes.* For any class certified under Rule 23(b)(1) or (b)(2), the court may direct appropriate notice to the class.

(B) *For (b)(3) Classes.* For any class certified under Rule 23(b)(3), the court must direct to class members the best notice that is practicable under the circumstances, including individual notice to all members who can be identified through reasonable effort. The notice must clearly and concisely state in plain, easily understood language:

(i) the nature of the action;

(ii) the definition of the class certified;

(iii) the class claims, issues, or defenses;

(iv) that a class member may enter an appearance through an attorney if the member so desires;

(v) that the court will exclude from the class any member who requests exclusion;

(vi) the time and manner for requesting exclusion; and

(vii) the binding effect of a class judgment on members under Rule 23(c)(3).

(3) *Judgment.* Whether or not favorable to the class, the judgment in a class action must:

(A) for any class certified under Rule (b)(1) or (b)(2), include and describe those whom the court finds to be class members; and

(B) for any class certified under Rule 23(b)(3), include and specify or describe those to whom the Rule 23(c)(2) notice was directed, who have not requested exclusion, and whom the court finds to be class members.

(4) *Particular Issues.* When appropriate, an action may be brought or maintained as a class action with respect to particular issues.

(5) *Subclasses.* When appropriate, a class may be divided into subclasses that are each treated as a class under this rule.

[Prior to the 2007 restyling, what now appears as subsections (c)(4) and (c)(5) of the rule appeared as subsections (c)(4)(A) and (c)(4)(B), respectively.]

(d) Conducting the Action.

(1) *In General.* In conducting an action under this rule, the court may issue orders that:

(A) determine the course of proceedings or prescribe measures to prevent undue repetition or complication in presenting evidence or argument;

(B) require—to protect class members and fairly conduct the action—giving appropriate notice to some or all class members of:

(i) any step in the action;

(ii) the proposed extent of the judgment; or

(iii) the members' opportunity to signify whether they consider the representation fair and adequate, to intervene and present claims or defenses, or to otherwise come into the action;

(C) impose conditions on the representative parties or on intervenors;

(D) require that the pleadings be amended to eliminate allegations about representation of absent persons and that the action proceed accordingly; or

(E) deal with similar procedural matters.

(2) **Combining and Amending Orders.** An order under Rule 23(d)(1) may be altered or amended from time to time and may be combined with an order under Rule 16.

(e) Settlement, Voluntary Dismissal, or Compromise. The claims, issues, or defenses of a certified class may be settled, voluntarily dismissed, or compromised only with the court's approval. The following procedures apply to a proposed settlement, voluntary dismissal, or compromise:

(1) The court must direct notice in a reasonable manner to all class members who would be bound by the proposal.

(2) If the proposal would bind class members, the court may approve it only after a hearing and on finding that it is fair, reasonable, and adequate.

(3) The parties seeking approval must file a statement identifying any agreement made in connection with the proposal.

(4) If the class action was previously certified under Rule 23(b)(3), the court may refuse to approve a settlement unless it affords a new opportunity to request exclusion to individual class members who had an earlier opportunity to request exclusion but did not do so.

(5) Any class member may object to the proposal if it requires court approval under this subdivision (e); the objection may be withdrawn only with the court's approval.

> [As originally enacted, Rule 23(e) provided simply that: "A class action shall not be dismissed or compromised without the approval of the court, and notice of the proposed dismissal or compromise shall be given to all members of the class in such manner as the court directs."]

(f) Appeals. A court of appeals may permit an appeal from an order granting or denying class-action certification under this rule if a petition for permission to appeal is filed with the circuit clerk within 14 days after the order is entered. An appeal does not stay proceedings in the district court unless the district judge or the court of appeals so orders.

> [As originally enacted, Rule 23 contained no discussion of appeals from district court class certification orders.]

(g) Class Counsel.

(1) **Appointing Class Counsel.** Unless a statute provides otherwise, a court that certifies a class must appoint class counsel. In appointing class counsel, the court:

(A) must consider:

> (i) the work counsel has done in identifying or investigating potential claims in the action;

> (ii) counsel's experience in handling class actions, other complex litigation, and the types of claims asserted in the action;

> (iii) counsel's knowledge of the applicable law; and

> (iv) the resources that counsel will commit to representing the class;

(B) may consider any other matter pertinent to counsel's ability to fairly and adequately represent the interests of the class;

(C) may order potential class counsel to provide information on any subject pertinent to the appointment and to propose terms for attorney's fees and nontaxable costs;

(D) may include in the appointing order provisions about the award of attorney's fees or nontaxable costs under Rule 23(h); and

(E) may make further orders in connection with the appointment.

(2) *Standard for Appointing Class Counsel.* When one applicant seeks appointment as class counsel, the court may appoint that applicant only if the applicant is adequate under Rule 23(g)(1) and (4). If more than one adequate applicant seeks appointment, the court must appoint the applicant best able to represent the interests of the class.

(3) *Interim Counsel.* The court may designate interim counsel to act on behalf of a putative class before determining whether to certify the action as a class action.

(4) *Duty of Class Counsel.* Class counsel must fairly and adequately represent the interests of the class.

> [As originally enacted, Rule 23 contained no discussion of class counsel.]

(h) Attorney's Fees and Nontaxable Costs. In a certified class action, the court may award reasonable attorney's fees and nontaxable costs that are authorized by law or by the parties' agreement. The following procedures apply:

(1) A claim for an award must be made by motion under Rule 54(d)(2), subject to the provisions of this subdivision (h), at a time the court sets. Notice of the motion must be served on all parties and, for motions by class counsel, directed to class members in a reasonable manner.

(2) A class member, or a party from whom payment is sought, may object to the motion.

(3) The court may hold a hearing and must find the facts and state its legal conclusions under Rule 52(a).

(4) The court may refer issues related to the amount of the award to a special master or a magistrate judge, as provided in Rule 54(d)(2)(D).

> [As originally enacted, Rule 23 contained no discussion of attorney's fee awards.]

NOTES AND QUESTIONS

1. *Comparing Class Actions and Consolidations.* What are the major differences between consolidations under Rule 42(a) and class actions under Rule 23? Consider this question from the standpoint of the court deciding whether to apply a non-contractual aggregation technique, the standpoint of the persons whose claims are to be aggregated, the standpoint of the law firm(s) representing (or that aspire to represent) such persons, and the standpoint of the defendant. Why does Rule 42(a) for consolidations call merely for the existence of "a common question of law or fact," with none of the additional demands made by Rule 23(b)? For a comparison along the foregoing lines, see Charles Silver, *Comparing Class Actions and Consolidations*, 10 Rev. Litig. 495 (1991).

2. *Aggregate Litigation Organized Along a Spectrum.* It is quite common to think about the different forms of aggregate litigation as though they lined up along a spectrum. The typical spectrum puts the individual suit with an attorney hired by a single client at one end, and the class action at the other. Consolidation is placed somewhere in between, closer to one end or the other depending on how the consolidation works. While this way of arranging aggregation techniques is intuitively attractive, it can be analytically helpful only if the dimension or dimensions that define the spectrum are clearly delineated.

One way of defining the spectrum is according to the degree of control a party has over his own lawsuit. It is the party who owns the claim, of course, but it is the lawyer who actually makes the litigation choices. In this sense, litigation involves the separation of ownership from control. While this is true of any lawsuit, it is especially important in large case aggregations where party control can be extremely weak and lawyer control very strong, creating serious risks of attorney self-dealing.

Litigation is not the only area where these problems arise, and it is useful to consult other examples for insights into the problems in litigation. Consider the following analogy to the corporation set forth in language from a preliminary draft of the American Law Institute's project entitled "Principles of the Law of Aggregate Litigation," language which was not ultimately adopted.*

§ 1.04   Separation of Ownership from Control

In all aggregate lawsuits, control of litigation of claims or defenses is separated from ownership of those claims or defenses. Different aggregate lawsuits endow participants with different levels of control over the proceedings.

Comment:

. . .This section focuses on a common structural feature of all [aggregate] lawsuits: the separation of ownership of an interest from

---

* ALI "Principles" track closely the form of the ALI "Restatements" already familiar to you from courses on torts or contracts. Like Restatements, ALI Principles set forth blackletter law followed by explanatory "Comments." When the ALI does blackletter law, it literally appears in black letters—the typographical equivalent, some might say, of the oracular voices of the ALI's distinguished former presidents and directors, such as Charles Alan Wright and Geoffrey Hazard. Unlike Restatements, however, ALI Principles do not purport to restate existing law but, instead, are explicitly normative. They aspire to set forth principles that *should* guide the law in a given area. The subjects selected for treatment by way of a Principles project rather than a Restatement project tend to consist of emerging areas of law. The term "Restatement," after all, implies that there has been some manner of "statement" already, something that may not be true in an emerging area of law.

the management of litigation concerning it. All aggregate lawsuits enable managers, typically attorneys, to influence or control the progress of litigation affecting the interests of diverse participants.. . .

A foundational insight of the economic literature on corporate governance is that ownership of assets and control of their disposition must often be separated to achieve economies of scale, to take advantage of the division and specialization of labor, to bear risks efficiently, and to realize other advantages. When diverse persons contribute assets to a joint undertaking, involving everyone in every decision is inefficient. Equally basic, however, is the understanding that when ownership and control of assets are divided, managers will predictably lack incentives to maximize asset values and may even gain by acting to owners' detriment. Managers' incentives will be defective because they neither bear all the costs of their decisions nor reap all the gains. Although market forces pressure companies to minimize the costs these defective incentives produce (known in the literature as agency costs), the prevailing view is that the costs remain inefficiently high.

Aggregate lawsuits resemble other economic undertakings in which ownership and control of assets rest in different hands. Claimants own the returns aggregate lawsuits generate, and respondents are subject to the liabilities, but agents, mainly attorneys, control or strongly influence the conduct of litigation. Consequently, aggregate lawsuits generate the same potential for agency costs as other economic undertakings in which ownership is separated from control.

The degree of managerial control varies across litigation contexts. In some aggregate lawsuits, managers enjoy considerable control and principals enjoy relatively little. In others, principals' power is greater. . . .

In aggregate lawsuits where the degree of control is high, participants possess the same powers and responsibilities as parties to conventional cases. In theory, they can set terms for collective action as well. When control is minimal, participants (sometimes including named parties) can decide neither how their individual claims or defenses will be litigated nor how the larger group will be run. Usually, represented persons can express themselves only by staying in or opting out, by filing or refusing to file claims, and by objecting or remaining silent. By comparison to the tools parties possess in conventional lawsuits, none of these options is especially efficacious. Cases with moderate control afford participants some important powers but deny them others. For example, they continue to be represented by their own attorneys, and they can accept settlement offers or reject them. But, in important respects, they also are at the mercy of others. They cannot escape aggregation, even when it occurs against their wishes, and, except when they serve as lead parties, they must accept services from and pay fees to lawyers and other persons they have little power to control. . . .

Lawsuits in which participants enjoy extensive or moderate control meet the minimum condition that each member of the aggregate proceeding was named in a lawsuit individually. Lawsuits in which control is minimal do not meet this condition.

For claimants, the condition of having been named in a lawsuit establishes that a person voluntarily decided to assert his or her legal rights. For defendants, being named establishes that a person received notice of a claim and freely chose to appear or default. One cannot be certain these fundamental decisions were made in lawsuits where control is minimal.

The decision to assert a legal right or to defend against a claim usually provides a reliable indication that a person has retained counsel. Although parties frequently represent themselves in some contexts, in aggregate lawsuits they do so rarely. In the case of plaintiffs, retained counsel usually is a lawyer hired pursuant to a contingent fee agreement. This may be a lawyer the client contacted directly or a lawyer to whom the client was referred after retaining a different attorney. Defendants' lawyers, by contrast, usually receive guaranteed fees. This is true when a defendant retains counsel directly and when defense counsel is appointed by an insurer.

When clients participate in ordinary attorney-client relationships with lawyers involved in litigation on their behalf, recognized rules of contract, agency, professional responsibility, and civil procedure enable them to address the many problems that can arise when principals rely on agents for help. Speaking generally, these rules enable clients to deploy incentives and other arrangements that encourage agents to serve their needs well. The clients can select good attorneys, choose fee arrangements that motivate the attorneys to work hard, observe how the attorneys handle their cases, discharge the attorneys for poor performance, sue the attorneys for malpractice, and use control of settlement and other decisions to protect themselves from opportunism and slacking. For plaintiffs, these arrangements encourage lawyers to maximize expected net recoveries, i.e., the amounts plaintiffs expect to retain after fees and other litigation expenses are paid. For defendants, they motivate lawyers to minimize expected total losses, i.e., the sum of payments to claimants and defense costs.

Internal arrangements differ enormously in lawsuits where individual control is low. In these cases, relationships between persons involved in aggregate proceedings and attorneys are creatures of law, not of fact. Participants neither select lawyers nor set payment terms. They are unlikely to monitor the lawyers, especially when claims are small relative to the cost of monitoring or the number of participants encourages free-riding. They cannot tell the lawyers how to handle their cases, they cannot fire the lawyers for disobedience or poor performance, they can rarely if ever sue for malpractice, and they have little control of settlement. Although they want the lawyers to pursue the same welfare-maximizing objectives as participants in cases where individual control is high, by and large they cannot use private orderings to bring this about. They must rely heavily on market forces they do not control and on judges acting as regulators and others acting as monitors to ensure that their interests are well represented.

American Law Institute, PRINCIPLES OF THE LAW OF AGGREGATE LITIGATION § 1.04, at 14–22 (Prelim. Draft No. 3, Aug. 25, 2005).

This account of a spectrum based on degree of party control offers a helpful framework for thinking about the agency-cost problems that haunt aggregate litigation. But it is also important to bear in mind that the paradigmatic attorney-client relationship can produce substantial agency costs of its own even in ordinary individual litigation. The lay client normally knows too little law to monitor and evaluate the attorney's decisions. If the case settles, as most cases do, the attorney is in a position to "sell" the settlement to the client and the client is in a poor position to make an independent judgment. To be sure, professional responsibility rules and malpractice suits control agency costs to some extent, at least when enough clients are able to detect attorney wrongdoing. Attorneys also have a reputational interest in treating clients well, especially when much of their business comes through word of mouth. Market competition exercises a disciplining force as well, although informational asymmetry can weaken market mechanisms. The point is that, while it makes sense to use individual litigation as the baseline for evaluating the agency costs of aggregate litigation, it is also important not to romanticize the baseline.

Moreover, even in a world of perfect agency, a party represented by an attorney of her own choice might still have very limited control over litigation that involves many other parties. When more than one plaintiff or defendant is involved in a lawsuit, each party has to share the litigation stage with the other parties. Moreover, the judge might have to limit the freedom of each party in order to coordinate the actions of the group. As we shall see, judges assigned to oversee large-scale consolidations created through multidistrict litigation often appoint lead counsel and a litigation committee to run the consolidated suit. Lawyers who are not selected for lead counsel or committee membership exercise very little control over the litigation as a practical matter. Therefore, one must be careful about relying on the existence of an attorney-client relationship as a proxy for client control.

One additional point is worth mentioning. Aligning the incentives of the attorney with those of the client can prevent the kind of attorney self-dealing that creates bad outcomes. But it also has another benefit independent of outcome quality: it furthers intrinsic participation values. Many jurists believe that participation through party control has value in itself and that this value promotes procedural justice by enhancing litigant satisfaction with the process and the outcome, respecting the dignity of individual litigants, or supporting the legitimacy of adjudication in a liberal democracy.

Distinguishing between outcome and participation perspectives is important for evaluating aggregation devices. For example, even if procedural controls and judicial supervision were able to guarantee reasonably good outcomes in class actions, one might still object on participation and autonomy grounds, arguing that the class action deprives absent class members of the right to control their own suits. See Martin H. Redish, WHOLESALE JUSTICE: CONSTITUTIONAL DEMOCRACY AND THE PROBLEM OF THE CLASS ACTION LAWSUIT 135-37 (2009).

In sum, aggregate litigation alters the distribution of control, and thus litigating power, within the group. When parties are allowed to litigate individually, they have decisional power over their own suits and freedom to make litigation choices even when those choices affect others adversely—such as by delaying other suits, exhausting a limited fund before other plaintiffs have a chance to recover from it, imposing high costs on the litigation system, and so on. When those same lawsuits are aggregated to avoid these adverse effects, litigating power is redistributed. Some persons, such as the representative party and the attorney in a class action and lead counsel in an MDL, have much more power than others. This redistribution of power must be justified. Other aspects of aggregation must be justified, too, such as forcing members of the group who benefit from the litigation choices of those in charge to contribute to the costs that produced those benefits—typically in the form of attorneys' fees—even when they did not actually consent and might have preferred to litigate on their own.

This problem of justification has a parallel in public governance. The formation of the state aggregates individuals, limits their freedom, and empowers some to govern others. The question of political legitimacy, what justifies the exercise of state power, has, of course, received a great deal of attention over the centuries. Political legitimacy involves some mix of consent, participation, representation, accountability, and other values. And as it turns out, the justifications for case aggregation in litigation depend on similar values. Thus, it can be helpful to draw on political theories of state legitimacy when considering whether a particular mode of aggregation is justified for litigation. Consider the following excerpt from a scholarly article that uses arrangements for public governance to shed light on the structure and legitimacy of the class action:

> [T]wo distinct questions [arise] in the class certification context: the necessity of class treatment to overcome collective action barriers to the prosecution of perceived group harms, and the question of who should control the class action and under what terms. Because these two questions are addressed jointly as part of the certification inquiry, courts have had great difficulty separating their particular attributes. Such disaggregation requires both doctrinal and theoretical sensitivity, and will hopefully shed light on the difficult field of class actions. . . .
>
> The first inquiry concerning the need for collective action follows a well-trod path in political theory. Hobbes and others point out that in the absence of collective security, the pitiable state of nature, there is no individual incentive to industry. Without assurance that each individual will secure the benefits of his or her own toil and initiative, all individuals are reduced jealously to warding off encroachments by potentially rapacious neighbors; each individual cannot invest in the development of property beyond that which can be immediately defended; and each individual is reduced to contracting only for what can be immediately exchanged as transactions into the future cannot be secured. While the existence of such a hypothesized state of nature may be questioned as a historical matter, the antidote to such disorder has been fairly clear. The primary solution has been the creation of a centralized authority, the state, capable of securing to each citizen a security interest in the guarantees of property and the enforceability of exchange. The cost of this centralized authority is then distributed among all the citizens through a system of taxation.
>
> Before moving on to the question of the governance of the state and the equity of the taxation mechanism, it is useful to draw the

analogy to the class action. For present purposes, it is useful to think of the class action mechanism as fundamentally a centralizing device designed to accomplish some of the same functions as performed by the state, particularly in those situations in which the state has not or cannot perform its regulatory function, or it would be inefficient for the state to undertake such regulation directly. In such circumstances, the class action delegates to private individuals the power to lead a diffuse group in a collective endeavor, provide internal equity in the treatment of the group's members, and spread the burden of collectively financing the endeavor across the entire group. It is a mechanism that assures that each individual member will have his interests protected and that each will be taxed for the collective undertaking. The taxation assessed through the class action allows for the selection of an agent, just as the taxation of the polity underwrites the apparatus of government. As expressed by the Supreme Court two decades ago:

> The aggregation of individual claims in a classwide suit is an evolutionary response to the existence of injuries unremedied by the regulatory action of the government. Where it is not economically feasible to obtain relief within the traditional framework of a multiplicity of small individual suits for damages, aggrieved persons may be without any effective redress unless they may employ the class action device.[6]

The analogy to the state then points to the second part of the inquiry: the question of the forms of governance. For Hobbes, recognition of the need for centralized power yielded the assumption that sovereign power must take the form of a monarchy. Without belaboring the point, political theory has progressed quite a bit in the intervening centuries as Locke, Montesquieu, and generations of democratic theorists have pondered the issue of the legitimacy of various forms of governance. All such theories accept the need for collective discipline, but all recognize that this is only the beginning of the inquiry for political legitimacy. The legitimacy of any particular governmental arrangement then turns on the ability to curb oppressive, abusive, or self-serving behavior that may emerge from within the newly created governing class.

This analogy then follows as well into the field of class actions. The very purpose of the class action mechanism is to discipline the individualized members so that they may be regulated and taxed and a governor appointed. . . .

That such an agent is necessary, however, does not answer the question whether any particular agent is acting properly, or whether a presumption of legitimacy should attach to that agent's decision making, or whether the system of taxation and the burdens of sacrifice are equitably distributed. As in democratic theory more broadly, that separate question of governmental legitimacy is extremely problematic. In fact, . . .it is the governance question that is emerging at the heart of the most troublesome class action cases . . ., even in cases in which the need for collective prosecution is relatively clear. . . . [I]t

---

[6] *Deposit Guaranty Bank v. Roper*, 445 U.S. 326, 339 (1980).

is the governmental structures of a class action that define whether representative litigation can satisfy the constitutional requirements of due process.

Samuel Issacharoff, *Governance and Legitimacy in the Law of Class Actions,* 1999 S. Ct. Rev. 337, 337–40.

These insights suggest other dimensions for defining aggregation spectrums. For example, one might order different types of aggregation according to how strongly they rely on consent, representation, or other values for legitimacy and justification. Thus, there could be a consent spectrum, a representation spectrum, and so on. Or one might model the spectrum as a multi-dimensional continuum with each dimension capturing a different value. For example, in individual litigation, consent, participation, and attorney representation with accountability all figure rather strongly in justifying the coercive imposition of an adverse result. At the other extreme lies the class action, which relies much more strongly on representation and accountability than on consent and participation.

Bearing in mind notions of contract in private law and governance in public law, one can go still further to lay out the landscape for aggregate litigation. As noted earlier in this Chapter, the hard fact of civil litigation today is that the vast majority of claims result in settlements of various sorts, not trials. Recognition of settlement as the dominant endgame of litigation, in turn, raises the question: By what authority is the procedure said to lend preclusive effect to a settlement binding on both sides? Consider one possible conceptualization of the continuum between "private" and "public" procedures for claims resolution here:

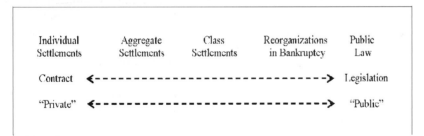

On the left edge are arrangements that draw their binding authority from notions of individual autonomy and consent under the private law of contracts. Conventional, individual settlements in litigation are the paradigm here, and the level of judicial scrutiny accorded to such settlements—none—accords with the premise that they simply are matters of private contract. On the right edge is public law—say, the federal compensation fund legislation enacted by Congress as an alternative to litigation against the airlines that operated the ill-fated flights of September 11, 2001. Air Transportation Safety and System Stabilization Act, Pub. L. No. 107–42, 115 Stat. 230 (2001). There is little debate at a fundamental level about the binding authority of public law (or administrative regulations issued under its auspices), just as there is little debate over the binding authority of a conventional, individual settlement. The authority of public law rests on notions of consent at the more abstract, collective level of legislation rather than the kind of consent involved in the private law of contracts.

The public-private continuum helps to pinpoint that the arrangements most interesting and, at the same time, most problematic consist of those between the two poles of contract and legislation. Moving from left to right among these middle-range options, one might locate the sorts of aggregate settlements mentioned earlier. The notion that supplies binding authority here is, once again, one of private contract, with the additional overlay of the aggregate settlement rule.

Class actions dispense with notions of contractual consent in private law, occupying a murky middle ground between the poles of "private" contract and "public" legislation. Might this account of the class action in institutional terms explain why that device has garnered so much attention—for some observers, such consternation?

Moving still further to the right from class actions, one might place bankruptcy proceedings—in particular, binding resolution of claims as part of a reorganization of the defendant under Chapter 11 of the Bankruptcy Code. These are explored—albeit, selectively—in Chapter 5. Unlike class actions that take the form of Article III cases, bankruptcy proceedings garner much of their authority to bind from an express grant of federal regulatory power to Congress in Article I of the Constitution. Unlike the most common form of class action, moreover, bankruptcy permits no opt outs. Rather, it approaches public legislation in its capacity to enforce on all creditors the terms of the reorganization plan upon judicial confirmation.

A continuum along the preceding lines highlights the difficulty with calls for abolition of the class action. Getting rid of class actions would not rid the civil justice system of the need for some means of collective resolution for the kinds of mass-dispersed claims that characterize modern industrial societies. Rather, abolition of class actions might well just move the ballgame to proximate means of aggregation along the continuum—to aggregate settlements or to bankruptcy. As we shall in Chapter 5, this is basically what has happened with asbestos litigation.

3. AGGREGATION NEITHER CONTRACTUAL NOR WHOLLY NON–CONTRACTUAL

Finally, one should not come away with the impression that the categories of aggregation by contract and aggregation that is entirely non-contractual cover the entire landscape. Rather, there are important hybrids between the two familiar forms—nooks, crannies, and cubbyholes, if you will, between the categories of the continuum.

As Chapter 5 shall elaborate, one way to inform the design of aggregate settlements for large numbers of related claimants is by—shockingly enough—actually conducting conventional, full-fledged individual trials for a small number of similar claims. Courts and commentators encapsulate this approach in the notion of "bellwether" trials. The term derives from a bellwether sheep—one with an actual bell around its neck so as to lead a larger flock. Alexandra D. Lahav, *Bellwether Trials*, 76 Geo. Wash. L. Rev. 576, 577 (2008). Here, the idea is not necessarily for the judgment in the bellwether cases to have preclusive effect upon other similar claimants. *Taylor*, of course, considerably restricts such preclusion with regard to nonparties to the tried actions. Rather, the notion is for the results in the tried cases to inform the design of a settlement "grid" for the much larger number of remaining actions. The grid then might form the basis for aggregate settlements that encompass those claimants. In practical effect, then, a bellwether trial—though formally an individual proceeding—can do more work than just the resolution of that particular case. In effect, bellwether trials can form the informational basis for subsequent aggregate settlements of similar claims.

One way to do this is to sort the bellwether cases by general type according to easily verifiable features (such as type of disease or injury) and then average the results of the bellwether trials for each type. The average figure serves as an estimate of the value of the corresponding type of claim. Each remaining claimant, in effect, gets the expected value of her claim. (For more on expected value, see Chapter 4.) One of the things this does is spread the risk of trial loss over all similar claims. This notion of a settlement grid that spreads the risk over the entire run of similar claims carries forward notions familiar to regimes such as workers' compensation. Widely implemented in the United States in the early twentieth century, workers' compensation effectively removed workplace-related injuries from the common-law tort system and placed them in an administrative, grid-like compensation framework that has continued in public law—primarily, at the state level—to the present day. On the intellectual affinity between workers' compensation and aggregate settlements for modern-day mass claims, see Samuel Issacharoff & John Fabian Witt, *The Inevitability of Aggregate Settlement: An Institutional Account of American Tort Law*, 57 Vand. L. Rev. 1571 (2004).

As you might guess, the plausibility of bellwether trials as a prelude to grid design turns upon the representativeness of the subset of cases in which full-fledged trials occur. If the tried cases consist of an unrepresentative sample of the overall run of claims—say, too many atypically strong claims—then the average of the trial outcomes will not reflect an accurate assessment of the value of the remaining claims. But even when sampling might not necessarily satisfy the rigorous standards of statistical analysis, the information revealed by way of bellwether trials might be sufficient—if only in a roughhewn way—to inform grid design. And, of course, there is generally no judicial review for fairness with respect to non-class settlements, just the ethical stricture of the aggregate settlement rule.

A related kind of hybrid builds further on the notion of bellwether trials. As noted, after such trials, one might seek to resolve the remaining, similar claims by way of aggregate settlements. And those settlements ultimately will take a contractual form: the release executed by the individual settling claimant in exchange for payment from the defendant. But this is not the only vehicle for resolution of the remaining claims. Rather, that vehicle instead might take another form: a contract not with the settling claimant (reflecting the ultimate cashing-out of her claim) but, rather, a contract with plaintiffs' law firms who represent such claimants in substantial numbers.

The usual move here is for the firms to agree to "recommend" to their individual clients that they settle their claims against the defendant according to the terms of the grid. The defendant then promises to pay claims presented to it by the signatory firms according to the terms agreed upon for the grid. In this way, the contract between the defendant and the plaintiffs' law firms effectively anticipates the terms of later, conventional settlement contracts that will resolve the claims of the clients those firms represent. As Chapter 5 shall discuss, the settlement that resolved litigation over the prescription pain reliever Vioxx took precisely this form—in part, interestingly enough, because of the difficulties that would have been presented by an effort to achieve closure by way of a class settlement.

CHAPTER 2

THE CLASS CERTIFICATION DECISION

This chapter explores in depth the judicial decision to certify a civil action to proceed as a class action—or, in the parlance of Rule 23, for "[o]ne or more members of a class" to sue "as representative parties on behalf of all" class members. Section A starts by analyzing the significance of the class certification decision for plaintiff class members and defendants, respectively, and for how procedural law should conceptualize the class itself. Section B discusses the general requirements for class certification in Rule 23(a). Section C delineates the different types of class actions authorized by Rule 23, starting with opt-out classes and then turning to the various forms of mandatory classes. Also discussed in Section C are class actions confined to a particular issue or issues within a larger litigation. These so-called issue classes may be either mandatory or opt-out in nature.

The later sections of the Chapter turn to a series of topics related to class certification. Section D discusses the debate over what the court may consider—in particular, the authority of the court to consider matters related to the substantive merits of the litigation—as part of its class certification decision, as well as the debate over the proper standard of proof for certification. Section E discusses various recent developments concerning the selection of class counsel as part of the class certification decision, including subsection (g) of Rule 23, added in 2003. Section F addresses defendant classes in which the persons aligned as defendants in the action may be sued on a class-wide basis. Finally, Section G concludes with a discussion of whether state-law limits on class certification should apply in federal class litigation.

A. THE SIGNIFICANCE OF THE CLASS CERTIFICATION DECISION

1. SIGNIFICANCE FOR PLAINTIFF CLASS MEMBERS

Hansberry v. Lee
311 U.S. 32 (1940)

■ MR. JUSTICE STONE delivered the opinion of the Court.

The question is whether the Supreme Court of Illinois, by its adjudication that petitioners in this case are bound by a judgment rendered in an earlier litigation to which they were not parties, has deprived them of the due process of law guaranteed by the Fourteenth Amendment.

Respondents brought this suit in the Circuit Court of Cook County, Illinois, to enjoin the breach by petitioners of an agreement restricting the use of land within a described area of the City of Chicago, which was alleged to have been entered into by some five hundred of the land owners.

The agreement stipulated that for a specified period no part of the land should be "sold, leased to or permitted to be occupied by any person of the colored race", and provided that it should not be effective unless signed by the "owners of 95 per centum of the frontage" within the described area. The bill of complaint set up that the owners of 95 per cent of the frontage had signed; that respondents are owners of land within the restricted area who have either signed the agreement or acquired their land from others who did sign and that petitioners Hansberry, who are Negroes, have, with the alleged aid of the other petitioners and with knowledge of the agreement, acquired and are occupying land in the restricted area formerly belonging to an owner who had signed the agreement.

To the defense that the agreement had never become effective because owners of 95 per cent of the frontage had not signed it, respondents pleaded that that issue was res judicata by the decree in an earlier suit. *Burke v. Kleiman*, 277 Ill. App. 519 (1934). To this petitioners pleaded, by way of rejoinder, that they were not parties to that suit or bound by its decree, and that denial of their right to litigate, in the present suit, the issue of performance of the condition precedent to the validity of the agreement would be a denial of due process of law guaranteed by the Fourteenth Amendment. It does not appear, nor is it contended that any of petitioners is the successor in interest to or in privity with any of the parties in the earlier suit.

The circuit court, after a trial on the merits, found that owners of only about 54 per cent of the frontage had signed the agreement, and that the only support of the judgment in the *Burke* case was a false and fraudulent stipulation of the parties that 95 per cent had signed. But it ruled that the issue of performance of the condition precedent to the validity of the agreement was res judicata as alleged and entered a decree for respondents. The Supreme Court of Illinois affirmed. We granted certiorari to resolve the constitutional question.

The Supreme Court of Illinois, upon an examination of the record in *Burke v. Kleiman*, supra, found that that suit, in the Superior Court of Cook County, was brought by a landowner in the restricted area to enforce the agreement which had been signed by her predecessor in title, in behalf of herself and other property owners in like situation, against four named individuals who had acquired or asserted an interest in a plot of land formerly owned by another signer of the agreement; that upon stipulation of the parties in that suit that the agreement had been signed by owners of 95 per cent of all the frontage, the court had adjudged that the agreement was in force, that it was a covenant running with the land and binding all the land within the described area in the hands of the parties to the agreement and those claiming under them including defendants, and had entered its decree restraining the breach of the agreement by the defendants and those claiming under them, and that the appellate court had affirmed the decree. It found that the stipulation was untrue but held, contrary to the trial court, that it was not fraudulent or collusive. It also appears from the record in *Burke v. Kleiman* that the case was tried on an agreed statement of facts which raised only a single issue, whether by reason of changes in the restricted area, the agreement had ceased to be enforceable in equity.

From this the Supreme Court of Illinois concluded in the present case that *Burke v. Kleiman* was a "class" or "representative" suit and that in such a suit "where the remedy is pursued by a plaintiff who has the right to represent the class to which he belongs, other members of the class are bound by the results in the case unless it is reversed or set aside on direct proceedings,"372 Ill. 369, that petitioners in the present suit were members of the class represented by the plaintiffs in the earlier suit and consequently were bound by its decree which had rendered the issue of performance of the condition precedent to the restrictive agreement res judicata, so far as petitioners are concerned. The court thought that the circumstance that the stipulation in the earlier suit that owners of 95 per cent of the frontage had signed the agreement was contrary to the fact as found in the present suit did not militate against this conclusion since the court in the earlier suit had jurisdiction to determine the fact as between the parties before it and that its determination, because of the representative character of the suit, even though erroneous, was binding on petitioners until set aside by a direct attack on the first judgment.

State courts are free to attach such descriptive labels to litigations before them as they may choose and to attribute to them such consequences as they think appropriate under state constitutions and laws, subject only to the requirements of the Constitution of the United States. But when the judgment of a state court, ascribing to the judgment of another court the binding force and effect of res judicata, is challenged for want of due process it becomes the duty of this Court to examine the course of procedure in both litigations to ascertain whether the litigant whose rights have thus been adjudicated has been afforded such notice and opportunity to be heard as are requisite to the due process which the Constitution prescribes.

It is a principle of general application in Anglo–American jurisprudence that one is not bound by a judgment in personam in a litigation in which he is not designated as a party or to which he has not been made a party by service of process. *Pennoyer v. Neff,* 95 U.S. 714 (1877). A judgment rendered in such circumstances is not entitled to the full faith and credit which the Constitution and statute of the United States prescribe, *id.* , and judicial action enforcing it against the person or property of the absent party is not that due process which the Fifth and Fourteenth Amendments require.

To these general rules there is a recognized exception that, to an extent not precisely defined by judicial opinion, the judgment in a "class" or "representative" suit, to which some members of the class are parties, may bind members of the class or those represented who were not made parties to it.

The class suit was an invention of equity to enable it to proceed to a decree in suits where the number of those interested in the subject of the litigation is so great that their joinder as parties in conformity to the usual rules of procedure is impracticable. Courts are not infrequently called upon to proceed with causes in which the number of those interested in the litigation is so great as to make difficult or impossible the joinder of all because some are not within the jurisdiction or because their whereabouts is unknown or where if all were made parties to the suit its continued abatement by the death of some would prevent or unduly delay a decree. In such cases where the interests of those not joined are of the same class as the interests of those who are, and where it is considered that the latter fairly represent the former in the prosecution of the litigation of the issues in which all have a common interest, the court will proceed to a decree.

It is evident that the considerations which may induce a court thus to proceed, despite a technical defect of parties, may differ from those which must be taken into account in determining whether the absent parties are bound by the decree or, if it is adjudged that they are, in ascertaining whether such an adjudication satisfies the requirements of due process and of full faith and credit. Nevertheless there is scope within the framework of the Constitution for holding in appropriate cases that a judgment rendered in a class suit is res judicata as to members of the class who are not formal parties to the suit. Here, as elsewhere, the Fourteenth Amendment does not compel state courts or legislatures to adopt any particular rule for establishing the conclusiveness of judgments in class suits; nor does it compel the adoption of the particular rules thought by this court to be appropriate for the federal courts. With a proper regard for divergent local institutions and interests, this Court is justified in saying that there has been a failure of due process only in those cases where it cannot be said that the procedure adopted, fairly insures the protection of the interests of absent parties who are to be bound by it.

It is familiar doctrine of the federal courts that members of a class not present as parties to the litigation may be bound by the judgment where they are in fact adequately represented by parties who are present, or where they actually participate in the conduct of the litigation in which members of the class are present as parties, or where the interest of the members of the class, some of whom are present as parties, is joint, or where for any other reason the relationship between the parties present and those who are absent is such as legally to entitle the former to stand in judgment for the latter.

In all such cases, so far as it can be said that the members of the class who are present are, by generally recognized rules of law, entitled to stand in judgment for those who are not, we may assume for present purposes that such procedure affords a protection to the parties who are represented though absent, which would satisfy the requirements of due process and full faith and credit. Nor do we find it necessary for the decision of this case to say that, when the only circumstance defining the class is that the determination of the rights of its members turns upon a single issue of fact or law, a state could not constitutionally adopt a procedure whereby some of the members of the class could stand in judgment for all, provided that the procedure were so devised and applied as to insure that those present are of the same class as those absent and that the litigation is so conducted as to insure the full and fair consideration of the common issue. We decide only that the procedure and the course of litigation sustained here by the plea of res judicata do not satisfy these requirements.

The restrictive agreement did not purport to create a joint obligation or liability. If valid and effective its promises were the several obligations of the signers and those claiming under them. The promises ran severally to every other signer. It is plain that in such circumstances all those alleged to be bound by the agreement would not constitute a single class in any litigation brought to enforce it. Those who sought to secure its benefits by enforcing it could not be said to be in the same class with or represent those whose interest was in resisting performance, for the agreement by its terms imposes obligations and confers rights on the owner of each plot of land who signs it. If those who thus seek to secure the benefits of the agreement were rightly regarded by the state Supreme Court as constituting a class, it is evident that those signers or their successors who are interested in challenging the validity of the agreement and resisting its performance are not of the same class in the sense that their interests are identical so that any group who had elected to enforce rights conferred by the agreement could be said to be acting in the interest of any others who were free to deny its obligation.

Because of the dual and potentially conflicting interests of those who are putative parties to the agreement in compelling or resisting its performance, it is impossible to say, solely because they are parties to it, that any two of them are of the same class. Nor without more, and with the due regard for the protection of the rights of absent parties which due process exacts, can some be permitted to stand in judgment for all.

It is one thing to say that some members of a class may represent other members in a litigation where the sole and common interest of the class in the litigation, is either to assert a common right or to challenge an asserted obligation. It is quite another to hold that all those who are free alternatively either to assert rights or to challenge them are of a single class, so that any group merely because it is of the class so constituted, may be deemed adequately to represent any others of the class in litigating their interests in either alternative. Such a selection of representatives for purposes of litigation, whose substantial interests are not necessarily or even probably the same as those whom they are deemed to represent, does not afford that protection to absent parties which due process requires. The doctrine of representation of absent parties in a class suit has not hitherto been thought to go so far. Apart from the opportunities it would afford for the fraudulent and collusive sacrifice of the rights of absent parties, we think that the representation in this case no more satisfies the requirements of due process than a trial by a judicial officer who is in such situation that he may have an interest in the outcome of the litigation in conflict with that of the litigants.

The plaintiffs in the *Burke* case sought to compel performance of the agreement in behalf of themselves and all others similarly situated. They did not designate the defendants in the suit as a class or seek any injunction or other relief against others than the named defendants, and the decree which was entered did not purport to bind others. In seeking to enforce the agreement the plaintiffs in that suit were not representing the petitioners here whose substantial interest is in resisting performance. The defendants in the first suit were not treated by the pleadings or decree as representing others or as foreclosing by their defense the rights of others, and even though nominal defendants, it does not appear that their interest in defeating the contract outweighed their interest in establishing its validity. For a court in this situation to ascribe to either the plaintiffs or defendants the performance of such functions on behalf of petitioners here, is to attribute to them a power that it cannot be said that they had assumed to exercise, and a responsibility which, in view of their dual interests it does not appear that they could rightly discharge.

Reversed.

NOTES AND QUESTIONS

1. The Constitutionality of Racially Restrictive Covenants. Today, the type of restrictive covenant at issue in *Hansberry* would be unenforceable under the Equal Protection Clause. The legal status of such covenants at the time of *Hansberry*, however, was uncertain. Decades earlier, the Court had invalidated racially restrictive zoning ordinances. *Buchanan v. Warley*, 245 U.S. 60 (1917). But the holding in *Buchanan* left open the possibility that property owners might impose similar sorts of racial restrictions by way of private contracts.

Indeed, in 1926, the Court itself had dismissed for want of a substantial federal question an appeal from a D.C. Circuit decision upholding the constitutionality of racially restrictive covenants. *Corrigan v. Buckley*, 299 F. 899 (D.C. Cir. 1924), appeal dismissed, 271 U.S. 323 (1926).

In *Hansberry*, the Supreme Court did not strike down racially restrictive covenants as unconstitutional, though the defendants had urged the Court to do so. Rather, the *Hansberry* Court left undisturbed the Illinois courts' determination that racially restrictive covenants were valid and enforceable as a matter of Illinois property law at the time—specifically, that such covenants "run with the land" and, as such, bind not only the original signatories but also those who purchase from such persons property covered by the covenant. A Supreme Court decision holding racially restrictive covenants unenforceable on constitutional grounds would come eight years later, in *Shelley v. Kraemer*, 334 U.S. 1 (1948).

2. *The Hansberry Family*. The Hansberry name should be familiar to those of you with a background in theater or American literature. Petitioner Carl Hansberry's daughter Lorraine went on to a distinguished literary career, authoring the play A RAISIN IN THE SUN and the personal memoir TO BE YOUNG, GIFTED, AND BLACK.

3. *The Proceedings in* Burke v. Kleiman. The issue in *Hansberry* concerns the asserted preclusive effect of the judgment entered in *Burke v. Kleiman*. In its opinion in *Hansberry*, the Illinois Supreme Court described the *Burke* complaint as follows:

> Olive Ida Burke, wife of James J. Burke, . . . was plaintiff. The complaint recited that she filed it "on behalf of herself and on behalf of all other property owners in the district covered and affected by the [restrictive covenant], and who are, or whose grantors, direct or otherwise, were parties to said indenture of agreement, and whose property interests will be adversely and injuriously affected by the violation hereinafter mentioned by the said defendants of the covenants and terms of said agreement."

Lee v. Hansberry, 24 N.E.2d 37, 39 (Ill. 1939). Does the reference to adverse effect upon "property interests" capture fully the reasons why a given white property owner might or might not favor the enforcement of a racially restrictive covenant in her neighborhood?

In *Burke*, the plaintiff class of property owners challenged a transaction whereby the defendant Kleiman had rented an apartment to an African–American. Did defense counsel make a tactical blunder by agreeing to stipulate that the precondition stated in the restrictive covenant—signature by 95 percent of the property owners in the neighborhood—had been satisfied? As a factual matter, there remains considerable uncertainty as to whether the requisite owners of 95% of the subdivision's frontage had signed the covenant, a question explored in Jay Tidmarsh, *The Story of* Hansberry: *The Rise of the Modern Class Action*, in CIVIL PROCEDURE STORIES 233, 265–67 (Kevin M. Clermont, 2nd ed. 2008). On the merits, the defense in *Burke* did not contend that the precondition stated in the restrictive covenant had not been satisfied; rather, the defense argued that circumstances in the neighborhood had so dramatically changed in the meantime as to make the covenant no longer binding. The *Hansberry* Court notes that the Illinois trial judge found the stipulation in

Burke to be "false and fraudulent." The Illinois Supreme Court, while agreeing that the stipulation was inaccurate, disagreed that it was false and fraudulent. There are some strong indications in the historical record that *Burke* was a fraudulent and collusive suit. Tidmarsh, *The Story of* Hansberry, at 267–70 (noting that whether *Burke* was a fraudulent and collusive suit is "the hardest question of all to answer," but expressing an opinion that it was not "fraudulent or collusive—or at least that the *Hansberry* defendants never proved it to be so at trial").

The proceedings in *Burke*, moreover, diverged from what is now familiar practice in modern class actions:

> . . . [I]llinois class-action decisions of the period required no fur-
> ther action beyond pleading a claim as a class action. In particular,
> the notion of an order certifying a class was unheard of; as long as the
> bill of complaint contained allegations that the case was brought on
> behalf of others, stated that the class had common rights that were in
> need of protection, and showed that the case was in the class's inter-
> ests, the case was regarded as a class action. Illinois courts often did
> not make the determination that a case was in fact a class action un-
> til a party in a second lawsuit argued that an opposing party was a
> class member bound by the judgment in the first case. Indeed, the
> *Hansberry* defendants never claimed that the trial court's failure to
> certify *Burke* as a class action was a legal defect in the case.

Id. at 265 (footnote omitted).

4.   *A Brief History of the Class Action.* What we now call the "class action" used to be called the "representative suit," and the Illinois practice described in the previous quotation was typical of representative suit procedure
at the time. The history is complex, too complex to recount in detail here. Nevertheless, it's important to understand some of the more salient aspects, especially distinctions between the representative suit and the modern class action,
in order to appreciate why the class action is so controversial today. Notwithstanding their historical connection, the representative suit and the modern
class action are, in fact, quite different devices.

There are several useful histories of the class action. Professor Stephen
Yeazell has written what is primarily a social and economic history of group
litigation and the representation idea. Stephen C. Yeazell, FROM MEDIEVAL
GROUP LITIGATION TO THE MODERN CLASS ACTION (1987). He describes how
eighteenth and nineteenth century representative suit law developed as a judicial response to the litigating needs of new groups, such as friendly societies
and joint stock companies, that became salient with the rise of market capital-
ism and other changing economic and social conditions. The result, he claims, is
an internally contradictory body of law anchored historically to particular
groups and social concerns and shaped by the tension between group litigation
and the commitment to individualism and party autonomy in litigation. Professor Robert Bone provides an intellectual history that focuses on the legal ideas
and beliefs that shaped the traditional representative suit and modern class
action. Robert G. Bone, *Personal and Impersonal Litigative Forms: Reconceiv-
ing the History of Adjudicative Representation (Review Essay)*, 70 B.U. L. Rev.
213 (1990). For other useful historical accounts of different aspects of class action history, see David Marcus, *Flawed but Noble: Desegregation Litigation and
Its Implications for the Modern Class Action*, 63 Fla. L. Rev. 657 (2011); Geof-

frey C. Hazard, Jr., John L. Gedid & Stephen Sowle, *An Historical Analysis of the Binding Effect of Class Suits*, 146 U. Pa. L. Rev. 1848 (1998).

The following brief summary is based on Professor Bone's work. The representative suit was created by the English courts of equity. Its primary purpose was not to bind absentees. Rather, it was to allow a plaintiff to proceed with his individual suit and obtain as complete a decree as possible without joining necessary parties when those parties were too numerous to be easily joined. In other words, the representative suit was an exception to the rather restrictive necessary-party rules in equity. See Bone, *Personal and Impersonal Litigative Forms*, 70 B.U. L. Rev. at 242–54.

According to this representative suit exception, absent necessary parties did not have to be joined when they and the representative plaintiff all shared "one common interest" in the suit. *Id.* at 245. "Common interest," however, did not refer to shared goals or preferences. Instead, it referred to formal relationships among legal rights, duties, and remedies. Roughly, absent necessary parties did not have to be joined when the representative plaintiff's legal right was formally identical to their legal rights, or connected in a technical way so that the plaintiff could be said to represent the absentees' rights as well as his own. *Id.* at 245–49. This was the sense in which the suit was "representative." The term "representative" referred to a relationship between lawsuits, not between parties. A suit was "representative" not because the plaintiff represented others in the sense of acting for them and taking their interests into account. Instead, the suit was representative in the sense that it was *like* the other suits "because it implicated the same abstract configuration of legal rights and duties." *Id.* at 242. For example, a taxpayer suit challenging a town's issuance of a bond as ultra vires qualified as a representative suit because each individual taxpayer's lawsuit alleged the identical legal right to lawful government action that all taxpayers shared in common. Accordingly, each suit was a formal replica of all the others insofar as right and remedy were concerned—and therefore "representative" in that sense. There was no need for a plaintiff to join other taxpayers because the plaintiff was able to bring the common right before the court.

Two important points emerge from this brief account. First, the fact that a suit qualified as a representative suit did not necessarily imply a res judicata effect. What it meant was that the plaintiff could proceed without joining necessary parties and the court could enter a decree that formally affected the rights of absentees. Whether those absent right holders were bound to the decree was a separate question determined in an absentee's later suit and decided by applying res judicata rules. As it turned out, some—though not all— representative suits did bind absentees, but they did so because of the nature of the legal rights involved and not because the plaintiff litigated for others in a fiduciary sense.

Second, the plaintiff triggered the representative suit exception by alleging that he sued "on behalf of" all those who shared the same "common interest." There was no special procedure, such as the certification stage of the modern class action. The chancellor got involved if the defendant raised an objection for failure to join necessary parties, thereby challenging the application of the representative suit exception. In that event, the chancellor decided whether the suit qualified as a "representative suit" by inspecting the formal structure of the legal rights. Since the representative suit determination had no necessary implications for res judicata, there was usually no need to check whether the plaintiff would litigate vigorously or whether the plaintiff shared the same goals or preferences for the litigation as the absent necessary parties.

If a party to a later suit relied on the earlier representative suit for a res judicata bar, the later judge had to determine whether the earlier suit qualified as the type of representative suit that had res judicata effect. But even then, the judge usually focused on the formal rights structure of the earlier lawsuit. In effect, the court relied on the self-interest of the representative to assure vigorous litigation of the legal rights he shared in common with everyone else. On occasion, judges did remark on representational adequacy, but usually only when there was some special reason to be concerned that the plaintiff might have failed to litigate in good faith. The important point is that there was no formal certification procedure, as there is today. *Id.* at 284–87.

The original version of Rule 23 was adopted in 1938, along with the rest of the Federal Rules of Civil Procedure. This version tracked the rights-based formalism of the eighteenth and nineteenth century representative suit prece- . dent. For example, Rule 23(a) stated:

> **(a) Representation**. If persons constituting a class are so numerous as to make it impracticable to bring them all before the court, such of them, one or more, as will fairly insure the adequate representation of all may, on behalf of all, sue or be sued, when the character of the right sought to be enforced for or against the class is
>
> > (1) joint or common, or secondary in the sense that the owner of a primary right refuses to enforce that right and a member of the class thereby becomes entitled to enforce it;
> >
> > (2) several, and the object of the action is the adjudication of claims which do or may affect specific property involved in the action; or
> >
> > (3) several, and there is a common question of law or fact affecting the several rights and a common relief is sought.

Moreover, the preclusive effect of the class action depended on the rights-based category to which it belonged. Class actions fitting in (a)(1)—so-called "true class actions"—bound everyone in the class. Class actions in (a)(2) involving several rights and specific property—so-called "hybrid class actions"— bound class members only with respect to the property at issue. Class actions in (a)(3)—so-called "spurious class actions"—had no binding effect at all, except for the representative parties and those class members who chose to intervene. See James Wm. Moore & Marcus Cohn, *Federal Class Actions–Jurisdiction and Effect of Judgment*, 32 Ill. L. Rev. 555, 556–63 (1938).

This was the state of class action law when *Hansberry v. Lee* was decided. Many states, like Illinois, still followed some version of traditional representative suit doctrine. The federal courts applied Rule 23, but without a clear understanding of its rights-based classifications. See Fed. R. Civ. P. 23, advisory committee's note (1966).

Thus, the Illinois courts treated *Burke v. Kleiman* as a representative suit in accordance with conventional representative suit law. The fact that the judge in *Burke* did not formally certify a class or check whether the plaintiffs were adequate representatives is hardly surprising, since that was not a regular part of the traditional representative suit procedure.

Many courts and commentators who cite *Hansberry* for the principle that absent class members can be precluded when their interests—meaning something like litigation preferences, goals, or stakes—are adequately represented ignore the opinion's more formalistic language. The Supreme Court makes a point of stating that the restrictive covenant at issue in *Burke* created "several" obligations and "did not purport to create a joint obligation or liability." *Hansberry*, 311 U.S. at 44. As a result, the property owners were not sufficiently unified *in a formal legal way* to "constitute a single class" justifying preclusion. *Id.* But the Court does not rely on the formal analysis alone, and this is, of course, why *Hansberry* is such an important opinion. The Court weaves the formalistic argument together with the interest representation idea. The Court refers to the jointness of the right, the joinder of a party, *or* adequate representation as alternative bases for binding a party to a judgment. While the 1938 version of Rule 23 also required the "adequate representation of all," it did so in conjunction with limiting the class action to particular types of formal legal rights. *Hansberry* suggested that adequate representation of interests itself might be sufficient to bind absentees consistent with due process, and thereby ushered in the modern class action. Robert G. Bone, *Rethinking the "Day in Court" Ideal and Nonparty Preclusion*, 67 N.Y.U. L. Rev. 193, 215 n.73 (1992) (arguing that *Hansberry* is best viewed as a transitional opinion "tentatively launch[ing] the interest representation idea at the same time as [holding] fast to the nineteenth century precedent.").

The class action did not assume its modern form in a clear and definitive way until the 1966 revision of Rule 23. The 1966 revision jettisoned the formalistic rights-based framework and replaced it with a more functional and pragmatic approach. Most importantly, it established the class action as an aggregation and preclusion device and placed the concept of representing common interests at its core.

5. *Olive and James Burke.* Hansberry came to purchase property in a neighborhood covered by a racially restrictive covenant not only through his own efforts but also with the assistance of various whites. According to the complaint in *Hansberry*, several whites—including James Burke—had, by "fraudulent concealment," led the First National Bank to convey title to straw purchasers for conveyance, in turn, to Hansberry. James Burke was none other than the husband of Olive Burke, the named plaintiff in *Burke v. Kleiman*.

Why might a white couple like the Burkes have changed their views on the enforcement of a racially restrictive covenant in their neighborhood? Note that the restrictive covenant in *Hansberry* purportedly went into effect in 1928 but that the conveyance to Hansberry did not take place until 1937. Note also that the record in *Hansberry* includes a casual remark, attributed to James Burke, to the effect that he had obtained a real estate license in early 1937. Tidmarsh, *The Story of* Hansberry, at 248.

6. *The Baseline of Individual Autonomy and the Nature of the Class.* Does *Hansberry* proceed from a faulty, or at least misleading, baseline of individual autonomy for class members? Here, recall the analogies to governance in its private-law and public-law forms discussed in Chapter 1. Is the class simply the sum of its constituent parts—the individual class members who comprise it—or does the class take on an existence of its own? One commentator suggests that the law should conceptualize the class itself as a distinct entity:

In the interest of oversimplification, take two models of "group litigation." The first—what might be called the aggregation model—sees the various joinder devices, including the class action, as essentially techniques for allowing individuals to achieve the benefits of pooling resources against a common adversary. Under this view, the individual who is part of the aggregate surrenders as little autonomy as possible (although some sacrifices are undoubtedly inevitable if the group effort is to have any utility and to afford any economies of scale). Thus the individual retains his own counsel, retains the right to leave the group before, during, and after the litigation, and can insist on playing a significant role in the operations of the group so long as he chooses to remain a part of that group.

The second . . . I call the "entity" model. In this view, which is clearly more appropriate in the class action context than in the context of such other joinder devices as consolidation or even massive intervention, the entity is the litigant and the client. Moreover, in the situations in which class action treatment is warranted, the individual who is a member of the class, for whatever purpose, is and must remain a member of that class, and as a result must tie his fortunes to those of the group with respect to the litigation, its progress, and its outcome. Of course, even this entity model does not deny the class member the opportunity to seek private advice, or to contribute in some way to the progress of the litigation, but it severely limits such aspects of individual autonomy as the range of choice to move in or out of the class or to be represented before the court by counsel entirely of one's own selection.

Neither of these models may exist in its unadulterated form in the real world of litigation at the present time, nor may they ever exist in such form. But they help to pose the conflict that in my view is both immanent and imminent—a conflict that has already engaged the energies of courts and commentators at least since the reemergence of the class action in the 1960s. . . .

As even the casual reader has probably already gleaned, my conclusion is that of the two models outlined above, the second (of the class as entity) is the more appropriate in the class action setting. . . .

This conclusion is not quite so radical as it may seem at first, since the idea of the collectivity as an entity is a familiar one in other settings. Thus, a whole range of voluntary private associations—congregations, trade unions, joint stock companies, corporations—and on a less "voluntary" level, municipalities and other governmental entities, have long been recognized as litigants in their own right—entities whose members may have at best only a limited say in what is litigated, in who represents the organization, and on what terms the controversy is ultimately resolved. Indeed, the rise of those organizations has been noted as one of the reasons for the decline of the class action from the mid-eighteenth to the mid-twentieth century.

The most helpful starting point may reside in the "small claim" class action—an action defined here to embrace those cases in which the claim of any individual class member for harm done is too small to provide any rational justification to the individual for incurring the

costs of litigation. As an example of such a case, take a claim on behalf of many purchasers that defendants have engaged in a price-
fixing conspiracy to violate the federal antitrust laws. . . .

In such cases, I submit—and some others who would certainly
not go beyond this point may well agree—that the soundest approach
is to view the cause of action as essentially a group claim fitting the
characteristics of the second model, with all the consequences that
entails. . . . The purpose of the action . . . is solely to deter the kind of
wrong that causes a small injury to a large number. . . . Although
some actions of this kind may not be justifiable except as a means of
contributing to the income of lawyers, surely others are fully warranted, and the question whether the action should be allowed to go
forward is quite different from the question of the nature of the action
once it is certified on behalf of a plaintiff class.

That it makes eminent sense to view the class as the aggrieved
claimant in such instances . . . strikes me as more than a trivial conclusion. It suggests that notions of individual choice, autonomy, and
participation—and their resonance in the constitutional guarantee of
due process—are not so rigid that they cannot yield to practical arguments about the nature of the case, the character of the wrong
complained of, and the individual interests at stake, as well as the
countervailing interests and preferences of others.

David L. Shapiro, Class Actions: The Class as Party and Client, 73 Notre Dame
L. Rev. 913, 918–19, 921, 923–25 (1998).* Is the *Hansberry* Court ultimately
saying that the *Burke* plaintiff class cannot realistically be conceived as an entity in any meaningful sense and, hence, that the *Burke* class judgment cannot
be binding? As you read the material in this book, think critically about Professor Shapiro's entity theory. What does it mean exactly, and which, if any, class
actions does it actually describe? Does the theory work better normatively than
descriptively?

2. SIGNIFICANCE FOR DEFENDANTS

In the Matter of Rhone–Poulenc Rorer, Inc.

51 F.3d 1293 (7th Cir. 1995)

■ POSNER, CHIEF JUDGE.

Drug companies that manufacture blood solids are the defendants in a
nationwide class action brought on behalf of hemophiliacs infected by the
AIDS virus as a consequence of using the defendants' products. The defendants have filed with us a petition for mandamus, asking us to direct
the district judge to rescind his order certifying the case as a class action.

The suit to which the petition for mandamus relates, *Wadleigh v.
Rhone–Poulenc Rorer Inc.*, 157 F.R.D. 410 (1994) arises out of the infection
of a substantial fraction of the hemophiliac population of this country by
the AIDS virus because the blood supply was contaminated by the virus

---

*Vol. 73 Notre Dame Law Review, Pages 918–19, 921, 923–25 (1998). Reprinted with
permission. © *Notre Dame Law Review*, University of Notre Dame. The casebook publisher
bears responsibility for any errors which have occurred in reprinting or editing.

before the nature of the disease was well understood or adequate methods of screening the blood supply existed. The AIDS virus (HIV—human immunodeficiency virus) is transmitted by the exchange of bodily fluids, primarily semen and blood. Hemophiliacs depend on blood solids that contain the clotting factors whose absence defines their disease. These blood solids are concentrated from blood obtained from many donors. If just one of the donors is infected with the AIDS virus the probability that the blood solids manufactured in part from his blood will be infected is very high unless the blood is treated with heat to kill the virus.

First identified in 1981, AIDS was diagnosed in hemophiliacs beginning in 1982, and by 1984 the medical community agreed that the virus was transmitted by blood as well as by semen. That year it was demonstrated that treatment with heat could kill the virus in the blood supply and in the following year a reliable test for the presence of the virus in blood was developed. By this time, however, a large number of hemophiliacs had become infected. Since 1984 physicians have been advised to place hemophiliacs on heat-treated blood solids, and since 1985 all blood donated for the manufacture of blood solids has been screened and supplies discovered to be HIV-positive have been discarded. Supplies that test negative still are heat-treated, because the test is not infallible and in particular may fail to detect the virus in persons who became infected within six months before taking the test.

The plaintiffs have presented evidence that 2,000 hemophiliacs have died of AIDS and that half or more of the remaining U.S. hemophiliac population of 20,000 may be HIV-positive. Unless there are dramatic breakthroughs in the treatment of HIV or AIDS, all infected persons will die from the disease. The reason so many are infected even though the supply of blood for the manufacture of blood solids (as for transfusions) has been safe since the mid–80s is that the disease has a very long incubation period; the median period for hemophiliacs may be as long as 11 years. Probably most of the hemophiliacs who are now HIV-positive, or have AIDS, or have died of AIDS were infected in the early 1980s, when the blood supply was contaminated.

Futures problem

Some 300 lawsuits, involving some 400 plaintiffs, have been filed, 60 percent of them in state courts, 40 percent in federal district courts under the diversity jurisdiction, seeking to impose tort liability on the defendants for the transmission of HIV to hemophiliacs in blood solids manufactured by the defendants. Obviously these 400 plaintiffs represent only a small fraction of the hemophiliacs (or their next of kin, in cases in which the hemophiliac has died) who are infected by HIV or have died of AIDS. One of the 300 cases is *Wadleigh*, filed in September 1993, the case that the district judge certified as a class action. Thirteen other cases have been tried already in various courts around the country, and the defendants have won twelve of them. All the cases brought in federal court (like *Wadleigh*)— cases brought under the diversity jurisdiction—have been consolidated for pretrial discovery in the Northern District of Illinois by the panel on multi-district litigation.

The plaintiffs advance two principal theories of liability. The first is that before anyone had heard of AIDS or HIV, it was known that Hepatitis B, a lethal disease though less so than HIV–AIDS, could be transmitted either through blood transfusions or through injection of blood solids. The plaintiffs argue that due care with respect to the risk of infection with Hepatitis B required the defendants to take measures to purge that virus from their blood solids, whether by treating the blood they bought or by screen-ing the donors—perhaps by refusing to deal with *paid* donors, known to be a class at high risk of being infected with Hepatitis B. The defendants' fail-ure to take effective measures was, the plaintiffs claim, negligent. Had the defendants not been negligent, the plaintiffs further argue, hemophiliacs would have been protected not only against Hepatitis B but also, albeit for-tuitously or as the plaintiffs put it "serendipitously," against HIV.

The plaintiffs' second theory of liability is more conventional. It is that the defendants, again negligently, dragged their heels in screening donors and taking other measures to prevent contamination of blood solids by HIV when they learned about the disease in the early 1980s. The plaintiffs have other theories of liability as well, including strict products liability, but it is not necessary for us to get into them.

The district judge did not think it feasible to certify *Wadleigh* as a class action for the adjudication of the entire controversy between the plaintiffs and the defendants. Fed. R. Civ. P. 23(b)(3). The differences in the date of infection alone of the thousands of potential class members would make such a procedure infeasible. Hemophiliacs infected before anyone knew about the contamination of blood solids by HIV could not rely on the second theory of liability, while hemophiliacs infected after the blood sup-ply became safe (not perfectly safe, but nearly so) probably were not infect-ed by any of the defendants' products. Instead the judge certified the suit "as a class action with respect to particular issues" only. Fed. R. Civ. P. 23(c)(4)(A). He explained this decision in an opinion which implied that he did not envisage the entry of a final judgment but rather the rendition by a jury of a special verdict that would answer a number of questions bearing, perhaps decisively, on whether the defendants are negligent under either of the theories sketched above. If the special verdict found no negligence un-der either theory, that presumably would be the end of all the cases unless other theories of liability proved viable. If the special verdict found negli-gence, individual members of the class would then file individual tort suits in state and federal district courts around the nation and would use the special verdict, in conjunction with the doctrine of collateral estoppel, to block relitigation of the issue of negligence.

With all due respect for the district judge's commendable desire to ex-periment with an innovative procedure for streamlining the adjudication of this "mass tort," we believe that his plan so far exceeds the permissible bounds of discretion in the management of federal litigation as to compel us to intervene and order decertification.

. . . [W]e shall assume in accordance with the judge's letter that even-tually there will be a final judgment to review. Only it will come too late to provide effective relief to the defendants. . . . The reason that an appeal will come too late to provide effective relief for these defendants is the sheer *magnitude* of the risk to which the class action, in contrast to the individual actions pending or likely, exposes them. Consider the situation that would obtain if the class had not been certified. The defendants would be facing 300 suits. More might be filed, but probably only a few more, because the statutes of limitations in the various states are rapidly expiring for poten-tial plaintiffs. The blood supply has been safe since 1985. That is ten years ago. The risk to hemophiliacs of having become infected with HIV has been widely publicized; it is unlikely that many hemophiliacs are unaware of it. Under the usual discovery statute of limitations, they would have to have taken steps years ago to determine their infection status, and having found out file suit within the limitations period running from the date of discovery, in order to preserve their rights.

Three hundred is not a trivial number of lawsuits. The potential damages in each one are great. But the defendants have won twelve of the first thirteen, and, if this is a representative sample, they are likely to win most of the remaining ones as well. Perhaps in the end, if class-action treatment is denied (it has been denied in all the other hemophiliac HIV suits in which class certification has been sought), they will be compelled to pay damages in only 25 cases, involving a potential liability of perhaps no more than $125 million altogether. These are guesses, of course, but they are at once conservative and usable for the limited purpose of comparing the situation that will face the defendants if the class certification stands. All of a sudden they will face thousands of plaintiffs. Many may already be barred by the statute of limitations, as we have suggested, though its further running was tolled by the filing of *Wadleigh* as a class action. *Am. Pipe & Constr. Co. v. Utah*, 414 U.S. 538, 554 (1974). (If the class is decertified, the statute of limitations will start running again.).

Suppose that 5,000 of the potential class members are not yet barred by the statute of limitations. And suppose the named plaintiffs in *Wadleigh* win the class portion of this case to the extent of establishing the defendants' liability under either of the two negligence theories. It is true that this would only be prima facie liability, that the defendants would have various defenses. But they could not be confident that the defenses would prevail. They might, therefore, easily be facing $25 billion in potential liability (conceivably more), and with it bankruptcy. They may not wish to roll these dice. That is putting it mildly. They will be under intense pressure to settle. If they settle, the class certification—the ruling that will have forced them to settle—will never be reviewed. Judge Friendly, who was not given to hyperbole, called settlements induced by a small probability of an immense judgment in a class action "blackmail settlements." Henry J. Friendly, FEDERAL JURISDICTION: A GENERAL VIEW 120 (1973). Judicial concern about them is legitimate, not "sociological," as it was derisively termed in *In re Sugar Antitrust Litig.*, 559 F.2d 481, 483 n.1 (9th Cir. 1977). . . .

We do not want to be misunderstood as saying that class actions are bad because they place pressure on defendants to settle. That pressure is a reality, but it must be balanced against the undoubted benefits of the class action that have made it an authorized procedure for employment by federal courts. We have yet to consider the balance. All that our discussion to this point has shown is that the first condition for the grant of mandamus—that the challenged ruling not be effectively reviewable at the end of the case—is fulfilled. The ruling will inflict irreparable harm; the next question is whether the ruling can fairly be described as usurpative. We have formulated this second condition as narrowly, as stringently, as can be, but even so formulated we think it is fulfilled. We do not mean to suggest that the district judge is engaged in a deliberate power-grab. We have no reason to suppose that he *wants* to preside over an unwieldy class action. We believe that he was responding imaginatively and in the best of faith to the challenge that mass torts, graphically illustrated by the avalanche of asbestos litigation, pose for the federal courts. But the plan that he has devised for the HIV-hemophilia litigation exceeds the bounds of allowable judicial discretion. Three concerns, none of them necessarily sufficient in itself but cumulatively compelling, persuade us to this conclusion.

The first is a concern with forcing these defendants to stake their companies on the outcome of a single jury trial, or be forced by fear of the risk of bankruptcy to settle even if they have no legal liability, when it is entirely feasible to allow a final, authoritative determination of their liability for the colossal misfortune that has befallen the hemophiliac population to emerge from a decentralized process of multiple trials, involving different juries, and different standards of liability, in different jurisdictions; and when, in addition, the preliminary indications are that the defendants are not liable for the grievous harm that has befallen the members of the class. These qualifications are important. In most class actions—and those . . . in which the rationale for the procedure is most compelling—individual suits are infeasible because the claim of each class member is tiny relative to the expense of litigation. That plainly is not the situation here. A notable feature of this case, and one that has not been remarked upon or encountered, so far as we are aware, in previous cases, is the demonstrated great likelihood that the plaintiffs' claims, despite their human appeal, lack legal merit. This is the inference from the defendants' having won 92.3 percent (12/13) of the cases to have gone to judgment. Granted, thirteen is a small sample and further trials, if they are held, may alter the pattern that the sample reveals. But whether they do or not, the result will be robust if these further trials are permitted to go forward, because the pattern that results will reflect a consensus, or at least a pooling of judgment, of many different tribunals.

[The court goes on to advance two additional reasons for decertification of the blood product class stemming, respectively, from choice-of-law considerations and the Reexamination Clause of the Seventh Amendment. Subsequent portions of this Chapter will explore those matters as they bear upon class certification.]

. . . The petition for a writ of mandamus is granted, and the district judge is directed to decertify the plaintiff class.

■ ROVNER, CIRCUIT JUDGE, dissenting.

. . . I . . . cannot agree with the majority's premise that [District] Judge Grady's order in fact will prompt a settlement. Contrary to the clear implication of the majority's opinion, the class portion of the anticipated trial in this case would not go so far as to establish defendants' *liability* to a class of plaintiffs; it would instead resolve *only* the question of whether defendants were negligent in distributing tainted clotting factor at any particular point in time. Even if defendants were faced with an adverse class verdict, then, a plaintiff still would be required to clear a number of hurdles before he would be entitled to a judgment. For example, defendants no doubt would contest at that stage whether a particular plaintiff could establish proximate causation or whether his or her claim is in any event barred by the statute of limitations. Thus, contrary to the majority's implication, a class verdict in favor of plaintiffs would not automatically entitle each member of the class to a seven-figure judgment. The defendants will thus have ample opportunity to settle should they lose the class trial. And that would seem to me an advisable strategy in light of the success they have had in earlier cases. That factor distinguishes this case from a more standard class action, where a non-bifurcated trial would resolve all relevant issues and conclusively establish liability to the class. Perhaps that explains why defendants' own arguments in support of their petition are based on the assumption that a class trial would ensue, rather than on the proposition that a settlement would follow inevitably from Judge Grady's order. . . .

NOTES AND QUESTIONS

1. *The Importance of Rhone–Poulenc.* Rhone–Poulenc has turned out to be a very important opinion in modern class action law. One reason has to do with the reputation of its author, Judge Richard Posner. Another reason has to do with its frank and open discussion of the relationship between class certification and settlement pressure. For example, one year after the *Rhone–Poulenc* decision, the Fifth Circuit reversed the certification of a nationwide class of cigarette smokers in *Castano v. Am. Tobacco Co.*, 84 F.3d 734, 746 (5th Cir. 1996). The *Castano* court relied on *Rhone–Poulenc* to support its argument that the massive nationwide class action the plaintiffs sought would impose undue settlement pressure on the defendants. Indeed, one commentator has described the *Rhone–Poulenc* decision as "a critical event" in the development of class action law and one that opened the door to a more restrictive approach to certification. Robert H. Klonoff, *The Decline of Class Actions*, 90 Wash. U. L. Rev. ___ (2013), available at http://papers.ssrn.com/sol3/papers.cfm?abstract_id=2038985, at. p.5 (Nov. 28, 2012 draft).

2. *Review of Class Certification Decisions Before and After 1998.* At the time of *Rhone–Poulenc*, appellate review of certification decisions was extremely limited. See generally C.A. Wright, A.R. Miller, M.K. Kane & R.L. Marcus, FEDERAL PRACTICE AND PROCEDURE § 1802 (2012) (discussing the limited avenues of appeal before Rule 23(f)). Since most class actions settle after certification, the obvious route, appealing from a final judgment at the end of the case, was seldom used. Moreover, Rule 23 contained no provision for interlocutory appeal, and the collateral order doctrine was not available. See *Coopers & Lybrand v. Livesay*, 437 U.S. 463, 469 (1978). There were also limitations on the availability of interlocutory review under 28 U.S.C. § 1292(b), and the writ of mandamus, the method used in *Rhone–Poulenc*, was limited as well: a writ of mandamus is supposed to be granted only in extraordinary circumstances (as Judge Posner readily acknowledges). This very narrow range for appellate review left the development of class action law largely in the hands of district judges without much by way of appellate supervision.

All of this changed in 1998 when subsection (f) was added to Rule 23. As further restyled in 2007 and amended in 2009, Rule 23(f) provides that:

> A court of appeals may permit an appeal from an order granting or denying class-action certification under this rule if a petition for permission to appeal is filed with the circuit clerk within 14 days after the order is entered. An appeal does not stay proceedings in the district court unless the district judge or the court of appeals so orders.

By making appeals more readily available, Rule 23(f) expanded the power of federal appellate courts over class action law, and as we shall see, many of these courts have used their new power to restrict class actions in significant ways. One commentator recently reviewed all the 23(f) appeals available on LEXIS and WESTLAW between November 30, 1998 and May 31, 2012. He found a strong pro-defendant trend both in the number of appeals taken and reversal rates. Klonoff, *The Decline of Class Actions*, *supra*, at p. 14 (reporting that about 69% of 23(f) appeals involved defendants appealing certification grants and only about 31% involved plaintiffs appealing certification denials, and also reporting that defendants succeeded in reversing a certification grant 70% of the time while plaintiffs succeeded in reversing a denial only 30% of the time).

  3. The Scope of Appellate Review under Rule 23(f). Explaining the operation of subsection (f), the advisory committee note states that:

> Appeal from an order granting or denying class certification is permitted in the sole discretion of the court of appeals. . . . The court of appeals is given unfettered discretion whether to permit the appeal, akin to the discretion exercised by the Supreme Court in acting on a petition for certiorari. . . . The Federal Judicial Center study supports the view that many suits with class-action allegations present familiar and almost routine issues that are no more worthy of immediate appeal than many other interlocutory rulings. Yet several concerns justify expansion of present opportunities to appeal. An order denying certification may confront the plaintiff with a situation in which the only sure path to appellate review is by proceeding to final judgment on the merits of an individual claim that, standing alone, is far smaller than the costs of litigation. An order granting certification, on the other hand, may force a defendant to settle rather than incur the costs of defending a class action and run the risk of potentially ruinous liability. These concerns can be met at low cost by establishing in the court of appeals a discretionary power to grant interlocutory review in cases that show appeal-worthy certification issues.
>
>   Permission to appeal may be granted or denied on the basis of any consideration that the court of appeals finds persuasive. Permission is most likely to be granted when the certification decision turns on a novel or unsettled question of law, or when, as a practical matter, the decision on certification is likely dispositive of the litigation.

  Relying on this advisory committee note for guidance, federal courts of appeals focus mainly on three factors to decide whether to take a Rule 23(f) appeal: (1) whether the denial of certification spells the death knell of the lawsuit; (2) whether the grant of certification imposes undue settlement pressure on the defendant; and (3) whether the certification decision raises a novel or unsettled question of law. Many circuits require, in addition to one of the first two factors, that the appellant also show that the district judge's certification decision is questionable on the merits. See FEDERAL PRACTICE AND PROCEDURE, *supra*, at § 1802.2. Moreover, some circuits allow appeals based on manifest error in the district court's certification decision, standing alone, and some are willing to take an appeal when it raises an unsettled and fundamental question of law even if there is no manifest error in the district court's decision. Finally, some courts limit the third factor—that the certification decision raises novel or unsettled questions—to those cases where the question is otherwise likely to evade review. See *id.* See also *In re Lorazepam & Clorozepate Antitrust Litig.*, 289 F.3d 98, 103–05 (D.C. Cir. 2002) (setting out three categories: "(1) when there is a death-knell situation for either the plaintiff or defendant that is independent of the merits of the underlying claims, coupled with a class certification decision by the district court that is questionable, taking into account the district court's discretion over class certification; (2) when the certification decision presents an unsettled and fundamental issue of law relating to class actions, important both to the specific litigation and generally, that is likely to evade end-of-the-case review; and (3) when the district court's class certification decision is manifestly erroneous").

4. *Estimating the Probability of Success.* In *Rhone–Poulenc*, is Judge Posner correct in looking only to blood product plaintiffs' win-rate in individual lawsuits *adjudicated at trial* as a basis for estimating the probability of successful litigation by the blood product class? What other data might bear upon that probability? In answering this question, consider how nonmutual issue preclusion can affect the mix of suits that go to trial. Given the possible preclusive effect of an adverse determination of common issues, wouldn't the defendant be inclined to settle the strongest cases? Also, consider the relative stakes of a plaintiff compared to a defendant facing multiple suits. When a defendant risks preclusion over multiple lawsuits, its stakes in early suits take account of future effects and thus should exceed the stakes of a plaintiff who is concerned only with her own suit. When stakes are asymmetric in this way, the party with the higher stakes usually invests more in the litigation. How is this likely to affect the win rate?

5. *The Litigation after Denial of Certification.* The Seventh Circuit's decertification of the class in *Rhone–Poulenc* did not mark the decline of the blood product litigation. Rather, counsel soon thereafter entered into a comprehensive settlement agreement, whereby defendants agreed to pay each HIV-positive hemophiliac the non-trivial sum of $100,000, exclusive of attorneys' fees. *In re Factor VIII or IX Concentrate Blood Prods. Litig.*, 159 F.3d 1016, 1018 (7th Cir. 1998) (noting that the settlement covered about 6,000 remaining cases). Adding to the irony of the result, this comprehensive settlement occurred through the vehicle of a second class action, certified by the same district judge who had certified the original class decertified in *Rhone–Poulenc*. Appeals concerning the validity of the class settlement were voluntarily dismissed. What does this subsequent behavior suggest about defendants' view of the likelihood of successful litigation by the plaintiffs?

In answering this question, you should bear in mind that a settlement reflects each party's estimate of its own likelihood of success, the expected trial award, and the costs of litigating the case through trial. The economic model of settlement provides a useful way to integrate these factors. According to the economic model, the most the defendant is willing to pay in settlement is whatever it expects to lose by going to trial, since a rational defendant would prefer to go to trial than pay anything more. By the same token, the least amount the plaintiff is willing to accept in settlement is whatever it expects to recover at trial net of its litigation costs, since a rational plaintiff would prefer to go to trial than take anything less. It follows that settlement is possible only if the defendant's expected trial loss (including its litigation costs) is greater than or equal to the plaintiff's expected trial recovery (net of its litigation costs). The difference between the defendant's expected loss and the plaintiff's expected recovery is called the settlement surplus and the range between the two values is called the settlement range. The settlement amount will lie somewhere in the settlement range and the parties will split the settlement surplus depending on the parties' relative bargaining power.

To illustrate, let's apply this model to the *Rhone–Poulenc* case. Judge Posner assumes that each plaintiff has about an 8% chance of winning on average (1 win in 13 past cases yields a 1/13 chance, which equals 0.0769). He also assumes that the average case is worth $5 million in damages. Some cases might be stronger and some weaker, and some might be worth more than $5 million and some less. But there's no way for the defendant to distinguish the cases without litigating each one, so the defendant calculates based on the average case. Judge Posner does not make any assumptions about the defendant's cost of litigating each individual case through trial. Let's assume that this cost is $400,000 on average. Given these figures, the defendant should be willing to offer each plaintiff as much as 0.08 x 5 million + $400,000 = $800,000. Compared to this figure, settling for $100,000 per case would seem a very good deal for the defendant.

It is much more difficult to explain why a plaintiff who knows she has one of the stronger or higher value cases would accept a settlement this low. The answer might have to do with agency costs. If the plaintiffs are represented en masse by a single set of attorneys, those attorneys have nothing to gain from settling cases individually. A higher recovery and thus larger percentage fee in a strong case is just offset by a lower fee in a weak case. Therefore, it's the average case that matters, just the same as for the defendant. And a $100,000 settlement might be attractive for the average case with a 0.08 probability of winning.

What does this analysis tell you about the reliability of inferring perceptions of case strength from settlement amounts?

6.   *The Mechanics of Class Settlement Pressure.* Judge Posner's argument that certification of the plaintiff class in *Rhone–Poulenc* would induce defendants to settle has two separable components: (i) certifying a class might increase the total number of claims that the defendant must face compared with litigating the controversy by way of conventional, individual lawsuits (from about 300 to about 5000 claims); and (ii) class certification in itself—apart from any change in the number of claims—increases the variance of outcomes.

These two components combine in Judge Posner's argument. The increase in variance due to class certification is magnified by the increase in the number of claims. Even so, it is worth considering the two components separately. Is the first concern—the possibility of an increased absolute number of claims in the event of a class action—a legitimate reason to decertify the class? Recall our earlier example of the antitrust class action involving consumers whose airline tickets were marked up in price by only $20 apiece pursuant to a price-fixing conspiracy. In these cases, class certification increases the number of claims from zero to some very large number. (Note too that Judge Posner refers favorably to the use of class actions in cases involving small claims.)

The second concern—that class certification increases the variance of outcomes—can be illustrated by way of a numerical example designed to isolate the variance point from the more-claims point. Suppose that in the no-class-action world, the defendant would face 1000 cases with an estimated 8 percent chance of being found negligent in any given case and with each finding of negligence resulting in $1 million in damages to the individual plaintiff due to the severity of the injury suffered. Given the large number of individual cases, one can be relatively confident that the defendant's loss rate over the entirety of the 1000 cases will closely approximate the 8 percent estimated probability of being found negligent in any given case. The result is that the defendant would expect to lose approximately 80 individual cases, resulting in a total payout of $80 million.

With a class action, the risks for the defendant are dramatically different. On the assumption that the negligence issue is the only substantial firewall standing between the defendant and liability, the defendant faces an 8 percent chance of being held liable to the class and thus paying $1 billion ($1 million payouts to each of 1000 class members) and a 92 percent chance of being held not liable to the class and thus paying nothing (based on a class-wide finding that defendants were not negligent). Why would a defendant be more inclined to settle in the class-action world than in the no-class-action world? The defendant's expected liability is the same in both: $80 million. The problem, however, is that the class action is a lot riskier. With individual litigation, the defendant knows that the chances are very good it will pay only $80 million in total damages because, with an 8 percent chance of losing each case, the most likely result is 80 losses and 920 wins. But with a class action, there are only two possible outcomes and one of them ($1 billion) is potentially catastrophic.

Let's take a closer look at this. One way to understand the point more clearly is to consider all the possible outcomes in the individual litigation scenario compared to the class action scenario, along with the probability each will occur. If all 1000 suits are litigated individually, the chance that all 1000 plaintiffs will win is very close to zero: $(.08)^{1000}$. The chance that all 1000 plaintiffs will lose, though a bit larger, is also vanishingly small: $(.92)^{1000}$. Each possibility in between—one plaintiff winning, two plaintiffs winning, three, four, and so on—happens with some probability. But the most probable outcome is that 80 plaintiffs will win and 920 will lose. Moreover, there is about a 95 percent probability that the actual number of plaintiff wins will fall somewhere between 62 and 98 (i.e., within two standard deviations of the mean of 80).

Contrast these predictions with those for the class action. With a class action, there are only two possible outcomes: 1000 plaintiffs win, or no plaintiffs win. Although the first possibility is not at all likely, it is a lot more likely than for individual litigation: a 0.08 probability compared to one that is virtually zero. More precisely, the outcome variance in the class action scenario is 1000 times greater than the outcome variance in the individual litigation scenario (a variance of 73,600 compared to 73.6), and greater variance means greater risk.

Why would this increased variance and risk necessarily induce settlement by the defendant? And even if settlement is more likely, why is that bad from a social perspective? Is the concern here more about the settlement amount than the settlement probability? How can we tell whether the amount of a settlement is bad? If the parties agree, what else is there to worry about? (Hint: Think about litigation as enforcing the substantive law.) Are both sides affected by increased variance? Does that change your conclusion in any way? For commentary parsing these questions, see Charles Silver, *We're Scared to Death: Class Certification and Blackmail*, 78 N.Y.U. L. Rev. 1357 (2003); J.B. Heaton, *The Risk Finance of Class Action Settlement Pressure*, 4 J. Risk Fin. 75 (2003); Robert G. Bone & David S. Evans, *Class Certification and the Substantive Merits*, 51 Duke L.J. 1251 (2002); Warren F. Schwartz, *Long–Shot Class Actions: Toward a Normative Theory of Legal Uncertainty*, 8 Legal Theory 297 (2002).

7.   *The Possible Reasons for the 8 Percent.* Assume, for the sake of argument, that Judge Posner's estimate of an 8 percent probability of success for the blood product plaintiffs represents an accurate estimate. Why might there be such a low probability of success? Recall that the class-wide trial contemplated in *Rhone–Poulenc* would—as Judge Rovner points out in her dissent—

have determined only the question whether defendants were negligent in the handling of their blood products in either, or both, of the respects alleged by the plaintiff class, *not* individual issues concerning the situations of particular hemophiliacs. The negligence question itself centered upon consideration of what blood product firms knew, or should have known, about the risks posed to the blood supply at relatively early stages of the AIDS crisis, when knowledge concerning the disease was in an underdeveloped and rapidly changing state.

Would the concerns expressed in *Rhone–Poulenc* be eliminated, or at least substantially reduced, if courts were routinely to rule on motions for summary judgment *prior to* deciding whether to certify a proposed class? For a proposal to mandate such an approach, see Randy J. Kozel & David Rosenberg, *Solving the Nuisance–Value Settlement Problem: Mandatory Summary Judgment*, 90 Va. L. Rev. 1849 (2004). If the district court in *Rhone–Poulenc* had granted summary judgment in favor of the defendants for lack of a triable issue on the breach element and thereby had eliminated the need for the court to rule on the plaintiffs' motion for class certification, then who on the plaintiffs' side of the blood product litigation would have been bound by that grant of summary judgment? For a critical analysis of the risk-aversion/settlement pressure argument in the class action context that makes the point that courts commonly reviewed the merits before certification by deciding dismissal or summary judgment motions, see Silver, *We're Scared to Death*, 78 N.Y.U. L. Rev. 1357.

8.   *Settlement Pressure and Statutory Damages.* The plaintiff class in *Rhone–Poulenc* sought the usual tort remedy of damages. Do concerns over class settlement pressure carry more or less weight with regard to claims for statutory damages—i.e., situations in which an underlying statute provides for a specific dollar amount in damages on a per-violation or per-claimant basis not linked to the actual loss suffered by the claimant? The Second Circuit confronted such a situation in *Parker v. Time Warner Entertainment Co.*, 331 F.3d 13 (2d Cir. 2003). *Parker* concerned claims under the Cable Communications Policy Act of 1984 (Cable Act), 47 U.S.C. §§ 52161 (2000). The class of Time Warner cable television customers—a class potentially numbering twelve million persons—alleged that Time Warner had violated the Cable Act by disclosing customer information to third parties but failing to inform customers of such disclosure. As a remedy for violations of this sort, the Cable Act provided for actual damages, but with a statutorily specified minimum recovery of the greater of $1000 per claimant or $100 for each day of violation. *Id.* § 551(f)(2)(A).

On the one hand, a class action seems well suited to this type of case. Each customer probably has too little at stake to justify an individual suit, so a class action might well be the only way to assure enforcement of the substantive law. On the other hand, with 12 million class members, certification can create a huge potential liability in the amount of 12 *billion* dollars (12 million customers × $1000 per customer). The district judge refused to certify because he thought 12 billion dollars might cripple Time Warner and because he believed that it was far out of proportion to the seriousness of the wrong.

The Second Circuit ultimately vacated the district court's refusal to certify the class and remanded for further proceedings, but not without expressing concern over the settlement pressure that class certification might exert:

> In denying class certification under Rule 23(b)(3), the District Court focused on the superiority of class litigation, the technical nature of the claimed violations of the Cable Act, and the impact of a po-

tentially huge class. The Court was particularly concerned about a damages award that would be disproportionately large compared to the harm actually suffered by the potential class members. "[A] class action is not the superior manner of proceeding where the liability defendant stands to incur is grossly disproportionate to any actual harm sustained by an aggrieved individual." *Parker*, 198 F.R.D. [374, 383 (E.D.N.Y. 2001)]. [District] Judge Glasser noted that there are due process concerns when the prospect of a stunningly large damages award looms as the result of technical violations of the Cable Act that affect potentially millions of subscribers. The District Court also noted that the case raised obvious manageability concerns: "Where a purported class promises to cause serious manageability problems, as would surely be the case where potential class members total 12 million subscribers in 23 states, defendants correctly point out that courts do not hesitate to dismiss based on manageability concerns alone." *Id.* at 384.

The difficulty we have with these conclusions is that they are based on assumptions of fact rather than on findings of fact. The District Court precluded any class discovery and even the filing of a motion for class certification. Thus, it remains unknown what class Parker would have sought to certify and the numbers of potential class members in that proposed class. Although the Amended Complaint alleges that the total number of Time Warner cable subscribers number about twelve million in twenty-three states, Parker has given no indication that he would actually seek to certify a class of *all* twelve million subscribers. Indeed, counsel for Parker stated ... that the number of potential class members could not be identified without discovery on the issue: "[T]here is simply no number because we've had no discovery as to the number of people who have actually been injured. We think it is a large number. We have no idea of whether it's thirteen million or one million or 1,000." Absent at least limited discovery concerning the composition of the class, the District Court had no evidence regarding the size of the recovery that Time Warner might face if the class claims were successful. Under the circumstances, the Court's conclusion that the size of the class would inevitably lead to "the financial demise" of Time Warner, *Parker*, 198 F.R.D. at 384, or even to significant manageability problems, was speculative.

We acknowledge Judge Glasser's legitimate concern that the potential for a devastatingly large damages award, out of all reasonable proportion to the actual harm suffered by members of the plaintiff class, may raise due process issues. Those issues arise from the effects of combining a statutory scheme that imposes minimum statutory damages awards on a per-consumer basis—usually in order to encourage the filing of individual lawsuits as a means of private enforcement of consumer protection laws—with the class action mechanism that aggregates many claims—often because there would otherwise be no incentive to bring an individual claim. Such a combination may expand the potential statutory damages so far beyond the actual damages suffered that the statutory damages come to resemble punitive damages—yet ones that are awarded as a matter of strict liability, rather than for the egregious conduct typically necessary to support a punitive damages award. It may be that the aggregation in a class action of large numbers of statutory damages claims potentially distorts the purpose of both statutory damages and class actions. If so, such a distortion could create a potentially enormous aggregate recovery for plaintiffs, and thus an *in terrorem* effect on defendants, which may induce unfair settlements. . . . At this point in this case, however, these concerns remain hypothetical.

Parker, 331 F.3d at 21–22.

In a concurring opinion, Judge Jon Newman agreed that the adding up of per-customer statutory damages by way of class certification would strain the bounds of credible congressional authorization in the Cable Act. *Id.* at 26 (Newman, J., concurring). But the solution for Judge Newman lay not in the withholding of class certification, but rather in the application on remand of the absurdity doctrine of statutory interpretation, whereby "statutes are not to be applied according to their literal terms when doing so achieves a result manifestly not intended by the legislature." *Id.* at 27. In Judge Newman's view, the district court on remand could properly exercise its discretion to certify the class while effectively reducing the statutory damages available on an aggregate basis below the $1000-per-customer amount expressly stated in the statute. *Id.* at 27–28.

What do you make of Judge Newman's suggestion in light of the observation that Congress itself addressed similarly an analogous problem under the Truth in Lending Act, amending that statute to cap the aggregate amount of statutory damages available in class actions as distinct from individual litigation? 15 U.S.C. § 1640(a)(2)(B) (2000) (capping the total recovery of statutory damages in "any class action or series of class actions arising out of the same failure to comply by the same creditor" at "the lesser of $500,000 or 1 per centum of the net worth of the [defendant] creditor"). See also Fair Debt Collection Practices Act, 15 U.S.C. § 1692k(a)(2) (allowing the judge to increase actual damages in an individual action to an amount "not exceeding $1,000" and also allowing the same for the named plaintiffs in a class action, but limiting liability to other class members to "such amount as the court may allow for all other class members, without regard to a minimum individual recovery, not to exceed the lesser of $500,000 or 1 per centum of the net worth of the [defendant"). Does Judge Newman's approach amount to rewriting the Cable Act? Suppose that instead of adjusting the amount on his own, the trial judge asks class counsel to waive any demand for statutory damages above a specified dollar amount in the aggregate as a condition for granting certification? Does the judge have the power to do this? How is this different from remittitur practice, in which a judge, convinced the verdict is too high, asks the defendant to agree to a lower verdict or face a new trial?

Similar problems have arisen under the Fair and Accurate Credit Transaction Act (FACTA). The purpose of FACTA is to help protect against identity theft. It requires sellers to truncate credit card numbers appearing on receipts so that only the last five digits appear. Any person who "willfully fails to comply" is liable for "actual damages sustained by the consumer as a result of the failure or [statutory] damages of not less than $100 and not more than $1,000" plus punitive damages and reasonable attorney's fees. 15 U.S.C. §§ 1681n(a) (2012).

In an unpublished opinion, the Fourth Circuit vacated a district judge's denial of class certification in a FACTA case, noting that all the requirements of Rule 23 were satisfied and that the small damages at stake were not likely to "result in enforcement . . . by individual actions of a scale comparable to the potential enforcement by way of class action." *Stillmock v. Weis Markets*, 385 Fed. Appx. 267, 274 (4th Cir. 2010). Judge Wilkinson concurred, but not without sounding a strong note of caution: "I worry that the exponential expansion of statutory damages through the aggressive use of the class action device is a real jobs killer that Congress has not sanctioned. . . . I see nothing in the statute . . . that mandates class action treatment of FACTA claims or precludes a district court from considering the prospect of annihilative liability in the certification calculus." *Id.* at 276.

The *Parker* litigation under the Cable Act ultimately resulted in—what else?—a class settlement. Time Warner cable subscribers received a choice among three kinds of benefits under the settlement: one free month of "any Time Warner service that is available on a monthly basis and to which the customer does not currently subscribe," two "free Movies on Demand," or a check for $5. See Stipulation and Agreement of Settlement, available at http://www.twcsettlement.com/sa.pdf. Do the class settlement terms suggest that the Second Circuit's concern over settlement pressure was well founded? Or do they suggest that, at the end of the day, the Cable Act claims in *Parker* were appropriately priced in the market for settlement? The class settlement also notes that, upon court approval, Time Warner will pay $5 million to cover class counsel's fees and costs. Does that alter your opinion on the settlement pressure question?

Later in this book, you'll read *Shady Grove Orthopedic Assocs., P.A. v. Allstate Ins. Co.*, 559 U.S. 393 (2010). This case involves similar issues, although it presents them in a different legal context. The plaintiff Shady Grove sued Allstate to recover unpaid statutory interest on overdue payments of insurance benefits. The plaintiff filed in federal court under diversity jurisdiction and sought class certification under Rule 23. A New York statute prohibited class actions for suits brought to "recover a penalty, or minimum measure of recovery created or imposed by statute." N. Y. Civ. Prac. Law Ann. § 901(b). Apparently, one purpose of this statute was to prevent "annihilating punishment of the defendant" resulting from aggregation of claims for statutory damages or fixed penalties. 130 S.Ct. at 1464 (Ginsburg, J., dissenting). The district judge denied certification on the strength of Section 901(b) and the Second Circuit affirmed. The Supreme Court reversed, holding that Rule 23 controlled the certification decision in federal court under *Hanna v. Plumer*—and not Section 901(b).

B. GENERAL REQUIREMENTS FOR CLASS CERTIFICATION

By its terms, Rule 23(a) sets forth requirements applicable to all forms of class actions. In determining whether a proposed class action should be certified, courts usually parse the four subsections of Rule 23(a) before turning to the particular form of class sought under Rule 23(b).

1. NUMEROSITY

Rule 23(a)(1) calls for a judicial finding that the class is "so numerous that joinder of all members is impracticable." This first general requirement for class certification has come to be known as one of "numerosity." This requirement, which embodies a preference for joining co-parties pursuant to Rule 20 when practical, reflects the class action's second-class status. In practice, the numerosity requirement is seriously contested only very rarely. In most instances in which class certification is sought, it will be readily apparent that this first requirement has been met—hence, the modest amount of space devoted to its parameters here.

The shorthand term "numerosity" somewhat misdirects one's attention, for the real bite of the rule comes not so much in its demand for numerous class members per se as in its insistence that their joinder must be "impracticable." When the would-be absent class members can readily be joined in the ordinary fashion of Rule 20—in practical terms, identified by name and served with legal process to participate in the action—there is no particular need for their legal rights to be adjudicated in abstentia by way of a class action. Instead, procedural law prefers that each person litigate on her own behalf.

As the authors of one prominent treatise observe, the word " 'impracticable' does not mean 'impossible.' The [class] representatives only need to show that it is extremely difficult or inconvenient to join all the members of the class." 7A FEDERAL PRACTICE AND PROCEDURE § 1762, at 176.

Given the focus upon the impracticability of joinder, it is not surprising that little in the way of absolute numerical rules has emerged from the cases applying the numerosity requirement. To be sure, proposed classes numbering in the single digits or teens have not been certified. But the case law becomes more mixed in the range between 30 and 100 class members. See *id*. at 188–205 (discussing illustrative cases). As one court summarizes the basic principles:

> Rule 23(a)(1) incorporates no bright-line test for determining numerosity. This determination rests on the court's practical judgment in light of the particular facts of the case. The class representative is not required to establish the exact number in the proposed class. "Plaintiffs must show some evidence of or reasonably estimate the number of class members." Estimates as to the size of the proposed class are sufficient for a class action to proceed. Mere speculation and unsubstantiated allegations as to numerosity, however, are insufficient to satisfy Rule 23(a)(1).

Wright v. Circuit City Stores, Inc., 201 F.R.D. 526, 537–38 (N.D. Ala. 2001).

2.   COMMONALITY AND TYPICALITY

As the Court notes in *Falcon* below, "[t]he commonality and typicality requirements of Rule 23(a) tend to merge." Both also "tend to merge" with the further requirement of adequate class representation, which is discussed in the next subsection. All three requirements, as the Court emphasizes, ask in various ways "whether the named plaintiff's claim and the class claims are so interrelated that the interests of the class members will be fairly and adequately protected in their absence." In short, these requirements ask whether the proposed class would be a sufficiently cohesive unit as to warrant deviation from the usual principle—recounted in *Hansberry*—that "one is not bound by a judgment in personam in a litigation in which he is not designated as a party or to which he has not been made a party by service of process."

The commonality requirement of subsection (a)(2) asks whether "there are questions of law or fact common to the class." The focus is on the relationship of the class members *to one another*. The typicality requirement of subsection (a)(3) focuses on the relationship *of the class representative to the absent members* of the proposed class, asking whether the claims of the former are "typical" of those of the latter. If there were no questions of law or fact common across the class as a whole, then it will be essentially impossible to find a class representative whose claims would typify those of the class as a group. In thinking about the commonality and typicality requirements, then, one might best think in terms of the cohesiveness of the proposed class and, only thereafter, translate one's conclusions as to the presence or absence of cohesiveness into the specific terms of subsections (a)(2)–(4).

General Telephone Co. v. Falcon

457 U.S. 147 (1982)

■ JUSTICE STEVENS delivered the opinion of the Court.

The question presented is whether respondent Falcon, who complained that petitioner did not promote him because he is a Mexican–American, was properly permitted to maintain a class action on behalf of Mexican–American applicants for employment whom petitioner did not hire.

I

In 1969 petitioner initiated a special recruitment and training program for minorities. Through that program, respondent Falcon was hired in July 1969 as a groundman, and within a year he was twice promoted, first to lineman and then to lineman-in-charge. He subsequently refused a promotion to installer-repairman. In October 1972 he applied for the job of field inspector; his application was denied even though the promotion was granted several white employees with less seniority.

Falcon thereupon filed a charge with the Equal Employment Opportunity Commission stating his belief that he had been passed over for promotion because of his national origin and that petitioner's promotion policy operated against Mexican–Americans as a class. In due course he received a right-to-sue letter from the Commission and, in April 1975, he commenced this action under Title VII of the Civil Rights Act of 1964. . . . His complaint alleged that petitioner maintained "a policy, practice, custom, or usage of: (a) discriminating against [Mexican–Americans] because of national origin and with respect to compensation, terms, conditions, and privileges of employment, and (b) . . . subjecting [Mexican–Americans] to continuous employment discrimination." Respondent claimed that as a result of this policy whites with less qualification and experience and lower evaluation scores than respondent had been promoted more rapidly. The complaint contained no factual allegations concerning petitioner's hiring practices.

Respondent brought the action "on his own behalf and on behalf of other persons similarly situated, pursuant to Rule 23(b)(2) of the Federal Rules of Civil Procedure." The class identified in the complaint was "composed of Mexican–American persons who are employed, or who might be employed, by GENERAL TELEPHONE COMPANY at its place of business located in Irving, Texas, who have been and who continue to be or might be adversely affected by the practices complained of herein."

After responding to petitioner's written interrogatories, respondent filed a memorandum in favor of certification of "the class of all hourly Mexican American employees who have been employed, are employed, or may in the future be employed and all those Mexican–Americans who have applied or would have applied for employment had the Defendant not practiced racial discrimination in its employment practices." His position was supported by the ruling of the United States Court of Appeals for the Fifth Circuit in *Johnson v. Georgia Highway Express, Inc.*, 417 F.2d 1122 (1969), that any victim of racial discrimination in employment may maintain an "across the board" attack on all unequal employment practices alleged to have been committed by the employer pursuant to a policy of racial discrimination. Without conducting an evidentiary hearing, the District Court certified a class including Mexican–American employees and Mexican–American applicants for employment who had not been hired.

Following trial of the liability issues, the District Court entered separate findings of fact and conclusions of law with respect first to respondent and then to the class. The District Court found that petitioner had not discriminated against respondent in hiring, but that it did discriminate against him in its promotion practices. The court reached converse conclusions about the class, finding no discrimination in promotion practices, but concluding that petitioner had discriminated against Mexican–Americans at its Irving facility in its hiring practices.

After various post-trial proceedings, the District Court ordered petitioner to furnish respondent with a list of all Mexican–Americans who had applied for employment at the Irving facility during the period between January 1, 1973, and October 18, 1976. Respondent was then ordered to give notice to those persons advising them that they might be entitled to some form of recovery. Evidence was taken concerning the applicants who responded to the notice, and backpay was ultimately awarded to 13 persons, in addition to respondent Falcon. The total recovery by respondent and the entire class amounted to $67,925.49, plus costs and interest.

. . . [W]e granted certiorari to decide whether the class action was properly maintained on behalf of both employees who were denied promotion and applicants who were denied employment.

II

The class-action device was designed as "an exception to the usual rule that litigation is conducted by and on behalf of the individual named parties only." *Califano v. Yamasaki*, 442 U.S. 682, 700–01 (1979). Class relief is "peculiarly appropriate" when the "issues involved are common to the class as a whole" and when they "turn on questions of law applicable in the same manner to each member of the class." *Id.* at 701. For in such cases, "the class-action device saves the resources of both the courts and the parties by permitting an issue potentially affecting every [class member] to be litigated in an economical fashion under Rule 23." *Id.*

Title VII of the Civil Rights Act of 1964, as amended, authorizes the Equal Employment Opportunity Commission to sue in its own name to secure relief for individuals aggrieved by discriminatory practices forbidden by the Act. See 42 U.S.C. § 2000e–5(f)(1). In exercising this enforcement power, the Commission may seek relief for groups of employees or applicants for employment without complying with the strictures of Rule 23. Title VII, however, contains no special authorization for class suits maintained by private parties. An individual litigant seeking to maintain a class action under Title VII must meet "the prerequisites of numerosity, commonality, typicality, and adequacy of representation" specified in Rule 23(a). These requirements effectively "limit the class claims to those fairly encompassed by the named plaintiff's claims."

We have repeatedly held that "a class representative must be part of the class and 'possess the same interest and suffer the same injury' as the class members." *East Texas Motor Freight System, Inc. v. Rodriguez*, 431 U.S. 395, 403 (1977) (quoting *Schlesinger v. Reservists Committee to Stop the War*, 418 U.S. 208, 216 (1974)). In *East Texas Motor Freight*, a Title VII action brought by three Mexican–American city drivers, the Fifth Circuit certified a class consisting of the trucking company's black and Mexican–American city drivers allegedly denied on racial or ethnic grounds transfers to more desirable line-driver jobs. We held that the Court of Appeals had "plainly erred in declaring a class action." 431 U.S. at 403. Because at the time the class was certified it was clear that the named plaintiffs were not qualified for line-driver positions, "they could have suffered no injury as a result of the allegedly discriminatory practices, and they were, therefore, simply not eligible to represent a class of persons who did allegedly suffer injury." *Id.* at 403–04.

Our holding in *East Texas Motor Freight* was limited; we noted that "a different case would be presented if the District Court had certified a class and only later had it appeared that the named plaintiffs were not class members or were otherwise inappropriate class representatives." *Id.* at 406 n.12. We also recognized the theory behind the Fifth Circuit's across-the-board rule, noting our awareness "that suits alleging racial or ethnic discrimination are often by their very nature class suits, involving classwide wrongs," and that "[c]ommon questions of law or fact are typically present." *Id.* at 405. In the same breath, however, we reiterated that "careful attention to the requirements of Fed. R. Civ. P. 23 remains nonetheless indispensable" and that the "mere fact that a complaint alleges racial or ethnic discrimination does not in itself ensure that the party who has brought the lawsuit will be an adequate representative of those who may have been the real victims of that discrimination." *Id.* at 405–06.

We cannot disagree with the proposition underlying the across-the-board rule—that racial discrimination is by definition class discrimination. But the allegation that such discrimination has occurred neither determines whether a class action may be maintained in accordance with Rule 23 nor defines the class that may be certified. Conceptually, there is a wide gap between (a) an individual's claim that he has been denied a promotion on discriminatory grounds, and his otherwise unsupported allegation that the company has a policy of discrimination, and (b) the existence of a class of persons who have suffered the same injury as that individual, such that the individual's claim and the class claims will share common questions of law or fact and that the individual's claim will be typical of the class claims.[13] For respondent to bridge that gap, he must prove much more than the validity of his own claim. Even though evidence that he was passed over for promotion when several less deserving whites were advanced may

---

[13] The commonality and typicality requirements of Rule 23(a) tend to merge. Both serve as guideposts for determining whether under the particular circumstances maintenance of a class action is economical and whether the named plaintiff's claim and the class claims are so interrelated that the interests of the class members will be fairly and adequately protected in their absence. Those requirements therefore also tend to merge with the adequacy-of-representation requirement, although the latter requirement also raises concerns about the competency of class counsel and conflicts of interest. . . .

support the conclusion that respondent was denied the promotion because of his national origin, such evidence would not necessarily justify the additional inferences (1) that this discriminatory treatment is typical of petitioner's promotion practices, (2) that petitioner's promotion practices are motivated by a policy of ethnic discrimination that pervades petitioner's Irving division, or (3) that this policy of ethnic discrimination is reflected in petitioner's other employment practices, such as hiring, in the same way it is manifested in the promotion practices. These additional inferences demonstrate the tenuous character of any presumption that the class claims are "fairly encompassed" within respondent's claim.

Respondent's complaint provided an insufficient basis for concluding that the adjudication of his claim of discrimination in promotion would require the decision of any common question concerning the failure of petitioner to hire more Mexican–Americans. Without any specific presentation identifying the questions of law or fact that were common to the claims of respondent and of the members of the class he sought to represent, it was error for the District Court to presume that respondent's claim was typical of other claims against petitioner by Mexican–American employees and applicants. If one allegation of specific discriminatory treatment were sufficient to support an across-the-board attack, every Title VII case would be a potential companywide class action. We find nothing in the statute to indicate that Congress intended to authorize such a wholesale expansion of class-action litigation.[15] . . .

III

The need to carefully apply the requirements of Rule 23(a) to Title VII class actions was noticed by a member of the Fifth Circuit panel that announced the across-the-board rule. In a specially concurring opinion in *Johnson v. Georgia Highway Express, Inc.*, 417 F.2d 1122., 1125–27 (1969), Judge Godbold emphasized the need for "more precise pleadings," for "without reasonable specificity the court cannot define the class, cannot determine whether the representation is adequate, and the employer does not know how to defend," *id.* at 1126. He termed as "most significant" the potential unfairness to the class members bound by the judgment if the framing of the class is overbroad. And he pointed out the error of the "tacit assumption" underlying the across-the-board rule that "all will be well for surely the plaintiff will win and manna will fall on all members of the class." *Id.* at 1127. With the same concerns in mind, we reiterate today that a Title VII class action, like any other class action, may only be certified if the trial court is satisfied, after a rigorous analysis, that the prerequisites of Rule 23(a) have been satisfied.

The judgment of the Court of Appeals affirming the certification order is reversed, and the case is remanded for further proceedings consistent with this opinion.

---

[15] If petitioner used a biased testing procedure to evaluate both applicants for employment and incumbent employees, a class action on behalf of every applicant or employee who might have been prejudiced by the test clearly would satisfy the commonality and typicality requirements of Rule 23(a). Significant proof that an employer operated under a general policy of discrimination conceivably could justify a class of both applicants and employees if the discrimination manifested itself in hiring and promotion practices in the same general fashion, such as through entirely subjective decisionmaking processes. In this regard it is noteworthy that Title VII prohibits discriminatory employment practices, not an abstract policy of discrimination. The mere fact that an aggrieved private plaintiff is a member of an identifiable class of persons of the same race or national origin is insufficient to establish his standing to litigate on their behalf all possible claims of discrimination against a common employer.

It is so ordered.

NOTES AND QUESTIONS

1. *The Practical Significance of Commonality and Typicality*. Why, as a practical matter, should the law condition class certification upon a showing of commonality across the class and typicality in the claims of the class representative by comparison to those of absent class members? What is the underlying theory of representation that makes such questions pertinent to the ultimate question of whether "[o]ne or more members of a class may sue . . . as representative parties on behalf of all members"? Does any such theory make sense as a basis for class action adjudication? What would be the troubling consequences, if any—whether for the judicial system or for the persons whose legal rights and obligations stand to be adjudicated in the action—if the law did not to require a showing of commonality and typicality as a precondition to class certification? To take the situation in *Falcon* specifically, what would be so bad about the idea of Mariano Falcon, who was hired but not promoted, litigating the claims of both current and prospective Mexican–American employees?

2. *Agency Action versus Class Action*. The *Falcon* Court takes care to note that the federal employment discrimination laws authorize the Equal Employment Opportunity Commission to bring enforcement actions against employers thought to have engaged in prohibited discrimination with regard to multiple employees, without having to satisfy the standards of Rule 23. Why should the law afford a public administrative agency more flexibility in this regard than private litigants?

3. *"Pattern-or-Practice" Cases*. The plaintiff in *Falcon* alleged disparate treatment of Mexican–Americans in their employment. Disparate treatment cases under Title VII call for proof of a discriminatory motive, unlike "disparate impact" cases that do not require such proof. Disparate impact cases focus on employment practices that are facially neutral but that fall more harshly on a Title VII-protected group and that are not justified on grounds of business necessity.

To this day, some disparate treatment cases involve situations in which the discriminatory motive is not hard to discern. Such cases involve flagrant, explicit animus on some ground prohibited by Title VII. But other disparate treatment cases involve discriminatory motives that are much more difficult to detect. Among the most vexing cases today are those in which the would-be class representative alleges that the defendant engaged in a "pattern or practice" of disparate treatment.

The Supreme Court has explained that the initial burden on the plaintiff in a pattern-or-practice case "is to demonstrate that unlawful discrimination has been a regular procedure or policy followed by an employer. . . ." *International Brotherhood of Teamsters v. United States*, 431 U.S. 324, 360 (1977). "At the initial, 'liability' stage of a pattern-or-practice suit the [plaintiff] is not required to offer evidence that each person for whom [the plaintiff] will ultimately seek relief was a victim of the employer's discriminatory policy. Its burden is to establish a prima facie case that such a policy existed." *Id.* "If an employer fails to rebut the inference that arises from the . . . prima facie case, a trial court may then conclude that a violation has occurred and determine the appropriate remedy. Without any further evidence . . . , a court's finding of a pattern or practice justifies an award of prospective relief," such as "an injunctive order against continuation of the discriminatory practice." *Id.* at 361. When individual relief is sought for the victims of the discriminatory practice, "a district court must usually conduct additional proceedings after the liability phase of the trial to determine the scope of individual relief." *Id.*

What if the pattern or practice consists of a nationwide employer's delegation of decisions regarding employee pay or promotions to its regional or local management—e.g., where the defendant sets baseline pay rates for particular jobs but permits local management to exercise wide-ranging, subjective discretion to depart from the baseline in individual instances, or where the defendant sets bare-bones, minimum standards for promotion and permits local management to exercise subjective discretion in choosing which workers to promote from among those who meet the minimum standards? Should the delegation of pay and promotion decisions to lower levels within the company give rise to common questions of law or fact such as would support the certification of a class consisting of company employees nationwide? Would such a view be tantamount to saying that the lack of a nationwide policy concerning pay and promotion amounts, in itself, to a nationwide policy? Would such a stance effectively give rise to a permutation of the "across-the-board" approach to class certification, what the Supreme Court in *Falcon* rejects? Conversely, would relegation of employees to the pursuit of litigation on a region-by-region or, perhaps, store-by-store basis effectively mask a larger culture of discrimination within the company on a nationwide basis?

The next case considers these issues in light of the certification of what was the largest employment discrimination class action in history against Wal–Mart on the theory that delegating decisions concerning the pay and promotion of hourly workers to managerial positions amounts to disparate treatment of its hourly female employees.

Wal–Mart Stores, Inc. v. Dukes

131 S.Ct. 2541 (2011)

■ JUSTICE SCALIA delivered the opinion of the Court in which JUSTICE GINSBURG, JUSTICE BREYER, JUSTICE SOTOMAYOR, and JUSTICE KAGAN joined as to Parts I and III.

We are presented with one of the most expansive class actions ever. The District Court and the Court of Appeals approved the certification of a class comprising about one and a half million plaintiffs, current and former female employees of petitioner Wal–Mart who allege that the discretion exercised by their local supervisors over pay and promotion matters violates Title VII by discriminating against women. In addition to injunctive and declaratory relief, the plaintiffs seek an award of backpay. We consider whether the certification of the plaintiff class was consistent with Federal Rules of Civil Procedure 23(a) and (b)(2).

I

A

Petitioner Wal–Mart is the Nation's largest private employer. It operates four types of retail stores throughout the country: Discount Stores, Supercenters, Neighborhood Markets, and Sam's Clubs. Those stores are divided into seven nationwide divisions, which in turn comprise 41 regions of 80 to 85 stores apiece. Each store has between 40 and 53 separate departments and 80 to 500 staff positions. In all, Wal–Mart operates approximately 3,400 stores and employs more than one million people.

Pay and promotion decisions at Wal–Mart are generally committed to local managers' broad discretion, which is exercised "in a largely subjective manner." Local store managers may increase the wages of hourly employees (within limits) with only limited corporate oversight. As for salaried employees, such as store managers and their deputies, higher corporate authorities have discretion to set their pay with-in preestablished ranges.

Promotions work in a similar fashion. Wal–Mart permits store managers to apply their own subjective criteria when selecting candidates as "support managers," which is the first step on the path to management. Admission to Wal–Mart's management training program, however, does require that a candidate meet certain objective criteria, including an above-average performance rating, at least one year's tenure in the applicant's current position, and a willingness to relocate. But except for those requirements, regional and district managers have discretion to use their own judgment when selecting candidates for management training. Promotion to higher office—*e.g.,* assistant manager, co-manager, or store manager—is similarly at the discretion of the employee's superiors after prescribed objective factors are satisfied.

B

The named plaintiffs in this lawsuit, representing the 1.5 million members of the certified class, are three current or former Wal–Mart employees who allege that the company discriminated against them on the basis of their sex by denying them equal pay or promotions, in violation of Title VII of the Civil Rights Act of 1964. . . .

These plaintiffs, respondents here, do not allege that Wal–Mart has any express corporate policy against the advancement of women. Rather, they claim that their local managers' discretion over pay and promotions is exercised disproportionately in favor of men, leading to an unlawful disparate impact on female employees. And, respondents say, because Wal–Mart is aware of this effect, its refusal to cabin its managers' authority amounts to disparate treatment. Their complaint seeks injunctive and declaratory relief, punitive damages, and backpay. It does not ask for compensatory damages.

Importantly for our purposes, respondents claim that the discrimination to which they have been subjected is common to *all* Wal–Mart's female employees. The basic theory of their case is that a strong and uniform "corporate culture" permits bias against women to infect, perhaps subconsciously, the discretionary decisionmaking of each one of Wal–Mart's thousands of managers—thereby making every woman at the company the victim of one common discriminatory practice. Respondents therefore wish to litigate the Title VII claims of all female employees at Wal–Mart's stores in a nationwide class action.

C

. . . Invoking [Rule 23's] provisions, respondents moved the District Court to certify a plaintiff class consisting of " '[a]ll women employed at any Wal–Mart domestic retail store at any time since December 26, 1998, who have been or may be subjected to Wal–Mart's challenged pay and management track promotions policies and practices.' " As evidence that there were indeed "questions of law or fact common to" all the women of Wal–Mart, as

[handwritten margin notes: "No policy but Discretion favors men." and "every woman at company"]

Rule 23(a)(2) requires, respondents relied chiefly on three forms of proof: statistical evidence about pay and promotion disparities between men and women at the company, anecdotal reports of discrimination from about 120 of Wal–Mart's female employees, and the testimony of a sociologist, Dr. William Bielby, who conducted a "social framework analysis" of Wal–Mart's "culture" and personnel practices, and concluded that the company was "vulnerable" to gender discrimination.

Wal–Mart unsuccessfully moved to strike much of this evidence. It also offered its own countervailing statistical and other proof in an effort to defeat Rule 23(a)'s requirements of commonality, typicality, and adequate representation. Wal–Mart further contended that respondents' monetary claims for backpay could not be certified under Rule 23(b)(2), first because that Rule refers only to injunctive and declaratory relief, and second because the backpay claims could not be manageably tried as a class without depriving Wal–Mart of its right to present certain statutory defenses. With one limitation not relevant here, the District Court granted respondents' motion and certified their proposed class.

D

A divided en banc Court of Appeals substantially affirmed the District Court's certification order. The majority concluded that respondents' evidence of commonality was sufficient to "raise the common question whether Wal–Mart's female employees nationwide were subjected to a single set of corporate policies (not merely a number of independent discriminatory acts) that may have worked to unlawfully discriminate against them in violation of Title VII." It also agreed with the District Court that the named plaintiffs' claims were sufficiently typical of the class as a whole to satisfy Rule 23(a)(3), and that they could serve as adequate class representatives . . .

Finally, the Court of Appeals determined that the action could be manageably tried as a class action because the District Court could adopt the approach the Ninth Circuit approved in *Hilao v. Estate of Marcos,* 103 F.3d 767, 782–87 (1996). There compensatory damages for some 9,541 class members were calculated by selecting 137 claims at random, referring those claims to a special master for valuation, and then extrapolating the validity and value of the untested claims from the sample set. The Court of Appeals "s[aw] no reason why a similar procedure to that used in *Hilao* could not be employed in this case." It would allow Wal–Mart "to present individual defenses in the randomly selected 'sample cases,' thus revealing the approximate percentage of class members whose unequal pay or non-promotion was due to something other than gender discrimination."

II

. . .

A

The crux of this case is commonality—the rule requiring a plaintiff to show that "there are questions of law or fact common to the class." Rule 23(a)(2). That language is easy to misread, since "[a]ny competently crafted class complaint literally raises common 'questions.'" Nagareda, *Class Certification in the Age of Aggregate Proof,* 84 N.Y.U. L. Rev. 97, 131–32 (2009). For example: Do all of us plaintiffs indeed work for Wal–Mart? Do our managers have discretion over pay? Is that an unlawful employment practice? What remedies should we get? Reciting these questions is not sufficient to obtain class certification. Commonality requires the plaintiff to demonstrate that the class members "have suffered the same injury," *Fal-*

con, supra, at 157. This does not mean merely that they have all suffered a violation of the same provision of law. Title VII, for example, can be violated in many ways—by intentional discrimination, or by hiring and promotion criteria that result in disparate impact, and by the use of these practices on the part of many different superiors in a single company. Quite obviously, the mere claim by employees of the same company that they have suffered a Title VII injury, or even a disparate-impact Title VII injury, gives no cause to believe that all their claims can productively be litigated at once. Their claims must depend upon a common contention—for example, the assertion of discriminatory bias on the part of the same supervisor. That common contention, moreover, must be of such a nature that it is capable of classwide resolution—which means that determination of its truth or falsity will resolve an issue that is central to the validity of each one of the claims in one stroke.

> "What matters to class certification . . . is not the raising of common 'questions'—even in droves—but, rather the capacity of a classwide proceeding to generate common *answers* apt to drive the resolution of the litigation. Dissimilarities within the proposed class are what have the potential to impede the generation of common answers." Nagareda, *supra,* at 132.

Rule 23 does not set forth a mere pleading standard. A party seeking class certification must affirmatively demonstrate his compliance with the Rule—that is, he must be prepared to prove that there are *in fact* sufficiently numerous parties, common questions of law or fact, etc. We recognized in *Falcon* that "sometimes it may be necessary for the court to probe behind the pleadings before coming to rest on the certification question," 457 U.S. at 160, and that certification is proper only if "the trial court is satisfied, after a rigorous analysis, that the prerequisites of Rule 23(a) have been satisfied." Frequently that "rigorous analysis" will entail some overlap with the merits of the plaintiff's underlying claim. That cannot be helped. "[T]he class determination generally involves considerations that are enmeshed in the factual and legal issues comprising the plaintiff's cause of action.'" *Falcon, supra,* at 160.[6] Nor is there anything unusual about that consequence: The necessity of touching aspects of the merits in order to resolve preliminary matters, *e.g.,* jurisdiction and venue, is a familiar feature of litigation.

In this case, proof of commonality necessarily overlaps with respondents' merits contention that Wal–Mart engages in a *pattern or practice* of discrimination. That is so because, in resolving an individual's Title VII

---

[6] A statement in one of our prior cases, *Eisen v. Carlisle & Jacquelin,* 417 U.S. 156, 177 (1974), is sometimes mistakenly cited to the contrary: "We find nothing in either the language or history of Rule 23 that gives a court any authority to conduct a preliminary inquiry into the merits of a suit in order to determine whether it may be maintained as a class action." But in that case, the judge had conducted a preliminary inquiry into the merits of a suit, not in order to determine the propriety of certification under Rules 23(a) and (b) (he had already done that, see *id.* at 165), but in order to shift the cost of notice required by Rule 23(c)(2) from the plaintiff to the defendants. To the extent the quoted statement goes beyond the permissibility of a merits inquiry for any other pretrial purpose, it is the purest dictum and is contradicted by our other cases.

Perhaps the most common example of considering a merits question at the Rule 23 stage arises in class-action suits for securities fraud. . . . To invoke this [fraud on the market] presumption, the plaintiffs seeking 23(b)(3) certification must prove that their shares were traded on an efficient market, *Erica P. John Fund, Inc. v. Halliburton Co.,* 563 U.S. ___, ___ (2011) (slip op., at 5), an issue they will surely have to prove *again* at trial in order to make out their case on the merits.

claim, the crux of the inquiry is "the reason for a particular employment decision," *Cooper v. Federal Reserve Bank of Richmond,* 467 U.S. 867, 876 (1984). Here respondents wish to sue about literally millions of employment decisions at once. Without some glue holding the alleged *reasons* for all those decisions together, it will be impossible to say that examination of all the class members' claims for relief will produce a common answer to the crucial question *why was I disfavored.*

employment Decisions are factual inquiries inquiries.

B

This Court's opinion in *Falcon* describes how the commonality issue must be approached. There an employee who claimed that he was deliberately denied a promotion on account of race obtained certification of a class comprising all employees wrongfully denied promotions and all applicants wrongfully denied jobs. We rejected that composite class for lack of commonality and typicality, explaining:

> "Conceptually, there is a wide gap between (a) an individual's claim that he has been denied a promotion [or higher pay] on discriminatory grounds, and his otherwise unsupported allegation that the company has a policy of discrimination, and (b) the existence of a class of persons who have suffered the same injury as that individual, such that the individual's claim and the class claim will share common questions of law or fact and that the individual's claim will be typical of the class claims."

Falcon suggested two ways in which that conceptual gap might be bridged. First, if the employer "used a biased testing procedure to evaluate both applicants for employment and incumbent employees, a class action on behalf of every applicant or employee who might have been prejudiced by the test clearly would satisfy the commonality and typicality requirements of Rule 23(a)." Second, "[s]ignificant proof that an employer operated under a general policy of discrimination conceivably could justify a class of both applicants and employees if the discrimination manifested itself in hiring and promotion practices in the same general fashion, such as through entirely subjective decisionmaking processes." We think that statement precisely describes respondents' burden in this case. The first manner of bridging the gap obviously has no application here; Wal–Mart has no testing procedure or other companywide evaluation method that can be charged with bias. The whole point of permitting discretionary decisionmaking is to avoid evaluating employees under a common standard.

The second manner of bridging the gap requires "significant proof" that Wal–Mart "operated under a general policy of discrimination." That is entirely absent here. Wal–Mart's announced policy forbids sex discrimination, and as the District Court recognized the company imposes penalties for denials of equal employment opportunity. The only evidence of a "general policy of discrimination" respondents produced was the testimony of Dr. William Bielby, their sociological expert. Relying on "social framework" analysis, Bielby testified that Wal–Mart has a "strong corporate culture," that makes it "vulnerable" to "gender bias." He could not, however, "determine with any specificity how regularly stereotypes play a meaningful role in employment decisions at Wal–Mart. At his deposition . . . Dr. Bielby conceded that he could not calculate whether 0.5 percent or 95 percent of the employment decisions at Wal–Mart might be determined by stereotyped thinking." The parties dispute whether Bielby's testimony even met the standards for the admission of expert testimony under Federal Rule of Civil Procedure 702 and our *Daubert* case, see *Daubert v. Merrell Dow Pharma-*

ceuticals, Inc., 509 U.S. 579 (1993). The District Court concluded that *Daubert* did not apply to expert testimony at the certification stage of class-action proceedings. We doubt that is so, but even if properly considered, Bielby's testimony does nothing to advance respondents' case. "[W]hether 0.5 percent or 95 percent of the employment decisions at Wal–Mart might be determined by stereotyped thinking" is the essential question on which respondents' theory of commonality depends. If Bielby admittedly has no answer to that question, we can safely disregard what he has to say. It is worlds away from "significant proof" that Wal–Mart "operated under a general policy of discrimination."

C

The only corporate policy that the plaintiffs' evidence convincingly establishes is Wal–Mart's "policy" of *allowing discretion* by local supervisors over employment matters. On its face, of course, that is just the opposite of a uniform employment practice that would provide the commonality needed for a class action; it is a policy *against having* uniform employment practices. It is also a very common and presumptively reasonable way of doing business—one that we have said "should itself raise no inference of discriminatory conduct," *Watson v. Fort Worth Bank & Trust,* 487 U.S. 977, 990 (1988).

To be sure, we have recognized that, "in appropriate cases," giving discretion to lower-level supervisors can be the basis of Title VII liability under a disparate-impact theory—since "an employer's undisciplined system of subjective decisionmaking [can have] precisely the same effects as a system pervaded by impermissible intentional discrimination." *Id.* at 990–91. But the recognition that this type of Title VII claim "can" exist does not lead to the conclusion that every employee in a company using a system of discretion has such a claim in common. To the contrary, left to their own devices most managers in any corporation—and surely most managers in a corporation that forbids sex discrimination—would select sex-neutral, performance-based criteria for hiring and promotion that produce no actionable disparity at all. Others may choose to reward various attributes that produce disparate impact—such as scores on general aptitude tests or educational achievements, see *Griggs v. Duke Power Co.,* 401 U.S. 424, 431–32 (1971). And still other managers may be guilty of intentional discrimination that produces a sex-based disparity. In such a company, demonstrating the invalidity of one manager's use of discretion will do nothing to demonstrate the invalidity of another's. A party seeking to certify a nationwide class will be unable to show that all the employees' Title VII claims will in fact depend on the answers to common questions.

Respondents have not identified a common mode of exercising discretion that pervades the entire company—aside from their reliance on Dr. Bielby's social frameworks analysis that we have rejected. In a company of Wal–Mart's size and geographical scope, it is quite unbelievable that all managers would exercise their discretion in a common way without some common direction. Respondents attempt to make that showing by means of statistical and anecdotal evidence, but their evidence falls well short.

The statistical evidence consists primarily of regression analyses performed by Dr. Richard Drogin, a statistician, and Dr. Marc Bendick, a labor economist. Drogin conducted his analysis region-by-region, comparing the number of women promoted into management positions with the percentage of women in the available pool of hourly workers. After considering regional and national data, Drogin concluded that "there are statistically significant disparities between men and women at Wal–Mart . . . [and] these disparities . . . can be explained only by gender discrimination." Bendick compared work-force data from Wal–Mart and competitive retailers and concluded that Wal–Mart "promotes a lower percentage of women than its competitors."

Even if they are taken at face value, these studies are insufficient to establish that respondents' theory can be proved on a classwide basis. In *Falcon,* we held that one named plaintiff's experience of discrimination was insufficient to infer that "discriminatory treatment is typical of [the employer's employment] practices." 457 U.S. at 158. A similar failure of inference arises here. As Judge Ikuta observed in her dissent, "[i]nformation about disparities at the regional and national level does not establish the existence of disparities at individual stores, let alone raise the inference that a company-wide policy of discrimination is implemented by discretionary decisions at the store and district level." A regional pay disparity, for example, may be attributable to only a small set of Wal–Mart stores, and cannot by itself establish the uniform, store-by-store disparity upon which the plaintiffs' theory of commonality depends.

There is another, more fundamental, respect in which respondents' statistical proof fails. Even if it established (as it does not) a pay or promotion pattern that differs from the nationwide figures or the regional figures in *all* of Wal–Mart's 3,400 stores, that would still not demonstrate that commonality of issue exists. Some managers will claim that the availability of women, or qualified women, or interested women, in their stores' area does not mirror the national or regional statistics. And almost all of them will claim to have been applying some sex-neutral, performance-based criteria—whose nature and effects will differ from store to store. In the landmark case of ours which held that giving discretion to lower-level supervisors can be the basis of Title VII liability under a disparate-impact theory, the plurality opinion *conditioned* that holding on the corollary that merely proving that the discretionary system has produced a racial or sexual disparity *is not enough.* "[T]he plaintiff must begin by identifying the specific employment practice that is challenged." *Watson,* 487 U.S. at 994. That is all the more necessary when a class of plaintiffs is sought to be certified. Other than the bare existence of delegated discretion, respondents have identified no "specific employment practice"—much less one that ties all their 1.5 million claims together. Merely showing that Wal–Mart's policy of discretion has produced an overall sex-based disparity does not suffice.

Respondents' anecdotal evidence suffers from the same defects, and in addition is too weak to raise any inference that all the individual, discretionary personnel decisions are discriminatory. In *Teamsters v. United States,* 431 U.S. 324 (1977), in addition to substantial statistical evidence of company-wide discrimination, the Government (as plaintiff) produced about 40 specific accounts of racial discrimination from particular individuals. That number was significant because the company involved had only 6,472 employees, of whom 571 were minorities, and the class itself consisted of around 334 persons. The 40 anecdotes thus represented roughly one account for every eight members of the class. Moreover, the Court of Appeals noted that the anecdotes came from individuals "spread throughout" the company who "for the most part" worked at the company's operational centers that employed the largest numbers of the class members. Here, by contrast, respondents filed some 120 affidavits reporting experiences of discrimination—about 1 for every 12,500 class members—relating to only some 235 out of Wal–Mart's 3,400 stores. More than half of these reports are concentrated in only six States (Alabama, California, Florida, Missouri, Texas, and Wisconsin); half of all States have only one or two anecdotes; and 14 States have no anecdotes about Wal–Mart's operations at all. Even if every single one of these accounts is true, that would not demonstrate that the entire company "operate[s] under a general policy of discrimination," *Falcon, supra,* at 159 n.15, which is what respondents must show to certify a companywide class.[9]

The dissent misunderstands the nature of the foregoing analysis. It criticizes our focus on the dissimilarities between the putative class members on the ground that we have "blend[ed]" Rule 23(a)(2)'s commonality requirement with Rule 23(b)(3)'s inquiry into whether common questions "predominate" over individual ones. That is not so. We quite agree that for purposes of Rule 23(a)(2) " '[e]ven a single [common] question' " will do, *post,* at 10 n.9 (quoting Nagareda, *The Preexistence Principle and the Structure of the Class Action,* 103 Colum. L. Rev. 149, 176, n.110 (2003)). We consider dissimilarities not in order to determine (as Rule 23(b)(3) requires) whether common questions *predominate,* but in order to determine (as Rule 23(a)(2) requires) whether there *is* "[e]ven a single [common] question." And there is not here. Because respondents provide no convincing proof of a companywide discriminatory pay and promotion policy, we have concluded that they have not established the existence of any common question.

In sum, we agree with Chief Judge Kozinski that the members of the class:

> "held a multitude of different jobs, at different levels of Wal–Mart's hierarchy, for variable lengths of time, in 3,400 stores, sprinkled across 50 states, with a kaleidoscope of supervisors (male and female), subject to a variety of regional policies that all differed. . . . Some thrived while others did poorly. They have little in common but their sex and this lawsuit." 603 F.3d at 652 (dissenting opinion). . . .

■ JUSTICE GINSBURG, with whom JUSTICE BREYER, JUSTICE SOTOMAYOR, and JUSTICE KAGAN join, concurring in part and dissenting in part. . . .

I

A

Rule 23(a)(2) establishes a preliminary requirement for maintaining a class action: "[T]here are questions of law or fact common to the class." The Rule "does not require that all questions of law or fact raised in the litigation be common," H. Newberg & A. Conte, NEWBERG ON CLASS ACTIONS § 3.10, pp. 3–48 to 3–49 (3d ed. 1992); indeed, "[e]ven a single question of law or fact common to the members of the class will satisfy the commonality requirement," Nagareda, *The Preexistence Principle,* 103 Colum. L. Rev. at 176 n.110.

A "question" is ordinarily understood to be "[a] subject or point open to controversy." AMERICAN HERITAGE DICTIONARY 1483 (3d ed.1992). Thus, a "question" "common to the class" must be a dispute, either of fact or of law,

---

[9] The dissent says that we have adopted "a rule that a discrimination claim, if accompanied by anecdotes, must supply them in numbers proportionate to the size of the class." *Post,* at ___, n. 4 (GINSBURG, J., concurring in part and dissenting in part). That is not quite accurate. A discrimination claimant is free to supply as few anecdotes as he wishes. But when the claim is that a company operates under a general policy of discrimination, a few anecdotes selected from literally millions of employment decisions prove nothing at all.

the resolution of which will advance the determination of the class members' claims.

B

The District Court, recognizing that "one significant issue common to the class may be sufficient to warrant certification," found that the plaintiffs easily met that test. Absent an error of law or an abuse of discretion, an appellate tribunal has no warrant to upset the District Court's finding of commonality.

The District Court certified a class of "[a]ll women employed at any Wal–Mart domestic retail store at any time since December 26, 1998." The named plaintiffs, led by Betty Dukes, propose to litigate, on behalf of the class, allegations that Wal–Mart discriminates on the basis of gender in pay and promotions. They allege that the company "[r]eli[es] on gender stereotypes in making employment decisions such as . . . promotion[s] [and] pay." Wal–Mart permits those prejudices to infect personnel decisions, the plaintiffs contend, by leaving pay and promotions in the hands of "a nearly all male managerial workforce" using "arbitrary and subjective criteria." Further alleged barriers to the advancement of female employees include the company's requirement, "as a condition of promotion to management jobs, that employees be willing to relocate." Absent instruction otherwise, there is a risk that managers will act on the familiar assumption that women, because of their services to husband and children, are less mobile than men.

Women fill 70 percent of the hourly jobs in the retailer's stores but make up only "33 percent of management employees." "[T]he higher one looks in the organization the lower the percentage of women." The plaintiffs' "largely uncontested descriptive statistics" also show that women working in the company's stores "are paid less than men in every region" and "that the salary gap widens over time even for men and women hired into the same jobs at the same time."

The District Court identified "systems for . . . promoting in-store employees" that were "sufficiently similar across regions and stores" to conclude that "the manner in which these systems affect the class raises issues that are common to all class members." The selection of employees for promotion to in-store management "is fairly characterized as a 'tap on the shoulder' process," in which managers have discretion about whose shoulders to tap. Vacancies are not regularly posted; from among those employees satisfying minimum qualifications, managers choose whom to promote on the basis of their own subjective impressions.

Wal–Mart's compensation policies also operate uniformly across stores, the District Court found. The retailer leaves open a $2 band for every position's hourly pay rate. Wal–Mart provides no standards or criteria for setting wages within that band, and thus does nothing to counter unconscious bias on the part of supervisors.

Wal–Mart's supervisors do not make their discretionary decisions in a vacuum. The District Court reviewed means Wal–Mart used to maintain a "carefully constructed . . . corporate culture," such as frequent meetings to reinforce the common way of thinking, regular transfers of managers between stores to ensure uniformity throughout the company, monitoring of stores "on a close and constant basis," and "Wal–Mart TV," "broadcas[t] . . . into all stores."

The plaintiffs' evidence, including class members' tales of their own experiences, suggests that gender bias suffused Wal–Mart's company culture. Among illustrations, senior management often refer to female associates as "little Janie Qs." One manager told an employee that "[m]en are here to make a career and women aren't." A committee of female Wal–Mart executives concluded that "[s]tereotypes limit the opportunities offered to women."

Finally, the plaintiffs presented an expert's appraisal to show that the pay and promotions disparities at Wal–Mart "can be explained only by gender discrimination and not by . . . neutral variables." Using regression analyses, their expert, Richard Drogin, controlled for factors including, *inter alia,* job performance, length of time with the company, and the store where an employee worked.[5] The results, the District Court found, were sufficient to raise an "inference of discrimination."

C

The District Court's identification of a common question, whether Wal–Mart's pay and promotions policies gave rise to unlawful discrimination, was hardly infirm. The practice of delegating to supervisors large discretion to make personnel decisions, uncontrolled by formal standards, has long been known to have the potential to produce disparate effects. Managers, like all humankind, may be prey to biases of which they are unaware. The risk of discrimination is heightened when those managers are predominantly of one sex, and are steeped in a corporate culture that perpetuates gender stereotypes. . . .

We have held that "discretionary employment practices" can give rise to Title VII claims, not only when such practices are motivated by discriminatory intent but also when they produce discriminatory results.

The plaintiffs' allegations state claims of gender discrimination in the form of biased decisionmaking in both pay and promotions. The evidence reviewed by the District Court adequately demonstrated that resolving those claims would necessitate examination of particular policies and practices alleged to affect, adversely and globally, women employed at Wal–Mart's stores. Rule 23(a)(2), setting a necessary but not a sufficient criterion for class-action certification, demands nothing further.

II

A

The Court gives no credence to the key dispute common to the class: whether Wal–Mart's discretionary pay and promotion policies are discriminatory. "What matters," the Court asserts, "is not the raising of common 'questions,'" but whether there are "[d]issimilarities within the proposed class" that "have the potential to impede the generation of common answers."

The Court blends Rule 23(a)(2)'s threshold criterion with the more demanding criteria of Rule 23(b)(3), and thereby elevates the (a)(2) inquiry so that it is no longer "easily satisfied." Rule 23(b)(3) certification requires, in

elevates a(2)
com. to a b(3)
heightened analysis

---

[5] The Court asserts that Drogin showed only average differences at the "regional and national level" between male and female employees. *Ante,* at 16 (internal quotation marks omitted). In fact, his regression analyses showed there were disparities *within* stores. The majority's contention to the contrary reflects only an arcane disagreement about statistical method—which the District Court resolved in the plaintiffs' favor. 222 F.R.D. 137, 157 (N.D. Cal. 2004). Appellate review is no occasion to disturb a trial court's handling of factual disputes of this order.

addition to the four 23(a) findings, de-terminations that "questions of law or fact common to class members predominate over any questions affecting only individual members" and that "a class action is superior to other available methods for . . . adjudicating the controversy."

The Court's emphasis on differences between class members mimics the Rule 23(b)(3) inquiry into whether common questions "predominate" over individual issues. And by asking whether the individual differences "impede" common adjudication, *ante,* at 10 (internal quotation marks omitted), the Court duplicates 23(b)(3)'s question whether "a class action is superior" to other modes of adjudication. Indeed, Professor Nagareda, whose "dissimilarities" inquiry the Court endorses, developed his position in the context of Rule 23(b)(3).[9] "The Rule 23(b)(3) predominance inquiry" is meant to "tes[t] whether proposed classes are sufficiently cohesive to warrant adjudication by representation." *Amchem Prods., Inc. v. Windsor,* 521 U.S. 591, 623 (1997). If courts must conduct a "dissimilarities" analysis at the Rule 23(a)(2) stage, no mission remains for Rule 23(b)(3).

Because Rule 23(a) is also a prerequisite for Rule 23(b)(1) and Rule 23(b)(2) classes, the Court's "dissimilarities" position is far reaching. Individual differences should not bar a Rule 23(b)(1) or Rule 23(b)(2) class, so long as the Rule 23(a) threshold is met. For example, in *Franks v. Bowman Transp. Co.,* 424 U.S. 747 (1976), a Rule 23(b)(2) class of African–American truckdrivers complained that the defendant had discriminatorily refused to hire black applicants. We recognized that the "qualification[s] and performance" of individual class members might vary. "Generalizations concerning such individually applicable evidence," we cautioned, "cannot serve as a justification for the denial of [injunctive] relief to the entire class."

B

The "dissimilarities" approach leads the Court to train its attention on what distinguishes individual class members, rather than on what unites them. Given the lack of standards for pay and promotions, the majority says, "demonstrating the invalidity of one manager's use of discretion will do nothing to demonstrate the invalidity of another's." *Ante,* at ___.

Wal–Mart's delegation of discretion over pay and promotions is a policy uniform throughout all stores. The very nature of discretion is that people will exercise it in various ways. A system of delegated discretion, *Watson* held, is a practice actionable under Title VII when it produces discriminatory outcomes. A finding that Wal–Mart's pay and promotions practices in fact violate the law would be the first step in the usual order of proof for plaintiffs seeking individual remedies for company-wide discrimination. That each individual employee's unique circumstances will ultimately determine whether she is entitled to backpay or damages, should not factor into the Rule 23(a)(2) determination.

* * *

The Court errs in importing a "dissimilarities" notion suited to Rule 23(b)(3) into the Rule 23(a) commonality inquiry. I therefore cannot join Part II of the Court's opinion.

---

[9] Cf. *supra,* at 2 (Rule 23(a) commonality prerequisite satisfied by "[e]ven a single question . . . common to the members of the class" (quoting Nagareda, *The Preexistence Principle,* 103 Colum. L. Rev. at 176 n.110)).

NOTES AND QUESTIONS

1. *Scope of the Decision.* The majority's opinion, which held that plaintiffs had not satisfied commonality under Rule 23(a), affects class certification across-the-board. For example, despite having certified a similar case in 2009, after *Dukes*, a federal court refused to certify a Rule 23(b)(3) class against title insurance companies for overcharging customers with a previous insurance policy because proving that a previous policy existed "is uniquely individualized; it cannot be established on a classwide basis." *Corwin v. Lawyers Title Ins. Co.*, 276 F.R.D. 484, 490 (E.D. Mich. Aug. 1, 2011). Thus, the proposed class failed under Rule 23(a)(2)'s commonality requirement before ever reaching what was previously the more daunting hurdle, whether common issues *predominated* over individual ones. What matters now is not whether plaintiffs can raise common questions, but whether "a classwide proceeding [can] generate common answers apt to drive the resolution of the litigation." Now, to clear Rule 23(a)'s commonality barrier, plaintiffs may have to propose bite-sized classes that target a specific supervisor, store, or plant. Less sprawling class definitions, however, may mean that plaintiffs will tend to be geographically concentrated and fewer in number. Consequently, while targeted classes may clear the commonality hurdle, they might find Rule 23(a)'s numerosity requirement more challenging.

2. *Reining in the Commonality Standard.* By its terms, subsection (a)(2) calls for common factual or legal "questions"—plural—across the class as a whole. The use of the plural form notwithstanding, the law of class actions had settled upon the principle that the existence of a single factual or legal question across the class as a whole would suffice to satisfy subsection (a)(2). See, e.g., *In re Am. Med. Sys., Inc.*, 75 F.3d 1069, 1080 (6th Cir. 1996); *Baby Neal ex rel. Kanter v. Casey*, 43 F.3d 48, 56 (3d Cir. 1994). In functional terms, therefore, one might have understood the commonality requirement of subsection (a)(2) simply as a demand for minimal commonality, as distinct from, say, subsection (b)(3), which calls explicitly for a finding that the questions common across the class predominate over "any questions affecting only individual members." Indeed, before *Dukes*, one might have plausibly said that the comparative nature of the inquiry in subsection (b)(3) virtually necessitates a minimalist conception of Rule 23(a)(2)'s commonality requirement. But, as Justice Ginsburg contends, the majority's treatment of commonality seems more in line with the then prevailing predominance standard (i.e., that common questions *predominate* over individual ones for a (b)(3) class). Given the commonality standard put forth by the majority, would plaintiffs fare any differently if they tried to certify their class under Rule 23(b)(3) rather than (b)(2) on remand? Could the court have reached the same decision—decertifying the class—on different grounds?

Courts have often reasoned that the commonality standard in Rule 23(a)(2) should mirror that used in Rule 42 consolidation, which calls for "a common question of law or fact," and in Rule 20 permissive joinder, which requires "any question of law or fact common" to all plaintiffs or defendants. Should the reasoning in *Dukes* extend to these rules as well or do they serve different purposes?

Given the high bar for commonality in *Dukes* one might come to the conclusion that no class could ever be certified, but that has not proven to be the case even though the decision has affected certification in a number of lawsuits. Compare *Ross v. RBS Citizens, N.A.*, 667 F.3d 900 (7th Cir. 2012) (certifying a

Fair Labor Standards Act class and distinguishing *Dukes* based on the class size (less than 2,000) and the proof required under Illinois Minimum Wage Law, which does not require proof of subjective, discriminatory intent); *In re Whirlpool Corp. Front–Loading Washer Prods. Liab. Litig.*, 678 F.3d 409 (6th Cir. 2012) (holding that commonality was satisfied because issues relating to design defects and adequate warnings were likely to result in common answers that were central to the validity of each class member's claim); *Gray v. Hearst Communications, Inc.*, 444 Fed. App'x 698 (2011) (certifying a Rule 23(b)(3) class and noting that the common issue satisfying (a)(2) was whether defendant had an obligation to distribute a phone book as widely as demanded by advertisers' uniform contractual term); *Sullivan v. DB Invs., Inc.*, 667 F.3d 273 (3d Cir. 2011) (certifying an antitrust class action for settlement purposes and noting that allegedly inflating diamond prices in violation of the antitrust laws was conduct common to all plaintiffs and resulted in a common injury); *Zurn Pex Plumbing Prods. Liab. Litig.*, 644 F.3d 604 (8th Cir. 2011) (holding that breach of warranty claims were certifiable as a class because interpreting the warranty provision created a common question that did not demand an individualized inquiry) with *M.D. ex rel Stukenberg v. Perry*, 675 F.3d 832 (5th Cir. 2012) (holding that a § 1983 class failed to satisfy (a)(2)'s commonality requirement and the cohesiveness required for a (b)(2) class because plaintiffs failed to demonstrate how systemic staffing deficiencies would resolve an issue "central to the validity of each of the [class member's] claims in one stroke"); *Bolden v. Walsh Constr. Co.*, 688 F.3d 893 (7th Cir. 2012) (ruling that a class of black construction workers could not satisfy the commonality requirement because the class encompassed different work sites run by different supervisors, all of whom had hiring discretion and operated under a policy forbidding discrimination); *Bennett v. Nucor Corp.*, 656 F.3d 802 (8th Cir. 2011) (holding that plaintiffs failed to prove commonality because statistical evidence of disparate impact did not demonstrate a single policy of hiring and promotion and because the disparate treatment occurred to different people, by different people, and in different ways).

Is Justice Ginsburg correct that the majority's interpretation of (a)(2) commonality overlaps with (b)(3) predominance? Is there an argument that *Wal–Mart*'s (a)(2) holding should be limited to class actions certified under 23(b)(2)?

3.   *Substance versus Procedure.* Is *Dukes* a case about substance—i.e., the law of Title VII—or procedure—i.e., class-certification standards? Part of the problem is that, as the Ninth Circuit observed in its opinion on *Dukes*, when plaintiffs present statistical evidence in pattern-or-practice employment discrimination cases, the evidence "does not *overlap* with the merits, it largely *is* the merits." As Professor Richard Nagareda explained in the article cited by both the majority and the minority, while EEOC enforcement actions can precipitate disputes over statistical proof,

> those disputes bear only on the merits, not on the permissible procedural format for the litigation. The insistence upon a class certification determination as a precondition for aggregation of private litigation, by contrast to public enforcement, puts statistical proof in the position of doing double-duty—of buttressing the plaintiffs' case on the merits but, first, of supporting their demand for class treatment. This double-duty is what makes for the overlap between the class certification inquiry and the merits.

Richard A. Nagareda, *Class Certification in the Age of Aggregate Proof*, 84 N.Y.U. L. Rev. 97, 152 (2009). On this central problem, both the majority and the minority invoke Professor Richard Nagareda, this casebook's first author, in support of their views. Does the following passage shed any light on this disagreement?

> [A] convincing account of what class certification must do—and what it may not do—situates motions on that topic as a distinctive mode of pre-trial analysis, in contrast to summary judgment. On this view, some lower-court decisions underreach, as does *Dukes*. Here, in the words of Judge Frank Easterbrook for the Seventh Circuit, courts "may not duck hard questions by observing that each side has some support" for its respective view that the class members are relevantly the same (on plaintiffs' account) or relevantly different (in the defendant's view); rather, those questions "must be faced and squarely decided." But, so, too, do some lower-court decisions overreach by subjecting to the more demanding preponderance standard for class certification disputes that are appropriately engaged under the more plaintiff-friendly metric for summary judgment.

Richard A. Nagareda, *Common Answers for Class Certification*, 63 Vand. L. Rev. En Banc 149, 170 (2010).

    4. Plaintiffs' Evidentiary Showing. If courts can look into the case's merits insofar as those merits bear on the certification requirements, how far should courts go in evaluating the reliability of parties' evidence? One might view the *Dukes* Court as rather demanding. After all, the plaintiffs offered evidence about Wal–Mart's corporate practices, policy, and culture; statistics on gender disparities; and anecdotal evidence of gender bias. To establish Wal–Mart's corporate culture, plaintiffs relied on expert testimony from a sociologist who used a social framework analysis to suggest that Wal–Mart's culture includes gender stereotyping. They also offered testimony from a statistician who ran regression analyses for each of Wal–Mart's forty-one regions, and a labor economics expert. Not surprisingly, Wal–Mart offered experts of its own. Yet the Court found the plaintiffs' evidence insufficient to demonstrate a common discriminatory policy sufficient for class certification. We shall return to the evidentiary burden for class certification below, in section D. of this chapter.

3. Adequate Representation

    As footnote 13 in *Falcon* suggests, subsection (a)(4)'s requirement that "the representative parties will fairly and adequately protect the interests of the class" remains closely tied, as a conceptual matter, to the subsection (a)(2)'s commonality requirement and the subsection (a)(3)'s typicality requirement. In parsing class certification's significance for the members of the proposed class by way of the Court's decision in *Hansberry v. Lee*, we already have encountered what remains to this day one of the leading cases on the adequate-representation requirement. Among other things, *Hansberry*—which was decided when the original version of Rule 23 was in effect and before the 1966 revision—serves as a reminder that the reference to adequate representation in subsection (a)(4) invokes a requirement that is not merely the creature of present-day procedural rules but, more importantly, a component of constitutional due process. As a result, decisions applying Rule 23(a)(4)'s adequate-representation requirement have the potential to place outer bounds on the ability of state procedural rules to take a different view of what constitutes adequacy. Moreover, as shall emerge in Chapter 4, adequate class representation's due process pedigree has significant implications for class members' ability to bring collateral attacks on class judgments—that is, to escape the preclusive effect of such a judgment by suing, for example, in a different judicial system than the one that rendered the class judgment and alleging that class counsel or the class representative inadequately represented the class members in the first lawsuit.

The principal Supreme Court cases discussing adequate class representation—not only *Hansberry*, but also two more recent cases, *Amchem Prods., Inc. v. Windsor*, 521 U.S. 591 (1997), and *Ortiz v. Fibreboard Corp.*, 527 U.S. 815 (1999)—are best examined not exclusively as cases about adequate class representation but within the context of other, closely related questions concerning the legitimacy and operation of the class-action device: in *Hansberry*, the preclusive effect of a class judgment upon absent class members; in *Amchem*, the appropriate parameters of opt-out class actions; and, in *Ortiz*, the appropriate parameters of mandatory class actions predicated upon the existence of a limited fund. This Chapter situates accordingly these three landmark Supreme Court cases. For now, however, it is worthwhile to sketch the two aspects of representational adequacy, with an acknowledgement that their details shall emerge in sharper relief after full-fledged treatment of *Amchem*, *Ortiz*, and related cases. The first aspect asks: adequate representation of the class members *by whom*? The second asks: *When and for what purpose* is the inquiry into representational adequacy being undertaken?

Start with the "by whom" question: One avenue of inquiry concerns the relationship between *the class representative* and the absent members of the class. This, of course, was the point of concern in *Hansberry*. Recall the discussion earlier of whether Olive Burke could represent adequately in litigation over a racially restrictive covenant the interests of all residents whose "property interests" might be adversely affected by a covenant breach. Or consider why Mariano Falcon, a current General Telephone Company employee, could not represent the interests of potential Mexican-American employees. Insofar as there are fissures *within* the class itself—insofar as there are divergent interests within the collective group, in other words—even a faithful and conscientious class representative assisted by faithful and conscientious class counsel would have difficulty fairly and adequately representing all persons within the class. To translate the point to the terms of principal-agent relationships: Even a faithful agent cannot serve multiple principals with divergent interests. Of course, this assumes that the representative is an agent in the sense of being required to take account of and protect the interests of the principal. A different view of representation that coexists in some tension with the agency view conceives of the representative as self-interested, who because her interests are typical of the group's interests, will benefit the group by selfishly pursuing her own agenda.

A second avenue of inquiry looks not to the alignment of interest within the class but, rather, to the alignment of interest between the class and *class counsel*. Put differently, adequate class representation also concerns the adequacy of the principal-agent relationship itself. This second dimension proceeds on the premise that, oftentimes, the class representative is largely a figurehead as a functional matter—someone in whose name the class action nominally proceeds but who exercises little, if any, meaningful control over the conduct of the litigation. Indeed, some commentators have gone so far as to argue that, "because the named plaintiff is a figurehead, the adequacy of representation would not be harmed if plaintiffs' attorneys could file 'Jane Doe' or 'Richard Roe' complaints on behalf of a fictitious absent class member without supplying an actual carcass for grilling over the hot coals of a deposition." Jonathan R. Macey & Geoffrey P. Miller, *The Plaintiffs' Attorney's Role in Class Action and Derivative Litigation: Economic Analysis and Recommendations for Reform*, 58 U. Chi. L. Rev. 1, 94 (1991). See also Jean Wegman Burns, *Decorative Figureheads: Eliminating Class Representatives in Class Actions*, 42 Hastings L.J. 165 (1990). Put bluntly, many class actions are lawyer-driven, not client-driven, lawsuits. Accordingly, as we shall see upon parsing cases like *Amchem* and *Ortiz*, courts in recent decades have come to apply the demand for adequate class representation to the attorney-client relationship on the plaintiff class side.

Now consider the "when and for what purpose" questions: As we shall elaborate in greater detail, the question of representational adequacy can arise in different settings and for different purposes. Rule 23(a)(4), for example, indicates that an inquiry into adequate representation is an essential part of the court's class certification determination—a ruling made at the litigation's outset as to whether the claims will proceed on a class-wide basis at all. As *Amchem* suggests, the focus under 23(a)(4) is on conflicts of interest within the class.

But the outset of the litigation is not necessarily the only time that courts inquire into adequate representation. For example, a court also might conceive adequate class representation as a minimum performance standard for class counsel with respect to conducting the litigation. Notice how an inquiry into the performance of counsel is not focused on the outset of the litigation, but rather on how the litigation turns out for the class. Given that the vast majority of cases certified to proceed on a class-wide basis and not otherwise resolved by dispositive motion end up settling, the idea of adequate representation as a performance standard for class counsel overlaps substantially with the inquiry into the fairness of the class settlement. How can one say that the class has been adequately represented, after all, if class counsel is trying to stick absent class members with an unfair deal? Rule 23, however, casts the inquiry into class settlement fairness as something worthy of distinct treatment in the structure of the rule itself (in Rule 23(e)), not in subsections (a) and (b). The overarching point, for now, is that the concept of adequate class representation has *multiple* meanings.

C. WHAT TYPE OF CLASS?

Every class action must satisfy the four requirements of Rule 23(a) and fit one of the types of class actions listed in Rule 23(b). Rule 23(b) identifies three general types (actually four because 23(b)(1) has two different parts), and lawyers refer to each type by the 23(b) pigeonhole in which it fits. Thus, there are "(b)(1) class actions", "(b)(2) class actions", and "(b)(3) class actions." Roughly speaking, the purpose of subsection 23(a) is to set out the minimum requirements for any class action: that joinder is impracticable, a homogenous enough class exists (commonality and typicality), and the representational nexus is sufficient to satisfy due process. Once these minimum requirements are satisfied, subsection 23(b) assures that there is a strong enough reason for proceeding as a class action. Thus, the best way to understand 23(b) is to map each of the different types of class actions it authorizes into the corresponding policy justification for class treatment.

As we have seen, the original version of Rule 23 was organized in a completely different way. It distinguished class actions by the "character of the right" involved and the preclusive effects depended on the formal nature of those legal rights. In particular, Rule 23(a) distinguished among cases in which the right was "joint or common," "secondary," or "several." Moreover, the so-called true class action—which included most cases involving joint or common rights—precluded class members, but the spurious class action— involving several rights united by a common question— functioned essentially as a joinder device. In spurious class actions, the fact that the lawsuit was a class action made it easier for absent class members to come into the suit and benefit from a favorable judgment if the plaintiff won, but those class members were not precluded if the plaintiff lost. Thus, only class members who actually joined were bound, a result that came to be known as "one-way intervention."

When the rule was revised in 1966, the advisory committee got rid of the conceptual categories in Rule 23 and rewrote the Rule along more pragmatic and functional lines. See Charles A. Wright, *Class Actions*, 47 F.R.D. 169, 176–77 (1970). They also redesigned the Rule so that *all* class actions had the potential to bind members of the class. Indeed, they rejected the whole idea of one-way intervention and reconceived the central purpose of the class action as preclusion.

The result is a Rule 23 that aims to connect the class action more directly to the policy reasons for class treatment. This is particularly true for the three subdivisions of Rule 23(b). Rule 23(b)(1) addresses situations where individual litigation might have a seriously unfair impact on other potential plaintiffs or on the defendant (some see this as Rule 19 mandatory joinder for cases where there are too many parties to actually join). Rule 23(b)(2) is based on remedial efficacy. It was designed originally to facilitate broad civil rights injunctions. See David Marcus, *Flawed but Noble: Desegregation Litigation and its Implications for the Modern Class Action*, 63 Fla. L. Rev. 657 (2011). More generally, (b)(2) targets cases where class treatment is needed for optimal injunctive or declaratory relief. Rule 23(b)(3) was entirely new with the 1966 revision. It extends preclusive effects to cases for monetary relief, which are generally considered quintessentially individual in character. It does this for several reasons, two of which loom large: to reap the judicial economy gains from litigating common issues of fact and law in one proceeding, and to reap the deterrence gains from facilitating private enforcement of the substantive law.

In addition, Rule 23(b) draws a major structural distinction between classes as to which class members have the opportunity to opt out and classes as to which membership is mandatory. In particular, Rule 23 makes (b)(1) and (b)(2) class actions mandatory, but it gives opt out rights in (b)(3). Subsection 1 of this section discusses opt-out classes under Rule 23(b)(3), starting with the grounding in the Due Process Clause of the opportunity to opt out and then turning to the application of the specific demands in Rule 23(b)(3). Subsection 2 then presents the various kinds of mandatory classes authorized by Rule 23(b)(1)–(2). Finally, subsection 3 treats issue classes under Rule 23(c)(4).

1. OPT–OUT CLASSES UNDER RULE 23

a. THE TWO FACES OF DUE PROCESS

Phillips Petroleum Co. v. Shutts

472 U.S. 797 (1985)

■ JUSTICE REHNQUIST delivered the opinion of the Court.

Petitioner is a Delaware corporation which has its principal place of business in Oklahoma. During the 1970s it produced or purchased natural gas from leased land located in 11 different States, and sold most of the gas in interstate commerce. Respondents are some 28,000 of the royalty owners possessing rights to the leases from which petitioner produced the gas; they reside in all 50 States, the District of Columbia, and several foreign countries. Respondents brought a class action against petitioner in the Kansas state court, seeking to recover interest on royalty payments which had been delayed by petitioner. They recovered judgment in the trial court, and the Supreme Court of Kansas affirmed the judgment over petitioner's contention[] that the Due Process Clause of the Fourteenth Amendment prevented Kansas from adjudicating the claims of all the respondents, and that the Due Process Clause and the Full Faith and Credit Clause of Article IV of the Constitution prohibited the application of Kansas law to all of the transactions between petitioner and respondents. 235 Kan. 195, 679 P.2d 1159 (1984). We granted certiorari to consider these claims. 469 U.S. 879 (1984). We reject petitioner's jurisdictional claim, but sustain its claim regarding the choice of law.

Because petitioner sold the gas to its customers in interstate commerce, it was required to secure approval for price increases from what was then the Federal Power Commission, and is now the Federal Energy Regulatory Commission. Under its regulations the Federal Power Commission permitted petitioner to propose and collect tentative higher gas prices, subject to final approval by the Commission. If the Commission eventually denied petitioner's proposed price increase or reduced the proposed increase, petitioner would have to refund to its customers the difference between the approved price and the higher price charged, plus interest at a rate set by statute. See 18 CFR § 154.102 (1984).

Although petitioner received higher gas prices pending review by the Commission, petitioner suspended any increase in royalties paid to the royalty owners because the higher price could be subject to recoupment by petitioner's customers. . . .

Respondents Irl Shutts, Robert Anderson, and Betty Anderson filed suit against petitioner in Kansas state court, seeking interest payments on their suspended royalties which petitioner had possessed pending the Commission's approval of the price increases. Shutts is a resident of Kansas, and the Andersons live in Oklahoma. Shutts and the Andersons own gas leases in Oklahoma and Texas. Over petitioner's objection the Kansas trial court granted respondents' motion to certify the suit as a class action under Kansas law. Kan. Stat. Ann. § 60-223 *et seq.* (1983). The class as certified was comprised of 33,000 royalty owners who had royalties suspended by petitioner. The average claim of each royalty owner for interest on the suspended royalties was $100.

After the class was certified respondents provided each class member with notice through first-class mail. The notice described the action and informed each class member that he could appear in person or by counsel; otherwise each member would be represented by Shutts and the Andersons, the named plaintiffs. The notices also stated that class members would be included in the class and bound by the judgment unless they "opted out" of the lawsuit by executing and returning a "request for exclusion" that was included with the notice. The final class as certified contained 28,100 members; 3,400 had "opted out" of the class by returning the request for exclusion, and notice could not be delivered to another 1,500 members, who were also excluded. Less than 1,000 of the class members resided in Kansas. Only a minuscule amount, approximately one quarter of one percent, of the gas leases involved in the lawsuit were on Kansas land.

After petitioner's mandamus petition to decertify the class was denied, *Phillips Petroleum v. Duckworth*, No. 82–54608 (Kan., June 28, 1982), cert. denied, 459 U.S. 1103 (1983), the case was tried to the court. The court found petitioner liable under Kansas law for interest on the suspended royalties. . . .

On appeal to the Supreme Court of Kansas, petitioner asserted [among other contentions] that the Kansas trial court did not possess personal jurisdiction over absent plaintiff class members as required by *International Shoe Co. v. Washington*, 326 U.S. 310 (1945), and similar cases. Related to this . . . claim was petitioner's contention that the "opt-out" notice to absent class members, which forced them to return the request for exclusion in order to avoid the suit, was insufficient to bind class members who were not residents of Kansas or who did not possess "minimum contacts" with Kansas. . . .

The Supreme Court of Kansas held . . . that the absent class members were plaintiffs, not defendants, and thus the traditional minimum contacts test of *International Shoe* did not apply. The court held that nonresident class-action plaintiffs were only entitled to adequate notice, an opportunity to be heard, an opportunity to opt out of the case, and adequate representation by the named plaintiffs. If these procedural due process minima were met, according to the court, Kansas could assert jurisdiction over the plaintiff class and bind each class member with a judgment on his claim. The court surveyed the course of the litigation and concluded that all of these minima had been met.

The court also rejected petitioner's contention that Kansas law could not be applied to plaintiffs and royalty arrangements having no connection with Kansas. The court stated that generally the law of the forum controlled all claims unless "compelling reasons" existed to apply a different law. The court found no compelling reasons, and noted that "[t]he plaintiff class members have indicated their desire to have this action determined under the laws of Kansas." The court affirmed as a matter of Kansas equity law the award of interest on the suspended royalties, at the rates imposed by the trial court. . . .

I

As a threshold matter we must determine whether petitioner has standing to assert the claim that Kansas did not possess proper jurisdiction over the many plaintiffs in the class who were not Kansas residents and had no connection to Kansas. . . .

Respondents claim that petitioner is barred by the rule requiring that a party assert only his own rights; they point out that respondents and petitioner are adversaries and do not have allied interests such that petitioner would be a good proponent of class members' interests. They further urge that petitioner's interference is unneeded because the class members have had opportunity to complain about Kansas' assertion of jurisdiction over their claim, but none have done so.

Respondents may be correct that petitioner does not possess standing *jus tertii*, but this is not the issue. Petitioner seeks to vindicate its own interests. As a class-action defendant petitioner is in a unique predicament. If Kansas does not possess jurisdiction over this plaintiff class, petitioner will be bound to 28,100 judgment holders scattered across the globe, but none of these will be bound by the Kansas decree. Petitioner could be subject to numerous later individual suits by these class members because a judgment issued without proper personal jurisdiction over an absent party is not entitled to full faith and credit elsewhere and thus has no res judicata effect as to that party. Whether it wins or loses on the merits, petitioner has a distinct and personal interest in seeing the entire plaintiff class bound by res judicata just as petitioner is bound. The only way a class action defendant like petitioner can assure itself of this binding effect of the judgment is to ascertain that the forum court has jurisdiction over every plaintiff whose claim it seeks to adjudicate, sufficient to support a defense of res judicata in a later suit for damages by class members. . . .

[handwritten margin note: △ has interest in making sure Kansas Ct. has pers. jur. over absent πs.]

II

Reduced to its essentials, petitioner's argument is that unless out-of-state plaintiffs affirmatively consent, the Kansas courts may not exert jurisdiction over their claims. Petitioner claims that failure to execute and return the "request for exclusion" provided with the class notice cannot constitute consent of the out-of-state plaintiffs; thus Kansas courts may exercise jurisdiction over these plaintiffs only if the plaintiffs possess the sufficient "minimum contacts" with Kansas as that term is used in cases involving personal jurisdiction over out-of-state defendants. *E.g., Int'l Shoe Co. v. Washington*, 326 U.S. 310 (1945); *Shaffer v. Heitner*, 433 U.S. 186 (1977); *World–Wide Volkswagen Corp. v. Woodson*, 444 U.S. 286 (1980). Since Kansas had no prelitigation contact with many of the plaintiffs and leases involved, petitioner claims that Kansas has exceeded its jurisdictional reach and thereby violated the due process rights of the absent plaintiffs.

In *International Shoe* we were faced with an out-of-state corporation which sought to avoid the exercise of personal jurisdiction over it as a defendant by a Washington state court. We held that the extent of the defendant's due process protection would depend "upon the quality and nature of the activity in relation to the fair and orderly administration of the laws. . . ." 326 U.S. at 319. We noted that the Due Process Clause did not permit a State to make a binding judgment against a person with whom the State had no contacts, ties, or relations. If the defendant possessed certain minimum contacts with the State, so that it was "reasonable and just, according to our traditional conception of fair play and substantial justice" for a State to exercise personal jurisdiction, the State could force the defendant to defend himself in the forum, upon pain of default, and could bind him to a judgment. *Id.* at 320.

The purpose of this test, of course, is to protect a defendant from the travail of defending in a distant forum, unless the defendant's contacts with the forum make it just to force him to defend there. As we explained in *Woodson*, the defendant's contacts should be such that "he should reasonably anticipate being haled" into the forum. 444 U.S. at 297. In *Ins. Corp. of Ireland v. Compagnie des Bauxites de Guinee*, 456 U.S. 694, 702–03 & n.10 (1982), we explained that the requirement that a court have personal jurisdiction comes from the Due Process Clause's protection of the defendant's personal liberty interest, and said that the requirement "represents a restriction on judicial power not as a matter of sovereignty, but as a matter of individual liberty." (Footnote omitted.)

Although the cases like *Shaffer* and *Woodson* which petitioner relies on for a minimum contacts requirement all dealt with out-of-state defendants or parties in the procedural posture of a defendant, cf. *New York Life Ins. Co. v. Dunlevy*, 241 U.S. 518 (1916); *Estin v. Estin*, 334 U.S. 541 (1948), petitioner claims that the same analysis must apply to absent class-action plaintiffs. In this regard petitioner correctly points out that a chose in action is a constitutionally recognized property interest possessed by each of the plaintiffs. *Mullane v. Central Hanover Bank & Trust Co.*, 339 U.S. 306 (1950). An adverse judgment by Kansas courts in this case may extinguish the chose in action forever through res judicata. Such an adverse judgment, petitioner claims, would be every bit as onerous to an absent plaintiff as an adverse judgment on the merits would be to a defendant. Thus, the same due process protections should apply to absent plaintiffs: Kansas should not be able to exert jurisdiction over the plaintiff's claims unless the plaintiffs have sufficient minimum contacts with Kansas.

We think petitioner's premise is in error. The burdens placed by a State upon an absent class-action plaintiff are not of the same order or magnitude as those it places upon an absent defendant. An out-of-state defendant summoned by a plaintiff is faced with the full powers of the forum State to render judgment *against* it. The defendant must generally hire counsel and travel to the forum to defend itself from the plaintiff's claim, or suffer a default judgment. The defendant may be forced to participate in extended and often costly discovery, and will be forced to respond in damages or to comply with some other form of remedy imposed by the court should it lose the suit. The defendant may also face liability for court costs and attorney's fees. These burdens are substantial, and the minimum contacts requirement of the Due Process Clause prevents the forum State from unfairly imposing them upon the defendant.

A class-action plaintiff, however, is in quite a different posture. The Court noted this difference in *Hansberry v. Lee*, 311 U.S. 32, 40–41 (1940), which explained that a "class" or "representative" suit was an exception to the rule that one could not be bound by judgment *in personam* unless one was made fully a party in the traditional sense. *Id.* citing *Pennoyer v. Neff*, 95 U.S. (5 Otto) 714 (1878). As the Court pointed out in *Hansberry*, the class action was an invention of equity to enable it to proceed to a decree in suits where the number of those interested in the litigation was too great to permit joinder. The absent parties would be bound by the decree so long as the named parties adequately represented the absent class and the prosecution of the litigation was within the common interest. 311 U.S. at 41.

Modern plaintiff class actions follow the same goals, permitting litigation of a suit involving common questions when there are too many plaintiffs for proper joinder. Class actions also may permit the plaintiffs to pool claims which would be uneconomical to litigate individually. For example, this lawsuit involves claims averaging about $100 per plaintiff; most of the plaintiffs would have no realistic day in court if a class action were not available.

In sharp contrast to the predicament of a defendant haled into an out-of-state forum, the plaintiffs in this suit were not haled anywhere to defend themselves upon pain of a default judgment. As commentators have noted, from the plaintiffs' point of view a class action resembles a "quasi-administrative proceeding, conducted by the judge." 3B J. Moore & J. Kennedy, MOORE'S FEDERAL PRACTICE ¶ 23.45[4.–5] (1984); Benjamin Kaplan, *Continuing Work of the Civil Committee: 1966 Amendments to the Federal Rules of Civil Procedure (I)*, 81 Harv. L. Rev. 356, 398 (1967).

A plaintiff class in Kansas and numerous other jurisdictions cannot first be certified unless the judge, with the aid of the named plaintiffs and defendant, conducts an inquiry into the common nature of the named plaintiffs' and the absent plaintiffs' claims, the adequacy of representation, the jurisdiction possessed over the class, and any other matters that will bear upon proper representation of the absent plaintiffs' interest. See, e.g., Kan. Stat. Ann. § 60–223 (1983); Fed. R. Civ. P. 23. Unlike a defendant in a civil suit, a class-action plaintiff is not required to fend for himself. See Kan. Stat. Ann. § 60–223(d) (1983). The court and named plaintiffs protect his interests. Indeed, the class-action defendant itself has a great interest in ensuring that the absent plaintiff's claims are properly before the forum. In this case, for example, the defendant sought to avoid class certification by alleging that the absent plaintiffs would not be adequately represented and were not amenable to jurisdiction. See *Phillips Petroleum v. Duckworth*, No. 82–54608 (Kan., June 28, 1982).

The concern of the typical class-action rules for the absent plaintiffs is manifested in other ways. Most jurisdictions, including Kansas, require that a class action, once certified, may not be dismissed or compromised without the approval of the court. In many jurisdictions such as Kansas the court may amend the pleadings to ensure that all sections of the class are represented adequately. Kan. Stat. Ann. § 60–223(d) (1983); see also, e.g., Fed. R. Civ. P. 23(d).

Besides this continuing solicitude for their rights, absent plaintiff class members are not subject to other burdens imposed upon defendants. They need not hire counsel or appear. They are almost never subject to counterclaims or cross-claims, or liability for fees or costs.[2] Absent plaintiff class members are not subject to coercive or punitive remedies. Nor will an adverse judgment typically bind an absent plaintiff for any damages, although a valid adverse judgment may extinguish any of the plaintiff's claims which were litigated.

Unlike a defendant in a normal civil suit, an absent class-action plaintiff is not required to do anything. He may sit back and allow the litigation to run its course, content in knowing that there are safeguards provided for his protection. In most class actions an absent plaintiff is provided at least with an opportunity to "opt out" of the class, and if he takes advantage of that opportunity he is removed from the litigation entirely. This was true of the Kansas proceedings in this case. The Kansas procedure provided for the mailing of a notice to each class member by first-class mail. The notice, as

None of the potential harms from out of state Jurisdiction in Int. Shoe are present w/ CA ∏s.

---

[2] Petitioner places emphasis on the fact that absent class members might be subject to discovery, counterclaims, cross-claims, or court costs. Petitioner cites no cases involving any such imposition upon plaintiffs, however. We are convinced that such burdens are rarely imposed upon plaintiff class members, and that the disposition of these issues is best left to a case which presents them in a more concrete way.

we have previously indicated, described the action and informed the class member that he could appear in person or by counsel, in default of which he would be represented by the named plaintiffs and their attorneys. The notice further stated that class members would be included in the class and bound by the judgment unless they "opted out" by executing and returning a "request for exclusion" that was included in the notice.

Petitioner contends, however, that the "opt out" procedure provided by Kansas is not good enough, and that an "opt in" procedure is required to satisfy the Due Process Clause of the Fourteenth Amendment. Insofar as plaintiffs who have no minimum contacts with the forum State are concerned, an "opt in" provision would require that each class member affirmatively consent to his inclusion within the class.

Because States place fewer burdens upon absent class plaintiffs than they do upon absent defendants in nonclass suits, the Due Process Clause need not and does not afford the former as much protection from state-court jurisdiction as it does the latter. The Fourteenth Amendment does protect "persons," not "defendants," however, so absent plaintiffs as well as absent defendants are entitled to some protection from the jurisdiction of a forum State which seeks to adjudicate their claims. In this case we hold that a forum State may exercise jurisdiction over the claim of an absent class-action plaintiff, even though that plaintiff may not possess the minimum contacts with the forum which would support personal jurisdiction over a defendant. If the forum State wishes to bind an absent plaintiff concerning a claim for money damages or similar relief at law,[3] it must provide minimal procedural due process protection. The plaintiff must receive notice plus an opportunity to be heard and participate in the litigation, whether in person or through counsel. The notice must be the best practicable, "reasonably calculated, under all the circumstances, to apprise interested parties of the pendency of the action and afford them an opportunity to present their objections." *Mullane*, 339 U.S. at 314–15; cf. *Eisen v. Carlisle & Jacquelin*, 417 U.S. 156, 174–75 (1974). The notice should describe the action and the plaintiffs' rights in it. Additionally, we hold that due process requires at a minimum that an absent plaintiff be provided with an opportunity to remove himself from the class by executing and returning an "opt out" or "request for exclusion" form to the court. Finally, the Due Process Clause of course requires that the named plaintiff at all times adequately represent the interests of the absent class members. *Hansberry*, 311 U.S. at 42–43.

We reject petitioner's contention that the Due Process Clause of the Fourteenth Amendment requires that absent plaintiffs affirmatively "opt in" to the class, rather than be deemed members of the class if they do not "opt out." We think that such a contention is supported by little, if any precedent, and that it ignores the differences between class-action plaintiffs, on the one hand, and defendants in nonclass civil suits on the other. Any plaintiff may consent to jurisdiction. *Keeton v. Hustler Magazine, Inc.*, 465 U.S. 770 (1984). The essential question, then, is how stringent the requirement for a showing of consent will be.

---

[3] Our holding today is limited to those class actions which seek to bind known plaintiffs concerning claims wholly or predominately for money judgments. We intimate no view concerning other types of class actions, such as those seeking equitable relief. Nor, of course, does our discussion of personal jurisdiction address class actions where the jurisdiction is asserted against a *defendant* class.

We think that the procedure followed by Kansas, where a fully de-scriptive notice is sent first-class mail to each class member, with an expla-nation of the right to "opt out," satisfies due process. Requiring a plaintiff to affirmatively request inclusion would probably impede the prosecution of those class actions involving an aggregation of small individual claims, where a large number of claims are required to make it economical to bring suit. See, e.g., *Eisen*, 417 U.S. at 161. The plaintiff's claim may be so small, or the plaintiff so unfamiliar with the law, that he would not file suit indi-vidually, nor would he affirmatively request inclusion in the class if such a request were required by the Constitution.[4] If, on the other hand, the plain-tiff's claim is sufficiently large or important that he wishes to litigate it on his own, he will likely have retained an attorney or have thought about fil-ing suit, and should be fully capable of exercising his right to "opt out."

In this case over 3,400 members of the potential class did "opt out," which belies the contention that "opt out" procedures result in guaranteed jurisdiction by inertia. Another 1,500 were excluded because the notice and "opt out" form was undeliverable. We think that such results show that the "opt out" procedure provided by Kansas is by no means *pro forma*, and that the Constitution does not require more to protect what must be the some-what rare species of class member who is unwilling to execute an "opt out" form, but whose claim is nonetheless so important that he cannot be pre-sumed to consent to being a member of the class by his failure to do so. Pe-titioner's "opt in" requirement would require the invalidation of scores of state statutes and of the class-action provision of the Federal Rules of Civil Procedure, and for the reasons stated we do not think that the Constitution requires the State to sacrifice the obvious advantages in judicial efficiency resulting from the "opt out" approach for the protection of the *rara avis* por-trayed by petitioner.

We therefore hold that the protection afforded the plaintiff class mem-bers by the Kansas statute satisfies the Due Process Clause. The interests of the absent plaintiffs are sufficiently protected by the forum State when those plaintiffs are provided with a request for exclusion that can be re-turned within a reasonable time to the court. Both the Kansas trial court and the Supreme Court of Kansas held that the class received adequate representation, and no party disputes that conclusion here. We conclude that the Kansas court properly asserted personal jurisdiction over the ab-sent plaintiffs and their claims against petitioner.

III

The Kansas courts applied Kansas contract and Kansas equity law to every claim in this case, notwithstanding that over 99% of the gas leases and some 97% of the plaintiffs in the case had no apparent connection to the State of Kansas except for this lawsuit. Petitioner protested that the Kansas courts should apply the laws of the States where the leases were located, or at least apply Texas and Oklahoma law because so many of the leases came from those States. The Kansas courts disregarded this conten-tion and found petitioner liable for interest on the suspended royalties as a

---

[4] In this regard the Reporter for the 1966 amendments to the Federal Rules of Civil Pro-cedure stated:

"[R]equiring the individuals affirmatively to request inclusion in the lawsuit would result in freezing out the claims of people—especially small claims held by small people—who for one reason or another, ignorance, timidity, unfamiliarity with business or legal matters, will simply not take the affirmative step."

Kaplan, *Continuing Work of the Civil Committee*, 81 Harv. L. Rev. at 397–98

matter of Kansas law, and set the interest rates under Kansas equity principles.

Petitioner contends that total application of Kansas substantive law violated the constitutional limitations on choice of law mandated by the Due Process Clause of the Fourteenth Amendment and the Full Faith and Credit Clause of Article IV, § 1. We must first determine whether Kansas law conflicts in any material way with any other law which could apply. There can be no injury in applying Kansas law if it is not in conflict with that of any other jurisdiction connected to this suit.

Petitioner claims that Kansas law conflicts with that of a number of States connected to this litigation, especially Texas and Oklahoma. These putative conflicts range from the direct to the tangential, and may be addressed by the Supreme Court of Kansas on remand under the correct constitutional standard. For example, there is no recorded Oklahoma decision dealing with interest liability for suspended royalties: whether Oklahoma is likely to impose liability would require a survey of Oklahoma oil and gas law. Even if Oklahoma found such liability, petitioner shows that Oklahoma would most likely apply its constitutional and statutory 6% interest rate rather than the much higher Kansas rates applied in this litigation.

Additionally, petitioner points to an Oklahoma statute which excuses liability for interest if a creditor accepts payment of the full principal without a claim for interest, Okla. Stat., Tit. 23, § 8 (1951). Petitioner contends that by ignoring this statute the Kansas courts created liability that does not exist in Oklahoma.

Petitioner also points out several conflicts between Kansas and Texas law. Although Texas recognizes interest liability for suspended royalties, Texas has never awarded any such interest at a rate greater than 6%, which corresponds with the Texas constitutional and statutory rate. Moreover, at least one court interpreting Texas law appears to have held that Texas excuses interest liability once the gas company offers to take an indemnity from the royalty owner and pay him the suspended royalty while the price increase is still tentative. Such a rule is contrary to Kansas law as applied below, but if applied to the Texas plaintiffs or leases in this case, would vastly reduce petitioner's liability.

The conflicts on the applicable interest rates, alone—which we do not think can be labeled "false conflicts" without a more thoroughgoing treatment than was accorded them by the Supreme Court of Kansas—certainly amounted to millions of dollars in liability. We think that the Supreme Court of Kansas erred in deciding on the basis that it did that the application of its laws to all claims would be constitutional. . . . .

Petitioner owns property and conducts substantial business in the State, so Kansas certainly has an interest in regulating petitioner's conduct in Kansas. Moreover, oil and gas extraction is an important business to Kansas, and although only a few leases in issue are located in Kansas, hundreds of Kansas plaintiffs were affected by petitioner's suspension of royalties; thus the court held that the State has a real interest in protecting "the rights of these royalty owners both as individual residents of [Kansas] and as members of this particular class of plaintiffs." The Kansas Supreme Court pointed out that Kansas courts are quite familiar with this type of lawsuit, and "[t]he plaintiff class members have indicated their desire to have this action determined under the laws of Kansas." Finally, the Kansas court buttressed its use of Kansas law by stating that this lawsuit was analogous to a suit against a "common fund" located in Kansas.

We do not lightly discount this description of Kansas' contacts with this litigation and its interest in applying its law. There is, however, no "common fund" located in Kansas that would require or support the application of only Kansas law to all these claims. As the Kansas court noted, petitioner commingled the suspended royalties with its general corporate accounts. There is no specific identifiable res in Kansas, nor is there any limited amount which may be depleted before every plaintiff is compensated. Only by somehow aggregating all the separate claims in this case could a "common fund" in any sense be created, and the term becomes all but meaningless when used in such an expansive sense.

We also give little credence to the idea that Kansas law should apply to all claims because the plaintiffs, by failing to opt out, evinced their desire to be bound by Kansas law. Even if one could say that the plaintiffs "consented" to the application of Kansas law by not opting out, plaintiff's desire for forum law is rarely, if ever controlling. In most cases the plaintiff shows his obvious wish for forum law by filing there. "If a plaintiff could choose the substantive rules to be applied to an action . . . the invitation to forum shopping would be irresistible." Even if a plaintiff evidences his desire for forum law by moving to the forum, we have generally accorded such a move little or no significance. . . . Thus the plaintiffs' desire for Kansas law, manifested by their participation in this Kansas lawsuit, bears little relevance.

The Supreme Court of Kansas in its opinion in this case expressed the view that by reason of the fact that it was adjudicating a nationwide class action, it had much greater latitude in applying its own law to the transactions in question than might otherwise be the case:

> "The general rule is that the law of the forum applies unless it is expressly shown that a different law governs, and in case of doubt, the law of the forum is preferred. . . . Where a state court determines it has jurisdiction over a nationwide class action and procedural due process guarantees of notice and adequate representation are present, we believe the law of the forum should be applied unless compelling reasons exist for applying a different law. . . . Compelling reasons do not exist to require this court to look to other state laws to determine the rights of the parties involved in this lawsuit." 235 Kan., at 221–22, 679 P.2d at 1181.

We think that this is something of a "bootstrap" argument. The Kansas class-action statute, like those of most other jurisdictions, requires that there be "common issues of law or fact." But while a State may, for the reasons we have previously stated, assume jurisdiction over the claims of plaintiffs whose principal contacts are with other States, it may not use this assumption of jurisdiction as an added weight in the scale when considering the permissible constitutional limits on choice of substantive law. It may not take a transaction with little or no relationship to the forum and apply the law of the forum in order to satisfy the procedural requirement that there be a "common question of law." The issue of personal jurisdiction over plaintiffs in a class action is entirely distinct from the question of the constitutional limitations on choice of law; the latter calculus is not altered by the fact that it may be more difficult or more burdensome to comply with the constitutional limitations because of the large number of transactions which the State proposes to adjudicate and which have little connection with the forum.

Kansas must have a "significant contact or significant aggregation of contacts" to the claims asserted by each member of the plaintiff class, contacts "creating state interests," in order to ensure that the choice of Kansas law is not arbitrary or unfair. *Allstate Ins. Co. v. Hague*, 449 U.S. 302, 312–13 (1981). Given Kansas' lack of "interest" in claims unrelated to that State, and the substantive conflict with jurisdictions such as Texas, we conclude that application of Kansas law to every claim in this case is sufficiently arbitrary and unfair as to exceed constitutional limits.

When considering fairness in this context, an important element is the expectation of the parties. There is no indication that when the leases involving land and royalty owners outside of Kansas were executed, the parties had any idea that Kansas law would control. Neither the Due Process Clause nor the Full Faith and Credit Clause requires Kansas "to substitute for its own [laws], applicable to persons and events within it, the conflicting statute of another state," *Pacific Employees Ins. Co. v. Indus. Accident Comm'n*, 306 U.S. 493, 502 (1939), but Kansas "may not abrogate the rights of parties beyond its borders having no relation to anything done or to be done within them." *Home Ins. Co. v. Dick*, 281 U.S. at 410.

Here the Supreme Court of Kansas took the view that in a nationwide class action where procedural due process guarantees of notice and adequate representation were met, "the law of the forum should be applied unless compelling reasons exist for applying a different law." 235 Kan. at 221, 679 P.2d at 1181. Whatever practical reasons may have commended this rule to the Supreme Court of Kansas, for the reasons already stated we do not believe that it is consistent with the decisions of this Court. We make no effort to determine for ourselves which law must apply to the various transactions involved in this lawsuit, and . . . in many situations a state court may be free to apply one of several choices of law. But the constitutional limitations [of due process] must be respected even in a nationwide class action.

We therefore affirm the judgment of the Supreme Court of Kansas insofar as it upheld the jurisdiction of the Kansas courts over the plaintiff class members in this case, and reverse its judgment insofar as it held that Kansas law was applicable to all of the transactions which it sought to adjudicate. We remand the case to that court for further proceedings not inconsistent with this opinion.

It is so ordered.

■ [JUSTICE STEVENS concurred in the holding as to personal jurisdiction but dissented as to the Court's choice-of-law analysis.]

NOTES AND QUESTIONS

1.   *Kansas Class Action Procedure. Shutts* arose under the equivalent in Kansas procedural law to a federal Rule 23(b)(3) opt-out class. In fact, the relevant portion of Kansas class action law contained no material differences in language as compared to federal Rule 23(b)(3). One accordingly may take the treatment in *Shutts* of what constitutional due process demands as applying equally to federal Rule 23(b)(3).

2.   *Due Process in Two Forms.* The *Shutts* Court speaks of due process as a limitation on both the Kansas court's assertion of personal jurisdiction over the absent members of the class (ultimately deemed permissible, in light of the procedural protections afforded) and that court's choice of the substantive law

to govern the nationwide class on the merits (deemed impermissible, at least without a more "thoroughgoing" choice-of-law analysis by the court).

The analysis of personal jurisdiction in the first half of *Shutts* facilitates considerably the certification of nationwide class actions. Think of what their fate would have been had the Court decided to require application of the same "minimum contacts" standard to absent class members as applies, per *International Shoe*, to a civil defendant. The personal jurisdiction analysis with respect to the Kansas state-court class action in *Shutts* effectively blesses the assertion of personal jurisdiction via nationwide, opt-out class actions in the federal courts as well, because constitutional limits on personal jurisdiction are no more stringent, and in some respects less stringent, in the federal courts than in the state courts.

But, once one says that a single court—state or federal—can assert personal jurisdiction over a class comprised of claimants spread across the nation, a further question arises: whose law governs the merits? That question is easy enough to answer in areas of uniform, national law—say, as to securities fraud, antitrust, or employment discrimination. The claims in *Shutts*, by contrast, were contractual claims governed by state law. But *which* state's law? As a subsequent portion of this Chapter shall elaborate, the need for the court to undertake a choice-of-law analysis for proposed nationwide class actions involving state-law claims has posed a formidable barrier to certification.

3. Personal Jurisdiction over Absent Class Members. As the *Shutts* Court points out, each plaintiff's claim is a chose in action, which qualifies as "property" within the meaning of the Due Process Clause and triggers the right not to be deprived of property without due process of law. The Court concludes that a showing that absent class members have minimum contacts with the forum is unnecessary provided absent class members receive (1) notice and an opportunity to be heard and participate in the litigation (2) the right to opt-out and (3) adequate representation. What is the basis for concluding that these procedural protections provide a basis for exercising personal jurisdiction over absent class members who lack minimum contacts with the forum?

One possible explanation is that failure to opt out—at least when accompanied by the other procedural protections identified by *Shutts*—implies consent to jurisdiction. Recall from your Civil Procedure class that consent provides a basis for personal jurisdiction separate from minimum contacts. In rejecting the defendants' argument that absent class members should be required to opt-*in*, the Court characterizes a class member "who is unwilling to execute an 'opt out' form, but whose claim is nonetheless so important that he cannot be presumed to consent to being a member of the class by his failure to do so" as rare.

But doesn't a failure to opt out provide a very thin basis from which to infer consent to jurisdiction? Consider the following: First, the Due Process Clause requires that reasonable notice be sent to the class, and Rule 23 requires that individual notice be sent to all those reasonably identifiable. Despite the literal language of *Shutts* to the contrary, however, it is generally agreed that neither the Constitution nor the Rule requires that notice actually be *received*. Second, even if notice is received, it is not always easy to read or understand without legal help—despite Rule 23(c)(2)(b)'s admonition that the notice be clear, concise, and easily understood. Finally, even if notice is both received and understood, why is it appropriate to treat a failure to opt out as consent to personal jurisdiction? There is, after all, no other circumstance in which a forum that lacks an appropriate territorial connection to a person may require a person to do anything.

Patrick Woolley has argued that the key justification for personal jurisdiction over absent class members who are unsophisticated and who lack minimum contacts with the forum is adequate representation, not the right to opt out:

> [A]dequate representation—properly understood—provides an absent class member with no less protection against the sovereign authority of the forum than does the [minimum contacts] requirement. Unless otherwise required by a forum [that has minimum contacts with a] class member, an adequate representative must pursue the claims of an absentee in the forum that would best serve the interests of the absent class member, all things considered. . . . [Thus,] assuming that the class member is adequately represented, he will not be prejudiced by having his claims resolved by a sovereign that lacks an appropriate connection with the class member.

Patrick Woolley, *Collateral Attack and the Role of Adequate Representation in Class Suits For Money Damages*, 58 Kansas L. Rev. 917, 970 (2010).

    4. Due Process in Money Damages Class Suits as Exit, Voice, and Loyalty. Recall that with respect to class actions involving claims for "money damages or similar relief at law," the Court identifies three "minimal due process protection[s]" to which an absent class member is entitled: (1) notice and an opportunity to be heard and participate in the litigation (2) the right to opt out and (3) adequate representation. The *Shutts* Court treats these protections as personal jurisdiction requirements. But it is also possible to think of them as more general due process safeguards applicable to all class suits for money damages. Indeed, the Supreme Court—or at least some Justices of the Court—sometimes suggests approval of this more general view. See, e.g., *Wal–Mart v. Dukes*, 131 S.Ct. 2541, 2559 (2011) (noting that "[i]n the context of a class action predominantly for money damages we have held that absence of notice and opt-out violates due process," citing *Shutts* for support and not limiting the statement to personal jurisdiction).

It is interesting to note that the due-process checklist provided in *Shutts* closely tracks the array of rights that individuals might have within collective organizations, such as a corporation or a polity. Setting forth a typology for such rights, political theorist Albert Hirschman observed that individuals might have exit rights (to leave the collective organization), voice rights (to have their say within the governing structure of the organization), and loyalty rights (to have those in charge of the organization deploy their governing power for the benefit of organization members rather than for themselves). Albert O. Hirschman, EXIT, VOICE, AND LOYALTY: RESPONSES TO DECLINE IN FIRMS, ORGANIZATIONS, AND STATES (1970).

For commentary highlighting the similarity between the *Shutts* due process checklist and Hirschman's three-part typology, see John C. Coffee, Jr., *Class Action Accountability: Reconciling Exit, Voice, and Loyalty in Representative Litigation*, 100 Colum. L. Rev. 370, 376–77 (2000); Samuel Issacharoff, *Governance and Legitimacy in the Law of Class Actions*, 1999 Sup. Ct. Rev. 337, 366.

5. *The Right to Opt–Out.* As mentioned in the previous note, *Shutts* might be understood as imposing a *constitutional* right to opt out only for absent class members who lack minimum contacts with the forum, or it might be better understood as identifying minimal due process requirements for *all* class actions predominately for money damages and holding that a "minimum contacts" requirement would be superfluous in light of these due process protections. If the Court in fact concluded in *Shutts* that *all* absent class members have the right to opt out of class suits predominately for money damages, then the Court would have in effect constitutionalized the opt-out right created by Rule 23.

The Advisory Committee Notes to Rule 23 provide the following justification for granting a right to opt out in (b)(3) litigation:

> [T]he interests of the individuals in pursuing their own litigation may be so strong here as to warrant denial of a class action altogether. Even when a class action is maintained under subdivision (b)(3), this individual interest is respected. Thus, the court is required to direct notice to the members of the class of the right of each member to be excluded from the class upon request.

Advisory Committee Note to 1966 Amendment of Rule 23. Does the Advisory Committee's reasoning provide a persuasive basis for distinguishing between class suits under Rule 23(b)(3) and class actions that lack an opt-out right? Does the reasoning provide any support for a *constitutional* right to opt out in *all* class suits predominately for money damages? Are there other reasons not identified by the Advisory Committee to give all absent class members a constitutional right to opt out of a class suit predominately for money damages? Some commentators have argued that opt out is valuable as a signal of inadequate representation on the theory that class members are more likely to opt out when they are dissatisfied with class representation. However, there is no indication that the 1966 Advisory Committee viewed opt out in this way or that the Supreme Court has adopted this understanding.

In any event, how important is the right to opt out as a practical matter? Consider the following findings of what is still the leading empirical study on opt-out rates, based on the 159 published class action decisions for the period 1993–2003 in which quantitative data were available concerning opt-outs:

> 1. Opt-outs from class participation . . . are rare: on average, less than 1 percent of class members opt-out. . . .

> 2. Opt-out rates vary by case type. Even in case categories in which the opt-out rates are highest, however, the percentage of class members who exclude themselves is quite low. The highest mean opt-out rate is 4.6 percent in the four mass tort cases for which data were available. Employment discrimination cases rank second with an opt-out rate of 2.2 percent for the three cases in our sample with the necessary data. The opt-out rate for thirty-nine consumer class action cases is less than 0.2 percent. . . .

Theodore Eisenberg & Geoffrey P. Miller, *The Role of Opt–Outs and Objectors in Class Action Litigation: Theoretical and Empirical Issues*, 57 Vand. L. Rev. 1529, 1532 (2004).

Indeed, in some class actions, the opt-out procedure is mainly a tool for lawyers to get larger fees. A lawyer who represents many members of the plaintiff class but who is not appointed class counsel might threaten to opt his clients out of the class unless class counsel agrees to give him a larger share of the fee award. If he is successful, the opt-out does not serve due-process values, but in fact, undermines those values by exacerbating agency problems. Rule 23(e)(3), which requires that parties seeking approval of a settlement "file a statement identifying any agreement made in connection with the proposal," might help to address this problem.

If the opt-out right is so difficult to exercise in a meaningful way and if opt-outs are rare in practice and might serve attorney interests more than client interests, then why place so much significance on the right to opt out? Indeed, why make the opt-out right a requirement of due process at all?

What about requiring absent class members to affirmatively opt in if they wish to benefit from the class action rather than requiring them to opt out if they wish to avoid the effects? Requiring opt in has the advantage of making it more likely that those who end up bound by the class action reflect on that possibility before participating. Would an opt-in procedure have any troubling consequences for would-be plaintiffs? For defendants? Do those consequences tend to arise in some substantive areas for class action litigation more so than others? For an argument in favor of an opt-in approach for class settlements, as distinct from class actions for actual litigation, see John Bronsteen, *Class Action Settlements: An Opt–In Proposal*, 2005 U. Ill. L. Rev. 903.

     6. The Right to be Heard and to Participate in the Litigation. Courts and commentators often ignore the fact that the right to be heard and participate in the litigation is part of *Shutts*'s due-process checklist. What does it mean for an individual class member to have the right to be heard and participate in the litigation? Since 1966 Rule 23 has afforded class members in a Rule 23(b)(3) suit the right to "enter an appearance through an attorney." Fed. R. Civ. P. 23(c)(2)(B)(iv). The Reporter for the Committee that drafted this language suggested that the right to appear is intended to afford absent class members the opportunity to receive pleadings and other papers in the case so that they may decide whether to seek intervention." B Kaplan, *Continuing Work of the Civil Committee*, 81 Harv. L. Rev. at 392 n.137. And courts have followed his lead. See, *e.g. Ramsey v. Arata*, 406 F. Supp 435, 442 (N.D. Texas 1975) (noting in dicta that the right to appear affords the opportunity to receive pleadings and papers in order to facilitate the decision to seek intervention).

Does *Shutts* mean anything more? For an argument that every class member who has not exercised her right to opt out or been severed from the litigation has a right to be heard and participate in class litigation as a full party, see Patrick Woolley, *Rethinking the Adequacy of Adequate Representation*, 75 Tex. L. Rev. 571 (1997). Of course, the participation even of full parties in complex litigation may be limited as appropriate. *Id.* at 603 (noting that while "*Shutts* leaves unclear the extent to which a court may properly regulate the participation of a party in complex, multiparty litigation[,] [a]ppropriate limitations on participation . . . must be consistent with the rationale for providing a right to participate."); *id* at 603 & n.148 (criticizing *In re San Juan DuPont Plaza Hotel Fire Litig.*, 768 F. Supp. 912, 918 (D.P.R. 1991), a case in which the district court purported to justify limits on participation because "[f]ull participation by each individual plaintiffs' counsel would likely result in numerous attorneys . . . zealously representing the interest of their individual cases and possibly leading to the presentation of confusing and conflicting theories," *vacated*, 982 F.2d 603 (1st Cir. 1992)).

7.   *The Significance of Footnote 3*. The Court seemingly goes out of its way to emphasize, in footnote 3 of *Shutts*, that "[o]ur holding today is limited to those class actions which seek to bind known plaintiffs concerning claims wholly or predominately for money judgments. We intimate no view concerning other types of class actions, such as those seeking equitable relief [e.g., an injunction or a declaratory judgment]." Footnote 3 surely should not be read to suggest that adequate representation is required only in class suits predominately for money damages. But what about the other due-process protections identified in *Shutts*? Should the notice and the right to be heard and participate in the litigation be limited to class suits predominately for money damages? Should the right to opt-out of class litigation be so limited?

Keep in mind that claims for money damages focus on the circumstances of the individual plaintiff and compensatory relief is tailored to the plaintiff's specific injury. Should the individualized nature of the claim and relief matter for due process? See *Wal–Mart Stores, Inc. v. Dukes*, 131 S. Ct. 2541, 2558–59 (2011) (tying mandatory versus opt-out class actions to the fact that (b)(2) involves a class seeking an "indivisible injunction benefitting all its members at once" while (b)(3) involves "individualized claims for money"). What about 23(b)(1)? As we shall see in the later part of this Chapter, Rule 23 makes (b)(1) class actions mandatory even when they produce monetary relief. Can a mandatory (b)(1) class action be squared with *Shutts*? The *Wal–Mart* Court had this to say about (b)(1): "Classes certified under (b)(1) . . . share the most traditional justifications for class treatment—that individual adjudications would be impossible or unworkable. . . . For that reason these are also mandatory classes. . . ." *Id.* at 2558. In this passage, the Court justifies depriving class members of an opt-out right (and even a right to notice of the class action) by citing the supposed practical necessity of a (b)(1) class action. But individual adjudications are not "impossible" in most (b)(1) situations, and they are "unworkable" only because the harmful consequences are unacceptable as a policy matter. Does this mean that the due-process rights of individual class members are conditioned on the policy reasons for class treatment? If that is so, then how do we tell which policy reasons are strong enough to justify forcing individuals to litigate their claims in a class action?

To illustrate, consider a limited-fund class action certified under (b)(1). These class actions must be mandatory, for otherwise some class members would exit and exhaust the fund before others are able to recover from it. But individual litigation is clearly not "impossible" in this situation. It might be "unworkable," but only because we have already decided that it is unfair for some plaintiffs to get full recovery at the expense of others. But why is this so unfair as to justify depriving class members of their traditional right to litigate their damages claims individually? And does the reason have any implications for other class actions? In mass-tort cases, for example, the number of claimants can be so huge that the delay from individual litigation greatly erodes the real value of recovery for those later in the lawsuit queue. This situation does not create a classic limited fund, so it must qualify under (b)(3) if it qualifies at all. As a result, all class members have opt-out rights. But does this make sense on policy grounds? If a class action can be made mandatory in order to prevent some plaintiffs from exhausting a limited fund and leaving others without meaningful recovery, then why can't a class action be made mandatory in order to prevent some plaintiffs from creating high delay costs that seriously undermine the real value of recovery for others?

8. *Due Process in Choice of Law.* What exactly is the due process defect in the Kansas court's application of Kansas substantive law to the entire nationwide class? Is the Supreme Court's analysis of choice of law consistent with its analysis of personal jurisdiction? Why not say that the failure of absent class members to opt out implies their consent not only to the jurisdiction of the Kansas court over their persons but also to the application of Kansas substantive law to govern their claims on the merits? *Whose* due process rights are at stake with regard to the choice of law?

9. *The Problem of Regulatory Mismatch.* Does it make sense for a court in a single state effectively to govern the nation by way of a nationwide class action? Note that, in *Shutts*, the scope of the underlying activity—there, the distribution of the royalty rights at issue—extended beyond the territorial authority of any one state. As Richard Nagareda and Samuel Issacharoff observe, the phenomenon of regulatory mismatch—a state exercising its power to regulate activities with nationwide effects—is a recurring feature of class action litigation involving activity on a national market:

> Forum matters. It may appear banal to observe that the court in which a case is situated, the rules and substantive laws that operate, and even the presiding judge all have important effects on the prospects of a case. As much as the choice of forum has become a signal issue in recent class action law, it is worth noting at the onset that this was not always the case.

> The modern class action has its antecedents in the need for coordinated disposition of confined conduct. [The traditional representative suit] pose[d] no question of forum. The case would be filed in the equity court for the affected jurisdiction, plain and simple.

> So long as the class action continued to be used primarily to challenge confined conduct, the same pattern would persist. Whatever the difficulties in *Hansberry v. Lee*, forum was not one of them. The case would challenge residential segregation in the South Side of Chicago, and either the state or the federal courts in Illinois would resolve the matter. Similarly, a landmark case such as *Brown v. Board of Education* would emerge from the federal court in Topeka, Kansas, or, as with its companion case from Wilmington, Delaware, from a local state court. But even in such landmark cases, rich with national significance, the immediate challenge would be local. Whether the subject matter was school desegregation, employment practices at a local steel mill, or voting rights, the forum for litigation followed from the local nature of the immediate actors responsible for the claimed harms.

> This pattern began to change with the advent of antitrust and securities class actions, a trend that would accelerate with the rise of consumer claims and mass harm cases. It is, therefore, no coincidence that an elaborated law of class actions should have emerged in this country in the twentieth century. The period saw not only the rise of the modern class action, but also—arguably, its antecedent—the emergence of integrated national markets for standardized goods and

services. National markets for undifferentiated products gave rise to a potential for harm on a mass scale, to which both class actions in private litigation and the modern regulatory state in the public sphere form the principal legal responses. National markets also broadened the fora within which a given plaintiff seeking to litigate a dispute concerning an undifferentiated, nationally marketed product might attempt to sue. So it is that, even in a world of conventional individual lawsuits, the broadened—if only modestly—array for forum selection contributed to the need for forum-selection rules to define where a case could be brought and for choice of law principles to enable the forum court to select the substantive law to govern the dispute.

Now, add to the picture aggregate procedure, layered on top of national markets. The mid-twentieth century saw the emergence of Rule 23 of the Federal Rules of Civil Procedure and the mimicking of its language by state counterpart rules in the vast majority of jurisdictions. This near-nationwide recognition of the class action in its modern form had the unanticipated effect of broadening further the array of potential fora. . . . Where both the disputed conduct and the would-be members of the class extend broadly, the range of potential fora expands commensurately. The range of possible locations for suit in a given instance might well extend to the various federal district courts in addition to their state trial-level counterparts spread across the nation. This practice received its formal approval in *Phillips Petroleum Co. v. Shutts*, where the nationwide class action was born of the minimal process requirements of notice and an ability to opt out, coupled with adequate representation. But *Shutts* would ask only whether a nationwide forum could be constituted; it did not ask whether the chosen forum was the dominant one, or even one that was particularly suitable.

Samuel Issacharoff & Richard A. Nagareda, *Class Settlements under Attack*, 156 U. Pa. L. Rev. 1649, 1660–63 (2008). As we shall see in Chapter 3, a variety of developments in the law of class actions—the Class Action Fairness Act of 2005 and the framework for consolidation of related lawsuits by the federal Judicial Panel on Multidistrict Litigation, among others—can be understood as partial, imperfect responses to the problem of regulatory mismatch.

b.   WHICH INTRA–CLASS CONFLICTS MATTER?

By its terms, Rule 23(b)(3) sets forth requirements in addition to the general requirements for class certification set forth in Rule 23(a). Specifically, Rule 23(b)(3)—as restyled in 2007—calls for a judicial finding that "the questions of law or fact common to class members predominate over any questions affecting only individual members, and that a class action is superior to other available methods for fairly and efficiently adjudicating the controversy." The same provision goes on to list four considerations that bear upon these required findings.

Consider the advisory committee's explanation of its handiwork in Rule 23(b)(3):

In the situations to which this subdivision relates, class-action treatment is not as clearly called for as in those described [in subdivisions (b)(1)–(2)], but it may nevertheless be convenient and desirable depending upon the particular facts. Subdivision (b)(3) encompasses those cases in which a class action would achieve economies of time, effort, and expense, and promote uniformity of decision as to persons similarly situated, without sacrificing procedural fairness or bringing about other undesirable results.

   The court is required to find, as a condition of holding that a class action may be maintained under this subdivision, that the questions common to the class predominate over the questions affecting individual members. It is only where this predominance exists that economies can be achieved by means of the class-action device. In this view, a fraud perpetrated on numerous persons by the use of similar misrepresentations may be an appealing situation for a class action, and it may remain so despite the need, if liability is found, for separate determination of the damages suffered by individuals within the class. On the other hand, although having some common core, a fraud case may be unsuited for treatment as a class action if there was material variation in the representations made or in the kinds or degrees of reliance by the persons to whom they were addressed. A "mass accident" resulting in injuries to numerous persons is ordinarily not appropriate for a class action because of the likelihood that significant questions, not only of damages but of liability and defenses of liability, would be present, affecting the individuals in different ways. In these circumstances an action conducted nominally as a class action would degenerate in practice into multiple lawsuits separately tried. Private damage claims by numerous individuals arising out of concerted antitrust violations may or may not involve predominating common questions.

The most significant guidance from the Supreme Court on the meaning of Rule 23(b)(3) and its relationship to the general requirements for class certification in Rule 23(a) comes in a 1997 decision striking down an ambitious attempt to use a settlement of an opt-out class action to resolve on a comprehensive basis the tort liabilities of several manufacturers of asbestos-containing products.

Amchem Products, Inc. v. Windsor

521 U.S. 591 (1997)

■ JUSTICE GINSBURG delivered the opinion of the Court.

   This case concerns the legitimacy under Rule 23 of the Federal Rules of Civil Procedure of a class-action certification sought to achieve global settlement of current and future asbestos-related claims. The class proposed for certification potentially encompasses hundreds of thousands, perhaps millions, of individuals tied together by this commonality: Each was, or some day may be, adversely affected by past exposure to asbestos products manufactured by one or more of 20 companies. Those companies, defendants in the lower courts, are petitioners here.

   The United States District Court for the Eastern District of Pennsylvania certified the class for settlement only, finding that the proposed settlement was fair and that representation and notice had been adequate. That court enjoined class members from separately pursuing asbestos-

settlement only

related personal-injury suits in any court, federal or state, pending the issuance of a final order. The Court of Appeals for the Third Circuit vacated the District Court's orders, holding that the class certification failed to satisfy Rule 23's requirements in several critical respects. We affirm the Court of Appeals' judgment.

I

A

The settlement-class certification we confront evolved in response to an asbestos-litigation crisis. See *Georgine v. Amchem Products, Inc.,* 83 F.3d 610, 618, and n.2 (C.A.3 1996) (citing commentary). A United States Judicial Conference Ad Hoc Committee on Asbestos Litigation, appointed by THE CHIEF JUSTICE in September 1990, described facets of the problem in a 1991 report:

> "[This] is a tale of danger known in the 1930s, exposure inflicted upon millions of Americans in the 1940s and 1950s, injuries that began to take their toll in the 1960s, and a flood of lawsuits beginning in the 1970s. On the basis of past and current filing data, and because of a latency period that may last as long as 40 years for some asbestos related diseases, a continuing stream of claims can be expected. The final toll of asbestos related injuries is unknown. Predictions have been made of 200,000 asbestos disease deaths before the year 2000 and as many as 265,000 by the year 2015.

> "The most objectionable aspects of asbestos litigation can be briefly summarized: dockets in both federal and state courts continue to grow; long delays are routine; trials are too long; the same issues are litigated over and over; transaction costs exceed the victims' recovery by nearly two to one; exhaustion of assets threatens and distorts the process; and future claimants may lose altogether." Report of The Judicial Conference Ad Hoc Committee on Asbestos Litigation 2–3 (Mar. 1991).

Real reform, the report concluded, required federal legislation creating a national asbestos dispute-resolution scheme. See *id.* at 3, 27–35; see also *id.* at 42 (dissenting statement of Hogan, J.) (agreeing that "a national solution is the only answer" and suggesting "passage by Congress of an administrative claims procedure similar to the Black Lung legislation"). As recommended by the Ad Hoc Committee, the Judicial Conference of the United States urged Congress to act. See Report of the Proceedings of the Judicial Conference of the United States 33 (Mar. 12, 1991). To this date, no congressional response has emerged.

In the face of legislative inaction, the federal courts—lacking authority to replace state tort systems with a national toxic tort compensation regime—endeavored to work with the procedural tools available to improve management of federal asbestos litigation. Eight federal judges, experienced in the superintendence of asbestos cases, urged the Judicial Panel on Multidistrict Litigation (MDL Panel), to consolidate in a single district all asbestos complaints then pending in federal courts. Accepting the recommendation, the MDL Panel transferred all asbestos cases then filed, but not yet on trial in federal courts to a single district, the United States District Court for the Eastern District of Pennsylvania; pursuant to the transfer order, the collected cases were consolidated for pretrial proceedings before Judge Weiner. See *In re Asbestos Prods. Liab. Litig. (No. VI),* 771 F. Supp.

[handwritten margin note: Cases aggregated were only ones that have been filed. Now those that have yet to be filed.]

415, 422–24 (Jud. Pan. Mult. Lit. 1991). The order aggregated pending cases only; no authority resides in the MDL Panel to license for consolidated proceedings claims not yet filed.

B

After the consolidation, attorneys for plaintiffs and defendants formed separate steering committees and began settlement negotiations. Ronald L. Motley and Gene Locks—later appointed, along with Motley's law partner Joseph F. Rice, to represent the plaintiff class in this action—cochaired the Plaintiffs' Steering Committee. Counsel for the Center for Claims Resolution (CCR), the consortium of 20 former asbestos manufacturers now before us as petitioners, participated in the Defendants' Steering Committee. Although the MDL Panel order collected, transferred, and consolidated only cases already commenced in federal courts, settlement negotiations included efforts to find a "means of resolving . . . future cases." [S]ee also *Georgine v. Amchem Prods., Inc.*, 157 F.R.D. 246, 266 (E.D. Pa. 1994) ("primary purpose of the settlement talks in the consolidated MDL litigation was to craft a national settlement that would provide an alternative resolution mechanism for asbestos claims," including claims that might be filed in the future).

In November 1991, the Defendants' Steering Committee made an offer designed to settle all pending and future asbestos cases by providing a fund for distribution by plaintiffs' counsel among asbestos-exposed individuals. The Plaintiffs' Steering Committee rejected this offer, and negotiations fell apart. CCR, however, continued to pursue "a workable administrative system for the handling of future claims." *Id.* at 270.

[handwritten margin note: Do want to settle / fund for all.]

To that end, CCR counsel approached the lawyers who had headed the Plaintiffs' Steering Committee in the unsuccessful negotiations, and a new round of negotiations began; that round yielded the mass settlement agreement now in controversy. At the time, the former heads of the Plaintiffs' Steering Committee represented thousands of plaintiffs with then-pending asbestos-related claims—claimants the parties to this suit call "inventory" plaintiffs. CCR indicated in these discussions that it would resist settlement of inventory cases absent "some kind of protection for the future." *Id.* at 294; see also *id.* at 295 (CCR communicated to the inventory plaintiffs' attorneys that once the CCR defendants saw a rational way to deal with claims expected to be filed in the future, those defendants would be prepared to address the settlement of pending cases).

Settlement talks thus concentrated on devising an administrative scheme for disposition of asbestos claims not yet in litigation. In these negotiations, counsel for masses of inventory plaintiffs endeavored to represent the interests of the anticipated future claimants, although those lawyers then had no attorney-client relationship with such claimants.

Once negotiations seemed likely to produce an agreement purporting to bind potential plaintiffs, CCR agreed to settle, through separate agreements, the claims of plaintiffs who had already filed asbestos-related lawsuits. In one such agreement, CCR defendants promised to pay more than $200 million to gain release of the claims of numerous inventory plaintiffs. After settling the inventory claims, CCR, together with the plaintiffs' lawyers CCR had approached, launched this case, exclusively involving persons outside the MDL Panel's province—plaintiffs without already pending lawsuits.[3]

C

The class action thus instituted was not intended to be litigated. Rather, within the space of a single day, January 15, 1993, the settling parties—CCR defendants and the representatives of the plaintiff class described below—presented to the District Court a complaint, an answer, a proposed settlement agreement, and a joint motion for conditional class certification.

The complaint identified nine lead plaintiffs, designating them and members of their families as representatives of a class comprising all persons who had not filed an asbestos-related lawsuit against a CCR defendant as of the date the class action commenced, but who (1) had been exposed—occupationally or through the occupational exposure of a spouse or household member—to asbestos or products containing asbestos attributable to a CCR defendant, or (2) whose spouse or family member had been so exposed. Untold numbers of individuals may fall within this description. All named plaintiffs alleged that they or a member of their family had been exposed to asbestos-containing products of CCR defendants. More than half of the named plaintiffs alleged that they or their family members had already suffered various physical injuries as a result of the exposure. The others alleged that they had not yet manifested any asbestos-related condition. The complaint delineated no subclasses; all named plaintiffs were designated as representatives of the class as a whole.

The complaint invoked the District Court's diversity jurisdiction and asserted various state-law claims for relief, including (1) negligent failure to warn, (2) strict liability, (3) breach of express and implied warranty, (4) negligent infliction of emotional distress, (5) enhanced risk of disease, (6) medical monitoring, and (7) civil conspiracy. Each plaintiff requested unspecified damages in excess of $100,000. CCR defendants' answer denied the principal allegations of the complaint and asserted 11 affirmative defenses.

A stipulation of settlement accompanied the pleadings; it proposed to settle, and to preclude nearly all class members from litigating against CCR companies, all claims not filed before January 15, 1993, involving compensation for present and future asbestos-related personal injury or death. An exhaustive document exceeding 100 pages, the stipulation presents in detail an administrative mechanism and a schedule of payments to compensate class members who meet defined asbestos-exposure and medical requirements. The stipulation describes four categories of compensable disease: mesothelioma; lung cancer; certain "other cancers" (colon-rectal, laryngeal, esophageal, and stomach cancer); and "non-malignant conditions" (asbestosis and bilateral pleural thickening). Persons with "exceptional" medical claims—claims that do not fall within the four described diagnostic categories—may in some instances qualify for compensation, but the settlement caps the number of "exceptional" claims CCR must cover.

For each qualifying disease category, the stipulation specifies the range of damages CCR will pay to qualifying claimants. Payments under the settlement are not adjustable for inflation. Mesothelioma claimants—

---

[3] It is basic to comprehension of this proceeding to notice that no transferred case is included in the settlement at issue, and no case covered by the settlement existed as a civil action at the time of the MDL Panel transfer.

Just like Heckler.

the most highly compensated category—are scheduled to receive between $20,000 and $200,000. The stipulation provides that CCR is to propose the level of compensation within the prescribed ranges; it also establishes procedures to resolve disputes over medical diagnoses and levels of compensation.

Compensation above the fixed ranges may be obtained for "extraordinary" claims. But the settlement places both numerical caps and dollar limits on such claims. The settlement also imposes "case flow maximums," which cap the number of claims payable for each disease in a given year.

Class members are to receive no compensation for certain kinds of claims, even if otherwise applicable state law recognizes such claims. Claims that garner no compensation under the settlement include claims by family members of asbestos-exposed individuals for loss of consortium, and claims by so-called "exposure-only" plaintiffs for increased risk of cancer, fear of future asbestos-related injury, and medical monitoring. "Pleural" claims, which might be asserted by persons with asbestos-related plaques on their lungs but no accompanying physical impairment, are also excluded. Although not entitled to present compensation, exposure-only claimants and pleural claimants may qualify for benefits when and if they develop a compensable disease and meet the relevant exposure and medical criteria. Defendants forgo defenses to liability, including statute of limitations pleas.

Class members, in the main, are bound by the settlement in perpetuity, while CCR defendants may choose to withdraw from the settlement after ten years. A small number of class members—only a few per year—may reject the settlement and pursue their claims in court. Those permitted to exercise this option, however, may not assert any punitive damages claim or any claim for increased risk of cancer. Aspects of the administration of the settlement are to be monitored by the AFL–CIO and class counsel. Class counsel are to receive attorneys' fees in an amount to be approved by the District Court.

D

On January 29, 1993, as requested by the settling parties, the District Court conditionally certified, under Federal Rule of Civil Procedure 23(b)(3), an encompassing opt-out class. The certified class included persons occupationally exposed to defendants' asbestos products, and members of their families, who had not filed suit as of January 15. . . .

Numerosity ✓
commonality

As to the specific prerequisites to certification, the District Court observed that the class satisfied Rule 23(a)(1)'s numerosity requirement, see *id.*, a matter no one debates. The Rule 23(a)(2) and (b)(3) requirements of commonality and preponderance were also satisfied, the District Court held, in that

> "[t]he members of the class have all been exposed to asbestos products supplied by the defendants and all share an interest in receiving prompt and fair compensation for their claims, while minimizing the risks and transaction costs inherent in the asbestos litigation process as it occurs presently in the tort system. Whether the proposed settlement satisfies this interest and is otherwise a fair, reasonable and adequate compromise of the claims of the class is a predominant issue for purposes of Rule 23(b)(3)." *Id.* at 316.

The District Court held next that the claims of the class representatives were "typical" of the class as a whole, a requirement of Rule 23(a)(3), and that, as Rule 23(b)(3) demands, the class settlement was "superior" to other methods of adjudication. See *id.*

Strenuous objections had been asserted regarding the adequacy of representation, a Rule 23(a)(4) requirement. Objectors maintained that class counsel and class representatives had disqualifying conflicts of interests. In particular, objectors urged, claimants whose injuries had become manifest and claimants without manifest injuries should not have common counsel and should not be aggregated in a single class. Furthermore, objectors argued, lawyers representing inventory plaintiffs should not represent the newly formed class.

Satisfied that class counsel had ably negotiated the settlement in the best interests of all concerned, and that the named parties served as adequate representatives, the District Court rejected these objections. See *id.* at 317–19, 326–32. Subclasses were unnecessary, the District Court held, bearing in mind the added cost and confusion they would entail and the ability of class members to exclude themselves from the class during the three-month opt-out period. See *id.* at 318–19. Reasoning that the representative plaintiffs "have a strong interest that recovery for *all* of the medical categories be maximized because they may have claims in *any*, or several categories," the District Court found "no antagonism of interest between class members with various medical conditions, or between persons with and without currently manifest asbestos impairment." *Id.* at 318. Declaring class certification appropriate and the settlement fair, the District Court preliminarily enjoined all class members from commencing any asbestos-related suit against the CCR defendants in any state or federal court. See *Georgine v. Amchem Prods., Inc.*, 878 F. Supp. 716, 726–27 (E.D. Pa. 1994).

The objectors appealed. The United States Court of Appeals for the Third Circuit vacated the certification, holding that the requirements of Rule 23 had not been satisfied. See 83 F.3d 610 (1996).

E

The Court of Appeals, in a long, heavily detailed opinion by Judge Becker, first noted several challenges by objectors to justiciability, subject-matter jurisdiction, and adequacy of notice. These challenges, the court said, raised "serious concerns." *Id.* at 623. However, the court observed, "the jurisdictional issues in this case would not exist but for the [class-action] certification." *id.* Turning to the class-certification issues and finding them dispositive, the Third Circuit declined to decide other questions.

On class-action prerequisites, the Court of Appeals referred to an earlier Third Circuit decision, *In re General Motors Corp. Pick–Up Truck Fuel Tank Prods.Liab.Litig.*, 55 F.3d 768, cert. denied, 516 U.S. 824 (1995) (hereinafter *GM Trucks*), which held that although a class action may be certified for settlement purposes only, Rule 23(a)'s requirements must be satisfied as if the case were going to be litigated. 55 F.3d at 799–800. The same rule should apply, the Third Circuit said, to class certification under Rule 23(b)(3). While stating that the requirements of Rule 23(a) and (b)(3) must be met "without taking into account the settlement," 83 F.3d, at 626, the Court of Appeals in fact closely considered the terms of the settlement as it examined aspects of the case under Rule 23 criteria. See *id.* at 630–34.

The Third Circuit recognized that Rule 23(a)(2)'s "commonality" requirement is subsumed under, or superseded by, the more stringent Rule 23(b)(3) requirement that questions common to the class "predominate over" other questions. The court therefore trained its attention on the "predominance" inquiry. See *id.* at 627. The harmfulness of asbestos exposure was indeed a prime factor common to the class, the Third Circuit observed. See *id.* at 626, 630. But uncommon questions abounded.

In contrast to mass torts involving a single accident, class members in this case were exposed to different asbestos-containing products, in different ways, over different periods, and for different amounts of time; some suffered no physical injury, others suffered disabling or deadly diseases. See *id.* at 626, 628. "These factual differences," the Third Circuit explained, "translate[d] into significant legal differences." *Id.* at 627. State law governed and varied widely on such critical issues as "viability of [exposure-only] claims [and] availability of causes of action for medical monitoring, increased risk of cancer, and fear of future injury." *Id.* "[T]he number of uncommon issues in this humongous class action," the Third Circuit concluded, *id.*, barred a determination, under existing tort law, that common questions predominated, see *id.* at 630.

The Court of Appeals next found that "serious intra-class conflicts preclude[d] th[e] class from meeting the adequacy of representation requirement" of Rule 23(a)(4). *Id.* Adverting to, but not resolving charges of attorney conflict of interests, the Third Circuit addressed the question whether the named plaintiffs could adequately advance the interests of all class members. The Court of Appeals acknowledged that the District Court was certainly correct to this extent: " '[T]he members of the class are united in seeking the maximum possible recovery for their asbestos-related claims.' " *Id.* (quoting 157 F.R.D. at 317). "But the settlement does more than simply provide a general recovery fund," the Court of Appeals immediately added; "[r]ather, it makes important judgments on how recovery is to be *allocated* among different kinds of plaintiffs, decisions that necessarily favor some claimants over others." 83 F.3d at 630.

In the Third Circuit's view, the "most salient" divergence of interests separated plaintiffs already afflicted with an asbestos-related disease from plaintiffs without manifest injury (exposure-only plaintiffs). The latter would rationally want protection against inflation for distant recoveries. See *id.* They would also seek sturdy back-end opt-out rights and "causation provisions that can keep pace with changing science and medicine, rather than freezing in place the science of 1993." *Id.* at 630–31. Already injured parties, in contrast, would care little about such provisions and would rationally trade them for higher current payouts. See *id.* at 631. These and other adverse interests, the Court of Appeals carefully explained, strongly suggested that an undivided set of representatives could not adequately protect the discrete interests of both currently afflicted and exposure-only claimants.

The Third Circuit next rejected the District Court's determination that the named plaintiffs were "typical" of the class, noting that this Rule 23(a)(3) inquiry overlaps the adequacy of representation question: "both look to the potential for conflicts in the class." *Id.* at 632. Evident conflict problems, the court said, led it to hold that "no set of representatives can be 'typical' of this class." *Id.*

The Court of Appeals similarly rejected the District Court's assessment of the superiority of the class action. The Third Circuit initially noted that a class action so large and complex "could not be tried." *Id.* The court elaborated most particularly, however, on the unfairness of binding exposure-only plaintiffs who might be unaware of the class action or lack sufficient information about their exposure to make a reasoned decision whether to stay in or opt out. See *id.* at 633. "A series of statewide or more narrowly defined adjudications, either through consolidation under Rule 42(a) or as class actions under Rule 23, would seem preferable," the Court of Appeals said. *Id.* at 634. . . .

We granted certiorari, 519 U.S. 957 (1996), and now affirm. . . .

III

. . . In the 1966 class-action amendments, Rule 23(b)(3), the category at issue here, was "the most adventuresome" innovation. See Kaplan, *A Prefatory Note*, 10 B.C. Ind. & Com. L. Rev. 497, 497 (1969) (hereinafter Kaplan, *Prefatory Note*). Rule 23(b)(3) added to the complex-litigation arsenal class actions for damages designed to secure judgments binding all class members save those who affirmatively elected to be excluded. Rule 23(b)(3) "opt-out" class actions superseded the former "spurious" class action, so characterized because it generally functioned as a permissive joinder ("opt-in") device.

Framed for situations in which "class-action treatment is not as clearly called for" as it is in Rule 23(b)(1) and (b)(2) situations, Rule 23(b)(3) permits certification where class suit "may nevertheless be convenient and desirable." Adv. Comm. Notes, 28 U.S.C. App., p. 697. To qualify for certification under Rule 23(b)(3), a class must meet two requirements beyond the Rule 23(a) prerequisites: Common questions must "predominate over any questions affecting only individual members"; and class resolution must be "superior to other available methods for the fair and efficient adjudication of the controversy." In adding "predominance" and "superiority" to the qualification-for-certification list, the Advisory Committee sought to cover cases "in which a class action would achieve economies of time, effort, and expense, and promote . . . uniformity of decision as to persons similarly situated, without sacrificing procedural fairness or bringing about other undesirable results." *Id.* Sensitive to the competing tugs of individual autonomy for those who might prefer to go it alone or in a smaller unit, on the one hand, and systemic efficiency on the other, the Reporter for the 1966 amendments cautioned: "The new provision invites a close look at the case before it is accepted as a class action. . . ." Kaplan, *Continuing Work*, at 390.

. . . [T]he Advisory Committee for the 1966 reform anticipated that in each case, courts would "consider the interests of individual members of the class in controlling their own litigations and carrying them on as they see fit." Adv. Comm. Notes, 28 U.S.C. App., p. 698. They elaborated:

> "The interests of individuals in conducting separate lawsuits may be so strong as to call for denial of a class action. On the other hand, these interests may be theoretic rather than practical; the class may have a high degree of cohesion and prosecution of the action through representatives would be quite unobjectionable, or the amounts at stake for individuals may be so small that separate suits would be impracticable." *Id.*

See also Kaplan, *Continuing Work*, at 391 ("Th[e] interest [in individual control] can be high where the stake of each member bulks large and his will and ability to take care of himself are strong; the interest may be no *[handwritten margin notes: "incl. cost of Damages — Higher [struck] more likely to opt out."]*

more than theoretic where the individual stake is so small as to make a separate action impracticable." (footnote omitted)). As the Third Circuit observed in the instant case: "Each plaintiff [in an action involving claims for personal injury and death] has a significant interest in individually controlling the prosecution of [his case]"; each "ha[s] a substantial stake in making individual decisions on whether and when to settle." 83 F.3d at 633.

While the text of Rule 23(b)(3) does not exclude from certification cases in which individual damages run high, the Advisory Committee had dominantly in mind vindication of "the rights of groups of people who individually would be without effective strength to bring their opponents into court at all." Kaplan, *Prefatory Note*, at 497. As concisely recalled in a recent Seventh Circuit opinion:

> "The policy at the very core of the class action mechanism is to overcome the problem that small recoveries do not provide the incentive for any individual to bring a solo action prosecuting his or her rights. A class action solves this problem by aggregating the relatively paltry potential recoveries into something worth someone's (usually an attorney's) labor." *Mace v. Van Ru Credit Corp.*, 109 F.3d 338, 344 (1997).

. . . In the decades since the 1966 revision of Rule 23, class-action practice has become ever more "adventuresome" as a means of coping with claims too numerous to secure their "just, speedy, and inexpensive determination" one by one. See Fed. R. Civ. P. 1. The development reflects concerns about the efficient use of court resources and the conservation of funds to compensate claimants who do not line up early in a litigation queue.

Among current applications of Rule 23(b)(3), the "settlement only" class has become a stock device. Although all Federal Circuits recognize the utility of Rule 23(b)(3) settlement classes, courts have divided on the extent to which a proffered settlement affects court surveillance under Rule 23's certification criteria.

In *GM Trucks*, 55 F.3d at 799–800, and in the instant case, 83 F.3d at 624–26, the Third Circuit held that a class cannot be certified for settlement when certification for trial would be unwarranted. Other courts have held that settlement obviates or reduces the need to measure a proposed class against the enumerated Rule 23 requirements. . . .

IV

We granted review to decide the role settlement may play, under existing Rule 23, in determining the propriety of class certification. The Third Circuit's opinion stated that each of the requirements of Rule 23(a) and (b)(3) "must be satisfied without taking into account the settlement." 83 F.3d at 626 (quoting *GM Trucks*, 55 F.3d at 799). That statement, petitioners urge, is incorrect.

[handwritten margin note: "Settlemnt is relevant to Cert."]

We agree with petitioners to this limited extent: Settlement is relevant to a class certification. The Third Circuit's opinion bears modification in that respect. But, as we earlier observed, see *supra*, at 2243, the Court of Appeals in fact did not ignore the settlement; instead, that court homed in on settlement terms in explaining why it found the absentees' interests inadequately represented. See 83 F.3d at 630–31. The Third Circuit's close inspection of the settlement in that regard was altogether proper.

[handwritten margin note: "Absentee's interest inadequately Represented!"]

Confronted with a request for settlement-only class certification, a district court need not inquire whether the case, if tried, would present intractable management problems, see Fed. R. Civ. P. 23(b)(3)(D), for the proposal is that there be no trial. But other specifications of the Rule—those designed to protect absentees by blocking unwarranted or overbroad class definitions—demand undiluted, even heightened, attention in the settlement context. Such attention is of vital importance, for a court asked to certify a settlement class will lack the opportunity, present when a case is litigated, to adjust the class, informed by the proceedings as they unfold. See Rule 23(c), (d).

Rule 23(e), on settlement of class actions, reads in its entirety: "A class action shall not be dismissed or compromised without the approval of the court, and notice of the proposed dismissal or compromise shall be given to all members of the class in such manner as the court directs." This prescription was designed to function as an additional requirement, not a superseding direction, for the "class action" to which Rule 23(e) refers is one qualified for certification under Rule 23(a) and (b). Cf. *Eisen*, 417 U.S. at 176177 (adequate representation does not eliminate additional requirement to provide notice). Subdivisions (a) and (b) focus court attention on whether a proposed class has sufficient unity so that absent members can fairly be bound by decisions of class representatives. That dominant concern persists when settlement, rather than trial, is proposed.

[handwritten margin note: 23 (e) Ct must approve Settlement]

The safeguards provided by the Rule 23(a) and (b) class-qualifying criteria, we emphasize, are not impractical impediments—checks shorn of utility—in the settlement-class context. First, the standards set for the protection of absent class members serve to inhibit appraisals of the chancellor's foot kind—class certifications dependent upon the court's gestalt judgment or overarching impression of the settlement's fairness.

Second, if a fairness inquiry under Rule 23(e) controlled certification, eclipsing Rule 23(a) and (b), and permitting class designation despite the impossibility of litigation, both class counsel and court would be disarmed. Class counsel confined to settlement negotiations could not use the threat of litigation to press for a better offer, see Coffee, Class Wars: The Dilemma of the Mass Tort Class Action, 95 Colum. L. Rev. 1343, 1379–80 (1995), and the court would face a bargain proffered for its approval without benefit of adversarial investigation, see, e.g., *Kamilewicz v. Bank of Boston Corp.*, 100 F.3d 1348, 1352 (7th Cir. 1996) (Easterbrook, J., dissenting from denial of rehearing en banc) (parties "may even put one over on the court, in a staged performance"), cert. denied, 520 U.S. 1204 (1997).

Federal courts, in any case, lack authority to substitute for Rule 23's certification criteria a standard never adopted—that if a settlement is "fair," then certification is proper. Applying to this case criteria the rulemakers set, we conclude that the Third Circuit's appraisal is essentially correct. Although that court should have acknowledged that settlement is a factor in the calculus, a remand is not warranted on that account. The Court of Appeals' opinion amply demonstrates why—with or without a settlement on the table—the sprawling class the District Court certified does not satisfy Rule 23's requirements.

A

We address first the requirement of Rule 23(b)(3) that "[common] questions of law or fact . . . predominate over any questions affecting only individual members." The District Court concluded that predominance was satisfied based on two factors: class members' shared experience of asbestos exposure and their common "interest in receiving prompt and fair compensation for their claims, while minimizing the risks and transaction costs inherent in the asbestos litigation process as it occurs presently in the tort system." 157 F.R.D. at 316. The settling parties also contend that the settlement's fairness is a common question, predominating over disparate legal issues that might be pivotal in litigation but become irrelevant under the settlement.

The predominance requirement stated in Rule 23(b)(3), we hold, is not met by the factors on which the District Court relied. The benefits asbestos-exposed persons might gain from the establishment of a grand-scale compensation scheme is a matter fit for legislative consideration, but it is not pertinent to the predominance inquiry. That inquiry trains on the legal or factual questions that qualify each class member's case as a genuine controversy, questions that preexist any settlement.[18]

The Rule 23(b)(3) predominance inquiry tests whether proposed classes are sufficiently cohesive to warrant adjudication by representation. See 7A FEDERAL PRACTICE AND PROCEDURE, at 518–19.[19] The inquiry appropriate under Rule 23(e), on the other hand, protects unnamed class members "from unjust or unfair settlements affecting their rights when the representatives become fainthearted before the action is adjudicated or are able to secure satisfaction of their individual claims by a compromise." See 7B FEDERAL PRACTICE AND PROCEDURE § 1797, at 340–41. But it is not the mission of Rule 23(e) to assure the class cohesion that legitimizes representative action in the first place. If a common interest in a fair compromise could satisfy the predominance requirement of Rule 23(b)(3), that vital prescription would be stripped of any meaning in the settlement context.

The District Court also relied upon this commonality: "The members of the class have all been exposed to asbestos products supplied by the defendants. . . ." 157 F.R.D. at 316. Even if Rule 23(a)'s commonality requirement may be satisfied by that shared experience, the predominance criterion is far more demanding. See 83 F.3d at 626–27. Given the greater number of questions peculiar to the several categories of class members, and to individuals within each category, and the significance of those uncommon questions, any overarching dispute about the health consequences of asbestos exposure cannot satisfy the Rule 23(b)(3) predominance standard.

The Third Circuit highlighted the disparate questions undermining class cohesion in this case:

> "Class members were exposed to different asbestos-containing products, for different amounts of time, in different

---

[18] In this respect, the predominance requirement of Rule 23(b)(3) is similar to the requirement of Rule 23(a)(3) that "claims or defenses" of the named representatives must be "typical of the claims or defenses of the class." The words "claims or defenses" in this context—just as in the context of Rule 24(b)(2) governing permissive intervention—"manifestly refer to the kinds of claims or defenses that can be raised in courts of law as part of an actual or impending law suit." *Diamond v. Charles*, 476 U.S. 54, 76–77 (1986) (O'CONNOR, J., concurring in part and concurring in judgment).

[19] This case, we note, involves no "limited fund" capable of supporting class treatment under Rule 23(b)(1)(B), which does not have a predominance requirement. See *Georgine v. Amchem Prods., Inc.*, 157 F.R.D. 246, 318 (E.D. Pa. 1994); see also *id.* at 291, & n. 40. The settling parties sought to proceed exclusively under Rule 23(b)(3).

ways, and over different periods. Some class members suffer no physical injury or have only asymptomatic pleural changes, while others suffer from lung cancer, disabling asbestosis, or from mesothelioma. . . . Each has a different history of cigarette smoking, a factor that complicates the causation inquiry.

"The [exposure-only] plaintiffs especially share little in common, either with each other or with the presently injured class members. It is unclear whether they will contract asbestos-related disease and, if so, what disease each will suffer. They will also incur different medical expenses because their monitoring and treatment will depend on singular circumstances and individual medical histories." *Id.* at 626.

Differences in state law, the Court of Appeals observed, compound these disparities. See *id.* at 627 (citing *Phillips Petroleum Co. v. Shutts*, 472 U.S. 797, 823 (1985)).

No settlement class called to our attention is as sprawling as this one. Predominance is a test readily met in certain cases alleging consumer or securities fraud or violations of the antitrust laws. See Adv. Comm. Notes, 28 U.S.C. App., p. 697. Even mass tort cases arising from a common cause or disaster may, depending upon the circumstances, satisfy the predominance requirement. The Advisory Committee for the 1966 revision of Rule 23, it is true, noted that "mass accident" cases are likely to present "significant questions, not only of damages but of liability and defenses of liability, . . . affecting the individuals in different ways." Adv. Comm. Notes, 28 U.S.C. App., p. 697. And the Committee advised that such cases are "ordinarily not appropriate" for class treatment. *Id.* But the text of the Rule does not categorically exclude mass tort cases from class certification, and District Courts, since the late 1970's, have been certifying such cases in increasing number. The Committee's warning, however, continues to call for caution when individual stakes are high and disparities among class members great. As the Third Circuit's opinion makes plain, the certification in this case does not follow the counsel of caution. That certification cannot be upheld, for it rests on a conception of Rule 23(b)(3)'s predominance requirement irreconcilable with the Rule's design.

B

Nor can the class approved by the District Court satisfy Rule 23(a)(4)'s requirement that the named parties "will fairly and adequately protect the interests of the class." The adequacy inquiry under Rule 23(a)(4) serves to uncover conflicts of interest between named parties and the class they seek to represent. See *General Telephone Co. of Southwest v. Falcon*, 457 U.S. 147, 157–58 n.13 (1982). "[A] class representative must be part of the class and 'possess the same interest and suffer the same injury' as the class members." *East Tex. Motor Freight System, Inc. v. Rodriguez*, 431 U.S. 395, 403 (1977). . .[20]

---

[20] The adequacy-of-representation requirement "tend[s] to merge" with the commonality and typicality criteria of Rule 23(a), which "serve as guideposts for determining whether . . . maintenance of a class action is economical and whether the named plaintiff's claim and the class claims are so interrelated that the interests of the class members will be fairly and adequately protected in their absence." *General Telephone Co. of Southwest v. Falcon*, 457 U.S. 147, 157 n.13 (1982). The adequacy heading also factors in competency and conflicts of class counsel. See *id.* at 157–58 n.13. Like the Third Circuit, we decline to address adequacy-of-counsel issues discretely in light of our conclusions that common questions of law or fact do

As the Third Circuit pointed out, named parties with diverse medical conditions sought to act on behalf of a single giant class rather than on behalf of discrete subclasses. In significant respects, the interests of those within the single class are not aligned. Most saliently, for the currently injured, the critical goal is generous immediate payments. That goal tugs against the interest of exposure-only plaintiffs in ensuring an ample, inflation-protected fund for the future. Cf. *General Telephone Co. of Northwest v. EEOC*, 446 U.S. 318, 331 (1980) ("In employment discrimination litigation, conflicts might arise, for example, between employees and applicants who were denied employment and who will, if granted relief, compete with employees for fringe benefits or seniority. Under Rule 23, the same plaintiff could not represent these classes.").

The disparity between the currently injured and exposure-only categories of plaintiffs, and the diversity within each category are not made insignificant by the District Court's finding that petitioners' assets suffice to pay claims under the settlement. See 157 F.R.D. at 291. Although this is not a "limited fund" case certified under Rule 23(b)(1)(B), the terms of the settlement reflect essential allocation decisions designed to confine compensation and to limit defendants' liability. For example, as earlier described, the settlement includes no adjustment for inflation; only a few claimants per year can opt out at the back end; and loss-of-consortium claims are extinguished with no compensation.

The settling parties, in sum, achieved a global compromise with no structural assurance of fair and adequate representation for the diverse groups and individuals affected. Although the named parties alleged a range of complaints, each served generally as representative for the whole, not for a separate constituency. In another asbestos class action, the Second Circuit spoke precisely to this point:

> "[W]here differences among members of a class are such that subclasses must be established, we know of no authority that permits a court to approve a settlement without creating subclasses on the basis of consents by members of a unitary class, some of whom happen to be members of the distinct subgroups. The class representatives may well have thought that the Settlement serves the aggregate interests of the entire class. But the adversity among subgroups requires that the members of each subgroup cannot be bound to a settlement except by consents given by those who understand that their role is to represent solely the members of their respective subgroups." *In re Joint Eastern and Southern Dist. Asbestos Litig.*, 982 F.2d 721, 742–43 (1992), modified on reh'g *sub nom. In re Findley*, 993 F.2d 7 (1993).

The Third Circuit found no assurance here—either in the terms of the settlement or in the structure of the negotiations—that the named plaintiffs operated under a proper understanding of their representational responsibilities. See 83 F.3d at 630–31. That assessment, we conclude, is on the mark.

C

Impediments to the provision of adequate notice, the Third Circuit emphasized, rendered highly problematic any endeavor to tie to a settle-

---

not predominate and that the named plaintiffs cannot adequately represent the interests of this enormous class.

ment class persons with no perceptible asbestos-related disease at the time of the settlement. *Id.* at 633. . . . Many persons in the exposure-only category, the Court of Appeals stressed, may not even know of their exposure, or realize the extent of the harm they may incur. Even if they fully appreciate the significance of class notice, those without current afflictions may not have the information or foresight needed to decide, intelligently, whether to stay in or opt out.

Family members of asbestos-exposed individuals may themselves fall prey to disease or may ultimately have ripe claims for loss of consortium. Yet large numbers of people in this category—future spouses and children of asbestos victims—could not be alerted to their class membership. And current spouses and children of the occupationally exposed may know nothing of that exposure.

Because we have concluded that the class in this case cannot satisfy the requirements of common issue predominance and adequacy of representation, we need not rule, definitively, on the notice given here. In accord with the Third Circuit, however, see 83 F.3d at 633–34, we recognize the gravity of the question whether class action notice sufficient under the Constitution and Rule 23 could ever be given to legions so unselfconscious and amorphous.

V

The argument is sensibly made that a nationwide administrative claims processing regime would provide the most secure, fair, and efficient means of compensating victims of asbestos exposure. Congress, however, has not adopted such a solution. And Rule 23, which must be interpreted with fidelity to the Rules Enabling Act and applied with the interests of absent class members in close view, cannot carry the large load CCR, class counsel, and the District Court heaped upon it. As this case exemplifies, the rulemakers' prescriptions for class actions may be endangered by "those who embrace [Rule 23] too enthusiastically just as [they are by] those who approach [the Rule] with distaste." Charles A. Wright, *Law of Federal Courts* 508 (5th ed. 1994); cf. 83 F.3d at 634 (suggesting resort to less bold aggregation techniques, including more narrowly defined class certifications).

* * *

For the reasons stated, the judgment of the Court of Appeals for the Third Circuit is

Affirmed.

■ JUSTICE O'CONNOR took no part in the consideration or decision of this case.

■ JUSTICE BREYER, with whom JUSTICE STEVENS joins, concurring in part and dissenting in part. . . .

I

First, I believe the majority understates the importance of settlement in this case. Between 13 and 21 million workers have been exposed to asbestos in the workplace—over the past 40 or 50 years—but the most severe instances of such exposure probably occurred three or four decades ago. See Report of The Judicial Conference Ad Hoc Committee on Asbestos Litigation, pp. 6–7 (Mar. 1991) (Judicial Conference Report). . . . This exposure has led to several hundred thousand lawsuits, about 15% of which involved claims for cancer and about 30% for asbestosis. See *In re Joint Eastern and Southern Dist. Asbestos Litig.*, 129 B.R. 710, 936–37 (E. and S.D.N.Y. 1991). About half of the suits have involved claims for pleural thickening and plaques—the harmfulness of which is apparently controversial. (One expert below testified that they "don't transform into cancer" and are not "predictor[s] of future disease," App. 781.) Some of those who suffer from the most serious injuries, however, have received little or no compensation. *In re School Asbestos Litig.*, 789 F.2d 996, 1000 (3d Cir. 1986); see also Christopher F. Edley & Paul C. Weiler, *Asbestos: A Multi–Billion–Dollar Crisis*, 30 Harv. J. Legis. 383, 384, 393 (1993) ("[U]p to one-half of asbestos claims are now being filed by people who have little or no physical impairment. Many of these claims produce substantial payments (and substantial costs) even though the individual litigants will never become impaired"). These lawsuits have taken up more than 6% of all federal civil filings in one recent year, and are subject to a delay that is twice that of other civil suits. Judicial Conference Report 7, 10–11.

Delays, high costs, and a random pattern of noncompensation led the Judicial Conference Ad Hoc Committee on Asbestos Litigation to transfer all federal asbestos personal-injury cases to the Eastern District of Pennsylvania in an effort to bring about a fair and comprehensive settlement. It is worth considering a few of the Committee's comments. See Judicial Conference Report 2 ("'Decisions concerning thousands of deaths, millions of injuries, and billions of dollars are entangled in a litigation system whose strengths have increasingly been overshadowed by its weaknesses.' The ensuing five years have seen the picture worsen: increased filings, larger backlogs, higher costs, more bankruptcies and poorer prospects that judgments—if ever obtained—can be collected" (quoting Rand Corporation Institute for Civil Justice)); *id.* at 13 ("The transaction costs associated with asbestos litigation are an unconscionable burden on the victims of asbestos disease." "[O]f each asbestos litigation dollar, 61 cents is consumed in transaction costs. . . . Only 39 cents were paid to the asbestos victims" (citing Rand finding)); *id.* at 12 ("Delays also can increase transaction costs, especially the attorneys' fees paid by defendants at hourly rates. These costs reduce either the insurance fund or the company's assets, thereby reducing the funds available to pay pending and future claimants. By the end of the trial phase in [one case], at least seven defendants had declared bankruptcy (as a result of asbestos claims generally")). . . .

Although the transfer of the federal asbestos cases did not produce a general settlement, it was intertwined with and led to a lengthy year-long negotiation between the cochairs of the Plaintiff's Multi–District Litigation Steering Committee (elected by the Plaintiff's Committee Members and approved by the District Court) and the 20 asbestos defendants who are before us here. *Georgine v. Amchem Prods., Inc.*, 157 F.R.D. 246, 266–67 (E.D. Pa. 1994); App. 660–62. These "protracted and vigorous" negotiations led to the present partial settlement, which will pay an estimated $1.3 billion and compensate perhaps 100,000 class members in the first 10 years. 157 F.R.D. at 268, 287. "The negotiations included a substantial exchange of information" between class counsel and the 20 defendant companies, including "confidential data" showing the defendants' historical settlement averages, numbers of claims filed and settled, and insurance resources. *Id.* at 267. "Virtually no provision" of the settlement "was not the subject of significant negotiation," and the settlement terms "changed substantially" during the negotiations. *Id.* In the end, the negotiations produced a settlement that, the District Court determined based on its detailed review of the process, was "the result of arms-length adversarial negotiations by extraordinarily competent and experienced attorneys." *Id.* at 335.

The District Court, when approving the settlement, concluded that it improved the plaintiffs' chances of compensation and reduced total legal fees and other transaction costs by a significant amount. Under the previous system, according to the court, "[t]he sickest of victims often go uncompensated for years while valuable funds go to others who remain unimpaired by their mild asbestos disease." *Id.* The court believed the settlement would create a compensation system that would make more money available for plaintiffs who later develop serious illnesses.

I mention this matter because it suggests that the settlement before us is unusual in terms of its importance, both to many potential plaintiffs and to defendants, and with respect to the time, effort, and expenditure that it reflects. All of which leads me to be reluctant to set aside the District Court's findings without more assurance than I have that they are wrong. I cannot obtain that assurance through comprehensive review of the record because that is properly the job of the Court of Appeals and that court, understandably, but as we now hold, mistakenly, believed that settlement was not a relevant (and, as I would say, important) consideration.

Second, the majority, in reviewing the District Court's determination that common "issues of fact and law predominate," says that the predominance "inquiry trains on the legal or factual questions that qualify each class member's case as a genuine controversy, questions that preexist any settlement." I find it difficult to interpret this sentence in a way that could lead me to the majority's conclusion. If the majority means that these pre-settlement questions are what matters, then how does it reconcile its statement with its basic conclusion that "settlement is relevant" to class certification, or with the numerous lower court authority that says that settlement is not only relevant, but important? See, e. g., *In re A.H. Robins Co.*, 880 F.2d 709, 740 (4th Cir. 1988), cert. denied *sub nom. Anderson v. Aetna Casualty & Surety Co.*, 493 U.S. 959 (1989); *In re Beef Indus. Antitrust Litig.*, 607 F.2d 167, 177–78 (5th C. 1979), cert. denied *sub nom. Iowa Beef Processors, Inc. v. Meat Price Investigators Assn.*, 452 U.S. 905 (1981); 2 Herbert B. Newberg & Alba Conte, NEWBERG ON CLASS ACTIONS § 11.27, pp. 11–54 to 11–55 (3d ed. 1992).

Nor do I understand how one could decide whether common questions "predominate" in the abstract—without looking at what is likely to be at issue in the proceedings that will ensue, namely, the settlement. Every group of human beings, after all, has some features in common, and some that differ. How can a court make a contextual judgment of the sort that Rule 23 requires without looking to what proceedings will follow? . . . I am not saying that the "settlement counts only one way." Rather, the settlement may simply "add a great deal of information to the court's inquiry and will often expose diverging interests or common issues that were not evident or clear from the complaint" and courts "can and should" look to it to enhance the "ability . . . to make informed certification decisions." *In re Asbestos Litig.*, 90 F.3d 963, 975 (5th Cir. 1996).

. . . The settlement is relevant because it means that these common features and interests are likely to be important in the proceeding that would ensue—a proceeding that would focus primarily upon whether or not the proposed settlement fairly and properly satisfied the interests class members had in common. That is to say, the settlement underscored the importance of (a) the common fact of exposure, (b) the common interest in receiving *some* compensation for certain rather than running a strong risk of *no* compensation, and (c) the common interest in avoiding large legal fees, other transaction costs, and delays.

Of course, as the majority points out, there are also important differences among class members. Different plaintiffs were exposed to different products for different times; each has a distinct medical history and a different history of smoking; and many cases arise under the laws of different States. The relevant question, however, is *how much* these differences matter in respect to the legal proceedings that lie ahead. Many, if not all, toxic tort class actions involve plaintiffs with such differences. And the differences in state law are of diminished importance in respect to a proposed settlement in which the defendants have waived all defenses and agreed to compensate all those who were injured.

These differences might warrant subclasses, though subclasses can have problems of their own. "There can be a cost in creating more distinct subgroups, each with its own representation. . . . [T]he more subclasses created, the more severe conflicts bubble to the surface and inhibit settlement. . . . The resources of defendants and, ultimately, the community must not be exhausted by protracted litigation." Jack B. Weinstein, INDIVIDUAL JUSTICE IN MASS TORT LITIGATION: THE EFFECT OF CLASS ACTIONS, CONSOLIDATIONS, AND OTHER MULTIPARTY DEVICES66 (1995). Or these differences may be too serious to permit an effort at group settlement. This kind of determination, as I have said, is one that the law commits to the discretion of the district court—reviewable for abuse of discretion by a court of appeals. I believe that we are far too distant from the litigation itself to reweigh the fact-specific Rule 23 determinations and to find them erroneous without the benefit of the Court of Appeals first having restudied the matter with today's legal standard in mind.

Third, the majority concludes that the "representative parties" will not "fairly and adequately protect the interests of the class." Rule 23(a)(4). It finds a serious conflict between plaintiffs who are now injured and those who may be injured in the future because "for the currently injured, the critical goal is generous immediate payments," a goal that "tugs against the interest of exposure-only plaintiffs in ensuring an ample, inflation-protected fund for the future."

I agree that there is a serious problem, but it is a problem that often exists in toxic tort cases. See id. at 64 (noting that conflict "between present and future claimants" "is almost always present in some form in mass tort cases because long latency periods are needed to discover injuries"); see also Judicial Conference Report 34–35 ("Because many of the defendants in these cases have limited assets that may be called upon to satisfy the judgments obtained under current common tort rules and remedies, there is a 'real and present danger that the available assets will be exhausted before those later victims can seek compensation to which they are entitled.' "). And it is a problem that potentially exists whenever a single defendant injures several plaintiffs, for a settling plaintiff leaves fewer assets available for the others. With class actions, at least, plaintiffs have the consolation that a district court, thoroughly familiar with the facts, is charged with the responsibility of ensuring that the interests of no class members are sacrificed.

But this Court cannot easily safeguard such interests through review of a cold record. "What constitutes adequate representation is a question of fact that depends on the circumstances of each case." 7A FEDERAL PRACTICE

AND PROCEDURE § 1765, at 271. That is particularly so when, as here, there is an unusual baseline, namely, the " 'real and present danger' " described by the Judicial Conference Report above. The majority's use of the lack of an inflation adjustment as evidence of inadequacy of representation for future plaintiffs, is one example of this difficulty. An inflation adjustment might not be as valuable as the majority assumes if most plaintiffs are old and not worried about receiving compensation decades from now. There are, of course, strong arguments as to its value. But that disagreement is one that this Court is poorly situated to resolve.

Further, certain details of the settlement that are not discussed in the majority opinion suggest that the settlement may be of greater benefit to future plaintiffs than the majority suggests. The District Court concluded that future plaintiffs receive a "significant value" from the settlement due to a variety of its items that benefit future plaintiffs, such as: (1) tolling the statute of limitations so that class members "will no longer be forced to file premature lawsuits or risk their claims being time-barred"; (2) waiver of defenses to liability; (3) payment of claims, if and when members become sick, pursuant to the settlement's compensation standards, which avoids "the uncertainties, long delays and high transaction costs [including attorney's fees] of the tort system"; (4) "some assurance that there will be funds available if and when they get sick," based on the finding that each defendant "has shown an ability to fund the payment of all qualifying claims" under the settlement; and (5) the right to additional compensation if cancer develops (many settlements for plaintiffs with noncancerous conditions bar such additional claims). 157 F.R.D. at 292. For these reasons, and others, the District Court found that the distinction between present and future plaintiffs was "illusory." *Id.* at 317–18.

I do not know whether or not the benefits are more or less valuable than an inflation adjustment. But I can certainly recognize an argument that they are. (To choose one more brief illustration, the majority chastises the settlement for extinguishing loss-of-consortium claims, *ante*, at 2251, 2252, but does not note that, as the District Court found, the "defendants' historical [settlement] averages, upon which the compensation values are based, include payments for loss of consortium claims, and, accordingly, the Compensation Schedule is not unfair for this ascribed reason," 157 F.R.D. at 278.) The difficulties inherent in both knowing and understanding the vast number of relevant individual fact-based determinations here counsel heavily in favor of deference to district court decisionmaking in Rule 23 decisions. Or, at the least, making certain that appellate court review has taken place with the correct standard in mind. . . .

Finally, I believe it is up to the District Court, rather than this Court, to review the legal sufficiency of notice to members of the class. The District Court found that the plan to provide notice was implemented at a cost of millions of dollars and included hundreds of thousands of individual notices, a wide-ranging television and print campaign, and significant additional efforts by 35 international and national unions to notify their members. *Id.* at 312–13, 336. Every notice emphasized that an individual did not currently have to be sick to be a class member. And in the end, the District Court was "confident" that Rule 23 and due process requirements were satisfied because, as a result of this "extensive and expensive notice procedure," "over six million" individuals "received actual notice materials," and "millions more" were reached by the media campaign. *Id.* at 312, 333, 336. Although the majority, in principle, is reviewing a Court of Appeals' conclusion, it seems to me that its opinion might call into question the fact-related determinations of the District Court. To the extent that it does so, I disagree, for such findings cannot be so quickly disregarded. And I do not think that our precedents permit this Court to do so.

II

The issues in this case are complicated and difficult. The District Court might have been correct. Or not. Subclasses might be appropriate. Or not. I cannot tell. And I do not believe that this Court should be in the business of trying to make these fact-based determinations. That is a job suited to the district courts in the first instance, and the courts of appeals on review. But there is no reason in this case to believe that the Court of Appeals conducted its prior review with an understanding that the settlement could have constituted a reasonably strong factor in favor of class certification. For this reason, I would provide the courts below with an opportunity to analyze the factual questions involved in certification by vacating the judgment, and remanding the case for further proceedings.

NOTES AND QUESTIONS

1. *Efforts to Streamline Asbestos Litigation Prior to* Amchem. Commentators trace the origins of litigation over asbestos on a mass scale to successful efforts in the early 1970s to establish a legal duty on the part of manufacturers—not just intermediate contractors in charge of industrial workplaces—to warn workers of the health hazards associated with asbestos exposure. Paul Brodeur, OUTRAGEOUS MISCONDUCT 73 (1985) (noting that the plaintiff's victory in *Borel v. Fibreboard Paper Prods. Corp.*, 493 F.2d 1076 (5th Cir. 1973) triggered the "avalanche" of litigation over asbestos). By the early–1990s, thousands of individual asbestos lawsuits were pending in both federal and state courts throughout the country.

It is important to bear in mind that the *Amchem* settlement class action arose only after other attempts over many years failed to deal with the avalanche of asbestos litigation. Judge Robert Parker, at the time a federal district judge in the Eastern District of Texas, was responsible for many of these efforts. After the Fifth Circuit reversed his lump sum damages plan in *In re Fibreboard Corp.*, 893 F.2d 706 (5th Cir. 1990), he took what was perhaps his boldest procedural step: the use of statistical sampling. See *Cimino v. Raymark Indus., Inc.*, 751 F. Supp. 649, 660–65 (E.D. Tex. 1990).

The *Cimino* litigation involved about three thousand aggregated asbestos cases. In the Eastern District and elsewhere, asbestos defendants had adopted a litigation strategy of "repeatedly contest[ing] . . . every contestable issue involving the same products, the same warnings, and the same conduct." *Id.* at 651–52. Lamenting the difficulties raised for the court by this strategy, Judge Parker observed that, even if he "could somehow close thirty cases a month, it would take six and one-half years to try [the existing] cases." Even then, "there would be pending over 5,000 [additional] untouched cases at the present rate of filing." *Id.*

Judge Parker responded to the challenge by using statistical sampling. In Chapter 5, we will examine some of the issues raised by the use of sampling in aggregate litigation. Briefly, Judge Parker's plan was to randomly sample a total of 160 cases drawing some cases from each of five disease categories. Each of the sampled cases would be tried and the sample average for the corresponding disease category would be given to plaintiffs in unsampled cases with that same disease. In effect, Judge Parker sought to generate by way of sample trials the kind of compensation grid that experienced asbestos lawyers negotiating a settlement might have constructed based on patterns of verdicts in past cases. Of course, Judge Parker's grid was not connected with any settlement. He used the grid to calculate final judgments imposed on the parties with or without their consent.

Judge Parker's trial plan met with reversal on appeal. The Fifth Circuit underscored that Texas tort law—the body of substantive law applicable in *Cimino*—afforded defendants certain protections as preconditions to the imposition of liability. Defendants could insist upon individualized proof not only of a causal link between their particular products and the injury suffered by a particular plaintiff but also of the damages to which each particular plaintiff is entitled. *Cimino v. Raymark Indus., Inc.*, 151 F.3d 297, 313 (5th Cir. 1998).

Do the compensation terms described in the *Amchem* class settlement agreement effectively replicate the grid that Judge Parker sought to generate in *Cimino* by way of statistical sampling of actual cases on file? What are the major differences—both procedural and strategic—between the grid envisioned in *Cimino* and the class settlement in *Amchem*? What explains asbestos defendants' embrace of the latter and their staunch opposition to the former?

2.   *The Design of the* Amchem *Class Settlement*. Who precisely was within the class definition proposed in *Amchem*? Why, as a practical or strategic matter, would class settlement negotiators so define the class?

What were the fundamental design features of the class settlement? Who was to receive cash compensation, and who was not? How do you think class counsel and defense counsel would have determined how much compensation to pay a given kind of claim? The compensation scheme of the *Amchem* class settlement resembles statutory workmen's compensation. Like workmen's compensation, the *Amchem* settlement sets out a schedule of fixed payments depending on injury type, eliminates certain defenses, and delivers compensation more quickly and less expensively than individual suits. Workmen's compensation is legislatively constructed and administered by an agency. The *Amchem* settlement would have been privately created, judicially approved, and administered by a private claims resolution facility created by the settlement. Does this give any reason to be concerned about the *Amchem* settlement? Is a settlement like this something courts should be involved with? Recall that Congress had been asked to set up an administrative compensation scheme for asbestos injuries, but it never did—and still has not. Should that matter? If so, which way does it cut? When federal courts got involved in the complex task of school desegregation during the 1960s and 1970s, some critics complained that designing and ordering this type of remedy was a legislative function and not one the courts should assume. In response, supporters of desegregation suits pointed to the fact that state legislatures were politically paralyzed or worse, and unlikely to do anything about the problem in the foreseeable future. Is desegregation different than asbestos litigation?

3.   *The Significance of a Class Settlement for Class Certification*. As between Justice Ginsburg for the majority and Justice Breyer in dissent, who has the better of the argument concerning the significance of a class settlement for the certification of the plaintiff class? Justice Ginsburg accurately observes that the portion of Rule 23 concerned with settlement (subsection (e), in its pre–

2003 form) is distinct within the structure of that rule from those portions that set forth the criteria for class certification (subsections (a) and (b)). But why, as a matter of first principles, would one want to separate the question of class certification from the question of class settlement approval in the way that the majority describes? The majority argues, among other things, that relaxing the certification requirements for a settlement class will reduce the class's bargaining power. It's not too difficult to flesh out this argument. The bargaining power that class counsel enjoys depends on what she can credibly threaten to do if a settlement is not reached. It follows that class counsel will have more power if the defendant believes the alternative to settlement is a litigating class action. But does this argument make sense? Bear in mind that if a litigating class cannot be certified, the suits might proceed individually—assuming individual suits are cost-justified—or through some other aggregation device such as joinder, MDL, or a smaller and differently structured class action. Presumably negotiations in the context of a settlement class would reflect these alternatives, just as any other negotiations would. How then are class members hurt by attorneys using whatever power they have to negotiate a resolution in the context of a settlement class?

In this connection, it is useful to recall that the *Amchem* Court does not require satisfaction of all certification requirements. It makes a point of stating that "a district court need not inquire whether the case, if tried, would present intractable management problems, see Fed. R. Civ. P. 23(b)(3)(D), for the proposal is that there be no trial." Does this undermine the bargaining power argument? If so, are there other reasons to impose at least some certification requirements on settlement class actions? There might be a good practical reason not to require manageability for settlement class certification. After all, how would a court determine manageability when none of the parties has any incentive to contest it and any trial plan is purely hypothetical?

The *Amchem* Court also notes that the Rule 23 certification requirements assure that "a proposed class has sufficient unity so that absent members can fairly be bound by decisions of class representatives," which it sees as a "dominant concern [that] persists when settlement, rather than trial, is proposed." What do you think the Court has in mind? Some commentators argue that because of the heightened risk that attorneys will sell out the class when settlement is negotiated before suit is filed, it is particularly important to make sure that a settlement class satisfies those certification requirements designed to provide structural assurances of adequate representation and no disabling conflicts of interest.

Many lower courts after *Amchem* have refused to certify or have decertified settlement class actions on the ground that they could not have been certified for litigation. See, e.g., *In Re Cmty. Bank of N. Va.*, 418 F.3d 277, 299–302 (3d Cir. 2005) (holding that the district court did not conduct the certification analysis required by *Amchem*, but also noting that certification might be appropriate); *In Re Grand Theft Auto Video Game Consumer Litig.*, 251 F.R.D. 139, 157–60 (S.D.N.Y. 2008) (decertifying a settlement class relying on *Amchem*'s holding and arguing that individual issues defeat predominance and undermine the cohesiveness of the class).

4.   Which Intra–Class Conflicts Warrant Subclassing? What are the outer limits of the insistence in *Amchem* upon subclassing? To parse that question—among the most vexing to arise in the aftermath of *Amchem*—consider first the line that the majority believed to require subclassing in that case: the line between asbestos-exposed workers with present-day impairments and those merely at an elevated risk of future disease. Can one articulate a principled legal standard that explains why that line warrants subclassing but why other sorts of divisions within a proposed class might not? Is it either desirable as a theoretical matter or feasible in practice to have class definitions that align perfectly the interests of persons within the class? If not, then what sorts of imperfections are permissible? Within any group of absent class members, one might imagine that there would be different risk preferences—i.e., differences in class members' willingness to forego a proposed settlement and take the risks of trial. Do differences in risk preferences warrant subclassing? Does the opportunity to opt out solve the problem of imperfect interest alignment within a proposed class? Recall from the notes after *Shutts* the Eisenberg—Miller data on the exceedingly low rates of opt-outs in most areas of class action litigation.

Two years after *Amchem*, the Court would offer further guidance on the limits of required subclassing. In a decision treated in greater depth later in this Chapter, the Court struck down as inconsistent with Rule 23(b)(1)(B) a mandatory class settlement that would have resolved future asbestos-related claims against Fibreboard Corporation, a firm not part of the *Amchem* deal. *Ortiz v. Fibreboard Corp.*, 527 U.S. 815 (1999). Although much of the Court's opinion in *Ortiz* concerns the parameters of Rule 23(b)(1)(B), the Court—speaking through Justice Souter—also noted that the single, undifferentiated class proposed in that case should have been subdivided.

Summarizing its analysis, the *Ortiz* Court noted that "the District Court took no steps at the outset to ensure that the potentially conflicting interests of easily identifiable categories of claimants be protected by provisional certification of subclasses under Rule 23(c)(4) [now restyled as Rule 23(c)(5)], relying instead on its *post hoc* findings at the fairness hearing that these subclasses in fact had been adequately represented." *Id.* at 831–32. Later in its opinion, the Court elaborated on what these "easily identifiable categories" were:

> First, it is obvious after *Amchem* that a class divided between holders of present and future claims (some of the latter involving no physical injury and attributable to claimants not yet born) requires division into homogeneous subclasses under Rule 23(c)(4)(B) [now Rule 23(c)(5)], with separate representation to eliminate conflicting interests of counsel. See *Amchem*, 521 U.S. at 627 (class settlements must provide "structural assurance of fair and adequate representation for the diverse groups and individuals affected"). As we said in *Amchem*, "for the currently injured, the critical goal is generous immediate payments," but "[t]hat goal tugs against the interest of exposure-only plaintiffs in ensuring an ample, inflation-protected fund for the future." 521 U.S. at 626. No such procedure was employed here. . . .
>
> Second, the class included those exposed to Fibreboard's asbestos products both before and after 1959. The date is significant, for that year saw the expiration of Fibreboard's insurance policy with Continental, the one that provided the bulk of the insurance funds for the settlement. Pre–1959 claimants accordingly had more valuable claims than post–1959 claimants, the consequence being a second in-

stance of disparate interests within the certified class. While at some point there must be an end to reclassification with separate counsel, these two instances of conflict are well within the requirement of structural protection recognized in *Amchem.*

It is no answer to say, as the Fifth Circuit said [below], that these conflicts may be ignored because the settlement makes no disparate allocation of resources as between the conflicting classes. See 134 F.3d at 669–70. The settlement decides that the claims of the immediately injured deserve no provisions more favorable than the more speculative claims of those projected to have future injuries, and that liability subject to indemnification is no different from liability with no indemnification. The very decision to treat them all the same is itself an allocation decision with results almost certainly different from the results that those with immediate injuries or claims of indemnified liability would have chosen.

Id. at 856–57. To the majority's analysis, Justice Breyer penned this response in dissent:

. . . To determine the "right" number of subclasses, a district court must weigh the advantages and disadvantages of bringing more lawyers into the case. The majority concedes as much when it says "at some point there must be an end to reclassification with separate counsel." The District Court said that if there had "been as many separate attorneys" as the objectors wanted, "there is a significant possibility that a global settlement would not have been reached. . . ." [The District Court opinion] lists the shared common interests among subclasses that argue for single representation, including "avoiding the potentially disastrous results of a loss . . . in [related litigation concerning the obligation of Fibreboard's insurers to provide coverage for the firm's asbestos-related liabilities]," "maximizing the total settlement contribution," "reducing transaction costs and delays," "minimizing . . . attorney's fees," and "adopting" equitable claims payment "procedures." Surely the District Court was within its discretion to conclude that "the point" to which the majority alludes was reached in this case.

I need not go into further detail here. Findings of Fact ¶ 347–354 explain why the alleged conflict between pre– and post–1959 claimants is not significant. *Id.* at 415a–418a (noting that "the decision as to how to divide the [class] settlement among class members" did not take place until after the [a separate settlement between Fibreboard and its insurers] was agreed to [with regard to insurers' indemnification obligations under their policies] at which point money was available equally to both pre– and post–1959 claimants). Findings of Fact ¶ 355–363 explain why the alleged conflict between claimants with, and those without, current illnesses is not significant. *Id.* at 419a–422a (explaining why "the interest of the two subgroups at issue here coincide to a far greater extent than they diverge"). The Fifth Circuit found that the District Court "did not abuse its discretion in finding that the class was adequately represented and that subclasses were not required." 90 F.3d at 982. This Court should not overturn these highly circumstance-specific judgments.

Id. at 880–81 (Breyer, J., dissenting, joined by Stevens, J.). Can one glean any additional guidance on the limits of required subclassing from the analysis in *Ortiz*? Or does the Court's decision in *Ortiz* just add to the confusion over when subclassing may end? In thinking about these questions, consider whether there is any relevant difference, insofar as conflicting interests and adequate representation are concerned, between present versus future claimants, on the one hand, and the pre–1959 versus post–1959 groups, on the other. Do class members have a right—either moral or legal—to greater recovery just because their injuries happened to manifest during the pre–1959 period? (Recall that the insurance policies were purchased by Fibreboard and not by the class members.)

5. Amchem *as a Manifestation of Rivalry Within the Asbestos Plaintiffs' Bar.* The successful legal campaign to derail the *Amchem* class settlement took place at the behest of the Dallas law firm of Baron & Budd—a firm, in many ways, quite similar to the two that served as class counsel. All three firms were among the most successful plaintiffs' law firms in the asbestos litigation. In this sense, the legal dispute in *Amchem* was the outgrowth not of a conflict between asbestos plaintiffs and defendants but, rather, of a fissure within the asbestos plaintiffs' bar. What explains why Baron & Budd would go to the trouble and considerable expense to defeat the *Amchem* class settlement? The district court in *Amchem* specifically found that asbestos plaintiffs' law firms other than class counsel, such as Baron & Budd, could have availed themselves of the same settlement terms for their "inventory" cases as class counsel were offered for theirs by the CCR defendants.

6. *The Relationship Between Class Structure and Class Settlement Content.* The implication of the *Amchem* Court's analysis seems to be that a differently constituted class—one that included sufficient subclasses—might have produced a better settlement for exposure-only plaintiffs. However, as Justice Breyer points out, it is very difficult to predict what kind of settlement would emerge from a different bargaining structure. Moreover, there's no assurance that all the parties would even be willing to settle on terms that made exposure-only plaintiffs better off. If the CCR refuses to invest more in the settlement and the lawyers representing the subclass of currently injured refuse to accept less, then there would be no settlement at all. If a global settlement were to fail with a restructured class, plaintiffs would be left to litigate individually or in smaller groups. Some might do better as a result, but many might do much worse. Given the huge uncertainty involved, is the majority's subclassing decision justified? Is the Court more concerned about the legitimacy of the process or the intrinsic participation rights of absent class members than with achieving an optimal outcome in the particular case? If you think so, does this sort of concern make sense in a case like this?

It's worth making an additional observation. Suppose, as seems likely, that the Court is concerned in part that attorneys for the class might enter into a sweetheart settlement with the defendant that sells out class members in return for a larger fee. When subclasses are created, different attorneys represent the different subclasses. So does subclassing reduce the risk? Won't it just end up spreading the large fee over more attorneys?

7. *Second Opt–Out.* In *Amchem*, the parties filed the class complaint in tandem with a proposed class settlement agreement, such that the class members could determine whether to opt out while aware of the content of the set-

tlement. But what if—as is more often the case—the parties settle *after* the opt-out period has run? The 2003 amendments to Rule 23 address this situation. As further restyled in 2007, Rule 23(e)(4) now provides: "If the class action was previously certified under Rule 23(b)(3), the court may refuse to approve a settlement unless it affords a new opportunity to request exclusion to individual class members who had an earlier opportunity to request exclusion but did not do so." Fed. R. Civ. P. 23(e)(4) (originally adopted as Rule 23(e)(3)). As the rules advisory committee explains:

> The opportunity to request exclusion from a proposed settlement is limited to members of a (b)(3) class. Exclusion may be requested only by individual class members; no class member may purport to opt out other class members by way of another class action.

> The decision whether to approve a settlement that does not allow a new opportunity to elect exclusion is confided to the court's discretion. . . . Many factors may influence the court's decision. Among these are changes in the information available to class members since expiration of the first opportunity to request exclusion, and the nature of the individual class members' claims.

> The terms set for permitting a new opportunity to elect exclusion from the proposed settlement of a Rule 23(b)(3) class action may address concerns of potential misuse. The court might direct, for example, that class members who elect exclusion are bound by rulings on the merits made before the settlement was proposed for approval. Still other terms or conditions may be appropriate.

8. *Sufficiency of the Notice Campaign.* In Part IV–C of its opinion, the *Amchem* Court raises concern, in dicta, about the sufficiency of the notice provided to class members. In relevant part, Rule 23(c)(2)(B) provides that, for opt-out class actions, "the court must direct to class members the best notice that is practicable under the circumstances, including individual notice to all members who can be identified through reasonable effort." (The operative language was part of Rule 23 at the time of *Amchem* and remains there—albeit, with some amplification as to the content of the notice provided—in the current, restyled version of the rule quoted here.)

Recall from *Shutts* that notice is a component of due process in class actions for damages. Indeed, the reference to "the best notice practicable" in *Shutts* and Rule 23(c)(2)(B) draws from language in the Supreme Court's opinion in *Mullane v. Central Hanover Bank & Trust Co.*, 339 U.S. 306, 314–15 (1950), a decision discussing the kind of notice sufficient to satisfy due process.

Now, consider the three categories of persons posited by the Court:

> (i) persons unaware of their exposure to asbestos and who are systematically unlikely to be reached on an individual basis through the notice campaign posited by the settling parties (e.g., the family members of asbestos-exposed workers);

> (ii) persons unaware of their exposure to asbestos but who were likely to receive individualized notice (or, at least, who would not lie outside the notice campaign in any systematic way); and

> (iii) persons aware of their exposure and who were likely to receive individual notice but who would not know now what the ulti-

mate health consequences, if any, of that exposure will be (i.e., what, if any, asbestos-related disease they will develop and what the severity of any such disease will be).

Given the language of Rule 23(c)(2)(B), should class action law be equally troubled about all three of these situations insofar as a given person so described did not receive actual notice? In some situations more than others? As a matter of first principles, is the standard for notice stated in Rule 23(c)(2)(B) the appropriate standard?

9. *The Aftermath of* Amchem. The desire to seek some vehicle to bring about comprehensive peace in the asbestos litigation has not abated since *Amchem*. It has, however, involved a shift from the class action setting to the bankruptcy context. The RAND Institute for Civil Justice observes:

> As of summer 2004, we identified 73 corporate asbestos defendants that had dissolved or filed for reorganization under Chapter 11 [of the Bankruptcy Code]: one in 1976, 20 in the 1980s, 15 in the 1990s, and at least 37 between January 2000 and summer 2004. Bankruptcy is more common today than in the past, with as many new petitions filed in the 2000s [i.e., the period after *Amchem*] as were filed in the previous two decades combined.

Stephen J. Carroll et al., ASBESTOS LITIGATION 109 (2005). During the same period, efforts to enact federal asbestos reform legislation have proven unsuccessful, the Court's suggestions notwithstanding.

In light of these developments, a segment of the scholarly literature has come to question whether *Amchem* ultimately has made for meaningful improvement in the situation of the persons of greatest concern to the Supreme Court: asbestos-exposed workers expected to bring tort actions over time. Consider the assessment of one prominent mass tort plaintiffs' lawyer:

> In the case of *Amchem*, the perfect was the enemy of the good: the multibillion-dollar settlement, rejected by the Supreme Court, was lost forever, and thousands of claimants who would gladly have traded their pristine due process rights for substantial monetary compensation have been consigned to the endless waiting that characterizes asbestos bankruptcies.

Elizabeth J. Cabraser, *The Class Action Counterreformation*, 57 Stan. L. Rev. 1475, 1476 (2005).

c.   CHOICE OF TEMPORAL PERSPECTIVE

The concept of class cohesiveness—the question of which fissures within the class call for subclassing—has proven elusive to the lower courts in the aftermath of *Amchem* and *Ortiz*. Consider the divergent approaches to the class cohesiveness question in the decisions that follow from the Second and Seventh Circuits, respectively:

Stephenson v. Dow Chemical Co.

273 F.3d 249 (2d Cir. 2001)

■ PARKER, CIRCUIT JUDGE.

This appeal requires us to determine the effect of the Supreme Court's landmark class action decisions in *Amchem Prods., Inc. v. Windsor*, 521 U.S. 591 (1997), and *Ortiz v. Fibreboard Corp.*, 527 U.S. 815 (1999), on a previously settled class action concerning exposure to Agent Orange during the Vietnam War. Daniel Stephenson and Joe Isaacson are two Vietnam War veterans who allege that they were injured by exposure to Agent Orange while serving in the military in Vietnam. In the late 1990s, Stephenson and Isaacson (along with their families) filed separate lawsuits against manufacturers of Agent Orange. These lawsuits were eventually transferred to Judge Jack B. Weinstein in the Eastern District of New York. . . .

In 1984, however, some twelve years before these suits, virtually identical claims against these defendants, brought by a class of military personnel who were exposed to Agent Orange while in Vietnam between 1961 and 1972, were globally settled [by way of a class settlement]. The Isaacson and Stephenson actions were brought in 1998 and 1999 respectively. Judge Weinstein, who presided over the 1984 [class] settlement, dismissed the claims of Stephenson and Isaacson, concluding that the prior settlement barred their suits. On appeal, plaintiffs chiefly contend, citing *Amchem* and *Ortiz*, that they were inadequately represented and, therefore, due process considerations prevent the earlier class action settlement from precluding their claims. Because we agree that *Amchem* and *Ortiz* prevent applying res judicata to bar plaintiffs' claim, we vacate the district court's dismissal and remand for further proceedings.

I. BACKGROUND

A. *Prior Agent Orange Litigation*

The Agent Orange class action litigation has a lengthy and complicated history, which we set forth in some detail below in order to convey the magnitude of this decision.

The first Agent Orange litigation began in the late 1970s, when individual veterans and their families filed class action suits in the Northern District of Illinois and Southern and Eastern Districts of New York, alleging that exposure to Agent Orange caused them injury. *In re "Agent Orange" Prod. Liab. Litig.*, 635 F.2d 987, 988 (2d Cir. 1980) ("*Agent Orange I*"). By order of the MDL Panel, these actions were transferred to the Eastern District of New York and consolidated for pretrial purposes. *Id.* Plaintiffs asserted claims of negligent manufacture, strict liability, breach of warranty, intentional tort and nuisance. *In re "Agent Orange" Prod. Liab. Litig.*, 597 F. Supp. 740, 750 (E.D.N.Y. 1984) ("*Agent Orange III*"); *aff'd* 818 F.2d 145 (2d Cir. 1987).

In 1983, the district court certified the following class under Federal Rule of Civil Procedure 23(b)(3):

> those persons who were in the United States, New Zealand or Australian Armed Forces at any time from 1961 to 1972 who were injured while in or near Vietnam by exposure to Agent Orange or other phenoxy herbicides, including those composed in whole or in part of 2, 4, 5–trichlorophenoxyacetic acid or containing some amount of 2, 3, 7, 8–tetrachlorodibenzo–p–dioxin. The class also includes spouses, parents, and children of the veterans born before January 1, 1984, directly or derivatively injured as a result of the exposure.

In re "Agent Orange" Prod. Liab. Litig., 100 F.R.D. 718, 729 (E.D.N.Y. 1983) ("*Agent Orange II*"). To support class certification, the district court specifically found:

> (1) that the affirmative defenses [including the "military contractor" defense] and the question of general causation are common to the class, (2) that those questions predominate over any questions affecting individual members, and (3) given the enormous potential size of plaintiffs' case and the judicial economies that would result from a class trial, a class action is superior to all other methods for a "fair and efficient adjudication of the controversy."

Id. at 724. The court also ordered notice by mail, print media, radio and television to be provided to class members, providing in part that persons who wished to opt out must do so by May 1, 1984. *Id.* at 729–32.

Trial of the class claims was to begin on May 7, 1984. *In re "Agent Orange" Prod. Liab. Litig.,* 818 F.2d 145, 154 (2d Cir. 1987) ("*Agent Orange V*"). On the eve of trial, the parties reached a settlement. *Agent Orange III,* 597 F. Supp. at 746. The settlement provided that defendants would pay $180 million into a settlement fund, $10 million of which would indemnify defendants against future state court actions alleging the same claims. See *id.* at 863–65. The settlement provided that "[t]he Class specifically includes persons who have not yet manifested injury." *Id.* at 865. Additionally, the settlement specifically stated that the district court would "retain jurisdiction over the Fund pending its final disposition." *Id.* at 866.

The district court held fairness hearings throughout the country, and approved the settlement as fair, reasonable and adequate. *See id.* at 746–47; see also *Ryan v. Dow Chem. Co. (In re "Agent Orange" Prod. Liab. Litig.),* 618 F. Supp. 623 (E.D.N.Y. 1985) (approving final settlement and dismissing merits). The court rejected the motion to certify a subclass of those class members who objected to terms of the settlement. *Agent Orange III,* 597 F. Supp. at 757. The court concluded that "[n]o purpose would have been served by appointing counsel for a subclass of disappointed claimants except to increase expenses to the class and delay proceedings." *Id.*

Seventy-five percent of the $180 million was to be distributed directly " 'to exposed veterans who suffer from long-term total disabilities and to the surviving spouses or children of exposed veterans who have died.' " *Agent Orange V,* 818 F.2d at 158. "A claimant would qualify for compensation by establishing exposure to Agent Orange and death or disability not 'predominately' caused by trauma. . . ." *Id.* Payments were to be made for ten years, beginning January 1, 1985 and ending December 31, 1994:

> No payment will be made for death or disability occurring after December 31, 1994. Payment will be made for compensable deaths occurring both before and after January 1, 1985. Payments will be made for compensable disability to the extent that the period of disability falls within the ten years of the program's operation.

Ryan v. Dow Chem. Co. (In re "Agent Orange" Prod. Liab. Litig.), 611 F. Supp. 1396, 1417 (E.D.N.Y. 1985) ("*Agent Orange IV*"), *rev'd in part on other grounds, In re "Agent Orange" Prod. Liab. Litig.,* 818 F.2d 179 (2d Cir. 1987) ("*Agent Orange VI*"). "Most of the remaining [25%] of the settlement fund established the Agent Orange Class Assistance Program, . . . which made grants to agencies serving Vietnam veterans and their families." *Ivy v. Diamond Shamrock Chems. Co. (In re "Agent Orange" Prod. Liab. Litig.),* 996 F.2d 1425, 1429–30 (2d Cir. 1993) ("*Ivy/Hartman II*"). Explaining the creation of this kind of fund, Judge Weinstein stated that it was "[t]he most practicable and equitable method of distributing benefits to" those claimants who did not meet eligibility criteria for cash payments. *Agent Orange IV*, 611 F. Supp. at 1431.

We affirmed class certification, settlement approval and much of the distribution plan. See *Agent Orange V*, 818 F.2d 145, 163–74 (approving settlement and class certification); *Agent Orange VI*, 818 F.2d 179, 184–86 (reversing only the portion of distribution plan that allowed an independent foundation to monitor the funding of projects to assist the class, but allowing district court to establish and supervise such a fund). We rejected challenges to class certification, concluding that "class certification was justified under Rule 23(b)(3) due to the centrality of the military contractor defense." *Agent Orange V*, 818 F.2d at 166–67. We specifically rejected an attack based on adequacy of representation, again based on the military contractor defense which, we reasoned, "would have precluded recovery by all plaintiffs, irrespective of the strengths, weaknesses, or idiosyncrasies of their claims." *Id.* at 167. We additionally concluded that the notice scheme devised by Judge Weinstein was the "best notice practicable" under Federal Rule of Civil Procedure 23(c)(2). *Id.* at 167–69. Finally, we affirmed the settlement as fair, reasonable and adequate, given the serious weaknesses of the plaintiffs' claims. See *id.* at 170–74.

In 1989 and 1990, two purported class actions, *Ivy v. Diamond Shamrock Chems. Co.* and *Hartman v. Diamond Shamrock Chems. Co.*, were filed in Texas state courts. *Ivy/Hartman II*, 996 F.2d at 1430. These suits, on behalf of Vietnam veterans exposed to Agent Orange, sought compensatory and punitive damages against the same companies as in the settled suit. See *Ivy/Hartman I*, 781 F. Supp. at 912–13. The plaintiffs alleged that their injuries manifested only after the May 7, 1984 settlement. See *id.* Additionally, the *Ivy/Hartman* plaintiffs expressly disclaimed any reliance on federal law, asserting only state law claims. See *id.* Nonetheless, the defendants removed the actions to federal court on the grounds that these claims had already been asserted and litigated in federal court. See *id.* at 913. The MDL Panel transferred the actions to Judge Weinstein in the Eastern District of New York. See *Ivy/Hartman II*, 996 F.2d at 1430.

The district court . . . turned to the plaintiffs' substantive arguments that it was unfair to bind them to the settlement when their injuries were not manifested until after the settlement had been reached. The district court rejected this argument, based on the following reasoning:

> All of the courts which considered the *Agent Orange* Settlement were fully cognizant of the conflict arguments now hypothesized by the plaintiffs and took steps to minimize the problem in the way they arranged for long-term administration of the Settlement Fund.

> In many cases the conflict between the interests of present and future claimants is more imagined than real. In the instant case, for example, the injustice wrought upon the plaintiffs is nonexistent. *These plaintiffs, like all class members who suffer death or disability before the end of 1994, are eligible for compensation from the Agent Orange Payment Fund.* The relevant latency periods and the age of the veterans ensure that almost all valid claims will be revealed before that time.

Even when it is proper and necessary for the courts to be so-licitous of the interests of future claimants, the courts cannot ig-nore the interests of presently injured plaintiffs as well as defend-ants in achieving a settlement. Class action settlements simply will not occur if the parties cannot set definitive limits on defend-ants' liability. Making settlement of Rule 23 suits too difficult will work harms upon plaintiffs, defendants, the courts, and the gen-eral public.

Res Judicata

Id. at 919–20 (emphasis added). The district court therefore dismissed the *Ivy/Hartman* litigation.

We affirmed the district court's dismissal. *Ivy/Hartman II*, 996 F.2d 1425, 1439. . . .

We . . . rejected plaintiffs' argument that their due process rights were violated because they were denied adequate representation and adequate notice in the prior action. See *id.* at 1435–36. We reasoned that "providing individual notice and opt-out rights to persons who are unaware of an inju-ry would probably do little good." *Id.* at 1435. We concluded that the plain-tiffs were adequately represented in the prior action, and that a subclass of future claimants was unnecessary " 'because of the way [the settlement] was structured to cover future claimants.' " *Id.* at 1436 (quoting *Ivy/Hartman I*, 781 F. Supp. at 919) (alteration in original).

Shortly before our decision in *Ivy/Hartman II*, the $10 million set aside for indemnification from state court Agent Orange judgments was transferred to the Class Assistance Program, because the district court deemed such a fund unnecessary. The distribution activities had begun in 1988, and concluded in June 1997. During the ten year period of the set-tlement, $196.5 million was distributed as cash payments to approximately 52,000 class members. The program paid approximately $52 million to "af-ter-manifested" claimants, whose deaths or disabilities occurred after May 7, 1984. Approximately $71.3 million of the fund was distributed through the Class Assistance Program.

B. *The Instant Litigation*

1. *The Parties*

Daniel Stephenson served in Vietnam from 1965 to 1970, serving both on the ground in Vietnam and as a helicopter pilot in Vietnam. He alleges that he was in regular contact with Agent Orange during that time. On February 19, 1998, he was diagnosed with multiple myeloma, a bone mar-row cancer, and has undergone a bone marrow transplant.

Joe Isaacson served in Vietnam from 1968 to 1969 as a crew chief in the Air Force, and worked at a base for airplanes which sprayed various herbicides, including Agent Orange. In 1996, Isaacson was diagnosed with non-Hodgkins lymphoma.

Defendants are chemical manufacturers who produced and sold to the United States Government the herbicide Agent Orange during the Vietnam War.

2. *Proceedings Below*

In August 1998, Isaacson filed suit in New Jersey state court, assert-ing claims only under state law. Defendants quickly removed the case to federal court and Isaacson's subsequent motion to remand was de-nied. . . . Thereafter, Isaacson's case was transferred to Judge Weinstein by the MDL Panel.

Stephenson filed his suit *pro se* in the Western District of Louisiana in February 1999, but he soon retained his current counsel. In April 1999, defendants moved for and were granted a Conditional Transfer Order by the MDL Panel, transferring this action to Judge Weinstein. After Stephenson's case was transferred, it was consolidated with the Isaacson case.

Defendants moved to dismiss under Federal Rule of Civil Procedure 12(b)(6), asserting that plaintiffs' claims were barred by the 1984 class action settlement and subsequent final judgment. Judge Weinstein granted this motion from the bench following argument, rejecting plaintiffs' argument that they were inadequately represented and concluding that plaintiffs' suit was an impermissible collateral attack on the prior settlement.

Because we disagree with this conclusion, based on the Supreme Court's holdings in *Amchem* and *Ortiz*, we must vacate the district court's dismissal and remand for further proceedings.

II. DISCUSSION

"We review a dismissal under Rule 12(b)(6) *de novo*, accepting all factual allegations in the complaint as true and drawing all reasonable inferences in the plaintiffs' favor." *Ganino v. Citizens Utilities Co.*, 228 F.3d 154, 161 (2d Cir. 2000). . . .

C.   *Due Process Considerations and Res Judicata*

The doctrine of res judicata dictates that "a final judgment on the merits of an action precludes the parties or their privies from relitigating issues that were or could have been raised in that action." *Kremer v. Chem. Constr. Corp.*, 456 U.S. 461, 466 n.6 (1982). Res judicata ordinarily applies "if the earlier decision was (1) a final judgment on the merits, (2) by a court of competent jurisdiction, (3) in a case involving the same parties or their privies, and (4) involving the same cause of action." *Anaconda–Ericsson Inc. v. Hessen (In re Teltronics Servs., Inc.)*, 762 F.2d 185, 190 (2d Cir. 1985).

Plaintiffs' argument focuses on element number three in the res judicata analysis: whether they are parties bound by the settlement. Plaintiffs rely primarily on the United States Supreme Court's decisions in *Amchem Prods., Inc. v. Windsor*, 521 U.S. 591 (1997), and *Ortiz v. Fibreboard Corp.*, 527 U.S. 815 (1999).

In *Amchem*, the Supreme Court confronted, on direct appeal, a challenge to class certification for settlement purposes in an asbestos litigation. The class defined in the complaint included both individuals who were presently injured as well as individuals who had only been exposed to asbestos. *Amchem*, 521 U.S. at 602 n.5. The Supreme Court held that this "sprawling" class was improperly certified under Federal Rules of Civil Procedure 23(a) and (b). *Id.* at 622–28. Specifically, the Court held that Rule 23(a)(4)'s requirement that the named parties " 'will fairly and adequately protect the interests of the class' " had not been satisfied. *Id.* at 625–26. . . .

In *Ortiz*, the Supreme Court again addressed a settlement-only class action in the asbestos litigation context. *Ortiz*, however, involved a settlement-only limited fund class under Rule 23(b)(1)(B). The Supreme Court ultimately held that the class could not be maintained under Rule 23(b)(1)(B), because "the limit of the fund was determined by treating the settlement agreement as dispositive, an error magnified" by conflicted counsel. *Ortiz*, 527 U.S. at 864. In so holding, *Ortiz* noted that "it is obvious after *Amchem* that a class divided between holders of present and future claims (some of the latter involving no physical injury and attributable to claimants not yet born) requires division into homogeneous subclasses under Rule 23(c)(4)(B), with separate representation to eliminate conflicting interests of counsel." *Id.* at 856.

Res judicata generally applies to bind absent class members except where to do so would violate due process. *Gonzales*, 474 F.2d at 74. Due process requires adequate representation "at all times" throughout the litigation, notice "reasonably calculated . . . to apprise interested parties of the pendency of the action," and an opportunity to opt out. *Shutts*, 472 U.S. at 811–12.

Both Stephenson and Isaacson fall within the class definition of the prior litigation: they served in the United States military, stationed in Vietnam, between 1961 and 1972, and were allegedly injured by exposure to Agent Orange. However, they both learned of their allegedly Agent Orange-related injuries only after the 1984 settlement fund had expired in 1994. Because the prior litigation purported to settle all future claims, but only provided for recovery for those whose death or disability was discovered prior to 1994, the conflict between Stephenson and Isaacson and the class representatives becomes apparent.[7] No provision was made for post–1994 claimants, and the settlement fund was permitted to terminate in 1994. *Amchem* and *Ortiz* suggest that Stephenson and Isaacson were not adequately represented in the prior Agent Orange litigation. Those cases indicate that a class which purports to represent both present and future claimants may encounter internal conflicts.

Defendants contend that there was, in fact, no conflict because all class members' claims were equally meritless and would have been defeated by the "military contractor" defense. This argument misses the mark. At this stage, we are only addressing whether plaintiffs' claims should be barred by res judicata. We are therefore concerned only with whether they were afforded due process in the earlier litigation. Part of the due process inquiry (and part of the Rule 23(a) class certification requirements) involves assessing adequacy of representation and intra-class conflicts. The ultimate merits of the claims have no bearing on whether the class previously certified adequately represented these plaintiffs.

Because these plaintiffs were inadequately represented in the prior litigation, they were not proper parties and cannot be bound by the settlement. We therefore must vacate the district court's dismissal and remand for further proceedings. We, of course, express no opinion as to the ultimate merits of plaintiffs' claims.

III. CONCLUSION

For the foregoing reasons, we hold that the prior *Agent Orange* settlement does not preclude these plaintiffs from asserting their claims alleging injury due to Agent Orange exposure. Because these plaintiffs were inadequately represented in the prior litigation, based on the Supreme Court's teaching in *Amchem* and *Ortiz*, they were not proper parties to the litigation. We therefore vacate the district court's dismissal and remand the case to the district court for further proceedings consistent with this opinion.

---

[7] Again, we distinguish the *Ivy/Hartman* cases, which held that pre 1994 claimants were adequately represented in the prior Agent Orange litigation. This conclusion was based, at least in part, on those claimants' eligibility for compensation from the settlement fund. See *Ivy/Hartman I*, 781 F. Supp. at 919; *Ivy/Hartman II*, 996 F.2d at 1435–36.

NOTES AND QUESTIONS

1. Settlement Design. We can assume that when the settlement was ne-gotiated, Stephenson, Isaacson, and other exposure-only class members did not know when, if ever, they would actually manifest injury. Stephenson and Isaacson were unlucky; they manifested after the 1994 cut off. But does that mean they received nothing from the settlement? Did the class members suffer-ing injury after 1994, in effect, sell the defendants their rights to sue in tort in exchange for nothing? What was the reason for choosing 1994 as the cutoff? Why would any rational class settlement designer wish to provide no cash com-pensation for veterans whose diseases manifested post–1994? Under the cir-cumstances, do you think it would be reasonable for an exposure-only victim to buy insurance coverage limited to diseases manifesting before 1994 (if the in-surance premiums increase with the duration of coverage)?

Notwithstanding the answers to these questions, one might still feel a bit troubled about compensating some injured parties while leaving others com-pletely uncompensated when all have the same legal claims and the reason for the different treatment has to do with the fortuity of when injury is manifested. The challenge, however, lies in explaining this intuition. Perhaps one reason to be troubled has to do with a lack of equal treatment. The settlement, however, treats class members equally in one respect; namely, they all receive the same insurance policy providing payment before 1994 but not after. Why is this not sufficient? Are class members entitled to a more individualized regard for their interests? Why? Does it matter that all class members have individual legal rights at stake? At the time the settlement was negotiated, class counsel knew with substantial certainty that some members would manifest injury after 1994 and thus receive no actual compensation at all. Is this a problem? To whom does the class attorney owe duties: the class as whole, class members individually, or some combination of the two? If the settlement is deficient, would it make a difference if it provided some small amount of compensation for post–1994 claimants, or must everyone receive the same amount? For a dis-cussion of some of these issues, see Patrick Woolley, *Collateral Attack and the Role of Adequate Representation in Class Suits for Money Damages*, 58 U. Kan. L. Rev. 917, 935–38 (2010).

Does the Second Circuit's holding mean that subclasses must be created whenever settlement payouts might vary with the date of manifestation, or does it apply only when there is an absolute cutoff? Does it mean as a practical matter that it is not possible to negotiate a settlement with a cut-off date? In thinking about this question, consider what is likely to happen if an attorney is appointed whose job it is to advocate for the interests of those who might mani-fest after 1994?

Should veterans with diseases that manifested post–1994 have been ex-cluded entirely from the class settlement, so as to leave intact their preexisting right to sue Dow Chemical? In practical terms, would it have been possible to exclude such persons from the class that stood to be bound by the Agent Orange class settlement? For criticism of the Agent Orange class settlement, see David A. Dana, *Adequacy of Representation after* Stephenson: *A Rawlsian/Behavioral Economics Approach to Class Action Settlements*, 55 Emory L.J. 279 (2006).

The decision to provide no cash compensation for post–1994 manifesta-tions of disease was the product not of class settlement negotiations but, rather, of a judicial determination. On the eve of trial, the settling counsel agreed on the overall dollar amount for the class settlement, albeit only after defendants were persuaded at the direction of the judge not to raise their settlement offer: "The real obstacle to a $200 million settlement, [one special master] soon realized, was not the chemical companies but Judge Weinstein. . . ." Peter H. Schuck, AGENT ORANGE ON TRIAL: MASS TOXIC DISASTERS IN THE COURTS 159–66 (1987) (noting that at the direction of the judge the special master told defendants to offer no more than $180 million and suggesting that defendants were prepared to settle the case for much more than Judge Weinstein engineered.).

The criteria for the allocation of the settlement amount were also set by Judge Weinstein, who drew on the recommendations of another special master, Kenneth Feinberg. Do these unusual features of the Agent Orange class settlement make the treatment of post–1994 manifestations of disease more or less suspect?

2.　*The Changing State of Science.* In his decision approving the class settlement, Judge Weinstein discussed at length the weakness of the then-available scientific support for the plaintiff class's asserted causal link between Agent Orange and various forms of latent disease. *In re "Agent Orange" Product Liability Litigation*, 597 F. Supp. 740, 777–95 (E.D.N.Y. 1984). Upholding Judge Weinstein's approval of the class settlement, the Second Circuit similarly noted that:

> [T]he clear weight of scientific evidence casts grave doubt on the capacity of Agent Orange to injure human beings. Epidemiological studies of Vietnam veterans, many of which were undertaken by the United States, Australian, and various state governments, demonstrate no greater incidence of relevant ailments among veterans or their families than among any other group.

In re "Agent Orange" Product Liability Litigation, 818 F.2d 145, 149 (2d Cir. 1987). Indeed, as to the few class members who exercised their right to opt out of the Agent Orange class so as to maintain conventional, individual tort actions, Judge Weinstein granted summary judgment for the defendant manufacturers for lack of a triable issue on the causation element. *In re "Agent Orange" Product Liability Litigation*, 611 F. Supp. 1223, 1259–60 (E.D.N.Y. 1985).

By the mid–1990s, however, the scientific literature concerning Vietnam-era defoliants had changed. A comprehensive review of the literature undertaken by the Institute of Medicine—a component of the National Academy of Sciences—suggested at least a possibility of causal links between Vietnam-era defoliants and some forms of latent disease, including multiple myeloma (Stephenson's diagnosis) and non-Hodgkins lymphoma (Isaacson's diagnosis). Institute of Medicine, *Veterans and Agent Orange: Health Effects of Herbicides Used in Vietnam* 6 (1994). The change in the scientific literature concerning Agent Orange may explain in practical terms why lawyers were so interested in representing plaintiffs such as Stephenson and Isaacson in tort actions. But does that change shed doubt upon the class settlement in such a way as to render it unenforceable?

3.　*Application of Supreme Court Precedent.* Does the Second Circuit's analysis represent a sound application of *Amchem* and *Ortiz*? Note that the Supreme Court's decisions in those two cases post-date not only the Second Circuit's original decision upholding the Agent Orange class settlement on direct review but also the Second Circuit's decision in *Ivy/Hartman II*. Was

Ivy/Hartman II rightly decided given what we now know—with the benefit of hindsight, to be sure—about class cohesiveness and adequate class representation? Did the Second Circuit err by trying to shoehorn the case into the subclassing analysis set forth in *Amchem* and *Ortiz*? Though the Second Circuit does not emphasize the Supreme Court's decision in *Phillips Petroleum v. Shutts*, does that decision nonetheless bear significantly on the adequate class representation question in *Stephenson*? In *Shutts*, the Court stated that the Due Process Clause requires that "the named plaintiff at all times adequately represent the interests of the absent class members" and appended in support of that statement a citation to *Hansberry*. What does the phrase "at all times" mean?

Recall from earlier in the chapter that the adequate representation requirement can be understood to impose a minimum performance standard for class counsel with respect to the conduct of the litigation. As several legal commentators have explained, the concept of adequate representation is formulated in various ways, including "whether the representatives . . . prosecute or defend the action with due diligence and reasonable prudence." Geoffrey C. Hazard, Jr. et al., *An Historical Analysis of the Binding Effect of Class Suits*, 146 U. Pa. L. Rev. 1849, 1855 (1998). See also *Gonzales v. Cassidy*, 474 F.2d 67, 75 (5th Cir. 1973) (defining adequacy of representation to include adequate performance by counsel).

By contrast, the American Law Institute has proposed that class counsel's performance should play no role in assessing whether a class member has been adequately represented for purposes of due process. PRINCIPLES OF AGGREGATE LITIGATION, § 2.07 (defining adequate representation for purposes of due process solely as the lack of structural conflicts of interest); see *also* Samuel Issacharoff & Richard Nagareda, *Class Settlements Under Attack*, 156 U. Pa. L. Rev. 1649, 1699–1700 (2008).

Should the Second Circuit in *Stephenson* have focused on the allegedly inadequate performance-of-counsel rather than the failure to subclass?

4.   The Supreme Court's Non–Decision in Stephenson. The Supreme Court granted Dow Chemical's petition for a writ of certiorari in *Stephenson*. Justice Stevens recused himself, and the remaining Justices deadlocked. The result was an affirmance by an equally divided Court of the judgment as to Stephenson—an outcome that has no precedential value outside the Second Circuit.* For discussion of the availability of collateral attack for inadequate representation, see Chapter 3.

5.   The Aftermath of Stephenson. In 2008, the Second Circuit affirmed the district court's grant of summary judgment for the defendants in *Stephenson* and related suits on the ground that liability was barred by the military contractor defense. *In re Agent Orange Prod. Liab. Litig.* 517 F.3d 76 (2d Cir. 2008). Also in 2008, the Second Circuit held against Vietnamese citizens, who had filed a separate suit to recover for their own Agent–Orange-related injuries, on the ground that the Alien Tort Claims Act did not confer jurisdiction and that in any event the military contractor defense barred recovery. *Vietnam Assoc. for Victims of Agent Orange v. Dow Chem. Co.*, 517 F.3d 104 (2d Cir. 2008).

---

* The Justices did agree, however, that Isaacson's case had been improperly removed from state to federal court.

* * *

Now, compare the analysis of class cohesiveness and adequate class representation in *Stephenson* with a roughly contemporaneous decision from the Seventh Circuit:

Uhl v. Thoroughbred Technology and Telecommunications, Inc.

309 F.3d 978 (7th Cir. 2002)

■ DIANE P. WOOD, CIRCUIT JUDGE.

This litigation arose after Thoroughbred Technology & Telecommunications, Inc. (T–Cubed) announced that it had the right to install conduits for fiber optic cables along railroad right-of-way corridors. Timothy Elzinga, a property owner along a right-of-way owned by the Norfolk Southern Railway, disagreed. In his view, such a use by T–Cubed without the permission of the adjacent landowners would amount to a slander of their title and a trespass. Discussions took place between Elzinga and T–Cubed, which eventually bore fruit in the form of a proposed class-wide settlement. This proposed settlement presumed that Elzinga would be certified as the representative of the putative class. With this much accomplished, Elzinga then filed suit and simultaneously sought certification of a settlement class, consisting of all the persons who owned real estate on either side of the railroad tracks along the route T–Cubed proposed to use for its cable.

One particular complication figures significantly in this appeal. At any given point, T–Cubed will lay fiber optic cable on only one side of the tracks. *Ex ante*, it is impossible to know which side that will be; detailed engineering surveys and technical criteria will govern the company's final choice. The settlement agreement attempts to deal with this uncertainty by dividing the class members into two categories: the Cable Side and the Non–Cable Side. (It does not address separately the possibility that one landowner might own land on both sides of the track; presumably such a person falls within both subgroups.) Under the terms of the agreement, the two groups will receive different forms of compensation. All class members, however, will become shareholders in Class Corridor, LLC (Class Corridor), a newly created limited liability company.

The appellant in this case, Cathy Mason, is an unnamed class member who claims that the settlement is unfair, and more formally, that it fails to satisfy the requirements of Fed. R. Civ. P. 23(a) and (b). (While a dispute remains as to whether Mason will be entitled to any benefits under the settlement agreement, the fact that she is claiming that she should receive something is enough to ensure that she has standing to intervene.) The district court granted Mason's motion to intervene, but it then overruled her objections and approved both the certification of the settlement class and the settlement agreement itself. We affirm. . . .

III

Satisfied that we may proceed to the merits, we turn next to the issue of class certification. We review the district court's certification of a class for an abuse of discretion. This is true even in the settlement context. *Amchem Prods., Inc. v. Windsor*, 521 U.S. 591, 630 (1997); *Retired Chicago Police Assoc. v. City of Chicago*, 7 F.3d 584, 596 (7th Cir. 1993). . . .

A. Class Representative

Much of Mason's argument centers around what she deems conflicting subgroups that were only assigned one representative. In *Amchem*, 521 U.S. at 619, and *Ortiz v. Fibreboard Corp.*, 527 U.S. 815, 828 n.6 (1999), the Supreme Court emphasized that although settlement is relevant to class certification, the requirements of Rule 23 must still be satisfied. Thus, a district court may not abandon the Federal Rules merely because a settlement seems fair, or even if the settlement is a "good deal." In some ways, the Rule 23 requirements may be even more important for settlement classes, for which (as this court has put it), the district court must act almost as a fiduciary of the class when approving settlements.

A class may not satisfy the requirements of Rule 23(a)(4) if the class representative does not "possess the same interest and suffer the same injury as the class members." *East Tex. Motor Freight Sys., Inc. v. Rodriguez*, 431 U.S. 395, 403 (1977) (citing *Schlesinger v. Reservists Committee to Stop the War*, 418 U.S. 208, 216 (1974)). This requires the district court to ensure that there is no inconsistency between the named parties and the class they represent. *Amchem*, 521 U.S. at 625. As the Supreme Court also noted in *Amchem*, some classes are more prone than others to intra-class conflicts that are not suitable for a single class representative—even if the single class representative believes "that the Settlement serves the aggregate interests of the entire class." 521 U.S. at 627.

Although Mason has expressed legitimate concerns about Elzinga's literal and figurative representation of both sides of the track, we think she misses the mark in the end. Her objection is premised on the idea that the class must be viewed solely from an *ex post* perspective. See John C. Coffee, Jr., *Class Wars: The Dilemma of the Mass Tort Class Action*, 95 Colum. L. Rev. 1343, 1435–36 (1995). Nothing in *Amchem* compels such an approach. In *Amchem*, the Court found the class to be overbroad in part because it contained both exposure-only and currently injured plaintiffs. In the instant case all members of the class are, for the most significant part of the feared damages, "exposure only": they have all been slandered and many have suffered a surveying trespass, but they are unaware if they will yet suffer trespass injuries from the installation of cable. Thus, if we view Elzinga's adequacy at the time of the settlement, he was in the same position as all class members. T–Cubed did not limit its claims to rights in Cable Side property; it claimed rights to all property adjacent to and beneath the railway.

Moreover, the fact that Cable Side and Non–Cable Side will receive different compensation under the settlement does not make it novel or unfair. See *Petrovic v. Amoco*, 200 F.3d 1140, 1147 (8th Cir. 1999) (holding differences in the amount of damages do not necessarily prohibit class certification). True, the district court could have appointed two representatives, one to represent the future Cable Side owners and one to represent the future Non–Cable Side owners. But we see no reason why it was compelled to do this, since the named representative had an equal incentive to represent both sides as long as he did not know where his property would end up. Until the cable has been laid, no "Cable Side" exists. In the end the Cable Side and Non–Cable Side may have diverging goals—the classes are mutually exclusive; by definition, Elzinga cannot be on both sides of the track. Cable Side's goal would be compensation for the conduits on their land, while the Non–Cable Side goal would be preparation for future infringement by telecommunications groups through the formation of Class Corridor.

. . . The important fact [here] is that Elzinga was not merely an uninterested neutral participant, unable to serve as an effective advocate for the class. He was someone who had a real stake in all aspects of the case: the slander of title claims, the surveying trespass claims, and the cable conduit trespass claims. See *Rand v. Monsanto Co.*, 926 F.2d 596, 599 (7th Cir. 1991). In light of the arguments presented to it, the district court did not abuse its discretion in finding Elzinga satisfied the requirements of Rule 23(a)(4). . . .

[The court went on to uphold the district court's approval of the class settlement terms.]

NOTES AND QUESTIONS

How does the Seventh Circuit's analysis of class conflicts in *Uhl* differ from the Second Circuit's in *Stephenson*? Which court is correct, either as a matter of first principles or as a matter of the faithful application of *Amchem* and *Ortiz*? Or can one distinguish *Uhl* from *Stephenson* based on the circumstances presented in those two cases?

d. CHOICE OF LAW

Recall that Rule 23(b)(3) requires a judicial finding that "questions of law or fact common to class members predominate over any questions affecting only individual members." One consideration that has the potential to bear significantly on the existence of such common questions is the underlying substantive law applicable in the action. Substantive law, after all, is what defines the relevant "questions of law or fact" in the litigation.

In many areas of class litigation, the underlying claims of class members arise primarily or exclusively under federal law—for instance, the federal antitrust laws or securities laws. In other areas, the underlying substantive law comes in the form of state, not federal, law—for instance, state tort law, contract law, or consumer protection law. State law, of course, is not necessarily uniform, and both the Constitution and state choice-of-law rules impose constraints on the ability of a court simply to apply the substantive law of the state in which it sits to all the claims in a multistate or nationwide class suit. Because materially different state laws do not pose a common question of law, differences in the substantive law of states can make it difficult to satisfy the predominance requirement in a multistate or nationwide class suit.

One should be careful about overstating the diversity of state law in the United States. As a noted Conflicts scholar has explained: "[W]hile in theory all fifty states could have different laws, in practice there are seldom more than two or three rules on any given question, each adopted by many states." Larry Kramer, *Choice of Law in the American Courts in 1990: Trends and Developments*, 39 Am. J. Comp. L. 465, 475 (1991). But even a few variations in state law may pose insuperable obstacles to certification. Thus, it should come as no surprise that class counsel in multistate and nationwide class suits often argue for the application of a single law in a class suit, and parties opposing the certification frequently argue that the laws of multiple states will apply.

What law or laws will apply in a suit is determined by applying the appropriate choice-of law principles. "Choice of law" is a fascinating and complex body of law that is discussed in detail in a separate course on Conflict of Laws. But because of its centrality to class litigation involving state law, some discussion of the subject is necessary here.

Recall that the Supreme Court insisted in *Shutts* that *if* there was a conflict between the law of Kansas and the laws of other states with a connection to the controversy, Kansas could apply its own law to all the claims only if it had a " 'significant contact or aggregation of contacts' to the claims asserted by each member of the plaintiff class, contacts 'creating state interests' in order to ensure that the choice of Kansas law is not arbitrary or unfair." When read in light of *Allstate Insurance Co. v. Hague*, 449 U.S. 302 (1981), it is clear that the constitutional standard set out in *Shutts* gives a state court wide latitude to apply its own substantive law.

Allstate involved an accident in Wisconsin between two vehicles insured in Wisconsin. All three persons involved in the accident, including the decedent Hague, were Wisconsin residents. Yet a majority of the United States Supreme Court concluded that Minnesota had not violated the Constitution when it decided to apply its own law in a suit brought against the Allstate Insurance Co. by Hague's widow. The plurality opinion in *Allstate* emphasized three factors which *taken together* justified application of Minnesota law, at least as a constitutional matter: (1) Hague had been employed in Minnesota, (2) Allstate was doing business in Minnesota, and (3) Hague's widow had moved to Minnesota after the accident for reasons unrelated to the lawsuit. *Id.* at 313–20.

The wide latitude that states have with respect to choice of law in class litigation is underscored by *Sun Oil Co. v. Wortman*, 486 U.S. 717 (1988). *Wortman* like *Shutts* involved a nationwide class suit brought in Kansas state court to recover interest on suspended royalty payments for the extraction of natural gas. After reversing in *Shutts*, the United States Supreme Court vacated the Kansas Supreme Court's decision in *Wortman* and remanded the case for reconsideration in light of *Shutts*. On remand, the Kansas courts found that the states whose substantive laws governed most of the claims would apply the same interest rate to suspended royalty payments as would Kansas. The United States Supreme Court affirmed, ignoring likely differences in the law that courts of the relevant states would have applied:

> [I]t is not enough that a state court misconstrue the law of another State. Rather, our cases make plain that the misconstruction must contradict law of the other State that is clearly established and has been brought to the court's attention.

486 U.S. 717 (1988). In other words, a state may presume that forum law is the same as the law of every other state with a connection to the controversy provided "clearly established" law that "contradict[s]" that presumption has not been "brought to the court's attention." Because the *Sun Oil* Court concluded that the class defendant had not met its burden of demonstrating that the law of Kansas was different from the law of other states, Kansas could apply its own law to the claims in the class suit, even though Kansas did not have "a significant contact or aggregation of contacts" with the claims. *Sun Oil* thus authorizes a state to apply a very strong presumption in favor of forum law, if the state chooses to do so. The dissent complained that

> [f]aced with the constitutional obligation to apply the substantive law of another State, a court that does not like that law apparently need take only two steps in order to avoid applying it. First, in-

vent a legal theory so novel or strange that the other State has never had an opportunity to reject it; then, on the basis of nothing but unsupported speculation, "predict" that the other State would adopt that theory if it had the chance.

486 U.S. at 749 (O'Connor, J., dissenting in part).

Shutts and *Wortman* together set out a two-step framework for evaluating whether a state may constitutionally apply its own law to claims in its courts. First, a court must determine whether the law of the forum state is different from the law of other states with a connection to the claim—in other words whether a "false conflict" exists. In deciding whether a false conflict exists, the Constitution permits a court to rely on the presumption in favor of forum law outlined in *Wortman*. Second, if a conflict exists between the law of the forum and the law of other states with a connection to the claims, the law of the forum may be applied to all of the claims only if the forum has a "significant contact or aggregation of contacts, creating state interests, such that choice of its law is neither arbitrary nor fundamentally unfair." *Shutts*, 472 U.S. at 818. Although *Shutts* does not explicitly address the issue, it seems clear that choice of any state's law—not just the law of the forum—must satisfy the *Shutts* test.

Within the capacious limits of the Constitution, states have followed and continue to follow a variety of approaches to choice of law.

> In the nineteenth century, choice of law questions were generally resolved by a system of "comity" under which the forum state applied the law of another state, according to generally accepted principles, as a matter of good will and harmonious interstate relations. For example, the law of the state in which a tort occurred would be followed, even if suit was brought in a different state. Further, the law of the state in which a contract was entered into would govern the validity of the contract. . . . The most important single source of nineteenth century choice of law rules was a treatise by Supreme Court Justice Joseph Story. J. Story, COMMENTARIES OF THE CONFLICT OF LAWS (1834).

> In the twentieth century, the comity-based system of Story was refined (many would say distorted) and incorporated into the first RESTATEMENT OF THE LAW OF CONFLICT OF LAWS (1934) for which the Reporter was Professor Joseph Beale. What had been a somewhat flexible and ultimately voluntary system under Story became, under the First Restatement, a rigid system based on a theory of obligation of the states to enforce the "vested rights" of parties under the Restatement's choice of law rules. In part because of the rigidity of Beale's system, in part because of the growing twentieth century insistence on realistic assessments of policy considerations underlying doctrinal rules, and in part because of an enormous increase in the number and complexity of interstate transactions, the First Restatement came under heavy attack.

> The most important attacker was Professor Brainerd Currie, who developed a complete system of "interest analysis," under which he sought to analyze the interests of the various states in the application of their law to the transaction in dispute. B. Currie, SELECTED ESSAYS ON THE CONFLICT OF LAWS (1963).

Hazard, Tait, Fletcher & Bundy, PLEADING AND PROCEDURE: STATE AND FEDERAL 369–70 (2009). Currie argued, for example, that the state in which an injury occurred sometimes had no "interest" in applying its law. The seminal case of *Babcock v. Jackson*, 191 N.E. 2d 279 (N.Y. 1963) provides a classic illustration. Babcock was injured in a one-car accident while he was a guest (i.e., a nonpaying passenger) in an automobile operated by Jackson. Ontario—where the accident took place—had a guest statute that protected even a negligent driver from liability to his guests. By contrast, New York—where Babcock and Jackson were domiciled—permitted a guest to recover from a negligent driver. The First Restatement would apply the guest statute of the state where the accident occurred, even if both the driver and the guest were domiciled in a state that would permit the guest to recover. Currie countered that in a case like *Babcock,* only the state of joint domicile has an interest in applying its policy because the effect of compensating or refusing to compensate the guest is felt where the parties are domiciled, not where the accident occurred. A case like *Babcock* involves what is known in interest analysis as a "false conflict" because *only one state has an interest* in applying its law. Cf. *Shutts* (using the term "false conflict" differently to mean there is no *difference* between the laws of states with a connection to the claim).

> Prompted by the many criticisms of the First Restatement, the American Law Institute published RESTATEMENT (SECOND) CONFLICT OF LAWS in 1971, after almost twenty years of discussion and debate. The Second Restatement is unabashedly policy-based and rule-eschewing, so much so that its formulations will often make it difficult to predict how a court applying the Second Restatement will decide any particular case. Many academics have criticized the Second Restatement, on almost as many grounds as there are critics. . . . Numerous [] academics have proposed their own systems that deviate in significant respect from the approach of the Second Restatement. See, e.g., Professor Robert Leflar's "choice-influencing considerations"; R. Leflar, AMERICAN CONFLICTS LAW (1968).

Hazard, Tait, Fletcher & Bundy, PLEADING AND PROCEDURE at 370. Both the Second Restatement and Professor Leflar's "choice-influencing considerations" were influenced by interest analysis.

The trend among the states has been to abandon the First Restatement. About ten states continue to adhere to the First Restatement (albeit often with more flexibility than Professor Beale had intended). The remaining states use a variety of modern approaches, including interest analysis, Professor Leflar's choice influencing considerations, and most importantly, the Second Restatement. Almost half of the states purport to follow the Second Restatement, but "Second Restatement courts evince wildly varying 'gradations of commitment to the Second Restatement, and perform many different choice-of-law analyses in its name.'" Brilmayer, Goldsmith & O'Hara O'Connor, Conflict of Laws 254–55 (2011) (quoting S. Symeonides, *The Judicial Acceptance of the Second Conflicts Restatement: A Mixed Blessing,* 56 Md. L. Rev. 1248, 1261–63 (1977)). "The result in the courts has been something close to chaos." Hazard, Tait, Fletcher & Bundy, PLEADING AND PROCEDURE at 370. The upshot of the wide discretion enjoyed by states with respect to choice of law is that the choice of *forum* has great influence on choice of law.

The chaos has not been limited to state courts because federal courts generally are required to apply the choice-of-law rules of the states in which they sit. See *Klaxon v. Stentor Elec.Mfg. Co.*, 313 U.S. 487 (1941).

Klaxon is an application of the policy of vertical uniformity between state and federal courts that was announced in cases following *Erie R.R. Co. v. Tompkins*, 304 U.S. 64 (1938). As the Supreme Court has explained, "[t]he nub of the policy that underlies *Erie R.R. Co. v. Tompkins* is that for the same transaction the accident of a suit . . . in a federal court instead of in a state court a block away, should not lead to a substantially different result." *Guaranty Trust Co. v. York*, 326 U.S. 99, 109 (1945). Congress— which is not bound by the *Erie* policy—may authorize federal courts to depart from applying the choice-of-law rules of the states in which they sit. An important question with respect to choice of law in federal class litigation is whether Rule 23, the Class Action Fairness Act of 2005, or both should be construed to authorize a federal court to depart even in a limited fashion from the *Klaxon* rule.

In practice, federal courts in class litigation have departed in limited ways from *Klaxon* without acknowledging (or perhaps even recognizing) that they have done so. Specifically, federal courts are often perceived as more willing than state courts to conclude that choice-of-law problems prevent class certification. For that reason, parties opposing class certification will often prefer to have a federal court make that decision. As we shall see in Chapter 3, the Class Action Fairness Act will often make it easier for defendants to remove such suits from state to federal court than does the general removal statute.

Class counsel might attempt to avoid choice-of-law questions altogether by asking the court to certify a class limited to persons within a single state. But a class suit of such limited scope may not justify the cost of representation. In multistate and nationwide class suits, plaintiffs have developed three major strategies to overcome the predominance issues that come to the fore because of the diversity of state law. The first strategy is to avoid state law altogether by pleading what might, at first glance, seem like state tort or contract claims as violations of federal law. For example, plaintiffs sometimes invoke the federal Racketeer Influenced and Corrupt Organizations Act (RICO). Use of the RICO statute to avoid choice-of-law problems is addressed later in this Chapter. See *Klay v. Humana, Inc.*, at 168. A second strategy relies on the contention that, although fifty nominally different bodies of state law may theoretically be relevant in a nationwide class suit, the laws at issue are functionally the same. In essence, this is a variation on the assertion that the case presents no conflict in the first place. The case that follows—*Cole v. General Motors Corp.*—and the accompanying notes address this second strategy. The third strategy relies on the argument that the Constitution and state choice-of-law principles authorize the application of a single body of law, notwithstanding the existence of conflicts among the laws of states with connections to the claims asserted in the proposed class suit. The plaintiffs typically argue in these cases that the law of the defendant's principal place of business should be applied to the claims of all of the class members. *In re St. Jude Medical* (which is found at the end of this section) and the accompanying notes address this third strategy. *

---

* In some cases, class counsel may be able to argue that a choice-of-law clause in a contract requires application of a single state's law to the claims of the class. But such a clause will not necessarily simplify class counsel's task. A choice-of-law clause, for example, may be denied effect if "the law of the chosen state would be contrary to a fundamental policy of the state" with "the most significant relationship" and "a materially greater interest . . . in the determination of the particular issue." RESTATEMENT (SECOND) CONFLICT OF LAWS § 187(2)(b). Litigation of the "fundamental policy" exception in a multistate or nationwide class suit may

Cole v. General Motors Corp.

484 F.3d 717 (5th Cir. 2007)

■ KING, CIRCUIT JUDGE:

Defendant-appellant General Motors Corporation appeals the district court's certification of a nationwide Rule 23(b)(3) class of Cadillac DeVille owners who allege breach of express and implied warranties. For the reasons that follow we REVERSE the district court's Ruling and REMAND for entry of an order denying class certification.

I.   FACTUAL AND PROCEDURAL BACKGROUND

General Motors Corporation ("GM") manufactured and sold over 200,000 1998 and 1999 model year Cadillac DeVilles ("DeVilles") in the United States. The DeVilles feature side-impact Air Bag Systems and Side Impact Sensing Modules ("SISMs"), the latter of which trigger inflation of the vehicle's side impact air bags under certain conditions. This class action centers on alleged defects in the SISMs.

In September 2000, GM sent a voluntary recall notice to all DeVille record owners and lessees explaining that GM

> has decided that a defect which relates to motor vehicle safety exists and may manifest itself in your 1998 or 1999 model year Cadillac DeVille. [GM] ha[s] learned of a condition that can cause the side impact air bags in your car to deploy unexpectedly, without a crash, as you start your car or during normal driving.

> . . . [GM added] that it would contact DeVille owners again when replacement SISMs were available so that owners could take their DeVilles to a dealership for the installation of two new SISMs.

Among the owners who received GM's voluntary recall notice were the named plaintiffs (and now class representatives) Beverly Cole, Anita S. Perkins, and Jewell P. Lowe (collectively, "plaintiffs"). Lowe is the mother of one of plaintiffs' counsel, Perkins is a paralegal for another of plaintiffs' counsel, and Cole is the paralegal's cousin. Each purchased a 1998 or 1999 DeVille equipped with the SISMs at issue; however, the SISMs in their vehicles were not among those that had deployed inadvertently.

> . . . [P]laintiffs moved for class certification pursuant to Rule 23(b)(3) of the Federal Rules of Civil Procedure on behalf of "[a]ll persons and legal entities who have acquired, whether by purchase, lease, donation or otherwise . . . anywhere in the United States, 1998 or 1999 Cadillac Devilles equipped with side impact air bag systems and side impact sensing modules." Their motion for class certification specifically excluded DeVille owners "who sustained bodily injury or death as the result of the unexpected or premature deployment of a side impact air bag."

> . . . According to GM, it completed mailing recall notices to all DeVille record owners and lessees on December 28, 2001, and the majority of those owners and lessees have had their SISMs replaced. Plaintiffs do not dispute that GM's recall is now complete.

---

require analysis of the public policy of multiple states. Thus, class counsel may face a choice-of-law headache whether or not she can invoke a choice-of-law clause calling for the application of single state's law.

In their [class complaint], plaintiffs allege that GM "promoted side im-pact air bags, which included so-called [SISMs], as an added safety feature" in its 1998 and 1999 DeVilles. Plaintiffs also allege that GM "has . . . admitted that a defect exists in the 1998 and the 1999 Cadillac Devilles which can cause the side impact air bags to deploy unexpectedly, without a crash, when the car is started or during normal driving." Plaintiffs further assert that GM "did not repair or replace the [SISMs] within a reasonable time after the sale and/or lease of the subject vehicles." Based on these al-legations, plaintiffs aver that GM

> has failed to deliver to plaintiffs and the class members the thing purchased, has delivered a thing other than the thing purchased, has breached express and implied warranties of sale, has sold and delivered to plaintiffs and the class members a thing containing defects under the redhibition laws of the State of Louisiana and the comparable provisions of the Uniform Commercial Code, and/or has breached contracts with plaintiffs and the class mem-bers, and such conduct has damaged plaintiffs and the class members.

> Plaintiffs seek recovery from GM for

> (1) return of the purchase or lease price, or, alternatively, for a re-duction of the purchase or lease price, (i.e., the loss of the benefit of the bargain, or the difference between the value of the vehicle as delivered and the value it would have had if it had been deliv-ered as warranted), and (2) for all other pecuniary and/or econom-ic damages as permitted by the redhibition laws of the State of Louisiana and/or the comparable provisions of the Uniform Com-mercial Code, (3) punitive damages, if permitted, (4) interest at the legal rate from the date(s) of purchase, or alternatively, from the date of judicial demand, until paid, together with (5) reasona-ble attorney's fees, and all costs. . . .

GM now brings this interlocutory appeal under Rule 23(f), asserting that the district court abused its discretion in certifying a nationwide class of plaintiffs bringing claims under the laws of fifty-one jurisdictions. . . .

III. CLASS CERTIFICATION

. . .

C. *Analysis*

. . . To satisfy the predominance requirement, plaintiffs must demon-strate that "questions of law or fact common to the members of the class predominate over any questions affecting only individual members." Fed. R. Civ. P. 23(b)(3). In a diversity class action, as is the case here, inherent in the predominance inquiry is a determination of which states' substantive laws will apply to the claims. This is because if multiple states' laws apply and those laws vary, the variations may impact whether common issues of law and fact predominate among the class members. . . .

Plaintiffs argued and the district court agreed that under Louisiana's choice of law rules, the laws governing plaintiffs' claims are "the laws of the state where the vehicle is used by its owner or lessee and in where [sic] the contract of repair is to be performed." Thus, the laws of all fifty-one jurisdictions (all fifty states plus the District of Columbia) apply to this class action.

We have recognized that in a class action governed by the laws of multiple states, such as this one, "variations in state law may swamp any common issues and defeat predominance." *Castano* [*v. Am. Tobacco Co.*, 84 F.3d 734,] 741 [(5th Cir. 1996)]. The party seeking certification of a nationwide class must therefore "provide an 'extensive analysis' of state law variations to reveal whether these pose 'insuperable obstacles.'" *Spence* [*v. Glock*, 227 F.3d 308,] 313 [(5th Cir. 2000)] (quoting *Walsh v. Ford Motor Co.*, 807 F.2d 1000, 1017 (D.C. Cir. 1986). . . . Failure to engage in an analysis of state law variations is grounds for decertification. See *Castano*, 84 F.3d at 741–44 (concluding that court abused its discretion in certifying class where plaintiffs had failed to properly address variations in state law such that conclusion of predominance was based on speculation); *Spence*, 227 F.3d at 316 (concluding that court abused its discretion in certifying class where plaintiffs had failed to carry their burden of providing an extensive analysis of applicable law).

Plaintiffs assert that they have analyzed the applicable laws of the fifty-one jurisdictions and they are "virtually the same." They conclude that predominance is unfettered in this case because any variations in the substantive law applicable to this case are "not significant and would not affect the result." They further conclude that "neither complex jury instructions nor multiple separate trials will be required to try the common issues in this proceeding under the laws of the 51 jurisdictions."

As support for their argument, plaintiffs provided the district court with an extensive catalog of the statutory text of the warranty and redhibition laws of the fifty-one jurisdictions implicated in this suit; included in this catalog is the text of the relevant provisions of the Louisiana Civil Code and the UCC provisions of forty-nine states and the District of Columbia. Plaintiffs additionally provided an overview of textual variations in the relevant UCC provisions as adopted by the fifty jurisdictions. Finally, plaintiffs submitted a report from an expert on contract law who opined, after analyzing some variations, that "the few variations in the provisions of UCC Article 2 relevant to this case are such that they do not affect the result" and that Louisiana law "does not differ from Article 2 in a manner that would affect the result."

GM, on the other hand, provided the district court with extensive charts of authority concerning express and implied warranty actions from the fifty-one jurisdictions showing, *inter alia*, variations among the states in regard to reliance, notice of breach, vertical privity, and presumptions of merchantability. Despite GM's showing, the district court concluded that applying the laws of fifty-one jurisdictions would not make the class unmanageable or cause individual issues to overcome common ones because Louisiana law and the relevant UCC provisions adopted by "virtually every other jurisdiction" provided similar protections for express and implied warranties. The district court adopted plaintiffs' assertion that common issues predominated over individual ones because all members of the class asserted the same "benefit of the bargain" warranty claim based on the fact that "they contracted for a vehicle that did not have a potentially defective side airbag system, but instead received a vehicle with a side airbag system that had the potential to deploy inadvertently."

We conclude that plaintiffs did not sufficiently demonstrate the predominance requirement because they failed both to undertake the required "extensive analysis" of variations in state law concerning their claims and to consider how those variations impact predominance. Plaintiffs' assertion of predominance relied primarily on the textual similarities of each jurisdiction's applicable law and on the general availability of legal protection in each jurisdiction for express and implied warranties. Plaintiffs' largely textual presentation of legal authority oversimplified the required analysis and glossed over the glaring substantive legal conflicts among the applicable laws of each jurisdiction.

As we explain below, there are numerous variations in the substantive laws of express and implied warranty among the fifty-one jurisdictions that the plaintiffs failed to "extensively analyze" for their impact on predominance. Although plaintiffs assert that the laws of the fifty-one jurisdictions are "virtually the same," such that "no complex jury instructions" or "multiple separate trials" would be necessary, we note that many of the variations in state law raise the potential for the application of multiple and diverse legal standards and a related need for multiple jury instructions. For some issues, variations in state law also multiply the individualized factual determinations that the court would be required to undertake in individualized hearings. Specifically, the laws of the jurisdictions vary with regards to (1) whether plaintiffs must demonstrate reliance, (2) whether plaintiffs must provide notice of breach, (3) whether there must be privity of contract, (4) whether plaintiffs may recover for unmanifested vehicle defects, (5) whether merchantability may be presumed and (6) whether warranty protections extend to used vehicles. Plaintiffs failed to articulate adequately how these variations in state law would not preclude predominance in this case.

1. *Reliance*

To create an express warranty under UCC § 2–313, an "affirmation of fact or promise" or a "description of the goods" by the seller must be part of the "basis of the bargain." UCC § 2–313. There is a clear split of authority among the jurisdictions as to whether a buyer must show reliance on a statement or representation for it to be considered part of the "basis of the bargain." Some jurisdictions require a strict showing of reliance. Other jurisdictions have no reliance requirement. And still other jurisdictions have applied a rebuttable presumption of reliance. But plaintiffs ignored these differences. Although plaintiffs' expert noted that some courts require reliance, instead of analyzing the variations among the jurisdictions for their effect on predominance, plaintiffs' expert dismissed the variations, contending that the promise of repair would always be relied upon by a buyer because it "always accompanies the purchase or rental of a new automobile." Without any supporting legal authority, plaintiffs' expert opined: "Never was a presumption of reliance, if reliance is necessary, more justified." The district court similarly concluded that it was reasonable to presume reliance on the part of all purchasers in this case. In doing so, the court distinguished law to the contrary from only one jurisdiction and cited no authority to support the validity of this presumption for the other jurisdictions.

Moreover, certain jurisdictions' requirement that plaintiffs show reliance as a condition for recovery greatly impacts the predominance inquiry. . . . In this class of more than 200,000 individuals, class members governed by the laws of states requiring strict reliance would be required to bring forth evidence of individualized reliance. This would require the court to undertake an inquiry that would turn on facts particular to each of those class members and raises the potential that the trial would break down into multiple individual hearings.

2. Notice of Breach

Section 2–607 of the UCC requires consumers wishing to bring a breach of warranty claim to notify the seller of an alleged breach "within a reasonable time." U.C.C. § 2–607(3)(2). Plaintiffs, however, did not address the UCC's notice requirement. In a fashion similar to its analysis of reliance, the district court presumed, without analyzing the law of any jurisdiction, that no jurisdiction would require that members of the class give GM notice of the alleged breach because GM had already acknowledged the problem.

We are not convinced, however, that all jurisdictions would adopt this presumption. We previously rejected the notion that notice is useless where a breach is apparent to both parties. . . . *Eastern Air Lines, Inc. v. McDonnell Douglas Corp.*, 532 F.2d 957, 972 (5th Cir. 1976). State law varies on what constitutes reasonable notice and to whom notice should be given, and other courts considering the issue in the class certification context have noted that these variations impact predominance. Given the variations among the states regarding the notice requirement, plaintiffs failed to adequately analyze the impact of these variations on predominance.

3. Privity of Contract

Plaintiffs similarly failed to "extensively analyze" the variations in the law of the fifty-one jurisdictions concerning the requirement of privity of contract. There is a "sharp split of authority" as to whether a purchaser may recover economic loss from a remote manufacturer when there is no privity of contract between the parties. The requirement of privity is more strictly enforced in claims involving implied warranties than those involving express warranties.

Plaintiffs' expert briefly addressed the privity requirement for express warranties in four states, concluding that any variations among the jurisdictions were "minor" and opining that regardless of variation, the privity requirement was inapplicable to the facts of this case. Plaintiffs' expert, however, entirely failed to address the privity requirement for implied warranties. . . .

GM has provided its own catalog of state law variations regarding privity, which indicates that a significant number of jurisdictions require vertical privity in an implied warranty action for direct economic loss. Other jurisdictions, however, have eliminated the privity of contract requirement and allow recovery of economic loss from remote manufacturers.

These state law variations are important, in part because they would require separate jury instructions. Additionally, for states that have a strict privity requirement for implied warranty claims, each class member would be required to prove individually that she purchased her DeVille from GM or its agent, as opposed to an independent dealer or another individual. Therefore, the privity of contract inquiry would turn on facts particular to each class member and thus would require individualized hearings. . . .

4. Recovery for Unmanifested Vehicle Defects

Plaintiffs additionally failed to demonstrate predominance because they did not address variations in state law regarding recovery for an unmanifested product defect. The vast majority of the members of this class never experienced any manifestation of the alleged defect. But many jurisdictions do not permit the recovery of economic loss in vehicle defect cases where the vehicle has performed satisfactorily and has never manifested the alleged defect. See, e.g., *Briehl v. Gen. Motors Corp.*, 172 F.3d 623, 627–28 (8th Cir. 1999) (collecting cases and dismissing claims brought under any theory for allegedly defective anti-lock braking systems where plaintiffs' brakes never malfunctioned or failed). . . .

5. *Presumptions of Merchantability*

Even among those jurisdictions that might allow recovery for an unmanifested vehicle defect, there are variations in their laws. In some jurisdictions, use of a vehicle for a certain period of time without experiencing a defect gives rise to a presumption that the vehicle is merchantable. Plaintiffs failed to address these presumptions, how they vary, and the potential individualized legal questions they present.

6. *Warranty Protections for Used Vehicles*

Finally, jurisdictions vary in regard to whether an implied warranty extends from a remote manufacturer to a purchaser of used goods. Compare *Gen. Motors Corp. v. Halco Instruments, Inc.*, 185 S.E.2d 619, 622 ([Ga. Ct. App.] 1971) (holding that purchaser of used goods has no implied warranty claim against manufacturer), with *Int'l Petroleum Servs., Inc. v. S & N Well Serv., Inc.*, 639 P.2d 29, 34 ([Kan.]1982) (stating that the extent of the implied warranty obligation in transactions involving used goods depends on the circumstances of the transactions). The class of plaintiffs here is composed of purchasers of both new and used cars. Plaintiffs again failed to analyze the impact of these variations in state law on the legal standards class members would be held to, the jury instructions, and trial management, (i.e., how the trial would be affected by the possible need to conduct individualized inquiries into whether class members bought used versus new cars).

IV. CONCLUSION

Plaintiffs have failed to adequately address, much less "extensively analyze," the variations in state law we discussed above and the obstacles they present to predominance. The district court was not in a position to determine that "questions of law and fact common to the members of the class predominate" in the vacuum created by plaintiffs' omission. See *Castano*, 84 F.3d at 742–43 & n. 15; *Spence*, 227 F.3d at 313. Given these significant variations in state law and the multiple individualized legal and factual questions they present, we conclude that plaintiffs have failed to carry their burden in establishing predominance and that the district court abused its discretion in certifying the class action.

Accordingly, the district court's Ruling granting class certification is REVERSED and the case is REMANDED for entry of an order denying class certification. . . .

NOTES AND QUESTIONS

1. *The Relevance of State Law Variations to Certification.* Because differences in the law applicable to claims of class members bear directly on the appropriateness of class certification, federal courts of appeal and state supreme courts now generally agree that determination of the applicable law

must *precede* certification. See, *e.g.*, *Walsh v. Ford Motor Co.*, 807 F.2d 1000, 1016 (D.C. Cir. 1986) (rejecting district court's conclusion that a class could be certified while "deferring" for "another day the question of which state's law applies."); *Compaq Computer Corp. v. LaPray*, 135 S.W.3d 657, 672 (Tex. 2004) ("[T]rial courts must abandon the practice of postponing choice-of-law questions until after certification, as courts can hardly evaluate the claims, defenses, or applicable law without knowing what that law is."); *Washington Mutual Bank v. Superior Court*, 15 P.3d 1071, 1082 (Cal. 2001) ("Although the involvement of more than one state's law does not make a class action per se unmanageable, any variances among state laws must be examined to determine whether common questions will predominate over individual issues and whether litigation of a nationwide class may be managed fairly and efficiently."). But there are outliers. In *Gen. Motors Corp. v. Bryant*, 374 Ark. 38 (2008), for example, the Arkansas Supreme Court affirmed the certification of a nationwide opt-out class action in a product-defect situation much like that in *Cole*:

> [W]e have previously rejected any requirement of a rigorous-analysis inquiry by our circuit courts [on motions for class certification.] Instead, we have given the circuit courts of our state broad discretion in determining whether the requirements for class certification have been met, recognizing the caveat that a class can always be decertified at a later date if necessary. . . .

> [I]t is possible that other states' laws might be applicable to the class members' claims. However, we cannot say that our class-action jurisprudence requires an Arkansas circuit court to engage in a choice-of-law analysis prior to certifying a class, as we have not hesitated to affirm a finding of predominance so long as a common issue to all class members predominated over individual issues.

Id. at 47. Is the reasoning of the Arkansas Supreme Court persuasive?

   2.   The Level of Generality for Choice-of-Law Analysis. The *Cole* court's description of the briefing on the choice-of-law question conveys an accurate sense of the usual moves by class counsel and defense counsel. "Advocates of class certification have an incentive to frame legal and factual issues at high levels of generality so as to argue for their commonality, whereas opponents of class certification have an incentive to catalogue in microscopic detail each legal or factual variation suggesting the existence of individual questions." Am. Law Institute., PRINCIPLES OF THE LAW OF AGGREGATE LITIGATION § 2.02 reporters' notes, comment a (2009).

   3.   Who Bears the Burden with Respect to Choice of Law? Although the plaintiffs in *Cole* conceded that the laws of fifty-one jurisdictions were applicable, the plaintiffs also insisted that the laws were "virtually the same." The Fifth Circuit responded "that plaintiffs did not sufficiently demonstrate that the predominance requirement because they failed both to undertake the required 'extensive analysis' of variations in state law concerning their claims and to consider how those variations impact predominance." There is wide support among federal courts for the insistence in *Cole* that a plaintiff cannot simply rest on the claim that there are no material variations in state law.

   Because a plaintiff seeking to certify a class bears the burden of demonstrating that the predominance requirement is satisfied, a plaintiff naturally bears the burden of demonstrating that *proven* variations in state law will not defeat predominance. But is it clear that the plaintiff in a case like *Cole* should bear the burden of providing an "extensive analysis" of variations of state law when the plaintiff claims that there are no material variations of state law? Note that the approach in *Cole*—whatever its merit—does not square with a presumption in favor of forum law.

    4.   *Class Actions in State Court and the Presumption in Favor of Forum Law.* State courts are split on whether a presumption in favor of forum law should be recognized in a class suit. With some qualifications, California law places the burden of demonstrating that foreign law applies on the party arguing for non-forum law in a class action. *Washington Mutual Bank v. Superior Court*, 15 P.3d at 1081–82 (Cal. 2001) (rejecting the argument that the claims of class members should presumptively be governed by the law of their residence "unless the proponent of class certification affirmatively demonstrates that California law is more properly applied"). It is only if the presumption in favor of forum law is overcome that a plaintiff must make a presentation "sufficient to permit the [superior] court, at the time of certification, to make a detailed assessment of how the difficulties posed by the variations in state law will be managed at trial." *Id.* at 1083. The New Mexico Supreme Court with some equivocation also applies a presumption in favor of forum law:

> Plaintiffs bear the initial burden of producing evidence of the various states' laws and demonstrating that class certification does not present insuperable obstacles. If the defendant wishes to contest the plaintiff's characterization of the laws of the relevant states, the defendant must "inform the district court of any errors they perceive. If the defendant fails to bring any clearly established contradictory law to the court's attention, the district court cannot be faulted if it concludes that the laws of the jurisdictions connected to the dispute do not conflict such that a single state's law may be applied to the entire class.

Ferrell v. Allstate Ins. Co., 144 N.M. 405, 412–13 (2008) (relying in part on *Wortman*). Indeed, the New Mexico Court held that the Second—rather than the First—Restatement should apply in class litigation of a contractual nature in part because a presumption in favor of forum law is not always consistent with the First Restatement's methodology. Cf. RESTATEMENT OF CONFLICT OF LAWS § 622 ("In the absence of evidence, the *common law* of another common-law state is presumed to be the same as the common law of the forum.") (emphasis added).

    By contrast, the Texas Supreme Court, following the Fifth Circuit's lead, has conflated the choice-of-law burden with the certification burden. *LaPray*, 135 S.W.3d at 672–73 ("A court may not accept 'on faith' a party's assertion that no variations in state laws exist; plaintiffs, as class action proponents, must show that it is accurate.") And in an ironic twist, the Kansas Supreme Court now has essentially repudiated its earlier decision in *Wortman* and aligned itself with courts that place the choice-of-law burden on the class proponent. *Dragon v. Vanguard Indus. Inc.*, 89 P.3d 908, 918 (Kansas 2004) (holding that the class proponent "has the burden to show that there are no significant differences in the various states' law or, if there are variations, that they can be managed by the trial court.").

Does it make sense for states to apply a presumption in favor of forum law in class suits that will inevitably determine claims with no connection to the forum?

5. *Is It Appropriate for a Federal Court to Place the Choice-of-Law Burden on the Plaintiff?* GM's extensive briefing in *Cole* and the nature of the substantive body of law at issue suggest that a presumption in favor of forum law would have made no difference in the case. But as *Wortman* makes clear, a presumption in favor of forum law may be decisive in some cases. In light of *Klaxon*, should we look to the choice-of-law rules of the state in which a federal district court sits to determine whether a plaintiff is entitled to a presumption in favor of forum law? *Cole* recognized that Louisiana choice-of-law rules governed, but never considered whether Louisiana would apply a presumption in favor of forum law. Did the *Cole* court simply ignore *Klaxon* on the assumption that placing the choice-of-law burden on a plaintiff was part and parcel of requiring a plaintiff to show that the predominance requirement of Rule 23 has been satisfied? Patrick Woolley has argued that the choice-of-law burden and the certification burden are separable:

> Determining whether common issues of law or fact predominate does not require displacing state choice-of-law rules. It requires only an evaluation of the impact of choice-of-law decisions on the viability of a class suit. . . . The predominance requirement does not speak to how a court should determine what laws will apply in a class suit, and th[e] [choice-of-law] question is logically antecedent to whether the need to apply more than one law should lead to denial of certification in any given case.

Woolley, *Erie and Choice of Law After the Class Action Fairness Act*, 80 Tulane L. Rev. 1723, 1741 (2006). Do you agree? If the choice-of-law and certification burdens are separable, *Shady Grove Orthopedic Associates v. Allstate*, 131 S. Ct. 2368 (2009), arguably requires that they be separated. As discussed later in this chapter, *Shady Grove* insists that ambiguities in the federal rules of civil procedure be read, when possible, to avoid interference with the *Erie* policy of vertical uniformity. Recall that *Klaxon* is an application of the *Erie* policy.

As discussed in Chapter 3, the legislative history (though not the text) of the Class Action Fairness Act arguably endorses the approach used in *Cole*. Given that Congress is not bound by the *Erie* policy, what bearing should this endorsement have on the availability of a presumption in favor of forum law in federal class litigation?

6. *Identification of Patterns in Substantive Law.* Recall the suggestion that "in practice there are seldom more than two or three rules on any given question, each adopted by many states." Thus, even if a single law cannot be applied to all of the claims, there may well exist a common body of law for identifiable subsets of claimants, with each subset representing a distinct variation. Keep in mind, however, that even a few variations in state law may make a class suit unmanageable. For judicial efforts at class treatment based upon the categorization of substantive law into manageable patterns, see *In re School Asbestos Litig.*, 789 F.2d 996, 1010 (3d Cir. 1986). See also *In re Telectronics Pacing Sys., Inc.*, 172 F.R.D. 271, 293–94 (S.D. Ohio 1997); *In re LILCO Sec. Litig.*, 111 F.R.D. 663, 670 (E.D.N.Y. 1986).

In re St. Jude Medical, Inc.

2006 WL 2943154 (D. Minn. October 13, 2006)

■ JOHN R. TUNHEIM, DISTRICT JUDGE.

Defendant St. Jude Medical produced the Silzone prosthetic heart valve. A test conducted by defendant showed a higher risk of paravalvular leaks at the site where the valves were implanted, and defendant voluntarily recalled all Silzone valves that had not yet been implanted. Numerous lawsuits were filed across the nation, and the cases filed in federal district courts were ultimately consolidated for joint pretrial proceedings in the District of Minnesota. On motions by the plaintiffs, this Court issued three orders that collectively had the result of certifying two classes. Defendant appealed the two class certifications, and the Eighth Circuit reversed and remanded for further proceedings. This matter is now before the Court on plaintiffs' renewed motion for certification of a nationwide consumer protection class. For the reasons discussed below, the Court grants plaintiffs' motion.

BACKGROUND

Plaintiffs alleged common law strict liability, breach of implied and express warranties, negligence, and medical monitoring, and claims under various consumer protection statutes in Minnesota. . . . On March 27, 2003, the Court. . . certified [(1) a medical monitoring class and (2) an injury class to pursue] claims under Minnesota's consumer protection and deceptive trade practices acts pursuant to Federal Rule of Civil Procedure 23(b)(3). . . .

On October 12, 2005, the Eighth Circuit issued an order reversing the class certifications and remanding for further proceedings. *In re St. Jude Medical, Inc., Silzone Heart Valves Prods. Liab. Litig.*, 425 F.3d 1116 (8th Cir.2005). The Eighth Circuit reversed the medical monitoring class, concluding that diverse factual and legal issues preclude class certification. Specifically, the Eighth Circuit found that each plaintiff's need for medical monitoring is highly individualized, and that states recognizing medical monitoring as a cause of action have different elements triggering culpability.

As for the consumer protection class, the Eighth Circuit reversed and remanded for more analysis. The Eighth Circuit stated that it could not determine whether this Court's choice of Minnesota law was constitutionally permissible because "the court did not analyze the contacts between Minnesota and each plaintiff class member's claims." The court remanded for the "proper choice-of-law analysis," citing *Phillips Petroleum Co. v. Shutts,* 472 U.S. 797, 822–23 (1985).

On January 10, 2006, plaintiffs filed a renewed motion for an Order certifying a nationwide consumer protection class under Minnesota's consumer protection statutes and the Private Attorney General Act. Specifically, plaintiffs request that the Court certify a class of "all Silzone prosthetic heart valve patients in the United States who have not undergone an explant of their Silzone valve or developed a manifest and diagnosed injury from their Silzone implant of degree or severity that would permit individual personal injury lawsuits to be commenced in their State of residence."

ANALYSIS

The Eighth Circuit reversed and remanded the consumer protection subclass for further analysis on two discrete issues. First, the Court must address whether Minnesota has sufficient contacts with each plaintiff's claims so that application of Minnesota law satisfies the constitutional requirements of the Due Process Clause and Full Faith and Credit Clause. Second, if Minnesota has sufficient contacts to satisfy the constitutional requirements, the Court must apply Minnesota's conflicts of law rules to determine whether application of Minnesota law is preferable over the law of other states with sufficient contacts. . . .

I.   Significant Contact Analysis Under The Due Process Clause And Full Faith And Credit Clause

The Due Process Clause and the Full Faith and Credit Clause provide "modest restrictions" on the application of forum law to class actions. *Shutts,* 472 U.S. at 818. The forum must have " 'significant contact or significant aggregation of contacts' to the claims asserted by each member of the plaintiff class, contacts 'creating state interests,' in order to ensure that the choice of [forum] law is not arbitrary or unfair." *Id.* at 821–22 quoting *Allstate Ins. Co. v. Hague,* 449 U.S. 302, 313 (1981). In many situations, there will be several constitutionally permissible choices of law. *Shutts,* 472 U.S. at 823.

The first step in this analysis is to determine whether the law of the forum "conflicts in any material way with any other law which could apply." *Shutts,* 472 U.S. at 816 (explaining that application of forum law causes no injury if it is not in conflict with that of any other jurisdiction connected to the lawsuit). Here, the forum state is Minnesota, and all fifty states are connected to this lawsuit because Silzone devices were implanted and individual class members reside in every state in the nation. As discussed below, the Court concludes that 18 states have substantive conflicts with the consumer protection laws of Minnesota.

Given these conflicts of law, the Court next considers whether applying the law of the forum would be fair. When making this assessment, the court must consider whether the forum has significant contacts to the litigation that support the forum state's interest in applying its law. *Id.* at 819, citing *Allstate,* 449 U.S. at 313–29. Another important consideration is the "expectation of the parties." *Shutts,* 472 U.S. at 822.

In its order reversing and remanding this case, the Eighth Circuit explained that application of the law of Minnesota "ultimately may be proper" but that this Court needed to conduct further analysis. *In re St. Jude Medical,* 425 F.3d 1116, 1119–20 (8th Cir.2005). Accordingly, the Court has analyzed the contacts between Minnesota and each class member's claims, and determines that application of Minnesota law is fair. Minnesota has significant contacts with each class member by virtue of the domicile and claims-related activities of defendant. *See Northwest Airlines v. Astraea Aviation Servs.,* 111 F.3d 1386, 1394 (8th Cir.1997) (holding that defendant's headquarters and conduct in Texas comprise "significant contacts" under the Due Process Clause). The Court need not specifically discuss Minnesota's contacts to each of over 11,000 class members' claims because each class member's claims have in common the following contacts with Minnesota.

First, defendant is incorporated, headquartered, and has its principal place of business in Minnesota. These physical and corporate domiciliary contacts support Minnesota's interest in applying its law. Minnesota has an interest in regulating its domestic corporations, and ensuring that out-of-state persons doing business with Minnesota firms may rely on their compliance with Minnesota statutes. See *CTS Corp. v. Dynamics Corp. of Am.,*

481 U.S. 69, 93 (1987) ("[The forum state] has a substantial interest in preventing the corporate forum from becoming a shield for unfair business dealing.").

Second, virtually all of the corporate acts implicated by each claim occurred in Minnesota. Cf. *Shutts,* 474 U.S. at 815 (reversing application of Kansas law to the entire class where over 99% of the gas leases at issue had no apparent connection to Kansas). Plaintiffs' claims are based on alleged false representations and material omissions regarding the safety and efficacy of the Silzone valves through defendant's global advertising, marketing, and product labeling. Importantly, all marketing and distribution efforts were based in Minnesota, and all labels and instructions were drafted in Minnesota.

Third, the Silzone heart valves were substantially created and manufactured in Minnesota. Specifically, defendant explains that the valves were "designed, researched, developed, engineered, manufactured, tested, [and] quality controlled in Minnesota." In addition, the related FDA and other regulatory affairs were managed and controlled from defendant's headquarters in Minnesota.

Finally, defendant invited heart valve purchasers and recipients to solicit more product information from Minnesota by including a Minneapolis, Minnesota telephone number in journal advertisements worldwide.

In addition, the invitation to place phone calls to Minnesota, along with the corporate and physical domiciliary contacts with Minnesota, affects the expectations of the parties on which law would apply to potential claims. Obviously, the application of Minnesota law to a Minnesota corporation could not be unexpected for defendant. To the extent that class members were even thinking about these issues when they received their heart valves, the Court finds that individual class members would have expected a plainly Minnesota-based corporation to be subject to the requirements of Minnesota statutes.

Given defendant's significant contacts with Minnesota, no one would doubt that an individual class member could sue defendant in Minnesota and apply Minnesota law. Similarly, the Court concludes that it is constitutionally permissible to apply Minnesota law in the class action context.

II. Application Of Minnesota's Conflict Of Laws Rules

Although the Court concludes that application of Minnesota law is constitutionally permissible, a conflict of laws analysis is necessary to determine if application of Minnesota law is preferable to the law of each plaintiff's home state, or state where the valve was implanted. The Court must therefore apply Minnesota's conflict of laws rules. This analysis requires consideration of [Professor Leflar's] five "choice-influencing" factors for each state where there is a substantive conflict of law. . . .

Before proceeding with the choice-of-law analysis, the Court needs to determine whether there are any conflicts of law, and whether those conflicts are substantive, rather than procedural. If there is no conflict of substantive law, then the law of the forum applies without further analysis. *Richie v. Paramount Pictures Corp.,* 544 N.W.2d 21, 29 (Minn.1996).

Plaintiffs have provided the Court with a detailed analysis of consumer protection statutes across the United States. Plaintiffs used an "outcome determinative" standard to see if a cause of action based on the facts they have alleged would be precluded under the laws of other states. See *Schu-*

macher v. Schumacher, 676 N.W. 2d 685, 689 (Minn.Ct.App.2004) ("A conflict of law exists if choosing the law of one state over the law of another state would be 'outcome determinative.' "). Based on this sound analysis, the Court concludes that 32 jurisdictions have no outcome determinative conflicts with Minnesota law. Application of Minnesota law to plaintiffs with significant contacts in these jurisdictions is therefore warranted without further analysis. The remaining 18 states have substantive conflicts of law, and thus require application of the five-factor test. . . .

III. Conclusion

The Court finds that Minnesota has significant contacts with each plaintiff's claims, such that application of Minnesota law to these claims is constitutionally permissible. After a detailed conflict of laws analysis, the Court concludes that Minnesota law should be applied to plaintiffs' claims over the laws of other jurisdictions with connections to this litigation. It is difficult for the Court to imagine how over 11,000 individual consumer fraud cases could be handled effectively against the defendant. It is equally difficult to try to apply the consumer protection statutes of the various states in a manner that can efficiently resolve this litigation. Certification of a consumer protection class clearly provides the most effective manner in which to resolve these misrepresentation and deceptive trade practices claims and it is clear to the Court that it is most fair to plaintiffs and to defendants to apply Minnesota law to these claims within the boundaries and restrictions of a class action. Based on these findings, and the Court's finding that class certification remains appropriate under Rule 23, the Court grants plaintiffs' renewed motion for class certification.

NOTES AND QUESTIONS

1. *Subsequent Developments in the St. Jude Medical Case.* On appeal, the Eighth Circuit once again reversed the district court's certification order, this time on the ground that even under the Minnesota Consumer Fraud statute, "St. Jude's potential liability to each plaintiff . . . will be dominated by individual issues of causation and reliance." 522 F.3d 836, 840 (2008). The Court of Appeals found it "unnecessary to consider the merits of the district court's choice-of-law analysis or the constitutionality of applying Minnesota law to a nationwide class in these circumstances." *Id.* at 841.

2. *The Constitutionality of Choosing the Law of the Defendant's Principal Place of Business.* Is choosing the law of a defendant's principal place of business consistent with *Shutts* as the district court in *St. Jude Medical* argues? Although *Shutts* makes clear that simply doing business in a state is not a sufficient basis for applying that state's law, the state in which a defendant has its principal place of business has more significant contacts with the defendant. The conclusion that the law of the place where the defendant has its principal place of business is constitutional is consistent with the widely held understanding that *Shutts* places only the most minimal limits on state choice of law. See, e.g., Samuel Issacharoff, *Getting Beyond Kansas*, 74 UMKC L. Rev. 613, 621 (2006) ("Shutts invites . . . application of a simple non-arbitrary choice of law rule, such as the law controlling the defendant at the time of the dispositive decision-making. . . ."). But that understanding of Shutts is not universally held. See, e.g., S. Rep. No. 109–14, at 23–27 (reporting on the Class Action Fairness Act of 2005) (citing *Shutts* for the proposition that the Supreme Court has "warned that courts should not attempt to apply the laws of one state to

behaviors that occurred in other jurisdictions"); Alison M. Grunewald, Note, *Rethinking Place of Business as Choice of Law in Class Action Lawsuits* 58 Vand. L. Rev. 1925, 195–46 (2005) ("[A]s a matter of fundamental fairness to the defendant, courts should not apply the law of the defendant's principal place of business in an individual suit, and should certainly not do so on an aggregate basis.").

    3. *The Bridgestone/Firestone Tire Products Litigation ("Bridgestone/Firestone I").* The Seventh Circuit rejected an effort by an Indiana federal district court in *Bridgestone/Firestone I* to apply Michigan and Tennessee law to claims in a nationwide class suit seeking compensation for the *risk* that Bridgestone/Firestone tires would fail:

> No class action is proper unless all litigants are governed by the same legal rules. . . . The district judge, well aware of this principle. . . concluded that Indiana law points to the headquarters of the defendants, because that is where the products are designed and important decisions about disclosures and sales are made. This ruling means that all claims by the Explorer class will be resolved under Michigan law and all claims by the tire class will be resolved under Tennessee law. . . .

> Indiana is a *lex loci delicti* state; in all but exceptional cases it applies the law of the place where harm occurred [as required by the First Restatement]. . . . Financial loss (if any . . .) was suffered in the places where the vehicles and tires were purchased at excessive prices or resold at depressed prices. Those injuries occurred in all 50 states . . . . The *lex loci delicti* principle points to the place of these injuries, not the defendants' corporate headquarters, as the source of law.

288 F.3d 1012, 1015–16 (7th Cir. 2002). The Court of Appeals ordered decertification of the class.

    Did the Court of Appeals engage in hyperbole when it flatly stated that "[n]o class action is proper unless all litigants are governed by the same legal rules . . . "? In any event, it is hard to quarrel with the Seventh Circuit's conclusion that a state which strictly applies the First Restatement will be unable to finesse choice-of-law complications by applying the law of the place in which the defendant has its principal place of business. In fact, as the Seventh Circuit itself made clear, the real dispute in *Bridgestone/Firestone* was whether Indiana had moved away from a strict First Restatement approach. The Court of Appeals rejected the plaintiffs' argument that a 1987 Indiana Supreme Court decision permitted consideration of the place of the *conduct* causing the injury and the residence of the parties. As *Bridgestone/Firestone I* demonstrates, the First Restatement's relative inflexibility can pose serious choice-of-law difficulties in class litigation. See *also Ferrell v. Allstate Insurance Co.*, 188 P.3d 1156, 1173 (N.M. 2008) (concluding "that the rigidity of the RESTATEMENT (FIRST) is particularly ill-suited for the complexities present in multi-state class actions" and holding that the Second Restatement is a more appropriate approach for a multistate contract class action).

    4. *Ysbrand v. Daimler Chrysler Corp.* By contrast, in a decision rendered after *Bridgestone/Firestone I*, the Oklahoma Supreme Court concluded that the law of the defendant's home state should be applied. See *Ysbrand v. DaimlerChrysler Corp.*, 81 P.3d 618 (Okla. 2003). *Ysbrand* upheld the certifica-

tion of a nationwide class suit with respect to breach-of-warranty claims. Plaintiffs alleged that defendants had manufactured minivans with defective front-passenger airbags. Purporting to apply the "most significant relationship test" of the Second Restatement, the Oklahoma Supreme Court held that the warranty law of Michigan—DaimlerChrysler's principal place of business—would govern the claims:

> All 50 states and the District of Columbia bear some relationship to the parties and transactions in this dispute by virtue of the nationwide sales of the minivans. The question becomes whether the relationship of each state where the vehicles were purchased is more significant to the parties and this litigation than that of Michigan, the principal place of business of DaimlerChrysler.

> . . . [T]he place of contracting, the place of negotiation and performance, and the location of the subject matter are of diminished significance to the sales of the minivans. The UCC[-based] warranties are not something which is negotiated in the purchase of a new car. Thus, the relative interest of each buyer's home state in applying its version of the UCC is more or less equal. By contrast, Michigan's interest in having its regulatory scheme applied to the conduct of a Michigan manufacturer is most significant. Michigan is where the decisions concerning the design, manufacture, and distribution of the minivans were made. Michigan is the only state where conduct relevant to all class members occurred. The principal place of DaimlerChrysler's business is the most important contact with respect to the UCC warranty claims.

> . . . The needs of the interstate system and the basic policies of predictability and uniformity of result require that the issue of product defect be determined in one forum with one result rather than in 51 jurisdictions with the very real possibility of conflicting decisions. While the interest of each home state in applying its local law is significant, Michigan's interest in the conduct of its manufacturer, and thus its connection to the warranty issues, is greater. Michigan law applies.

Id. at 625–26. Note that *Ysbrand* reaches a different choice-of-law result than likely would have been reached in the absence of aggregation:

> Imagine that one of the class members [in *Ysbrand*] live[d] in Norman, Oklahoma and purchased his minivan at the local Chrysler dealership. Had he sued DaimlerChrysler on his own, it seems very unlikely that any Oklahoma court would have displaced presumptively applicable Oklahoma law in favor of Michigan law. Indeed, the reasons for displacing Oklahoma law in the *Ysbrand* class action—the fact that Oklahoma did not have an interest in regulating out of state transactions and the benefits of having a single law apply—would not even be present in a suit brought by a single Oklahoma plaintiff. Thus . . . the Oklahoma class members in *Ysbrand* will have their warranty claims decided under a different law in the class action than they would have had as individual litigants.

Stephen S. Gensler, *Civil Procedure: Class Certification and the Predominance Requirement Under Oklahoma Section 2023(B)(3)* 56 Okla. L. Rev. 289, 300–01 (2003).

5. *Should States Modify Choice-of-Law Rules to Facilitate Certification?* Are choice-of-law principles that call for applying the law of the defendant's principal place of business a desirable thing in a world of national markets for undifferentiated goods and services?

There has been vigorous debate about whether it is appropriate to apply different choice of law rules to class suits (and other aggregate litigation) than would apply in ordinary litigation. Russell Weintraub, the distinguished Conflicts scholar, noted with approval that "courts utilizing interest and most-significant-relationship analysis have sometimes facilitated certification of a national class action by applying to all claims the law of the state that was the center of defendant's wrongful conduct." See R. Weintraub, COMMENTARY ON THE CONFLICT OF LAWS 57 (Supp. 2005). And the American Law Institute almost two decades ago proposed a set of choice-of-law rules for complex litigation premised on the view "that it would be highly desirable if a single state's law could be applied to a particular issue that is common to all the claims and parties involved in the litigation." Am. Law Inst., COMPLEX LITIGATION: STATUTORY RECOMMENDATIONS AND ANALYSIS 316 (1994). By contrast, Larry Kramer has objected that

> No one seems to notice the irony of advocating a choice-of-law rule that selects the law of a single state on the ground that complex litigation is national in character. I would have thought that the more "national" the case, the less appropriate it is for any single state's standard to govern. . . . [T]he appropriate solution surely cannot be to apply the law of one state—a law that may be quirky or obsolete and that, in any event, reflects the political judgment of only a fraction of the nation.

Kramer, *Choice of Law in Complex Litigation*, 71 N.Y.U.L. Rev. 547, 578–79 (1996).

6. *Is the Use of Different Choice-of-Law Rules in Class Litigation Constitutional?* Richard Nagareda has identified a potential constitutional obstacle to applying different choice-of-law rules than would otherwise be applied to facilitate class certification. He underlines that *Shutts* rejected as a "bootstrap argument" the Kansas Supreme Court's contention that "[w]here a state court determines it has jurisdiction over a nationwide class action and procedural due process guarantees of notice and adequate representation are present . . . the law of the forum should be applied unless compelling reasons exist for applying a different law." 472 U.S. at 821. Honing in on the Court's criticism of "bootstrap[ping]," Professor Nagareda suggests that the Constitution should be read to prohibit reliance on the class device to support application of a single body of substantive law in a case like *Ysbrand*:

> Choice of law . . . must rest upon matters that preexist the class action itself. . . . The important point remains that choice of law in the absence of bootstrapping results in the same choice being made for purposes of a class action as would be made in an individual action brought in the forum state.

Nagareda, *Bootstrapping in Choice of Law After the Class Action Fairness Act*, 74 UMKC L. Rev. 661, 665–66 (2006). Do you agree? Whatever the merit of Professor Nagareda's argument, it is at least in tension with the conventional understanding that constitutional limits on state choice of law are about the appropriateness of the *law* selected, not the appropriateness of a state's choice-of-law methodology.

e.   PUTTING THE RULE 23(b)(3) INQUIRY TOGETHER

Thus far, we have considered each requirement individually. The following opinion pulls it all together by walking through the Rule 23 analysis for a (b)(3) opt-out class action.

Klay v. Humana, Inc.

382 F.3d 1241 (11th Cir. 2004)

■ TJOFLAT, CIRCUIT JUDGE:

This is a case of almost all doctors versus almost all major health maintenance organizations (HMOs). . . . The plaintiffs are a putative class of all doctors who submitted at least one claim to any of the defendant HMOs between 1990 and 2002. They allege that the defendants conspired with each other to program their computer systems to systematically underpay physicians for their services. We affirm the district court's certification of the plaintiffs' federal claims, though we strongly urge the district court to revisit the definition of these classes, and reverse the district court's certification of the plaintiffs' state claims. . . .

I.

The plaintiffs are physicians who were reimbursed by one or more of the defendant HMOs for treating patients covered by those HMOs. The plaintiffs allege that the backbone of their relationship with the HMOs is that they "will be paid, in a timely manner, for the covered, medically necessary services they render." In a phrase that will undoubtedly play well with a jury, the doctors alliteratively claim that the defendants systematically "deny, delay and diminish the payments due to [them]," and fail to tell doctors that they are being underpaid. The complaint alleges that the defendants' reimbursement system is based on covertly denying payments to physicians based on financially expedient cost and actuarial criteria rather than medical necessity, processing physicians' bills using automated programs which manipulate standard coding practices to artificially reduce the amount they are paid, and . . . systematically delaying payments to gain increased use of the physicians' funds. [Second Amended Complaint] ¶ 6.

If an agreement between a physician and an HMO exists, its terms govern the physician's reimbursement. The HMOs also "represent to the medical profession at large" that when a physician treats a patient who belongs to an HMO with which the physician does not have a contract, the HMO will still reimburse him. Among the ways in which the defendants allegedly convey this information are "[b]y disseminating billing information to the profession at large," "confirming coverage for medically necessary services when contacted by doctors prior to treatment," and "explaining payments so as to make it appear that doctors are being paid for the covered, medically necessary services they render."

The complaint alleges that physicians under contract with HMOs are compensated through one of two different methods—fee-for-service or capitation. Physicians who do not have a contractual relationship with an HMO are reimbursed only under a fee-for-service regime. Although the plaintiffs allege that they are being systematically underpaid under both payment methods, the exact ways in which this is purportedly accomplished differ; we will consider each reimbursement scheme in turn.

A.

Under a fee-for-service plan, an HMO agrees to reimburse doctors for any medically necessary services they perform on covered individuals, whether or not those doctors are under contract with the HMO. This gives doctors an incentive to perform as many tests and procedures as they can convince the HMO are medically necessary; HMOs, in contrast, have an incentive to approve as few procedures as possible. Both parties claim they are acting in their patients' best medical interests.

To claim reimbursement, physicians are required to fill out an HCFA–1500 form, developed by the federal government and the American Medical Association. These forms employ a "current procedural terminology" coding procedure ("CPT coding") whereby medical procedures are identified by standardized designators. Each designator is comprised of two components: a "base code" that identifies the nature of the procedure and a series of modifiers "for the degree of difficulty, complexity and multiplicity." Each HCFA–1500 form is processed by the defendants' computer systems, which specify the amount that the physician should be paid.

The plaintiffs allege that these computer systems are programmed to systematically underpay the plaintiffs through a variety of methods. First, the plaintiffs allege that the systems are programmed to simply deny reimbursement for certain base codes that insurance companies feel are too expensive, notwithstanding their contractual obligations to both physicians and patients. Second, the plaintiffs allege that when the systems read certain base codes on HCFA–1500 forms, they are programmed to interpret them as requesting reimbursement for less expensive procedures ("downcoding"). Third, the plaintiffs contend that the system is programmed to simply group certain base codes together, so that if the system reads certain combinations of codes on the forms, they will be interpreted as being only a single code ("grouping").

Fourth, the system is allegedly programmed to ignore certain modifiers that would drive up physicians' reimbursements. Fifth, the plaintiffs assert that the system is designed to unnecessarily put their reimbursement claims in a "state of suspense before they are processed even though no additional information is needed or requested. . . . The end result is that average payment times exceed by multiples the time provided for by law in most states as well as the time set by contract and industry practice." Finally, the plaintiffs allege that the forms the HMOs send to physicians explaining the amounts of their reimbursements, called "explanation of benefits" forms ("EOBs"), "misrepresent or conceal the actual manner in which Plaintiffs' . . . payment requests were processed so as to induce them to accept reduced payments in reliance thereon."

B.

Even plaintiffs whose contracts establish a capitation payment plan are not free from the defendants' alleged manipulation. Under a capitation agreement, each patient specifies a physician as his "primary care provider." The HMO is obligated to pay each physician a small monthly fee, called a capitation payment, for each patient registered to him. The physician, in turn, is obligated to provide whatever medical services each registered patient requires. Thus, a capitation system is a flat-rate scheme in which a physician's payments are "based on the number of patients they agree to treat rather than on the services they actually render." A capitation method gives a physician an incentive to provide as few services as possible to each patient, whether or not medically necessary, because his payments are not tied to the quality or extent of services he provides. The HMOs, in turn, have an incentive to register as few patients as possible with each physician, so as to reduce their monthly per-patient outlays.

The plaintiffs contend that the HMOs are underpaying physicians by failing to pay capitation fees for many patients who have registered with a physician but never visited him. Consequently, plaintiffs allege, they are receiving capitation payments based on a much smaller pool of patients than that to which they are entitled. . . .

C.

The plaintiffs sued a variety of large HMOs because they claim that these practices are not occurring in isolation, but are instead the end-product of a decades-long nefarious conspiracy to undermine the American health care system. The plaintiffs assert that such a conspiracy was necessary to permit these practices to continue, because "[i]f only one Defendant engaged in these activities, physicians could and would refuse to do business with that Defendant, but together Defendants have the power and influence necessary to affect and perpetuate their scheme." To support this allegation, the plaintiffs point to the fact that most of the HMOs run their reimbursement processes in substantially the same way, and participate in various industry groups, trade associations, and standards-promulgation projects.

D.

This case originated when lawsuits were filed in four federal judicial districts against Humana, Inc., for underpaying doctors in the manners described above. These suits were consolidated by the Judicial Panel on Multidistrict Litigation . . . in the Southern District of Florida. . . .

Once the cases were consolidated, the plaintiffs filed an amended complaint against all of the defendants. It requested that the district court certify three classes. First, the plaintiffs requested certification of a Global Class, including "[a]ll medical doctors who provided services to any person insured by any defendant from August 14, 1990 to [the date of certification]," to pursue their claims that the defendants conspired to violate the Racketeer Influenced and Corrupt Organizations Act (RICO), and aided and abetted each other in doing so. Second, the plaintiffs sought recognition of a National Subclass, comprised of all "[m]edical doctors who provided services to any person insured by a Defendant, when the doctor has a claim against such Defendant and is not bound to arbitrate the claim," to pursue various state-law claims against the defendants, as well as claims based on "direct" (substantive, as opposed to inchoate) RICO violations. Finally, the plaintiffs requested certification of a California Subclass, comprised of "[m]edical doctors who provided services to any person insured in California by any defendant, when the doctor was not bound to arbitrate the claim being asserted," to pursue alleged violations of Cal. Bus. & Prof. Code

§ 17200. The district court certified all three classes, *In re Managed Care Litig.*, 209 F.R.D. 678 (S.D. Fla. 2002), and the HMOs now appeal. . . .

II.

The defendants' first claim is that the district court erred in certifying a Global Class to pursue federal RICO claims based on conspiracy and aiding-and-abetting, and a National Class to pursue federal claims based on "direct" RICO violations, because the common issues of fact and law these claims involve do not predominate over individualized issues. . . .

A.

To understand the plaintiffs' RICO claims, it is necessary to first examine two of the central elements upon which they are predicated—the "pattern of racketeering activity" in which the defendants allegedly engaged, and the "enterprise" to which this racketeering activity was allegedly related. To violate RICO, a defendant must engage in a pattern of racketeering activities. RICO designates the violation of certain federal criminal laws as "racketeering activities," see 18 U.S.C. § 1961(1). The plaintiffs contend that the defendants committed racketeering activities by [among other things] engaging in mail and wire fraud, in violation of 18 U.S.C. §§ 1341 and 1343 [and engaging in] extortion, in violation of 18 U.S.C. §§ 1951(a) and (b)(2). . . .

The defendants allegedly committed mail and wire fraud by withholding from the plaintiffs information concerning the various practices described above in Sections I.A and I.B. For example, the plaintiffs allege that the "Defendants misrepresented to Plaintiffs and class members that Defendants would pay Plaintiffs and class members for medically necessary services and procedures according to the CPT codes for the services and procedures they provided." The plaintiffs further contend that the defendants "have concealed and have failed to disclose that they deliberately delay payments . . . [and] that they have developed or purchased claims systems designed to manipulate CPT codes. . . ."

The defendants allegedly engaged in extortion by

> forc[ing] Plaintiffs and members of the class to accept capitation contracts, accept the loss of compensation for treating Defendants' insureds which results from their misrepresentation and manipulation of the workings of the capitation payment system, and accept the denial, reduction and delay of payments for covered, medically necessary services . . . through fear of economic loss. Defendants create this fear through threats, both veiled and explicit, that doctors will lose the patient base Defendants control, be blacklisted, and in the case of noncontract doctors, not be paid at all.

[Third Amended Complaint] ¶ 150–51. . . .

Having laid out the various racketeering activities in which the defendants allegedly engaged, we now turn to the enterprise to which these activities were ostensibly related. The plaintiffs assert that the defendants belonged to a shadowy, mysterious "Managed Case Enterprise" that included other health insurance companies not named as defendants, the companies that developed the claims-processing software the defendants use, companies that review claims for the defendants, and several trade, standards-setting, and industry organizations and associations to which the defendants belong or with which the defendants work. This enterprise is a "system that allows [the defendants] to manipulate and control reimbursements to physicians and conceal the manner in which that is done."

. . . The plaintiffs assert that the defendants operated the Managed Care Enterprise by engaging in racketeering activity because the enterprise itself was created to systematically underpay doctors for the services they provide.

[T]he plaintiffs [also] contend that the defendants violated 18 U.S.C. § 1962(d), which prohibits conspiracies to violate other provisions of RICO by conspiring with each other to violate 18 U.S.C. §§ 1962(a) and (c), as discussed above. The plaintiffs further assert that the defendants violated 18 U.S.C. § 2 by aiding and abetting each other in violating 18 U.S.C. §§ 1962(a) and (c), as discussed above. . . .

B.

The defendants' main contention is that the district court erred in certifying classes to litigate the RICO claims discussed above because the common issues of fact and law these claims involve do not predominate over the individualized issues involved that are specific to each plaintiff. . . .

"Whether an issue predominates can only be determined after considering what value the resolution of the class-wide issue will have in each class member's underlying cause of action." *Rutstein v. Avis Rent–A–Car Sys.*, 211 F.3d 1228, 1234 (11th Cir. 2000). Common issues of fact and law predominate if they "ha[ve] a direct impact on every class member's effort to establish liability and on every class member's entitlement to injunctive and monetary relief." *Ingram v. Coca–Cola Co.*, 200 F.R.D. 685, 699 (N.D. Ga. 2001). Where, after adjudication of the classwide issues, plaintiffs must still introduce a great deal of individualized proof or argue a number of individualized legal points to establish most or all of the elements of their individual claims, such claims are not suitable for class certification under Rule 23(b)(3). See *Perez v. Metabolife Int'l, Inc.*, 218 F.R.D. 262, 273 (S.D. Fla. 2003) (declining class certification in part because "any efficiency gained by deciding the common elements will be lost when separate trials are required for each class member in order to determine each member's entitlement to the requested relief").

An alternate formulation of this test was offered in *Alabama v. Blue Bird Body Co.*, 573 F.2d 309 (5th Cir. 1978). In that case, we observed that if common issues truly predominate over individualized issues in a lawsuit, then "the addition or subtraction of any of the plaintiffs to or from the class [should not] have a substantial effect on the substance or quantity of evidence offered." *Id.* at 322. Put simply, if the addition of more plaintiffs to a class requires the presentation of significant amounts of new evidence, that strongly suggests that individual issues (made relevant only through the inclusion of these new class members) are important. *Id.* ("If such addition or subtraction of plaintiffs does affect the substance or quantity of evidence offered, then the necessary common question might not be present."). If, on the other hand, the addition of more plaintiffs leaves the quantum of evidence introduced by the plaintiffs as a whole relatively undisturbed, then common issues are likely to predominate.

C.

In certifying the plaintiffs' RICO claims, the district court found that common questions of fact and law predominate because this case "involves a conspiracy and joint efforts to monopolize and restrain trade." *Managed Care Litig.*, 209 F.R.D. at 696. . . . We agree with this analysis.

1.

The plaintiffs here allege the type of nationwide conspiracy which we [previously have] intimated . . . would probably be appropriate for nationwide class certification. . . . [I]n this case, . . . all of the defendants operate nationwide and allegedly conspired to underpay doctors across the nation, so the numerous factual issues relating to the conspiracy are common to all plaintiffs.

This case stands in stark contrast to many others in which we found individualized issues to predominate. For example, in *Jackson v. Motel 6 Multipurpose, Inc.*, 130 F.3d 999 (11th Cir. 1997), a putative class of African–American plaintiffs sued Motel 6, alleging that the chain either denied African–Americans accommodations altogether, or rented them only dirty rooms. We declined to certify the class because the plaintiffs' claims would have "require[d] distinctly case-specific inquiries into the facts surrounding each alleged incident of discrimination." *Id.* at 1006. . . .

We came to the same conclusion in *Rutstein* [*v. Avis Rent-a-Car Sys.*], 211 F.3d 1228 (11th Cir. 2000), where we denied class certification to a group of plaintiffs alleging that Avis refused to establish corporate accounts for Jewish companies. We held that each plaintiff's individualized allegations necessarily predominated over the issue of whether Avis had discriminatory policies because "[e]ach plaintiff [would] have to bring forth evidence demonstrating that the defendant had an intent to treat him or her less favorably because of the plaintiff's Jewish ethnicity." *Id.* at 1235. We explained that individual claims for discrimination are inextricably bound up in innumerable case-specific facts, for "even if [the] plaintiffs [could] demonstrate that a general policy or practice of discrimination was applied in their cases, Avis [could] escape liability by showing that an individual plaintiff would have been denied or terminated even if no such policy or practice had existed." *Id.* at 1236.

Motel 6 and *Rutstein* were both cases in which individuals were seeking to litigate separate discrimination claims that arose from a variety of individual incidents together in the same class action simply because they alleged that the acts of discrimination occurred pursuant to corporate policies. In the instant case, however, the plaintiffs' RICO claims are not simply individual allegations of underpayments lumped together, and the allegation of an official corporate policy or conspiracy is not simply a piece of circumstantial evidence being used to support such individual underpayment claims. Instead, the very gravamen of the RICO claims is the "pattern of racketeering activities" and the existence of a national conspiracy to underpay doctors. These are not facts from which jurors will be asked to infer the commission of wrongful acts against individual plaintiffs; these very facts constitute essential elements of each plaintiff's RICO claims. While the existence of a policy of discrimination did not constitute an element of any of the causes of action in *Rutstein* or *Motel 6*, the existence of a general conspiracy to violate certain federal laws, or a pattern and practice of aiding and abetting other HMOs' violations of those laws, is an essential element of each individual plaintiff's RICO-related claims. Cf. *Rutstein*, 211 F.3d at 1235 ("Whether Avis maintains a policy or practice of discrimination may be relevant in a given case, but it certainly cannot establish that the company intentionally discriminated against every member of the putative class."). Thus, while corporate policies were only circumstantially relevant in the discrimination cases, and insufficient to overcome the tremendous individualized issues of fact that remained in those cases, they constitute the very heart of the plaintiffs' RICO claims here, and would necessarily have to be re-proven by every plaintiff if each doctor's claims were tried separately.

2.

The defendants contend that class certification is inappropriate because the RICO claims are based, in large part, on allegations of mail and wire fraud. Under *Sikes v. Teleline, Inc.*, reliance may not be presumed in fraud-based RICO actions; instead, the evidence must demonstrate that each individual plaintiff actually relied upon the misrepresentations at issue. 281 F.3d 1350, 1360, 1362 (11th Cir. 2002) (holding that, to make out a civil RICO claim based on mail or wire fraud, a plaintiff must demonstrate that he "relied on a misrepresentation made in furtherance of [a] fraudulent scheme" because "[i]t would be unjust to employ a presumption to relieve a party of its burden of production when that party has all the evidence regarding that element of the claim"). The defendants contend that, because each individual plaintiff must specifically show that he, personally, relied on the misstatements at issue, this individualized issue necessarily predominates. . . .

Under well-established Eleventh Circuit precedent, the simple fact that reliance is an element in a cause of action is not an absolute bar to class certification. . . .

[W]hile each plaintiff must prove his own reliance in this case, we believe that, based on the nature of the misrepresentations at issue, the circumstantial evidence that can be used to show reliance is common to the whole class. That is, the same considerations could lead a reasonable factfinder to conclude beyond a preponderance of the evidence that each individual plaintiff relied on the defendants' representations.

The alleged misrepresentations in the instant case are simply that the defendants repeatedly claimed they would reimburse the plaintiffs for medically necessary services they provide to the defendants' insureds, and sent the plaintiffs various EOB forms claiming that they had actually paid the plaintiffs the proper amounts. While the EOB forms may raise substantial individualized issues of reliance, the antecedent representations about the defendants' reimbursement practices do not. It does not strain credulity to conclude that each plaintiff, in entering into contracts with the defendants, relied upon the defendants' representations and assumed they would be paid the amounts they were due. A jury could quite reasonably infer that guarantees concerning physician pay—the very consideration upon which those agreements are based—go to the heart of these agreements, and that doctors based their assent upon them. This is a far cry from the type of "presumed" reliance we invalidated [under RICO] in *Sikes*. Consequently, while each plaintiff must prove reliance, he or she may do so through common evidence (that is, through legitimate inferences based on the nature of the alleged misrepresentations at issue). For this reason, this is not a case in which individualized issues of reliance predominate over common questions.

3.

The defendants point out that individualized determinations are necessary to determine the extent of damages allegedly suffered by each plaintiff. While this is undoubtedly true, it is insufficient to defeat class certification under Rule 23(b)(3). "[N]umerous courts have recognized that the presence of individualized damages issues does not prevent a finding that the common issues in the case predominate." *Allapattah Servs. v. Exxon Corp.*, 333 F.3d 1248, 1261 (11th Cir. 2003), *reh'g en banc denied*, 362 F.3d 739 (11th Cir. 2004); see, e.g., *In re Tri–State Crematory Litig.*, 215 F.R.D. 660, 692 n.20 (N.D. Ga. 2003) ("The requirement of determination of damages on an individual basis does not foreclose a finding of predominance or defeat certification of the class.").

"[I]n assessing whether to certify a class, the Court's inquiry is limited to whether or not the proposed methods [for computing damages] are so insubstantial as to amount to no method at all. . . . [Plaintiffs] need only come forward with plausible statistical or economic methodologies to demonstrate impact on a class-wide basis." *In re Terazosin Hydrochloride Antitrust Litig.*, 220 F.R.D. 672, 698 (S.D. Fla. 2004) (quotation marks omitted). Particularly where damages can be computed according to some formula, statistical analysis, or other easy or essentially mechanical methods, the fact that damages must be calculated on an individual basis is no impediment to class certification.

It is primarily when there are significant individualized questions going to liability exist that the need for individualized assessments of damages is enough to preclude 23(b)(3) certification. See, e.g., *Sikes*, 281 F.3d at 1366 ("These claims will involve extensive individualized inquiries on the issues of injury and damages—so much so that a class action is not sustainable."); *Rutstein*, 211 F.3d at 1234, 1240 (declining to certify a class because "most, if not all, of the plaintiffs' claims will stand or fall . . . on the resolution of . . . highly case-specific factual issues" and "liability for damages is a necessarily individualized inquiry"). Of course, there are also extreme cases in which computation of each individual's damages will be so complex, fact-specific, and difficult that the burden on the court system would be simply intolerable, see, e.g., *Windham v. Am. Brands, Inc.*, 565 F.2d 59, 70 (4th Cir. 1977) ("The district court estimated—conservatively, we think—that in the absence of a practical damage formula, determination of individual damages in this case could consume ten years of its time. The propriety of placing such a burden on already strained judicial resources seems unjustified."), but we emphasize that such cases rarely, if ever, come along.

In this case, even though individualized damage inquiries are necessary, many of them can be accomplished simply through reference to the HCFA–1500 forms or the HMO's records of which patients registered with doctors who are reimbursed through a capitation system. In addition, even if many plaintiffs' claims require corroboration and individualized consideration, such inquiries are outweighed by the predominating fact that the defendants allegedly conspired to commit, and proceeded to engage in, a pattern of racketeering activities to further their Managed Care Enterprise. It is ridiculous to expect 600,000 doctors across the nation to repeatedly prove these complicated and overwhelming facts.

D.

Because we are reviewing the district court's certifications under an abuse of discretion standard, we affirm. Nevertheless, it seems that the plaintiffs could comfortably be split into two Subclasses based on their reimbursement scheme: those operating on a fee-for-service basis and those with capitation contracts. While the existence of the conspiracy is equally relevant to both groups of plaintiffs, it seems that the capitation providers' claims revolve around some additional common issues that are not relevant to the fee-for-service providers. Moreover, because the capitation providers' primary allegation is that the HMOs did not pay them for all the patients actually registered to them, their individualized damage inquiries seem to be limited to an examination of the HMOs' records, and do not require as much potentially in-depth analysis as the fee-for-service providers' claims. Because this issue was not raised on appeal, however, we leave it to the district court to consider in the first instance whether the creation of these Subclasses might be a superior way of proceeding.

III.

. . .

A.

The plaintiffs' breach of contract claims are not amenable to class certification under Rule 23(b)(3) because, although they are based on questions of contract law that are common to the whole class, the individualized issues of fact they entail will probably predominate. These claims allege that "Defendants have breached their obligation to pay Plaintiffs and class members for medically necessary services in accordance with their contractual obligations."

. . . It goes without saying that class certification is impossible where the fifty states truly establish a large number of different legal standards governing a particular claim. . . .

On the other hand, if a claim is based on a principle of law that is uniform among the states, class certification is a realistic possibility. . . .

Similarly, if the applicable state laws can be sorted into a small number of groups, each containing materially identical legal standards, then certification of subclasses embracing each of the dominant legal standards can be appropriate. In such a case, of course, a court must be careful not to certify too many groups. "If more than a few of the laws of the fifty states differ, the district judge would face an impossible task of instructing a jury on the relevant law. . . ." *In re Am. Med. Sys.*, 75 F.3d 1069, 1085 (6th Cir. 1996).

The burden of showing uniformity or the existence of only a small number of applicable standards (that is, "groupability") among the laws of the fifty states rests squarely with the plaintiffs. . . .

In this case, the plaintiffs allege that the only real legal issue pertinent to their breach of contract claims is the definition of "breach," which does not differ from state to state. . . . "Whether [a] contract[ ] . . . has been breached is a pure and simple question of contract interpretation which should not vary from state to state." *Indianer v. Franklin Life Ins. Co.*, 113 F.R.D. 595, 607 (S.D. Fla. 1986), *overruled in part on other grounds by Ericsson GE Mobile Communs., Inc. v. Motorola Communs. & Elecs., Inc.*, 120 F.3d 216, 219 n.12 (11th Cir. 1997). . . . [W]e are inclined to agree. A breach is a breach is a breach. . . .See *Black's Law Dictionary* 200 (8th ed. 2004) (defining "breach of contract" as "[v]iolation of a contractual obligation by failing to perform one's own promise").

Moreover, while the plaintiffs' breach of contract claims necessarily implicate the contract law of all fifty states (since members of the putative class practice in every jurisdiction in the country), the defendants fail to argue on appeal that there are any relevant differences in the applicable laws among these jurisdictions. Their brief fails to point to any material differences among state laws addressing breaches of contract. Consequently, we accept the proposition that the applicable state laws governing contract interpretation and breach are sufficiently identical to constitute common legal issues in this case.

While this relatively simple issue of law is common to all the breach of contract claims, it is far outweighed by the individualized issues of fact pertinent to these claims. The plaintiffs contend that all of the agreements at issue require that doctors be reimbursed at a "reasonable rate" for the "medically necessary" services they provide. We nevertheless recognize that this case involves the actions of many defendants over a significant period of time and that each defendant throughout this period utilized many different form contracts. Indeed, each defendant contracted with different types of care-providing entities, including individual physicians, partnerships, medical practice groups, and the like, each of which necessitated a different type of contract. The sheer number of contracts involved is one factor that makes us hesitant to conclude that common issues of fact predominate; this is not a situation in which all plaintiffs signed the same form contract. . . .

The facts that the defendants conspired to underpay doctors, and that they programmed their computer systems to frequently do so in a variety of ways, do nothing to establish that any individual doctor was underpaid on any particular occasion. The evidence that each doctor must introduce to make out each breach claim is essentially the same whether or not a general conspiracy or policy of breaching existed. For example, regardless of whether facts about the conspiracy or computer programs are proven, each doctor, for each alleged breach of contract (that is, each alleged underpayment), must prove the services he provided, the request for reimbursement he submitted, the amount to which he was entitled, the amount he actually received, and the insufficiency of the HMO's reasons for denying full payment. There are no common issues of fact that relieve each plaintiff of a substantial portion of this individual evidentiary burden. While allegations concerning the defendants' conspiracy to underpay doctors, or their policy of and aiding and abetting each other in underpaying doctors, went directly to material elements of each individual plaintiff's RICO claim, here they are, at best, merely circumstantial evidence tangentially relevant to each individual plaintiff's breach of contract claim.

Another crucial reason why the plaintiffs cannot establish predominance of classwide facts on their breach of contract claims is that, although each of the defendants allegedly breached their contracts in the same general ways, they did so through a variety of specific means that are not subject to generalized proof for a large number of physicians. . . .

The algorithms by which the computer programs allegedly groups procedures appear to be . . . varied and complicated. . . . Instead of applying one specific universal rule to cheat all doctors (e.g. automatically deducting $100 from everyone's claim), the reimbursement programs are instead alleged to apply a variety of more individually tailored rules, each of which applies to only a subset of the plaintiff class. For example, if the doctors proved that the programs automatically grouped together all lung transplants with all heart transplants, reimbursing all doctors who submitted a claim for both only for heart transplants, this fact would be irrelevant to the breach of contract claims of most members of the plaintiff class. Instead, such proof would be relevant only to those doctors who submitted a reimbursement request for both a heart transplant and lung transplant on the same patient. . . .

The same reasoning applies to the plaintiffs' claim that the programs used by the defendants sometimes improperly drop modifiers from doctors' reimbursement requests. . . .

Because the program does not always automatically drop all modifiers, however, or always ignore a particular modifier under a set of circumstances applicable to most or all applicants (e.g., if it automatically dropped modifiers whenever the total amount of reimbursement sought in a claim was over $200), this allegation is not susceptible to classwide proof. Even if the plaintiffs were to prove that the computer systems "sometimes" improperly drops "certain" modifiers, this fact would do nothing to further any of the plaintiffs' individual breach of contract claims. Each plaintiff would still have to establish that he submitted a claim containing a modifier warranting increased payment, that use of the modifier was justified in that particular situation, and that the HMO's computer program improperly dropped it. Generalized evidence that the programs sometimes drops modifiers would not help each plaintiff in satisfying his burden of proof of demonstrating that a modifier was improperly dropped in his particular case. Furthermore, even if the plaintiffs were able to establish that modifiers were automatically dropped in particular situations not applicable to most of the 600,000 plaintiffs involved in this case (e.g., the program automatically dropped "complex" modifiers whenever the underlying procedure was a hysterectomy), such proof would be irrelevant to the large majority of doctors who had not submitted a claim for that particular procedure with the particular modifier at issue.

Similar reasoning applies to the other ways in which the HMOs allegedly breached their contracts with the fee-for-service providers, such as the defendants' alleged downcoding and denial of payment practices. While some of the capitation claims may have been suitable for class treatment, no capitation provider subclasses were requested or certified. . . .

For these reasons, we conclude that, even though the plaintiffs' breach of contract claims involve some relatively simple common issues of law and possibly some common issues of fact, individualized issues of fact predominate. Consequently, the district court abused its discretion in certifying these claims for classwide treatment.

[The court went on to overturn class certification as to the plaintiffs' state-law claims for unjust enrichment and violation of various "prompt-pay" statutes.]

IV.

The preceding Parts focused exclusively on whether common issues of fact and law stemming from the plaintiffs' federal and state claims predominate over individualized issues. We held that while the plaintiffs' federal claims satisfy this requirement, their state claims do not. We now turn to whether the plaintiffs' federal claims satisfy the second prong of the Rule 23(b)(3) test—that "a class action is superior to other available methods for the fair and efficient adjudication of the [claims]." Our focus is not on the convenience or burden of a class action suit *per se*, but on the relative advantages of a class action suit over whatever other forms of litigation might be realistically available to the plaintiffs.

In many respects, the predominance analysis of Part II has a tremendous impact on the superiority analysis of this Part for the simple reason that, the more common issues predominate over individual issues, the more desirable a class action lawsuit will be as a vehicle for adjudicating the plaintiffs' claims. Rule 23(b)(3) contains a "non exhaustive" list of four factors courts should take into account in making this determination:

> (A) the class members' interests in individually controlling the prosecution or defense of separate actions;

> (B) the extent and nature of any litigation concerning the controversy already begun by or against class members;

> (C) the desirability or undesirability of concentrating the litigation of the claims in the particular forum; and

> (D) the likely difficulties in managing a class action.

Fed. R. Civ. P. 23(b)(3). There is no reason to believe that the putative class members in this case have any particular interest in controlling their own litigation, so the first factor does not counsel against class certification. Similarly, there are no class members separately pursuing other cases involving the same claims and parties, so the second specified factor does not aid the defendants, either. The parties focus most of their discussion on the remaining two factors—the desirability of litigating these claims in a single forum, and the manageability of such a large case. We address each of these concerns in turn. We then turn to two additional arguments against class certification raised by the defendants.

A.

The first factor the parties seriously contest is whether it is desirable to concentrate this litigation in a single forum. Once the plaintiffs establish that common issues of fact and law predominate over individualized issues, there are typically three main reasons why it is desirable to litigate multiple parties' claims in a single forum. First, class actions "offer[ ] substantial economies of time, effort, and expense for the litigants . . . as well as for the [c]ourt." *Terazosin Litig.*, 220 F.R.D. at 700. Holding separate trials for claims that could be tried together "would be costly, inefficient, and would burden the court system" by forcing individual plaintiffs to repeatedly prove the same facts and make the same legal arguments before different courts. *Id.* Where predominance is established, this consideration will almost always mitigate in favor of certifying a class.

Second, as the Supreme Court has recognized in a related context, class actions often involve "an aggregation of small individual claims, where a large number of claims are required to make it economical to bring suit. The plaintiff's claim may be so small, or the plaintiff so unfamiliar with the law, that he would not file suit individually. . . ." *Phillips Petroleum Co. v. Shutts*, 472 U.S. 797, 813 (1985). . . . This consideration supports class certification in cases . . . where, as here, the amounts in controversy would make it unlikely that most of the plaintiffs, or attorneys working on a contingency fee basis, would be willing to pursue the claims individually. This is especially true when the defendants are corporate behemoths with a demonstrated willingness and proclivity for drawing out legal proceedings for as long as humanly possible and burying their opponents in paperwork and filings.

Third, it is desirable to concentrate claims in a particular forum when that forum has already handled several preliminary matters. In this case, various individual claims were consolidated before the district court by the Panel on Multidistrict Litigation, and the court has done a fine job in addressing a wide range of pretrial motions. While such extensive work is by no means necessary for us to conclude that concentration of the claims in a class action in a single forum is desirable, in this case it is impossible to overlook the significant efforts that have already been put into these proceedings. Consequently, the most common factors for assessing whether it is desirable for the plaintiffs' claims to be litigated in a single forum point to class certification in this case.

. . . At least one district court in our circuit has suggested that, in considering whether it is desirable to have all putative class members' claims litigated in a single forum, we should consider whether the theories under which they seek relief are "immature"—that is, relatively new or innovative. In *Jacobs v. Osmose, Inc.*, the district court held,

> Class action treatment is not the superior method for handling this matter. A mass tort such as this cannot properly be certified without a prior track record from which this Court would be able to draw the information necessary to make the predominance analysis required under Rule 23. Certification of an "immature" tort results in a higher than normal risk that the class action may not be superior to individual adjudication. Any savings in judicial resources in this case is speculative. . . .

213 F.R.D. 607, 618 (S.D. Fla. 2003); see also *Castano*, 84 F.3d at 749 ("In the context of an immature tort, any savings in judicial resources is speculative, and any imagined savings would be overwhelmed by the procedural problems that certification of a *sui generis* cause of action brings with it.").

None of our cases has ever held the "maturity" of a tort to be a proper consideration in the certification decision. Without delving into whether the plaintiffs' claims in this case are sufficiently new or innovative to count as an "immature" tort under the *Osmose* standard, we reject this as a legitimate consideration in making a "superiority" determination. There is no reason why, even with so-called "immature torts," district and circuit courts cannot make the necessary determinations under Rule 23 based on the pleadings and whatever evidence has been gathered through discovery. Moreover, there is no basis in Rule 23 for arbitrarily foreclosing plaintiffs from pursuing innovative theories through the vehicle of a class action lawsuit. Particularly when the considerations discussed at the beginning of this Section would preclude most plaintiffs from individually litigating their personal claims, a class action may be the only way that most people can have their rights—even "innovative" or "immature" rights—enforced. Furthermore, if an "immature tort" truly raises a variety of new or complicated legal questions, then those questions constitute significant common issues of law. Their resolution in a single class-action forum would greatly foster judicial efficiency and avoid unnecessary, repetitious litigation. For these reasons, it is desirable to litigate the plaintiffs' federal claims in a single forum.

B.

The final factor expressly specified in Rule 23(b)(3) that courts must weigh in deciding to certify a class action is whether certification will cause manageability problems. . . .

In this case, the district court concluded that there were no "unsurmountable difficulties" with managing the case. *Managed Care Litig.*, 209 F.R.D. at 696. While recognizing that "[r]eliance, causation and damages *may* create complications during the course of this litigation," the court found that "the potential difficulties are nowhere near the magnitude of problems that could arise from 600,000 separate actions." *Id.* at 696–97.

In reviewing this determination, we recall two points generally applicable throughout this "superiority" analysis. First, we are not assessing whether this class action will create significant management problems, but instead determining whether it will create relatively more management problems than any of the alternatives (including, most notably, 600,000 separate lawsuits by the class members). Second, where a court has already made a finding that common issues predominate over individualized issues, we would be hard pressed to conclude that a class action is less manageable than individual actions. . . .

[W]e hold that the district court acted well within its discretion in concluding that it would be better to handle this case as a class action instead of clogging the federal courts with innumerable individual suits litigating the same issues repeatedly. The defendants have failed to point to any specific management problems—aside from the obvious ones that are intrinsic in large class actions—that would render a class action impracticable in this case.

C.

Moving beyond the factors enumerated in Rule 23(b)(3), the defendants offer two additional reasons why a class action is inferior to a host of individual suits in resolving these disputes. First, they maintain that "a single jury, in a single trial, should not decide the fate of the managed care industry." Courts have occasionally found the impact that a class action suit could potentially have on an industry to be a persuasive reason to prohibit a class action from proceeding. [Citing *Rhone–Poulenc*.]

We find such reasoning unpersuasive and contrary to the ends of justice. This trial is not about the managed care industry; it is about whether several large HMOs conspired to systematically underpay doctors. The issue is not whether managed care is wrong, but whether particular managed care companies failed to live up to their agreements. The plaintiffs are seeking nothing more than the compensatory damages to which they are contractually entitled, and the treble damages to which they are statutorily entitled [under RICO].

We have nothing but the defendants' conclusory, self-serving speculations to support their claim that this trial could devastate the managed care industry. [I]f their fears are truly justified, the defendants can blame no one but themselves. It would be unjust to allow corporations to engage in rampant and systematic wrongdoing, and then allow them to avoid a class action because the consequences of being held accountable for their misdeeds would be financially ruinous. We are courts of justice, and can give the defendants only that which they deserve; if they wish special favors such as protection from high—though deserved—verdicts, they must turn to Congress.

D.

Second, the defendants contend that a class action creates "unfair and coercive pressures on [them]" to settle that are unrelated to the merits of the plaintiffs' claims. . . .

Mere pressure to settle is not a sufficient reason for a court to avoid certifying an otherwise meritorious class action suit. See *MasterMoney Antitrust Litig.*, 280 F.3d at 145 ("The effect of certification on parties' leverage in settlement negotiations is a fact of life for class action litigants. While the sheer size of the class in this case may enhance this effect, this alone cannot defeat an otherwise proper certification."); *Waste Mgmt. Holdings, Inc. v. Mowbray*, 208 F.3d 288, 295 (1st Cir. 2000) ("[N]o matter how strong the economic pressure to settle, a Rule 23(f) application, in order to succeed, also must demonstrate some significant weakness in the class certification decision.").

Indeed, settlement pressures have already been taken into account in the structure of Rule 23; such pressures were the main reason behind the enactment of Rule 23(f), which allowed the defendants to pursue this appeal in the first place. Having already used settlement pressure as a basis for getting into this court on interlocutory appeal, the defendants cannot continue to rely upon it as the basis for overturning the underlying certification ruling.

Moreover, while affirming certification may induce some defendants to settle, overturning certification may create similar "hydraulic" pressures on the plaintiffs, causing them to either settle or—more likely—abandon their claims altogether. Because one of the parties will generally be disadvantaged regardless of how a court rules on certification, this factor should not be weighed.

V.

For the reasons articulated above, we affirm the district court's grants of class certification as to all RICO-related claims, though we urge it to reconsider the precise scope of the classes, and reverse the district court's grant of class certification as to [the] state-law [breach-of-contract, unjust enrichment, and prompt-pay] claims. . . .

Given the number of parties involved in this case, it threatens to degenerate into a Hobbesian war of all against all. Nevertheless, we feel that the district court—a veritable Leviathan—will be able to prevent the parties from regressing to a state of nature. One can only hope that, on remand, the proceedings will be short, though preferably not nasty and brutish.

SO ORDERED.

NOTES AND QUESTIONS

1.   *Civil RICO Claims.* Why, as a strategic matter, would class counsel find attractive the notion of challenging the payment practices of the defendant managed care industry as a violation of RICO? Consider the overview of RICO provided in a leading treatise on federal criminal law:

> Passed in 1970 as part of a major crime fighting bill, RICO's stated goal is to protect the public from "parties who conduct organizations affecting interstate commerce through a pattern of racketeering activity." According to legislative history a statute like RICO is needed because of the "insulation" crime chieftains have developed: "Their operating methods, carefully and cleverly evolved during decades of this century, generally are highly effective foils against diligent police efforts to obtain firm evidence that would lead to prosecution and conviction."
>
> One of the unique features of RICO is that it authorizes both criminal and civil claims for a violation of its provisions. Thus, the

United States Department of Justice may seek a criminal indictment or file a civil complaint alleging RICO violations. In addition, private parties may file a complaint alleging the same RICO violations. RICO has become renown, in part, because of the stiff sanctions it provides for violations[,] . . .[including] criminal convictions, treble damages and attorneys fees for civil judgments.

2 Sarah N. Welling, Sara Sun Beale & Pamela H. Bucy, FEDERAL CRIMINAL LAW AND RELATED ACTIONS § 21.1, at 233 (1998). The Supreme Court has described the legal framework for civil claims under RICO as follows:

RICO's private right of action is contained in 18 U.S.C. § 1964(c), which provides in relevant part that "[a]ny person injured in his business or property by reason of a violation of section 1962 of this chapter may sue therefor in any appropriate United States district court and shall recover threefold the damages he sustains and the cost of the suit, including a reasonable attorney's fee." Section 1962 contains RICO's criminal prohibitions. [Among other prohibitions within this section,] § 1962(c) . . . makes it "unlawful for any person employed by or associated with" an enterprise engaged in or affecting interstate or foreign commerce "to conduct or participate, directly or indirectly, in the conduct of such enterprise's affairs through a pattern of racketeering activity." The term "racketeering activity" is defined to include a host of so-called predicate acts, including "any act which is indictable under . . . section 1341 (relating to mail fraud)." § 1961(1)(B).

The upshot is that RICO provides a private right of action for treble damages to any person injured in his business or property by reason of the conduct of a qualifying enterprise's affairs through a pattern of acts indictable as mail fraud. Mail fraud, in turn, occurs whenever a person, "having devised or intending to devise any scheme or artifice to defraud," uses the mail "for the purpose of executing such scheme or artifice or attempting so to do." § 1341. The gravamen of the offense is the scheme to defraud, and any "mailing that is incident to an essential part of the scheme satisfies the mailing element," *Schmuck v. United States*, 489 U.S. 705, 712 (1989), even if the mailing itself "contain[s] no false information," *id.* at 715.

. . . [Section] 1964(c)'s "language can, of course, be read to mean that a plaintiff is injured 'by reason of' a RICO violation, and therefore may recover, simply on showing that the defendant violated § 1962, the plaintiff was injured, and the defendant's violation was a 'but for' cause of plaintiff's injury." [*Holmes v. Sec. Investor Prot. Corp.*, 503 U.S. 258, 265–66 (1992).] We nonetheless held that not "all factually injured plaintiffs" may recover under § 1964(c). *Id.* at 266. Because Congress modeled § 1964(c) on other provisions that had been interpreted to "requir[e] a showing that the defendant's violation not only was a 'but for' cause of his injury, but was the proximate cause as well," we concluded that § 1964(c) likewise requires the plaintiff to establish proximate cause in order to show injury "by reason of" a RICO violation. *Id.* at 268.

. . . [W]e "use[d] 'proximate cause' to label generically the judicial tools used to limit a person's responsibility for the consequences of that person's own acts," *Holmes*, 503 U.S. at 268, with a particular emphasis on the "demand for some direct relation between the injury asserted and the injurious conduct alleged," *id*. . . . The direct-relation requirement avoids the difficulties associated with attempting "to ascertain the amount of a plaintiff's damages attributable to the violation, as distinct from other, independent, factors," [*id.*] at 269; prevents courts from having "to adopt complicated rules of apportioning damages among plaintiffs removed at different levels of injury from the violative acts, to obviate the risk of multiple recoveries," *id.*; and recognizes the fact that "directly injured victims can generally be counted on to vindicate the law as private attorneys general, without any of the problems attendant upon suits by plaintiffs injured more remotely," *id.* at 269–70.

Bridge v. Phoenix Bond & Indemnity Co., 553 U.S. 639, 647, 653–54 (2008). See also *Hemi Group, LLC v. City of New York*, 130 S.Ct. 983 (2010) (reaffirming *Bridge* but also distinguishing it on the ground that the causation theory in *Bridge* was "straightforward").

2.   *Reliance under RICO Since* Klay. At the time of *Klay*, Eleventh Circuit precedents—indeed, the decisions of several other circuits—read civil RICO to include a reliance element. The Supreme Court subsequently held otherwise. In *Bridge*, the Court clarified that "a plaintiff asserting a RICO claim predicated on mail fraud need not show, either as an element of its claim or as a prerequisite to establishing proximate causation, that it relied on the defendant's alleged misrepresentations." *Id.* at 661. Writing for a unanimous Court, Justice Thomas grounded the holding in *Bridge* squarely on the statutory language of RICO, which nowhere states a reliance element. To the contrary, the relevant language lists mail fraud among the possible predicate acts of racketeering under RICO "even if no one relied on any misrepresentations," and the statute then goes on to confer a private right of action to all persons injured "by reason of" such acts. *Id.* at 649. "[A] person can be injured 'by reason of' a pattern of mail fraud even if he has not relied on any misrepresentations." *Id.* at 640.

3.   *Reliance under State Consumer Fraud Statutes*. The observation that civil RICO includes no reliance element does not mean that the class certification analysis in *Klay* is somehow irrelevant. The treatment of the reliance element of *state*-law claims sounding in fraud or misrepresentation forms a recurring question in much class action litigation involving consumer rights. Samuel Issacharoff, *The Vexing Problem of Reliance in Consumer Class Actions*, 74 Tul. L. Rev. 1633 (2000). Whether the reliance element should prevent class certification in a given instance may well depend upon how the applicable substantive law conceptualizes that element. Consider the following variations, among others that one might posit:

	Applicable Substantive Law Uses a Subjective Standard for Reliance	Applicable Substantive Law Uses an Objective, Reasonable–Person Standard for Reliance
Differences in Defendant's Alleged Conduct via-à-vis Individual Class Members	Scenario 1	Scenario 2
Defendant's Alleged Conduct Takes the Form of Standardized Representations	Scenario 3	Scenario 4

Which of these scenarios would be most amenable to class treatment?

4. *The Treatment of Damages in the Predominance Analysis.* Why does the court ultimately conclude that the need to determine damages on an individual basis nevertheless does not undermine the predominance of common issues with regard to the plaintiffs' RICO claims? In what other contexts for class action litigation would you expect a similar analysis of the damage calculus to hold sway?

5. *Contrasting the RICO Analysis and the State–Law Breach-of-Contract Analysis.* What ultimately explains the amenability of the RICO claims to class treatment under Rule 23(b)(3), in contrast to the non-amenability of the state-law breach-of-contract claims to such treatment? Are the RICO claims, in some sense, inherently focused upon the defendants' alleged misconduct in the aggregate in a way that the state-law breach-of-contract claims are not?

6. *The Significance of a Common Body of Evidence.* The court in *Klay* holds that class treatment is appropriate for the federal RICO claims because the plaintiff class sought to rely on a common body of evidence to prove the (supposed) reliance element. Contrast the result in *Klay* with respect to certification of the federal RICO claims with the result in *Poulos v. Caesars World, Inc.*, 379 F.3d 654 (9th Cir. 2004). In *Poulos*, the proposed plaintiff class of casino patrons sued the manufacturers of video gaming equipment under RICO, alleging that the manufacturers had made various misrepresentations concerning the mathematical gambling odds applicable to their machines. The court noted that the plaintiff class sought to rely on a common body of evidence but nonetheless deemed class certification to be inappropriate. Even if the jury were to conclude that the defendants had made the misrepresentations attributed to them by the plaintiff class and, further, that all class members suffered concrete injuries as a result of losing money on the contested video gambling machines, those conclusions on the jury's part still would not have necessitated a finding that the plaintiffs' injuries were causally linked to the defendants' misrepresentations. *Id.* at 665. The court observed:

> [G]ambling is not a context in which we can assume that potential class members are always similarly situated. Gamblers do not share a common universe of knowledge and expectations—one motivation does not "fit all." Some players may be unconcerned with the odds of winning, instead engaging in casual gambling as entertainment or a social activity. Others may have played with absolutely no knowledge or information regarding the odds of winning such that the appearance and labeling of the machines is irrelevant and did nothing to influence their perceptions. Still others, in the spirit of taking a calculated risk, may have played fully aware of how the machines operate. Thus, to prove proximate causation *in this case*, an individualized showing of reliance is required.

Id. at 665–66. Is the outcome on the class certification question in *Poulos* inconsistent with *Klay*?

7. *Rethinking Predominance.* Perhaps the most practical observation advanced by the court in *Klay* is that "the predominance analysis [under Rule 23(b)(3)] has a tremendous impact on the superiority analysis . . . for the simple

reason that, the more common issues predominate over individual issues, the more desirable a class action lawsuit will be as a vehicle for adjudicating the plaintiffs' claims." If that is true, then what does the superiority analysis add to the Rule 23(b)(3) class certification decision? One can ask the same question in the opposite way: What does predominance add to the superiority requirement? If a class action is superior to other available methods for adjudicating the claims, then why not certify a class? Consider the following critique of the predominance requirement:

> The basic problem with the predominance test is that it requires elaborate efforts to answer a question that is not worth asking. . . . The predominance inquiry fixates on the notion that class actions are viable when class members share similar factual circumstances and raise similar legal questions. However, similarity among claims is an unhelpful concept when one thinks about the practical consequences of certifying a class and the procedural principles to which class adjudication should conform. A more relevant concept is *dis*similarity. The existence of some similarity within the class is what makes class actions potentially efficient and appealing, but it is the lack of substantial dissimilarity that makes class actions a fair and procedurally viable means of rendering judgment for or against the class and its members. The predominance concept conflates the similarity and dissimilarity inquiries into a single balancing test, thus obscuring the practical and theoretical importance of dissimilarity standing alone.

> . . . When individual questions of law or fact unique to particular class members raise insurmountable obstacles to class adjudication, then the number and importance of common questions is irrelevant. On the other hand, if the proposed class action would be "superior" to possible alternative forms of litigation even accounting for the efforts needed to cope with difficult—yet manageable—individualized issues, then denying certification based on an arbitrary notion of whether common questions "predominate" would be gratuitous. Individualized questions of law or fact viewed in isolation thus either should or should not preclude certification in any particular case; their relative "predominance" with respect to common questions should neither salvage an otherwise uncertifiable class nor derail a class that should otherwise be certified. Certification rules relying on the "predominance" test thus enshrine a pointless concept that obscures the need to evaluate individual questions of law and fact directly rather than in comparison to common questions.

> Having rejected the predominance test, I propose . . . a "resolvability" test that would reconcile the practical demands of class litigation with theoretical constraints. The new test would permit certification only when the court has a feasible plan to answer all disputed questions of law and fact that must be resolved before entering judgment for or against class members under the law governing each class member's claim and applicable defenses. . . . The new resolvability approach to dissimilarity would channel the inherent subjectivity of certification decisions along more clearly defined paths and would realign certification analysis with principled constraints from which the predominance test has drifted. Rules should ideally facilitate the

implementation of guiding principles, but the predominance test does the opposite, interposing a meaningless and distracting wedge between principle and practice.

Allan Erbsen, *From "Predominance" to "Resolvability": A New Approach to Regulating Class Actions*, 58 Vand. L. Rev. 995, 1005–06 (2005).

Do you agree with Professor Erbsen's critique? He seems puzzled by the predominance requirement. But doesn't it track an efficiency analysis fairly closely? If common questions are associated with cost savings and individual questions with cost increases, predominance could measure the net overall efficiency gains from class adjudication. Does that make sense?

Still, Professor Erbsen is correct that the idea of superiority can be construed to subsume this sort of efficiency analysis. Why then does (b)(3) include both predominance and superiority? Recall that the majority in *Amchem* referred to the predominance inquiry as "test[ing] whether proposed classes are sufficiently cohesive to warrant adjudication by representation." Moreover, when contrasting Rule 23(e), the Court said that predominance "assures the class cohesion that legitimizes representative action in the first place." Is the Court referring to efficiency? If not, what does it mean by class cohesiveness and why is cohesiveness important?

8. *Treatment of the Settlement Pressure Argument.* Is the Eleventh Circuit persuasive in its rejection of the settlement pressure argument advanced in such decisions as that of the Seventh Circuit in *Rhone–Poulenc*? Note, in particular, the inference drawn from the existence today of Rule 23(f).

9. *The Significance of Rule 23(c)(1)(B).* Added as part of the 2003 rule amendments and then restyled in 2007, Rule 23(c)(1)(B) provides that "[a]n order that certifies a class action must define the class and the class claims, issues, or defenses. . . ." In *Wachtel v. Guardian Life Ins. Co.*, 453 F.3d 179 (3d Cir. 2006), the Third Circuit addressed the practical importance of this provision. Like *Klay*, *Wachtel* concerned reimbursement practices in connection with health care services. The proposed plaintiff class in *Wachtel*, however, consisted not of physicians but, rather, of beneficiaries under various health insurance plans. The class challenged the defendants' use of, among other things, certain databases that allegedly resulted in systematic under-reimbursement of their health care bills. The district court certified the proposed class, but the Third Circuit reversed. In its opinion, the Third Circuit offered the first detailed judicial exposition of the meaning and importance of Rule 23(c)(1)(B):

> [W]e conclude that the plain text of the Subdivision, especially when considered in light of the text and structure of parallel provisions in Rule 23, indicate that Rule 23(c)(1)(B) requires district courts to include in class certification orders a clear and complete summary of those claims, issues, or defenses subject to class treatment.
>
> Current practice often falls short of that standard. . . . Although examples of common claims, issues, or defenses presented by the case may be discussed as part of the court's commonality, typicality, or predominance analysis, certification orders and memoranda are most often devoid of any clear statement regarding the full scope and parameters of the claims, issues or defenses to be treated on a class basis as the matter is litigated.

We conclude that the plain text of Rule 23(c) as amended requires more specific and more deliberate treatment of the class issues, claims, and defenses than the practice described above has usually reflected. More specifically, in our view, the proper substantive inquiry for an appellate tribunal reviewing a certification order for Rule 23(c)(1)(B) compliance is whether the precise parameters defining the class and a complete list of the claims, issues, or defenses to be treated on a class basis are readily discernible from the text either of the certification order itself or of an incorporated memorandum opinion.

We arrive at this conclusion primarily through textual analysis of Rule 23(c)(1)(B) itself. To "define" a thing or concept is "to state precisely or determinately [its boundaries]; to specify" or "[t]o frame or give a precise description" of a thing. *Oxford English Dictionary* (2d ed. 1989). According to the Rule, those things to be defined in a certification order include the "class *and* the class claims, issues, or defenses. . . ."

The substantive standard that we have laid out above also comports with and facilitates compliance with the textual requirements and apparent purpose of other provisions of Rule 23. For instance, Rule 23(c)(2) indicates that for any class certified under Rule 23(b)(1) or (2), "the court may direct appropriate notice to the class," Fed. R. Civ. P. 23(c)(2)(A), and that for any class certified under Rule 23(b)(3), "the court *must* direct to class members the best notice practicable under the circumstances." Fed. R. Civ. P. 23(c)(2)(B) (emphasis added). That notice must, *inter alia*, "concisely and clearly state . . . the definition of the class certified" and "the class claims, issues or defenses." *Id.* Clear and complete treatment of both the class and the class claims, issues, or defenses at the class certification stage will unquestionably facilitate the timely execution of what is almost always the next step—In fact, often a mandatory next step, see Fed. R. Civ. P. 23(c)(2)(B)—in class action litigation, namely the court-supervised distribution of class notice to class members.

Furthermore, compliance with the requirements of Rule 23(c)(1)(B) as we have defined them today will significantly aid appellate review of a district court's decision to certify a matter as a class action. Most significantly, it seems self-evident that a clear and complete statement of the claims, issues, or defenses to be treated on a class basis will shed light on a district court's numerosity, commonality, typicality, and predominance analysis under Rule 23(a) and (b). In addition, Rule 23(c)(4)(A) [restyled in 2007 as Rule 23(c)(4)] states that "[w]hen appropriate (A) an action may be brought or maintained as a class action with respect to particular issues. . . ." *Id.* Not only is there overlap between compliance with Rule 23(c)(1)(B) and compliance with Rule 23(c)(4)(A), but compliance with the former as we define it today will greatly facilitate meaningful appellate review of complex certification decisions regarding the latter.

Although we regard the plain text argument outlined above as sufficient to support our holding, we note that in addition to comporting with the text of the Rule itself, the standard for compliance with

Rule 23(c)(1)(B) that we outline today dovetails with the apparent purpose and goals of amending the Rule as expressed in the Advisory Committee Notes. . . .

In summary, we hold that the requirement of Rule 23(c)(1)(B) that a certification order "define the class and the class claims, issues, or defenses," means that the text of the order or an incorporated opinion must include (1) a readily discernible, clear, and precise statement of the parameters defining the class or classes to be certified, and (2) a readily discernible, clear, and complete list of the claims, issues or defenses to be treated on a class basis. . . .

Applying the above standard, we conclude that the Certification Order and accompanying Memorandum Opinion (collectively, the "Order") in the instant case fail to meet the substantive requirements of Rule 23(c)(1)(B). . . .

[T]he Order's discussion of class claims, issues, or defenses is unclear, intermittent, and incomplete, and nothing in the Order evidences an intent to explicitly define which claims, issues, or defenses are to be treated on a class basis for the remainder of the litigation. [Ed. Note: The court goes on to say that identification of some common issues in an exemplary fashion does not satisfy the requirement, nor do "general, non-exclusive statements" used to support a predominance finding. The court faults the district court for making these statements "in the course of analysis that is distinct from analysis meant to define class claims, issues, or defenses" and for making statements that do not "[address] with any precision or formality which claims, issues, or defenses will be litigated on a class basis moving forward."]

It is conceivable that we could cobble together the various statements quoted above and reach a general inference as to some categories of issues that the District Court believes are appropriate for class treatment. . . A certification order or opinion that requires a reviewing appellate court to comb the entirety of its text searching for isolated statements that may add up to a partial list of class claims, issues, or defenses falls short of the readily discernible and complete list of class claims, issues, or defenses required by the Rule. Under Rule 23(c)(1)(B), a sufficient certification order must, in some clear and cogent form, define the claims, issues, or defenses to be treated on a class basis. The instant Order fails to meet that requirement.

453 F.3d at 184–89. The Third Circuit continues to apply its strict interpretation of 23(c)(1)(B). See *In re Constar Int'l Inc. Sec. Litig.*, 585 F.3d 774, 782 (3d Cir. 2009) (concluding that the certification order complied with *Wachtel*'s requirements). Other circuits have also followed *Wachtel*'s interpretation of 23(c)(1)(B). See *Ross v. RBS Citizens*, 667 F.3d 900 (7th Cir. 2012) (adopting *Wachtel*'s interpretation but concluding that the putative class satisfied its requirements); *In re Pharm. Indus. Average Wholesale Price Litig.*, 588 F.3d 24, 38–41 (1st Cir. 2009) (citing *Wachtel* approvingly).

Is this all an exercise in hypertechnicality? Do the functional justifications offered by the court for Rule 23(c)(1)(B) arguably omit the *most* important justification? (Consider the language of Rule 23(c)(4), which is examined more extensively later in this Chapter.) Should Rule 23(c)(1)(B)'s requirements vary with the type of class action? For example, are 23(b)(2) class actions likely to benefit from definitional precision and specificity as much as 23(b)(3) class actions? See MANUAL FOR COMPLEX LITIGATION (FOURTH) § 22.222 (2004). For a criticism of the trend toward more stringent requirements for class definition, see Robert H. Klonoff, *The Decline of Class Actions*, 90 Wash. U. L. Rev. ___ (2013), available at http://papers.ssrn.com/sol3/papers.cfm?abstract_id=2038985, at pp. 34–41 (Nov. 28, 2012 draft).

2. MANDATORY CLASSES UNDER RULE 23(b)(1)–(2)

a. WHY MANDATORY CLASSES?

Given the Supreme Court's statement in *Shutts* that the opportunity to opt out is a component of constitutional due process with regard to class treatment of claims for legal relief (at least for those class members without minimum contacts), when—if ever—should class membership be mandatory? The phrasing of footnote 3 in *Shutts* itself implies the existence of at least one situation where mandatory class treatment is permissible: when the class seeks only equitable relief, such as an injunction to stop an ongoing course of conduct and/or a declaratory judgment to establish the illegality of such conduct. Subsection (b)(2) of Rule 23—as restyled in 2007—fits this category, providing for the certification of a mandatory class when "the party opposing the class has acted or refused to act on grounds that apply generally to the class, so that final injunctive relief or corresponding declaratory relief is appropriate respecting the class as a whole." Discussing subsection (b)(2), the rules advisory committee states:

> The subdivision does not extend to cases in which the appropriate final relief relates exclusively or predominantly to money damages. Action or inaction is directed to a class within the meaning of this subdivision even if it has taken effect or is threatened only as to one or a few members of the class, provided it is based on grounds which have general application to the class.

> Illustrative are various actions in the civil-rights field where a party is charged with discriminating unlawfully against a class, usually one whose members are incapable of specific enumeration. [Citing numerous such cases from the 1950s and 60s.] Subdivision (b)(2) is not limited to civil-rights cases. Thus an action looking to specific or declaratory relief could be brought by a numerous class of purchasers, say retailers of a given description, against a seller alleged to have undertaken to sell to that class at prices higher than those set for other purchasers, say retailers of another description, when the applicable law forbids such a pricing differential. So also a patentee of a machine, charged with selling or licensing the machine on condition that purchasers or licensees also purchase or obtain licenses to use an ancillary unpatented machine, could be sued on a class basis by a numerous group of purchasers or licensees, or by a numerous group of competing sellers or licensors of the unpatented machine, to test the legality of the "tying" condition.

As we shall see, much controversy has arisen from the advisory committee's statement that mandatory class treatment under subsection (b)(2) does not reach cases "in which the appropriate final relief relates exclusively *or pre-*

dominantly to money damages"—a statement implying that mandatory classes under subsection (b)(2) may encompass damage claims, to some non-predominant degree.

Unlike subsection (b)(2), subsection (b)(1)(A) does not refer by its terms to injunctive or declaratory relief. As restyled in 2007, subsection (b)(1)(A) does provide for the certification of a mandatory class when the prosecution of "separate actions by or against individual class members would create a risk of . . . inconsistent or varying adjudications with respect to individual class members that would establish incompatible standards of conduct for the party opposing the class." Speaking of subsection (b)(1)(A), the rules advisory committee states:

> One person may have rights against, or be under duties toward, numerous persons constituting a class, and be so positioned that conflicting or varying adjudications in lawsuits with individual members of the class might establish incompatible standards to govern his conduct. The class action device can be used effectively to obviate the actual or virtual dilemma which would thus confront the party opposing the class. The matter has been stated thus: "The felt necessity for a class action is greatest when the courts are called upon to order or sanction the alteration of the status quo in circumstances such that a large number of persons are in a position to call on a single person to alter the status quo, or to complain if it is altered, and the possibility exists that [the] actor might be called upon to act in inconsistent ways." Louisell & Hazard, *Pleading and Procedure: State and Federal* 719 (1962). . . . To illustrate: Separate actions by individuals against a municipality to declare a bond issue invalid or condition or limit it, to prevent or limit the making of a particular appropriation or to compel or invalidate an assessment, might create a risk of inconsistent or varying determinations. In the same way, individual litigations of the rights and duties of riparian owners, or of landowners' rights and duties respecting a claimed nuisance, could create a possibility of incompatible adjudications. Actions by or against a class provide a ready and fair means of achieving unitary adjudication. . . .

In practical operation, mandatory class treatment under subsection (b)(2) has converged substantially with mandatory class treatment under subsection (b)(1)(A). Describing "the type of class action context most likely to qualify for class treatment under Rule 23(b)(1)(A)," one leading treatise points to "a broad spectrum of class actions seeking declaratory or injunctive relief against a party opposing the class." 2 Alba Conte & Herbert B. Newberg, NEWBERG ON CLASS ACTIONS § 4:8, at 31–32 (4th ed. 2002). The same source adds that "[m]ost of these examples, particularly in the civil rights area, will also qualify as Rule 23(b)(2) class actions." *Id.* "Rule 23(b)(1)(A) class actions are not limited to those suits seeking primarily declaratory or injunctive relief. Monetary damages may be a major if not predominant form of relief sought." *Id.* § 4:8, at 32–33. This too is seemingly a feature of mandatory classes under subsection (b)(2), per the language of the rules advisory committee on that provision—at least insofar as monetary relief is not predominant. Recognizing this convergence in practice, this Chapter treats together, under the label of classes seeking "indivisible" relief, the authorization for mandatory class treatment provided in subsections (b)(1)(A) and (b)(2).

Does the convergence of practice under subsections (b)(1)(A) and (b)(2) shed light on the justification for mandatory class treatment in the situations described therein? What would happen if the kinds of actions described in those subsections were *not* treated by way of mandatory classes? Who stands to be protected by those subsections—the would-be class members or the defendant? On these questions, consider the law of issue preclusion in its current form, under which issue preclusion is not permissible *against* a non-party to the proceeding said to have preclusive effect but may be wielded *for* the benefit of a non-party against a party to the earlier proceeding, per *Parklane* from Chapter 1.

Rule 23 also provides for mandatory class treatment in the situations described in its subsection (b)(1)(B), when the prosecution of "separate actions by or against individual class members would create a risk of . . . adjudications with respect to individual class members that, as a practical matter, would be dispositive of the interests of the other members not parties to the individual adjudications or would substantially impair or impede their ability to protect their interests." As to subsection (b)(1)(B), the rules advisory committee explains:

This clause takes in situations where the judgment in a nonclass action by or against an individual member of the class, while not technically concluding the other members, might do so as a practical matter. The vice of an individual action would lie in the fact that the other members of the class, thus practically concluded, would have had no representation in the lawsuit. In an action by policy holders against a fraternal benefit association attacking a financial reorganization of the society, it would hardly have been practical, if indeed it would have been possible, to confine the effects of a validation of the reorganization to the individual plaintiffs. Consequently a class action was called for with adequate representation of all members of the class. . . . The same reasoning applies to an action which charges a breach of trust by an indenture trustee or other fiduciary similarly affecting the members of a large class of security holders or other beneficiaries, and which requires an accounting or like measures to restore the subject of the trust.

In various situations an adjudication as to one or more members of the class will necessarily or probably have an adverse practical effect on the interests of other members who should therefore be represented in the lawsuit. This is plainly the case when claims are made by numerous persons against a fund insufficient to satisfy all claims. A class action by or against representative members to settle the validity of the claims as a whole, or in groups, followed by separate proof of the amount of each valid claim and proportionate distribution of the fund, meets the problem. . . . The same reasoning applies to an action by a creditor to set aside a fraudulent conveyance by the debtor and to appropriate the property to his claim, when the debtor's assets are insufficient to pay all creditors' claims.

Does the rationale for mandatory class treatment under subsection (b)(1)(B) ultimately rest on considerations similar to those that support mandatory class treatment under subsections (b)(1)(A) and (b)(2)? Whom does subsection (b)(1)(B) stand to protect?

b. CLASSES FOR INDIVISIBLE RELIEF UNDER RULE 23(B)(1)(A) OR (B)(2)

As underscored earlier, the advisory committee notes on subsection (b)(2) explicitly recognize the possibility that the mandatory classes authorized thereunder might encompass damage claims to some non-predominant degree. And, as the passages from the Newberg treatise reflect, case law under subsection (b)(1)(A) has developed along similar lines. Is mandatory class treatment of damage claims, even to a non-predominant degree, constitutionally permissible in light of the due process checklist in *Shutts*? The following materials address this question and also explore some of the more difficult issues that arise when certifying mandatory class actions, especially in connection with claims for medical monitoring in tort litigation and for employment discrimination under Title VII of the Civil Rights Act.

(1) Mandatory Classes for Medical Monitoring

Barnes v. American Tobacco Co.

161 F.3d 127 (3d Cir. 1998)

■ SCIRICA, CIRCUIT JUDGE.

In this suit against the major American tobacco companies, we must decide whether a medical monitoring class should be certified under Federal Rule of Civil Procedure 23(b)(2). The District Court decertified a proposed class of cigarette smokers on the grounds that significant individual issues precluded certification. . . . We will affirm the District Court's decertification order. . . .

I.

FACTS AND PROCEDURAL HISTORY

Named plaintiffs . . . are Pennsylvania residents who began smoking cigarettes before the age of 15 and have smoked for many years. Plaintiffs filed suit against the defendant tobacco companies . . . on behalf of a purported class of over one million Pennsylvania cigarette smokers. In their prayer for relief, plaintiffs asked (1) that defendants fund a court-supervised or court approved program providing medical monitoring to class members; (2) for punitive damages to create a fund for common class-wide purposes, including medical research, public education campaigns, and smoking cessation programs; and (3) for other monetary and injunctive relief the court deemed just and proper.

A.

The District Court found the class did not meet the requirements of Rule 23(b)(2) or (b)(3). See *Arch v. The Am. Tobacco Co.*, 175 F.R.D. 469 (E.D. Pa. 1997). The District Court rejected Rule 23(b)(2) certification because plaintiffs had not primarily sought injunctive or equitable relief, finding that "[p]laintiffs' medical monitoring claim is merely a thinly disguised claim for future damages" and that "the overwhelming majority of relief sought by plaintiffs in their entire complaint is monetary in nature." *Id.* at 484. The court also found certification improper under Rule 23(b)(3) because issues common to the class did not predominate over plaintiffs' individual issues. . . .

The District Court suggested, however, that plaintiffs' request for a court-supervised program of medical monitoring to detect the latent diseases caused by smoking was the "paradigmatic" request for injunctive relief under a medical monitoring claim. . . .

Accordingly, the District Court granted plaintiffs leave to file an amended complaint. In their Second Amended Complaint, plaintiffs brought only one claim against defendants—medical monitoring. Moreover, plaintiffs eliminated all requests for smoking cessation programs, medical treatment programs, punitive damages, and restitutional damages; the only relief they sought was a court-supervised fund that would pay for medical examinations designed to detect latent diseases caused by smoking. Plaintiffs sought certification under Rule 23(b)(2) for "[a]ll current residents of Pennsylvania who are cigarette smokers as of December 1, 1996 [the day the amended complaint was filed in federal court] and who began smoking before age 19, while they were residents of Pennsylvania."

The Second Amended Complaint alleged that plaintiffs and other class members had been exposed to proven hazardous substances through the intentional or negligent actions of the defendants and/or through defective products for which defendants are strictly liable. Plaintiffs alleged that as a proximate result of this exposure, they and other class members suffer significantly increased risks of contracting serious latent diseases and therefore need periodic diagnostic medical examinations. Specifically, plaintiffs contended that classwide expert evidence would prove that: (1) when cigarettes are used as defendants intended them to be used, the vast majority of those who use cigarettes become addicted and (2) cigarettes are the leading cause in the nation of cardiovascular disease, lung cancer, and chronic obstructive pulmonary disease, due to the exposure of the throat, heart, and lungs to tobacco smoke.

Plaintiffs' physician experts designed the monitoring program using objective medical tests and age-graded criteria. They stated that cigarette smoking was the principal cause of lung cancer, cardiovascular disease, and chronic obstructive pulmonary disease, the three diseases to be monitored.

On August 22, 1997, the District Court conditionally certified the class under Rule 23(b)(2). . . .

Subsequently, defendants asked the court to certify the class certification order for interlocutory appeal or, in the alternative, to reconsider the order . The District Court denied defendants' request to certify or reconsider the class certification order but decertified the class under Rule 23(c)(1). . . .

Specifically, the court found three individual issues precluded class certification: addiction, causation, and affirmative defenses. . . .

III. DISCUSSION

A.   Medical Monitoring

The crucial issue is whether plaintiffs' medical monitoring claim requires inquiry into individual issues. We begin by briefly describing the evolution of this cause of action and its elements.

In *In re Paoli R.R. Yard PCB Litig.*, 916 F.2d 829 (3d Cir. 1990) (*Paoli I*), we predicted the Pennsylvania Supreme Court would recognize a cause of action for medical monitoring. We reaffirmed that prediction in *In re Paoli R.R. Yard PCB Litig.*, 35 F.3d 717 (3d Cir. 1994) (*Paoli II*). The issue of medical monitoring first reached the Pennsylvania Supreme Court in

Simmons v. Pacor, Inc., 543 Pa. 664, 674 A.2d 232 (Pa. 1996), where the unanimous court recognized medical monitoring as a viable cause of action under Pennsylvania law. In *Simmons*, the court permitted plaintiffs with asbestos-related asymptomatic pleural thickening to recover for medical monitoring. It was not until *Redland Soccer Club v. Dept. of the Army*, 548 Pa. 178, 696 A.2d 137 (Pa. 1997), however, that the Pennsylvania Supreme Court had the opportunity to articulate the specific elements of a claim for medical monitoring. Building on this court's decisions in *Paoli I* and *Paoli II*, the Supreme Court found that plaintiffs must prove the following elements:

[handwritten: Med Monitoring Claim]

> (1) exposure greater than normal background levels; (2) to a proven hazardous substance; (3) caused by the defendant's negligence; (4) as a proximate result of the exposure, plaintiff has a significantly increased risk of contracting a serious latent disease; (5) a monitoring procedure exists that makes the early detection of the disease possible; (6) the prescribed monitoring regime is different from that normally recommended in the absence of the exposure; and (7) the prescribed monitoring regime is reasonably necessary according to contemporary scientific principles.

Redland, 696 A.2d at 145–46.

[handwritten: Damages Remedy]

The injury in a cause of action for medical monitoring is the "costs of periodic medical examinations necessary to detect the onset of physical harm." *Id.* at 144. It is evident that this injury is somewhat different from an injury in a traditional tort, which rests on physical harm. In recognizing medical monitoring as a compensable injury, the Pennsylvania Supreme Court quoted at length from our distinction in *Paoli I* between a cause of action for increased risk of future harm and a cause of action for medical monitoring. We concluded that a claim for medical monitoring is different from a claim for increased risk of harm because the medical monitoring plaintiff has an identifiable rather than a speculative injury. We explained:

> The injury in an enhanced risk claim is the anticipated harm itself. The injury in a medical monitoring claim is the cost of the medical care that will, one hopes, detect that injury. The former is inherently speculative because courts are forced to anticipate the probability of future injury. The latter is much less speculative because the issue for the jury is the less conjectural question of whether the plaintiff needs medical surveillance.

Paoli I, 916 F.2d at 850–851.

In *Redland*, the court cited four important policy reasons for recognizing a cause of action for medical monitoring. First, medical monitoring promotes "early diagnosis and treatment of disease resulting from exposure to toxic substances caused by a tortfeasor's negligence." Second, "[a]llowing recovery for such expenses avoids the potential injustice of forcing an economically disadvantaged person to pay for expensive diagnostic examinations necessitated by another's negligence," and "affords toxic-tort victims, for whom other sorts of recovery may prove difficult, immediate compensation for medical monitoring needed as a result of exposure." Third, medical monitoring "furthers the deterrent function of the tort system by compelling those who expose others to toxic substances to minimize risks and costs of exposure." Finally, such recovery is "in harmony with 'the important public health interest in fostering access to medical testing for individuals

whose exposure to toxic chemicals creates an enhanced risk of disease.' "
Redland, 696 A.2d at 145 (citations omitted).

B.   Certification . . .

    2.   Fed. R. Civ. P. 23(b)(2). . .

While 23(b)(2) class actions have no predominance or superiority requirements, it is well established that the class claims must be cohesive.
Discussing the requirements for 23(b)(2) classes in *Wetzel v. Liberty Mutual
Ins. Co.,* 508 F.2d 239 (3d Cir. 1975), we noted, "[b]y its very nature, a (b)(2)
class must be cohesive as to those claims tried in the class action. . . . Because of the cohesive nature of the class, Rule 23(c)(3) contemplates that all members of the class will be bound. Any resultant unfairness
to the members of the class was thought to be outweighed by the purposes
behind class actions: eliminating the possibility of repetitious litigation and
providing small claimants with a means of obtaining redress for claims too
small to justify individual litigation." *Id.* at 248–49 (citations omitted). . . .[18]

    . . .In decertifying the class, the District Court decided that "too many
individual issues exist which prevent this case from proceeding as a class
action." *Barnes,* 176 F.R.D. at 500. As noted, the District Court found that
addiction, causation, and affirmative defenses all presented individual issues not properly decided in a class action. We believe that addiction, causation, the defenses of comparative and contributory negligence, the need
for medical monitoring and the statute of limitations present too many individual issues to permit certification. . . .[19]

    a.   Nicotine addiction and causation

    The District Court found nicotine addiction plays a central role in the
case and that addiction is a "highly individualistic inquiry." The District
Court noted that when plaintiffs were "compelled to discuss the substantive
issues in the case on defendants' motion for summary judgment, [they]
primarily focused on 'addiction' and purported nicotine 'manipulation. . . .' "
While plaintiffs do not seem to dispute that addiction requires an individual inquiry, they maintain nonetheless that addiction plays no part in the
case.

        Plaintiffs contend that throughout the litigation, they have

        asserted that defendants' *knowledge* and *intentional misuse* of the
        addictive properties of nicotine—their intentional design of ciga-
        rettes to contain a level of nicotine they knew would be addic-
        tive—went to their intentional misconduct and liability for design-
        ing a defective product. Plaintiffs do not contend that all smokers
        are addicted, that addiction is a pre-requisite to class member-
        ship, or that addiction is determinant of a need for medical moni-
        toring. Addiction is a term and concept that is difficult to avoid in
        any smoking case. The documents show that defendants intended

---

    [18] "At base, the (b)(2) class is distinguished from the (b)(3) class by class cohesive-
ness. . . . Injuries remedied through (b)(2) actions are really group, as opposed to individual
injuries. The members of a (b)(2) class are generally bound together through 'preexisting or
continuing legal relationships' or by some significant common trait such as race or gender."
Holmes v. Continental Can Company, 706 F.2d 1144, 1155 (11th Cir.1983) (quoting Note, *Notice in Rule 23(b)(2) Class Actions for Monetary Relief: Johnson v. General Motors Corp.,* 128
U. Pa. L. Rev. 1236, 1252–53 (1980) (footnotes omitted)).

    [19] We note that the individual issues raised by cigarette litigation often preclude class cer-
tification. See, e.g., *Castano v. The Am. Tobacco Co.,* 84 F.3d 734 (5th Cir.1996) (decertifying
23(b)(3) class because individual issues predominated). . . .

and designed cigarettes to be addictive. That they have largely succeeded may be all too apparent. But the addiction of any particular smoker—much less the class as a whole—is simply *not* an element of plaintiffs' claims.

Brief of Appellant at 41.

We disagree. Addiction remains an essential part of plaintiffs' claim. In order to prevail on their medical monitoring claim—under any of their three theories of liability (negligence, strict products liability, and intentional exposure to a hazardous substance)—plaintiffs must demonstrate that defendants *caused* their exposure to tobacco. Indeed, plaintiffs' Second Amended Complaint alleges "[p]laintiffs and class members have been significantly exposed to proven hazardous substances through the intentional or negligent actions of the Defendants, and/or through defective products for which Defendants are strictly liable" and that "[a]s a proximate result of this exposure, Plaintiffs and class members suffer significantly increased risks of contracting serious latent diseases." Second Amended Complaint ¶ 20–21.

It is apparent from plaintiffs' Second Amended Complaint . . . that addiction is the linchpin of causation in this case. . . .

Plaintiffs asserted the evidence will establish *inter alia* that (1) defendants intentionally designed cigarettes to addict smokers; (2) defendants allowed the number of addicted smokers to grow, knowing full well that the smoke caused cancer and lung disease; and (3) defendants intentionally manipulated and controlled nicotine levels. As we understand plaintiffs' theory, defendants' actions caused plaintiffs to become addicted to cigarettes and thereby rendered their choice to smoke nonvoluntary.

Plaintiffs suggest that causation can be proved on a class-wide basis, contending they need to show only that smoking cigarettes was a "substantial factor" in "causing" the three diseases to be monitored in the program. Plaintiffs point to the Surgeon General's Reports conclusively determining that cigarette smoking is the major cause of the diseases for which the medical monitoring program was constructed. This evidence, they claim, more than satisfies their burden on the issue of causation.

But plaintiffs cannot prove causation by merely showing that smoking cigarettes causes cancer and other diseases. They must demonstrate that defendants' intentional or negligent nicotine manipulation caused each individual plaintiff to have a significantly increased risk of contracting serious latent diseases thereby demonstrating the need for medical monitoring. Alternatively, under a strict products liability theory, as the District Court found, "each class member will have to establish that the type of cigarettes he or she smoked contained a defect at the time he or she smoked them." *Barnes*, 176 F.R.D. at 501 (citation omitted). According to plaintiffs, the alleged defect is that defendants intentionally designed these cigarettes to be addictive. But whether defendants caused the injury depends on whether each individual actually is addicted. These are all issues that must be determined on an individual basis.

We note that plaintiffs do not contest the District Court's conclusion that "whether or not an individual is addicted is a highly individualistic inquiry." *Barnes*, 176 F.R.D. at 500. Instead, plaintiffs suggested to the District Court that once the general issue whether cigarettes can cause addiction is resolved, they could resolve the issue of individual addiction by

[handwritten margin note: π must show that Δ caused π's exposure to harmful substance]

having each class member answer a questionnaire consisting of six questions. The District Court noted that

> even if the questionnaire were used to determine nicotine dependence, defendants would be permitted to cross-examine each and every class member as to their alleged dependence. Plaintiffs admittedly acknowledge that the plan they propose would be, at most, a *prima facie* indication of addiction. Plaintiffs' own experts concede that addiction is necessarily an individual inquiry. To refute plaintiffs' *prima facie* case, defendants would be permitted to cross-examine each individual about his specific choices, decisions and behavior, and defendants would be entitled to offer expert testimony about each person's specific circumstances and diagnosis.

Arch, 175 F.R.D. at 488.

Because nicotine addiction must be determined on an individual basis and remains an essential part of plaintiffs' medical monitoring claim, we agree with the District Court that class treatment is inappropriate.

b.   The need for medical monitoring

We also believe the requirement that each class member demonstrate the need for medical monitoring precludes certification. In order to state a claim for medical monitoring, each class member must prove that the monitoring program he requires is "different from that normally recommended in the absence of exposure." *Redland*, 696 A.2d at 146. To satisfy this requirement, each plaintiff must prove the monitoring program that is prescribed for the general public and the monitoring program that would be prescribed for him. Although the general public's monitoring program can be proved on a classwide basis, an individual's monitoring program by definition cannot. In order to prove the program he requires, a plaintiff must present evidence about his individual smoking history and subject himself to cross-examination by the defendant about that history. This element of the medical monitoring claim therefore raises many individual issues.

c.   Defenses

The District Court also held that defenses raise individual issues precluding certification. . . .

As noted, plaintiffs asserted three theories of liability. They claimed that they were significantly exposed to proven hazardous substances through defendants' intentional actions, negligent actions, and defective products (strict liability). Defendants assert the defenses of consent, comparative negligence, and assumption of risk. Plaintiffs contend that these defenses are not available and that individual issues relating to these defenses should not preclude class certification. Plaintiffs maintain that "comparative negligence" is only available in actions for damages resulting in death or injury, that assumption of risk is not available because the defendants will not be able to show that any plaintiff assumed the risk of the specific defect, and that consent requires a full awareness of defendants' specific conduct and there is no record evidence of such awareness in this case.

The District Court found defendants could raise the defense of comparative negligence, predicting the Pennsylvania Supreme Court would apply Pennsylvania's Comparative Negligence Act rather than contributory negligence to a medical monitoring claim. . . .

We need not decide whether the Pennsylvania Supreme Court would apply the Comparative Negligence Act to plaintiffs' negligence claim. If the Comparative Negligence Act does not apply, defendants still have the defense of contributory negligence available to them.

Under Pennsylvania law, the tort of intentional exposure to hazardous substances is predicated on a theory of battery. Express consent may be given by words or affirmative conduct and implied consent may be manifested when a person takes no action, indicating an apparent willingness for the conduct to occur. The consent must be to the "defendant's conduct, rather than to its consequences." *Prosser & Keeton* § 18, at 118. A plaintiff's consent is not effective if "the consenting person was mistaken about the nature and quality of the invasion intended by the conduct." *Prosser & Keeton* § 18, at 114.

Plaintiffs argued in the District Court that the court should use its equitable powers to bar defendants from asserting their affirmative defenses because of defendants' intentional and fraudulent conduct. See *Barnes*, 984 F. Supp. at 864–65. But the District Court rejected this argument and plaintiffs do not press it on appeal. Instead, plaintiffs argue there is no record evidence they consented to defendants' specific conduct. Defendants maintain plaintiffs knew they were exposing themselves to a hazardous substance yet continued to smoke. There is some evidence on the record, including plaintiffs' own deposition testimony, to support defendants' position that despite warnings, plaintiffs continued to smoke. See *id.* ("By her own admission, Potts learned 'for sure' that cigarette smoking created an increased risk of disease in 1966, when the Surgeon General's warnings were put on cigarette packages. In addition, and more importantly, Ms. Potts was informed by her cardiologist in the late 1980s that she was at a significantly increased risk of contracting heart disease, in the form of clogged arteries, from smoking.").

Under Pennsylvania law, plaintiffs may recover on a theory of strict liability where a product in a defective condition unreasonably dangerous to the consumer or user causes harm to the plaintiff. Plaintiff must prove the product was defective and the defect was a substantial factor in causing the injury. While a defendant may not assert comparative negligence in a strict products liability action, Pennsylvania courts allow defendants to introduce "evidence of a plaintiff's voluntary assumption of the risk, misuse of a product, or highly reckless conduct . . . insofar as it relates to the element of causation." *Charlton v. Toyota Indus. Equip.*, 714 A.2d 1043, 1047 (Pa. Super. 1998). To demonstrate that a plaintiff's actions are highly reckless, defendants must show plaintiff "knew or had reason to know of facts which created a high degree of risk of physical harm to himself or that he deliberately proceeded to act, or failed to act, in conscious disregard of that risk." *Id.* (citation omitted).

Assumption of risk is also available in negligence claims. In a negligence action, a defendant is relieved of his duty to protect the plaintiff when the plaintiff was aware of the risk and faced it voluntarily. . . .

d.   Statute of Limitations

Finally, we believe that determining whether each class member's claim is barred by the statute of limitations raises individual issues that prevent class certification. It is fundamental that a plaintiff must bring a claim before the applicable statute of limitations expires. Determining whether the statute of limitations has expired necessarily involves determining when it began to run. Under Pennsylvania law, the statute of limitations starts running when the plaintiff's cause of action accrues; a medical monitoring claim accrues when the plaintiff suffers a "significantly increased risk of contracting a serious latent disease." *Redland*, 696 A.2d at 145. Under plaintiffs' analysis, a cigarette smoker suffers this risk when he reaches the ten or twenty "pack-year" level. A "pack-year" is equivalent to a year in which a person smokes a pack of cigarettes per day. To calculate a particular plaintiff's pack-year history, the court multiplies the number of packs of cigarettes the plaintiff smokes daily by the number of years he has smoked. . . . Under the pack-year approach to claim accrual, determining when a plaintiff's claim accrued necessitates two individual inquiries for each plaintiff: when he began smoking and how much he has smoked since then. The need to conduct such a determination for each plaintiff augurs that a class action will devolve into a lengthy series of individual trials and therefore makes a class action an improper method for resolving these claims.

Because of the individual issues involved in this case—nicotine addiction, causation, the need for medical monitoring, contributory/comparative negligence and the statute of limitations—we believe class treatment is inappropriate.[29]

NOTES AND QUESTIONS

1.   *The Strategy of Medical Monitoring Classes.* Why, as a strategic matter, would class counsel wish to seek certification of a medical-monitoring class? Are medical-monitoring claims similar to breach-of-warranty claims when consumers have purchased a product with some manner of defect that nonetheless has yet to manifest itself, à la the allegations in *Cole v. General Motors Corp.*?

In *Barnes*, the court looks to Pennsylvania tort law, because the proposed class consisted of smokers in Pennsylvania. Would the result as to class certification under Rule 23(b)(2) be the same if the class action were brought on behalf of smokers across the country?

2.   *State Recognition of Medical Monitoring.* One court recently summarized the doctrinal landscape for medical monitoring:

> The law of medical monitoring varies from state to state. Some states recognize medical monitoring as an element of damages when liability is otherwise established, while other states recognize medical monitoring as an independent cause of action; some states require proof of a present, physical injury to obtain medical monitoring, and some do not; and some states do not provide for medical monitoring at all.

In re Welding Fume Prods. Liab. Litig., 245 F.R.D. 279, 291–92 (N.D. Ohio 2007); *see also* PRINCIPLES OF THE LAW OF AGGREGATE LITIGATION § 2.04 illus-

---

[29] In support of certification, plaintiffs point to other medical monitoring claims that have been certified under Rule 23(b)(2) or 23(b)(3). See, e.g., *Gibbs v. E.I. DuPont De Nemours & Co.*, 876 F. Supp. 475 (W.D.N.Y. 1995) (exposure to chemicals); *Yslava v. Hughes Aircraft Co.*, 845 F. Supp. 705, 713 (D. Ariz. 1993) (class alleging long-term exposure to contaminated ground water certified); *Boggs v. Divested Atomic Corp.*, 141 F.R.D. 58, 67 (S.D. Ohio 1991) (long term exposure to radioactive materials and hazardous waste). Plaintiffs' case, however, presents numerous individual issues not involved in those cases. In addition, the cases plaintiffs cite all involve involuntary exposure to hazardous materials rather than the voluntary exposure involved in this case.

tration 2 (2010) ("Initial acceptance of medical monitoring has waned, and the last decade has seen more states decline to recognize it than adopt it.").

What if the governing law is unclear and the contending sides on the question of class certification under Rule 23(b)(2) were to present conflicting opinions from prominent, well-credentialed professors of tort law, one of whom concludes that medical monitoring is appropriately characterized under governing state law as akin to damages and the other of whom concludes that it is properly characterized as akin to an injunction? The question of how to handle competing expert opinions on matters of class certification generally is addressed later in this Chapter.

Is the notion of medical monitoring really all that newfangled? Consider the account presented by two tort theorists:

> [D]efendants who are ordered to underwrite medical tests for those whom they have put at risk of physical injury should not be understood as providing a compensatory payment for injuries already realized, economic or otherwise. . . . Of course, when one sees money changing hands in the context of a tort suit, one naturally thinks in terms of compensation. Ordinarily, payment is made in satisfaction of what is sometimes described as a secondary duty of repair. It is described as secondary, because it attaches as the result of a violation of a primary duty not to cause an injury through wrongful conduct. In this instance, however, appearances are misleading. Payment in a tort context need not always be in satisfaction of a secondary duty to compensate for a completed wrong. Rather, payment might also be a way of performing a certain kind of primary duty owed by a defendant to a plaintiff. And this is more likely to be the case when payment comes in the form of a fund issuing periodic payments rather than a lump-sum transfer: The mode of payment bespeaks an ongoing obligation, rather than a one time satisfaction of a debt owed in light of a wrong already done.

> Recasting payment of medical monitoring expenses as the performance of a primary duty of conduct rather than the fulfillment of a secondary duty to compensate might seem to get us out of the frying pan and into the fire. If such payments constitute the performance of a primary duty, then the duty in question must be one of affirmative aid, as opposed to a duty to take care to avoid causing injury. Notoriously, the common law of tort is, and has long been, quite stingy about recognizing such affirmative duties. There is no general duty to protect or rescue through affirmative conduct, as opposed to a duty to refrain from acts that injure a person. Why, given the paucity of affirmative duties recognized by the common law, should we suppose that we have found an adequate ground for medical monitoring claims by reconceiving them in terms of an affirmative primary duty?

> The answer lies in the fact that one of the well-recognized exceptions to the general rule against affirmative duties is the duty owed by one who has created a dangerous condition that renders another in peril and hence in need of affirmative aid. . . . [S]uppose D, driving his car at night, runs another driver, P, off the road without causing injury to P or his car. D then drives off without attempting to help P by, for example, shining his headlights in P's direction so that P can

assess the situation. P falls down a steep embankment and is injured, and can show that he would not have fallen had D shone his head-lights on the accident scene. D will be liable to P because, once having placed him in peril, he was obligated to take steps to protect P from the peril.

John C.P. Goldberg & Benjamin C. Zipursky, *Unrealized Torts*, 88 Va. L. Rev. 1625, 1709–10 (2002).

3. *The Importance of Context.* To what extent do the barriers to certify-ing a Rule 23(b)(2) medical monitoring class in *Barnes* stem from unusual fea-tures of the tobacco litigation? Would such a class face the same sorts of certifi-cation barriers if the exposure in question had been entirely involuntary—say, to hazardous chemicals that had seeped under the plaintiff class members' property from a nearby industrial facility? Put differently, do the constraints articulated in *Barnes* necessarily doom Rule 23(b)(2) medical-monitoring clas-ses?

4. *The Design of the Medical–Monitoring Regimen.* Consider the guid-ance provided by an oft-cited district court decision concerning the design of the medical-monitoring program:

> Relief in the form of medical monitoring may be by a number of means. First, a court may simply order a defendant to pay a plaintiff a certain sum of money. The plaintiff may or may not choose to use that money to have his medical condition monitored. Second, a court may order the defendants to pay the plaintiffs' medical expenses di-rectly so that a plaintiff may be monitored by the physician of his choice. Neither of these forms of relief constitute injunctive relief as required by Rule 23(b)(2).
>
> However, a court may also establish an elaborate medical moni-toring program of its own, managed by court-appointed court-supervised trustees, pursuant to which a plaintiff is monitored by particular physicians and the medical data produced [is] utilized for group studies. In this situation, a defendant, of course, would finance the program as well as being required by the Court to address issues as they develop during [the] program administration. Under these circumstances, the relief constitutes injunctive relief as required by Rule 23(b)(2).

Day v. NLO, Inc., 144 F.R.D. 330, 335–36 (S.D. Ohio 1992). Why should these distinctions make a difference to the class certification question?

5. *Class Cohesiveness.* Notice that the *Barnes* court uses the concept of class "cohesiveness" to justify examining individual versus common questions, even though (b)(2) itself does not say anything about such an examination. The court says "[w]hile 23(b)(2) class actions have no predominance or superiority requirements, it is well established that the class claims must be cohesive" and noted that class members can be bound because the class is cohesive. Where does this cohesiveness requirement come from? Is it an interpretation of 23(b)(2), an implicit requirement of Rule 23 in general, or a constitutional due process requirement? We have seen it before. Recall that the Supreme Court in *Amchem* described the (b)(3) predominance inquiry as testing "whether pro-posed classes are sufficiently cohesive to warrant adjudication by representa-tion" and tied cohesiveness to "legitimacy." What does "cohesiveness" mean and

how does one tell whether a class is sufficiently cohesive? Bear these questions in mind as you read the rest of the material on mandatory class actions.

(2) Mandatory Classes and the Supreme Court's Non–Decision in Ticor

Brown v. Ticor Title Insurance Co.

982 F.2d 386 (9th Cir. 1992)

■ T.G. NELSON, CIRCUIT JUDGE.

Appellants Brown and Dziewit (hereinafter "Brown") are representatives of the Arizona and Wisconsin classes of consumers of title insurance. After the approval of a settlement agreement in a class action in Pennsylvania involving the same parties, Brown filed the present action in the district court of Arizona alleging a conspiracy to fix price levels for title search and examination services.

RELATED CASES

In 1985, following enforcement proceedings initiated by the Federal Trade Commission ("FTC"), twelve separate class action lawsuits were filed in five federal district courts in four states. The complaints alleged price fixing by various title insurance companies, encompassing the defendants in the present case, in thirteen affected states, including Arizona and Wisconsin. The class actions were consolidated as MDL 633 in the Eastern District of Pennsylvania by the Judicial Panel on Multidistrict Litigation pursuant to 28 U.S.C. § 1407. The complaints alleged that Ticor had violated the antitrust laws by participating in state-licensed rating bureaus which filed collective rates for real estate title search and examination services with state insurance regulatory bodies.

[In the district court, Ticor asserted a state action immunity defense, a doctrine that insulates from antitrust liability conduct undertaken under the auspices of state law—in this instance, state rating bureaus with regulatory authority over the title insurance industry. Before the district court could rule on the applicability of this defense], the parties reached a settlement. . . .

The settlement dropped the monetary claims against Ticor and provided for (1) an injunction against Ticor's participation in rating bureaus for a specified time period in five states, including Arizona and Wisconsin, (2) an increased dollar amount of each title insurance policy issued to class members in all thirteen states during the class period, (3) additional coverage for new title insurance policies purchased by class members, and (4) payment of the costs of lawsuit and attorneys' fees as approved by the MDL 633 court.

The MDL 633 court certified the class under Federal Rules of Civil Procedure 23(b)(1) and (b)(2) and accepted the settlement. In doing so, the court considered and rejected objections to the settlement, including an attempt by the Arizona attorney general to opt out of the class. . . .

Brown filed the present action in the Arizona district court on behalf of Arizona and Wisconsin title insurance consumers alleging a combination and conspiracy by Ticor to fix, maintain and stabilize rates in Arizona and Wisconsin for title search and examination services in violation of the federal antitrust laws, codified at 15 U.S.C. § 1, et seq. (the Sherman Act). Ticor moved for summary judgment dismissing the action based on *res judicata*, claiming that Brown, as a party to the MDL 633 settlement, was bound by the settlement. Relying on *res judicata* as well as state action immunity, the district court granted Ticor's summary judgment motion. . . .

DUE PROCESS VIOLATION

Brown . . .argues that minimal procedural due process must be provided in a class action lawsuit in order "to bind known plaintiffs concerning claims wholly or predominately" for monetary damages. See *Phillips Petroleum Co. v. Shutts*, 472 U.S. 797, 811 n.3 (1985). Brown asserts that certifying the MDL 633 class pursuant to Federal Rules of Civil Procedure 23(b)(1) and (b)(2), which do not provide for the right to opt out, would be a violation of minimum due process if the class judgment precluded future recovery of damages, and therefore *res judicata* is not applicable to his case.

In order to bind an absent plaintiff concerning a claim for monetary damages, the court must provide minimal due process. *Shutts* is limited to claims "wholly or predominately for money judgments." The Third Circuit held that the MDL 633 litigation was a "hybrid suit that involved the *foreclosure of substantial damage claims*." *In re Real Estate*, 869 F.2d at 768 (emphasis added). We follow the Third Circuit's holding.

According to *Shutts*, minimal due process requires that "an absent plaintiff be provided with an opportunity to remove himself from the class by executing and returning an 'opt out' or 'request for exclusion' form to the court," if monetary claims are involved. 472 U.S. at 812. Because Brown had no opportunity to opt out of the MDL 633 litigation, we hold there would be a violation of minimal due process if Brown's damage claims were held barred by *res judicata*. Brown will be bound by the injunctive relief provided by the settlement in MDL 633, and foreclosed from seeking other or further injunctive relief in this case, but *res judicata* will not bar Brown's claims for monetary damages against Ticor.

[The court went on to hold that Ticor was not entitled to state action immunity.]

NOTES AND QUESTIONS

1. *The Supreme Court's Non–Decision in* Ticor Title. The Supreme Court initially granted the writ of certiorari in *Ticor Title* but later dismissed the writ as improvidently granted. (As we will see shortly, the Supreme Court dealt with the opt-out issue later in *Wal–Mart Stores, Inc. v. Dukes*, although as a matter of Rule 23 interpretation rather than due process.) The result is to leave in place the Ninth Circuit's decision. In a per curiam opinion, the Supreme Court explained:

> [I]n this Court, petitioners present only a single question—viz., "[w]hether a federal court may refuse to enforce a prior federal class action judgment, properly certified under Rule 23, on grounds that absent class members have a constitutional due process right to opt out of any class action which asserts monetary claims on their behalf. . . .
>
> That certified question is of no general consequence if, whether or not absent class members have a constitutional right to opt out of such actions, they have a right to do so under the Federal Rules of Civil Procedure. Such a right would exist if, in actions seeking mone-

tary damages, classes can be certified only under Rule 23(b)(3), which permits opt-out, and not under Rules 23(b)(1) and (b)(2), which do not. That is at least a substantial possibility—and we would normally resolve that preliminary nonconstitutional question before proceeding to the constitutional claim. The law of res judicata, however, prevents that question from being litigated here. It was conclusively determined in the MDL No. 633 litigation that respondents' class fit within Rules 23(b)(1)(A) and (b)(2); even though that determination may have been wrong, it is conclusive upon these parties, and the alternative of using the Federal Rules instead of the Constitution as the means of imposing an opt-out requirement for this settlement is no longer available.

The most obvious consequence of this unavailability is, as we have suggested, that our resolution of the posited constitutional question may be quite unnecessary in law, and of virtually no practical consequence in fact, except with respect to these particular litigants. Another consequence, less apparent, is that resolving the constitutional question on the assumption of proper certification under the Rules may lead us to the wrong result. If the Federal Rules, which generally are not affirmatively enacted into law by Congress, see 28 U.S.C. §§ 2072(a), (b), 2074(a), are not entitled to that great deference as to constitutionality which we accord federal statutes, they at least come with the *imprimatur* of the rulemaking authority of this Court. In deciding the present case, we must assume either that the lack of opt-out opportunity in these circumstances was decreed by the Rules or that it was not (though the parties are bound by an erroneous holding that it was). If we make the former assumption we may approve, in the mistaken deference to prior Supreme Court action and congressional acquiescence, action that neither we nor Congress would independently think constitutional. If we make the latter assumption, we may announce a constitutional rule that is good for no other federal class action. Neither option is attractive.

. . . Moreover, as matters have developed it is not clear that our resolution of the constitutional question will make any difference even to these litigants. On the day we granted certiorari we were informed that the parties had reached a settlement designed to moot the petition, which now awaits the approval of the District Court.

In these circumstances, we think it best to dismiss the writ as improvidently granted.

Ticor Title Ins. Co. v. Brown, 511 U.S. 117, 121–22 (1994) (per curiam). Justice O'Connor, joined by Chief Justice Rehnquist and Justice Kennedy, vigorously dissented from the dismissal of the writ of certiorari:

The lower courts have consistently held that the presence of monetary damages claims does not preclude class certification under Rules 23(b)(1)(A) and (b)(2). Whether or not those decisions are correct (a question we need not, and indeed should not, decide today), they at least indicate that there are a substantial number of class members in exactly the same position as respondents. Under the Ninth Circuit's rationale in this case, every one of them has the right to go into federal court and relitigate their claims against the defendants in the original action. The individuals, corporations, and governments that have successfully defended against class actions or reached appropriate settlements, but are now subject to relitigation of the same claims with individual class members, will rightly dispute the Court's characterization of the constitutional rule in this case as inconsequential.

Id. at 124 (O'Connor, J., dissenting from dismissal of writ).

    2.   The Ticor Title *Class Settlement.* What are the possible explanations—both sinister and benign—for the raising of damage claims in the antitrust actions consolidated by the MDL Panel against Ticor Title but the dropping of such claims in connection with the class settlement agreement? Were the damage claims effectively settled for nothing?

    3.   Damages Claims in Mandatory Class Actions. How should the Supreme Court, in a case properly before it, resolve on the merits the issue raised by *Ticor Title*? Does *Shutts* simply replicate in its footnote 3 the ambiguity created by the advisory committee's statement that mandatory classes may encompass damage claims as long as they do not predominate in the litigation? Should, or must, the existing Rule 23(b) be amended to address this matter?

(3) Mandatory Classes Under Title VII of the Civil Rights Act

    In framing the core situations for mandatory class treatment under subsection (b)(2), the rules advisory committee refers to several civil-rights class actions well known to the committee members at the time they crafted Rule 23. At the time that Rule 23 became law, in 1966, relief in civil-rights cases consisted principally of injunctive or declaratory relief—hence, the reference thereto in the text of Rule 23(b)(2). Not until the late 1960s did early cases under the then-recently-enacted Title VII of the Civil Rights Act of 1964 award backpay to victims of unlawful employment discrimination—i.e., relief designed to compensate them for the economic losses they suffered as a result of such discrimination. Not until the mid–1970s, in *Albemarle Paper Co. v. Moody*, 422 U.S. 405 (1975), would the Supreme Court firmly establish a presumption in favor of a backpay award upon proof of unlawful employment discrimination. On these developments, see George Rutherglen, *Notice, Scope, and Preclusion in Title VII Class Actions*, 69 Va. L. Rev. 11 (1983).

    During the same period, courts routinely certified mandatory class actions under Rule 23(b)(2) in employment discrimination cases notwithstanding the inclusion of demands for backpay. Then, Congress enacted the Civil Rights Act of 1991, which extended the remedies available for violations of Title VII by authorizing a damages remedy for intentional discrimination that is no prohibited by 42 U.S.C. § 1981—a Reconstruction-era statute that had long been interpreted to provide a damages remedy to those who suffer *racial* discrimination in the "mak[ing] or enforce[ment] of contracts." The 1991 Civil Rights Act for the first time authorized victims of intentional sex discrimination to recover compensatory and punitive damages under federal law. In the wake of these changes, courts began to raise the question posed but not decided by *Ticor*: to what extent can a mandatory class action under Rule 23(b)(2) include demands for backpay, emotional, compensatory, and punitive damages—relief that sounds a lot like monetary, divisible relief? As one commentator has explained, understanding why this question matters necessitates an understanding of both the procedural and substantive aspects of this puzzle:

> The first half of this puzzle is procedure; it's explained in the language of Rule 23(b)(2). Rule 23(b)(2) speaks in terms of equitable relief and permits class certification when "the party opposing the class has acted or refused to act on grounds that apply generally to the class, so that final injunctive relief or corresponding declaratory relief is appropriate respecting the class as a whole." By contemplating equitable remedies and presuming class cohesion, this standard avoids monetary remedies and the due process rights that attach to property. It thereby paves the way for a mandatory, non-opt out class, which was precisely what the 1966 Advisory Committee had in mind to further desegregation litigation.

> The second half of the puzzle is substantive. When Congress enacted Title VII of the 1964 Civil Rights Act, its menu of remedies included a declaratory judgment that the defendant violated the Act in its employment practices and an injunction to prevent the defendant from continuing to discriminate—both clearly equitable remedies. But as civil-rights litigation evolved, the Supreme Court added back pay to the list of available remedies. This payment compensated plaintiffs for the difference between their current position and the position they would have been in absent the employer's discriminatory practices. Courts and litigants were careful to argue that back pay was different from ordinary monetary damages because it flows automatically from the defendant's violation of Title VII. However dubious this distinction is, casting back pay as something other than a legal remedy avoided the right to a jury trial under the Seventh Amendment, a result that 1960s-era civil-rights plaintiffs in the South preferred.

Elizabeth Chamblee Burch, *Introduction:* Dukes v. Wal–Mart Stores, Inc., 63 Vand. L. Rev. En Banc 91, 99 (2010) (citations omitted).

Two events, one judicial and one legislative, threatened to disrupt this delicate balance of certifying Title VII claims as Rule 23(b)(2) class actions even though they contained requests for backpay. First, in 1985, the Supreme Court's decision in *Phillips Petroleum v. Shutts* held that class members have the right to opt out of a class when their claims involve legal relief—i.e., money. Money constitutes property within the meaning of the Due Process Clause, yet footnote three in *Shutts* limited the Court's holding "to those class actions which seek to bind known plaintiffs concerning claims wholly or *predominately* for money judgments. We intimate no view concerning other types of class actions, such as those seeking equitable relief." The word "predominately," first mentioned in an Advisory Committee Note on Rule 23(b)(2), became the key to maintaining the pre-*Shutts* balance and, as we'll see, the cornerstone of Wal–Mart's petition for a writ of certiorari. So long as equitable relief predominated over backpay, courts could avoid triggering due process rights, including the right to opt out.

Second, in 1991, Congress changed the law to authorize compensatory damages for emotional distress and punitive damages for violations of Title VII to the extent those remedies were not already available to a plaintiff under § 1981. Although backpay could plausibly be characterized as equitable, compensatory and punitive damages were a different matter. So, the

Civil Rights Act of 1991, which Congress passed to encourage civil rights litigation, had the ironic consequence of making a Rule 23(b)(2) employment discrimination class harder to certify and class relief harder to obtain.

Given this turmoil, one might wonder why plaintiffs would choose a (b)(2) class at all, why not use (b)(3) instead? But from plaintiffs' attorneys' perspective, (b)(2) offers two comparative advantages over (b)(3) classes: plaintiffs don't automatically have the right to receive notice or opt out (which avoids diminishing attorneys' fees), and, more importantly, common issues don't have to predominate over individual ones. The latter point is of particular importance when the class definition includes everyone from hourly "demo girls," a women's-only job handing out free food samples, to cashiers, greeters, and salaried managers as it did in *Wal-Mart Stores, Inc. v. Dukes*. It likewise shifts the focus to a common, but complex, array of company-wide discriminatory practices that could be cured through a declaratory judgment and injunctive relief.

The Court's *Shutts* opinion and the Civil Rights Act of 1991 plus the added confusion from the Court's non-decision in *Ticor Title*, have caused the lower courts to split mightily over what "predominantly" means, when due process requires the right to opt out, and whether to certify (b)(2) classes requesting backpay, compensatory damages for emotional distress, and punitive damages. Although courts have often suggested that the 1991 amendments had the ironic effect of making Title VII classes harder to certify, remember that equitable relief (under Title VII) and compensatory damages (under § 1981) were available in race discrimination cases before the 1991 amendments. Consequently, it is possible that the cases may simply reflect changing judicial attitudes rather than a changed statutory landscape.

To get a sense of the lower courts' split over the "predominance" requirement, consider this excerpt from the Fifth Circuit's decision in *Allison v. Citgo Petroleum Co.*:

> [M]onetary relief predominates in (b)(2) class actions unless it is incidental to requested injunctive or declaratory relief. By incidental, we mean damages that flow directly from liability to the class *as a whole* on the claims forming the basis of the injunctive or declaratory relief. Ideally, incidental damages should be only those to which class members automatically would be entitled once liability to the class (or subclass) as a whole is established. That is, the recovery of incidental damages should typically be concomitant with, not merely consequential to, class-wide injunctive or declaratory relief. Moreover, such damages should at least be capable of computation by means of objective standards and not dependent in any significant way on the intangible, subjective differences of each class member's circumstances. Liability for incidental damages should not require additional hearings to resolve the disparate merits of each individual's case; it should neither introduce new and substantial legal or factual issues, nor entail complex individualized determinations. Thus, incidental damages will, by definition, be more in the nature of a group remedy, consistent with the forms of relief intended for (b)(2) class actions.

> . . . We have little trouble affirming the district court's finding that the plaintiffs' claims for compensatory and punitive damages are not sufficiently incidental to the injunctive and declaratory relief being sought to permit them in a (b)(2) class action. We start with the

premise that, in this circuit, compensatory damages for emotional distress and other forms of intangible injury will not be presumed from mere violation of constitutional or statutory rights. Specific individualized proof is necessary, and testimony from the plaintiff alone is not ordinarily sufficient. Compensatory damages may be awarded only if the plaintiff submits proof of actual injury, often in the form of psychological or medical evidence, or other corroborating testimony from a third party. The very nature of these damages, compensating plaintiffs for emotional and other intangible injuries, necessarily implicates the subjective differences of each plaintiff's circumstances; they are an individual, not class-wide, remedy.

Allison v. Citgo Petroleum Corp., 151 F.3d 402, 415–17 (5th Cir. 1998).

By *Allison's* reasoning, the additional remedies made available to employment discrimination plaintiffs under the Civil Rights Act of 1991 make mandatory class treatment under Rule 23(b)(2) harder for such plaintiffs to obtain. Is that result legally sound? In an ordinary tort case, how would one classify a remedy that provided the plaintiff a sum of money equivalent to the earnings she lost from being unable to work due to the defendant's tortious misconduct? Why does the same remedy suddenly get categorized differently when the underlying misconduct is employment discrimination under Title VII? The theory that backpay is equitable is based on the longstanding notion that restitution is a form of equitable relief. Is it possible to distinguish between restitution and compensatory damages with respect to lost wages? Does the historical context shed light on this question?

In contrast to the Fifth Circuit's decision in *Allison*, consider the legal standard formulated by the Second Circuit:

We decline to adopt the . . . approach set out by the Fifth Circuit in *Allison* and followed by the district court below. Rather, we hold that when presented with a motion for (b)(2) class certification of a claim seeking both injunctive relief and non-incidental monetary damages, a district court must "consider[] the evidence presented at a class certification hearing and the arguments of counsel," and then assess whether (b)(2) certification is appropriate in light of "the relative importance of the remedies sought, given all of the facts and circumstances of the case." [*Hoffman v. Honda of Am. Mfg., Inc.*, 191 F.R.D. 530, 536 (S.D. Ohio 1999).] The district court may allow (b)(2) certification if it finds in its "informed, sound judicial discretion" that (1) "the positive weight or value [to the plaintiffs] of the injunctive or declaratory relief sought is predominant even though compensatory or punitive damages are also claimed," *Allison*, 151 F.3d at 430 (Dennis, J., dissenting), and (2) class treatment would be efficient and manageable, thereby achieving an appreciable measure of judicial economy.

Although the assessment of whether injunctive or declaratory relief predominates will require an ad hoc balancing that will vary from case to case, before allowing (b)(2) certification a district court should, at a minimum, satisfy itself of the following: (1) even in the absence of a possible monetary recovery, reasonable plaintiffs would bring the suit to obtain the injunctive or declaratory relief sought; and (2) the injunctive or declaratory relief sought would be both reasonably necessary and appropriate were the plaintiffs to succeed on the merits.

Insignificant or sham requests for injunctive relief should not provide cover for (b)(2) certification of claims that are brought essentially for monetary recovery.

Robinson v. Metro–North Commuter R.R. Co., 267 F.3d 147, 164 (2d Cir. 2001). Is the Second Circuit's standard in *Robinson* an improvement on the Fifth Circuit's approach in *Allison*? Or does it countenance an even more dramatic departure from the premises of Rule 23(b)(2)? As you read the Supreme Court's decision on this topic in *Wal–Mart Stores, Inc. v. Dukes*, consider whether it adopts reasoning akin to that in *Allison* or *Robinson*, or if it adopts an entirely different standard.

Wal–Mart Stores, Inc. v. Dukes

131 S Ct. 2541 (2011)

■ JUSTICE SCALIA delivered the opinion of the Court in which JUSTICE GINSBURG, JUSTICE BREYER, JUSTICE SOTOMAYOR, and JUSTICE KAGAN joined as to Parts I and III.

[Recall that current and former female employees of Wal–Mart sued the company for gender discrimination, alleging that the discretion exercised by their local supervisors over pay and promotion violated Title VII. They requested injunctive and declaratory relief as well as an award of backpay and wanted the court to certify a class under Rule 23(b)(2). A divided Court held, in Part II, that the Plaintiffs failed to meet Rule 23(a)'s commonality requirement. All justices concurred with the opinion in Part III, below.]

III

We also conclude that respondents' claims for backpay were improperly certified under Federal Rule of Civil Procedure 23(b)(2). Our opinion in *Ticor Title Ins. Co. v. Brown*, 511 U.S. 117 (1994) (per curiam) expressed serious doubt about whether claims for monetary relief may be certified under that provision. We now hold that they may not, at least where (as here) the monetary relief is not incidental to the injunctive or declaratory relief.

A

Rule 23(b)(2) allows class treatment when "the party opposing the class has acted or refused to act on grounds that apply generally to the class, so that final injunctive relief or corresponding declaratory relief is appropriate respecting the class as a whole." One possible reading of this provision is that it applies *only* to requests for such injunctive or declaratory relief and does not authorize the class certification of monetary claims at all. We need not reach that broader question in this case, because we think that, at a minimum, claims for *individualized* relief (like the backpay at issue here) do not satisfy the Rule. The key to the (b)(2) class is "the indivisible nature of the injunctive or declaratory remedy warranted—the notion that the conduct is such that it can be enjoined or declared unlawful only as to all of the class members or as to none of them." Nagareda, 84 N.Y.U. L. Rev. at 132. In other words, Rule 23(b)(2) applies only when a single injunction or declaratory judgment would provide relief to each member of the class. It does not authorize class certification when each individual class member would be entitled to a *different* injunction or declaratory judgment against the defendant. Similarly, it does not authorize class certification when each class member would be entitled to an individualized award of monetary damages.

That interpretation accords with the history of the Rule. Because Rule 23 "stems from equity practice" that predated its codification, in determining its meaning we have previously looked to the historical models on which the Rule was based. *Ortiz v. Fibreboard Corp.,* 527 U.S. 815, 841–45 (1999). As we observed in *Amchem,* "[c]ivil rights cases against parties charged with unlawful, class-based discrimination are prime examples" of what (b)(2) is meant to capture. In particular, the Rule reflects a series of decisions involving challenges to racial segregation—conduct that was remedied by a single classwide order. In none of the cases cited by the Advisory Committee as examples of (b)(2)'s antecedents did the plaintiffs combine any claim for individualized relief with their classwide injunction.

Permitting the combination of individualized and classwide relief in a (b)(2) class is also inconsistent with the structure of Rule 23(b). Classes certified under (b)(1) and (b)(2) share the most traditional justifications for class treatment—that individual adjudications would be impossible or unworkable, as in a (b)(1) class, or that the relief sought must perforce affect the entire class at once, as in a (b)(2) class. For that reason these are also mandatory classes: The Rule provides no opportunity for (b)(1) or (b)(2) class members to opt out, and does not even oblige the District Court to afford them notice of the action. Rule 23(b)(3), by contrast, is an "adventuresome innovation" of the 1966 amendments, framed for situations "in which 'class-action treatment is not as clearly called for.' " It allows class certification in a much wider set of circumstances but with greater procedural protections. Its only prerequisites are that "the questions of law or fact common to class members predominate over any questions affecting only individual members, and that a class action is superior to other available methods for fairly and efficiently adjudicating the controversy." And unlike (b)(1) and (b)(2) classes, the (b)(3) class is not mandatory; class members are entitled to receive "the best notice that is practicable under the circumstances" and to withdraw from the class at their option.

Given that structure, we think it clear that individualized monetary claims belong in Rule 23(b)(3). The procedural protections attending the (b)(3) class—predominance, superiority, mandatory notice, and the right to opt out—are missing from (b)(2) not because the Rule considers them unnecessary, but because it considers them unnecessary *to a (b)(2) class.* When a class seeks an indivisible injunction benefitting all its members at once, there is no reason to undertake a case-specific inquiry into whether class issues predominate or whether class action is a superior method of adjudicating the dispute. Predominance and superiority are self-evident. But with respect to each class member's individualized claim for money, that is not so—which is precisely why (b)(3) requires the judge to make findings about predominance and superiority before allowing the class. Similarly, (b)(2) does not require that class members be given notice and opt-out rights, presumably because it is thought (rightly or wrongly) that notice has no purpose when the class is mandatory, and that depriving people of their right to sue in this manner complies with the Due Process Clause. In the context of a class action predominantly for money damages we have held that absence of notice and opt-out violates due process. See *Phillips Petroleum Co. v. Shutts,* 472 U.S. 797, 812 (1985). While we have never held that to be so where the monetary claims do not predominate, the serious possibility that it may be so provides an additional reason not to read Rule 23(b)(2) to include the monetary claims here.

B

Against that conclusion, respondents argue that their claims for backpay were appropriately certified as part of a class under Rule 23(b)(2) because those claims do not "predominate" over their requests for injunctive and declaratory relief. They rely upon the Advisory Committee's statement that Rule 23(b)(2) "does not extend to cases in which the appropriate final relief relates *exclusively or predominantly* to money damages." The negative implication, they argue, is that it *does* extend to cases in which the appropriate final relief relates only partially and nonpredominantly to money damages. Of course it is the Rule itself, not the Advisory Committee's description of it, that governs. And a mere negative inference does not in our view suffice to establish a disposition that has no basis in the Rule's text, and that does obvious violence to the Rule's structural features. The mere "predominance" of a proper (b)(2) injunctive claim does nothing to justify elimination of Rule 23(b)(3)'s procedural protections: It neither establishes the superiority of *class* adjudication over *individual* adjudication nor cures the notice and opt-out problems. We fail to see why the Rule should be read to nullify these protections whenever a plaintiff class, at its option, combines its monetary claims with a request—even a "predominating request"—for an injunction.

Respondents' predominance test, moreover, creates perverse incentives for class representatives to place at risk potentially valid claims for monetary relief. In this case, for example, the named plaintiffs declined to include employees' claims for compensatory damages in their complaint. That strategy of including only backpay claims made it more likely that monetary relief would not "predominate." But it also created the possibility (if the predominance test were correct) that individual class members' compensatory-damages claims would be *precluded* by litigation they had no power to hold themselves apart from. If it were determined, for example, that a particular class member is not entitled to backpay because her denial of increased pay or a promotion was *not* the product of discrimination, that employee might be collaterally estopped from independently seeking compensatory damages based on that same denial. That possibility underscores the need for plaintiffs with individual monetary claims to decide *for themselves* whether to tie their fates to the class representatives' or go it alone—a choice Rule 23(b)(2) does not ensure that they have.

The predominance test would also require the District Court to reevaluate the roster of class members continually. The Ninth Circuit recognized the necessity for this when it concluded that those plaintiffs no longer employed by Wal–Mart lack standing to seek injunctive or declaratory relief against its employment practices. The Court of Appeals' response to that difficulty, however, was not to eliminate *all* former employees from the certified class, but to eliminate only those who had left the company's employ by the date the complaint was filed. That solution has no logical connection to the problem, since those who have left their Wal–Mart jobs *since* the complaint was filed have no more need for prospective relief than those who left beforehand. As a consequence, even though the validity of a (b)(2) class depends on whether "final injunctive relief or corresponding declaratory relief is appropriate respecting the class *as a whole,*" Rule 23(b)(2) (emphasis added), about half the members of the class approved by the Ninth Circuit have no claim for injunctive or declaratory relief at all. Of course, the alternative (and logical) solution of excising plaintiffs from the class as they leave their employment may have struck the Court of Appeals as wasteful of the District Court's time. Which indeed it is, since if a backpay action were properly certified for class treatment under *(b)(3)*, the ability to litigate a plaintiff's backpay claim as part of the class would not turn on the irrelevant question whether she is still employed at Wal–Mart. What follows from this, however, is not that some arbitrary limitation on class membership should be imposed but that the backpay claims should not be certified under Rule 23(b)(2) at all.

Finally, respondents argue that their backpay claims are appropriate for a (b)(2) class action because a backpay award is equitable in nature. The latter may be true, but it is irrelevant. The Rule does not speak of "equitable" remedies generally but of injunctions and declaratory judgments. As Title VII itself makes pellucidly clear, backpay is neither.

C

In *Allison v. Citgo Petroleum Corp.*, 151 F.3d 402, 415 (5th Cir. 1998), the Fifth Circuit held that a (b)(2) class would permit the certification of monetary relief that is "incidental to requested injunctive or declaratory relief," which it defined as "damages that flow directly from liability to the class *as a whole* on the claims forming the basis of the injunctive or declaratory relief." In that court's view, such "incidental damages should not require additional hearings to resolve the disparate merits of each individual's case; it should neither introduce new and substantial legal or factual issues, nor entail complex individualized determinations." We need not decide in this case whether there are any forms of "incidental" monetary relief that are consistent with the interpretation of Rule 23(b)(2) we have announced and that comply with the Due Process Clause. Respondents do not argue that they can satisfy this standard, and in any event they cannot.

Contrary to the Ninth Circuit's view, Wal–Mart is entitled to individualized determinations of each employee's eligibility for backpay. Title VII includes a detailed remedial scheme. If a plaintiff prevails in showing that an employer has discriminated against him in violation of the statute, the court "may enjoin the respondent from engaging in such unlawful employment practice, and order such affirmative action as may be appropriate, [including] reinstatement or hiring of employees, with or without backpay . . . or any other equitable relief as the court deems appropriate." But if the employer can show that it took an adverse employment action against an employee for any reason other than discrimination, the court cannot order the "hiring, reinstatement, or promotion of an individual as an employee, or the payment to him of any backpay."

We have established a procedure for trying pattern-or-practice cases that gives effect to these statutory requirements. When the plaintiff seeks individual relief such as reinstatement or backpay after establishing a pattern or practice of discrimination, "a district court must usually conduct additional proceedings . . . to determine the scope of individual relief." *Teamsters,* 431 U.S. at 361. At this phase, the burden of proof will shift to the company, but it will have the right to raise any individual affirmative defenses it may have, and to "demonstrate that the individual applicant was denied an employment opportunity for lawful reasons." *Id.* at 362.

The Court of Appeals believed that it was possible to replace such proceedings with Trial by Formula. A sample set of the class members would be selected, as to whom liability for sex discrimination and the backpay owing as a result would be determined in depositions supervised by a master. The percentage of claims determined to be valid would then be applied to the entire remaining class, and the number of (presumptively) valid claims thus derived would be multiplied by the average backpay award in the sample set to arrive at the entire class recovery—without further individualized proceedings. We disapprove that novel project. Because the Rules Enabling Act forbids interpreting Rule 23 to "abridge, enlarge or modify any substantive right," a class cannot be certified on the premise that Wal–Mart will not be entitled to litigate its statutory defenses to individual claims. And because the necessity of that litigation will prevent backpay from being "incidental" to the classwide injunction, respondents' class could not be certified even assuming, *arguendo,* that "incidental" monetary relief can be awarded to a 23(b)(2) class.

* * *

The judgment of the Court of Appeals is

Reversed.

■ JUSTICE GINSBURG, with whom JUSTICE BREYER, JUSTICE SOTOMAYOR, and JUSTICE KAGAN join, concurring in part and dissenting in part.

The class in this case, I agree with the Court, should not have been certified under Federal Rule of Civil Procedure 23(b)(2). The plaintiffs, alleging discrimination in violation of Title VII, seek monetary relief that is not merely incidental to any injunctive or declaratory relief that might be available. A putative class of this type may be certifiable under Rule 23(b)(3), if the plaintiffs show that common class questions "predominate" over issues affecting individuals—*e.g.,* qualification for, and the amount of, backpay or compensatory damages—and that a class action is "superior" to other modes of adjudication.

Whether the class the plaintiffs describe meets the specific requirements of Rule 23(b)(3) is not before the Court, and I would reserve that matter for consideration and decision on remand. The Court, however, disqualifies the class at the starting gate, holding that the plaintiffs cannot cross the "commonality" line set by Rule 23(a)(2). In so ruling, the Court imports into the Rule 23(a) determination concerns properly addressed in a Rule 23(b)(3) assessment.

NOTES AND QUESTIONS

1.   *Due Process.* Recall that before *Dukes,* the appellate courts split over the extent to which a mandatory Rule 23(b)(2) class could include requests for backpay, compensatory damages for emotional distress, and punitive damages. These monetary remedies easily fall under the "property" portion of the Due Process Clause's protection against deprivation of "life, liberty, or property, without due process of law," and, although the Supreme Court did not tackle the issue directly until *Dukes,* its decision in *Phillips Petroleum v. Shutts* suggested that opt-out rights were required only in actions "concerning claims *wholly or predominately* for money judgments." 472 U.S. 797, 811 n.3 (1985) (emphasis added). The *Dukes* Court's decision on the issue was far stricter than any the appellate courts imagined—even the Fifth Circuit's strict approach in *Allison.* Though it did not go so far as to allow *only* requests for injunctive or declaratory relief, it did not permit backpay or any situation in which "each class member would be entitled to an individualized award of monetary dam-

ages." 131 S. Ct. 2541, 2557. Did the Supreme Court reach the right result over backpay? Can a reasonable line be drawn between backpay on one hand and compensatory and punitive damages on the other?

How should lower courts interpret the majority's standard in (b)(2) classes outside of Title VII? For example, suppose plaintiffs claim that defendant disposed of a carcinogen into a lagoon, which seeped into an underground aquifer, evaporated into the air, and spread throughout their neighborhood. They seek to certify a Rule 23(b)(2) class for medical monitoring. Assuming they can satisfy Rule 23(a)(2)'s commonality requirement, which may be difficult given the individualized nature of proving causation and medical necessity, would the screening regime and costs (which will vary from person to person) run afoul of *Dukes* prohibition on non-incidental monetary damages? See *Gates v. Rohm & Haas Co.*, 655 F.3d 255 (3d Cir. 2011) (holding that (b)(2) medical monitoring claims failed because individual issues of proof prevented classwide, common relief and speculating that these claims might not be cognizable under (b)(2) after *Dukes* because screening regimes and costs will vary from person to person).

Alternatively, assume that plaintiffs sue a generic drug manufacturer for failing to disclose numerous differences between its depression drug and the name brand "equivalent." If the court finds that commonality is satisfied because defendant's business practices harmed class members uniformly, how should it analyze (b)(2) if plaintiffs request restitution and injunctive relief under a uniform law that includes a $5,000 statutory penalty per class member? See *In re Budeprion XL Marketing & Sales Litig.*, MDL No. 2107 (E.D. Pa.) (July 2, 2012) (certifying a (b)(2) class for settlement purposes only and noting that the (b)(2) question was "a close question" but holding that plaintiffs' injunctive relief would benefit the entire Class identically," statutory damages "would avoid an individualized calculation of damages," and plaintiffs' proposed "mechanism whereby restitution damages could be calculated for the entire class" made certification permissible).

2. *Employment Discrimination Claims under Rule 23(b)(3).* Justice Ginsburg suggests in dissent that plaintiffs might proceed under Rule 23(b)(3) as opposed to Rule 23(b)(2), but does the first half of the Court's opinion on commonality permit plaintiffs to proceed in this way?

3. *The Possibility of "Hybrid" Classes in Employment Discrimination.* Should the courts certify the indivisible aspects of a case like *Allison* or *Dukes* for mandatory class treatment under Rule 23(b)(2)—as earlier Fifth Circuit cases such as *Pettway* permitted—and certify the divisible aspects seeking monetary relief for opt-out class treatment under Rule 23(b)(3)? In *Allison*, the Fifth Circuit went on to consider this possibility but ultimately rejected (b)(3) certification on the facts of the case:

> [D]eciding whether common issues predominate and whether the class action is a superior method to resolve the controversy requires an understanding of the relevant claims, defenses, facts, and substantive law presented in the case. . . . [T]he recovery of compensatory and punitive damages in Title VII cases requires individualized and independent proof of injury to, and the means by which discrimination was inflicted upon, each class member. The plaintiffs' claims for compensatory and punitive damages must therefore focus almost entirely on facts and issues specific to individuals rather than

the class as a whole: what kind of discrimination was each plaintiff subjected to; how did it affect each plaintiff emotionally and physically, at work and at home; what medical treatment did each plaintiff receive and at what expense; and so on and so on. Under such circumstances, an action conducted nominally as a class action would "degenerate in practice into multiple lawsuits separately tried."

The predominance of individual-specific issues relating to the plaintiffs' claims for compensatory and punitive damages in turn detracts from the superiority of the class action device in resolving these claims. These manageability problems are exacerbated by the fact that this action must be tried to a jury and involves more than a thousand potential plaintiffs spread across two separate facilities, represented by six different unions, working in seven different departments, and alleging discrimination over a period of nearly twenty years.

Allison, 151 F.3d at 419.

Other courts, however, have found that compensatory damages "do not automatically negate the finding that common issues predominate in a (b)(3) class action." *Taylor v. District of Columbia Water & Sewer Auth.*, 205 F.R.D. 43, 50 (D.C. Cir. 2002).

Does the Supreme Court's reasoning in *Dukes* shed any light on this question? Does it support the refusal to certify a mandatory class under subsection (b)(2) as to equitable claims *only*, or just the refusal to certify a (b)(2) class that includes the legal, monetary claims authorized by the 1991 amendments? After completing the discussion of mandatory classes under Rule 23(b), this Chapter shall return to the question of when a court should certify a class action with regard to particular issues within a larger constellation of issues in a given case. See Fed. R. Civ. P. 23(c)(4).

4.   *Litigating Plaintiffs' Claims Post–Dukes.* Given the widely understood prohibition on claim splitting, how should counsel proceed after *Dukes*? She could ask the court to certify the Rule 23(b)(2) class for indivisible relief as an issue class and then permit each class member to proceed with requests for divisible remedies individually. Or, as explained in the previous Note, she might request a hybrid class where indivisible relief proceeds under Rule 23(b)(2) and divisible relief, such as backpay, compensatory damages, and punitive damages, proceeds under Rule 23(b)(3). But would requesting compensatory and punitive damages cause individual issues to predominate over common ones? As we saw in the previous Note, courts split on whether compensatory damages negate a finding of predominance.

The same uncertainty—whether a damage assessment would undermine the predominance of common questions—arises with regard to punitive damages. The Civil Rights Act of 1991 allows each employee who is a victim of intentional discrimination prohibited by Title VII to receive up to $300,000 in punitive damages, but requires an employee to show that the employer engaged in a pattern or practice of discrimination "with malice or with reckless indifference to the federally protected rights of an aggrieved individual." 42 U.S.C. § 1981a(b)(1), (b)(3). (Note that the punitive-damage cap does not apply to punitive damage claims for race discrimination, which must be asserted under § 1981.) When pre-*Dukes* courts considered whether Title VII allowed punitive damages on a classwide basis, several of them, including the Ninth Circuit in *Dukes*, suggested that punitive damages might clear the predominance hurdle if liability was predicated on a class-wide theory. But other courts thought that Title VII required a fact-specific inquiry into whether each class member would be entitled to backpay and punitive damages, which kept common questions from predominating under Rule 23(b)(3). The same quandary presents itself in a variety of punitive-damage contexts: should the court focus on the defendant's conduct as a whole or how that conduct affected each individual plaintiff? Moreover, *Dukes* suggested that class members be allowed to opt out of the punitive-damage claims. Is that required in all punitive-damage claims or should it depend on the character of the underlying right at stake—that is, whether it is an individual or an aggregate right? See Elizabeth Chamblee Burch, *Adequately Representing Groups*, Fordham L. Rev. (forthcoming, 2013), *available at* http://ssrn.com/abstract=2247751.

If counsel eschews damages and requests only declaratory or injunctive relief to facilitate certification under Rule 23(b)(2), is counsel opening herself up to claims of inadequate representation under Rule 23(a)(4)? Courts considering this issue before *Dukes* were split. Compare *Miller v. Baltimore Gas & Elec. Co.*, 202 F.R.D. 195, 203 (D. Md. 2001) (denying plaintiffs leave to amend the complaint and remove damages claims because it raised "serious questions regarding the ability of the named plaintiffs to represent the putative class adequately"); *Zachery v. Texaco Exploration & Production, Inc.*, 185 F.R.D. 230, 243 (W.D. Tex. 1999) (abandoning claims to facilitate certification raises questions as to whether the named plaintiffs would adequately represent the interests of other putative class members); with *Sullivan v. Chase Inv. Servs. of Boston, Inc.*, 79 F.R.D. 246, 258 (N.D. Cal. 1978) ("The fact that counsel have not tried to press claims against CIS which they believe (and justifiably so) are unsuitable for class treatment does not make them inadequate."); see also Edward F. Sherman, *"Abandoned Claims" in Class Actions: Implications for Preclusion and Adequacy of Counsel*, 79 Geo. Wash. L. Rev. 483, 491–92 (2011).

5. *Individual Defenses.* Once a plaintiff establishes a discriminatory pattern or practice, the employer then has the right to raise individual affirmative defenses. As Justice Scalia explained, under Title VII, "if the employer can show that it took an adverse employment action against an employee for any reason other than discrimination"—showing up late, poor customer service, false information on an application, or insubordination—"the court cannot order the 'hiring, reinstatement, or promotion of an individual as an employee, or the payment to him of any backpay." 131 S. Ct. 2541, 2560–61. Litigating those defenses en masse, explained the Court, would alter the substantive right to raise defenses in individual proceedings and would thus violate the Rules Enabling Act. How then should affirmative, individual defenses affect class certification? Does the Court's explanation mean that a defendant can inject individuality into an otherwise cohesive class and undermine the predominance of common questions? Individual defenses are not unique to Title VII cases; one need not think too creatively to name a few—waiver, statute-of-limitations, assumption of the risk, and contributory negligence all come readily to mind.

To defeat certification on the ground that defenses must be adjudicated individually, must a defendant offer any evidence showing that the alleged defenses are good? Or may the defendant simply assert that it will raise the defenses? If the latter, won't defendants claim to have defenses in all cases, and thereby always defeat certification?

6.   *Certifying a Class Post–Dukes.* Does *Dukes* sound the death knell for class actions as some commentators predicted? Not necessarily. As Note 2 after the first half of the *Dukes* opinion in the commonality section explained, a number of courts have not found commonality to be as much of a stumbling block as one might have suspected after reading the opinion. And even though *Dukes* has posed a hurdle in certifying some Rule 23(b)(2) classes that might have been certified before it, *Dukes* has certainly not been the death knell for (b)(2) class actions. Compare *McReynolds v. Merrill Lynch, Pierce, Fenner & Smith, Inc.*, 672 F.3d 482 (7th Cir. 2012) (reversing the denial of class certification in an employment discrimination case and noting that the lawfulness of the company policy and the availability of injunctive relief can be determined under Rule 23(c)(4) (issues classes) and (b)(2) but that separate trials may be necessary to determine the effect of the policy on individual earnings); *Gooch v. Life Invs. Ins. Co. of Am.*, 672 F.3d 402 (6th Cir. 2012) (upholding the certification of a (b)(2) class of plaintiffs seeking to have the court issue a declaratory judgment interpreting a cancer-insurance contract term that applied uniformly to each class member); *Ellis v. Costco Wholesale Corp.*, 2012 WL 4371817 (N.D. Cal. Sept. 25, 2012) (certifying a gender-discrimination class action under Rule 23(b)(2) for liability and injunctive relief and (b)(3) for backpay, compensatory, and punitive damages); with *M.D. ex rel Stukenberg v. Perry*, 675 F.3d 832 (5th Cir. 2012) (holding that a § 1983 action involving children in Texas's long-term foster care system was improperly certified under (b)(2) because some of the 12 injunctions sought would have affected only subgroups within the class); *Jamie S. v. Milwaukee Pub. Schs.*, 668 F.3d 481 (7th Cir. 2012) (holding that a (b)(2) class of special-education public-school students alleging systemic IDEA violations in Milwaukee public schools was inappropriate because a single remedial injunction failed to provide relief to the class as a whole). If a subclass could have been certified, why should the relief have to go to the class as a whole rather than to a particular subclass?

7.   Wal–Mart Stores, Inc. v. Dukes *Postscript.* The Supreme Court's decertification of the *Dukes* class did not end the litigation against Wal–Mart. After that decision, plaintiffs filed a fourth amended complaint that: reduced the proposed class size from 1.5 million women to between one and several-hundred thousand, added information about Wal–Mart's corporate structure, and included additional, specific examples of discriminatory conduct. Wal–Mart moved to dismiss this complaint, claiming that the new complaint suffered from the same deficiencies that derailed it in the Supreme Court. Although Judge Charles Breyer of the Northern District of California (Justice Stephen Breyer's brother) voiced concerns about whether the complaint could stand during oral argument, he denied Wal–Mart's motion to dismiss. He explained:

> With rare exceptions, the appropriate vehicle for testing the sufficiency of class allegations is a motion for class certification. This case is not one of the exceptions. Because Plaintiffs have proposed a class that could be certified if a showing consistent with the Supreme Court's decision were made, this Order reserves for later determination whether Plaintiffs' evidence suffices under Rule 23.

Dukes v. Wal–Mart Stores, Inc., 2012 WL 4329009, at *1 (N.D. Cal. Sept. 21, 2012). In addition, the Civil Rules Advisory Committee has recently appointed a Rule 23 subcommittee to examine the proper role of individual monetary awards in Rule 23(b)(2) mandatory classes as well as how courts should consider the merits in ruling on class certification. The minutes of these meetings (the first report was in March of 2012) are available on the Advisory Committee on Rules of Civil Procedure's website: http://www.uscourts.gov/RulesAndPolicies/rules/archives/meeting-minutes/meeting-minutes-rules-civil-procedure.aspx.

c. LIMITED FUND CLASSES UNDER RULE 23(b)(1)(B)

Ortiz v. Fibreboard Corp.

527 U.S. 815 (1999)

■ JUSTICE SOUTER delivered the opinion of the Court.

This case turns on the conditions for certifying a mandatory settlement class on a limited fund theory under Federal Rule of Civil Procedure 23(b)(1)(B). We hold that applicants for contested certification on this rationale must show that the fund is limited by more than the agreement of the parties, and has been allocated to claimants belonging within the class by a process addressing any conflicting interests of class members.

I

Like *Amchem Prods., Inc. v. Windsor*, 521 U.S. 591 (1997), this case is a class action prompted by the elephantine mass of asbestos cases, and our discussion in *Amchem* will suffice to show how this litigation defies customary judicial administration and calls for national legislation. . . .

As the tide of asbestos litigation rose, Fibreboard found itself litigating on two fronts. On one, plaintiffs were filing a stream of personal injury claims against it, swelling throughout the 1980's and 1990's to thousands of new claims for compensatory damages each year. On the second front, Fibreboard was battling for funds to pay its tort claimants. From May 1957 through March 1959, respondent Continental Casualty Company had provided Fibreboard with a comprehensive general liability policy with limits of $1 million per occurrence, $500,000 per claim, and no aggregate limit. Fibreboard also claimed that respondent Pacific Indemnity Company had insured it from 1956 to 1957 under a similar policy. Beginning in 1979, Fibreboard was locked in coverage litigation with Continental and Pacific in a California state trial court, which in 1990 held Continental and Pacific responsible for indemnification as to any claim by a claimant exposed to Fibreboard asbestos products prior to their policies' respective expiration dates. The decree also required the insurers to pay the full cost of defense for each claim covered. The insurance companies appealed.

With asbestos case filings continuing unabated, and its secure insurance assets almost depleted, Fibreboard in 1988 began a practice of "structured settlement," paying plaintiffs 40 percent of the settlement figure up front with the balance contingent upon a successful resolution of the coverage dispute. By 1991, however, the pace of filings forced Fibreboard to start settling cases entirely with the assignments of its rights against Continental, with no initial payment. To reflect the risk that Continental might prevail in the coverage dispute, these assignment agreements generally carried a figure about twice the nominal amount of earlier settlements. Continental challenged Fibreboard's right to make unilateral assignments, but in 1992 a California state court ruled for Fibreboard in that dispute.

Meanwhile, in the aftermath of a 1990 Federal Judicial Center conference on the asbestos litigation crisis, Fibreboard approached a group of leading asbestos plaintiffs' lawyers, offering to discuss a "global settlement" of its asbestos personal-injury liability. Early negotiations bore relatively little fruit, save for the December 1992 settlement by assignment of a significant inventory of pending claims. This settlement brought Fibreboard's deferred settlement obligations to more than $1.2 billion, all contingent upon victory over Continental on the scope of coverage and the validity of the settlement assignments.

In February 1993, after Continental had lost on both issues at the trial level, and thus faced the possibility of practically unbounded liability, it too joined the global settlement negotiations. Because Continental conditioned its part in any settlement on a guarantee of "total peace," ensuring no unknown future liabilities, talks focused on the feasibility of a mandatory class action, one binding all potential plaintiffs and giving none of them any choice to opt out of the certified class. Negotiations continued throughout the spring and summer of 1993, but the difficulty of settling both actually pending and potential future claims simultaneously led to an agreement in early August to segregate and settle an inventory of some 45,000 pending claims, being substantially all those filed by one of the plaintiffs' firms negotiating the global settlement. The settlement amounts per claim were higher than average, with one-half due on closing and the remainder contingent upon either a global settlement or Fibreboard's success in the coverage litigation. This agreement provided the model for settling inventory claims of other firms.

With the insurance companies' appeal of the consolidated coverage case set to be heard on August 27, the negotiating parties faced a motivating deadline, and about midnight before the argument, in a coffee shop in Tyler, Texas, the negotiators finally agreed upon $1.535 billion as the key term of a "Global Settlement Agreement." $1.525 billion of this sum would come from Continental and Pacific, in the proportion established by the California trial court in the coverage case, while Fibreboard would contribute $10 million, all but $500,000 of it from other insurance proceeds. The negotiators also agreed to identify unsettled present claims against Fibreboard and set aside an as-then unspecified fund to resolve them, anticipating that the bulk of any excess left in that fund would be transferred to class claimants. The next day, as a hedge against the possibility that the Global Settlement Agreement might fail, plaintiffs' counsel insisted as a condition of that agreement that Fibreboard and its two insurers settle the coverage dispute by what came to be known as the "Trilateral Settlement Agreement." . . .

On September 9, 1993, as agreed, a group of named plaintiffs filed an action in the United States District Court for the Eastern District of Texas, seeking certification for settlement purposes of a mandatory class comprising three groups: all persons with personal injury claims against Fibreboard for asbestos exposure who had not yet brought suit or settled their claims before the previous August 27; those who had dismissed such a claim but retained the right to bring a future action against Fibreboard; and "past, present and future spouses, parents, children, and other relatives" of class members exposed to Fibreboard asbestos. The class did not include claimants with actions presently pending against Fibreboard or claimants "who filed and, for cash payment or some other negotiated value, dismissed claims against Fibreboard, and whose only retained right is to sue Fibreboard upon development of an asbestos-related malignancy." The complaint pleaded personal injury claims against Fibreboard, and, as justification for class certification, relied on the shared necessity of ensuring insurance funds sufficient for compensation. After Continental and Pacific had obtained leave to intervene as party-defendants, the District Court provisionally granted class certification, enjoined commencement of further separate litigation against Fibreboard by class members, and appointed a guardian ad litem to review the fairness of the settlement to the class members.

As finally negotiated, the Global Settlement Agreement provided that in exchange for full releases from class members, Fibreboard, Continental, and Pacific would establish a trust to process and pay class members' asbestos personal injury and death claims. Claimants seeking compensation would be required to try to settle with the trust. If initial settlement attempts failed, claimants would have to proceed to mediation, arbitration, and a mandatory settlement conference. Only after exhausting that process could claimants go to court against the trust, subject to a limit of $500,000 per claim, with punitive damages and prejudgment interest barred. Claims resolved without litigation would be discharged over three years, while judgments would be paid out over a 5– to 10–year period. The Global Settlement Agreement also contained spendthrift provisions to conserve the trust, and provided for paying more serious claims first in the event of a shortfall in any given year.

After an extensive campaign to give notice of the pending settlement to potential class members, the District Court allowed groups of objectors, including petitioners here, to intervene. After an 8–day fairness hearing, the District Court certified the class and approved the settlement as "fair, adequate, and reasonable" under Rule 23(e). Satisfied that the requirements of Rule 23(a) were met, the District Court certified the class under Rule 23(b)(1)(B), citing the risk that Fibreboard might lose or fare poorly on appeal of the coverage case or lose the assignment-settlement dispute, leaving it without funds to pay all claims. The "allowance of individual adjudications by class members," the District Court concluded, "would have destroyed the opportunity to compromise the insurance coverage dispute by creating the settlement fund, and would have exposed the class members to the very risks that the settlement addresses." In response to intervenors' objections that the absence of a "limited fund" precluded certification under Rule 23(b)(1)(B), the District Court ruled that although the subdivision is not so restricted, if it were, this case would qualify. It found both the "disputed insurance asset liquidated by the $1.535 billion Global Settlement," and, alternatively, "the sum of the value of Fibreboard plus the value of its insurance coverage," as measured by the insurance funds' settlement value, to be relevant "limited funds."

[handwritten margin note: D.C. says ind. adjudications would destroy assets.]

On appeal, the Fifth Circuit affirmed both as to class certification and adequacy of settlement. . . .

Shortly thereafter, this Court decided *Amchem* and proceeded to vacate the Fifth Circuit's judgment and remand for further consideration in light of that decision. On remand, the Fifth Circuit again affirmed, in a brief *per curiam* opinion, distinguishing *Amchem* on the grounds that the instant action proceeded under Rule 23(b)(1)(B) rather than (b)(3), and did not allocate awards according to the nature of the claimant's injury. *In re Asbestos Litig.*, 134 F.3d 668, 669–70 (5th Cir. 1998). Again citing the findings on certification under Rule 23(b)(1)(B), the Fifth Circuit affirmed as "incontestable" the District Court's conclusion that the terms of the subdivision had been met. *Id.* at 670. . . .

We granted certiorari, 524 U.S. 936 (1998), and now reverse. . . .

III

A

. . . Rule 23(b)(1)(B) speaks from "a vantage point within the class, [from which the Advisory Committee] spied out situations where lawsuits conducted with individual members of the class would have the practical if not technical effect of concluding the interests of the other members as well, or of impairing the ability of the others to protect their own interests." Benjamin Kaplan, *Continuing Work of the Civil Committee: 1966 Amendments of the Federal Rules of Civil Procedure (I)*, 81 Harv. L. Rev. 356, 388 (1967). Thus, the subdivision (read with subdivision (c)(2)) provides for certification of a class whose members have no right to withdraw, when "the prosecution of separate actions . . . would create a risk" of "adjudications with respect to individual members of the class which would as a practical matter be dispositive of the interests of the other members not parties to the adjudications or substantially impair or impede their ability to protect their interests." Fed. R. Civ. P. 23(b)(1)(B). . . .

Among the traditional varieties of representative suit encompassed by Rule 23(b)(1)(B) were those involving "the presence of property which call[ed] for distribution or management," J. Moore & J. Friedman, 2 FEDERAL PRACTICE 2240 (1938). One recurring type of such suits was the limited fund class action, aggregating "claims . . . made by numerous persons against a fund insufficient to satisfy all claims." Adv. Comm. Notes 697; cf. 1 NEWBERG § 4.09, at 4–33 ("Classic" limited fund class actions "include claimants to trust assets, a bank account, insurance proceeds, company assets in a liquidation sale, proceeds of a ship sale in a maritime accident suit, and others"). The Advisory Committee cited *Dickinson v. Burnham*, 197 F.2d 973 (2d Cir. 1952), cert. denied, 344 U.S. 875 (1952), as illustrative of this tradition. In *Dickinson*, investors hoping to save a failing company had contributed some $600,000, which had been misused until nothing was left but a pool of secret profits on a fraction of the original investment. In a class action, the District Court took charge of this fund, subjecting it to a constructive trust for division among subscribers who demonstrated their claims, in amounts proportional to each class member's percentage of all substantiated claims. The Second Circuit approved the class action and the distribution of the entire pool to claimants, noting that "[a]lthough none of the contributors has been paid in full, no one . . . now asserts or suggests that they should have full recovery . . . as on an ordinary tort liability for conspiracy and defrauding. The court's power of disposition over the fund was therefore absolute and final." *Id.*, at 980. As the Advisory Committee recognized in describing *Dickinson*, equity required absent parties to be represented, joinder being impractical, where individual claims to be satisfied from the one asset would, as a practical matter, prejudice the rights of absent claimants against a fund inadequate to pay them all.

Equity, of course, recognized the same necessity to bind absent claimants to a limited fund when no formal imposition of a constructive trust was entailed. In *Guffanti v. Nat'l Surety Co.*, 196 N.Y. 452, 458, 90 N.E. 174, 176 (1909), for example, the defendant received money to supply steamship tickets and had posted a $15,000 bond as required by state law. He converted to personal use funds collected from more than 150 ticket purchasers, was then adjudged bankrupt, and absconded. One of the defrauded ticket purchasers sued the surety in equity on behalf of himself and all others like him. Over the defendant's objection, the New York Court of Appeals sustained the equitable class suit, citing among other considerations the fact that all recovery had to come from a "limited fund out of which the aggregate recoveries must be sought" that was inadequate to pay all claims, and subject to pro rata distribution. *Id.* at 458, 90 N.E. 174, 90 N.E. at 176. See Hazard, Gedid, & Sowle 1915 ("[*Guffanti*] explained that when a debtor's assets were less than the total of the creditors' claims, a binding class action was not only permitted but was required; otherwise some creditors (the parties) would be paid and others (the absentees) would not"). See also *Morrison v. Warren* 174 Misc. 233, 234, 20 N.Y.S.2d 26, 27 (1940) (suit on behalf of more than 400 beneficiaries of an insurance policy following a fire appropriate where "the amount of the claims . . . greatly exceeds the amount of the insurance"); *Nat'l Surety Co. v. Graves*, 211 Ala. 533, 534, 101 So. 190 (1924) (suit against a surety company by stockholders "for the benefit of themselves and all others similarly situate who will join the suit" where it was alleged that individual suits were being filed on surety bonds that "would result in the exhaustion of the penalties of the bonds, leaving many stockholders without remedy").

Ross v. Crary, 1 Paige Ch. 416, 417–18 (N.Y. Ch. 1829), presents the concept of the limited fund class action in another incarnation. "[D]ivers suits for general legacies," *id.* at 417, were brought by various legatees against the executor of a decedent's estate. The *Ross* court stated that where "there is an allegation of a deficiency of the fund, so that an account of the estate is necessary," the court will "direc[t] an account in one cause only" and "stay the proceeding[s] in the others, leaving all the parties interested in the fund, to come in under the decree." *Id.* at 417–18. Thus, in equity, legatee and creditor bills against the assets of a decedent's estate had to be brought on behalf of all similarly situated claimants where it was clear from the pleadings that the available portion of the estate could not satisfy the aggregate claims against it.

B

The cases forming this pedigree of the limited fund class action as understood by the drafters of Rule 23 have a number of common characteristics, despite the variety of circumstances from which they arose. The points of resemblance are not necessarily the points of contention resolved in the particular cases, but they show what the Advisory Committee must have assumed would be at least a sufficient set of conditions to justify binding absent members of a class under Rule 23(b)(1)(B), from which no one has the right to secede.

The first and most distinctive characteristic is that the totals of the aggregated liquidated claims and the fund available for satisfying them, set definitely at their maximums, demonstrate the inadequacy of the fund to pay all the claims. The concept driving this type of suit was insufficiency, which alone justified the limit on an early feast to avoid a later famine. The equity of the limitation is its necessity.

Inadequacy of fund to pay all claims

Second, the whole of the inadequate fund was to be devoted to the overwhelming claims. It went without saying that the defendant or estate or constructive trustee with the inadequate assets had no opportunity to benefit himself or claimants of lower priority by holding back on the amount distributed to the class. The limited fund cases thus ensured that the class as a whole was given the best deal; they did not give a defendant a better deal than *seriatim* litigation would have produced.

Whole fund must go to paying claims.

individual suits

Third, the claimants identified by a common theory of recovery were treated equitably among themselves. The cases assume that the class will comprise everyone who might state a claim on a single or repeated set of facts, invoking a common theory of recovery, to be satisfied from the limited fund as the source of payment. Each of the people represented in *Ross*, for example, had comparable entitlement as a legatee under the testator's will. Those subject to representation in *Dickinson* had a common source of claims in the solicitation of funds by parties whose subsequent defalcation left them without their investment, while in *Guffanti* the individuals represented had each entrusted money for ticket purchases. In these cases the hope of recovery was limited, respectively, by estate assets, the residuum of profits, and the amount of the bond. Once the represented classes were so identified, there was no question of omitting anyone whose claim shared the common theory of liability and would contribute to the calculated shortfall of recovery. . . .[18] Once all similar claims were brought directly or by representation before the court, these antecedents of the mandatory class action presented straightforward models of equitable treatment, with the simple equity of a pro rata distribution providing the required fairness, see 1 J. Pomeroy, *Equity Jurisprudence* § 407, pp. 764–65 (4th ed. 1918) ("[I]f the fund is not sufficient to discharge all claims upon it in full . . . equity will incline to regard all the demands as standing upon an equal footing, and will decree a *pro rata* distribution or payment").

In sum, mandatory class treatment through representative actions on a limited fund theory was justified with reference to a "fund" with a definitely ascertained limit, all of which would be distributed to satisfy all those with liquidated claims based on a common theory of liability, by an equitable, pro rata distribution.

C

The Advisory Committee, and presumably the Congress in approving subdivision (b)(1)(B), must have assumed that an action with these characteristics would satisfy the limited fund rationale cognizable under that subdivision. The question remains how far the same characteristics are necessary for limited fund treatment. While we cannot settle all the details of a subdivision (b)(1)(B) limited fund here (and so cannot decide the ultimate question whether settlements of multitudes of related tort actions are amenable to mandatory class treatment), there are good reasons to treat these characteristics as presumptively necessary, and not merely sufficient, to satisfy the limited fund rationale for a mandatory action. At the least, the burden of justification rests on the proponent of any departure from the traditional norm.

It is true, of course, that the text of Rule 23(b)(1)(B) is on its face open to a more lenient limited fund concept, just as it covers more historical antecedents than the limited fund. But the greater the leniency in departing from the historical limited fund model, the greater the likelihood of abuse in ways that will be apparent when we apply the limited fund criteria to the case before us. The prudent course, therefore, is to presume that when

---

[18] Professor Chafee explained, in discussing bills of peace, that where a case presents a limited fund, "it is impossible to make a fair distribution of the fund or limited liability to all members of the multitude except in a single proceeding where the claim of each can be adjudicated with due reference to the claims of the rest. The fund or limited liability is like a mince pie, which cannot be satisfactorily divided until the carver counts the number of persons at the table." Zechariah Chafee Jr., *Bills of Peace with Multiple Parties*, 45 Harv. L. Rev. 1297, 1311 (1932).

subdivision (b)(1)(B) was devised to cover limited fund actions, the object was to stay close to the historical model. As will be seen, this limiting construction finds support in the Advisory Committee's expressions of understanding, minimizes potential conflict with the Rules Enabling Act, and avoids serious constitutional concerns raised by the mandatory class resolution of individual legal claims, especially where a case seeks to resolve future liability in a settlement-only action.

To begin with, the Advisory Committee looked cautiously at the potential for creativity under Rule 23(b)(1)(B), at least in comparison with Rule 23(b)(3). Although the Committee crafted all three subdivisions of the Rule in general, practical terms, without the formalism that had bedeviled the original Rule 23, see Kaplan, *Continuing Work*, at 380–86, the Committee was consciously retrospective with intent to codify pre-Rule categories under Rule 23(b)(1), not forward looking as it was in anticipating innovations under Rule 23(b)(3). Thus, the Committee intended subdivision (b)(1) to capture the " 'standard' " class actions recognized in pre-Rule practice, *id.* at 394.

Consistent with its backward look under subdivision (b)(1), as commentators have pointed out, it is clear that the Advisory Committee did not contemplate that the mandatory class action codified in subdivision (b)(1)(B) would be used to aggregate unliquidated tort claims on a limited fund rationale. None of the examples cited in the Advisory Committee Notes or by Professor Kaplan in explaining Rule 23(b)(1)(B) remotely approach what was then described as a "mass accident" case. While the Advisory Committee focused much attention on the amenability of Rule 23(b)(3) to such cases, the Committee's debates are silent about resolving tort claims under a mandatory limited fund rationale under Rule 23(b)(1)(B). It is simply implausible that the Advisory Committee, so concerned about the potential difficulties posed by dealing with mass tort cases under Rule 23(b)(3), with its provisions for notice and the right to opt out, see Rule 23(c)(2), would have uncritically assumed that mandatory versions of such class actions, lacking such protections, could be certified under Rule 23(b)(1)(B). We do not, it is true, decide the ultimate question whether Rule 23(b)(1)(B) may ever be used to aggregate individual tort claims, cf. *Ticor Title Ins. Co. v. Brown*, 511 U.S. 117, 121 (1994) (per curiam). But we do recognize that the Committee would have thought such an application of the Rule surprising, and take this as a good reason to limit any surprise by presuming that the Rule's historical antecedents identify requirements.

The Rules Enabling Act underscores the need for caution. As we said in *Amchem*, no reading of the Rule can ignore the Act's mandate that "rules of procedure 'shall not abridge, enlarge or modify any substantive right,' " *Amchem*, 521 U.S. at 613 (quoting 28 U.S.C. § 2072(b)); cf. *Guaranty Trust Co. v. York*, 326 U.S. 99, 105 (1945) ("In giving federal courts 'cognizance' of equity suits in cases of diversity jurisdiction, Congress never gave, nor did the federal courts ever claim, the power to deny substantive rights created by State law or to create substantive rights denied by State law"). Petitioners argue that the Act has been violated here, asserting that the Global Settlement Agreement's priorities of claims and compromise of full recovery abrogated the state law that must govern this diversity action under 28 U.S.C. § 1652. Although we need not grapple with the difficult choice-of-law and substantive state-law questions raised by petitioners' assertion, we do need to recognize the tension between the limited fund class action's pro rata distribution in equity and the rights of individual tort victims at law.

Even if we assume that some such tension is acceptable under the Rules Enabling Act, it is best kept within tolerable limits by keeping limited fund practice under Rule 23(b)(1)(B) close to the practice preceding its adoption.

. . . [M]andatory class actions aggregating damages claims implicate the due process "principle of general application in Anglo–American jurisprudence that one is not bound by a judgment *in personam* in a litigation in which he is not designated as a party or to which he has not been made a party by service of process," *Hansberry v. Lee*, 311 U.S. 32, 40 (1940), it being "our 'deep-rooted historic tradition that everyone should have his own day in court,'" *Martin v. Wilks*, 490 U.S. 755, 762 (1989) (quoting 18 C. Wright, A. Miller, & E. Cooper, FEDERAL PRACTICE AND PROCEDURE § 4449, p. 417 (1981)). . . . Although " '[w]e have recognized an exception to the general rule when, in certain limited circumstances, a person, although not a party, has his interests adequately represented by someone with the same interests who is a party,'" or "where a special remedial scheme exists expressly foreclosing successive litigation by nonlitigants, as for example in bankruptcy or probate," *Martin,* 490 U.S. at 762 n.2 (citations omitted), the burden of justification rests on the exception.

The inherent tension between representative suits and the day-in-court ideal is only magnified if applied to damages claims gathered in a mandatory class. Unlike Rule 23(b)(3) class members, objectors to the collectivism of a mandatory subdivision (b)(1)(B) action have no inherent right to abstain. The legal rights of absent class members (which in a class like this one would include claimants who by definition may be unidentifiable when the class is certified) are resolved regardless of either their consent, or, in a class with objectors, their express wish to the contrary.[23] And in settlement-only class actions the procedural protections built into the Rule to protect the rights of absent class members during litigation are never invoked in an adversarial setting, see *Amchem,* 521 U.S. at 620. . . .

IV

The record on which the District Court rested its certification of the class for the purpose of the global settlement did not support the essential premises of mandatory limited fund actions. It failed to demonstrate that the fund was limited except by the agreement of the parties, and it showed exclusions from the class and allocations of assets at odds with the concept of limited fund treatment and the structural protections of Rule 23(a) explained in *Amchem*.

A

The defect of certification going to the most characteristic feature of a limited fund action was the uncritical adoption by both the District Court and the Court of Appeals of figures agreed upon by the parties in defining the limits of the fund and demonstrating its inadequacy. When a district court, as here, certifies for class action settlement only, the moment of certification requires "heightene[d] attention," *Amchem,* 521 U.S. at 620, to the justifications for binding the class members. This is so because certifi-

[handwritten margin note: The idea of parties Defining the fund and agreeing that its inadequate is inconsistent.]

---

[23] It is no answer in this case that the settlement agreement provided for a limited, back-end "opt out" in the form of a right on the part of class members eventually to take their case to court if dissatisfied with the amount provided by the trust. The "opt out" in this case requires claimants to exhaust a variety of alternative dispute mechanisms, to bring suit against the trust, and not against Fibreboard, and it limits damages to $500,000, to be paid out in installments over 5 to 10 years, despite multimillion-dollar jury verdicts sometimes reached in asbestos suits, *In re Asbestos Litig.*, 90 F.3d, at 1006–07 n.30 (Smith, J., dissenting). Indeed, on approximately a dozen occasions, Fibreboard had settled for more than $500,000.

cation of a mandatory settlement class, however provisional technically, effectively concludes the proceeding save for the final fairness hearing. And, as we held in *Amchem*, a fairness hearing under Rule 23(e) is no substitute for rigorous adherence to those provisions of the Rule "designed to protect absentees," *id.*, among them subdivision (b)(1)(B). Thus, in an action such as this the settling parties must present not only their agreement, but evidence on which the district court may ascertain the limit and the insufficiency of the fund, with support in findings of fact following a proceeding in which the evidence is subject to challenge.

The "fund" in this case comprised both the general assets of Fibreboard and the insurance assets provided by the two policies, see 90 F.3d at 982 (describing the fund as Fibreboard's entire equity and $2 billion in insurance assets under the Trilateral Settlement Agreement). As to Fibreboard's assets exclusive of the contested insurance, the District Court and the Fifth Circuit concluded that Fibreboard had a then-current sale value of $235 million that could be devoted to the limited fund. While that estimate may have been conservative,[28] at least the District Court heard evidence and made an independent finding at some point in the proceedings. The same, however, cannot be said for the value of the disputed insurance.

The insurance assets would obviously be "limited" in the traditional sense if the total of demonstrable claims would render the insurers insolvent, or if the policies provided aggregate limits falling short of that total; calculation might be difficult, but the way to demonstrate the limit would be clear. Neither possibility is presented in this case, however. Instead, any limit of the insurance asset here had to be a product of potentially unlimited policy coverage discounted by the risk that Fibreboard would ultimately lose the coverage dispute litigation. This sense of limit as a value discounted by risk is of course a step removed from the historical model, but even on the assumption that it would suffice for limited fund treatment, there was no adequate finding of fact to support its application here. Instead of undertaking an independent evaluation of potential insurance funds, the District Court (and, later, the Court of Appeals), simply accepted the $2 billion Trilateral Settlement Agreement figure as representing the maximum amount the insurance companies could be required to pay tort victims, concluding that "[w]here insurance coverage is disputed, it is appropriate to value the insurance asset at a settlement value."

Settlement value is not always acceptable, however. One may take a settlement amount as good evidence of the maximum available if one can assume that parties of equal knowledge and negotiating skill agreed upon the figure through arms-length bargaining, unhindered by any considerations tugging against the interests of the parties ostensibly represented in the negotiation. But no such assumption may be indulged in this case, or probably in any class action settlement with the potential for gigantic fees. In this case, certainly, any assumption that plaintiffs' counsel could be of a mind to do their simple best in bargaining for the benefit of the settlement class is patently at odds with the fact that at least some of the same lawyers representing plaintiffs and the class had also negotiated the separate settlement of 45,000 pending claims, 90 F.3d at 969–71, the full payment of which was contingent on a successful Global Settlement Agreement or the

---

[28] The District Court based the $235 million figure on evidence provided by an investment banker regarding what a "financially prudent buyer" would pay to acquire Fibreboard free of its personal injury asbestos liabilities, less transaction costs. In 1997, however, Fibreboard was acquired for about $515 million, plus $85 million of assumed debt.

successful resolution of the insurance coverage dispute (either by litigation or by agreement, as eventually occurred in the Trilateral Settlement Agreement). Class counsel thus had great incentive to reach any agreement in the global settlement negotiations that they thought might survive a Rule 23(e) fairness hearing, rather than the best possible arrangement for the substantially unidentified global settlement class. The resulting incentive to favor the known plaintiffs in the earlier settlement was, indeed, an egregious example of the conflict noted in *Amchem* resulting from divergent interests of the presently injured and future claimants. See 521 U.S. at 626–27 (discussing adequacy of named representatives under Rule 23(a)(4)). . . .

B

The explanation of need for independent determination of the fund has necessarily anticipated our application of the requirement of equity among members of the class. There are two issues, the inclusiveness of the class and the fairness of distributions to those within it. On each, this certification for settlement fell short.

The definition of the class excludes myriad claimants with causes of action, or foreseeable causes of action, arising from exposure to Fibreboard asbestos. While the class includes those with present claims never filed, present claims withdrawn without prejudice, and future claimants, it fails to include those who had previously settled with Fibreboard while retaining the right to sue again "upon development of an asbestos related malignancy," plaintiffs with claims pending against Fibreboard at the time of the initial announcement of the Global Settlement Agreement, and the plaintiffs in the "inventory" claims settled as a supposedly necessary step in reaching the global settlement, see 90 F.3d at 971. . . . [T]here can be no question that such a mandatory settlement class will not qualify when in the very negotiations aimed at a class settlement, class counsel agree to exclude what could turn out to be as much as a third of the claimants that negotiators thought might eventually be involved, a substantial number of whom class counsel represent.

Might such class exclusions be forgiven if it were shown that the class members with present claims and the outsiders ended up with comparable benefits? The question is academic here. On the record before us, we cannot speculate on how the unsettled claims would fare if the global settlement were approved, or under the trilateral settlement. As for the settled inventory claims, their plaintiffs appeared to have obtained better terms than the class members. They received an immediate payment of 50 percent of a settlement higher than the historical average, and would get the remainder if the global settlement were sustained (or the coverage litigation resolved, as it turned out to be by the Trilateral Settlement Agreement); the class members, by contrast, would be assured of a 3–year payout for claims settled, whereas the unsettled faced a prospect of mediation followed by arbitration as prior conditions of instituting suit, which would even then be subject to a recovery limit, a slower payout, and the limitations of the trust's spendthrift protection. Finally, as discussed below, even ostensible parity between settling nonclass plaintiffs and class members would be insufficient to overcome the failure to provide the structural protection of independent representation as for subclasses with conflicting interests. . . .

[Citing *Amchem*, the Court then went on to criticize the inclusion in a single class of both presently impaired and presently unimpaired persons as well as the inclusion of both pre– and post–1959 claims. These passages were reproduced earlier in this Chapter, in the notes following *Amchem*.]

C

A third contested feature of this settlement certification that departs markedly from the limited fund antecedents is the ultimate provision for a fund smaller than the assets understood by the Court of Appeals to be available for payment of the mandatory class members' claims; most notably, Fibreboard was allowed to retain virtually its entire net worth. Given our treatment of the two preceding deficiencies of the certification, there is of course no need to decide whether this feature of the agreement would alone be fatal to the Global Settlement Agreement. To ignore it entirely, however, would be so misleading that we have decided simply to identify the issue it raises, without purporting to resolve it at this time.

Fibreboard listed its supposed entire net worth as a component of the total (and allegedly inadequate) assets available for claimants, but subsequently retained all but $500,000 of that equity for itself.[34] On the face of it, the arrangement seems irreconcilable with the justification of necessity in denying any opportunity for withdrawal of class members whose jury trial rights will be compromised, whose damages will be capped, and whose payments will be delayed. With Fibreboard retaining nearly all its net worth, it hardly appears that such a regime is the best that can be provided for class members. Given the nature of a limited fund and the need to apply its criteria at the certification stage, it is not enough for a District Court to say that it "need not ensure that a defendant designate a particular source of its assets to satisfy the class' claims; [but only that] the amount recovered by the class [be] fair." *Ahearn*, 162 F.R.D. at 527. . . .

VI

In sum, the applicability of Rule 23(b)(1)(B) to a fund and plan purporting to liquidate actual and potential tort claims is subject to question, and its purported application in this case was in any event improper. The Advisory Committee did not envision mandatory class actions in cases like this one, and both the Rules Enabling Act and the policy of avoiding serious constitutional issues counsel against leniency in recognizing mandatory limited fund actions in circumstances markedly different from the traditional paradigm. Assuming, *arguendo*, that a mandatory, limited fund rationale could under some circumstances be applied to a settlement class of tort claimants, it would be essential that the fund be shown to be limited independently of the agreement of the parties to the action, and equally essential under Rules 23(a) and (b)(1)(B) that the class include all those with claims unsatisfied at the time of the settlement negotiations, with intraclass conflicts addressed by recognizing independently represented subclasses. In this case, the limit of the fund was determined by treating the

---

[34] We need not decide here how close to insolvency a limited fund defendant must be brought as a condition of class certification. While there is no inherent conflict between a limited fund class action under Rule 23(b)(1)(B) and the Bankruptcy Code, cf., e.g., *In re Drexel Burnham Lambert Group, Inc.*, 960 F.2d 285, 292 (2d Cir. 1992), it is worth noting that if limited fund certification is allowed in a situation where a company provides only a *de minimis* contribution to the ultimate settlement fund, the incentives such a resolution would provide to companies facing tort liability to engineer settlements similar to the one negotiated in this case would, in all likelihood, significantly undermine the protections for creditors built into the Bankruptcy Code. We note further that Congress in the Bankruptcy Reform Act of 1994, Pub. L. 103–394, § 111(a), amended the Bankruptcy Code to enable a debtor in a Chapter 11 reorganization in certain circumstances to establish a trust toward which the debtor may channel future asbestos-related liability, see 11 U.S.C. §§ 524(g), (h).

settlement agreement as dispositive, an error magnified by the representation of class members by counsel also representing excluded plaintiffs, whose settlements would be funded fully upon settlement of the class action on any terms that could survive final fairness review. Those separate settlements, together with other exclusions from the claimant class, precluded adequate structural protection by subclass treatment, which was not even afforded to the conflicting elements within the class as certified.

The judgment of the Court of Appeals, accordingly, is reversed, and the case is remanded for further proceedings consistent with this opinion.

It is so ordered.

■ JUSTICE BREYER, with whom JUSTICE STEVENS joins, dissenting. . . .

I

A

Four special background circumstances underlie this settlement and help to explain the reasonableness and consequent lawfulness of the relevant District Court determinations. First, as the majority points out, the settlement comprises part of an "elephantine mass of asbestos cases," which "defies customary judicial administration. . . ."

Judge Parker, the experienced trial judge who approved this settlement, noted in one 3,000–member asbestos class action over which he presided that 448 of the original class members had died while the litigation was pending. *Cimino v. Raymark Indus., Inc.*, 751 F. Supp. 649, 651 (E.D. Tex. 1990). And yet, Judge Parker went on to state, if the District Court could close "thirty cases a month, it would [still] take six and one-half years to try these cases and [due to new filings] there would be pending over 5,000 untouched cases" at the end of that time. *Id.* at 652. His subsequent efforts to accelerate final decision or settlement through the use of sample cases produced a highly complex trial (133 trial days, more than 500 witnesses, half a million pages of documents) that eventually closed only about 160 cases because efforts to extrapolate from the sample proved fruitless. The consequence is not only delay but also attorney's fees and other "transaction costs" that are unusually high, to the point where, of each dollar that asbestos defendants pay, those costs consume an estimated 61 cents, with only 39 cents going to victims.

Second, an individual asbestos case is a tort case, of a kind that courts, not legislatures, ordinarily will resolve. It is the number of these cases, not their nature, that creates the special judicial problem. The judiciary cannot treat the problem as entirely one of legislative failure, as if it were caused, say, by a poorly drafted statute. Thus, when "calls for national legislation" go unanswered, judges can and should search aggressively for ways, within the framework of existing law, to avoid delay and expense so great as to bring about a massive denial of justice.

Third, in that search the district courts may take advantage of experience that appellate courts do not have. Judge Parker, for example, has written of "a disparity of appreciation for the magnitude of the problem," growing out of the difference between the trial courts' "daily involvement with asbestos litigation" and the appellate courts' "limited" exposure to such litigation in infrequent appeals. *Cimino*, 751 F. Supp. at 651.

Fourth, the alternative to class-action settlement is not a fair opportunity for each potential plaintiff to have his or her own day in court. Unusually high litigation costs, unusually long delays, and limitations upon the total amount of resources available for payment together mean that most potential plaintiffs may not have a realistic alternative. And Federal Rule of Civil Procedure 23 was designed to address situations in which the historical model of individual actions would not, for practical reasons, work. . . .

II

. . . The [present] case falls within Rule [23(b)(1)(B)]'s language as long as there was a significant "risk" that the total assets available to satisfy the claims of the class members would fall well below the likely total value of those claims, for in such circumstances the money would go to those claimants who brought their actions first, thereby " 'substantially impair[ing]' " the " 'ability' " of later claimants " 'to protect their interests.' " And the District Court found there was indeed such a " 'risk.' "

Conceptually speaking, that "risk" was no different from the risk inherent in a classic pre-Rules "limited fund" case. Suppose a broker agrees to invest the funds of 10 individuals who each give the broker $100. The broker misuses the money, and the customers sue. (1) Suppose their claims total $1,000, but the broker's total assets amount to $100. (2) Suppose the same broker has no assets left, but he does have an insurance policy worth $100. (3) Suppose the broker has both $100 in assets and a $100 insurance policy.

Same Risk.

The first two cases are classic limited fund cases [of the sort to which the majority points]. The third case simply combines the first two, and that third case is the case before us.

Of course the value of the insurance policies in our case is not as precise as the $100 in my example, nor was it certain at the time of settlement. But that uncertainty makes no difference. It was certain that the insurance policies' value was limited. And that limitation was created by the likelihood of an independent judicial determination of the meaning of words in the policy, in respect to which the merits or value of the underlying tort claims against Fibreboard were beside the point.

Nor does it matter that the value of the insurance policies in our case might have fluctuated over time. Long before the Federal Rules of Civil Procedure, courts permitted actions by one group of insurance policyholders to bind all policyholders, even where the group proceeded against an insurance-company-administered fund that fluctuated over time. See *Hartford Life Ins. Co. v. Ibs*, 237 U.S. 662, 672 (1915) (life insurance fund which, like the fund before us, was administered through court-ordered rules that bound all policyholders).

Neither does it matter that the insurance policies *might* be worth much more money *if* the California court decided the coverage dispute in Fibreboard's favor. A trust worth, say, $1 million (faced with $2 million in claims) is a limited fund, despite the possibility that a company whose stock it holds *might* strike oil and send the value of the trust skyrocketing. Limitation is a matter of present value, which takes appropriate account of such future possibilities. . . .

There is no doubt in this case that the settlement made far more money available to satisfy asbestos claims than was likely to occur in its absence. And the District Court found that administering the fund would involve transaction costs of only 15%. A comparison of that 15% figure with the 61% transaction costs figure applicable to asbestos cases in general suggests hundreds of millions of dollars in savings—an amount greater than Fibreboard's net worth. And, of course, not only is it better for the injured plaintiffs, it is far better for Fibreboard, its employees, its creditors, and the communities where it is located for Fibreboard to remain a working enterprise, rather than slowly forcing it into bankruptcy while most of its money is spent on asbestos lawyers and expert witnesses. . . .

NOTES AND QUESTIONS

1.   *The Relationship of* Amchem *and* Ortiz. Does the reasoning of the Court's decision two years earlier as to the opt-out class settlement in *Amchem* foreordain the outcome as to the mandatory class settlement in *Ortiz*? The objectors to the *Ortiz* class settlement certainly thought so. Once again, counsel for the objectors consisted of Baron & Budd, the same asbestos plaintiffs' law firm that successfully challenged the *Amchem* class settlement. Their petition for the writ of certiorari in *Ortiz* began with the line: "Some people just can't take a hint."

Recall one of the core holdings of *Amchem*: that the existence of a proposed class settlement cannot, in itself, supply the predominant common issue required for certification of an opt-out class. Does the Court's approach to the purported limited fund in *Ortiz* flow from a similar principle?

2.   *Identifying a Limited Fund*. As between Justice Souter for the majority and Justice Breyer for the dissenters, who has the better of the argument on whether there existed a limited fund in *Ortiz*? Limited at what time?

3.   *Limited–Fund Class Action versus Chapter 11 Bankruptcy*. Why did Fibreboard pursue the class settlement ultimately struck down in *Ortiz* rather than initiate a corporate reorganization proceeding under the auspices of Chapter 11 of the Bankruptcy Code? Consider that a reorganization proceeding in bankruptcy would have triggered the application of the absolute priority rule. On its face, the absolute priority rule requires that, as a precondition to confirmation under Chapter 11, a reorganization plan must pay debt holders (a category that includes tort claimants against the debtor firm) before equity holders (such as corporate shareholders). 11 U.S.C. § 1129(b)(2). Two commentators explain that reorganization plans under Chapter 11 often deviate from notions of absolute priority. These commentators contend that these seeming deviations stem from uncertainty over the valuation of the debtor firm and the concomitant need to account for that uncertainty in the division of resources between debt holders and equity holders. Douglas G. Baird & Donald S. Bernstein, *Absolute Priority, Valuation Uncertainty, and the Reorganization Bargain*, 115 Yale L.J. 1930 (2006).

4.   *Limited–Fund Class Action versus Legislation*. At bottom, the deal struck down in *Ortiz* sought to confine future tort claimants essentially to the insurance coverage of the defendant. Lest one think that this kind of deal has faded from the legal landscape, consider the legislation enacted by Congress in the aftermath of the terrorist attacks of September 11, 2001. Air Transportation Safety and System Stabilization Act, Pub. L. No. 107–42, 115 Stat. 230 (2001). Victims of the attacks and their survivors have two options: They may seek compensation from a government-run fund backed by the resources of the United States Treasury (popularly known as the 9/11 Fund). Or they may sue the airlines that operated the ill-fated flights. As to this second option, however, the 9/11 Fund legislation caps the potential liability of the airlines at the limits of their insurance coverage. (In addition, the legislation confines such

litigation to a particular federal district court.) Why should Congress be able to cap the liability of the airlines at the limits of their insurance coverage in the 9/11 Fund legislation? The settling parties in *Ortiz* were unable to cap the liability of Fibreboard to the limits of its insurance coverage by way of Rule 23(b)(1)(B).

5.   *The Limits of a Limited–Fund Class*. After *Ortiz*, other than Judge Weinstein's decision in *In re Simon II Litigation* (below), courts generally have not certified "limited-fund" class actions involving unliquidated damages. The Sixth Circuit's decision in *In re Telectronics Pacing Sys., Inc.*, 221 F.3d 870 (6th Cir. 2000) is one of the leading and best-known post-*Ortiz* opinions. The case involved around 40,000 class members who alleged that they received defective pacemakers and brought tort claims against the pacemaker manufacturer and its foreign parent companies. The district court certified a $57–million limited-fund class action under Rule 23(b)(1)(B) and explained that the payment included all of the manufacturer's assets, but none of the parent companies' because personal jurisdiction over those companies was unlikely. In reversing this decision, the Sixth Circuit explained that even though the manufacturer's assets did constitute a limited fund, it was "undisputed that the two [parent] companies do not have 'limited funds' in the traditional sense and would be able to bear the expense of litigation and pay damages if found liable." *Id.* at 878. Thus, the district court erred by "approv[ing] a settlement releasing the parent companies from all liability. . . ." *Id.* at 879.

6. *Limited–Fund Class Actions for Punitive Damages*. In the aftermath of *Ortiz*, one of the most significant developments on the subject of Rule 23(b)(1)(B) consisted of an effort to seek the certification of a nationwide mandatory class action with regard to punitive damage claims against the tobacco industry. The limited fund said, at the time, to support mandatory class treatment consisted not of the net worth of the tobacco industry but, rather, of a constitutional limit on the punitive damages that may be awarded in the aggregate, consistent with due process, with regard to a single course of tortious misconduct. The notion of such a due process limit on aggregate punitive damages arose from decisions of the Supreme Court itself in non-class litigation.

At the outset, it is crucial to note that the constitutional law of punitive damages itself has been in a state of flux in the period since *Ortiz*. The Second Circuit's decision in *In re Simon II* Litigation—presented below as a main case—notably dates from the period between 1999 (when the Court decided *Ortiz*) and 2007. In that period, the constitutional discourse on punitive damages stood roughly as follows:

Both lower courts and commentators pointed with consternation to the prospect that a widespread course of tortious misconduct might result in multiple punitive damage awards that, in the aggregate, would excessively punish the defendant. Important early recognitions of the problem include *Roginsky v. Richardson–Merrell, Inc.*, 378 F.2d 832 (2d Cir. 1967), and Richard A. Seltzer, *Punitive Damages in Mass Tort Litigation: Addressing the Problems of Fairness, Efficiency and Control*, 52 Fordham L. Rev. 37 (1983). In an oft-quoted passage from *Roginsky*, Judge Henry Friendly expressed "the gravest difficulty in perceiving how claims for punitive damages in such a multiplicity of actions throughout the nation can be so administered as to avoid overkill." 378 F.2d at 839.

Pleas along the foregoing lines from defendants in product liability lawsuits over asbestos garnered expressions of concern from some lower-court judges. *Dunn v. HOVIC*, 1 F.3d 1371, 1400–05 (Weis, J., dissenting), modified on other grounds, 13 F.3d 58 (3d Cir. 1993); *id.* at 1405 (Becker, J., dissenting); *Juzwin v. Amtorg Trading Corp.*, 705 F. Supp. 1053, 1060–64 (D.N.J. 1989), modified, 718 F. Supp. 1233 (D.N.J. 1989). But those same courts nonetheless concluded that the "overkill" problem lay beyond their capacity to solve, for any solution would entail the coordination of tort litigation nationwide. *Dunn,* 1 F.3d at 1386 (recognizing that "no single court can fashion an effective response"); *Juzwin,* 718 F. Supp. at 1236 (stating that "multiple awards of punitive damages for a single course of conduct violate the fundamental fairness requirement of the Due Process Clause," but adding that "equitable and practical concerns prevent [courts] from fashioning a fair and effective remedy").

To date, the Supreme Court has yet to opine directly upon the application of due process constraints to punitive damage awards over the course of multiple, similar lawsuits. The Supreme Court's decisions up to the time of *Simon II*, however, did imply the existence of an outer constitutional limit upon the aggregate amount of punitive damages that may be awarded based upon a single course of misconduct. After referring in decisions from the early 1990s to the existence of substantive due process constraints on punitive damages, the Court in *BMW of N. Am., Inc. v. Gore*, 517 U.S. 559 (1996), finally struck down a punitive-damage award as unconstitutional. *Gore* consisted of a consumer-fraud action centered upon the defendant manufacturer's undisclosed repainting of a BMW automobile prior to its delivery from the factory to the plaintiff. An Alabama jury had returned a punitive-damage award 500 times more than the modest diminution in market value suffered by the plaintiff Gore, as reflected in the jury's compensatory damage award. The Supreme Court held that the Due Process Clause prohibits a state from advancing its legitimate ends of punishment and retribution by way of a punitive-damage award so excessive in amount that the defendant would not have had "fair notice" of the prospect that its misconduct would meet with such severity. 517 U.S. at 574.

The Court elaborated this due process constraint in *State Farm Mut. Auto. Ins. Co. v. Campbell*, 538 U.S. 408 (2003). There, the defendant automobile insurer had failed to settle an earlier lawsuit against its insureds, the Campbells, for an amount within the insurance policy limits. When the lawsuit resulted in a damage award against the Campbells well in excess of their auto insurance coverage, they sued State Farm for bad-faith failure to settle, fraud, and intentional infliction of emotional distress. A Utah jury returned a punitive damage award 145 times the Campbells' actual losses. Overturning the award, the Supreme Court declined to set any "rigid benchmarks" or "bright-line ratio" for the relationship between punitive and compensatory damages. The Court nonetheless opined that, "in practice, few awards exceeding a single-digit ratio between punitive and compensatory damages, to a significant degree, will satisfy due process," *id.* at 425—a rough rule of thumb that the 145–to–1 ratio in Campbell exceeded dramatically.

Simply as a mathematical matter, the existence of a constitutional outer limit on the amount of punitive damages that a jury may award an individual plaintiff based upon a given course of misconduct by the defendant implied the existence of a limit upon the aggregate amount of punitive damages that multiple actions may impose for those same misdeeds. Should such a constitutionally limited fund have fared any better under Rule 23(b)(1)(B) than the fund limited only by the agreement of the parties—what the *Ortiz* Court held not to satisfy that rule? United States District Judge Jack Weinstein thought so and accordingly certified a mandatory, limited fund class for the punitive damage claims of smokers nationwide suffering from smoking-related disease. The defendant tobacco companies appealed and, in 2005, the Second Circuit ultimately decertified the class:

In re Simon II Litigation

407 F.3d 125 (2d Cir. 2005)

■ OAKES, SENIOR CIRCUIT JUDGE.

Defendant-appellant tobacco companies appeal from the . . . order of the United States District Court for the Eastern District of New York, Jack B. Weinstein, *Judge*, which certified a nationwide non-opt-out class of smokers seeking only punitive damages under state law for defendants' alleged fraudulent denial and concealment of the health risks posed by cigarettes. Having granted permission to appeal pursuant to Federal Rule of Civil Procedure 23(f), we must decide whether the district court properly certified this class under Rule 23(b)(1)(B).

Defendant-appellants challenge the propriety of certifying this action as a limited fund class action pursuant to a "limited punishment" theory. The theory postulates that a constitutional limit on the total punitive damages that may be imposed for a course of fraudulent conduct effectively limits the total fund available for punitive awards.

We hold that the order certifying this punitive damages class must be vacated because there is no evidence by which the district court could ascertain the limits of either the fund or the aggregate value of punitive claims against it, such that the postulated fund could be deemed inadequate to pay all legitimate claims, and thus plaintiffs have failed to satisfy one of the presumptively necessary conditions for limited fund treatment under *Ortiz v. Fibreboard Corp.*, 527 U.S. 815 (1999).

While we expressly limit our holding to the conclusion that class certification is incompatible with *Ortiz*, the circumstances warrant some discussion of whether the order is incompatible with the Supreme Court's intervening decision in *State Farm Mut. Auto. Ins. Co. v. Campbell*, 538 U.S. 408 (2003). As we discuss in Part II, Section F, of this opinion, it appears that the order fails to ensure that a potential punitive award in this action would bear a sufficient nexus, and be both reasonable and proportionate, to the harm or potential harm to the plaintiff class and to the general damages to be recovered, as required by *State Farm*.

Based on our holding, we vacate the district court's certification order and remand for further proceedings.

I.

FACTS AND PROCEDURAL HISTORY

. . . Plaintiffs sought certification to determine defendants' fraudulent course of conduct and total punitive damages liability to a class consisting of those who suffered from, or had died from, diseases caused by smoking. Plaintiffs did not seek a class-wide determination or allocation of compensatory damages or seek certification of subclasses. . . .

A.

The industry conspiracy prompting this litigation is described briefly in the allegations of the Third Amended Complaint and in considerable detail in the Certification Order. We will simply excerpt a relevant portion of the district court's description of the allegations:

> Plaintiffs allege, and can provide supporting evidence, that, beginning with a clandestine meeting in December 1953 at the Plaza Hotel in New York City among the presidents of Philip Morris, R.J. Reynolds, American Tobacco, Brown & Williamson, Lorillard and U.S. Tobacco, tobacco companies embarked on a systematic, half-century long scheme to . . . : (a) stop competing with each other in making or developing less harmful cigarettes; (b) continue knowingly and willfully to engage in misrepresentations and deceptive acts by, among other things, denying knowledge that cigarettes caused disease and death and agreeing not to disseminate harmful information showing the destructive effects of nicotine and tobacco consumption; (c) shut down research efforts and suppress medical information that appeared to be adverse to the Tobacco Companies' position that tobacco was not harmful; (d) not compete with respect to making any claims relating to the relative health-superiority of specific tobacco products; and (e) to confuse the public about, and otherwise distort, whatever accurate information about the harmful effects of their products became known despite their "[efforts to conceal such information.]"

211 F.R.D. at 114. . . .

Plaintiffs sought certification of a single class of smokers suffering from various diseases which the medical community attributes to smoking . . . for the sole purpose of determining defendants' total liability for punitive damages.

B.

Upon considering the class proposed[,] . . . the district court certified a punitive damages non-opt-out class pursuant to Rule 23(b)(1)(B). The class definition included current and former smokers of defendants' cigarettes who are U.S. residents, or who resided in the U.S. at time of death, and were first diagnosed between April 9, 1993, and the date of dissemination of class notice, with one or more [smoking-related] diseases. . . . The class excluded persons who had obtained judgment or settlement against any defendant, persons against whom defendants had obtained judgment, members of the certified class in *Engle v. R.J. Reynolds Tobacco Co.*, No. 94–08273 CA–22, 2000 WL 33534572 (Fla. Cir. Ct. Nov. 6, 2000),[4] persons who reasonably should have realized they had the disease prior to April 9,

---

[4] In *Engle*, a class action by Florida smokers against cigarette manufacturers, a jury determined punitive damages in the aggregate for the entire class. The evidence indicated the class could comprise up to several hundred thousand people; the court found that a punitive damages award of approximately $145 billion bore a reasonable relationship to damages proved and injuries suffered, and that the award was in keeping with the degree of the wrongful conduct without "sending the defendant into bankruptcy." 2000 WL 33534572, at *31. The trial court therefore denied the defendants' motion for a new trial or, in the alternative, a remittitur, on the grounds of excessiveness of the punitive damages award. On May 31, 2003, however, the Florida District Court of Appeal reversed, with instructions to decertify the class. . . . *Liggett Group Inc. v. Engle*, 853 So.2d 434 (Fla. Dist. Ct. App. 2003). The Supreme Court of Florida recently granted review . . . , and to this date the appeal is still pending. [That court subsequently overturned the punitive damage verdict for the *Engle* class, per the notes after this case—Ed.]

1993, and persons whose diagnosis or reasonable basis for knowledge pre-dated tobacco use.

The district court determined that the class action would proceed in three stages. In the first stage, a jury would make "a class-wide determination of liability and estimated total value of national undifferentiated compensatory harm to all members of the class." *Id.* at 100. The sum of compensatory harm would "not be awarded but will serve as a predicate in determining non-opt-out class punitive damages." *Id.* The same jury would determine compensatory awards, if any, for individual class representatives, although the class itself did not seek compensatory damages. In the second stage, the same jury would determine whether defendants engaged in conduct that warrants punitive damages. In the third stage, the same jury would determine the amount of punitive damages for the class and decide how to allocate damages on a disease-by-disease basis. The court would then distribute sums to the class on a pro-rata basis by disease to class members who submit appropriate proof. Any portion not distributed to class members would be "allocated by the court on a *cy pres* basis to treatment and research organizations working in the field of each disease on advice of experts in the fields." *Id.* The order specified that the jury would apply New York law according to conflicts of laws principles, and reiterated that the court was not presented with and did not rule upon a compensatory class. The district court noted that although plaintiffs chose the more limited course in pursuing a punitive class only, certification "for determination of compensatory damages to be distributed using an appropriate matrix would be possible and might be desirable in coordination with the class now certified." *Id.*

II.

DISCUSSION

A.   Standard of Review

We review the district court's order granting class certification for abuse of discretion, a deferential standard. . . .

D.   Limited Fund Class Action Based on the "Limited Punishment" Theory

The district court, in certifying the punitive damages class under Rule 23(b)(1)(B), cited recent scholarship and court decisions that "have concluded that the theory of limited punishment supports a punitive damages class action." 211 F.R.D. at 184. "Under this theory," the district court stated, "the limited fund involved would be the constitutional cap on punitive damages, set forth in *BMW v. Gore* [517 U.S. 559 (1996)] and related cases." *Id.*

The premise for this theory is that there is a constitutional due process limitation on the total amount of punitive damages that may be assessed against a defendant for the same offending conduct. Whether the limitation operates to prejudice the respective parties, it seems, turns on two contrary assumptions. For the potential plaintiff, piecemeal individual actions or successive class actions for punitive damages would operate to his disadvantage if punitive awards in earlier-filed suits subtract from the constitutional total and thereby reduce or preclude punitive damages for future claimants. This proposition assumes that courts identify and successfully enforce the postulated total limit, and that plaintiffs have an interest in a ratable portion of the permissible damages. For defendants, piecemeal individual or successive class actions would pose a threat of excessive punishment in violation of their due process rights if successive juries assess awards that exceed the limit of what is necessary for deterrence and retribution. This proposition, to the contrary, assumes that early suits exhaust or exceed the constitutional limit and successive trial or appellate courts fail to enforce it by either reducing or barring awards. It is not clear whether the theory supposes that successive individual awards, which considered alone may be constitutionally permissible if they are reasonable and proportionate to the given plaintiff's harm and bear a sufficient nexus to that harm, may reach a point where the goals of punitive damages have been served, and successive victims of the same tortious course of conduct by the tortfeasor should be unable to recover punitive damages. . . .

Despite the long-recognized possibility that defendants may be subjected to large aggregate sums of punitive damages if large numbers of victims succeed in their individual punitive damages claims . . . , the United States Supreme Court has not addressed whether successive individual or class action punitive awards, each passing constitutional muster under the relevant precedents, could reach a level beyond which punitive damages may no longer be awarded.

E.   The Traditional "Limited Fund" Class Action Under *Ortiz v. Fibreboard Corp.*

This brings us to appellants' chief argument—that class certification under Rule 23(b)(1)(B) is precluded by the Supreme Court's decision in *Ortiz v. Fibreboard Corp.*, 527 U.S. 815 (1999), because the proposed class plaintiffs have failed to demonstrate what the Supreme Court identified as the "presumptively necessary" conditions for certification in limited fund cases. Although *Ortiz* considered a set of circumstances quite unlike those in the instant case when it reviewed the certification of a Rule 23(b)(1)(B) mandatory settlement class on a limited fund theory, it identified, in the historical antecedents to Rule 23, the characteristic conditions that justified binding absent class members. It summarized those characteristics as "a 'fund' with a definitely ascertained limit, all of which would be distributed to satisfy all those with liquidated claims based on a common theory of liability, by an equitable, pro rata distribution." *Id.* at 841. Given the presumptive necessity of these characteristics, "the burden of justification rests on the proponent of any departure from the traditional norm." *Id.* at 842. . . .

Keeping in mind that the Court has thus counseled "against leniency in recognizing mandatory limited fund actions in circumstances markedly different from the traditional paradigm," *id.* at 864, we hold that the first fundamental requisite for limited fund treatment is lacking here, because there was no "evidence on which the district court may ascertain the limit and the insufficiency of the fund." *Id.* at 849.

The proposed fund in this case, the constitutional "cap" on punitive damages for the given class's claims, is a theoretical one, unlike any of those in the cases cited in *Ortiz*, where the fund was either an existing res or the total of defendants' assets available to satisfy claims. The fund here is—in essence—postulated, and for that reason it is not easily susceptible to proof, definition, or even estimation, by any precise figure. It is therefore fundamentally unlike the classic limited funds of the historical antecedents of Rule 23.

Not only is the upper limit of the proposed fund difficult to ascertain, but the record in this case does not evince a likelihood that any given number of punitive awards to individual claimants would be constitutionally excessive, either individually or in the aggregate, and thus overwhelm the available fund.[9]

Without evidence indicating either the upper limit or the insufficiency of the posited fund, class plaintiffs cannot demonstrate that individual plaintiffs would be prejudiced if left to pursue separate actions without having their interests represented in this suit, as Rule 23(b)(1)(B) would require.

Defendant-appellants also argue that there are two ways in which the class certified fails to exhibit the third presumptively necessary characteristic of a limited fund case, namely, that "the claimants identified by a common theory of recovery were treated equitably among themselves." *Ortiz*, 527 U.S. at 839. First, they argue that the class is fatally under-inclusive, and, second, they argue that the Certification Order fails to provide for equitable treatment among class members. The *Ortiz* Court found that these same two issues undermined the requirement of equity among class members for the settlement class in that case. Because we de-certify the class on other grounds, we need not resolve the equity question, which would be relevant only if the class were going forward as certified.

F.   Punitive Awards After *State Farm Mutual Automobile Life Ins. Co. v. Campbell*

While our holding in this case rests exclusively on the conclusion that certification is incompatible with *Ortiz*, we have an additional concern that warrants some discussion. It seems that a punitive award under the circumstances articulated in the Certification Order is likely to run afoul of the Supreme Court's admonitions in *State Farm*, a decision handed down several months after the Certification Order issued. See *State Farm Mut. Auto. Ins. Co. v. Campbell*, 538 U.S. 408 (2003). In certifying a class that seeks an assessment of punitive damages prior to an actual determination and award of compensatory damages, the district court's Certification Order would fail to ensure that a jury will be able to assess an award that, in the first instance, will bear a sufficient nexus to the actual and potential harm to the plaintiff class, and that will be reasonable and proportionate to those harms. . . .

Furthermore, with respect to the evidence to be considered at the punitive damages stage, *State Farm* indicates that a jury could not consider acts of as broad a scope as the district court in this case anticipated. The Certification Order in this case provides:

> This class action is intended to cover all punitive damages nationwide. This could include punitive damages due to outrageous conduct by defendants towards non-class members. The punitive function served by this certified class could be utilized in part for persons outside the class as, for example, passive breathers of the smoke exuded by others, those with diseases other than those represented by this certified class, and future diseased persons. . . . Allowing the jury to consider evidence of damage to others at this stage in setting the punitive award is appropriate in a

---

[9] We are not here presented with what might be a closer question—that is, if a standard class action had resulted in a verdict for compensatory damages for the class in one stage of a trial, and the mandatory class proponent wished to bind absent class members to any determination of a punitive award in a subsequent stage, because the given number of outstanding individual claims and the anticipated punitive award could demonstrably result in an unconstitutionally large punitive award.

nationwide class action where a portion of the harmful behavior may not be correlatable with class members.

211 F.R.D. at 186.

State Farm made clear that conduct relevant to the reprehensibility analysis must have a nexus to the specific harm suffered by the plaintiff, and that it could not be independent of or dissimilar to the conduct that harms the plaintiff. 538 U.S. at 422–23. Harmful behavior that is not "correlatable" with class members and the harm or potential harm to them would be precluded under *State Farm*.

G.   Defendant–Appellants' Other Arguments

Defendant-appellants also contend the Certification Order runs afoul of the Rules Enabling Act, 28 U.S.C. § 2072(b) (2000), because, on a number of counts, it alters or abridges the parties' substantive rights. Defendant-appellants challenge the imposition of class-wide liability for punitive damages in the absence of individualized proof of the elements of the causes of action on which punitive damages would be predicated. They also claim that the trial plan to resolve individual compensatory claims in separate follow-on actions to the class-wide punitive damages determination would subject the facts underlying the compensatory claims to re-examination by successive juries in violation of the Seventh Amendment.

Because we have held that certification is incompatible with *Ortiz*, we need not address whether the district court's proposed statistical aggregation of proof, or its invocation of a "fraud-on-the-market" theory, would have been appropriate for a class-wide approximation of compensatory liability in this case, or for proof of any given element going toward actual liability in a conventional class action for compensatory and punitive damages. Our holding also disposes of any need to address the controversy surrounding the challenged follow-on actions.

Defendant-appellants also challenge the Certification Order's determination that "the single law of New York's compensatory and punitive damages will apply." 211 F.R.D. at 167. The district court did not certify the class to determine compensatory damages but, rather, called for New York law to be applied "to determine compensatory damages primarily as a predicate for punitive damages. . . ." *Id.* at 174. Because it is unclear what course plaintiffs may ultimately seek on remand regarding class certification, we need not address the hypothetical question of whether the district court could apply only New York law to a yet-undefined potential compensatory and/or punitive damages class.

III.

CONCLUSION

The proposed class having failed to satisfy the threshold requirements for certification set forth in *Ortiz* and Rule 23(b)(1)(B), we must vacate the district court's certification order and remand for further proceedings.

NOTES AND QUESTIONS

1.   *Subsequent Developments in the Constitutional Law of Punitive Damages.* Much of the debate in *Simon II* concerned the relationship between certifying a Rule 23(b)(1)(B) mandatory, limited-fund class and the constitutional limitations on punitive damages in *Campbell* as well as in earlier Supreme Court decisions. Since *Simon II*, the Supreme Court has elaborated still

further on the latter subject—quite arguably, in a way that puts the certification dispute in *Simon II* in a dramatically different light. In *Philip Morris USA v. Williams*, 549 U.S. 346 (2007), the Court overturned a punitive-damage award in an individual tort action in which the Oregon trial court had permitted the jury to consider evidence concerning the alleged misconduct of Philip Morris vis-à-vis smokers other than the plaintiff, most of whom were from states other than Oregon. In the Court's words:

> Evidence of actual harm to nonparties can help to show that the conduct that harmed the plaintiff also posed a substantial risk of harm to the general public, and so was particularly reprehensible. . . . Yet . . . a jury may not go further than this and use a punitive damages verdict to punish a defendant directly on account of harms it is alleged to have visited on nonparties.

Id. at 1064. Consideration for purposes of punishment violates due process, said the Court, because "[a] defendant threatened with punishment for injuring a non-party victim has no opportunity to defend against the charge, by showing, for example in a case such as this, that the other victim was not entitled to damages because he or she knew that smoking was dangerous or did not rely upon the defendant's statements to the contrary." *Id.* at 1063.

Distinguishing between the effects on third parties for purposes of reprehensibility (permitted by *Williams*) but not for purposes of punishment (forbidden by *Williams*) is delicate, to say the least. Cf. *id.* at 1067 (Stevens, J., dissenting) ("This nuance eludes me."). For the foreseeable future, however, *Williams* states the constitutional law of punitive damages. In 2008, the Supreme Court decided *Exxon Shipping Co. v. Baker*, 554 U.S. 471 (2008), which involved a $507.5 million compensatory-damage award and a $5 billion punitive-damage award in conjunction with a massive oil spill from a tanker on the Alaskan coast. The Court held that, as a matter of federal common law of maritime torts, a punitive-damage award in an admiralty case may not exceed the compensatory award (a 1:1 ratio). *Id.* at 514. Attempts to rely on this rationale to define the outermost limit of due process in non-admiralty cases, however, has not met with much success. Most circuit courts have distinguished *Exxon* based on the particular features of maritime law. See, e.g., *Myers v. Cent. Fl. Invs., Inc.*, 592 F.3d 1201, 1221 (11th Cir. 2010) ("In *Exxon*, the Supreme Court was quite explicit that it was dealing with maritime law, and not due process of law."); *Kunz v. DeFelice*, 538 F.3d 667, 678 (7th Cir. 2008) (same).

Does *Williams* effectively mean that *Simon II* must be understood as a historical artifact? If *Williams* had been part of the constitutional law of punitive damages at the time of *Simon II*, would the argument for class certification there have been strengthened or weakened—or eviscerated? On the significance of *Williams* for class treatment of punitive damages, compare Elizabeth J. Cabraser & Robert J. Nelson, *Class Action Treatment of Punitive Damages Issues after* Philip Morris v. Williams*: We Can Get There from Here*, 2 Charleston L. Rev. 407 (2008), with Byron G. Stier, *Now It's Personal: Punishment and Mass Tort Litigation after* Philip Morris v. Williams, 2 Charleston L. Rev. 433 (2008).

    2.   *The Relationship of the Limited Punishment Theory to the Constraints on Punitive Damages in Individual Cases.* For the sake of argument, consider the state of the law concerning constitutional limits on punitive damages as it stood at the time of *Simon II*—that is, without the additional guidance provid-

ed by the Supreme Court in *Williams*. Seen in the context of its time, does class counsel's argument for certifying the *Simon II* class rest upon "contrary assumptions," to borrow the Second Circuit's words? Is the argument for certifying a mandatory, limited-fund class strengthened or weakened if one assumes that courts in individual tobacco cases faithfully will apply the constitutional constraints upon punitive-damage awards previously set forth in cases like *Campbell*? Does the positing of presumptive ratio of punitive damages to compensatory damages in *Campbell* make the argument for certifying a class under Rule 23(b)(1)(B) easier or harder? (The Supreme Court decided *Campbell* between the time Judge Weinstein certified the *Simon II* class and the Second Circuit decertified it. Judge Weinstein thus made his certification decision without the guidance of *Campbell*.)

What explains the tobacco industry's inclination to fight the certification of a nationwide mandatory class for punitive damages in *Simon II*? The justification advanced for certifying the proposed class seemingly is more solicitous of the defendants' interests—it purportedly protects them against the prospect of excessive punishment—than of class members. Why, then, are class counsel urging certification in *Simon II* and defendants opposing it?

3. *Evidence versus Theory*. At several points, the *Simon II* court suggests that the deficiency in class counsel's class-certification argument is evidentiary in nature—that class counsel did not muster sufficient proof of the fund's limited nature to justify mandatory class treatment. As a practical matter, what more—if anything—could class counsel have done to bolster the case for class certification, given the constitutional law of punitive damages at the time? Is the real problem an evidentiary one, or is there a deeper conceptual obstacle to certification of mandatory classes for punitive-damage claims based upon the limited punishment theory (again, on the premise that it had a constitutional basis, at least at the time of *Simon II*)? Is the purported limited fund in *Simon II* as much the creation of the proposed class itself as the purported limited fund found not to warrant mandatory class treatment in *Ortiz*?

4. *The Diversity of the Tobacco Plaintiffs' Bar*. At times roughly contemporaneous with *Simon II*, there were several instances of multimillion-dollar punitive-damage awards returned in other lawsuits against the tobacco industry—specifically, in a Florida state-court class action confined to smokers in that jurisdiction and in a series of individual actions in California. The group of plaintiffs' lawyers who sought to serve as class counsel in *Simon II* conspicuously did not include the lawyers who had garnered those punitive-damage awards. Think strategically: why not? Are the would-be class counsel in *Simon II* pursuing a different business strategy than the other plaintiffs' lawyers bringing suits against the tobacco industry? How would the requested class certification in *Simon II* have served that strategy and affected other, parallel lawsuits?

3. ISSUE CLASSES

In addition to the description of mandatory and opt-out classes in subsection (b), Rule 23(c)(4) also provides that, "[w]hen appropriate, an action may be brought . . . as a class action with respect to particular issues." This language originally appeared in Rule 23 as subsection (c)(4)(A), before the 2007 restyling of the rule broke out what was previously subsection (c)(4)(B) concerning subclasses into a subsection of its own—new subsection (c)(5). Bear in mind that, as a result, the extant case law on issue classes will, for some time, reflect the previous numbering rather than the 2007 restyling. Just remember: Current subsection (c)(4) concerning issue classes is what was previously subsection (c)(4)(A); and current subsection (c)(5) on subclasses is what was previously subsection (c)(4)(B). The introductory discussion here speaks in terms of the rule in its present form.

Subsection (c)(4) does not supply a separate basis for class certification in addition to those set forth in subsection (b). Rather, subsection (c)(4) simply purports to clarify that the various kinds of class actions described in subsection (b) may—"when appropriate"—be certified only as to "particular issues" within a larger array of issues in a given litigation.

There are many ways in which one might attempt to separate a given issue or constellation of issues arguably suited for class treatment from other, individual issues not so suited. Consider this admittedly non-exhaustive list:

> Liability versus Remedy: One might attempt to separate all questions concerning the defendant's liability from questions concerning the selection and the allocation of an appropriate remedy (e.g., how much in damages individual class members shall receive, if liability is shown).

> Particular Elements of Liability versus Other Liability Elements or Affirmative Defenses: Liability generally turns upon proof of multiple elements of the plaintiffs' cause of action, some of which focus exclusively upon the defendant's conduct and others of which entail examining a particular plaintiffs' conduct. One might attempt to separate the former for class treatment while leaving the latter to individual proceedings. Similarly, one might attempt to separate particular elements of liability from issues concerning the application of an affirmative defense.

> Claims for Divisible Relief versus Claims for Indivisible Relief: A given course of conduct may give rise to both claims for divisible relief (e.g., for damages and some forms of equitable relief) and claims for indivisible relief (e.g., for classwide injunctive or declaratory relief). As we have seen, employment discrimination presents particular challenges in this regard. Rule 23(b)(2) makes claims for indivisible relief more suited for class treatment— indeed, mandatory class treatment—than claims for divisible relief. Per *Dukes*, for example, damage claims generally must proceed under Rule 23(b)(3), if class treatment is to be afforded at all.

The materials here initially ask whether the Constitution— specifically, the Reexamination Clause of the Seventh Amendment— imposes any constraints upon the use of issue classes. The materials then turn to the relationship, as a matter of Rule 23, between issue classes under subsection (c)(4) and the class certification requirements of subsection (b)—in particular, the demand of subsection (b)(3) that common questions predominate over individual ones with regard to an opt-out class.

Issue classes have become a topic of much discussion in the wake of *Wal–Mart Stores, Inc. v. Dukes* and both practitioners and academics have explored them as a way to aggregate and resolve common issues. The Advisory Committee on Civil Rules recently appointed a Rule 23 Subcommittee to consider issue classes and the relationship between Rule 23(b)(3) and (c)(4), specifically whether predominance is always required, but to date no changes have been made to Rule 23.

a.   THE REEXAMINATION CLAUSE

The Seventh Amendment provides:

> In suits at common law, where the value in controversy shall exceed twenty dollars, the right of trial by jury shall be preserved, and no fact tried by a jury, shall be otherwise reexamined in any court of the United States, than according to the rules of the common law.

The first part of the Seventh Amendment confers a right to jury trial in specified cases. The second part of the Amendment is known as the Reexamination Clause and forms the focus of the materials that follow.

In the Matter of Rhone–Poulenc Rorer, Inc.

51 F.3d 1293 (7th Cir. 1995)

■ POSNER, CHIEF JUDGE.

[Recall that the district court had certified a nationwide class of HIV-positive hemophiliacs suing the defendant manufacturers in tort for their alleged negligent handling of blood in connection with their blood products. In addition to concerns over settlement pressure and choice of law, the court went on to describe a third obstacle grounded in the Reexamination Clause.]

The third respect in which we believe that the district judge has exceeded his authority concerns the point at which his plan of action proposes to divide the trial of the issues that he has certified for class-action treatment from the other issues involved in the thousands of actual and potential claims of the representatives and members of the class. Bifurcation and even finer divisions of lawsuits into separate trials are authorized in federal district courts. Fed. R. Civ. P. 42(b). And a decision to employ the procedure is reviewed deferentially. However, as we have been at pains to stress recently, the district judge must carve at the joint. Of particular relevance here, the judge must not divide issues between separate trials in such a way that the same issue is reexamined by different juries. The problem is not inherent in bifurcation. It does not arise when the same jury is to try the successive phases of the litigation. But most of the separate "cases" that compose this class action will be tried, after the initial trial in the Northern District of Illinois, in different courts, scattered throughout the country. The right to a jury trial in federal civil cases, conferred by the Seventh Amendment, is a right to have juriable issues determined by the first jury impaneled to hear them (provided there are no errors warranting a new trial), and not reexamined by another finder of fact. This would be obvious if the second finder of fact were a judge. But it is equally true if it is another jury. In this limited sense, a jury verdict can have collateral estoppel effect.

The plan of the district judge in this case is inconsistent with the principle that the findings of one jury are not to be reexamined by a second, or third, or nth jury. The first jury will not determine liability. It will determine merely whether one or more of the defendants was negligent under one of the two theories. The first jury may go on to decide the additional issues with regard to the named plaintiffs. But it will not decide them with regard to the other class members. Unless the defendants settle, a second (and third, and fourth, and hundredth, and conceivably thousandth) jury will have to decide, in individual follow-on litigation by class members not named as plaintiffs in the *Wadleigh* case, such issues as comparative negligence—did any class members knowingly continue to use unsafe blood solids after they learned or should have learned of the risk of contamination with HIV?—and proximate causation. Both issues overlap the issue of the defendants' negligence. Comparative negligence entails, as the name implies, a comparison of the degree of negligence of plaintiff and defendant. Proximate causation is found by determining whether the harm to the plaintiff followed in some sense naturally, uninterruptedly, and with reasonable probability from the negligent act of the defendant. It overlaps the issue of the defendants' negligence even when the state's law does not (as many states do) make the foreseeability of the risk to which the defendant subjected the plaintiff an explicit ingredient of negligence. A second or subsequent jury might find that the defendants' failure to take precautions against infection with Hepatitis B could not be thought the *proximate* cause of the plaintiffs' infection with HIV, a different and unknown blood-borne virus. How the resulting inconsistency between juries could be prevented escapes us.

NOTES AND QUESTIONS

1.   *The Relationship of the Right to Jury Trial and the Reexamination Clause.* Many in the Founding generation regarded the jury as an institution that would reinforce the democratic character of the system of governance set forth in the original Constitution. Specifically, they saw juries as an important check not just upon abuse of power by the judiciary (in its administration of the justice system) but also abuse by the legislature (with its potential to enact oppressive legislation at the behest of interest groups that then would seek to enforce such legislation in court). Akhil Reed Amar, THE BILL OF RIGHTS: CREATION AND RECONSTRUCTION (1998). The constraint imposed by the Reexamination Clause is closely related to the basic guarantee of a right to jury trial "[i]n suits at common law, where the value in controversy shall exceed twenty dollars." The concern was that, absent something like the Reexamination Clause, a jury's decision could effectively be eviscerated through reexamination in a subsequent proceeding. Put simply, both the Trial-by-Jury Clause and the Reexamination Clause were intended to safeguard the right to a jury trial. For discussion of the right to a jury trial in federal court, see 9 FEDERAL PRACTICE AND PROCEDURE §§ 2301–16.

2.   *The Reexamination Clause and Article III.* The Reexamination Clause also has a close relationship with Article III—specifically, the language in Article III that conferred "appellate jurisdiction, both as to law and fact" on the Supreme Court. See Edith Guild Henderson, *The Background of the Seventh Amendment*, 80 Harv. L. Rev. 289, 294 (1966). Concern arose among anti-Federalists that Article III's grant of appellate jurisdiction with respect to questions of "fact" might be taken to authorize the newly-created Supreme Court to retry before a jury in Washington, D.C. facts originally tried in *state* courts sitting in local communities across the country—that is, to empower a federal court on appellate review of state trials to do what the judicial systems of some states themselves authorized as part of their own appellate practices at the time of the Founding. See Wilfred J. Ritz, REWRITING THE JUDICIARY ACT OF 1789, at 42 (1990) ("In three of the New England states—Massachusetts, New

Hampshire, and Rhode Island—there was [during the period 1787–89] an opportunity for multiple trials. The decision, real or sham, resulting from a trial in an inferior tribunal could be appealed to a superior tribunal, where a second and entirely new trial could be had. And this in turn could be appealed in Massachusetts and a new third trial could be had."); THE FEDERALIST No. 83, at 502–03 (Alexander Hamilton) (Clinton Rossiter ed. 1961) (noting the possibility of appeal "from one jury to another" in Rhode Island, Connecticut, Massachusetts, New Hampshire, and Georgia).

3.   *The Text of the Clause.* The Reexamination Clause prohibits only the reexamination in a federal court of a "fact tried by a jury." What precisely does the phrase "fact tried by a jury" mean? Note that the reference is to a "fact tried by a jury" as distinct from Article III's grant of judicial power over a "case or controversy."

Why does the Reexamination Clause speak of the reexamination of facts "in" any federal court? How might the meaning of the Clause have been changed if the word "by" instead of "in" had been used?

The concluding words of the Reexamination Clause make clear that reexamination of a "fact tried by a jury" may take place "in" a federal court if done "according to the rules of the common law." There is considerable debate in the scholarly literature about whether the reference to "the rules of the common law" should be understood to refer only to those common-law rules in place at the time of the Founding (a static reading) or to permit the subsequent emergence of rules through the ordinary evolution of the common law that might then form additional exceptions to the general prohibition of the Reexamination Clause (a dynamic reading).

4.   *The Seventh Circuit.* What "fact" was the jury in *Rhone–Poulenc* asked to determine under the trial plan designed by the district court for the class proceeding? Would that "fact" have been "reexamined" in the subsequent proceedings envisioned by the district court? Or did the Seventh Circuit improperly conflate the Seventh Amendment stricture against reexamining a fact tried by jury with the concern that the jury in a follow-on proceeding would have to decide an issue that overlapped with a previously decided issue? For an argument that overlapping issues do not necessarily create a problem under the Reexamination Clause, see Patrick Woolley, *Mass Tort Litigation and the Seventh Amendment Reexamination Clause*, 83 Iowa L. Rev. 499 (1998).

The Seventh Circuit recognizes that "[t]he prohibition is not against having two juries review the same evidence, but rather against having two juries decide the same essential issues." *Houseman v. U.S. Aviation Underwriters*, 171 F.3d 1117, 1128 (7th Cir. 1999). Overlapping issues present the *risk* that a later jury will disregard authoritative findings of an earlier jury.

Recall the discussion of *Parklane Hosiery Co. v. Shore* in Chapter 1. If *Rhone–Poulenc*'s reasoning is accepted, is nonmutual collateral estoppel potentially unconstitutional in cases involving overlapping issues?

Putting aside the proper interpretation of the Reexamination Clause, were there practical reasons for not going forward with the proposed class suit in *Rhone–Poulenc*?

5.   *The Views of Other Circuits.* At least two other circuits have agreed with the Seventh Circuit's analysis in *Rhone–Poulenc*. See *Blyden v. Mancusi*, 186 F.3d 252 (2d Cir. 1999); *Castano v. Am. Tobacco Co.*, 84 F.3d 734 (5th Cir.

1996); see also *Olden v. LaForge Corp.*, 383 F.3d 495, 509 n.6 (6th Cir. 2004) (stating that the bifurcation plan in the case *might* violate the Seventh Amendment and citing *Rhone–Poulenc* for the proposition that when a court bifurcates a case, it must "divide issues between separate trials in such a way that the same issue is [not] reexamined by different juries."). Cf. *Valentino v. Carter–Wallace, Inc.* 97 F.3d 1227, 1232 (9th Cir. 1996) (noting that the Seventh Amendment concern in *Rhone–Poulenc* "may not be fully in line with the law of this circuit.").

In *Blyden*, the Second Circuit addressed the application of the Reexamination Clause in the context of a civil rights class action brought on behalf of prisoners in the aftermath of the infamous 1971 riot at Attica prison. Bifurcating liability from damages, the district court had called upon the jury for the liability phase to answer the following question, among others on a multi-part verdict form designed by the court: "(A) Have the plaintiffs proven by a preponderance of the pertinent evidence that, after the retaking and liberation [of the prison] but prior to the time when the plaintiffs had been relocked in cells, officers engaged in reprisals constituting cruel and unusual punishment against the plaintiffs or any of them by using unnecessary or excessive force?" The jury answered "yes" to the question posed in part (A) as well as to a subsequent question inquiring whether a particular Attica prison official, Karl Pfeil, had "directed or ordered" such reprisals. *Blyden*, 186 F.3d at 260.

Citing *Rhone–Poulenc*, the Court of Appeals concluded that the damages phase of the proceedings entailed prohibited reexamination of a fact tried by the liability-phase jury. The court explained:

> It can hardly be disputed that in the instant matter both the liability jury and the damages juries were asked to determine whether the same acts constituted "reprisals." That was the issue to be resolved in part (A) of the verdict sheet in the liability trial. However, [part] (A) did not ask the jury to specify which acts were found to be "reprisals" and which were not. The damages juries were not, therefore, given a list of acts constituting "reprisals" and asked to award damages to particular plaintiffs injured by them. Instead, the jurors in the damages trials were told that there had been "reprisals" but were asked to determine for themselves which particular acts constituted such "reprisals." . . .

> The damages juries were therefore left free to determine whether any particular act constituted a "reprisal"—[the damages jury for one particular plaintiff] was even asked to revisit Pfeil's supervisory liability for "solitary and unrepeated" acts of "renegade officers"— without regard to how the liability jury viewed that particular act. This of course created the real possibility—amounting to a probability—that acts found to be "reprisals" by the liability jury were different from the acts found to be "reprisals" by the damages juries. This procedure clearly violated the Seventh Amendment.

Id. at 268–69.

b.   ISSUE CLASSES WITHIN THE FRAMEWORK OF RULE 23

Aside from possible constitutional obstacles, certifying issue classes presents difficult questions simply as a matter of Rule 23. Issue classes under subsection (c)(4) are seemingly designed to add to the trial judge's flexibility under Rule 23. But, at the same time, subsection (c)(4) arguably is in tension with subsection (b).

Consider initially subsection (b)(3)'s demand for a finding that common questions predominate over individual questions as a precondition to certifying an opt-out class. The precise relationship between subsection (b)(3)'s predominance requirement and subsection (c)(4)'s authorization for issue classes has caused considerable confusion in the courts. Compare, e.g., *Castano v. Am. Tobacco Co.*, 84 F.3d 734, 745 n.21 (5th Cir. 1996) ("Reading rule 23(c)(4) as allowing a court to sever issues until the remaining common issue predominates over the remaining individual issues would eviscerate the predominance requirement of rule 23(b)(3); the result would be automatic certification in every case where there is a common issue, a result that could not have been intended"), with *Valentino v. Carter–Wallace, Inc.*, 97 F.3d 1227, 1234 (9th Cir. 1996) ("Even if the common questions do not predominate over the individual questions so that class certification of the entire action is warranted, Rule 23 authorizes the district court in appropriate cases to isolate the common issues under Rule [23(c)(4)] and proceed with class treatment of these particular issues."). Academic commentary divides along similar lines. Compare Laura J. Hines, *Challenging the Issue Class Action End–Run*, 52 Emory L.J. 709 (2003) (criticizing the use of issue classes as undermining the class certification requirements of Rule 23(b)(3)), with Jon Romberg, *Half a Loaf is Predominant and Superior to None: Class Certification of Particular Issues Under Rule 23(c)(4)(A)*, 2002 Utah L. Rev. 249 (advocating expanded use of issue classes).

In addition, the relationship between subsection (c)(4) and subsection (b)(2) is unclear. Can a trial judge simply carve out claims for injunctive or declaratory relief in order to certify them for mandatory class treatment under subsection (b)(2) and leave claims for monetary relief for subsequent individual proceedings (or perhaps certification under (b)(3))? Would that mean that any litigation involving claims for equitable relief could give rise to a mandatory class as to those issues? Recall that courts are split on this issue in the employment-discrimination context.

The materials that follow address these two questions in turn. Again, recall that the portion of Rule 23 concerning issue classes was previously numbered as subsection (c)(4)(A) and is cited accordingly in the case law on the subject prior to December 2007.

(1) The Relationship of Issue Classes and the Predominance Requirement

In re Nassau County Strip Search Cases

461 F.3d 219 (2d Cir. 2006)

■ STRAUB, CIRCUIT JUDGE.

This appeal is the latest installment in a series of litigations over the Nassau County Correctional Center's ("NCCC") blanket strip search policy for newly admitted, misdemeanor detainees ("the policy"). Plaintiffs, who were strip searched pursuant to the policy, appeal from a series of orders entered in the District Court . . . denying their repeated motions for class certification on the ground that individual issues predominated over common ones.

During the course of class certification motion practice, plaintiffs requested that the District Court certify a Rule 23(b)(3) class solely on the issue of liability, as permitted by Rule 23(c)(4)(A). In response, defendants conceded their liability to plaintiffs. The District Court denied the motion. As an initial matter, the District Court expressed serious doubt over whether it could certify a class on the issue of liability since it already had determined that plaintiffs' claims, as a whole, failed the predominance test. Even if it could do so, the District Court reasoned that defendants' concession removed common liability issues from the predominance analysis. With common liability issues so excised, the Court concluded that individual liability issues, such as the application of an affirmative defense, predominated. The Court thus denied plaintiffs' motions for class certification on the issue of liability.

The precise issues on appeal are whether (1) a court may certify a Rule 23(b)(3) class as to a particular issue when it already has determined that the claim as a whole fails the predominance test; (2) common issues that are conceded remain part of the predominance analysis; and (3) the District Court exceeded its allowable discretion by failing to certify a class on the issue of liability. As set forth more fully below, we hold that (1) a court may employ rule 23(c)(4)(A) to certify a class as to an issue regardless of whether the claim as a whole satisfies the predominance test; (2) the District Court erred when it concluded that defendants' concession eliminated liability issues from the predominance analysis; and (3) the District Court exceeded its allowable discretion by failing to certify a class on the issue of liability pursuant to Rules 23(b)(3) and (c)(4)(A). Accordingly, we reverse the District Court's orders . . . to the extent that they deny certification as to the issue of liability, and we remand for proceedings consistent with this opinion.

BACKGROUND

[This case centers on allegations] that plaintiffs were arrested on misdemeanor charges unrelated to weapons or drugs and thereafter strip searched, without individualized suspicion, pursuant to the policy. Plaintiffs claimed that the strip searches violated 42 U.S.C. § 1983, the Fourth, Fifth, Eighth, and Fourteenth Amendments to the United States Constitution, and Article 1, section 12 of the New York State Constitution. They sought compensatory and punitive damages, a declaration that the policy was unconstitutional, and an injunction barring enforcement of the policy. They also sought to maintain each litigation as a class action. . . .

The Court recognized certain common questions, namely, (1) whether defendants maintained a blanket strip search policy; (2) whether that policy was unconstitutional; and (3) whether some or all defendants may be held liable. Nonetheless, it determined that individualized issues predominated. . . .

Plaintiffs moved for reconsideration . . . [and] asserted that the Court should certify a class on the issue of liability pursuant to Rule 23(c)(4)(A). They again defined the class as "all persons arrested for or charged with non-felony offenses who have been admitted to the [Nassau County Correctional Center] and strip searched without particularized reasonable suspicion."

The District Court again noted its "concern that partial certification might not be appropriate in the first instance where the cause of action, as a whole, does not satisfy the predominance requirement of Rule 23(b)(3)."

"Even assuming" that Rule 23(c)(4)(A) could be used in that fashion, the Court denied the motion because plaintiffs' proposed class definition "would necessitate mini-trials just to determine class membership." In order to determine class membership, the Court believed, each would-be class member would have to show affirmatively that he was strip searched without particularized reasonable suspicion—a criterion that the definition incorporated. This burden was complicated by the fact that defendants claimed that they had ceased the blanket strip search policy after the Eastern District's 1999 decision in *Shain*, and thereafter conducted strip searches only *with* particularized reasonable suspicion.

In January 2003, plaintiffs renewed their motion for class certification as to liability and offered a new definition of the class as follows: "[A]ll persons arrested for misdemeanors or noncriminal offenses in Nassau County who thereafter were strip-searched at the NCCC pursuant to defendants' blanket policy, practice and custom which required that all arrestees be strip searched upon admission to the facility. . . ." By referring only to the "blanket policy," this new definition did not require plaintiffs to show that reasonable suspicion was absent in each case, and it excluded individuals strip searched after the 1999 *Shain* decision, when defendants ceased implementing the policy. . . .

In response, defendants conceded "the one common issue" that in their view "might be appropriate for class certification . . . namely, whether the NCCC's strip search policy during the class period was constitutional." Specifically, defendants recognized that they "are bound by *Shain* under the doctrine of collateral estoppel."

The District Court denied the renewed motion. . . . [T]he Court determined that defendants' concession removed all common liability issues from its predominance analysis. Accordingly, the only liability issue that remained was an individual one: whether, notwithstanding the policy, some plaintiffs were searched based upon "reasonable and contemporaneously held suspicion." "With the liability issue thus circumscribed," the Court wrote, "certification as to that issue would not serve any purpose." Interestingly, the Court recognized that the individualized " 'reasonable suspicion inquiries' will be de minimis" for two reasons: because defendants conceded that "such an inquiry will only be sought regarding a limited number of plaintiffs," and because pursuant to *United States v. Colon*, 250 F.3d 130, 138 (2d Cir. 2001), reasonable suspicion must be possessed by some law enforcement officer at the time of the search and may not be retroactively imputed. . . .

DISCUSSION

. . .

III. The District Court Erred in Failing to Certify a Class on the Issue of Liability Pursuant to Rules 23(b)(3) and (c)(4)(A) . . .

A. *A District Court May Certify a Class as to Specific Issues Regardless of Whether the Entire Claim Satisfies Rule 23(b)(3)*

Whether a court may employ Rule 23(c)(4)(A) to certify a class as to a specific issue where the entire claim does not satisfy Rule 23(b)(3)'s predominance requirement is a matter of first impression in this Circuit. It also is a matter as to which the Circuits have split.

The Fifth Circuit has adopted a "strict application" of Rule 23(b)(3)'s predominance requirement. Under this view, "[t]he proper interpretation of the interaction between subdivisions (b)(3) and (c)(4) is that a cause of action, as a whole, must satisfy the predominance requirement of (b)(3) and that (c)(4) is a housekeeping rule that allows courts to sever the common issues for a class trial." *Castano v. Am. Tobacco Co.*, 84 F.3d 734, 745 n.21 (5th Cir. 1996).

The Ninth Circuit holds a different view. Pursuant to that court's precedent, "[e]ven if the common questions do not predominate over the individual questions so that class certification of the entire action is warranted, Rule 23 authorizes the district court in appropriate cases to isolate the common issues under Rule 23(c)(4)(A) and proceed with class treatment of these particular issues." *Valentino v. Carter–Wallace, Inc.*, 97 F.3d 1227, 1234 (9th Cir. 1996); *cf. Gunnells v. Healthplan Servs., Inc.*, 348 F.3d 417, 439 (4th Cir. 2003) (holding that courts may employ Rule 23(c) to certify a class as to one claim even though all of plaintiffs' claims, taken together, do not satisfy the predominance requirement).

We agree with the Ninth Circuit's view of the matter. First, the plain language and structure of Rule 23 support the Ninth Circuit's view. Rule 23(c)(4) provides as follows:

> When appropriate (A) an action may be brought or maintained as a class action *with respect to particular issues*, or (B) a class may be divided into subclasses and each subclass treated as a class, *and* the provisions of this rule shall *then* be construed and applied accordingly.

Fed. R. Civ. P. 23(c)(4) (emphases added).

As the rule's plain language and structure establish, a court must first identify the issues potentially appropriate for certification "and . . . then" apply the other provisions of the rule, *i.e.*, subsection (b)(3) and its predominance analysis. See *Gunnells*, 348 F.3d at 439 (reasoning that the rule's language provides this "express command" that "courts have no discretion to ignore").

Second, the Advisory Committee Notes confirm this understanding. With respect to subsection (c)(4), the notes set forth that, "[f]or example, in a fraud or similar case the action may retain its 'class' character *only* through the adjudication of liability to the class; the members of the class may thereafter be required to come in individually and prove the amounts of their respective claims." Fed. R. Civ. P. 23(c)(4) adv. comm. n. to 1966 amend. (emphasis added). As the notes point out, a court may employ Rule 23(c)(4) when it is the "only" way that a litigation retains its class character, *i.e.*, when common questions predominate only as to the "particular issues" of which the provision speaks. Further, the notes illustrate that a court may properly employ this technique to separate the issue of liability from damages.

In addition, as the Fourth Circuit has noted, the Fifth Circuit's view renders subsection (c)(4) virtually null, which contravenes the "well-settled" principle "that courts should avoid statutory interpretations that render provisions superfluous." *State St. Bank & Trust Co. v. Salovaara*, 326 F.3d 130, 139 (2d Cir. 2003). Pursuant to the Fifth Circuit's view, "a court considering the manageability of a class action—a requirement for predominance under Rule 23(b)(3)(D)—[would have] to pretend that subsection (c)(4)–a provision specifically included to make a class action more manageable—does not exist until after the manageability determination [has been] made." *Gunnells*, 348 F.3d at 439. Accordingly, "a court could only use subsection (c)(4) to manage cases that the court had already determined would be manageable *without* consideration of subsection (c)(4)." *Id.* . . .

B. The District Court Erred When It Concluded that Defendants' Concession Eliminates Common Liability Issues from Rule 23(b)(3)'s Predominance Analysis

As noted above, the District Court reasoned that the major liability issues common to the class—whether defendants implemented a blanket strip search policy, and if so, whether they are liable for it—were eliminated from the predominance analysis by defendants' concession. Whether a concession can limit the predominance analysis in that fashion also is a question of first impression. For three reasons, we conclude that a concession does not eliminate a common issue from the predominance calculus, and that the District Court erred in holding otherwise.

First, because the predominance analysis tests whether the class is a " 'sufficiently cohesive' " unit, *In re Visa Check*, 280 F.3d at 136, all factual or legal issues that are common to the class inform the analysis. See *Amchem Prods., Inc. v. Windsor*, 521 U.S. 591, 621 (1997) ("Subdivisions (a) and (b) focus court attention on whether a proposed class has sufficient unity so that absent members can fairly be bound by decisions of class representatives."). In turn, an issue is common to the class when it is susceptible to generalized, class-wide proof. *In re Visa Check*, 280 F.3d at 136 ("In order to meet the predominance requirement . . . a plaintiff must establish that the issues in the class action that are subject to generalized proof, and thus applicable to the class as a whole, predominate over those issues that are subject only to individualized proof." (internal quotation marks omitted and alteration incorporated)) . . . That the class-wide proof comes in the form of a simple concession rather than contested evidence certainly shortens the time that the court must spend adjudicating the issue, but it does nothing to alter the fundamental cohesion of the proposed class, which is the central concern of the predominance requirement. See 2 Alba Conte & Herbert B. Newberg, NEWBERG ON CLASS ACTIONS § 4:25 (4th ed. 2002) ("[T]he predominance test does not involve a comparison of court time needed to adjudicate common issues weighed against time needed to dispose of individual issues. . . ."); 7AA Wright & Miller, FEDERAL PRACTICE AND PROCEDURE § 1778 (3d ed. 2005) ("[C]lockwatching is not very helpful in ascertaining whether class-action treatment would be desirable in a particular case."). Similarly, the fact that an issue is conceded or otherwise resolved does not mean that it ceases to be an "issue" for the purposes of predominance analysis. Even resolved questions continue to implicate the "common nucleus of operative facts and issues" with which the predominance inquiry is concerned. See *Waste Mgmt. Holdings, Inc. v. Mowbray*, 208 F.3d 288, 299 (1st Cir. 2000) ("[T]he fact that an issue has been resolved on summary judgment does not remove it from the predominance calculus."). Just as much as do contested issues, resolved issues bear on the key question that the analysis seeks to answer: whether the class is a legally coherent unit of representation by which absent class members may fairly be bound.

Second, Rule 23 seeks greater efficiency via collective adjudication and, relatedly, greater uniformity of decision as to similarly situated parties. See Fed. R. Civ. P. 23(b)(3) adv. comm. n. to 1966 amend. For these reasons we have written that when plaintiffs are "allegedly aggrieved by a single policy of defendants," such as the blanket policy at issue here, the case presents "precisely the type of situation for which the class action device is suited" since many nearly identical litigations can be adjudicated in unison. *In re Visa Check*, 280 F.3d at 146.

Eliminating conceded issues from Rule 23(b)(3)'s predominance calculus would undermine the goal of efficiency by requiring plaintiffs who share a "commonality of the violation and the harm," nonetheless to pursue separate and potentially numerous actions because, ironically, liability is so clear. *Id.* (noting that class action management "problems pale in comparison to the burden on the courts that would result from trying the cases individually").

Such a result also undermines the goal of uniformity by creating the risk of inconsistent decisions through the repeated litigation of the same question; here, for example, each individual plaintiff would have to establish anew that defendants were collaterally estopped by their prior concession and, if not, that defendants were liable on the merits. Cf. *Waste Mgmt. Holdings, Inc.*, 208 F.3d at 299 (concluding that because certification was "necessary to determine whether the prior resolution carries res judicata effect with respect to purported class members," the district court properly took account of "the common nucleus of operative facts and issues, even though certain of these already had been resolved"). Although defendants have conceded liability to these plaintiffs, there is no guarantee that they would concede liability in a case or series of cases involving significantly higher damages. Further, courts might differ as to whether, in light of the settlement, the requirements of collateral estoppel were met, specifically, whether the issue of liability was "actually litigated and decided" and whether its "resolution . . . was necessary to support a valid and final judgment on the merits." *Ball v. A.O. Smith Corp.*, 451 F.3d 66, 69 (2d Cir. 2006); cf. *In re Tamoxifen Citrate Antitrust Litig.*, 429 F.3d 370, 387 n.15 (2d Cir. 2005) ("[I]t is clearly a permissible byproduct of settlement that future hypothetical plaintiffs might be forced to relitigate the same issues involved in the settled cases."). . . .

Finally, we find further support for our view in the specific circumstances of this case. Defendants possess, but have not disclosed, records of all the newly-admitted misdemeanor detainees strip searched pursuant to the blanket policy. Absent class certification and its attendant class-wide notice procedures, most of these individuals—who potentially number in the thousands—likely never will know that defendants violated their clearly established constitutional rights, and thus never will be able to vindicate those rights. As a practical matter, then, without use of the class action mechanism, individuals harmed by defendants' policy and practice may lack an effective remedy altogether. Further, if defendants may utilize their concession to defeat class certification, it would work the perverse result of allowing them to escape the cost of their unconstitutional behavior precisely because their liability is too plain to be denied. No other court has sanctioned such a result; nor shall we.

C. *The District Court Erred in Determining that, as to Liability, Individual Issues Predominated*

. . . The class definition . . . implicated two broad common liability issues: whether the blanket [strip search] policy existed and whether defendants are liable for its implementation. The only countervailing, individualized liability issue was whether, regardless of the policy, some plaintiffs were strip searched based upon "reasonable and contemporaneously held

suspicion." The existence of this defense does "not . . . foreclose class certification." [*In re Visa Check*, 280 F.3d] at 138 (internal quotation marks omitted). Further, as the District Court recognized, "any such 'reasonable suspicion inquiries' will be de minimis"; indeed, defendants set forth that "such
an inquiry will only be sought regarding a limited number of plaintiffs." In
light of the pervasive character of the common liability issues and the admittedly *de minimis* nature of individualized liability issues, we conclude
that the District Court erred by holding that individual liability issues predominated over common ones. . . .

D.   *The District Court Erred in Concluding that the Class Action Device Is
      Not a Superior Litigation Mechanism*

For Rule 23(b)(3) certification to be proper, a class action also must be
the most "fair and efficient" method of resolving this case. In analyzing that
question, courts must consider four nonexclusive factors: (1) the interest of
the class members in maintaining separate actions; (2) "the extent and nature of any litigation concerning the controversy already commenced by or
against members of the class"; (3) "the desirability or undesirability of concentrating the litigation of the claims in the particular forum"; and (4) "the
difficulties likely to be encountered in the management of a class action."
See Fed. R. Civ. P. 23(b)(3). Contrary to the District Court's conclusion in
its decision dated November 7, 2003, all of these factors—as well as the
reasons set forth above regarding efficiency and fairness—favor class certification.

First, the class members have little interest in maintaining separate
actions since there already exists a concession of liability in this action and,
without class notification, most putative class members will not even know
that they suffered a violation of their constitutional rights. Second, this action already has progressed substantially and, again, offers the benefit of a
liability phase that can be resolved quickly and conclusively. Third, concentrating the litigation in one forum simplifies and streamlines the litigation
process. Fourth, we perceive little difficulty in managing a class action on
the issue of liability, especially since the District Court already has noted
that any individualized inquiries will be few and far between. Accordingly,
we conclude that the District Court erred in holding that a class action was
not the most fair and efficient litigation vehicle under these circumstances.

CONCLUSION

. . . In light of our direction to certify a class on the issue of liability
pursuant to the definition set forth in the September 23 decision, we also
instruct the District Court to consider anew whether to certify a class as to
damages as well. . . .

(2) Mandatory Versus Opt–Out Issue Classes

Must the issue class in *Nassau County* afford class members the opportunity to opt out of the class? Or could the court have mandated membership in the class-wide proceedings? *Should* class membership be mandated? Recall here the justification for mandatory class treatment in the
existing Rule 23(b)(1)–(2).

On the relationship between issue classes under Rule 23(c)(4) and
mandatory class treatment under Rule 23(b)(2), consider an opinion from
the Seventh Circuit:

McReynolds v. Merrill Lynch, Pierce, Fenner & Smith, Inc.

672 F.3d 482 (7th Cir. 2012)

■ POSNER, CIRCUIT JUDGE.

The plaintiffs have filed a class action suit that charges Merrill Lynch with racial discrimination in employment in violation of Title VII of the Civil Rights Act of 1964 and 42 U.S.C. § 1981. The plaintiffs ask that a class be certified for two purposes: deciding a common issue, Rule 23(c)(4)—whether the defendant has engaged and is engaging in practices that have a disparate impact (that is, a discriminatory effect, though it need not be intentional) on the members of the class, in violation of federal antidiscrimination law—and providing injunctive relief. Rule 23(b)(2). They also want damages. But while they asked the district court to certify the class for purposes of seeking compensatory and punitive damages, at argument the plaintiffs' lawyer said she wasn't asking—not yet anyway—for such certification, though her opening brief had suggested that if we found that the district court had erred in refusing to certify for class treatment the disparate impact issue and injunctive relief, we should order the court to "consider [on remand] the extent to which damages issues also could benefit from class treatment, consistent with *Allen v. Int'l Truck & Engine Corp.,* 358 F.3d 469 (7th Cir. 2004)." We defer that question to the end of our opinion. But we note here that without proof of intentional discrimination, which is not an element of a disparate impact claim, the plaintiffs cannot obtain damages, whether compensatory or punitive, but only equitable relief (which might however include backpay, and thus have a monetary dimension).

The district court denied certification. . . .

Wal–Mart Stores, Inc. v. Dukes holds that if employment discrimination is practiced by the employing company's local managers, exercising discretion granted them by top management (granted them as a matter of necessity, in Wal–Mart's case, because the company has 1.4 million U.S. employees), rather than implementing a uniform policy established by top management to govern the local managers, a class action by more than a million current and former employees is unmanageable; the incidents of discrimination complained of do not present a common issue that could be resolved efficiently in a single proceeding. Rule 23(a)(2). Not that the employer would be immune from liability even in such a case; if the local managers are acting within the scope of their employment in discriminating against their underlings on a forbidden ground (sex, alleged in *Wal–Mart,* race in our case), the employer is liable for their unlawful conduct under the doctrine of respondeat superior. But because there was no company-wide policy to challenge in *Wal–Mart*—the only relevant corporate policies were a policy *forbidding* sex discrimination and a policy of delegating employment decisions to local managers—there was no common issue to justify class treatment.

The district judge thought this case like *Wal–Mart* because Merrill Lynch, accused of discriminating against 700 black brokers currently or formerly employed by it, delegates discretion over decisions that influence the compensation of all the company's 15,000 brokers ("Financial Advisors" is their official title) to 135 "Complex Directors." Each of the Complex Directors supervises several of the company's 600 branch offices, and within each branch office the brokers exercise a good deal of autonomy, though only within a framework established by the company.

Two elements of that framework are challenged: the company's "teaming" policy and its "account distribution" policy. The teaming policy permits brokers in the same office to form teams. They are not required to form or join teams, and many prefer to work by themselves. But many others prefer to work as part of a team. Team members share clients, and the aim in forming or joining a team is to gain access to additional clients, or if one is already rich in clients to share some of them with brokers who have complementary skills that will secure the clients' loyalty and maybe persuade them to invest more with Merrill Lynch. As we said, there are lone wolves, but there is no doubt that for many brokers team membership is a plus; certainly the plaintiffs think so.

The teams are formed by brokers, and once formed a team decides whom to admit as a new member. Complex Directors and branch-office managers do not select the team's members.

Account distributions are transfers of customers' accounts when a broker leaves Merrill Lynch and his clients' accounts must therefore be transferred to other brokers. Accounts are transferred within a branch office, and the brokers in that office compete for the accounts. The company establishes criteria for deciding who will win the competition. The criteria include the competing brokers' records of revenue generated for the company and of the number and investments of clients retained.

The Complex Directors, as well as the branch-office managers, have a measure of discretion with regard to teaming and account distribution; they can veto teams and can supplement the company criteria for distributions. And to the extent that these regional and local managers exercise discretion regarding the compensation of the brokers whom they supervise, the case is indeed like *Wal–Mart*. But the exercise of that discretion is influenced by the two company-wide policies at issue: authorization to brokers, rather than managers, to form and staff teams; and basing account distributions on the past success of the brokers who are competing for the transfers. Furthermore, team participation and account distribution can affect a broker's performance evaluation, which under company policy influences the broker's pay and promotion. The plaintiffs argue that these company-wide policies exacerbate racial discrimination by brokers.

The teams, they say, are little fraternities (our term but their meaning), and as in fraternities the brokers choose as team members people who are like themselves. If they are white, they, or some of them anyway, are more comfortable teaming with other white brokers. Obviously they have their eyes on the bottom line; they will join a team only if they think it will result in their getting paid more, and they would doubtless ask a superstar broker to join their team regardless of his or her race. But there is bound to be uncertainty about who will be effective in bringing and keeping shared clients; and when there is uncertainty people tend to base decisions on emotions and preconceptions, for want of objective criteria.

Suppose a police department authorizes each police officer to select an officer junior to him to be his partner. And suppose it turns out that male police officers never select female officers as their partners and white officers never select black officers as their partners. There would be no intentional discrimination at the departmental level, but the practice of allowing police officers to choose their partners could be challenged as enabling sexual and racial discrimination—as having in the jargon of discrimination law a "disparate impact" on a protected group—and if a discriminatory effect was proved, then to avoid an adverse judgment the department would have to prove that the policy was essential to the department's mission. That case would not be controlled by *Wal–Mart* (although there is an undoubted resemblance), in which employment decisions were delegated to local managers; it would be an employment decision by top management.

Merrill Lynch's broker teams are formed by brokers, not managers, just as in our hypothetical example police officers' partners are chosen by police officers, not supervisors. If the teaming policy causes racial discrimination and is not justified by business necessity, then it violates Title VII as "disparate impact" employment discrimination—and whether it causes racial discrimination and whether it nonetheless is justified by business necessity are issues common to the entire class and therefore appropriate for class-wide determination.

And likewise with regard to account distributions: if as a result of racial preference at the team level black brokers employed by Merrill Lynch find it hard to join teams, or at least good teams, and as a result don't generate as much revenue or attract and retain as many clients as white brokers do, then they will not do well in the competition for account distributions either; and a kind of vicious cycle will set in. A portion of a team's pre-existing revenues are transferred within a team to a new recruit, who thus starts out with that much "new" revenue credited to him or her—an advantage, over anyone who is not on a team and thus must generate all of his own "new" revenue, that translates into a larger share of account distributions, which in turn helps the broker do well in the next round of such distributions. This spiral effect attributable to company-wide policy and arguably disadvantageous to black brokers presents another question common to the class, along with the question whether, if the team-inflected account distribution system does have this disparate impact, it nevertheless is justified by business necessity.

There is no indication that the corporate level of Merrill Lynch (or its parent, Bank of America) *wants* to discriminate against black brokers. Probably it just wants to maximize profits. But in a disparate impact case the presence or absence of discriminatory intent is irrelevant; and permitting brokers to form their own teams and prescribing criteria for account distributions that favor the already successful—those who may owe their success to having been invited to join a successful or promising team—are practices of Merrill Lynch, rather than practices that local managers can choose or not at their whim. Therefore challenging those policies in a class action is not forbidden by the *Wal–Mart* decision; rather that decision helps (as the district judge sensed) to show on which side of the line that separates a company-wide practice from an exercise of discretion by local managers this case falls.

Echoing the district judge, the defendant's brief states that "any discrimination here would result from local, highly-individualized implementation of policies rather than the policies themselves." That is too stark a dichotomy. Assume that with no company-wide policy on teaming or account distribution, but instead delegation to local management of the decision whether to allow teaming and the criteria for account distribution, there would be racial discrimination by brokers or local managers, like the discrimination alleged in *Wal–Mart*. But assume further that company-wide policies authorizing broker-initiated teaming, and basing account distributions on past success, increase the amount of discrimination. The incremental causal effect (overlooked by the district judge) of those company-wide policies—which is the alleged disparate impact—could be most efficiently determined on a class-wide basis.

We are not suggesting that there is in fact racial discrimination at any level within Merrill Lynch, or that management's teaming and account distribution policies have a racial effect. The fact that black brokers have on average lower earnings than white brokers may have different causes altogether. The only issue at this stage is whether the plaintiffs' claim of disparate impact is most efficiently determined on a class-wide basis rather than in 700 individual lawsuits.

The district judge exaggerated the impact on the feasibility and desirability of class action treatment of the fact that the exercise of discretion at the local level is undoubtedly a factor in the differential success of brokers, even if not a factor that overwhelms the effect of the corporate policies on teaming and on account distributions. Obviously a single proceeding, while it might result in an injunction, could not resolve class members' claims. Each class member would have to prove that his compensation had been adversely affected by the corporate policies, and by how much. So should the claim of disparate impact prevail in the class-wide proceeding, hundreds of separate trials may be necessary to determine which class members were actually adversely affected by one or both of the practices and if so what loss each class member sustained—and remember that the class has 700 members. But at least it wouldn't be necessary in each of those trials to determine whether the challenged practices were unlawful. Rule 23(c)(4) provides that "when appropriate, an action may be brought or maintained as a class action with respect to particular issues." The practices challenged in this case present a pair of issues that can most efficiently be determined on a class-wide basis, consistent with the rule just quoted.

As said in *Mejdrech v. Met–Coil Sys. Corp.*, 319 F.3d 910, 911 (7th Cir. 2003),

> class action treatment is appropriate and is permitted by Rule 23 when the judicial economy from consolidation of separate claims outweighs any concern with possible inaccuracies from their being lumped together in a single proceeding for decision by a single judge or jury. Often, and as it seems to us here, these competing considerations can be reconciled in a "mass tort" case by carving at the joints of the parties' dispute. If there are genuinely common issues, issues identical across all the claimants, issues moreover the accuracy of the resolution of which is unlikely to be enhanced by repeated proceedings, then it makes good sense, especially when the class is large, to resolve those issues in one fell swoop while leaving the remaining, claimant-specific issues to individual follow-on proceedings.

The kicker is whether "the accuracy of the resolution" would be "unlikely to be enhanced by repeated proceedings." If resisting a class action requires betting one's company on a single jury verdict, a defendant may be forced to settle; and this is an argument against definitively resolving an issue in a single case if enormous consequences ride on that resolution. *In re Bridgestone/Firestone, Inc.*, 288 F.3d 1012, 1020 (7th Cir. 2002); *In re Rhone–Poulenc Rorer, Inc.*, 51 F.3d 1293, 1299–1300 (7th Cir. 1995); contra, *Klay v. Humana, Inc.*, 382 F.3d 1241, 1274 (11th Cir. 2004). But Merrill Lynch is in no danger of being destroyed by a binding class-wide determination that it has committed disparate impact discrimination against 700 brokers, although an erroneous injunction against its teaming and account distribution policies could disadvantage it in competition with brokerage firms that employ similar policies—though we have no information on whether others do.

The *Mejdrech* decision, and *Bridgestone/Firestone* and *Rhone–Poulenc* more fully, discuss the danger that resolving an issue common to hundreds of different claimants in a single proceeding may make too much turn on the decision of a single, fallible judge or jury. The alternative is multiple proceedings before different triers of fact, from which a consensus might emerge; a larger sample provides a more robust basis for an inference. But that is an argument for separate trials on pecuniary relief, and the only issue of relief at present is whether to allow the plaintiffs to seek class-wide injunctive relief. There isn't any feasible method—certainly none has been proposed in this case—for withholding injunctive relief until a series of separate injunctive actions has yielded a consensus for or against the plaintiffs.

As far as pecuniary relief is concerned, there may be no common issues (though then again there may be, see *Allen v. Int'l Truck & Engine Corp.*, 358 F.3d at 472), and in that event the next stage of the litigation, should the class-wide issue be resolved in favor of the plaintiffs, will be hundreds of separate suits for backpay (or conceivably for compensatory damages and even punitive damages as well, if the plaintiffs augment their disparate-impact claim with proof of intentional discrimination). The stakes in each of the plaintiffs' claims are great enough to make individual suits feasible. Most of Merrill Lynch's brokers earn at least $100,000 a year, and many earn much more, and the individual claims involve multiple years. But the lawsuits will be more complex if, until issue or claim preclusion sets in, the question whether Merrill Lynch has violated the antidiscrimination statutes must be determined anew in each case.

We have trouble seeing the downside of the limited class action treatment that we think would be appropriate in this case, and we conclude that the district judge erred in deciding to the contrary (with evident misgivings, however). The denial of class certification under Rules 23(b)(2) and (c)(4) is therefore

REVERSED.

NOTES AND QUESTIONS

1. *Issue Class Treatment for Employment Discrimination.* Does the approach to issue-class certification in *McReynolds* solve the problems sketched earlier in this Chapter concerning Rule 23(b)(2) class treatment of employment-discrimination litigation in light of the mixture of equitable and legal remedies available therein? Is the approach sketched in *McReynolds* superior to the Supreme Court's analysis in *Wal–Mart Stores, Inc. v. Dukes* in this regard?

Does this opinion square with the Supreme Court's decision in *Wal–Mart Stores, Inc. v. Dukes*? Merrill Lynch certainly did not think so. It, along with the U.S. Chamber of Commerce and the Equal Employment Advisory Council, tried unsuccessfully to have the Supreme Court review the opinion. Merrill Lynch's petition asserted that the Seventh Circuit's opinion was "irreconcilable" with *Dukes* and argued that delegating discretion to local managers and co-workers with regard to the "teaming" and account distribution policies was indistinguishable from the policies at issue in *Dukes*. Merrill Lynch also contended that the class failed to meet Rule 23(a)'s commonality standard and argued that the Seventh Circuit's approach to issue classes "exacerbates the problem of blackmail settlements, allowing the threat of a class trial and injunctive relief to coerce settlement of meritless claims."

2. *Issue Classes and the Settlement Pressure Debate.* Are the reasons cited by Judge Posner for mandatory class treatment of equitable claims under subsection (b)(2) confined to that particular subsection? Or do some or all of them justify mandatory class treatment of defendant-centered aspects of liability in litigation for damages? To put the question somewhat differently: Can one reconcile the analysis in *McReynolds* with the same court's earlier opinion in *Rhone–Poulenc*?

If the law of class actions were to embrace issue classes more frequently, what would prevent class counsel from routinely seeking the certification of such classes and the settlement leverage that they might bring vis-à-vis defendants? Can issue classes be certified as to any insignificant or tangential issue that is nonetheless common in the sense of satisfying the minimal standard for commonality under Rule 23(a)(2)? Or can issue classes realistically be confined only to "important" or "decisive" issues within the panoply of all issues in a given area of litigation? Does the predominance inquiry in Rule 23(b)(3) seek to pose this question, if only inartfully and indirectly? Might one lend more precision to the class certification inquiry for issue classes by instructing courts to ask whether the aggregate treatment of common issues would materially advance the resolution of multiple civil claims by comparison to other realistic procedural alternatives? Or is that formulation amorphous as well?

3. *Issues Classes and the Seventh Amendment.* Does Judge Posner's opinion in *McReynolds* square with his earlier opinion in *Rhone–Poulenc* on the Seventh Amendment's Reexamination Clause? After the Seventh Circuit decided *Rhone–Poulenc*, it decided *Allen v. Int'l Truck and Engine Corp.*, 358 F.3d 469 (7th Cir. 2004), in which Judge Easterbrook, writing for the majority wrote:

> Certifying a class for injunctive purposes, while handling damages claims individually, does not transgress the seventh amendment. Just as in a single-person (or 27–person) suit, a jury will resolve common factual disputes, and its resolution will control when the judge takes up the request for an injunction. International Truck will enjoy its jury-trial right either way; and once *one* jury (in individual or class litigation) has resolved a factual dispute, principles of issue preclusion can bind the defendant to that outcome in future litigation consistently with the seventh amendment. See *Parklane Hosiery Co. v. Shore*, 439 U.S. 322 (1979); cf. *Blonder–Tongue Labs., Inc. v. Univ. of Illinois Found.*, 402 U.S. 313 (1971). The other 323 employees' right to jury trial can be protected in either or both of two ways: By offering them the opportunity to opt out, or by denying them (in any later damages proceedings) both the benefits and the detriments of issue and claim preclusion. See *Lytle v. Household Mfg., Inc.*, 494 U.S. 545 (1990); *Premier Elec. Constr. Co. v. Nat'l Elec. Contractors Ass'n, Inc.*, 814 F.2d 358 (7th Cir. 1987). Thus a class proceeding for equitable relief vindicates the seventh amendment as fully as do individual trials, is no more complex than individual trials, yet produces benefits compared with the one-person-at-a-time paradigm. The

district court erred in concluding that seventh-amendment concerns foreclose certification of a class under Rule 23(b)(2).

4. Interlocutory Appeal of the Certified Issue on the Merits. If courts were to certify issue classes more frequently, then the class-wide proceeding, by definition, would not generate a final judgment unless plaintiffs lost on a dispositive motion. The remaining issues not encompassed in the class action would have to be resolved in follow-on cases, typically brought on an individual basis. As a practical matter, is it tolerable to await the entry of final judgments in those follow-on cases before an appeal can be taken as to a determination on the merits of the common issue in the class-wide proceeding? Or should procedural law *require* that an opportunity for interlocutory appeal on the merits of the common issue *must* be provided in connection with the certification of any issue class? For such a recommendation, see Am. Law Inst., PRINCIPLES OF THE LAW OF AGGREGATE LITIGATION § 2.09(a)(2) (2010). Such an interlocutory appeal on the merits would be *in addition to* the existing interlocutory appeal under Rule 23(f) of the decision to certify the issue class in the first place. As comment *b* to § 2.09(a)(2) explains:

> In practical terms, unitary appellate review of a merits determination of the common issue prevents the waste of judicial resources that would occur if subsequent proceedings were to go forward but only thereafter to reveal some defect in the merits determination of the common issue. Unitary merits review also avoids the possibility of multiple appeals—potentially, to multiple courts—concerning the common issue in the aftermath of other proceedings that do, ultimately, yield final judgments. Authorization of an aggregate interlocutory appeal thereby preserves the efficiency and equity gains to be realized through the treatment of the common issue in a single proceeding.

> The conditioning of aggregate treatment on the availability of an interlocutory appeal on the merits serves an additional purpose. The expectation is that such an appeal will serve as an added backstop against efforts to seek aggregate treatment as to trivial or insignificant issues that nonetheless are common in a given litigation. Part of this backstop effect already comes through the specification in § 2.02(a)(1) that the court should determine whether aggregate treatment of a common issue by way of a class action will "materially advance the resolution of multiple civil claims by addressing the core of the dispute in a manner superior to other realistic procedural alternatives, so as to generate significant judicial efficiencies." . . .

> The practical effect of subsection § 2.09(a)(2) is that those seeking aggregate treatment of a common issue should be prepared to face the possibility of an aggregate interlocutory appeal on the merits of that issue in addition to the possibility of an interlocutory appeal with respect to the initial decision whether to aggregate. The disposition of both appeals should precede the disposition of the remaining issues raised by the underlying claims—for example, the obtaining of damage awards for particular claimants.

Does § 2.09(a)(2) provide enough of a "backstop"? Too much of one? Would plaintiffs' counsel, in fact, be unduly discouraged from pursuing issue classes under the foregoing parameters for fear that they might lose control over the litigation when the time came for follow-on individual cases?

Does increased use of issue classes portend messy and amorphous judicial efforts to supervise the division of the spoils from litigation as between class counsel and other plaintiffs' lawyers who bring follow-on cases built upon the class-wide determination of the common issue? Or would plaintiffs' lawyers effectively coordinate their efforts beforehand—e.g., with would-be class counsel entering into arrangements with other plaintiffs' law firms to divide responsibility (and the anticipated financial rewards) for the issue class and the follow-on cases, respectively?

5. *Turning a Decertified Class as to All Issues Into an Issue Class on Appeal.* In *Engle v. Liggett Group, Inc.*, 945 So.2d 1246 (Fla. 2006), the Florida Supreme Court overturned a $145 billion—yes, $145 *billion*—punitive damage award to a plaintiff class comprised of smokers in Florida. In so doing, however, the court distinguished between the class-wide treatment of *all* issues raised by the punitive damage claims of Florida smokers against the tobacco industry (which the court held not to warrant class treatment as a matter of Florida procedure) and the determination of common issues raised by those claims. The court identified several specific factual determinations made by the jury in the class proceeding in favor of the plaintiff class:

> We approve the Phase I findings for the class as to Questions 1 (that smoking cigarettes causes aortic aneurysm, bladder cancer, cerebrovascular disease, cervical cancer, chronic obstructive pulmonary disease, coronary heart disease, esophageal cancer, kidney cancer, laryngeal cancer, lung cancer (specifically, adenocarcinoma, large cell carcinoma, small cell carcinoma, and squamous cell carcinoma), complications of pregnancy, oral cavity/tongue cancer, pancreatic cancer, peripheral vascular disease, pharyngeal cancer, and stomach cancer), 2 (that nicotine in cigarettes is addictive), 3 (that the defendants placed cigarettes on the market that were defective and unreasonably dangerous), 4(a) (that the defendants concealed or omitted material information not otherwise known or available knowing that the material was false or misleading or failed to disclose a material fact concerning the health effects or addictive nature of smoking cigarettes or both), 5(a) (that the defendants agreed to conceal or omit information regarding the health effects of cigarettes or their addictive nature with the intention that smokers and the public would rely on this information to their detriment), 6 (that all of the defendants sold or supplied cigarettes that were defective), (7) (that all of the defendants sold or supplied cigarettes that, at the time of sale or supply, did not confirm to representations of fact made by said defendants), and 8 (that all of the defendants were negligent). Therefore, these findings in favor of the *Engle* Class can stand.

> The class consists of all Florida residents fitting the class description as of the trial court's order dated November 21, 1996. However, we conclude for the reasons explained in this opinion that continued class action treatment is not feasible and that upon remand the class must be decertified. Individual plaintiffs within the class will be permitted to proceed individually with the findings set forth above given res judicata effect in any subsequent trial between indi-

vidual class members and the defendants, provided such action is filed within one year of the mandate in this case.

Id. at 1276–77. Is it legitimate for a court to afford issue-preclusive effect to class-wide determinations of common issues even while decertifying the class that formed the procedural predicate for those determinations? Is the Florida Supreme Court in *Engle* effectively saying that the case could have—and should have—proceeded as an issue class and that one can salvage the legitimate, issue-class aspects of the proceeding on appeal? Does it matter whether the common issues as to which the Florida Supreme Court afforded issue-preclusive effect were seriously contested? Does it matter whether the individual smokers who file within one year might, simply as a strategic matter, wish to present to their respective juries evidence on many of the points described by the Florida Supreme Court—indeed, the same evidence that the *Engle* class jury considered?

In the aftermath of *Engle*, a federal district court sitting in Florida was faced with the prospect of actually applying the issue-preclusive effect of the findings as to common issues in the decertified class action. This proved quite difficult. The court initially reasoned that it could not afford issue-preclusive effect merely upon the say-so of the Florida Supreme Court. *Brown v. R.J. Reynolds Tobacco Co.*, 576 F. Supp. 2d 1328 (M.D. Fla. 2008). Upon conducting an independent inquiry, the court ultimately concluded that none of the findings as to common issues in *Engle* were issue preclusive in subsequent, individual actions by smokers:

> The apparent flaw with the [special verdict] jury form, and any verdict delivered from the form, is its nonspecificity with respect to what acts or omissions committed by what Defendant breached what duty to which Plaintiff causing what injury. As such, this Court "would have to embark on sheer speculation" to determine what issues were actually decided during the Phase I trial [in *Engle*] and how to apply them to the individual claims before this Court. *Hoag* [*v. New Jersey*, 356 U.S. 464, 472 (1958)]. At most, these findings establish that at some time the Defendants sold a defective product, concealed their tortious behavior, acted negligently, breached an express or implied warranty, and engaged in a conspiracy to misrepresent information relating to the health effects of smoking. While these findings demonstrate that the Defendants engaged in tortious behavior at some point in the past, such findings are insufficient to establish any element of the Engle plaintiffs' claims. Rather, the Phase I findings merely establish conduct as a broad abstraction, and conduct in the abstract fails to meet the identity requirement [i.e., the requirement of the same issue across the proceeding said to yield issue-preclusive effect and the present proceeding] to apply such findings in the specific cases before this Court.

Id. at 1342. The Eleventh Circuit took the case on interlocutory appeal and examined the issue preclusive effect of the earlier class-wide jury trial. Although there was little question that the Phase I approved findings had an issue-preclusive effect:

> The disagreement is about what the jury actually did find. The defendants, taking a narrow view, insist that the only facts found by the jury are those framed by the specific factual issue set out in the ques-

tions posed to them on the verdict form. The plaintiffs, by contrast, take a broader view of what facts the jury decided, arguing that the language of the questions, and hence the jury's answers, can and should be fleshed out using the record as a whole and apparently by going outside the record.

Brown v. R.J. Reynolds Tobacco Co., 611 F.3d 1324, 1334–35 (11th Cir. 2010). The court then observed that "[u]nder Florida law the issue preclusion standard requires the asserting party to show with a 'reasonable degree of certainty' that the specific factual issue was determined in its favor. The entire trial record may be considered for that purpose, although the burden is on the asserting party to point to specific parts of it to support its position . . . " Accordingly, it was up to the parties and the district court to determine which facts Phase I's approved findings actually established. In 2012, the United States Supreme Court denied R.J. Reynolds's petition to consider whether affording these issues preclusive effect violated the Due Process Clause. *R.J. Reynolds Tobacco Co. v. Clay*, 2012 WL 4009438 (Nov. 26, 2012).

Did the district court's insistence upon a precise and specific special verdict form so as to satisfy the same-issue requirement for issue preclusion actually operate as a welcome additional brake upon efforts to obtain issue class certification? In which sorts of cases would it be more likely for the court in the issue-class proceeding to be able to craft a special verdict form that would satisfy the district court's issue-preclusion analysis in *Brown*?

D. THE PARAMETERS OF JUDICIAL INQUIRY IN CLASS CERTIFICATION

Given the consequences of a decision to certify an action to proceed on a class-wide basis, it comes as little surprise that much attention has focused on what precisely the court may, should, or must consider in connection with the class certification decision. At the most basic level, of course, the court is to decide whether the requirements for class certification have been satisfied. But, as earlier portions of this Chapter have shown, this seemingly simple inquiry has the potential to enmesh the court in the possible fissures within the proposed class, the substantive law potentially applicable to class members' claims, and the relief that would be appropriate in the event of successful litigation by the class on the merits. All of these considerations touch, in one sense or another, upon the substance of class members' claims.

The historical starting point for this debate consists of a brief passage in the Supreme Court's opinion in *Eisen v. Carlisle & Jacquelin*, 417 U.S. 156 (1974). The *Eisen* litigation involved claims for damages under the federal antitrust and securities laws brought on behalf of a proposed class of about six million odd-lot traders on the New York Stock Exchange against various brokerage firms that handled odd-lot business.[*] Most, if not all, of the individual claims were for small amounts (Eisen himself had about $70 at stake). Rule 23(c)(2) at the time, and today, called for individualized notice to all class members who could be "identified through reasonable effort." Since roughly 2,250,000 class members were identifiable, individual mail notice would have cost the plaintiffs about $250,000 at the then-prevailing postage rate, an amount that the class representative and class

---

[*] "Odd lots are shares traded in lots of fewer than a hundred." *Eisen*, 417 U.S. at 159.

attorney were not willing to bear. The district court was concerned that a meritorious small-claim class action would be stymied due simply to the cost of the notice campaign. So the judge tried a novel approach. He ordered individual notice to all class members with ten or more odd-lot trades and to 5000 others chosen at random, as well as publication notice in prominent newspapers. The judge estimated that this truncated notice scheme would cost $22,000, and he allocated 90% of that total to the defendants based on a conclusion, formed after a preliminary hearing on the merits, that the class "was 'more than likely' to prevail at trial."

The Supreme Court disagreed. It held that the truncated notice scheme was inconsistent with the language of Rule 23(c)(2) and that the district judge had no power to allocate 90% of the notice costs to the defendants. As to the latter, the Court explained:

> [The district court's] decision [to impose 90 percent of the notice costs on defendants] was predicated on the court's finding, made after a preliminary hearing on the merits of the case, that petitioner was "more than likely" to prevail on his claims. Apparently, that court interpreted Rule 23 to authorize such a hearing as part of the determination whether a suit may be maintained as a class action. We disagree.

> We find nothing in either the language or history of Rule 23 that gives a court any authority to conduct a preliminary inquiry into the merits of a suit in order to determine whether it may be maintained as a class action. . . . This procedure is directly contrary to the command of subdivision (c)(1) that the court determine whether a suit denominated a class action may be maintained as such "(a)s soon as practicable after the commencement of (the) action. . . ."

> Additionally, we might note that a preliminary determination of the merits may result in substantial prejudice to a defendant, since of necessity it is not accompanied by the traditional rules and procedures applicable to civil trials. The court's tentative findings, made in the absence of established safeguards, may color the subsequent proceedings and place an unfair burden on the defendant.

Id. at 177–78.

After *Eisen*, many lower courts focused on the statement in the opinion that nothing in Rule 23 authorizes a court "to conduct a preliminary inquiry into the merits of a suit in order to determine whether it may be maintained as a class action." They tore this statement from its context and made it into a general rule—the so-called "*Eisen* rule"—that barred any inquiry into the merits to determine Rule 23's certification requirements.

Still, it became apparent relatively quickly that the *Eisen* rule was unworkable in pure form. While some Rule 23 requirements, such as 23(a)(1) numerosity, have nothing do with the merits, others, such as 23(b)(3) predominance, can overlap significantly with merits issues. For example, to determine predominance, the judge must project how the lawsuit will unfold and sort between issues likely to be central to the litigation and those too weak or marginal to figure prominently. In a later case, *Gen. Tel. Co. v. Falcon*, 457 U.S. 147 (1982), which you read in section 2.B. of this Chapter, the Supreme Court recognized the entanglement of certification with merits issues:

> As we noted in *Coopers & Lybrand* v. *Livesay*, 437 U.S. 463, "the class determination generally involves considerations that are 'enmeshed in the factual and legal issues comprising the plaintiff's cause of action.'" *Id.*, at 469 (quoting *Mercantile Nat. Bank* v. *Langdeau*, 371 U.S. 555, 558). Sometimes the issues are plain enough from the pleadings to determine whether the interests of the absent parties are fairly encompassed within the named plaintiff's claim, and sometimes it may be necessary for the court to probe behind the pleadings before coming to rest on the certification question. . . . We reiterate today that a Title VII class action, like any other class action, may only be certified if the trial court is satisfied, after a rigorous analysis, that the prerequisites of Rule 23(a) have been satisfied.

Id. at 160–61.

The *Falcon* Court did not even mention the *Eisen* rule, let alone explain how a merits inquiry could be squared with its requirements. As a result, the lower courts struggled with the obvious tension. Sometimes they probed the merits rather carefully, citing *Falcon* in support. At other times they relied mostly on the complaint's factual allegations or required only a minimal evidentiary presentation, citing the *Eisen* rule in support. Many courts declared that doubts should be resolved in favor of certification, especially for small claim class actions, because a failure to certify might mean no lawsuit at all and because an erroneous certification decision could be reversed later in the litigation. For an analysis of the *Falcon–Eisen* tension and a brief survey of the different approaches up to 2001, see Robert G. Bone & David S. Evans, *Class Certification and the Substantive Merits*, 51 Duke L.J. 1251, 1268–76 (2002).

The Supreme Court finally put an end to the *Eisen* rule in *Wal–Mart Stores, Inc.* v. *Dukes*, 131 S. Ct. 2541 (2011). After noting that the "rigorous analysis" required by *Falcon* frequently "will entail some overlap with the merits of the plaintiff's underlying claim," the Court took direct aim at the *Eisen* rule itself:

> A statement in one of our prior cases, *Eisen* v. *Carlisle & Jacquelin*, 417 U.S. 156, 177 (1974), is sometimes mistakenly cited to the contrary. . . . But in that case, the judge had conducted a preliminary inquiry into the merits of a suit, not in order to determine the propriety of certification under Rules 23(a) and (b) . . . , but in order to shift the cost of notice required by Rule 23(c)(2) from the plaintiff to the defendants. To the extent the quoted statement goes beyond the permissibility of a merits inquiry for any other pretrial purpose, it is the purest dictum and is contradicted by our other cases.

Id. at 2551, 2552 n.6.

While it removes an obstacle to merits inquiries at the certification stage, the *Wal–Mart* Court's rejection of the *Eisen* rule leaves another question unresolved. When a substantive issue is relevant to a certification requirement, how convinced must the judge be that the plaintiff's position on that issue is correct before granting certification? Stated more simply, what is the standard of proof for certification? Since about 2001, when the Seventh Circuit tightened up on the certification inquiry in *Szabo* v. *Bridgeport Mach., Inc.*, 249 F.3d 672 (7th Cir. 2001), many courts of appeals have adopted stricter standards of proof than they had applied previously. The following opinion, written before the Supreme Court's *Wal–Mart* decision, is a particularly important example of this trend:

In re Hydrogen Peroxide Antitrust Litigation
552 F.3d 305 (3d Cir. 2008)

■ SCIRICA, CHIEF JUDGE.

At issue in this antitrust action are the standards a district court applies when deciding whether to certify a class. We will vacate the order certifying the class in this case and remand for proceedings consistent with this opinion.

In deciding whether to certify a class under Fed. R. Civ. P. 23, the district court must make whatever factual and legal inquiries are necessary and must consider all relevant evidence and arguments presented by the parties. See *Newton v. Merrill Lynch, Pierce, Fenner & Smith, Inc.*, 259 F.3d 154, 166, 167 (3d Cir. 2001) (citing *Szabo v. Bridgeport Machs., Inc.*, 249 F.3d 672, 676 (7th Cir. 2001)); MANUAL FOR COMPLEX LITIGATION (THIRD) § 30.1 (1995)). In this appeal, we clarify three key aspects of class certification procedure. First, the decision to certify a class calls for findings by the court, not merely a "threshold showing" by a party, that each requirement of Rule 23 is met. Factual determinations supporting Rule 23 findings must be made by a preponderance of the evidence. Second, the court must resolve all factual or legal disputes relevant to class certification, even if they overlap with the merits—including disputes touching on elements of the cause of action. Third, the court's obligation to consider all relevant evidence and arguments extends to expert testimony, whether offered by a party seeking class certification or by a party opposing it.

I.

Purchasers of hydrogen peroxide and related chemical products brought this antitrust conspiracy action against chemical manufacturers. An inorganic liquid, hydrogen peroxide is used most prominently as a bleach in the pulp and paper industry with smaller amounts appearing in chemicals and laundry products, environmental applications, textiles, and electronics. Hydrogen peroxide is available in solutions of different concentrations and grades depending on its intended use. Major concentrations are 35, 50, and 70 percent. The grades, roughly in order from least-to most-expensive, are: standard, food/cosmetic (which must meet FDA standards), electronic, and propulsion. All defendants sold the standard grade, but not all defendants sold all other grades. Defendants sold different amounts of each of the grades. Each grade has different supply and demand conditions because the grades are sold to end-users in a variety of industries with different economic characteristics. According to defendants, the different grades are not economic substitutes for each other, but plaintiffs disagree. Prices diverge dramatically among grades; electronic or propulsion grade can be as much as five times more expensive than standard grade.

The other two products at issue are sodium percarbonate and sodium perborate, together known as persalts, which are granular solids containing hydrogen peroxide used primarily as detergents. . . .

After the United States Department of Justice and the European Commission began investigating possible violations of the antitrust laws in the hydrogen peroxide industry, several plaintiffs filed class action complaints against producers of hydrogen peroxide and persalts under § 4 of the Clayton Act, 15 U.S.C. § 15, alleging a conspiracy in restraint of trade violating § 1 of the Sherman Act, 15 U.S.C. § 1. The Judicial Panel on Multidistrict Litigation transferred all cognate federal actions to the United States District Court for the Eastern District of Pennsylvania, which consolidated the cases. The consolidated amended complaint alleged that during an eleven-year class period (January 1, 1994–January 5, 2005) defendants (1) communicated about prices they would charge, (2) agreed to charge prices at certain levels, (3) exchanged information on prices and sales volume, (4) allocated markets and customers, (5) agreed to reduce production capacity, (6) monitored each other, and (7) sold hydrogen peroxide at agreed prices.

The District Court denied defendants' motion to dismiss the complaint for failure to state a claim. Following extensive discovery, plaintiffs moved to certify a class of direct purchasers of hydrogen peroxide, sodium perborate, and sodium percarbonate, over an eleven-year class period. In support of class certification, plaintiffs offered the opinion of an economist. Defendants, opposing class certification, offered the opinion of a different economist. Defendants separately moved to exclude the opinion of plaintiffs' economist as unreliable under *Daubert v. Merrell Dow Pharm., Inc.*, 509 U.S. 579 (1993). Concluding plaintiffs' expert's opinion was admissible and supported plaintiffs' motion for class certification, the District Court certified a class of direct purchasers of hydrogen peroxide, sodium perborate, and sodium percarbonate under Fed. R. Civ. P. 23(b)(3). The District Court identified seven issues to be tried on a class-wide basis: (1) whether defendants and others engaged in a combination and conspiracy to fix, raise, maintain, or stabilize prices; allocate customers and markets; or control and restrict output of hydrogen peroxide, sodium perborate, and sodium percarbonate sold in the United States; (2) the identity of the participants in the alleged conspiracy; (3) the duration of the alleged conspiracy and the nature and character of defendants' acts performed in furtherance of it; (4) the effect of the alleged conspiracy on the prices of hydrogen peroxide and persalts during the class period; (5) whether the alleged conspiracy violated the Sherman Act; (6) whether the activities alleged in furtherance of the conspiracy or their effect on the prices of hydrogen peroxide and persalts during the class period injured named plaintiffs and the other members of the class; and (7) the proper means of calculating and distributing damages. The class was defined as:

> All persons or entities, including state, local and municipal government entities (but excluding defendants, their parents, predecessors, successors, subsidiaries, and affiliates as well as federal government entities) who purchased hydrogen peroxide, sodium perborate, or sodium percarbonate in the United States, its territories, or possessions, or from a facility located in the United States, its territories, or possessions, directly from any of the defendants, or from any of their parents, predecessors, successors, subsidiaries, or affiliates, at any time during the period from September 14, 1994 to January 5, 2005.

We granted defendants' petition for an interlocutory appeal under Fed. R. Civ. P. 23(f).

II.

Class certification is proper only "if the trial court is satisfied, after a rigorous analysis, that the prerequisites" of Rule 23 are met. *Gen. Tel. Co. of Sw. v. Falcon*, 457 U.S. 147, 161 (1982); see also *Amchem Prods., Inc. v.*

Windsor, 521 U.S. 591, 615 (1997) (Rule 23(b)(3) requirements demand a "close look"). "A class certification decision requires a thorough examination of the factual and legal allegations." *Newton*, 259 F.3d at 166.[6]

The trial court, well-positioned to decide which facts and legal arguments are most important to each Rule 23 requirement, possesses broad discretion to control proceedings and frame issues for consideration under Rule 23. But proper discretion does not soften the rule: a class may not be certified without a finding that each Rule 23 requirement is met. Careful application of Rule 23 accords with the pivotal status of class certification in large-scale litigation, because

> denying or granting class certification is often the defining moment in class actions (for it may sound the "death knell" of the litigation on the part of plaintiffs, or create unwarranted pressure to settle nonmeritorious claims on the part of defendants). . . .

Newton, 259 F.3d at 162; see *id.* at 167 ("Irrespective of the merits, certification decisions may have a decisive effect on litigation."); see also *Coopers & Lybrand v. Livesay*, 437 U.S. 463, 476 (1978). In some cases, class certification "may force a defendant to settle rather than incur the costs of defending a class action and run the risk of potentially ruinous liability." Accordingly, the potential for unwarranted settlement pressure "is a factor we weigh in our certification calculus." *Newton*, 259 F.3d at 168 n.8. The Supreme Court recently cautioned that certain antitrust class actions may present prime opportunities for plaintiffs to exert pressure upon defendants to settle weak claims. See *Bell Atl. Corp. v. Twombly*, 550 U.S. 544 (2007).

III.

Here, the District Court found the Rule 23(a) requirements were met, a determination defendants do not now challenge. Plaintiffs sought certification under Rule 23(b)(3) . . . Only the predominance requirement [of (b)(3)] is disputed in this appeal. Predominance "tests whether proposed classes are sufficiently cohesive to warrant adjudication by representation," *Amchem*, 521 U.S. at 623, a standard "far more demanding" than the commonality requirement of Rule 23(a), *id.* at 623–24, "requiring more than a common claim," *Newton*, 259 F.3d at 187. "Issues common to the class must predominate over individual issues. . . ." *In re The Prudential Ins. Co. of Am. Sales Practices Litig.*, 148 F.3d 283, 313–14 (3d Cir. 1998). Because the "nature of the evidence that will suffice to resolve a question determines whether the question is common or individual," *Blades v. Monsanto Co.*, 400 F.3d 562, 566 (8th Cir. 2005), " 'a district court must formulate some prediction as to how specific issues will play out in order to determine whether common or individual issues predominate in a given case,' " *In re New Motor Vehicles Can. Exp. Antitrust Litig.*, 522 F.3d 6, 20 (1st Cir. 2008) [hereinafter *New Motor Vehicles*] (quoting *Waste Mgmt. Holdings, Inc. v. Mowbray*, 208 F.3d 288, 298 (1st Cir. 2000)). "If proof of the essential elements of the cause of action requires individual treatment, then class certification is unsuitable." Accordingly, we examine the elements of plaintiffs' claim "through the prism" of Rule 23 to determine whether the District Court properly certified the class.

---

[6] . . . Class certification under Rule 23 has two primary components. The party seeking class certification must first establish the four requirements of Rule 23(a) . . . If all four requirements of Rule 23(a) are met, a class of one of three (each with additional requirements) may be certified. See Fed. R. Civ. P. 23(b)(1)-(3). (Rule 23 received stylistic revisions effective December 1, 2007. Fed. R. Civ. P. 23 Advisory Committee's note. 2007 Amendment. We quote the restyled version; its changes are immaterial to this appeal.)

A.

The elements of plaintiffs' claim are (1) a violation of the antitrust laws—here, § 1 of the Sherman Act, (2) individual injury resulting from that violation, and (3) measurable damages. 15 U.S.C. § 15. Importantly, individual injury (also known as antitrust impact) is an element of the cause of action; to prevail on the merits, every class member must prove at least some antitrust impact resulting from the alleged violation. *Bogosian v. Gulf Oil Corp.*, 561 F.2d 434, 454 (3d Cir. 1977); see *Newton*, 259 F.3d at 188 (In antitrust and securities fraud class actions, "[p]roof of injury (whether or not an injury occurred at all) must be distinguished from calculation of damages (which determines the actual value of the injury)").

In antitrust cases, impact often is critically important for the purpose of evaluating Rule 23(b)(3)'s predominance requirement because it is an element of the claim that may call for individual, as opposed to common, proof. See *New Motor Vehicles*, 522 F.3d at 20 ("In antitrust class actions, common issues do not predominate if the fact of antitrust violation and the fact of antitrust impact cannot be established through common proof"); *Bell Atl. Corp. v. AT & T Corp.*, 339 F.3d 294, 302 (5th Cir. 2003) ("[W]here fact of damage cannot be established for every class member through proof common to the class, the need to establish antitrust liability for individual class members defeats Rule 23(b)(3) predominance.").

Plaintiffs' burden at the class certification stage is not to prove the element of antitrust impact, although in order to prevail on the merits each class member must do so. Instead, the task for plaintiffs at class certification is to demonstrate that the element of antitrust impact is capable of proof at trial through evidence that is common to the class rather than individual to its members. Deciding this issue calls for the district court's rigorous assessment of the available evidence and the method or methods by which plaintiffs propose to use the evidence to prove impact at trial.

Here, the District Court found the predominance requirement was met because plaintiffs would be able to use common, as opposed to individualized, evidence to prove antitrust impact at trial. On appeal, defendants contend the District Court erred in three principal respects in finding plaintiffs satisfied the predominance requirement: (1) by applying too lenient a standard of proof for class certification, (2) by failing meaningfully to consider the views of defendants' expert while crediting plaintiffs' expert, and (3) by erroneously applying presumption of antitrust impact under *Bogosian*, 561 F.2d at 454–55.

We review a class certification order for abuse of discretion, which occurs if the district court's decision "rests upon a clearly erroneous finding of fact, an errant conclusion of law or an improper application of law to fact." *Newton*, 259 F.3d at 165. "[W]hether an incorrect legal standard has been used is an issue of law to be reviewed *de novo*." *In re Initial Pub. Offerings Sec. Litig.*, 471 F.3d 24, 32 (2d Cir. 2006) [hereinafter *IPO*] (citation omitted).

B.

We summarize briefly the evidence and arguments offered to the District Court. As noted, both plaintiffs and defendants presented the opinions of expert economists. Importantly, the experts disagreed on the key disputed predominance issue—whether antitrust impact was capable of proof at trial through evidence common to the class, as opposed to individualized evidence.

Plaintiffs' expert, John C. Beyer, Ph.D., offered an opinion purporting to show that "there is common proof that can be used to demonstrate that the alleged conspiracy to raise prices, restrict output and allocate customers would have impacted all purchasers of hydrogen peroxide, sodium perborate, and sodium percarbonate." Beyer's "market analysis" suggested that conditions in the hydrogen peroxide industry favored a conspiracy that would have impacted the entire class. First, hydrogen peroxide and persalts are fungible, undifferentiated commodity products, which means producers compete on price, not quality or other features. Second, production is heavily concentrated in a small group of manufacturers. Third, there are high barriers to entry in the industry and no close economic substitutes, preventing any competitors from entering the market and undercutting prices. Fourth, defendants' geographic markets overlapped, so that purchasers would have benefitted from price competition if not for the alleged conspiracy.

. . . Beyer also observed a "pricing structure" in the hydrogen peroxide industry which, he contended, showed prices across producers, grades and concentrations of hydrogen peroxide, and end uses moved similarly over time. This, according to Beyer, suggested a conspiracy would have impacted all class members . . .

Beyer identified two "potential approaches" to estimating damages on a class-wide basis: (1) benchmark analysis, which would compare actual prices during the alleged conspiracy with prices that existed before the class period; and (2) regression analysis, through which it "may be possible . . . to estimate the relationship between price of hydrogen peroxide, sodium perborate, and sodium percarbonate and the various market forces that influence prices, including demand and supply variables." These methods, according to Beyer, could be used to estimate the prices plaintiffs would have faced but for the conspiracy. . . .

Defendants offered the opinion of their own expert economist, Janusz A. Ordover, Ph.D., to "provide an independent expert assessment of whether certification of the proposed class of Plaintiffs is appropriate in this matter." Specifically, Ordover set out to address "whether, assuming a conspiracy of the kind described in the Complaint, the Plaintiffs will be able to show, through common proof, that all or virtually all of the members of the proposed class suffered economic injury caused by the alleged conspiracy." Ordover also "opine[d] on whether a formulaic approach exists by which impact could be demonstrated and damages to the class could be reasonably calculated." Ordover responded to and disputed many of Beyer's opinions.

First, Ordover disputed Beyer's finding that hydrogen peroxide and persalts are fungible, contending that the "various grades of hydrogen peroxide . . . [and persalts] have different supply characteristics and face different demand conditions. The existence of supply and demand characteristics that are specific to the various grades and uses requires individualized assessment of the impact of the alleged conspiracy at least across these different grades and uses. Consequently, a finding of class-wide impact from the alleged conspiracy cannot be inferred from the mere fact of the conspiracy and from common evidence." Second, . . . Ordover disputed Beyer's pricing structure analysis, contending "there is no tendency for prices charged to individual customers to move together, which indicates that the alleged conspiracy cannot be shown to have had class-wide impact," necessitating individualized inquiries to determine whether a customer incurred impact.

Ordover also found some of defendants' price-increase announcements were ineffective—actual prices did not follow the purported announcements—suggesting list prices could not be used to measure antitrust impact on a basis common to the class. Ordover observed that a number of contracts for the sale of hydrogen peroxide were individually negotiated, with a variety of contract terms. And deposition testimony from named plaintiffs indicated list prices were sometimes disregarded. Ordover opined that the statistical methods by which Beyer proposed to demonstrate common impact and damages were not feasible. . . .

Significantly, Ordover presented empirical analysis of the data on individual sales transactions and found that different customers purchasing the two most common grades and three most common concentrations from the same hydrogen peroxide producer in a given year were as likely to experience a decline in actual prices over the year as an increase, while other similarly situated customers experienced no change in price. Defendants contend this disparity goes to the core of the predominance issue—plaintiffs and their expert, Beyer, failed to "explain . . . how or which common proof could be used to determine that the alleged conspiracy impacted customers whose prices declined, as well as customers whose prices increased or stayed the same, over the same time period." Beyer, according to defendants, only "promised" to come up with a method to overcome this obstacle, without showing or even suggesting how it might be done. . . . The theme of defendants' argument is that the data, which Ordover analyzed, rebut Beyer's "theory" that common proof was feasible. Beyer's and Ordover's analyses are irreconcilable.

In addition to presenting Ordover's testimony, defendants moved to exclude Beyer's testimony as unreliable, citing *Daubert v. Merrell Dow Pharm., Inc.*, 509 U.S. 579 (1993). The District Court denied the *Daubert* motion in its memorandum and order certifying the class.

C.

The District Court concluded the predominance requirement was met. It held that "[e]ither [Beyer's] market analysis or the pricing structure analysis would likely be independently sufficient at this stage. Plaintiffs and Dr. Beyer have provided us with both. Despite defendants' claims to the contrary, we should require no more of plaintiffs in a motion for class certification." . . . The District Court held that it was sufficient that Beyer proposed reliable methods for proving impact and damages; it did not matter that Beyer had not completed any benchmark or regression analyses, and the court would not require plaintiffs to show at the certification stage that either method would work.

IV.

A.

Defendants contend the District Court applied too lenient a standard of proof with respect to the Rule 23 requirements by (1) accepting only a "threshold showing" by plaintiffs rather than making its own determination, (2) requiring only that plaintiffs demonstrate their "intention" to prove impact on a class-wide basis, and (3) singling out antitrust actions as appropriate for class treatment even when compliance with Rule 23 is "in doubt."

Although it is clear that the party seeking certification must convince the district court that the requirements of Rule 23 are met, little guidance is available on the subject of the proper standard of "proof" for class certification. The Supreme Court has described the inquiry as a "rigorous analysis," *Falcon*, 457 U.S. at 161, and a "close look," *Amchem*, 521 U.S. at 615, but it has elaborated no further.

1.

The following principles guide a district court's class certification analysis. First, the requirements set out in Rule 23 are not mere pleading rules. The court may 'delve beyond the pleadings to determine whether the requirements for class certification are satisfied.' "[15]

An overlap between a class certification requirement and the merits of a claim is no reason to decline to resolve relevant disputes when necessary to determine whether a class certification requirement is met. Some uncertainty ensued when the Supreme Court declared in *Eisen v. Carlisle & Jacquelin*, 417 U.S. 156, 177 (1974), that there is "nothing in either the language or history of Rule 23 that gives a court any authority to conduct a preliminary inquiry into the merits of a suit in order to determine whether it may be maintained as a class action." . . . As we explained in *Newton*, 259 F.3d at 166–69, *Eisen* is best understood to preclude only a merits inquiry that is not necessary to determine a Rule 23 requirement. Other courts of appeals have agreed. Because the decision whether to certify a class "requires a thorough examination of the factual and legal allegations," *id.* at 166, the court's rigorous analysis may include a "preliminary inquiry into the merits," *id.* at 168, and the court may "consider the substantive elements of the plaintiffs' case in order to envision the form that a trial on those issues would take," *id.* at 166. A contested requirement is not forfeited in favor of the party seeking certification merely because it is similar or even identical to one normally decided by a trier of fact. Although the district court's findings for the purpose of class certification are conclusive on that topic, they do not bind the fact-finder on the merits.

The evidence and arguments a district court considers in the class certification decision call for rigorous analysis. A party's assurance to the court that it intends or plans to meet the requirements is insufficient. . . . Support for our analysis is drawn from amendments to Rule 23 that took effect in 2003. First, amended Rule 23(c)(1)(A) altered the timing requirement for the class certification decision. The amended rule calls for a decision on class certification "[a]t an early practicable time after a person sues or is sued as a class representative," while the prior version had required that decision be made "as soon as practicable after commencement of an action." We recognized in *Weiss v. Regal Collections*, 385 F.3d 337, 347 (3d Cir. 2004), that this change in language, though subtle, reflects the

---

[15] See 5 James Wm. Moore et al., MOORE'S FEDERAL PRACTICE § 23.61[1] (3d ed. 2008) ("Pleading requirements are distinct from the requirements for certifying a case as a class action. A court may not and should not certify a class action without a rigorous examination of the facts to determine if the certification requirements of Rule 23(a) and (b) have been met." (citation omitted));. . . . In *Szabo*, the Court of Appeals for the Seventh Circuit offered this persuasive explanation:

> The reason why judges accept a complaint's factual allegations when ruling on motions to dismiss under Rule 12(b)(6) is that a motion to dismiss tests the legal sufficiency of a pleading. Its *factual* sufficiency will be tested later—by a motion for summary judgment under Rule 56, and if necessary by trial. By contrast, an order certifying a class usually is the district judge's last word on the subject; there is no later test of the decision's factual premises (and, if the case is settled, there could not be such an examination even if the district judge viewed the certification as provisional).

249 F.3d at 675–76.

need for a thorough evaluation of the Rule 23 factors—for this reason the rule does not "require or encourage premature certification determinations." [Ed. Note: The court emphasizes in this regard the possibility that time would be needed for pre-certification discovery, citing the Advisory Committee's Note to the 2003 amendments as well as the report of the Standing Committee on Rules of Practice and Procedure.] . . . Relatedly, in introducing the concept of a "trial plan," the Advisory Committee's 2003 note focuses attention on a rigorous evaluation of the likely shape of a trial on the issues:

> A critical need is to determine how the case will be tried. An increasing number of courts require a party requesting class certification to present a "trial plan" that describes the issues likely to be presented at trial and tests whether they are susceptible of class-wide proof.

Fed. R. Civ. P. 23 advisory committee's note, 2003 Amendments.

Additionally, the 2003 amendments eliminated the language that had appeared in Rule 23(c)(1) providing that a class certification "may be conditional."[21] The Advisory Committee's note explains: "A court that is not satisfied that the requirements of Rule 23 have been met should refuse certification until they have been met." The Standing Committee on Rules of Practice and Procedure advised:

> The provision for conditional class certification is deleted to avoid the unintended suggestion, which some courts have adopted, that class certification may be granted on a tentative basis, even if it is unclear that the rule requirements are satisfied.

While these amendments do not alter the substantive standards for class certification, they guide the trial court in its proper task—to consider carefully all relevant evidence and make a definitive determination that the requirements of Rule 23 have been met before certifying a class. To summarize: because each requirement of Rule 23 must be met, a district court errs as a matter of law when it fails to resolve a genuine legal or factual dispute relevant to determining the requirements.

2.

. . . Factual determinations necessary to make Rule 23 findings must be made by a preponderance of the evidence. In other words, to certify a class the district court must find that the evidence more likely than not establishes each fact necessary to meet the requirements of Rule 23.

In reviewing a district court's judgment on class certification, we apply the abuse of discretion standard. A district court abuses its discretion in deciding whether to certify a class action if its "decision rests upon a clearly erroneous finding of fact, an errant conclusion of law or an improper application of law to fact." Under these Rule 23 standards, a district court exercising proper discretion in deciding whether to certify a class will resolve factual disputes by a preponderance of the evidence and make findings that each Rule 23 requirement is met or is not met, having considered all relevant evidence and arguments presented by the parties. The abuse of discretion standard requires the judge to exercise sound discretion—failing that,

---

[21] Although the language allowing for "conditional" certification has been removed, Fed. R. Civ. P. 23(c)(1)(C) provides that "[a]n order that grants or denies class certification may be altered or amended before final judgment."

the judge's decision is not entitled to the deference attendant to discretionary rulings.

If a class is certified, "the text of the order or an incorporated opinion must include (1) a readily discernible, clear, and precise statement of the parameters defining the class or classes to be certified, and (2) a readily discernible, clear, and complete list of the claims, issues or defenses to be treated on a class basis." *Wachtel*, 453 F.3d at 187; see Fed. R. Civ. P. 23(c)(1)(B).

B.

Although the District Court properly described the class certification decision as requiring "rigorous analysis," some statements in its opinion depart from the standards we have articulated. The District Court stated, "So long as plaintiffs demonstrate their intention to prove a significant portion of their case through factual evidence and legal arguments common to all class members, that will now suffice. It will not do here to make judgments about whether plaintiffs have adduced enough evidence or whether their evidence is more or less credible than defendants'." With respect to predominance, the District Court stated that "[p]laintiffs need only make a threshold showing that the element of impact will predominantly involve generalized issues of proof, rather than questions which are particular to each member of the plaintiff class." As we have explained, proper analysis under Rule 23 requires rigorous consideration of all the evidence and arguments offered by the parties. It is incorrect to state that a plaintiff need only demonstrate an "intention" to try the case in a manner that satisfies the predominance requirement. Similarly, invoking the phrase "threshold showing" risks misapplying Rule 23. A "threshold showing" could signify, incorrectly, that the burden on the party seeking certification is a lenient one (such as a prima facie showing or a burden of production) or that the party seeking certification receives deference or a presumption in its favor. So defined, "threshold showing" is an inadequate and improper standard. "[T]he requirements of Rule 23 must be met, not just supported by some evidence." *IPO*, 471 F.3d at 33; see e.g., *id*. at 40, 42 (rejecting the view that a party seeking certification need only make "some showing" with respect to the Rule 23 requirements).

Citing *Cumberland Farms, Inc. v. Browning–Ferris Indus.*, 120 F.R.D. 642, 645 (E.D. Pa. 1988), the District Court reasoned, "[i]t is well recognized that private enforcement of [antitrust] laws is a necessary supplement to government action. With that in mind, in an alleged horizontal price-fixing conspiracy case when a court is in doubt as to whether or not to certify a class action, the court should err in favor of allowing the class." See also *Eisenberg v. Gagnon*, 766 F.2d 770, 785 (3d Cir. 1985) (citing *Kahan v. Rosenstiel*, 424 F.2d 161, 169 (3d Cir. 1970)) (advising that in a "doubtful" case when presented with a putative securities class action, court should err, if at all, in favor of certification). These statements invite error. Although the trial court has discretion to grant or deny class certification, the court should not suppress "doubt" as to whether a Rule 23 requirement is met—no matter the area of substantive law. Accordingly, *Eisenberg* should not be understood to encourage certification in the face of doubt as to whether a Rule 23 requirement has been met. *Eisenberg* predates the recent amendments to Rule 23 which, as noted, reject tentative decisions on certification and encourage development of a record sufficient for informed analysis. We recognize the Supreme Court has observed that "[p]redominance is a test readily met in certain cases alleging consumer or securities fraud or violations of the antitrust laws." *Amchem*, 521 U.S. at 625. But it does not follow that a court should relax its certification analysis, or presume a requirement for certification is met, merely because a plaintiff's claims fall within one of those substantive categories.

To the extent that the District Court's analysis reflects application of incorrect standards, remand is appropriate. We recognize that the able District Court did not have the benefit of the standards we have articulated. Faced with complex, fact-intensive disputes, trial courts have expended considerable effort to interpret and apply faithfully the requirements of Rule 23. One important reason for granting interlocutory appeals under Fed. R. Civ. P. 23(f) is to address "novel or unsettled questions of law" like those presented here.

C.

Defendants contend the District Court erred as a matter of law in failing to consider the expert testimony of defendants' expert, Ordover, instead deferring to the opinion of plaintiffs' expert, Beyer. Plaintiffs do not dispute that a district court may properly consider expert opinion with respect to Rule 23 requirements at the class certification stage, but maintain that in this case the District Court considered and rejected Ordover's opinion and defendants' arguments based on it.

In addressing defendants' *Daubert* motion to exclude Beyer's opinion, the court discussed whether it should consider Ordover's opinion in deciding whether Beyer's opinion was admissible. The court stated it would be improper to "weigh the relative credibility of the parties' experts"—in other words, to weigh Ordover's opinion against Beyer's—for the purpose of deciding whether to admit or exclude Beyer's opinion. Concluding Beyer's opinion was admissible, the court denied the *Daubert* motion. But in addressing the Rule 23 requirements, the court did not confront Ordover's analysis or his substantive rebuttal of Beyer's points. Nor did the court address Ordover's finding of substantial price disparities among similarly situated purchasers of hydrogen peroxide. The court appears to have assumed it was barred from weighing Ordover's opinion against Beyer's for the purpose of deciding whether the requirements of Rule 23 had been met. This was erroneous.

1.

Expert opinion with respect to class certification, like any matter relevant to a Rule 23 requirement, calls for rigorous analysis. It follows that opinion testimony should not be uncritically accepted as establishing a Rule 23 requirement merely because the court holds the testimony should not be excluded, under *Daubert* or for any other reason. See *IPO*, 471 F.3d at 42 (rejecting the view that "an expert's testimony may establish a component of a Rule 23 requirement simply by being not fatally flawed" and instructing that "[a] district judge is to assess all of the relevant evidence admitted at the class certification stage and determine whether each Rule 23 requirement has been met, just as the judge would resolve a dispute about any other threshold prerequisite for continuing a lawsuit"). . . . Like any evidence, admissible expert opinion may persuade its audience, or it may not. This point is especially important to bear in mind when a party opposing certification offers expert opinion. The district court may be persuaded by the testimony of either (or neither) party's expert with respect to whether a certification requirement is met. Weighing conflicting expert testimony at the certification stage is not only permissible; it may be integral to the rigorous analysis Rule 23 demands. See *West*, 282 F.3d at 938 (cautioning that neglecting to resolve disputes between experts "amounts to a delegation of judicial power to the plaintiffs, who can obtain class certification just by hiring a competent expert").

Resolving expert disputes in order to determine whether a class certification requirement has been met is always a task for the court—no matter whether a dispute might appear to implicate the "credibility" of one or more experts, a matter resembling those usually reserved for a trier of fact. Rigorous analysis need not be hampered by a concern for avoiding credibility issues; as noted, findings with respect to class certification do not bind the ultimate fact-finder on the merits. A court's determination that an expert's opinion is persuasive or unpersuasive on a Rule 23 requirement does not preclude a different view at the merits stage of the case.

That weighing expert opinions is proper does not make it necessary in every case or unlimited in scope. As the Court of Appeals for the Second Circuit instructed,

> To avoid the risk that a Rule 23 hearing will extend into a protracted mini-trial of substantial portions of the underlying litigation, a district judge must be accorded considerable discretion to limit both discovery and the extent of the hearing on Rule 23 requirements. But even with some limits on discovery and the extent of the hearing, the district judge must receive enough evidence, by affidavits, documents, or testimony, to be satisfied that each Rule 23 requirement has been met.

IPO, 471 F.3d at 41. In its sound discretion, a district court may find it unnecessary to consider certain expert opinion with respect to a certification requirement, but it may not decline to resolve a genuine legal or factual dispute because of concern for an overlap with the merits. Genuine disputes with respect to the Rule 23 requirements must be resolved, after considering all relevant evidence submitted by the parties. See *West*, 282 F.3d at 938 ("Tough questions must be faced and squarely decided, if necessary by holding evidentiary hearings and choosing between competing perspectives."); *Szabo*, 249 F.3d at 676 (district court must "resolve the disputes before deciding whether to certify the class"); *IPO*, 471 F.3d at 41 (Rule 23 calls for "definitive assessment" of its requirements); *id.* at 42 (rejecting the view that "a district judge may not weigh conflicting evidence and determine the existence of a Rule 23 requirement just because that requirement is identical to an issue on the merits").

2.

. . . We do not question plaintiffs' general proposition, which the District Court accepted, that a conspiracy to maintain prices could, in theory, impact the entire class despite a decrease in prices for some customers in parts of the class period, and despite some divergence in the prices different plaintiffs paid. But the question at class certification stage is whether, if such impact is plausible in theory, it is also susceptible to proof at trial through available evidence common to the class. When the latter issue is genuinely disputed, the district court must resolve it after considering all relevant evidence. Here, the District Court apparently believed it was barred from resolving disputes between the plaintiffs' and defendants' experts. Rule 23 calls for consideration of all relevant evidence and arguments, including relevant expert testimony of the parties. Accordingly, we will vacate the order certifying the class and remand for proceedings consistent with this opinion.[26]. . .

NOTES AND QUESTIONS

1. Hydrogen Peroxide's Standard of Proof. Quoting from the Supreme Court's opinion in *General Telephone v. Falcon,* the Third Circuit insists on a "rigorous analysis" of all certification requirements. According to the court, the plaintiff must demonstrate all the Rule 23 certification requirements by a preponderance of the evidence, including any merits issues relevant to certification. However, the court also makes clear that any merits determinations made for certification purposes are not binding on the trier of fact at trial, and it quotes the Second Circuit in *IPO Securities* for the proposition that "a district judge must be accorded considerable discretion to limit both discovery and the extent of the hearing on Rule 23 requirements" to avoid turning the certification hearing into a full-blown "mini-trial."

The *Hydrogen Peroxide* court draws support for its stricter approach from the 2003 amendments to Rule 23. Do those amendments dictate the court's choice? Does its choice make sense as a policy matter? The court adopts a preponderance of the evidence standard, but what must be proved by this standard? That the claims asserted in the complaint have merit? That the claims asserted in the complaint are capable of being proved for everyone in the class on the basis of common evidence? In thinking about these questions, it is useful to compare the court's choice of standard of proof to other possible formulations. The options can be arrayed along a spectrum. At one extreme, all the plaintiff need do is state in a conclusory fashion (but subject to Rule 11 sanctions) that all the certification requirements are met. A slightly more onerous burden would require the plaintiff to present a plausible theory of class-wide proof but without any need for supporting evidence. A stricter approach would require evidentiary support but only enough to meet a liberal summary judgment standard. (This appears to be the approach that the *Hydrogen Peroxide* district court used.) Going one step further, a court might weigh the evidence on both sides but subject it to a weaker burden than a preponderance standard. And so on. Viewed in the context of this spectrum of possibilities, it is apparent that the Third Circuit chose a rather strict standard of proof. What reasons does the court give for making this choice?

2. The Fraud-on-the-Market Theory. Hydrogen Peroxide is an antitrust class action, involving the question whether antitrust impact can be proved on a class-wide basis for each class member. A parallel problem arises in securities-fraud class actions. To establish liability for securities fraud, a plaintiff must prove that she actually relied on the misrepresentation. Reliance is an individual issue that, like antitrust impact, can scuttle a finding of 23(b)(3) predominance. However, the Supreme Court eased the way for plaintiffs in *Basic Inc. v. Levinson,* 485 U.S. 224, 245–47 (1988), by recognizing a presumption of reliance when investors trade in an efficient market, provided the information is material and sufficiently public to affect the share price. This so-called fraud-on-the-market theory is based on the efficient-capital-markets hypothesis, which holds that share price should reflect all available information

---

[26] The current record suggests it may be possible to overcome some obstacles to class certification by shortening the class period or by fashioning sub-classes. See Fed. R. Civ. P. 23(c)(5).

when the market is efficient. As a result, an investor who purchases at the market price necessarily relies on all such information (though indirectly), including the misrepresentations that form the basis of the securities fraud suit. Plaintiffs bringing securities-fraud class actions typically appeal to the fraud-on-the-market presumption to convert reliance into a common question and satisfy the predominance requirement.

But there is a catch. As a condition to using the presumption, the plaintiff must prove that the market is efficient. If it is, the presumption is available (assuming the other requirements are satisfied); if it isn't, the presumption is not available. Thus, a critical issue at the class certification stage is what burden the plaintiff must meet to prove that the market is efficient.

The Second Circuit in *In re IPO Sec. Litig.*, 471 F.3d 24 (2d Cir. 2006), adopted a rather strict approach. The district judge had relied on two previous Second Circuit decisions, *Caridad v. Metro–North Commuter RR*, 191 F.3d 283 (2d Cir. 1999) and *In re Visa Check/MasterMoney Antitrust Litig.*, 280 F.3d 124 (2d Cir. 2001), to require only "some showing" of an efficient market based on expert testimony that was not "fatally flawed." The Second Circuit reversed, holding that this was too lax, and outlining the approach that should be used:

> (1) a district judge may certify a class only after making determinations that each of the Rule 23 requirements has been met; (2) such determinations can be made only if the judge resolves factual disputes relevant to each Rule 23 requirement and finds that whatever underlying facts are relevant to a particular Rule 23 requirement have been established and is persuaded to rule, based on the relevant facts and the applicable legal standard, that the requirement is met; (3) the obligation to make such determinations is not lessened by overlap between a Rule 23 requirement and a merits issue, even a merits issue that is identical with a Rule 23 requirement; (4) in making such determinations, a district judge should not assess any aspect of the merits unrelated to a Rule 23 requirement; and (5) a district judge has ample discretion to circumscribe both the extent of discovery concerning Rule 23 requirements and the extent of a hearing to determine whether such requirements are met in order to assure that a class certification motion does not become a pretext for a partial trial of the merits.

> In drawing these conclusions, we add three observations. First, our conclusions necessarily preclude the use of a "some showing" standard, and to whatever extent *Caridad* might have implied such a standard for a Rule 23 requirement, that implication is disavowed. Second, we also disavow the suggestion in *Visa Check* that an expert's testimony may establish a component of a Rule 23 requirement simply by being not fatally flawed. A district judge is to assess all of the relevant evidence admitted at the class certification stage and determine whether each Rule 23 requirement has been met, just as the judge would resolve a dispute about any other threshold prerequisite for continuing a lawsuit. Finally, we decline to follow the dictum in *Heerwagen* [*v. Clear Channel Communications*, 435 F.3d 219 (2d Cir. 2006)] suggesting that a district judge may not weigh conflicting evidence and determine the existence of a Rule 23 requirement just because that requirement is identical to an issue on the merits.

471 F.3d at 41–42.

Applying its stricter approach, the *IPO* court concluded that the market for IPO shares was not efficient and therefore the fraud-on-the-market presumption was not available. Although the *IPO* court did not clearly specify any particular quantum of proof, the Second Circuit filled this gap two years later. In *Teamsters Local 445 Freight Div. Pension Fund v. Bombardier, Inc.*, 546 F.3d 196, 202 (2d Cir. 2008), it held that "the preponderance of the evidence standard applies to evidence proffered to establish Rule 23's requirements."

3.   *Developments in Other Circuits. Hydrogen Peroxide* and *IPO* are examples of a trend in the circuits toward stricter evidentiary burdens. For cases from other circuits that have contributed to this trend, see *Vega v. T–Mobile USA, Inc.*, 564 F.3d 1256, 1266 (11th Cir. 2009); *In Re New Motor Vehicles Canadian Export Antitrust Litig.*, 522 F.3d 6, 17, 24–26 (1st Cir. 2008); *Oscar Private Equity Invs. v. Allegiance Telecom., Inc.*, 487 F.3d 261, 266–68 (5th Cir. 2007); *Gariety v. Grant Thornton, LLP*, 368 F.3d 356, 366 (4th Cir. 2004); and *Szabo v. Bridgeport Machs., Inc.*, 249 F.3d 672, 675–76 (7th Cir. 2001).

4.   *Prove the Issue or Demonstrate the Issue Can Be Proved?* According to *Hydrogen Peroxide*, the plaintiff need not actually prove the element in question, but only demonstrate that it is capable of proof at trial through evidence common to the class. But what does this mean exactly? How can a plaintiff demonstrate that an ostensibly individual element is capable of proof through common evidence without actually proving it in that way? If the plaintiff musters her common evidence, the defendant will almost certainly contest it, and then the judge will have to weigh the competing evidence. This much is clear from *Hydrogen Peroxide*, isn't it? But how can the judge weigh evidence without actually determining the issue? The judge might conclude that the plaintiff's showing is good enough on balance to warrant certification, but after *Hydrogen Peroxide*, doesn't "good enough" have to mean "by a preponderance"?

In this connection, consider a more recent decision, which like *Hydrogen Peroxide*, comes from the Third Circuit: *Behrend v. Comcast Corp.*, 655 F.3d 182 (3d Cir. 2011), rev'd *Comcast Corp. v. Behrend*, 2013 WL 1222646. Although *Behrend* has been reversed, see note 7 below, it is still a good example of how differing views on the underlying issues support different approaches to the standard of proof, even among judges on the same circuit. The plaintiffs in *Behrend* were Comcast subscribers, and they alleged that Comcast acquired facilities from competing cable providers (so-called "Transaction Parties") as part of a scheme to monopolize the Philadelphia regional market in violation of federal antitrust laws. The plaintiffs sought to certify a 23(b)(3) class action consisting of Comcast subscribers. To satisfy the predominance requirement, the plaintiffs introduced evidence to demonstrate that both antitrust impact and individual damage could be proved on a class-wide basis. The district judge gave serious consideration to the voluminous evidence on both sides and analyzed it in light of *Hydrogen Peroxide*'s principles before holding that (b)(3) predominance was satisfied. Comcast appealed, and the Third Circuit affirmed.

Stressing that Comcast "bears a heavy burden in convincing us that the District Court's factually findings were clearly erroneous," *id.* at 197, the Third Circuit panel reviewed the plaintiffs' expert evidence and concluded:

> Based on this evidence, we determine that the antitrust impact Plaintiffs allege is "plausible in theory" and "susceptible to proof at

trial through available evidence common to the class." *Hydrogen Peroxide*, 552 F.3d at 325. We are satisfied that the District Court's findings were supported by the evidence and were not clearly erroneous. . . .

. . . At bottom, Comcast misconstrues our role at this stage of the litigation. Comcast would have us decide on the merits whether there was actual or potential competition among the Transaction Parties, the reason [a potential competitor] abandoned the Philadelphia market, and whether Plaintiffs' experts proved antitrust impact. We are not the jury. Although in Hydrogen Peroxide we heightened the inquiry a district court must perform on the issue of class certification, nothing in that opinion indicated that class certification hearings were to become actual trials in which factual disputes are to be resolved. . . . We allow preliminary merits inquiries when necessary for Rule 23 because of the potentially "decisive effect on litigation" of a certification decision, but those inquiries remain limited and nonbinding on the merits at trial. Nothing in *Hydrogen Peroxide* requires plaintiffs to prove their case at the class certification stage; to the contrary, they must establish by a preponderance that their case is one that meets each requirement of Rule 23. To require more contravenes *Eisen* and runs dangerously close to stepping on the toes of the Seventh Amendment by preempting the jury's factual findings with our own.

Id. at 198–200 (also citing "recent scholarship" critical of the "trend towards converting certification decisions into mini trials").

Are the *Behrend* court's conclusions and assertions consistent with *Hydrogen Peroxide*? See also *Messner v. Northshore Univ. HealthSystems*, 669 F.3d 802, 818–19 (7th Cir. 2012) (district judge denied certification on the ground that the plaintiffs' expert's method for proving antitrust impact on a class-wide basis was flawed, but the Seventh Circuit reverses, citing *Behrend* and criticizing the district judge for applying too strict an approach that "asked not for a showing of common questions, but for a showing of common answers to those questions").

5. *Class Certification and the Merits.* Does *Hydrogen Peroxide* go far enough? Should procedural law call for a merits inquiry not just when the merits are related to a certification requirement but also when they are not? In other words, should the law condition class certification on a global determination that the plaintiff class is likely to succeed on the merits? In reflecting on this question, consider again the policy reasons why the *Hydrogen Peroxide* court adopted a stricter approach, and ask whether these policy reasons are adequately served by restricting the analysis to certification-related merits issues. For an argument supporting a broader merits inquiry, see Robert G. Bone & David S. Evans, *Class Certification and the Substantive Merits*, 51 Duke L.J. 1251 (2002). For a more modest proposal in line with current case law trends, see Geoffrey P. Miller, *Review of the Merits in Class Action Certification*, 33 Hofstra L. Rev. 51, 87 (2004) (arguing against a requirement that the court "inquire into the plaintiff's ultimate probability of success at trial" but in favor of an approach that would "permit[ ] the trial court to investigate the merits provided that doing so is convenient and useful to analyzing the certification requirements of Rule 23").

6.   *Abuse of Discretion and the Scope of Review*. The courts of appeals in both *Hydrogen Peroxide* and *IPO* reversed because the district judge applied the wrong legal standard. When the question is whether the district judge applied the correct law, the scope of review of a certification decision is *de novo*. However, in other respects, it is highly deferential. Factual determinations can be overturned only if they are clearly erroneous, and determinations of law applied to fact can be reversed only for abuse of discretion. This means that a district judge has wide latitude to grant or deny certification as long as she makes plain that she is applying the proper legal standards and considers all relevant evidence.

7.   *The Implications of* Wal–Mart v. Dukes. The Supreme Court did not clearly specify the certification burden in *Wal–Mart Stores, Inc. v. Dukes*, 131 S.Ct. 2541 (2011), but one can infer quite a lot from the Court's opinion. Recall the situation in the *Wal–Mart* case. The plaintiffs sought class certification under 23(b)(2). To satisfy Rule 23(a)(2)'s common question requirement, they relied on a central merits issue in the case: whether Wal–Mart had a company-wide policy of discrimination. They argued that while Wal–Mart did not have any formal policy of discrimination against women, it did have a "policy" of delegating excessively subjective discretion to local mangers, and this policy interacted with background gender stereotypes and Wal–Mart's internal company culture to create a framework conducive to discriminatory decisions at the local level with regard to pay and promotion. The plaintiff's theory was in line with the approaches used in several other pattern-or-practice class actions brought against large, nationwide employers.

The Wal–Mart plaintiffs didn't just offer a theory; they also provided evidence to support that theory. This included expert statistical evidence as well as sociological and anecdotal evidence. In response, Wal–Mart offered its own statistical expert, challenged the plaintiffs' sociologist, and argued that the anecdotes were too few in number given Wal–Mart's size.

There is something remarkable about the class certification battle in *Wal–Mart*. The common question—the existence of a company-wide discriminatory policy—is also the plaintiff's entire prima facie case. This was not true for *Hydrogen Peroxide* or *IPO Securities*. In those two cases, the issue—antitrust impact or reliance—was just one of several liability issues. The centrality of the common question in *Wal–Mart* places the relationship between certification and trial proof in particularly stark relief: If the plaintiff has to prove the existence of a company-wide discriminatory policy to obtain class certification, the court would be deciding the prima facie case under the auspices of a preliminary, pre-trial ruling.

The Supreme Court did not directly address this question or discuss exactly what evidentiary burden a plaintiff must meet to obtain certification. However, the Court ended up applying a fairly stiff standard and along the way made some significant pronouncements relevant to the standard of proof in general. The majority clearly rejected what it called "a mere pleading standard" and stated that "[a] party seeking class certification must affirmatively demonstrate his compliance with the Rule—that is, he must be prepared to prove that there are *in fact* sufficiently numerous parties, common questions of law or fact, etc." *Id*. at 2551 (emphasis in original).

As for the 23(a)(2) commonality requirement, the Court made clear that it is not enough for plaintiffs simply to identify a common question. They must actually *demonstrate* that all class members' claims depend upon the common question. *Id.* at 2545 (holding the plaintiffs must demonstrate that all the class claims "depend upon a common contention" that is "capable of class-wide resolution," in the sense that "determination of its truth or falsity will resolve an issue that is central to the validity of each one of the claims in one stroke"). However, the Court did not clearly state how strong the plaintiff's demonstration must be. The majority reiterated the importance of a "rigorous analysis," *id.*, adopted *Falcon*'s "significant proof" language for claims, like those in *Wal-Mart*, based on "a general policy of discrimination," and at one point, described the burden as "convincing proof." *Id.* at 2551–67. But it left considerable uncertainty about what "significant" and "convincing" actually mean.

Nevertheless, the Court found that the plaintiffs' evidence was too weak to satisfy the (a)(2) common question requirement. The Court questioned whether plaintiffs' statistics could possibly show company-wide gender disparity given their focus at the regional and national level. *Id.* at 2555. Moreover, the Court reasoned that proof of company-wide disparities alone would not be enough because gender disparity can result from perfectly lawful decisions. *Id.* The Court also dismissed the plaintiffs' sociological evidence as insufficiently specific to Wal–Mart, *id.* at 2553–54; and concluded that the plaintiffs' anecdotal evidence was "too weak to raise any inference that all the individual, discretionary personnel decisions are discriminatory." *Id.* at 2556.

How would you characterize the *Wal–Mart* Court's standard of proof? How does it compare to the standard adopted by the Third Circuit in *Hydrogen Peroxide*? Does it matter whether the plaintiffs would be entitled to a jury as the fact finder in the event of trial on the merits? 42 U.S.C. § 1981a(c) (right to jury trial in employment discrimination actions seeking compensatory or punitive damages). Does the crux of the dispute over class certification in *Wal-Mart*, properly understood, pertain to the role of the jury at all?

In *Comcast Corp. v. Behrend*, 2013 WL 1222646, the Supreme Court reversed the Third Circuit. (For more on *Behrend*, see note 4 *supra*.) The five-Justice majority concluded that the plaintiffs' econometric model fell "far short of establishing that damages are capable of measurement on a classwide basis." *Id.* at *5. The plaintiffs' model estimated damages attributable to four theories of antitrust impact, but the district judge decided that the plaintiffs could rely on only one of those theories. After rendering this decision, the district judge considered whether it adversely affected the viability of plaintiffs' model and concluded that it did not, that the model was still capable of measuring damages on a classwide basis. Despite this district court determination and the Third Circuit's affirmance, the Supreme Court majority held that the plaintiffs' model failed because it did not "even attempt to" focus in on those damages specifically attributable to the single surviving theory of antitrust impact. *Id.* In the majority's view, the Court of Appeals was too reluctant to examine the merits and should have looked more closely at whether the plaintiffs' model was adequate. *Id.* In reaching this conclusion, the majority repeated *Wal-Mart*'s insistence that Rule 23 "does not set forth a mere pleading standard;" that the party seeking certification "'must affirmatively demonstrate his compliance' with Rule 23," and that the judge must conduct a "rigorous analysis" that probes behind the pleadings and "will frequently entail 'overlap with the merits of the plaintiff's underlying claim." *Id.* at *4. The Court also noted that the party seeking certification must satisfy "through evidentiary proof" the requirements of Rule

23(b), *id.*, and that courts have a duty "to take a 'close look'" at (b)(3) predominance. *Id.*

8.   Daubert *at the Certification Stage.* One important question is whether a judge must conduct a *Daubert* analysis of expert testimony at the certification stage. In *Wal–Mart Stores, Inc. v. Dukes*, the Supreme Court hinted that a *Daubert* analysis might be required, but it did not so hold. 131 S. Ct. at 2553–54 (after noting that the district judge was of the opinion that *Daubert* did not apply at the certification stage, the Court states "we doubt that is so"). The lower courts have taken different approaches to answering this question. Compare *Ellis v. Costco Wholesale Corp.*, 657 F.3d 970, 982 (9th Cir. 2011) (holding that "the district court correctly applied the evidentiary standard in [*Daubert*]"); *Am. Honda Motor Co., Inc. v. Allen*, 600 F.3d 813, 815–16 (7th Cir. 2010) (holding that *Daubert* must be applied "when an expert's report or testimony is critical to class certification"), with *Zurn Pex Plumbing Prods. Liab. Litig.*, 644 F.3d 604, 613 (8th Cir. 2011) (holding that a district judge need not conduct a "full and conclusive *Daubert* inquiry" at the certification stage).

E. CLASS COUNSEL

In its original 1966 form, Rule 23 did not speak directly to the selection or compensation of class counsel. The original rule demanded a judicial finding that the class representative—the named plaintiff—will "fairly and adequately protect the interests of the class," Fed. R. Civ. P. 23(a)(4), a requirement that remains in place today. In keeping with pre-Rule 23 cases such as *Hansberry*, the ostensible focus of subsection (a)(4) remained within the class, on the alignment of interest between the class representative and absent class members.

Over time, both commentators and courts came to recognize that the class representative often is a mere figurehead who exercises little, if any, supervision over the conduct of the class action. There emerged, in short, a widespread recognition that class actions are usually lawyer-driven, not client-driven, lawsuits, because class counsel bears the risks and costs of litigation and has a larger stake in the outcome than any individual claimant. As a result, recent cases like *Ortiz v. Fibreboard Corp.* focus as much or more on the alignment of interest between the proposed class and class counsel (the principal-agent relationship in the class action) than on the alignment of interest within the class itself (the relationship amongst the principals, if you will).

This Section focuses on the two main judicial checkpoints with respect to class counsel—what one might describe colloquially as the "front end" (class certification) and the "back end" (a fee award upon a verdict or settlement beneficial to the class). At both points, the court acts as the ultimate decision maker.

1. SELECTION METHODS

Ordinarily, clients hire lawyers directly at the start of litigation and, when doing so, provide contractually for lawyers' fees. In a class action, the named plaintiff has a contract with the lawyer offered to represent the class ("class counsel"), but the absent class members do not. Given the size of class members' claims and other impediments, the cost of direct bargaining is prohibitive. If class members are to be represented, both the choice of class counsel and class counsel's fees must be determined by non-contractual means.

The class action rules used in state and federal courts fill the gaps left by the absence of client-lawyer contracts. The rules (and judicial decisions made pursuant to them) determine who the class members are, identify the claims on which a class action may proceed, fix the lawyers for the class, and establish the terms on which the representation occurs. In federal courts, when the requirements for certification are met, provisions (g) and (h) of Rule 23 govern the selection and compensation of class counsel. State courts may follow rules similar to these or may have common law procedures. As you will see, common law also matters in federal courts because it (in particular, the law of restitution and unjust enrichment) provides the substantive legal basis for paying lawyers who represent plaintiff classes.

a. SELECTION AND COMPENSATION OF CLASS COUNSEL UNDER RULES 23(g) AND (h)

As amended in 2003 and further restyled in 2007, subsection (g) of Rule 23 requires a federal district court judge to appoint class counsel when certifying a class and sets out factors a judge must consider when making this appointment. Subsection (h) establishes procedures to govern fee awards, including notice to class members, who may file objections.

(g) Class Counsel.

(1) *Appointing Class Counsel.* Unless a statute provides otherwise, a court that certifies a class must appoint class counsel. In appointing class counsel, the court:

>   (A) must consider:

>   (i) the work counsel has done in identifying or investigating potential claims in the action;

>   (ii) counsel's experience in handling class actions, other complex litigation, and the types of claims asserted in the action;

>   (iii) counsel's knowledge of the applicable law; and

>   (iv) the resources that counsel will commit to representing the class;

>   (B) may consider any other matter pertinent to counsel's ability to fairly and adequately represent the interests of the class;

>   (C) may order potential class counsel to provide information on any subject pertinent to the appointment and to propose terms for attorney's fees and nontaxable costs;

>   (D) may include in the appointing order provisions about the award of attorney's fees or nontaxable costs under Rule 23(h); and

>   (E) may make further orders in connection with the appointment.

(2) *Standard for Appointing Class Counsel.* When one applicant seeks appointment as class counsel, the court may appoint that applicant only if the applicant is adequate under Rule 23(g)(1) and (4). If more than one adequate applicant seeks appointment, the court must appoint the applicant best able to represent the interests of the class.

(3) *Interim Counsel.* The court may designate interim counsel to act on behalf of a putative class before determining whether to certify the action as a class action.

(4) *Duty of Class Counsel.* Class counsel must fairly and adequately represent the interests of the class.

(h) Attorney's Fees and Nontaxable Costs.

In a certified class action, the court may award reasonable attorney's fees and nontaxable costs that are authorized by law or by the parties' agreement. The following procedures apply:

(1) A claim for an award must be made by motion under Rule 54(d)(2), subject to the provisions of this subdivision (h), at a time the court sets. Notice of the motion must be served on all parties and, for motions by class counsel, directed to class members in a reasonable manner.

(2) A class member, or a party from whom payment is sought, may object to the motion.

(3) The court may hold a hearing and must find the facts and state its legal conclusions under Rule 52(a).

(4) The court may refer issues related to the amount of the award to a special master or a magistrate judge, as provided in Rule 54(d)(2)(D).

One should not infer that subsection (g) called for drastic change in Rule 23 practice; rather, as the advisory committee explains, subsection (g) largely wrote into the rule many of the best practices that had emerged under Rule 23 in its original form. (Note that the advisory committee's explanation tracks subsection (g) in the form of its original enactment in 2003, not as modestly restyled in 2007.)

> **Subdivision (g).** Subdivision (g) is new. It responds to the reality that the selection and activity of class counsel are often critically important to the successful handling of a class action. Until now, courts have scrutinized proposed class counsel as well as the class representative under Rule 23(a)(4). This experience has recognized the importance of judicial evaluation of the proposed lawyer for the class, and this new subdivision builds on that experience rather than introducing an entirely new element into the class certification process. Rule 23(a)(4) will continue to call for scrutiny of the proposed class representative, while this subdivision will guide the court in assessing proposed class counsel as part of the certification decision. . . .

> **Paragraph (1)** sets out the basic requirement that class counsel be appointed if a class is certified and articulates the obligation of class counsel to represent the interests of the class, as opposed to the potentially conflicting interests of individual class members. It also sets out the factors the court should consider in assessing proposed class counsel.

> **Paragraph (1)(A)** requires that the court appoint class counsel to represent the class. Class counsel must be appointed for all classes, including each subclass that the court certifies to represent divergent interests.

> **Paragraph (1)(A)** does not apply if "a statute provides otherwise." This recognizes that provisions of the Private Securities Litigation Reform Act of 1995, Pub. L. No. 104–67, 109 Stat. 737

(1995) (codified in various sections of 15 U.S.C.), contain directives that bear on selection of a lead plaintiff and the retention of counsel. This subdivision does not purport to supersede or to affect the interpretation of those provisions, or any similar provisions of other legislation.

Paragraph 1(B) recognizes that the primary responsibility of class counsel, resulting from appointment as class counsel, is to represent the best interests of the class. The rule thus establishes the obligation of class counsel, an obligation that may be different from the customary obligations of counsel to individual clients. Appointment as class counsel means that the primary obligation of counsel is to the class rather than to any individual members of it. The class representatives do not have an unfettered right to "fire" class counsel. In the same vein, the class representatives cannot command class counsel to accept or reject a settlement proposal. To the contrary, class counsel must determine whether seeking the court's approval of a settlement would be in the best interests of the class as a whole.

Paragraph (1)(C) articulates the basic responsibility of the court to appoint class counsel who will provide the adequate representation called for by paragraph (1)(B). . . .

The court may direct potential class counsel to provide additional information about the topics mentioned in paragraph (1)(C) or about any other relevant topic. For example, the court may direct applicants to inform the court concerning any agreements about a prospective award of attorney fees or nontaxable costs, as such agreements may sometimes be significant in the selection of class counsel. The court might also direct that potential class counsel indicate how parallel litigation might be coordinated or consolidated with the action before the court.

The court may also direct counsel to propose terms for a potential award of attorney fees and nontaxable costs. Attorney fee awards are an important feature of class action practice, and attention to this subject from the outset may often be a productive technique. Paragraph (2)(C) therefore authorizes the court to provide directions about attorney fees and costs when appointing class counsel. Because there will be numerous class actions in which this information is not likely to be useful, the court need not consider it in all class actions.

Some information relevant to class counsel appointment may involve matters that include adversary preparation in a way that should be shielded from disclosure to other parties. An appropriate protective order may be necessary to preserve confidentiality.

In evaluating prospective class counsel, the court should weigh all pertinent factors. No single factor should necessarily be determinative in a given case. For example, the resources counsel will commit to the case must be appropriate to its needs, but the court should be careful not to limit consideration to lawyers with the greatest resources.

If, after review of all applicants, the court concludes that none would be satisfactory class counsel, it may deny class certification, reject all applications, recommend that an application be modified, invite new applications, or make any other appropriate order regarding selection and appointment of class counsel.

Paragraph (2). This paragraph sets out the procedure that should be followed in appointing class counsel. Although it affords substantial flexibility, it provides the framework for appointment of class counsel in all class actions. For counsel who filed the action, the materials submitted in support of the motion for class certification may suffice to justify appointment so long as the information described in paragraph (g)(1)(C) is included. If there are other applicants, they ordinarily would file a formal application detailing their suitability for the position. . . .

Paragraph (2)(A) authorizes the court to designate interim counsel during the pre-certification period if necessary to protect the interests of the putative class. Rule 23(c)(1)(B) directs that the order certifying the class include appointment of class counsel. Before class certification, however, it will usually be important for an attorney to take action to prepare for the certification decision. The amendment to Rule 23(c)(1) recognizes that some discovery is often necessary for that determination. It also may be important to make or respond to motions before certification. Settlement may be discussed before certification. Ordinarily, such work is handled by the lawyer who filed the action. In some cases, however, there may be rivalry or uncertainty that makes formal designation of interim counsel appropriate. Rule 23(g)(2)(A) authorizes the court to designate interim counsel to act on behalf of the putative class before the certification decision is made. Failure to make the formal designation does not prevent the attorney who filed the action from proceeding in it. Whether or not formally designated interim counsel, an attorney who acts on behalf of the class before certification must act in the best interests of the class as a whole. For example, an attorney who negotiates a pre-certification settlement must seek a settlement that is fair, reasonable, and adequate for the class.

Rule 23(c)(1) provides that the court should decide whether to certify the class "at an early practicable time," and directs that class counsel should be appointed in the order certifying the class. In some cases, it may be appropriate for the court to allow a reasonable period after commencement of the action for filing applications to serve as class counsel. The primary ground for deferring appointment would be that there is reason to anticipate competing applications to serve as class counsel. Examples might include instances in which more than one class action has been filed, or in which other attorneys have filed individual actions on behalf of putative class members. The purpose of facilitating competing applications in such a case is to afford the best possible representation for the class. Another possible reason for deferring appointment would be that the initial applicant was found inadequate, but it seems appropriate to permit additional applications rather than deny class certification.

Paragraph (2)(B). . . .

If there are multiple adequate applicants, paragraph (2)(B) directs the court to select the class counsel best able to represent the interests of the class. This decision should also be made using

the factors outlined in paragraph (1)(C), but in the multiple applicant situation the court is to go beyond scrutinizing the adequacy
of counsel and make a comparison of the strengths of the various
applicants. As with the decision whether to appoint the sole applicant for the position, no single factor should be dispositive in selecting class counsel in cases in which there are multiple applicants. The fact that a given attorney filed the instant action, for
example, might not weigh heavily in the decision if that lawyer
had not done significant work identifying or investigating claims.
Depending on the nature of the case, one important consideration
might be the applicant's existing attorney-client relationship with
the proposed class representative.

Paragraph (2)(C) builds on the appointment process by authorizing the court to include provisions regarding attorney fees in
the order appointing class counsel. Courts may find it desirable to
adopt guidelines for fees or nontaxable costs, or to direct class
counsel to report to the court at regular intervals on the efforts
undertaken in the action, to facilitate the court's later determination of a reasonable attorney fee.

Neither subsection (g) nor subsection (h) requires judges to set fee
terms in any particular way. Both leave them free to pick either of the two
most common compensation formulas: the contingent-percentage approach,
on which class counsel receives a fraction of a class' recovery; and the lodestar method, which pays class counsel an hourly rate with certain en-
hancements. In recent years, judges have employed the contingent-
percentage approach increasingly often in cases with cash recoveries. They
have reserved the lodestar method for class actions that seek injunctive
remedies. Such class actions are often brought pursuant to statutes that
entitle prevailing plaintiffs to recover fee awards.

The choice of the contingent-percentage approach in damages cases
comports with Seventh Circuit doctrine, which requires district court judges to "mimic the market" when awarding fees. Judges must estimate the
fees class members would have agreed to pay in direct bargaining with
their lawyers. Because contingent-percentage arrangements predominate
in actual transactions between plaintiffs and lawyers, the "mimic-the-
market" approach encourages judges presiding over class actions to base
fee awards on contingent percentages of class members' recoveries. See *In
re Synthroid Mktg. Litig.*, 264 F.3d 712, 718 (7th Cir. 2001), ("courts must
do their best to award counsel the market price for legal services, in light of
the risk of nonpayment and the normal rate of compensation in the market
at the time."); *Cont'l Illinois Sec.*, 962 F.2d at 568 (7th Cir. 1992) ("[I]t is
not the function of judges in fee litigation to determine the equivalent of
the medieval just price. It is to determine what the lawyer would receive if
he were selling his services in the market rather than being paid by court
order.").

Although only the Seventh Circuit is formally committed to the "mimic-the-market" approach, district court judges in other federal circuits
sometimes also employ it when setting fees. See, e.g., *In re Enron Corp.
Sec., Derivative & ERISA Litig.*, 586 F. Supp. 2d 732 (S.D. Tex. 2008) (invoking the mimic-the-market approach in support of a fee award of $668
million); *Connectivity Sys. Inc. v. Nat'l City Bank*, 2011 WL 292008, at *12
(S.D. Ohio, Jan, 26, 2011) ("The Court's function is to determine what the
lawyer would receive in the market and to compensate counsel at the fair

market value."). They can do this because most other circuits use a multi-factor reasonableness approach that permits trial judges to consider evidence of lawyers' usual and customary fees.

Of course, the multi-factor approach allows judges to deviate from market-based fee awards as well. The Ninth Circuit uses a benchmark approach, according to which 25 percent of the common fund recovery is the presumptively reasonable fee which district court judges must adjust upward or downward in light of particular case characteristics, including: (1) the results achieved; (2) the risks of litigation; (3) the skill required and the quality of work; (4) the contingent nature of the fee; (5) the burdens carried by class counsel; and (6) the awards made in similar cases. See *Six (6) Mexican Workers v. Ariz. Citrus Growers*, 904 F.2d 1301, 1311 (9th Cir. 1990); *In re Bluetooth Headset Prods. Liab. Litig.*, 654 F.3d 935, 943–45 (9th Cir. 2011).

Regardless of the methodology employed, empirical studies find that the size of the class recovery is overwhelmingly the most important determinant of the size of the fee. Theodore Eisenberg & Geoffrey P. Miller, *Attorney Fees and Expenses in Class Action Settlements: 1993–2008*, 7 J. Empirical Legal Stud. 248, 250 (2010).

b. DETERMINING THE FEE

In recognizing the authority of the court to award "reasonable" attorneys fees, subsection (h) consciously sidesteps the difficult question of how to determine those fees. As the advisory committee explains:

> [Subsection (h)] authorizes an award of "reasonable" attorney fees and nontaxable costs. This is the customary term for measurement of fee awards in cases in which counsel may obtain an award of fees under the "common fund" theory that applies in many class actions, and is used in many fee-shifting statutes. Depending on the circumstances, courts have approached the determination of what is reasonable in different ways. In particular, there is some variation among courts about whether in "common fund" cases the court should use the lodestar or a percentage method of determining what fee is reasonable. The rule does not attempt to resolve the question whether the lodestar or percentage approach should be viewed as preferable.

The case that follows offers an overview of the lodestar and percentage methods as well as guidance on who has standing to challenge the fee award to class counsel.

In re Cendant Corp. PRIDES Litigation

243 F.3d 722 (3d Cir. 2001)

■ GARTH, CIRCUIT JUDGE:

This appeal arises out of a class action filed on behalf of investors in Cendant Corporation (Cendant) after Cendant disclosed prior accounting irregularities. . . . Several actions were filed as a result of this disclosure, including an action commenced . . . on behalf of purchasers of Cendant's Feline PRIDES shares. The PRIDES litigation was subsequently consolidated with the other pending Cendant actions. However, . . . the District Court ruled that separate lead plaintiffs and lead counsel were to represent the interests of the PRIDES shareholders, as distinct from the rest of the Cendant class.

The firm of Kirby, McInerney & Squire, formerly Kaufman, Malchman, Kirby & Squire, ("Kirby") was appointed as lead counsel of the Cendant PRIDES class. . . . Kirby filed a motion for class certification, for summary judgment on the claims under § 11 of the Securities Act, and for injunctive relief. On behalf of the PRIDES class, Kirby entered into a proposed settlement agreement with Cendant on March 17, 1999—three and a half months after Kirby's motions were filed and no more than nine months after the action had been started.

Under the settlement agreement, Cendant agreed to issue Rights to new PRIDES, with a stated value of $11.71. Those rights were in trade for existing PRIDES. The total possible number and amount of Rights to be distributed pursuant to the agreement was 29,161,474, with an approximate stated value of $341,500,000. Regarding Kirby's attorneys' fees, the settlement agreement provided: "Cendant . . . will take no position on an application by Lead Counsel for an award of fees and expenses provided that such application shall not request fees in excess of 10% percent [sic] of the aggregate Stated Value of 29,161,474 Rights, which is approximately $341,500,000, plus reasonable expenses incurred by Lead Counsel in connection with this Action."

The Notice of Pendency of Class Action summarized the proposed settlement of the PRIDES litigation. In connection with "Lead Counsel's fees and expenses," the Notice stated: "Lead Counsel has notified the other signatories hereto that it intends to apply to the Court for an award of fees, in an amount not to exceed 10% of the aggregate Stated Value of 29,161,474 Rights, or approximately $34.1 million, plus reasonable expenses." . . .

[T]he Joanne A. Aboff Trust ("Trust") filed several objections to the notice of settlement, all of which pertained to Kirby's representation and fee request. . . .

[T]he District Court signed an Opinion and Order approving the settlement, stating: "The Court considers the settlement to be eminently fair and reasonable. The class is made completely whole by such compensation. There are no objections voiced to the settlement—only to the request for attorney fees. The proposed settlement is approved subject to the following modifications to the attorneys' fees." *In re Cendant Corp. Prides Litig.*, 51 F. Supp. 2d 537, 541 (D.N.J. 1999).

The District Court granted Kirby's request for expenses, finding that the requested expenses of $2,367,493 were "reasonable and necessary to the prosecution of this litigation." 51 F. Supp. 2d at 542. Then the Court found that, for attorneys' fees, Kirby should receive a number of Rights equivalent to 5.7% of the balance of Rights received by the Class. That percentage amounts to 1,650,680 Rights, valued at approximately $19,329,463. The District Court directed "Lead Counsel to seek to satisfy payment of these awards of expenses and fees from any unclaimed Rights. Then, and only then, to the extent that such fees and expenses have not been satisfied by unclaimed Rights, shall any deficiency be assessed against and borne by the class." 51 F. Supp. 2d at 542. The Court went on to instruct that "[a]ny rights unclaimed after authorized class claimants and Lead Counsel have been issued their entitled Rights shall be canceled by Cendant Corporation." 51 F. Supp. 2d at 542.

I.

Before we consider the merits of the Trust's appeal, a threshold question must be answered: does the Trust have standing to challenge the District Court's award of attorneys' fees to Kirby? . . .

"Ordinarily, only a party *aggrieved* by a judgment or order of a district court may exercise the statutory right to appeal therefrom. A party who receives all that he has sought generally is not aggrieved by the judgment affording the relief and cannot appeal from it." *Deposit Guar. Nat'l Bank v. Roper*, 445 U.S. 326, 333 (1980) (emphasis added).

The standing question in this case is troublesome, because it appears as if the PRIDES settlement has provided the class members with full recovery and because any reduction in the amount of attorneys' fees to Kirby will not be distributed among the class members, but instead those rights will be returned to and canceled by Cendant. Therefore, Kirby argues, the Trust is not aggrieved by the award of attorneys' fees and has no standing to appeal. [Editor's Note: As the court explained above, any unclaimed rights not used to compensate class counsel for expenses and fees were to be destroyed by Cendant, the issuer. Given this, the court seemed to think that class members had no stake in the amount of fees and costs awarded because a reduction would not benefit them. The truth of the conclusion is debatable. Rights entitle their holders to purchase securities at a set price in a given time. When the set price is below the market price, rights have positive value because holders can buy securities and immediately sell them at a profit. Valuable rights thus cost issuers money—the difference between the price received from a rights holder and the price that could be obtained by selling securities in the market. Consequently, companies become more valuable when rights are cancelled. This causes share prices to rise and also makes purchase rights more valuable. Class members could therefore have gained if rights given to class counsel were cancelled instead.]

While this argument admittedly has a superficial attraction because the PRIDES class members will seemingly recover a "dollar-for-dollar" return for their claims and Kirby's fees will not reduce their recovery, we nevertheless hold that the Trust does have standing to appeal the award of attorneys' fees. We base this holding on two related concepts: 1) the nature of the relationship between class plaintiffs, class counsel, and defendants in class actions requires that the "aggrieved" requirement be construed broadly in class action cases; and 2) the judiciary's independent authority over the appointment of class counsel, the grant of attorneys' fees, and the review of attorneys' fee awards in class actions. In connection with these two principles, we require that district courts conduct an extensive analysis and inquiry before determining the amount of fees, because we have an independent interest in monitoring district courts' fee awards, particularly those awards stemming from Rule 23 class actions. See, e.g., *Zucker v. Occidental Petroleum Corp.*, 192 F.3d 1323, 1328 (9th Cir. 1999); see generally Advisory Committee's Notes on Fed. R. Civ. P. 23, 28 U.S.C., Notes following Rule 23 (addressing, *inter alia*, "the question of the measures that might be taken during the course of the action to assure procedural fairness"). Indeed, we are in effect third parties to the fee award process, albeit silent parties for the most part until the award is finalized and reviewed.

A.

Ostensibly, lead class counsel represents all class plaintiffs. However, in attempting to settle a large class action, class counsel must often spend more time negotiating with and interacting with the defendants than with their own clients. This situation presents several dangers. First, as we observed in *Prandini v. Nat'l Tea Co.*, "a defendant is interested only in disposing of the total claims asserted against it[, and] the allocation between the class payment and the attorneys' fees is of little or no interest to the defense." 557 F.2d 1015, 1020 (3d Cir. 1977). Moreover, the "divergence in [class members' and class counsel's] financial incentives . . . creates the 'danger . . . that the lawyers might urge a class settlement at a low figure or on a less-than-optimal basis in exchange for red-carpet treatment for fees.'" *In re Gen. Motors Corp. Pick–Up Truck Fuel Tank Prod. Liab. Litig.* (hereinafter *"In re GM Trucks"*), 55 F.3d 768, 820 (3d Cir. 1995) (quoting *Weinberger v. Great Northern Nekoosa Corp.*, 925 F.2d 518, 524 (1st Cir. 1991)).

This unique relationship among plaintiffs' counsel, plaintiffs, and defendants in class actions imposes a special responsibility upon appellate courts to hear challenges to fee awards by class members whose claims may have been reduced or in some way affected in exchange for large fee awards. See *In re GM Trucks*, 55 F.3d at 819–21. This is so even in this case, where the Trust presumably will not benefit from a reduction in Kirby's attorneys' fees, because the PRIDES settlement was structured so that any remaining Rights will be returned to Cendant.

The Ninth Circuit addressed a similar situation in *Zucker v. Occidental Petroleum Corp.*, 192 F.3d 1323 (9th Cir. 1999), pointing out in its discussion that, even where the plaintiff "gets the same money whether the fee is cut or not, . . . a client whose attorney accepts payment, without his consent, from the defendants he is suing, may have a remedy, and this remedy may extend to a plaintiff class whose class attorneys accept payment from the defendants the class is suing." 192 F.3d at 1326.

The Ninth Circuit took this reasoning a step further in *Lobatz v. U.S. West Cellular of Calif.*, in which the court, holding that a class member had standing to appeal an attorneys' fee award "even though that award was payable independent of the class settlement," stated:

> If . . . class counsel agreed to accept excessive fees and costs to the detriment of class plaintiffs, then class counsel breached their fiduciary duty to the class[, and] any excessive award could be considered property of the class plaintiffs, and any injury they suffered could be at least partially redressed by allocating to them a portion of that award.

Lobatz, 222 F.3d 1142, 1147 (9th Cir. 2000).

Under the Ninth Circuit's analysis, therefore, the Trust need not benefit from a reduction in Kirby's fee to have standing to appeal. Moreover, the Ninth Circuit suggested in *Zucker* that the requirement that class plaintiffs be aggrieved should be construed broadly, citing Judge Sneed's observation in his dissent in *In re First Capital Holdings* "that '[a]rguably, a class member always retains an interest in attorney fees, even when her claims have been met in full.'" *Zucker*, 192 F.3d at 1328 (quoting *In re First Capital Holdings Corp. Fin. Prods. Sec. Litig.*, 33 F.3d 29, 31 (9th Cir. 1994) (Sneed, J., dissenting)).

B.

As indicated above, we are convinced of our obligation to vacate the District Court's order awarding fees by the special position of the courts in connection with class action settlements and attorneys' fee awards. As we observed in *In re GM Trucks*, "a thorough review of fee applications is required in all class action settlements." 55 F.3d at 819. Specifically, the danger inherent in the relationship among the class, class counsel, and defendants "generates an especially acute need for close judicial scrutiny of fee arrangements" in class action settlements. 55 F.3d at 820. In discussing this duty of district courts to oversee class settlements in *In re GM Trucks*, we explained:

> the court's oversight task is considerably complicated by the fact that these attorney-class conflicts are often difficult to discern in the class action context, "where full disclosure and consent are many times difficult and frequently impractical to obtain." Finally, we emphasize that the court's oversight function serves not only to detect instances of "the actual abuse [that potential attorney-class conflicts] may cause, but also [the] potential public misunderstandings they may cultivate in regard to the interests of class counsel."

55 F.3d at 820 (quoting *In re Agent Orange Prod. Liab. Litig.*, 818 F.2d 216, 224, 225 (2d Cir. 1987)). In other words, we indicated in *In re GM Trucks* the importance of the judicial role in finalizing class action settlements, and we suggested that this importance derived from general concerns about "potential public misunderstandings" as much as from a desire to protect the plaintiffs in the particular class.

In *Zucker*, in asserting that the district court was required to review the award of attorneys' fees regardless of whether anyone had standing to challenge the award, the Ninth Circuit stated:

> In a class action, whether the attorneys' fees come from a common fund or are otherwise paid, the district court must exercise its inherent authority to assure that the amount and mode of payment of attorneys' fees are fair and proper. This duty of the court exists independently of any objection. Therefore it exists, *a fortiori*, regardless of whether an objector has a remediable economic stake in the court's decision. Because the district court had the authority and duty to pass upon the fairness of the attorneys' fees settlement independently of whether there was objection, we need not decide whether the objector had standing.

192 F.3d at 1328–29.

The court in *Zucker* further explained that "[n]o Article III case or controversy is needed with regard to attorneys' fees as such, because they are but an ancillary matter over which the district court retains equitable jurisdiction." 192 F.3d at 1329. The Ninth Circuit found support for this proposition in the reasoning of the Eighth Circuit that "because 'the reasonableness of attorneys' fees is within the overall supervisory authority' of the court in a class action, the court did not need to reach the question of whether an objector has standing." *Zucker*, 192 F.3d at 1329 (quoting *Grunin v. Int'l House of Pancakes*, 513 F.2d 114, 127 n. 13 (8th Cir. 1975)).

While the statements in *In re GM Trucks* and *Zucker* refer to the authority of district, not appellate, courts in connection with class action settlements, the cases make clear that reviewing courts retain an interest—a

most special and predominant interest—in the fairness of class action settlements and attorneys' fee awards. Accordingly, our interest as a reviewing court in ensuring that district courts fulfill their obligations and comply
with the instructions and guidelines in this area bolsters our determination
that the Trust has standing to challenge Kirby's fee award. . . .

II.

There are two primary methods for calculating attorneys' fees: the percentage-of-recovery method[10] and the lodestar method.[11] "The percentage-
of-recovery method is generally favored in cases involving a common fund,[12]
and is designed to allow courts to award fees from the fund 'in a manner
that rewards counsel for success and penalizes it for failure.'" *In re Prudential*, 148 F.3d at 333. "The lodestar method is more commonly applied in
statutory fee-shifting cases, and is designed to reward counsel for undertaking socially beneficial litigation in cases where the expected relief has a
small enough monetary value that a percentage-of-recovery method would
provide inadequate compensation." 148 F.3d at 333.

The total settlement in this case was valued at $341,500,000, and the
District Court granted attorneys' fees in the amount of $19,329,463. As the
District Court noted, this amount constitutes 5.7% of the class's total recovery. In connection with the lodestar calculation, the District Court observed
that "Lead Counsel, through its principal partners, associates, and paralegals expended approximately 5,600 hours, and its senior partners have a
regular hourly rate of $495." 51 F. Supp. 2d at 542. Using the $495 hourly
rate, the lodestar multiplier[14] for the District Court's fee award is 7.[15]

Two primary principles govern our review of the District Court's fee
award to Kirby: 1) did the District Court provide sufficient explanation for
granting the fee award of $19.3 million?; and 2) was the award so unrea-
sonably high that the District Court abused its discretion in granting that
amount in attorneys' fees?

A.

In *Gunter v. Ridgewood Energy Corp.*, we considered a district court's
award of attorneys' fees in a class action settlement. 223 F.3d 190 (3d Cir.
2000). That case involved a $9.5 million settlement, out of which the dis-
trict court allowed attorneys' fees amounting to 18% of the settlement fund,

---

[10] This method has been described as follows: "The percentage of recovery method resembles a contingent fee in that it awards counsel a variable percentage of the amount recovered
for the class." *In re GM Trucks*, 55 F.3d 768, 819 n.38 (3d Cir. 1995).

[11] The lodestar method was initially set forth in *Lindy Bros. Builders, Inc. of Philadelphia
v. Am. Radiator & Standard Sanitary Corp.*, 487 F.2d 161 (3d Cir. 1973), *appeal following
remand*, 540 F.2d 102 (3d Cir. 1976). As this court explained in *Gunter v. Ridgewood Energy
Corp.*, "[a] court determines an attorney's lodestar by multiplying the number of hours he or
she reasonably worked on a client's case by a reasonable hourly billing rate for such services
given the geographical area, the nature of the services provided, and the experience of the
lawyer." 223 F.3d 190, 195 n.1 (3d Cir. 2000).

[12] "[T]he common-fund doctrine . . . allows a person who maintains a lawsuit that results
in the creation, preservation, or increase of a fund in which others have a common interest, to
be reimbursed from that fund for litigation expenses incurred." *Court Awarded Attorney Fees,
Report of the Third Circuit Task Force*, 108 F.R.D. 237, 241 (1985) (hereinafter "*Task Force
Report*").

[14] The Task Force Report explained that, after the lodestar is calculated, "[t]he 'lodestar'
then could be increased or decreased based upon the contingent nature or risk in the particular case involved and the quality of the attorney's work. An increase or decrease of the lodestar
amount is referred to as a 'multiplier.'" *Task Force Report*, 108 F.R.D. 237, 243.

[15] 5,600 hours x $495 = 2,772,000. $19,329,463 divided by 2,772,000 = 6.97. . . .

significantly less than the one-third requested by the attorneys. 223 F.3d at 191. The district court in *Gunter* explained its decision as follows: "The nature of this litigation, its resolution at this stage without the necessity of trial, the nature of the settlement, and its value, convince the court that it would place a reasonable burden on the class to award attorneys' fees of 18% of the Settlement Fund, or $1,700,000." 223 F.3d at 192 (citing *Gunter v. Ridgewood Energy Corp.*, Civ. No. 95–438(WHW), at 3 (D.N.J. Nov. 16, 1999)). The attorneys appealed the district court's reduction of their fee request.

In reviewing the district court's fee award in *Gunter*, we stated that "[w]e give [a] great deal of deference to a district court's decision to set fees." 223 F.3d at 195. However, we noted, "[n]otwithstanding our deferential standard of review, it is incumbent upon a district court to make its reasoning and application of the fee-awards jurisprudence clear, so that we, as a reviewing court, have a sufficient basis to review for abuse of discretion." 223 F.3d at 196. Therefore, "if the district court's fee-award opinion is so terse, vague, or conclusory that we have no basis to review it, we must vacate the fee-award order and remand for further proceedings." 223 F.3d at 196. In addition, "if a district court does not fulfill its duty to apply the relevant legal precepts to a fee application, it abuses its discretion by not exercising it." 223 F.3d at 196.

In *Gunter*, we vacated the district court's fee award because the district court "dealt with the fee-award issue in a cursory and conclusory fashion" and did not employ the factors which this Court has stated that district courts should consider in awarding fees using the percentage-of-recovery method in common-fund class actions. See *Gunter*, 223 F.3d at 196–97. These factors were set forth in *Gunter* in a footnote:

> Among other things, these factors include: (1) the size of the fund created and the number of persons benefitted; (2) the presence or absence of substantial objections by members of the class to the settlement terms and/or fees requested by counsel; (3) the skill and efficiency of the attorneys involved; (4) the complexity and duration of the litigation; (5) the risk of nonpayment; (6) the amount of time devoted to the case by plaintiffs' counsel; and (7) the awards in similar cases.

Gunter, 223 F.3d at 195 n.1 (citing *In re Prudential*, 148 F.3d 283, 336–40 (3d Cir. 1998); *In re GM Trucks*, 55 F.3d 768, 819–22 (3d Cir. 1995)).

As in *Gunter*, the District Court's fee opinion in this case was too cursory for us to "have a sufficient basis to review for abuse of discretion." *Gunter*, 223 F.3d at 196. The District Court did not even specify whether it was using the percentage-of-recovery method or the lodestar method to set attorneys' fees. Nor, if the District Court intended to utilize the lodestar method, did it calculate the lodestar multiplier. . . .

[T]he court did not even address the percentage-of-recovery method, except to the extent that it calculated that the fee award constituted 5.7% of the total class recovery. . . .

B.

Because the District Court failed to consider the *Gunter* factors that we deem essential to a proper exercise of discretion and to an appropriate consideration of attorneys' fee awards, we will discuss those factors here.

1. *Complexity and Duration of Litigation*

. . . In setting Kirby's fee award, the District Court apparently turned a blind eye to the following factors: 1) the case was relatively simple in terms of proof, in that Cendant had conceded liability and no risks pertaining to liability or collection were pertinent; 2) the case was settled at a very early stage of the litigation, with an agreement being announced two months after Kirby filed for class certification and a proposed settlement being submitted to the District Court two months after that; 3) there was a minimal amount of motion practice in this case—before settlement, Kirby submitted only the Complaint and three motions, all on the same day; 4) discovery was virtually nonexistent—indeed the District Court did not mention any depositions taken or document review conducted by Kirby; and 5) Kirby spent a relatively small amount of time on this case compared to the amount of time expended in most other large class actions.

2. *Range of Awards*

Before reviewing specific awards in other large class settlements, we will review generally the range of attorneys' fee awards in common fund settlements of class actions. In *In re GM Trucks*, we observed that "[o]ne court has noted that the fee awards have ranged from nineteen percent to forty-five percent of the settlement fund." 55 F.3d 768, 822 (3d Cir. 1995) (citing *In re SmithKline Beckman Corp. Sec. Litig.*, 751 F. Supp. 525, 533 (E.D. Pa. 1990)). We also noted in *In re Prudential* that "[t]he district court . . . examined the fee awards in class actions with recoveries exceeding $100 million and found the fee percentages ranged from 4.1% to 17.92%." 148 F.3d 283, 339 (3d Cir. 1998). . . . These varying ranges of attorneys' fees confirm that a district court may not rely on a formulaic application of the appropriate range in awarding fees but must consider the relevant circumstances of the particular case.

One important consideration is the size of the settlement. The Task Force Report stated, with reference to fee awards in common fund cases: "The negotiated fee, and the procedure for arriving at it, should be left to the court's discretion. In most instances, it will involve a sliding scale dependent upon the ultimate recovery, the expectation being that, absent unusual circumstances, the percentage will decrease as the size of the fund increases." 108 F.R.D. 237, 256 (1985). We called attention to this statement in *In re Prudential*, explaining that "[t]he basis for this inverse relationship is the belief that '[i]n many instances the increase [in recovery] is merely a factor of the size of the class and has no direct relationship to the efforts of counsel.'" *In re Prudential*, 148 F.3d at 339 (quoting *In re First Fidelity Bancorporation Sec. Litig.*, 750 F. Supp. 160, 164 n.1 (D.N.J. 1990)). Accordingly, district courts setting attorneys' fees in cases involving large settlements must avoid basing their awards on percentages derived from cases where the settlement amounts were much smaller.

3. *Other Awards*

The District Court did not undertake to review the fees granted in other class action settlement cases, particularly in other large settlement cases, *i.e.*, cases in which the common fund exceeded $100 million. Had it conducted such a review, the District Court should have looked specifically at cases in which the percentage-of-recovery method, not the lodestar method, was employed to set the fee award, and it should have examined the reasoning behind the district courts' fee awards in cases of similar size.

Below, we have set forth a chart of fee awards given in federal courts since 1985 in class actions in which the settlement fund exceeded $100 million and in which the percentage of recovery method was used . . .

Case	Settlement	Fees as % of Recovery	Lodestar Multiplier
In re Cendant Corp. PRIDES Litig., 51 F. Supp. 2d 537 (D.N.J. 1999) The instant case under review here.	$341.5 million	5.7% ($19.3 mil.)	7–10
In re Cendant Corp. Litig., 109 F. Supp. 2d 285 (D.N.J. 2000)	$3.16 billion	8.275% ($262 mil.)	32.7
In re Auction Houses Antitrust Litig., 2001 WL 170792 (S.D.N.Y. Feb. 22, 2001)	$512 million	5.2% ($27 mil.)	Inf. not available
In re Orthopedic Bone Screw Prod. Liab. Litig., 2000 WL 1622741(E.D. Pa. Oct. 23, 2000)	$100 million	12%	Inf. not available
In re Prudential, 106 F. Supp. 2d 721 (D.N.J. 2000)	$1.8 billion	5% ($90 mil.)	2.13
In re Ikon Office Solutions, Inc. Sec. Litig., 194 F.R.D. 166 (E.D. Pa. 2000)	$111 million	30%	2.7
Shaw v. Toshiba America Inf. Sys., Inc., 91 F. Supp. 2d 942 (E.D. Tex. 2000)	$2.1 billion	7% ($147 mil.)	Inf. not available
In re Sumitomo Copper Litig., 74 F. Supp. 2d 393 (S.D.N.Y. 1999)	$116 million	27.5% ($32 mil.)	2.5
Kurzweil v. Philip Morris Co., 1999 WL 1076105 (S.D.N.Y. Nov. 30, 1999)	$123.8 million	30% ($37.1 mil.)	2.46
In re Lease Oil Antitrust Litig., 186 F.R.D. 403 (S.D. Tex. 1999)	$190 million	25%	1.35
In re Copley Pharm., Inc., 1 F. Supp. 2d 1407 (D. Wyo. 1998)	$150 million	13% ($19.5 mil.)	2
In re PaineWebber Ltd. P'ships Litig., 999 F. Supp. 719 (S.D.N.Y. 1998)	$200 million	13% ($25.9 mil.)	1.4
Walco Investments, Inc. v. Thenen, 975 F. Supp. 1468 (S.D.Fla. 1997)	$141 million	15% ($21 mil.)	1.8
In re Combustion Inc., 968 F. Supp. 1116 (W.D.La. 1997)	$127 million	36%	2.99

Local 56, United Food & Commercial Workers Union v. Campbell Soup Co., 954 F. Supp. 1000 (D.N.J. 1997)	$114.5 million	2.8% ($3 mil.)	2.39
Bowling v. Pfizer, Inc., 922 F. Supp. 1261 (S.D. Ohio 1996), aff'd 102 F.3d 777 (6th Cir. 1996)	$102.5 million	10% ($10.2 mil.)	Inf. not available
In re Domestic Air Transportation Antitrust Litig., 148 F.R.D. 297 (N.D. Ga. 1993)	$305 million	5.25% ($14.3 mil.)	Inf. not available
In re MGM Grand Hotel Fire Litig., 660 F. Supp. 522 (D. Nev. 1987)	$205 million	7%	1–2.95

In the charted cases, the attorneys' fee awards ranged from 2.8% to 36% of the total settlement fund. Looking at the percentage of recovery in this case (5.7%), it appears that it is in line with the other cases and even at the low end of the range. However, a brief review of the facts and posture of these other cases makes clear that, when examined through the seven-factor lens of *Gunter*, the higher fees awarded in the other cases were far more justified than the high award in this case. [The court then proceeded to summarize the cited cases.]

[I]n case after case, the same factors recur: complex and/or novel legal issues, extensive discovery, acrimonious litigation, and tens of thousands of hours spent on the case by class counsel. Because none of these factors which increase the complexity of class litigation was present here, it makes sense that the fee awarded in this case should be far lower than those awarded in the charted cases, which fees ranged from 2.8% to 36% of the total settlement.

Also relevant to the District Court's analysis in this case is our holding in *In re Prudential* remanding the case to the district court. In that case, we rejected an award of 6.7% of the settlement fund in a case with a fund of $1 billion to $2 billion because the district court had failed to explain adequately why it had applied such a high percentage to the settlement figure and because the court had not explained why the 5.1 lodestar multiplier was justified. We also warned in *In re Prudential* against overemphasizing counsel's role in recovery, in the context of our criticism of the district court's assumption that counsel had been a catalyst for a plan authored by the Multi State Life Insurance Task Force, which facilitated the class action settlement in that it established Prudential's liability. We explained that "[a]llowing private counsel to receive fees based on the benefits created by public agencies would undermine the equitable principles which underlie the concept of the common fund, and would create an incentive for plaintiffs attorneys to 'minimize the costs of failure . . . by free riding on the monitoring efforts of others.'" *In re Prudential*, 148 F.3d at 337. Similarly, as we have consistently observed, Cendant's liability and consequent collectability had been conceded at the outset of the PRIDES controversy, and that fact should have been given major consideration by the District Court when setting Kirby's attorneys' fees.

Our review of the lack of complexity of this case and of awards in other large class action settlements, all of which involved more complex issues, more time invested by the attorneys, and, with only a few exceptions, smaller total settlements, leads us to the conclusion that the District Court abused its discretion in granting a 5.7% attorneys' fee award in this case.

4.   *Checking Against Lodestar*

The District Court's abuse of discretion in this case is magnified when one looks at the lodestar multiplier. As we stated above, "we have . . . suggested that district courts cross-check the percentage award at which they arrive against the 'lodestar' award method." *Gunter v. Ridgewood Energy Corp.*, 223 F.3d 190, 195 n.1 (3d Cir. 2000); see also *In re Prudential*, 148 F.3d at 333 (stating that " 'it is sensible for a court to use a second method of fee approval to cross check' its initial fee calculation"). Even when the lodestar method is used only as a cross-check, "courts must take care to explain how the application of a multiplier is justified by the facts of a particular case." *In re Prudential*, 148 F.3d at 340–41.

In this case, the lodestar multiplier is 7 at a minimum (using Kirby's senior partner rate as the rate for all hours), and the Trust calculates the lodestar multiplier as 10. Either of these multipliers (Kirby's multiplier of 7 or the Trust's multiplier of 10) is substantially higher than any of the multipliers in the cases charted above, which range from 1.35 to 2.99, and is also significantly higher than the "large" 5.1 multiplier in *In re Prudential*, which we questioned because "the court offer[ed] little explanation as to why a multiplier was necessary or appropriate." 148 F.3d at 340–41. In allowing such a high multiplier in this case without even calculating it, much less explaining how it is justified, the District Court strayed from all responsible discretionary parameters in the awarding of Kirby's attorneys' fees.

In all the cases in which high percentages were applied to arrive at attorneys' fees, the courts explained the extensive amount of work that the attorneys had put into the case, and appropriately the lodestar multiplier in those cases never exceeded 2.99. This range is consistent with the principle that " '[m]ultiples ranging from one to four are frequently awarded in common fund cases when the lodestar method is applied.' " *In re Prudential*, 148 F.3d at 341 (quoting 3 Herbert Newberg & Alba Conte, NEWBERG ON CLASS ACTIONS, § 14.03 at 14–5 (3d ed. 1992)). In this case, the District Court judge made clear that he wanted to reward Kirby for Kirby's quick and beneficial settlement of the case, and that may be a good reason for the fee award to exceed the lodestar, but not to the exclusion of all other factors. On remand of this case to the District Court, we strongly suggest that a lodestar multiplier of 3 (the highest multiplier of the cases reviewed above) is the appropriate ceiling for a fee award, although a lower multiplier may be applied in the District Court's discretion. The 3 multiplier would result in an award of no more than $8.3 million for Kirby (calculating the lodestar at $495/hour). . . .

NOTES AND QUESTIONS

1.   *Standing to Challenge the Fee Award*. Does the expansive application of standing principles in *Cendant PRIDES* flow from the same considerations that support a fiduciary role for the courts generally with regard to class actions? Is there a practical downside to the lenient application of standing principles in the fee award context?

2.   *The Choice Between Lodestar and Percentage Methods*. *Cendant PRIDES* illustrates how a court may use both lodestar and percentage methods

of fee calculation to double-check one another. As a descriptive matter, does the difference in methods ultimately translate into a difference in actual fee awards? Empirical research suggests not. The leading empirical study on class counsel fee awards finds that the choice of fee award formulas has little impact on the size of the fee. Theodore Eisenberg & Geoffrey P. Miller, *Attorneys Fees in Class Action Settlements: An Empirical Study*, 1 J. Empirical Legal Stud. 27, 53 (2004).

McKenzie v. Federal Express Corp.

2012 WL 2930201 (C.D.Cal.)

■ FEESS, DISTRICT JUDGE

I.

INTRODUCTION & BACKGROUND

On February 19, 2010, Plaintiff filed this class and representative action lawsuit in California state court against Defendants Federal Express Corporation ("FedEx") and "Does" 1–50, inclusive, alleging claims under California Labor Code 226(a) in connection with Plaintiff's 16–year employment as a courier with FedEx. Plaintiff alleged that FedEx failed to provide required information on wage statements issued to hourly employees, including the beginning date of the pay period, the sum of the total hours worked by the employee, and all applicable hourly rates and the number of hours worked at each hourly rate. These omissions prevented hourly employees from readily determining whether they were paid correctly for all days and hours worked, and what pay period was covered by the paycheck. . . . On April 14, 2011, this Court granted summary judgment in favor of Plaintiff on her first cause of action for civil penalties pursuant to the California Labor Code Private Attorney General Act ("PAGA"), Cal. Lab.Code section 2698*et seq.,* for Defendant's violation of Section 226(a).

This Court certified the plaintiff class, all current and former hourly employees employed by FedEx in California from February 19, 2009 to the present, on June 16, 2011, and Defendant's motion for reconsideration of the certification decision and Rule 23(f) petition to the Ninth Circuit were denied. In October 2011, the Parties reached agreement on a settlement [according to which] FedEx [will] pay a non-reversionary Gross Settlement Amount ("GSA") of $8.25 million, from which payments are to be made for: (1) attorney fees in an amount up to $2,749,725 (33.33 percent of the GSA); (2) litigation costs incurred by class counsel estimated at $12,000; (3) a class representative service award of $5,000 to Plaintiff McKenzie; (4) settlement administration costs estimated at $100,000 payable to Simpluris, Inc. . . . ; and (5) the payment of $82,500 for civil penalties under PAGA. . . . The Net Settlement Amount ("NSA") of more than $5.3 million is to be distributed to Class Members, in proportion to the number of wage statements each received during the Covered Period and pursuant to an agreed-upon formula detailed in the Settlement Agreement. Any remaining balance will be redistributed to Class Members and/or paid into a *cy pres* fund and then distributed to a charitable organization approved by the Parties and the Court. . . .

Based on an NSA figure of more than $5.3 million and a total of 14,344 participating Class Members, the highest settlement share to be paid is $585.00, and the average settlement share to be paid is $372.00. . . .

B. *MOTION FOR ATTORNEY FEES AND COSTS*

Plaintiff additionally seeks this Court's approval of an attorney fee payment of $2,749,725, which represents 33.33 [percent] of the common fund . . .

1. ATTORNEY FEES

a. *Legal Standard*

Circuit law teaches that class action plaintiffs' attorney fees may be based on a percentage recovery from a common fund. If an attorney seeks a percentage recovery in a class action, twenty-five percent of the common fund has been established as the "benchmark" award in the Ninth Circuit. However, the "benchmark percentage should be adjusted, or replaced by a lodestar calculation, when special circumstances indicate that the percentage recovery would be either too small or too large in light of the hours devoted to the case or other relevant factors." *Six Mexican Workers v. Ariz. Citrus Growers,* 904 F.2d 1301, 1311 (9th Cir.1990). . . .

b. *Application*

i. Results Achieved

Applying the benchmark percentage of 25 percent in this case would generate an attorney fee award of $2,062,500. Plaintiff submits that an upward adjustment from the benchmark, to 33.33 percent, is justified in this case by the injunctive and monetary relief achieved by class counsel. With regard to the monetary relief, class counsel argues that the average settlement payment of $372.00 is a good result in view of the minimal injury suffered and the fact that Class Members have not been required to release any wage claims. Indeed, class counsel states that he is unaware of any other wage statement case that has achieved such a high monetary settlement. [The Court then described changes FedEx made to its pay stubs so employees could more easily verify their pay.]

The result is no doubt favorable, but it can hardly be described as "exceptional" within the meaning of applicable jurisprudence. For example, in *Vizcaino [v. Microsoft Corp.,* 290 F.3d 1043 (9th Cir.2002),] the class action litigation challenged the classification of more than 3,000 persons whose status as "freelancers" rendered them ineligible for employee benefits. Even though class members had signed written agreements waiving such benefits, class counsel successfully litigated a modification to their classification to make them employees who would be hired as W–2 workers who received all benefits normally available to Microsoft employees. In addition to obtaining these benefits for employees nationwide, a change that was valued at over $100 million, Microsoft paid a cash settlement to class members of $96,885,000. *Vizcaino,* 290 F.3d at 1046, 1048–49. Finally, the ruling also clarified employment law regarding the classification of temporary workers, to the benefit of employers and workers nationwide. *Id.* at 1049. These were indeed "exceptional results" which resulted in a 28 percent attorney fee award to counsel.

Although class counsel here achieved a positive result for class members, the issue on which the settlement was based was substantially less complex than that at stake in *Vizcaino,* and much more technical. Indeed, there was never a shred of evidence that any employee was actually deprived of his or her overtime pay, only that determining the amount was difficult. Moreover, though difficult, the computation was not impossible. Here, an employee could have determined his or her wages and overtime payments and rates of pay with modest effort and the application of simple arithmetic. Even so, the law says that such efforts are not required, which is why Plaintiffs prevailed. But to state that this is an exceptional result mistakes litigation success with extraordinary performance, particularly when the issue and the result are compared with those attained in *Vizcaino* where counsel were awarded only 28 percent of the common fund. In that case, the monetary relief was far more substantial; the changes to Microsoft's personnel practices also had significant monetary value to class members; and the benefits from the clarification in the law accrued to employers and workers nationwide. Comparable circumstances are not present in this case. Accordingly, this factor does not weigh in favor of enhancing the benchmark award.

ii. Risks of Litigation and the Contingent Nature of the Fee

Plaintiff submits that class counsel has taken considerable risk in litigating this case, because the litigation was undertaken on a contingency basis over the course of two years against a well-funded adversary, and because wage statement claims are an emerging area under both state and federal law. In particular, the issues raised by FedEx's defenses included whether the company's wage statements violated Labor Code section 226; whether Plaintiff was required to prove an injury pursuant to section 226(e) to recover PAGA penalties; whether the section 226(e) injury requirement prevented class certification of the section 226 claim; whether the U.S. Supreme Court's decision in *Dukes v. Wal–Mart* prevented class certification; and whether Plaintiff's PAGA claim required class certification under Rule 23.

Although class counsel in this litigation were required to confront unsettled legal issues, this circumstance does not distinguish this case from most others that proceed before this Court. Plaintiff concedes that this case was not factually complex. (See Mem. Final Settlement Approval at 15.) Moreover, unlike class counsel in *Vizcaino,* here, counsel did not face adverse decisions by this Court that were successfully challenged on appeal, reviving the class claims. . . Accordingly, this factor does not weigh in favor of enhancing the benchmark award.

iii. Skill Required and the Quality of the Work

This factor does not weigh in favor of enhancing the benchmark award. Although class counsel is experienced in class actions and has skillfully performed their duties, as the Court has previously noted, wage and hour litigation is not as legally complex as other types of litigation that often generate a common fund, notably securities class action litigation. . . . Class counsel . . . has billed more than 1,000 hours for the work performed on this case over more than two years, and expects to bill an additional 50 to 100 hours to obtain final approval, monitor the distribution process, and to resolve any problems that arise during settlement administration after final approval. Billing at hourly rates of $550 to $600 per hour, which Plaintiff states are consistent with the prevailing market rates for attorneys handling this type of litigation, class counsel has generated fees of approximately $640,695. Thus, a benchmark award of $2,062,500 represents a multiplier of roughly 3.2. Plaintiff's requested award of $2,749,725 represents a multiplier of 4.3. In a case cited by Plaintiff, *Wershba v. Apple Computer, Inc.,* 91 Cal.App.4th 224, 110 Cal.Rptr.2d 145 (Ct.App.2001), the California Court of Appeal observed that courts using the lodestar method to calculate attorney fees awards in civil class actions typically apply multipliers in the range of 2 to 4. *Id.* at 170. Accordingly, the Court is satisfied that the benchmark figure, which falls within the higher end of this range, appropriately accounts for the skill required and the quality of work performed by class counsel in this case.

v.   Burdens Carried by Counsel

Class counsel's law firm is a small plaintiff's firm consisting of two attorneys. It has worked on this case since 2009 on contingency, dedicating approximately 1,000 hours of work that have been unpaid to date; has turned away other paying clients from its two-attorney firm; and has incurred $10,755 in of out-of-pocket expenses. Its retainer agreement with Plaintiff provides for a 33.33 percent contingency payment in the event of success in this action. Class counsel states that the loss of this case would have dealt a devastating financial blow to its law firm. However, beyond conclusory statements to the effect that paying clients have been turned away and that a loss would have severely damaged the firm's financial stability, counsel's declaration is short on specifics. Indeed, this portion of the declaration is somewhat inconsistent with other portions identifying the numerous other class actions in which Plaintiff's firm currently serves as class counsel. The argument also ignores that, at the 25 percent benchmark rate, counsel will realize a substantial premium over the typical hourly billing rate of $550 to $600 per hour for comparable work.

Class counsel's circumstances are a commonplace with all attorneys who serve as plaintiffs class counsel. It is a risk that counsel voluntarily undertook and is not worthy of an exceptional award. . . .

vi.   Awards Made in Similar Cases

Class counsel offers four examples of attorney fee awards in wage and hour class action settlements that met or exceeded the percentage requested here. In two of these cases, California Superior Courts awarded 33.33 percent of the common fund on settlements totaling in the hundreds of thousands of dollars, and provided little analysis. In the other two cases, the District Court for the Southern District of California awarded 40 percent on settlements in the millions of dollars. One of these awards was made to present class counsel. These authorities are not, of course, binding on this Court. Moreover, they represent only a very small percentage of the total universe of successful wage and hour class action litigations. The Court finds those cases unpersuasive when compared with the vast majority of cases addressing fee awards. Accordingly, this factor does not weigh in favor of enhancing the benchmark award.[1]

vii. Conclusion

The Court finds that Plaintiff's attorneys have competently performed their expected duties as class counsel, but that there is no justification for enhancing the benchmark award. Accordingly, the Court approves the award of attorney fees at the benchmark rate of 25 percent, for a total award of $2,062,500.

---

[1] The Court observes that Plaintiff's argument that the requested percentage "approximates the legal marketplace by awarding a fee comparable to what clients and counsel would have likely negotiated at the outset of the matter" and did negotiate in this case (see Mem. Final Settlement Approval at 18–19) was rejected in *Vizcaino*. In that case, the Ninth Circuit stated that the retainer agreements between plaintiffs and class counsel "although somewhat probative of a reasonable rate, are not particularly helpful." 290 F.3d at 1049. The court explicitly rejected the marketplace approach to determining fee awards in common fund cases, under which a reasonable fee is determined by attempting to replicate the market rate. *Id.* at 1049–50.

NOTES AND QUESTIONS

1. When Should Judges Set Fees? Although both subsection (g) and sub-section (h) give judges the power to set fees early in class actions, judges have done so only exceptionally. They normally decide the terms on which class counsel will be paid when approving settlements, as Judge Feess did in *McKenzie v. Federal Express Corp.* Might this practice discourage lawyers from investing resources in lawsuits by making their returns uncertain? In *McKenzie*, the lawyers hoped to receive 33 percent of the recovery, wound up with only 25 percent, and could conceivably have recovered less had Judge Feess decided that a downward adjustment of the benchmark was proper. Might they have been more willing to put their time and money into the lawsuit had they known from the beginning how large the contingent fee would be?

The Ninth Circuit's benchmark approach can be viewed as a form of advance fee setting. A lawyer who files a class action can be reasonably confident of receiving a 25 percent fee. The degree of confidence would reflect the frequency with which district court judges in the Ninth Circuit depart from the 25 percent benchmark. The Seventh Circuit's "mimic-the-market" approach is a weak form of advance fee setting as well. Lawyers know their fees will be based on contingent percentages prevailing in the private market for legal services. Although the percentage cannot be known precisely until the presiding judge rules, market-based fees typically fall in the 25 to 40 percent range.

When viewed as approaches that set fees in advance, the approaches taken by the Seventh and Ninth Circuits run afoul of the views of commentators who believe that judges should set fees when class litigation ends, because only then can judges know how much labor lawyers expended and how much they bore in costs. The Task Force on the Contingent Fee created by the Tort Trial and Insurance Practice Section of the American Bar Association divided on this point. Although most of the members supported back-end fee setting, one argued that fees should be set in advance. Compare Task Force on Contingent Fees, Tort Trial and Insurance Practice Section of the American Bar Association, Report on Contingent Fees in Class Action Litigation, 25 Rev. of Litig. 459 (2006) (supporting practice of setting fees when class actions settle), with Charles Silver, *Dissent from Recommendation to Set Fees Ex Post*, 25 Rev. of Litig. 497 (2006) (encouraging judges to set fee terms at or near the start of class litigation).

2. Should Judges Investigate Lawyers' Ability to Finance Class Actions? Although subsection (g) gives judges discretion to consider lawyers' ability to finance litigation when choosing class counsel, judges rarely make a serious investigation of putative class counsel's ability to tolerate financial costs and risks. Should they care about this consideration more than they do? In the class action brought on behalf of Vietnam War veterans allegedly harmed by exposure to the herbicide known as "Agent Orange," the veterans' lawyers eventually ran out of money and had to obtain help from investors, who demanded sizeable returns. See Peter H. Shuck, AGENT ORANGE ON TRIAL: MASS TOXIC DISASTERS IN THE COURTS (1987); John C. Coffee, Jr., *The Unfaithful Champion: The Plaintiff as Monitor in Shareholder Litigation*, 48 Law & Contemp. Probs. 5 (1985). Because class members depend on lawyers to finance lawsuits, lawyers who cannot afford the commitments class actions require can easily be outspent by wealthy corporate defendants or convinced to avoid the risk of losing by accepting inadequate settlements.

By the same token, outside the context of securities fraud litigation, discussed further below, competition for the role of class counsel appears to be rare. Shouldn't judges appoint even impecunious attorneys instead of allowing class members to remain unrepresented?

3. Should Judges Use the Contingent Percentage Method or the Lodestar Method? From class members' perspective, judges should regulate fees in ways calculated to maximize net expected recoveries, that is, the amounts class members are likely to take home after paying their lawyers and reimbursing expenses. If class members could monitor their lawyers perfectly, a contingent hourly rate would achieve this result. Class members would order their attorneys to work just long enough to maximize their net expected recoveries, and would then tell them to stop. In reality, class members are poor monitors: they are often unsophisticated; their financial interests are too small to motivate them to follow class actions closely; and they would rather free-ride on the efforts of others than bear the cost of monitoring themselves. Given this, what fee arrangement would they use if they could set fees directly?

In *Kirchoff v. Flynn*, 786 F.2d 320 (1986), Judge Frank Easterbrook, a leading member of the law and economics school, pointed out that contingent percentage fees dominate the market for plaintiff representations. It does so, he contends, because, by rewarding lawyers for securing larger recoveries, it minimizes the amount of monitoring clients must perform. This does not mean that contingent percentage fees work perfectly. With faulty monitoring, no compensation arrangement that pays a lawyer less than 100 percent of the marginal return on effort will encourage the lawyer to exert optimal effort. Easterbrook's point is just that the contingent-percentage method works better than other approaches in the market contexts where it is employed. This is why the Seventh Circuit requires district court judges to mimic the market when awarding fees in class actions. Judges should give class members the same benefits they would have obtained had they been able to hire lawyers directly, including the strong harmony of interests contingent percentage fee arrangements confer.

On the basic economics of contingent percentage fee arrangements, see Bruce L. Hay, *Contingent Fees and Agency Costs*, 25 J. Leg. Stud. 503 (1996); Herbert M. Kritzer, *Seven Dogged Myths Concerning Contingency Fees*, 80 Wash. U. L.Q. 739 (2002); Herbert M. Kritzer, RISKS, REPUTATIONS, AND REWARDS: CONTINGENCY FEE LEGAL PRACTICE IN THE UNITED STATES (2004). For criticisms of contingent percentage fees charged in mass tort cases, see Lester Brickman, *The Market for Contingent Fee-Financed Tort Litigation: Is It Price Competitive?*, 25 Cardozo L. Rev. 65 (2003).

The alternative to the contingent-percentage approach is the lodestar method, which bases fees on the lodestar (time reasonably expended multiplied by a lawyer's reasonable hourly rate) and a few enhancement factors combined into a multiplier. Proponents argue that the lodestar method protects class members from excessive fees because it compensates lawyers only for time they reasonably expend. It also eliminates windfall fees generated by enormous settlements that sometimes pay lawyers effective rates equal to thousands of dollars an hour. Critics of the lodestar approach contend that it encourages cheap settlements because it weakens the connection between the size of the recovery and class counsel's fee. A lawyer has no reason to care whether a class action settles for $5 million or $10 million if she will be paid $400 an hour in either event. An hourly rate lawyer may therefore accept a cheap settlement that, if approved by the court, will cover her hourly rate in full instead of holding out for a larger one, when hard bargaining would require her to incur a risk of non-payment. See John C. Coffee, Jr., *The Unfaithful Champion: The Plaintiff as Monitor in Shareholder Litigation*, 48 Law & Contemp. Probs. 5 (1985).

Suppose one concedes for the sake of argument that contingent-percentage fees are generally preferable to lodestar-based fees. Wouldn't it have been better to use the lodestar method in *McKenzie* even so? The central question in the litigation was simple: Either FedEx's pay stubs contained the information required by Section 226(a) or they did not. When the court granted summary judgment in favor of the class on this question, wasn't the litigation effectively over? Why pay a lawyer a contingent percentage of the entire class' recovery for litigating a straightforward question of law? The lawyers also claim to have devoted 1,000 hours to the case. That's about half a year of lawyer-time, assuming 2,000 billable hours a year. Can a lawsuit decided on summary judgment really have required that much time?

4.   *How Large Should Lodestar Multipliers Be?* Courts that use the lodestar method when awarding fees from class members' recoveries usually enhance lawyers' hourly rates by applying multipliers to the lodestar basis. In *McKenzie*, class counsel requested a multiplier of 4.3, the court awarded a multiplier of 3.2, and the court observed that multipliers typically fall between 2 and 4. Recent empirical scholarship suggests that multipliers at the low end of the range have become more common. See Theodore Eisenberg & Geoffrey P. Miller, *Attorney Fees and Expenses in Class Action Settlements: 1993–2008*, 7 J. Empirical Legal Stud. 248, 273 (2010) (finding an average multiplier of 1.96 in common fund class actions); Brian T. Fitzpatrick, *An Empirical Study of Class Action Settlements and Their Fee Awards*, 7 Journal of Empirical Legal Studies 811, 834 (2010) (reporting that lodestar multipliers "ranged from 0.07 to 10.3, with a mean of 1.65 and a median of 1.34").

In *McKenzie*, class counsel attempted to persuade the court that a large multiplier was warranted by pointing out that their small law firm would have suffered a crippling loss had the case ended without a recovery. Should Judge Feess have been more sympathetic to this argument than he was? The authors of an article that examined both the normative foundation of lodestar multipliers and the empirics of lawyers' willingness to accept litigation risks contended that multipliers as large as 10 may be needed to encourage small firm lawyers to handle class actions. Normally, small firms act in a risk-averse manner: they diversify their risks by handling large numbers of matters, each of which individually requires a small commitment of resources and all of which collectively generate a predictable revenue stream. Think of making a thousand small bets on the toss of a fair coin and you'll get the idea. Class actions, by contrast, saddle lawyers with large, undiversifiable risks. They require lots of resources, and they often end badly. To encourage risk averse lawyers to bear these risks, multipliers should be large. See James H. Stock and David A. Wise, *Market Compensation in Class Action Suits: A Summary of Basic Ideas and Results*, 16 Class Action Reports 584 (1993).

Conceding for the sake of argument that small multipliers fail to motivate lawyers to handle class actions, should judges really use multipliers to encourage lawyers to bring class actions like the one in *McKenzie*, where the plaintiffs sued over a harmless, technical violation of a statute? As Judge Feess observed, "there was never a shred of evidence that any employee was actually deprived of his or her overtime pay, only that determining the amount was difficult" because FedEx's pay stubs lacked certain information required by law. Should lawyers who sue to correct technical violations earn a substantial premium over their regular hourly rates?

5. *Objections to Fee Requests.* Subsection (h)(2) permits defendants to object to fee requests when they pay fees directly. In practice, objections by defendants are rare, however, because settlement agreements usually resolve any fee-related responsibilities defendants may possess. Once an agreement liquidates a defendant's total exposure to a class, the defendant will care more about ending the litigation than about how the money it must pay is divided between class members and class counsel. If the settlement is a sell-out, in which the defendant bribed class counsel by offering a large fee award in exchange for a cheap resolution, the defendant's support for the proposal will be even stronger. Finally, settlement agreements often contain "clear sailing" provisions that memorialize defendants' promises not to object as long as class counsel's fee request remains at or below an identified amount. Many judges and commentators view "clear sailing" agreements with suspicion. Should they?

Class members can also object to fee requests, and often do. Their actions may seem economically irrational. The cost of objecting usually exceeds the gain any class member can hope to realize by reducing class counsel's fee, especially because only class members who retain attorneys to appear at fairness hearings are likely to object effectively. The logic of collective action should also discourage objections. All class members benefit when fees are reduced because, in most cases, the savings enlarge the settlement fund, which is divided among everyone in a class. Consequently, the economically rational choice would seem to be to avoid the cost of objecting by free-riding on objections filed by others.

In fact, objecting can be profitable, so much so that many lawyers make a good living off the practice. After having their objections denied by trial judges, these lawyers, known as professional objectors, file appeals, thereby preventing settlements from becoming final, delaying the payment of fees to class counsel, and exposing class counsel to the risk that the fee award will be reduced or reversed. Wanting to be paid promptly, lawyers representing plaintiff classes often find it advisable to pay fee objectors to go away. Although Rule 23(e) of the Federal Rules of Civil Procedure requires side agreements with objectors to be reported to the trial judge when the settlement review process is underway, the rule seems not to apply to agreements that resolve post-approval appeals. In a dissenting opinion in *Devlin v. Scardelletti*, 536 U.S. 1, 21–22 (2002), Justice Scalia, joined by Justices Kennedy and Thomas, took note of the problem posed by professional objectors, who appeal settlement approvals even though their objections lack merit.

c.   AUCTION–BASED TECHNIQUES

Subsection (g) of Federal Rule of Civil Procedure 23 takes no position concerning what once appeared to be a major innovation relating to the choice and compensation of class counsel: the use of auctions to determine who class counsel will be and how much class counsel will be paid. The materials in this section trace the history of class counsel auctions and ask whether (and, if so, when) that technique merits application. The materials in the following section flesh out subsection (g)'s proviso that the procedures it creates do not apply when an applicable statute "provides otherwise." As the advisory committee mentions, this caveat was included in subsection (g) so as not to disturb the method for class counsel selection set forth for federal securities class actions in the Private Securities Litigation Reform Act of 1995 ("PSLRA").

In re Auction Houses Antitrust Litigation
197 F.R.D. 71 (S.D.N.Y. 2000)

■ KAPLAN, DISTRICT JUDGE.

Class action lawsuits protect plaintiffs' rights and promote accountability by permitting dispersed, disorganized plaintiffs who may have suffered only small injuries to find redress by acting as a group where they would lack sufficient incentive to do so individually. At the same time, however, the relationship between a plaintiff class and its attorney may suffer from a structural flaw, a divergence of economic interests of the class and its counsel. The class action mechanism can redound more to the benefit of the attorney than to that of the class, as counsel has an incentive to act in its own best interest, rather than that of the class. Thus, the class action mechanism on occasion has proved to be Janus-faced.

This case has presented an occasion to seek to ease this tension and improve the class action as an instrument of justice. The Court, over the objection of some of plaintiffs' counsel, employed an auction in selecting lead counsel. This opinion sets forth the basis for the Court's decision to conduct an auction and the reasoning behind the manner in which it was conducted.

I

A.   Background

Defendants Sotheby's Holding, Inc. and its subsidiary Sotheby's Inc. (collectively "Sotheby's") and Christie's International PLC and its subsidiary Christie's, Inc. (collectively "Christie's") are in the business of providing auction services of fine and applied arts, furniture, antiques, automobiles, collectibles and other items. The primary sources of revenues of the defendant auction houses are so-called buyers' premiums and sellers' commissions. A buyer's premium is, typically, a percentage of the price at which the buyer successfully bids on an item at auction that is added to the auction sales price and retained by the auction house. The seller's commission is a percentage of the auction sales price deducted from the sale proceeds paid to the seller and retained by the auction house.

On December 24, 1999, Christie's International's former chief executive officer, Christopher Davidge, resigned abruptly. Subsequently, Christie's reportedly provided evidence of price fixing with Sotheby's to the Department of Justice and is said to have received conditional amnesty from criminal prosecution in exchange for providing evidence.

In late January and February 2000, following press reports of these events, a large number of individual and class action complaints were filed in this District against Christie's and Sotheby's. All were referred to the undersigned as related cases. The complaints allege that the auction house defendants, beginning at least as early as January 1, 1993, conspired to manipulate the prices at which they provided non-Internet auction services. The conspiracy allegedly began in 1993 with an agreement to employ a common rate schedule for the premiums charged to buyers. It allegedly was expanded in 1995, when they allegedly agreed to use substantially similar rates for sellers' commissions. Further, plaintiffs maintain that the auction houses agreed in 1995 to terminate the previous practice of negotiating the amounts of sellers' commissions with some of their customers.

The first status conference in this case was held on February 23, 2000. Dozens of plaintiffs' attorneys attended, and a consortium of five law firms immediately proposed themselves as plaintiffs' executive committee or co-lead counsel in the case. The group of five represented that it had been selected in an earlier meeting attended by all of the plaintiffs' lawyers, that all possessed the highest credentials, and that the selection was unopposed. . . .

On April 20, 2000, the Court certified the plaintiff class. In a separate order, the Court announced that it was considering the use of an auction to select lead counsel. The order set forth a tentative set of procedures governing the auction and solicited bids from interested counsel. The Court solicited also *amicus* briefs from a number of well-respected academic authorities in the field and invited counsel to submit briefs commenting on the merits of the proposed auction procedure.

B.   First Proposed Fee Structure

The bids contemplated by the Court's initial order were to contain three parts. First, each bid was to include information concerning the bidder's qualifications and evidence that the bidder had evaluated fully the risks and potential rewards of the litigation. Second, each bid was to contain two figures, X and Y, on the basis of which the bidder was prepared to serve as lead counsel. The X and Y figures were to be determined based on the bidder's evaluation of the case and the following fee structure: One hundred percent of any gross recovery obtained by the class or class members up to and including X would go entirely to the class or class members, free of attorney's fees. One hundred percent of any gross recovery in excess of X, up to and including Y, would go to lead counsel. One fourth of any recovery in excess of Y would be paid to lead counsel as additional compensation and three fourths to the class. Third, each bidder was to submit a brief memorandum setting forth the basis for and supporting the bid. The briefs were to explain the bidders' respective evaluations of the case, including their assumptions as to possible and likely recoveries in the event liability were established, and the bases therefore. The order stated that, if the Court decided to use the bids in selecting lead counsel, lead counsel would be selected on the basis of both the economic terms of the bids and the qualifications of the bidder.[9]

On the appointed day, twenty law firms submitted bids for the position of lead counsel. Several included affidavits by economists supporting their bids. The Court received also three briefs *amicus curiae* and several submissions from bidders commenting on the merits of the auction procedure.

---

[9] In addition to submitting the X and Y figures, each bidder was required to submit a sworn certification that the bidder had not, directly or indirectly, communicated with (1) any other bidder concerning the terms of the bid or its position with respect to whether the Court should adopt this method, (2) any defendant or prospective defendant following the issuance of the order concerning settlement or possible settlement of any or all of the actions, or (3) any other attorney or firm concerning its possible performance of legal or other services for the bidder in connection with this litigation in the event the bidder were selected as lead counsel.

C.   Second Proposed Fee Structure

After considering the comments of the *amici* and bidders, the Court issued a second order revising the fee structure and soliciting a new round of bids. This second proposed fee structure included only one variable, X, rather than two. One hundred percent of any gross recovery up to and including X was to go to the class. And twenty-five percent of any recovery in excess of X would be paid to counsel, with the remainder going to the class. Each bid was to state the value of X pursuant to which the bidder was prepared to serve as lead counsel. As before, bidders were required to submit explanatory memoranda and sworn certifications. As with the previous round of bidding, the Court stated that it would select lead counsel based on its judgment as to which bidder was likely best to serve the interests of the class, taking into account the economic terms of the bids as well as the bidder's qualifications.

All additional terms contained in the first proposed fee structure were included in the Court's second proposal as well, including the provision that the attorney's fee would be inclusive of all costs, disbursements and other charges incurred in connection with the litigation. The Court noted further that it did not intend to disclose any of the bids prior to the earlier of (a) final adjudication of the action, or (b) notice to the class of a proposed settlement, and it ordered that lead counsel thus selected not disclose the terms of its bid to defendants or anyone else without approval of the Court.

D.   Disclosure of Interim Committee's Expert Analysis

Prior to the submission of final bids, it became apparent that interim lead counsel had engaged in settlement discussions with defendants in the course of which they obtained information that their experts used to prepare studies of potential damages. Accordingly, the Court granted a motion by a prospective bidder and gave all counsel access to the damage studies solely for the purpose of preparing bids. . . .

F.   Selection of Lead Counsel for the Class

By May 25, 2000, the final day for submission of the bids, the Court had received twenty-one sealed bids for the position of lead counsel, of which seventeen complied with the Court's proposed fee structure. After careful review, the Court selected David Boies and Richard B. Drubel of Boies, Schiller & Flexner, LLP as lead counsel in the case.

II

A.   Problems of Choosing and Compensating Counsel

The modern class action device undoubtedly has proved an important innovation for plaintiffs' rights. It provides a means of redress to dispersed and disorganized plaintiffs who may have suffered only small injuries and who, in its absence, likely would lack sufficient incentives to bring their own claims. By serving as a vehicle for these claims, the class action plays an important part in enforcement policy in many areas, including securities regulation and antitrust. Nonetheless, the class action mechanism is not free of problems, foremost among them for purposes of this case difficulties in obtaining counsel who will manage the case efficiently and effectively on behalf of the class and the mismatch of economic incentives between the plaintiff class and its attorney.

When, as here, multiple related claims are filed by different plaintiffs' attorneys, a case may threaten quickly to become unmanageable, as coordination and strategy problems arise. To remedy the problem of unmanageability, courts traditionally select lead counsel from among the attorneys representing the individual plaintiffs. Lead counsel typically is responsible for working with other counsel to develop positions on substantive and procedural issues in the case, presenting arguments to the court, initiating discovery requests and responses, employing expert witnesses, conducting depositions and insuring that schedules are met. By placing these responsibilities in the hands of one or a small group of counsel, the selection of lead counsel is meant to permit large numbers of cases in which common questions predominate to be prosecuted simultaneously as consolidated or class actions, thereby avoiding duplicated efforts, wasted resources and inconsistent or preclusive judgments. Nevertheless, problems of coordination and duplication of effort may exist.

Lead counsel generally litigates a class action case on behalf of dozens, hundreds or thousands of individual plaintiffs, all of whom seek to recover from defendants. Given the potential for massive plaintiffs' recoveries in such cases, the lead counsel position may involve a potentially large attorney's fee. The role therefore has become a coveted prize to be fought over or bargained for among competing plaintiff's attorneys. This process typically occurs in one of two ways, neither of which necessarily leads to an optimal outcome. Often, interested counsel jockey for the lead counsel position, leaving the court to choose one of the contenders, sometimes with little guidance. Counsel thus selected is not necessarily the most qualified or that who will best protect the interests of the class. Alternatively, the plaintiffs' lawyers negotiate among themselves to select lead counsel or a team of lead counsel, and the choice is presented as a *fait accompli* for the court summarily to endorse. Here again, the choice is not necessarily in the plaintiffs' best interests. These two scenarios threatened to replay themselves almost exactly in this case.

B. Compensation–Drawbacks of Commonly Utilized Fee Structures

Plaintiffs' attorney is, of course, duty bound to act in the best interests of the class. However, because of the manner in which attorney's fees in class actions frequently are calculated, the optimal recovery for the class often does not yield the highest attorney's fee. Likewise, the result yielding the highest attorney's fee is not necessarily in the class' best interests. This tension can lead counsel to neglect the class' interests in pursuit of a higher fee. These mismatched incentives predominate when the fee is determined by using either of the two most common fee structures used in common fund cases, the lodestar method and the percentage-of-recovery method.

1. Lodestar Method

The lodestar method essentially compensates plaintiffs' counsel for the time expended in litigating the case, with the final result sometimes adjusted by application of a multiplier to reflect the risk assumed. It is determined by "multiplying the number of hours expended by each attorney involved in each type of work on the case by the hourly rate normally charged for similar work by attorneys of like skill in the area," and "[o]nce this base or 'lodestar' rate [is] established," calculating the final fee by then deciding whether to take into account "other less objective factors, such as the 'risk of litigation,' the complexity of the issues, and the skill of the attorneys." [*City of Detroit v. Grinnell Corp.*, 560 F.2d 1093, 1098 (2d Cir. 1977)] Because this figure takes no account of the size of plaintiffs' recovery, any of several perverse results can obtain.

First, the lodestar method may induce lead counsel to prolong the litigation beyond the optimal point from plaintiffs' perspective simply in order to accrue more hours.

Second, despite incentives to prolong the litigation to a certain point, counsel compensated by the lodestar method has also an incentive to settle the case before it reaches the trial stage, even if trial is in plaintiffs' best interests. This stems from the fact that, while these attorneys share with their clients the downside risk associated with trial (*i.e.*, a finding of no liability and therefore no attorney's fee), they do not necessarily share the potential economic upside (*i.e.*, a substantial plaintiffs' judgment), as trial usually requires few attorney hours relative to pretrial preparation.

Third, the lodestar fee structure creates an incentive for the attorney to do unnecessary work such as filing motions with little merit, taking unnecessary depositions, or demanding production of huge volumes of documents, solely in order to accrue more hours. This risk is exacerbated where the class is represented by a committee of attorneys, rather than a single firm. The involvement of numerous counsel can create pressure to generate sufficient attorney hours to compensate all participating attorneys, and work may be allocated in order to further this objective, rather than in the most efficient and cost-effective manner. Appointment of a committee can lead also to administrative and cost problems, as coordination among committee members is time consuming and costly. All of these factors may result in a higher lodestar without commensurate benefit to the class.

Finally, the lodestar method can lead plaintiffs' attorney to agree to a less-than-favorable settlement for the class while counsel collects a substantial fee. In the most egregious cases, such settlements have involved non-monetary consideration of virtually no value to all or part of the class while counsel received substantial fees in cash. Although the Court is responsible for assessing the fairness of the settlement and fee application, this task often is difficult. As soon as the parties to a class action lawsuit arrive at a settlement, all have an interest in seeing it approved by the court. This is particularly true in cases in which defendants face potentially enormous damages and therefore are inclined to settle quickly and comparatively cheaply, even if the fee application is unjustifiably high. Further, because attorney's fees are taken from the common fund, rather than paid separately by defendants, defendants have little interest in contesting the amount of the fee. Instead, once a settlement is agreed upon, the adversary system typically abandons the judge, as plaintiffs' lawyers and defendants band together to convince the court to approve the settlement and the fee award. This creates substantial difficulties for the court in evaluating the fairness of both the settlement and the fee application.

Evaluation of the fee application can be complicated further where the class is represented by a committee, rather than a single firm. The process of reviewing retrospectively numerous time records and determining appropriate remuneration therefore is arduous, particularly when multiple firms are involved. More seriously, committees of counsel have been known to break down and submit separate contested fee applications to the Court, making accurate retrospective analysis almost impossible.

2.   The Percentage-of-Recovery Method

The percentage-of-recovery method, in contrast, "is a simpler calculation of the fee award as some percentage of the fund created for the benefit of the class," frequently twenty to thirty percent. This method allows the attorney to share in both the upside and the downside risk of the litigation and thereby attempts to re-align the interests of plaintiffs' and their attorney. Although eliminating incentives to prolong the litigation unnecessarily or accumulate needless hours, however, this method creates perverse incentives of its own. In particular, the percentage-of-recovery method might lead the plaintiffs' attorney to settle the case prematurely as soon as counsel's opportunity costs begin to mount. Early settlement allows counsel to collect a large fee after investing relatively little time in the case, rather than continuing the litigation in order to maximize plaintiffs' recovery but receiving a lower marginal rate of return on his or her work. Again, from the plaintiffs' perspective, this outcome is suboptimal.

3. Collective Action Dilemma in Class Actions

These problems of mismatched incentives are present not only in class actions, but also in traditional attorney-client relationships where both the hourly rate fee structure and the contingency fee can motivate the attorney to pursue his or her own economic interest at the expense of the client. However, they often can be far more severe in the class action context, primarily because classes tend to be large, dispersed and disorganized and therefore suffer from a collective action dilemma not faced by individual litigants. This collective action dilemma leads to significantly less monitoring of the attorney by the class and consequential higher agency costs. The danger of a suboptimal result for plaintiffs, therefore, is far more severe in the class action context than in traditional litigation.

4. Procedural Disadvantages for Class Action Plaintiffs

Plaintiffs are prohibited from exerting the same supervisory control over the litigation as exists in the non-class action context. They usually lack control even over the selection of counsel, giving rise to a situation in which a poorly qualified lawyer may be chosen to represent the class when few individuals in the class would have selected that lawyer in an open market. These problems further contribute to suboptimal outcomes in the class action context.

In consequence of these drawbacks, the class action mechanism cannot work wholly in the interests of the litigants. Under either of the most common fee structures, attorney/client agency costs are extraordinarily high. In some cases, they allow the class action device to serve the interests of the lawyers more than those of their clients. A few courts recently have begun to experiment with reform.

C. Use of Auctions to Select Lead Counsel

1. First Experiment with Lead Counsel Auction

Judge Vaughan Walker in the Northern District of California was the first to experiment with an auction to select and compensate lead counsel in a class action. In *In re Oracle Sec.Litig.*, [131 F.R.D. 688 (N.D. Cal. 1990); 132 F.R.D. 538 (N.D. Cal. 1990);136 F.R.D. 639 (N.D. Cal. 1991),] he declined to ratify the selection of two firms as co-lead counsel by a group fifteen plaintiffs' lawyers involved in the case. Noting that although many among the fifteen were experienced antitrust attorneys, they displayed "cavalier indifference" to the spirit of the antitrust laws in their selection of counsel, Judge Walker instead ordered the two selected firms and two others that jointly had contested the selection to submit budgets for the litigation, on the basis of which he proposed to choose lead counsel. On the appointed day, however, rather than submitting separate budgets, two of the four firms, one from each of the opposing camps, submitted a joint proposal to serve as lead counsel, thereby frustrating the court's effort to inject competition into the process.

Judge Walker flatly rejected this proposal and instead ordered all interested counsel to submit bids, from among which the court would select lead counsel. The bids were required to state the bidder's qualifications for the position and specify the percentage of any recovery the firm would charge as fees and costs. The court prohibited the competing firms from submitting joint proposals and demanded that each bidder certify that its bid was prepared independently and that no part thereof had been revealed to any other bidder.

Following Judge Walker's order, four firms submitted bids for the position of lead counsel. The bid selected proposed a sliding contingency fee arrangement with an early settlement discount and an expense cap of $325,000. Under the sliding fee arrangement, the percentage of plaintiffs' recovery that would constitute the attorney's fee was to decrease as the amount of recovery increased. The court selected this bid because, in its view, (1) the declining percentage-of-recovery fee, unlike a flat or increasing percentage-of-recovery fee, would prevent a windfall recovery by lead counsel and instead would share counsel's "economies of effort" with the class, (2) the expense cap would prevent depletion of the common fund through inordinate litigation expenses, (3) the early settlement discount would guard against cheap, collusive, early settlement, (4) the bid was the most competitive in rates, and (5) the successful bidder was at least as well qualified as the other bidders.

Some significant time after the selection of counsel, the parties in the *Oracle* case arrived at a settlement. Calculation of attorney's fees based on the schedule proposed in the successful bid yielded an attorney's fee of $4.8 million, or 19.2 percent of the settlement recovery. This compared favorably to what counsel would have been awarded using a standard 25 percent recovery method—$6.25 million. It is, of course, impossible to determine what counsel would have received using the lodestar method, as attorney time records are unavailable, and any multiplier the court would have used is unknown. Further, it is impossible to ascertain whether the compensation schedule had any effect, positive or negative, on the overall amount of the settlement.

2.   Subsequent Experiments with Lead Counsel Auctions

Since Judge Walker first experimented with a lead counsel auction, several other courts have followed suit. A number have embraced fee structures with built-in incentives similar to those endorsed in *Oracle*, including the declining percentage-of-recovery fee and the expense cap. Others have endorsed a cap on attorney's fees, presumably in order to prevent windfall recovery by plaintiffs' counsel. Some have adopted Judge Walker's notion of a fee discount for early settlement and requested bids that would adjust the fee based on the stage of the litigation at which the case is resolved, ranging from pleading to motions to dismiss, to summary judgment, to verdict after trial, to appeal. This approach doubtless is based on the view that lead counsel should be encouraged to eschew cheap early settlement and rewarded for the risk attendant to continuing the litigation into a later stage. Still other courts have asked bidders to submit their evaluations of the case, including the probability of success, in order better to compare the competing proposals. Finally, some courts have given a right of first refusal to counsel for the lead plaintiff, allowing counsel to match the terms of the winning bid if it so chooses. This undoubtedly reflects a presumption, *ceteris paribus*, in favor of counsel for the lead plaintiff.

The fee structures adopted in many of these cases attempt to address the high agency costs that pervade the traditional lodestar and percentage-of-recovery methods. Some of them, however, create perverse incentives of their own. The attorney's fee cap, for example, addresses a major concern of the lodestar method—the investment of needless attorney hours in the case, including unnecessarily prolonging the litigation. However, the fee cap creates an incentive for lead counsel to settle the case exactly at the level at which the fee reaches its maximum, even if that level is suboptimal from plaintiffs' perspective. If disclosed to defendants, the fee cap also can lead defendants to exploit the disjuncture of interests between plaintiffs' and their counsel by making a firm settlement offer in the amount that would exactly maximize counsel's fee, even if defense counsel otherwise would be prepared to go higher. Again, lead counsel would have an incentive to agree to settlement in this amount and not press for an award more favorable to plaintiffs.

The same problem arises with the use of a cap on expenses. Although doubtless reducing runaway litigation expenses, the expense cap encourages lead counsel to cease prosecuting the case as soon as expenses have reached the cap level.

The early settlement discount addresses a central risk of the traditional percentage-of-recovery method—early and cheap collusive settlements—by providing lead counsel with increasing marginal returns to effort over time. However, this method risks falling short, as it motivates counsel not to maximize the class' recovery, but merely to extend the duration of the litigation, even if doing so is not in plaintiffs' best interests. Therefore, although this arrangement might improve upon the flat percentage-of-recovery method, it does not align counsel's interests fully with those of the class.

The declining percentage-of-recovery fee structure adopted in *Oracle* and other cases likewise addresses some of the concerns associated with the traditional flat percentage-of-recovery arrangement, yet contains its own problems. By adjusting downward the percentage of the recovery awarded to counsel as plaintiffs' recovery increases, this arrangement arguably limits windfall attorney's fee awards. However, this method may give rise to an attorney incentive problem by creating declining marginal returns to effort for counsel. If counsel's opportunity costs begin to exceed the economic benefit to counsel of continuing to litigate, counsel may be more likely to settle the case and exit the litigation rather than prolonging the litigation and pushing for a higher recovery for the class, even if the added effort would be in plaintiffs' best interest. Again, this method can create an incentive to settle quickly and cheaply, when the returns to effort are highest, rather than investing additional time and maximizing plaintiffs' recovery.

An increasing percentage-of-recovery method likewise does not eliminate fully the disjuncture of interests between plaintiffs and lead counsel. As a rule, this method awards lead counsel a marginally greater percentage of plaintiffs' recovery as the recovery incrementally increases, giving counsel an incentive to avoid premature settlement and push for a higher plaintiffs' recovery. In theory, this approach can reduce agency costs by limiting the circumstances in which costs would outweigh the benefits of continuing to prosecute the litigation. Indeed, it gives counsel an incentive to push any settlement offer higher, as counsel's marginal returns increase with plaintiffs' recovery. However, this fee structure might have the effect of encouraging plaintiffs' lawyers to eschew settlement in search of a very high recovery, even if this strategy is overly risky from plaintiffs' perspective. Further, it is not clear *a priori* how to demarcate the increments of plaintiffs' recovery according to which counsel's fee correspondingly will increase. Setting the increments too low might eliminate the positive effect of the increasing percentage-of-recovery method on counsel's incentives because the opposing parties, after some discovery, will come to value the case in the highest range, eliminating some of the upside benefit to lead counsel of a higher settlement. Conversely, if the increments are set too high, it might become apparent after some discovery that the case will be valued only in the lowest range. This in turn can make the litigation too costly for lead counsel, thereby encouraging premature cheap settlement in order to extricate counsel quickly from the case.

3.   *Possible Drawbacks of Lead Counsel Auctions*

The use of auctions to select lead counsel in class actions has been the subject of much criticism. It has been argued that a simple auction that awards the lead counsel position to the bidder proposing the lowest fee carries substantial risks. Although this approach may keep attorney's fees at a minimum, it limits the potential upside gain for counsel of a substantial award to plaintiff and consequently can encourage quick and cheap settlements. Further, use of price as the sole criterion for selection does nothing to ensure that plaintiffs receive quality representation.

The lead counsel auction unwittingly may undermine also the efficacy of the class action device. Courts in certain cases have been known to award the lead counsel position to the attorney that files the first complaint in the case or to a group of which that attorney is a part. The rationale behind this first-to-file rule is that it creates an incentive for attorneys to ferret out wrongs that may be difficult or impossible for individual plaintiffs ever to identify. By rewarding attorneys that incur these search costs, the award of the lead counsel position to the first attorney to file arguably makes the class action mechanism a more vital means of redress for injured plaintiffs. This, in turn, benefits society by creating a deterrent to wrongful behavior by others.

The routine selection of lead counsel by auction, in contrast, may discourage attorneys from searching out and identifying illegal activity, as the attorney who takes this initiative is not necessarily compensated for his or her effort. This casts doubt on the desirability of holding any auction at all, at least in cases in which attorney initiative played an important role in uncovering the alleged wrong.

Granting counsel to the lead plaintiff a right of first refusal conceivably might address this concern by promising the attorney that incurred the search costs, if willing to offer his or her services at a competitive price, a reward for this action. However, a right of first refusal takes control over the selection of lead counsel out of the court's hands and thereby undermines the court's ability to ensure that the class receives the highest quality representation.

Mindful of these considerations, the Court in this case undertook to establish a method of counsel selection and a fee structure that, in the context of this case, would begin to address some of these concerns and seek to align counsel's and plaintiffs' interests more fully.

III

The Court was mindful of these considerations when considering the possibility of an auction for the position of lead counsel. It concluded that this case is singularly appropriate for the use of an auction for several reasons.

Unlike many class actions, no attorney initiative was required here to ferret out the alleged wrong committed by defendants. Rather, the alleged wrong came to light only after it was announced that the Department of Justice had begun to investigate defendants and that Christie's had sought conditional amnesty from criminal prosecution. The attorney who filed the first complaint in this case therefore is not necessarily any more deserving of the lead counsel position than is any other attorney involved, and selection as lead counsel of someone other than the first-to-file did not deprive an investigating attorney of his or her just reward or dissuade attorneys in other cases from searching out a wrong.

This case is well suited for a lead counsel auction also because several factors are present that permit an auction nearly to approximate an efficient market. First, this case has received extensive media attention and consequently attracted large numbers of able plaintiffs' attorneys. Indeed, whereas most previous experiments with lead counsel auctions have involved bids from very few attorneys, the Court in this case received bids from upward of twenty firms in each of two rounds of bidding. As larger markets lead to more competition, and as competition leads to more efficient results, the number of prospective qualified bidders in this case undoubtedly contributed to the submission of many high quality bids from which to choose.

Second, the form of relief sought in this case is monetary damages, rather than equitable relief. This makes the case easier to evaluate, simplifies the bidding process and permits the Court more easily to compare the bids.

The circumstances in this case allowed the lead counsel auction to approach an efficient market for legal services for a third reason as well—the bidding attorneys had far more information with which to evaluate the case, both as to liability and damages, than typically is available. With respect to liability, this case differs from those in which plaintiffs simply make a claim that defendants deny, or even cases in which the government is undertaking a criminal investigation of defendants. Rather, Christie's reportedly had sought to take advantage of the government's amnesty program and allegedly has received conditional amnesty from prosecution. Although this alone certainly does not establish liability or speak to the scope or temporal duration of the alleged conspiracy, it appears to give plaintiffs a better prospect for success on the merits than is often the case.

With respect to damages, too, there are fewer unknowns here than often is the case. The essence of plaintiffs' claim is that Christie's and Sotheby's acted as duopolists to rig prices in what is principally a two firm market. Significant information is available regarding the market shares of the two companies, and Sotheby's is a publicly held company, the financial statements of which are available and informative. This information alone provided bidders with a strong base of information from which to calculate potential damages. Further, as the case developed, it became clear that there had been at least preliminary settlement negotiations in which defendants furnished financial information to Interim Lead Counsel, and they had ordered expert analysis of this information. The Court ordered that the expert analysis be made available to all bidders prior to the time the bids were due in order to equalize the information base and create the most competitive process possible. In consequence, there was an unusually substantial base of information from which bidders intelligently could evaluate the case.

A.   Reasoning Behind the Court's First Proposed Fee Structure

The Court's first proposed fee structure was designed to avoid the agency pitfalls that characterize many of the fee structures discussed above. In order to create a disincentive to cheap, premature settlement, any recovery less than X was to go entirely to the class, depriving lead counsel of a fee. Although bidders presumably would choose a value for X below their expected value of the case, the pressure of competition would tend to drive X toward the expected recovery, appropriately discounted for the passage of time. Once the potential recovery surpassed X, however, counsel's marginal returns to effort would increase dramatically, as all recovery between X and Y would go entirely to counsel. This was designed to motivate counsel to prosecute the case as effectively as possible. As lead counsel's returns to effort would be greatest if the case were resolved for exactly Y, bidders presumably would tend to choose a value for Y close to the expected value of the case. Finally, twenty-five percent of any recovery in excess of Y was to go to counsel, with the remainder going to the class. This flat percentage-of-recovery arrangement was designed to provide added motivation to counsel to continue to prosecute the case while avoiding the risk of over-prosecution that might result from an increasing percentage-of-recovery fee.

Two other features of the Court's first proposal are worthy of note. The proposal provided that the successful bidder would be required to absorb all litigation expenses. This was intended to create an incentive to keep costs at a minimum and to avoid difficult problems in evaluating *post hoc* the propriety and utility of expenses. Further, the bids were to be kept confidential so as to prevent collusion by bidding attorneys.

B.   Amicus Briefs

On the day the bids were due, the Court received also several *amicus* briefs and submissions from bidders commenting on the proposed fee structure. These submissions raised two principal issues with respect to the proposed auction structure.

First, one of the *amici* rightly pointed out that the initial proposed fee structure, that, by awarding one hundred percent of any recovery between X and Y to counsel, could create a stark conflict of interest between counsel and the class.[52] If, for example, the winning bid placed X at $20 million and Y at $40 million, and if defendants were willing to settle only at $20 million, lead counsel would have an incentive to take the case to trial, even if the likelihood of verdict high of enough to bring added benefit the class (in excess of $40 million) were very small. Trial in such an instance clearly would not be in plaintiffs' best interests. And indeed, were lead counsel to reject such an offer and take the case to trial, as the proposed fee structure implicitly encouraged it to do, counsel well might be in violation of counsel's fiduciary duty to the class.

A second *amicus* pointed out that evaluation of the bids by the Court would be particularly complex by virtue of there being two variables, X and

---

[52] This point was raised by Professor [John] Coffee as well as one of the plaintiffs' counsel.

Y, rather than just one.[53] Without some relatively firm information on the distribution of possible recoveries, it would be difficult intelligently to compare two bids, one of which set slightly lower values on both X and Y than did the other.

C. Reasoning Behind the Court's Second Proposed Fee Structure

In light of these comments, the Court revised the proposed fee structure to better align counsel's and plaintiffs' interests and facilitate ready comparison of the bids. The use of a single variable, X, rather than two, as in the first proposal, was meant to eliminate the potential conflict of interest created by the first proposal. As counsel will receive no fee if plaintiffs' recovery falls below X, counsel clearly is discouraged from settling prematurely and has an incentive to pursue a recovery higher than X. This effort will accrue to the benefit of both counsel and the class. As the value of the case surpasses X, counsel's marginal returns to effort will increase steadily, as they will receive twenty-five percent of any amount in excess of X. Again, this creates an incentive for counsel to litigate the case aggressively. Insofar as the Y variable has been eliminated, so too has the conflict of interest.[55]

The Court's prohibition in the second proposal of disclosure of the terms of the successful bid was designed also to reduce perverse incentives that may have been created under the first proposal. Were defendants apprised of the amount of the bid, they might be inclined to formulate settlement offers in order best to take advantage of any perverse attorney incentives created by the fee structure.

D. Disclosure of Interim Committee's Expert Analysis

The Court's ruling that certain documents in possession of the Interim Committee be disclosed to all plaintiffs' counsel also was intended to improve the quality of the auction process. This expert analysis contained damage assessments that materially would have assisted counsel in the formulation of bids that accurately took into account the value of the case. In consequence, these documents were ordered disclosed so as to even the playing field, facilitate bidders in assessing accurately the value of the case, and improve the overall quality of the bids submitted.

---

[53]This issue was raised by Professors Randall S. Thomas and Robert G. Hansen as well as one of plaintiffs' counsel.

[55]Although generally critical of lead counsel auctions, Professor Coffee in his *amicus* submission to the Court voiced his approval of the use of an auction to select lead counsel in this case. As discussed above, he questioned the Court's first proposed bid structure on the ground that allocating one hundred percent of any recovery between X and Y to counsel would create an unnecessary conflict of interest. He suggested that the Court revise its proposal and employ instead an increasing percentage-of-recovery fee structure in which counsel would be awarded a marginally greater percentage of plaintiffs' recovery as the recovery increased. He proposed the increasing percentage-of-recovery method because, by giving counsel an increasingly large stake in a higher plaintiffs' recovery, such a fee structure would encourage plaintiffs' attorney to "expend the additional effort, accept the additional risk, and wait out the greater delay to obtain such a recovery." See also Coffee, *"Auction Houses": Legal Ethics and the Class Action*, N.Y.L.J. 223, May 18, 2000, at 5. Professor Coffee's position was well taken, and the Court's second proposed fee structure endeavors to do just that. By depriving counsel of a fee for any recovery below X and awarding counsel twenty-five percent of any recovery in excess of X, the Court's second proposed fee structure effectively institutes a two-tier, increasing percentage-of-recovery fee. By giving counsel no stake in any recovery below X and a substantial stake in any recovery in excess thereof, the second proposed fee structure encourages lead counsel to expend the effort, accept the risk and seek to obtain a recovery in excess of X.

E.   Selection of Lead Counsel

After careful review of the bids, the Court selected David Boies and Richard B. Drubel of Boies, Schiller & Flexner, LLP as lead counsel in the case. This choice does not reflect adversely on the capability or integrity of other bidders, many of whom are known to and respected by the Court. It merely reflects the Court's judgment as to which bidder, in all the circumstances, likely would best serve the interests of the plaintiff class. In short, the Court sought to act as a fiduciary to the class in selecting counsel. In light of the pendency of the litigation, the Court is not prepared at this time to disclose the terms of the winning bid.

F.   Potential Agency Costs of Second Proposed Fee Structure

At least one potential incentive problem with the attorney's fee structure remains. Under the bid structure ultimately adopted, it theoretically might become apparent at some point that the case cannot be resolved in an amount greater than X, in which case counsel would receive no compensation. If that occurs, lead counsel will have an incentive to settle the case immediately and make a hasty exit. This may not be in plaintiffs' interests and in any event, certainly raises the specter of an attorney-client conflict of interest. The potential conflict is exacerbated by the fact that lead counsel is required to pay all expenses out of the fee award, raising even further the opportunity costs for counsel of continued prosecution. Nonetheless, it appears that the unique circumstances of this case make this scenario unlikely for several reasons.

First, as in any class action, the Court is vested with authority to reject an inadequate settlement. The Court is fully prepared to do this were it apparent that counsel had failed to represent adequately the class.

Second, the Court in this case was in a uniquely advantageous position from which to evaluate the bids, helping to ensure that the bid selected was not unreasonably high. Following a motion by the government to stay discovery with respect to twelve key documents furnished by Christie's to the Department of Justice, the Court ordered that these documents be made available for *in camera* inspection. The information provided therein gave the Court with an additional tool with which to evaluate the bids, as did the plaintiffs' damage analysis.

Third, the Court has required that notice to the class explain the manner in which lead counsel was selected and the risk for the class that may result from the manner in which lead counsel will be compensated. This is designed to give class members sufficient information with which to evaluate the fee structure, allowing those who oppose it to opt out.

Finally, if the parties arrive at a proposed settlement, the Court will order notice to the class to disclose the fee arrangement. By revealing to the class the incentive structure under which counsel has been working, disclosure of the fee structure should permit class members adequately to evaluate any settlement and encourage any objectors to come forward if that proves appropriate.

IV

The benefits of any auction for lead counsel are difficult to assess. It is simple to compare *post facto* the fee awarded to counsel selected by auction to that which would have been awarded using a traditional percentage-of-recovery method. Likewise, ready comparison can be made with the fees that would have been awarded to other bidders, had their bids been selected. However, the relative value of the attorney's fee does not adequately measure the success of the auction. Instead, the true value of the auction lies in its effect, if any, on the net recovery obtained by plaintiffs. In this respect, the jury on the lead counsel auction in this case is still out, but it is anticipated that the fee structure and the auction process will function as they were intended—to align attorney-client interests more closely, reduce agency costs, and help ensure that the class action mechanism acts as an effective mechanism of justice. . .

NOTES AND QUESTIONS

1. *The Merits of Auction–Based Techniques.* The operation of judicially administered class counsel auctions has garnered significant attention in the academic literature. E.g., Lucian Arye Bebchuk, *The Questionable Case for Using Auctions to Select Lead Counsel,* 80 Wash. U. L.Q. 889 (2002); Jill E. Fisch, *Lawyers on the Auction Block: Evaluating the Selection of Class Counsel by Auction,* 102 Colum. L. Rev. 650 (2002); *Third Circuit Task Force Report on Selection of Class Counsel,* reprinted in 74 Temp. L. Rev. 689 (2001); Randall S. Thomas & Robert G. Hansen, *Auctioning Class Action and Derivative Lawsuits: A Critical Analysis,* 87 Nw. U. L. Rev. 423 (1993).

In an auction as popularly understood—say, for an original Picasso painting—bidders bid based on the price they are willing to pay for the item being auctioned. How were the bids in *Auction Houses* structured? Should the percentage fee for class counsel rise or fall as the recovery for the class increases?

How confident should one be that the winning bidder in an auction structured in the manner of the one in *Auction Houses* will consist of the law firm that is the best representative of the class? In selecting a surgeon to perform a difficult medical procedure on you or a family member—say, an innovative but risky form of surgery—would you select the surgeon who will give you the best price for that procedure? Is there anything about the nature of the auction itself that might lead one to doubt whether the winning bidder has accurately estimated the expected value of the class litigation? Consider here that the winning bidder for a Picasso painting is the person whose bid is more—perhaps, dramatically more—in dollar terms than that of the next-highest bidder.

A class counsel auction takes place after a class action has already been filed. If you were a plaintiffs' law firm, how would the prospect of a class counsel auction—if such a procedure were to become a regular part of the class action landscape—affect your incentive to invest in the development of new areas of class action litigation? Is there an inherent tradeoff between ex ante investment incentives and ex post quality of representation?

2. *The Class Counsel Auction in* Auction Houses. What features of the situation in *Auction Houses* arguably make that case a stronger one for the use of a class counsel auction than other class actions? Put yourself in the position of a law firm considering whether to bid as part of such an auction and, if so, how to structure your bid. How would you go about answering those questions?

3. *Other Proposals.* The class counsel auction in *Auction Houses* auctioned the right to represent the class at the outset of the class action. But auction-based techniques need not necessarily take this form. Consider one proposal that would operate not at the outset of the class action but, instead, after a proposed class settlement agreement is on the table:

. . . Under an ex post bid approach, an objecting class member would guarantee that the class will be no worse off if lead counsel rights are transferred. If an acceptable guarantee is provided, the court would presumptively assign lead counsel rights to the attorney for the dissenting party. The court would mandate that the litigation files be transferred from prior counsel to the new lead counsel. The court could either reject the prior settlement or provisionally approve it but defer a final decision until the results of the litigation under new counsel are known. The case would then proceed as before.

To take a simple example, imagine that counsel seeks judicial approval of a settlement under which the defendant will pay $10 million in exchange for a general release. Out of this amount, counsel requests a fee award of $3 million, leaving $7 million for the class. We assume that these amounts will actually be paid. Suppose further that a class member (or, more realistically, her attorney) believes that the defendant could have been induced to pay more. In such a case the dissenting party would be allowed to post a bond or other form of guarantee for the proposed recovery ($10 million plus any amounts necessary to adjust for delay in payment). If such a bond is posted and found to equal or exceed the relief obtained in the proposed settlement, the court would presumptively transfer lead counsel rights to the dissenter's attorney.

Now suppose that new lead counsel achieves a settlement of $16 million, with a request for $4 million in counsel fees and expenses. Notice of the new settlement would be distributed to the class and the matter would be set for a hearing. In reviewing the fairness of this settlement, the court would take account of the fact that the class has been made better off by the new counsel's actions (by a net of $5 million). The court would also evaluate the requested fee. If the fee is found to be reasonable, the court would distribute the amount between new and old counsel, attempting to make a fair allocation reflecting the respective contributions of both while recognizing that the first counsel did not achieve the best result for the class. The matter could be left to the discretion of the trial court, or the court could experiment with a formula. . . .

What happens if the new counsel obtains an inferior result for the class? Say the new counsel eventually settles the matter for $8 million. The shortfall of $2 million would be taken from the bond. The court would revisit and approve the initial settlement, this time armed with the information that the value obtained for the class in the initial settlement has been tested in an adversarial context and proven to be substantial. The first counsel would revive her request for the originally-negotiated fee of $3 million, which the court would evaluate in light of the fact that the second counsel tried and failed to obtain a better result.

Geoffrey P. Miller, *Competing Bids in Class Action Settlements*, 31 Hofstra L. Rev. 633, 639–41 (2003).

Another proposal would act at the outset of the class litigation but would involve the auctioning not of the right to represent the class but, instead, of the underlying claims of the class members themselves. Class members would receive immediately the funds offered by the winning bidder. And the winning bidder then would litigate, and keep any proceeds from, the underlying claims against the defendant. See Jonathan R. Macey & Geoffrey P. Miller, *The Plaintiffs' Attorney's Role in Class Action and Derivative Litigation: Economic Analysis and Recommendations for Reform*, 58 U. Chi. L. Rev. 1 (1991).

d.   THE PSLRA

The second major innovation in class counsel selection in recent years consists of the enactment of the Private Securities Litigation Reform Act of 1995. As summarized in one early decision:

> The PSLRA, which altered the procedures for bringing class actions under the federal securities laws, was enacted in response to a variety of perceived abuses of the class action procedure. H.R. Rep. No. 104-369, at 31 (1995) *reprinted in* 1996 U.S.C.C.A.N. 730. Among other things Congress was concerned that the lead plaintiff in class action lawsuits was being determined by plaintiffs' lawyers' race to the courthouse. See S. Rep. No. 104-98 (1995) *reprinted in* 1996 U.S.C.C.A.N. 679. In enacting the PSLRA, Congress intended to "increase the likelihood that parties with significant holdings in issuers, whose interests are more strongly aligned with the class of shareholders, will participate in the litigation and exercise control over the selection and actions of plaintiffs counsel." H.R. Rep. No. 104-369, at 32 (1995) *reprinted in* 1996 U.S.C.C.A.N. at 731.

> The PSLRA directs the Court to "appoint as lead plaintiff the *member or members* of the purported plaintiff class that the court determines to be most capable of adequately representing the interests of class members." 15 U.S.C. § 78u–4(a)(3)(B)(i) (emphasis added). The Act creates a "rebuttable presumption . . . that the most adequate plaintiff . . . is the person or group of persons that (aa) has either filed the complaint or made a motion in response to a notice . . . (bb) in the determination of the court, has the largest financial interest in the relief sought by the class; and (cc) otherwise satisfies the requirements of Rule 23 of the Federal Rules of Civil Procedure." 15 U.S.C. § 78u–4(a)(3)(B)(iii)(I).

> The presumption may be rebutted "only upon proof by a member of the purported plaintiff class that the presumptively most adequate plaintiff—(aa) will not fairly and adequately represent the interests of the class; or (bb) is subject to unique defenses that render such plaintiff incapable of adequately representing the class." 15 U.S.C. § 78u–4(a)(3)(B)(iii)(II). Before obtaining discovery in this regard, the objecting plaintiff must demonstrate a reasonable basis for a finding "that the presumptively most adequate plaintiff is incapable of representing the class." 15 U.S.C. § 78u–4(a)(3)(B)(iv).

> Finally, the PSLRA states that "[t]he most adequate plaintiff shall, subject to the approval of the court, select and retain counsel to represent the class." 15 U.S.C. § 78u–4(a)(3)(B)(v).

In re Oxford Health Plans, Inc., Sec. Litig., 182 F.R.D. 42, 43–44 (S.D.N.Y. 1998). The provisions of the PSLRA concerning the selection of class counsel stem from an influential law review article: Elliott J. Weiss & John S. Beckerman, *Let the Money Do the Monitoring: How Institutional Investors*

[handwritten margin note: Rebuttable Presumption Standard for Class Rep]

Can Reduce Agency Costs in Securities Class Actions, 104 Yale L.J. 2053 (1995).

Early litigation under the PSLRA raised the question whether the lead plaintiff provisions of that Act permit the court, on its own initiative, to select class counsel by way of an auction. Appellate courts have said "no," reasoning that a judicially-supervised auction is inconsistent with the specification in the PSLRA that "[t]he most adequate plaintiff shall, subject to the approval of the court, select and retain counsel to represent the class." *In re Cavanaugh*, 306 F.3d 726 (9th Cir. 2002); *In re Cendant Corp. Litig.*, 264 F.3d 201 (3d Cir. 2001).

The PSLRA, if anything, marks a return—if only in the context of securities litigation—to the ideal expressed in early class action decisions: that the class representative might exercise meaningful supervision over class counsel. The "lead plaintiff" provisions of the PSLRA seek to invigorate this kind of supervision. But is that a realistic aspiration? The sorts of large institutional investors likely to have the largest financial stake in a given securities class action are preferred as lead plaintiffs by the PRLRA, in keeping with the notion of "let[ting] the money do the monitoring." But such investors are not required by the PSLRA to serve as lead plaintiffs, as the following empirical research underscores based upon experience in the post-PSLRA period:

James D. Cox & Randall S. Thomas, *With the Assistance of Dana Kiku, Does the Plaintiff Matter? An Empirical Analysis of Lead Plaintiffs in Securities Class Actions*

106 Colum. L. Rev. 1587, 1587–90, 1602–10 (2006)

[M]ore than ten years after the enactment of the lead plaintiff provision, the claim that the lead plaintiff, and particularly the lead plaintiff that is an institutional investor, is a more effective monitor of class counsel in securities fraud class actions continues to be intuitively appealing, but remains unproven. In this study, we inquire empirically whether the lead plaintiff provision has performed as projected. . . .

Disturbingly, many institutions have been reluctant to assume the role of lead plaintiff, especially in smaller cases. The available evidence suggests that, as late as 2001, institutions had appeared in only 5 to 10% of all securities fraud class actions, although there are indications that they are getting involved more frequently in recent years. Indeed, in our study of 388 settlements, pension funds and other financial institutions represented a very small percentage of the post-PSLRA plaintiffs. As our data reveals, by any metric—for example, the number of settled cases, the dollar amount of settlements, or the provable losses suffered by the class—a securities class action suit's representative is far more likely to be an aggregation of nonfinancial institutional investors or even a single individual.

. . . Th[e] reluctance [of institutional investors to serve as lead plaintiffs] may be explained by the costs of doing so. The SEC's study of the first year's experience under the PSLRA found that institutional investors identified a number of concerns about the costs and potential liability that they would face if they became lead plaintiffs. In particular, they identified the threat of discovery into the institutional investor's business, the amount of time that they would need to spend to manage the case, the potential for disclosure of proprietary nonpublic information, and the threat of suit by other disgruntled plaintiffs. Others have noted that activist institutions also need to worry about the effects of potential access to inside information on their trading activity, their loss of preferential access to information from defendant companies, as well as possible political pressure. Our conversations with attorneys active in securities litigation suggest that the potential hardships of being a lead plaintiff are an important factor that institutional investors are still considering before acting as lead plaintiffs, although the benefits of doing so may have become increasingly apparent to them. We discuss some of these costs below.

1.   *Discovery into the Lead Plaintiff's Business Practices.*—The possibility that defendants—and other plaintiffs' law firms competing to obtain the lead plaintiff position—might seek to engage in disruptive discovery about institutional investors' internal business practices and trading activities was well understood prior to the passage of PSLRA. . . .

[T]he PSLRA conditions the ability of other potential class representatives to conduct discovery to challenge whether a petitioner should be appointed lead plaintiff to first demonstrating "a reasonable basis for a finding that the presumptively most adequate plaintiff is incapable of adequately representing the class." [15 U.S.C. § 78u–4(a)(3)(B)(iv).]

Our discussions with attorneys in this area lead us to believe that discovery issues, while initially of some concern to institutions, have not proved to be too onerous. Defendants' counsel have quickly learned that the investment advisors who advise institutional investors regarding securities transactions are extremely knowledgeable about the company's securities filings and its financial statements. In this sense, the lead plaintiff may well have more of the characteristics of a reasonable investor than do many of the class members. As defendants contemplate their lack of success in demonstrating that the plaintiffs were not acting in reliance on the company's statements or did not understand the meaning of its disclosures, their interest in pursuing discovery about the institutional investors' actions has declined.

2.   *Greater Recoveries for Institutions That Pursue Their Own Actions.*—Institutional investors with large potential claims have sometimes found it more advantageous to act for themselves rather than on behalf of all other investors. Institutional investors with such claims may believe that their claims are better pursued as individual claims than as part of a class action. They may believe that, in a class action, their stronger claims will be combined with weaker claims to dilute their ultimate share of the settlement value. Some evidence that has been gathered supports this point. Moreover, institutions, with their cadres of analysts, may be in a better position than other investors to sue under section 18 of the Securities Exchange Act of 1934, where they can likely meet its double reliance standard and thereby escape the necessity of pleading scienter.

On the other hand, institutions that opt out of a class action to pursue their own individual action do face risks. Mainly, such institutions are no longer able to control the class action litigation. But this should not be a major deterrent. To be sure, an inadequate record and a poor settlement in a parallel class are likely to affect adversely the institution's individual action. However, many of the public pension funds that have been most active in this area want to try to fix the system. They desire not only to improve the effectiveness of class action litigation, but also to strengthen the financial reporting process through corporate governance changes and to encourage recoveries from individual corporate officers and directors so that institutional plaintiffs do not bear indirectly some of the cost of the suit's successful prosecution. These institutions may be limited in the number of cases in which they can get involved and would prefer to deploy their resources in class actions where they can have a broader impact.

3. *Disincentives to Becoming a Lead Plaintiff.*—Institutional lead plaintiffs incur costs when monitoring the actions of lead counsel. These costs include investigating the claims made, selecting lead counsel, reading any complaint or pleadings filed by counsel, and expending time and resources to monitor the prosecution and possible settlement of the action. Related to such costs are potential "free rider problems, because institutions, particularly those concerned about minimizing administrative costs generally, are rationally apt to prefer that another investor take the initiative to become involved." In fact, one attorney who represents institutional investors in securities fraud class actions told us that the first question his clients ask before considering undertaking a lead plaintiff position is whether any other institution is willing to do it.

Free rider problems have been a barrier to institutional investor activism in almost every area of corporate governance. The fact remains that, in the United States, even the largest institutional investors rarely own more than 5% of a company's stock, making it imperative that they act as part of a group of investors if they wish to have a significant impact. In all these situations, the costs of initiating and sponsoring action are borne by the activists, while any benefits fall proportionately among all members of the group. Lead plaintiff proponents claim that free rider problems should not pose the same problems for institutions choosing to pursue that position because an institution does not need any other institution's support to do so. In fact, the passivity of other institutions enhances the chances of the selection of activist funds as lead plaintiff, assuming such an institution chooses to act.

However, institutional investors' initial unwillingness to participate as lead counsel could well have been attributable to free rider problems. Acting as an effective lead plaintiff can be a very time-consuming task in complex, aggressively litigated cases, where multiple suits against different sets of defendants at different points in time may be necessary in order to maximize the class recovery. Of course, some cases are much more straightforward and require less oversight, and some institutions will devote less time than is needed to achieve the most appropriate client-driven litigation goals. But, in general, an institutional investor lead plaintiff will probably *I.I. aren't compensated for time lost.* need to devote significant amounts of out-of-pocket expenses, legal staff time, and investment staff time. While out-of-pocket expenses are reimbursed in successful actions, the courts have only sometimes agreed to compensate institutions for the time spent by their in-house professional staff at market rates.

A number of our survey respondents identified monitoring costs as an important issue in their decisionmaking process, although their estimates of the total time involved ranged widely from 40 to 100 hours to as much as 250 to 1000 hours. . . . [W]e obtained very complete estimates from the general counsel of a leading institutional investor. Using these estimates and valuing the institution's average personnel cost at $100 per hour, which seems quite low to us, then the cost of a reasonable case management effort by an institutional investor lead plaintiff in an "average" case would total between $25,000 and $100,000. Even though some institutional investors believe that they can double or even quadruple their recovery by serving as active lead plaintiffs, these are substantial upfront costs to bear relative to the incremental benefits institutions expect their involvement to yield. Moreover, several of our survey respondents stated that they had very limited manpower to staff cases and therefore chose not to become involved as lead plaintiff in many cases.

An individual investor, or even an aggregation of individuals, is not likely to engage in the extensive involvement described in the preceding paragraphs at each of many stages of litigation by an institution. Our data set reflects that the individual investor is not a repeat player in the process as is the case with some public pension funds. Moreover, the individual investor is not likely to have an internal staff to involve it in the monitoring assessments that occur at multiple stages of the suit's life. Hence, these monitoring costs are not sunk costs, as they are in large part with institutions, but rather require the individuals to devote new resources to the enterprise. In light of these facts, individuals are likely to underinvest in monitoring. We therefore do not believe it is likely that lead plaintiffs who are not such a financial institution are likely to produce gains that approach those associated with a lead plaintiff who is a financial institution. . . .

Finally, we would be remiss if we did not mention two other important obstacles to institutional investors becoming lead plaintiffs. First, a number of our survey respondents noted the lack of information about the case at the very early stage of the litigation—when they are forced to decide whether to become lead plaintiffs—as a barrier to serving as class counsel. In essence, PSLRA gives institutions a maximum of sixty days to make this choice, which essentially limits the information on which they base their decision to the complaint, the publicly available information about the company, and the size of their estimated loss. [15 U.S.C. § 77z–1(a)(3)(A)(i)(II).] Sixty days appears to be a relatively brief time for institutional investors to inform themselves fully enough to decide whether to become a lead plaintiff, especially where the loss estimates generated at this stage can vary wildly.

Second, many institutions have commercial relationships that may be jeopardized if they become lead plaintiffs. Even though financial institutions are not monolithic in their missions or operations, many institutions' managers face conflicts of interest when considering whether to become a lead plaintiff. Banks, mutual funds, and insurance companies—three of the five largest classes of financial institutions—are each vendors of financial services and products. Their customers include the corporations and accounting firms who are the grist of securities class actions. And, to the extent that public pension funds and endowments appear not to have the same conflicts as other types of institutions, those conflicts appear when the public pension fund or endowment depends on outside money managers who have such conflicts. These relationships are jeopardized if the institution becomes the lead plaintiff in a class action focused on its customers or benefactors.

[In addition,] financial service providers are not eager to become, or to align themselves with, antagonists of their clientele. This observation likely explains why our data contains no settlement where a bank, mutual fund, or insurance company has served as a lead plaintiff in a securities class action. Our intuition is that such institutions are generally unwilling to lead the assault on executives who have issued misleading reports if such visibility could pose problems in selling financial services to other executives who likely share the view that most securities class action suits are strike suits. Consorting with "class action lawyers" does not win one friends in the executive suites of America or at the club. Furthermore, there is only the thinnest social divide between executives of banks, insurance companies, and mutual funds and executives of industrial firms. These are groups of individuals who understand one another and who are aware of the price to be incurred by failing to honor that understanding. By default, therefore, it is the public or union pension fund that is most likely to serve as a lead plaintiff because it is the type of institution not likely to have such a commercial interest that would be jeopardized by aligning itself with the plaintiffs' bar. [T]hese are the overwhelming majority of institutional investors that are appearing as lead plaintiffs in our sample. Thus, there are distinct imputed costs to becoming a lead plaintiff when the institution is also a vendor of commercial products to those who may become the targets of future securities class actions.

NOTES AND QUESTIONS

1.   *Limits on Incentive Awards to Lead Plaintiffs.* The PSLRA permits court-ordered awards to class representatives but limits such awards to "reasonable costs and expenses (including lost wages) directly relating to the representation of the class." 15 U.S.C. § 78u–4(a)(4). The PSLRA also requires class representatives to swear that they "will not accept any payment" beyond their "pro rata share of any [class] recovery." 15 U.S.C. § 78u–4(a)(2)(A)(vi). The Conference Committee Report on the PSLRA flatly states that "[l]ead plaintiffs are not entitled to a bounty for their services," reasoning that "bounty payments or bonuses" in the pre-PSLRA period "encouraged the filing of abusive cases." H.R. Rep. No. 104–39, at 33 (1995), *reprinted in* 1995 U.S.C.C.A.N. 730, 732.

Is there a mismatch between the forward-looking prescription of the PSLRA for class representation (invigoration of institutional investors as presumptive lead plaintiffs) and the backward-looking ban on "bonuses" that would provide such investors with financial rewards beyond their pro rata share of any class recovery plus costs and expenses? Remember that, outside of litigation, we are talking here about institutions that spend their time chasing after big financial rewards.

2.   *Leaving Money on the Table.* Additional empirical research by Professors Cox and Thomas documents that "less than thirty percent of institutional investors with provable losses perfect their claims in [securities class action] settlements." James D. Cox & Randall S. Thomas, *Letting Billions Slip Through Your Fingers: Empirical Evidence and Legal Implications of the Failure of Financial Institutions to Participate in Securities Class Action Settlements*, 58 Stan. L. Rev. 411, 413 (2005). Put less formally, institutional investors appear to be leaving unclaimed considerable sums of money to which they are entitled under class settlements. In light of the $5.45 billion distributed by way of securities class settlements in 2004, a "back-of-the-envelope" calculation based on the Cox–Thomas data suggests that "each year slightly more than $1 billion is left on the settlement table by nonfiling financial institutions." *Id.* at 412. Does this suggest that institutional investors are falling down on the job or that they are appropriately scouring the financial world for new, high-yield investment opportunities rather than shifting money around to address past losses?

3.   The Institutional Investor Model Matures. Although institutional investors rarely served as lead plaintiffs in the years immediately following the enactment of the PSLRA, their participation eventually increased. Today, they are fixtures of the securities class action landscape. As researchers studied the impact of their participation, it initially seemed that they "cherry picked" the cases, taking control of the best ones while leaving the weaker ones to others.

It now seems clear that institutional investors do improve class action performance. According to Professor Michael Perino, cases led by institutional investors generate larger recoveries and recover higher fractions of investors' losses. Institutional investors reduce lawyers' fees too. Fee requests in cases led by these investors were 5.3 percent lower than requests in cases led by other investors. Michael Perino, *Institutional Activism Through Litigation: An Empirical Analysis of Public Pension Fund Participation in Securities Class Actions*, 9 Journal of Empirical Legal Stud. 368 (2012).

e.   WHY SHOULD CLASS COUNSEL RECEIVE A FEE AWARD?

Although subsections (g) and (h) of Rule 23 establish procedures for awarding fees in class actions, they do not empower judges to transfer dollars from class members to lawyers serving as class counsel. That authority comes from a body of substantive common law that, today, seems somewhat obscure: the law of restitution, which governs the allocation of benefits in the absence of contracts. Because class members and class counsel cannot bargain directly, the law of restitution sets the terms of their financial relationship. This is true even when a statute entitles a class that prevails in litigation to a fee award from a defendant. The class, not class counsel, holds the right to the fee award. *Evans v. Jeff D.*, 475 U.S. 717 (1986). The law of restitution transfers the proceeds generated by the exercise of that right to the class' attorney.

Subsection 1 begins with the basic question of why class counsel should receive a fee award. Subsection 2 addresses situations in which class action litigation takes place under statutes that contain fee-shifting provisions. Subsection 3 concludes with the interplay between fee award considerations and class settlement design.

(1) The Restitutionary Basis of Fee Awards

Boeing Co. v. Van Gemert

444 U.S. 472 (1980)

■ MR. JUSTICE POWELL delivered the opinion of the Court.

The question presented in this class action is whether a proportionate share of the fees awarded to lawyers who represented the successful class may be assessed against the unclaimed portion of the fund created by a judgment.

I

In March 1966, The Boeing Co. called for the redemption of certain convertible debentures. Boeing announced the call through newspaper notices and mailings to investors who had registered their debentures. The notices, given in accordance with the indenture agreement, recited that each $100 amount of principal could be redeemed for $103.25 or converted into two shares of the company's common stock. They set March 29 as the deadline for the exercise of conversion rights. Two shares of the company's common stock on that date were worth $316.25. When the deadline expired, the holders of debentures with a face value of $1,544,300 had not answered the call. These investors were left with the right to redeem their debentures for slightly more than face value.

Van Gemert and several other nonconverting debenture holders brought a class action against Boeing in the United States District Court for the Southern District of New York. They claimed that Boeing had violated federal securities statutes as well as the law of New York by failing to give them reasonably adequate notice of the redemption. As damages, they sought the difference between the amount for which their debentures could be redeemed and the value of the shares into which the debentures could have been converted. . . .

[handwritten: Failed to give Reasonable Adequate Notice]

The [district] court [ultimately] established the amount of Boeing's liability to the class as a whole. It provided that respondents, "in behalf of all members of the plaintiff class, . . . shall recover as their damages . . . the principal sum of $3,289,359 together with [prejudgment] interest. . . ." The court then fixed the amount that each member of the class could recover on a principal amount of $100 in debentures. Each individual recovery was to carry its proportionate share of the total amount allowed for attorney's fees, expenses, and disbursements. That share, the court declared, "shall bear the same ratio to all such fees, expenses and disbursements as such class member's recovery shall bear to the total recovery" awarded the class. Finally, the court ordered Boeing to deposit the amount of the judgment into escrow at a commercial bank, and it appointed a Special Master to administer the judgment and pass on the validity of individual claims. The court retained jurisdiction pending implementation of its judgment.

Boeing appealed only one provision of the judgment. It claimed that attorney's fees could not be awarded from the unclaimed portion of the judgment fund for at least two reasons. First, the equitable doctrine that allows the assessment of attorney's fees against a common fund created by the lawyers' efforts was inapposite because the money in the judgment fund would not benefit those class members who failed to claim it. Second, because Boeing had a colorable claim for the return of the unclaimed money, awarding attorney's fees from those funds might violate the American rule against shifting fees to the losing party. Therefore, Boeing contended, the District Court should award attorney's fees from only the portion of the fund actually claimed by class members. [The Second Circuit affirmed.]

[handwritten: Atty fees could not be awarded from unclaimed funds]

[handwritten: Boeing says it has claim to unclaimed funds]

We granted certiorari, and we now affirm.

II

Since the decisions in *Trustees v. Greenough*, 105 U.S. 527 (1882), and *Central R.R. & Banking Co. v. Pettus*, 113 U.S. 116 (1885), this Court has recognized consistently that a litigant or a lawyer who recovers a common fund for the benefit of persons other than himself or his client is entitled to a reasonable attorney's fee from the fund as a whole. The common-fund doctrine reflects the traditional practice in courts of equity, and it stands as a well-recognized exception to the general principle that requires every litigant to bear his own attorney's fees. The doctrine rests on the perception that persons who obtain the benefit of a lawsuit without contributing to its cost are unjustly enriched at the successful litigant's expense. Jurisdiction over the fund involved in the litigation allows a court to prevent this inequity by assessing attorney's fees against the entire fund, thus spreading fees proportionately among those benefited by the suit.

. . .Once the class representatives have established the defendant's liability and the total amount of damages, members of the class can obtain their share of the recovery simply by proving their individual claims against the judgment fund. This benefit devolves with certainty upon the identifiable persons whom the court has certified as members of the class. Although the full value of the benefit to each absentee member cannot be determined until he presents his claim, a fee awarded against the entire judgment fund will shift the costs of litigation to each absentee in the exact proportion that the value of his claim bears to the total recovery. See generally John P. Dawson, *Lawyers and Involuntary Clients in Public Interest Litigation*, 88 Harv. L. Rev. 849, 916–22 (1975).

In this case, the named respondents have recovered a determinate fund for the benefit of every member of the class whom they represent. Boeing did not appeal the judgment awarding the class a sum certain. Nor does Boeing contend that any class member was uninjured by the company's failure adequately to inform him of his conversion rights. Thus, the damage to each class member is simply the difference between the redemption price of his debentures and the value of the common stock into which they could have been converted. To claim their logically ascertainable shares of the judgment fund, absentee class members need prove only their membership in the injured class. Their right to share the harvest of the lawsuit upon proof of their identity, whether or not they exercise it, is a benefit in the fund created by the efforts of the class representatives and their counsel. Unless absentees contribute to the payment of attorney's fees incurred on their behalves, they will pay nothing for the creation of the fund and their representatives may bear additional costs. The judgment entered by the District Court and affirmed by the Court of Appeals rectifies this inequity by requiring every member of the class to share attorney's fees to the same extent that he can share the recovery. Since the benefits of the class recovery have been "traced with some accuracy" and the costs of recovery have been "shifted with some exactitude to those benefiting," we conclude that the attorney's fee award in this case is a proper application of the common-fund doctrine.

III

The common-fund doctrine, as applied in this case, is entirely consistent with the American rule against taxing the losing party with the victor's attorney's fees. The District Court's judgment assesses attorney's fees against a fund awarded to the prevailing class. Since there was no appeal from the judgment that quantified Boeing's liability Boeing presently has no interest in any part of the fund. The members of the class, whether or not they assert their rights, are at least the equitable owners of their respective shares in the recovery. Any right that Boeing may establish to the return of money eventually unclaimed is contingent on the failure of absentee class members to exercise their present rights of possession. Although Boeing itself cannot be obliged to pay fees awarded to the class lawyers, its latent claim against unclaimed money in the judgment fund may not defeat each class member's equitable obligation to share the expenses of litigation.

The judgment of the Court of Appeals is

Affirmed.

■ [The dissenting opinion of JUSTICE REHNQUIST is omitted.]

NOTES AND QUESTIONS

1. *The Common–Fund Theory and Restitution.* The *Boeing* Court grounds the fee award to class counsel squarely in restitutionary principles— specifically, the notion that, absent such an award, class members would be unjustly enriched by the efforts of class counsel to create a common fund for their benefit by way of the class litigation. One commentator explains the logic behind this restitutionary conception of the fee award:

> It is difficult to explain why absent plaintiffs are obligated to pay attorneys who represent plaintiff classes for the same reason it is difficult to explain why it is proper to tax people in order to pay the salaries of government officials. In both instances, people are charged without their consent. They are forced to pay even though, if asked, they might and probably would prefer to keep the money for themselves.

> People sometimes attempt to justify taxation by arguing that forced exchanges of money and governmental services leave citizens better off. The underlying premise is that the benefits citizens receive are more valuable than the taxes they pay. Unfortunately, this simple argument is inadequate to generate an obligation on the part of absent class members to pay attorneys' fees as restitution. The law of restitution disfavors forced exchanges, even exchanges that leave the parties better off. Although the mandate to cure unjust enrichment is clear, a basic principle of restitution is that a person who receives a benefit voluntarily conferred in the absence of mistake, coercion, request, or emergency is not unjustly enriched and has no obligation to pay. The presumption is that recipient R incurs a duty to pay provider P only when P bargains for compensation in advance and R agrees to pay. The presumption would survive a showing that a forced exchange of benefits for compensation would leave R better off.

> Absent plaintiffs do not hire attorneys; the truth is more nearly the reverse. Attorneys acting for named plaintiffs draw absent plaintiffs into class actions involuntarily and absent plaintiffs cannot always extricate themselves once they are joined. Nor do absent plaintiffs exert much control over the way class actions are run. In many cases, they cannot even reject the benefits class actions provide. Absent plaintiffs are passive parties who "sit back and allow the litigation to run its course."

> Given the passivity of absent plaintiffs, the law of restitution would presume that they have no obligation to pay for the benefits class actions provide. A restitutionary theory of attorneys' fees in class actions must overcome that presumption. It must show that "accepting or even simply receiving the benefits of a [class action] can . . . obligate an individual to contribute" toward the expenses of litigation, "even though the individual has not actually consented" to pay in advance.

> [A]ccording to the law of restitution, it is appropriate to require absent class members to pay attorneys' fees when all of the following conditions are met:

(1) It is impracticable for a group of absent plaintiffs to organize a group lawsuit by voluntary means;

(2) As a result of successful class litigation, absent plaintiffs enjoy benefits they would not otherwise receive;

(3) Absent plaintiffs do not receive the benefits as gifts;

(4) Absent plaintiffs either voluntarily accept the benefits they receive or have no opportunity to decline them; and

(5) Absent plaintiffs are better off receiving benefits and paying attorneys' fees than doing without the benefits entirely.

I contend that when these conditions are met, the law of restitution requires absent plaintiffs to pay attorneys' fees. They have a duty to compensate attorneys who litigate class actions for them because, under the circumstances, it is just and practicable to require them to pay.

Charles Silver, *A Restitutionary Theory of Attorneys' Fees in Class Actions*, 76 Cornell L. Rev. 656, 663–66 (1991).

f.   FEE–SHIFTING STATUTES

In *Cendant PRIDES*, the court distinguished fee awards from a "common fund" created by the class action and fee awards made pursuant to a "fee-shifting" statute. As typically formulated in federal law, fee-shifting statutes authorize the court to award attorneys' fees and costs to the "prevailing party." Fee-shifting statutes with this wording are a widespread feature of federal civil rights legislation, appearing in Titles II and VII of the Civil Rights Act of 1964, 42 U.S.C. §§ 2000a–3(b) and 2000e5(k) (addressing discrimination in public accommodations and employment, respectively), the Voting Rights Act Amendments of 1975, 42 U.S.C. § 1973l(e), the Civil Rights Attorney's Fees Awards Act of 1976, 42 U.S.C. § 1988, the Fair Housing Amendments Act of 1988, 42 U.S.C. § 3613(c)(2), and the Americans with Disabilities Act of 1990, 42 U.S.C. § 12205, among other statutes. When a fee-shifting statute applies, that statute governs the making of a fee award, not restitutionary principles such as the common-fund theory.

As interpreted, the reference to "prevailing party" in many statutes essentially means prevailing plaintiff. However, in other statutes, such as the Copyright Act, which provide for bilateral fee-shifting, the same language is taken to mean either party. Absent "special circumstances," a prevailing plaintiff qualifies for a fee award pursuant to a fee-shifting statute, whereas a prevailing defendant may obtain a fee award only if the plaintiff's lawsuit is "frivolous, unreasonable, or without foundation." *Christiansburg Garment Co. v. EEOC*, 434 U.S. 412, 417, 421 (1978). Most importantly, an award made pursuant to a fee-shifting statute shifts financial responsibility for attorneys' fees from the plaintiff (as under the common-fund theory) to the defendant.

In a significant decision overturning the practices of many federal circuits under fee-shifting statutes, the Supreme Court in *Buckhannon Board & Care Home, Inc. v. West Virginia Dep't of Health & Human Res.*, 532 U.S. 598 (2001), held that the term "prevailing plaintiff" means "one who has been awarded some relief by the court," such as through a judgment on the merits or a court-ordered consent decree. *Id.* at 603. Given that class actions may be settled only upon the issuance of a judgment, per Rule 23(e), class settlements too would suffice to trigger the application of fee-shifting statutes. The term "prevailing plaintiff," however, does not encompass situations in which there has been "no judicially sanctioned change in the legal relationship of the parties." See *id.* at 603–05.

In *Buckhannon Board*, for example, a plaintiff class had sued for injunctive and declaratory relief against certain West Virginia regulatory requirements governing assisted living residences, alleging that those requirements violated the federal Fair Housing Amendments Act and the Americans with Disabilities Act. While the class action was pending, the West Virginia legislature repealed the requirements in question. Although the state's action effectively gave the plaintiff class members what they were seeking—relief from the allegedly invalid regulatory requirements— the Court held that the class members nonetheless did not constitute "prevailing plaintiff[s]" within the meaning of the applicable fee-shifting statutes, for the change in West Virginia law had not come by way of *judicially sanctioned* relief.

g. STRATEGIC EFFECTS OF FEE CONSIDERATIONS ON CLASS SETTLEMENTS

Given the coexistence of both lodestar and percentage fee methods and both the common-fund theory and fee-shifting statutes, is there a dangerous potential for what one might describe as arbitrage across the various categories? Consider the following case:

Staton v. Boeing Co.

327 F.3d 938 (9th Cir. 2003)

■ BERZON, CIRCUIT JUDGE.

This case involves a consent decree in an employment discrimination class lawsuit. The action was brought in 1998 by a class of approximately 15,000 African–American employees of the Boeing Company ("Boeing or the Company") against the Company. The decree requires Boeing to pay $7.3 million in monetary relief to the class, less [various adjustments], and releases Boeing from race discrimination-related and other claims. It further provides for certain injunctive relief, although much of this relief appears to be largely precatory in nature. Finally, the decree awards to the lawyers for the class ("class counsel") $4.05 million in attorneys' fees.

A group of class members objected to the proposed consent decree, arguing that the class fails to meet the certification requirements . . . for class actions and that the settlement contained in the decree is unfair, inadequate and unreasonable. . . . The district court approved the decree despite the objections, and the objectors appealed to this court. . . .

We hold that the district court acted within its discretion in certifying the case as a class action. . . . We agree with the objectors, however, that the district court should not have approved the settlement agreement under Rule 23(e), because of several considerations relating to the award of attorneys' fees . . .

II. DISCUSSION

. . .

B. *The Settlement . . .*

2. *The Settlement as a Whole*

In this case, we are somewhat uneasy, reading the settlement as a whole, about whether in reaching the settlement, class counsel adequately pursued the interests of the class as a whole. Provisions giving rise to this unease include the extent of Boeing's release from liability, which includes any breach of contract action by any class member; [a] stipulation that the prohibition on race discrimination cannot be enforced in individual cases; the numerous instances in which Boeing is permitted to develop its own remedial schemes (and, in some instances, unilaterally to abandon such schemes as infeasible), with an obligation only to consult with class counsel but with no obligation to submit to any enforcement or dispute resolution mechanism if the schemes are unsatisfactory; the limited role for the consultant Boeing is required to hire; and the incorporation in the agreement of promotion and complaint programs Boeing had already developed and implemented, with no obligation on the part of the Company to continue those programs in their present form or alternatively to substitute programs of the same efficacy.

Further, the district court did not entirely appreciate the limited scope of many of the injunctive provisions of the decree. For example, the court opined that "changes *will be made* in the procedure for resolving discrimination related complaints." (Emphasis added.) In fact, the changes in the complaint procedure had already been implemented, and, while the agreement indicates that the implementation appeared adequate, Boeing made no commitment in the decree to continue the same process in effect during the term of the agreement (or even to assure that any replacement process would be as effective as the present one).

We also note that, unlike the district court, we decline to rely in our assessment of the injunctive provisions upon "the approval of several disinterested experts in race discrimination, the Reverend Jesse Jackson first among them." The experts' positive assessments all rely heavily on the assertion that the decree provides all members of the class with three years of free legal assistance to, as one declaration put it, "review their employment history, review proposed or actual job opportunities, . . . assist them with job applications, and . . . challenge the selection of someone else for the jobs." As noted above, Boeing has expressed its skepticism that the decree embodies any obligation on the part of class counsel to provide such free individualized legal assistance or on the part of Boeing to respond to such individualized representation by attorneys. Reading the decree carefully, we share that skepticism.

The attorneys' fees provision provides $750,000 to class counsel for "monitoring, administration, implementation and defense of the Decree," including, in particular, "Class Counsel's time and expenses involved in the processing of claims under [the Decree] and the distribution of all monetary awards . . . including expenditures by Class Counsel in regard to compensating the Claims Arbitrator. . . ." That language hardly encompasses the individualized representation for future claims of discrimination the experts' declarations assume. Nor does any provision in the decree specifically require Boeing to confer with class counsel about individuals' promotion applications. It may be that class counsel, commendably, intend to attempt to provide such individual representation, although nothing in the factual record indicates a commitment to do so. If so, $750,000 is unlikely to go very far in compensating class counsel for such representation, given the size of the class and the other representational duties for which the decree specifically earmarks the money. Since the experts' understanding of the proposed settlement appears less than precise, the district court should not have relied so heavily upon those assessments, and we do not do so.

Despite all of the foregoing concerns, we would not overturn the district court's determination to approve the settlement as fair were the release and injunctive provisions the only aspects of the decree that are troublesome. As the district court noted, plaintiffs' risk of losing the case on the merits was quite high; Boeing had an unbroken history of prevailing in discrimination cases; maintaining the class action was not a foregone conclusion; promotion decisions, a primary focus of the litigation, are largely discretionary; and discovery was likely to be extremely expensive for the plaintiffs and class counsel, whose resources are undoubtedly more limited than those of Boeing. The total monetary relief provided in the proposed settlement agreement is not insubstantial, either in total or on a pro rata basis given the number of claimants, and the balance between retrospective and prospective relief is usually one for the litigants to determine. Nor do the injunctive provisions themselves raise any flags regarding favoritism for some members of the class over others. No class member is assured a promotion or any other future privilege not accorded to others, nor are certain groups of class members treated more favorably than others for purposes of future relief. . . .

Furthermore, we are told that the decree in large part incorporates already-existing Boeing programs rather than creating new ones because Boeing determined once the lawsuit was filed to devise new, more effective promotion and complaint policies so as to avoid similar charges in the future. Although the failure of the consent decree to assure continuation of these same or equally effective programs in the future remains troubling, we cannot reject out of hand this explanation for crediting existent programs as part of the prospective relief attained by the proposed decree.

In short, the injunctive aspects of the proposed settlement neither directly reflect pursuit of self-interest by favored members of the class nor, standing alone, strike us as being so beyond the pale as a compromise of claims to merit reversal of the district court's fairness assessment. At the same time, the questionable factors we have noted do suggest the possibility that class counsel and the IIRs *could* have agreed to relatively weak prospective relief because of other inducements offered to them in the course of the negotiations. We therefore scrutinize with particular care the aspects of the proposed settlement that provide monetary benefits directly to class counsel and to the IIRs: [particularly,] the attorneys' fees . . . provisions.[15]

---

[15] Also contributing to our determination to scrutinize the attorneys' fees provisions with special care is the nature of the notice to the class with respect to fees. The class notice did not break out the amount of attorneys' fees provided for in the settlement agreement, although an alert class member could have calculated those fees from the information provided. . . .

Where the class was informed of the amount of fees only indirectly and where the failure to give more explicit notice could itself be the result of counsel's self-interest, the courts must be all the more vigilant in protecting the interests of class members with regard to the fee award.

3.   *Attorneys' Fees*

a.   *Necessity of Scrutiny*: Attorneys' fees provisions included in proposed class action settlement agreements are, like every other aspect of such agreements, subject to the determination whether the settlement is "fundamentally fair, adequate, and reasonable." Fed. R. Civ. P. 23(e). There is no exception in Rule 23(e) for fees provisions contained in proposed class action settlement agreements. Thus, to avoid abdicating its responsibility to review the agreement for the protection of the class, a district court must carefully assess the reasonableness of a fee amount spelled out in a class action settlement agreement.

That the defendant in form agrees to pay the fees independently of any monetary award or injunctive relief provided to the class in the agreement does not detract from the need carefully to scrutinize the fee award. Ordinarily, "a defendant is interested only in disposing of the total claim asserted against it . . . the allocation between the class payment and the attorneys' fees is of little or no interest to the defense. . . ." *In re GMC*, 55 F.3d at 819–20 (internal quotation marks and citation omitted); see also *Evans v. Jeff D.*, 475 U.S. 717, 732, 734 (1986) (recognizing that "the possibility of a tradeoff between merits relief and attorney's fees" is often implicit in class action settlement negotiations, because "[m]ost defendants are unlikely to settle unless the cost of the predicted judgment, discounted by its probability, plus the transaction costs of further litigation, are greater than the cost of *the settlement package*.") (emphasis added).

Given these economic realities, the assumption in scrutinizing a class action settlement agreement must be, and has always been, that the members of the class retain an interest in assuring that the fees to be paid class counsel are not unreasonably high. If fees are unreasonably high, the likelihood is that the defendant obtained an economically beneficial concession with regard to the merits provisions, in the form of lower monetary payments to class members or less injunctive relief for the class than could otherwise have obtained. . . .

b.   *Substantive Scrutiny of Statutory Fees*: Generally, litigants in the United States pay their own attorneys' fees, regardless of the outcome of the proceedings. In order to encourage private enforcement of the law, however, Congress has legislated that in certain cases prevailing parties may recover their attorneys' fees from the opposing side. When a statute provides for such fees, it is termed a "fee-shifting" statute. Under a fee-shifting statute, the court "must calculate awards for attorneys' fees using the 'lodestar' method," which involves "multiplying the number of hours the prevailing party reasonably expended on the litigation by a reasonably hourly rate," and, "if circumstances warrant, adjust[ing] the lodestar to account for other factors which are not subsumed within it." The rules governing both reduction and enhancement have become increasingly refined over time, and we have therefore required careful explanations by district courts of statutory fee determinations.

Both Title VII [of the Civil Rights Act] and [42 U.S.C.] § 1981—the two federal statutes under which this suit was brought—have fee-shifting provisions. The parties therefore could have negotiated an award of fees under [those provisions]. Had they done so, the district court's review would have focused on the reasonableness of the fee request under the lodestar calculation method. . . . Absent some unusual explanation, a defendant would not agree in a class action settlement to pay out of its own pocket fees measurably higher than it could conceivably have to pay were the fee amount litigated, unless there was some non-fee benefit the defendant received thereby.

In fact, no lodestar-based scrutiny of the fees awarded class counsel in the settlement agreement ever took place. Boeing and class counsel did not attempt to explain the award of fees provided in the consent decree as negotiated under the applicable fee-shifting statutes. Further, the record as it stands would not have been sufficient for such an inquiry, as it contains only the barest estimate of hours expended, with no detail. Not even a summary of the billing records was submitted.

Of course, in the context of a settlement, the fees provided for in the agreement are as subject to compromise as are the merits provisions. Consequently, . . . the fee amount in a class action settlement agreement can be *less* than would be awarded by a court. And, since the proper amount of fees is often open to dispute and the parties are compromising precisely to avoid litigation, the court need not inquire into the reasonableness of the fees even at the high end with precisely the same level of scrutiny as when the fee amount is litigated. But here, there was no such inquiry at all. Nor is the record adequate for an inquiry, even one employing a less-than-stringent standard that recognizes the settlement context.

We are therefore in no position to determine whether the fees Boeing agreed to pay are reasonable lodestar fees under the applicable fee-shifting statutes and do not do so. On remand, the parties are free to attempt such justification, based on the principles outlined in this opinion and in the extensive lodestar fees case law.

c.   *The Common Fund Justification*: Rather than justifying the attorneys' fees provisions of the settlement agreement on the statutory fee-shifting basis that would properly have applied, the parties sought to justify the fee amount according to the principles applicable to common funds. They did so by constructing a hypothetical "fund" by adding together the amount of money Boeing would pay in damages to members of the class under the agreement, the amount of fees provided to various counsel, the cost of the class action notices paid for by Boeing, and a gross amount of money ascribed to all the injunctive relief contained in the agreement. For clarity, we will call the total of all those monetary amounts the "putative fund," for, as we shall see, it is not properly viewed as a common fund as that term is used in attorneys' fees law. (We will continue, also for clarity, to call the doctrine by its usual name, "common fund.") The parties portrayed the total fee award as 28% of the putative fund, and maintained that such a percentage is well within the percentage permitted under our common fund fee cases. The district court viewed the fee award as the parties requested and approved it, and the consent decree as a whole, on that basis. For several reasons, that approval was not appropriate.

i.   *Availability of common fund fees*

Before we can decide whether the attempted common fund justification in this case was adequate, we must resolve whether the existence of potentially applicable fee-shifting statutory provisions precludes class counsel from recovering attorneys' fees under the common fund doctrine. We conclude, as have the two other circuits that have addressed the issue [the Third and Seventh Circuits] that there is no preclusion on recovery of common fund fees where a fee-shifting statute applies.

Under the "common fund" doctrine, "a litigant or a lawyer who recovers a common fund for the benefit of persons other than himself or his client is entitled to a reasonable attorney's fee from the fund as a whole." *Boeing Co. v. Van Gemert*, 444 U.S. 472, 478 (1980). . . . In contrast to fee-shifting statutes, which enable a prevailing party to recover attorneys' fees from the vanquished party, the common fund doctrine permits the court to award attorneys' fees from monetary payments that the prevailing party recovered in the lawsuit. Put another way, in common fund cases, a variant of the usual rule applies and the winning party pays his or her own attorneys' fees; in fee-shifting cases, the usual rule is rejected and the losing party covers the bill.

The procedures used to determine the amount of reasonable attorneys' fees differ concomitantly in cases involving a common fund from those in which attorneys' fees are sought under a fee-shifting statute. As in a statutory fee-shifting case, a district court in a common fund case can apply the lodestar method to determine the amount of attorneys' fees. . . .

Alternatively, in a common fund case, the district court can determine the amount of attorneys' fees to be drawn from the fund by employing a "percentage" method. . . . "This circuit has established 25% of the common fund as a benchmark award for attorney fees."

That common fund fees can be awarded where statutory fees are available follows from the equitable nature of common fund fees. . . . [U]nless Congress has forbidden the application of the common fund doctrine in cases in which attorneys could potentially recover fees under the type of fee-shifting statutes at issue here, the courts retain their equitable power to award common fund attorneys' fees.

Congress did not explicitly forbid the use of the common fund doctrine in cases potentially involving [litigation brought under Title VII or § 1981], and we see no reason to infer that it did so implicitly. The intent of the fee-shifting provisions at issue here is not countered by the application of common fund principles.

The fees available under a fee-shifting statute are part of the plaintiff's recovery and are not dependent upon any explicit fee arrangements between the plaintiffs and their counsel. For that reason, contingent fee agreements between counsel and client are valid in cases where statutory fees are available. See *Venegas v. Mitchell*, 495 U.S. 82, 86–89 (1990). Common fund fees are essentially an equitable substitute for private fee agreements where a class benefits from an attorney's work, so the same general principles outlined in *Venegas* should apply.

Application of the common fund doctrine to class action settlements does not compromise the purposes underlying fee-shifting statutes. In settlement negotiations, the defendant's determination of the amount it will pay into a common fund will necessarily be informed by the magnitude of its potential liability for fees under the fee-shifting statute, as those fees will have to be paid after successful litigation and could be treated at that point as part of a common fund against which the attorneys' fees are measured. Conversely, the prevailing party will expect that part of any aggregate fund will go toward attorneys' fees and so can insist as a condition of settlement that the defendants contribute a higher amount to the settlement than if the defendants were to pay the fees separately under a fee-shifting statute.

The district court did not, therefore, err in treating this case as one that *could* fall under the common fund doctrine rather than under the potentially applicable fee-shifting provisions, *if* the parties properly so agreed, the resulting fee was reasonable, and other requisites applicable to common fund fees were met.

The possibility that a prevailing party could recover fees either under the court's equitable powers or under its statutory authority does not, however, give the parties or the court free rein once either the common fund or the statutory rubric is selected. Fees sought or awarded under a fee-shifting statute require the application of the standards and procedures crafted for such statutes, discussed above. Similarly, if the parties invoke common fund principles, they must follow common fund procedures and standards, designed to protect class members when common fund fees are awarded. We turn next to the specific procedure employed in the negotiation and award of the attorneys' fees in this case.

ii.   *Inclusion in the settlement of the attorneys' fees*

The parties negotiated the amount of attorneys' fees awarded class counsel as a term of the settlement agreement and thus conditioned the merits settlement upon judicial approval of the agreed-upon fees. See *Hanlon*, 150 F.3d at 1026 ("Neither the district court nor this court ha[s] the ability to 'delete, modify or substitute certain provisions.' The settlement must stand or fall in its entirety.") (citations omitted). By proceeding in this fashion with respect to attorneys' fees and then attempting to justify the fees not as statutory fees but as common fund fees, the parties followed an irregular and, as we hold below, improper procedure.

Under regular common fund procedure, the parties settle for the total amount of the common fund and shift the fund to the court's supervision. The plaintiffs' lawyers then apply to the court for a fee award from the fund.

In setting the amount of common fund fees, the district court has a special duty to protect the interests of the class. . . .

When the ordinary procedure is not followed and instead the parties explicitly condition the merits settlement on a fee award justified on a common fund basis, the obvious risk arises that plaintiffs' lawyers will be induced to forego a fair settlement for their clients in order to gain a higher award of attorneys' fees. That risk is, if anything, exacerbated where, as here, the agreement provides for payment of fees by the defendant, as in a statutory fee-shifting situation, but the parties choose to justify the fee as coming from a putative common fund. Where that is the case, courts have to be alert to the possibility that the parties have adopted this hybrid course precisely because the fee award is in fact higher than could be supported on a statutory fee-shifting basis, yet the deal is so dependent upon class counsel receiving a greater-than-lodestar amount of fees that the parties were not willing to give the court supervisory discretion to determine the distribution of the total settlement package between counsel and the class.

We recognize that in *Evans* [*v. Jeff D.*], 475 U.S. at 720, the [Supreme] Court held that the parties to a class action may simultaneously negotiate merits relief and an award of attorneys' fees under a fee-shifting statute, and may condition the entire settlement upon a waiver of fees. The Court explained:

> [A] general proscription against negotiated waiver of attorney's fees in exchange for a settlement on the merits would itself impede vindication of civil rights, at least in some cases, by reducing the attractiveness of settlement.

Id. at 732; see also *id.* at 733 ("If defendants are not allowed to make lump-sum offers that would, if accepted, represent their total liability, they would understandably be reluctant to make settlement offers.") (quoting *Marek v. Chesny*, 473 U.S. 1, 6–7 (1985)). Thus, to facilitate settlement by providing defendants with assurances as to the limits of their liability exposure, the parties to a lawsuit may, in conjunction with their merits negotiation, properly negotiate statutory fees to be paid by the defendant.

The concern motivating the decision in *Evans*—that prohibiting simultaneous negotiations and agreements as to merits and fees will discourage settlements—simply does not exist, however, in a case, such as this one, in which the parties to the negotiations seek to justify attorneys' fees as coming from a putative fund and to apply common fund principles. Usually, an agreement that provides lawyers fees on a common fund basis constitutes a "lump-sum" agreement, *Evans*, 475 U.S. at 733, one that enables defendants to know the precise extent of their liability regardless of the amount of attorneys' fees eventually awarded from the fund. Thus, the parties *could* have simply agreed upon the total amount of the putative fund, as well as the damages and injunctive relief, and left the division of that fund as between the class and counsel to the district court, as is usual in common fund cases.[21] Requiring the parties to so proceed or, in the alternative, to agree to a fee award as part of the settlement agreement in an amount no higher than could be justified by statutory fee-shifting principles, fully serves the defendant's only legitimate interest in class counsel's fee award. That requirement thereby provides the requisite impetus to settlement on the defendant's part while protecting against a maldistribution of the total settlement package between the class and its counsel.

Further, the effect of conditioning the settlement on a set amount of attorneys' fees based on an actual or putative common fund can be to inhibit district courts from engaging in independent determinations of reasonable fees, as required by law. The parties' all-or-nothing approach imposes pressure to approve otherwise acceptable and desirable settlements in spite of built-in attorneys' fees provisions. While this same dynamic may exist where fees can be justified on a statutory fee basis, the more precise lodestar standards for adjudging the reasonableness of such fees, summarized above, make the influence of such pressure much less forceful.

We hold, therefore, that in a class action involving both a statutory fee-shifting provision and an actual or putative common fund, the parties may negotiate and settle the amount of statutory fees along with the merits of the case, as permitted by *Evans*. In the course of judicial review, the amount of such attorneys' fees can be approved if they meet the reasonableness standard when measured against statutory fee principles. Alternatively, the parties may negotiate and agree to the value of a common fund (which will ordinarily include an amount representing an estimated hypothetical award of statutory fees) and provide that, subsequently, class counsel will apply to the court for an award from the fund, using common fund fee principles. In those circumstances, the agreement as a whole does not stand or fall on the amount of fees. Instead, after the court determines the reasonable amount of attorneys' fees, all the remaining value of the fund belongs to the class rather than reverting to the defendant.

---

[21] The description of the total amount of the fund need not take any particular form and could result from adding up separately-enumerated amounts in the agreement.

The parties in this case did not follow either of these procedures, or any other that adequately protected the class from the possibility that class counsel were accepting an excessive fee at the expense of the class.[22] The district court therefore erred in approving the consent decree.

iii. *Injunctive relief as part of the district court's putative fund*

Even if the fee award had been determined in a procedurally proper way, approval of the amount of the attorneys' fees on common fund principles would still have been mistaken as a matter of law, because the actual percentage award was much higher than the 28% the district court recognized.

In order for attorneys to obtain an award of fees from a common fund, the court must be able to: (1) sufficiently identify the class of beneficiaries; (2) accurately trace the benefits; and (3) shift the fee to those benefiting with some exactitude. *Van Gemert*, 444 U.S. at 478–79. "[T]he criteria are satisfied when each member of a certified class has an undisputed and mathematically ascertainable claim to part of a lump-sum judgment recovered on his behalf," whereas they are not satisfied when "litigants simply vindicate a general social grievance." *Id.* at 479.

Under these requirements, the monetary relief for the plaintiff class (including attorneys' fees) provided for in the consent decree could be converted as described above so as to qualify as a common fund from which class counsel could obtain an award of attorneys' fees. The class consists of the approximately 15,000 African–American Boeing employees and so is sufficiently identifiable. The benefits from the monetary relief provided for in the decree would be distributed according to its terms and so can be accurately traced. Finally, the fees could be shifted with exactitude to the benefiting class if taken properly from the fund.

In approving the award of attorneys' fees provided for in the consent decree, the district court employed the percentage method to determine that the award was fair. The court found that the fees constituted 28% of the putative fund, just above the 25% benchmark. To make this calculation, however, the court included in the amount of the putative fund an estimated value of $3.65 million for injunctive relief, the amount that the decree required Boeing to spend on approval and implementation of this component.

Although the injunctive relief falls somewhere between the permissible and the prohibited bases for fees set forth in *Van Gemert*—the relief neither produces "an undisputed and mathematically ascertainable" amount for each class member, nor merely "vindicate[s]" a general social grievance— we have no difficulty here deciding that the district court abused its discretion in counting the parties' estimated value of that relief towards the putative fund.

The injunctive relief included in the consent decree requires Boeing only to "meet and confer" with class counsel or to discuss certain issues. Although Boeing must participate in such conferences and discussions, there is no requirement that Boeing take any action with respect to what the

---

[22] By spelling out these alternatives, we do not mean to preclude all others. Rather, the parties have flexibility in negotiating class action settlement agreements, including the attorneys' fee provisions. The alternatives outlined in the text are paradigms. Any variants, to be reasonable, would have to provide equivalent assurance that the inherent tensions among class representation, defendant's interests in minimizing the cost of the total settlement package, and class counsel's interest in fees are being adequately policed by the court.

Company learns. The conferences and discussions may not result in tangible relief to class members. Moreover, a diversity consultant may not benefit the class to a degree commensurate with his or her cost.

Additionally, while the injunctive relief (along with the cost of obtaining approval of the decree) is to cost Boeing a fixed minimum amount, $3.65 million, some of the injunctive relief described in the consent decree consists of steps Boeing had apparently decided to take on its own, even before it entered the settlement. The decree also permits Boeing to credit expenditures towards the injunctive relief amount without regard to whether such expenditures are in addition to the cost of Boeing's prior outlays for administering similar programs. Thus, the true cost of the injunction to the defendant—and the true benefit to the plaintiff class—is a matter of speculation and may be far less than $3.65 million. That amount of money cannot be accurately traced to the decree, let alone to the beneficiaries making up the class. Without the estimated value of the injunctive relief, the fund is reduced to only $10.55 million, and the fee award of $4.05 million constitutes 38%—well above the 25% benchmark—of the putative fund.

We do not hold that a district court can never consider the value of injunctive relief in determining the reasonableness of a common fund fee. For instance, in *Hanlon*, 150 F.3d at 1029, we upheld the use of the common fund doctrine to award attorneys' fees after the parties reached a settlement agreement under which Chrysler would replace defective latches on minivans that it had manufactured. Although the replacement of latches is injunctive in nature, the agreement bestowed upon each beneficiary a clearly measurable benefit: one replacement latch for each minivan owned. The court could therefore, with some degree of accuracy, value the benefits conferred. Even so, in *Hanlon* the district court used its valuation of the fund only as a cross-check of the lodestar amount, "reject[ing] the idea of a straight percentage recovery because of its uncertainty as to the valuation of the settlement," *id.*, and it was on that basis that we affirmed the fee award.

Precisely because the value of injunctive relief is difficult to quantify, its value is also easily manipulable by overreaching lawyers seeking to increase the value assigned to a common fund. We hold, therefore, that only in the unusual instance where the value to individual class members of benefits deriving from injunctive relief can be accurately ascertained may courts include such relief as part of the value of a common fund for purposes of applying the percentage method of determining fees. When this is not the case, courts should consider the value of the injunctive relief obtained as a "relevant circumstance" in determining what percentage of the common fund class counsel should receive as attorneys' fees, rather than as part of the fund itself. Alternatively, particularly where obtaining injunctive relief likely accounted for a significant part of the fees expended, courts can use the common fund version of the lodestar method either to set the fee award or as a cross-check to assist in the determination of how the "relevant circumstance" of the injunctive relief should affect a percentage award.

The district court did not employ either of these procedures here. Nor can we determine on the record before us that considering the injunctive relief as a "relevant circumstance" or employing the common fund lodestar method would have justified the award of $4.05 million as a reasonable fee.

On this ground, also, the district court erred in approving the proposed attorneys' fees award. . .

■ TROTT, CIRCUIT JUDGE, dissenting:

. . . My colleagues' problems with the attorneys' fees stem from getting lost in unfamiliar trees and a consequent failure to see the forest for what it is. This settlement promises clear future value to African–Americans working for one of our nation's largest and most important employers. Measured against this value, much of which is intangible, the modest attorneys' fees agreement appears to me on the record to be quite appropriate. . . . In dollar terms, it does not subtract from the value of the settlement, which is only a small part of what the settlement accomplishes. The merits settlement itself was (1) free of collusion and chicanery, (2) generous in its opt-out provisions, (3) fair in its monetary provisions, (4) forthcoming in its look to the future, and (5) vigorously litigated. Nevertheless, the attorneys' fees issue ends up as the proverbial tail wagging the dog to death, even though the dog is not a dog at all, but a viable solution to a serious problem demanding prompt resolution. If the settlement itself were truly suspicious and indicative of a betrayal, then a different approach might be in order; but if the settlement stands, in my view, so do these fees. It may not match up perfectly with other methods of measuring whether fees are appropriate, but no matter whether fees here are low or high, they do not subtract from the relief obtained by the plaintiffs. My colleagues say that the method used in this case to determine attorneys' fees "allows too much leeway for lawyers representing a class to spurn a fair, adequate and reasonable settlement for their clients in favor of inflated attorneys' fees." This problem is *not* part of this case, and I do not see how something that might have happened but did not must torpedo *this* hard-bargained positive outcome. In the end, this case has been decided based on possibilities, not realities.

The standard of review we are bound to employ is highly deferential, as it should be. . . . Here, not only do the majority fail to adhere to this deferential standard, adopting instead a standard of "somewhat uneasy with the settlement as a whole"; but in my view, they do so in a case where the district court's approval of the settlement and of the attorneys' fees was clearly an appropriate exercise of discretion. The district court judge responsible for this case is highly experienced, capable, and astute, one over whose eyes no one pulls the wool. It is a rare settlement that will delight all parties, but this settlement has much to say for it. Accordingly, I dissent from a decision that will have the effect of unnecessarily delaying full implementation of this efficacious solution for four years—if not more—from the date the district court found it to be appropriate.

NOTES AND QUESTIONS

1. *The Relationship of Class Settlement Substance and Class Counsel Fees.* Given the unwillingness of the majority in *Staton* to overturn the district court's approval of the consent decree—in practical effect, a class settlement—based simply upon the content of its substantive provisions, why should the majority take issue with the manner in which the settling parties chose to handle attorneys' fees? Is Judge Trott correct in his dissent, when he contends that, "if the settlement stands, . . . so do these fees"? Is Judge Trott correct to criticize the majority for deciding the case "based on possibilities, not realities"? Is

that not what courts *always* must do when scrutinizing the fairness of a class settlement?

Why as a strategic matter might class counsel have been disinclined to invoke the applicable fee-shifting provisions, complete with submission of the usual kinds of documentation of class counsel's hours worked on the litigation?

2. *The Problems of Employment Discrimination Class Settlements.* The concerns catalogued by the Ninth Circuit panel majority in *Staton* are by no means atypical or the consequence simply of the particular fee arrangements in that case. As one commentator observes:

> The last decade saw an explosion of employment discrimination class action lawsuits that were resolved through record breaking settlements. The best known of these cases is the $176 million settlement involving Texaco, one that came on the heels of the much publicized discovery of tape-recorded meetings that seemingly indicated the use of explicit racial epithets by management-level employees. There have also been substantial settlements involving Coca–Cola ($192 million), Home Depot ($104 million), Shoney's ($105 million), Publix Markets ($81 million), and State Farm Insurance Co. ($157 million). The tide likely shifted in favor of employers as a result of the decision in Wal–Mart Stores, Inc. v. Dukes, 131 S.Ct. 2541 (2011), which decertified a nationwide class of female employees who claimed to be victims of job discrimination.

> Despite the proliferation of these high profile cases, we know surprisingly little about their effects on either the firms that have been sued or the plaintiff classes. . . . [I have sought] to expand our knowledge by analyzing the effect these large class action lawsuits have on firms and plaintiffs [through] an empirical analysis designed to assess whether the lawsuits or their settlements affect shareholder value, as measured by their effect on stock prices [and] three case studies of lawsuits involving Texaco, Home Depot and Denny's to explore whether the lawsuits produce substantial changes within the corporations or provide meaningful benefits to the plaintiff class.

> This study challenges many of the prevailing views on employment discrimination class action litigation. The statistical study demonstrates that the lawsuits do not substantially influence stock prices, either at their filing or their settlement, and when there is an effect, it tends to be short-lived. Yet, although the lawsuits do not result in significant financial losses to shareholder value, managers still often take them seriously. . . . Taking the lawsuits seriously, however, does not mean that the managers implement meaningful reform; on the contrary, . . . the settlements frequently produce little to no substantive change within the corporations. Moreover, many of the changes that are implemented tend to be cosmetic in nature and are primarily designed to address public relations problems. As demonstrated in the case studies, many companies, such as Texaco and Home Depot, fail to enact meaningful changes in their employment practices, and monetary recoveries generally constitute the primary direct benefit the lawsuits provide to the plaintiff class.

When divided by the size of the class, these benefits tend to be relatively modest, averaging about $10,000 per class member—well below what a plaintiff could expect to recover in a successful individual suit. Furthermore, given the size of the defendant corporations, the damages also fail to pose a significant deterrent threat to firms. To give but one example, the record-setting settlement involving Coca–Cola amounted to less than 0.15% of the firm's capitalization. Although the damage amounts are often insufficient to compensate plaintiffs or deter defendants, other parties involved in the litigation fare significantly better. Attorneys routinely receive fee awards that are four to six times their actual fees, and a host of groups loosely tied to the diversity industry are likewise collecting a disproportionate share of the settlement funds through diversity training, purchases from minority suppliers, and contributions to various minority groups either as part of the settlement or to repair public relations damage. . . .

These findings reflect a substantial shift in the nature of employment discrimination litigation, and indeed in the nature of discrimination itself. Not so long ago, class action employment discrimination suits were defined as a quintessential form of public law litigation where monetary relief was generally viewed as one component of necessary remedial relief, and a far less important component than the institutional reform the suit ultimately produced. Yet today the lawsuits have largely become just another variation of a tort claim where monetary relief is the principal, and often the only, goal of the litigation. Along with this shift in emphasis has come a dramatic change in our perspective on the persistence of discrimination. There is no longer any concerted effort to eliminate discrimination; instead, efforts are directed at providing monetary compensation for past discrimination without particular concern for preventing future discrimination, or even remedying past discrimination, through injunctive relief. For firms, discrimination[] claims are now like accidents—a cost of doing business, which necessarily implies that a certain level of discrimination will persist.

Michael Selmi, *The Price of Discrimination: The Nature of Class Action Employment Discrimination Litigation and Its Effects*, 81 Tex. L. Rev. 1249, 1249–52 (2003).

3. *Market–Based Techniques Recalled.* Are the difficulties associated with the determination of class counsel fees at the conclusion of class action litigation ultimately a testament to the wisdom of proposals for simultaneous selection of class counsel and determination of the method for calculation of their fees as part of the class certification determination? Consider Judge Easterbrook's remarks for the Seventh Circuit in *In re Synthroid Mktg.Litig.*, 264 F.3d 712, 718–19 (7th Cir. 2001):

[In the usual fee determination scenario,] the district court must estimate the terms of the contract that private plaintiffs would have negotiated with their lawyers, had bargaining occurred at the outset of the case (that is, when the risk of loss still existed). The best time to determine this rate is the beginning of the case, not the end (when hindsight alters the perception of the suit's riskiness, and sunk costs make it impossible for the lawyers to walk away if the fee is too low). This is what happens in actual markets. Individual clients and their lawyers *never* wait until after recovery is secured to contract for fees. They strike their bargains before work begins. Ethically lawyers must do this, but the same thing happens in markets for other professional services with different (or no) ethical codes. Many district judges have begun to follow the private model by setting fee schedules at the outset of class litigation—sometimes by auction, sometimes by negotiation, sometimes for a percentage of recovery, sometimes for a lodestar hourly rate and a multiplier for riskbearing. (The greater the risk of loss, the greater the incentive compensation required.) Timing is more important than the choice between negotiation and auction, or between percentage and hourly rates, for all of these systems have their shortcomings. Only *ex ante* can bargaining occur in the shadow of the litigation's uncertainty; only *ex ante* can the costs and benefits of particular systems and risk multipliers be assessed intelligently. Before the litigation occurs, a judge can design a fee structure that emulates the incentives a private client would put in place. At the same time, both counsel and class members can decide whether it is worthwhile to proceed with that compensation system in place. But in this case the district judge let the opportunity slip away, turning to fees only *ex post*. Now the court must set a fee by approximating the terms that would have been agreed to *ex ante*, had negotiations occurred.

F. DEFENDANT CLASSES

This Chapter has focused thus far on class actions in the form of a plaintiff class suing a conventional named defendant or multiple named defendants. By its terms, however, Rule 23 contemplates the possibility of defendant classes—that is, litigation by a conventional plaintiff against a class. Rule 23(a) specifically states that "[o]ne or more members of a class may sue *or be sued* as representative parties on behalf of all members." The materials in this section explore the special issues presented by the proposed certification of a defendant class—first, on an opt-out basis and, second, on a mandatory basis.

Thillens, Inc. v. Community Currency Exchange Association

97 F.R.D. 668 (N.D. Ill. 1983)

■ WILLIAM T. HART, DISTRICT JUDGE.

Plaintiff Thillens, Inc. ("Thillens") filed this action in 1981 against the Community Currency Exchange Association of Illinois ("Association"), former and current members of the Association ("individual defendants") and the community currency exchanges owned by those members ("exchange defendants"). Also named are three former Illinois officials ("public defendants"). Thillens alleges that over the past twenty-three years the Association and the individual defendants conspired with the public defendants to restrain Thillens' trade as an ambulatory currency exchange, in violation of federal and state antitrust laws, 42 U.S.C. § 1983, and 18 U.S.C. § 1961

("RICO"). Also included are various pendent claims. Thillens seeks compensatory and punitive damages, injunctive relief and attorneys' fees.

Thillens is an Illinois corporation, licensed as an "ambulatory currency exchange" providing "mobile check cashing services" within the greater Chicago metropolitan area. Thillens claims to be the only ambulatory currency exchange operating in the Chicago area and perhaps in all of Illinois. Thillens has never belonged to the Association. The Association is an Illinois not-for-profit corporation serving as the trade association for approximately 300 persons who own or control at least 500 "community currency exchanges" in Illinois. Most Chicago area community currency exchanges allegedly belong to the Association. All currency exchanges are required to be licensed by the Illinois Department of Financial Institutions ("DFI").

The gist of Thillens' complaint is that the alleged conspiracy caused the DFI since 1958 to (1) deny Thillens 400 license applications to operate ambulatory currency exchanges in the relevant markets; (2) deprive Thillens of fair hearings to protest the denial of the licenses sought by Thillens; and (3) promulgate unreasonable rules and regulations substantially to Thillens' detriment.

. . . This Opinion and Order considers . . . Thillens' motion for certification of a defendant class. The proposed class includes 17 named individual defendants, approximately 350 unnamed individual past and current members of the Association and the more than 500 community currency exchanges owned by those members and represented by the Association. Neither the Association nor the public defendants is named as a class member. Thillens, however, nominates the Association as class representative.

Thillens argues that the class proposed is highly cohesive. In its view, the Association is the logical choice for class representative, precisely because it is the self-selected industry representative of the individual and exchange defendants. Thillens also claims that the Association is financially able to perform representational duties. Finally, Thillens notes that at least 95 individual defendants are represented by the law firm which represents the Association and 16 named defendants.

Thillens also supports its motion for certification of a defendant class by arguing that no unfairness would result: Supposedly each proposed defendant member paid dues to the Association during the relevant period. All of the defendants in the proposed class are alleged to have knowingly participated or acquiesced in the conspiracy and political bribery fund. In light of what Thillens characterizes as virtually identical behaviors, giving rise to identical defenses, Thillens claims that certification will result in substantial savings of judicial and personal resources, without significant sacrifice by class members.

The Association and various individual defendants oppose the motion for certification of a defendant class. They argue that defendant classes are uncommon, especially in antitrust actions. Their primary objection is that certification would be inconsistent with each defendant's due process rights. The defendants also claim that the Association would be an inadequate representative of the class' interests because it formerly pled guilty to mail fraud and acknowledged the existence of a political bribery fund, acts which Thillens seeks to prove in this action. According to the Association, it would be collaterally estopped from denying those acts, to the detriment of the class members.

For the reasons stated below, Thillens' motion for certification of a defendant class is granted. The class is certified under Fed. R. Civ. P. 23(b)(3). Each member of the class must be notified personally of its status as a class member consistent with the requirements of Fed. R. Civ. P. 23(c)(2). In the event that liability is determined in Thillens' favor, each member of the class who has not opted out may attempt to prove its non-participation in any conspiracy or nonperformance of any unlawful act. Furthermore, each member of the class may be represented by the counsel of its choice.

DISCUSSION

A. *A Defendant Class May Be Certified If Due Process is Satisfied*

As a preliminary matter, the Court considers whether and under what conditions a defendant class may be certified. Rule 23 of the Federal Rules of Civil Procedure clearly contemplates both plaintiff *and* defendant class actions. For example, its very first clause provides "[o]ne or more members of a class may sue *or be sued* as representative parties on behalf of all." (emphasis added). Fed. R. Civ. P. 23(a). That Rule 23 was designed to permit both plaintiff classes and defendant classes is underscored by the appearance in the Rule of phrases such as "the claims *or defenses* of the representative parties" (emphasis added), Fed. R. Civ. P. 23(a)(3), and "the prosecution of separate action by *or against* individual members of the class." (emphasis added). Fed. R. Civ. P. 23(b)(1). Unquestionably, a defendant class *may* be certified.

The analysis of *when* a defendant class will be certified is more complicated than the consideration of *if* such certification is ever possible. Regardless of whether a plaintiff or defendant class is certified, the class action device yields substantial economic and practical savings. Many parties may be brought before the court in a single suit. Each class member will be bound by the ultimate decision. Furthermore, a class action expands, by collateral estoppel effect, the scope of the decision by binding parties not before the court in the class action. Thus, the need to relitigate the same questions in multiple suits, at the risk of inconsistent judgments, is avoided.

Simultaneously, the binding nature of the class action poses a dilemma. Fundamental fairness to absentee members must be balanced against judicial savings. Where representative adjudication occurs pursuant to a defendant class, due process concerns not inherent in plaintiff class actions arise. The crux of the distinction is: the unnamed plaintiff stands to gain while the unnamed defendant stands to lose.

It is the hallmark of our system of justice that personal rights cannot be compromised without due process. See, e.g., *Int'l Shoe Co. v. Washington*, 326 U.S. 310 (1945) (foreign defendant must have certain minimum contacts with forum state); *Mullane v. Central Hanover Bank & Trust Co.*, 339 U.S. 306 (1950) (no binding adjudication without reasonable attempts to notify defendant). If, however, a binding judgment depended on the assertion of *in personam* jurisdiction over each member of a class, the action's economies would be dissipated. The Supreme Court has resolved the apparent tension by holding that due process is satisfied and absent members of a class are bound so long as the interests of the absentees are adequately represented. *Hansberry v. Lee*, 311 U.S. 32, 42 (1940) (plaintiff class); *Sam Fox Publ'g Co. v. United States*, 366 U.S. 683, 691 (1961) (defendant class).

Arguably, therefore, a finding that a defendant class is adequately represented should resolve the due process dilemma which attaches to certification of a defendant class. Nonetheless the concern lingers. Defendant classes seldom are certified. If at all, such certification most commonly occurs (1) in patent infringement cases; (2) in suits against local public officials challenging the validity of state laws; or (3) in securities litigation. Attempts to certify defendant classes in antitrust actions generally are unsuccessful. . . .

Several rules . . . emerge from [the case law]: (1) A defendant class will not be certified unless each named plaintiff has a colorable claim against each defendant class member; (2) A defendant class will not be certified under Fed. R. Civ. P. 23(b)(3) without a clear showing that common questions do *in fact* predominate over individual issues; (3) The requirement that each named plaintiff must have a claim against each defendant may be waived where the defendant members are related by a conspiracy or "juridical link."

A "juridical link" is some legal relationship which relates all defendants in a way such that single resolution of the dispute is preferred to a multiplicity of similar actions. . . .

[Here], a single plaintiff, Thillens, alleges that it has been injured by each member of the proposed defendant class. Instead of being an amorphous entity, the proposed defendant class of currency exchanges and their individual owners is highly cohesive and self-organized. It is juridically linked at least by allegations that each defendant class member voluntarily joined a conspiracy to harm Thillens. Additionally, this Court has subject matter jurisdiction over the claims made.

There are no theoretical roadblocks to certification of this defendant class antitrust action so long as due process safeguards are imposed. However, the proposed class still must be tested by the provisions of Fed. R. Civ. P. 23(a) and (b).

B. *The Defendant Class Proposed Meets the Requirements of Fed. R. Civ. P. 23(a)*

. . . 4. *The Association is an Adequate Representative*

Because of the serious due process problems which attend the certification of a defendant class, the 23(a)(4) mandate for an adequate representative must be strictly observed. The test of adequacy of representation proposed by Fed. R. Civ. P. 23(a)(4) is two-pronged: (1) the representative must be able to conduct the litigation and (2) the representative's interests must not be antagonistic to those of the class members. Although the representative need not be a member of the class, see, e.g., *Truckee–Carson Irrigation District*, 71 F.R.D. 10 (D. Nev. 1975), there is the further requirement that the class representative must have injured the plaintiff in the same way as other defendants have injured him. *Aleknagik Natives Ltd. v. Andrus*, 648 F.2d 496, 505 (9th Cir. 1980), *relying on Sosna v. Iowa*, 419 U.S. 393, 403 (1975).

The Association allegedly has injured Thillens in precisely the same way as did every individual defendant, exchange defendant and public defendant. All defendants allegedly conspired to ruin Thillens' ambulatory currency exchange business, maintained a secret bribery fund for that purpose and engaged in antitrust and common law violations to Thillens' detriment.

Nonetheless, the Association is an unwilling class representative. That fact alone should not deter a court from naming it as representative, however. In *In re Gap*, the court observed that "[i]ronically the best defendant class representative may well be the one who most vigorously and persuasively opposes certification since he is the one most likely to guarantee an adversary presentation of the issues." 79 F.R.D. at 290. If the sheer volume of the briefs which have been filed by the Association (and Thillens) in this case are any indication, adversary presentation of all issues by the Association is guaranteed.

The real concern with a reluctant representative should be for his ability to carry the expense and other practical burdens of a class defense. . . .

Here, no serious suggestion can be raised that the Association either is financially unable or without requisite skills to act as the class representative. In fact, the Association does not argue the point. Presumably, the Association is fiscally sound. It owns a bank and at least one currency exchange. No individual defendant could better afford the role of class representative. Furthermore, the Association, through its attorneys, has considerable litigation experience. It has sued to protect the rights of the Association in matters of common interest to its members. The lawyers currently representing the Association, represented the Association and certain individual defendants in the criminal action which prompted Thillens to bring this suit.

Moreover, the Association's directors coincidentally are defendant class members. They have a clear channel of communication from the defendant class to the proposed representative. No doubt the director/defendants will consult on trial strategy and concerns of class members with the Association. Furthermore, the defendant class members fund the Association and, therefore, to some extent control it.

Finally, the Association is the self-selected representative of the member defendants. Each named and unnamed class member allegedly has voluntarily joined the Association seeking to have its business interests represented by the Association. The defendant members pay dues for the very purpose of having the Association represent their interests. . . .

The second prong of 23(a)(4) also is met. The Association's interests are not antagonistic to the interests of the members of the class. Certification of a class on the grounds of antagonism should be denied only if that antagonism goes to the subject matter of the litigation.

The main subject matter in this case is antitrust. All parties, the representative, defendant class members and public defendants are expected to try to avoid liability by disclaiming an antitrust conspiracy. Arguably, the Association will not passively raise that defense. In defending itself vigorously, the Association necessarily will raise all defenses of the class members except for individual members' claims of nonparticipation in the conspiracy. See *Rosado v. Wyman*, 322 F. Supp. 1173, 1193 (S.D.N.Y. 1970), *aff'd on other grounds*, 437 F.2d 619 (2d Cir. 1970), *cert. denied*, 397 U.S. 397 (1970). In fact, this Association has an added incentive to vigorously defend the interests of the members. The Association's by-laws provide that it will indemnify, on request, Association members who are found liable for actions arising out of membership in the Association. Clearly, the interests of the Association are not antagonistic to the interests of the class members.

Nonetheless, the Association raises a troublesome point in opposition to its adequacy. The Association claims that it cannot adequately represent the members of the class since it has pled guilty to several counts of mail fraud and has admitted the existence of a political bribery fund. The argument runs that defendant class members would be prejudiced because the Association will be collaterally estopped from denying those actions.

In the offensive use of collateral estoppel, a plaintiff seeks to prevent a defendant from relitigating an issue which the defendant unsuccessfully litigated in an action with another party. *Parklane Hosiery Co., Inc. v. Shore*, 439 U.S. 322 (1979). In order to give collateral estoppel effect in a civil proceeding to matters decided in a criminal adjudication, the matter must have actually been decided or have been necessary to the resolution of the matter decided in the prior proceedings. *Von Lusch v. C & P Telephone Co.*, 457 F. Supp. 814 (D. Md. 1978). The matter decided in the former criminal action may have resulted from a guilty plea. *Brazzell v. Adams*, 493 F.2d 489 (5th Cir. 1974).

Unlike *res judicata*, collateral estoppel does not apply to matters which *could have been* litigated. If there is a reasonable doubt as to what was decided in a prior judgment, that doubt should be resolved against using collateral estoppel unless the issue clearly appears on the face of the former complaint.

The Association entered a guilty plea . . . in which it admitted keeping and using a secret cash fund for making political contributions to Illinois public officials. The purpose of the "bribes" was to influence actions affecting the currency exchange industry and its members. The Association also pled guilty to five counts of mail fraud in furtherance of that scheme. The Court supposes, without deciding, that the Association will be collaterally estopped from denying the existence of the fund. Consistent with the guilty plea, the Association also likely would be estopped from denying use of the fund to bribe public defendants McAvoy and Wall and from denying mail fraud.

The Association's forced admission in this action of political bribery and mail fraud, however, would not result in an automatic finding of a conspiracy in violation of the antitrust laws. Nor would such admissions necessarily indicate that Thillens was the target of the conspiracy. At a minimum, Thillens still must prove the existence of a conspiracy, its focus on Thillens and an anticompetitive effect of the conspiracy in the relevant markets. Undoubtedly the Association intends to vehemently oppose Thillens' effort to establish the antitrust claims or any of the other claims it raises in this case. Based on the history of the relationship between the parties thus far, the Court is sure that the Association's defense will be rigorous and spirited. All members of the defendant class proposed will be adequately represented by the Association regardless of any collateral estoppel effect which might be imposed to coerce admissions against the Association's interest. The due process rights of the defendant class members will not be offended by naming the Association as class representative. All the requirements of 23(a), therefore, are satisfied.

C.   *The Defendant Class Proposed Meets the Requirements of Fed. R. Civ. P. 23(b)(3)*

. . . The determination required by 23(b)(3) is different than that sought under 23(a). Rule 23(a) asks whether there are common questions of law or fact, whereas 23(b)(3) expands 23(a) by requiring that the common questions must predominate.

Most antitrust class actions are certified under 23(b)(3). However, the Court must not perfunctorily find predominance, for only where predominance exists will the economic utility of the class action device be realized. Advisory Committee's Note, 39 F.R.D. 69, 103 (1966). "[P]rivate damage claims by numerous individuals arising out of concerted antitrust violations [even those alleging conspiracy] may or may not involve predominate common questions." *Id.*

As noted throughout, the primary common issue is to prove the existence of a conspiracy against Thillens in violation of antitrust laws. Clearly that issue will predominate the litigation. In fact, all the issues common to establishing antitrust violations are overriding. The only noncommon issue will be the individual members' defenses of nonparticipation. Given the complexity of the antitrust matters, the individual defenses will occupy only a minor portion of the trial time.

Rule 23(b)(3) also requires a finding that a class action is superior to other available methods of adjudication. For Thillens, a class action is superior, if not the only way, by which all its claims can be litigated. The cost of individual service and suits would be high if not prohibitive. If forced to separately litigate, Thillens likely would forego actions against numerous defendant class members.

From the defendants' perspective, the class action also is superior to other forms of dispute resolution. No individual defendant will have to carry the whole cost of this litigation. Although dues to the Association might increase as the suit progresses, any one defendant's proportionate share would be far smaller than his cost for a separate action. Individual class members would not be expected to take time from their business or personal pursuits to continuously appear at what no doubt will be a lengthy trial.

Furthermore, because their Association is the representative, class members will not relinquish total control over the management of the case. Since some class members serve as Association directors they undoubtedly will advise the Association in this matter. Presumably, even nondirector class members are in contact with the Association and can assist with and be apprised of the Association's defense through membership meetings, elections and newsletters. In the event that some members desire additional counsel, they will be permitted to seek such assistance.

Finally, this class action is especially superior from a judicial standpoint. Most of the defendant class members reside in the Cook County area and the effect of the alleged conspiracy was centered in that area. If Thillens sued all 900 or so defendants individually, most of the suits would be brought in the United States District Court for the Northern District of Illinois. An already busy docket would be further taxed. Precisely because most defendants are local, this Court does not contemplate any serious problems in the management of the action. In sum, absent voluntary agreement to arbitrate their differences or to settle, the class action is the superior method by which to adjudicate Thillens' claims.

Although this defendant class meets all the relevant requirements of 23(b)(3) and most defendant classes are certified under 23(b)(3), certification of a defendant class thereunder is questionable. Sometimes called the "exclusionary section," Fed. R. Civ. P. 23(c)(2)(A) expressly permits any defendant in a class certified under 23(b)(3) to opt-out of the class if he does so by a specific date. Thus, the risk in certifying a defendant class under 23(b)(3) is that all or many class members will "jump ship." The risk is minimized, however, because opting-out defendants are at risk of "losing" the effect of a favorable decision in the event that this action is determined against Thillens. Opting-out defendants also may have to underwrite much of the cost of a separate litigation should Thillens decide to sue them individually. Those risks may be sufficient incentive to cause most defendants to stay in the class action.

Despite the exclusionary limitation, 23(b)(3) certification is the best way to address the serious due process concerns which pervade the prosecution of a defendant class. All class members will be given notice of Thillens' intent to include them in the class and of their right to opt-out. Each defendant who elects to remain may seek individual counsel. Any defendant class member who does not timely quit the class cannot, therefore, argue in good faith that certification of the class was a violation of its due process rights . . .

IT IS THEREFORE ORDERED that

(1) A defendant class will be certified under Fed. R. Civ. P. 23(b)(3) to consist of: 17 named individual defendants, approximately 350 unnamed individual past and current members of the Community Currency Exchange Association of Illinois, Inc., and the more than 500 community currency exchanges owned by those members and represented by the Association. . . .

NOTES AND QUESTIONS

1. *Opt–Out Defendant Classes.* As the *Thillens* court underscores, defendant classes, even on an opt-out basis, might be considered especially problematic, for they force aggregate treatment upon class members at the behest not of class counsel (who, at least nominally, have the interests of class members at heart) but of the party on the opposite side of the litigation (who, as such, has little reason to be concerned with the interests of class members). Why, simply as a strategic matter, would a party like Thillens want to propose the Community Currency Exchange Association as the representative of the defendant class?

Is the treatment of class cohesiveness in *Thillens*—an oft-cited illustration of defendant classes—consistent with the constitutional constraints articulated in *Shutts* for conventional, plaintiff classes? Recall that the *Shutts* Court takes care to note that its checklist of exit, voice, and loyalty rights does not speak to due process in the context of a defendant class. Should the process due differ here?

2. *Mandatory Defendant Classes.* *Thillens* involved the certification of an opt-out defendant class under subsection (b)(3). But what about the certification of a mandatory defendant class? Consider the chilly reception given to that possibility in the following case under subsection (b)(2).

Henson v. East Lincoln Township

814 F.2d 410 (7th Cir. 1987)

■ POSNER, CIRCUIT JUDGE.

The question for decision is whether classes of defendants are permissible in actions governed by Rule 23(b)(2) of the Federal Rules of Civil Procedure. The district judge said "no," 108 F.R.D. 107 (C.D. Ill. 1985), and we must decide whether he was right.

Following *Goldberg v. Kelly*, 397 U.S. 254 (1970), this court, in *White v. Roughton*, 530 F.2d 750 (7th Cir. 1976) (per curiam), held that the due process clause of the Fourteenth Amendment requires local welfare departments in Illinois to establish written standards for welfare ("general assistance") eligibility, and notice-and-hearing procedures for the grant or denial of applications for welfare. The *White* case involved the welfare department of the township of Champaign, and the consent decree that was entered in the wake of our decision . . . provided no state-wide relief. A downstate legal-aid bureau, the Land of Lincoln Legal Assistance Foundation, filed the present suit in 1980. The purpose of the suit is to make other welfare departments in Illinois comply with the principles laid down in our 1976 decision. The suit is on behalf of one named plaintiff, Henson, a resident of East Lincoln Township, and every other person in 65 downstate Illinois counties (the counties served by the Foundation) who has been denied due process of law in connection with an application for welfare. The suit is against East Lincoln Township and its welfare supervisor—they are the named defendants—plus every other local welfare department (and its supervisor) in the 65 counties that does not receive any state aid. The defendant departments are all what are called "non-receiving" departments; welfare departments that receive state aid are bound by state procedural regulations that comply with the principles of *White v. Roughton*. Henson believes there are 770 "non-receiving" departments in the 65 counties, and they and their supervisors are the members of the defendant class. The suit seeks only injunctive relief, and the Foundation asked for certification of the defendant class only under subsection (b)(2) of Rule 23.

The Foundation notified each of the 770 departments of the suit. . . . Most of the 525 departments that answered at least some of the Foundation's questions acknowledged that they were not complying with one or more of the principles announced in *White v. Roughton*—at least that is the construction that the Foundation places on their answers and for purposes of this appeal we shall assume it is correct.

The district judge denied the plaintiff's motion under Fed. R. Civ. P. 23(c)(1) to certify the defendant class, on the ground that Rule 23(b)(2) does not permit defendant classes. He certified his ruling for an immediate appeal under 28 U.S.C. § 1292(b), and we agreed to hear it. . . .

It is apparent from the words of Rule 23(a) ("sue or be sued as representative parties") that suits against a defendant class are permitted. But it does not follow that they are permitted under all three subsections of Rule 23(b). They plainly are permitted under (b)(1), which speaks of "separate actions by or against individual members of the class." Nor is there anything to preclude them under (b)(3). Henson (realistically, the Foundation) cannot fit his case under (b)(1), however, because that subsection contemplates a joint right or obligation. An example would be a suit against members of an unincorporated association naming the officers of the association as the representatives of the defendant class. See Advisory Committee's Notes to 1966 Amendment of Rule 23. And Henson is not interested in bringing the action under (b)(3). Any member of a defendant (as of a plaintiff) class in a (b)(3) suit can "opt out" and thus not be bound by the judgment. See Rule 23(c)(3). Henson fears that every member of the defendant class would do just that. It is (b)(2) or nothing.

The question whether there can be a defendant class in a Rule 23(b)(2) suit cannot be answered by reference to authority. Although the question was declared "settled" in favor of permitting a defendant class in *Marcera v. Chinlund*, 595 F.2d 1231, 1238 (2d Cir.), vacated on other grounds under the name of *Lombard v. Marcera*, 442 U.S. 915 (1979), in neither of the cases that the court in *Marcera* cited for this proposition—*Washington v. Lee*, 263 F. Supp. 327 (M.D. Ala. 1966) (3–judge court), aff'd without opinion, 390 U.S. 333 (1968), and *Lynch v. Household Finance Corp.*, 360 F. Supp. 720, 722 n. 3 (D. Conn. 1973) (3–judge court)—had the issue been discussed. *Lee* had been filed before the 1966 amendments to Rule 23 that added (b)(2) (though it was decided after); the opinion does not even mention (b)(2). According to a count by the defendants in this case that Henson does not suggest is inaccurate, district courts have certified a defendant class in 45 cases under (b)(2) since 1966. . . . But the only courts of appeals to discuss the permissibility of such actions (there is decision but no discussion in *Marcera*) have held that they are not permissible. See *Thompson v. Board of Education*, 709 F.2d 1200, 1203–04 (6th Cir. 1983); *Paxman v. Campbell*, 612 F.2d 848, 854 (4th Cir. 1980) (per curiam). . . .

And then there are those 45 district court cases in which a defendant class was certified under (b)(2)—but their aggregate precedential significance is small. In most there is no discussion of the lawfulness of the certification; the court just does it. In some the issue is discussed but the discussion is perfunctory; the best explanation for these cases is that "the courts are simply unwilling to deprive the plaintiff of this useful measure." *Doss v. Long*, 93 F.R.D. 112, 119 (N.D. Ga. 1981). Some of the 45 cases may be distinguishable from this one. For example, in *DeAllaume v. Perales*, 110 F.R.D. 299, 304 (S.D.N.Y. 1986), and perhaps in *Marcera* itself (see 595 F.2d at 1238), the members of the defendant class were acting in concert. The plaintiffs in *DeAllaume* alleged that local officials were carrying out the policy directive of a state official. The members of the plaintiff class may therefore have had a dispute with all the members of the defendant class, viewed as agents of the state official and thus as the spokes of a conspiracy of which he was the hub. And in *Technograph Printed Circuits, Ltd. v. Methode Electronics, Inc.*, 285 F. Supp. 714, 723 (N.D. Ill. 1968), the defendant class wanted declaratory and injunctive relief against the plaintiffs, making the defendant class in effect a plaintiff class. Finally, not all district judges think that a defendant class can be certified in a suit governed by Rule 23(b)(2); besides the district court opinion in the present case see, e.g., *Coleman v. McLaren*, 98 F.R.D. 638, 651–52 (N.D. Ill. 1983).

Henson appeals to the language of Rule 23, which begins, "One or more members of a class may sue or be sued as representative parties on behalf of all. . . ." But the next word is "only," and is followed by a list of prerequisites to maintaining a suit as a class action. The first sentence does not authorize defendant classes but merely states limitations common to all class action. Nowhere does it imply that defendant class actions are possible under every subsection of Rule 23(b).

Henson points out that (b)(2) speaks of "the party opposing the class" and that the draftsmen could easily have said "the defendant" instead if they had meant to limit (b)(2) to plaintiff classes. But (b)(2) speaks of declaratory as well as injunctive relief, and in a declaratory judgment action the parties frequently get reversed. A debtor for example might bring a suit against a class of creditors, seeking a declaration of nonliability. In such a case it could be argued that the "real" plaintiffs were the creditors and the "real" defendant the debtor—that it was the debtor who had "acted or refused to act on grounds generally applicable to the class." In such a case a (b)(2) "defendant" class might conceivably be permissible, though that is not an issue we need resolve today. *Blake v. Arnett*, 663 F.2d 906, 911–13 (9th Cir. 1981), may have been such a case.

Actually the language of (b)(2) is against Henson. Always it is the alleged wrongdoer, the defendant—never the plaintiff (except perhaps in the reverse declaratory suit)—who will have "acted or refused to act on grounds generally applicable to the class." In this case, for example, the plaintiff class is complaining about the conduct of the named defendants and of the unnamed defendant class members in not promulgating written standards for welfare eligibility and in otherwise not complying with the requirements of due process of law spelled out in *White v. Roughton*. No one is complaining about any act or refusal to act by Henson or by any member of the plaintiff class.

The drafting history is also against Henson. The Advisory Committee's Notes make no reference to defendant class actions in connection with (b)(2). They describe the (b)(2) class action as an action by a plaintiff class against a defendant who has done something injurious to the class as a whole. "Illustrative are various actions in the civil-rights field where a party is charged with discriminating against a class, usually one whose members are incapable of specific enumeration." Henson's counsel acknowledged at oral argument that the draftsmen of (b)(2) did not contemplate defendant classes but he argued that nevertheless the language they used brought such actions (perhaps inadvertently) under the rule. It does not, as we have shown; so we need not decide whether draftsmen of rules or statutes should ever be held to meanings that are inadvertent—the product of the ambiguities inherent in language.

Henson's main argument is that to interpret Rule 23(b)(2) as excluding defendant class actions would create a remedial gap so large that the draftsmen's failure to provide for such actions must be ascribed to oversight. The premise of this argument is not persuasive. The ease and speed with which the Federal Rules of Civil Procedure can be amended by those whom Congress entrusted with the responsibility for doing so should make federal judges hesitate to create new forms of judicial proceeding in the teeth of the existing rules. Neither the rules committee nor any of its advisors has ever considered whether actions such as the present should be maintainable and if so under what conditions and with what limitations; and the fact that in 45 out of almost two million civil lawsuits filed in federal district courts since 1966 a defendant class has been certified under (b)(2) does not prove that the (b)(2) defendant class action fills an essential need. Such an action creates as we shall see severe problems of manageability and due process, and if the need for such actions is nonetheless an urgent one, the problems they create should be addressed by the persons charged with primary responsibility for formulating the rules of procedure for the federal courts.

The Foundation points out that if this suit cannot be maintained against a class of defendants, the plaintiff class will shrink to welfare applicants in East Lincoln Township—for they alone have a quarrel with the named defendants. To get all the relief this suit seeks the Foundation will have to find a plaintiff in each of the other 770 townships (or in however many actually are violating the Fourteenth Amendment)—and one suit will become several hundred and clog the overcrowded dockets of the federal district courts in central and southern Illinois. The Foundation paints with too vivid a palette. Any township that is violating the principles of *White v. Roughton* has strong incentives to bring itself voluntarily into prompt and full compliance (and all or most of them may, for all we know, have done so during the five-year course of this litigation). By virtue of 42 U.S.C. § 1988, the plaintiff in a federal civil rights suit is normally entitled to the award of a reasonable attorney's fees if he prevails, so townships that prove obdurate in defending the indefensible will pay not only their own legal expenses but those of their adversaries. Furthermore, it may be that in many of these townships either there are no denials of due process or the denials aren't hurting anyone who cares to step forward and be a class representative, in which event the number of separate suits that would replace this two-sided class action might be many fewer than the Foundation predicts. (Indeed, it acknowledged at argument that the difficulty of lining up plaintiffs in the other townships was one of its motivations for seeking to certify a defendant class.) Even if several hundred cases are filed, they can be consolidated for pretrial discovery and for trial in one court, before one judge, and all but the lead case stayed until that case is resolved, and then the others resolved summarily. See 28 U.S.C. § 1407. The practical difference between class treatment and individual-case treatment, so far as securing the constitutional rights of welfare recipients in Illinois is concerned, could turn out to be small.

It is relevant to our consideration to note that a double class action would be unwieldy, or worse, in the circumstances disclosed by this case, and probably generally. The law firm retained by one Illinois township of modest size is being asked to shoulder responsibility for defending the interests of hundreds of others, which by the same token are being asked to place the responsibility for a litigation vital to the discharge of their essential and financially burdensome public functions in lawyers they may never have heard of. Indeed, "told" rather than "asked"; for not only is there no provision in (b)(2) for a class member to opt out of the suit, but there is no requirement of notifying the members of the class, though such notice was provided here. It would be odd if the rule permitted a defendant class without requiring notice; this is one more bit of evidence against Henson's reading of the statute.

And because the defendant class consists of local governments and their officials, in effect the federal district court is being asked to override the state's allocation of powers among local governmental bodies and treat the welfare system as if it were a state system rather than a local system—though it really is local, except for those townships that receive state aid, and they are not involved in this case. It is only an accident, moreover, that this litigation is limited to 65 counties in Illinois. On the Foundation's reading of (b)(2), as it acknowledged at argument, this suit could have been brought as a nationwide class action pitting all welfare applicants in the United States who are being denied due process of law against all the welfare departments in the United States that are thought to be denying those benefits. The welfare department of Eugene, Oregon might find itself an unnamed defendant in the Central District of Illinois, represented by the law firm retained by the township of East Lincoln, Illinois. True, it might be able to interpose objections based on lack of personal jurisdiction. See 3B MOORE'S FEDERAL PRACTICE ¶ 23.40[6], at p. 23–313 n. 8 (2d ed. 1985). But this would not solve the deeper problems of such a suit. By the very definition of a double class action there is no controversy between most plaintiffs and most defendants. Residents of East Lincoln have no quarrel with any defendant except East Lincoln; East Lincoln has no quarrel with any plaintiff except Henson. And so it goes for all the members of the plaintiff and defendant classes. The double class action is a legislative or regulatory device for bringing about general compliance with law (the injunction issued at the end of the action corresponding to a statute or regulation that binds all persons within its scope, whether or not they have been guilty of any wrongdoing in the past), rather than an adjudicative device for resolving a dispute. Indeed, as we have said, the Foundation's fear of not being able to enlist a plaintiff against each and every one of the allegedly noncomplying townships was one of the motivations behind seeking the certification of a defendant class. It is possible that in a double class action with thousands of parties only two would have a dispute—Henson and East Lincoln Township. Without having to decide whether Article III permits a federal court to assert jurisdiction over a mass of parties that may not be engaged in an actual controversy with anyone, we believe that a federal court should not claim such jurisdiction on the basis of a rule of procedure not intended by its draftsmen to confer it.

An influential current in contemporary legal thought believes that the old-fashioned bipolar model of adjudication is hopelessly outmoded and that the federal courts should embrace with enthusiasm a newer model of adjudication, in which federal district courts carry out ambitious restructurings of public institutions, such as state and local welfare systems, in the manner of a regulatory agency. See, e.g., Chayes, *The Role of the Judge in Public Law Litigation*, 89 Harv. L. Rev. 1281 (1976). Whatever the abstract merits of this approach (and maybe it should not be evaluated in the abstract), we do not find it embodied in Rule 23(b)(2), and we have no authority to amend the rule.

One might argue that concerns about a nationwide (b)(2) defendant class action or about the use of the (b)(2) defendant class action to get around an absence of willing plaintiffs should be addressed on a case-by-case basis rather than used to create an absolute rule against such an action. We disagree. Our job is to interpret the existing rule, and the fact that the rule does not set forth the explicit limitations that would be necessary and appropriate to prevent such a class action from becoming a monstrous perversion of the principles of civil procedure is evidence that the rule does not authorize such actions. Nothing in the structure or history of the rule suggests that it was intended as a broad delegation to the courts of a power that judges would domesticate by bringing to bear limiting principles found elsewhere in Rule 23, or in the Constitution, or in the Judicial Code.

Granted, such limiting principles abound. We have mentioned one already—the limitations on a court's personal jurisdiction. There are others, so that even if (b)(2) double class actions were possible in principle, the present class action or our hypothetical nationwide class action might be precluded—whether by Rule 11, which requires that counsel inquire before rather than after bringing suit whether his client has a claim against the defendant (including we suppose members of a defendant class), or by Rule 23(a)(4), which requires that "the representative parties will fairly and adequately protect the interests of the class," see *La Mar v. H & B Novelty & Loan Co.*, 489 F.2d 461, 466 (9th Cir. 1973). At the very least, such actions might be trimmed down to manageability by orders issued under Rule 23(d), such as an order permitting the district court to allow each member of the defendant class to intervene in the suit with the full rights of a named party. But the managerial burdens placed on the district court would be great, and the potential for litigation over rulings under these provisions considerable. We are loath to embark on these uncharted and, as it seems to us, perilous seas without some indication that the framers of Rule 23 would have wanted us to do so; there is no such indication. Previous judicial experience with such class actions is too limited to persuade us that our fears are chimerical or our interpretation of the rule unsound. If as we doubt there is a great need for defendant classes in Rule 23(b)(2) suits, we do not doubt that the Advisory Committee on the Federal Rules of Civil Procedure will repair the gap left by our interpretation by the present rule. It is more likely that the Committee can come up with a rule that will solve (if they are soluble) the notice and management problems that suits such as this pose than that ad hoc decisions by federal district judges around the country will produce a satisfactory standard.

Our conclusion is supported not only by the cases cited earlier but by the Wright and Miller treatise, see 7A Wright, Miller & Kane, FEDERAL PRACTICE AND PROCEDURE § 1775, at pp. 461–62 (2d ed. 1986), and by the thorough discussion in Comment, *Defendant Class Actions and Federal Civil Rights Litigation*, 33 UCLA L. Rev. 283, 316–25 (1985). Professor Moore, though sympathetic to allowing (b)(2) suits against classes, admits that it would require stretching the language of the rule and would create a variety of problems; why he nevertheless favors the device is unclear. See 3B MOORE'S FEDERAL PRACTICE, *supra*, ¶ 23.40[6]. The case for the (b)(2) defendant class is well argued in Note, *Certification of Defendant Classes Under Rule 23(b)(2)*, 84 Colum. L. Rev. 1371 (1984), stressing the utility of the device in a case such as the present where local officials are alleged to be unwilling to comply with decisional law; but for reasons explained earlier we are less impressed than the note's author is by the practical arguments for the device. We note, finally, that double class actions remain possible under (b)(3), as in *Appleton Electric Co. v. Advance–United Expressways*, 494 F.2d 126, 137 & n.22 (7th Cir. 1974).

The district court's order declining to certify a defendant class is

AFFIRMED.

NOTES AND QUESTIONS

1. *Rule Text.* Is the Seventh Circuit correct that the text of subsection (b)(2) counsels against the certification of the proposed defendant class in *Henson*? Given the previously-noted convergence in practice between subsection (b)(2) and subsection (b)(1)(A) with regard to *plaintiff* classes, is the court correct to dismiss so casually the textual argument for certification of defendant classes based on the language at the outset of subsection (b)(1)?

Given the text of subsection (b)(2) specifically, is it appropriate for the court to consider the viability of non-class litigation to bring the townships in addition to East Lincoln into compliance with their legal obligations? In particular, is it appropriate for the court to consider the existence of a fee-shifting statute designed to facilitate civil rights lawsuits of the sort in *Henson*?

Reconsider the underlying justification for mandatory class treatment under subsection (b)(2), discussed earlier in this Chapter. Are there situations in which a conventional defendant would *want* to sue (albeit, nominally aligned as the plaintiff) multiple persons in the aggregate (nominally aligned as a defendant class)? What if the substance of the litigation in *Henson* had concerned not the townships' compliance with previously established legal obligations but, rather, the existence of such obligations—if any—under the federal Constitution in the first place?

2. *Defendant Class or Double (a.k.a. Bilateral) Class?* Does the *Henson* court's real quarrel lie with the nature of the proposed class as a "double class" or "bilateral class" (phrases used equivalently by courts to describe the situation of a plaintiff class suing a defendant class) rather than with the basic notion of a defendant class under subsection (b)(2)?

The Seventh Circuit in *Henson* cites an earlier Ninth Circuit decision in *La Mar v. H & B Novelty & Loan Co.*, 489 F.2d 461 (9th Cir. 1973), on the problems raised by double classes. The *La Mar* court observed:

> . . . [T]o reduce the incidence of proceedings in which the trial judge and the representative plaintiff's counsel become a part-time regulatory agency, we assert that a plaintiff who has no cause of action against the defendant cannot "fairly and adequately protect the interests" of those who do have such causes of action. This is true even though the plaintiff may have suffered an identical injury at the hands of a party other than the defendant and even though his attorney is excellent in every material respect. Obviously this position does not embrace situations in which all injuries are the result of a conspiracy or concerted schemes between the defendants at whose hands the class suffered injury. Nor is it intended to apply in instances in which all defendants are juridically related in a manner that suggests a single resolution of the dispute would be expeditious.

489 F.2d at 466.

G. FEDERAL CLASS ACTIONS AND STATE LAW

The Diversity Jurisdiction Clause of Article III gives federal courts no authority to create substantive law. *Erie R.R. Co. v. Tompkins*, 304 U.S. 64 (1938). For that reason, unless there is some other basis in the Constitution for applying federal law, "state law must govern [in a federal court] because there can be no other law." *Hanna v. Plumer*, 380 U.S. 460, 471–72 (1965). Conversely, when federal substantive law—a statute enacted under the Commerce Clause, for example—is on point, federal law governs in both state and federal court.

The rules are more complex for matters that can be characterized as procedural. As a general matter, the United States and the states individually all have the authority to use their respective laws of procedure in their own courts, and federal courts have some power to make common law for procedural matters not already covered by a federal constitutional or statutory provision or an official Federal Rule promulgated pursuant to the Rules Enabling Act. In fact, the Supreme Court has made clear that federal courts are required to apply a valid federal procedural statute or Federal Rule on point. *Hanna*, 380 U.S. at 469–74. But in the absence of a federal constitutional provision, a valid procedural statute, or a valid Federal Rule, the power of federal courts to use their common law powers to make procedural law in the face of a contrary state procedural rule is limited by the *Erie* policy when the federal court adjudicates a state-created claim. Recall that "[t]he nub of the [*Erie*] policy . . . is that for the same transaction the accident of a suit . . . in a federal court instead of in a state court a block away, should not lead to a substantially different result." *Guaranty Trust Co. v. York*, 326 U.S. 99, 109 (1945). *Hanna* further established that the outcome determination test of *York* must be understood in the light of the "twin aims of the *Erie rule*: discouragement of forum shopping [between state and federal court] and avoidance of inequitable administration of the laws." *Hanna*, 380 U.S. at 468.* Federal courts may also be required to defer to state procedural law if a Federal Rule of Civil Procedure would be *invalid as applied* in a diversity case. The validity of a Federal Rule of Civil Procedure is governed by the Rules Enabling Act, which provides in relevant part:

> (a) The Supreme Court shall have the power to prescribe general rules of practice and procedure and rules of evidence for cases in the United States district courts (including proceedings before magistrate judges thereof) and courts of appeals.
>
> (b) Such rules shall not abridge, enlarge or modify any substantive right. . . .

28 U.S.C. § 2072. Lower courts have never found a Federal Rule of Civil Procedure invalid on its face and only *rarely* invalid as applied to adjudication of a state claim in the face of a contrary state rule. And the Supreme Court has never found a Federal Rule of Civil Procedure invalid even as applied.

In the case that follows, a sharply divided Supreme Court addresses (1) whether Rule 23 purports to cover the point at issue, and (2) whether Rule 23 can validly be applied in the case, thereby ousting conflicting New York state law.

Shady Grove Orthopedic Associates, P.A. v. Allstate Insurance Co.

559 U.S. 393 (2010)

■ JUSTICE SCALIA announced the judgment of the Court and delivered the opinion of the Court with respect to Parts I and II–A [and] an opinion with respect to Part[] II–B[,] . . . in which THE CHIEF JUSTICE, JUSTICE THOMAS, and JUSTICE SOTOMAYOR join. . . .

New York law prohibits class actions in suits seeking penalties or statutory minimum damages.[1] We consider whether this precludes a federal district court sitting in diversity from entertaining a class action under Federal Rule of Civil Procedure 23.

I

The petitioner's complaint alleged the following: Shady Grove Orthopedic Associates, P.A., provided medical care to Sonia E. Galvez for injuries she suffered in an automobile accident. As partial payment for that care, Galvez assigned to Shady Grove her rights to insurance benefits under a

---

* The *Erie* policy may be outweighed in limited circumstances by other federal policies. See, e.g., *Byrd v. Blue Ridge Rural Electric Cooperative*, 356 U.S. 525 (1958).

[1] N.Y. Civ. Prac. Law Ann. § 901 (West 2006) provides: . . .

"(b) Unless a statute creating or imposing a penalty, or a minimum measure of recovery specifically authorizes the recovery thereof in a class action, an action to recover a penalty, or minimum measure of recovery created or imposed by statute may not be maintained as a class action."

policy issued in New York by Allstate Insurance Co. Shady Grove tendered a claim for the assigned benefits to Allstate, which under New York law had 30 days to pay the claim or deny it. Allstate apparently paid, but not on time, and it refused to pay the statutory interest that accrued on the overdue benefits (at two percent per month).

Shady Grove filed this diversity suit in the Eastern District of New York to recover the unpaid statutory interest. Alleging that Allstate routinely refuses to pay interest on overdue benefits, Shady Grove sought relief on behalf of itself and a class of all others to whom Allstate owes interest. The District Court dismissed the suit for lack of jurisdiction. It reasoned that N.Y. Civ. Prac. Law Ann. § 901(b), which precludes a suit to recover a "penalty" from proceeding as a class action, applies in diversity suits in federal court, despite Federal Rule of Civil Procedure 23. Concluding that statutory interest is a "penalty" under New York law, it held that § 901(b) prohibited the proposed class action. And, since Shady Grove conceded that its individual claim (worth roughly $500) fell far short of the amount-in-controversy requirement for individual suits under 28 U.S.C. § 1332(a), the suit did not belong in federal court.[3]

The Second Circuit affirmed. . . .

II

The framework for our decision is familiar. We must first determine whether Rule 23 answers the question in dispute. *Burlington Northern R.R.. Co. v. Woods*, 480 U.S. 1, 4–5 (1987). If it does, it governs—New York's law notwithstanding—unless it exceeds statutory authorization or Congress's rulemaking power. See *Hanna v. Plumer*, 380 U.S. 460, 463–64 (1965). . . .

A

The question in dispute is whether Shady Grove's suit may proceed as a class action. Rule 23 provides an answer. It states that "[a] class action may be maintained" if two conditions are met: The suit must satisfy the criteria set forth in subdivision (a) (i.e., numerosity, commonality, typicality, and adequacy of representation), and it also must fit into one of the three categories described in subdivision (b). By its terms this creates a categorical rule entitling a plaintiff whose suit meets the specified criteria to pursue his claim as a class action. (The Federal Rules regularly use "may" to confer categorical permission, as do federal statutes that establish procedural entitlements.) Thus, Rule 23 provides a one-size-fits-all formula for deciding the class-action question. Because § 901(b) attempts to answer the same question—i.e., it states that Shady Grove's suit "may *not* be maintained as a class action" (emphasis added) because of the relief it seeks—it cannot apply in diversity suits unless Rule 23 is *ultra vires*.

The Second Circuit believed that § 901(b) and Rule 23 do not conflict because they address different issues. Rule 23, it said, concerns only the criteria for determining whether a given class can and should be certified; section 901(b), on the other hand, addresses an antecedent question: whether the particular type of claim is eligible for class treatment in the first place—a question on which Rule 23 is silent. Allstate embraces this analysis.

---

[3] Shady Grove had asserted jurisdiction under 28 U.S.C. § 1332(d)(2), which relaxes, for class actions seeking at least $5 million, the rule against aggregating separate claims for calculation of the amount in controversy.

We disagree. To begin with, the line between eligibility and certifiability is entirely artificial. Both are preconditions for maintaining a class action. Allstate suggests that eligibility must depend on the "particular cause of action" asserted, instead of some other attribute of the suit. But that is not so. Congress could, for example, provide that only claims involving more than a certain number of plaintiffs are "eligible" for class treatment in federal court. In other words, relabeling Rule 23(a)'s prerequisites "eligibility criteria" would obviate Allstate's objection—a sure sign that its eligibility-certifiability distinction is made-to-order.

There is no reason, in any event, to read Rule 23 as addressing only whether claims made eligible for class treatment by some other law should be certified as class actions. Allstate asserts that Rule 23 neither explicitly nor implicitly empowers a federal court "to certify a class in each and every case" where the Rule's criteria are met. But that is exactly what Rule 23 does: It says that if the prescribed preconditions are satisfied "[a] class action *may be maintained*" (emphasis added)—not "a class action may be permitted." Courts do not maintain actions; litigants do. The discretion suggested by Rule 23's "may" is discretion residing in the plaintiff: He may bring his claim in a class action if he wishes. And like the rest of the Federal Rules of Civil Procedure, Rule 23 automatically applies "in all civil actions and proceedings in the United States district courts," Fed. R. Civ. P. 1.

Allstate points out that Congress [through statute] has carved out some federal claims from Rule 23's reach—which shows, Allstate contends, that Rule 23 does not authorize class actions for all claims, but rather leaves room for laws like § 901(b). But Congress, unlike New York, has ultimate authority over the Federal Rules of Civil Procedure; it can create exceptions to an individual rule as it sees fit—either by directly amending the rule or by enacting a separate statute overriding it in certain instances. The fact that Congress has created specific exceptions to Rule 23 hardly proves that the Rule does not apply generally. In fact, it proves the opposite. If Rule 23 did *not* authorize class actions across the board, the statutory exceptions would be unnecessary. . . .

The dissent argues that § 901(b) has nothing to do with whether Shady Grove may maintain its suit as a class action, but affects only the *remedy* it may obtain if it wins. . . .

We need not decide whether a state law that limits the remedies available in an existing class action would conflict with Rule 23; that is not what § 901(b) does. By its terms, the provision precludes a plaintiff from "maintain[ing]" a class action seeking statutory penalties. Unlike a law that sets a ceiling on damages (or puts other remedies out of reach) in properly filed class actions, § 901(b) says nothing about what remedies a court may award; it prevents the class actions it covers from coming into existence at all. Consequently, a court bound by § 901(b) could not certify a class action seeking both statutory penalties and other remedies even if it announces in advance that it will refuse to award the penalties in the event the plaintiffs prevail; to do so would violate the statute's clear prohibition on "maintain[ing]" such suits as class actions. . . .

The dissent all but admits that the literal terms of § 901(b) address the same subject as Rule 23—*i.e.*, whether a class action may be maintained—but insists the provisions's *purpose* is to restrict only remedies. . . . [The dissent argued that the purpose of § 901(b) was to protect defendants from excessive damages that might result from allowing each class member to recover statutory penalties in a class action.—Ed.]

[The dissent's] evidence of the New York Legislature's purpose is pretty sparse. But even accepting the dissent's account of the Legislature's objective at face value, it cannot override the statute's clear text. Even if its aim is to restrict the remedy a plaintiff can obtain, § 901(b) achieves that end by limiting a plaintiff's power to maintain a class action. The manner in which the law "could have been written" has no bearing; what matters is the law the Legislature did enact. We cannot rewrite that to reflect our perception of legislative purpose. The dissent's concern for state prerogatives is frustrated rather than furthered by revising state laws when a potential conflict with a Federal Rule arises; the state-friendly approach would be to accept the law as written and test the validity of the Federal Rule. . . .

But while the dissent does indeed artificially narrow the scope of § 901(b) by finding that it pursues only substantive policies, that is not the central difficulty of the dissent's position. The central difficulty is that even artificial narrowing cannot render § 901(b) compatible with Rule 23. *Whatever* the policies they pursue, they flatly contradict each other. Allstate asserts (and the dissent implies that we can (and must) *interpret* Rule 23 in a manner that avoids overstepping its authorizing statute.[7] If the Rule were susceptible of two meanings—one that would violate § 2072(b) and another that would not—we would agree. But it is not. Rule 23 unambiguously authorizes any plaintiff, in any federal civil proceeding, to maintain a class action if the Rule's prerequisites are met. We cannot contort its text, even to avert a collision with state law that might render it invalid. What the dissent's approach achieves is not the avoiding of a "conflict between Rule 23 and § 901(b)," but rather the invalidation of Rule 23 (pursuant to § 2072(b) of the Rules Enabling Act) to the extent that it conflicts with the substantive policies of § 901. There is no other way to reach the dissent's destination. We must therefore confront head-on whether Rule 23 falls within the statutory authorization.

B

Erie involved the constitutional power of federal courts to supplant state law with judge-made rules. In that context, it made no difference whether the rule was technically one of substance or procedure; the touchstone was whether it "significantly affect[s] the result of a litigation." *Guaranty Trust Co. v. York,* 326 U.S. 99, 109 (1945). That is not the test for either the constitutionality or the statutory validity of a Federal Rule of Procedure. Congress has undoubted power to supplant state law, and un-

---

[7] The dissent also suggests that we should read the Federal Rules " 'with sensitivity to important state interests' " and " 'to avoid conflict with important state regulatory policies.' " (quoting *Gasperini v. Center for Humanities, Inc.*, 518 U.S. 415, 427 n.7, 438, n.22 (1996)). The search for state interests and policies that are "important" is just as standardless as the "important or substantial" criterion we rejected in *Sibbach v. Wilson & Co.*, to define the state-created rights a Federal Rule may not abridge.

If all the dissent means is that we should read an ambiguous Federal Rule to avoid "substantial variations [in outcomes] between state and federal litigation," *Semtek Int'l Inc. v. Lockheed Martin Corp.*, 531 U.S. 497, 504 (2001) (internal quotation marks omitted), we entirely agree. We should do so not to avoid doubt as to the Rule's validity—since a Federal Rule that fails *Erie*'s forum-shopping test is not ipso facto invalid, see *Hanna v. Plumer,* 380 U.S. 460, 469–72, (1965)—but because it is reasonable to assume that "Congress is just as concerned as we have been to avoid significant differences between state and federal courts in adjudicating claims," *Stewart Organization, Inc. v. Ricoh Corp.*, 487 U.S. 22, 37–38 (1988) (Scalia, J., dissenting). The assumption is irrelevant here, however, because there is only one reasonable reading of Rule 23.

doubted power to prescribe rules for the courts it has created, so long as those rules regulate matters "rationally capable of classification" as procedure. *Hanna*, 380 U.S. at 472. In the Rules Enabling Act, Congress authorized this Court to promulgate rules of procedure subject to its review, 28 U.S.C. § 2072(a), but with the limitation that those rules "shall not abridge, enlarge or modify any substantive right," § 2072(b).

We have long held that this limitation means that the Rule must "really regulat[e] procedure—the judicial process for enforcing rights and duties recognized by substantive law and for justly administering remedy and redress for disregard or infraction of them," *Sibbach*, 312 U.S. at 14. The test is not whether the rule affects a litigant's substantive rights; most procedural rules do. *Mississippi Publ'g Corp. v. Murphree*, 326 U.S. 438, 445 (1946). What matters is what the rule itself *regulates*: If it governs only "the manner and the means" by which the litigants' rights are "enforced," it is valid; if it alters "the rules of decision by which [the] court will adjudicate [those] rights," it is not.

Applying that test, we have rejected every statutory challenge to a Federal Rule that has come before us. We have found to be in compliance with § 2072(b) rules prescribing methods for serving process and requiring litigants whose mental or physical condition is in dispute to submit to examinations. Likewise, we have upheld rules authorizing imposition of sanctions upon those who file frivolous appeals or who sign court papers without a reasonable inquiry into the facts asserted. Each of these rules had some practical effect on the parties' rights, but each undeniably regulated only the process for enforcing those rights; none altered the rights themselves, the available remedies, or the rules of decision by which the court adjudicated either.

Applying that criterion, we think it obvious that rules allowing multiple claims (and claims by or against multiple parties) to be litigated together are also valid. See, e.g., Fed. R. Civ. P. 18 (joinder of claims), 20 (joinder of parties), 42(a) (consolidation of actions). Such rules neither change plaintiffs' separate entitlements to relief nor abridge defendants' rights; they alter only how the claims are processed. For the same reason, Rule 23—at least insofar as it allows willing plaintiffs to join their separate claims against the same defendants in a class action—falls within § 2072(b)'s authorization. A class action, no less than traditional joinder (of which it is a species), merely enables a federal court to adjudicate claims of multiple parties at once, instead of in separate suits. And like traditional joinder, it leaves the parties' legal rights and duties intact and the rules of decision unchanged.

Allstate contends that the authorization of class actions is not substantively neutral: Allowing Shady Grove to sue on behalf of a class "transform[s] [the] dispute over a five hundred dollar penalty into a dispute over a five million dollar penalty." Allstate's aggregate liability, however, does not depend on whether the suit proceeds as a class action. Each of the 1,000 plus members of the putative class could (as Allstate acknowledges) bring a freestanding suit asserting his individual claim. It is undoubtedly true that some plaintiffs who would not bring individual suits for the relatively small sums involved will choose to join a class action. That has no bearing, however, on Allstate's or the plaintiffs' legal rights. The likelihood that some (even many) plaintiffs will be induced to sue by the availability of a class action is just the sort of "incidental effec[t]" we have long held does not violate § 2072(b), *Mississippi Publ'g*, 326 U.S. at 445.

Allstate argues that Rule 23 violates § 2072(b) because the state law it displaces, § 901(b), creates a right that the Federal Rule abridges—namely, a "substantive right . . . not to be subjected to aggregated class-action liability" in a single suit. To begin with, we doubt that that is so. Nothing in the text of § 901(b) (which is to be found in New York's procedural code) confines it to claims under New York law; and of course New York has no power to alter substantive rights and duties created by other sovereigns. As we have said, the consequence of excluding certain class actions may be to cap the damages a defendant can face in a single suit, but the law itself alters only procedure. In that respect, § 901(b) is no different from a state law forbidding simple joinder. As a fallback argument, Allstate argues that even if § 901(b) is a procedural provision, it was enacted "for *substantive reasons*" (emphasis added). Its end was not to improve "the conduct of the litigation process itself" but to alter "the outcome of that process."

The fundamental difficulty with both these arguments is that the substantive nature of New York's law, or its substantive purpose, *makes no difference*. A Federal Rule of Procedure is not valid in some jurisdictions and invalid in others—or valid in some cases and invalid in others—depending upon whether its effect is to frustrate a state substantive law (or a state procedural law enacted for substantive purposes). . . .

In sum, it is not the substantive or procedural nature or purpose of the affected state law that matters, but the substantive or procedural nature of the Federal Rule. We have held since *Sibbach*, and reaffirmed repeatedly, that the validity of a Federal Rule depends entirely upon whether it regulates procedure. See *Sibbach*, 312 U.S. at 14, 61; *Hanna*, 380 U.S. at 464, *Burlington*, 480 U.S. at 8, If it does, it is authorized by § 2072 and is valid in all jurisdictions, with respect to all claims, regardless of its incidental effect upon state-created rights.

[Parts II–C and II–D of Justice Scalia's opinion are omitted.]

The judgment of the Court of Appeals is reversed, and the case is remanded for further proceedings.

It is so ordered.

■ JUSTICE STEVENS, concurring in part and concurring in the judgment.

The New York law at issue, N.Y. Civ. Prac. Law Ann. (CPLR) § 901(b) is a procedural rule that is not part of New York's substantive law. Accordingly, I agree with Justice SCALIA that Federal Rule of Civil Procedure 23 must apply in this case and join Parts I and II-A of the Court's opinion. But I also agree with Justice GINSBURG that there are some state procedural rules that federal courts must apply in diversity cases because they function as a part of the State's definition of substantive rights and remedies.

I

. . . Congress has provided for a system of uniform federal rules under which federal courts sitting in diversity operate as "an independent system for administering justice to litigants who properly invoke its jurisdiction," *Byrd v. Blue Ridge Rural Elec. Cooperative, Inc.*, 356 U.S. 525, 537 (1958), and not as state-court clones that assume all aspects of state tribunals but are managed by Article III judges. But while Congress may have the constitutional power to prescribe procedural rules that interfere with state substantive law in any number of respects, that is not what Congress has done. Instead, it has provided in the Enabling Act that although "[t]he Supreme Court" may "prescribe general rules of practice and procedure," § 2072(a), those rules "shall not abridge, enlarge or modify any substantive right," § 2072(b). Therefore, "[w]hen a situation is covered by one of the Federal Rules . . . the court has been instructed to apply the Federal Rule" unless doing so would violate the Act or the Constitution. *Hanna*, 380 U.S. at 471.

. . . The Enabling Act does not invite federal courts to engage in the "relatively unguided *Erie* choice," but instead instructs only that federal rules cannot "abridge, enlarge or modify any substantive right," § 2072(b). The Enabling Act's limitation does not mean that federal rules cannot displace state policy judgments; it means only that federal rules cannot displace a State's definition of its own rights or remedies.

Congress has thus struck a balance: "[H]ousekeeping rules for federal courts" will generally apply in diversity cases, notwithstanding that some federal rules "will inevitably differ" from state rules. *Hanna*, 380 U.S. at 473. But not every federal "rul[e] of practice or procedure," § 2072(a), will displace state law. To the contrary, federal rules must be interpreted with some degree of "sensitivity to important state interests and regulatory policies," *Gasperini* 518 U.S. at 427 n.7, and applied to diversity cases against the background of Congress' command that such rules not alter substantive rights and with consideration of "the degree to which the Rule makes the character and result of the federal litigation stray from the course it would follow in state courts," *Hanna*, 380 U.S. at 473. This can be a tricky balance to implement.

It is important to observe that the balance Congress has struck turns, in part, on the nature of the state law that is being displaced by a federal rule. And in my view, the application of that balance does not necessarily turn on whether the state law at issue takes the form of what is traditionally described as substantive or procedural. Rather, it turns on whether the state law actually is part of a State's framework of substantive rights or remedies. See § 2072(b); *cf. Hanna*, 380 U.S. at 471 ("The line between 'substance' and 'procedure' shifts as the legal context changes"); *Guaranty Trust Co. v. York*, 326 U.S. 99, 108 (1945) (noting that the words " 'substance' " and " 'procedure' " "[e]ach impl[y] different variables depending upon the particular problem for which [they] are used").

Applying this balance, therefore, requires careful interpretation of the state and federal provisions at issue. "The line between procedural and substantive law is hazy," *Erie R.R. Co. v. Tompkins*, 304 U.S. 64, 92 (1938) (Reed, J., concurring), and matters of procedure and matters of substance are not "mutually exclusive categories with easily ascertainable contents," *Sibbach*, 312 U.S. at 17 (Frankfurter, J., dissenting). Rather, "[r]ules which lawyers call procedural do not always exhaust their effect by regulating procedure," *Cohen v. Beneficial Ind. Loan Corp.*, 337 U.S. 541, 555 (1949), and in some situations, "procedure and substance are so interwoven that rational separation becomes well-nigh impossible," *id.* at 559 (Rutledge, J., dissenting). A "state procedural rule, though undeniably 'procedural' in the ordinary sense of the term," may exist "to influence substantive outcomes," *S.A. Healy Co. v. Milwaukee Metropolitan Sewerage Dist.*, 60 F.3d 305, 310 (7th Cir. 1995) (Posner, J.), and may in some instances become so bound up with the state-created right or remedy that it defines the scope of that substantive right or remedy. Such laws, for example, may be seemingly procedural rules that make it significantly more difficult to bring or to prove a claim, thus serving to limit the scope of that claim. See, e.g., *Cohen*, 337 U.S. at 555 (state "procedure" that required plaintiffs to post bond before suing); *Guaranty Trust Co.*, 326 U.S. 99 (state statute of limitations). Such "procedural rules" may also define the amount of recovery. See, e.g., *Gasperini*, 518 U.S. at 427 (state procedure for examining jury verdicts as means of capping the available remedy); Moore § 124.07[3][a] (listing examples of federal courts' applying state laws that affect the amount of a judgment).

In our federalist system, Congress has not mandated that federal courts dictate to state legislatures the form that their substantive law must take. And were federal courts to ignore those portions of substantive state law that operate as procedural devices, it could in many instances limit the ways that sovereign States may define their rights and remedies. When a State chooses to use a traditionally procedural vehicle as a means of defining the scope of substantive rights or remedies, federal courts must recognize and respect that choice. Cf. *Ragan v. Merchants Transfer & Warehouse Co.*, 337 U.S. 530, 533 (1949) ("Since th[e] cause of action is created by local law, the measure of it is to be found only in local law. . . . Where local law qualifies or abridges it, the federal court must follow suit").

II

When both a federal rule and a state law appear to govern a question before a federal court sitting in diversity, our precedents have set out a two-step framework for federal courts to negotiate this thorny area. At both steps of the inquiry, there is a critical question about what the state law and the federal rule mean.

The court must first determine whether the scope of the federal rule is " 'sufficiently broad' " to " 'control the issue' " before the court, "thereby leaving no room for the operation" of seemingly conflicting state law. See *Burlington Northern R. Co. v. Woods*, 480 U.S. 1, 4–5 (1987). If the federal rule does not apply or can operate alongside the state rule, then there is no "Ac[t] of Congress" governing that particular question, 28 U.S.C. § 1652, and the court must engage in the traditional Rules of Decision Act inquiry under *Erie* and its progeny.* In some instances, the "plain meaning" of a federal rule will not come into " 'direct collision' " with the state law, and both can operate. *Walker*, 446 U.S. at 750 n.9. In other instances, the rule "when fairly construed," *Burlington Northern R.R.. Co.*, 480 U.S. at 4, with "sensitivity to important state interests and regulatory policies," *Gasperini*, 518 U.S. at 427 n.7, will not collide with the state law.[5]

If, on the other hand, the federal rule is "sufficiently broad to control the issue before the Court," such that there is a "direct collision," *Walker*, 446 U.S. at 749–50, the court must decide whether application of the federal rule "represents a valid exercise" of the "rulemaking authority . . . bestowed on this Court by the Rules Enabling Act." *Burlington Northern R.R.. Co.*, 480 U.S. at 5. That Act requires, inter alia, that federal rules "not abridge, enlarge or modify *any* substantive right." 28 U.S.C. § 2072(b) (emphasis added). Unlike Justice SCALIA, I believe that an application of a

---

* [The Rules of Decision Act provides in relevant part: "The laws of the several states, except where the Constitution or treaties of the United States or Acts of Congress otherwise require or provide, shall be regarded as rules of decision in civil actions in the courts of the United States, in cases where they apply." 28 U.S.C. § 1652. The *Erie* policy is widely but not universally understood to be required by the Rules of Decision Act.—Ed.]

[5] I thus agree with Justice GINSBURG that a federal rule, like any federal law, must be interpreted in light of many different considerations, including "sensitivity to important state interests," and "regulatory policies." I disagree with Justice GINSBURG, however, about the degree to which the meaning of federal rules may be contorted, absent congressional authorization to do so, to accommodate state policy goals.

federal rule that effectively abridges, enlarges, or modifies a state-created right or remedy violates this command. Congress may have the constitutional power "to supplant state law" with rules that are "rationally capable of classification as procedure," but we should generally presume that it has not done so. Indeed, the mandate that federal rules "shall not abridge, enlarge or modify any substantive right" evinces the opposite intent, as does Congress' decision to delegate the creation of rules to this Court rather than to a political branch.

Thus, the second step of the inquiry may well bleed back into the first. When a federal rule appears to abridge, enlarge, or modify a substantive right, federal courts must consider whether the rule can reasonably be interpreted to avoid that impermissible result. See, e.g., *Semtek Int'l Inc. v. Lockheed Martin Corp.*, 531 U.S. 497, 503 (2001) (avoiding an interpretation of Federal Rule of Civil Procedure 41(b) that "would arguably violate the jurisdictional limitation of the Rules Enabling Act" contained in § 2072(b)).[6] And when such a "saving" construction is not possible and the rule would violate the Enabling Act, federal courts cannot apply the rule. See 28 U.S.C. § 2072(b) (mandating that federal rules "shall not" alter "*any* substantive right" (emphasis added)).

Justice SCALIA believes that the sole Enabling Act question is whether the federal rule "really regulates procedure," which means, apparently, whether it regulates "the manner and the means by which the litigants' rights are enforced." I respectfully disagree. This interpretation of the Enabling Act is consonant with the Act's first limitation to "general rules of practice and procedure," § 2072(a). But it ignores the second limitation that such rules also "not abridge, enlarge or modify *any* substantive right," § 2072(b) (emphasis added), and in so doing ignores the balance that Congress struck between uniform rules of federal procedure and respect for a State's construction of its own rights and remedies. It also ignores the separation-of-powers presumption, and federalism presumption, that counsel against judicially created rules displacing state substantive law.[9] . . .

---

[6] See also *Ortiz* v. *Fibreboard Corp.*, 527 U. S. 815, 842, 845 (1999) (adopting "limiting construction" of Federal Rule of Civil Procedure 23 that, *inter alia*, "minimizes potential conflict with the Rules Enabling Act"); *Amchem Prods., Inc.* v. *Windsor*, 521 U. S. 591, 612–13 (1997) (observing that federal rules "must be interpreted in keeping with the Rules Enabling Act, which instructs that rules of procedure 'shall not abridge, enlarge or modify any substantive right' ").

[9] The plurality's interpretation of the Enabling Act appears to mean that no matter how bound up a state provision is with the State's own rights or remedies, any contrary federal rule that happens to regulate "the manner and the means by which the litigants' rights are enforced" must govern. There are many ways in which seemingly procedural rules may displace a State's formulation of its substantive law. For example, statutes of limitations, although in some sense procedural rules, can also be understood as a temporal limitation on legally created rights; if this Court were to promulgate a federal limitations period, federal courts would still, in some instances, be required to apply state limitations periods. Similarly, if the federal rules altered the burden of proof in a case, this could eviscerate a critical aspect—albeit one that deals with how a right is enforced-of a State's framework of rights and remedies. Or if a federal rule about appellate review displaced a state rule about how damages are reviewed on appeal, the federal rule might be pre-empting a state damages cap. Cf. *Gasperini*, 518 U.S. at 427.

Justice SCALIA responds that some of these federal rules might be invalid under his view of the Enabling Act because they may not "really regulat[e] procedure." (internal quotation marks omitted). This response, of course, highlights how empty the plurality's test really is. The response is also limited to those rules that can be described as "regulat[ing]" substance, it does not address those federal rules that alter the right at issue in the litigation, see *Sibbach* v. *Wilson & Co.*, 312 U.S. 1, 13–14 (1941), only when they displace particular state laws. Justice Scalia speculates that "Congress may well have accepted" the occasional alteration of sub-

III

. . .

Rule 23 Controls Class Certification

When the District Court in the case before us was asked to certify a class action, Federal Rule of Civil Procedure 23 squarely governed the determination whether the court should do so. That is the explicit function of Rule 23. Rule 23, therefore, must apply unless its application would abridge, enlarge, or modify New York rights or remedies. . . .

At bottom, the dissent's interpretation of Rule 23 seems to be that Rule 23 covers only those cases in which its application would create no *Erie* problem. The dissent would apply the Rules of Decision Act inquiry under *Erie* even to cases in which there is a governing federal rule, and thus the Act, by its own terms, does not apply. But "[w]hen a situation is covered by one of the Federal Rules, the question facing the court is a far cry from the typical, relatively unguided *Erie* choice." *Hanna*, 380 U.S. at 471. The question is only whether the Enabling Act is satisfied. Although it reflects a laudable concern to protect "state regulatory policies," Justice GINSBURG's approach would, in my view, work an end run around Congress' system of uniform federal rules, see 28 U.S.C. § 2072, and our decision in *Hanna*. Federal courts can and should interpret federal rules with sensitivity to "state prerogatives"; but even when "state interests . . . warrant our respectful consideration," federal courts cannot rewrite the rules. If my dissenting colleagues feel strongly that § 901(b) is substantive and that class certification should be denied, then they should argue within the Enabling Act's framework. Otherwise, "the Federal Rule applies regardless of contrary state law." *Gasperini*, 518 U.S. at 427 n.7.

Applying Rule 23 Does Not Violate the Enabling Act

As I have explained, in considering whether to certify a class action such as this one, a federal court must inquire whether doing so would abridge, enlarge, or modify New York's rights or remedies, and thereby violate the Enabling Act. This inquiry is not always a simple one because "[i]t is difficult to conceive of any rule of procedure that cannot have a significant effect on the outcome of a case," and almost "any rule can be said to have . . . 'substantive effects,' affecting society's distribution of risks and rewards," Faced with a federal rule that dictates an answer to a traditionally procedural question and that displaces a state rule, one can often argue that the state rule was really some part of the State's definition of its rights or remedies.

In my view, however, the bar for finding an Enabling Act problem is a high one. The mere fact that a state law is designed as a procedural rule suggests it reflects a judgment about how state courts ought to operate and not a judgment about the scope of state-created rights and remedies. And for the purposes of operating a federal court system, there are costs involved in attempting to discover the true nature of a state procedural rule and allowing such a rule to operate alongside a federal rule that appears to govern the same question. The mere possibility that a federal rule would alter a state-created right is not sufficient. There must be little doubt.

---

stantive rights "as the price of a uniform system of federal procedure." Were we forced to speculate about the balance that Congress struck, I might very well agree. But no speculation is necessary because Congress explicitly told us that federal rules "shall not" alter "any" substantive right. § 2072(b).

The text of CPLR § 901(b) expressly and unambiguously applies not only to claims based on New York law but also to claims based on federal law or the law of any other State. And there is no interpretation from New York courts to the contrary. It is therefore hard to see how § 901(b) could be understood as a rule that, though procedural in form, serves the function of defining New York's rights or remedies. . . .

The legislative history, moreover, does not clearly describe a judgment that § 901(b) would operate as a limitation on New York's statutory damages. In evaluating that legislative history, it is necessary to distinguish between procedural rules adopted for some policy reason and seemingly procedural rules that are intimately bound up in the scope of a substantive right or remedy. Although almost every rule is adopted for some reason and has some effect on the outcome of litigation, not every state rule "defines the dimensions of [a] claim itself." New York clearly crafted § 901(b) with the intent that only certain lawsuits—those for which there were not statutory penalties—could be joined in class actions in New York courts. That decision reflects a policy judgment about which lawsuits should proceed in New York courts in a class form and which should not. As Justice GINS-BURG carefully outlines, § 901(b) was "apparently" adopted in response to fears that the class-action procedure, applied to statutory penalties, would lead to "annihilating punishment of the defendant." V. Alexander, PRACTICE COMMENTARIES, C901:11, *reprinted in* 7B McKINNEY'S CONSOLIDATED LAWS OF NEW YORK ANN., p. 104 (2006) (internal quotation marks omitted). But statements such as these are not particularly strong evidence that § 901(b) serves to define who can obtain a statutory penalty or that certifying such a class would enlarge New York's remedy. Any device that makes litigation easier makes it easier for plaintiffs to recover damages.

In addition to the fear of excessive recoveries, some opponents of a broad class-action device "argued that there was no *need* to permit class actions in order to encourage litigation . . . when statutory penalties . . . provided an aggrieved party with a sufficient economic incentive to pursue a claim." *Id.* at 211 (emphasis added). But those opponents may have felt merely that, for any number of reasons, New York courts should not conduct trials in the class format when that format is unnecessary to motivate litigation. Justice GINSBURG asserts that this could not be true because "suits seeking statutory damages are arguably best suited to the class device because individual proof of actual damages is unnecessary." But some people believe that class actions are inefficient or at least unfair, insofar as they join together slightly disparate claims or force courts to adjudicate unwieldy lawsuits. It is not for us to dismiss the possibility that New York legislators shared in those beliefs and thus wanted to exclude the class vehicle when it appeared to be unnecessary.

The legislative history of § 901 thus reveals a classically procedural calibration of making it easier to litigate claims in New York courts (under any source of law) only when it is necessary to do so, and not making it too easy when the class tool is not required. This is the same sort of calculation that might go into setting filing fees or deadlines for briefs. There is of course a difference of degree between those examples and class certification, but not a difference of kind; the class vehicle may have a greater practical effect on who brings lawsuits than do low filing fees, but that does not transform it into a damages "proscription."[18] . . .

---

[18] Justice GINSBURG asserts that class certification in this matter would "transform a $500 case into a $5,000,000 award." But in fact, class certification would transform 10,000

Because Rule 23 governs class certification, the only decision is whether certifying a class in this diversity case would "abridge, enlarge or modify" New York's substantive rights or remedies. § 2072(b). Although one can argue that class certification would enlarge New York's "limited" damages remedy, such arguments rest on extensive speculation about what the New York Legislature had in mind when it created § 901(b). But given that there are two plausible competing narratives, it seems obvious to me that we should respect the plain textual reading of § 901(b), a rule in New York's procedural code about when to certify class actions brought under any source of law, and respect Congress' decision that Rule 23 governs class certification in federal courts. In order to displace a federal rule, there must be more than just a possibility that the state rule is different than it appears.

Accordingly, I concur in part and concur in the judgment.

■ JUSTICE GINSBURG, with whom JUSTICE KENNEDY, JUSTICE BREYER, and JUSTICE ALITO join, dissenting.

The Court today approves Shady Grove's attempt to transform a $500 case into a $5,000,000 award, although the State creating the right to recover has proscribed this alchemy. If Shady Grove had filed suit in New York state court, the 2% interest payment authorized by New York Ins. Law Ann. § 5106(a) (West 2009) as a penalty for overdue benefits would, by Shady Grove's own measure, amount to no more than $500. By instead filing in federal court based on the parties' diverse citizenship and requesting class certification, Shady Grove hopes to recover, for the class, statutory damages of more than $5,000,000. The New York Legislature has barred this remedy, instructing that, unless specifically permitted, "an action to recover a penalty, or minimum measure of recovery created or imposed by statute may not be maintained as a class action." N.Y. Civ. Prac. Law Ann. (CPLR) § 901(b) (West 2006). The Court nevertheless holds that Federal Rule of Civil Procedure 23, which prescribes procedures for the conduct of class actions in federal courts, preempts the application of § 901(b) in diversity suits.

The Court reads Rule 23 relentlessly to override New York's restriction on the availability of statutory damages. Our decisions, however, caution us to ask, before undermining state legislation: Is this conflict really necessary? Cf. Roger J. Traynor, *Is This Conflict Really Necessary?* 37 Tex. L.Rev. 657 (1959). Had the Court engaged in that inquiry, it would not have read Rule 23 to collide with New York's legitimate interest in keeping certain monetary awards reasonably bounded. I would continue to interpret Federal Rules with awareness of, and sensitivity to, important state regulatory policies. Because today's judgment radically departs from that course, I dissent.

I

A

. . . The Rules Enabling Act, enacted in 1934, authorizes us to "prescribe general rules of practice and procedure" for the federal courts, but with a crucial restriction: "Such rules shall not abridge, enlarge or modify

---

$500 cases into one $5,000,000 case. It may be that without class certification, not all of the potential plaintiffs would bring their cases. But that is true of any procedural vehicle; without a lower filing fee, a conveniently located courthouse, easy-to-use federal procedural rules, or many other features of the federal courts, many plaintiffs would not sue.

any substantive right." 28 U.S.C. § 2072. Pursuant to this statute, we have adopted the Federal Rules of Civil Procedure. In interpreting the scope of the Rules, including, in particular, Rule 23, we have been mindful of the limits on our authority. See, e.g., *Ortiz v. Fibreboard Corp.*, 527 U.S. 815, 845 (1999) (The Rules Enabling Act counsels against "adventurous application" of Rule 23; any tension with the Act "is best kept within tolerable limits."); *Amchem Prods., Inc. v. Windsor*, 521 U.S. 591, 612–613 (1997).

If a Federal Rule controls an issue and directly conflicts with state law, the Rule, so long as it is consonant with the Rules Enabling Act, applies in diversity suits. See *Hanna*, 380 U.S. at 469–474. If, however, no Federal Rule or statute governs the issue, the Rules of Decision Act, as interpreted in *Erie*, controls. That Act directs federal courts, in diversity cases, to apply state law when failure to do so would invite forum-shopping and yield markedly disparate litigation outcomes. See *Gasperini*, 518 U.S. at 428. Recognizing that the Rules of Decision Act and the Rules Enabling Act simultaneously frame and inform the *Erie* analysis, we have endeavored in diversity suits to remain safely within the bounds of both congressional directives.

B

In our prior decisions in point, many of them not mentioned in the Court's opinion, we have avoided immoderate interpretations of the Federal Rules that would trench on state prerogatives without serving any countervailing federal interest. . . .

In pre-*Hanna* decisions, the Court vigilantly read the Federal Rules to avoid conflict with state laws. In *Palmer v. Hoffman*, 318 U.S. 109, 117 (1943), for example, the Court read Federal Rule 8(c), which lists affirmative defenses, to control only the manner of pleading the listed defenses in diversity cases; as to the burden of proof in such cases, *Palmer* held, state law controls. . . .

In all of these cases, the Court stated in *Hanna*, "the scope of the Federal Rule was not as broad as the losing party urged, and therefore, there being no Federal Rule which covered the point in dispute, *Erie* commanded the enforcement of state law." 380 U.S. at 470. In *Hanna* itself, the Court found the clash "unavoidable." . . . Even as it rejected the Massachusetts prescription in favor of the federal procedure, however, "[t]he majority in Hanna recognized . . . that federal rules . . . must be interpreted by the courts applying them, and that the process of interpretation can and should reflect an awareness of legitimate state interests." R. Fallon, J. Manning, D. Meltzer, & D. Shapiro, HART AND WECHSLER'S THE FEDERAL COURTS AND THE FEDERAL SYSTEM 593 (6th ed.2009) (hereinafter HART & WECHSLER).

Following *Hanna*, we continued to "interpre[t] the federal rules to avoid conflict with important state regulatory policies." HART & WECHSLER 593. . . .

In sum, both before and after *Hanna*, the above-described decisions show, federal courts have been cautioned by this Court to "interpre[t] the Federal Rules . . . with sensitivity to important state interests," *Gasperini*, 518 U.S. at 427 n.7 and a will "to avoid conflict with important state regulatory policies," *id.* at 438 n.22.[2] The Court veers away from that ap-

---

[2] Justice STEVENS stakes out common ground on this point: "[F]ederal rules," he observes, "must be interpreted with some degree of 'sensitivity to important state interests and regulatory policies,' . . . and applied to diversity cases against the background of Congress' command that such rules not alter substantive rights and with consideration of 'the degree to

proach—and conspicuously, its most recent reiteration in *Gasperini*—in favor of a mechanical reading of Federal Rules, insensitive to state interests and productive of discord. . . .

D

Shady Grove contends—and the Court today agrees—that Rule 23 unavoidably preempts New York's prohibition on the recovery of statutory damages in class actions. . . .

The Court, I am convinced, finds conflict where none is necessary. Mindful of the history behind § 901(b)'s enactment, the thrust of our precedent, and the substantive-rights limitation in the Rules Enabling Act, I conclude, as did the Second Circuit and every District Court to have considered the question in any detail that Rule 23 does not collide with § 901(b). As the Second Circuit well understood, Rule 23 prescribes the considerations relevant to class certification and postcertification proceedings—but it does not command that a particular remedy be available when a party sues in a representative capacity. Section 901(b), in contrast, trains on that latter issue. Sensibly read, Rule 23 governs procedural aspects of class litigation, but allows state law to control the size of a monetary award a class plaintiff may pursue.

In other words, Rule 23 describes a method of enforcing a claim for relief, while § 901(b) defines the dimensions of the claim itself. In this regard, it is immaterial that § 901(b) bars statutory penalties in wholesale, rather than retail, fashion. The New York Legislature could have embedded the limitation in every provision creating a cause of action for which a penalty is authorized; § 901(b) operates as shorthand to the same effect. It is as much a part of the delineation of the claim for relief as it would be were it included claim by claim in the New York Code.

The Court single-mindedly focuses on whether a suit "may" or "may not" be maintained as a class action. Putting the question that way, the Court does not home in on the reason *why*. Rule 23 authorizes class treatment for suits satisfying its prerequisites because the class mechanism generally affords a fair and efficient way to aggregate claims for adjudication. Section 901(b) responds to an entirely different concern; it does not allow class members to recover statutory damages because the New York Legislature considered the result of adjudicating such claims en masse to be exorbitant. The fair and efficient *conduct* of class litigation is the legitimate concern of Rule 23; the remedy for an infraction of state law, however, is the legitimate concern of the State's lawmakers and not of the federal rulemakers. Cf. Ely, *The Irrepressible Myth of Erie*, 87 Harv. L.Rev. 693, 722 (1974) (It is relevant "whether the state provision embodies a substantive policy or represents only a procedural disagreement with the federal rulemakers respecting the fairest and most efficient way of conducting litigation.").

Suppose, for example, that a State, wishing to cap damages in class actions at $1,000,000, enacted a statute providing that "a suit to recover more

---

which the Rule makes the character and result of the federal litigation stray from the course it would follow in state courts,' *Hanna*, 380 U.S. at 473." . . . Nevertheless, Justice STEVENS sees no reason to read Rule 23 with restraint in this particular case; the Federal Rule preempts New York's damages limitation, in his view, because § 901(b) is "a procedural rule that is not part of New York's substantive law." This characterization of § 901(b) does not mirror reality. . . . But a majority of this Court, it bears emphasis, agrees that Federal Rules should be read with moderation in diversity suits to accommodate important state concerns.

CH.2 THE CLASS CERTIFICATION DECISION 377

than $1,000,000 may not be maintained as a class action." Under the Court's reasoning—which attributes dispositive significance to the words "may not be maintained"—Rule 23 would preempt this provision, nevermind that Congress, by authorizing the promulgation of rules of procedure for federal courts, surely did not intend to displace state-created ceilings on damages. The Court suggests that the analysis might differ if the statute "limit[ed] the remedies available in an existing class action," such that Rule 23 might not conflict with a state statute prescribing that "no more than $1,000,000 may be recovered in a class action." There is no real difference in the purpose and intended effect of these two hypothetical statutes. The notion that one directly impinges on Rule 23's domain, while the other does not, fundamentally misperceives the office of Rule 23.

The absence of an inevitable collision between Rule 23 and § 901(b) becomes evident once it is comprehended that a federal court sitting in diversity can accord due respect to both state and federal prescriptions. Plaintiffs seeking to vindicate claims for which the State has provided a statutory penalty may pursue relief through a class action if they forgo statutory damages and instead seek actual damages or injunctive or declaratory relief; any putative class member who objects can opt out and pursue actual damages, if available, and the statutory penalty in an individual action. In this manner, the Second Circuit explained, "Rule 23's procedural requirements for class actions can be applied along with the substantive requirement of CPLR 901(b)." 549 F.3d at 144. In sum, while phrased as responsive to the question whether certain class actions may begin, § 901(b) is unmistakably aimed at controlling how those actions must end. On that remedial issue, Rule 23 is silent.

Any doubt whether Rule 23 leaves § 901(b) in control of the remedial issue at the core of this case should be dispelled by our *Erie* jurisprudence, including *Hanna*, which counsels us to read Federal Rules moderately and cautions against stretching a rule to cover every situation it could conceivably reach. . . .

Notably, New York is not alone in its effort to contain penalties and minimum recoveries by disallowing class relief; Congress, too, has precluded class treatment for certain claims seeking a statutorily designated minimum recovery. See, e.g.,15 U.S.C. § 1640(a)(2)(B) (Truth in Lending Act) ("[I]n the case of a class action. . . no minimum recovery shall be applicable."); § 1693m(a)(2)(B) (Electronic Fund Transfer Act) (same); 12 U.S.C. § 4010(a)(2)(B)(i) (Expedited Fund Availability Act) (same). Today's judgment denies to the States the full power Congress has to keep certain monetary awards within reasonable bounds. States may hesitate to create determinate statutory penalties in the future if they are impotent to prevent federal-court distortion of the remedy they have shaped.[11]

By finding a conflict without considering whether Rule 23 rationally should be read to avoid any collision, the Court unwisely and unnecessarily retreats from the federalism principles undergirding *Erie*. Had the Court reflected on the respect for state regulatory interests endorsed in our decisions, it would have found no cause to interpret Rule 23 so woodenly—and every reason not to do so. Cf. Traynor, 37 Tex. L.Rev. at 669 ("It is bad

---

[11] States have adopted a variety of formulations to limit the use of class actions to gain certain remedies or to pursue certain claims, as illustrated by the 96 examples listed in Allstate's brief. The Court's "one-size-fits-all" reading of Rule 23 . . . likely prevents the enforcement of all of these statutes in diversity actions—including the numerous state statutory provisions that, like § 901(b), attempt to curb the recovery of statutory damages.

enough for courts to prattle unintelligibly about choice of law, but unforgiveable when inquiry might have revealed that there was no real conflict.").

II

Because I perceive no unavoidable conflict between Rule 23 and § 901(b), I would decide this case by inquiring "whether application of the [state] rule would have so important an effect upon the fortunes of one or both of the litigants that failure to [apply] it would be likely to cause a plaintiff to choose the federal court." . . .

In short, Shady Grove's effort to characterize § 901(b) as simply "procedural" cannot successfully elide this fundamental norm: When no federal law or rule is dispositive of an issue, and a state statute is outcome affective in the sense our cases on *Erie* (pre and post-*Hanna*) develop, the Rules of Decision Act commands application of the State's law in diversity suits. As this case starkly demonstrates, if federal courts exercising diversity jurisdiction are compelled by Rule 23 to award statutory penalties in class actions while New York courts are bound by § 901(b)'s proscription, "substantial variations between state and federal [money judgments] may be expected." *Gasperini*, 518 U.S. at 430 (quoting *Hanna*, 380 U.S. at 467–68). The "variation" here is indeed "substantial." Shady Grove seeks class relief that is ten thousand times greater than the individual remedy available to it in state court. As the plurality acknowledges forum shopping will undoubtedly result if a plaintiff need only file in federal instead of state court to seek a massive monetary award explicitly barred by state law. See *Gasperini*, 518 U.S. at 431 ("*Erie* precludes a recovery in federal court significantly larger than the recovery that would have been tolerated in state court."). The "accident of diversity of citizenship," *Klaxon Co. v. Stentor Elec. Mfg. Co.*, 313 U.S. 487, 496, should not subject a defendant to such augmented liability. See *Hanna*, 380 U.S. at 467 ("The *Erie* rule is rooted in part in a realization that it would be unfair for the character or result of a litigation materially to differ because the suit had been brought in a federal court."). . . .

III

The Court's erosion of *Erie*'s federalism grounding impels me to point out the large irony in today's judgment. Shady Grove is able to pursue its claim in federal court only by virtue of the recent enactment of the Class Action Fairness Act of 2005 (CAFA), 28 U.S.C. § 1332(d). . . . By providing a federal forum, Congress sought to check what it considered to be the overreadiness of some state courts to certify class actions. In other words, Congress envisioned fewer—not more—class actions overall. Congress surely never anticipated that CAFA would make federal courts a mecca for suits of the kind Shady Grove has launched: class actions seeking state-created penalties for claims arising under state law—claims that would be barred from class treatment in the State's own courts.

NOTES AND QUESTIONS

1.   The Proper Interpretation of Rule 23. The Second Circuit opinion in *Shady Grove* concludes that Rule 23 does not address what substantive claims may be asserted using the class device. Justice Ginsburg in dissent relatedly argues that "Rule 23 describes a method of enforcing a claim for relief, while § 901(b) defines the dimensions of the claim itself." By contrast, the Court insists that Rule 23 is unambiguous: It allows certification of *any* class suit that satisfies the requirements of Rule 23(a) and (b). Which understanding of Rule 23 is most persuasive?

Although the Justices vigorously debate the proper scope of Rule 23, the opinions suggest that the Justices essentially are in agreement (though with differences in detail) that, *when possible*, federal rules should be read to avoid significant conflict with state law. From this perspective, the crux of the dispute between the majority and the dissent is about whether the text of Rule 23 reasonably can be read as narrowly as the dissent suggests.

What are the implications for other class-action issues of the Court's apparent unanimity that Rule 23 should be read, when possible, to avoid substantial conflict with state law?

2.   *The Rules Enabling Act ("REA") Analysis.* The majority's conclusion that Rule 23 covers the point in question means that Rule 23 must be applied to the case unless it is invalid under the REA. Justice Scalia and Justice Stevens provide separate analyses of the REA question. By contrast, the dissent does not opine on what the REA requires because the dissent denies that Rule 23 covers the point at issue. The dissenting Justices conclude instead that the *Erie* policy requires application of New York law.

Writing for the plurality, Justice Scalia has no difficulty concluding that Rule 23 satisfies the requirements of the Rules Enabling Act. He insists that "[w]hat matters is what the rule itself regulates: If it governs only 'the manner and the means' by which the litigants' rights are 'enforced,' it is valid. . . . " The plurality concludes that Rule 23 is valid under this standard because like a joinder rule, Rule 23 "leaves the parties' legal rights and duties intact and the rules of decision unchanged." Is Justice Scalia's analysis persuasive?

Justice Stevens, for his part, agrees that Justice Scalia's "interpretation of the Enabling Act is consonant with the Act's first limitation to 'general rules of practice and procedure.'" But Justice Stevens refuses to join Justice Scalia's plurality opinion because he believes that the plurality's reasoning "ignores the second limitation that such rules also "not abridge, enlarge or modify *any* substantive right[.]" While he upholds the application of Rule 23 to this case, Justice Stevens leaves open the possibility that a Federal Rule valid on its face might still "abridge, enlarge, or modify" a substantive right, and thus violate the REA as applied, if there was "little doubt" that it "altered a state-created right."

3.   *The Contested Role of State Law.* The debate between Justices Scalia and Stevens is about the proper role of state law in an REA analysis. Justice Stevens argues that a federal rule of civil procedure cannot displace a state substantive right. In so concluding, he emphasizes that § 2072(b) is intended to protect state substantive law. John Hart Ely, in a remarkably influential article, reached the same conclusion in 1974 and argued that the federal rules should give way to state law enacted for "one or more nonprocedural reasons, for some purpose or purposes not having to do with the fairness or efficiency of the litigation process." John Hart Ely, *The Irrepressible Myth of* Erie, 87 Harv. L. Rev. 693, 725 (1974). Justice Stevens apparently would impose a higher standard for displacing state law. He argues that a federal rule cannot displace a state law that "is part of a State's framework of substantive rights or remedies," insisting that "whether the state law at issue takes the form of what is traditionally described as substantive or procedural" is irrelevant. He nonethe-

less concludes that § 901(b)—the provision of New York law at issue—is not part of the state's framework of substantive rights or remedies. Putting aside for the moment Justice Stevens' approach to the Rules Enabling Act, do you agree with his characterization of New York law?

Justice Scalia, writing for the plurality, argues that the validity of the federal rules simply does not depend on state law. "A Federal Rule of Procedure is not valid in some jurisdictions and invalid in others—or valid in some cases and invalid in others—depending upon whether its effect is to frustrate a state substantive law (or a state procedural law enacted for substantive purposes)." The plurality's approach appears to be consistent with the intent of the Act's drafters. As Stephen Burbank, the leading historian of the Rules Enabling Act, has noted, Justice Scalia's "insistence on a test for validity that does not depend on idiosyncratic aspects of state law rings true for a statute that was designed primarily to allocate federal lawmaking power *ex ante*, rather than to protect policy choices (let alone only state law policies) *ex post*." Stephen B. Burbank & Tobias B. Wolff, *Redeeming the Missed Opportunities of Shady Grove* 159 U. Pa. L. Rev. 17, 51 (2010); see also Stephen Burbank, *The Rules Enabling Act of 1934*, 130 U. Pa. L. Rev. 1015 (1982).

The lack of a majority opinion on the role of state law in an REA analysis predictably has led to disagreement among the lower courts. As two commentators have explained:

> Lower courts have applied both tests but have not yet achieved consensus on which opinion controls. Some courts have applied the "narrowest grounds" rule to conclude that the test of Justice Stevens should take precedence. According to that rule, "[w]hen a fragmented Court decides a case and no single rationale explaining the result enjoys the assent of five Justices, the holding of the Court may be viewed as that position taken by those Members who concurred in the judgments on the narrowest grounds."

Jack E. Pace III & Rachel J. Feldman, *From Shady to Dark: One Year Later, Shady Grove's Meaning Remains Unclear*, 25–SPG Antitrust 75, 76 (2011). A few courts applying Justice Stevens' approach have held Rule 23 invalid as applied to a particular issue. See, e.g. *McKinney v. Bayer Corp.*, 744 F. Supp. 2d 733 (N.D. Ohio 2010) (applying the Ohio Consumer Sales Practice Act, which allows a consumer to bring a class suit under the statute only when a supplier acted in the face of prior notice that its conduct was deceptive or unconscionable). For discussion of the "narrowest grounds rule"—also known as the *Marks* doctrine—see Berkelow, *Much Ado About Pluralities: Pride and Precedent Amidst the Cacophony of Concurrences, and Re–Percolation after* Rapanos, 15 Va. J. Soc. Pol. & Law 299, 320–33 (2008).

Which approach to the Rules Enabling Act—Justice Scalia's or Justice Stevens'—is more persuasive?

Recall that the dissenters did not opine on the appropriate interpretation of the REA and that Justice Stevens is no longer on the Court. If the Court were to address the same issue today, is it clear that it would adopt either the plurality approach or Justice Stevens' approach?

CHAPTER 3

THE COORDINATION OF AGGREGATE LITIGATION

This Chapter addresses a range of procedural issues concerning aggregate litigation, some of which stem from the combination of a federal court system and 50 semi-autonomous state court systems in the United States. Section A addresses two federal subject matter jurisdiction statutes that focus on aggregate litigation: The Class Action Fairness Act of 2005, the most significant and controversial procedural reform affecting class litigation since the adoption of Rule 23 itself, and the Multiparty Multiforum Trial Jurisdiction Act of 2002, which authorizes federal subject matter jurisdiction in certain mass accident cases. Section B presents the constellation of procedural mechanisms and doctrines that police the relationship between various courts—federal-to-federal, federal-to-state, and state-to-state.

A. FEDERAL SUBJECT MATTER JURISDICTION

1. THE CLASS ACTION FAIRNESS ACT

The enactment of the Class Action Fairness Act of 2005 ("CAFA") represents the culmination of longstanding political efforts—predominantly, on the part of Republican members of Congress and defense-side interests in the private sector—to address perceived problems with state-court class actions by making it considerably easier for defendants to remove such lawsuits to federal court. The House of Representatives repeatedly passed predecessor bills to CAFA, but those bills met with opposition in the Senate. The increase in the Republican Senate majority as a result of the 2004 election put the supporters of CAFA in position to bring the legislation to a vote on the merits. The final vote in the Senate was 72–26 in favor of the legislation, with several prominent Democrats, including then-Senator Barack Obama siding with Republican supporters.

a. THE PERCEIVED PROBLEMS

Senate Report No. 109–14
109th Cong. (2005)

. . .

IV. BACKGROUND AND NEED FOR LEGISLATION

As set forth in Article III of the Constitution, the Framers established diversity jurisdiction to ensure fairness for all parties in litigation involving persons from multiple jurisdictions, particularly cases in which defendants from one state are sued in the local courts of another state. Interstate class actions[—]which often involve millions of parties from numerous states—present the precise concerns that diversity jurisdiction was designed to prevent: frequently in such cases, there appears to be state court provincialism against out-of-state defendants or a judicial failure to recognize the interests of other states in the litigation. Yet, because of a technical glitch in the diversity jurisdiction statute (28 U.S.C. § 1332), such cases are usually excluded from federal court. This glitch is not surprising given that class actions as we now know them did not exist when the statute's concept was crafted in the late 1700s.

This Committee believes that the current diversity and removal standards as applied in interstate class actions have facilitated a parade of abuses, and are thwarting the underlying purpose of the constitutional requirement of diversity jurisdiction. [CAFA] addresses these concerns by . . . allowing a larger number of class actions into federal courts, while continuing to preserve primary state court jurisdiction over primarily local matters. . . .

B.   Federal Diversity Jurisdiction and Removal Provisions

1.   The Basics of Diversity Jurisdiction

The Constitution extends federal court jurisdiction to cases of a distinctly federal character—for instance, cases raising issues under the Constitution or federal statutes, or cases involving the federal government as a party—and generally leaves to state courts the adjudication of local questions arising under state law. However, the Constitution specifically extends federal jurisdiction to encompass one category of cases involving issues of state law: "diversity" cases, or suits "between Citizens of different States."

According to the Framers, the primary purpose of diversity jurisdiction was to protect citizens in one state from the injustice that might result if they were forced to litigate in out-of-state courts. . . .

In addition to protecting individual litigants, diversity jurisdiction has two other important purposes. In testimony several years ago . . . Prof. E. Donald Elliott of the Yale Law School expressed the view that diversity jurisdiction was designed not only to protect against actual discrimination, but also "to shore up confidence in the judicial system by preventing even the appearance of discrimination in favor of local residents." In addition, several legal scholars have noted that the Framers were concerned that state courts might discriminate against interstate businesses and commercial activities, and thus viewed diversity jurisdiction as a means of ensuring the protection of interstate commerce. As former Acting Solicitor General Walter Dellinger testified before the Committee, "diversity jurisdiction has served to guarantee that parties of different state citizenship have a means of resolving their legal differences on a level playing field in a manner that nurtures interstate commerce." Both of these concerns—judicial integrity and interstate commerce—are strongly implicated by class actions. . . .

C.   How Diversity Jurisdiction and Removal Statutes Are Abused

The current rules governing federal jurisdiction have the unintended consequence of keeping most class actions out of federal court, even though most class actions are precisely the type of case for which diversity jurisdiction was created. In addition, current law enables plaintiffs' lawyers who prefer to litigate in state courts to easily "game the system" and avoid removal of large interstate class actions to federal court.

This gaming problem exists for two reasons. The first is the "complete diversity" requirement. Although the Supreme Court has held that only the named plaintiffs' citizenship should be considered for purposes of determining if the parties to a class action are diverse, the "complete" diversity rule still mandates that all named plaintiffs must be citizens of different states from all the defendants. In interstate class actions, plaintiffs' counsel frequently and purposely evade federal jurisdiction by adding named plaintiffs or defendants simply based on their state of citizenship in order to defeat complete diversity. One witness at the Committee's 2002 hearing on class actions testified that her drug store was named as a defendant in "hundreds of lawsuits" so that "the lawyers could keep the case in a place known for its lawsuit-friendly environment." If all it takes to keep a class action in state court is to name one local retailer, it is no surprise that few interstate class actions meet the complete diversity requirement.

The second problem is created by the amount-in-controversy requirement. . . . The Committee believes that requiring each plaintiff to reach the $75,000 mark makes little sense in the class action context. After all, class actions frequently involve tens of millions of dollars even though each individual plaintiff's claims are far less than that. Moreover, class action lawyers typically misuse the jurisdictional threshold to keep their cases out of federal court. For example, class action complaints often include a provision stating that no class member will seek more than $75,000 in relief, even though they can simply amend their complaints after the removal to seek more relief and even though the class action seeks millions of dollars in the aggregate. Under current law, that is frequently enough to keep a major class action in state court.

This leads to the nonsensical result under which a citizen can bring a "federal case" by claiming $75,001 in damages for a simple slip-and-fall case against a party from another state, while a class action involving 25 million people living in all fifty states and alleging claims against a manufacturer that are collectively worth $15 billion must usually be heard in state court (because each individual class member's claim is for less than $75,000). Put another way, under the current jurisdictional rules, federal courts can assert diversity jurisdiction over a typical state law claim arising out of an auto accident between a driver from one state and a driver from another, or a typical trespass claim involving a trespasser from one state and a property owner from another, but they cannot assert jurisdiction over claims encompassing large-scale, interstate class actions involving thousands of plaintiffs from multiple states, defendants from many states, the laws of several states, and hundreds of millions of dollars—cases that have obvious and significant implications for the national economy. . . .

D. Other Abuses of the Class Action Rules

The ability of plaintiffs' lawyers to evade federal diversity jurisdiction has helped spur a dramatic increase in the number of class actions litigated in state courts—an increase that is stretching the resources of the state court systems. According to studies, federal class action filings over the past ten years have increased by more than 300 percent. At the same time, class action filings in state courts have grown more than three times faster—by more than 1,000 percent.

Notably, many of these cases are being filed in improbable jurisdictions. A study conducted in three venues with reputations as hotbeds for class action activity found exponential increases in the numbers of class actions filed in recent years. For example, in the Circuit Court of Madison County, Illinois, a mostly rural county that covers 725 square miles and is home to less than one percent of the U.S. population, the number of class actions filed annually grew from 2 in 1998 to 39 in 2000—an increase of 3,650 percent. A follow-up study found that the number of class actions filed in the county continued to grow dramatically in 2001 and 2002. And in 2003, class action filings there catapulted to 106, up more than 5,000 percent since 1998. According to the president of the Illinois Trial Lawyers Association (an association representing plaintiffs' lawyers), the reason for the 2003 jump in filings was an effort to beat this legislation; plaintiffs' lawyers were "playing it safe" and rushing to get suits filed in case the legislation was enacted in 2004. The same studies also found that most of the class actions brought in Madison County and other magnet courts had little—if anything—to do with the venues where they were brought.

The reason for this dramatic increase in state court class actions cannot be found in variations in class action rules; after all, the rules governing the decision whether cases may proceed as class actions are basically the same in federal and state courts—and of course, they are the same within states, i.e., the same in "magnet" jurisdictions such as Madison County and St. Clair County, Illinois, as they are in more easily accessible jurisdictions such as Cook County, Illinois. In fact, thirty-six states have adopted the basic federal class action rule (Rule 23), sometimes with minor revisions. Of the remaining states, most have rules that are guided by federal court class action policy and contain similar requirements. (Two states, Mississippi and West Virginia, do not have rules or statutes authorizing class actions.) Thus, there are no wide variations between federal and state court class action policies.

The Committee finds, however, that one reason for the dramatic explosion of class actions in state courts is that some state court judges are less careful than their federal court counterparts about applying the procedural requirements that govern class actions. In particular, many state court judges are lax about following the strict requirements of Rule 23 (or the state's parallel governing rule), which are intended to protect the due process rights of both unnamed class members and defendants. In contrast, federal courts generally scrutinize proposed settlements much more carefully and pay closer attention to the procedural requirements for certifying a matter for class treatment.

Another problem is that a large number of state courts lack the necessary resources to supervise proposed class settlements properly. Many state judges do not have law clerks, and the explosion of state court class actions has simply overwhelmed their dockets. Not surprisingly, abuses are much more likely to occur when state court judges are unable to give class action cases and settlements the attention they need. Federal judges, in contrast, have access to magistrates and can appoint special masters when they are faced with complex litigation like class actions. Moreover, the average state court judge is assigned 1,568 new cases each year, compared to federal judges, who are assigned, on average, fewer than 500.

The lack of a federal forum for most interstate class actions and the inconsistent administration of class actions in state courts have led to several forms of abuse. First, lawyers, not plaintiffs, may benefit most from settlements. Second, corporate defendants are forced to settle frivolous claims to avoid expensive litigation, thus driving up consumer prices. Third, constitutional due process rights are often ignored in class actions. Fourth, expensive and predatory copy-cat cases force defendants to litigate the same case in multiple jurisdictions, driving up consumer costs. . . .

. . . Sometimes these duplicative actions are filed by lawyers who hope to wrest the potentially lucrative lead role away from the original lawyers. In other instances, the "copy-cat" class actions are blatant forum shopping—the original class lawyers file similar class actions before different courts in an effort to find a receptive judge who will rapidly certify a class. When these similar, overlapping class actions are filed in State courts of different jurisdictions, there is no way to consolidate or coordinate the cases. The "competing" class actions must be litigated separately in an uncoordinated, redundant fashion because there is no state court mechanism for consolidating state court cases. The result is enormous waste—multiple judges of different courts must spend considerable time adjudicating precisely the same claims asserted on behalf of precisely the same people. As a result, state courts and class counsel may "compete" to control the cases, often harming all the parties involved. In contrast, when overlapping cases are pending in different federal courts, they can be consolidated under one single judge to promote judicial efficiency and ensure consistent treatment of the legal issues involved.

E.   *National Class Actions Belong in Federal Court under Traditional Notions of Federalism*

. . . The effect of class action abuses in state courts is being exacerbated by the trend toward "nationwide" class actions, which invite one state court to dictate to 49 others what their laws should be on a particular issue, thereby undermining basic federalism principles. . . . Clearly, a system that allows state court judges to dictate national policy on these and numerous other issues from the local courthouse steps is contrary to the intent of the Framers when they crafted our system of federalism. In one case, for example, plaintiffs filed suit in an Alabama county court on behalf of more than 20 million people alleging that the design of federally mandated airbags is faulty.[104] From the standpoint of federalism, this suit defies logic. Why should an Alabama state court tell 20 million people in all 50 states what kind of airbags they can have in their cars?

The most egregious of such cases are those in which one state court issues nationwide rulings that actually contradict the laws of other states. This problem is particularly prevalent in insurance cases, which are being filed in increasingly greater number. As District of Columbia Insurance Commissioner Lawrence Mirel has testified before this Committee, class actions "frequently go[] around or simply ignore[] the role of state regulators."

One case reported in the New York Times, for example, involved a longstanding practice of the State Farm Insurance Companies (shared by other insurers) of using non-original equipment manufacturer (OEM) parts to repair cars. The practice was fully disclosed to policyholders, and the majority of states expressly permit insurers to specify non-OEM parts. Indeed, two states, Hawaii and Massachusetts, actually require the specification of non-OEM parts. Nonetheless, plaintiffs brought suit in Illinois state court claiming that all non-OEM parts used by policyholders were inferior to OEM parts, and that State Farm had breached its contractual obligation to policyholders and committed fraud each time it specified such parts. Even though the plaintiffs eventually dropped their claim that all non-OEM parts were inferior, and conceded that this could only be determined on a

---

[104] See *Smith v. General Motors Corp., et al.*, Civ. A. No. 97–39 (Cir. Ct. Coosa County, AL).

part-by-part basis, the trial court still permitted the jury to reach a group judgment on the class action. The court was not even deterred by the fact that the plaintiffs in the class came from states throughout the nation with widely varying laws regarding the use of non-OEM parts, including the two states—Hawaii and Massachusetts—that strongly embraced the very practice condemned by plaintiffs. Indeed, in affirming a $1.3 billion verdict against State Farm in this case, an Illinois state appellate court acknowledged that it had disregarded "state insurance commissioners [w]ho testified that the laws of many of our sister states permit and in some cases . . . . [even] encourage" usage of non-OEM parts.[108]

The State Farm case is not unique. This state court interference with the laws of other jurisdictions is becoming disturbingly common . . .

NOTES AND QUESTIONS

1. *Do State and Federal Courts Differ in Their Treatment of Class Actions?* Whether the stated grounds for the enactment of CAFA accurately reflect underlying class action practice remains a disputed question. The authors of one significant study conducted under the auspices of the Federal Judicial Center in the aftermath of CAFA observe that "there is little empirical evidence supporting the belief that state and federal courts differ generally in their treatment of class actions." Thomas E. Willging & Shannon R. Wheatman, *Attorney Choice of Forum in Class Action Litigation: What Difference Does It Make?*, 81 Notre Dame L. Rev. 591, 593 (2006).

2. *The Anomalous State Court Problem.* One way of understanding the problem addressed by CAFA focuses not on categorical differences between state and federal courts with respect to class certification but rather on the existence of anomalous state courts that might be inclined to certify when the vast majority of other courts—federal courts, other states' courts and, indeed, many other courts within the same state judicial system—would not be so inclined. Writing for the Seventh Circuit in a pre-CAFA case, Judge Frank Easterbrook described the problem:

> Suppose that every state in the nation would as a matter of first principles deem inappropriate a nationwide class covering these claims and products. What this might mean in practice is something like "9 of 10 judges in every state would rule against certifying a nationwide class". . . . Although the 10% that see things otherwise are a distinct minority, one is bound to turn up if plaintiffs file enough suits—and, if one nationwide class *is* certified, then all the no-certification decisions fade into insignificance. A single positive trumps all the negatives. Even if just one judge in ten believes that a nationwide class is lawful, then if the plaintiffs file in ten different states the probability that at least one will certify a nationwide class is 65%. Filing in 20 states produces an 88% probability of national class certification. This happens whenever plaintiffs can roll the dice as many times as they please—when nationwide class certification sticks (because it subsumes all other suits) while a no-certification decision has no enduring effect.

---

[108] *Avery v. State Farm Mut. Auto. Ins. Co.*, 746 N.E.2d 1242, 1254 (Ill. App. Ct. 2001). [Editor's note: In a decision rendered after the enactment of CAFA, the Illinois Supreme Court overturned the certification of this class. *Avery v. State Farm Mut. Auto. Ins. Co.*, 835 N.E.2d 801 (Ill. 2005).]

In re Bridgestone/Firestone, Inc., Tires Prods. Liab. Litig., 333 F.3d 763, 766–67 (7th Cir. 2003).*

b. JURISDICTION AND REMOVAL

CAFA in Context. The basic idea behind CAFA is easily summarized: Get more class actions involving state-law claims—especially, nationwide class actions—out of state court and into federal court. CAFA does so by adding a new section, 28 U.S.C. § 1332(d), to the diversity jurisdiction statute. But keep in mind that CAFA is not the only basis for federal subject matter jurisdiction over a class suit premised on state law. Before CAFA, federal courts had the power to exercise diversity jurisdiction over a class suit under § 1332(a) when (1) the *named* plaintiffs were completely diverse from the class defendants and (2) *each* class member had claims in excess of $75,000 against each defendant that he or she sued. Federal courts still have that power after the enactment of CAFA.

The supplemental jurisdiction statute (28 U.S.C. § 1367)—in combination with § 1332(a)—may also provide a basis for subject matter jurisdiction over class actions that would not qualify for jurisdiction solely under § 1332(a). In *Exxon Mobil v. Allapattah*, 545 U.S. 546 (2005), the Supreme Court held that a federal district court has the power to exercise subject matter jurisdiction over a plaintiff class action when (1) the named plaintiffs are completely diverse from the class defendant, and (2) at least *one* class member has claims against the class defendant that satisfy the amount-in-controversy requirement of § 1332(a).

Why does it matter that CAFA is not the sole basis for diversity jurisdiction over class actions? Because § 1332(a)—especially in conjunction with the supplemental jurisdiction statute—may authorize subject matter jurisdiction in a few cases that CAFA does not reach. To take a simple example, CAFA does not apply when "the number of members of all proposed plaintiff classes in the aggregate is less than 100," 28 U.S.C. § 1332(d)(5)(B); neither § 1332(a) nor § 1367 includes any such limitation.

The Jurisdictional Grant. Section 1332(d)(2) provides:

> The district courts shall have original jurisdiction of any civil action in which the matter in controversy exceeds the sum or value of $5,000,000, exclusive of interest and costs, and is a class action in which—
>
> (A) any member of a class of plaintiffs is a citizen of a State different from any defendant;

---

* This case is commonly known as *Bridgestone/Firestone II* in contrast to *Bridgestone/Firestone I*, which is discussed in Chapter 2 in connection with choice of law. Recall that, in *Bridgestone/Firestone I*, the Seventh Circuit—speaking via Judge Easterbrook—decertified a nationwide class comprised of the owners of automobiles equipped with the disputed Bridgestone/Firestone tires. That ruling effectively foreclosed the prospect of such a nationwide class in federal court, as the MDL Panel previously had consolidated all federal litigation in a district court within the Seventh Circuit.

Undaunted, class counsel thereafter sought the certification of the same proposed nationwide class—this time, in state court. The defendants responded by asking the Seventh Circuit to enjoin the state-court proceedings. At oral argument in *Bridgestone/Firestone II*, Judge Easterbrook had these candid words to explain what was really going on: "The argument that is obviously being made in state court is: Our decision counts for nothing; any state court is free to 'flip the bird' to the Seventh Circuit." The authority of the federal courts to address such tactics is a complicated question that is discussed later in this Chapter.

(B) any member of a class of plaintiffs is a foreign state or a citizen or subject of a foreign state and any defendant is a citizen of a State; or

(C) any member of a class of plaintiffs is a citizen of a State and any defendant is a foreign state or a citizen or subject of a foreign state.

The jurisdictional grant relaxes the requirements of diversity jurisdiction in two especially important ways. First, complete diversity (between the named plaintiffs and the defendants) is no longer a prerequisite for federal subject matter jurisdiction over a class suit founded on state law. So long as *one* class member—not even necessarily a named plaintiff—is diverse from *one* defendant, the minimal diversity requirement of Section 1332(d) is satisfied.*

Second, so long as the claims in the class suit—taken together—exceed $5 million, the amount-in-controversy requirement is satisfied. In most other contexts, the claims of individual plaintiffs cannot be added together to satisfy the amount-in-controversy requirement. See, e.g., *Exxon Mobil v. Allapattah* (finding supplemental jurisdiction only because at least one class member had claims against the defendant in excess of $75,000). But as § 1332(d)(6) makes clear, "the claims of the individual class members shall be aggregated to determine whether the matter in controversy exceeds the sum or value of $5,000,000, exclusive of interests and costs." Thus, CAFA represents a significant relaxation of the aggregation rules that ordinarily govern the amount-in-controversy requirement.

Jurisdiction under CAFA does not depend on certification of a class. § 1332(d)(8) ("[Section 1332(d)] shall apply to any class action before or after the entry of a class certification order by the court with respect to that action."). CAFA jurisdiction attaches when a case is *filed* as a class action. . . ." In re *Burlington Northern Santa Fe Railway*, 606 F.3d 379, 381 (7th Cir. 2010) (emphasis in original). And courts have held that" denial of class certification does not divest federal courts of jurisdiction." *Metz v. Unizan Bank*, 649 F.3d492, 500 (6th Cir. 2011) (collecting cases).

The Constitutionality of the Jurisdictional Grant. The Supreme Court has stated that Article III of the Constitution "poses no obstacle to the legislative extension of federal jurisdiction, founded on diversity, so long as any two adverse parties are not co-citizens." *State Farm Fire & Casualty Co. v. Tashire*, 386 U.S. 523, 531 (1967). *Tashire* is widely understood to stand for the proposition that "complete diversity" is simply a requirement of § 1332(a) and that Congress is free to authorize federal subject matter jurisdiction on the basis of minimal diversity. But not everyone agrees. See C. Douglas Floyd, *The Limits of Minimal Diversity*, 55 Hastings L.J. 613, 614–15 (2004). Professor Floyd argues that a statute permitting jurisdiction on the basis of minimal diversity is constitutional only if "the joinder of the non-diverse state law claims reasonably might be thought to serve the purposes underlying Article III's grant of federal jurisdiction over controversies between 'Citizens of different States.' "*Id.* at 615. He contends that *Ta-*

---

* CAFA also makes it easier to establish diverse citizenship in a case involving an unincorporated association. For purposes of § 1332(a), an *unincorporated* association takes the citizenship of all of its members; the National Governor's Association, for example, would be a citizen of *every* state. Section 1332(d)(10) provides that for purposes of CAFA an unincorporated association is "a citizen of the State where it has its principal place of business and the State under whose laws it is organized." In effect, CAFA treats corporations and unincorporated associations the same for purposes of determining citizenship.

shire—an action brought under the Federal Interpleader Act—presented "the clearest case for the assertion of federal jurisdiction based on 'minimal diversity.'" *Id.* at 633. By contrast, CAFA

> authorize[s] the federal courts to exercise jurisdiction over non-diverse state law claims in circumstances where that is not necessary to permit the federal courts fairly and efficiently to dispose of cases properly pending before them. Moreover, . . . the ends that Congress sought to achieve frequently bear little or no relationship to the purposes of the Diversity Clause. And, where legitimate ends are identified, the means employed frequently have no apparent connection to those ends, or sweep far beyond what would be necessary to achieve them. . . .

> The conventional justification for that clause—the prevention of bias against out-of-state litigants—does not address alleged inadequacies and inefficiencies in the state courts in general, but rather bias against out-of-state litigants in those courts.

Id. at 651–652 (writing before CAFA's enactment). What do you make of Professor Floyd's effort to limit the scope of the Diversity Jurisdiction Clause? For an article questioning whether it is constitutional to consider the citizenship of absent class members prior to certification, see Mark Moller, *A New Look at the Original Meaning of the Diversity Clause*, 51 Wm. & Mary L. Rev. 1113 (2009).

Exclusions from Jurisdiction. In addition to providing that § 1332(d)(2) does "not apply" to class suits with less than 100 class members, § 1332(d)(5) also states that CAFA does not authorize jurisdiction over any class action in which "the primary defendants are States, State officials, or other governmental entities against whom the district court may be foreclosed from ordering relief." § 1332(d)(5)(A). Section 1332(d)(9), for its part, makes clear that CAFA's jurisdictional grant does not apply to any class action that "solely" involves specified claims under the federal securities laws or claims "that relate to the internal affairs or governance of a corporation or other form of business enterprise and that arises under or by virtue of the laws of the State in which such corporation or business enterprise is incorporated or organized." In a nutshell, corporate-governance litigation (a specialty of Delaware state courts) and certain federal securities litigation (already the subject of federal reform legislation in the guise of the Private Securities Litigation Reform Act, discussed in Chapter 2) remain largely unaffected.

The Removal Provision. CAFA includes a removal provision—28 U.S.C. § 1453—designed to make it easier to remove qualifying actions from state to federal court. The provision can be understood only in the context of the generally applicable removal provisions found at 28 U.S.C. §§ 1441 and 1446. Section 1441 generally authorizes removing a suit from state to federal court *if* the suit could have been brought originally in federal court. But § 1441 does not authorize removal in diversity cases if "any of the parties in interest properly joined and served as defendants is a citizen of the State in which such action is brought." § 1441(b)(2). Section 1446—which sets forth the procedure for removing civil actions—provides (1) that a defendant has only thirty days to file a notice of removal after "receipt . . . of the initial pleading" or "other paper" that indicates the suit is removable, and (2) that all the defendants must consent to removal. § 1446(b). Section 1446 also generally requires that removal of a diversity action occur within a year of the action's commencement. § 1446(c)(1). Cross-referencing § 1446, CAFA's removal provision provides that

> A class action may be removed to a district court of the United States in accordance with section 1446 (except that the 1–year limitation under section 1446(c)(1) shall not apply), without re-gard to whether any defendant is a citizen of the State in which the action is brought, except that such action may be removed by any defendant without the consent of all defendants.

28 U.S.C. § 1453(b). In short, § 1453(b) clears away several obstacles that might otherwise prevent removal of class suits founded on state law.

Was it wise as a policy matter for CAFA to have left the removal power in the hands of the same side with which that power resides in non-class litigation—that is, with the defendant rather than the plaintiffs? Does CA-FA provide absent class members with *any* protection against class-action abuses in state court when class counsel and defendants agree that the suit should remain there? See Robert H. Klonoff & Mark Hermann, *The Class Action Fairness Act: An Ill–Conceived Approach to Class Settlements*, 80 Tul. L. Rev. 1695, 1710 (2006) (noting that because "the interests of class counsel and defendants are aligned in the settlement context," the inability of class members to remove creates the "potential for settlement forum-shopping.").

Does a removing defendant bear the burden of demonstrating that re-moval is proper? Although the burden was indisputably placed on the de-fendant before CAFA was enacted, the Senate Report sought to make re-moval easier by shifting the burden in CAFA cases: "If a purported class action is removed pursuant to the jurisdictional provisions [of CAFA], the named plaintiff(s) should bear the burden of demonstrating that the re-moval was improvident (i.e., that the applicable jurisdictional requirements are not satisfied)." S. Rep. No. 109–14, at 42 (2005). Courts of appeals have nonetheless continued to require the removing party to demonstrate that removal is proper. In refusing to give effect to the legislative history on this point, the Seventh Circuit, for example, insisted that

> [t]his passage does not concern any text in the bill that even-tually became law. When a law sensibly could be read in multiple ways, legislative history may help a court understand which of these received the political branches' imprimatur. But when the legislative history stands by itself, as a naked expression of "in-tent" unconnected to any enacted text, it has no more force than an opinion poll of legislators—less, really, as it speaks for few-er. . . .

> . . . [N]aked legislative history has no legal effect, as the Su-preme Court held in *Pierce v. Underwood*, 487 U.S. 552, 566–68 (1988). A Committee of Congress attempted to alter an estab-lished legal rule by a forceful declaration in a report; the Justices [in *Pierce*] concluded however, that because the declaration did not correspond to any new statutory language that would change the rule, it was ineffectual. Just so here. The rule that the propo-nent of federal jurisdiction bears the [burden of demonstrating ju-risdiction] has been around for a long time. To change such a rule, Congress must enact a statute. . . .

Brill v. Countrywide Home Loans, Inc. 427 F.3d 446, 448 (2005). *Brill* cited the Supreme Court's decision earlier that year in *Exxon Mobil Corp. v. Al-*

lapattah, 545 U.S. 546 (2005). In construing the supplemental jurisdiction statute, the Court had noted that "judicial reliance on legislative materials like committee reports, which are not themselves subject to the requirements of Article I, may give unrepresentative committee members—or, worse yet, unelected staffers and lobbyists—both the power and the incentive to attempt strategic manipulations of legislative history to secure results they were unable to achieve through the statutory text." *Id.* at 568.* The Senate Report's authoritativeness is further clouded by uncertainty about whether it was available when the full Senate voted on the Class Action Fairness Act. For discussion of this uncertainty, see Guyon Knight, Note, *The CAFA Mass Action Numerosity Requirement: Three Problems With Counting to 100*, 78 Fordham L. Rev. 1875, 1891–92 (2010).

For an argument that courts have erred in placing the burden on the removing party in CAFA cases, see H. Hunter Twiford, III, Anthony Rollo & John T. Rouse, *CAFA's New "Minimal Diversity" Standard for Interstate Class Actions Creates a Presumption That Jurisdiction Exists, with the Burden of Proof Assigned to the Party Opposing Jurisdiction*, 25 Miss. C. L. Rev. 7 (2005).

Section 1453 obviously applies to suits over which the federal courts have original jurisdiction under § 1332(d). But as Adam Steinman has noted, § 1453's text is not so limited. See Adam N. Steinman, *Sausage Making, Pigs' Ears, and Congressional Expansions of Federal Jurisdiction: Exxon Mobil v. Allapattah and Its Lessons for the Class Action Fairness Act*, 81 Wash. L. Rev. 279 (2006). See also Lauren D. Fredericks, Note, *Developments in the Law: II. Removal, Remand, and Other Procedural Issues Under the Class Action Fairness Act of 2005*, 39 Loy. L.A. L. Rev. 995, 1023–24 (2006). Should § 1453(b) be read to relax the requirements for removal of *any* class action—not expressly excepted by § 1453(d)—over which a federal court has subject matter jurisdiction? Should Section 1453(b) be read even more expansively to itself provide a basis for federal subject matter jurisdiction over *any* class action (not expressly excepted by § 1453(d)) that is removed from state court and falls within Article III's grant of judicial power to the United States? Does § 1453(d)—which lists precisely the same exceptions as § 1332(d)(9)—strengthen or weaken the textual argument that § 1453 authorizes removal of some class actions over which a federal court does not have original jurisdiction under § 1332(d)?

To date, courts of appeals have addressed only whether § 1453(c)—not § 1453(b)—is available when the defendant makes no claim to jurisdiction under CAFA. Section 1453(c) relaxes the general prohibition on appellate review of orders granting or denying motions to remand a suit from federal to state court. Cf. 28 U.S.C § 1447(d). The courts of appeal have not been receptive to a broad reading of Section 1453(c). See In re *UPS Supply Chain Solutions*, No. 08-0513, 2008 WL 4767817 (6th Cir. Oct. 27, 2008); *Wallace v. Louisiana Prop. Ins. Corp.*, 444 F.3d 697 (5th Cir. 2006); *Saab v. Home Depot, U.S.A. Inc.*, 469 F.3d 758 (8th Cir. 2006). In *Saab*, the Eighth Circuit explained:

> CAFA added section § 1453(c), "Review of remand orders," which applies "to any removal of a case under this section." Saab suggests that "this section" must refer to § 1453, which, according to

---

* *But see Garcia v. United States*, 469 U.S. 70, 76 (1984) ("[T]he authoritative source for finding the Legislature's intent lies in the Committee Reports on the bill, which represent the considered and collective understanding of those Congressmen involved in drafting and studying proposed legislation.").

> petitioner, does not limit its scope to class actions removed under § 1332(d). Section 1453(a), however, defines "class," "class action," "class certification order," and "class member" by reference to § 1332(d)(1), the diversity jurisdiction provision added by CAFA.
>
> Thus, we do not interpret "class action" as it is employed in § 1453(c) to encompass *all* class actions. Rather, we must limit § 1453(c)'s review provisions to those class actions brought under CAFA. Our reading is consistent with the legislative history of CAFA, which includes the observation that, "[n]ew subsection 1453(c) provides discretionary appellate review of remand orders *under this legislation* but also imposes time limits." S.Rep. No. 109–14, at 49 (emphasis added).

469 F.3d at 759–60. Is the court's reference to § 1332(d)(1)—CAFA's definition section—helpful? After all, § 1332(d)(1) nowhere limits the definition of class action to actions over which there is original jurisdiction under § 1332(d)(2). Is the court's reliance on legislative history persuasive? In construing the supplemental jurisdiction statute, the Supreme Court insisted that

> the authoritative statement is the statutory text, not the legislative history or any other extrinsic material. Extrinsic materials have a role in statutory interpretation only to the extent they shed a reliable light on the enacting Legislature's understanding of otherwise ambiguous terms.

Exxon Mobil Corp. v. Allapattah, 545 U.S. 546, 568 (2005). Is *Saab*'s approach consistent with *Allapattah*'s insistence that legislative history should matter only when the statute's text is ambiguous?

c. MANDATORY AND DISCRETIONARY DECLINATION OF JURISDICTION

The exercise of jurisdiction under CAFA is subject to important limits and qualifications. Recall, for example, that CAFA's jurisdictional grant requires that the aggregate value of the class claims be in excess of $5 million. Moreover, § 1332(d) includes two provisions noted in the previous subpart—§§ 1332(d)(5) and 1332(d)(9)—that limit CAFA's broad jurisdictional grant. This subpart discusses two CAFA provisions that require or authorize federal district courts to decline to exercise jurisdiction: § 1332(d)(3), which gives federal courts *discretion* to refuse to exercise jurisdiction in certain circumstances, and § 1332(d)(4), which *requires* federal courts to decline to exercise jurisdiction in some cases. The main purpose of these provisions is to keep cases with a particularly strong tie to the forum in state court. But note that these provisions also may afford class counsel an opportunity to structure the class suit so as to lock it into state court.

Section 1332(d)(3)—the "interest of justice" exception—provides that a federal district "*may* in the interests of justice and looking at the totality of the circumstances" decline to exercise jurisdiction in a class action when more than one-third but less than two-thirds of class members and all of the primary defendants are citizens of the state where the suit was originally filed. § 1332(d)(3) (emphasis added). The subdivision specifically identifies six factors that a district court is to consider in deciding whether declining to exercise jurisdiction would be in the interests of justice.[*]

---

[*] Section 1332(d)(3) sets out the following factors:

Section 1332(d)(4), by contrast, provides that the court "shall decline" to exercise jurisdiction when the requirements of *either* § 1332(d)(4)(A) *or* (d)(4)(B) are met. Section 1332(d)(4)(B)—known as the "home state" exception—requires a court to decline to exercise jurisdiction if "*two-thirds or more*" of class members and "the primary defendants are citizens of the State in which the action was originally filed."§ 1332(d)(4)(B) (emphasis added). Cf. § 1332(d)(3) (authorizing a court to consider declining to exercise jurisdiction in certain circumstances in a class action when "*greater than one-third but less than two-thirds*" of class members and "the primary defendants are citizens of the State in which the action was originally filed") (emphasis added).

Section 1332(d)(4)(A)—known as the "local controversy" exception—requires a district court to decline to exercise jurisdiction in some cases in which more than two-thirds of the class members are citizens of the state in which the action was originally filed, *but not all the primary defendants are citizens of the state in which the action was originally filed*. At least one of the defendants must be a party (1) "from whom significant relief is sought," (2) "whose alleged conduct forms a significant basis for the claims asserted" by the class, *and* (3) "who is a citizen of the State in which the action was originally filed." § 1332(d)(4)(A)(i)(II). Other conditions must also be satisfied before a court is required to decline to exercise jurisdiction under § 1332(d)(4)(A). See § 1332(d)(4)(A)(i)(III) (requiring that the " principal injuries resulting from the alleged conduct or any related conduct of each defendant [have been] incurred in the State in which the action was originally filed"); § 1332(d)(4)(A)(ii) (requiring a court to decline jurisdiction under Section 1332(d)(4)(A) only if "during the 3–year period preceding the filing of [the] class action, no other class action has been filed asserting the same or similar factual allegations against any of the defendants on behalf of the same or other persons").

Who bears the burden of demonstrating that jurisdiction should be declined under § 1332(d)(3) or (d)(4)? In *Hart v. FedEx Ground Package Sys. Inc.*, 457 F.3d 675 (7th Cir. 2006), the Seventh Circuit held that a class seeking a remand to state court has the burden of showing that jurisdiction should be declined. *Id.* at 680–81. The Seventh Circuit cited the Supreme Court's conclusion in *Breuer v. Jim's Concrete of Brevard, Inc.*, 538 U.S. 691 (2003), that the opponent of removal "must prove that there is an express exception to removability." The *Hart* court explained that it is reasonable to understand §§ 1332(d)(3) and (d)(4) as " 'express exceptions' to CAFA's

---

(A) whether the claims asserted involve matters of national or interstate interest;

(B) whether the claims asserted will be governed by laws of the State in which the action was originally filed or by the laws of other States;

(C) whether the class action has been pleaded in a manner that seeks to avoid Federal jurisdiction;

(D) whether the action was brought in a forum with a distinct nexus with the class members, the alleged harm, or the defendants;

(E) whether the number of citizens of the State in which the action was originally filed in all proposed plaintiff classes in the aggregate is substantially larger than the number of citizens from any other State, and the citizenship of the other members of the proposed class is dispersed among a substantial number of States; and

(F) whether, during the 3–year period preceding the filing of that class action, 1 or more other class actions asserting the same or similar claims on behalf of the same or other persons have been filed.

§ 1332(d)(3).

normal jurisdictional rule, as the Supreme Court used that term in *Breuer.*" *Id.* at 681. The Seventh Circuit further reasoned that placement of the burden on the plaintiffs as to the carve-out provisions was consistent with the stated purposes of CAFA and noted that the Senate Report also called for placement of the burden on a plaintiff class seeking remand.

d. MASS ACTIONS—JURISDICTION AND REMOVAL

Given that CAFA clamps down on nationwide class actions in state court that involve state-law claims, what latitude do plaintiffs' lawyers have to avoid the strictures of CAFA simply by using aggregation techniques other than the class action? Recall from Chapter 1 that the class action is just one of several vehicles for aggregate litigation. In light of the potential for evasion, CAFA adds still more language to the diversity jurisdiction statute:

(d) . . .

(11)(A) For purposes of this subsection and section 1453, a mass action shall be deemed to be a class action removable under paragraphs (2) through (10) if it otherwise meets the provisions of those paragraphs.

(B)(i) As used in subparagraph (A), the term "mass action" means any civil action . . . in which monetary relief claims of 100 or more persons are proposed to be tried jointly on the ground that the plaintiffs' claims involve common questions of law or fact, except that jurisdiction shall exist only over those plaintiffs whose claims in a mass action satisfy the jurisdictional amount requirements under subsection (a).

(ii) As used in subparagraph (A), the term "mass action" shall not include any civil action in which—

(I) all of the claims in the action arise from an event or occurrence in the State in which the action was filed, and that allegedly resulted in injuries in that State or in States contiguous to that State;

(II) the claims are joined upon motion of a defendant;

(III) all of the claims in the action are asserted on behalf of the general public (and not on behalf of individual claimants or members of a purported class) pursuant to a State statute specifically authorizing such action; or

(IV) the claims have been consolidated or coordinated solely for pretrial proceedings.

28 U.S.C. § 1332(d)(11).

The Eleventh Circuit has remarked that "CAFA's mass action provisions present an opaque, baroque maze of interlocking cross-references that defy easy interpretation, even though they are contained in a single paragraph of the amended diversity statute, 28 U.S.C. § 1332(d)(11), and are comprised of but four sub-paragraphs. . . ." *Lowery v. Alabama Power Co.*, 483 F.3d 1184, 1198 (11th Cir. 2007). The core idea of § 1332(d)(11), of course, is that a qualifying mass action is treated as a class action for purposes of applying §§ 1332(d) and 1453. But beyond that basic point, § 1332(d)(11)'s text seems to raise more questions than it answers.

Take, for example, the uncertain interaction between §§ 1332(d)(11)(A) and 1332(d)(11)(B)(i) with respect to the amount-in-controversy requirement. Section 1332(d)(11)(A) indicates that jurisdiction should be available over a mass action so long as the aggregate amount in controversy is in excess of $5 million. On the other hand, § 1332(d)(11)(B)(i) specifically provides that "jurisdiction shall exist only over those plaintiffs whose claims in a mass action satisfy the jurisdictional amount requirements under [Section 1332(a)]"—in other words, only over plaintiffs who *individually* have claims in excess of $75,000 against each defendant.

How should these provisions be reconciled when 100 or more plaintiffs have more than $5 million at stake in the aggregate, but less than 100 satisfy the amount-in-controversy mandated by § 1332(a)? The legislative history indicates that a court must remand the claims of an individual plaintiff who does not have claims in excess of $75,000 against each defendant that he or she sues. But so long as 100 or more persons had more than $5 million at stake when the action was removed, the federal court retains jurisdiction even if the number of plaintiffs falls below 100. S. Rep. No. 109-14 at 47. The Eleventh Circuit read the provisions in accordance with the legislative history, while leaving open the possibility that plaintiffs have the burden of showing that at least one plaintiff will satisfy § 1332(a)'s amount-in-controversy requirement. *See Lowery*, 483 F.3d 1203–07.

The case that follows—and the accompanying notes and questions— address some of the other questions raised by the mass action provision.

Anderson v. Bayer Corp.

610 F.3d 390 (7th Cir. 2010)

■ FLAUM, CIRCUIT JUDGE.

Defendants (collectively referred to as "Bayer") have petitioned for leave to appeal the remand orders issued by the district court. . . . In five separate, mostly identical complaints in state court, plaintiffs sued Bayer for personal injuries they allege were caused by Trasylol, a prescription medication manufactured by Bayer. Defendants removed, invoking the "mass action" provision of the Class Action Fairness Act ("CAFA"), which allows the removal of cases joining the claims of at least 100 plaintiffs that otherwise meet CAFA's jurisdictional requirements. The district court remanded four of the five cases because they contained fewer than 100 plaintiffs (in the fifth case plaintiffs meant to include 99 plaintiffs, but actually named two co-executors in the same paragraph for a total of 100 plaintiffs). Bayer asks us to grant its petitions for review in the four cases remanded to state court and hold that (1) plaintiffs cannot avoid federal diversity jurisdiction by carving their filings into five separate pleadings, and (2) there is diversity jurisdiction over most plaintiff's claims because the claims of the small number of non-diverse plaintiffs were fraudulently misjoined and should be severed. Because we agree with the district court on the first question, we conclude that we are without jurisdiction to reach the second.

In August and September of 2009, plaintiffs' counsel filed in St. Clair County, Illinois, claims on behalf of 57 unrelated plaintiffs, dividing the claims between four virtually identical complaints, using verbatim language, alleging that the plaintiffs (or their decedents) suffered injuries as a result of being administered Trasylol during heart surgery. Bayer removed, invoking the district court's diversity jurisdiction over the diverse plaintiffs' claims by arguing that the few non-diverse plaintiffs had been fraudulently misjoined. The district court remanded *sua sponte*.

After remand to St. Clair County, plaintiffs' counsel amended the complaints to add 111 new plaintiffs, spread across the four existing suits. This resulted in a total of 100 plaintiffs in Gilmore,[1] 5 in *Brown*, 45 in *Bancroft*, and 18 in *Lecker*. Plaintiffs' counsel also filed a fifth complaint, *Anderson*, naming three plaintiffs, one of whom was non-diverse. Defendants once again removed. The district court remanded *Bancroft, Brown, Lecker,* and *Anderson,* rejecting defendants' argument that they should be treated as a single mass action and defendants' alternative argument that the non-diverse plaintiffs should have been severed from the action as fraudulently misjoined. Defendants then filed this petition for permission to appeal under 28 U.S.C. § 1453(c), a provision of CAFA that creates an exception for class actions to the general rule that remand orders are not reviewable.

Bayer first argues that plaintiffs' cases meet CAFA's definition of a "mass action" and thus the district court erred in remanding the cases. 28 U.S.C. § 1332(d)(11)(B)(i) defines a mass action as "any civil action . . . in which the monetary relief claims of 100 or more persons are proposed to be tried jointly on the ground that the plaintiffs' claims involve common questions of law or fact." Under CAFA, such mass actions "shall be deemed to be a class action" removable to federal court, so long as CAFA's other jurisdictional requirements are met. *Id.* § 1332(d)(11)(A). There is no dispute that the other requirements—amount in controversy and minimal diversity— are met in each of the four cases that Bayer appealed.

Of course, none of the instant four cases actually involve the claims of more than 100 plaintiffs. Bayer, however, urges us not to place "too much weight on form" in the CAFA context. *See Marshall v. H & R Block Tax Servs., Inc.,* 564 F.3d 826, 828 (7th Cir.2009). They argue that plaintiffs' five separate pleadings are a transparent attempt to circumvent CAFA, and, as such, should be treated as a single mass action. In support of this argument, they cite *Freeman v. Blue Ridge Paper Products, Inc.,* 551 F.3d 405 (6th Cir.2008). In *Freeman,* the Sixth Circuit considered an appeal from the remand of five related cases that had separated the plaintiffs' claims for nuisance into six-month periods in order to avoid meeting CA- FA's $5 million jurisdictional amount. The Sixth Circuit found that "there was no colorable reason for breaking up the lawsuit in this fashion, other than to avoid federal jurisdiction," and thus held that the damages sought in each suit "must be aggregated" for the purpose of determining whether the amount-in-controversy requirement had been met.

Freeman, however, did not address the mass action provision of CAFA. This distinction is important because CAFA states that "the term 'mass action' shall not include any civil action in which the claims are joined upon motion of a defendant." 28 U.S.C. § 1332(d)(11)(B)(ii)(II). By excluding cas- es in which the claims were consolidated on a defendant's motion, Congress appears to have contemplated that some cases which could have been brought as a mass action would, because of the way in which the plaintiffs chose to structure their claims, remain outside of CAFA's grant of jurisdic- tion. This is not necessarily anomalous; after all, the general rule in a di-

---

[1] Because it joined the claims of 100 or more plaintiffs, *Gilmore v. Bayer Corp.,* No. 09– 986–GPM, (S.D. Ill. 2009), was not remanded by the district court and thus is not part of this appeal.

versity case is that "plaintiffs as masters of the complaint may include (or omit) claims or parties in order to determine the forum." *See Garbie v. DaimlerChrysler Corp.*, 211 F.3d 407, 410 (7th Cir.2000) (citing *Caterpillar Inc. v. Williams*, 482 U.S. 386, 392 (1987)).

The only appellate court to have addressed an argument similar to Bayer's has rejected its approach. [*Tanoh v. Dow Chemical Co.*, 561 F.3d 945 (9th Cir. 2009)]. . . .

We agree with our colleagues on the Ninth Circuit. The mass action provision gives plaintiffs the choice to file separate actions that do not qualify for CAFA jurisdiction. The instant cases contain fewer than 100 plaintiffs and thus are not removable under the plain language of the statute. Bayer's argument that these separate lawsuits be treated as one action is tantamount to a request to consolidate them—a request that Congress has explicitly stated cannot become a basis for removal as a mass action.

Of course, subsequent action by the plaintiffs in state court might render these claims removable. *See Bullard v. Burlington Northern Santa Fe Railway Co.*, 535 F.3d 759, 762 (7th Cir. 2008) (holding that a case in state court may become a removable mass action "long after filing" if the claims of more than 100 plaintiffs are subsequently proposed to be tried jointly). In *Bullard*, we specifically described as removable a hypothetical set of "15 suits" with "10 plaintiffs each" that are proposed to be tried together. *Id.* We also noted that the § 1332(d)(11) extended to a situation where only a few representative plaintiffs would actually go to trial, with claim or issue preclusion to be used to dispose of the remaining claims without trial. *Id.* Such a request from the plaintiffs seems possible (perhaps even likely) at some future point in these cases, given the similarity of their claims. But it is not yet a certainty, and Congress has forbidden us from finding jurisdiction based on Bayer's suggestion that the claims be tried together. So long as plaintiffs (or perhaps the state court) do not propose to try these cases jointly in state court, they do not constitute a mass action removable to federal court.[2] . . .

Defendants' petition for leave to appeal under 28 U.S.C. § 1453(c) is DENIED.

NOTES AND QUESTIONS

1. *The Meaning of "Proposed to be Tried Jointly."* Courts have had no difficulty concluding that "claims are proposed to be tried jointly" when the plaintiffs join in a single complaint. But what if the plaintiffs are not joined in a single complaint? Is § 1332(d)(11) triggered only if the plaintiffs propose to try the claims jointly, or is it sufficient that a state court consolidates the claims *sua sponte*? *Anderson*, of course, expressly reserved the question of whether a state court's *sua sponte* joinder of claims would qualify, while holding that a mass action does not arise when "the claims are joined upon motion of a defendant." Relatedly, how should claims that are never formally consolidated for trial be treated? Recall that *Anderson* in dicta stated that: "§ 1332(d)(11) extend[s] to a situation where only a few representative plaintiffs would actually go to trial, with claim or issue preclusion to be used to dispose of the remaining

---

[2] Like the Ninth Circuit in *Tanoh*, we express no opinion as to whether a state court's *sua sponte* joinder of claims might allow a defendant to remove separately filed state court claims to federal court as a single "mass action."

claims without trial." Does this represent an appropriate reading of the mass action provision?

2. Is Jurisdictional Gamesmanship Permitted? Recall that in *Anderson* the removing defendants characterized the multiple pleadings as a "transparent effort" to avoid jurisdiction under CAFA. Without contesting defendants' characterization, the court refused to treat the separately filed actions as the functional equivalent of one civil action, concluding that the legislative text suggests that Congress intended that plaintiffs should be able to structure their lawsuits to fall below the 100 person threshold. Do you agree? The Fifth Circuit took a different approach in resolving a similar question. In *Louisiana ex. rel. Caldwell v. Allstate Insurance Co.*, 536 F.3d 418 (5th Cir. 2008), the court of appeals pierced the pleadings and concluded that the state Attorney General—who had brought the suit as the sole plaintiff (and who was assisted by private counsel)—was merely a nominal party with respect to some of the claims and that the true parties in interest with respect to those claims were more than 100 policyholders. Quoting the Senate Report, the Fifth Circuit noted that Congress had emphasized that "jurisdictional gamesmanship" should not be permitted. *Id.* at 424. Cf. *LG Display Co. v. Madigan*, 665 F.3d 768 (7th Cir. 2011) (rejecting the Fifth Circuit's approach). For a thoughtful discussion of this and other issues raised by § 1332(d)(11), see Guyon Knight, Note, *The CAFA Mass Action Numerosity Requirement: Three Problems With Counting to 100*, 78 Fordham L. Rev. 1875, 1891–92 (2010).

e. CAFA, *KLAXON*, AND CHOICE OF LAW

Although CAFA expressly finds that state courts have improperly made "judgments that impose their view of the law on other States," Class Action Fairness Act § 2(a)(4)(C), the operative provisions of the Act do not provide a choice-of-law rule for class actions. For its part, the Senate Report states that "the Act does not change the application of the Erie Doctrine, which requires federal courts to apply the substantive law dictated by applicable choice-of-law principles in actions arising under diversity jurisdiction." S. Rep. No. 109–14, at 49. As discussed in Chapter 2, *Klaxon Co. v. Stentor Electric Mfg. Co.*, 313 U.S. 487 (1941), implements the *Erie* policy by requiring a federal court to apply the choice-of-law rules of the state in which it sits. *Id.* at 496–97. But if a federal court applies *Klaxon* in cases covered by CAFA, does the legislation actually do anything to address the alleged choice-of-law abuses that the Act decried?

Recall from Chapter 2 that the Oklahoma Supreme Court is on record as applying the law of the defendant's principal place of business to a nationwide breach-of-warranty class action. *Ysbrand v. DaimlerChrysler Corp.*, 81 P.3d 618 (Okla. 2003). The Senate Report specifically cites *Ysbrand* as an example of the courts of one state improperly imposing their view of the law on the other 49. See S. Rep. No. 109–14, at 25. What should a federal court sitting in Oklahoma do if faced with a choice-of-law decision in a nationwide breach-of-warranty class action indistinguishable from *Ysbrand*? Is not a federal court faithful to *Klaxon* required to replicate the result in *Ysbrand*? For an argument that courts attentive to the "congressional policy objectives [of CAFA] will have to consider whether modest relaxation of the *Klaxon* rule would be appropriate" in cases like *Ysbrand*, see Patrick Woolley, Erie *and Choice of Law After the Class Action Fairness Act*, 80 Tul. L. Rev. 1723, 1756 (2006).

As a practical matter, does the failure to include a choice-of-law provision in CAFA actually undermine the objectives of the drafters? Recall the observation in Chapter 2 that, "in practice, federal courts in class litigation have departed in limited ways from *Klaxon* without acknowledging (or perhaps even recognizing) that they have done so." David Marcus has suggested that

> [s]ince the mid–1990s, federal courts have demonstrated a systematic impatience with the aggressive use of Rule 23 in multistate cases with state law causes of action. This hostility, which is traceable through federal courts' choice-of-law decisions, does not directly result from a formal change in the law but instead appears to reflect an emerging consensus against certain uses of the class action device. CAFA supporters' confidence in federalization rests in large measure on a perception of this shared hostility.

David Marcus, *Erie, the Class Action Fairness Act, and Some Federalism Implications of Diversity Jurisdiction*, 48 Wm. & Mary L. Rev. 1247, 1281 (2007). If Professor Marcus's assessment is correct, did the drafters of CAFA need a choice-of-law provision to achieve their objectives?

Even if federal courts assiduously respect *Klaxon*, will CAFA nonetheless lead to what might be called the "backdoor federalization" of substantive law in areas ostensibly still the province of the states? Samuel Issacharoff and Catherine Sharkey have argued:

> Although CAFA declared its intent to leave *Erie* untouched, once national-market cases are jurisdictionally isolated in federal courts, the need to develop incremental decisional law to address the particular concerns of these cases will be inescapable. And if federal courts are the only courts hearing these cases, then the most relevant source of authority for how to handle similar problems will be the common experience of federal courts in other CAFA cases. The likely effect of CAFA will then be to allow a body of national law to develop that corresponds to the demands of an undifferentiated market in which products are manufactured and sent to consumers across a distributional chain of ever-expanding geographic reach.

Samuel Issacharoff & Catherine M. Sharkey, *Backdoor Federalization*, 53 UCLA L. Rev. 1353, 1419–20 (2006). One federal district judge similarly has noted that "[t]o the extent that "some areas of state substantive law are only adjudicated in the form of class actions, CAFA will. . . work to preclude state courts from any opportunity to address certain areas of law." *In re Welding Fume Prod. Liab. Litig.*, 245 F.R.D. 279 (N.D. Ohio 2007). Should federal courts certify choice-of-law questions to state courts when possible to avoid "backdoor federalization"?

Some welcome federalization in this context. Suzanna Sherry, for example, flatly argues that "CAFA should be read as overruling *Erie Railroad Co. v. Tompkins*, at least for the national-market cases that it places within federal court jurisdiction" and suggests that this would be a good result. Suzanna Sherry, *Overruling Erie: Nationwide Class Actions and National Common Law*, 156 U. Pa. L. Rev. 2135, 2136 (2008). Do you agree?

2. THE MULTIPARTY, MULTIFORUM TRIAL JURISDICTION ACT

A precursor to the Class Action Fairness Act was the Multiparty, Multiforum Trial Jurisdiction Act of 2002 ("MMTJA"), which is codified in §§ 1369 and 1441(e) of Title 28. The Act was intended to facilitate the aggregate treatment in federal court of cases arising from a mass accident. See *Wallace v. Louisiana Citizens Property Ins. Corp.*, 444 F.3d 697, 702 (5th Cir. 2006) (stating that the Act "was designed to ameliorate the restrictions on the exercise of federal jurisdiction that ultimately forced parties in multiple suits arising from the same disaster to litigate in several fora"). Indeed, the MMTJA specifically requires a district court in which an action under § 1369 is pending to "promptly notify the judicial panel on multidistrict litigation of the pendency of the action." § 1369(e).

Section 1369 grants the federal district courts

"original jurisdiction of any civil action involving minimal diversity between adverse parties that arises from a single accident, where at least 75 natural persons have died in the accident at a discrete location if—

(1) a defendant resides in a State and a substantial part of the accident took place in another State or other location, regardless of whether that defendant is also a resident of the State where a substantial part of the accident took place;

(2) any two defendants reside in different States, regardless of whether such defendants are also residents of the same State or States; *or*

(3) substantial parts of the accident took place in different States."

§ 1369(a) (emphasis added).* The Act defines "accident" as "a sudden accident, or a natural event culminating in an accident, that results in death incurred at a discrete location by at least 75 natural persons,"§ 1369(c)(4)." For discussion of the case law exploring what qualifies as an "accident" within the meaning of the statute, see Construction and Application of Multiparty, Multiforum, Trial Jurisdiction Act of 2002 (MMTJA), 28 U.S.C.A. § 1369, 32 A.L.R. Fed. 2d 263 §§ 8–10 (2008).

---

* The influential article that proposed the Act explains that the restrictions later codified in subdivisions (a)(1)–(a)(3) are crucial and notes that subdivisions (a)(2) and (a)(3) are, for the most part, redundant given the breadth of subdivision (a)(1):

[The restrictions] attempt[] to capture . . . the condition that . . . should be necessary (but not sufficient) for the exercise of a federal multiparty, multiforum jurisdiction— any defendant's residency in a state other than one in which a substantial part of the acts or omissions giving rise to the action occurred. Because that condition is covered in subpart [(a)(1)], for most purposes subpart [(a)(2)] would be superfluous. It is included primarily for clarity and administrative ease . . . Subpart [(a)(2)] does, however, deal with one situation not covered by subpart [(a)(1)]: cases in which all events took place abroad but litigation in American courts is possible because defendants reside in different American states. For a somewhat converse and probably also unusual situation, subpart [(a)(3)] confers subject matter jurisdiction in cases involving nonresident defendants and events that occurred in two or more American states.

Thomas D. Rowe, Jr. & Kenneth D. Sibley, *Beyond Diversity: Federal Multiparty, Multiforum Jurisdiction*, 135 U. Pa. L. Rev. 7, 50 (1986). "A corporation. . . is deemed to be a resident of any State in which it is incorporated or licensed to do business or is doing business." § 1369(c)(2).

In addition to authorizing and limiting jurisdiction, the Act requires a district court to "abstain" from exercising jurisdiction under Section 1369(a) over "a civil action" in which

(1) the substantial majority of all plaintiffs are citizens of a single State of which the primary defendants are also citizens; *and*

(2) the claims asserted will be governed primarily by the laws of that State.

§ 1369(b) (emphasis added). At least one district court has held that the term "all plaintiffs" in § 1369(b)(1) "must include all potential plaintiffs, meaning all those who have died or suffered injury as a result of the tragedy at issue." *Passa v. Derderian*, 308 F. Supp. 2d 43, 60 (D.R.I. 2004). Is the court's holding consistent with the language of 1369(b)? Does a civil action that is not certified as a class suit include more than the parties before the court in the particular action?

The MMTJA also includes a removal provision that sweeps more broadly than § 1369. In addition to authorizing removal of actions over which a federal district court may exercise jurisdiction under § 1369, see § 1441(e)(1)(A), § 1441(e) authorizes removal of actions over which a federal district court could not have exercised jurisdiction under § 1369. Specifically, § 1441(e)(1)(B) authorizes removal of an action by a defendant who is "a party to an action which is or could have been brought, in whole or in part, under section 1369 in a United States district court and arises from the same accident as the action in State court *even if the action to be removed could not have been brought in a district court as an original matter.*" § 1441(e)(1)(B) (emphasis added). In other words, as long as there is a civil action in a federal court over which a federal court may exercise jurisdiction under § 1369, state court actions that arise out of the same accident may be removed. *Wallace*, 444 F.3d at 702 ("When the requirements of § 1441(e)(1)(B) are met, defendants need not establish the existence of independent subject matter jurisdiction under any other provision, including under § 1369(a), because supplemental jurisdiction has been established").* This grant of supplemental jurisdiction has been held to authorize removal of a state action even if the federal court would have been required to abstain from exercising original jurisdiction under § 1369(b). *Wallace*, 444 F.3d at 702 ("§ 1369(b) is not an independent bar to the exercise of jurisdiction over a case removed pursuant to § 1441(e)(1)(B), as it applies only to the exercise of original jurisdiction under § 1369(a)."). Does the conclusion that § 1369(b) does not apply to cases removed under Section 1441(e)(1)(B) make any difference if courts read § 1369(b) as broadly as *Passa* suggests?

In addition to authorizing removal of civil actions over which federal courts cannot exercise original jurisdiction under § 1369, the MMTJA's removal provision has other noteworthy features. Section 1441(e)—like the removal provision of the Class Action Fairness Act—tweaks the ordinary

---

* Section 1369(d) provides a similar basis for supplemental jurisdiction when a plaintiff rather than a defendant seeks aggregation in a mass accident case. Section 1369(d) provides that "[i]n any action in a district court which is or could have been brought, in whole or in part, under this section, any person with a claim arising from the accident described in subsection (a) shall be permitted to intervene as a party plaintiff in the action, *even if that person could not have brought an action in a district court as an original matter.*" § 1369(d) (emphasis added). Because minimal diversity is a constitutional requirement for the exercise of diversity jurisdiction, § 1441(e)(1)(B) poses the question of whether, as a constitutional matter, the existence of minimal diversity may be established by consolidating an action in which minimal diversity does not exist with other actions. Section 1369(d) avoids that question by allowing intervention in a civil action that meets the requirements of the Constitution.

requirements of removal procedure to make it easier to remove a qualifying action. Compare § 1441(e)(1) with § 1446. Actions removed under § 1441(e) must be remanded back to state court after the federal court makes "a liability determination" if "further proceedings as to damages" are required. § 1441(e)(2). But the federal district court may retain the action if "the court finds that, for the convenience of the parties and witnesses and in the interest of justice, the action should be retained for the determination of damages." *Id.*

B. COORDINATION OF PARALLEL PROCEEDINGS

This section addresses the procedural issues that arise when related civil lawsuits, which may be class actions, mass actions, or large numbers of individual cases, proceed in different courts across the country—perhaps, in different courts within the federal judicial system, in courts of different states, or simultaneously in both the federal system and various state-court systems. Even in the post-CAFA world, there will continue to be some class actions and mass actions litigated in state courts, whether because such actions are not removable at all or because the defendant chooses not to remove. There will also be instances in which related conventional lawsuits are brought in state courts in volume, for example, by consumers who claim to have taken defective drugs or to have been injured by defective products. This section focuses on the techniques for coordination of related lawsuits and the doctrinal limitations upon such coordination.

1. COORDINATION WITHIN THE FEDERAL COURTS: THE MDL PANEL

In 1968, Congress passed the Multidistrict Litigation Act, 28 U.S.C. § 1407, largely in response to thousands of antitrust actions brought in the federal courts against the electrical equipment industry. As reflected in the excerpts that follow, the central innovation of the Act consists of its creation of the Judicial Panel on Multidistrict Litigation ("MDL Panel") to coordinate related lawsuits within the federal judicial system:

Multidistrict Litigation Act
28 U.S.C. § 1407

(a) When civil actions involving one or more common questions of fact are pending in different districts, such actions may be transferred to any district for coordinated or consolidated pretrial proceedings. Such transfers shall be made by the judicial panel on multidistrict litigation authorized by this section upon its determination that transfers for such proceedings will be for the convenience of parties and witnesses and will promote the just and efficient conduct of such actions. Each action so transferred shall be remanded by the panel at or before the conclusion of such pretrial proceedings to the district from which it was transferred unless it shall have been previously terminated: *Provided, however,* That the panel may separate any claim, cross-claim, counterclaim, or third-party claim and remand any of such claims before the remainder of the action is remanded.

(b) Such coordinated or consolidated pretrial proceedings shall be conducted by a judge or judges to whom such actions are assigned by the judicial panel on multidistrict litigation. For this purpose, upon request of the panel, a circuit judge or a district judge may be designated and assigned temporarily for service in the transferee district by the Chief Justice of the United States or the chief judge of the circuit, as may be required. . . . With the consent of the transferee district court, such actions may be assigned by the panel to a judge or judges of such district. The judge or judges to whom such actions are assigned, the members of the judicial panel on multidistrict litigation, and other circuit and district judges designated when needed by the panel may exercise the powers of a district judge in any district for the purpose of conducting pretrial depositions in such coordinated or consolidated pretrial proceedings.

(c) Proceedings for the transfer of an action under this section may be initiated by—

(i) the judicial panel on multidistrict litigation upon its own initiative, or

(ii) motion filed with the panel by a party in any action in which transfer for coordinated or consolidated pretrial proceedings under this section may be appropriate. . . .

The panel shall give notice to the parties in all actions in which transfers for coordinated or consolidated pretrial proceedings are contemplated, and such notice shall specify the time and place of any hearing to determine whether such transfer shall be made. . . . The panel's order of transfer shall be based upon a record of such hearing at which material evidence may be offered by any party to an action pending in any district that would be affected by the proceedings under this section, and shall be supported by findings of fact and conclusions of law based upon such record. . . .

(d) The judicial panel on multidistrict litigation shall consist of seven circuit and district judges designated from time to time by the Chief Justice of the United States, no two of whom shall be from the same circuit. The concurrence of four members shall be necessary to any action by the panel.

(e) No proceedings for review of any order of the panel may be permitted except by extraordinary writ. . . . Petitions for an extraordinary writ to review an order of the panel to set a transfer hearing and other orders of the panel issued prior to the order either directing or denying transfer shall be filed only in the court of appeals having jurisdiction over the district in which a hearing is to be or has been held. Petitions for an extraordinary writ to review an order to transfer or orders subsequent to transfer shall be filed only in the court of appeals having jurisdiction over the transferee district. There shall be no appeal or review of an order of the panel denying a motion to transfer for consolidated or coordinated proceedings. . . .

The MDL Panel started transferring and consolidating related lawsuits immediately, and has been busy ever since. "Since its inception, the Panel has considered motions for centralization in almost 2,400 dockets involving nearly 400,000 cases and millions of claims therein. These dockets encompass litigation categories as diverse as airplane crashes; other single accidents, such as train wrecks or hotel fires; mass torts, such as those involving asbestos, drugs and other products liability cases; patent validity and infringement; antitrust price fixing; securities fraud; and employment practices." United States Judicial Panel on Multidistrict Litigation, Overview of Panel, http://www.jpml.uscourts.gov/panel-info/overview-panel (last visited Feb. 7, 2013). The MDL Panel is extremely fond of centralization. One study found that related products liability cases were overwhelmingly likely to be transferred and consolidated whenever the defendant supported the motion. Mark Herrmann & Pearson Bownas, *Making Book on the MDL Panel: Will It Centralize Your Products Liability Cases?*, 8 Class Action Litig. Rep. (BNA) 110 (Feb. 9, 2007). Another author wrote of the MDL Panel's "maximalist" use of its powers. Richard L. Marcus, *Cure–All for an Era of Dispersed Litigation? Toward a Maximalist Use of the Multidistrict Litigation Panel's Transfer Power*, 82 Tul. L. Rev. 2245, 2249 (2008). In late 2012, 284 MDL dockets were pending in 55 federal transferee courts. United States Judicial Panel on Multidistrict Litigation, MDL Statistics Report—Distribution of Pending MDL Dockets (Nov. 14, 2012).

According to the statute, related cases are supposed to be transferred to an MDL court for "pretrial proceedings." When the cases are ready for trial, the MDL judge is supposed to notify the MDL Panel, which must remand each case "to the district from which it was transferred." The remand requirement rankled MDL judges. By preventing them from trying cases transferred to their courts, it limited their control of the cases and impeded their ability to encourage global settlements. MDL judges therefore sought to circumvent the statute by, among other means, engaging in a practice known as "self-transfer": the transfer of the consolidated cases to themselves for purposes of trial—in practical terms, for comprehensive settlement negotiations—upon the conclusion of pre-trial proceedings. The Supreme Court brought this practice to a halt in *Lexecon, Inc. v. Milberg Weiss Bershad Hynes & Lerach*, 523 U.S. 26 (1998).

Even so, and despite *Lexecon*, remands are rare. MDL judges hold onto cases so tenaciously that even they describe MDLs as "black hole[s], into which cases are transferred never to be heard from again." Eldon E. Fallon, Jeremy T. Grabill & Robert Pitard Wynne, *Bellwether Trials in Multidistrict Litigation*, 82 Tul. L. Rev. 2323, 2330 (2008). (The lead author, Eldon E. Fallon, is a federal district court judge who has handled several MDLs.) Of the 393,682 civil actions sent to MDL courts for pretrial proceedings since 1968, 12,419 had been remanded for trial as of late 2011, a remand rate of 3 percent. Even this figure exaggerates the likelihood of remand. A mere 4 MDLs account for the vast majority of the remanded non-asbestos cases. Emery G. Lee, Margaret S. Williams, Richard A. Nagareda, Joe S. Cecil, Thomas E. Willging & Kevin M. Scott, *The Expanding Role of Multidistrict Consolidation in Federal Civil Litigation: An Empirical Investigation* 17–18 (Aug. 3, 2009), *available at* http://ssrn.com/abstract=1443375. The rarity of remands is also discussed in Elizabeth Chamblee Burch, *Disaggregating*, Wash. U. L. Rev. (forthcoming 2013), *available at* http://ssrn.com/abstract=2137782 .

a.　SELECTING THE TRANSFEREE COURT

In practical terms, much of the action surrounding the MDL Panel concerns the selection of the district court in which a given body of related litigation is to be consolidated. Formally, the law permits the MDL Panel to select any federal district court for this purpose. In practice, the Panel's choice of transferee fora appears to be strongly influenced by the location of the filed cases and the defendant's forum preference. The Panel's composition may also influence its decisions. Having a member judge on the MDL Panel increases the likelihood that a particular district court will be chosen. Margaret S. Williams & Tracey E. George, *Between Cases and Classes: The Decision to Consolidate Multidistrict Litigation* (August 3, 2009) (unpublished research),*available at* http://ssrn.com/abstract=1443377).

The MDL Panel's preference for transferee courts preferred by defendants suggests that a good deal turns on the choice of MDL forum. Defendants naturally prefer courts that are pro-defendant over those that are pro-plaintiff. Consequently, by favoring defendants the Panel may affect the balance of power between parties, giving defendants more power in settlement negotiations than they might have if plaintiff-friendly courts were preferred. The choice of transferee forums also has implications for plaintiffs' attorneys, who compete for lead positions in consolidated proceeding or have other priorities. As the following case illustrates, the choice of district court can be a surrogate for rivalries amongst plaintiffs' law firms seeking control of the litigation:

In re Silicone Gel Breast Implants Products Liability Litigation

793 F. Supp. 1098 (J.P.M.L. 1992)

■ Before NANGLE, CHAIRMAN, DILLIN, MILTON POLLACK, LOUIS H. POLLAK, MERHIGE, and ENRIGHT, JUDGES OF THE PANEL.

The record before us suggests that more than a million women have received silicone gel breast implants. Since the Food and Drug Administration held highly publicized hearings a few months ago about the safety of this product, a rush to the courthouse has ensued, although some litigation concerning the product has periodically been filed in the federal courts in the last several years.

This litigation presently consists of the 78 actions . . . pending in 33 federal districts. . . .

Before the Panel are four separate motions pursuant to 28 U.S.C. § 1407: 1) motion of plaintiffs in three Northern District of California actions to centralize all actions in the Northern District of California or any other appropriate transferee forum (these plaintiffs now favor centralization in the Southern District of Ohio); 2) motion of plaintiffs in one Northern District of California action to centralize all actions in that district; 3) motion of plaintiffs in seven actions to centralize all actions in either the Northern District of California or the District of Kansas; and 4) motion of plaintiffs in the Eastern District of Virginia action . . . to centralize in that district the medical monitoring claims that are presented in seven purported class actions.

The overwhelming majority of the more than 200 responses received by the Panel supports transfer. The major issue presented in the responses is selection of the transferee forum, with two large groups of parties aligned in favor of opposing views. The first large group of parties favors selection of either the Northern District of California (Judge Thelton E. Henderson or Judge Marilyn H. Patel) or the District of Kansas (Judge Patrick F. Kelly). This group includes 1) plaintiffs in at least 65 of the 78 actions before the Panel; 2) plaintiffs in at least 69 potential tag-along actions; and 3) approximately 250 attorneys who are purportedly investigating claims of more than 2,000 potential plaintiffs. The second large group of parties favors selection of the Southern District of Ohio (Judge Carl B. Rubin). This group includes 1) plaintiffs in nine of the 78 actions before the Panel; 2) plaintiffs in at least nine potential tag-along actions; 3) approximately 75 law firms that purport to represent approximately 4,000 actual and potential plaintiffs; and 4) sixteen defendants, including major silicone gel breast implant manufacturers Dow Corning Corporation (Dow Corning), Baxter Healthcare Corporation, McGhan Medical Corporation (McGhan), Bristol–Meyers Squibb Company and Mentor Corporation (Mentor). . . .

Selection of the transferee court and judge for this litigation has been a challenging task. The parties' arguments in their briefs and at the Panel hearing in this matter have focused primarily on the relative merits of the suggested California and Ohio forums. Proponents of the California forum stress that i) both Judge Henderson and Judge Patel have tried breast implant actions and are thus very familiar with the issues raised in this docket, ii) several implant manufacturers, including McGhan and Mentor, have their principal places of business in California, and iii) California is presumptively the state with the largest number of actual and potential claimants in the breast implant litigation. Meanwhile, proponents of the Ohio forum emphasize Judge Rubin's familiarity with the litigation, gained by presiding over the consolidated breast implant action . . . in his district since January 1992. During that time, Judge Rubin has conditionally certified a nationwide, opt-out class of breast implant recipients; established a document depository; appointed a Plaintiffs' Lead Counsel Committee consisting of seven members; scheduled trial on common issues for June 1993; and initiated the dissemination of notice to class members.

We observe that either the Northern District of California or the Southern District of Ohio could be an appropriate forum for this docket and certainly the judges referred to are experienced and well-qualified to handle this litigation. We are troubled, however, by the volume and tone of the negative arguments with which opposing counsel have sought to denigrate each other's forum choices, litigation strategies and underlying motives. A brief recitation of a few of these arguments sufficiently conveys their flavor. For example, various parties argue that 1) parties in the Ohio forum have engendered a flurry of pretrial activity in an effort to dictate our decision on selection of the transferee court; 2) the class in the Southern District of Ohio was certified in a precipitous fashion, without according adequate notice or opportunity to be heard to interested parties nationwide; 3) defendants oppose the California forum only because the two trials there resulted in substantial verdicts against one of them; and 4) the plaintiffs who favor the California forum are forum shopping for a judge who has tried a breast implant action in which plaintiffs prevailed.

Essentially, these arguments are fueled by an acrimonious dispute among counsel, relating to control of the litigation as well as to how it should proceed (class versus individual treatment). It is neither our function nor our inclination to take sides in this dispute. But we are indeed persuaded that the level of acrimony has caused the parties and counsel on each side to harbor a perception that they would be unfairly affected by selection of any of the suggested forums. This perception of "unfairness" is unwarranted, because this Panel believes that all of the federal judges involved in these 78 actions would conduct these proceedings in a fair and impartial manner. Nevertheless, we recognize that in a mega-tort docket of this nature, involving claimants who may be experiencing litigation for the first time, such a perception could become a dark cloud over these proceedings and threaten their just and efficient conduct.

In light of these considerations, we have determined to look beyond the preferences of the parties in our search for a transferee judge with the ability and temperament to steer this complex litigation on a steady course that will be sensitive to the concerns of all parties. Because no single location stands out as the geographic focal point for this nationwide docket, the scope of our search embraced the universe of federal district judges. By selecting Chief Judge Pointer [of the Northern District of Alabama], a former member of our Panel, Chairman of the Board of Editors of the MANUAL FOR COMPLEX LITIGATION, Chairman of the Judicial Conference's Advisory Committee on Civil Rules, and an experienced multidistrict transferee judge, we are confident that we are entrusting this important and challenging assignment to a distinguished jurist. We urge all parties and counsel to work cooperatively with one another and with Judge Pointer toward the goal of a just, efficient and expeditious resolution of the litigation. . . .

NOTES AND QUESTIONS

1. *Was the Plaintiffs' Preference for California Reasonable?* In *In re Silicone Gel Breast Implants Products Liability Litigation*, the MDL Panel reported the assertion, presumably made by the defendants, that some plaintiffs' attorneys preferred a California court because they wanted the cases handled by a judge who had presided over a trial that produced a pro-plaintiff result. Given that the MDL court cannot try any cases transferred to it, why might the plaintiffs' attorneys have wanted the California judge? Why did they not prefer Judge Rubin, who seemed to have demonstrated his plaintiff-friendly bona fides by certifying a class action? Could Judge Rubin's decision to certify a class have made him unpopular with plaintiffs' attorneys who were not chosen as class counsel?

Could the preference of many plaintiffs (or their lawyers) for a California district court have an innocent explanation? For example, might it reflect the convenience of California as a forum? Why should a California resident whose implant surgery was performed in California by a physician licensed in California and who is represented by a California attorney in a lawsuit properly filed in a California court have to bear the added cost and inconvenience of litigating in Alabama? Does the federal judiciary's desire to reduce its own costs by putting the entire litigation in the hands of a single judge justify imposing additional costs on personal injury claimants? Could the MDL Panel have reduced plaintiffs' costs by selecting three or four courts located near large populations of breast implant recipients and ordering the judges in those courts to cooperate? " '[T]he convenience of parties and witnesses' is a relevant consideration in the centralization decision under § 1407." Daniel A. Richards, Note. *An Analysis of the Judicial Panel on Multidistrict Litigation's Selection of Transferee District and Judge*, 78 Fordham L. Rev. 311. 316 (2009).

California plaintiffs may also have preferred a California federal district court because their cases could have been tried there after pre-trial preparations were completed. Settlement negotiations in a California MDL court would therefore have been informed by the knowledge that California plaintiffs' cases would be tried by the MDL judge if the negotiations failed. By contrast, California plaintiffs' cases could not have been tried by an MDL judge sitting in Ohio, Alabama or any other state because the cases would have had to be remanded to the transferee fora when pretrial preparations were complete. Assuming that the pretrial process educates the presiding judge about the merits, weren't California plaintiffs justified in wanting a California judge to handle the MDL?

2.   *What Matters Do MDL Judges Handle?* The statute authorizes transfer and consolidation of related cases for pretrial purposes. The matters that MDL judges handle pretrial include motions to dismiss, motions for summary judgment, class certification motions, and discovery motions (including motions for sanctions). MDL judges also choose the plaintiffs' attorneys (and sometimes the defense attorneys) who will hold lead positions. These lawyers run the consolidated proceeding and may receive enormous awards of attorneys' fees. Finally, MDL judges also preside over settlement negotiations and, in some instances, review proposed settlements for fairness and reasonableness. MDL procedures are described in the MANUAL FOR COMPLEX LITIGATION, FOURTH (2004).

It is important to understand that even though MDL judges cannot try transferred cases, their rulings on pretrial matters are binding throughout the litigation, including post-remand. Were this not so, the efficiency gains from coordinated pretrial processing would be lost. Given the rarity of remands, the matter is of mainly academic interest, except insofar as rulings on pretrial matters may affect settlement negotiations in an MDL.

b.   THE MDL STATUTE AND CHOICE OF LAW

(1) Choice of State Law

The *Klaxon* rule—which requires a federal court to apply the choice-of-law rules of the state in which it sits—typically does not apply when a suit is transferred from a federal district court in one state ("the transferor court") to a federal district court in another state ("the transferee court"). In cases in which the transferor federal court had personal jurisdiction over the parties and venue was properly laid in the transferor district, the Supreme Court has held that the "change of courtrooms" that results from transfer should not lead to the application of different state law. In other words, the transferee court should apply the choice-of-law rules of the state in which the transferor court sits. See *Van Dusen v. Barrack*, 376 U.S. 612 (1964); *Ferens v. John Deere Co.*, 494 U.S. 516 (1990).

Section 1404(a), which *Van Dusen* construes, provides that "[f]or the convenience of parties and witnesses, in the interest of justice, a district court may transfer any civil action to any other district or division where it might have been brought or to any district or division to which all parties have consented." 28 U.S.C. § 1404(a). The Court in *Van Dusen* explained:

> If a change of law were in the offing, the parties might well regard the section primarily as a forum-shopping instrument. And, more importantly, courts would at least be reluctant to grant transfers,

[Handwritten margin note: Klaxon - Fed Ct. Must apply choice of law Rules of the state in which it Sits]

despite considerations of convenience, if to do so might conceivably prejudice the claim of a plaintiff who had initially selected a permissible forum.

376 U.S. at 636. The Court stressed that its holding was consistent with the *Erie* policy: "What *Erie* and the cases following it have sought was an identity or uniformity between federal and state courts; and the fact that in most instances this could be achieved by directing federal courts to apply the laws of the states 'in which they sit' should not obscure that, in applying the same reasoning to § 1404(a), the critical identity to be maintained is between the federal district court which decides the case and the courts of the State in which the action was filed." *Id.* at 638–39.

Courts also apply *Van Dusen* to suits transferred for pretrial proceedings pursuant to the 28 U.S.C. § 1407, the MDL statute. *Van Dusen* can lead to serious complications in an MDL proceeding, given the number of cases and the consequent number of transferor courts that tend to be involved. But at least in theory, a transfer under Section 1407 will not work a change in the applicable law.

How should an MDL court applying *Van Dusen* decide a motion for class certification of state claims when the choice of substantive law affects the certification decision? Recall from Chapter 2 that choice-of-law analysis can make a huge difference to certification when the plaintiff seeks to represent a multistate or nationwide class alleging state-law claims. In particular, when the choice-of-law analysis dictates application of different law to the claims of different class members, it can be difficult or impossible for the plaintiff to meet the Rule 23 (b)(3) predominance requirement.

To explore this question, suppose that P files suit in the Central District of California and the suit is subsequently transferred to a large MDL proceeding in the Southern District of New York. After transfer, P files a motion with the MDL judge for certification of a nationwide class action (or more precisely, the plaintiffs' steering committee decides to seek certification of a class and to have P file the motion). Should the MDL judge apply New York choice-of-law rules, as would be appropriate had the case been filed in the MDL forum originally? Or should the judge apply California choice-of- law rules, which would have been applied to P's case in the absence of transfer? A straightforward application of *Van Dusen* would support the application of California choice-of-law rules because P's suit was transferred from California. See *In re Propulsid Product Liability Litigation*, 208 F.R.D. 133, 140–42 (E.D. La. 2002) (holding that the choice-of-law rules of the plaintiff's original forum, not the MDL forum, apply to a plaintiff's motion to certify a nationwide class).

Should an MDL judge always apply the choice-of-law rules of the forum in which the named plaintiff's suit was brought (i.e., the transferor forum) when deciding whether to certify a multistate or nationwide class action? What if the forum in which the named plaintiff's suit was brought would apply a choice-of-law rule that greatly facilitates certification by reducing or eliminating intra-class variation in the applicable law? What if that choice-of-law rule would select law that is particularly plaintiff-friendly? And what if it is clear that the MDL plaintiffs' lead counsel and steering committee acted strategically in choosing the actions for which certification is sought. This was the situation in *In re Toyota Motor Corp. Unintended Acceleration Marketing, Sales Practices, and Products Liability Litigation*, 785 F. Supp. 2d 925 (C.D. Cal. 2011), and it is useful to examine how the MDL judge reacted.

Toyota Motor Corp. was an MDL proceeding involving claims for damages caused by the sudden, unintended acceleration of Toyota vehicles. The MDL consisted of cases filed in courts throughout the nation. A subset of plaintiffs, all of whom filed originally in California (the "Moving Plaintiffs"), brought a motion for the application of California choice of law to a putative nationwide class action limited to claims for economic loss (i.e., the lost value due to the defective condition of their vehicles). The plaintiffs argued that since their cases were originally filed in California, California choice of law rules applied and that the relevant California choice-of-law rule would choose California substantive law for all of the class claims. The court denied the plaintiffs' motion, reasoning as follows:

> Here, the Moving Plaintiffs represent, and the Toyota Defendants have not disputed, that all the Moving Plaintiffs filed their actions in California. Thus, in the first instance, long-standing federal principles lead to the application of California's law. . . .

> But other considerations, some unique to multidistrict litigation, convince the Court that a fuller analysis compels a different result. . . . [G]ranting the relief sought by Plaintiffs here would undermine the purposes of the present MDL because it fails to take into account the requirement that the cases retain their separate and distinct identities in a manner that facilitates their statutorily mandated return to their home states for trial. . . .

> At oral argument, Plaintiffs analogized the current procedural posture to a case that had been filed in the first instance just by the Moving Plaintiffs in California state court. . . .

> Accepting . . . counsel's statement that "[t]here is no rule that says that one set of cases can't advance ahead of another set of cases," the basic facts are different here. Such hypothetical parallel state proceedings are just that: [s]eparate, but parallel proceedings that are not ever coupled with, and thus, would not ever need to be separated from the hypothesized proceeding. Stated differently, the state court analogy removes the non-Moving Plaintiffs from the radar screen. The Court cannot do that. Rather, this Court must consider the separate and distinct identities of the member cases to this MDL. . . .

> Undeniably, an MDL court has substantial discretion with regard to "phasing, timing and coordination of . . . cases." Indeed, the power of an MDL court with respect to such issues "is at its peak." However, despite this broad discretion on issues that are at the peak of the Court's power, the Court does not have the power to override the application of substantive legal standards. . . .

> Were the Court to grant the relief sought by the Moving Plaintiffs, the result would allow the non-moving Plaintiffs to avail themselves of California's [choice-of-law rules] by piggybacking upon their brother and sister Plaintiffs who filed in California. They do so in a manner designed to alter, and indeed expand the substantive rights of some Plaintiffs and to diminish the substantive rights of the Toyota Defendants, at times producing vastly different results as to the non-moving Plaintiffs who filed in other states.

Id. at 928–32. In the absence of an MDL proceeding, there is no question that California choice-of-law rules would have been applied to determine whether a nationwide class suit filed in California should be certified. Does the court adequately justify a different result just because plaintiffs sought class certification in the context of an MDL proceeding?

Note that the court frowned on what it saw as a strategic ploy to pick out named plaintiffs from the MDL who had filed in California, thereby invoking the California choice-of-law rule. *Id.* at 928 ("Plaintiffs' strategy has been crafted—thoughtfully and candidly—to maximize the case for adopting California's choice-of-law rules."). Should this kind of strategic maneuvering count against the plaintiffs? Would strategic motivation matter if there had been no MDL and these plaintiffs had filed in California to secure California choice-of-law rules for certification? Why should the MDL make a difference?

The concerns expressed by the *Toyota* court likely explain why some courts have refused to apply the choice-of-law rules of a *single* state when considering class certification in the course of an MDL proceeding. Rather, these courts insist that the choice-of-law rules of *all* of the states from which suits in the MDL were brought be considered on a motion for class certification. *See, e.g., In re Mercedes Benz Tele Aid Contract Litigation*, 257 F.R.D. 46, 56 (D.N.J. 2009) (holding in connection with a motion for class certification that the court would "apply the choice of law rules of [*all*] the states from which the various cases that make up this multi-district litigation were transferred when deciding what substantive law governs . . . "). Is application of the choice-of-law rules of multiple states in a class suit consistent with *Van Dusen*? Is it workable?

(2) When Federal Circuits Interpret Federal Law Differently

Federal circuits differ, often in nuanced and sometimes in dramatic ways, with respect to the meaning and application of federal substantive and procedural law. When such differences exist, is the transferee district court obliged to apply the interpretation of federal law that would be binding on the courts of transferor district? The Supreme Court has yet to resolve this question, but federal courts generally have adhered to the view that an MDL court should apply the law of its circuit. The leading case is *In 're Korean Air Lines Disaster of September 1, 1983*, 829 F.2d 1171 (D.C. Cir. 1987). As then-Judge Ruth Bader Ginsburg explained in that case:

> [T]he *Erie* policies served by the *Van Dusen* decision do not figure in the calculus when the law to be applied is federal, not state. Given the reality of conflict among the circuits on the proper interpretation of federal law, however, why deny to a plaintiff with a federal claim the "venue privilege" a diversity claimant enjoys? Plaintiffs in the *Van Dusen* situation could effectively pick [the applicable law by filing in a particular court]. Why deny a similar right of selection and retention to plaintiffs [with respect to federal law]?
>
> [V]enue provisions are designed with geographical convenience in mind, and not to "guarantee that the plaintiff will be able to select the law that will govern the case." In diversity cases, however, federal courts are governed by *Klaxon* and therefore may not compose federal choice-of-law principles; instead, they must look to state prescriptions in determining which state's law applies. With "no federal choice-of-law principles that favor the application of the law of one state over the law of another," the diversity

plaintiff's opening move or "venue privilege" ordinarily fills the gap—it "prevails by default." For the adjudication of federal claims, on the other hand, "[t]he federal courts comprise a single system [in which each tribunal endeavors to apply] a single body of law"; there is no compelling reason to allow plaintiff to capture the most favorable interpretation of that law simply and solely by virtue of his or her right to choose the place to open the fray.

Id. at 1174–75 (relying in part on Richard L. Marcus, *Conflicts Among Circuits and Transfers Within the Federal Judicial System*, 93 Yale L.J. 677 (1984)).

Consider the court's reasoning. *Korean Airlines* recognized that the *Erie* policy is irrelevant when federal law is the source of the applicable law. But did the court give enough weight to the other policies identified in *Van Dusen*, specifically that transfer statutes should not create or multiply opportunities for forum shopping and that judicial decisions to transfer should not turn on choice-of-law considerations?

Did the court give enough weight to the fact that § 1407 requires the MDL court to remand a case back to the district from which it was transferred at the conclusion of pretrial proceedings? Keep in mind that at the time *Korean Airlines* was decided, MDL courts often retained for trial suits that had initially been transferred to the MDL court for pretrial proceedings, a practice the Supreme Court later rejected in *Lexecon Inc. v. Milberg Weiss Bershad Hynes & Lerach*, 523 U.S. 26 (1998). But even when *Korean Airlines* was decided, it was clear that some cases would be transferred back to the district from which they came for trial. After remand, decisions made in an MDL may be reviewed in a circuit with a different understanding of federal law than the circuit in which the MDL court sits. A concurring opinion in *Korean Airlines* expressed concern about this possibility, but ultimately concluded that the problems created would be slight:

> A series of inconsistent appellate judgments is not a desirable outcome ... particularly since the result in some cases might be to require renewed pretrial or trial proceedings. This whole course of case development, starting with divergent paths of appeal and ending with either conflicting or duplicative results, would clearly frustrate the primary goals of section 1407 (a) "to promote the just and efficient conduct" of multi-district actions.

> Having a transferee court apply the norm of independent judgment in ruling on transferred cases, therefore, does pose some risk of undermining on appeal the interests served by section 1407(a). ... I believe that, although there is some risk of cases unraveling upon review by transferor circuits, it is not significant. First, relatively few cases ever return to the transferor courts. Second, most transferee court rulings will not be outcome-determinative, but instead will involve routine matters, such as discovery orders, that will not provide grounds for a transferor circuit court to reverse a pretrial ruling by the transferee district court.

> Third, as to those few outcome-determinative rulings of the transferee district court, there exists the possibility of interlocutory appeal to the transferee circuit, pursuant to 28 U.S.C. 1292(b), as indeed occurred in this case. ... By reviewing the ruling, the transferee circuit probably will have insured that, if the cases are

retransferred to the transferor courts, they will not unravel on later appeal. That is because . . . the interlocutory decisions of a coordinate court of appeals are likely to be accepted as binding, under the doctrine of law of the case, in the courts of appeals reviewing the final decision of the district court.

Id. at 1180 (D.H. Ginsburg, J., concurring). Did the concurrence—and, for that matter, the majority—underestimate the costs of the rule it adopted? For an argument that *Korean Airlines* is wrong, see Robert A. Ragazzo, *Transfer and Choice of Federal Law: The Appellate Model*, 93 Mich. L. Rev. 703, 706 (1995) (arguing that "transferee federal law should apply after permanent [transfers under § 1404] but not MDL transfers [under § 1407]").

c.   THE EFFECT OF MDL CONSOLIDATION ON SETTLEMENT

Does the MDL consolidation process unfairly advantage defendants in settlement negotiations? Can any such effect be tempered or exaggerated, depending on the transferee court's rigor in its application of the Supreme Court's decision in *Lexecon*? Consider the assessment offered by United States District Judge William G. Young.*

DeLaventura v. Columbia Acorn Trust

417 F. Supp. 2d 147 (D. Mass. 2006)

■ YOUNG, J.

It is the province of the Congress so to allocate jurisdiction and venue among the 94 United States District Courts. . . . It is the province of the competent attorney to shop for a forum believed best suited to the client's cause. It is the province of the federal judiciary fairly to mediate between the aspiration and the reality.

Since all 94 district courts follow identical rules concerning discovery and trial preparation, one excellent innovation in civil practice is the idea that a single judge might manage a number of "related" cases, getting them all ready for trial in a uniform manner and returning the "trial-ready" cases from whence they came (i.e., to the district courts with proper jurisdiction and venue) for trials before local juries.

I.   Multi–District Litigation.

This excellent innovation has been codified by [the MDL statute.]. . .

The Judicial Panel on Multidistrict Litigation acted upon 22,516 civil actions pursuant to 28 U.S.C. 1407 during the 12–month period ending September 30, 2004. The Panel transferred 10,681 cases originally filed in 91 district courts to 46 transferee districts for inclusion in coordinated or consolidated pretrial proceedings for 11,835 actions previously initiated in the transferee districts. . . . The Panel did not order transfer in 29 newly docketed litigations involving 268 actions.

---

* As reproduced here, the edited version of Judge Young's opinion omits the portions dealing with the specific MDL-related removal issue before the court. The opinion is noteworthy less for what it says about that particular issue and more for Judge Young's explanation of what he regards as larger systemic problems with the MDL Panel and its operations.

Since the Panel's creation in 1968, it has centralized 211,317 civil actions for pretrial proceedings. As of September 30, 2004, a total of 10,899 actions had been remanded for trial, 389 actions had been reassigned within the transferee districts, and 136,070 actions had been terminated in the transferee courts. At the end of this fiscal year, 63,959 actions were pending throughout 54 transferee district courts.

Leonidas Ralph Mecham, *Judicial Business of the United States Courts, 2004 Annual Report of the Director* 25, available at http://www.uscourts. gov/judbususc/judbus.html (last visited Jan. 29, 2006). Certain conclusions follow obviously from these statistics:

First, the MDL panel itself overwhelmingly favors the procedure it administers. Thus, once the MDL panel decides to consider a matter pursuant to Section 1407(a), transfer is more than likely.

Second, as compared to the processing time of an average case, MDL practice is slow, very slow. See Christopher J. Roche, *A Litigation Association Model to Aggregate Mass Tort Claims for Adjudication*, 91 Va. L. Rev. 1463, 1469 (2005) ("[D]elay is a common feature of mass tort litigation. Resolution of cases may take years, in some cases effectively precluding plaintiffs from any meaningful recovery."). Despite the assumption that "transfer and consolidation will promote judicial efficiency which will result in convenience to the parties and witnesses", Stanley J. Levy, *Complex Multidistrict Litigation and the Federal Courts*, 40 Fordham L. Rev. 41, 47 (1971), the purported "efficiency gains of consolidated trial are not supported by reality", Benjamin W. Larson, Lexecon Inc. v. Milberg Weiss Bershad Hynes & Lerach: *Respecting the Plaintiff's Choice of Forum*, 74 Notre Dame L. Rev. 1337, 1364 (1999).

Third, as MDL practice flourishes, many cases are transferred out of their home courts and away from local juries, but few—very few—ever return for trial. The reasons are twofold. Most cases settle, and this is as it should be. MDL cases settle at approximately the same rate as cases handled in their home courts. Yet the "settlement culture" for which the federal courts are so frequently criticized is nowhere more prevalent than in MDL practice. . . .

[I]t is almost a point of honor among transferee judges acting pursuant to Section 1407(a) that cases so transferred shall be settled rather than sent back to their home courts for trial. This, in turn, reinforces the unfortunate tendency to hang on to transferred cases to enhance the likelihood of settlement. Indeed, MDL practice actively encourages retention even of trial-ready cases in order to "encourage" settlement. See, e.g., MDL No. 875 (subjecting thousands of asbestosis cases to MDL practice for over fourteen years). "The Panel is reluctant to order remand absent a suggestion of remand from the transferee district court." R. Proc. Jud. Panel Multidistrict Litig. 7.6(d). There are no public figures evidencing how often, if ever, the Panel has remanded a case over the objection of the transferee judge.

Although the Supreme Court has made clear that it was never the statutory intent that Section 1407(a) be interpreted as a super-venue statute allowing transfer for all purposes to the transferee judge, *Lexecon Inc. v. Milberg Weiss Bershad Hynes & Lerach*, 523 U.S. 26 (1998), the Federal Judicial Center has long considered it "[a] major deficiency in MDL procedure . . . that the panel does not have statutory authority to transfer cases for trial." Thomas E. Willging, Report, *Trends in Asbestos Litigation*, Federal Judicial Center (1987). The Judicial Conference has lobbied for legislation "which would effectively over-rule *Lexecon* by statutory amendment." Hon. Wm. Terrell Hodges, *Chair of Judicial Panel Sees Role as Gatekeeper*, The Third Branch, Nov. 2005, at 10. Indeed, the chair of the MDL Panel could not be more straightforward:

> We're hopeful that in this Congress the legislation will pass and that *Lexecon* will be a thing of the past. It's hard to know how many multidistrict dockets actually have been affected in some substantial way by the requirement of *Lexecon* that constituent actions be remanded to the transferor courts as soon as the case is ready for trial. A number of devices, frankly, have been utilized by innovative judges since *Lexecon* to minimize its effect.

Id. at 12.

. . . The . . . important point is that the pursuit of settlement without offering a trial is both unwise—and a defense ploy.

Some, believing that any settlement is preferable to any trial, may consider this a desirable outcome. In actuality, however, this marginalization of juror fact finding perversely and sharply skews the MDL bargaining process in favor of defendants. Consider: All litigants bargain in the shadow of trial. Those averse to the inevitable uncertainties of the direct democracy of the American jury will factor the risks of trial into their settlement postures. Failure to arrive at a mutually acceptable settlement should, and in most cases does, result in a trial. In MDL practice, however, it is solely the transferee judge who controls the risk of trial. The litigant who refuses to settle can never get back to his home court to go before a local jury unless the transferee judge agrees.

Once trial is no longer a realistic alternative, bargaining shifts in ways that inevitably favor the defense. After all, a major goal of nearly every defendant is to avoid a public jury trial of the plaintiff's claims. Fact finding is relegated to a subsidiary role, and bargaining focuses instead on ability to pay, the economic consequences of the litigation, and the terms of the minimum payout necessary to extinguish the plaintiff's claims. Commentators generally agree that MDL practice favors the defense.

MDL proceedings are described as a "delaying tactic used by defendants" which "consume a great deal of time." Benjamin W. Larson, Comment, Lexecon, Inc. v. Milberg Weiss Bershad Hynes and Lerach: *Respecting the Plaintiff's Choice of Forum*, 74 Notre Dame L. Rev. 1337, 1364 (1999). . . . Plaintiffs lose control over the management of their case.

> [A] plaintiff's motive in pleading to secure a particular jurisdiction may not be evaluated in the removal versus remand struggle. In response to this forum shopping, defense counsel have often filed a notice of removal alleging fraudulent joinder of the nondiverse defendant. *Before a plaintiff has the opportunity to file a motion to remand, defense counsel often initiates a reference to the Judicial Panel* averring that the case is pending in a United States district court. *If, as a result of this reference, the Judicial Panel enters a transfer order, or a conditional transfer order, the plaintiff's counsel may face a David and Goliath situation.* Upon receipt of a conditional transfer order or a tag-along transfer order, many plaintiffs' counsel certainly understand David's fears in the face of Goliath.

Mike Roberts, *Multidistrict Litigation and the Judicial Panel, Transfer and Tag–Along Orders Prior to a Determination of Remand: Procedural and Substantive Problem or Effective Judicial Public Policy?*, 23 Memphis St. U.L. Rev. 841, 842–43 (1993) (emphasis added, footnotes omitted). This "strategy allows the defense counsel to attempt to secure a transfer order or conditional transfer order before the original federal district court determines, and in some cases even hears, the anticipated motion to remand." *Id.* at 843. . . .

It is precisely because MDL practice is perceived so clearly to favor the defense that Congress appears to have lost confidence in a judicial management mechanism that once had such great promise. The Class Action Fairness Act of 2005, itself thought to be legislation that favors business defendants, *see Natale v. Pfizer, Inc.*, 379 F. Supp. 2d 161, 164–68 (D. Mass. 2005), contains an unmistakable rebuke to the Panel on Multi–District Litigation in Section 4, which provides that no class action removed to federal court under its provisions shall thereafter be transferred to another district pursuant to Title 28, Section 1407(a) of the U.S. Code without the request of a majority of plaintiffs. *See* 28 U.S.C. § 1332(d)(11)(C)(i).

Were transferee judges content to work-up transferred cases for trial on a reasonably short time schedule, sensitive to the fact-finding contributions to be made by the American jury in the district where congressionally mandated venue is proper—while at the same time exerting every effort to settle all those cases amenable to settlement—perhaps MDL practice might earn back the respect it has lost.

[An example of a judge who has used this technique] is Judge Eldon Fallon of the Eastern District of Louisiana, the transferee judge for the federal lawsuits involving Vioxx:

> At last count, Merck faced close to 7,000 lawsuits related to Vioxx, and the number keeps growing. Two judges will play critical roles in how these cases play out. One is . . . U.S. District Judge Eldon Fallon of New Orleans.
>
> Fallon has control of all the federal Vioxx lawsuits, and he is hearing the case that starts in Houston today. . . . Today's trial is the first of four Vioxx trials Judge Fallon has scheduled for the next few months. The four cases are intended to represent the range of alleged harms caused by Vioxx.
>
> Fallon is following a strategy he's used before to push plaintiffs and drug makers to the settlement table, by *trying* representative cases and letting their outcomes *in court* set a price tag for an overall settlement. He's doing this despite Merck's insistence that it will not settle and that the company will take every case to court.
>
> Judge Fallon has promised a speedy trial.

Snighda Prakash, *Federal Trial on Vioxx Opens in Houston*, NPR Morning Edition, Nov. 29, 2005 (emphasis added). . . .

NOTES AND QUESTIONS

1. *Bellwether Trials.* Judge Young praised Judge Fallon for conducting bellwether trials in the Vioxx MDL. Are bellwethers a good means of setting prices for other cases, as he contends? Or are bellwether trials unimportant unless paired with a credible threat that all cases in an MDL will be remanded

for trials in the courts from which they were transferred? Why should Merck (or the Vioxx plaintiffs, for that matter) have cared about the outcomes of bellwether trials if the prospects for trying any cases other than the bellwethers were remote? Moreover, doesn't a bellwether trial show conclusively that the judge presiding over an MDL is violating § 1407, according to which cases are supposed to be remanded to the federal districts from which they were transferred when pretrial preparations are complete? Pretrial activities must end before bellwether trials can occur, mustn't they?

2.   *Do MDLs Deny Parties Due Process?* Widely accepted economic reasoning suggests that parties settle for the expected values of claims at trial to avoid litigation costs. This implies that delays usually benefit defendants. The farther off the trial date, the less the expected judgment is worth today, so the less the defendant has to pay to settle a claim. (The basic economics of settlement values are covered in Chapter 4.A.) Delays can sometimes harm defendants; for example, the defendant might face ongoing negative publicity from the lawsuit, or the prospect of a huge potential liability might impede its access to the capital markets. However, often it is the plaintiff who suffers the most.

Judge Young contends that MDLs delay trial dates indefinitely because transferee judges are loathe to let go of cases. This is why, in his view, settlement bargaining in MDLs focuses on the collateral effects of litigation instead of the expected trial verdict: the prospect of an indefinite delay renders the present value of any trial verdict close to zero. There is an important exception: An MDL judge can validate or dismiss an entire group of claims on a pretrial motion by finding, for example, that one party deserves to win as a matter of law or that the epidemiological evidence is too weak to establish causation between a product and the injury it assertedly caused. Thus, Judge Young's view focuses mainly on cases in which the outcome turns on disputed facts, which include most cases won by plaintiffs. On the frequency with which plaintiffs and defendants prevail on summary judgment motions, see Joe S. Cecil, Rebecca N. Eyre, Dean Miletich, and David Rindskopf, *A Quarter–Century of Summary Judgment Practice in Six Federal District Courts*, 4 J. of Empirical Legal Stud. 861 (2007).

The extent to which MDLs alter settlement values by delaying trial dates is, of course, an empirical matter. But assuming that MDL judges rarely remand cases (even when settlement is very unlikely) and that the resulting delay harms plaintiffs much more than defendants, a question arises: Do MDL judges deny plaintiffs due process of law by failing to remand cases whose outcomes depend on disputed facts? In *Amchem Products, Inc. v. Windsor*, we noted the Supreme Court's concern that plaintiffs who could not credibly threaten to try a case as a class action could also not bargain for appropriate relief in settlement. *Amchem Products, Inc. v. Windsor*, 521 U.S. 591, 593 (1997) ("Class counsel confined to settlement negotiations could not use the threat of litigation to press for a better offer.") To be sure, the Court made this observation in the context of reviewing a settlement class action and interpreting the requirements of Rule 23. Nevertheless, the *Amchem* Court's interpretation of Rule 23 was clearly influenced by its view of adequate representation and other constitutional due process requirements in the class setting. Isn't a similar concern raised by a practice of delaying MDL proceedings in order to induce settlements if doing so in effect strips plaintiffs of any credible threat to try their cases? And what of defendants who, instead of settling, would rather obtain trial vindications? Do MDL judges deprive them of due process by denying them their day in court?

3.   *What's Wrong with Settling?* Judge Young doesn't oppose settlements in general. To the contrary, he writes: "Most cases settle, and this is as it should be." He also observes that "MDL cases settle at approximately the same rate as cases handled in their home courts." Given this, why is he so irate about the settlement culture that imbues MDLs? One might add to his observations the fact that MDLs sometimes produce enormous global resolutions. Merck paid $4.85 billion to settle pending *Vioxx* cases. BP offered over $7 billion to settle claims cases arising out of the oil spill that followed the Deepwater Horizon explosion. Ideally, one would like hard evidence that MDLs take too long or settle too cheaply, but the matter has not been rigorously studied.

4.   *State–Law Counterparts to the Federal MDL Panel.* Following the example of the federal MDL statute, some state judicial systems have counterpart mechanisms for the transfer of related cases to a single trial-level court. E.g., Tex. R. Jud. Admin. 13. For more detailed treatment of the state mechanisms, see Mark Herrmann, Geoffrey J. Ritts & Katherine Larson, *Statewide Coordinated Proceedings: State Court Analogues to the Federal MDL Process* (2d ed. 2004).

2.   COORDINATION ACROSS DIFFERENT JUDICIAL SYSTEMS

a.   FULL FAITH AND CREDIT

The Full Faith and Credit Clause of the Constitution, which governs the relationship between state judicial systems, provides: "Full faith and credit shall be given in each state to the public acts, records, and judicial proceedings of every other state." Art. IV, § 1. The Full Faith and Credit Statute, 28 U.S.C. § 1738, implements the Full Faith and Credit Clause *and* also imposes an obligation *on federal* courts to give state judgments full faith and credit. The Full Faith and Credit Clause and its implementing statute together *ordinarily* require that a state judgment be given the same preclusive effect as the state which rendered the judgment would give it. The case excerpted below both discusses the general rule and considers whether it should apply with respect to a judgment in a class action that settles claims within the federal courts' exclusive subject matter jurisdiction.

Matsushita Electric Industrial Co. v. Epstein

516 U.S. 367 (1996)

■ JUSTICE THOMAS delivered the opinion of the Court.

This case presents the question whether a federal court may withhold full faith and credit from a state-court judgment approving a class-action settlement simply because the settlement releases claims within the exclusive jurisdiction of the federal courts. The answer is no. Absent a partial repeal of the Full Faith and Credit Act, 28 U.S.C. § 1738, by another federal statute, a federal court must give the judgment the same effect that it would have in the courts of the State in which it was rendered.

I

In 1990, petitioner Matsushita Electric Industrial Co. made a tender offer for the common stock of MCA, Inc., a Delaware corporation. The tender offer not only resulted in Matsushita's acquisition of MCA, but also precipitated two lawsuits on behalf of the holders of MCA's common stock. First, a class action was filed in the Delaware Court of Chancery against MCA and its directors for breach of fiduciary duty in failing to maximize shareholder value. The complaint was later amended to state additional claims against MCA's directors for, *inter alia*, waste of corporate assets by exposing MCA to liability under the federal securities laws. In addition, Matsushita was added as a defendant and was accused of conspiring with MCA's directors to violate Delaware law. The Delaware suit was based purely on state-law claims.

While the state class action was pending, the instant suit was filed in Federal District Court in California. The complaint named Matsushita as a defendant and alleged that Matsushita's tender offer violated Securities Exchange Commission (SEC) Rules 10b–3 and 14d–10. These Rules were created by the SEC pursuant to the 1968 Williams Act Amendments to the Securities Exchange Act of 1934 (Exchange Act). Section 27 of the Exchange Act confers exclusive jurisdiction upon the federal courts for suits brought to enforce the Act or rules and regulations promulgated thereunder. See 15 U.S.C. § 78aa. The District Court declined to certify the class, entered summary judgment for Matsushita, and dismissed the case. The plaintiffs appealed to the Court of Appeals for the Ninth Circuit.

After the federal plaintiffs filed their notice of appeal but before the Ninth Circuit handed down a decision, the parties to the Delaware suit negotiated a settlement.[2] In exchange for a global release of all claims arising out of the Matsushita–MCA acquisition, the defendants would deposit $2 million into a settlement fund to be distributed *pro rata* to the members of the class. As required by Delaware Chancery Rule 23, which is modeled on Federal Rule of Civil Procedure 23, the Chancery Court certified the class for purposes of settlement and approved a notice of the proposed settlement. The notice informed the class members of their right to request exclusion from the settlement class and to appear and present argument at a scheduled hearing to determine the fairness of the settlement. In particular, the notice stated that "[b]y filing a valid Request for Exclusion, a member of the Settlement Class will not be precluded by the Settlement from individually seeking to pursue the claims alleged in the . . . California Federal Actions, . . . or any other claim relating to the events at issue in the Delaware Actions." Two such notices were mailed to the class members and the notice was also published in the national edition of the Wall Street Journal. The Chancery Court then held a hearing. After argument from several objectors, the Court found the class representation adequate and the settlement fair.

The order and final judgment of the Chancery Court incorporated the terms of the settlement agreement, providing:

> "All claims, rights and causes of action (state or federal, including but not limited to claims arising under the federal securities law, any rules or regulations promulgated thereunder, or otherwise), whether known or unknown that are, could have been or might in

---

[2] A previous settlement was rejected by the Court of Chancery as unfair to the class. See *In re MCA, Inc. Shareholders Litigation*, 598 A.2d 687 (1991).

the future be asserted by any of the plaintiffs or any member of the Settlement Class *(other than those who have validly requested exclusion therefrom)*, . . . in connection with or that arise now or hereafter out of the Merger Agreement, the Tender Offer, the Distribution Agreement, the Capital Contribution Agreement, the employee compensation arrangements, the Tender Agreements, the Initial Proposed Settlement, this Settlement . . . *and including without limitation the claims asserted in the California Federal Actions*. . . are hereby compromised, settled, released and discharged with prejudice by virtue of the proceedings herein and this Order and Final Judgment."

The judgment also stated that the notice met all the requirements of due process. The Delaware Supreme Court affirmed.

Respondents were members of both the state and federal plaintiff classes. Following issuance of the notice of proposed settlement of the Delaware litigation, respondents neither opted out of the settlement class nor appeared at the hearing to contest the settlement or the representation of the class. On appeal in the Ninth Circuit, petitioner Matsushita invoked the Delaware judgment as a bar to further prosecution of that action under the Full Faith and Credit Act, 28 U.S.C. § 1738.

The Ninth Circuit rejected petitioner's argument, ruling that § 1738 did not apply. *Epstein v. MCA, Inc.*, 50 F.3d 644, 661–66 (1995). Instead, the Court of Appeals fashioned a test under which the preclusive force of a state court settlement judgment is limited to those claims that "could . . . have been extinguished by the issue preclusive effect of an adjudication of the state claims." *Id.*, at 665. The lower courts have taken varying approaches to determining the preclusive effect of a state court judgment, entered in a class or derivative action, that provides for the release of exclusively federal claims. We granted certiorari to clarify this important area of federal law.

II

The Full Faith and Credit Act mandates that the "judicial proceedings" of any State "shall have the same full faith and credit in every court within the United States . . . as they have by law or usage in the courts of such State . . . from which they are taken." 28 U.S.C. § 1738. The Act thus directs all courts to treat a state court judgment with the same respect that it would receive in the courts of the rendering state. Federal courts may not "employ their own rules . . . in determining the effect of state judgments," but must "accept the rules chosen by the State from which the judgment is taken." *Kremer v. Chemical Constr. Corp.*, 456 U.S. 461, 481–82 (1982). Because the Court of Appeals failed to follow the dictates of the Act, we reverse.

A

The state court judgment in this case differs in two respects from the judgments that we have previously considered in our cases under the Full Faith and Credit Act. As respondents and the Court of Appeals stressed, the judgment was the product of a class action and incorporated a settlement agreement releasing claims within the exclusive jurisdiction of the federal courts. Though respondents urge "the irrelevance of section 1738 to this litigation," we do not think that either of these features exempts the judgment from the operation of § 1738.

That the judgment at issue is the result of a class action, rather than a suit brought by an individual, does not undermine the initial applicability of § 1738. The judgment of a state court in a class action is plainly the product of a "judicial proceeding" within the meaning of § 1738. Therefore, a judgment entered in a class action, like any other judgment entered in a state judicial proceeding, is presumptively entitled to full faith and credit under the express terms of the Act.

Further, § 1738 is not irrelevant simply because the judgment in question might work to bar the litigation of exclusively federal claims. Our decision in *Marrese v. American Academy of Orthopaedic Surgeons*, 470 U.S. 373 (1985), made clear that where § 1738 is raised as a defense in a subsequent suit, the fact that an allegedly precluded "claim is within the exclusive jurisdiction of the federal courts *does not necessarily make § 1738 inapplicable.*" *Id.*, at 380 (emphasis added). In so holding, we relied primarily on *Kremer v. Chemical Constr. Corp., supra*, which held, without deciding whether Title VII claims are exclusively federal, that state court proceedings may be issue preclusive in Title VII suits in federal court. *Kremer*, we said, "implies that absent an exception to § 1738, state law determines at least the . . . preclusive effect of a prior state judgment in a subsequent action involving a claim within the exclusive jurisdiction of the federal courts." *Marrese*, 470 U.S., at 381. Accordingly, we decided that "a state court judgment may in some circumstances have preclusive effect in a subsequent action within the exclusive jurisdiction of the federal courts." *Id.*, at 380.

. . . In accord with these precedents, we conclude that § 1738 is generally applicable in cases in which the state court judgment at issue incorporates a class action settlement releasing claims solely within the jurisdiction of the federal courts.

B

Marrese provides the analytical framework for deciding whether the Delaware court's judgment precludes this exclusively federal action. When faced with a state court judgment relating to an exclusively federal claim, a federal court must first look to the law of the rendering State to ascertain the effect of the judgment. See *id.*, at 381–82. If state law indicates that the particular claim or issue would be barred from litigation in a court of that state, then the federal court must next decide whether, "as an exception to § 1738," it "should refuse to give preclusive effect to [the] state court judgment." *Id.*, at 383. See also *Migra v. Warren City School Dist. Bd. of Ed.*, 465 U.S. 75, 80 (1984) ("[I]n the absence of federal law modifying the operation of § 1738, the preclusive effect in federal court of [a] state-court judgment is determined by [state] law").

[handwritten margin note: Look to law of state to Determine its preclusive effects.]

1

We observed in *Marrese* that the inquiry into state law would not always yield a direct answer. Usually, "a state court will not have occasion to address the specific question whether a state judgment has issue or claim preclusive effect in a later action that can be brought only in federal court." 470 U.S., at 381–82. Where a judicially approved settlement is under consideration, a federal court may consequently find guidance from general state law on the preclusive force of settlement judgments. Here, in addition to providing rules regarding the preclusive force of class-action settlement judgments in subsequent suits in state court, the Delaware courts have also spoken to the particular effect of such judgments in federal court.

Delaware has traditionally treated the impact of settlement judgments on subsequent litigation in state court as a question of claim preclusion. Early cases suggested that Delaware courts would not afford claim preclusive effect to a settlement releasing claims that could not have been presented in the trial court. See *Ezzes v. Ackerman*, 234 A.2d 444–46 (Del. 1967) ("[A] judgment entered either after trial on the merits or upon an approved settlement is *res judicata* and bars subsequent suit on the same claim. . . . [T]he defense of *res judicata*. . . is available if the pleadings framing the issues in the first action would have permitted the raising of the issue sought to be raised in the second action, and if the facts were known or could have been known to the plaintiff in the second action at the time of the first action"). As the Court of Chancery has perceived, however, "the *Ezzes* inquiry [was] modified in regard to class actions," *In re Union Square Associates Securities Litigation*, C.A. No. 11028, 1993 WL 220528, *3 (June 16, 1993), by the Delaware Supreme Court's decision in *Nottingham Partners v. Dana*, 564 A.2d 1089 (1989).

In *Nottingham*, a class action, the Delaware Supreme Court approved a settlement that released claims then pending in federal court. In approving that settlement, the *Nottingham* Court appears to have eliminated the *Ezzes* requirement that the claims could have been raised in the suit that produced the settlement, at least with respect to class actions:

> " '[I]n order to achieve a comprehensive settlement that would prevent relitigation of settled questions at the core of a class action, a court may permit the release of a claim based on the identical factual predicate as that underlying the claims in the settled class action even though the claim was not presented and might not have been presentable in the class action.' " 564 A.2d, at 1106 (quoting *TBK Partners, Ltd. v. Western Union Corp.*, 675 F.2d 456, 460 (C.A.2 1982)).

See *Union Square*, C.A. No. 11028, 1993 WL 220528, *3 (relying directly on *Nottingham* to hold that a Delaware court judgment settling a class action was res judicata and barred arbitration of duplicative claims that could not have been brought in the first suit). These cases indicate that even if, as here, a claim could not have been raised in the court that rendered the settlement judgment in a class action, a Delaware court would still find that the judgment bars subsequent pursuit of the claim.

The Delaware Supreme Court has further manifested its understanding that when the Court of Chancery approves a global release of claims, its settlement judgment should preclude on-going or future federal court litigation of any released claims. In *Nottingham*, the Court stated that "[t]he validity of executing a general release in conjunction with the termination of litigation has long been recognized by the Delaware courts. More specifically, the Court of Chancery has a history of approving settlements that have implicitly or explicitly included a general release, which would also release federal claims." 564 A.2d, at 1105 (citation omitted). Though the Delaware Supreme Court correctly recognized in *Nottingham* that it lacked actual authority to order the dismissal of any case pending in federal court, it asserted that state-court approval of the settlement would have the collateral effect of preventing class members from prosecuting their claims in federal court. Perhaps the clearest statement of the Delaware Chancery Court's view on this matter was articulated in the suit preceding this one: "When a state court settlement of a class action releases all claims which arise out of the challenged transaction and is determined to be fair and to have met all due process requirements, the class members are bound by the release or the doctrine of issue preclusion. Class members cannot subsequently relitigate the claims barred by the settlement in a federal court." *In re MCA, Inc. Shareholders Litigation*, 598 A.2d 687, 691 (1991).[4] We are aware of no Delaware case that suggests otherwise.

Given these statements of Delaware law, we think that a Delaware court would afford preclusive effect to the settlement judgment in this case, notwithstanding the fact that respondents could not have pressed their Exchange Act claims in the Court of Chancery. The claims are clearly within the scope of the release in the judgment, since the judgment specifically refers to this lawsuit. As required by Delaware Court of Chancery Rule 23, see *Prezant v. De Angelis*, 636 A.2d 915, 920 (1994), the Court of Chancery found, and the Delaware Supreme Court affirmed, that the settlement was "fair, reasonable and adequate and in the best interests of the . . . Settlement class" and that notice to the class was "in full compliance with . . . the requirements of due process." *In re MCA, Inc. Shareholders Litigation*, C.A. No. 11740 (Feb. 22, 1993). The Court of Chancery "further determined that the plaintiffs[,] . . . as representatives of the Settlement Class, have fairly and adequately protected the interests of the Settlement Class." *In re MCA, Inc. Shareholders Litigation, supra*, reprinted in App. to Pet. for Cert. 73a. Cf. *Phillips Petroleum Co., supra*, at 812 (due process requires "that the named plaintiff at all times adequately represent the interests of the absent class members").[5] Under Delaware Rule 23, as under Federal Rule of Civil Procedure 23, "[a]ll members of the class, whether of a plaintiff or a defendant class, are bound by the judgment entered in the action unless, in a Rule 23(b)(3) action, they make a timely election for exclusion." 2 H. Newberg, CLASS ACTIONS § 2755, p. 1224 (1977). See also *Cooper v. Federal Reserve Bank of Richmond*, 467 U.S. 867, 874 (1984) ("There is of course no dispute that under elementary principles of prior adjudication a judgment in a properly entertained class action is binding on class members in any subsequent litigation"). Respondents do not deny that, as shareholders of MCA's common stock, they were part of the plaintiff class and that they never opted out; they are bound, then, by the judgment.

2

Because it appears that the settlement judgment would be res judicata under Delaware law, we proceed to the second step of the *Marrese* analysis and ask whether § 27 of the Exchange Act, which confers exclusive jurisdic-

---

[4] In fact, the Chancery Court rejected the first settlement, which contained no opt-out provision, as unfair to the class precisely because it believed that the settlement would preclude the class from pursuing their exclusively federal claims in federal court. See *In re MCA Inc. Shareholders Litigation*, 598 A.2d 687, 692 (1991) ("[I]f this Court provides for the release of all the claims arising out of the challenged transaction, the claims which the Objectors have asserted in the federal suit will likely be forever barred").

[5] Apart from any discussion of Delaware law, respondents contend that the settlement proceedings did not satisfy due process because the class was inadequately represented. Respondents make this claim in spite of the Chancery Court's express ruling, following argument on the issue, that the class representatives fairly and adequately protected the interests of the class. Cf. *Prezant v. De Angelis*, 636 A.2d 915, 923 (Del. 1994) ("[The] constitutional requirement [of adequacy of representation] is embodied in [Delaware] Rule 23(a)(4), which requires that the named plaintiff 'fairly and adequately protect the interests of the class' "). We need not address the due process claim, however, because it is outside the scope of the question presented in this Court. While it is true that a respondent may defend a judgment on alternative grounds, we generally do not address arguments that were not the basis for the decision below.

tion upon the federal courts for suits arising under the Act, partially repealed § 1738. Section 27 contains no express language regarding its relationship with § 1738 or the preclusive effect of related state court proceedings. Thus, any modification of § 1738 by § 27 must be implied. In deciding whether § 27 impliedly created an exception to § 1738, the "general question is whether the concerns underlying a particular grant of exclusive jurisdiction justify a finding of an implied partial repeal of § 1738." *Marrese*, 470 U.S., at 386. . . .

As an historical matter, we have seldom, if ever, held that a federal statute impliedly repealed § 1738. The rarity with which we have discovered implied repeals is due to the relatively stringent standard for such findings, namely, that there be an " 'irreconcilable conflict' " between the two federal statutes at issue. *Kremer v. Chemical Constr. Corp., supra*, at 468 (quoting *Radzanower v. Touche Ross & Co.*, 426 U.S. 148, 154 (1976)).

Section 27 provides that "[t]he district courts of the United States . . . shall have exclusive jurisdiction . . . of all suits in equity and actions at law brought to enforce any liability or duty created by this chapter or the rules and regulations thereunder." 15 U.S.C. § 78aa. There is no suggestion in § 27 that Congress meant for plaintiffs with Exchange Act claims to have more than one day in court to challenge the legality of a securities transaction. Though the statute plainly mandates that suits alleging violations of the Exchange Act may be maintained only in federal court, nothing in the language of § 27 "remotely expresses any congressional intent to contravene the common-law rules of preclusion or to repeal the express statutory requirements of . . . 28 U.S.C. § 1738." *Allen v. McCurry, supra*, at 97–8.

Nor does § 27 evince any intent to prevent litigants in state court— whether suing as individuals or as part of a class—from voluntarily releasing Exchange Act claims in judicially approved settlements. While § 27 prohibits state courts from adjudicating claims arising under the Exchange Act, it does not prohibit state courts from approving the release of Exchange Act claims in the settlement of suits over which they have properly exercised jurisdiction, *i.e.*, suits arising under state law or under federal law for which there is concurrent jurisdiction. In this case, for example, the Delaware action was not "brought to enforce" any rights or obligations under the Act. The Delaware court asserted judicial power over a complaint asserting purely state law causes of action and, after the parties agreed to settle, certified the class and approved the settlement pursuant to the requirements of Delaware Rule of Chancery 23 and the Due Process Clause. Thus, the Delaware court never trespassed upon the exclusive territory of the federal courts, but merely approved the settlement of a common-law suit pursuant to state and nonexclusive federal law. While it is true that the state court assessed the general worth of the federal claims in determining the fairness of the settlement, such assessment does not amount to a judgment on the merits of the claims. . . .

The legislative history of the Exchange Act elucidates no specific purpose on the part of Congress in enacting § 27. We may presume, however, that Congress intended § 27 to serve at least the general purposes underlying most grants of exclusive jurisdiction: "to achieve greater uniformity of construction and more effective and expert application of that law." *Murphy v. Gallagher*, [761 F.2d 878, 885 (C.A.2 1985).] When a state court upholds a settlement that releases claims under the Exchange Act, it threatens neither of these policies. There is no danger that state court judges who are not fully expert in federal securities law will say definitively what the Exchange Act means and enforce legal liabilities and duties thereunder. And the uniform construction of the Act is unaffected by a state court's approval of a proposed settlement because the state court does not adjudicate the Exchange Act claims but only evaluates the overall fairness of the settlement, generally by applying its own business judgment to the facts of the case. . . .

In the end, §§ 27 and 1738 "do not pose an either-or proposition." *Connecticut Nat. Bank v. Germain*, 503 U.S. 249, 253 (1992). They can be reconciled by reading § 1738 to mandate full faith and credit of state court judgments incorporating global settlements, provided the rendering court had jurisdiction over the underlying suit itself, and by reading § 27 to prohibit state courts from exercising jurisdiction over suits arising under the Exchange Act. . . . We conclude that the Delaware courts would give the settlement judgment preclusive effect in a subsequent proceeding and, further, that § 27 did not effect a partial repeal of § 1738.

C

The Court of Appeals did not engage in any analysis of Delaware law pursuant to § 1738. Rather, the Court of Appeals declined to apply § 1738 on the ground that where the rendering forum lacked jurisdiction over the subject matter or the parties, full faith and credit is not required. . . .

. . . [T]he state court in this case clearly possessed jurisdiction over the subject matter of the underlying suit and over the defendants. Only if this were not so—for instance, if the complaint alleged violations of the Exchange Act and the Delaware court rendered a judgment on the merits of those claims—would the exception to § 1738 for lack of subject-matter jurisdiction apply. Where, as here, the rendering court in fact had subject-matter jurisdiction, the subject-matter jurisdiction exception to full faith and credit is simply inapposite. In such a case, the relevance of a federal statute that provides for exclusive federal jurisdiction is not to the state court's possession of jurisdiction *per se,* but to the existence of a partial repeal of § 1738.

* * *

The judgment of the Court of Appeals is reversed and remanded for proceedings consistent with this opinion.

It is so ordered.

■ JUSTICE GINSBURG, with whom JUSTICE STEVENS joins, and with whom JUSTICE SOUTER joins as to Part II–B, concurring in part and dissenting in part.

I join the Court's judgment to the extent that it remands the case to the Ninth Circuit. I agree that a remand is in order because the Court of Appeals did not attend to this Court's reading of 28 U.S.C. § 1738 in a controlling decision, *Kremer v. Chemical Constr. Corp.,* 456 U.S. 461 (1982). But I would not endeavor, as the Court does, to speak the first word on the content of Delaware preclusion law. Instead, I would follow our standard practice of remitting that issue for decision, in the first instance, by the lower federal courts. See, *e.g., Marrese v. American Academy of Orthopaedic Surgeons,* 470 U.S. 373, 387 (1985).

I write separately to emphasize a point key to the application of § 1738: A state-court judgment generally is not entitled to full faith and credit unless it satisfies the requirements of the Fourteenth Amendment's

Due Process Clause. See *Kremer*, 456 U.S., at 482–83. In the class action setting, adequate representation is among the due process ingredients that must be supplied if the judgment is to bind absent class members. See *Phillips Petroleum Co. v. Shutts*, 472 U.S. 797, 808, 812 (1985); *Prezant v. De Angelis*, 636 A.2d 915, 923–24 (Del. 1994).

Suitors in this action (called the "Epstein plaintiffs" in this opinion), respondents here, argued before the Ninth Circuit, and again before this Court, that they cannot be bound by the Delaware settlement because they were not adequately represented by the Delaware class representatives. They contend that the Delaware representatives' willingness to release federal securities claims within the exclusive jurisdiction of the federal courts for a meager return to the class members, but a solid fee to the Delaware class attorneys, disserved the interests of the class, particularly, the absentees. The inadequacy of representation was apparent, the Epstein plaintiffs maintained, for at the time of the settlement, the federal claims were *sub judice* in the proper forum for those claims—the federal judiciary. Although the Ninth Circuit decided the case without reaching the due process check on the full faith and credit obligation, that inquiry remains open for consideration on remand. See *ante*, n. 5 (due process "w[as] not the basis for the decision below," so the Court "need not address [it]"). . . .

II

. . .

B

Every State's law on the preclusiveness of judgments is pervasively affected by the supreme law of the land. To be valid in the rendition forum, and entitled to recognition nationally, a state court's judgment must measure up to the requirements of the Fourteenth Amendment's Due Process Clause. *Kremer*, 456 U.S., at 482–83. "A State may not grant preclusive effect in its own courts to a constitutionally infirm judgment, and other state and federal courts are not required to accord full faith and credit to such a judgment." *Id.*, at 482 (footnote omitted).

In *Phillips Petroleum Co. v. Shutts*, this Court listed minimal procedural due process requirements a class action money judgment must meet if it is to bind absentees; those requirements include notice, an opportunity to be heard, a right to opt out, and adequate representation. 472 U.S., at 812. "[T]he Due Process Clause of course requires that the named plaintiff at all times adequately represent the interests of the absent class members." *Ibid.* (citing *Hansberry v. Lee*, 311 U.S. 32, 42–43, 45 (1940)). As the *Shutts* Court's phrase "at all times" indicates, the class representative's duty to represent absent class members adequately is a continuing one. 472 U.S., at 812; see also *Gonzales v. Cassidy*, 474 F.2d 67, 75 (C.A.5 1973) (representative's failure to pursue an appeal rendered initially adequate class representation inadequate, so that judgment did not bind the class).

Although emphasizing the constitutional significance of the adequate representation requirement, this Court has recognized the first line responsibility of the states themselves for assuring that the constitutional essentials are met. See *Hansberry*, 311 U.S., at 42.[5] Final judgments, however,

---

[5] Many States, including Delaware, have class action rules corresponding to Federal Rule of Civil Procedure 23, a rule ranking adequacy of representation as a prerequisite to maintaining a class action. See 3 H. Newberg & A. Conte, NEWBERG ON CLASS ACTIONS, App. 13–1 (3d ed. 1992) (listing 39 States and the District of Columbia with rules comparable to the amended Federal Rule of Civil Procedure 23). . . .

remain vulnerable to collateral attack for failure to satisfy the adequate representation requirement. See *id.*, at 40, 42; see also RESTATEMENT (SECOND) OF JUDGMENTS §§ 42(1)(d) and (e), Comments *e* and *f*, pp. 406, 410–12 (1982) (noting, *inter alia*, that judgment is not binding on purportedly represented person where, to the knowledge of the opposing party, the representative seeks to advance his own interest at the expense of the represented person); see also *id.*, § 41, Comment *a*, p. 394 (if § 42 circumstances exist, "the represented person may avoid being bound *either* by appearing in the action before rendition of the judgment *or* by attacking the judgment by subsequent proceedings"). (Emphasis added.) A court conducting an action cannot predetermine the res judicata effect of the judgment; that effect can be tested only in a subsequent action. See 7B C. Wright, A. Miller, & M. Kane, FEDERAL PRACTICE AND PROCEDURE § 1789, p. 245 (2d ed. 1986).

In Delaware, the constitutional due process requirement of adequate representation is embodied in Delaware Court of Chancery's Rule 23, a class action rule modeled on its federal counterpart. *Prezant*, 636 A.2d, at 923, 920. Delaware requires, as a prerequisite to class certification, that the named plaintiffs "fairly and adequately protect the interests of the class." Del. Ch. Rule 23(a)(4). In *Prezant*, the Delaware Supreme Court considered whether adequate class representation was "a *sine qua non* for approval of a class action settlement," and concluded that it was. *Prezant*, 636 A.2d, at 920, 926. The state high court overturned a judgment and remanded a settlement because the Court of Chancery had failed to make an explicit finding of adequate representation. *Id.*, at 926.

The Delaware Supreme Court underscored that due process demands more than notice and an opportunity to opt-out; adequate representation, too, that court emphasized, is an essential ingredient. *Id.*, at 924 (citing *Phillips Petroleum Co. v. Shutts*, 472 U.S., at 812). Notice, the Delaware Supreme Court reasoned, cannot substitute for the thorough examination and informed negotiation an adequate representative would pursue. *Prezant*, 636 A.2d, at 924. The court also recognized that opt-out rights "are infrequently utilized and usually economically impracticable." *Ibid.*

The Vice Chancellor's evaluation of the merits of the settlement could not bridge the gap, the Delaware Supreme Court said, because an inadequate representative "taint[s]" the entire settlement process. *Id.*, at 925. "[A]n adequate representative," the Delaware Supreme Court explained, "vigorously prosecuting an action without conflict and bargaining at arms-length, may present different facts and a different settlement proposal to the court than would an inadequate representative." *Ibid.* Consequently, the Delaware Supreme Court held, "in every class action settlement, the Court of Chancery is required to make an explicit determination on the record of the propriety of the class action according to the requisites of Rule 23(a) and (b)." *Ibid.*

In the instant case, the Epstein plaintiffs challenge the preclusive effect of the Delaware settlement, arguing that the Vice Chancellor never in fact made the constitutionally required determination of adequate representation. See *id.*, at 923.[7] They contend that the state court left unresolved key questions: notably, did the class representatives share substantial common interests with the absent class members, and did counsel in Dela-

---

[7] The Vice Chancellor did not have the benefit of the Delaware Supreme Court's clear statement in *Prezant*, decided one year after this settlement was approved. In *Prezant*, however, the Delaware Supreme Court largely reiterated and applied what this Court had stated almost a decade earlier in *Phillips Petroleum Co. v. Shutts*, 472 U.S. 797, 808, 812 (1985).

ware vigorously press the interests of the class in negotiating the settle-ment.[8] In particular, the Epstein plaintiffs question whether the Delaware class representatives—who filed the state lawsuit on September 26, 1990, two months before the November 26 tender offer announcement—actually tendered shares in December, thereby enabling them to litigate a Rule 14d–10 claim in federal court. They also suggest that the Delaware repre-sentatives undervalued the federal claims—claims they could only settle, but never litigate, in a Delaware court. Finally, the Epstein plaintiffs con-tend that the Vice Chancellor improperly shifted the burden of proof; he rejected the Delaware objectors' charges of "collusion" for want of evidence while acknowledging that "suspicions [of collusion] abound." *In re MCA, Inc. Shareholders Litigation*, 1993 WL 43024, at *5.

Mindful that this is a court of final review and not first view, I do not address the merits of the Epstein plaintiffs' contentions, or Matsushita's counterargument that the issue of adequate representation was resolved by full and fair litigation in the Delaware Court of Chancery. These arguments remain open for airing on remand. I stress, however, the centrality of the procedural due process protection of adequate representation in class action lawsuits, emphatically including those resolved by settlement. See general-ly J. Coffee, Suspect Settlements in Securities Litigation, N.Y.L.J., March 28, 1991, p. 5, col. 1.

NOTES AND QUESTIONS

1.   *The Soundness of Delaware Preclusion Law.* Does it make sense for Delaware to treat a class settlement as resolving claims within the exclusive subject matter jurisdiction of the federal courts? Should one regard with suspi-cion the willingness of the Delaware courts to take such an expansive view of state preclusion law *only* in the context of class settlements, as distinct from settlements of individual lawsuits? Do decisions like *Nottingham* increase or decrease the cost of class settlements as compared to a world in which class settlements could resolve only those claims that could be litigated in Delaware state court? Does Delaware's willingness to extinguish claims over which its courts have no subject matter jurisdiction create a structural conflict of interest between class counsel and the class? Would it be desirable for Congress to amend the federal securities laws to override the Full Faith and Credit Act—something that federal securities laws in their present form do not do according to *Matsushita*? For discussion of whether Delaware preclusion law creates a structural conflict of interest between class counsel and the class, see the dis-cussion of *Matsushita* on remand in Chapter 4.

2.   *What is the Significance of the Court's Discussion of Due Process?* Does the Court's opinion amount to a determination that the Delaware class action satisfied the requirements of due process? Recall that after noting that the Delaware Chancery Court had found that due process had been satisfied, the Court states that the Epstein plaintiffs "do not deny that, as shareholders of MCA's common stock, they were part of the plaintiff class and that they nev-er opted out; they are bound, then, by the judgment." But the Court later in-

---

[8] The order approving the class for settlement purposes, the Epstein plaintiffs urge, con-tains no discussion of the adequacy of the representatives, and the order and final judgment approving the settlement contains only boilerplate language referring to the adequacy of rep-resentation, see *id.*, at 204–05. The Delaware Supreme Court approved the Court of Chan-cery's judgment in a one paragraph order. See *In re MCA, Inc. Shareholders Litigation*, 633 A.2d 370 (1993) (judgment order).

sists in footnote 5 that it "need not address the due process claim, however, because it is outside the scope of the question presented in this Court." How should these two statements be reconciled? As discussed in Chapter 4, that question was debated at length on remand.

b.   COORDINATION ACROSS STATE AND FEDERAL JUDICIAL SYSTEMS

In addition to the Full Faith and Credit Act, two other bodies of procedural doctrine govern the coordination of litigation across state and federal judicial systems: the Anti–Injunction Act and the *Rooker–Feldman* doctrine. The Anti–Injunction Act, as its name suggests, is a creation of federal statutory law. By its terms, the Act provides:

> A court of the United States may not grant an injunction to stay proceedings in a State court except as expressly authorized by Act of Congress, or where necessary in aid of its jurisdiction, or to protect or effectuate its judgments.

JPML an exception?

28 U.S.C. § 2283. The Anti–Injunction Act in its present form builds upon limitations that date from the earliest years of the nation. See Act of March 2, 1793, § 5, 1 Stat. 335 (predecessor provision barring federal courts from issuing "a writ of injunction . . .to stay proceedings in any court of a State"). Discussing the origins of the Act outside the class action context, the Supreme Court has observed that:

> . . . While all the reasons that led Congress to adopt this restriction on federal courts are not wholly clear, it is certainly likely that one reason stemmed from the essentially federal nature of our national government. When this Nation was established by the Constitution, each State surrendered only a part of its sovereign power to the national government. But those powers that were not surrendered were retained by the States and unless a State was restrained by "the supreme Law of the Land" as expressed in the Constitution, laws, or treaties of the United States, it was free to exercise those retained powers as it saw fit. One of the reserved powers was the maintenance of state judicial systems for the decision of legal controversies. Many of the Framers of the Constitution felt that separate federal courts were unnecessary and that the state courts could be entrusted to protect both state and federal rights. Others felt that a complete system of federal courts to take care of federal legal problems should be provided for in the Constitution itself. This dispute resulted in compromise. One "supreme Court" was created by the Constitution, and Congress was given the power to create other federal courts. In the first Congress this power was exercised and a system of federal trial and appellate courts with limited jurisdiction was created by the Judiciary Act of 1789, 1 Stat. 73.

> While the lower federal courts were given certain powers in the 1789 Act, they were not given any power to review directly cases from state courts, and they have not been given such powers since that time. Only the Supreme Court was authorized to review on direct appeal the decisions of state courts. Thus from the beginning we have had in this country two essentially separate legal systems. Each system proceeds independently of the other with ultimate review in this Court of the federal questions raised in either system. Understandably this dual court system was bound to

lead to conflicts and frictions. Litigants who foresaw the possibility of more favorable treatment in one or the other system would predictably hasten to invoke the powers of whichever court it was believed would present the best chance of success. Obviously this dual system could not function if state and federal courts were free to fight each other for control of a particular case. Thus, in order to make the dual system work and "to prevent needless friction between state and federal courts," *Oklahoma Packing Co. v. Oklahoma Gas & Electric Co.*, 309 U.S. 4, 9 (1940), it was necessary to work out lines of demarcation between the two systems. Some of these limits were spelled out in the 1789 Act. Others have been added by later statutes as well as judicial decisions. The 1793 [A]nti-injunction Act was at least in part a response to these pressures.

Atlantic Coast Line R.R. v. Brotherhood of Locomotive Engineers, 398 U.S. 281, 285–86 (1970).

Blanket Rule w/ 3 exceptions

The Act's structure consists of a background rule—federal courts have no power to enjoin state-court proceedings—followed by three important exceptions. The first exception—permitting injunctions of state-court proceedings that Congress has "expressly authorized" the federal courts to issue by statute—has little significance for class litigation outside of some limited cases. The real action instead has centered upon the scope of the last two exceptions—respectively, for injunctions "necessary in aid of [the federal court's] jurisdiction" and for injunctions "to protect or effectuate its judgments." Traditionally, the "necessary in aid of [the federal court's] jurisdiction" exception has applied only where a case is removed from state to federal court but the state does not relinquish its jurisdiction, or more frequently, where a federal court acquires in rem or quasi in rem jurisdiction over real property. The "protect or effectuate [a federal court's] judgments" exception has traditionally allowed federal courts to enjoin state-court proceedings when doing so is necessary to ensure the preclusive effect of an earlier federal-court judgment. Consequently, it typically required a final judgment on the merits. As you read the following cases, particularly those that demonstrate how these exceptions have applied in the class-action context, think about whether and how courts tether their reasoning to these traditional uses and requirements.

RF: Only S.C. S.C. Only. Can hear appeals of state S.C.

The *Rooker–Feldman* doctrine takes its name from the two Supreme Court cases in which it has been articulated: *Rooker v. Fidelity Trust Co.*, 263 U.S. 413 (1923), and *District of Columbia Court of Appeals v. Feldman*, 460 U.S. 462 (1983). The doctrine provides that only the United States Supreme Court—not the federal district courts nor courts of appeal—has power to hear a case that in effect (if not form) is an appeal of a state judicial decision.

The first case in this section—*In re General Motors Corp. Pick–Up Truck Fuel Tank Products Liability Litigation*—illustrates the interplay of the Full Faith and Credit Act, the Anti–Injunction Act, and the *Rooker–Feldman* doctrine in the class-action context. The second case, *Smith v. Bayer*, then addresses whether a federal judge can use an exception to the Anti–Injunction Act to enjoin plaintiffs from bringing a second class action in state court after a federal court declined to certify the first class. That is, how many times may plaintiffs move to certify a class when a previous court has denied class certification? Subsequent cases then turn to the particulars of the Anti–Injunction Act exceptions.

(1) An Overview of Coordination Doctrines in Action

In re General Motors Corp. Pick–Up Truck Fuel Tank Products Liability Litigation

134 F.3d 133 (3d Cir. 1998)

■ BECKER, CIRCUIT JUDGE.

This is a sequel to our opinion in *In re General Motors Corp. Pick–Up Truck Fuel Tank Prod. Liab. Litig.*, 55 F.3d 768 (3d Cir.), *cert. denied sub nom. General Motors Corp. v. French*, 516 U.S. 824 (1995) [hereinafter *GM I*], in which we held that the District Court for the Eastern District of Pennsylvania had erred in certifying a nationwide settlement class of General Motors ("GM") truck owners who sought damages and injunctive relief as the result of the allegedly defective design of the fuel system in certain GM Trucks, which is said to have created a high risk of fire following side collisions. The Eastern District of Pennsylvania litigation was made up of a large number of cases transferred to that court by the Judicial Panel on Multidistrict Litigation ("JPML") pursuant to 28 U.S.C. § 1407 for consolidated pretrial proceedings (the "MDL cases"). In *GM I*, we vacated the class certification order and set aside the settlement but left open the possibility that the defect in the certification procedure might be cured, the class certified, and a revised settlement approved on remand. However, instead of proceeding further in the Eastern District of Pennsylvania, the parties to the settlement repaired to the 18th Judicial District for the Parish of Iberville, Louisiana, where a similar suit had been pending, restructured their deal, and submitted it to the Louisiana court, which ultimately approved it.

The action before us is an appeal from an order of the district court denying emergency applications by a number of GM truck owners who were members of the Eastern District of Pennsylvania class for an injunction against further class action proceedings in the Louisiana case. At the time of the district court's order, the Louisiana state court was considering whether to approve a settlement between GM and a certified settlement class of GM pickup truck owners, though it stayed entry of its final order until the district court could rule on the request for injunction.

The Louisiana settlement class is composed of persons who purchased over a fifteen-year period certain mid- and full-size GM pickup trucks . . . with fuel tanks located outside the frame rails. Like the federal plaintiffs, the Louisiana plaintiffs allege that the fuel system design leads to an increased risk of fire following side collisions. Appellants are members of that settlement class, and none of them has chosen to opt out of that class. Following the conditional certification of the settlement class by the Louisiana court, the present appellants, truck owners who were never parties but were successful objectors to the proposed Eastern District of Pennsylvania settlement, moved to intervene in the on-going proceedings in the MDL cases and requested the court to enjoin the Louisiana state court from considering the settlement agreement before it. The district court . . . denied appellants' motion for intervention as untimely, and also denied the motion for injunctive relief. Appellants then filed Emergency Motions with this Court requesting injunctions against the Louisiana court proceedings. We denied those motions and ordered full briefing. Thereafter, the Louisiana state court entered final judgment approving the settlement. The present appellants also filed notices of appeal from that judgment in

the Louisiana appellate system, so that they were proceeding simultaneously with their appeal from the district court's denial of their motion for
injunction and their Louisiana appeal.

Appellants' claim centers on their argument that the Louisiana settlement is little changed from the one previously rejected by us in *GM I*.
Accordingly, they view the settlement as an "end run" around, and a flagrant violation of, the jurisdiction of the Eastern District of Pennsylvania
MDL court to which we had remanded the case for further proceedings.
Although the procedure followed by appellees gives us pause, the precedent
of this Court and the Supreme Court compels us to disagree with appellants and to affirm the district court's decision on several grounds.

. . . [N]ow that the Louisiana court has entered a final judgment on the
settlement, our review is barred by both the Full Faith and Credit Act and
the *Rooker–Feldman* doctrine, which prevents intermediate federal appellate review of state court decisions. [In addition], appellants' requested injunction does not fall under any of the three exceptions to the Anti–
Injunction Act, which authorize a federal court to stay state court proceedings only when "expressly authorized by an Act of Congress, or where necessary in aid of its jurisdiction, or to protect or effectuate its judgments." 28
U.S.C. § 2283.

I.   FACTS AND PROCEDURAL HISTORY

A.   The MDL Proceedings

. . . Between 1973 and 1991, GM sold over 6.3 million pickup trucks
with fuel tanks mounted outside of the frame rails. These trucks are allegedly defective because they are subject to an increased risk of fire in the
event of a side collision. In late October 1992, counsel filed claims on behalf
of plaintiffs in 26 federal courts and 11 state courts, including Louisiana.
On February 26, 1993, the JPML transferred all related federal actions to
the District Court for the Eastern District of Pennsylvania for coordinated
discovery and pre-trial proceedings. . . .

On March 5, 1993, pursuant to an order of the transferee judge, plaintiffs filed a Consolidated Amended Class Action Complaint with 277 named
plaintiffs seeking equitable relief and damages. Specifically, the complaint
alleged violations of the Magnuson–Moss Warranty Act, the Lanham
Trademark Act, as well as a variety of state common law claims including
negligence, strict liability, fraud, unfair practices, and breach of written
and implied warranty.

Also on March 5, 1993, plaintiffs filed a consolidated motion for nationwide class certification. The district court set July 19, 1993, as the date
for the hearing on this motion. . . . By the date of the hearing, the parties
had reached a settlement in principle and petitioned the court for approval.
Without prejudice to GM's opposition to class certification, the parties
agreed to certification of a settlement class of GM pickup truck owners.

While the provisional settlement included many detailed terms, the
most important term provided for a coupon with limited transferability and
redeemability provisions. Basically, class members would receive a $1,000
coupon, redeemable toward the purchase of any new GMC truck or Chevrolet light duty truck for a fifteen month period. Under its terms, the approved settlement would have had no effect on any accrued or future claims
for personal injury or death, and would not have affected the rights of class
members to participate in any future remedial action that might be required by the National Traffic and Motor Safety Act of 1966.

The district court reviewed the substantive terms of the settlement, and on July 20, 1993, preliminarily determined that the settlement was reasonable. The court also provisionally certified the class of GM truck owners as a settlement class pursuant to Fed. R. Civ. P. 23(b)(3). . . .

In response to the notices mailed to almost 5.7 million registered truck owners and published nationally, over 5,200 truck owners elected to opt out of the class, and approximately 6,500 truck owners objected to the settlement. On October 26, 1993, the district court held a fairness hearing and approved the settlement as fair, reasonable, and adequate.

The objectors appealed, and we reversed. We held that . . . a finding that the settlement was "fair and reasonable", which was all that the district court had made, was not a surrogate for the Rule 23 class findings. Then, identifying potential problems with meeting the commonality, typicality, and predominance requirements, we vacated the orders that had certified the settlement class and had approved the settlement, and remanded the case for further proceedings.

Following remand, plaintiffs amended their complaint, filed a renewed motion for class certification, and proceeded with discovery pursuant to our opinion. . . . [A]ccording to the district court, no settlement is pending, and the motion for class certification is not yet ripe.

B.   The Louisiana Proceedings

In addition to the litigation that had been consolidated and was progressing in the district court, plaintiffs had concurrently filed actions in 11 state courts, including Louisiana. . . . On May 18, 1993, a Louisiana trial court granted plaintiffs' motion for class certification of a statewide class as the basis for litigation. This decision was stayed by a Louisiana appellate court on August 8, 1993, based upon the preliminary nationwide settlement reached in the Eastern District of Pennsylvania MDL cases.

After we vacated the order creating the settlement class, a new round of negotiations between Louisiana class counsel and GM began. On June 27, 1996, these negotiations came to fruition. The parties filed their new provisional settlement agreement in the 18th District Court for the Parish of Iberville, where the statewide litigation class had previously been certified. The Louisiana court preliminarily approved the new settlement and provisionally certified a nationwide class. The court ordered individual notices disseminated to the 5.7 million class members, scheduled a formal fairness hearing for November 6, 1996, and requested objections and notices of exclusions. 200 of the 277 plaintiffs in the federal MDL successfully moved to intervene in the Louisiana proceedings.

The new Louisiana settlement, while similar in content to the original settlement provisionally approved by the MDL court in 1993 and later rejected by this Court, differs in several ways, all responsive to our comments in *GM I* about perceived problems with the earlier settlement. First, the Louisiana settlement extends the period during which class members could validly redeem their $1,000 coupons (from 15 to 33 months for consumers and from 15 to 50 months for fleet and government owners). Second, the settlement provides for greater transferability of the coupons. Third, the settlement would allow class members to apply the coupon value toward the purchase of any GM vehicle (except Saturn automobiles), rather than just GM pickup trucks. Fourth, the settlement stipulates that GM and plaintiffs' counsel will fund two new safety programs, researching the safety of general fuel systems and testing proposed retrofits for safety and feasibility, purported to be worth a combined $5.1 million. Fifth, commitments have apparently been made by a major bank to purchase the transferable coupons, thereby creating a secondary market.

Appellants and appellees strongly dispute the viability and significance of the differences between the two settlements. Appellees contend that these changes satisfy most, if not all, of this Court's problems with the original agreement. They note significantly that all the governmental and fleet entities, as well as the Public Citizen Litigation Group and the Center for Auto Safety, which objected to the original settlement, support the Louisiana settlement. Appellants, conversely, assert that class counsel and GM have essentially repackaged the agreement that had been rejected in Philadelphia, made purely cosmetic changes, and have run off to Louisiana for approval. . . .

III. *FULL FAITH AND CREDIT AND THE* ROOKER–FELDMAN *DOCTRINE.*

Appellees contend that . . . now that the Louisiana court has entered a final judgment, we can no longer simply enjoin the Louisiana court from entering judgment on the provisional settlement. In their submission, we would have to first direct the district court to vacate the Louisiana court's final judgment and then enjoin it from entering any new judgment on the settlement. Appellees contend that both the Full Faith and Credit Act, 28 U.S.C. § 1738, and the *Rooker–Feldman* doctrine prevent us from vacating the final judgment of the Louisiana court.

A. *The Full Faith and Credit Act*

28 U.S.C. § 1738 provides in pertinent part:

> The . . . judicial proceedings of any court of any such State, Territory, or Possession . . . shall have the same full faith and credit in every court within the United States and its Territories and Possessions as they have by law or usage in the courts of such State, Territory, or Possession from which they are taken.

As interpreted by the Supreme Court, § 1738 "directs all courts to treat a state court judgment with the same respect that it would receive in the courts of the rendering state." *Matsushita Elec. Indus. Co. v. Epstein*, 516 U.S. 367, 373 (1996). We may not " 'employ [our] own rules . . . in determining the effect of state judgments,' but must 'accept the rules chosen by the State from which the judgment is taken.' " *Id. (citing Kremer v. Chemical Const. Corp.*, 456 U.S. 461, 481–82 (1982)). . . .

Under Louisiana law, the class action settlement that appellants seek to enjoin here is a final judgment. Facially, therefore, § 1738 leaves us no choice but to decline appellants' request. This conclusion is confirmed by the Supreme Court's recent decision in *Matsushita.* . . .

. . . [T]he present appellants are members of the Louisiana class who did not exercise their opt out rights. They are active participants in the settlement approval process there, and have timely appealed the adverse judgment there as well. Especially under these circumstances, the Full Faith and Credit Act prevents this Court from vacating the now final judgment of the Louisiana court.

B. *The Rooker–Feldman Doctrine*

Under the *Rooker–Feldman* doctrine, "federal district courts lack subject matter jurisdiction to review final adjudications of a state's highest court or to evaluate constitutional claims that are 'inextricably intertwined with the state court's [decision] in a judicial proceeding.' " *Blake v. Papa-dakos*, 953 F.2d 68, 71 (3d Cir. 1992) (*quoting District of Columbia Court of Appeals v. Feldman*, 460 U.S. 462, 483 n. 16 (1983)); *see also Rooker v. Fidelity Trust Co.*, 263 U.S. 413, 416 (1923). The concerns that underlie the doctrine are respect for the state courts and concerns over finality of judgments. District courts lack subject matter jurisdiction once a state court has adjudicated an issue because Congress has conferred only original jurisdiction, not appellate jurisdiction, on the district courts. We have interpreted the doctrine to encompass final decisions of lower state courts.

As was discussed *supra* with respect to the Full Faith and Credit Act, the Louisiana court has entered a valid final judgment. The decision by that Court was clearly an adjudicative and not a legislative or ministerial act. Therefore, in order for us to grant appellants' requested relief, we would first have to "determine that the state court judgment was erroneously entered." *Rooker–Feldman* bars exactly this sort of intermediate appellate review of state court judgments and divests this Court of subject matter jurisdiction of this appeal.

IV. *THE ANTI–INJUNCTION ACT*

Under the terms of the Anti–Injunction Act, "[a] court of the United States may not grant an injunction to stay proceedings in a State court except as expressly authorized by Act of Congress, or where necessary in aid of its jurisdiction, or to protect or effectuate its judgments." 28 U.S.C. § 2283. If an injunction falls within one of these three exceptions, the All–Writs Act provides the positive authority for federal courts to issue injunctions of state court proceedings.[5] The two statutes act in concert, and the parallel "necessary in aid of jurisdiction" language is construed similarly. Appellees assert that even assuming that this case was not barred for all of the reasons discussed above, the Anti–Injunction Act would still frustrate appellants' prayers for relief.

Our judgment in *GM I* concerning the requirements that a settlement class must meet under Rule 23, which would have applied in the MDL action on remand had the parties sought to forge a new settlement in the district court, became final when the Supreme Court denied GM's petition for *certiorari*. According to appellants, this precludes all other courts (state and federal) from adopting any other interpretation of class settlement requirements, under either state or federal law. Therefore, they say, under the principles of collateral estoppel and "law of the case", the settlement class issue is insulated from reevaluation in other forums.

Translated into a statutory context, appellants argue that this situation falls under an exception to the Anti–Injunction Act, and therefore under the positive force of the All–Writs Act, the district court had the power to enjoin the Louisiana proceedings either "in aid of its jurisdiction" or "to protect and effectuate its judgments". As we will now explain, however, the exceptions to the Anti–Injunction Act are very narrow indeed, and the Act serves as an absolute bar to district court injunctive action here.

The Anti–Injunction Act is "an absolute prohibition against enjoining State Court proceedings, unless the injunction falls within one of three specifically defined exceptions." *Atlantic Coast Line R. Co. v. Brotherhood of Locomotive Eng'rs*, 398 U.S. 281, 286 (1970). . . . This prohibition applies

---

[5] The All–Writs Act provides: "The Supreme Court and all courts established by Act of Congress may issue all writs necessary or appropriate in aid of their jurisdiction and agreeable to the usages and principles of law." 28 U.S.C. § 1651.

whether appellants seek to enjoin the parties to the action or the state court itself. Moreover, these three exceptions are to be rigorously construed and "should not be enlarged by loose statutory construction." *Atlantic Coast*, 398 U.S. at 287. "[A] federal court does not have inherent power to ignore the limitations of § 2283 and to enjoin state court proceedings merely because those proceedings interfere with a protected federal right or invade an area preempted by federal law, even when the interference is unmistakably clear." *Id.* at 294.

Narrow interp. of exceptions

Finally, "[a]ny doubts as to the propriety of a federal injunction against state court proceedings should be resolved in favor of permitting the state court to proceed in an orderly fashion to finally determine the controversy." *Id.* at 297. With this background, we now proceed with the relevant exceptions to the Act.

A.   *"Necessary in Aid of Its Jurisdiction"*

Appellants' primary argument for injunctive relief is that this action falls under the "in aid of its jurisdiction" exception to the Anti–Injunction Act. Appellants argue that because the same attorneys representing the same class of plaintiffs were once pursuing settlement in the Eastern District in the MDL and now, having had their proposed settlement rejected by this Court, are pursuing a similar settlement in Louisiana, they are engaged in forum shopping, evading the dictates of this Court, and ultimately, impeding the federal court's ability to exercise its jurisdiction.

First, we note that the "necessary in aid of its jurisdiction" exception applies only "to prevent a state court from so interfering with a federal court's consideration or disposition of a case as to seriously impair the federal court's flexibility and authority to decide that case." *Atlantic Coast*, 398 U.S. at 295. No such interference or impairment appears in this record. Indeed, in those cases cited by appellants where a state action has been enjoined, the federal court had already approved or conditionally approved its own settlement or the approval was imminent. That is not the case here. The MDL court is not considering a nationwide settlement pursuant to our remand in *GM I*. Moreover, the Louisiana settlement contained opt out provisions, thereby protecting the rights of the 277 remaining MDL plaintiffs . . . .

. . . There is no classwide settlement pending before the district court (indeed, the conditional class certification by the district court no longer subsists), and no stipulation of settlement or prospect of settlement in that court is imminent. Furthermore, it simply cannot be said that the Louisiana court is attempting to dictate to the district court the scope and terms of a settlement, since none is pending before the district court. Finally, there can be no confusion by class members, for only one set of notices has been sent out (from the Louisiana court).

In fact, if the settlement is ultimately approved by the Louisiana appellate system (and the United States Supreme Court, if necessary), then the nationwide class will be certified (in Louisiana), and (excepting opt outs) no court will have any plaintiffs left with which to proceed. If disapproved, then the district court (or any other court) can continue with discovery. . . .

B.   *"To Protect or Effectuate Its Judgments"* *Relitigation exception*

Appellants alternatively argue that appellees are purposefully attempting to avoid our decision in *GM I*, 55 F.3d at 768, which vacated the class certification. Under the so-called "relitigation exception" of the Anti–

Injunction Act, this is, according to appellants, precisely the sort of situation where an injunction is in order "to protect or effectuate [the] judgments" of this Court. While the district court would have been bound on remand to apply the precepts we announced about the requisites for class certification and the anatomy of the class (including subclassing), appellants nonetheless are incorrect when they attempt to attach res judicata or collateral estoppel effect to our *GM I* decision in other jurisdictions. . . .

First, denial of class certification is not a "judgment" for the purposes of the Anti–Injunction Act while the underlying litigation remains pending. See *J.R. Clearwater Inc. v. Ashland Chem. Co.*, 93 F.3d 176, 179 (5th Cir. 1996). We endorse the Fifth Circuit's rationale that denial of class certification under these circumstances lacks sufficient finality to be entitled to preclusive effect. Second, the decision by this Court to reject the provisional settlement class is not a "judgment" with respect to the Louisiana settlement agreement, and our interpretation of Rule 23 is not binding on the Louisiana court. All that we did in *GM I* was hold that the district court had erred in certifying the settlement class without making factual findings to support class certification under Rule 23(a) and (b)(3), and require that certain problems with meeting the Rule 23(a) and (b) requirements be corrected by the MDL court on remand. We held open the possibility that on remand, settlement "in either [] original or a renegotiated form" might later be approved. Moreover, our construction of Rule 23 and application to the provisional settlement class is not controlling on the Louisiana court, because it is not bound by our interpretation of Rule 23. Rather, the Louisiana court properly applied La. Code Civ. Proc. Ann. arts. 591 and 592, the parallel Louisiana class certification rule.

Since appellants have failed to show that an exception to the Anti–Injunction Act [applies here], neither this Court nor the district court has the authority to enjoin the Louisiana proceedings.

The order of the district court will be affirmed.

NOTES AND QUESTIONS

1. The Rooker–Feldman *Doctrine Today.* The court in *General Motors* relied on the full faith and credit statute, the *Rooker–Feldman* doctrine, and the Anti–Injunction Act to conclude that it should not interfere with the Louisiana judgment. As should be obvious from the decision, the full faith and credit and Rooker–Feldman doctrines have important similarities. For a comparative discussion of the two, see Dustin E. Buehler, Jurisdiction, *Abstention, and Finality: Articulating a Unique Role for the* Rooker–Feldman *Doctrine*, 42 Seton Hall L. Rev. 553 (2012). When *General Motors* was decided in 1998, the Third Circuit's interpretation of the *Rooker–Feldman* doctrine was not unusual. But the Supreme Court in 2005 made clear that the doctrine should be read narrowly: "The *Rooker–Feldman* doctrine, we hold today, is confined to cases of the kind from which the doctrine acquired its name: cases brought by state-court losers complaining of injuries caused by state-court judgments rendered *before* the district court proceedings commenced and inviting district court review and rejection of those judgments." *Exxon Mobil Corp. v. Saudi Basic Industries Corp.*, 544 U.S. 280, 284 (2005) (emphasis added). If *General Motors* were decided today, *Rooker–Feldman* would be irrelevant because the Louisiana state court had not entered judgment *before* the actions consolidated in the Eastern District of Pennsylvania commenced. Cf. *General Motors* 134 F.3d at 143 ("District courts lack subject matter jurisdiction once a state court has adjudicated an issue because Congress has conferred only original jurisdiction, not appellate jurisdiction, on the district courts").

    2.   *The Coupon Settlement.* Why might class counsel and General Motors agree to a class settlement structured in terms of coupons for owners of the implicated trucks, as opposed to cash payouts for the reduction in truck value arising from the fuel tank design? How should a court go about determining the value of a class settlement structured in terms of coupons for class members for purposes of making a fee award to class counsel based upon a percentage of the overall class recovery? The difficulties presented by coupon settlements have garnered detailed analysis in the scholarly literature. See Christopher R. Leslie, *A Market–Based Approach to Coupon Settlements in Antitrust and Consumer Class Action Litigation,* 49 UCLA L. Rev. 991 (2002); Geoffrey P. Miller & Lori S. Singer, *Nonpecuniary Class Action Settlements,* 60 Law & Contemp. Prob. 97 (Autumn 1997).

    CAFA addresses coupon settlements in federal-court class actions. In pertinent part, CAFA provides:

> (a) CONTINGENT FEES IN COUPON SETTLEMENTS.—If a proposed settlement in a class action provides for a recovery of coupons to a class member, the portion of any attorney's fee award to class counsel that is attributable to the award of the coupons shall be based on the value to class members of the coupons that are redeemed. . . .

> (e) JUDICIAL SCRUTINY OF COUPON SETTLEMENTS.—In a proposed settlement under which class members would be awarded coupons, the court may approve the proposed settlement only after a hearing to determine whether, and making a written finding that, the settlement is fair, reasonable, and adequate for class members. The court, in its discretion, may also require that a proposed settlement agreement provide for the distribution of a portion of the value of unclaimed coupons to 1 or more charitable or governmental organizations, as agreed to by the parties. The distribution and redemption of any proceeds under this subsection shall not be used to calculate attorneys' fees under this section.

28 U.S.C. § 1712.

Smith v. Bayer Corp.

564 U.S. ___, 131 S.Ct. 2368 (June 16, 2011), No. 09–1205

■ JUSTICE KAGAN delivered the opinion of the Court in which JUSTICE THOMAS joined as to Parts I and II.A.

    In this case, a Federal District Court enjoined a state court from considering a plaintiff's request to approve a class action. The District Court did so because it had earlier denied a motion to certify a class in a related case, brought by a different plaintiff against the same defendant alleging similar claims. The federal court thought its injunction appropriate to prevent relitigation of the issue it had decided.

    We hold to the contrary. In issuing this order to a state court, the federal court exceeded its authority under the "relitigation exception" to the Anti–Injunction Act. That statutory provision permits a federal court to enjoin a state proceeding only in rare cases, when necessary to "protect or effectuate [the federal court's] judgments." 28 U.S.C. § 2283. Here, that standard was not met for two reasons. First, the issue presented in the state court was not identical to the one decided in the federal tribunal. And second, the plaintiff in the state court did not have the requisite connection to the federal suit to be bound by the District Court's judgment.

I

Because the question before us involves the effect of a former adjudication on this case, we begin our statement of the facts not with this lawsuit, but with another. In August 2001, George McCollins sued respondent Bayer Corporation in the Circuit Court of Cabell County, West Virginia, asserting various state-law claims arising from Bayer's sale of an allegedly hazardous prescription drug called Baycol (which Bayer withdrew from the market that same month). McCollins contended that Bayer had violated West Virginia's consumer-protection statute and the company's express and implied warranties by selling him a defective product. And pursuant to West Virginia Rule of Civil Procedure 23 (2011), McCollins asked the state court to certify a class of West Virginia residents who had also purchased Baycol, so that the case could proceed as a class action.

Approximately one month later, the suit now before us began in a different part of West Virginia. Petitioners Keith Smith and Shirley Sperlazza (Smith for short) filed state-law claims against Bayer, similar to those raised in McCollins' suit, in the Circuit Court of Brooke County, West Virginia. And like McCollins, Smith asked the court to certify under West Virginia's Rule 23 a class of Baycol purchasers residing in the State. Neither Smith nor McCollins knew about the other's suit.

In January 2002, Bayer removed McCollins' case to the United States District Court for the Southern District of West Virginia on the basis of diversity jurisdiction. The case was then transferred to the District of Minnesota pursuant to a preexisting order of the Judicial Panel on Multi–District Litigation, which had consolidated all federal suits involving Baycol (numbering in the tens of thousands) before a single District Court Judge. Bayer, however, could not remove Smith's case to federal court because Smith had sued several West Virginia defendants in addition to Bayer, and so the suit lacked complete diversity.[6] Smith's suit thus remained in the state courthouse in Brooke County.

Over the next six years, the two cases proceeded along their separate pretrial paths at roughly the same pace. By 2008, both courts were preparing to turn to their respective plaintiffs' motions for class certification. The Federal District Court was the first to reach a decision.

Applying Federal Rule of Civil Procedure 23,[7] the District Court declined to certify McCollins' proposed class of West Virginia Baycol purchasers. The District Court's reasoning proceeded in two steps. The court first ruled that, under West Virginia law, each plaintiff would have to prove "actual injury" from his use of Baycol to recover. The court then held that because the necessary showing of harm would vary from plaintiff to plaintiff,

---

[6] The Class Action Fairness Act of 2005, 119 Stat. 4, which postdates and therefore does not govern this lawsuit, now enables a defendant to remove to federal court certain class actions involving nondiverse parties. See 28 U.S.C. §§ 1332(d), 1453(b); see also *infra*, at ___.

[7] Although McCollins had originally sought certification under West Virginia Rule of Civil Procedure 23 (2011), federal procedural rules govern a case that has been removed to federal court. See *Shady Grove Orthopedic Associates, P.A. v. Allstate Ins. Co.*, 559 U.S. ___ (2010).

"individual issues of fact predominate[d]" over issues common to all members of the proposed class, and so the case was not suitable for class treatment. In the same order, the District Court also dismissed McCollins' claims on the merits in light of his failure to demonstrate physical injury from his use of Baycol. McCollins chose not to appeal.

Although McCollins' suit was now concluded, Bayer asked the District Court for another order based upon it, this one affecting Smith's case in West Virginia. In a motion—receipt of which first apprised Smith of McCollins' suit—Bayer explained that the proposed class in Smith's case was identical to the one the federal court had just rejected. Bayer therefore requested that the federal court enjoin the West Virginia state court from hearing Smith's motion to certify a class. According to Bayer, that order was appropriate to protect the District Court's judgment in McCollins' suit denying class certification. The District Court agreed and granted the injunction.

The Court of Appeals for the Eighth Circuit affirmed. The court noted that the Anti–Injunction Act generally prohibits federal courts from enjoining state court proceedings. But the court held that the Act's relitigation exception authorized the injunction here because ordinary rules of issue preclusion barred Smith from seeking certification of his proposed class. According to the court, Smith was invoking a similar class action rule as McCollins had used to seek certification "of the same class" in a suit alleging "the same legal theories;" the issue in the state court therefore was "sufficiently identical" to the one the federal court had decided to warrant preclusion. In addition, the court held, the parties in the two proceedings were sufficiently alike: Because Smith was an unnamed member of the class McCollins had proposed, and because their "interests were aligned," Smith was appropriately bound by the federal court's judgment.

We granted certiorari, 561 U.S. ___ (2010), because the order issued here implicates two circuit splits arising from application of the Anti–Injunction Act's relitigation exception. The first involves the requirement of preclusion law that a subsequent suit raise the "same issue" as a previous case. The second concerns the scope of the rule that a court's judgment cannot bind nonparties.[4] We think the District Court erred on both grounds when it granted the injunction, and we now reverse.

II

The Anti–Injunction Act, first enacted in 1793, provides that

"A court of the United States may not grant an injunction to stay proceedings in a State court except as expressly authorized by Act of Congress, or where necessary in aid of its jurisdiction, or to protect or effectuate its judgments." 28 U.S.C. § 2283.

The statute, we have recognized, "is a necessary concomitant of the Framers' decision to authorize, and Congress' decision to implement, a dual system of federal and state courts." *Chick Kam Choo v. Exxon Corp.*, 486

---

[4] Compare 593 F.3d, at 724 ("[T]he denial of class certification is binding on unnamed [putative] class members" because they are "in privity to [the parties] in the prior action") and *In re Bridgestone/Firestone, Inc., Tires Prods. Liability Litigation*, 333 F.3d 763, 768–69 (C.A.7 2003) (same), with *In re Ford Motor Co.*, 471 F.3d 1233, 1245 (C.A.11 2006) (holding that "[t]he denial of class certification" prevents a court from "binding" anyone other than "the parties appearing before it") and *In re General Motors Corp. Pick–Up Truck Fuel Tank Prods. Liability Litigation*, 134 F.3d 133, 141 (C.A.3 1998) (holding that putative "class members are not parties" and so cannot be bound by a court's ruling when "there is no class pending").

U.S. 140, 146 (1988). And the Act's core message is one of respect for state courts. The Act broadly commands that those tribunals "shall remain free from interference by federal courts." *Atlantic Coast Line R. Co. v. Locomotive Engineers,* 398 U.S. 281–82 (1970). That edict is subject to only "three specifically defined exceptions." And those exceptions, though designed for important purposes, "are narrow and are 'not [to] be enlarged by loose statutory construction.'" Indeed, "[a]ny doubts as to the propriety of a federal injunction against state court proceedings should be resolved in favor of permitting the state courts to proceed."

This case involves the last of the Act's three exceptions, known as the relitigation exception. That exception is designed to implement "well-recognized concepts" of claim and issue preclusion. The provision authorizes an injunction to prevent state litigation of a claim or issue "that previously was presented to and decided by the federal court." But in applying this exception, we have taken special care to keep it "strict and narrow." After all, a court does not usually "get to dictate to other courts the preclusion consequences of its own judgment." Deciding whether and how prior litigation has preclusive effect is usually the bailiwick of the *second* court (here, the one in West Virginia). So issuing an injunction under the relitigation exception is resorting to heavy artillery.[5] For that reason, every benefit of the doubt goes toward the state court; an injunction can issue only if preclusion is clear beyond peradventure.

The question here is whether the federal court's rejection of McCollins' proposed class precluded a later adjudication in state court of Smith's certification motion. For the federal court's determination of the class issue to have this preclusive effect, at least two conditions must be met. First, the issue the federal court decided must be the same as the one presented in the state tribunal. And second, Smith must have been a party to the federal suit, or else must fall within one of a few discrete exceptions to the general rule against binding nonparties. In fact, as we will explain, the issues before the two courts were not the same, and Smith was neither a party nor the exceptional kind of nonparty who can be bound. So the courts below erred in finding the certification issue precluded, and erred all the more in thinking an injunction appropriate.[7]

A

In our most recent case on the relitigation exception, *Chick Kam Choo v. Exxon,* we applied the "same issue" requirement of preclusion law to invalidate a federal court's injunction. 486 U.S., at 151. The federal court had dismissed a suit involving Singapore law on grounds of *forum non conveniens.* After the plaintiff brought the same claim in Texas state court, the federal court issued an injunction barring the plaintiff from pursuing relief in that alternate forum. We held that the District Court had gone too far. "[A]n essential prerequisite for applying the relitigation exception," we explained, "is that the . . . issues which the federal injunction insulates from litigation in state proceedings actually have been decided by the federal

---

[5] That is especially so because an injunction is not the only way to correct a state trial court's erroneous refusal to give preclusive effect to a federal judgment. As we have noted before, "the state appellate courts and ultimately this Court" can review and reverse such a ruling. See *Atlantic Coast Line R. Co. v. Locomotive Engineers,* 398 U.S. 281, 287 (1970).

[7] Because we rest our decision on the Anti–Injunction Act and the principles of issue preclusion that inform it, we do not consider Smith's argument, based on *Phillips Petroleum Co. v. Shutts,* 472 U.S. 797 (1985), that the District Court's action violated the Due Process Clause.

court." That prerequisite, we thought, was not satisfied because the issue to be adjudicated in state court was not the one the federal court had resolved. The federal court had considered the permissibility of the claim under federal *forum non conveniens* principles. But the Texas courts, we thought, "would apply a significantly different *forum non conveniens* analysis;" they had in prior cases rejected the strictness of the federal doctrine. Our conclusion followed: "[W]hether the Texas *state* courts are an appropriate forum for [the plaintiff's] Singapore law claims has not yet been litigated." Because the legal standards in the two courts differed, the issues before the courts differed, and an injunction was unwarranted.

The question here closely resembles the one in *Chick Kam Choo*. The class Smith proposed in state court mirrored the class McCollins sought to certify in federal court: Both included all Baycol purchasers resident in West Virginia. Moreover, the substantive claims in the two suits broadly overlapped: Both complaints alleged that Bayer had sold a defective product in violation of the State's consumer protection law and the company's warranties. So far, so good for preclusion. But not so fast: a critical question—the question of the applicable legal standard—remains. The District Court ruled that the proposed class did not meet the requirements of Federal Rule 23 (because individualized issues would predominate over common ones). But the state court was poised to consider whether the proposed class satisfied *West Virginia* Rule 23. If those two legal standards differ (as federal and state *forum non conveniens* law differed in *Chick Kam Choo*)— then the federal court resolved an issue not before the state court. In that event, much like in *Chick Kam Choo*, "whether the [West Virginia] *state* cour[t]" should certify the proposed class action "has not yet been litigated."

The Court of Appeals and Smith offer us two competing ways of deciding whether the West Virginia and Federal Rules differ, but we think the right path lies somewhere in the middle. The Eighth Circuit relied almost exclusively on the near-identity of the two Rules' texts. That was the right place to start, but not to end. Federal and state courts, after all, can and do apply identically worded procedural provisions in widely varying ways. If a State's procedural provision tracks the language of a Federal Rule, but a state court interprets that provision in a manner federal courts have not, then the state court is using a different standard and thus deciding a different issue. At the other extreme, Smith contends that the source of law is all that matters: a different sovereign must in each and every case "have the opportunity, if it chooses, to construe its procedural rule differently." But if state courts have made crystal clear that they follow the same approach as the federal court applied, we see no need to ignore that determination; in that event, the issues in the two cases would indeed be the same. So a federal court considering whether the relitigation exception applies should examine whether state law parallels its federal counterpart. But as suggested earlier, the federal court must resolve any uncertainty on that score by leaving the question of preclusion to the state courts.

Under this approach, the West Virginia Supreme Court has gone some way toward resolving the matter before us by declaring its independence from federal courts' interpretation of the Federal Rules—and particularly of Rule 23. In *In re W. Va. Rezulin Litigation*, 214 W.Va. 52, 585 S.E.2d 52 (2003), the West Virginia high court considered a plaintiff's motion to certify a class—coincidentally enough, in a suit about an allegedly defective pharmaceutical product. The court made a point of complaining about the parties' and lower court's near-exclusive reliance on federal cases about

Federal Rule 23 to decide the certification question. Such cases, the court cautioned, " 'may be persuasive, but [they are] not binding or controlling.' " And lest anyone mistake the import of this message, the court went on: The aim of "this rule is to avoid having our legal analysis of our Rules 'amount to nothing more than Pavlovian responses to federal decisional law.' " Of course, the state courts might still have adopted an approach to their Rule 23 that tracked the analysis the federal court used in McCollins' case. But absent clear evidence that the state courts had done so, we could not conclude that they would interpret their Rule in the same way. And if that is so, we could not tell whether the certification issues in the state and federal courts were the same. That uncertainty would preclude an injunction.

But here the case against an injunction is even stronger, because the West Virginia Supreme Court has *disapproved* the approach to Rule 23(b)(3)'s predominance requirement that the Federal District Court embraced. Recall that the federal court held that the presence of a single individualized issue—injury from the use of Baycol—prevented class certification. The court did not identify the common issues in the case; nor did it balance these common issues against the need to prove individual injury to determine which predominated. The court instead applied a strict test barring class treatment when proof of each plaintiff's injury is necessary.[8] By contrast, the West Virginia Supreme Court in *In re Rezulin* adopted an all-things-considered, balancing inquiry in interpreting its Rule 23. Rejecting any "rigid test," the state court opined that the predominance requirement "contemplates a review of many factors." Indeed, the court noted, a " 'single common issue' " in a case could outweigh " 'numerous . . . individual questions.' " That meant, the court further explained (quoting what it termed the "leading treatise" on the subject), that even objections to certification " 'based on . . . causation, or reliance' "—which typically involve showings of individual injury—" 'will not bar predominance satisfaction.' " So point for point, the analysis set out in *In re Rezulin* diverged from the District Court's interpretation of Federal Rule 23. A state court using the *In re Rezulin* standard would decide a different question than the one the federal court had earlier resolved.[9]

This case, indeed, is little more than a rerun of *Chick Kam Choo*. A federal court and a state court apply different law. That means they decide distinct questions. The federal court's resolution of one issue does not preclude the state court's determination of another. It then goes without saying that the federal court may not issue an injunction. The *Anti*–Injunction Act's *re*-litigation exception does not extend nearly so far.

---

[8] The District Court's approach to the predominance inquiry is consistent with the approach employed by the Eighth Circuit. See *In re St. Jude Medical, Inc.*, 522 F.3d 836, 837–40 (2008) (holding that most commercial misrepresentation cases are "unsuitable for class treatment" because individual issues of reliance necessarily predominate). We express no opinion as to the correctness of this approach.

[9] Bayer argues that *In re Rezulin* does not preclude an injunction in this case because the West Virginia court there decided that common issues predominated over individual issues of damages, not over individual issues of liability (as exist here). See Brief for Respondent 25–26. We think Bayer is right about this distinction, but wrong about its consequence. Our point is not that *In re Rezulin* dictates the answer to the class certification question here; the two cases are indeed too dissimilar for that to be true. The point instead is that *In re Rezulin* articulated a general approach to the predominance requirement that differs markedly from the one the federal court used. Minor variations in the application of what is in essence the same legal standard do not defeat preclusion; but where, as here, the State's courts "would apply a significantly different . . . analysis," *Chick Kam Choo v. Exxon Corp.*, 486 U.S. 140, 149 (1988), the federal and state courts decide different issues.

B

The injunction issued here runs into another basic premise of preclusion law: A court's judgment binds only the parties to a suit, subject to a handful of discrete and limited exceptions. The importance of this rule and the narrowness of its exceptions go hand in hand. We have repeatedly "emphasize[d] the fundamental nature of the general rule" that only parties can be bound by prior judgments; accordingly, we have taken a "constrained approach to nonparty preclusion." *Taylor v. Sturgell*, 553 U.S. 880, 898 (2008). Against this backdrop, Bayer defends the decision below by arguing that Smith—an unnamed member of a proposed but uncertified class—qualifies as a party to the McCollins litigation. Alternatively, Bayer claims that the District Court's judgment binds Smith under the recognized exception to the rule against nonparty preclusion for members of class actions. We think neither contention has merit.

Bayer's first claim ill-comports with any proper understanding of what a "party" is. In general, "[a] 'party' to litigation is '[o]ne by or against whom a lawsuit is brought,'" *United States ex rel. Eisenstein v. City of New York*, 556 U.S. ___ (2009), or one who "become[s] a party by intervention, substitution, or third-party practice," *Karcher v. May*, 484 U.S. 72, 77 (1987). And we have further held that an unnamed member of a *certified* class may be "considered a 'party' for the [particular] purpos[e] of appealing" an adverse judgment. *Devlin v. Scardelletti*, 536 U.S. 1, 7 (2002). But as the dissent in *Devlin* noted, no one in that case was "willing to advance the novel and surely erroneous argument that a nonnamed class member is a party to the class-action litigation *before the class is certified*." Still less does that argument make sense *once certification is denied*. The definition of the term "party" can on no account be stretched so far as to cover a person like Smith, whom the plaintiff in a lawsuit was denied leave to represent. If the judgment in the McCollins litigation can indeed bind Smith, it must do so under principles of *non* party preclusion.

As Bayer notes, one such principle allows unnamed members of a class action to be bound, even though they are not parties to the suit. See *Cooper v. Federal Reserve Bank of Richmond*, 467 U.S. 867, 874 ("[U]nder elementary principles of prior adjudication a judgment in a properly entertained class action is binding on class members in any subsequent litigation"); see also *Taylor*, 553 U.S., at 894 (stating that nonparties can be bound in "properly conducted class actions"). But here Bayer faces a conundrum. If we know one thing about the McCollins suit, we know that it was *not a* class action. Indeed, the very ruling that Bayer argues ought to be given preclusive effect is the District Court's decision that a class could not properly be certified. So Bayer wants to bind Smith as a member of a class action (because it is only as such that a nonparty in Smith's situation can be bound) to a determination that there could not be a class action. And if the logic of that position is not immediately transparent, here is Bayer's attempt to clarify: "[U]ntil the moment when class certification was denied, the *McCollins* case *was* a properly conducted class action." That is true, according to Bayer, because McCollins' interests were aligned with the members of the class he proposed and he "act[ed] in a representative capacity when he sought class certification."

But wishing does not make it so. McCollins sought class certification, but he failed to obtain that result. Because the District Court found that individual issues predominated, it held that the action did not satisfy Federal Rule 23's requirements for class proceedings. In these circumstances,

[handwritten margin note: unnamed class member is not a "party" until class is certified]

we cannot say that a properly conducted class action existed at any time in the litigation. Federal Rule 23 determines what is and is not a class action in federal court, where McCollins brought his suit. So in the absence of a certification under that Rule, the precondition for binding Smith was not met. Neither a proposed class action nor a rejected class action may bind nonparties. What does have this effect is a class action approved under Rule 23. But McCollins' lawsuit was never that.

No preclusion until certified.

We made essentially these same points in *Taylor v. Sturgell* just a few Terms ago. The question there concerned the propriety of binding nonparties under a theory of "virtual representation" based on "identity of interests and some kind of relationship between parties and nonparties." 553 U.S., at 901. We rejected the theory unanimously, explaining that it "would 'recogniz[e], in effect, a common-law kind of class action.'" Such a device, we objected, would authorize preclusion "shorn of [Rule 23's] procedural protections." *Ibid.* Or as otherwise stated in the opinion: We could not allow "circumvent[ion]" of Rule 23's protections through a "virtual representation doctrine that allowed courts to 'create *de facto* class actions at will.'" We could hardly have been more clear that a "properly conducted class action," with binding effect on nonparties, can come about in federal courts in just one way—through the procedure set out in Rule 23. Bayer attempts to distinguish *Taylor* by noting that the party in the prior litigation there did not propose a class action. But we do not see why that difference matters. Yes, McCollins wished to represent a class, and made a motion to that effect. But it did not come to pass. To allow McCollins' suit to bind nonparties would be to adopt the very theory *Taylor* rejected.

Bayer's strongest argument comes not from established principles of preclusion, but instead from policy concerns relating to use of the class action device. Bayer warns that under our approach class counsel can repeatedly try to certify the same class "by the simple expedient of changing the named plaintiff in the caption of the complaint." And in this world of "serial relitigation of class certification," Bayer contends, defendants "would be forced in effect to buy litigation peace by settling."

But this form of argument flies in the face of the rule against nonparty preclusion. That rule perforce leads to relitigation of many issues, as plaintiff after plaintiff after plaintiff (none precluded by the last judgment because none a party to the last suit) tries his hand at establishing some legal principle or obtaining some grant of relief. We confronted a similar policy concern in *Taylor*, which involved litigation brought under the Freedom of Information Act (FOIA). The Government there cautioned that unless we bound nonparties a "'potentially limitless'" number of plaintiffs, perhaps coordinating with each other, could "mount a series of repetitive lawsuits" demanding the selfsame documents. But we rejected this argument, even though the payoff in a single successful FOIA suit—disclosure of documents to the public—could "trum[p]" or "subsum[e]" all prior losses, just as a single successful class certification motion could do. *In re Bridgestone/Firestone,* 333 F.3d, at 766–67. As that response suggests, our legal system generally relies on principles of *stare decisis* and comity among courts to mitigate the sometimes substantial costs of similar litigation brought by different plaintiffs. We have not thought that the right approach (except in the discrete categories of cases we have recognized) lies in binding nonparties to a judgment.

And to the extent class actions raise special problems of relitigation, Congress has provided a remedy that does not involve departing from the usual rules of preclusion. In the Class Action Fairness Act of 2005 (CAFA), Congress enabled defendants to remove to federal court any sizable class action involving minimal diversity of citizenship. Once removal takes place, Federal Rule 23 governs certification. And federal courts may consolidate multiple overlapping suits against a single defendant in one court (as the Judicial Panel on Multi–District Litigation did for the many actions involving Baycol). Finally, we would expect federal courts to apply principles of comity to each other's class certification decisions when addressing a common dispute. CAFA may be cold comfort to Bayer with respect to suits like this one beginning before its enactment. But Congress's decision to address the relitigation concerns associated with class actions through the mechanism of removal provides yet another reason for federal courts to adhere in this context to longstanding principles of preclusion.[12] And once again, that is especially so when the federal court is deciding whether to go so far as to enjoin a state proceeding. . . .

The Anti–Injunction Act prohibits the order the District Court entered here. The Act's relitigation exception authorizes injunctions only when a former federal adjudication clearly precludes a state-court decision. As we said more than 40 years ago, and have consistently maintained since that time, "[a]ny doubts . . . should be resolved in favor of permitting the state courts to proceed." *Atlantic Coast Line,* 398 U.S., at 297. Under this approach, close cases have easy answers: The federal court should not issue an injunction, and the state court should decide the preclusion question. But this case does not even strike us as close. The issues in the federal and state lawsuits differed because the relevant legal standards differed. And the mere proposal of a class in the federal action could not bind persons who were not parties there. For these reasons, the judgment of the Court of Appeals is

Reversed.

NOTES AND QUESTIONS

1. *The Parties and the Procedural History.* What was at stake in *Smith v. Bayer*? Start by mapping out the parties and the various lawsuits. The first lawsuit by the McCollins plaintiffs was filed in West Virginia state court, but the defendant then removed it to federal court where it was transferred to the pending multidistrict litigation in Minnesota. Why did the Minnesota district court deny class certification? Does a court send a message about adequate representation when it denies class certification?

Keith Smith and Shirley Sperlazza filed the second suit (the one pending before the Supreme Court in *Smith v. Bayer*) in West Virginia state court, too. Did Smith and Sperlazza know about the McCollins's earlier lawsuit? Had notice been sent out in the first suit? Smith and Sperlazza argued that they did not know about the first lawsuit and were not parties to that case. Had the Supreme Court reached the opposite decision and precluded Smith and Sperlazza from relitigating the class certification decision, would that have been defensible under *Taylor v. Sturgell*? Finally, would the Court's reasoning have been

---

[12] By the same token, nothing in our holding today forecloses legislation to modify established principles of preclusion should Congress decide that CAFA does not sufficiently prevent relitigation of class certification motions. Nor does this opinion at all address the permissibility of a change in the Federal Rules of Civil Procedure pertaining to this question. Cf. n. 7, *supra* (declining to reach Smith's due process claim).

different if the second action was filed in (or removed to) federal court under CAFA?

2.   *The Preclusion Question.* How do Smith and Sperlazza argue that they should not be precluded by the decision in the first lawsuit? Having identified the grounds that prevent the use of the preclusion doctrines, how does the Anti–Injunction Act issue arise? Notice that Bayer wants to avoid class certification, but to gain the benefits of classwide preclusion. Is it possible to have it both ways?

3.   *Relitigating the Class Certification Decision.* Before the Supreme Court decided *Smith v. Bayer*, the Seventh Circuit came out differently in *Thorogood v. Sears Roebuck & Co.*, 624 F.3d 842 (7th Cir. 2010). The named plaintiff in that case, Steven Thorogood, had obtained certification of a nationwide class suit in an Illinois federal court. The suit alleged that Sears had misled consumers about the metal used in Kenmore clothes dryers—that it had falsely labeled them as made of "stainless steel," although the drums were in fact made of a ceramic-coated "mild" steel, which might rust and thereby stain clothes. The Seventh Circuit reversed the grant of certification in what it called a "near frivolous class action." Undeterred, class counsel in the Illinois action then filed a nearly identical suit in California, albeit with a different named plaintiff and a class limited to California purchasers. After a federal district court sitting in California rejected Sears's argument that the certification decision was barred by collateral estoppel, Sears returned to Illinois federal district court to ask that any further class proceedings in federal or state court with respect to the claims at issue be enjoined.* The Seventh Circuit ordered the district court to grant the request, but the Supreme Court granted certiorari and remanded the case for reconsideration in light of *Smith v. Bayer*. In a harshly-worded opinion, the Seventh Circuit observed on remand:

> We unsay nothing we said in that opinion, and in our other opinions in this protracted litigation, in criticism of the suits and of lawyer Krislov and his co-counsel . . . ; nothing we said about the susceptibility of class action litigation to abuse; and no part of our statement that abuse of litigation is a proper ground for the issuance of an injunction under the All Writs Act . . . Without such an injunction a defendant might have to plead the defense of res judicata or collateral estoppel in a myriad of jurisdictions in order to ward off a judgment, and would be helpless against settlement extortion if a valid defense were mistakenly rejected by a trial court—a mistake we thought (and think) the district judge in California had committed. . . .
>
> The Supreme Court noted in *Smith v. Bayer Corp.* that "Bayer's strongest argument [for enjoining the . . . class action in that case] comes not from established principles of preclusion, but instead from policy concerns relating to use of the class action device." 131 S.Ct. at 2381. Indeed it's a strong argument because the policy concerns are acute, as explained at length and with many references in our previous opinions in this and other cases. But the Court rejected "this form

---

* The Anti–Injunction Act was not implicated by Sears' request in *Thorogood*. The Act has no bearing on an injunction barring further proceedings in a federal court. And, although the Seventh Circuit apparently overlooked the point, the Anti–Injunction Action Act is similarly inapplicable to an injunction barring state court proceedings that have not yet commenced. See generally, 17A Wright et. al. FEDERAL PRACTICE AND PROCEDURE § 4222.

of argument" (policy) as a justification for enjoining class action suits by class members who had never become parties because it "flies in the face of the rule against nonparty preclusion." *Id.* The Court, which not infrequently bases decision on policy concerns, for they are legitimate tools for making rules of law, could have changed the rule of nonparty preclusion but decided to stick with it, and instead listed alternatives to preclusion: stare decisis, comity, consolidation of overlapping suits by the Panel on Multidistrict Litigation (not—yet—available in the dryer saga, because [the litigation in the California federal court] is the only pending suit, as far as we know, and available when filed in a state court only if the suit is removed to federal court, as [the California] suit was), changes to the Federal Rules of Civil Procedure, and federal legislation. Sears will have to tread one or more of these paths if it wants relief from this copycat class action and perhaps more such actions to come; we can't save it.

678 F.3d 546, 550, 552 (7th Cir. 2012) (Posner. J.). Does this suggest that something more is needed than the alternatives to preclusion that the Supreme Court recommends?

The American Law Institute in its Principles of the Law of Aggregate Litigation proposes the following solution: "A judicial decision to deny aggregate treatment for a common issue or for related claims by way of a class action should raise a rebuttable presumption against the same aggregate treatment in other courts as a matter of comity." American Law Institute, PRINCIPLES OF THE LAW OF AGGREGATE LITIGATION § 2.11. How would this operate in *Thorogood*? Would the Supreme Court have reached the same decision in *Smith v. Bayer* using this approach? What does it mean to employ a "rebuttable presumption"?

(2) The Anti–Injunction Act Exceptions Applied

In *GM Pick–Up Truck* and *Smith v. Bayer*, the Third Circuit and the Supreme Court, respectively, determined that none of the exceptions to the Anti–Injunction Act applied. The materials here parse the class action situations in which courts have found an applicable exception. The first and, in many ways, most straightforward situation is when state-court litigation is filed in the face of a federal-court class judgment. A second situation concerns the pending certification in federal court of a mandatory, limited-fund class action. A third situation arises when a federal opt-out class settlement is pending approval and state-court proceedings would interfere with the federal court's consideration of the settlement. Three lower-court cases illustrate these situations, in turn.

In re Corrugated Container Antitrust Litigation
659 F.2d 1332 (5th Cir. 1981)

■ CLARK, CIRCUIT JUDGE:

This is an appeal from an order of the United States District Court for the Southern District of Texas enjoining certain of the plaintiffs in this class action from pursuing a lawsuit pending in a South Carolina state court in which these same persons are also plaintiffs and from pursuing any claims relating to this class action in any court other than the United States District Court in Texas. For the reasons stated herein, we affirm.

The litigation that is the basis of this appeal is an enormous class action in which more than fifty private treble damage actions brought on behalf of all purchasers of corrugated containers and sheets against thirty-seven manufacturers, alleging an antitrust conspiracy, were consolidated by the Judicial Panel on Multidistrict Litigation and transferred to the United States District Court for the Southern District of Texas (the multidistrict court). . . .

The South Carolina state court plaintiffs (South Carolina Plaintiffs) against whom the injunction issued are also members of the plaintiff class in the case still pending in the multidistrict court. On June 30, 1978, Three J Farms, Inc., and three other corporations filed a complaint in the Court of Common Pleas for Spartanburg County, South Carolina, (South Carolina Complaint) purporting to represent the class of all persons injured during the alleged conspiracy in the corrugated industry by actions that violated the antitrust laws of South Carolina. The same attorneys who represented the named plaintiffs in filing the South Carolina Complaint represent these parties in the multidistrict court. That complaint is similar to the Unified Complaint filed in the multidistrict case. . . . The South Carolina litigation has been stayed by agreement of the parties pending the outcome of the instant appeal.

The South Carolina Plaintiffs . . . argue that the injunction violates the federal Anti–Injunction Act. . . .

The [Anti–Injunction Act] excepts from its interdict injunctions necessary (1) to aid the court's jurisdiction and (2) to protect or effectuate its judgments. It is undisputed that the multidistrict court has jurisdiction of the class action before it. The multidistrict court perceived that the actions of the appellants in pursuing substantially similar state law claims in the South Carolina court would be a challenge to that jurisdiction. We agree. As the Supreme Court has explained, this exception to the Anti–Injunction Act means that injunctions may be issued where "necessary to prevent a state court from so interfering with a federal court's consideration or disposition of a case as to seriously impair the federal court's flexibility and authority to decide that case." *Atlantic Coastline R. R. v. Brotherhood of Locomotive Engineers*, 398 U.S. 281, 295 (1970) (dicta). This complicated antitrust action has required a great deal of the district court's time and necessitates its ability to maintain a flexible approach in resolving the various claims of the many parties. Further, the presiding judge of the Seventh Judicial Circuit, Court of Common Pleas of Spartanburg County, South Carolina, entered a temporary restraining order on October 23, 1978, enjoining the defendants in the Three J Farms suit, many of whom are also defendants in the federal multidistrict action, from "preparing, disseminating or utilizing any settlement document in connection with any action pending in any Court wherein such settlement document contains any release of any antitrust claims under the laws of the State of South Carolina without the prior approval of this Court." Such a limitation on the terms of settlement would clearly interfere with the multidistrict court's ability to dispose of the broader action pending before it.

The entry of an appealable order is generally considered a prerequisite to invocation of the relitigation or "protection of judgment" exception. The judgments involved in the multidistrict action which are sought to be protected are those approving settlements executed between the class plaintiffs and most of the defendants. They are appealable. These judgments were entered shortly after the order appealed from here. However, when the injunction order was issued, the multidistrict court had approved the settlements and the final judgments were predictable if not assured. Since such an objection would most probably be moot, the state court plaintiffs do not complain that the injunction preceded final judgment.

An exception to the general rule that a federal forum may not enjoin the prosecution of a simultaneous in personam action on the same cause of action in state court comes into play once judgment is entered. Unless the judgment is set aside on appeal, state proceedings seeking to relitigate issues covered by the federal judgment may be enjoined under the "protection" exception. . . . [T]he exception applies where the state proceeding would be precluded by res judicata. . . . [Here,] [r]es judicata would bar the South Carolina litigation. Since there are federal judgments that approve some of the settlements and that control the further litigation of the appellant's cause of action, the injunction was and is not precluded by 28 U.S.C. § 2283.

Moreover, the policies of federalism are not flouted by this injunction. In this case, the multidistrict court found that [some of the plaintiffs' attorneys] "have taken, and manifested an intention to continue to take, actions threatening this court's exercise of its proper jurisdiction and the effectuation of its judgments, by filing and threatening to file duplicative and harassing litigation in the courts of various states and by seeking therein orders disrupting the proceedings in M.D.L. 310." The appellants have not attacked the multidistrict court's characterization of the motivation behind the actions taken by these attorneys. Under these circumstances, the South Carolina court could not be offended by losing the opportunity to entertain an harassing lawsuit. . .

The order of the district court is

AFFIRMED.

NOTES AND QUESTIONS

1.   *The Strategy Behind State–Court Proceedings in the Face of a Federal Class Judgment.* What would motivate plaintiffs' counsel to file state-court litigation in the face of a federal class judgment of the sort described in *Corrugated Container*? What might the attorneys for the South Carolina plaintiffs hope to accomplish? Why might such attorneys not be satisfied with the opportunity to opt out their clients from the federal class settlement (assuming that the opt-out period remains open)?

2.   *The Effect of the "Relitigation" Exception on Class Settlements.* What practical problems would arise if the federal courts could not enjoin state-court proceedings in situations like *Corrugated Container*? In particular, what would be the effect on the value of class settlements for defendants?

3.   *The Alternative to Seeking a Federal–Court Injunction.* From the defendant's standpoint, what is so good about obtaining a federal-court injunction in a situation like *Corrugated Container*? Insofar as the federal class settlement is claim preclusive, why could the defendant not simply assert claim preclusion as a defense in the state-court proceedings? In fact, a defendant *could* do so. But what might happen then—particularly, in the sort of state that would be an attractive forum for plaintiffs to file? (You might refer back to the earlier discussion of the Seventh Circuit's opinion in *Thorogood v. Sears Roebuck & Co.* for a federal-court example.)

In re Joint Eastern and Southern District Asbestos Litigation (In re Eagle–Picher Industries, Inc.)

134 F.R.D. 32 (E.D.N.Y. 1990)

■ WEINSTEIN, DISTRICT JUDGE:

This Memorandum describes the authority of a federal court to stay proceedings in all other courts to prevent the inequitable distribution of a limited pool of assets after a "limited fund" class action has been conditionally certified in accordance with a proposed settlement agreement. . . .

II.   PROCEDURAL BACKGROUND

Eagle–Picher, a manufacturer of asbestos-containing insulation products, typifies the experiences of other asbestos manufacturers.

Some 130,000 asbestos-related personal injury and wrongful death cases have been filed against it; approximately half of these are currently pending in state and federal courts nationwide. . . . No downturn in asbestos-related claims against Eagle–Picher can be expected.

Eagle–Picher's financial condition has steadily deteriorated. Operating income—while substantial—is insufficient to pay asbestos-related claims. The company has been forced to sell a large part of its assets to raise cash for payment of these claims. Insurance coverage has been all but exhausted.

Seeking an alternative to bankruptcy, Eagle–Picher moved for certification of a class pursuant to Rule 23(b)(1)(B) of the Federal Rules of Civil Procedure. The class would consist of all persons who currently, or may at any time in the future, assert or claim to have asbestos-related personal injury or wrongful death claims against Eagle–Picher based upon exposure to its asbestos-containing products.

On August 13, 1990, at the initial hearing on Eagle–Picher's motion, the court appointed [one] Special Master to determine whether the financial assets of Eagle–Picher are so limited that payment of asbestos-related personal injury and wrongful death claims, cross-claims and third-party claims are in jeopardy and whether there is a substantial probability that the claims of earlier litigants would exhaust Eagle–Picher's assets—preventing payment to later litigants. [The court appointed a second Special Master] to review the availability of insurance coverage and related matters on August 16, 1990. . .

On October 1, 1990, in view of [the Special Masters'] findings and the entire record to date, the court determined that it was "necessary and in the best interests of the proposed class to expedite resolution of this matter to prevent further financial deterioration of Eagle–Picher and thus secure prompt and equitable payments to eligible present and future claimants." In view of the need for continuing settlement discussions, additional counsel on behalf of class members were appointed on November 19, 1990.

Appointed counsel and Eagle–Picher conducted intensive settlement negotiations during October and November of 1990. These negotiations have produced the Memorandum of Understanding of Proposed Settlement ("settlement agreement") executed by counsel for Eagle–Picher, representative counsel for future claimants and one of the representative counsel for present claimants. . .

Upon conclusion of the hearings on the status of the settlement negotiations, the court conditionally certified a class action and stayed any pending asbestos-related proceedings brought on behalf of class members.

III. LEGAL ANALYSIS

. . .

A. *Effect of Class Certification*

Conditional certification of a national mandatory class action pursuant to Rule 23(b)(1)(B) of the Federal Rules of Civil Procedure will super[s]ede all litigation against Eagle–Picher pending in federal and state forums. *See In re Federal Skywalk Cases*, 680 F.2d 1175, 1180–82 (8th Cir.), *cert. denied*, 459 U.S. 988 (1982) (certification order will enjoin prosecution of pending state court actions). . . . The effect of conditional class certification will be for all pending state and federal cases to become part of the mandatory class and cease to exist as independent cases. If the settlement agreement is approved by the court, all pending actions will be adjudicated according to the settlement's terms—saving scarce funds for distribution among all class members.

To permit pending actions against Eagle–Picher to proceed in their present form would substantially impair or impede the interests of other asbestos claimants and would significantly deplete the assets available to resolve all pending and future cases. These pending cases, if allowed to continue independently, will seriously hinder the ability of the court to evaluate the adequacy and fairness of the proposed settlement of the class action by constantly depleting Eagle–Picher's assets. The need to end this drain of Eagle–Picher's assets is especially acute in view of [the Special Masters'] limited fund findings and the rate at which new claims are being filed.

The court was informed that no cases are actually on trial. Halting present litigation will save a great deal of legal expenses. It is also efficient and reflects the growing cooperation among federal and state courts in adjudicating asbestos cases. Should any court, for special circumstances, desire to continue with scheduled trials or hearings, an application for an exception may be made.

B. *Operation of Anti–Injunction Act*

. . . The Anti–Injunction Act only prohibits a federal court from staying pending state court proceedings and does not affect a federal court's power to enjoin future state actions or any actions in other federal courts. . . . While the policy underlying the Anti–Injunction Act is avoidance of "disharmony between federal and state systems, the exception in Section 2283 reflects congressional recognition that injunctions may sometimes be necessary in order to avoid that disharmony." *Amalgamated Sugar Co. v. NL Industries*, 825 F.2d 634, 639 (2d Cir. 1987). Under the present circumstances, the power to enjoin the pending state cases falls within the "necessary in aid of jurisdiction" exception to the Anti–Injunction Act.

Courts have interpreted the "necessary in aid of jurisdiction" exception liberally "to prevent a state court from . . . interfering with a federal court's flexibility and authority" to decide the case before it. *Atlantic Coast Line R.R. v. Brotherhood of Locomotive Eng'rs*, 398 U.S. 281, 295 (1970). . . .

The Second Circuit has recognized that a stay of proceedings in state court is appropriate under the "necessary in aid of jurisdiction" exception "where a federal court is on the verge of settling a complex matter, and state court proceedings undermine its ability to achieve that objective."

Standard Microsystems Corp. v. Texas Instruments Inc., 916 F.2d 58, 60 (2d Cir. 1990). . . .

A mandatory national class action certified pursuant to Rule 23(b)(1)(B) falls squarely within the rationale of these controlling Second Circuit precedents. The court is in the process of reviewing the settlement agreement of the proposed class action encompassing all asbestos-related claims against Eagle–Picher. At this critical juncture, the court can only continue its evaluation if the assets available to settle the case remain intact. An injunction of all proceedings is necessary to implement the terms of the settlement and to protect the court's jurisdiction over the class action. . . .

The All-Writs Act empowers a federal court to issue an injunction against actions in state court "even before a federal judgment is reached. . . ." *In re Baldwin–United Corp.*, 770 F.2d 328, 335 (2d Cir. 1985). Such an injunction allows the court to protect its settlement efforts.

The court has before it a settlement agreement purporting to resolve all present and future asbestos-related claims asserted against Eagle–Picher. Conditional certification of the class is a necessary first step on the road to its possible approval and implementation. Rule 23 of the Federal Rules of Civil Procedure mandates exercise of power to maintain the status quo during the trial and appellate process. Fairness hearings, for example, must now be conducted. A stay of all proceedings must be entered now to protect Eagle–Picher's assets during these hearings—assets the settlement assumes will be available—and to ensure an equitable result for all present and future persons injured by asbestos-containing products. Thus, the rationale of *Baldwin–United* requires interpretation of the Anti–Injunction Act to permit operation of Rule 23.

The "in aid of jurisdiction" exception would also authorize a stay of state court proceedings when the "federal court's jurisdiction is *in rem* and the state court action may effectively deprive the federal court of the opportunity to adjudicate as to the *res*. . . ." *Standard Microsystems Corp. v. Texas Instruments Inc.*, 916 F.2d 58, 60 (2d Cir. 1990). . . .

Several courts have considered class action litigation analogous to *in rem* actions given their magnitude and complexity. In *Baldwin–United* the class action proceeding was "so far advanced that it was the virtual equivalent of a res over which the district judge required full control." *In re Baldwin–United Corp.*, 770 F.2d 328, 337 (2d Cir. 1985); see *Battle v. Liberty National Life Ins. Co.*, 877 F.2d 877, 882 (11th Cir. 1989) ("makes sense to consider this case, involving years of litigation and mountains of paperwork, as similar to a *res* to be administered").

It is readily apparent, in view of Special Master Frankel's report, that parallel court proceedings may produce inconsistent and inequitable results. Some judgments may be paid in full while others will receive nothing or less than full value. Under these circumstances, the *in rem* nature of the court's jurisdiction over the class action and the limited fund provides an additional ground for concluding that a stay of all existing proceedings is consistent with the Anti–Injunction Act.

Federal courts have also relied upon the "in aid of jurisdiction" exception to the Anti–Injunction Act to justify a stay of existing state proceedings in interpleader actions pursuant to Rule 22 of the Federal Rules of Civil Procedure. Interpleader is traditionally employed when two or more persons claim an interest in a fund, and the claims to the fund may exceed the total value of that fund.

Limited fund class actions closely resemble an interpleader action. In light of the severely limited assets of Eagle–Picher, the class members here are virtually identical to interpleader claimants. The class members, like interpleader claimants, must recover from Eagle–Picher's limited assets or not recover at all.

Given the similarity of the present class action to an interpleader action, a stay of state proceedings would be warranted under the "necessary in aid of jurisdiction" exception. Only by staying all other proceedings can the class action achieve the goal of adjudicating all asbestos claims against Eagle–Picher in one action and preventing recovery from its assets in an inequitable or inconsistent manner.

Under the circumstances of this case, it seems apparent that the Anti–Injunction Act would permit certification of a mandatory class action. Nevertheless, two courts, *In re Temple (Raymark Industries)*, 851 F.2d 1269, 1272 (11th Cir. 1988) and *Waldron v. Raymark Indus., Inc.*, 124 F.R.D. 235 (N.D. Ga. 1989), have denied certification of mandatory class actions relying in part on dicta in *In re Federal Skywalk Cases*. While these cases are contrary to controlling Second Circuit precedent, they have sparked significant commentary and merit discussion.

In *Skywalk*, the Eighth Circuit vacated certification of a limited fund class action primarily on the ground that the finding of a limited fund was inadequate and unsupported as a matter of law. The Eleventh Circuit, in dicta [in its *Temple* decision cited above], construed the *Skywalk* decision as holding that the Anti–Injunction Act bars certification of a mandatory class action if state cases have been started. The district court, on remand, never reached the "in aid of jurisdiction" exception to the Anti–Injunction Act because it summarily concluded that the *Temple* dicta precluded certification of a non-opt-out class action when state cases are pending.

The *Temple* court's interpretation of *Skywalk* and its subsequent application in *Waldron*, however, ignore the fact that the basis for vacating certification in *Skywalk* was the absence of a limited fund. Without the limited fund—such as exists in the present case—as a jurisdictional predicate, a court cannot proceed with a limited fund class action as a basis for enjoining existing state actions. The "necessary in aid of jurisdiction" exception to the Anti–Injunction Act would not apply because the court is without jurisdiction to aid. Properly construed, *Skywalk* stands only for the proposition that where class certification is improper because no limited fund exists, a court cannot rely upon the "necessary in aid of jurisdiction" exception to the Anti–Injunction Act to justify a stay of existing state proceedings. . . .

NOTES AND QUESTIONS

1.   *The "Jurisdiction" that an Injunction Would "Aid."* How far does a federal court have to go in determining the viability of a federal class action so as to give rise to "jurisdiction" over that class that an injunction against state-court proceedings then would "aid"? What if there is merely a class complaint on file in the federal court—i.e., not yet any certification of the class? Does it make a difference whether that complaint seeks the certification of a mandatory or an opt-out class? If so, why? If not, then does the "jurisdiction" to be protected by the issuance of an injunction stem principally from the class certification decision, not so much from the nature of the class certified? Consider

whether CAFA changes any of your answers. Does CAFA portend a substantial expansion of injunctions "in aid of" the federal-court jurisdiction provided under that statute?

2. The Analogy to Proceedings In Rem. How far should the federal courts go in comparing class actions to proceedings *in rem*? Does the analogy extend only to mandatory, limited-fund classes? Or does it reach further, to opt-out or other non-opt out classes? Can you come up with an argument that it should extend to properly certified Rule 23(b)(2) classes?

3. State–Court Injunctions of Federal Proceedings. The Anti–Injunction Act regulates only the enjoining of state proceedings by federal courts. What about the converse situation of a state court attempting to enjoin a federal proceeding? In *Donovan v. City of Dallas*, 377 U.S. 408 (1964), the Supreme Court held such an injunction to be impermissible:

> Early in the history of our country a general rule was established that state and federal courts would not interfere with or try to restrain each other's proceedings. . . . It may be that a full hearing in an appropriate court would justify a finding that the state-court judgment in favor of [the city of] Dallas in the first suit barred the issues raised in the second suit, a question as to which we express no opinion. But plaintiffs in the second suit chose to file that case in the federal court. They had a right to do this, a right which is theirs by reason of congressional enactments passed pursuant to congressional policy. And whether or not a plea of res judicata in the second suit would be good is a question for the federal court to decide. While Congress has seen fit to authorize courts of the United States to restrain state-court proceedings in some special circumstances, it has in no way relaxed the old and well-established judicially declared rule[11] that state courts are completely without power to restrain federal-court proceedings in in personam actions like the one here. And it does not matter that the prohibition here was addressed to the parties rather than to the federal court itself. . . .
>
> Petitioners being properly in the federal court had a right granted by Congress to have the court decide the issues they presented, and to appeal to the Court of Appeals from the District Court's dismissal.

377 U.S. at 412–13. State-court proceedings *in rem*, however, are among the very few exceptions to this general principle.

Carlough v. Amchem Products, Inc.

10 F.3d 189 (3d Cir. 1993)

■ MANSMANN, CIRCUIT JUDGE.

The appellants, the "*Gore* plaintiffs," are absent members of a purported federal plaintiff class in an action brought pursuant to Federal Rule of Civil Procedure 23(b)(3) for asbestos-related tort damages in the United States District Court for the Eastern District of Pennsylvania. [The federal

---

[11] See, e.g., *United States ex rel. v. Council of Keokuk*, 6 Wall. 514, 517; *Weber v. Lee County*, 6 Wall. 210; *Riggs v. Johnson County*, 6 Wall. 166, 194–96; *M'Kim v. Voorhies*, 7 Cranch 279.

class action here is the same one ultimately decertified by the Supreme Court in *Amchem Products, Inc. v. Windsor*—Ed.] Simultaneously with the federal class action, but prior to the establishment of an opt out period in the federal suit, the *Gore* plaintiffs initiated a class action in the State Circuit Court of Monongalia County, West Virginia, against the same defendants named in the federal class action. The federal district court issued a preliminary injunction pursuant to the Anti–Injunction Act and the All–Writs Act, enjoining the *Gore* plaintiffs from prosecuting their state claims on the ground that the injunction was "necessary in aid" of the federal court's jurisdiction. The *Gore* plaintiffs appeal that injunction. . . .

The appellees, numerous asbestos producers jointly represented by the Center For Claims Resolution (the "CCR") and named as defendants in both actions, assert that the district court may consider the merits of the proposed settlement agreement filed simultaneously with the federal class action complaint before the state court entertains the *Gore* plaintiffs' request for declaratory judgment, when such a declaration allegedly would threaten to undermine the district court's oversight of the settlement. . . .

I.

A.

. . . [The *Gore* class action in West Virginia state court] names the same CCR defendants as in the [*Amchem*] federal class action, was commenced prior to the impending "opt out" period of the federal action . . . , and seeks as relief a declaration that the proposed [*Amchem*] settlement is unenforceable and not entitled to full faith and credit in the West Virginia courts and is not binding on members of the purported West Virginia class. It further seeks a declaration that the *Gore* plaintiffs are adequate representatives of the purported West Virginia class and are authorized to "opt out" of the purported federal class in [*Amchem*] on behalf of the entire West Virginia class. Finally, the *Gore* action seeks compensatory damages for each member of the West Virginia class for injury caused by the defendants' conduct in violation of West Virginia law, as well as punitive damages. The class of persons defined in the West Virginia suit parallels that defined in the federal [*Amchem*] suit, except that the West Virginia class is limited to persons whose claims are based on asbestos exposure occurring in West Virginia and is further limited to persons "who do not presently have a diagnosed medical condition related to asbestos." . . .

IV.

. . . [W]e turn now to the . . . question of the propriety of the court's application of the "necessary in aid" exception to the Anti–Injunction and All–Writs Acts. . . .

[S]imultaneous federal and state adjudications of the same in personam cause of action do not of themselves trigger the necessary in aid exception, and the letter and spirit of the Anti–Injunction Act and All–Writs Act counsel a restrictive application of that exception. . . .

Despite the deference paid to the independence of the state courts and principles of comity, there are instances in which courts of appeals have determined that state actions must be enjoined to allow the federal court to proceed ably with pending matters. . . .

Here the prospect of settlement was . . . imminent, as in other cases in which federal courts have issued injunctions. Additionally, as the district court found, the nature of the *Gore* suit provides further justification for the injunction. The *Gore* plaintiffs are not requesting relief strictly parallel to that sought in the federal forum. Rather than requesting damages for exposure to asbestos, the stated purpose of the *Gore* suit is to challenge the propriety of the federal class action, which the district court characterized as a preemptive strike against the viability of the federal suit, and to obtain rulings from the West Virginia state court regarding the West Virginia class members' right to opt out of the federal action. In addition, [*Amchem*] is an opt out federal class action posing no impediment to the *Gore* plaintiffs' individual exercise of their opt out right and option to commence their own respective lawsuits in the forum of their choice. Cf. *In re Real Estate Title*, 869 F.2d 760, 769 (injunction not proper where no opportunity to opt out); *In re Glenn Turner*, 521 F.2d 775, 778–79 (injunction precluded for non-class members but not precluded as against members of an opt out class where necessary to orderly and efficient federal class management). Thus, we agree with the district court findings that judicial precedent as well as the preemptive cast of the *Gore* suit and the recent establishment of the opt out period overcome the reluctant disposition of the courts to issue a necessary in aid injunction.

We hold that given the establishment of an opt out period and the *Gore* plaintiffs' ability to opt out, it is within the sound discretion of the district court to enjoin their action in state court. The *Gore* plaintiffs individually are at liberty to pursue litigation of their asbestos-related injury claims in the forum of their choice. This ability abrogates any argument of the *Gore* plaintiffs that their West Virginia rights are not adequately addressed by the federal court settlement. Injunction of that portion of the *Gore* suit seeking a ruling from the West Virginia court permitting a mass opting out of all West Virginia plaintiffs is also necessary in aid of the district court's jurisdiction. At this mature phase of the settlement proceedings and after years of pre-trial negotiation, a mass opting out of West Virginia plaintiffs clearly would be disruptive to the district court's ongoing settlement management and would jeopardize the settlement's fruition. In addition, a mass opting out presents a likelihood that the members of the West Virginia class will be confused as to their membership status in the dueling lawsuits. All members of the *Gore* class are only now receiving notice of the federal suit. A declaration by the West Virginia court at this time that all West Virginia members of the federal class are now in the West Virginia suit (and we make no comment as to the legal authority of the West Virginia court to so rule) could cause havoc. . . .

We find it difficult to imagine a more detrimental effect upon the district court's ability to effectuate the settlement of this complex and far-reaching matter than would occur if the West Virginia state court was permitted to make a determination regarding the validity of the federal settlement. Challenges that the settlement violates West Virginia law can be presented to the district court, and those plaintiffs wishing to preserve their claims for West Virginia adjudication may opt out of the federal class.

Given the concerns of the district court to finalize the settlement and given the time invested in reaching that goal, we find that the district court did not abuse its discretion in determining that the injunction should issue. . . .

NOTES AND QUESTIONS

1. *The Strategic Underpinnings of the* Gore *Class Action.* What is the strategic motivation for the *Gore* class action in West Virginia amidst the fed-

eral court's consideration of the *Amchem* class settlement? Given what you know of the *Amchem* class settlement terms from the discussion in Chapter 2, why do you suppose the *Gore* lawsuit was filed in West Virginia and, in particular, "limited to persons 'who do not presently have a diagnosed medical condition related to asbestos' "? Why, as a strategic matter, was the opportunity eventually to opt out of the federal *Amchem* class settlement not satisfactory to the would-be counsel for the West Virginia class in *Gore*?

2.   *Comparison to* Corrugated Container. Why couldn't the federal court in *Carlough* enjoin the *Gore* litigation in West Virginia state court on the same basis as its counterpart enjoined the South Carolina state-court litigation in *Corrugated Container*?

3.   *The Relationship of the Injunction to the Opportunity to Opt Out.* In *Carlough*, the Third Circuit emphasizes that the West Virginia plaintiffs in *Gore* remained free to opt out of the *Amchem* class settlement. Recall that the *Amchem* class complaint was filed in federal court simultaneously with a proposed class settlement, such that class members could consider the settlement terms in the course of deciding whether to opt out. But what should happen in a more typical Rule 23(b)(3) situation? Specifically, suppose that the class complaint is filed in federal court, actual adversarial litigation (e.g., discovery) takes place for some time thereafter, the federal court certifies the class under Rule 23(b)(3) and affords class members the opportunity to opt out, the opt-out period ends, and then the parties reach a class settlement agreement that they present to the federal court for approval. At that point, could the federal court enjoin a state-court lawsuit brought by one or more of the absent members of the federal class? To rephrase the question: Does the application of the "in aid of its jurisdiction" exception turn on the availability of an opportunity for those who are the subject of the state-court action to opt out of the federal class? Does it turn on whether the federal class at least has been certified?

Note, again, that the cases presented here on the exceptions to the Anti–Injunction Act all arose pre-CAFA. The courts have yet to consider in depth the interplay between the two statutes. Does CAFA change the landscape for federal-court injunctions, especially for injunctions "in aid of [the federal court's] jurisdiction"? What if a class action is removed to federal court pursuant to CAFA and then, prior to any decision on class certification by the federal court, a state-court lawsuit is filed? Can the federal court enjoin that state-court lawsuit? Or, again, does it matter whether the federal court at least has certified the class?

Is the proper focal point what the federal court has done, or should it concern what the state court has done? Would the logic of *Carlough* support an injunction in the following situation: A state court certifies an opt-out class action under its applicable state procedural rule and accordingly provides notice to the class members. After the state-court class certification, the defendant purports to settle the underlying claims of the class members, but by way of a parallel opt-out class action in federal court. The proposed class settlement thus is "on the table" in the federal court, along with a motion seeking class certification simply for the purpose of settlement. Does *Carlough* mean that the federal court may enjoin the *already-certified* state-court class action? The law of the Anti–Injunction Act aside, would such injunctive power raise practical concerns?

(3) Federal-on-Federal Injunctive Power and MDL Consolidation

The Anti–Injunction Act regulates only a federal-court injunction of state proceedings. Can a federal court enjoin another federal court in the class-action context? Given the existence of the MDL Panel to consolidate related litigation within the federal system, how could such a federal-on-federal injunctive scenario arise at all?

Consider three examples. First, think back to *Thorogood v. Sears*, 678 F.3d 546 (7th Cir. 2012), where plaintiffs' counsel filed a second class action in California state court (which was then removed to California federal court) after the Seventh Circuit decertified an earlier, nearly identical action in Illinois. Although Sears pleaded collateral estoppel in the California case, the district judge denied the subsequent motion. The Seventh Circuit then ordered the Illinois federal district court to enjoin class counsel and class members from proceeding with the California class action, a move that it later reversed after the Supreme Court's opinion in *Smith v. Bayer*.

Second, in *Smentek v. Dart*, 683 F.3d 373 (7th Cir. 2012), the Seventh Circuit examined some of the means "besides preclusion" suggested by *Smith v. Bayer* for limiting "copycat class action litigation" in the context of a § 1983 claim brought by former inmates of Cook County Jail. This action was the third lawsuit and third request (though each by a different former inmate) to certify a class of former inmates who requested but did not receive timely dental treatment while in jail. The first two judges denied class certification, but the third reversed her ruling that the plaintiff was collaterally estopped from relitigating the class-certification question after *Smith v. Bayer*. As Judge Posner explained, "We don't understand why all three cases were not assigned to the same judge." *Id.* at 375. Nevertheless, the court was thus tasked with interpreting the Supreme Court's remark in *Smith v. Bayer* that "we would expect federal courts to apply principles of comity to each other's class certification decisions when addressing a common dispute." 131 S.Ct. 2368, 2382 (2011). Finding that comity did nothing to alleviate the situation, the court observed, "Without a rule of preclusion, class action lawyers can do what the lawyer here (and the lawyer in *Thorogood*) did: keep bringing identical class actions with new class representatives until they draw a judge who is willing to certify the class." *Smentek*, 683 F.3d at 376–77. Judge Posner concluded:

> We are left with the weak notion of "comity" as requiring a court to pay respectful attention to the decision of another judge in a materially identical case, but no more than that even if it is a judge of the same court or a judge of a different court within the same judiciary. We emphasize, however, the qualification in "materially identical." Even two class actions involving the same class may differ materially, for example in the suitability of the class representative or the adequacy of class counsel, and where they do the judge in the second, or third, or nth class action is on his own. This is not such a case. . . .

Id. at 377. What, if anything, is the solution to the "judge-shopping problem" that the Seventh Circuit identifies?

Finally, *Grider v. Keystone Health Plan Central, Inc.*, 500 F.3d 322 (3d Cir. 2007), provides a third example of a federal injunction barring parties from proceeding in another federal court. *Grider* consisted of a certified class action in the United States District Court for the Eastern District of Pennsylvania. The plaintiff class included "approximately 6,000 doctors in

Central Pennsylvania who were [health care] providers with the Keystone health maintenance organization . . . , which operates exclusively in Central Pennsylvania." *Id.* at 324. Along much the same lines already familiar to you from the massive class litigation against the managed care industry in *Klay v. Humana, Inc.* (featured in Chapter 2 in connection with Rule 23(b)(3)), the plaintiff class of doctors in *Grider* challenged two aspects of Keystone's reimbursement process. The first aspect concerned Keystone's reimbursement of doctors on a fee-for-service basis and sounded themes on the merits similar to those in *Klay*—e.g., alleged "bundling" and "downcoding" of claims to lessen the reimbursement provided. A second aspect concerned additional reimbursement due under "capitation" arrangements, whereby doctors are paid on a per-capita basis for providing care to groups of patients, all of whom work for the same large employer.

Not surprisingly, a motion was filed to consolidate the *Grider* class action with the many similar lawsuits against the managed care industry consolidated by the MDL Panel in the United States District Court for the Southern District of Florida—the proceedings that ultimately yielded the *Klay* class. The MDL Panel, however, declined to consolidate *Grider* with the other managed care cases, explaining that:

> while *Grider* shares some questions of fact with actions in this litigation previously centralized in the Southern District of Florida, inclusion of *Grider* in MDL . . . proceedings in the Southern District of Florida will not necessarily serve the convenience of the parties and witnesses and promote the just and efficient conduct of this litigation. We point out that *Grider* is nearly three years old with a discovery cutoff date of less than five months away. Moreover, alternatives to Section 1407 transfer exist that can minimize whatever possibilities there might be of duplicate discovery, inconsistent pretrial rulings, or both.

Id. at 326 (quoting MDL order denying transfer). In the Southern District of Florida—i.e., the MDL transferee court—settlement efforts ultimately yielded a deal that would encompass the claims in *Grider*. Upon learning of the pendency of such a proposed class settlement, class counsel in *Grider* persuaded the district court for the Eastern District of Pennsylvania to enjoin the settlement of the *Grider* claims in the Southern District of Florida. On appeal, however, the Third Circuit reversed the injunction barring the "parties from participating in or reaching a bona fide settlement in another federal court":

> [T]he lack of cases in which the All Writs Act has been used to enjoin settlement efforts in another federal court is telling. It is clear that the Act is generally used to prohibit activities in another court that threaten to undermine a pending settlement in the enjoining court. . . . When the Act has been used to *block* settlement efforts in another court, it is typically because a party was deliberately using that forum to circumvent a pending settlement agreement in the enjoining court. . . .

> Based on the limited precedent in this area, there does not appear to be any basis for the injunction in this case. Although significant resources have been invested in the *Grider* litigation to this point, there is simply no support for the proposition that a court may enjoin parties from participating in or reaching a bona fide settlement in another federal court that may dispose of claims before it—particularly when there is no pending settlement in the

enjoining court and the other federal court is an MDL court charged with attempting to reach a global settlement.

First, . . . there is no evidence of any collusion or wrongdoing by the *Grider* Defendants. Rather, there is a consolidated MDL in Florida that appears to have reached a settlement on claims similar to the ones in *Grider* after court-ordered mediation. . . .

Second, "[a]n injunction under the All Writs Act invokes the equitable power of the court; thus, as is similarly the case for traditional injunctions, a court may not issue an injunction under the All Writs Act if adequate remedies at law are available." *[Alabama v.] U.S. Army Corps of Eng'rs*, 424 F.3d [1117, 1132 (11th Cir. 2005). . . . Under this standard, the general rule is that "if a party will have opportunity to raise its claims in the concurrent federal proceeding sought to be enjoined, that concurrent proceeding is deemed to provide an adequate remedy at law." *Id.*. . .

Here, that adequate remedy at law is Federal Rule of Civil Procedure 23(e). . . . To the extent that the actual proposed settlement . . . affects the *Grider* class members unfairly, those class members may object, and Judge Moreno [for the Southern District of Florida] can deal with the objections. . . .

The Appellees have not explained why Rule 23(e) is not an adequate remedy at law that would militate against injunctive relief under the All Writs Act. They have argued instead that they cannot avail themselves of the protections of Rule 23(e) because they are not members of the [MDL settlement] class. But if it is true that the *Grider* class members are not members of the . . . settlement class, any settlement reached [there] would not affect the *Grider* case at all because the *Grider* class members would not have to sign a release of claims. Under these circumstances, there would be no need for an injunction.

This is not to say that there are not valid concerns with allowing the *Grider* Defendants to proceed with the Florida settlement discussions, even though there is no evidence of collusion to this point. Although everyone involved in this case admits there is overlap between the claims in *Grider* and the claims [before the MDL transferee court], there are aspects of the *Grider* claims that are not at issue [there]. Primarily, the [MDL] claims do not cover the Defendants' behavior with respect to capitation payments that is at issue in *Grider*. Rather, [the proceeding in the MDL transferee court] is limited to the Defendants' procedures for paying fee-for-service reimbursements. In addition, the relevant dates of the class periods differ. In *Grider*, the class includes anyone who rendered services from January 1, 1996 through October 5, 2001, whereas the [MDL] settlement class period is from May 22, 1999 through the date when the settlement is preliminarily approved. But any fear that the Defendants may use future settlement discussions in Florida to release themselves from liability without ever having to answer for certain claims that are unique to the *Grider* litigation is assuaged by the protections contained in Rule 23(e).

Finally, our conclusion that the injunction issued by the District Court was an abuse of discretion is buttressed by the fact that the court it sought to enjoin is the site of a multidistrict consolidation on the matters at issue in *Grider*. The very purpose of such a consolidation is to conserve judicial resources by resolving as many claims as possible. Thus, although the *Grider* case itself is not part of the MDL, to the extent that the MDL court can achieve a global settlement that appropriately and fairly deals with a range of claims, other federal courts should be willing to let it do so absent some indication of collusion.

Id. at 330–33.

Is *Grider* rightly decided? Is the result the natural and sensible implication of the general notion that mere parallel litigation in multiple fora is no basis for an injunction of one forum by another? Should one be concerned by the recognition that the *Grider* class claims could not have been tried in the MDL transferee court? Does that feature distinguish the *Grider* class claims from the vast majority of cases consolidated in the MDL transferee court? (Recall here the holding in *Lexecon* and the related practical concerns raised by Judge Young in *DeLaventura*.)

Is Rule 23(e) review in the MDL transferee court really an adequate remedy at law, such as to make the discretionary, equitable remedy of an injunction inappropriate? Would the *Grider* class members be able to object in the MDL transferee court?

Would an injunction effectively have gutted the MDL Panel's decision not to transfer *Grider* so as to join the other managed care litigation in the Southern District of Florida for pre-trial proceedings? Or do the injunction proceedings actually suggest that the MDL Panel erred in declining to exercise its discretion to transfer *Grider*?

CHAPTER 4

CLASS SETTLEMENT REVIEW AND DESIGN

The vast majority of class actions not resolved by dispositive motion result in settlements, not trials. Thomas E. Willging et al., *An Empirical Analysis of Rule 23 to Address the Rulemaking Challenges*, 71 N.Y.U. L. Rev. 74, 143 (1996). The recognition that settlement plays such a significant role in class action lawsuits hardly sets those suits apart from civil litigation along more conventional lines, in which rates of settlement also are extremely high. The class action does stand apart, however, in its requirement of judicial approval for any class settlement. Settlements of ordinary civil lawsuits generally need not be approved by the court.

This Chapter examines the constellation of issues surrounding the review, enforcement, and design of class settlements. Section A considers class settlement review in its most obvious form: direct review, initially by the trial-level court and then on direct appeal. Section B examines the debate over collateral attacks on class settlements—that is, efforts to challenge the binding effect of a class settlement not upon direct review but, instead, through the bringing of another lawsuit. Sections C and D turn to questions of class settlement design, discussing, respectively, the design of opt-out class settlements to discourage class members from actually exercising their right to opt out and the applicability of cy pres principles to the allocation of class funds. Section E speaks to the handling of conflicts between the class and class counsel with regard to the merits of a settlement.

A. DIRECT REVIEW OF CLASS SETTLEMENTS UNDER RULE 23(e)

As originally enacted in 1966, Rule 23(e) provided simply that: "A class action shall not be dismissed or compromised without the approval of the court, and notice of the proposed dismissal or compromise shall be given to all members of the class in such manner as the court directs." The 2003 amendments to Rule 23 elaborate upon the basic requirement of judicial approval for class settlements by writing into the rule text widely-followed judicial practices with regard to the original version of subsection (e). The restyling of the rule in 2007 effected some renumbering of the subsections from their 2003 form.

Subsection (e)(2), for example, provides that: "If the proposal would bind class members, the court may approve it only after a hearing and on finding that it is fair, reasonable, and adequate." As the advisory committee observes, such hearings were "already common practice." Likewise, the substantive standard for settlement approval—a finding that the settlement is "fair, reasonable, and adequate"—builds upon judicial precedents under the original subsection (e).

Subsection (e)(3) provides that: "The parties seeking approval must file a statement identifying any agreement made in connection with the proposal." The advisory committee explains that this provision "aims . . . at related undertakings that, although seemingly separate, may have influenced the terms of the settlement by trading away possible advantages for the class in return for advantages for others." What sorts of advantages might those be? Here, recall the discussion of *Amchem* and *Ortiz* in Chapter 2.

Perhaps the most notable addition made as part of the 2003 amendments to subsection (e) comes in what is now numbered as subsection (e)(4), which provides that: "If the class action was previously certified under Rule 23(b)(3), the court may refuse to approve a settlement unless it affords a new opportunity to request exclusion to individual class members who had an earlier opportunity to request exclusion but did not do so." The advisory committee explains that:

> Often there is an opportunity to opt out at th[e] point [that a settlement is reached] because the class is certified and settlement is reached in circumstances that lead to simultaneous notice of certification and notice of settlement. In these cases, the basic opportunity to elect exclusion applies without further complication. In some cases, particularly if settlement appears imminent at the time of certification, it may be possible to achieve equivalent protection by deferring notice and the opportunity to elect exclusion until actual settlement terms are known. This approach avoids the cost and potential confusion of providing two notices and makes the single notice more meaningful. But notice should not be delayed unduly after certification in the hope of settlement.

> [Rule 23(e)(4)] authorizes the court to refuse to approve a settlement unless the settlement affords a new opportunity to elect exclusion in a case that settles after a certification decision if the earlier opportunity to elect exclusion provided with the certification notice has expired by the time of the settlement notice. A decision to remain in the class is likely to be more carefully considered and is better informed when settlement terms are known.

> The opportunity to request exclusion from a proposed settlement is limited to members of a (b)(3) class. Exclusion may be requested only by individual class members; no class member may purport to opt out other class members by way of another class action.

> The decision whether to approve a settlement that does not allow a new opportunity to elect exclusion is confided to the court's discretion. The court may make this decision before directing notice to the class under [Rule 23(e)(1)] or after the [Rule 23(e)(2)] hearing. Many factors may influence the court's decision. Among these are changes in the information available to class members since expiration of the first opportunity to request exclusion, and the nature of the individual class members' claims.

> The terms set for permitting a new opportunity to elect exclusion from the proposed settlement of a Rule 23(b)(3) class action may address concerns of potential misuse. The court might direct, for example, that class members who elect exclusion are bound by rulings on the merits made before the settlement was proposed for approval. Still other terms or conditions may be appropriate.

The advisory committee's specification that "no class member may purport to opt out other class members by way of another class action" is consistent with earlier case law rejecting the possibility of what one might call a mass class opt out—that is, an effort to opt out the members of a class action in court X by virtue of their membership in a rival class action brought in court Y. E.g., *Carlough v. Amchem Prod., Inc.*, 10 F.3d 189, 204 (3d Cir. 1993) (discussed in Chapter 3 with regard to the Anti–Injunction Act).

Finally, what is now subsection (e)(5) requires judicial approval for the withdrawal of an objection to a class settlement. As the advisory committee notes:

> Review follows automatically if the objections are withdrawn on terms that lead to modification of the settlement with the class. Review also is required if the objector formally withdraws the objections. If the objector simply abandons pursuit of the objection, the court may inquire into the circumstances.

In addition to the 2003 amendments to Rule 23, CAFA also speaks to class settlements. CAFA provides that:

> Not later than 10 days after a proposed settlement of a class action is filed in court, each defendant that is participating in the proposed settlement shall serve upon the appropriate State official of each State in which a class member resides and the appropriate Federal official, a notice of the proposed settlement. . . .

28 U.S.C. § 1715(b). The idea is to enhance the potential for regulatory officials to comment on the fairness of a proposed class settlement—for example, by filing amicus briefs with the reviewing court. The "appropriate Federal official" usually will be the Attorney General of the United States. *Id.* § 1715(a)(1)(A). The "appropriate State official of each State" is defined to mean "the person in the State who has the primary regulatory or supervisory responsibility with respect to the defendant, or who licenses or otherwise authorizes the defendant to conduct business in the State, if some or all of the matters alleged in the class action are subject to regulation by that person. If there is no primary regulator, supervisor, or licensing authority, or the matters alleged in the class action are not subject to regulation or supervision by that person, then the appropriate State official shall be the State attorney general." *Id.* § 1715(a)(2). See Catherine M. Sharkey, *CAFA Settlement Notice Provisions: Optimal Regulatory Policy?*, 156 U. Pa. L. Rev. 1971 (2008).

1. STANDARD OF REVIEW

To say that the reviewing court should approve a class settlement if it is "fair, reasonable, and adequate" is still to leave open fundamental questions about the institutional posture of the court under subsection (e). One influential statement of the court's institutional role in settlement review comes in the case that follows.

Reynolds v. Beneficial National Bank

288 F.3d 277 (7th Cir. 2002)

■ POSNER, CIRCUIT JUDGE.

We have consolidated for decision a number of appeals from orders by the district court approving a settlement of consumer-finance class action litigation, denying petitions to intervene, and awarding attorneys' fees. . . . The principal issue presented by these appeals is whether the district judge discharged the judicial duty to protect the members of a class in class action litigation from lawyers for the class who may, in derogation of their professional and fiduciary obligations, place their pecuniary self-interest ahead of that of the class. This problem, repeatedly remarked by judges and scholars, requires district judges to exercise the highest degree of vigilance in scrutinizing proposed settlements of class actions. We and other courts have gone so far as to term the district judge in the settlement phase of a class action suit a fiduciary of the class, who is subject therefore to the high duty of care that the law requires of fiduciaries. *Culver v. City of Milwaukee,* 277 F.3d at 915; *Stewart v. General Motors Corp.,* 756 F.2d 1285, 1293 (7th Cir. 1985); *In re Cendant Corp. Litigation,* 264 F.3d 201, 231 (3d Cir. 2001); *Grant v. Bethlehem Steel Corp.,* 823 F.2d 20, 22 (2d Cir. 1987).

[margin handwriting: Judges must exercise Highest Degree of scrutiny.]

We do not know whether the $25 million settlement that the district judge approved is a reasonable amount given the risk and likely return to the class of continued litigation; we do not have sufficient information to make a judgment on that question. What we do know is that . . . the judge did not give the issue of the settlement's adequacy the care that it deserved.

This litigation arose out of refund anticipation loans made jointly by the two principal defendants, Beneficial National Bank and H & R Block, the tax preparer. When H & R Block files a refund claim with the Internal Revenue Service on behalf of one of its customers, the customer can expect to receive the refund within a few weeks unless the IRS decides to scrutinize the return for one reason or another. But even a few weeks is too long for the most necessitous taxpayers, and so Beneficial through Block offers to lend the customer the amount of the refund for the period between the filing of the claim and the receipt of the refund. The annual interest rate on such a loan will often exceed 100 percent—easily a quarter of the refund, even though the loan may be outstanding for only a few days. Block arranges the loan but Beneficial puts up the money for it. Not disclosed to the customer is the fact that Beneficial pays Block a fee for arranging the loan and also that Block owns part of the loan.

Beginning in 1990, more than twenty class actions were brought against the defendants on behalf of the refund anticipation borrowers. The suits charged a variety of violations of state and federal consumer-finance laws and also breach of fiduciary duty under state law. . . . The most damaging charge appears to be that Block's customers are led to believe that Block is acting as their agent or fiduciary, much as if they had hired a lawyer or accountant to prepare their income tax returns, as affluent people do, whereas Block is, without disclosure to them, engaged in self-dealing.

Most of the suits failed on one ground or another; none has resulted in a final judgment against Beneficial or Block. But in the late 1990s several withstood motions to dismiss or motions for summary judgment, and at least one, a Texas suit, was slated for trial.

On September 3, 1997, two lawyers who had prosecuted two of the unsuccessful class actions, Howard Prossnitz and Francine Schwartz, had lunch in Chicago with Burt Rublin, who was and remains Beneficial's lead lawyer in defending against the class-action avalanche. Prossnitz and Schwartz brought with them to the lunch another lawyer, Daniel Harris. Although neither Prossnitz nor Schwartz, nor their friend Harris, had a pending suit against Beneficial (or against Block, which was not represented at the lunch), they discussed "a global RAL settlement" with Rublin. It is doubtful whether Prossnitz or Schwartz even had a client at this time; and certainly Harris did not. Schwartz later "bought" a client from another lawyer, to whom she promised a $100,000 referral fee. The necessity for such a transaction, when the class contains 17 million members, eludes our understanding.

In the hearing before the district judge on the adequacy of the settlement (the "fairness hearing," as it is called), Harris testified that at the lunch Rublin "'threw out' a number, for purposes of illustration, of $24 or $25 million." The judge described this testimony (which he elsewhere describes as "Harris believes he heard Rublin say the case was worth $23 or $24 million"), though it is vociferously denied by Rublin, as "credible." There was, however, no actual settlement negotiation at the lunch.

Prossnitz, Schwartz, and Harris, all solo practitioners, brought a substantial law firm, Miller Faucher and Cafferty LLP, into the picture. In April of the following year the foursome filed two class action suits against Beneficial similar to the others that had been filed and that were (those that hadn't flopped) wending their way through the courts of various states. One of the two suits filed also named as defendants H & R Block and three affiliated Block entities, but three of those, including Block itself, were voluntarily dismissed from the suit by the plaintiffs in October 1998 and the fourth was dismissed in February 1999. Shortly after the suits were filed, Harris made a settlement offer to Beneficial that was rejected, but after a hiatus negotiations began. Block was included in the settlement negotiations, despite the fact that there were by then no claims pending against it. It was included because Beneficial was reluctant to settle without Block, having promised to indemnify it for any liability resulting from Block's role in Beneficial's refund anticipation loans.

In October of 1999, a class jointly represented by the three solo practitioners and the Miller firm (we'll call these the "settlement class lawyers"), plus Beneficial and Block, entered into a settlement agreement which they submitted to the district court for its approval. The agreement contemplated the filing of an amended complaint naming H & R Block as a defendant, and by its terms covered claims against five Block entities, of which four were the entities originally named but subsequently dismissed as defendants in one of the two original class action complaints. The agreement defined the class as all persons who had obtained refund anticipation loans from Beneficial between January 1, 1987, and October 26, 1999, and provided for the release of all claims "arising out of or in any way relating to the tax refund anticipation loans ('RALs,' sometimes erroneously referred to as 'Rapid Refunds') obtained by the Class at any time up to and through" that date. The defendants agreed to create a fund of $25 million against which members of the class could file a claim not to exceed $15. Any money left in the fund after the expiration of the period for filing claims was to revert to the defendants, who also agreed to injunctive relief in the form of certain required disclosures to future customers, primarily of the financial arrangements between Beneficial and Block, and to bear the cost of notice to class members and of the class counsel's legal fees out of their own pockets rather than out of the settlement fund. One RAL class action, the *Basile* suit pending in the Pennsylvania courts, was excluded from the agreement, apparently because Block thought it could get the supreme court of that state to reverse a lower court decision that had gone against the company. Beneficial and Block agreed to split the expense of the settlement 50–50.

The district judge approved the settlement except for the reversion and the $15 cap, which at his insistence the parties raised to $30 for those members of the class (apparently the vast majority) who had received two or more tax refund anticipation loans from Block. With these changes the settlement was approved and notices mailed to 17 million persons—most of whom ignored them; several million of the notices, moreover, were undeliverable, presumably because the addressees had moved and left no forwarding address. Only 1 million of the recipients filed claims, which would be enough, however, to exhaust the settlement fund. Only about 6,000 of the recipients opted out of the class action so that they could seek additional relief against the defendants. . . .

In finding that $25 million was an adequate settlement, the judge relied in part on an unsworn report by James Adler, an accountant who purported to estimate the damages caused by the defendants' alleged violations of law. He was not deposed or subjected to cross-examination and the judge did not discuss the adequacy of his methodology. Adler came up with a figure of $60 million, but it is unclear whether this was intended to be an estimate of the entire damages that the class might hope to recover if the case was tried and went to judgment and what legal assumptions underpinned the estimates.

The various objectors to the settlement, primarily intervening or would-be intervening plaintiffs who have claims that the settlement will release, contend that the settlement agreement is the product of a "reverse auction," the practice whereby the defendant in a series of class actions picks the most ineffectual class lawyers to negotiate a settlement with in the hope that the district court will approve a weak settlement that will preclude other claims against the defendant. The ineffectual lawyers are happy to sell out a class they anyway can't do much for in exchange for generous attorneys' fees, and the defendants are happy to pay generous attorneys' fees since all they care about is the bottom line—the sum of the settlement and the attorneys' fees—and not the allocation of money between the two categories of expense. The defendants agreed to pay attorneys' fees in this case, to the three solo practitioners and the law firm that negotiated the settlement, of up to $4.25 million.

Although there is no proof that the settlement was actually collusive in the reverse-auction sense, the circumstances demanded closer scrutiny than the district judge gave it. He painted with too broad a brush, substituting intuition for the evidence and careful analysis that a case of this magnitude, and a settlement proposal of such questionable antecedents and circumstances, required. The initial agreement submitted for the judge's approval, remember, had provided for a reversion and also capped each class member's recovery at $15. If the parties had an inkling that only 1 million class members would file claims, they were agreeing to a settlement worth only $15 million, and probably less; for if 1 million class members filed claims capped at $30, fewer would have filed claims capped at $15. Yet according to a credibility determination by the district judge that we are not in a position to second guess, two and half years earlier, *before* RAL plaintiffs began having some success in the courts, Beneficial's counsel had indicated that $23 to $25 million were ballpark figures for a settlement with Beneficial alone. Beneficial's share of a $15 million settlement in which Block was a codefendant would be only $7.5 million (remember that Beneficial and Block agreed to split the cost of the settlement 50–50)—yet that is the settlement the lawyers for the settlement class agreed to, plus injunctive relief the value of which no one has attempted to monetize and which is barely discussed in the briefs or by the judge. The injunctive relief signally does not include a requirement that H & R Block disclose its interest in Beneficial's refund anticipation loans.

Moreover, H & R Block appears to have faced substantial exposure in a Texas class action in which it was accused of breach of fiduciary obligations to its customers. The class in that suit was seeking disgorgement of all the fees paid to Block by the banks that made refund anticipation loans through it. The class argued that such a forfeiture was mandatory if Block was found to have violated its fiduciary duties. Disgorgement was also sought of all other fees that Block had received "in connection with each RAL transaction"—that is, the tax-preparation and electronic-filing fees that Block had charged its RAL customers to file their taxes for them—a form of relief that the class claimed was within the trial court's equitable discretion. The total amount sought could have reached $2 billion. The class had been certified, the case was proceeding in the Texas courts, and the theory of liability and damages could not be dismissed as frivolous; indeed, the case had been set for trial. Even if the class had only a 1 percent chance of prevailing, the expected value of its suit might reach $20 million. (This is on the unrealistic assumption that the only possible outcomes were a $2 billion judgment and a zero judgment. Realistic intermediate possibilities would make the $20 million estimate expand.)

Remarkably in view of the progress and promise of the Texas suit relative to the half-hearted efforts of the settlement class counsel, the district judge enjoined the Texas suit on the authority of the All Writs Act, 28 U.S.C. § 1651(a), reasoning that the suit might upend the settlement. *In re VMS Securities Litigation*, 103 F.3d 1317, 1323–24 (7th Cir. 1996); *In re Agent Orange Product Liability Litigation*, 996 F.2d 1425, 1431–32 (2d Cir. 1993); *In re Baldwin–United Corp. (Single Premium Deferred Annuities Ins. Litigation)*, 770 F.2d 328, 335–38 (2d Cir. 1985). The effect of the injunction is that the settlement release, if upheld, would release the claims in the Texas suit. For this release of potentially substantial claims against H & R Block the settlement class received no consideration. In fact the settlement class received no consideration for the release of *any* claims against Block. The only effect of bringing Block into the settlement was to allow Beneficial to cut its own expense of the settlement in half. The lawyers for the settlement class were richly rewarded for negotiations that greatly diminished the cost of settlement to Beneficial from the level that it had considered to be in the ballpark years earlier when the cases were running more in its favor than when the settlement agreement was negotiated. In effect, the settlement values the Texas and all other claims against Block at zero.

The district judge enjoined the lawyers for the Texas class from notifying the members of that class of the status of the Texas litigation to assist them in deciding whether to opt out of the settlement that the settlement class counsel had negotiated with Beneficial and Block and continue to litigate in the Texas courts. The judge should not have done this, especially since opting out was likely to be the sensible course of action given the ungenerosity of the settlement to the Texas class. A pattern of withholding information likely to undermine the settlement emerged when, after approving the settlement, the district judge encouraged the solo practitioners to submit their fee applications in camera, lest the paucity of the time they had devoted to the case (for which the judge awarded them more than $2 million in attorneys' fees) be used as ammunition by objectors to the adequacy of the representation of the class. There was no sound basis for sealing the fee applications, let alone for sealing the number of hours each of the settlement class counsel had devoted to the case. The applications are not in the appellate record and we do not know what the total number of hours devoted by the class counsel to this litigation was, but apparently it was a small number. This is not surprising, since the lawyers' efforts between the filing of the complaint and the settlement negotiations were singularly feeble, illustrated by their responding to the Block defendants' motion to dismiss for lack of personal jurisdiction with a voluntary dismissal of the claims against those defendants. Their representation of the class was almost certainly inadequate, an independent reason for disapproving a settlement. *Ortiz v. Fibreboard Corp.*, 527 U.S. 815, 856 and n. 31 (1999). . . . But in addition it reinforces our concern with the adequacy of the district judge's consideration of the settlement.

The judge approved the settlement primarily because he thought the prospects for the class if the litigation continued were uncertain. They might lose in the end, or win little; and even if they won a lot, the delay in winning would make the relief eventually awarded the class worth much less in present-value terms. To most people, a dollar today is worth a great deal more than a dollar ten years from now. It is especially likely to be worth more to the members of the class in this litigation. Only a person with a very high discount rate (that is, a strong preference for present over future dollars—a preference that may reflect desperation rather than fecklessness or shortsightedness) would borrow at an astronomical interest rate in order to get a sum of money now rather than a few weeks from now.

All this is true, but in the suspicious circumstances that we have recited the judge should have made a greater effort (he made none) to quantify the net expected value of continued litigation to the class, since a settlement for less than that value would not be adequate. Determining that value would require estimating the range of possible outcomes and ascribing a probability to each point on the range, though as just noted those outcomes must be discounted to the present using a reasonable, and in this case perhaps a steep, interest rate. We say "perhaps" because even a person with a high discount rate may not care much whether he receives $15 to $30 now or in the future, since it is such a trivial amount of money even to a person who is usually strapped for funds. If, moreover, the court would award prejudgment interest in a case litigated to judgment, discounting might wash out of the picture altogether.

A high degree of precision cannot be expected in valuing a litigation, especially regarding the estimation of the probability of particular outcomes. Still, much more could have been done here without (what is obviously to be avoided) turning the fairness hearing into a trial of the merits. For example, the judge could have insisted that the parties present evidence that would enable four possible outcomes to be estimated: call them high, medium, low, and zero. High might be in the billions of dollars, medium in the hundreds of millions, low in the tens of millions. Some approximate range of percentages, reflecting the probability of obtaining each of these outcomes in a trial (more likely a series of trials), might be estimated, and so a ballpark valuation derived.

Some arbitrary figures will indicate the nature of the analysis that we are envisaging. Suppose a high recovery were estimated at $5 billion, medium at $200 million, low at $10 million. Suppose the midpoint of the percentage estimates for the probability of victory at trial was .5 percent for the high, 20 percent for the medium, and 30 percent for the low (and thus 49.5 percent for zero). Then the net expected value of the litigation, before discounting, would be $68 million; discounting, depending on an estimate of the likely duration of the litigation, would bring this figure down, though probably not to $25 million—and any discounting might be inappropriate, as we explained. These figures are arbitrary; our point is only that the judge made no effort to translate his intuitions about the strength of the plaintiffs' case, the range of possible damages, and the likely duration of the litigation if it was not settled now into numbers that would permit a responsible evaluation of the reasonableness of the settlement. . . .

All things considered, we conclude that the district judge abused his discretion in approving the settlement. . . .

NOTES AND QUESTIONS

1. *Court as Fiduciary. Reynolds* is perhaps most famous for its conception of the court in class settlement review as serving in a fiduciary capacity. As Judge Posner readily acknowledges, a similar conception also appears in other cases. To what extent does the fiduciary conception of judicial review under Rule 23(e) accurately describe the relationship between the court (the would-be fiduciary) and absent class members (the beneficiaries, to continue the fiduciary analogy)?

2. *Post–Reynolds Developments.* The Seventh Circuit continues to follow the *Reynolds* approach. See, e.g., *Williams v. Rohm and Haas Pension Plan,* 658 F.3d 629, 634 (7th Cir. 2011) (following *Reynolds* and specifically noting that a "district court must take special care in performing [an expected value] assessment when the proposed settlement evinces certain warning signs"); *Synfuel Technologies, Inc. v. DHL Express, Inc.,* 463 F.3d 646, 652–53 (7th Cir. 2006) (following *Reynolds*). However, the Ninth Circuit, while recognizing the importance of examining settlements with care, endorsed a somewhat less rigorous approach in *Rodriguez v. West Publishing Corp.,* 563 F.3d 948, 965 (9th Cir. 2009):

> This circuit has long deferred to the private consensual decision of the parties. . . . As we have emphasized,

> > the court's intrusion upon what is otherwise a private consensual agreement negotiated between the parties to a lawsuit must be limited to the extent necessary to reach a reasoned judgment that the agreement is not the product of fraud or overreaching by, or collusion between, the negotiating parties, and that the settlement, taken as a whole, is fair, reasonable and adequate to all concerned.

> [*Hanlon v. Chrysler Corp.,* 150 F.3d 1011 (9th Cir. 1998)](quoting *Officers for Justice,* 688 F.2d at 625). . . .

> We are not persuaded . . . by Objectors' further submission that the court should have specifically weighed the merits of the class's case against the settlement amount and quantified the expected value of fully litigating the matter. For this they rely on the Seventh Circuit . . . However, our approach, and the factors we identify, are somewhat different. We put a good deal of stock in the product of an arms-length, non-collusive, negotiated resolution . . . and have never

prescribed a particular formula by which that outcome must be tested. As we explained in *Officers for Justice*, "[u]ltimately, the district court's determination is nothing more than an amalgam of delicate balancing, gross approximations and rough justice."

Given the informational demands of judicial review along the lines described in *Reynolds*, is the Ninth Circuit's approach more sensible? Even if there are serious practical limits to what a judge can do—a fact that even Judge Posner recognizes—are there still benefits to a rule like the Seventh Circuit's that demands a systematic analytic approach? In the end, though, can such a review do more than catch the most egregiously unfair sorts of class settlements? Can or should procedural law aspire to anything more than that? For further discussion of the court's fiduciary role with regard to both class settlement review and class certification, see Chris Brummer, Note, *Sharpening the Sword: Class Certification, Appellate Review, and the Role of the Fiduciary Judge in Class Action Lawsuits*, 104 Colum. L. Rev. 1042 (2004).

3.   *Evaluating the Settlement.* Judge Posner takes the district judge to task for not evaluating the settlement's fairness in light of the expected value of trial and the present value of a future trial award. It is important to have a working understanding of the concepts Judge Posner employs because they are basic to any settlement analysis.

a.   *Expected Value.* Let's take a simple example. Suppose you represent the plaintiff in a medical malpractice case. The defendant has offered $750,000 to settle, and you must decide whether to accept the offer. You believe your case is moderately strong—certainly not weak, but also not a sure thing. You figure the chance of success in proving liability is greater than 50% but not as high as 70%. So you average between the two and estimate a 60% likelihood of successfully proving liability. You've also had a doctor examine your client's injuries, and you have enough experience with other cases involving similar injuries to predict that a jury is likely to award $2 million if it decides that the defendant is liable. This looks like a fairly substantial case but you still have to consider litigation costs. Even a strong case with very serious injuries might not be worth taking to trial if the cost of litigating the case is too high. Once again, you draw on your experience litigating similar cases to estimate litigation costs in this case. You figure you'll need at least one trial expert for liability and one for damages, and you also know that discovery will be costly. So you estimate the total cost of litigating the case through trial at $300,000. (For simplicity, we shall assume that the plaintiff has hired you on a fee-for-services rather than a contingency fee basis and therefore the plaintiff must pay the full cost of litigating the case, win or lose.)

How do you combine these three variables—60% chance of proving liability, $2 million award conditional on proving liability, and litigation costs of $300,000—to generate a single trial value for the case that can be compared with the $750,000 settlement offer? It would be a mistake to use the $2 million figure because there's a 40% chance that your client will be out of pocket $300,000 (i.e., win nothing but still have to pay $300,000 in litigation costs). Trial is a gamble when viewed at the time the settlement offer is made. Therefore, what we need is some way to assign a value to a gamble. We can't just choose one of the possible outcomes because other outcomes are possible, too. We need some way to combine all the outcomes into a single value. This is what expected value does.

The expected value of a gamble is the sum of all the possible outcome values, each discounted by the probability it will occur.[*] In our medical malpractice example, the gamble is a trial, and there are two possible outcomes: either the plaintiff wins, or the plaintiff loses (i.e., the defendant wins). If the plaintiff wins, she nets $1,700,000: i.e., she wins $2 million but she has to pay $300,000 in litigation costs. A loss has a negative value equal to –$300,000: i.e., the plaintiff gets nothing but she must still pay $300,000 in litigation costs. The probability of a winning outcome is 60%, and it follows that the probability of a losing outcome must be 40% (since there are only two possible outcomes and their probabilities must add up to 100%).

So we calculate the expected value of this trial gamble by adding up the two possible outcome values, each discounted by the probability that the particular outcome will occur. This gives us: 0.6 [the probability of a winning outcome] × $1,700,000 [the value of a winning outcome] + 0.4 [the probability of a losing outcome] × –$300,000 [the value of a losing outcome] = 0.6 × $1,700,000 – 0.4 × $300,000 = $900,000. Thus, you, as plaintiff's attorney, should compare this expected trial value of $900,000 with the settlement offer of $750,000. Trial is obviously more valuable than the offer, so you should reject the offer (unless your client is quite risk averse). In fact, you should reject any offer less than $900,000.

Now let's turn to Judge Posner's discussion in *Reynolds*. He applies the same expected value analysis, but in a slightly more complicated way. In the simple analysis above, we assumed that the only source of uncertainty was proof of liability; that once liability was proved, the jury would award $2 million in damages. But this is a simplification. In fact, the jury might award less than or more than $2 million and a good lawyer should be able to assign rough probabilities to different possible awards. The way to handle this complication is to assign probabilities to each of the possible trial awards and combine them with the probability of proving liability. From this perspective, an award of zero is equivalent to the plaintiff failing to prove liability, and the probability of obtaining each nonzero award is just the probability of proving liability combined with the probability of obtaining an award in that amount if liability is proven.

This is the way Judge Posner sets up his expected value analysis in *Reynolds*. He supposes that the trial judge can obtain sufficient information about probability and outcome value (and presumably cost) for four possible trial outcomes: a high jury award, a medium jury award, a low jury award, and a zero award (i.e., no liability). In his hypothetical, the high award is valued at $5 billion and the probability that a jury will award it is 0.5% (which includes the probability that a jury will find liability *coupled with* the probability that the same jury will award the amount of $5 billion if it finds liability). The medium award is valued at $200 million and its probability is 20%. The low award is valued at $10 million and its probability is 30%. And the probability of failing to prove liability—and thus of obtaining nothing—is 49.5%. (All these probabilities must add up to 100%, since Judge Posner assumes these are the only possible outcomes.) The expected value of trial without subtracting for litigation costs (Posner doesn't consider litigation costs in his calculation) is: 0.005×5 bil-

---

[*] In mathematical terms, let $w_1, w_2, \ldots, w_n$ be n possible outcomes and let $p_1, p_2, \ldots, p_n$ be the probabilities of obtaining each of these outcomes, respectively. Then the expected value of the lawsuit is equal to: $p_1 \times w_1 + p_2 \times w_2 + \ldots + p_n \times w_n$.

lion + 0.2×200 million + 0.3×10 million + 0.495×0 = $25 million + $40 million + $3 million + $0 = $68 million.

     b.   *Present Value.* Judge Posner also incorporates present value into his analysis. The concept of present value is based on the intuitively sensible proposition that a dollar paid today is worth more than a dollar paid sometime in the future. This means that one must discount the face value of money promised at some future date in order to compare it to money received today. Present value is relevant to a settlement analysis because a settlement is money received today whereas a trial award is money received at some future date (i.e., the date that the case ends). We say that money to be received in the future must be "discounted to its present value."

     The reason money received in the future is not worth as much as the same sum received today is quite straightforward. If you receive one dollar today, you can invest that dollar at the prevailing interest rate and receive one dollar plus interest in a year's time. It follows that a dollar received today is worth more in one year than a dollar received one year from now (because today's dollar will gain interest over the year). Conversely, one dollar to be received in a year's time is worth less today than a dollar received today.

     For example, suppose the interest rate is 5% and assume that interest is compounded annually. One dollar received today and invested at 5% is worth $1.05 one year from now. Moreover, all one needs is about 95 cents today to generate $1 in a year's time (because 95 cents invested at 5% will yield interest of about 5 cents, which when combined with the 95 cents gives a total of $1 next year). Therefore, one dollar promised one year from now is worth about 95 cents when it is discounted to present value. For a slightly more realistic example, suppose someone is entitled to receive $1000 in five years and suppose the prevailing interest rate is 5% compounded annually. The present value of the $1000 (i.e., the value today of $1000 to be received five years from now) is about $783.51. Again, this means that $783.51 will yield $1000 if invested at 5% for five years (compounded annually). We should note one additional complication. For people with few resources, the value of money received today is a function of much more than the interest rate. If someone needs money desperately and needs it now, the cost of waiting for it is likely to be much greater than foregone interest payments. Thus, the amount someone in dire straits discounts a dollar received in the future is likely to be greater than the discount a person would apply if all she cared about was receiving interest.

     Judge Posner says two things about present value. First, he says that someone must have a very high discount rate to be willing to pay huge interest to receive a refund a few weeks sooner. This makes sense. Suppose John Jones expects to receive a $300 refund in three weeks. If Jones is willing to accept $150 now rather than wait, it follows that $300 must be worth at most $150 to Jones when discounted to present value. Given that the discount is only for a three week period, the discount rate must be extremely high.

     Judge Posner also invokes present value in a different context. The $20 million settlement is money received now, whereas the expected trial value of $68 million is money received in the future after a possibly protracted lawsuit. Thus the $68 million must be discounted to present value. If class members have very high discount rates, it is conceivable that $68 million is worth no more than $20 million when discounted to present value. Judge Posner argues, however, that even class members in tough financial straits are not likely to

apply a high discount rate to the very small individual recoveries they are likely to receive. And the interest rate component of any discount will wash out if
the court awards prejudgment interest at market rates.

4. *Judicial Competence.* Is it realistic to ask trial judges to estimate expected values and take account of present value in the process? From what
sources can trial judges obtain the information about likely success, possible
trial verdicts, and expected litigation costs with which to evaluate the expected
value of continued litigation? When considering these questions, bear in mind
that many successful attorneys do rough expected value analysis in an intui-
tive, nonmathematical way whenever they evaluate settlements, just as our
medical malpractice attorney did in the hypothetical above. However, we expect
attorneys to know a lot more about their clients and the case than the judge
knows. Can we trust settling attorneys to be honest with the judge and present
information accurately at a fairness hearing? What can the judge do to encourage an accurate presentation?

5. *Mapping the Available Tools.* What tools are potentially available to
the court tasked with review of a proposed class settlement? Consider the menu
of options—not all of which are part of current law—suggested by Professor
William Rubenstein:

> Everyone agrees that class action lawyers must be kept in check,
> but no one knows quite how to do it. The goal is to identify procedural
> rules that will encourage plaintiffs' attorneys to file cases when indi-
> vidual litigation externalities justify representative litigation, but
> that will simultaneously discourage the agency problems—
> particularly strike suits and sell-out deals—that afflict class litiga-
> tion. The ideal mechanism would provide real supervision of class ac-
> tion attorneys without stifling their entrepreneurial instincts. During
> the past two decades, scholars have nominated a variety of candi-
> dates to serve as that ideal. These proposals generally fall into two
> categories: private market-based mechanisms meant to monitor class
> counsel throughout the proceedings and public court-focused mecha-
> nisms meant to strengthen judicial oversight at the moment of set-
> tlement. Despite the range and ingenuity of these proposals, agency
> issues persist. And their persistence bleeds over into beguiling doc-
> trinal and theoretical questions investigated in a second strain of
> class action scholarship concerning whether and when later courts
> should revisit counsel's adequacy collaterally.

> The bridge linking the agency-cost literature's concern with
> monitoring class counsel and the collateral-attack literature's concern
> about revisiting this monitoring is the peculiar juridical moment
> known as the fairness hearing. . . . [C]lass action lawsuits are trans-
> actions in which absent parties' rights to sue are traded for finality.
> But, like a same-sex couple attempting themselves to reproduce, the
> buyers and sellers of finality cannot alone produce the bartered prod-
> uct: Given that the purchase of preclusion is the key aspect of the
> deal, at the end of every class action lawsuit, of any type or any size,
> in any court in any state, under any given body of law, invariably lies
> a person named a judge—the only actor capable of providing finali-
> ty—holding a proceeding called a fairness hearing.

Nonetheless, both strands of scholarly literature have essentially given up on the judiciary's ability to provide real class action oversight; indeed the literature is largely motivated by this failure. Market-focused scholars locate monitoring outside of the judiciary and then rarely ponder what effect their proposals ought to have on the fairness hearing that will inevitably take place; it appears implicit that if the monitoring mechanism works, it does not really matter what the judge does at the end of the show, so long as she simply lowers the curtain. Court-focused scholars emphasize judicial oversight, but their proposals are therefore confined to familiar judicial mechanisms like special masters and guardian ad litem, mechanisms that inspire hopes for success akin to those with which one attends a grade school production of, say, Hamlet. The collateral-attack literature, having seen that show, looks away, vesting its hopes in the idea that the second act will be better than the first, despite the fact that the cast and stage remain largely unchanged.

Rather than averting our gaze from the first act, tempting as that may be, we should, I argue, give the inescapable fairness hearing more, not less, attention. To that end, [there are] four (more or less) new mechanisms that might assist the judge at the fairness hearing. These are:

The Devil's Advocate. When a class action settlement is proposed, the court could appoint a "devil's advocate" to argue against the reasonableness of the settlement or fee, thereby using public funds to ensure an adversarial fairness hearing.

Bonds. When a class settlement is proposed, the settling parties could be required to post a bond with the court. The bond could be utilized as security so that if the settlement failed to win approval, the bond would be forfeited; more modestly, the bond could be used to pay the attorneys' fees of objectors who brought reasonable concerns to the court's attention. Both versions utilize market incentives to monitor class counsel.

Labels. A public agency could passively require that class action settlements be labeled with a simple chart identifying their key characteristics, much like the Food and Drug Administration requires food to be labeled. Alternatively, a public agency could actively investigate, assess, and label class action settlements with a grade, like health departments rate restaurant sanitation. Or a public agent could simply review and report on the nature of the settlement, like a probation officer reports sentencing facts. Any of these approaches would help make more transparent to courts and class members the elements and quality of the settlement.

Trademarks. A private independent agency could register a certification mark, similar to the Good Housekeeping Seal of Approval, and provide that mark to class action settlements meeting its guidelines. Such a mark would, like its public counterpart, signal to class members and judges the quality of the settlement terms.

The devil's advocate and bonding ideas are, respectively, public and private adversarial approaches; the labeling and marking ideas are, respectively, public and private regulatory ideas.

Examining this new set of disparate proposals enables an assessment of the underlying question of institutional design: namely, whether adversarial or regulatory, public or private, approaches are likely to be most efficacious at identifying and curtailing problematic settlements and hence controlling class counsel. Given that at a fairness hearing a judge is charged with reviewing two distinct sets of concerns—the process by which the settlement was achieved and the content of the settlement in light of the strengths or weaknesses of the plaintiffs' claims— . . . these roles require a combination of adversarial and regulatory approaches. For review of the substance and value of the class's legal claims, adversarial presentation of issues is the preferred procedure and a judge the favored decisionmaker. For review of the settlement process, regulatory oversight is required and an administrative inquisitor the ideal agent. Thus, the proposed settlement of a class action should trigger a two-part fairness hearing, involving both judicial assessment of the value of the claims and regulatory assessment of the process of settlement.

William B. Rubenstein, *The Fairness Hearing: Adversarial and Regulatory Approaches*, 53 UCLA L. Rev. 1435, 1436–40 (2006).

2. WHO MAY SEEK APPELLATE REVIEW OF CLASS SETTLEMENT APPROVAL

Devlin v. Scardelletti

536 U.S. 1 (2002)

■ JUSTICE O'CONNOR delivered the opinion of the Court.

Petitioner, a nonnamed member of a class certified under Federal Rule of Civil Procedure 23(b)(1), sought to appeal the approval of a settlement over objections he stated at the fairness hearing. The Court of Appeals for the Fourth Circuit held that he lacked the power to bring such an appeal because he was not a named class representative and because he had not successfully moved to intervene in the litigation. We now reverse.

I

Petitioner Robert Devlin, a retired worker represented by the Transportation Communications International Union (Union), participates in a defined benefits pension plan (Plan) administered by the Union. In 1991, on the recommendation of the Plan's trustees, the Plan was amended to add a cost of living adjustment (COLA) for retired and active employees. As it turned out, however, the Plan was not able to support such a large benefits increase. To address this problem, the Plan's new trustees sought to freeze the COLA. Because they were concerned about incurring Employee Retirement Income Security Act of 1974 (ERISA) liability by eliminating the COLA for retired workers, the trustees froze the COLA only as to active employees. Because the Plan still lacked sufficient funds, the new trustees obtained an equitable decree from the United States District Court for the District of Maryland in 1995 declaring that the former trustees had breached their fiduciary duties and that ending the COLA for retired workers would not violate ERISA. Accordingly, in a 1997 amendment, the new trustees eliminated the COLA for all Plan members.

In October 1997, those trustees filed the present class action in the United States District Court for the District of Maryland, seeking a declaratory judgment that the 1997 amendment was binding on all Plan members or, alternatively, that the 1991 COLA amendment was void. Originally, petitioner was proposed as a class representative for a subclass of retired workers because of his previous involvement in the issue. He refused to become a named representative, however, preferring to bring a separate action in the United States District Court for the Southern District of New York, arguing, among other things, that the 1997 Plan amendment violated the Age Discrimination in Employment Act of 1967. The New York District Court dismissed petitioner's claim involving the 1997 amendment, which was later affirmed by the Second Circuit because:

> "The exact COLA issue that the appellants are pursuing . . . is being addressed by the district court in Maryland. . . . It seems eminently sensible that the Maryland district court should resolve fully the COLA amendment issue." *Devlin v. Transportation Communications Int'l Union*, 175 F.3d 121, 132 (C.A.2 1999).

At the time petitioner's claim was dismissed, the District Court in Maryland had already conditionally certified a class under Federal Rule of Civil Procedure 23(b)(1), dividing it into two subclasses: a subclass of active employees and a subclass of retirees. On April 20, 1999, petitioner's attorney sent a letter to the District Court informally seeking to intervene in the class action. On May 12, 1999, petitioner sent another letter repeating this request. He did not, however, formally move to intervene at that time.

Also in May, the Plan's trustees and the class representatives agreed on a settlement whereby the COLA benefits would be eliminated in exchange for the addition of other benefits. On August 27, 1999, the trustees filed a motion for preliminary approval of the settlement. On September 10, 1999, petitioner formally moved to intervene pursuant to Federal Rule of Civil Procedure 24. On November 12, 1999, the District Court denied petitioner's intervention motion as "absolutely untimely." It then heard objections to the settlement, including those advanced by petitioner, and, concluding that the settlement was fair, approved it.

Shortly thereafter, petitioner noted his appeal, challenging the District Court's dismissal of his intervention motion as well as its decision to approve the settlement. The Court of Appeals for the Fourth Circuit affirmed the District Court's denial of intervention under an abuse of discretion standard. It further held that, because petitioner was not a named representative of the class and because he had been properly denied the right to intervene, he lacked standing to challenge the fairness of the settlement on appeal.

Petitioner sought review of the Fourth Circuit's holding that he lacked the ability to appeal the District Court's approval of the settlement. We granted certiorari, 534 U.S. 1064 (2001), to resolve a disagreement among the Circuits as to whether nonnamed class members who fail to properly intervene may bring an appeal of the approval of a settlement.

II

Although the Fourth Circuit framed the issue as one of standing, 265 F.3d, at 204, we begin by clarifying that this issue does not implicate the jurisdiction of the courts under Article III of the Constitution. As a member of the retiree class, petitioner has an interest in the settlement that creates a "case or controversy" sufficient to satisfy the constitutional requirements of injury, causation, and redressability.

Nor do appeals by nonnamed class members raise the sorts of concerns that are ordinarily addressed as a matter of prudential stand-ing. . . . Because petitioner is a member of the class bound by the judgment, there is no question that he satisfies these three requirements. The legal rights he seeks to raise are his own, he belongs to a discrete class of inter-ested parties, and his complaint clearly falls within the zone of interests of the requirement that a settlement be fair to all class members. Fed. Rule Civ. Proc. 23(e).

What is at issue, instead, is whether petitioner should be considered a "party" for the purposes of appealing the approval of the settlement. We have held that "only parties to a lawsuit, or those that properly become parties, may appeal an adverse judgment." *Marino v. Ortiz*, 484 U.S. 301, 304 (1988) *(per curiam)*. Respondents argue that, because petitioner is not a named class representative and did not successfully move to intervene, he is not a party for the purposes of taking an appeal. . . .

Petitioner objected to the settlement at the District Court's fairness hearing, as nonnamed parties have been consistently allowed to do under the Federal Rules of Civil Procedure. The District Court's approval of the settlement—which binds petitioner as a member of the class—amounted to a "final decision of [petitioner's] right or claim" sufficient to trigger his right to appeal. And . . . petitioner will only be allowed to appeal that aspect of the District Court's order that affects him—the District Court's decision to disregard his objections. Petitioner's right to appeal this aspect of the Dis-trict Court's decision cannot be effectively accomplished through the named class representative—once the named parties reach a settlement that is approved over petitioner's objections, petitioner's interests by definition diverge from those of the class representative.

Marino v. Ortiz, supra, is not to the contrary. In that case, we refused to allow an appeal of a settlement by a group of white police officers who were not members of the class of minority officers that had brought a racial discrimination claim against the New York Police Department. Although the settlement affected them, the District Court's decision did not finally dispose of any right or claim they might have had because they were not members of the class.

Nor does considering nonnamed class members parties for the purpos-es of bringing an appeal conflict with any other aspect of class action proce-dure. In a related case, the Seventh Circuit has argued that nonnamed class members cannot be considered parties for the purposes of bringing an appeal because they are not considered parties for the purposes of the com-plete diversity requirement in suits under 28 U.S.C. § 1332. See *Navigant Consulting*, 275 F.3d, at 619; see also *Snyder v. Harris*, 394 U.S. 332, 340 (1969). According to the Seventh Circuit, "[c]lass members cannot have it both ways, being non-parties (so that more cases can come to federal court) but still having a party's ability to litigate independently." 275 F.3d, at 619. Nonnamed class members, however, may be parties for some purposes and not for others. The label "party" does not indicate an absolute characteris-tic, but rather a conclusion about the applicability of various procedural rules that may differ based on context.

Nonnamed class members are, for instance, parties in the sense that the filing of an action on behalf of the class tolls a statute of limitations against them. See *American Pipe & Constr. Co. v. Utah*, 414 U.S. 538 (1974). Otherwise, all class members would be forced to intervene to preserve their claims, and one of the major goals of class action litigation—to simplify litigation involving a large number of class members with similar claims—would be defeated. The rule that nonnamed class members cannot defeat complete diversity is likewise justified by the goals of class action litigation. Ease of administration of class actions would be compromised by having to consider the citizenship of all class members, many of whom may even be unknown, in determining jurisdiction. Perhaps more importantly, considering all class members for these purposes would destroy diversity in almost all class actions. Nonnamed class members are, therefore, not parties in that respect.

What is most important to this case is that nonnamed class members are parties to the proceedings in the sense of being bound by the settlement. It is this feature of class action litigation that requires that class members be allowed to appeal the approval of a settlement when they have objected at the fairness hearing. To hold otherwise would deprive nonnamed class members of the power to preserve their own interests in a settlement that will ultimately bind them, despite their expressed objections before the trial court. Particularly in light of the fact that petitioner had no ability to opt out of the settlement, see Fed. Rule Civ. Proc. 23(b)(1), appealing the approval of the settlement is petitioner's only means of protecting himself from being bound by a disposition of his rights he finds unacceptable and that a reviewing court might find legally inadequate. . . .

Respondents argue that, nonetheless, appeals from nonnamed parties should not be allowed because they would undermine one of the goals of class action litigation, namely, preventing multiple suits. See *Guthrie v. Evans*, 815 F.2d, at 629 (arguing that allowing nonnamed class members' appeals would undermine a "fundamental purpose of the class action": "to render manageable litigation that involves numerous members of a homogenous class, who would all otherwise have access to the court through individual lawsuits"). Allowing such appeals, however, will not be as problematic as respondents claim. For one thing, the power to appeal is limited to those nonnamed class members who have objected during the fairness hearing. This limits the class of potential appellants considerably. As the longstanding practice of allowing nonnamed class members to object at the fairness hearing demonstrates, the burden of considering the claims of this subset of class members is not onerous.

III

The Government, as *amicus curiae*, admits that nonnamed class members are parties who may appeal the approval of a settlement, but urges us nonetheless to require class members to intervene for purposes of appeal. See Brief for United States et al. as *Amici Curiae* 12–27. To address the fairness concerns to objecting nonnamed class members bound by the settlement they wish to appeal, however, the Government also asserts that such a limited purpose intervention generally should be available to all those, like petitioner, whose objections at the fairness hearing have been disregarded. Federal Rule of Civil Procedure 24(a)(2) provides for intervention as of right:

> "Upon timely application . . . when the applicant claims an interest relating to the property or transaction which is the sub-

ject of the action and the applicant is so situated that the disposition of the action may as a practical matter impair or impede the applicant's ability to protect that interest, unless the applicant's interest is adequately represented by existing parties."

According to the Government, nonnamed class members who state objections at the fairness hearing should easily meet these three criteria. . . .

Given the ease with which nonnamed class members who have objected at the fairness hearing could intervene for purposes of appeal, however, it is difficult to see the value of the Government's suggested requirement. It identifies only a limited number of instances where the initial intervention motion would be of any use: where the objector is not actually a member of the settlement class or is otherwise not entitled to relief from the settlement, where an objector seeks to appeal even though his objection was successful, where the objection at the fairness hearing was untimely, or where there is a need to consolidate duplicative appeals from class members. In such situations, the Government argues, a district court can disallow such problematic and unnecessary appeals.

This seems to us, however, of limited benefit. In the first two of these situations, the objector stands to gain nothing by appeal, so it is unlikely such situations will arise with any frequency. Justice SCALIA argues that if such objectors were undeterred by this fact at the time they filed their original objections, they will be undeterred at the appellate level. This misunderstands the point. As to the first group—those who are not actually entitled to relief—one would not expect them to have filed objections in the district court in the first place. The few irrational persons who wish to pursue one round of meaningless relief will, I agree, probably be irrational enough to pursue a second. But there should not be many of such persons in any case. As for the second—those whose objections were successful at the district court level—they were far from irrational in the filing of their initial objections, and they should not generally be expected to lose this level of sensibility when faced with the prospect of a meaningless appeal. Moreover, even if such cases did arise with any frequency, such concerns could be addressed by a standing inquiry at the appellate level.

The third situation—dealing with untimely objections—implicates basic concerns about waiver and should be easily addressable by a court of appeals. A court of appeals also has the ability to avoid the fourth by consolidating cases raising duplicative appeals. Fed. Rule App. Proc. 3(b)(2). If the resolution of any of these issues should turn out to be complex in a given case, there is little to be gained by requiring a district court to consider these issues, which are the type of issues (standing to appeal, waiver of objections below, and consolidation of appeals) typically addressed only by an appellate court. As such determinations still would most likely lead to an appeal, such a requirement would only add an additional layer of complexity before the appeal of the settlement approval may finally be heard.

Nor do we agree with the Government that, regardless of the desirability of an intervention requirement for effective class management, the structure of the rules of class action procedure requires intervention for the purposes of appeal. According to the Government, intervention is the method contemplated under the rules for nonnamed class members to gain the right to participate in class action proceedings. We disagree. Just as class action procedure allows nonnamed class members to object to a settlement at the fairness hearing without first intervening, it should similarly allow them to appeal the District Court's decision to disregard their objections.

Moreover, no federal statute or procedural rule directly addresses the question of who may appeal from approval of class action settlements, while the right to appeal from an action that finally disposes of one's rights has a statutory basis. 28 U.S.C. § 1291.

IV

We hold that nonnamed class members like petitioner who have objected in a timely manner to approval of the settlement at the fairness hearing have the power to bring an appeal without first intervening. We therefore reverse the judgment of the Court of Appeals for the Fourth Circuit and remand the case for further proceedings consistent with this opinion.

It is so ordered.

■ JUSTICE SCALIA, with whom JUSTICE KENNEDY and JUSTICE THOMAS join, dissenting.

"The rule that only parties to a lawsuit, or those that properly become parties, may appeal an adverse judgment, is well settled." *Marino v. Ortiz*, 484 U.S. 301, 304 (1988) *(per curiam)*; Fed. Rule App. Proc. 3(c)(1) ("The notice of appeal must . . . specify the party or parties taking the appeal"). This is one well-settled rule that, thankfully, the Court leaves intact. Other chapters in the hornbooks are not so lucky.

I

The Court holds that petitioner, a nonnamed member of the class in a class action litigated by a representative member of the class, is a "party" to the judgment approving the class settlement. This is contrary to well-established law. The "parties" to a judgment are those named as such—whether as the original plaintiff or defendant in the complaint giving rise to the judgment, or as "[o]ne who [though] not an original party . . . become[s] a party by intervention, substitution, or third-party practice," *Karcher v. May*, 484 U.S. 72, 77 (1987). As the Restatement puts it, "[a] person who is named as a party to an action and subjected to the jurisdiction of the court is a party to the action," RESTATEMENT (SECOND) OF JUDGMENTS § 34(1), p. 345 (1980) (hereinafter RESTATEMENT); "[t]he designation of persons as parties is usually made in the caption of the summons or complaint but additional parties may be named in such pleadings as a counterclaim, a complaint against a third party filed by a defendant, or a complaint in intervention," *id.*, § 34, Comment a, Reporter's Note, at 347. As was the case here, the only members of a class who are typically named in the complaint are the class representatives; thus, it is only these members of the class, and those who intervene or otherwise enter through third-party practice, who are parties to the class judgment. This is confirmed by the application of those Federal Rules of Civil Procedure that confer upon "parties" to the litigation the rights to take such actions as conducting discovery and moving for summary judgment, e.g., Fed. Rules Civ. Proc. 30(a)(1), 31(a)(1), 33(a), 34(a), 36(a), 45(a)(3), 56(a), 56(b), 56(e). It is undisputed that the class representatives are the only members of the class who have such rights.

Petitioner was offered the opportunity to be named the class representative, but he declined; nor did he successfully intervene. Accordingly, he is not a party to the class judgment. . . .

B

. . . [The Court] contends that petitioner should be considered a party to the judgment because, as a member of the class, he is bound by it. *Ante*, at 2011 ("What is most important to this case is that nonnamed class members are parties to the proceedings in the sense of being bound by the settlement"). This will come as news to law students everywhere. There are any number of persons who are not parties to a judgment yet are nonetheless bound by it. See RESTATEMENT § 41(1), at 393 (listing examples); *id.*, § 75, Comment a, at 210 ("A person is bound by a judgment in an action to which he is not a party if he is in 'privity' with a party"). Perhaps the most prominent example is precisely the one we have here. Nonnamed members of a class are bound by the class judgment, even though they are not parties to the judgment, because they are represented by class members who are parties. . . .

Petitioner here, in the words of the Restatement, "is not a party" but "is bound by [the] judgment as though he were a party." Because our "well-settled" rule allows only "parties" to appeal from a judgment, petitioner may not appeal the class settlement. . . .

II

. . . The Court does not dispute that nonnamed class members will typically meet the requirements for intervention as of right under Federal Rule of Civil Procedure 24, including intervention only for the purpose of appeal, and even after the class judgment has been entered.

The Court *does* dispute whether there is any "value" in requiring nonnamed class members who object to the settlement to intervene in order to take an appeal. In my view, avoiding the reduction to indeterminacy of the hitherto clear rule regarding who is a party is "value" enough. But beyond that, it makes sense to require objectors to intervene before appealing, for the reason advanced by the Government: to enable district courts "to perform an important screening function." Brief for United States et al. as *Amici Curiae* 23. For example, when considering whether to allow an objector to intervene, a district court can verify that the objector does not fall outside the definition of the settlement class and is otherwise entitled to relief in the class action, that the objection has not already been resolved in favor of the objector in the approved settlement, and that the objection was presented in a timely manner. *Id.* at 23–24. The Court asserts that there is no "value" to these screening functions because a court of appeals can pass on those matters just as easily, and in any event an objector who is unable to obtain relief from the class settlement will not seek to appeal "with any frequency," as he "stands to gain nothing by appeal."

As to the last point: The person who has nothing to gain from an appeal also had nothing to gain from filing his objection in the first place, but was undeterred (as many are), see, e.g., *Shaw v. Toshiba America Information Systems, Inc.*, 91 F. Supp. 2d 942, 973–974, and nn. 17–18 (E.D. Tex. 2000). The belief that meritless objections, undeterred the first time, will be deterred the second, surely suggests the triumph of hope over experience.[5] And as for the suggestion that the court of appeals can pass on the-

---

[5]   The Court assures us that these appeals will be "few" because, like the objections on which they are based, they are "irrational." To say that the substance of an objection (and of the corresponding appeal) is irrational is not to say that it is irrational to make the objection and file the appeal. See *Shaw*, 91 F. Supp. 2d at 973–974, and n. 18 (noting "'canned' objections filed by professional objectors who seek out class actions to simply extract a fee by lodg-

se questions just as easily: Since when has it become a principle of our judicial administration that what *can* be left to the appellate level *should* be left to the appellate level? Quite the opposite is true. District judges, who issue their decrees in splendid isolation, can be multiplied *ad infinitum*. Courts of appeals cannot be staffed with too many judges without destroying their ability to maintain, through en banc rehearings, a predictable law of the circuit. In any event, the district court, being intimately familiar with the facts, *is* in a better position to rule initially upon such questions as whether the objections to the settlement were procedurally deficient, late filed, or simply inapposite to the case. If it denies interventions on such grounds, and if the denials are not appealed, the court of appeals will be spared the trouble of considering those objections altogether. And even when the denials are appealed, the court of appeals will have the benefit of the district court's opinion on these often fact-bound questions. (Typically, the only occasion the district court would have had to pass on these questions is in the course of considering the motion to intervene; when considering whether to approve the class settlement, district courts typically do not treat objections individually even on substance, let alone form.) . . .

For these reasons, I would affirm the Court of Appeals.

NOTES AND QUESTIONS

1.   *The Strategic Implications of* Devlin. Consider a post-*Devlin* advertisement in *The American Lawyer*, a widely-circulated news magazine for practicing lawyers. The advertisement is for an organization called The Class Action Fairness Group and contains a photograph of a baseball umpire calling a runner "safe" at home plate after the runner has knocked over the catcher. The wording next to the photo reads as follows:

> If judging is like calling balls and strikes, *sometimes the judge needs glasses.*
>
> Preliminary approval does not mean final approval.
>
> Going to bat for you, one fairness hearing at a time.

The Class Action Fairness Group, Am. Lawyer, Oct. 2006, at 144 (emphasis in original). Does this suggest that *Devlin* might have undesirable consequences as a strategic matter?

Given the holding in *Devlin*, is there any way for the lawyers who design class settlements to disempower, or at least reduce the bargaining leverage of, the sorts of objectors to which Justice Scalia alludes in his footnote 5? Empirical research in the aftermath of *Devlin* documents the emergence of "quick pay" in class settlement agreements:

> The quick-pay provision is special wording inserted by class counsel, with the consent of the defendants, into class action settlement agreements. These provisions permit class counsel to receive the fees awarded to them by district courts as soon as those courts approve the class action settlements, regardless of whether the settlements or fees are appealed. These provisions deal with the possibility of ap-

---

ing generic, unhelpful protests"). The Court cites nothing to support its sunny surmise that the appeals will be few.

peals by obligating class counsel to repay the fees if the settlements or their fees are later overturned or modified. . . .

The purpose of quick-pay provisions is to greatly reduce the leverage objecting class members have over class counsel by removing the ability of their appeals to delay the point at which class counsel receive fee awards. If class counsel have already received their fee awards, then there is no reason for them to pay a premium to objectors with meritless appeals merely to avoid the delay caused by their appeals. In this regard, quick-pay provisions may discourage objectors from filing meritless appeals in the first place because the provisions increase the ability of class counsel to credibly threaten to ride an appeal out to fruition. Of course, counsel may still be willing to pay objectors with meritless appeals a relatively small sum to avoid the expense of defending against the appeal.

Brian T. Fitzpatrick, *The End of Objector Blackmail?*, 62 Vand. L. Rev. 1623, 1641–42 (2009). Upon examination of all federal-court class action settlements in 2006, the same source found quick-pay provisions in over one third of all such settlements that year—in particular, in nearly 80 percent of all securities fraud class settlements. *Id.* at 1626.

Are quick-pay provisions desirable? Recall from Chapter 2 the conventional justification for fee awards to class counsel, grounded in notions of unjust enrichment and restitution.

2. *Absent Class Members as Parties.* Even if an absent class member need not intervene in order to object to the fairness of a proposed class settlement in district court (or to appeal an adverse ruling on that question), might there nonetheless be strategic advantages to intervention? By intervening, the objector would gain what everyone agrees to be "party" status under any definition. What can parties do that non-parties cannot and that might be especially valuable to someone challenging a proposed class settlement? Recall here the informational disadvantages that Professor Rubenstein's proposals seek to overcome.

Though absent class members may object, they are "not entitled, as a matter of right, to an evidentiary hearing during a settlement hearing." *Jones v. Nuclear Pharm., Inc.*, 741 F.2d 322, 325 (10th Cir. 1984). Rather, with regard to such matters as the opportunity to cross-examine witnesses presented by proponents of the class settlement or to present evidence to rebut such witnesses, the latitude available to an objector remains in the discretion of the district court. *Rutter & Wilbanks Corp. v. Shell Oil Co.*, 314 F.3d 1180, 1187 (10th Cir. 2002).

3. *Implications.* Does consideration of class members as parties for purposes of seeking direct appellate review have any implications for the claim preclusive effect of a final judgment approving a class settlement upon such review? This last question implicates the longstanding debate over the appropriate latitude, if any, for collateral attacks on class settlements—the subject of the next section.

B. Collateral Attacks on Class Settlements

Among the most controversial issues surrounding class settlements today is the latitude available to class members to collaterally attack a class judgment—in other words, to attack the binding effect of the judgment in *subsequent* litigation. The controversy over the availability of collateral attack extends, of course, to judgments rendered as a result of a class-wide trial. But the prevalence of class settlements as the endgame of class litigation—and the heightened potential for abuse in the settlement context—have focused particular attention on whether judgments that approve class settlements are vulnerable to collateral attack.

As a general rule, a party is bound by a judgment unless the judgment is reversed on direct appeal. But while direct appeal ordinarily is the only avenue available to review a judgment, the law has long recognized that a collateral attack on a judgment may be appropriate in limited circumstances and that federal and state courts are not required to give full faith and credit to judgments in those circumstances. The question addressed in this section is whether class judgments embodying settlements based on inadequate representation fall within the general rule or an exception. Two decisions of the Ninth Circuit in *Epstein v. MCA, Inc.* starkly frame the debate and elucidate the stakes for defendants and class members alike. The first (known as *Epstein II*), upheld the right of a plaintiff to collaterally attack a class judgment and found that that the Epstein plaintiffs had been inadequately represented. The second (known as Epstein *III*) vacated Epstein *II* and rejected the argument that plaintiffs had the right to collaterally attack the judgment.

Epstein II and *III* were decided on remand from the Supreme Court in *Matsushita Electric Industrial Co. v. Epstein* (discussed in Chapter 3). Recall that a class settlement in Delaware state court had purported to resolve both Delaware fiduciary duty claims and federal securities claims arising from Matsushita's acquisition of MCA by approving a settlement of the claims. The question before the Court in *Matsushita* was whether the release of the federal securities claims as part of a settlement of the Delaware state claims was entitled to full faith and credit even though the Delaware courts had *no* subject matter jurisdiction to *adjudicate* the federal claims. The Court held that the federal statute that gave federal courts exclusive jurisdiction over the federal securities claims did not impliedly repeal the requirements of the Full Faith and Credit Statute. The Court, however, did not resolve whether the Delaware judgment could be denied full faith and credit on a different ground. The Court stated that it "need not address" the plaintiffs' due process claim, because it was "outside the scope of the question presented to this Court" and "not the basis for the decision" of the Ninth Circuit.

There is no doubt that a failure of due process *sometimes* renders a judgment vulnerable to collateral attack and prevents courts from giving binding effect to the judgment. A default judgment, for example, is not binding on a party against whom judgment was entered *if* the court that rendered the judgment lacked personal jurisdiction over the party. *Insurance Corp. of Ireland, Ltd. v. Compagnie des Bauxites de Guinée*, 456 U.S. 694, 706 (1982) ("A defendant is always free to ignore the judicial proceedings, risk a default judgment, and then challenge that judgment on jurisdictional grounds in a collateral proceeding."). But if the party contesting jurisdiction made an appearance in the first action—even if only for the purpose of contesting jurisdiction—lack of jurisdiction over the person does not subject the judgment to collateral attack. *Baldwin v. Iowa State Traveling Men's Ass'n*, 283 U.S. 522 (1931). Similarly, in *Kremer v. Chemical Construction Corp.*, 456 U.S. 451 (1982), the Court insisted that a party who had appeared in the state proceedings was entitled only to a "full and fair opportunity to litigate." *Id.* at 481. *Epstein II* and *III* grapple with whether an *absent* class member—who by definition did not appear in the class suit—has a right to collaterally attack the class judgment for inadequate representation.

Epstein v. MCA, Inc. ("*Epstein II*")

126 F.3d 1235 (1997)

■ WILLIAM A. NORRIS, CIRCUIT JUDGE:

This case is before us on remand from the United States Supreme Court. . . .

The case is a class action brought by former MCA shareholders who surrendered their stock in response to a tender offer by Matsushita. In *Epstein I*, the named plaintiffs ("the Epstein plaintiffs") contended, inter alia, that Matsushita's tender offer violated the so-called "all-holder, best-price" rule of SEC Rule 14d–10 by paying a premium for the stock of MCA's chairman and chief executive officer, Lew Wasserman, and MCA's chief operating officer, Sidney Sheinberg. The district court awarded summary judgment to the defendants, and the Epstein plaintiffs appealed. . . .

On remand, the Epstein plaintiffs press anew an argument that we found unnecessary to address in *Epstein I*: that we should withhold full faith and credit from the Delaware judgment because it was entered into in violation of the due process right of the absent class members to adequate representation at all times. We now turn to that question.

I.

Matsushita contends that we are barred from addressing the merits of the Epstein plaintiffs' claims of inadequate representation. Matsushita makes three arguments in support of this contention:

(1) The Supreme Court's decision in *Matsushita* did not leave the issue open on remand;

(2) The issue of the adequacy of representation was fully and fairly litigated in the Delaware Court of Chancery;

(3) The Epstein plaintiffs are estopped from raising the adequacy of their representation collaterally because they did not raise it by intervening in the Delaware proceeding.

A

In arguing that the "[t]he opinion of the Supreme Court leaves no issue open on remand," Matsushita either mischaracterizes or disregards the unambiguous statements in the record to the contrary. . . .

B

Next we address Matsushita's argument that the Delaware settlement judgment precludes the Epstein plaintiffs from "relitigating" the issue of adequacy of representation under Delaware issue preclusion law. It claims that adequacy of representation was actually litigated by objectors at the Delaware fairness hearing, and that other Delaware courts would therefore give preclusive effect to the Chancery Court's determination that representation of the absent class members was adequate. Therefore, Matsushita argues, under 28 U.S.C. § 1738, we too must attach issue preclusion. . . .

2.

Even if adequacy of representation had actually been litigated by objectors at the fairness hearing, and even if Delaware law would allow an individual objector to bind an absentee on the issue of adequacy of representation—however improbable that might seem—we still could not give full faith and credit to such a judgment because it would violate due process of law. As the Epstein plaintiffs aptly put it, "*[o]bjectors are objectors, not class representatives.*" Binding absentees to any part of a class action judgment "is an act of judicial power," *Epstein I*, 50 F.3d at 667, and that power can only be exercised over absentees when their interests have, in fact, been adequately represented by parties lawfully authorized to represent them. See, e.g., *Richards v. Jefferson Cty.*, Ala., 517 U.S. 793, 798, (1996) ("[O]ne is not bound by a judgment *in personam* in a litigation in which he is not designated as a party . . . [except, in a class action, where he] has his interests adequately represented."). It would defy this fundamental principle of our jurisprudence to allow the due process right of absent class members to adequate representation to be litigated by random, volunteer objectors.

. . . The only case Matsushita cites that offers any help on its proposition that volunteer objectors can litigate the due process rights of absent class members is *Grimes v. Vitalink Communications,* 17 F.3d 1553 (3d Cir.1994). In *Grimes*, the Third Circuit held that objectors may litigate the due process rights of absent class members who have sufficient minimum contacts to support an exercise of personal jurisdiction over them by the forum. It reasons that, so long as an absentee has "minimum contacts" with the forum, he can be bound by the judgment without receiving *Shutts'* safeguards. There is nothing in *Shutts*, however—or in any other case—to suggest that *Shutts* offers protection only to those absentees who are beyond the *in personam* reach of the forum. Because *Grimes* conflates the requirements of *in personam* jurisdiction with the due process safeguards that *Shutts* guarantees to absent class members, we respectfully decline to follow it.

Finally, Matsushita raises the alarmist cry that it will sound the death knell to finality in class actions if individual objectors cannot bind absentees on the issue of adequate representation. We of course reject this hyperbole. . . .

C

. . . Matsushita argues that because of the procedures used in the Delaware Chancery Court, the Epstein plaintiffs cannot bring a collateral attack on adequacy of representation. This argument comes in two parts. First, Matsushita argues, the settlement hearing provided a "full and fair opportunity" for absentees to contest the adequacy of their representation. The absentees had a duty to intervene in that hearing if they wished to protect their rights, Matsushita claims, and having failed to do so, they are estopped from bringing a collateral challenge. Second, and more broadly, Matsushita argues that the procedures Delaware had in place foreclose us from *ever* hearing a collateral challenge to adequacy of representation. Matsushita argues that we are limited to reviewing the sufficiency of the *procedures* that Delaware had in place to ensure adequate representation, rather than the adequacy of the representation itself. "[T]he Chancery Court's adherence to Rule 23 procedures satisfies the Due Process Clause as a matter of law," Matsushita continues, and an absent class member's claim on "the merits" of inadequate representation "is far outside the scope of the [collateral] review permitted by . . . the case law of this Court." We agree with the Epstein plaintiffs that both of these arguments are meritless.

1

Matsushita argues that class members who wish to contest adequacy of representation must intervene during the course of the class action proceedings and do battle with their own representatives in an adversarial contest over the way they are discharging their fiduciary duties. This argument ignores the clear teaching of *Phillips Petroleum Co. v. Shutts,* 472 U.S. 797 (1985), that a class member is not required to do anything during the course of a class-action proceeding. He is free to sit it out, assured that he will be bound by the result if, but only if, the proceeding comports with the special due process requirements designed to safeguard the interests of absent class members. As the Court put it in *Shutts,* "Unlike a defendant in a normal civil suit, an absent class-action plaintiff is not required to do anything. He may sit back and allow the litigation to run its course, *content in knowing that there are safeguards provided for his protection.*" *Id.* at 810, (emphasis added). Those "safeguards," as enumerated in *Shutts,* are (1) "notice," (2) "an opportunity to be heard and participate in the litigation," (3) "an opportunity to remove himself from the class" by opting out, and (4) "adequate represent[ation]" "*at all times.*" *Id.* at 812 (emphasis added). Thus, *Shutts* admonishes absent class members that they will be bound by the merits of a judgment—including the fairness of a court-approved settlement—if it is a product of adequate representation and their other due process safeguards. But *Shutts* promises in return that they need not monitor this proceeding from afar: if the litigation culminating in the judgment violated their due process rights, then absent class members will not be bound by it.

Gonzales v. Cassidy, 474 F.2d 67 (5th Cir.1973)—a precursor to *Shutts*—is square authority against Matsushita's intervene-or-be-estopped argument. In *Gonzales,* the Fifth Circuit rejected the very argument that Matsushita now urges upon us: "[The defendants] advance an estoppel-type argument to support the proposition that [the absent class member] cannot raise the inadequate representation issue [on collateral review]. Their position is that [the absent class member] is estopped to attack the judgment because he should have intervened."

In rejecting this argument and holding that an absent class member may collaterally attack a judgment on the ground that he was not adequately represented, the Fifth Circuit reasoned that the question "whether counsel's conduct of the entire suit was such that due process would not be violated by giving res judicata effect to the judgment in that suit *necessarily requires a hindsight approach.*" (emphasis added). As the court went on to say, "The purpose of Rule 23 would be subverted by requiring a class member who learns of a pending suit involving a class of which he is a part to monitor that litigation to make certain that his interests are being protected. . . ."

A hypothetical based on the facts of our case serves to illustrate the common sense soundness of *Shutts* and *Gonzales* and the impracticality of Matsushita's argument that the Epstein plaintiffs are now estopped from challenging the adequacy of representation because they failed to intervene at the fairness hearing. Suppose a class member did appear as an objector at the hearing and challenged the fairness of the settlement on the ground that it had not taken into account the claim that a $21–million payment to

Sheinberg was in reality a premium for his stock. Suppose further that the objector produced evidence in the form of deposition testimony and documents—perhaps discovered in a parallel federal class action—casting doubt on the real purpose of the $21–million payment. Suppose still further that Delaware counsel had never heard of the $21–million payment before the objector reported it at the fairness hearing.

The question is: how should class counsel have responded to this new evidence about the Sheinberg payment during the middle of the fairness hearing, given their fiduciary duty to look after the interests of all members of the class? The obvious answer would seem to be to ask the Vice Chancellor to continue the fairness hearing until they had a chance to learn more about the Sheinberg payment and consider its potential settlement value. After all, if there was evidence to prove that the $21–million payment was a premium to get Mr. Sheinberg to support the tender offer, it would take only a simple calculation to determine that other shareholders would be entitled to a substantial recovery.

Let us suppose, however, that for whatever reason—perhaps the irre-sist[i]bility of a quick fee on claims they could not litigate—counsel stuck to their guns and got the proposed settlement—2 [cents] per share (less attorneys fees)—approved and cast into a judgment. Could the law possibly be that all the class members who failed to intervene at the fairness hearing are estopped from challenging the judgment collaterally on the ground that they were not provided adequate representation? Common sense as well and *Shutts* and *Gonzales* dictate that the answer must be that they are not.

This dilemma is the driving force behind *Gonzales'* reasoning. The impracticality of assessing the adequacy of ongoing representation "live-time" is the very reason that the Fifth Circuit in *Gonzales* insisted that the challenge must be conducted with a "hindsight" approach, as on collateral review. Matsushita attempts to turn this around and limit *Gonzales'* scope to cases in which it was "impossible to raise" the constitutional claim in the original proceeding. See Appellees' Br. at 35–26 ("*Gonzales* also turns on the impossibility of participation in the original proceeding. . . . *Gonzales* thus stands for the limited proposition that [collateral attack is limited to] due process violations that could not have been presented in the rendering court prior to the entry of judgment.").

This is not what *Gonzales* held. On the contrary, it held that even claims that were not "impossible" to have been raised in the initial proceedings are entirely appropriate for collateral review:

> To answer the question whether the class representatives adequately represented the class so that the judgment in the class suit will bind the absent members of the class requires a two-pronged inquiry: (1) did the trial court in the first suit correctly determine, initially, that the representative would adequately represent the class? and (2) Does it appear, after the termination of the suit, that the class representative adequately protected the interest of the class?

Gonzales, 474 F.2d at 72.

To hold otherwise—with respect to either prong of the inquiry—would be to require absent class members to monitor the proceedings in order to secure their rights to adequate representation. Absent class members are not required to bear this burden. See *Shutts*, 472 U.S. at 810; *Gonzales*, 474 F.2d at 76 ("The [adequate representation safeguard] would be subverted by requiring a class member . . . to monitor the litigation. . . ."). They may rest secure in the knowledge that they can attack the judgment in a subsequent action if their due process rights are in fact violated. "Due process of law would be violated for the judgment in a class action suit to be res judicata to the absent class members *unless the court applying res judicata* can conclude that the class was adequately represented in the first suit." *Gonzales*, 474 F.2d at 74 (citing H*ansberry v. Lee*, 311 U.S. 32 (1940)) (emphasis added). Indeed, to permit such a due process challenge to be definitively resolved in the initial proceeding would effectively permit an initial court to pronounce the preclusive effect of its own judgment. See *Matsushita*, 516 U.S. at ___ (Ginsburg, J., concurring in part and dissenting in part) ("A court conducting an action cannot predetermine the res judicata effect of the judgment; that effect can be tested only in a subsequent action.") (citing 7B Charles A. Wright, Arthur R. Miller & Mary Kay Kane, FEDERAL PRACTICE AND PROCEDURE § 1789, at 245 (2d ed.1986)).

In adopting *Gonzales*' reasoning (and rejecting Matsushita's spin on it), we bring our circuit into line with settled law that forecloses Matsushita's intervene-or-be-estopped theory. As the Court stated in *Shutts*, "an absent class-action plaintiff is not required to do anything." *Shutts*, 472 U.S. at 810. Rather, it is the prerogative of absentees to remain just that: absent from a proceeding in which they are "parties" only virtually, through their class representatives. The "continuing solicitude for their rights" entitles absent class members to refrain from intervening, "content in knowing that there are safeguards provided for [their] protection." *Id.* at 810. By forcing an absent class member to monitor a proceeding and intervene to challenge the adequacy of representation that he is still in the process of receiving would defeat the purpose of having such safeguards. As Justice Ginsburg further made clear in her separate opinion in *Matsushita*: "[An absent class member] may avoid being bound *either* by appearing in the action before rendition of the judgment *or by attacking the judgment by subsequent proceedings*." *Matsushita*, 516 U.S. at ___ (Ginsburg, J., concurring in part and dissenting in part) (first emphasis in original, second emphasis added) (quoting RESTATEMENT (SECOND) OF JUDGMENTS § 41, Comment a, p. 394); see also 18 Charles A. Wright, Arthur R. Miller & Edward H. Cooper, FEDERAL PRACTICE AND PROCEDURE § 4455, at 479 (1981) ("[Adequate representation] ordinarily is . . . determin[ed] in defining any class that is certified. *The question remains open to redetermination in a subsequent action*, however, since nonparties can be bound only if some party adequately represented their interests.") (emphasis added); *Gonzales*, 474 F.2d at 76 (absent class member has no duty to monitor class action proceeding); cf. M*artin v. Wilks,* 490 U.S. 755, 762–65 (failure to intervene did not estop non-parties from suing parties to consent decree that adversely affected their interests).

2

Matsushita attempts to avoid *Shutts* by arguing that K*remer v. Chemical Constr. Corp.*, 456 U.S. 461 (1982) prevents absentees from ever collaterally challenging adequacy of representation when the forum state uses a procedure like Delaware Chancery Court Rule 23. This attempt gets Matsushita nowhere. We reiterate the fundamental principle that *Shutts* established: absent class members have a right to adequate representation "at all times," and they have no duty to intervene in the initial proceeding in order to protect that right. There is nothing in *Kremer* to the contrary.

In *Kremer*, the Court reaffirmed the bedrock principle that a judgment must satisfy the requirements of due process in order to receive full faith and credit. In the specific case before it, the Court held that a New York administrative proceeding was entitled to full faith and credit because the procedures it employed satisfied due process. Matsushita argues that *Kremer* likewise limits absent class members to a "procedures only" approach when they seek to challenge adequacy of representation. It points to passages in *Kremer* that ask whether the New York administrative proceeding provided the "minimum procedural requirements" of due process. Kremer, 456 U.S. at 481. It then argues that the mere existence of Rule 23 satisfies the "minimum procedural requirements" for protecting adequacy of representation. That being so, Matsushita concludes, *Kremer* never permits a collateral challenge that alleges that absent class members in fact received inadequate representation.

We categorically reject this simplistic application of *Kremer* to the class action context. The Court fashioned *Kremer*'s "procedures only" approach to apply to collateral challenges of judgments in traditional litigation, where individual parties are bound by virtue of their *presence* before the court. *Kremer* was not a class action and did not address the special due process problems of binding persons not parties to the action. *Shutts*, in contrast, which was a class action, held that absentees have a right to adequate representation "at all times," and that they need not intervene to enforce that right. No procedure can reliably protect an absent plaintiff who does not *in fact* have an adequate representative in court championing his cause. The Court recognized this salutary principle in *Hansberry v. Lee*, 311 U.S. 32 (1940), and it has never retreated from it. *Id.* at 41–42 ("members of a class not present as parties to the litigation may be bound by the judgment where they are *in fact* adequately represented") (emphasis added).

Nonetheless, Matsushita argues, the absent class members in this case received notice, an opportunity to be heard (at the objection hearing), and the right to opt out of both the class action proceeding and the proposed settlement. Surely, Matsushita complains, these protections fully satisfied the "minimum procedural requirements" of *Kremer*, and due process does not require anything more.

The Supreme Court, however, could not have been more clear in requiring more. Indeed, if settled law defeats Matsushita's contention that absent class members have a duty to intervene or be estopped from challenging the adequacy of their representation, then this contention faces a veritable fortress of authority. In *Shutts*, the Court echoed the language of *Kremer* when it laid out the "minimum procedural due process protection" due to absent class members, including "adequate represent[ation]" "at all times." *Shutts*, 472 U.S. at 811–12. In addition to *Shutts,* the case law is consistent that adequate representation *in fact* is required to bind absent class members. . . .

In sum, neither caselaw nor common sense supports Matsushita's position that the mere existence of procedures like Rule 23 can foreclose an absentee from receiving his day in court on the issue of adequacy of representation. . . .

II

We now turn to the merits of the adequacy of representation issue. Following the model provided by *Gonzales*, we conduct a "two-pronged inquiry," *Gonzales*, 474 F.2d at 72. First, we determine whether there was a disabling conflict of interest between Delaware counsel and the MCA shareholders who tendered their shares. Second, we review the actual conduct of Delaware counsel in discharging their fiduciary duty to protect the interests of those shareholders.

A

The essence of the Epstein plaintiffs' position on the claimed conflict of interest is that the Delaware settlement was the product of a one-sided bargaining process because their representatives went to the table with no credible bargaining power. Not surprisingly, Matsushita makes no serious attempt to challenge this position, relying almost exclusively on their arguments as to why we cannot reach the merits. It is axiomatic that a plaintiff's power to negotiate a reasonable settlement derives from the threat of going to trial with a credible chance of winning. As the Supreme Court has said, permitting class-action settlements in which class counsel are disabled from litigating the case renders:

> both class counsel and court . . . disarmed. Class counsel confined to settlement negotiations could not use the threat of litigation to press for a better offer, see Coffee, *Class Wars: The Dilemma of the Mass Tort Class Action*, 95 Colum. L. Rev. 1343, 1379–1380 (1995), and the court would have to face a bargain proffered for its approval without the benefit of adversarial investigation, see, e.g., *Kamilewicz v. Bank of Boston Corp.*, 100 F.3d 1348, 1352 (C.A.7 1996) (Easterbrook, J., dissenting from denial of rehearing en banc) (parties "may even put one over on the court, in a staged performance")

Amchem, 521 U.S. at ___ (1997) (per Ginsburg, J.); see also *Kamilewicz*, 100 F.3d at 1352 (Easterbrook, J., joined by Posner, C.J., and Manion, Rovner, and Diane P. Wood, JJ., dissenting from denial of rehearing en banc) ("The lawyers support the settlement to get fees; the defendants support it to evade liability; the court can't vindicate the class's rights because the friendly presentation means that it lacks essential information.").

The Delaware class plaintiffs and their counsel could not carry out a threat to litigate the federal claims in this case, and Matsushita knew it.

The inability of the class representatives to exercise any leverage on behalf of the Epstein plaintiffs was the result of three basic facts. First, they could not litigate the federal claims because Congress has said that Exchange Act claims may not be litigated in state courts. Thus, the claims that Matsushita violated SEC Rule 14d–10 by paying premiums to Messrs. Wasserman and Sheinberg were not and could not have been pleaded in the Delaware action. Moreover, there was no discovery on those claims; indeed, the Delaware plaintiffs probably were unable to conduct any discovery on the federal claims because the facts relevant to those claims had no apparent relevance to the subject matter of the state law claim that the MCA directors had breached their fiduciary duties in failing to maximize shareholder value upon a change of corporate control. Finally, Matsushita would have had reason to discount the value of any settlement made with the state plaintiffs against the risk that a state court judgment releasing Exchange Act claims would not survive a collateral attack on the ground that the Delaware courts had no jurisdiction to release exclusively federal claims especially in light of the absence of any overlapping issues of fact between the state and federal claims. Matsushita must have recognized that it would subject itself to a substantial risk by settling the federal claims in state court rather than federal court, and would have had to discount its bottom line in the state settlement negotiations accordingly. The denouement was predictable: Matsushita used its infinitely superior bargaining power vis-a-vis the state class representatives to settle the Exchange Act claims at a rock bottom price.[13]

Second, the class representatives not only lacked the bargaining power that comes with a credible threat of going to trial and winning, they also lacked the ability to make a credible threat that they could put Matsushita at risk by going to trial on the state claims and proving facts material to the federal claims that would be binding upon Matsushita through issue preclusion. Because the state and federal claims shared no common issues of material fact, a judgment on the state claims could not be used as an "offensive" estoppel in future litigation of the federal claims. While the Delaware class representatives lacked the muscle to put Matsushita at risk on the federal claims, the existence of their state class action, however worthless standing alone, served to provide Matsushita with an opportunity to try to get rid of the federal claims at a bargain basement price. If the parties could get court approval of a settlement that released the federal claims, Matsushita would have at least a fair shot of using the judgment to block the federal action with a full faith and credit argument. That is, of course, exactly what Matsushita did as soon as the judgment became final. We had the Epstein plaintiffs' appeal of the district court's summary judgment under submission when Matsushita notified us of the Delaware settlement judgment and argued that we should give it preclusive effect.

Third, Matsushita had a further bargaining advantage, quite apart from its knowledge that the Delaware plaintiffs could not put it at risk on the federal claims. Matsushita also knew that class counsel had an extraordinary incentive to settle and settle quickly because that was the only way they could extract a fee out of the federal claims. Class counsel could not benefit from the federal claims by going to trial for the obvious reason that the federal claims could not be litigated in state court. Moreover, the pendency of a parallel action in federal court—the *Epstein* case—meant that Delaware class counsel were at risk of being "beaten to the punch" and getting no return on the federal claims at all. Matsushita knew that it was negotiating a release of the federal claims with class counsel who could not litigate those claims and whose self-interest gave them an incentive to settle and settle fast.

What all this demonstrates is that there was a jarring misalignment of interests between class counsel and members of the federal class. It was plainly in the best interest of counsel to settle the federal claims at any price. For them, any settlement was better than no settlement because settlement was the only way they could make any money on the federal claims—indeed, given that the state claims were essentially worthless, it was the only way that Delaware counsel could get any compensation at all.

---

[13] Indeed, it would not be an exaggeration to say that the Delaware plaintiffs were kept in state court entirely at the sufferance of Matsushita. As we discuss below, the Delaware Vice Chancellor, in rejecting the first settlement, determined that the state law claims were "extremely weak" and had "little or no value" because no such state cause of action existed. See In re MCA Shareholders Litigation, 598 A.2d 687, 694 (Del.Ch.1991). Matsushita could have, but did not move the Chancery Court to dismiss the state action. Rather, it chose to use it as a vehicle for seeking an inexpensive release of the federal claims. See also 18 Charles A. Wright, Arthur R. Miller & Edward H. Cooper, FEDERAL PRACTICE AND PROCEDURE § 4470, at 526 (Supp.1997) ("In approving the settlement, the Delaware Vice Chancellor observed that the defendants seemed more bent on escaping potential liability under federal law than on avoiding state-law claims that the Vice Chancellor had earlier characterized as extremely weak.").

Delaware counsel were not, after all, serving as pro bono counsel to the MCA shareholders who tendered their shares.

It was not, in contrast, in the best interest of the clients—the MCA shareholders—to settle their Exchange Act claims at any price. Their interest lay in settling those claims for a sufficient amount to make it imprudent to take the risk of litigation. That risk, of course, would have to be realistically assessed in terms of the chances of prevailing on either or both of their claims that Matsushita had violated SEC Rules 10b–13 and 14d–10 in paying premiums to Messrs. Wasserman and Sheinberg. Indeed, the misalignment of interests and incentives between class counsel and their clients in these extraordinary circumstances was so great that it is fair to say that counsel's interests were more in line with the interests of Matsushita than those of their clients.

This was not the adequate representation of absent class members that due process requires "at all times." *Shutts*, 472 U.S. at 812. As we have said, "An adequate representative must . . . be free from economic interests that are antagonistic to the interests of the class." The interests of Delaware counsel in this case were nothing but antagonistic to the interests of the MCA shareholders who tendered their shares. As a result of the three factors described above, which make this case extraordinary on its facts, Delaware counsel's overriding economic interest lay in settling the federal claims at any price and winning the race to judgment. The interests of the MCA shareholders who tendered their shares, in contrast, lay in pursuing those claims vigorously and either obtaining a reasonable settlement or litigating the claims in federal court. Their interests certainly did not lie in agreeing to a settlement that gave the attorneys a $1,000,000 fee but nothing for themselves—the settlement originally proposed by Delaware counsel—nor in agreeing to a settlement of 2 [cents] per share, inclusive of attorneys' fees—the settlement Delaware counsel ultimately persuaded the Vice Chancellor to approve. . . . Here, there is no question that there was antagonism between the interests of the lawyers and the interests of their clients. That antagonism made their representation of the MCA shareholders who tendered their shares inadequate as a matter of law.

In addition to the argument that Delaware counsel had a disabling conflict of interest, the Epstein plaintiffs contend that the actual conduct of Delaware counsel in settling the federal claims fell far short of the representation that due process requires. Rather, they claim, Delaware counsel completely failed to investigate or develop their federal claims and basically "rolled over" during settlement negotiations, ultimately entering into a settlement that was essentially worthless except for their own fees. This course of conduct, they conclude, falls well below the level of representation that is required to bind absentees. We agree.

Adequate representation requires that counsel "vigorously and tenaciously protect[] the interests of the class." *Gonzales*, 474 F.2d at 75. "Vigorous" and "tenacious" protection requires, at a minimum, that counsel pursue their clients' claims, make a reasonable effort to assess the fair settlement value of those claims, and pursue a settlement that approximates that value, always taking into account the ever-present risks of litigation. The inadequacy of Delaware counsel's representation is brought into sharp focus by their vigorous disparagement of the federal claims throughout the course of the settlement proceedings. Indeed, Delaware counsel's representation of those claims surpassed inadequacy and sank to the level of subversion. Counsel consistently sought to convince, not only their clients, but their adversaries and the Chancery Court itself that the federal claims had no merit. They repeatedly and summarily dismissed those claims as "frivolous" without ever conducting any discovery or any meaningful analysis of the legal issues, much less presenting the claims in a favorable light. In sharp contrast, the *Epstein* counsel earnestly pursued those same claims in federal court, recognizing their merit and successfully demonstrating that merit in persuading this court to reverse an adverse summary judgment ruling below. This contrast makes it all the more clear that Delaware counsel's representation of the MCA shareholders who tendered their shares fails even the most minimal standards of adequacy. . . .

In sum, the only "vigorous" and "tenacious" work, that Delaware counsel performed on behalf of the Epstein plaintiffs was to convince the Chancery Court to adopt their adversary's position and view the federal claims as essentially worthless. This was not merely "inadequate" representation, it was hostile representation that served the interests of counsel in getting a fee, but did not serve the interests of the MCA shareholders in getting a settlement based upon a thorough and fair assessment of their Exchange Act claims. To bind the Epstein plaintiffs to the Delaware judgment under these circumstances would violate their due process right to have their interests adequately represented at all times.

CONCLUSION

Our decision that the Delaware judgment deprived the Epstein plaintiffs of their due process rights to adequate representation is the product of an extraordinary set of circumstances. Delaware counsel suffered from a conflict of interest: they could not litigate the Exchange Act claims of the absent class members, could not extinguish those claims by the issue preclusive effect of a judgment based upon the state claims, and were in competition with a parallel class action in federal court which threatened to destroy their chances of securing a fee. Not surprisingly, their conduct in the Delaware action reflected this disabling conflict. Delaware counsel disparaged the Exchange Act claims of their own clients at every turn—to the clients themselves, to their adversaries, and even to the Chancery Court.

These extraordinary circumstances provide a sufficient answer to Matsushita's concern that our decision will pose a grave threat to the finality of class action judgments. The reality of the matter is that it is the rare exception for representation in a class action even to approach the point where an absentee will have a colorable claim for inadequacy. The small handful of cases that have come to our attention in which absentees have successfully challenged adequacy of representation bears this observation out. The paucity of such cases is to be expected. With rare exceptions, trial judges do their jobs and certify class representatives capable of representing the interests of absent class members. And, again with rare exceptions, the class representatives (including their counsel) faithfully discharge their fiduciary duties to the class. This case presents one of those rare exceptions.

■ [JUDGE O'SCANNLAIN'S dissenting opinion is omitted.]

Epstein v. MCA, Inc. (*"Epstein III"*)

179 F.3d 641 (9th Cir. 1999)

■ O'SCANNLAIN, CIRCUIT JUDGE:

We reconsider our decision in this case which is still before us on remand from the United States Supreme Court. . . .

On October 24, 1997, two days after the filing of *Epstein II*, Judge Norris, the author of both *Epstein I* and *Epstein II*, resigned from this court. Matsushita filed a petition for rehearing on November 5, 1997. On January 9, 1998, Judge Thomas was drawn to replace Judge Norris and the reconstituted panel granted the petition for rehearing on June 8, 1998. Following rehearing, we now withdraw our opinion in *Epstein II* and consider anew whether the Epstein appellants are bound by the Delaware judgment.

II

The Epstein appellants assert that, despite the Supreme Court's holding in *Matsushita,* we cannot accord full faith and credit to the Delaware judgment because it violated their due process rights to adequate representation in and judicial supervision of the Delaware proceedings. We are somewhat perplexed by this contention, because *Matsushita*'s holding was explicitly and implicitly premised upon the validity of the Delaware judgment. The Supreme Court stated in *Matsushita* that the Epstein appellant's were "bound . . . by the judgment," 516 U.S. at 379, and held that the exclusively federal claims released by that judgment were not exempted from full faith and credit, *see id.* at 385–87. It should go without saying that we are not free to ignore the Court's determinations in *Matsushita* by holding that the Epstein appellants are *not* bound by the judgment. . . .

B

While the Court's explicit consideration in *Matsushita* of the due process requirements to bind absent class members admittedly did not include an express statement that the Delaware judgment in question did not violate due process, that conclusion was logically necessary to the Court's holding. In *Kremer v. Chemical Construction Corp.,* the Supreme Court made plain that "[a] State may not grant preclusive effect in its own courts to a constitutionally infirm judgment, and other state and federal courts are not required to accord full faith and credit to such a judgment." 456 U.S. 461, 482, (1982). Thus in *Matsushita,* any resolution of the preclusive effect to be afforded under Delaware law to the Delaware judgment necessarily entailed a determination of whether the judgment was "constitutionally infirm." If the judgment were constitutionally infirm, the judgment could not be binding under Delaware law, nor could a federal court accord it full faith and credit. . . .

III

Apart from any statements in *Matsushita*[,] . . . the Epstein appellants assert that *Phillips Petroleum Co. v. Shutts*, 472 U.S. 797 (1985), and *Kremer [v. Chemical Construction Corp.*, 456 U.S. 461 (1982)] create a largely unfettered right to challenge collaterally the adequacy of representation in class actions. . . .

Shutts does not support the broad collateral review that the Epstein appellants seek. In *Shutts*, the Court identified various procedural safeguards that are necessary to bind absent class members, including notice, the opportunity to be heard, the opportunity to opt out, and adequate representation. 472 U.S. at 812. However, nowhere in *Shutts* did the Court state or imply that where the certifying court makes a determination of the adequacy of representation in accord with *Shutts*, this determination is subject to collateral review. *Shutts* in fact implies that such review is unwarranted by emphasizing that the certifying court is charged with protecting the interests of the absent class members. See *id.* at 809.

Simply put, the absent class members' due process right to adequate representation is protected not by collateral review, but by the certifying court initially, and thereafter by appeal within the state system and by direct review in the United States Supreme Court. See, e.g., *Grimes v. Vitalink Communications Corp.*, 17 F.3d 1553, 1558 (3d Cir. 1994) (refusing to allow absent class members collaterally to challenge adequacy of representation because the opportunity to challenge that determination by appeal to Delaware Supreme Court, and thereafter to the United States Supreme Court, "granted all the process that was due"); *Nottingham Partners v. Trans–Lux Corp.*, 925 F.2d 29, 33 (1st Cir. 1991) (holding that so long as procedural safeguards were employed, objections to the determinations of a certifying court had to be remedied on appeal to the state supreme court or the United States Supreme Court, and not by recourse to the "federal courts in the vain pursuit of back-door relief").

As the Court stated in *Hansberry v. Lee*, "there has been a failure of due process only in those cases where it cannot be said that *the procedure adopted*, fairly insures the protection of the interests of absent parties who are to be bound by it." 311 U.S. 32, 42 (1940) (emphasis added). Due process requires that an absent class member's right to adequate representation be protected by the adoption of the appropriate procedures by the certifying court and by the courts that review its determinations; due process does not require collateral second-guessing of those determinations and that review.

B

Kremer does not indicate otherwise. . . . *Kremer* held that neither state nor federal courts are required to give full faith and credit to a constitutionally infirm judgment. See *Kremer*, 456 U.S. at 482. The extent of collateral review is, however, limited.

Kremer merely recognized that a judgment is not entitled to full faith and credit "if there is reason to doubt the quality, extensiveness, or fairness of *procedures* followed in prior litigation." *Id.* at 481 (emphasis added). Limited collateral review would be appropriate, therefore, to consider whether the procedures in the prior litigation afforded the party against whom the earlier judgment is asserted a "full and fair opportunity" to litigate the claim or issue. *Id.* at 480. This review would not, however, include reconsideration of the merits of the claim or issue, see *id.* at 483–85, (declining to reexamine the facts underlying or the merits of Kremer's claim, and instead examining the procedures provided), and such a challenge would most likely fail because "state proceedings need do no more than satisfy the minimum procedural requirements of the Fourteenth Amendment's Due Process Clause in order to qualify for the full faith and credit guaranteed by federal law." *Id.* at 481.

C

Matsushita itself indicates that broad collateral review of the adequacy of representation (or of the other due process requirements for binding absent class members) is not available. *Matsushita* made plain that class action judgments are accorded full faith and credit like other judgments. . . .

The Court did, of course, address the additional due process requirements for binding absent class members, stating, by way of example, that "due process for class action plaintiffs requires 'notice plus an opportunity to be heard and participate in the litigation,'" and "'that the named plaintiff at all times adequately represent the interests of the absent class members.'" *Id.* at 378–79 (quoting *Shutts*, 472 U.S. at 812). The Court, however, satisfied itself that these requirements had been met *by referencing the Delaware courts' findings on these matters*, rather than by independently determining whether the requirements were met. . . .

IV

For the foregoing reasons, the Delaware judgment was not constitutionally infirm and must be accorded full faith and credit. . . .

■ Wiggins, Circuit Judge, concurring:

I concur in the result of Judge O'Scannlain's majority opinion. I write separately to explain why I changed my vote in this appeal. . . .

I now believe that, while the Supreme Court did not conclusively resolve the due process issue before the remand, it did send unmistakable signals on that very issue. In three separate passages, the Court indicated that the Delaware courts likely had already conclusively resolved the due process issue.[1] Our original majority disposition in this appeal did not give sufficient weight to these admonitions

The Supreme Court's conclusion is clearly supported by the record. One of the objectors, William Krupman, explicitly opposed the proposed settlement because "the purported class representatives . . . had proposed a settlement that benefitted no one but their own attorneys. *They did not provide adequate representation to the class.*" (emphasis added). In considering Krupman's objection, the Chancery Court felt that his objection concerning the adequacy of the class representatives' representation of the class members was similar to the objection raised by another objector, Pamela Minton de Ruiz, who objected to the settlement "on the basis that the settlement is collusive." The Chancery Court nonetheless approved the settlement because the settlement was "in the best interest of the class," notwithstanding these objections to the adequacy of the class representatives' representation.

Because the adequacy of representation issue was fully and fairly litigated and necessarily decided in the Chancery Court, the Delaware courts would give preclusive effect to that determination. See *Messick v. Star Enter.*, 655 A.2d 1209, 1211 (Del. 1995). The Full Faith and Credit Act, 28

---

[1] First, in Part I of its opinion, as it described the procedural posture of the case it stated that "[a]fter argument from several objectors, the [Chancery] court found the class representation adequate. . . ." *Matsushita*, 516 U.S. at 371. Later, in explaining why it believed that the Delaware courts would afford preclusive effect to the settlement judgment, the Supreme Court explained that "[t]he Court of Chancery 'further determined that the plaintiffs[,] . . . as representatives of the Settlement Class, have fairly and adequately protected the interests of the Settlement Class.'" *Id.* at 378.

Finally, the Court expressed its astonishment at plaintiffs' decision to assert their due process claim "in spite of the Chancery Court's express ruling, following argument on the issue, that the class representatives fairly and adequately protected the interests of the class." *Id.* at 379 n. 5.

U.S.C. § 1738, requires that we "treat a state court judgment with the same respect that it would receive in the courts of the rendering state." *Matsushita*, 516 U.S. at 373. As such, we are required to give preclusive effect to the Chancery Court's judgment that class representation was adequate irrespective of whether we agree with that determination. I therefore concur.

■ [Judge Thomas wrote a dissenting opinion, a part of which stated that "[i]nsofar as is possible, I shall not repeat Judge Norris's forceful analysis, as detailed in the panel opinion on remand. It demands an independent and careful examination and is, in my view, dispositive." *Id.* at 651 n.1.]

NOTES AND QUESTIONS

1.   *The Collateral Attack Debate in Context.* From at least 1940 (when *Hansberry* was decided) through the 1990's, there was wide agreement among courts and commentators that an absent class member had the right to collaterally attack a class judgment for inadequate representation. In fact, the availability of collateral attack for inadequate representation was so well-established that the leading civil procedure treatise flatly stated that *Epstein II* "seemed surprising only by taking such great effort to reach conclusions that many students would have thought clearly required by long tradition." 18A Charles Alan Wright et al., FEDERAL PRACTICE AND PROCEDURE § 4455, at 485 (2002).

There was substantial authority supporting FEDERAL PRACTICE AND PROCEDURE's observation. As early as 1942, the first Restatement of Judgments stated:

> Where a person is not a party to a class action, the judgment therein has *conclusive effect against him only if his interests were adequately represented.* . . . [A] person as to whom a class action is ineffective is not required to seek relief during the continuance of the action. . . .

RESTATEMENT OF JUDGMENTS § 116 cmt. b, at 563–64 (1942). Citing to § 116 of the First Restatement, the Advisory Committee Notes prepared in conjunction with the 1966 Revision of Rule 23 similarly state that the revised Rule "does not disturb the recognized principle that the court conducting the [class] action cannot predetermine the res judicata effect of the judgment; this can be tested only in a subsequent action." The Second Restatement is in accord. RESTATEMENT (SECOND) JUDGMENTS § 42 cmt. b (1982); see also *id.* at cmt. e reporter's note (citing *Hansberry* for the proposition that "[t]he finding of divergence of interest may, *of course*, be made on collateral challenge" (emphasis added)).

But in the years since *Epstein III*, the trend among federal courts of appeal and state supreme courts has been to limit the availability of collateral attack, although courts remain split and commentators have come down on both sides of the debate. By 2009, the tide of professional opinion had shifted to the point that the American Law Institute could recommend a substantial narrowing of the traditional view that an absent class member may collaterally attack a class judgment for inadequate representation. Specifically, the American Law Institute argues that collateral attack should be prohibited unless the class court "failed to make the necessary findings of adequate representation, or failed to afford class members reasonable notice and an opportunity to be heard as required by applicable law." American Law Institute, PRINCIPLES OF THE LAW OF AGGREGATE LITIGATION § 3.14(a)(2). For citations to courts and commentators on all sides of the debate, see Patrick Woolley, *Collateral Attack and the Role of Adequate Representation in Class Suits for Money Damages*, 58 U. Kan. L. Rev. 917, 917–918, nn. 1–7 (2010).

Why the shift? One part of the answer has to do with the increasing importance of settlement. Those most focused on encouraging class settlements tend to favor stricter limitations on the availability of collateral attack. To be sure, settlement proponents are concerned about agency costs and inadequate representation, but they prefer to deal with these risks in the original litigation, through the district judge's Rule 23 review and appeals from the class court's determinations. Centralizing the representational adequacy inquiry in the original proceeding supports the certainty benefits of settlement and thus facilitates successful settlement negotiations. Allowing absent class members to collaterally attack a class judgment for inadequate representation renders class settlements vulnerable to later challenge at the behest of absent class members (or their attorneys), and the enhanced uncertainty makes settlements more difficult to achieve. In short, the availability of collateral attack imposes a greater burden today than when *Hansberry*, for example, was decided because of the greater importance of class actions and class settlements.

Those who favor a more expansive right to collaterally attack a judgment for inadequate representation tend to focus instead on agency problems and abuse in the class setting, including the possibility of collusion between class counsel and class defendants with respect to settlement. Defenders of a more expansive right to collateral attack are also more skeptical of the ability of absent class members and class courts to catch these problems in the class suit itself, and they worry about the negative effects of collusive settlements in massive nationwide class actions. Given these risks, the argument goes, collateral attack serves as a crucial safeguard against abuse and provides an incentive to all concerned to ensure that due process values are respected in the original suit. From this perspective, an expansive right to collaterally attack a class judgment for inadequate representation is particularly important today because of the serious risks associated with class settlements.

2. *The Conceptual Debate over Collateral Attack.* Recall that in nonclass litigation, a defendant who does not appear may collaterally attack a default judgment for lack of personal jurisdiction. Since absent class members do not appear in the class action, it might seem to follow that they should be able to attack the class judgment on the ground that the class court did not have personal jurisdiction over them. Recall that the U.S. Supreme Court in *Phillips Petroleum Co. v. Shutts* held that courts may exercise personal jurisdiction over an absent class member who lacks minimum contacts with the forum. The Court explained that "if the forum state wishes to bind an absent class member concerning a claim for money damages or similar relief at law," 472 U.S. at 811, the forum court must provide notice and the right to opt out, *and* the named plaintiffs must adequately represent the absent class members. Suppose that a class court provides notice, allows opt outs and determines that the absent class members were adequately represented. May absent class members nonetheless collaterally challenge the adequacy of representation?

Judge Norris in his opinion in *Matsushita* mentioned and refused to follow the Third Circuit decision in *Grimes v. Vitalink*, 17 F.3d 1553 (3d Cir.1994). *Grimes* held that an absent class member who has minimum contacts with the forum can be denied the right to collaterally attack a judgment for inadequate representation when that issue was litigated in the class court. In later decisions, the Third Circuit extended *Grimes* by holding that an absent class member who receives notice and fails "to opt out "consent[s] to the jurisdiction of the class action court . . . even when that member lacks minimum contacts with the forum," and may be bound by a finding of adequate representation. *In re Diet Drugs Products Liability Litigation*, 431 F.3d 141, 146 (3d Cir.2005) (summarizing the law of the circuit).

Is the Third Circuit correct that a class court has personal jurisdiction over absent class members who received notice and failed to opt out, thereby binding them to the class court's determination of adequate representation and barring collateral attack? Is this consistent with *Shutts*? For a negative answer, see Patrick Woolley, *The Jurisdictional Nature of Adequate Representation in Class Litigation*, 79 Geo. Wash. L. Rev. 410 (2011) (arguing that a class court lacks power to bind an absent class member to a finding of adequate representation in the same way that a court in nonclass litigation lacks power to bind an absentee to a finding of personal jurisdiction); see also Henry Paul Monaghan, *Antisuit Injunctions and Preclusion Against Absent Nonresident Class Members*, 98 Colum. L. Rev. 1148, 1154 (1998) (arguing that courts do not have jurisdiction over absent class members who lack minimum contacts with the forum and have not been adequately represented). For a very different view of the jurisdictional question, see Samuel Issacharoff & Richard Nagareda, *Class Settlements under Attack*, 156 U. Pa. L. Rev. 1649, 1702 (2008) (arguing that "national markets give rise to . . . demands for closure that are national in scope" and "[w]here jurisdiction realistically cannot turn on some vestigial notion of territoriality, the basis for the rendering court's assertion of authority over absent class members must proceed on some other basis—in *Shutts*, implied consent to a process that combines rights in the vein of self-help (exit and voice rights) with a right to oversight by fiduciaries (loyalty rights)").

Another way to approach the question of collateral attack is to focus, not on personal jurisdiction, but on whether it is "fair" in a broader sense to bind an absent class member to a finding of adequate representation. In *Wolfert ex. rel. Estate of Wolfert v. Transamerica Home First Inc.*, 439 F.3d 165 (2d Cir. 2006), for example, the Second Circuit insisted that an absent class member could be bound if others had litigated the question in the class court, and it did so without addressing whether the class court had personal jurisdiction over the class member:

> [I]f the class action court ruled only in general terms that representation was adequate, without any adversarial consideration of the claim now advanced by Mrs. Wolfert that New York law affords her substantial rights beyond those afforded by California law, it would be manifestly unfair to preclude her collateral attack. On the other hand, if, in the class action, *a defendant opposing class certification or an objector to the settlement* had made a serious argument that a subclass was required because of claims substantially similar to hers, and that argument had been considered and rejected by the class action court, it would not be unfair to preclude collateral review of that ruling and relegate Mrs. Wolfert to her direct review remedies. It would not be a denial of due process to give full faith and credit to the class action court's ruling on adequacy of representation unless that ruling was made in the absence of an adversarial presentation of the claim that interests substantially similar to those of Mrs. Wolfert's required the designation of a sub-class.

Id. at 172 (emphasis added). Recall as well that, without mentioning the question of personal jurisdiction, Judge Wiggins concluded in *Epstein III* that the Epstein Plaintiffs could be bound by the Delaware class judgment because two objectors to the settlement had argued in Delaware state court that the representation of the class was inadequate. Judge O'Scannlain relied on the actions of the same objectors in his dissent in *Epstein II*, but omitted the argument from his opinion in *Epstein III*.

Is it appropriate to bind absent class members when class objectors have raised questions about adequate representation on which the class court rules? Is the Second Circuit's decision in *Wolfert* based on the theory of "virtual representation"? Recall the discussion of virtual representation and *Taylor v. Sturgell* in Chapter 1. Is *Wolfert* consistent with *Taylor*?

In contrast to *Wolfert*, Professors Issacharoff and Nagareda justify limitations on collateral attack based, not on challenges to adequacy by other litigants in the class court, but on the duty of the class court to ensure adequate representation. Issacharoff & Nagareda, *Class Settlements under Attack*, 156 U. Pa. L. Rev. at 1716 (arguing that "[a] fiduciary conception of direct review suggests that what should matter for a collateral attack is the rigor of the rendering court's determination of [whether] structural [conflicts exist], not necessarily whether that question has been 'actually litigated' by someone in the familiar, adversarial litigation sense."). How adequate is this safeguard? Recall the discussion of Judge Weinstein's role in the Agent Orange settlement in the notes after the *Stephenson* case in Chapter 2. Was Judge Weinstein's conduct in *Agent Orange* consistent with that of a fiduciary for the class?

3.   *Is* Epstein III's *reading of* Matsushita *Correct?* Judge Wiggins was the deciding vote in both *Epstein II* and *III*. He justified his change of position in *Epstein III* substantially on the ground that he had not given sufficient weight in *Epstein II* to *Matsushita*'s discussion of due process. Recall footnote 1 of Judge Wiggins' opinion in *Epstein III*. Putting aside his speculation that the Supreme Court was "astonished" that the *Epstein* plaintiffs raised due process objections "in spite of the Chancery Court's ruling," does he make a persuasive case that the Court in *Matsushita* signaled that the due process issue had been definitively resolved?

Judge O'Scannlain, for his part, argues that the Court in *Matsushita* "satisfied itself that [the due process] requirements [of *Shutts*] had been met *by referencing the Delaware courts' findings on these matters*, rather than by independently determining whether the requirements were met." Because a judgment is entitled to full faith and credit only if due process is satisfied, Judge O'Scannlain concludes that the Court's reliance on the findings of the Delaware courts meant that the Ninth Circuit should not independently determine the Epstein Plaintiffs due process objections. Do you agree with Judge O'Scannlain that resolving the due process question was "logically necessary" to the Supreme Court's holding in *Matsushita*? In this connection, recall Justice Ginsburg's observation in her separate opinion: "[T]his Court has recognized the first line responsibility of the states themselves for assuring that the constitutional essentials are met. Final judgments, however, remain vulnerable to collateral attack for failure to satisfy the adequate representation requirement."

4.   *Did Delaware Class Counsel Adequately Represent the Class?* Note that every judge who participated in *Epstein II* and *III* expressed concern about the adequacy of the representation provided by Delaware counsel. Even Judge

O'Scannlain—who twice rejected the Epstein Plaintiffs' efforts to collaterally attack the class judgment—wrote that Delaware counsel's "act of referring, in a single breath, to their own clients' claims as 'fraught with uncertainty,' 'weak,' and 'horrendous' suggests less than dynamic advocacy." *Epstein II*, 126 F.3d at 1256 (O'Scannlain, J., dissenting).

In the settlement negotiations for the Delaware class litigation, what leverage did class counsel have to extract settlement value for the relinquishing of the federal securities claims? Was Judge Norris correct that class counsel in the Delaware action were, in effect, disarmed in class settlement negotiations with regard to the federal securities claims? Or did Delaware class counsel have at least some leverage based upon the possibility that they might refile their lawsuit in federal district court in Delaware and, in so doing, avail themselves of the grant of exclusive subject matter jurisdiction to adjudicate the federal securities claims? For a suggestion along these lines, see an article by William T. Allen, *Finality in Judgments in Class Actions: A Comment on* Epstein v. MCA, Inc., 73 N.Y.U. L. Rev. 1149, 1162 (1998) ("Knowing that the plaintiff could quickly file a 1934 Act claim in the federal court if necessary makes it unnecessary for the plaintiff to do so in order to have the leverage that a 1934 Act claim provides."). But see *Epstein III*, 179 F.3d at 652 (Thomas, J., dissenting) ("By the time settlement occurred, the statute of limitations prevented the Delaware class from litigating the federal claims in any court.").

Why, as a strategic matter, might Delaware class counsel have resisted the notion of withdrawing their Delaware state-court action and refiling it in federal district court in Delaware even before the statute of limitations had run? Put differently, would a threat to refile in federal court have been a credible threat on Delaware class counsel's part? What might have happened if Delaware class counsel had refiled in federal court? Recall here the discussion earlier in this Chapter of the MDL Panel decision in *In re Silicone Gel Breast Implants Product Liability Litigation*.

What effect, if any, should the quality of the representation provided by Delaware class counsel have on the debate with respect to collateral attack?* Does the quality of representation afforded the class in Delaware affect your understanding of the costs and benefits of collateral attack?

5.   *The Decisions of the Epstein Plaintiffs and their Counsel.* The Epstein plaintiffs had an opportunity to opt out of the Delaware settlement, but chose not to take it. Why do you suppose the Epstein Plaintiffs chose not to simply opt out of the litigation? Why did class counsel in the California federal action not appear in Delaware to contest the class settlement reached in that forum? What would class counsel have gained if they had succeeded in persuading the Delaware court that the proposed settlement was unfair? Would Delaware counsel simply have renegotiated the settlement once again? Or might Califor-

---

*Another well-known collateral attack involved even more egregious "representation" by class counsel. Pursuant to a settlement of a class suit filed in Alabama, refunds were credited to and class counsel's attorneys' fees were deducted from the escrow accounts of class members. The formula prescribed by the settlement meant that some class members *lost* money as a result of the settlement. One class member received a refund of $2.19, but paid an attorneys' fee of $91! In a scathing critique of the settlement, two commentators note that "[a]ny class member who paid more in attorney's fees than he or she recovered 'would have been better off if class counsel had lost the case.'" Susan P. Koniak & George M. Cohen, *Under Cloak of Settlement*, 82 Va. L. Rev. 1051, 1068 (1996). Fortunately for class members residing in Vermont, the Vermont Supreme Court approved a collateral attack on the settlement. *State v. Homeside Lending, Inc.*, 826 A.2d 997 (Vt. 2003).

nia counsel have persuaded the Delaware court to decertify or stay the Delaware action?

6. *The Significance of CAFA.* Should the enactment of CAFA influence how courts think about the parameters for collateral attacks? Recall the discussion of regulatory mismatch in the notes following *Shutts* in Chapter 2. In a national market for undifferentiated goods and services, where should a collateral attack be brought?

C. DETERRENCE OF OPT–OUTS THROUGH CLASS SETTLEMENT DESIGN

With this Section, we shift from judicial review of class settlements to constraints on how those settlements are designed. As we have seen, one of the important differences between (b)(1) and (b)(2) class actions, on the one hand, and (b)(3) class actions on the other is that the former are mandatory and the latter gives parties a right to opt out. This section examines the extent to which class settlement designers can press at the boundaries between mandatory and opt-out class actions by structuring opt-out class settlements in such a way as to discourage class members from actually opting out. The two cases that follow present variations on this general theme.

In re Prudential Insurance Co. of America Sales Practice Litigation
261 F.3d 355 (3d Cir. 2001)

■ McKEE, CIRCUIT JUDGE.

This appeal arises in the wake of the settlement of a nationwide class action against The Prudential Insurance Company of America. Two policyholders who were members of the class appeal the district court's order enjoining them from prosecuting suits they filed in state court in Florida based upon policies that were eligible for inclusion in the nationwide class, but which the plaintiffs excluded from the terms of the class settlement. For the reasons that follow, we will affirm.

I. FACTUAL BACKGROUND

A large group of policy holders started a nationwide class action against Prudential Life Insurance Company alleging that Prudential agents had engaged in deceptive sales practices.

The class is comprised of [over 8 million] Prudential policyholders who allegedly were the victims of fraudulent and misleading sales practices employed by Prudential's sales force. The challenged sales practices consisted primarily of churning,[2] vanishing premiums[3] and fraudulent investment plans,[4] and each cause of action is based on fraud or deceptive conduct.

---

[2] The district court explained that "[i]n the life insurance context, the term 'churning' refers to the removal, through misrepresentations or omissions, of the cash value, including dividends, of an existing life insurance policy or annuity to acquire a replacement policy. The value of the first policy may be reduced either by borrowing against the policy or by virtue of the policy's lapse. Churning often results in financial detriment to the policyholder, a financial benefit to the agent by virtue of a large commission on the first year premium, and administrative charges being paid to the insurer." *In re Prudential Ins. Co. of America Sales Practices Litigation*, 962 F. Supp. 450, 474 (E.D. Pa. 1997). . . .

On October 28, 1996, the class representatives entered into a Stipulation of Settlement with Prudential. That same day, the district court entered an Order Conditionally Certifying the Class for Settlement Purposes, Designating Class Counsel and Class Representatives, Staying Pending Motions, Directing Issuance of Notice, Issuing Injunction and Scheduling Settlement Hearing (the "Certification Order"). In that Certification Order, the district court also conditionally certified the following for purposes of settlement:

> a class that consists of all persons who own or owned at termination an individual permanent whole life insurance policy issued by Prudential or any of its United States Life insurance subsidiaries during the Class Period of January 1, 1982 through December 31, 1995 (the "Policy" or "Policies"), except as specifically described below [not relevant here] ("Policyholders"), and do not timely exclude themselves from participating in the settlement ("Class Members" or the "Class").

. . . The Class Notice . . . advised class members of the effect of the proposed settlement and referenced a Release that was attached as Appendix A. The Release stated in relevant part that "Class Members hereby expressly agree that they shall not . . . institute, maintain or assert . . . any and all causes of action, claims . . . that have been, [or] could have been, asserted by Plaintiffs or any Class Member against [Prudential] in any other court action . . . connected with . . . The Released Transactions[5]. . . ."

The Class Notice also told the Class Members how they could exclude themselves from the class and explained that policyholders who owned more than one policy could "choose to remain a Class Member with respect to some Policies, but . . . exclude [themselves] from the Class with respect to other Policies."

Following the mailing of the Class Notice and the Fairness Hearing, the district court entered a Final Order and Judgment certifying a settlement and approving the settlement as fair, reasonable and adequate. *In re Prudential Ins. Co. of America Sales Practices Litigation*, 962 F. Supp. 450 (D.N.J. 1997). The Final Order also clearly informed all class members of the preclusive effect of the Settlement. It stated:

---

[3] The district court found that "Prudential agents used . . . 'vanishing premium' policies, often in conjunction with churning, to sell permanent life insurance policies to class members; Prudential agents misrepresented that policyholders would have to pay no out-of-pocket premiums after a certain number of premium payments during the initial years of the policies. . . . Prudential's standardized sales presentations and policy illustrations failed to disclose that the policy premiums would not vanish and that Prudential did not expect the policies to pay for themselves as illustrated. Prudential's illustrations also did not inform policyholders of the assumptions on which the policy illustrations were based, assumptions which had no reasonable basis in fact. . . ." 962 F. Supp. at 476.

[4] The district court explained that "Prudential fraudulently marketed life insurance policies as 'investment plans,' 'retirement plans,' or similar investment vehicles. Plaintiffs allege that Prudential agents failed to disclose that these purported 'investment plans' were really standard life insurance policies, which carried costs and other components that materially and adversely differed from true investment or retirement plans. . . ." 926 F. Supp. at 476–77.

[5] "Released Transactions" are defined in the Release to "mean the marketing, solicitation, application, underwriting, acceptance, sale, purchase, operation, retention, administration, servicing, or replacement by means of surrender, partial surrender, loans respecting, withdrawal and/or termination of the Policies or any insurance policy or annuity sold in connection with, or relating in any way directly or indirectly to the sale or solicitation of, the Policies. . . ."

The terms of the Stipulation of Settlement and of this Final Order and Judgment, including all exhibits and supplemental exhibits thereto, shall forever be binding on, and shall have res judicata and claim preclusive effect in all pending and future lawsuits maintained by or on behalf of, the plaintiffs and all other class members, as well as their heirs, executors and administrators, successors and assigns. All claims for compensatory or punitive damages on behalf of class members are hereby extinguished, except as provided for in the Stipulation of Settlement.

In addition, the district court expressly incorporated the Release into the Final Order.

The Certification Order also contained the following injunction:

Prudential has offered evidence showing the existence of multiple class actions which could act to seriously impair this Court's ability to oversee the orderly and efficient management of the proposed nationwide class action settlement, and have demonstrated that without preliminary injunctive relief, many similar actions could proceed. Based on its familiarity with the issues in this lawsuit and the complexity of the proposed settlement, the Court finds that such actions may substantially impair the ability of this Court and the parties to implement the proposed settlement . . . Therefore, based on the record, including the legal and factual support for an injunction submitted by Prudential, this Court finds that an injunction is necessary to protect its jurisdiction, and hereby issues the following injunction, effective upon the mailing of the Class Notice, with Policyholders having been thus afforded the opportunity to exclude themselves from the Class:

All Policyholders and all persons acting on behalf of or in concert or participation with any Policyholder, are hereby enjoined from filing, commencing, prosecuting, continuing, litigating, intervening in or participating as class members in, any lawsuit in any jurisdiction based on or related to the facts and circumstances underlying the claims and causes of action in this lawsuit, unless and until such Policyholder has timely excluded herself or himself from the Class.

The district court invoked the authority of the All–Writs Act, 28 U.S.C. § 1651(a), and the Anti–Injunction Act, 28 U.S.C. § 2283, in entering this injunction. The court reasoned that the injunction was "necessary in aid of its jurisdiction in order to effectuate the proposed settlement," and therefore permissible under the Anti–Injunction Act and authorized by the All–Writs Act. . . .

We affirmed the district court's certification of the class and approval of the settlement in *In re Prudential Ins. Co. of America Sales Practices Litigation*, 148 F.3d 283 (3d Cir. 1998). . . .

II.   THE FLORIDA SUIT

Marvin and Alice Lowe, the appellants here, are members of the class because they purchased five Prudential insurance policies between 1981 and 1989. Four of those policies were class eligible. The Lowes requested that two of the policies be excluded from the class (the "Excluded Policies"), but they remained class members as to two other policies (the "Class Policies").

Ten months after the district court certified the class and approved the nationwide settlement, the Lowes started an action in state court in Broward County Florida. There, they initially alleged that a Prudential agent had engaged in deceptive and fraudulent practices in connection with their purchase of all five insurance policies. However, because the Class Policies constituted Released Transactions under the terms of the class settlement, the Lowes filed an amended complaint in which they limited their claims to the two Excluded Policies. The Lowes' First Amended Complaint asserts a cause of action against Prudential for breach of fiduciary duty, violations of Florida's RICO statute, negligent misrepresentation, fraudulent inducement, common law fraud, constructive fraud, reckless and wanton supervision, negligent supervision, and unjust enrichment.

Prudential claimed that the First Amended Complaint continued to rely on, and enumerate, all of the circumstances surrounding the purchase of the two Class Policies. In fact, Prudential insisted that the Lowes merely deleted the policy numbers of the two Class Policies from their original complaint then refiled that same complaint as the Amended Complaint. For example, the Class Action complaint alleged that:

> Prudential engaged in a systematic fraudulent marketing scheme in which its agents wrongfully induced policyholders to purchase certain Prudential life insurance policies. Second Am. Compl. at ¶ 5.

> Prudential implemented its scheme through the use of false and misleading sales presentations, policy illustrations, marketing materials, and other information that Prudential approved, prepared, and disseminated to its nationwide sales force. Second Am. Compl. at ¶ 5. . . .

> Beginning in the early 1980's, Prudential used its centralized marketing system to implement a scheme to sell new insurance policies to existing and new customers through three deceptive sales tactics: "churning," "vanishing premium," and "investment plan" techniques.

962 F. Supp. at 473–74. The Lowes' First Amended Complaint alleged:

> Sometime prior to 1982, the exact date being unknown to the [Lowes], Prudential devised a sales scheme and artifice to deprive its insureds and potential customers, including the [Lowes], of their property, in which Prudential trained its sales force, . . . , to induce and persuade current and potential customers, including the [Lowes], to purchase life insurance policies based on false and misleading policy illustrations and sales presentations, involving, *inter alia*, "churning" and "vanishing premiums." . . .

> Prudential embarked upon a scheme, plan, and common course of conduct through its agency system within Florida to sell high commission whole life polices to residents of the State of Florida through false and misleading sales presentations and policy illustrations based upon the vanishing premium concept. In this regard, Prudential targeted [the Lowes] in a scheme that included inter alia: (1) the sale of . . . vanishing premium policies, and (2) churning prior existing "in force" polices. [The Lowes] were induced to purchase various life insurance policies based on sales presentations and policy illustrations and promises that, if they made "out-of-pocket" premium payments for a designated

number of years, the interest earned on the polices would be sufficient to pay the premiums thereon for life, and thus, they would not have to come out-of-pocket to pay premiums after the designated number of years.

The First Amended Complaint and the Class Complaint both alleged senior management involvement in the "scheme." Compare 962 F. Supp. at 473–478 and 148 F.3d at 294 (describing Class allegations, including allegations of senior management involvement) with Lowe's First Amended Complaint at ¶ 26 ("[a]fter training and encouraging its agents to engage in the fraudulent scheme outlined above, Prudential turned a blind eye toward the fraudulent practices of its agents.").

The Lowes, however, insisted that their First Amended Complaint deleted their claims for damages stemming from the purchase of the Released Transactions as well as any reference to the Released Transactions. They argued that the First Amended Complaint was not based on, and did not seek damages for, the claims underlying the two Class Policies.

In a letter to Prudential's counsel dated January 13, 1999, the Lowes' counsel explained "while we do not intend to seek damages based upon the non-opted out policies, *the facts surrounding them were relevant to our claims*, including but not limited to our claim of a pattern and practice by Prudential justifying not only the imposition of liability, but additionally an assessment of punitive damages." (emphasis added). Prudential concluded that this letter established that the Lowes intended to rely upon evidence relating to the Class Policies in their suit on the Excluded Policies. Thus, argued Prudential, the Lowes intended to establish a pattern and practice of defrauding policyholders by relying upon facts relevant to the Class Policies and to use that evidence as a basis for their state claims for punitive and compensatory damages in relation to the sale of the Excluded Policies. Prudential argued that the Lowes' state court action would therefore force Prudential to defend the very matters covered by the Class Release. Accordingly, Prudential asked the district court to rule that the Lowes' action in Florida on the Excluded Policies violated the terms of the class settlement.

The district court agreed and held that

permitting litigation of [Excluded Policies] claims through the use of evidence of those sales practices and patterns that were the subject of the class action would impair the finality of the class settlement to an unacceptable degree. In effect, this would permit the relitigation of the released claims.

Therefore, on March 29, 2000, the district court issued an order specifically enjoining the Lowes

from engaging in motion practice, pursuing discovery, presenting evidence or undertaking any other action in furtherance [of their state court action] that is based on, relates to or involves facts and circumstances underlying the Released Transactions in the Class Action. . . .

This appeal followed.

III. DISCUSSION

. . . The Lowes contend that the injunction was not authorized under the All–Writs Act and was barred by the Anti–Injunction Act. They argue in the alternative that the injunction should be vacated because it is overbroad, vague, ambiguous, beyond the scope of the Final Judgment and Order, and otherwise an abuse of discretion.

It is now settled that a judgment pursuant to a class settlement can bar later claims based on the allegations underlying the claims in the settled class action. This is true even though the precluded claim was not presented, and could not have been presented, in the class action itself. See, *TBK Partners, Ltd. v. Western Union Corp.*, 675 F.2d 456, 460 (2d Cir. 1982). *TBK Partners* appears to be the first case firmly establishing this principle. However, that rule has since been applied in other cases in the Second Circuit, see also *In re Baldwin–United Corp. (Single Premium Deferred Annuities Insurance Litigation)*, 770 F.2d 328, 336 (2d Cir. 1985), and it has been accepted by the Ninth Circuit. . . . See, e.g., *Class Plaintiffs v. City of Seattle*, 955 F.2d 1268 (9th Cir. 1992). In *Class Plaintiffs*, the court held that a federal court may release claims over which it has no subject matter jurisdiction if the state claims arise from the same nucleus of operative facts as the claims properly before it.

Admittedly, it "may seem anomalous at first glance . . . that courts without jurisdiction to hear certain claims have the power to release those claims as part of a judgment." *Grimes v. Vitalink Communications Corp.*, 17 F.3d 1553, 1563 (3d Cir. 1994). However, we have endorsed the rule because it "serves the important policy interest of judicial economy by permitting parties to enter into comprehensive settlements that 'prevent relitigation of settled questions at the core of a class action.'" *Id.* (quoting *TBK Partners*, 675 F.2d at 460). We cited this principle approvingly when we affirmed the district court's approval of the class action settlement here.

That does not, however, end our inquiry. Although this principle is well established, we must examine the text of the Class Notice and, more particularly, the Class Release to determine the propriety of this injunction. We must determine whether settlement of claims the Lowes had under the Class Policies precludes them from pursuing claims in Florida purportedly arising from the Excluded Policies.

The Class Notice specifically referred to the Class Release and informed class members:

> If the proposed settlement is approved by the Court, and affirmed on appeal, the lawsuit will be dismissed with prejudice, and Prudential will be released from all claims that have been or could have been asserted by Class Members. *The release encompasses any matter relating to the marketing, solicitation, application, underwriting, acceptance, sale, purchase, operation, retention, administration, servicing, or replacement, by means of surrender, partial surrender, loans respecting withdrawal and/or terminations of Policies or any insurance policy or annuity sold in connection with or relating in any way directly or indirectly to the sale or solicitation of, the Policies. The release is intended to be very broad.* The release is a critical element of the proposed settlement, and accordingly, the entire text has been included in Appendix A to this Notice (except for certain defined terms that appear elsewhere in this Notice). Because it will affect your rights if you remain in the Class, you should read this paragraph and the entire release.

(emphasis added). As noted earlier, the Release was attached as Appendix A to the Class Notice, and provided, in relevant part:

Plaintiffs and all Class Members hereby expressly agree that they shall not now or hereafter institute, maintain or assert against any of the Releasees, either directly or indirectly, on their own behalf, on behalf of the Class or any other person, and release and discharge the Releasees from, any and all causes of action, claims, damages, equitable, legal and administrative relief, interest, demands or rights, of any kind or nature whatsoever, whether based on federal, state or local statute or ordinance, regulation contract, common law, or any other source, that have been, could have been, may be or could be alleged or asserted now or in the future by Plaintiffs or any Class Member against the Releasees in the Actions or in any other court action or before any administrative body (including any state Department of Insurance or other regulatory commission), tribunal or arbitration panel on the basis of, connected with, arising out of, or related to, in whole or in part, the Released Transactions and servicing relating to the Released Transactions. . . .

(emphasis added).

The Class Policies constitute Released Transactions and the Lowes do not argue to the contrary. Accordingly, the Lowes clearly released Prudential from any claims "based on," "connected with," "arising out of," "or related to, in whole or in part" their two Class Policies. Inasmuch as the Class Release was expressly incorporated into the Final Order and Judgment, it has both claim preclusive and issue preclusive effect, and class members were specifically advised of this. The Class Release also precludes class members from relying upon the common nucleus of operative facts underlying claims on the Class Policies to fashion a separate remedy against Prudential outside the confines of the Released Claims. Consequently, the Lowes, as class members on two Class Polices, are precluded from using the sales practices and factual predicates pertaining to their Class Policies in their state court action on the Excluded Policies.

The district court concluded that allowing the Lowes to prosecute their civil claims in the Florida court would allow an end run around the Class settlement by affording them (and other class members who might later attempt the same strategy) an opportunity for "relitigation of the released claims." Indeed, it would. In fact, the position urged by the Lowes here would seriously undermine the possibility for settling any large, multi district class action. Defendants in such suits would always be concerned that a settlement of the federal class action would leave them exposed to countless suits in state court despite settlement of the federal claims. Here, such state suits could number in the millions. . . .

The Lowes also argue that the Class Injunction precludes them, and all others who elected to opt-out of only some Class Eligible Policies "from pursuing any claims whatever on their" Excluded Policies. Essentially, they argue that the district court's order "render[s] meaningless the opt-out provisions upon which [they] and all others who chose to exclude their Policies from the Class Settlement relied." They contend that they should have at least been advised that anyone who opted-out on some of their class eligible policies but remained in the class on others, ran the risk that their right to pursue independent claims on the excluded policies was illusory and meaningless.

This argument is not without force. However, the Lowes exaggerate the effect of the district court's order. That order only prevents them from using evidence common to the purchase and sale of their Class Policies and their Excluded Policies in their state action on their Excluded Policies. It does not prohibit them from pursuing any and all claims on the Excluded Policies in the state court as they suggest. The district court made the distinction very clear in its carefully worded opinion. The court scrutinized the Lowes' Florida action, compared it with the Released Transactions and concluded:

> Certain of their substantive causes of action appear amenable to proof by evidence that is relevant exclusively to the Excluded Policies. The Lowes claims for breach of fiduciary duty and fraud are examples. Other counts . . . such as Lowes' claim that Prudential violated the Florida state RICO statute, or practiced reckless and wanton supervision, are different. To prosecute these claims the Lowes would presumably seek to discover and submit broader evidence of wrongful activity. Indeed, the language of their complaint leaves no room for doubt as to the Lowes' intention in that regard.

It is difficult to imagine how the Lowes' could prosecute their claims under Florida's RICO statute, or pursue their allegations of reckless and wanton supervision, without relying upon evidence that is relevant to the Class Policies as well as the Excluded Policies. Nevertheless, the district court's injunction does not prevent them from attempting to prove those claims if they can do it in a manner that is consistent with the Class Release and their status as class members. "The Lowes are free to attempt proving their RICO and other claims without the use of such evidence. . . . [T]o the extent those claims cannot survive without the evidence excluded by the [district court], such a result could only bolster the conclusion that the failing claims were part of the class settlement." We agree that if the Lowes cannot meet their burden on the Excluded Policies absent this evidence, that will be proof of the injunctive pudding. Thus, we do not believe that the Class Notice was deficient or that class members were blindsided by this injunction. We have previously affirmed the adequacy of that Notice against other attacks, see *In re Prudential Ins. of America Sales Practices Litigation*, 148 F.3d 283, and we again affirm the adequacy of that Notice against the specific issues raised by the Lowes.[8] . . .

IV.

We conclude that the district court was well within its authority in enforcing the Class Injunction in the manner that it did, and that it did not abuse its discretion. The court had carefully managed this vast and intricate settlement in a manner that allowed for its fair and reasonable resolution while protecting the interests of all of the parties involved. As part of the settlement agreement class members such as the Lowes agreed to release certain claims against Prudential. The agreement could not have been enforced without the injunction that the Lowes now challenge. The district

---

[8] We do, however, take this opportunity to add a note of caution. The Class Notice adequately informed potential class members of the right to opt-out of the class as to some policies and remain in the class as to other policies. It also gave adequate notice of the rights that would be surrendered as to any policies not excluded from the class. In the future, however, it may be advisable for district courts to consider adding more specific language to settlement documents. Any such language would advise class members that, even though they retain certain claims as to transactions excluded from a settlement, their ability to pursue those claims may be hindered by the terms of the release of claims that remain part of any class settlement.

court's order did nothing more than enforce that agreement. Accordingly, for all the reasons set forth above, we will affirm order of the district court.

NOTES AND QUESTIONS

1. *Settlement Interpretation and Notice.* Is the Prudential class settlement properly read to support the evidentiary injunction issued by the district court? The court's footnote 8 aside, were class members like the Lowes adequately notified of the prospect that any lawsuits brought as to excluded insurance policies would be subject to the evidentiary constraints ultimately imposed by the district court injunction? As a strategic matter, why might counsel for the Lowes wish to present evidence concerning policies covered by the class settlement in litigation concerning the policies that the Lowes excluded?

2. *Preclusion Principles.* Suppose that the class settlement agreement and the notice provided to absent class members indicated in explicit, unmistakable terms that any lawsuits as to excluded insurance policies would be subject to evidentiary constraints of the sort imposed by the district court's injunction. Is the *Prudential* court correct in framing its analysis of those constraints in largely pragmatic terms—i.e., whether using evidence concerning the released insurance policies in lawsuits dealing with excluded policies will "undermine the possibility for settling any large, multi district class action"?

Does the court ask the right questions in light of claim and issue preclusion principles, as discussed in Chapter 1? Consider what would happen to a class member who opted out with regard to her one and only Prudential insurance policy. Could the district court enjoin such a person from presenting evidence concerning the released policies of other persons in an individual lawsuit concerning her one excluded policy?

Consider two different class members with multiple Prudential insurance policies: Ann bought multiple insurance policies in a single business transaction with Prudential at the same time and in the same jurisdiction. As permitted by the class settlement, Ann opts out with regard to one of her policies— say, the one of higher dollar value—but remains in the class as to the other. By contrast, Betty also bought multiple Prudential insurance policies but did so ten years apart, with the first policy purchased in, say, Texas and the second purchased in Florida. Betty opts out as to her earlier Texas policy but stays in as to her later Florida policy. Do Ann and Betty stand on the same footing with regard to the evidentiary constraints that can be imposed on their individual lawsuits over their respective excluded policies?

In re Inter–Op Hip Prosthesis Liability Litigation

204 F.R.D. 330 (N.D. Ohio 2001)

■ O'MALLEY, J.

Sulzer Orthopedics, Inc. ("Sulzer Orthopedics") is a designer, manufacturer and distributor of orthopedic implants for hips, knees, shoulders, and elbows. One of its products is known as the "Inter–Op[] shell," which is one component of a system used for complete hip replacements. Specifically, the Inter–Op shell is a socket-like device, which is inserted into . . . the pelvis; the shell is designed to receive a separate, ball-like device, which is inserted into the . . . thigh bone. The two components thereby replace the articulating ball-and-socket structure of the hip joint. The Inter–Op shell is regulated by the federal Food and Drug Administration ("FDA").

Proper surgical attachment of these replacement components in the body is critical. Orthopedic implants are often cemented or screwed into position. Some implants are also designed to allow the bone to grow into and around them, holding them securely in place. The Inter–Op . . . shell was designed to bond with the natural bone.

Unfortunately, a manufacturing defect apparently prevented some of Sulzer Orthopedics' Inter–Op shells from bonding with the [bone]. In early December of 2000, Sulzer Orthopedics announced a voluntary recall of certain manufacturing lots of its Inter–Op shells. Most of the recalled products were manufactured during or after October of 1999, but a limited number were produced as early as June of 1997. The recall stated that Sulzer Orthopedics had "received reports of post-operative loosening" of some of the Inter–Op shells, apparently "related to a reaction of the body to a slight residue of lubricant used in the manufacturing process." Sulzer Orthopedics recalled approximately 40,000 units of its Inter–Op shell, of which about 26,000 had already been implanted in patients. About 90% of these implants occurred in the United States. . . .

In fact, to date about 2,400 of the patients who received implants of the Inter–Op shells have undergone "revision surgery"—removal of the defective implant and replacement with a new one. For a variety of reasons, not all of the patients who were implanted with recalled Inter–Op shells will undergo revision surgery. For example, some patients will not experience any bone-bonding failure; other patients may suffer severe failure but be medically ineligible for revision surgery. Ultimately, Sulzer Orthopedics estimates that approximately 4,500 patients will undergo revision surgery to replace the defective Inter–Op acetabular shells, and that the need for revision surgery will, in virtually all instance, become manifest within the next two years.

Shortly after Sulzer Orthopedics issued its voluntary recall in December of 2000, a number of plaintiffs around the country filed lawsuits, in both state and federal courts. To date, there are pending about 1,300 civil suits nationwide, about 200 of which are in federal court. These cases involve about 2,000 named plaintiffs, primarily including implant recipients and their spouses. Over 90% of the state court actions have been filed in California, Texas, Florida, or New York. About 19 of the state court cases are styled as class actions, as are about 34 of the federal court cases. The defendants named in these lawsuits include not only Sulzer Orthopedics, but also: (1) Sulzer Medica USA Holding Company ("Sulzer Medica USA"), a holding company that owns Sulzer Orthopedics; (2) Sulzer Medica Ltd., a Swiss holding company that owns Sulzer Medica USA; (3) Sulzer AG, a Swiss company that previously owned a majority of the stock of Sulzer Medica Ltd., (4) various other Sulzer-related entities; and (5) various surgeons, hospitals, and medical supply companies connected to the distribution or implantation of the defective product. The causes of action in these lawsuits include claims for defective design, marketing and manufacture; breach of express and implied warranties; negligence; strict liability; and other legal theories of recovery. Trial proceedings have already begun in at least one state court case.[4]

---

[4] Trial began on August 20, 2001 in the Nueces County, Texas state court case of *Rupp v. Sulzer Orthopedics, Inc.*, ending in a verdict exceeding $15 million. . . . Notably, these state

Pursuant to 28 U.S.C. § 1407, three different federal plaintiffs filed motions with the Federal Judicial Panel on Multi–District Litigation ("MDL Panel"), seeking to consolidate and centralize 30 of the federal lawsuits.[5] On June 19, 2001, the MDL Panel granted these motions, consolidating and transferring all related pending federal litigation to the Northern District of Ohio.

IV. Fairness of the Proposed Settlement Agreement . . .

B. The Terms of the Settlement Agreement.

[O]n August 24, 2001, the parties submitted [a] proposed settlement agreement [to be implemented through a judgment in a Rule 23(b)(3) class action. The proposed class of Inter–Op shell implantees is subdivided into two subclasses, each with separate representation. The two subclasses consist of those implantees who have not yet had revision surgery and those who have.] . . . The provisions of the [settlement] agreement are lengthy and complex. Thus, the Court sets out only the basic elements of the agreement here, in simplified fashion.

- The parties will create a "Settlement Trust," which will administer a Research Fund, a Medical Monitoring Fund, a Patient Benefit Fund, and an Extraordinary Injury Fund.

- The defendants will put $4 million in cash into the Research Fund, which will be used for "medical research relating to reconstructive orthopedic implants . . . for the benefit of Class Members."

- The defendants will put $20 million in cash into the Medical Monitoring Fund, which will be used to monitor the implants of claimants who have not yet had revision surgery, by paying for "the reasonable unreimbursed costs of one physicians visit and one set of x-rays associated therewith during each of the annual periods ending on the second year, third year and fifth year following the date of" the original implantation.

- The defendants will put at least $361.5 million in cash and stock into the Patient Benefit Fund (more if required), to pay compensation to implantees and their associated consortium claimants, as follows:

   —to claimants who do not have revision surgery, $750 in cash, $2,000 in stock,[21] and $500 to their spouses.

---

court proceedings involved only Sulzer Orthopedics, Inc. as a defendant, and did not involve claims against Sulzer Medica, Sulzer AG, or any other related entity.

[5] Interestingly, Richard Heimann [of Lieff, Cabraser, Heimann & Bernstein] is one of the attorneys who filed a motion with the MDL Panel for consolidation. Mr. Heimann asked that the MDL Panel transfer all federal "Sulzer hip implant" cases to the Northern or Central Districts of California; Mr. Heimann had filed a putative class action, in the Northern District of California, seeking to represent a nation-wide class of persons who received Inter–Op hip implants. Mr. Heimann is now one of the most vocal objectors to class certification and the proposed class settlement agreement.

[21] Actually, the claimant receives a certain number of shares of "stock" in Sulzer Medica Ltd.—that is, a certain number of American Depositary Receipts ("ADRs"), valued at $5.10 per ADR. If the ADRs have a higher value when issued, that value goes to the benefit of the claimant. The value of a share of Sulzer Medica at the market's close on August 30, 2001 was $7.95. Participating class members and their counsel will ultimately receive about a third of all the outstanding stock in Sulzer Medica Ltd.

—to claimants who have one revision surgery, $37,500 in cash, $20,000 in stock, and $5,000 to their spouses.

—to claimants who have more than one revision surgery, $63,500 in cash, $34,000 in stock, and $5,000 to their spouses.

- The defendants will put another $125 million in cash into the Patient Benefit Fund, to pay for any medical expenses a claimant incurred in connection with revision surgery (or to pay related subrogation claims).

- The defendants will also provide $33.3 million in cash and stock as payment of attorney fees to claimants' individual attorneys, at the rate of 1/3 of the claimants' compensation.

- The defendants will also provide $4.5 million in cash to cover the costs of administration of the Settlement Trust.

- The defendants will put a minimum of $30 million in cash and stock into the Extraordinary Injury Fund, to pay for additional compensation to implantees and their associated consortium claimants.

- Any amounts not paid out of the other Funds will be transferred into the Extraordinary Injury Fund, so that this Fund may ultimately exceed $100 million in cash and stock.

- None of the money or stock placed into the Settlement Trust will revert to the defendants; rather, it will all eventually be paid to participating class members.

- There will not be any reduction of the amounts that the defendants must pay into the Settlement Trust based on claimants who opt out of the class.[22]

- The defendants will place liens on virtually all of their assets in favor of the Settlement Trust, to secure all of their obligations; these liens will not be released until the defendants have met all of their obligations.[23]

- To pay the amounts listed above, the defendants will: (a) put all available insurance proceeds into the Settlement Trust; (b) put all available cash into the Settlement Trust, except for one month's working capital; (c) put the required number of stock shares into the Settlement Trust, and (d) put 50% of their net annual income into the Settlement Trust.

- If the defendants settle a case with an opt-out claimant on terms more favorable than are received under the Settlement Agreement by participating claimants, then the defendants agree to pay all participating claimants the increment.

---

[22] The effect of this provision is that the more claimants who opt out of the class, the higher will be the amounts ultimately paid to claimants who do not opt out.

[23] It is predicted that the Settlement Agreement will have paid out all amounts owed within about six years. Accordingly, the Court refers to these liens, below as "six-year liens." [The class settlement agreement nonetheless provides that, in the interim, Sulzer may sell assets "for business purposes" free and clear of the lien, as long as the proceeds from those sales are not used to pay opt-out claimants.—Ed.]

C.   *Analysis. . . .*

The Availability of Opt–Out Rights

Under the terms of the proposed settlement agreement, any claimant may choose to "opt out" of class membership and not participate in the agreement. By doing so, that claimant forgoes all of the benefits guaranteed to participating class members. If the claimant timely and properly exercises his opt-out right, he may initiate, continue with, or otherwise prosecute any legal claim against the defendants, without any limitation, impediment or defense arising from the terms of the settlement agreement. Of course, the defendants may then assert against the opt-out claimant any defenses and rights they would otherwise have, in the absence of the settlement agreement.

The calculus an opt-out claimant would make in this particular case is similar to the calculus an opt-out claimant would make in any Rule 23(b)(3) class action: the claimant can decide to take the risk of foregoing *certain* benefits guaranteed to him by the settlement agreement, and instead take the risk of suing the defendants "on his own," with the hope of obtaining *uncertain* but possibly greater benefits. In this case, the certain benefits the opt-out claimant would decide to forego include: (1) payment of all medical expenses associated with revision surgery; (2) freedom from any subrogation claims seeking reimbursement of medical expense payments already made on his behalf; (3) receipt of compensation in the form of amounts certain in stock and cash, for himself, his spouse, and his attorney; (4) the opportunity to receive additional compensation for "extraordinary injuries;" (5) medical monitoring, if needed; (6) the knowledge that certain of the "Sulzer-related" defendants have effectively dropped possibly meritorious defenses (e.g., Sulzer Medica, Ltd.); and (7) substantially reduced time and expense in connection with pursuing his claims. On the other hand, a claimant could possibly obtain even greater benefits by opting out of the settlement and, for example: (1) obtaining a judgment for a greater amount; (2) obtaining a judgment against certain "Sulzer-related" defendants that may not have contributed settlement funds in an amount satisfactory to the claimant (e.g., Sulzer AG); and (3) obtaining a judgment against certain other defendants that have not contributed to the settlement (e.g., the surgeon or medical supply company).

That a claimant may undertake this calculus and choose to opt out of the settlement speaks to the fairness of the proposed agreement—if a claimant does not believe the agreement is reasonable, adequate, or equitable, he may sue the defendants, just as he could in the complete absence of the settlement agreement. In this case, however, many of the objectors argue that the proposed settlement agreement leaves them with an unacceptable calculus, because the possible benefits of opting out are too low. The objectors note that, under the proposed settlement agreement, the defendants will place preferential six-year liens on their assets in favor of the class; this means that an opt-out plaintiff would have to "stand in line" behind participating class members for several years before he could collect on a successful judgment. The objectors also note that, under the proposed settlement agreement, any settlement funds allocated to claimants who opt out will be awarded to participating class members; this means that an opt-out plaintiff who succeeds in obtaining a judgment might have fewer assets against which to collect, since the settlement share allocated to him was not retained by the defendants. In addition, the objectors note that, if the defendants settle with an opt-out claimant on terms more favorable than are received under the Settlement Agreement by participating claimants, then the defendants agree to pay all participating claimants the excess financial consideration; objectors assert this gives the defendants a strong disincentive to afford them "better" settlements. The objectors go so far as to argue that the proposed agreement does such a thorough job of ensuring all of the defendants' assets will be paid to the settlement class, the settlement class is really the sort of Rule 23(b)(1)(B) "mandatory" class that has been disallowed by the Supreme Court in *Amchem* and *Ortiz*.

The Court rejects this argument completely. The essence of this complaint is that the settlement agreement is "too good" to opt out of. If true, this is an extremely strong indication that the settlement is fair. These objectors, however, push their position even farther, asserting that so minuscule a benefit is left to an opt-out claimant that opting out is "illusory" or "hollow" or "a sham;" that, ultimately, the Sulzer-related defendants have collected virtually all of their assets, created a "limited fund," and arranged to make conditions so onerous to an opt-out claimant that participation in the settlement agreement is effectively mandatory.

This argument, however, ignores the reality that opt-out claimants are entirely free to: (1) pursue their own litigation, wherein they can name their "own" defendants and follow their own strategy; (2) secure an immediately-collectible judgment against those defendants whom they have most objected should not be released from liability, including Sulzer AG, physicians and hospitals, and medical suppliers; (3) also secure a judgment against those defendants that placed six-year liens on their assets; and (4) enjoy the accumulation of post-judgment interest on any such judgments until the liens are released, and then fully collect on those judgments. Indeed, given the likelihood that any successful judgment may be appealed, having to wait for release of the "six-year liens" does not really represent a substantial delay. This list of benefits may not be as long as an opt-out claimant would like, but it is not "illusory." Moreover, there is currently no impediment preventing any claimant from pursuing their [sic] own case; the Court has not enjoined any related litigation. Thus, at this juncture, a claimant who wants to opt out does not even have to actually do so before proceeding with his own lawsuit. . . .

The Sixth Circuit Court of Appeals has recently reaffirmed the viability of class action settlements in mass tort cases where opt-out rights are preserved. *In re Telectronics Pacing Systems, Inc.*, 221 F.3d 870 (6th Cir. 2000). In *Telectronics*, the Court examined the question of "how far the courts should go in allowing class action, mass tort cases to deviate from th[e] tradition" of allowing for an "adversary trial by an individual plaintiff claiming redress for a particular wrong." *Id.* at 872. The Court noted that "[c]lass certification, whether mandatory or not, necessarily compromises various rights of absent class members." *Id.* at 881. Accordingly, "class members' rights to notice and an opportunity to opt out should be preserved whenever possible." *Id.* at 881 (quoting *Jefferson v. Ingersoll Int'l Inc.*, 195 F.3d 894, 899 (7th Cir. 1999)). This means that certification of a class under Rule 23(b)(1)(B) should be "carefully scrutinized and sparingly utilized." *Id.* On the other hand, the Sixth Circuit emphasized that "Rule 23(b)(3), with its notice and opt-out provisions, strikes a balance between the value of aggregating similar claims and the right of an individual to have his or her day in court." *Id.* The Court of Appeals noted, moreover, that this balance is maintained as long as opt-out rights exist, even if, as practical matter, an opt-out claimant would have little chance of actually collecting on an individual judgment. See *id.* at 877 ("[c]learly any potentially large judgment creates the risk of depletion of a defendant's assets and sets up the possibility that, as a practical matter, adjudication may be 'dispositive of the interest of other members not parties to the adjudications' or may 'substantially impair or impede their ability to protect their interests'") (quoting Fed. R. Civ. P. 23(b)(1)(B)). Thus, despite the contention of some objectors that *Telectronics* prohibits the use of all class action settlements in mass tort cases, *Telectronics*, instead, simply steers district courts away from Rule 23(b)(1)(B) and toward Rule 23(b)(3) as the appropriate vehicle for such settlements. *Telectronics*, quite correctly, followed the Supreme Court's lead in *Amchem* on this point. See *Amchem*, 521 U.S. at 625 (holding that Rule 23(b)(3) is the "Rule's growing edge" for class treatment of mass tort litigation). This Court does the same.

The proposed settlement agreement in this case, repeatedly characterized by even its detractors as inventive, simply is not a mandatory class action. Rather, it appears to be on the "growing edge" of Rule 23(b)(3)'s provisions for an opt-out class action. The opt-out provisions provided to the class are not illusory, and present a calculus not very different from that which a claimant in any opt-out class action must undertake. The opt-out structure of the proposed settlement agreement passes the test for preliminary fairness and is within the range of reasonableness. . . .

NOTES AND QUESTIONS

1.   *The Background of the Sulzer Hip Implant Class Settlement.* As its class settlement negotiator, Sulzer retained Richard "Dickie" Scruggs, a noted personal injury plaintiffs' lawyer from Mississippi who had previously taken a leading role in litigation against the tobacco industry, among other targets of mass-tort lawsuits. (Scruggs recently served a prison sentence in connection with criminal charges related to an effort to bribe a Mississippi state judge, a subsequent matter entirely unrelated to the Sulzer hip implant class settlement.) As part of the Sulzer litigation, Scruggs reportedly stood to be paid "a 'low seven-figure number,' plus a 'success fee' of about $20 million should the [hip implant class] settlement be approved." Jess Bravin, *Sulzer Medica Offers Novel Deal To Resolve Patients' Lawsuits*, Wall St. J., Aug. 16, 2001, at A3, available at http://online.wsj.com/article/SB997912715925918012.html. As Scruggs himself summarized the class settlement to the *Wall Street Journal*: "[I]f anybody opts out, they still have to try their case, win their case, win their appeal, and then there would be no assets to satisfy their judgment, because they are all pledged to the class." *Id.*

Given the content of the proposed class settlement, why would a defendant like Sulzer wish to use the services of a prominent lawyer usually involved on the plaintiffs' side of mass-tort litigation?

2.   *Subsequent Developments.* Counsel for the objectors to the Sulzer hip implant class settlement consisted of mass tort plaintiffs' law firms that already had obtained as their individual clients substantial numbers of hip implant recipients in need of revision surgery. Petitioners' Consolidated Brief in Support of Appeal Pursuant to FRCP 23(f) and FRAP 5 at 3–4, *In re Inter–Op Hip Prosthesis Prod. Liab. Litig.* (6th Cir. Feb. 2002) (Nos. 01–303 & 01–304). The objectors appealed the district court's settlement approval decision to the Sixth Circuit, which expressed "serious doubts as to the legitimacy of the proposed class settlement" in the course of granting a preliminary motion to lift a

stay imposed by the district court on related litigation. *In re Inter-Op Hip Prosthesis Prod. Liab. Litig.*, 2001 WL 1774017, at *1 (6th Cir. Oct. 29, 2001). The efforts of the objectors ultimately led class counsel and their defense counterpart Scruggs to fashion a substantially different class settlement agreement before the Sixth Circuit could rule on the original one.

The final class settlement eliminated the lien and trust fund in the original deal. Moreover, the final class settlement boosted the benefits to class members for remaining in the class—in particular, those provided to class members who undergo revision surgery. Not only did the final settlement boost the overall dollar value of the benefits for these high-value claims—and, to a lesser extent, for low-value claims as well—it also restructured those benefits by providing them almost entirely in cash rather than stock. The boost in benefits to class members was funded primarily by Sulzer Medica, Ltd., the Swiss parent corporation of the defendant product manufacturer Sulzer Orthopedics. Sulzer Medica, Ltd. previously had not devoted cash (as distinct from shares of its stock) to the class settlement.

3.   The Merits of the Original Class Settlement. Is there such a thing as a Rule 23(b)(3) opt-out class settlement that veers impermissibly close to a Rule 23(b)(1)(B) mandatory class settlement? If so, how are courts supposed to know one when they see one? For that matter, why didn't the designers of the original Sulzer class settlement simply use Rule 23(b)(1)(B)? Would the assets provided to the trust under the original Sulzer class settlement have satisfied the standards of *Ortiz* for a limited fund?

Absent a class settlement, any given hip implant recipient stood at risk that Sulzer might convey a security interest in some or all of its assets to other creditors pursuant to Article 9 of the Uniform Commercial Code. Given that risk, how can there be anything objectionable about the creation of the lien in favor of the class settlement trust?

In opposing the original Sulzer hip implant settlement, the objectors pointed to *In re General Motors Engine Interchange Litigation*, 594 F.2d 1106 (7th Cir. 1979). There, General Motors had initiated a practice of using Chevrolet engines in certain of its new Oldsmobile, Buick, and Pontiac automobiles for the 1977 model year. This practice led to a series of lawsuits across the country under federal statutes such as the Magnuson–Moss Act (a major federal consumer-protection statute) and state law (e.g., breach of warranty). Upon consolidation of pending lawsuits in the federal courts by the MDL Panel, the district court certified a Rule 23(b)(3) class action for all persons who had purchased the affected automobiles. At the same time that the court certified the class, the court "dismissed all federal claims except for the Magnuson–Moss claim and declined to exercise its power to take pendant jurisdiction over the related state law claims." *Id.* at 1115. Settlement negotiations ensued and ultimately bore fruit. "The proposed settlement provided that GM would provide to each consumer who had purchased a 1977 Oldsmobile, Buick or Pontiac equipped with a Chevrolet engine . . . $200 plus a 36–month or 36,000–mile extended warranty on the power train. In return each purchaser would be required to sign a release of all state and federal claims concerning the substitution of engines, components, parts, and assemblies in the car." *Id.* at 1116.

The district court conducted a fairness hearing on the proposed class settlement and thereafter issued a curious order. The order approved the class settlement as fair under Rule 23(e). But the order also dismissed the Magnuson–Moss claims of the plaintiff class based upon a finding by the district court that "the engines and other parts included in the [affected automobiles] were 'comparable' to those warranted." *Id.* at 1117. This finding apparently represented the district judge's resolution of a conflict in the evidence presented at the fairness hearing by GM and the class settlement objectors concerning the engineering characteristics of the Chevrolet engines.

On appeal, the Seventh Circuit overturned the district court's order:

> . . . [E]ven if the subclass member refuses to accept GM's offer and refuses to sign the release, the order nevertheless dismisses with prejudice the subclass member's federal claim. The subclass member is presented with an accept-or-else situation: if he does not accept, his federal claim is lost even though he cannot receive the benefits of the settlement package. We have searched the reported decisions in vain for precedent for such a settlement. Finding none and being of the opinion that the dismissal of the action is fundamentally unfair to nonconsenting subclass members, we cannot permit the settlement in its present form to stand. . . .

> We do not think that it follows . . . that the trial court has the power under Rule 23 to dismiss with prejudice the Magnuson–Moss claims of those subclass members who refuse to accept the settlement package. As to them, the "settlement" is not a settlement; it is merely an offer to settle with a penalty, the dismissal of their federal claims, if they do not accept. We decline to put every subclass member to such an unfair choice.

> This court on two occasions has noted that the essence of a settlement is a bilateral exchange. By the terms of the order of the trial court, [the class] members who do not sign the release give up their Magnuson–Moss claims and the opportunity to be represented in the class action in return for nothing. . . . GM gains the dismissal of each subclass member's federal claim, but surrenders nothing in return. . . .

> Even if the subclass member does pursue his state remedies, he is still prejudiced by the dismissal of his Magnuson–Moss claim. "From a consumer protection point of view, the [Magnuson–Moss] Act is clearly preferable to the Uniform Commercial Code, which is difficult to apply to consumer sales transactions and is full of pitfalls for consumers seeking recovery for defective products." Smith, *The Magnuson–Moss Warranty Act: Turning the Tables on Caveat Emptor*, 13 Cal. W. L. Rev. 391, 429 (1977). In addition to providing a more certain path to recovery, the Magnuson–Moss Act provides the consumer with a more adequate remedy. It provides that the successful plaintiff may also recover the costs of litigation (subject to the court's discretion not to award attorneys' fees). 15 U.S.C. § 2310(d)(2). Thus, the dismissal of the subclass member's Magnuson–Moss claim, leaving him to pursue his state remedies individually, reduces both the probability that the consumer will pursue those remedies and, if he does, the probability that his remedy will be adequate.

Id. at 1133–37. Does *GM Engine Interchange* stand as pertinent authority with regard to the permissibility of the original Sulzer hip implant class settlement?

Or is the situation presented in *GM Engine Intercharge* fundamentally different? For that matter, is *GM Engine Interchange* correctly decided in its own right?

    4.   Other Techniques to Deter Opt–Outs. Consider the following additional techniques that might discourage class members from opting out:

> A "right-to-withdraw" clause, whereby the defendant may choose to withdraw from the class settlement if it determines that an excessive number of class members have opted out.

> A "most-favored-nation" clause, whereby the class settlement assures class members of additional benefits in the event that comparable opt-out cases receive judgments or settlements higher in value than the benefits described in the class settlement agreement.

Are either of these techniques impermissible? In the Sulzer hip implant litigation, the class-settlement designers added a "right-to-withdraw" clause when they switched from the original class settlement agreement to the final version. Indeed, both types of clauses are relatively common features of opt-out class settlements. For economic analysis of "most-favored-nation" clauses in civil settlements generally, see Kathryn E. Spier, *The Use of "Most–Favored–Nation" Clauses in Settlement of Litigation*, 34 RAND J. Econ. 78 (2003).

    5.   Back–End Opt–Out Rights. In contrast to the original Sulzer hip implant class settlement, a $3.75 billion class settlement in litigation over the diet drug combination fen-phen entailed the provision of additional opt-out rights to class members beyond the initial opportunity to exit the class required by procedural rule. Specifically, diet drug users could decide to opt out—and, in so doing, to sue the settling defendant in tort—at any of three points: (1) during an initial 120–day period following official notice of the class settlement terms—i.e., the opt-out period required by Rule 23; (2) upon diagnosis of a mild heart valve abnormality, as revealed by an echocardiogram administered pursuant to a medical screening program established by the class settlement; or (3) upon diagnosis of severe heart valve disease. Class members who opted out at point (2) or (3), however, could not seek punitive damages in their tort actions. In effect, their punitive damage claims comprised the "price" for the additional opt-out rights—colloquially known as "back-end" opt-out rights—provided by the class settlement. The district court approved the fen-phen class settlement, and the Third Circuit affirmed without opinion. *In re Diet Drugs (Phentermine/Fenfluramine/Dexfenfluramine) Prods. Liab. Litig.*, 2000 WL 1222042 (E.D. Pa. 2000), *aff'd without opinion*, 275 F.3d 34 (3d Cir. 2001).

    The fen-phen class settlement proved an unwieldy arrangement for both class members and the settling defendant American Home Products, now named Wyeth Corporation. The major practical difficulty in the administration of the settlement consisted of an influx of claims in numbers wildly in excess of those projected at the time of class settlement approval—in particular, low-dollar-value claims at the cusp between abnormality and valvular regurgitation within normal parameters. The unanticipated number of claims ultimately ground the settlement regime to a halt, with consequent delays for class members with the most severe heart valve injuries.

    In a series of amendments over several years, the peacemaking lawyers desperately sought to shore up the credibility of the class settlement. The seventh amendment to the class settlement agreement, approved by the district court in early 2005, created a new administrative regime funded by an additional $1.275 billion from Wyeth. The new regime continues to pay the sums to high-value claims promised in the original class settlement. But it reduces dramatically the sums for persons with the least severe valvular problems, albeit while preserving their preexisting right to seek additional compensation under the settlement should their condition worsen. Most significantly, this seventh amendment eliminates the back-end opt-out rights that were the signature feature of the original deal. In their place, the seventh amendment provides for class members either to accept the new compensation terms or to opt out within a confined time period and thereby preserve their opportunity to seek compensatory damages in the tort system. *In re Diet Drugs (Phentermine/Fenfluramine/Dexfenfluramine) Prods. Liability Litig.*, 226 F.R.D. 498, 515 (E.D. Pa. 2005). In effect, the seventh amendment converts the structure of the fen-phen class settlement into that of a conventional opt-out class, whereby class members must make a one-time choice between private administration and the tort system.

For back-end opt-outs, moreover, the prohibition against punitive damage claims proved to be porous. After the Supreme Court decisions tightening judicial review of punitive damage awards, observers on the defense side began to warn of efforts by tort plaintiffs to seek such awards under the rubric of compensatory damages for pain and suffering. In the fen-phen litigation, the district court attempted to enforce the terms of the class settlement by enjoining back-end opt-outs not only from seeking punitive damages but also from presenting in support of their permitted claims for compensatory damages any evidence "related directly or indirectly" to punitive damages or extreme misconduct on Wyeth's part. *In re Diet Drugs (Phentermine/Fenfluramine/Dexfenfluramine) Prods. Liability Litig.*, 369 F.3d 293, 303 (3d Cir. 2004). On appeal, the Third Circuit acknowledged the "justifiable fear . . . that plaintiffs were seeking to obtain through the back door what they were barred from receiving through the front." *Id.* at 300. But the Third Circuit still lifted the injunction, observing that the class settlement barred back-end opt-outs from seeking punitive damages but contained no restrictions on the evidence that they might seek to admit at trial in support of demands for compensatory damages. At most, Wyeth could call upon trial courts to exercise their existing discretion to exclude particular items of evidence as tangential or unduly prejudicial. *Id.* at 312–15.

All together, the difficulties encountered by the fen-phen class settlement made for an estimated 60,000 back-end opt-outs and an overall cost to Wyeth of $21 billion as of September 2006. 226 F.R.D. at 522 (estimate of opt-outs); *How Deep Do Merck's Wounds Go?*, Wall St. J., Sept. 30, 2006 (estimate of costs to Wyeth). To put these numbers into perspective: The 60,000 back-end opt-outs *by themselves* exceed the projected total of just over 35,500 fen-phen users that scientific experts had estimated would develop compensable heart valve problems based upon the application of "conservative assumptions likely to overstate [claimant] demands." 2000 WL 1222042, *28.

Do the problems associated with the administration of the fen-phen class settlement demonstrate that the provision of back-end opt-out rights makes for an *inherently* unstable arrangement? Or do the problems experienced by the fen-phen class settlement stem from idiosyncratic aspects of the fen-phen situation? As we will see when we discuss the Vioxx litigation in Chapter 5, provisions for limiting plaintiffs' practical ability to exclude themselves from a settlement are not limited to class actions.

D. CY PRES DISTRIBUTIONS

The class settlements discussed thus far involved the distribution of money to class members in exchange for their damage claims—sometimes over an extended time span, to be sure, but ultimately to the persons within the class. What happens when distribution to persons within the class is not realistically possible? This Section discusses the potential for application of cy pres principles to govern the allocation of funds made available by class action litigation. Some of you already may have encountered the term "cy pres" in connection with trusts and estates.

> "The term 'cy pres' is derived from the Norman French expression *cy pres comme possible*, which means 'as near as possible.'" *Democratic Cent. Comm. v. Washington Metro. Area Transit Comm'n*, 84 F.3d 451, 455 n.1 (D.C. Cir. 1996). The cy pres doctrine originated as a rule of construction to save a testamentary charitable gift that would otherwise fail, allowing "the next best use of the funds to satisfy the testator's intent as near as possible." *Id.* (internal quotation omitted). Courts have also utilized cy pres distributions where class members "are difficult to identify or where they change constantly," or where there are unclaimed funds. *Powell* [*v. Georgia–Pacific Corp.*, 119 F.3d 703, 706 (8th Cir. 1997)]. "In these cases, the court, guided by the parties' original purpose, directs that the unclaimed funds be distributed 'for the indirect prospective benefit of the class.'" *Id.* (quoting 2 Newberg and A. Conte, NEWBERG ON CLASS ACTIONS, § 10.17 at 10–41 (3d ed. 1992)). . . .

In re Airline Ticket Comm. Antitrust Litig., 268 F.3d 619, 625 (8th Cir. 2001). Consider the application of cy pres principles in the following case.

Nachsin v. AOL, LLC

663 F.3d 1034 (9th Cir. 2011)

■ N. R. SMITH, CIRCUIT JUDGE:

The *cy pres* doctrine allows a court to distribute unclaimed or nondistributable portions of a class action settlement fund to the "next best" class of beneficiaries. See *Six (6) Mexican Workers v. Ariz. Citrus Growers*, 904 F.2d 1301, 1307–08 (9th Cir. 1990). *Cy pres* distributions must account for the nature of the plaintiffs' lawsuit, the objectives of the underlying statutes, and the interests of the silent class members, including their geographic diversity. The *cy pres* distributions here do not comport with our *cy pres* standards. While the donations were made on behalf of a nationwide plaintiff class, they were distributed to geographically isolated and substantively unrelated charities.

I.

In August 2009, four named plaintiffs . . . brought a class action lawsuit against America Online, LLC (AOL) on behalf of a putative class consisting of more than 66 million paid AOL subscribers. Plaintiffs alleged that AOL wrongfully inserted footers containing promotional messages into e-mails sent by AOL subscribers. The amended complaint asserted six causes of action [including invasion of privacy, unjust enrichment, breach of contract, and others].

The parties entered into voluntary mediation to settle their dispute. Working with retired U.S. District Court Judge Dickran Tevrizian, AOL and Plaintiffs eventually reached a class settlement (the Settlement). The Settlement calls for the certification of a settlement class consisting of "all current AOL members," or about 66 million subscribers. It further provides that (1) AOL will notify its members of the existence of the e-mail footer advertisements and their ability to opt out of the footers; (2) if AOL continues to append footer advertisements to members' outgoing e-mails, AOL will re-send the same email notification to members every six months for a period of two years; and (3) AOL will inform future members of the e-mail footers and provide a link enabling members to opt out of the footer advertisements.

The Settlement also addressed Plaintiffs' claims for monetary damages. All parties agreed monetary damages were small and difficult to ascertain. The maximum recovery at trial would have been the unjust enrichment AOL received as a result of its footer advertisement sales, or about $2 million. Divided among the more than 66 million AOL subscribers, each member of the class would receive only about 3 cents. The cost to distribute these payments would far exceed the maximum potential recovery.

In lieu of a cost-prohibitive distribution to the plaintiff class and at Judge Tevrizian's suggestion, the parties agreed that AOL would make a series of charitable donations. Because the 66,069,441 plaintiffs were geographically and demographically diverse, the parties claimed they could not identify any charitable organization that would benefit the class or be specifically germane to the issues in the case. At the parties' request, Judge Tevrizian suggested and the parties agreed that AOL would donate $25,000 to three charitable beneficiaries: (1) the Legal Aid Foundation of Los Angeles, (2) the Federal Judicial Center Foundation, and (3) the Boys and Girls Club of America (shared between the chapters in Los Angeles and Santa Monica).

In addition and at the suggestion of Judge Tevrizian, the parties agreed to compensate the named class representatives (for bringing the action) by awarding $35,000 to four charities of the class representatives' choice (rather than providing direct financial compensation). The Settlement provides that AOL will donate $8,750 to a charity designated by each named representative. These designated charities include the (1) New Roads School of Santa Monica, (2) Oklahoma Indian Legal Services; and (3) the Friars Foundation. Each entity is a non-profit organization with tax deductible status under 26 U.S.C. § 501(c)(3).

The district court granted preliminary approval of the Settlement and provisionally certified the settlement class. Shortly thereafter, AOL sent an e-mail to over 60 million members of the class notifying them of the Settlement (the Notice). The Notice (1) explained that AOL will make donations to several charities totaling $110,000; (2) notified class members that the full settlement agreement is available at the district court or online at the internet addresses provided in the Notice; and (3) provided contact information, including phone numbers and an e-mail address, where inquiries could be sent. Two members of the class objected to the Settlement . . . An additional 4,525 AOL subscribers opted out of the Settlement, but 1,037 failed to provide their names for the opt-out as required by the district court's instructions, and seven failed to submit opt-out requests before the opt-out deadline.

[The Court of Appeals explains further that a class member filed a formal Objection to the Proposed Settlement, arguing among other things that "the charitable award does not meet the standard for *cy pres*, because the charities selected by the parties do not relate to the issue in the case and are not geographically diverse." The district court denied the objections and approved the settlement, holding in particular that "the charities that have been chosen are [not] inappropriate or out of line with other class actions settlements that I have seen approved in this court and in other courts."]

II.

We review a district court's approval of a proposed class action settlement, including a proposed *cy pres* settlement distribution, for abuse of discretion. A court abuses its discretion when it fails to apply the correct legal standard or bases its decision on unreasonable findings of fact.

We have recognized that federal courts frequently use the *cy pres* doctrine "in the settlement of class actions where the proof of individual claims would be burdensome or distribution of damages costly." *Six Mexican Workers*, 904 F.2d at 1305. . . .

However, as a growing number of scholars and courts have observed, the *cy pres* doctrine—unbridled by a driving nexus between the plaintiff class and the *cy pres* beneficiaries—poses many nascent dangers to the fairness of the distribution process. See, e.g., *S.E.C. v. Bear, Stearns & Co.*, 626 F. Supp. 2d 402, 414–17 (S.D.N.Y. 2009); Martin H. Redish et al., Cy Pres *Relief and the Pathologies of the Modern Class Action: A Normative and Empirical Analysis*, 62 Fla. L. Rev. 617 (2010). Some courts appear to have abandoned the "next best use" principle implicit in the *cy pres* doctrine. These courts have awarded *cy pres* distributions to myriad charities which, though no doubt pursuing virtuous goals, have little or nothing to do with the purposes of the underlying lawsuit or the class of plaintiffs involved. See, e.g., *In re Motorsports Merch. Antitrust Litig.*, 160 F. Supp. 2d 1392, 1396–99 (N.D. Ga. 2001) (distributing $1.85 million remaining from a price fixing class action settlement relating to merchandise sold at professional stock car races to ten organizations including the Duke Children's Hospital and Health Center, the Make-a-Wish Foundation, the American Red Cross, and the Susan G. Komen Breast Cancer Foundation); *Superior Beverage Co., Inc. v. Owens–Illinois, Inc.*, 827 F. Supp. 477, 480 (N.D. Ill. 1993) (awarding $2 million from an antitrust class action settlement to fifteen applicants, including the San Jose Museum of Art, the American Jewish Congress, a public television station, and the Roger Baldwin Foundation of the American Civil Liberties Union of Illinois).

When selection of *cy pres* beneficiaries is not tethered to the nature of the lawsuit and the interests of the silent class members, the selection process may answer to the whims and self interests of the parties, their counsel, or the court. Moreover, the specter of judges and outside entities dealing in the distribution and solicitation of settlement money may create the appearance of impropriety. *Bear Stearns*, 626 F. Supp. 2d at 415; see George Krueger & Judd Serotta, Op–Ed., *Our Class–Action System is Unconstitutional*, Wall St. J., Aug. 6, 2008 ("Judges, in their unlimited discretion, have occasionally been known to order a distribution to some place like their own alma mater or a public interest organization that they happen to favor."); Editorial, *When Judges Get Generous*, Wash. Post, Dec. 17, 2007, at A20 ("Federal judges are permitted to find other uses for excess funds, . . . giving the money away to favorite charities with little or no relation to the underlying litigation is inappropriate and borders on distasteful."); Adam Liptak, *Doling out Other People's Money*, N.Y. Times, Nov. 26, 2007 ("Lawyers and judges have grown used to controlling these pots of money, and they enjoy distributing them to favored charities, alma maters and the like.").

To remedy some of these concerns, we held in *Six Mexican Workers* that *cy pres* distribution must be guided by (1) the objectives of the underlying statute(s) and (2) the interests of the silent class members.[2] *Six Mexican Workers*, 904 F.2d at 1307. The proposed *cy pres* distribution in *Six Mexican Workers* failed to meet this standard. In that case, the district court awarded a class of 1,349 undocumented Mexican workers $1,846,500 for their Fair Labor Contractor Registration Act claims against a conglomerate of fruit farmers. The district court ordered that any unclaimed funds be distributed through a *cy pres* award to the Inter–American Fund (IAF) for indirect humanitarian assistance in Mexico. We rejected this award, explaining that (1) the "proposal benefits a group far too remote from the plaintiff class," (2) "[t]he plan . . . fails to provide adequate supervision over distribution," and (3) although "the plan permits distribution to areas where the class members may live . . . there is no reasonable certainty that any member will be benefited." We directed the district court on remand to consider escheating the funds [to the government] pursuant to 28 U.S.C. § 2042 if the court could not develop an appropriate *cy pres* distribution.

The *cy pres* distribution in this case fails to meet any of the guiding standards in *Six Mexican Workers*. The proposed awards fail to (1) address the objectives of the underlying statutes, (2) target the plaintiff class, or (3) provide reasonable certainty that any member will be benefitted. Plaintiffs in this case brought claims against AOL for breach of electronic communications privacy, unjust enrichment, and breach of contract, among others, relating to AOL's provision of commercial e-mail services. Yet none of the *cy pres* donations—$25,000 each to the Legal Aid Foundation of Los Angeles, the Boys and Girls Clubs of Santa Monica and Los Angeles, and the Federal Judicial Center Foundation—have anything to do with the objectives of the underlying statutes on which Plaintiffs base their claims.

The *cy pres* distribution also fails to target the plaintiff class, because it does not account for the broad geographic distribution of the class. See *In re Airline Ticket Comm'n Antitrust Litig.*, 307 F.3d 679, 683 (8th Cir. 2002) (reversing a district court's *cy pres* distribution because it "failed to consider the full geographic scope of the case"); *Houck on Behalf of U.S. v. Folding Carton Admin. Comm.*, 881 F.2d 494, 502 (7th Cir. 1989) (remanding a proposed *cy pres* award in a nationwide class action so the district court could consider "a broader nationwide use of its *cy pres* discretion"). Although the class includes more than 66 million AOL subscribers throughout the United States, two-thirds of the donations will be made to local charities in Los Angeles, California. Even among the small percentage of plaintiffs located in Los Angeles, there is also no indication that any would benefit from donations to the Boys and Girls Clubs of Los Angeles and Santa

---

[2] We also note that the American Law Institute has adopted a rule for *cy pres* awards requiring parties "to identify a recipient whose interests reasonably approximate those being pursued by the class." PRINCIPLES OF THE LAW OF AGGREGATE LITIGATION § 3.07(c) (Am. L. Inst. 2010).

Monica or Los Angeles Legal Aid. The proposed donation to the Federal Judicial Center Foundation at least conceivably benefits a national organization, but this organization has no apparent relation to the objectives of the underlying statutes, and it is not clear how this organization would benefit the plaintiff class. We therefore conclude that the district court applied the incorrect legal standard in approving the proposed *cy pres* distribution and, therefore, abused its discretion.

We are not persuaded by AOL's argument that courts must defer to the parties' freely-negotiated settlement, or AOL's reliance on the statement from *Rodriguez* that judicial review "must be limited to the extent necessary to reach a reasoned judgment that the agreement is not the product of fraud or overreaching by, or collusion between, the negotiating parties, and that the settlement, taken as a whole, is fair, reasonable and adequate to all concerned." *Rodriguez*, 563 F.3d at 965. This argument conflates two separate inquiries relating to class settlements: (1) whether the *class settlement*, "taken as a whole, is fair, reasonable, and adequate to all concerned," *id.*; and (2) whether the *distribution* of the approved class settlement complies with our standards governing *cy pres* awards. [The appealing Objector] does not argue that the Settlement fails to adequately compensate Plaintiffs' injuries; instead, he argues that the (presumptively adequate) Settlement fails to comport with our established standards for *cy pres* distribution in *Six Mexican Workers*. A proposed *cy pres* distribution must meet these standards regardless of whether the award was fashioned by the settling parties or the trial court.

We are also not persuaded by the parties' claims that the size and geographic diversity of the plaintiff class make it "impossible" to select an adequate charity. It is clear that all members of the class share two things in common: (1) they use the internet, and (2) their claims against AOL arise from a purportedly unlawful advertising campaign that exploited users' outgoing email messages. The parties should not have trouble selecting beneficiaries from any number of non-profit organizations that work to protect internet users from fraud, predation, and other forms of online malfeasance. If a suitable *cy pres* beneficiary cannot be located, the district court should consider escheating the funds to the United States Treasury. See *Six Mexican Workers*, 904 F.2d at 1309. . . .

REVERSED in part, AFFIRMED in part, and REMANDED.

NOTES AND QUESTIONS

1. The Distribution Problem. Assume that a class action has been litigated to final judgment and damages properly awarded in light of the facts and the substantive law, or assume that a class action has settled and the settlement is fair, adequate and reasonable. If individual shares of the total award or settlement can be determined and distributed to class members in a reasonably practical way, then the court will distribute those shares without any need to use cy pres. But what if individual distributions are not practically feasible? For example, what if individual class members are not identifiable or cannot be located with reasonable effort. Or what if it is too difficult to calculate their individual shares or, as in *Nachshin*, the cost of distributing those shares exceeds the share's value?

Consider the facts of the Ninth Circuit case, *Six (6) Mexican Workers v. Arizona Citrus Growers*, 904 F.2d 1301 (9th Cir. 1990), on which the *Nachsin* court relies. The case was a class action brought on behalf of 1349 undocumented Mexican workers employed by the defendant. The plaintiffs alleged violations of the Farm Labor Contractor Registration Act (FLCRA) and sought statutory damages. The district judge found liability after a bench trial and entered a class judgment of $1,836,500. The problem was how to distribute the total class award to individual class members, who, as undocumented workers, might be very difficult to locate.

Distribution problems can arise in class actions, like *Six Mexican Workers*, that are litigated to final judgment or class actions, like *Nachshin*, that are settled. What options are available to the court and the parties when the trial award or settlement cannot be fully distributed to individual class members in a practically feasible way? One option is to make a cy pres distribution of unclaimed funds to a charitable organization. There are four other possibilities, each of which has its own problems.

First, when distribution problems are foreseeable in advance, the judge might simply deny (b)(3) certification on manageability grounds. The Ninth Circuit rejected this approach in *Six Mexican Workers*, noting that "where the statutory objectives include enforcement, deterrence, or disgorgement, the class action may be the 'superior' and only viable method to achieve these objectives, even despite the prospect of unclaimed funds." A second possibility is to give any unclaimed funds back to the defendant (i.e., reversion to the defendant). The *Six Mexican Workers* court rejected this alternative on the ground that it would undermine the deterrence goals of the FLCRA's statutory damages provision.

This leaves two other possibilities besides cy pres. In cases where distribution to some but not all class members is feasible, any unclaimed funds might be distributed pro rata to those class members who also receive regular distributions. This approach distributes all of the class recovery to class members but it gives some members a windfall. Finally, any unclaimed funds might escheat to the government as unclaimed property. This approach benefits the public, but it confers no benefit on the class as such.

Which of these options is the best? Should it depend on the type of case? Should a court use cy pres only when it is superior to the other four alternatives? One study of reported cases from 1974 through 2008 found a marked increase in the use of cy pres, especially after 2000. Martin H. Redish, Peter Julian & Samantha Zyontz,. Cy Pres *Relief and the Pathologies of the Modern Class Action: A Normative and Empirical Analysis*, 62 Fla. L. Rev. 617, 653 (2010) (finding that courts granted or approved cy pres awards to third-party charities in 30 class actions from 1974 to 2000 and 65 class actions from 2001 through 2008).

2. *Constraints on the Application of Cy Pres Principles.* As noted above, cy pres is limited to cases presenting serious obstacles to individual distribution. Moreover, even when cy pres is appropriate, there are constraints on the choice of cy pres beneficiary. In particular, there must be a sufficiently close nexus between the beneficiary and the lawsuit. The *Nachshin* court identifies three nexus requirements: "*Cy pres* distributions must account for the nature of the plaintiffs' lawsuit, the objectives of the underlying statutes, and the interests of the silent class members, including their geographic diversity." Applying these requirements, the *Nachshin* court found that the parties' choice of charities was inadequate, noting that the parties could easily have identified national non-profits with a closer relationship to the lawsuit.

The Ninth Circuit in *Six Mexican Workers* also rejected the district judge's selection of a beneficiary. Since many of the undocumented workers probably lived in Mexico, the district judge chose the Inter–American Fund as a vehicle for distribution of the unclaimed funds in Mexico. On appeal, the Ninth Circuit held that this choice "does not adequately target the plaintiff class"—noting that there was no assurance that any class member in Mexico would benefit—and "fails to provide adequate supervision over distribution"—noting that the IAF did not have a substantial record of service and the plan did not limit its choice of projects. *Six Mexican Workers, supra,* at 1308–09.

In employment discrimination litigation, the Eighth Circuit has upheld the application of cy pres principles to authorize the distribution of unclaimed funds to support scholarships for African–American high school students in communities located around the industrial facility that had been the focal point for the class litigation. *Powell v. Georgia–Pacific Corp.,* 119 F.3d 703 (8th Cir. 1997). In antitrust litigation over the fixing of commissions by various professional modeling agencies, the Second Circuit upheld the use of cy pres principles to support the distribution of unclaimed funds to various charities that—in the court's words—"would directly or indirectly benefit members of the class." *Masters v. Wilhelmina Model Agency, Inc.,* 473 F.3d 423, 432 (2d Cir. 2007). Specifically, the charities consisted of: "Beth Israel Medical Center's Continuum Women's Cardiac Care Network; Columbia Presbyterian Medical Center's Eating Disorders Program; Columbia Presbyterian Medical Center's Division on Substance Abuse; Columbia Presbyterian Medical Center's Ovarian Cancer Repository; New York University Medical Center; Civil Division of the Legal Aid Society; and The Heart Truth." *Id.*

Are there meaningful differences among these cases? Are the distributions in *Powell* and *Masters* proper given the results and the standards set out in *Nachsin* and *Six American Workers*? What if the distributions had gone to a geographically proximate law school to establish an endowed program for the study of employment discrimination law or antitrust law, as the case may be? How about if they funded the study of civil litigation generally? Class actions specifically? What if class counsel were alumni of the recipient law school? What if the approving trial-level judge was an alumnus? A parent of a current student?

In *Lane v. Facebook, Inc.,* 696 F.3d 811 (9th Cir. 2012), a class action suit brought by Facebook users alleging violations of privacy rights in connection with Facebook's Beacon program, the Ninth Circuit approved, over a sharp dissent by Judge Kleinfeld, a cy pres distribution to an entirely new entity created by the settlement, the Digital Trust Foundation, dedicated to funding and sponsoring programs related to protecting online identity, privacy, and the like. Should a court approve a cy pres beneficiary created by the parties? By creating their own non-profit entity, the parties can shape the beneficiary in a way that meets nexus requirements. But is there also a greater risk of self-dealing? Should it matter that the entity has no proven record of service or a reputation for actually achieving its goals?

Why does it matter where the unclaimed funds go if they can't be distributed to the class members who are entitled to them? The *Nachsin* court mentions two concerns: that the choice of cy pres beneficiary might serve the self-interest of the parties, their counsel, or the court, and that leaving the choice to the court without constraints might create the appearance of impropriety. Are these concerns serious enough to justify nexus constraints? Are there any other reasons to be concerned about unfettered discretion in the choice of cy pres beneficiary? If some constraints on the choice of cy pres beneficiary are justified, how strict should those constraints be? What if the goals of the underlying substantive law focus mainly on deterrence? Should it matter that class members have legal rights at stake? If so, how should this fact matter?

    3.   *Cy Pres and Fluid Class Recovery.* Fluid class recovery is a close cousin of cy pres. Both involve distributing class recovery in a second best way. The difference between the two devices has been described in the following way:

> . . .cy pres refers to the designation of a portion of unclaimed damage or settlement funds to a charitable use that is in some way related to the subject of the suit. . . . [F]luid class recovery applies to an effort—either in a class settlement or as part of a class award—to approximate the injured class of consumers through the provision of relief to future consumers. The assumption is that the class of future users will likely substantially overlap with the injured class of past consumers.

Redish et al. 62 Fla. L. Rev., *supra* at 662.

    Daar v. Yellow Cab Co., 433 P.2d 732 (Cal. 1967), is a good example of fluid class recovery. *Daar* was a California state court class action brought to recover overcharges on taxi fares. The case settled, but the parties faced a serious distribution problem. There was no practical way to identify the customers who had taken taxi rides in the past and thus had been overcharged. The court approved a settlement that applied the fund to reduce fares for future taxi passengers. If past riders are likely to ride in taxis again, this distribution plan would benefit many injured class members, albeit imperfectly.

    Even though it closely resembles cy pres in many respects, fluid class recovery is more controversial. See, e.g., *Windham v. American Brands, Inc.*, 565 F.2d 59, 72 (4th Cir. 1977), *cert. denied*, 435 U.S. 968 (1978); Redish et al. 62 Fla. L. Rev., *supra* at 661 ("In contrast to cy pres, the fluid class recovery concept has had a most difficult time in the courts.").

    4.   *Litigated Judgment Versus Settlement. Nachshin* involved a class settlement, while *Six Mexican Workers* involved a litigated class judgment. Should it matter whether the cy pres plan is formulated by the judge as part of a litigated judgment or formulated by the parties as part of a class settlement? Notice that the *Nachshin* court rejects the defendant's argument that the trial judge should defer to the parties' choices when a case settles. The court states: "This argument conflates two separate inquiries relating to class settlements: (1) whether the *class settlement*, "taken as a whole, is fair, reasonable, and adequate to all concerned" and (2) whether the *distribution* of the approved class settlement complies with our standards governing *cy pres* awards. . . . A proposed *cy pres* distribution must meet these standards regardless of whether the award was fashioned by the settling parties or the trial court." Does this make sense? What if the defendant is willing to settle for a larger amount if the cy pres beneficiary is an organization that the defendant prefers? Isn't a larger class settlement better than a smaller one? What about agency costs? Would deferential cy pres standards in the context of class settlements facilitate collu-

sion between class counsel and the defendant? Consider this last question in connection with the following Note.

5.   *Effect on Class Counsel Fees.* Should funds distributed to recipients other than the class members by way of cy pres principles count as part of the common fund for purposes of the determination of class counsel's fee award? Would a stricture against inclusion of such distributions in the common fund effectively police unwarranted use of the cy pres idea? Should one differentiate between cy pres distributions to non-class members of leftover, unclaimed settlement funds and such distributions due to the impracticality of any distribution to the class?

6.   *Criticism of Cy Pres Distributions.* As the *Nachshin* court notes, the use of cy pres distributions is controversial and it has elicited critical attention from the press in recent years. In addition to the articles cited by the court, see Amanda Bronstad, *Cy Pres Awards Under Scrutiny*, Nat'l L.J., Aug. 11, 2008, at 1.

In his concurring opinion in *Six Mexican Workers*, Judge Fernandez attacked cy pres, especially as ordered by a judge after a litigated judgment, and he also criticized the majority for categorically rejecting the option of reverting unclaimed funds to the defendant:

> [The] use [of cy pres] may well amount to little more than an exercise in social engineering by a judge, who finds it offensive that defendants have profited by some wrongdoing, but who has no legitimate plaintiff to give the money to. It is a very troublesome doctrine, which runs the risk of being a vehicle to punish defendants in the name of social policy, without conferring any particular benefit upon any particular wronged person. . . .
>
> The outcome of this litigation establishes that the defendants' rights to their own money are not superior to the rights of the plaintiffs. However, defendants' rights remain superior to those of anyone else.

Six (6) Mexican Workers v. Ariz. Citrus Growers, 904 F.2d 1301, 1312–13 (9th Cir. 1990).

Is cy pres really an "exercise in social engineering"? An article cited by the *Nachshin* court is even more critical of cy pres in the class action context. Redish et al., 62 Fla. L. Rev., *supra*, 617. The authors of this article object to cy pres on a number of grounds, including that it contravenes Article III's case-or-controversy requirement by introducing a third party into the litigation (the cy pres beneficiary) whose rights have not been violated and who has not suffered injury from the defendant's wrong; that it violates separation of powers and the Rules Enabling Act by "effectively transform[ing] [the substantive law] from a compensatory remedial structure to the equivalent of a civil fine," and that it threatens to violate the due process rights of the defendant and absent class members. *Id.* at 641–51. Is there really a constitutional problem with the use of cy pres to distribute damages? Would there be a constitutional problem if the use of cy pres were not constrained in the way it is?

7.   *Cy Pres and the ALI's Principles of the Law of Aggregate Litigation.* The *Nachshin* court remarks in footnote 2 that section 3.07 of the American Law Institute's Principles of the Law of Aggregate Litigation approves the use of cy pres. Section 3.07 addresses cy pres in the context of a class settlement

and states that "[a] court may approve a settlement that proposes a cy pres remedy even if such a remedy could not be ordered in a contested case." Nevertheless, section 3.07 embodies a strong presumption in favor of individual distribution and therefore restricts the use of cy pres in significant ways. According to section 3.07(a),"[i]f individual class members can be identified through reasonable effort, and the distributions are sufficiently large to make individual distributions economically viable, settlement proceeds should be distributed directly to individual class members." Moreover, section 3.07(b) creates a preference for distributing any unclaimed funds to those class members who participated in the distribution: "the settlement should presumptively provide for further distributions to participating class members unless the amounts involved are too small to make individual distributions economically viable or other specific reasons exist that would make such further distributions impossible or unfair." Finally, when cy pres is otherwise justified, section 3.07(c) limits the choice of designated beneficiary:

> The court, when feasible, should require the parties to identify a recipient whose interests reasonably approximate those being pursued by the class. If, and only if, no recipient whose interests reasonably approximate those being pursued by the class can be identified after thorough investigation and analysis, a court may approve a recipient that does not reasonably approximate the interests being pursued by the class.

Comment b to § 3.07 explains:

> This Section begins from the premise that funds generated through the aggregate prosecution of divisible claims are presumptively the property of the class members (and that the settlement has not been structured so that any funds remaining revert to the defendant). Starting from this vantage point, this Section generally permits cy pres awards only when direct distributions to class members are not feasible—either because class members cannot be reasonably identified or because distribution would involve such small amounts that, because of the administrative costs involved, such distribution would not be economically viable. In such circumstances, there should be a presumed obligation to award any remaining funds to an entity that resembles, in either composition or purpose, the class members or their interests.

American Law Institute, PRINCIPLES OF THE LAW OF AGGREGATE LITIGATION § 3.07 cmt. b.

How approximate may a "reasonabl[e] approximat[ion]" be? How much "investigation and analysis" must be done by parties before they can choose a beneficiary whose interests do not "reasonably approximate those being pursued by the class"? Isn't it always possible to find some organization that, in some way, "resembles, in either composition or purpose, the class members or their interests"? How would the cases and examples in the Notes above fare under section 3.07?

E. ATTORNEY–CLIENT CONFLICTS IN THE CLASS SETTLEMENT CONTEXT

We have already seen that the relationship between class counsel and the members of the class differs in significant respects from the relationship between lawyers and clients in non-class litigation. The many differences between class members and ordinary clients having been noted, it can nonetheless be helpful to conceive of Rule 23 as an implied-at-law contract for the representation of the class, that is, as a substitute for the actual contracts that run between lawyers and signed clients. Under the rule, a judge presiding over a motion for certification decides whether an at-law relationship will exist between a lawyer and a class. The judge also decides who the class members will be, what claims may be asserted on their behalf, whether the class members are entitled to opt out, and how much they will pay in fees. When a settlement is proposed, judicial review also substitutes for individual client consent. Considering the many functions Rule 23 serves that are ordinarily performed by contracts highlights the differences between class members and ordinary clients.

1. CONFLICT OF INTEREST RULES

To what extent should ordinary conflict-of-interest principles apply to class counsel? In one sense, we already have seen significant concern with class counsel conflicts of interest in the context of class settlements—e.g., in the Supreme Court's decisions in *Amchem* and *Ortiz*. In another sense, however, the application of ordinary conflict-of-interest principles may not suit the class action device. For example, the adequate representation requirement may necessitate subclasses outfitted with separate lawyers even though state bar rules permit joint representations in mass actions. Equally, conflicts that are prohibited outside of class actions may have to be accepted in them, lest the proliferation of subclasses render class litigation inefficient or uneconomical. In general, state bar rules were not made with class actions in mind and "should not be mechanically applied to the problems that arise in the settlement of class action litigation." In re *Agent Orange Prod. Liab. Litig.*, 800 F.2d 14, 19 (2d. Cir. 1986).

One set of ethical difficulties arises when the named plaintiff who originally hired class counsel becomes dissatisfied with a resulting class settlement to the point of becoming an objector to the deal. May class counsel continue to represent the class—in particular, to stand by the settlement that class counsel wrought—when the person who originally hired them now opposes the settlement? An important decision from the Third Circuit grapples with such a scenario.

Lazy Oil Co. v. Witco Corp.

166 F.3d 581 (3d Cir. 1999)

■ BECKER, CHIEF JUDGE.

This is an appeal from an order of the District Court approving a class action settlement of an antitrust case. Ironically, the lead objector, Lazy Oil Co., is also the lead plaintiff, whose principal, Bennie G. Landers, conceived the suit but later became disaffected with its management and direction and ultimately with its fruits—the settlement. All the objectors are producers of Penn Grade Crude Oil, i.e., crude oil drawn from the western side of the Appalachian Basin. . . . The objectors contend that the settlement is not fair, at least to the producer plaintiffs in contrast to the investor plaintiffs. The objectors distinguish between these two types of class members in making their objections to the settlement, alleging that producer plaintiffs, as full-time oil-producing enterprises, have distinct interests and, particularly, unique losses, as compared to investor plaintiffs, who simply invest funds in oil-producing businesses.

The objectors maintain that producer plaintiffs lost not only revenues from the lower prices paid for their oil (a loss they share with investor plaintiffs), but also suffered the compounded losses from their inability to invest these lost funds in drilling new oil wells or upgrading their existing ones—losses allegedly not applicable to investor plaintiffs. This alleged distinction is also at the heart of the other two issues raised by objectors in this appeal. They contend that the District Court erred in not certifying a subclass of producer plaintiffs to ensure that their unique interests were adequately represented. Finally, they contend that the Class Counsel— originally hired to bring this suit by the lead plaintiffs, who are now objectors—should have been disqualified from representing the remaining class representatives and the entire class once the objectors chose to attack the settlement.

. . . [T]he District Court filed an omnibus order overruling objections to the settlement, approving the terms of the settlement, denying objectors' motion to remove or disqualify Class Counsel, denying objectors' motion for certification of a subclass, and denying approval of the plan for allocating the settlement proceeds.

From the objectors' point of view, our opinion should be devoted largely to a merits analysis of their objections to the settlement. However, we dispose of that aspect of the case summarily, concluding that . . . the District Court did not abuse its discretion in approving the settlement. Neither do we have difficulty with the District Court's order refusing to remove or disqualify Class Counsel, which we also affirm. We do, however, expound on this point to clarify the standard for adjudicating such claims in the class action context. More specifically, drawing on the concurring opinion in *In re Corn Derivatives Antitrust Litigation*, 748 F.2d 157, 162 (3d Cir. 1984) (Adams, J., concurring), we adopt a balancing approach to motions to remove or disqualify class counsel on conflict-of-interest grounds once former class representatives, i.e., former clients of class counsel, become objectors and therefore adversaries to class counsel's remaining clients. . . .

I. *Background*

The subject of this appeal began as two separate class actions, each brought in the District Court for the Western District of Pennsylvania, by sellers of Penn Grade crude against three purchasers and refiners of this crude, Quaker State, Pennzoil, and Witco. The plaintiffs in both actions alleged that the defendants conspired to depress the price of Penn Grade Crude, in violation of the Sherman Antitrust Act. The cases were consolidated and, in June 1995, the District Court certified the consolidated case as a class action under Rule 23(b)(3), with the class comprising all "direct sellers of Penn Grade Crude" who sold oil to the defendants between January 1, 1981, and June 30, 1995. Shortly thereafter, the plaintiffs settled with Quaker State for $4.4 million. This settlement was approved by the District Court, and no issues relating to it are before us.

In early 1997, after several months of negotiations, plaintiffs reached a settlement with the remaining defendants, under which Pennzoil would pay approximately $9.7 million and Witco would pay approximately $4.8 million, with neither defendant admitting any liability or wrongdoing. Upon presentation of the settlement to the class representatives, two of them, Lazy Oil Co. and Thomas A. Miller Oil Co., objected to the settlement. At least 384 class members joined Lazy Oil et al. in objecting to the terms of the settlement after receiving notice of its terms. Class Counsel thereafter moved to withdraw from representing the objectors.

In February 1997, the District Court directed that notice of the proposed settlement be sent to all class members and published in local and national newspapers. The objectors filed motions, *inter alia*, requesting that the Court disapprove the settlement, for establishment of a producer subclass, and for disqualification of Class Counsel. As noted above, . . . the Court approved the settlement and denied the objectors' motions. With extensive findings of fact, the Court found that plaintiffs faced substantial obstacles to proving that defendants had violated the antitrust laws, as well as serious problems with their theory of damages. The Court . . . concluded that the settlement was fair and reasonable, and that the objectors' primary concern, i.e., that producer plaintiffs were not adequately represented or compensated by the settlement, was based on a speculative and unsupported argument (that had been raised very late in the litigation). Therefore, it overruled all of the relevant objections and approved the settlement. This appeal followed. . . .

V.   *Disqualification of Class Counsel*

The objectors contend that Class Counsel should be disqualified because they are now representing a party (i.e., the plaintiffs) adverse to one they previously represented (i.e., the objectors), creating an impermissible conflict of interest. This contention raises an interesting threshold question as to the standard a district court should apply to the conflict determination.

The most extensive discussion of the conflict-of-interest issue within our jurisprudence is found in *In re Corn Derivatives Antitrust Litigation*, 748 F.2d 157 (3d Cir. 1984). In *Corn Derivatives*, we granted a motion to disqualify an attorney who had formerly represented several class representatives; some of the class representatives approved of a proposed settlement and others did not. Unlike the present case, in *Corn Derivatives* counsel had withdrawn from representing the parties approving of the settlement and sought only to represent one objector on appeal. After consulting the relevant portions of the ABA's Model Rules of Professional Conduct and Model Code of Professional Responsibility,[12] we concluded that the prejudice to the former clients would be too great to justify counsel's continued representation of the objector. See *id.* at 162. We focused on the policies underlying the rules against an attorney representing a party in a matter in which a former client is now an adversary, including preventing "even the potential that a former client's confidences and secrets may be

---

[12] Currently, the ABA's Model Rules of Professional Conduct provide that "[a] lawyer who has formerly represented a client in a matter shall not thereafter represent another person in the same or a substantially related matter in which that person's interests are materially adverse to the interests of the former client unless the former client consents after consultation." Model Rules of Professional Conduct Rule 1.9(a) (1983); see also *id.* cmt. ("The underlying question is whether the lawyer was so involved in the matter that the subsequent representation can be justly regarded as a changing of sides in the matter in question.").

used against him"; maintaining "public confidence in the integrity of the bar" and upholding the duty of loyalty that a client has the right to expect. *Id.*

Our opinion also discussed countervailing considerations, such as whether the counsel at issue represented the entire class (which was not the case in *Corn Derivatives*, but is true here), and the interest of the party who wishes to retain the counsel in avoiding increased costs and keeping "counsel who has extensive familiarity with the factual and legal issues involved." *Id.* Overall, however, we analyzed the situation no differently than we would have a non-class action case in which "two clients retained the same law firm to file suit, and where, later, that law firm chose to represent one of those clients against the other in the course of the same litigation." *Id.* at 161.

In his concurring opinion, Judge Adams more explicitly endorsed a balancing approach to attorney-disqualification motions in the class action context. Judge Adams argued that the rules for attorney disqualification could not be "mechanically transpose[d]" to the class action context and that the more appropriate means of addressing such issues was through "a balancing process." *Id.* at 163 (Adams, J., concurring). After discussing the rationale behind these points, he noted that, "[i]f a class attorney is automatically prevented from continuing to represent the named parties or a majority of a class which supports a settlement, the minority dissenting class members might obtain considerable leverage in the litigation by being able to force the majority to seek new counsel." *Id.* at 164 (Adams, J., concurring).

We agree with Judge Adams's concerns. In many class actions, one or more class representatives will object to a settlement and become adverse parties to the remaining class representatives (and the rest of the class). If, by applying the usual rules on attorney-client relations, class counsel could easily be disqualified in these cases, not only would the objectors enjoy great "leverage," but many fair and reasonable settlements would be undermined by the need to find substitute counsel after months or even years of fruitful settlement negotiations. "Moreover, the conflict rules do not appear to be drafted with class action procedures in mind and may be at odds with the policies underlying the class action rules." Bruce A. Green, *Conflicts of Interest in Litigation: The Judicial Role*, 65 Fordham L. Rev. 71, 127 (1996).

As the Second Circuit noted, in a case factually similar to *Corn Derivatives*:

> Automatic application of the traditional principles governing disqualification of attorneys on grounds of conflict of interest would seemingly dictate that whenever a rift arises in the class, with one branch favoring a settlement or a course of action that another branch resists, the attorney who has represented the class should withdraw entirely and take no position. Were he to take a position, either favoring or opposing the proposed course of action, he would be opposing the interests of some of his former clients in the very matter in which he has represented them.
>
> . . . [W]hen an action has continued over the course of many years, the prospect of having those most familiar with its course and status be automatically disqualified whenever class members

have conflicting interests would substantially diminish the efficacy of class actions as a method of dispute resolution.

In re "Agent Orange" Prod. Liab. Litig., 800 F.2d 14, 18–19 (2d Cir. 1986) (citations omitted). The court then concluded "that the traditional rules that have been developed in the course of attorneys' representation of the interests of clients outside of the class action context should not be mechanically applied to the problems that arise in the settlement of class action litigation." *Id.* at 19. Rather, it held, a balancing approach like that advocated by Judge Adams in *Corn Derivatives* was more appropriate in the class action context.

The *Agent Orange* court listed a number of relevant factors in this balancing inquiry, including some from Judge Adams's opinion: the information in the attorney's possession, the availability of the information elsewhere, the importance of this information to the disputed issues, actual prejudice that could flow from the attorney's possession of the information, the costs to class members of obtaining new counsel and the ease with which they might do so, the complexity of the litigation, and the time needed for new counsel to familiarize himself with the case. See *Agent Orange*, 800 F.2d at 19.

We are persuaded by the well-reasoned opinions in *Agent Orange* and *Corn Derivatives*. We therefore hold that, in the class action context, once some class representatives object to a settlement negotiated on their behalf, class counsel may continue to represent the remaining class representatives and the class, as long as the interest of the class in continued representation by experienced counsel is not outweighed by the actual prejudice to the objectors of being opposed by their former counsel. In making this determination, the district court may consider the factors discussed in *Agent Orange* and in both the majority and concurring opinions in *Corn Derivatives*.

Turning to the present case, we note that the situation here differs from that in *Corn Derivatives* in that counsel there sought to represent only one party, an objector, and not the remaining class members. In a case such as the present one, the balance weighs heavily in favor of denying a motion for disqualification of class counsel that is made on the basis of nothing more than the fact that the objectors include former clients (in the same case) of class counsel, without any showing of impropriety or prejudice. See also *Bash v. Firstmark Standard Life Ins. Co.*, 861 F.2d 159, 161 (7th Cir. 1988) ("Recognizing that strict application of rules on attorney conduct that were designed with simpler litigation in mind might make the class-action device unworkable in many cases, the courts insist that a serious conflict be shown before they will take remedial or disciplinary action."); cf. *Saylor v. Lindsley*, 456 F.2d 896, 900 (2d Cir. 1972) (noting that plaintiff's counsel in a derivative action "remains bound . . ., if the client has objected [to a settlement], to inform the court of this when presenting the settlement, so that it may devise procedures whereby the plaintiff, with a new attorney, may himself conduct further inquiry if so advised").

Objectors contend that Class Counsel in this case did not adequately represent all of the class members because they failed to consider the unique interests and damages of the producer plaintiffs. Given our agreement with the District Court that the objectors' distinction between producer and investor plaintiffs is not supported by the record in this case, we find no clear error in the District Court's finding that Class Counsel adequately represented the interests of all class members, even if some class members and some of the class representatives are unsatisfied with the results of Class Counsel's efforts. See *Walsh v. Great Atl. & Pac. Tea Co.*, 726 F.2d 956, 964 (3d Cir. 1983) ("Class counsel's duty to the class as a whole frequently diverges from the opinion of either the named plaintiff or other objectors.").

Applying the standard we have outlined above, we are satisfied that the District Court weighed the competing interests appropriately and did not abuse its discretion in denying the motion for disqualification of Class Counsel.

NOTES AND QUESTIONS

1. *Strategic Considerations.* What if the court in *Lazy Oil* had come out the opposite way—that is, had disqualified class counsel from continuing to represent the class? What strategic leverage would such a decision afford to a named plaintiff like Lazy Oil?

2. *The Relationship of Settlement Fairness and Conflicts of Interest.* Does it make a difference to the conflict-of-interest analysis that the court finds unpersuasive Lazy Oil's argument, as one of many objectors, that there should have been additional subclassing? If the court is correct that the named plaintiffs could adequately represent the entire plaintiff class as defined, then what explains the opposition of Lazy Oil and other named plaintiffs to the deal struck by class counsel?

3. *Whose Class Is It Anyway?* Did the court attach appropriate significance to Lazy Oil's active involvement in the initiation of the litigation in a way that made it much more than a "decorative figurehead" and to the opposition to the class settlement by a *majority* of the named plaintiffs (a fact not entirely apparent from the court's account)? One commentator observes:

> [I]t is possible to find the Third Circuit's analysis persuasive on many of its factual conclusions and yet still feel that the broader question has been largely missed (or politely suppressed). That question is: What control should sophisticated class representatives have over a class action? Can class counsel simply ignore their preferences, even when a clear majority of the representatives wants the settlement rejected? Effectively, class counsel did that in *Lazy Oil* by resigning as counsel to seventy-five percent of the class representatives (who opposed the proposed settlement), but remaining as counsel to the fourth representative and to the class generally....
>
> ... Whose lawsuit was it? If a substantial group of individuals sued together in a consolidated proceeding, their ability to change counsel would seem beyond question and could not be denied simply because their attorney was more realistic than they were about the action's merit. Yet, the practical impact of the Third Circuit's holding in *Lazy Oil* was clearly to imply that class counsel had effective control of the class action (indeed, possibly even if all the class representatives were to oppose the settlement). Such a result can be rationalized on the ground that the attorney represents all class members, and not simply the representatives, but the implicit assumption here that the rest of the class would side with the attorney (and not the class representatives) simply because they did not opt out or because the court approved the settlement as fair and adequate assumes precisely what

is to be proven. Such an approach makes judicial approval of the settlement's fairness the exclusive test, and this is precisely the approach that *Amchem* rejected, because it would "eclipse" the other protections of Rule 23.

John C. Coffee, Jr., *Class Action Accountability: Reconciling Exit, Voice, and Loyalty in Representative Litigation*, 100 Colum. L. Rev. 370, 408–09 (2000).

4. The Significance of Timing. Would the result in *Lazy Oil* remain the same if the conflict between class counsel and the objecting named plaintiffs had emerged prior to class certification? Between class certification and the completion of class settlement negotiations? To ask these questions in a different way: Is the key fact of *Lazy Oil* the completion of the class settlement agreement?

2. POST–SETTLEMENT SUITS BY CLASS MEMBERS AGAINST CLASS COUNSEL FOR LEGAL MALPRACTICE

An ordinary plaintiff can sue a lawyer for malpractice, and a legal malpractice claim can be based on a lawyer's recommendation that a client settle for an unreasonably low sum. Should class members be allowed to sue class counsel for the same thing, that is, for supporting a settlement that they have good reason to believe was too low? Or should post-settlement malpractice suits be barred on the ground that judicial review and approval of settlements and fee awards under Rule 23(e) conclusively establishes that class counsel acted reasonably? What about a middling position, on which post-settlement malpractice suits would be barred absent a showing that class counsel withheld material information from class members and the court?

In the following case, Texas billionaire Sam Wyly sued Milberg Weiss and other law firms that served as class counsel in securities fraud litigation against Computer Associates. Wyly accused the lawyers of settling the class action cheaply and prematurely so they could collect $30–$40 million in fees. In support of this charge, Wyly pointed out that the lawyers failed to conduct discovery into certain allegations and refused to seek to reopen the case after learning that Computer Associates' defense lawyers withheld 23 boxes of documents in discovery. He also argued that the deal was a bad one for the class. After the settlement was approved, Computer Associates restated $2.2 billion in revenue and, in connection with a federal criminal investigation, several of its high-level officers admitted to participating in a fraud. Because the class settlement released the company and its employees from further liability, these development entitled investors to no more relief than they had already received.

Wyly filed his malpractice lawsuit in a New York state court after the federal district court judge who approved the settlement dismissed his motion to set aside the judgment under Rule 60(b). The lawyers responded by asking the federal judge to enjoin the state court prosecution. The court issued the order, finding that both the "in aid of jurisdiction" and "relitigation" exceptions to the Anti–Injunction Act applied. (The Anti–Injunction Act is discussed in detail in Chapter 3.C.) The Second Circuit reversed on the applicability of the former exception but affirmed on the applicability of the latter. Only the discussion of the "relitigation" exception appears below.

Wyly v. Weiss

697 F.3d 131 (2nd Cir. 2012)

■ JOSE A. CABRANES, CIRCUIT JUDGE:

A. Factual Background

1. The 1998 and 2002 Class Actions

Beginning in July 1998, eleven putative class action complaints were filed in the United States District Court for the Eastern District of New York against Computer Associates International, Inc. ("Computer Associates" or "CA") and certain of its then-current and former officers and directors, alleging violations of the federal securities laws and Generally Accepted Accounting Principles ("GAAP"). By Order dated October 9, 1998, the District Court consolidated those complaints into a single action, *In re Computer Assocs. Class Action Sec. Litig.*, No. 98–cv–4839 (TCP) (E.D.N.Y.) (the "1998 Class Action"), and appointed the law firms of Milberg Weiss LLP and Stull, Stull & Brody as co-lead counsel for the class. The plaintiffs in the 1998 Class Action alleged that officers and directors of Computer Associates participated in a scheme to artificially inflate the price of CA stock, artificially inflate its reported revenues, and conceal the deterioration of its business. The class period in the 1998 Class Action spanned approximately six months, from January 20, 1998 through July 22, 1998.

Between February and May 2002, thirteen additional putative class action complaints were filed against Computer Associates and certain of its then-current and former officers and directors, again alleging violations of the federal securities laws and GAAP. By Order dated July 25, 2002, the cases were consolidated into a single action, *In re Computer Assocs. 2002 Class Action Sec. Litig.*, No. 02–cv–1226 (TCP) (E.D.N.Y.) (the "2002 Class Action"), and Milberg Weiss LLP and Schiffrin & Barroway, LLP were appointed co-lead counsel for the class. The class period in the 2002 Class Action spanned approximately two years and nine months, from May 28, 1999 through February 25, 2002. In connection with the 2002 Class Action, class counsel decided not to conduct any discovery and instead elected to rely exclusively on the discovery conducted in the 1998 Class Action.

2. The Government Investigation

In February 2002, the United States Attorney's Office for the Eastern District of New York and the Securities & Exchange Commission (jointly, the "Government") launched a joint investigation into CA's accounting practices. In July 2003, CA's defense counsel in the Government investigation, Wachtell, Lipton, Rosen & Katz ("WLRK"), informed the CA Board of Directors (the "CA Board" or the "Board") that up to $200 million of revenue was prematurely or improperly recognized in one quarter of fiscal year 2000 alone. WLRK further informed the Board that anything less than an independent internal investigation would be viewed by the Government as non-cooperation. As a result, the CA Board authorized its Special Litigation Committee ("SLC") to conduct an internal investigation. The SLC then retained Sullivan & Cromwell LLP to assist in that investigation.

3. The Class Action Settlement

In early 2003, with the trial of the 1998 Class Action approaching and at the direction of the District Court, the parties entered into mediation. In August 2003, following approximately seven months of mediation, the parties reached a global settlement of the 1998 and 2002 Class Actions by which the class members were to receive 5.7 million shares of CA common stock, valued at approximately $130 to 150 million at the time of the settlement. [The Government investigation ultimately resulted in payment of an additional $225 million in restitution to CA shareholders, as well as other structural and non-monetary relief.] As its fee, class counsel would receive approximately 1.4 million shares of CA common stock, valued at approximately $30 to 40 million. In return, CA and its officers and directors were to receive broad-based liability releases.

On December 5, 2003, the District Court conducted a fairness hearing on the projected global settlement, as required by Federal Rule of Civil Procedure 23(e)(2). No class member objected to the settlement. At the fairness hearing, class counsel stated that:

> As we all are aware, there is a criminal investigation [of CA] that is ongoing, and I just wanted the Court to understand, as we have stated in our papers, that we've [taken] all of that into account in coming to the conclusions we did as to what would be a fair, reasonable and adequate settlement for the class members.

Joint App'x 1: 270 at 5:5–5:10. On December 8, 2003, the District Court certified a single class encompassing the 1998 Class Action and the 2002 Class Action and approved the settlement. On December 16, 2003, the District Court issued an Amended Order and Final Judgment (the "Settlement Order"), which (1) held that the settlement was "fair, reasonable[,] and adequate," (2) awarded class counsel fees, which the Court held to be "fair and reasonable," and (3) retained exclusive jurisdiction "over the parties and the Settlement Class Members for all matters relating to the[se] Actions."

4. Subsequent Discoveries

Within months of the District Court's approval of the global settlement, several CA executives pleaded guilty to federal securities violations and obstruction of justice. On April 26, 2004, Computer Associates announced that it was restating more than $2.2 billion in revenue. On September 22, 2004, CA's general counsel, Steven Woghin, pleaded guilty to conspiracy to commit securities fraud and obstruction of justice, and CA entered into a Deferred Prosecution Agreement ("DPA") in order to avoid criminal prosecution. In the DPA, CA admitted that many of its senior executives participated in a multi-billion dollar accounting fraud and cover-up.

On September 24, 2004, the *Wall Street Journal* reported that CA had improperly withheld 23 boxes of documents (the "23 boxes") during the class actions and the Government investigation. See Charles Forelle & Joann S. Lublin, *In CA Probe: Recovered E-mails, Surprise Cache of Documents,* The Wall St. J., Sept. 24, 2004, at A1. Although the 23 boxes were not produced during discovery in the class actions, CA had turned over the 23 boxes to Sullivan & Cromwell in connection with the internal investigation in September 2003—prior to the approval of the global settlement.

5. The Rule 60(b) Motion

In light of the foregoing developments, Sam Wyly and other members of the Settlement Class (jointly, the "Wyly Appellants") contacted class counsel on October 18, 2004, and requested that they move to vacate the Settlement Order pursuant to Federal Rule of Civil Procedure 60(b). On November 24, 2004, class counsel declined. On December 7, 2004, the Wyly Appellants moved for relief from the Settlement Order under Rule 60(b).

Nearly three years of discovery and motion practice followed. During that time, the District Court ordered that the 23 boxes be produced to counsel for the Wyly Appellants for their review. Although the Wyly Appellants continue to attach great significance to the 23 boxes on appeal, the U.S. Attorney's Office and the SLC stressed to the District Court that "the 23 boxes . . . rendered *no* additional evidence of fraud beyond that which [the Wyly Appellants] already had." Joint App'x 4: 902 (SLC Report) (internal quotation marks omitted).

At a discovery conference on August 1, 2007, the District Court dismissed the Rule 60(b) motion *sua sponte.* The next day, the District Court entered an order memorializing its ruling (the "Rule 60(b) Order"), holding that "the moving parties have failed to set forth cause to permit further discovery to be conducted in conjunction with the 60(b) motions." *In re Computer Assocs.,* 2007 WL 2261683, at *1 (E.D.N.Y. Aug. 2, 2007). Specifically, the District Court concluded that "in the three years since the filing of the original 60(b) motions in 2004, the parties have failed to produce any 'new' evidence of fraud upon th[e] Court . . . and have failed to establish that the contents of the '23 boxes' allegedly withheld during discovery . . . warrant granting further discovery and reopening the 2003 settlement." *Id.,*2007 WL 2261683 at *2. The Wyly Appellants appealed, and on July 23, 2009, we affirmed the District Court's order on procedural grounds. See *Federman v. Artzt,* 339 Fed.Appx. 31, 33–34 (2d Cir.2009).

B.   Procedural History

The Wyly Appellants filed an initial complaint in the Supreme Court of New York on November 26, 2007, and an amended complaint on December 11, 2007, alleging that class counsel placed its own financial interests before those of the class. The amended complaint, captioned *Wyly v. Milberg Weiss LLP,* No. 07/603883 (N.Y.Sup.Ct.), asserted claims for, *inter alia,* breach of fiduciary duty, legal malpractice, unjust enrichment, and fraud.

On January 2, 2008, the movants-appellees—Melvyn I. Weiss, Milberg Weiss LLP, Lee A. Weiss, Barry A. Weprin, George A. Bauer, III, Jules Brody, Schiffrin Barroway Topaz & Kessler LLP, Richard Schiffrin, Andrew Barroway, Stull, Stull & Brody, and Andrew L. Barroway (jointly, the "Appellees" or "class counsel")—moved in the District Court for an order permanently enjoining the Wyly Appellants from prosecuting the state court action. The Appellees argued that the District Court's holdings at the fairness hearing, its approval of the global settlement, and its dismissal of the Rule 60(b) motion permitted the issuance of an injunction under the All Writs Act, 28 U.S.C. § 1651, barring the state court proceedings against class counsel.

On September 29, 2010, the District Court granted the injunction and directed class counsel to submit a proposed order. The District Court entered the proposed order on November 3, 2010, holding, *inter alia,* that "this Court's determination of Class Counsel's entitlement to fees necessarily determined the adequacy of their representation of the class members (including Wyly) and collaterally estops claims of attorney malpractice or misconduct in connection with the Settlement." *Barroway v. Computer Assocs.,* No. 98–cv–4839 (TCP)(ETB) (E.D.N.Y. Nov. 3, 2010), Doc. No. 402. The District Court further held that the state court action "seeks to relitigate and nullify [its] findings as to the adequacy of [class counsel's] representation of the plaintiff class," as reflected in the Settlement Order and the Rule 60(b) Order. *Id.*

This appeal followed.

DISCUSSION

The sole issue on appeal is whether the District Court's injunction against the state court action was proper under the All Writs Act, 28 U.S.C. § 1651, and the Anti–Injunction Act, 28 U.S.C. § 2283.

The All Writs Act, 28 U.S.C. § 1651, authorizes federal courts to "issue all writs necessary or appropriate in aid of their respective jurisdictions and agreeable to the usages and principles of law." *Id.* § 1651(a). "This grant of authority is limited by the Anti–Injunction Act, 28 U.S.C. § 2283, which bars a federal court from enjoining a proceeding in state court unless that action is 'expressly authorized by Act of Congress, or where necessary in aid of its jurisdiction, or to protect or effectuate its judgments.'" . . . [T]he District Court held that a permanent injunction of the state court action was "necessary in aid of its jurisdiction" (the "in aid of jurisdiction" exception) and was needed to "protect or effectuate its judgments" (the "relitigation" exception). . . .

B. The "Relitigation" Exception

Having determined that the "in aid of jurisdiction" exception is inapplicable, we now turn to the Anti–Injunction Act's so-called "relitigation" exception, which permits a federal court to enjoin a state court proceeding "to protect or effectuate its judgments." 28 U.S.C. § 2283. The relitigation exception . . . authorizes a federal court to enjoin "state litigation of a claim or issue 'that previously was presented to and decided by the federal court.'" *Smith v. Bayer Corp.*, ___ U.S. ___, 131 S.Ct. 2368, 2375, 180 L.Ed.2d 341 (2011) (quoting *Chick Kam Choo v. Exxon Corp.*, 486 U.S. 140, 147, 108 S.Ct. 1684, 100 L.Ed.2d 127 (1988)). . . .

The preclusive effect of a federal court's judgment issued pursuant to its federal-question jurisdiction is governed by the federal common law of preclusion. . . .

The Appellees . . . focus their argument on *issue* preclusion, see Appellees' Br. 34–36 (arguing that state court suit raises the "same issue" as previously decided).

The Supreme Court has listed the various requirements of issue preclusion . . . Our summary of the four requirements for issue preclusion is in harmony with these various Supreme Court statements: "(1) the identical issue was raised in a previous proceeding; (2) the issue was actually litigated and decided in the previous proceeding; (3) the part[ies] had a full and fair opportunity to litigate the issue; and (4) the resolution of the issue was necessary to support a valid and final judgment on the merits." *Marvel Characters, Inc.*, 310 F.3d at 288–89.

Before applying the elements of issue preclusion to this case, we begin with a preliminary observation about the Appellees' argument. In the course of the federal class action litigation, the District Court did not "actually decide" whether the Appellees committed legal malpractice; that claim was not presented, and therefore the Court had no reason to address malpractice as such. The Appellees' issue-preclusion argument is focused not on whether the District Court previously adjudicated a malpractice *claim,* however, but on whether the Court resolved one of the *elements* of a malpractice claim—namely, counsel's deficient performance. See *AmBase Corp. v. Davis Polk & Wardwell*, 8 N.Y.3d 428, 434, 834 N.Y.S.2d 705, 866 N.E.2d 1033 (2007) (a plaintiff alleging malpractice under New York law must show, *inter alia,* that "the defendant attorney failed to exercise the ordinary *reasonable skill* and knowledge commonly possessed by a member of the legal profession. . . ." (emphasis supplied)). If the Appellees can show that issue preclusion prevents a future court from finding this *element* satisfied, then any malpractice claim that would require a finding that counsel's performance was deficient is precluded under federal law. See *Parklane Hosiery Co. v. Shore,* 439 U.S. 322, 337, 99 S.Ct. 645, 58 L.Ed.2d 552 (1979) (judge-made findings may bind the parties in a subsequent action at law).

We begin by examining the issue raised and decided in the federal class action proceedings—elements one and two of our preclusion analysis. The Settlement Order held, *inter alia,* that the global settlement of the 1998 and 2002 class actions was "fair, reasonable[,] and adequate," and that class counsel was entitled to an award of fees that the District Court found to be "fair and reasonable." Whether an award of "fair and reasonable" attorneys' fees necessarily decides the deficient-performance prong of a legal malpractice claim is an issue of first impression in this Circuit. We conclude that the deficient-performance prong of New York's legal malpractice rule is identical to the reasonable-performance issue that the District Court decided as a necessary component of the Settlement Order.

Even a cursory review of the allegations in the amended complaint belies the Wyly Appellants' contention that the state court action does not seek to relitigate the District Court's determination that class counsel's representation was reasonable. The amended complaint alleges, *inter alia,* that:

- Class counsel "abandoned their fiduciary duties owed to [the Wyly Appellants] and the other class members" by settling the 2002 Class Action prior to discovery. Joint App'x 2: 426–27 (¶ 5).

- The 2002 Class Action was "jettison[ed]" to obtain a settlement that "yielded pennies for the victimized public shareholders, but over $40 million in attorneys' fees for [class counsel]." Joint App'x 2: 456 (¶ 132).

- The releases given to the CA defendants were overly broad. Joint App'x 2: 448 (¶ 99).

- The attorneys' fees awarded to class counsel constitute unjust enrichment and should be disgorged. Joint App'x 2: 458 (¶¶ 146–48), 467–68 (¶ b).

- Class counsel breached their duty of loyalty to the plaintiff class by refusing to support the Wyly Appellants' Rule 60(b) motion. Joint App'x 2: 450 (¶ 104).

These allegations, which are designed to state a claim that the Appellees "failed to exercise the ordinary *reasonable skill* and knowledge commonly possessed by a member of the legal profession," *AmBase Corp.,* 8 N.Y.3d at 434, 834 N.Y.S.2d 705, 866 N.E.2d 1033 (emphasis supplied), constitute a collateral attack on the District Court's findings that the Settlement was "fair, reasonable and adequate," that class counsel was entitled to an award of attorneys' fees, and that those fees were "fair and reasonable." Those findings were possible only if counsel's performance met or exceeded the minimal standards of professional competence—otherwise an award of fees would not have been fair and reasonable in the circumstances. We therefore conclude that the state court action seeks to relitigate the same issue that the District Court already resolved. See *Achtman v. Kirby, McInerney & Squire, LLP,* 464 F.3d 328, 336 (2d Cir. 2006) ("In the course of approving those settlements and the resulting fee awards, the court found [counsel's] representation reasonable and adequate. . . .").

The limited case law from other Courts of Appeals on the relitigation exception accords with our conclusion that a district court's finding regarding the adequacy of counsel may have preclusive effect in a future malpractice action. See, e.g., *Thomas v. Powell*, 247 F.3d 260, 264 (D.C.Cir. 2001) (upholding the injunction of class plaintiffs' post-settlement malpractice action because the district court had "squarely decided" that the attorneys acted in the interests of the class); see also *Koehler v. Brody*, 483 F.3d 590, 598 (8th Cir. 2007) (rejecting class plaintiffs' post-settlement malpractice claim because "[i]mplicit within the court's approval [of the settlement] were findings that the case had not settled for an amount that was too low, and that class counsel fairly and adequately protected the interests of the class" (internal citation and quotation marks omitted)); *Laskey v. Int'l Union*, 638 F.2d 954, 957 (6th Cir. 1981) ("Since appellants had the opportunity to object to the legal representation at the prior settlement hearing and since a finding that the class was adequately represented is necessary for finding the settlement was fair and reasonable, which in turn was essential to approving the settlement, appellants are collaterally estopped from now asserting that the legal representation was not adequate and that [class counsel] committed legal malpractice." (internal citation omitted)); *Achtman v. Kirby, McInerney & Squire, LLP*, 404 F. Supp. 2d 540, 545 (S.D.N.Y. 2005) (holding that "[i]f the threatened malpractice litigation against the law firms based on the representation they provided in the underlying action was brought before another court," the court's prior findings "based on the quality of the representation before this Court would be relitigated and essentially undone by another court").

The Wyly Appellants seek to distinguish the foregoing authority by contesting the third element of issue preclusion—in other words, by arguing that they were deprived of a "full and fair opportunity" to litigate the issue of their counsel's representation. The Appellants point to the fact that, unlike the plaintiffs in the foregoing cases, they were not physically present or represented by separate counsel at the fairness hearing. This argument is unavailing.

"It is a violation of due process for a judgment to be binding on a litigant who was not a party or a privy and therefore has never had an opportunity to be heard." *Parklane Hosiery Co.*, 439 U.S. at 327 n. 7, 99 S.Ct. 645. This rule, however, does not prevent preclusive effect from applying to suits by members of a certified class action. See *Bayer Corp.*, 131 S.Ct. at 2380 (noting that "unnamed members of a class action [may] be bound, even though they are not parties to the suit"). There is no dispute that the Wyly Appellants were members of the certified Settlement Class, and were therefore bound by both the Settlement Order and the Rule 60(b) Order. The Wyly Appellants also were fully aware of the date and time of the fairness hearing, and it was their choice not to attend. As members of a certified class, they are bound by the judgment of the District Court. See *In re Am. Exp. Fin. Advisors Sec. Litig.*, 672 F.3d 113, 129 (2d Cir. 2011) ("Absent a violation of due process or excusable neglect for failure to timely opt out, a class-action settlement agreement binds all class members who did not do so."). They cannot now, by dint of their decision not to attend the fairness hearing, assume a capacity they would otherwise lack to challenge the outcome of that proceeding.

The Wyly Appellants further contend that the relitigation exception does not apply here because many of the facts and events giving rise to claims alleged in the state court action "were unknown, or had not yet occurred, at the time the District Court approved the 2003 Settlement." Appellants' Br. 35. This argument might have more force were it not for the fact that the Wyly Appellants litigated their fraud allegations for nearly three years in connection with their Rule 60(b) motion—and lost. See *Greene v. United States*, 79 F.3d 1348, 1352 (2d Cir. 1996) (noting that issue preclusion may be inappropriate if "'controlling facts or legal principles have changed significantly' since the initial decision" (quoting *Montana v. United States*, 440 U.S. 147, 155, 99 S.Ct. 970, 59 L.Ed.2d 210 (1979))). In the Rule 60(b) Order, the District Court held that the Wyly Appellants "failed to produce any 'new' evidence of fraud," notwithstanding the "[a]mple opportunity . . . given to the parties to illuminate and bring to th[e] Court's attention any fraud or reasonable basis for a finding of fraud upon th[e] Court." The Court further held that the Wyly Appellants "failed to establish that the contents of the '23 boxes' allegedly withheld during discovery and prior to the settlement warrant granting further discovery and reopening the 2003 settlement." Given that the District Court was fully aware of the pending Government investigation at the time of the fairness hearing, see Joint App'x 1: 270 at 5:5–5:10, and that the parties exhaustively litigated further allegations of fraud in connection with the Rule 60(b) motion, we conclude that the relitigation exception applies notwithstanding the alleged subsequent discoveries.

Finally, we note that the District Court's finding regarding class counsel's adequacy was necessary to its judgment accepting the settlement and fees award. See *In re Am. Int'l Grp., Inc. Sec. Litig.*, 689 F.3d 229, 238 (2d Cir.2012) ("Before approving a class settlement agreement, a district court . . . *must* separately evaluate whether the settlement agreement is 'fair, reasonable, and adequate' under Rule 23(e)." (emphasis supplied)). The fourth element of issue preclusion, requiring "the resolution of the issue [that] was necessary to support a valid and final judgment on the merits," *Marvel Characters, Inc.*, 310 F.3d at 289, is therefore satisfied as well.

In sum, we hold that where, as here, the parties had a full and fair opportunity to litigate the reasonableness of counsel's representation, a district court's award of "fair and reasonable" attorneys' fees precludes a subsequent action for legal malpractice for counsel's advocating the settlement. We conclude that the District Court's decision to issue an injunction in these circumstances was "within the range of permissible decisions" and therefore was not an abuse of its discretion. *Sims*, 534 F.3d at 132 (quotation marks omitted).

We note that the traditional "principles of equity, comity, and federalism that must restrain a federal court when asked to enjoin a state court proceeding" support this result. *Mitchum*, 407 U.S. at 243, 92 S.Ct. 2151. Prior to filing their malpractice suit, Appellants had already filed a Rule 60(b) motion, and the District Court ultimately concluded that in three years of litigation, they "failed to produce any 'new' evidence of fraud" or any other valid reason to reopen the case. The Court therefore had legitimate concerns that the Appellants' malpractice action in state court might simply be an end-run around its prior decisions. See *Travelers Indem. Co. v. Sarkisian*, 794 F.2d 754, 760–61 (2d Cir.1986) (courts enjoy wider discretion to enjoin litigation when the enjoined party may be abusing the court system); *In re Martin-Trigona*, 737 F.2d 1254, 1261–62 (2d Cir. 1984) (same). The District Court's decision finds further support in a justified fear that allowing malpractice suits in state court against these Appellees might "unleash such suits upon class counsel in fora far and wide" and thereby undermine the class action system as a whole. *Achtman*, 404 F. Supp. 2d at 546. Moreover, complex class action suits present relatively unusual circumstances with respect to comity toward state courts, since the risk of vexatious litigation by dissatisfied litigants is higher, and since the federal court is often in a better position to quickly appraise the merits of a preclusion argument regarding a complex suit that it has already adjudicated. See *Browning Debenture Holders' Committee v. DASA Corp.*, 605 F.2d 35, 40 (2d Cir. 1978) ("While comity requires respect for the ability of the state courts to decide the issue of res judicata properly, it also requires sympathy for their calendar problems and for the task that would confront them were this litigation to be imposed upon them." (quotation marks omitted)).

In light of the preclusive effect of the District Court's award of "fair and reasonable" attorneys' fees, as well as the foregoing equitable considerations, we affirm the judgment of the District Court.

NOTES AND QUESTIONS

1.   *What Options are Available to Class Members when Class Counsel Commits Malpractice?* Wyly argued that he should not be bound by any findings the district court made when approving the class settlement because he wasn't at the fairness hearing. The Second Circuit rejected this argument, finding that Wyly was bound because he received notice of the hearing and waived the opportunity to appear. Doesn't this mean that class members must object at fairness hearings or forever lose their rights?

Wyly argued that the malpractice action represented a "collateral attack" on the class judgment and insisted that the plaintiffs in the malpractice suit were bound by the earlier class judgment. Recall the discussion of collateral attack earlier in this chapter; that discussion considered whether a class judgment binds an absent class member who has been inadequately represented in other litigation against the class defendant(s). *Wyly*, by contrast, asks whether class counsel may use the class judgment as a shield against a malpractice suit by an absent class member who claims that he was inadequately represented. Similar arguments for and against permitting an inadequately represented class member to sue can be deployed in both contexts. But there is one important difference: allowing an inadequately represented class member to bring further litigation against class defendants might have the effect of unraveling the finality of a settlement, a result that may harm the class defendants and other class members, even if only class counsel is to blame for the inadequate representation. So, the argument against allowing further litigation has greater force when additional litigation would be directed against class defendants. In this vein, the Principles of Aggregate Litigation argued that "[w]hen class members are permitted to bring collateral challenges to a settlement on grounds that were, or could have been, raised during the settlement process, the very integrity of the settlement process is undermined," § 3.14 cmt a, but sought to "leave[ ] unchanged existing law governing class members' ability to pursue claims of malpractice or breach of fiduciary duty against class counsel," § 3.14(b).

Does it make sense to deprive class members who fail to object of the right to sue later? The Second Circuit's position seems to give class members credit for having more information than they usually possess. Class members are passive, as the US Supreme Court observed in *Phillips Petroleum v. Shutts*, 472 US 797 (1985). They rely on others to represent their interests. Consequently, they know little about the litigation's merits or the quality of class counsel's efforts. Settlement notices give them some information, but notices never tell class members that class counsel may have acted improperly. Class counsel draft settlement notices, after all. As a practical matter, class members are likely to learn about misconduct mainly through media coverage, as Wyly did here. But it may be too late to object to a settlement when media coverage appears.

If the preceding is right, class members seem to face a strange choice. They may object to settlements for the purpose of investigating class counsel's conduct and learning whether class counsel acted improperly. Or they may sit on their hands. By objecting without evidence, they will irritate judges and possibly subject themselves to sanctions. By keeping quiet, they will lose their rights. They will also lose time, either way. In an ordinary case, a disappointed client has the amount of time allowed by the statute of limitations, usually a year or more, to investigate a lawyer's actions. Fairness hearings normally occur within a few months of the date on which a proposed settlement is submitted for preliminary approval. Class members must therefore decide whether to allege malpractice much more quickly than other plaintiffs.

2.   *Do Large Fee Awards Provide Evidence of Misconduct?* Wyly claimed that class counsel settled quickly in order to receive $30–$40 million in fees. In effect, he used the opportunity to collect a large fee as evidence that class counsel was bribed. Supposing this argument had been made at a fairness hearing, how should the presiding judge have responded? Given that class counsel works on a contingency basis and that settlement size strongly influences the size of fee awards, does an enormous fee indicate anything other than an enormous recovery? Is there reason to think that class counsel would have left millions of dollars on the table when deciding to settle, if doing so would also have cost class counsel millions in fees? What other evidence could Wyly have adduced to show that the settlement was inadequate or premature?

When the class action against Computer Associates settled, the Milberg Weiss lawsuit was embroiled in a federal investigation of its own. Over many years, lawyers in the firm paid kickbacks to certain investors who served as lead plaintiffs. Eventually, many of the lawyers involved in the scheme—including lead partners Melvyn Weiss and William Lerach—pled guilty to criminal charges and served time in prison. See Patrick Dillon, CIRCLE OF GREED: THE SPECTACULAR RISE AND FALL OF THE LAWYER WHO BROUGHT CORPORATE AMERICA TO ITS KNEES (2010). What role, if any, should Milberg Weiss' difficulties have played in assessing the fairness of the class settlement with Computer Associates? Did the participation of other law firms alleviate the need to worry that Milberg Weiss may have been more concerned about funding its defense and continuing its operations than obtaining the largest possible recovery for investors? Should the trial court have appointed an independent expert to evaluate the proposed settlement because Milberg Weiss' opinion may have been tainted?

3. *Did the Pot Call the Kettle Black?* Although the matter received no mention in the Second Circuit's opinion, in 2010 the SEC indicted Sam Wyly and his brother, Charles, for orchestrating a $550 million scheme of securities fraud and insider trading. After investigating the brothers for six years, the SEC accused them of using sham offshore trusts located in the Isle of Man and the Cayman Islands to hide "13 years of stock sales in four companies they founded or where they served as directors." The brothers allegedly hid the sales "to eliminate the risk that disclosure would send a bearish signal to the market and cause share prices to fall while they were selling." Although the Wylys and their lawyers contend the SEC's allegations are meritless, the suit survived a motion dismiss. Jonathan Stempel, *Wyly Brothers Lose Bid to Dismiss SEC Fraud Suit*, Reuters.com, Mar 31, 2011, available at http://www.reuters.com/article/2011/03/31/us-wyly-sec-idUSTRE72 U6E820110331.

Whatever one thinks of the merits of the SEC's case against the Wylys, like most people they seem to want to make money. Assuming this to be so, why did Sam Wyly attempt to reopen the lawsuit? If he had succeeded in having the judgment set aside, the gain from a subsequent, larger settlement (assuming one was negotiated) would have been divided among all investors in the class. Wouldn't Wyly's portion have been small?

In fact, Sam Wyly's stake was unusually large. After selling Sterling Software to Computer Associates in 2000, he retained a large financial interest in Computer Associates' performance. When Computer Associates revealed that it would miss its earnings estimates, Wyly and his family trusts supposedly lost $50 million in one day. Seeing no point in impoverishing the company (which would harm him and other investors by reducing its stock price), Wyly wanted the company's managers to bear the cost. So he sued them. Some of the insiders were extraordinarily rich. In 1999, Computer Associates paid Charles Wang $655 million and Sanjay Kumar $330 million. He also wanted the culpable insiders to bear the litigation costs. Wyly's efforts to reopen the class action litigation and his suit against class counsel appear to have been part of his effort to extract money from the insiders who participated in the fraud. See Elizabeth MacDonald, *Wyly's War*, Forbes.com, April 25, 2005, available at http://www.forbes.com/forbes/2005/0425/036.html.

Given the size of Wyly's loss and his interest in saddling the responsible insiders with the costs of the fraud, why did he remain in the investor class instead of opting out and proceeding on his own? Professor Coffee contends that large investors who hire separate counsel fare better than absent class members in litigation. John C. Coffee, Jr., *Accountability and Competition in Securities Class Actions: Why "Exit" Works Better than "Voice"*, 30 Cardozo L. Rev. 407 (2008).

4. *What Would Have Happened had the Federal District Court Granted Wyly's Motion to Set Aside the Judgment?* As you know, the federal district court judge denied Wyly's Rule 60(b) motion. Suppose the judge had granted it. What then? By the time the motion was decided, the money in the settlement fund had been distributed to investors and paid to class counsel as fees. Would the court have had to order the funds returned? If so, wouldn't the burden on the investors and class counsel have been intolerable? After all, the reason for setting aside the judgment was that Computer Associates (or its counsel) committed discovery fraud. Perhaps Computer Associates should suffer on account

of this misconduct, but why should investors or class counsel be required to give up their gains?

CHAPTER 5

Non–Class Vehicles for Settlement

This Chapter fills out the continuum of aggregate litigation initially presented in Chapter 1. Recall that class actions comprise only one of several vehicles for aggregation that lie between the poles of "private" contracts (in the manner of conventional individual settlements of civil lawsuits) and "public" legislation. This Chapter initially discusses aggregate settlements (between individual settlements and class settlements along the continuum) and bankruptcy proceedings under § 524(g) of the Bankruptcy Code for asbestos-related reorganizations (between class actions and legislation). The category of aggregate settlements itself encompasses much within it—not only the aggregate settlement rule in the law of professional responsibility but also related questions concerning judicial oversight of fees and bellwether trials as an informational basis for settlement design.

The Chapter concludes with an overview of an overtly "public" vehicle for the resolution of mass civil claims: litigation and settlement by the government itself, acting on behalf of the public generally.

A. Aggregate Settlements

Chapter 1 introduced the notion of an aggregate settlement and the principal ethical limitation applicable to such settlements, the Aggregate Settlement Rule (ASR), which is Rule 1.8(g) of the Model Rules of Professional Responsibility. The materials that follow explore in greater detail the content of the ASR and the ongoing debate concerning its application.

1. What Is an Aggregate Settlement?

Lawyer Proposing to Make or Accept an Aggregate Settlement or Aggregated Agreement, American Bar Association Formal Ethics Opinion 06–438 (2006)

This opinion considers the subject of aggregate settlements or aggregated agreements addressed in Rule 1.8(g).[3] . . .

---

[3] Rule 1.8(g) states:

A lawyer who represents two or more clients shall not participate in making an aggregate settlement of the claims of or against the clients, or in a criminal case an aggregated agreement as to guilty or nolo contendere pleas, unless each client gives informed consent, in a writing signed by the client. The lawyer's disclosure shall include the existence and nature of all the claims or pleas involved and of the participation of each person in the settlement. . . .

This opinion does not treat as aggregate settlements those settlements made in certified class action cases or derivative actions. . . . Neither does this opinion address multi-party representation in bankruptcy cases.

Because the terms "aggregate settlement" and "aggregated agreement" are not defined in the Model Rules of Professional Conduct, it first is necessary to explain those terms before identifying the disclosures required to satisfy Rule 1.8(g). An aggregate settlement or aggregated agreement occurs when two or more clients who are represented by the same lawyer together resolve their claims or defenses. . . . It is not necessary that all of the lawyer's clients . . . having claims against the same parties, or having defenses against the same claims, participate in the matter's resolution for it to be an aggregate settlement or aggregated agreement. The rule applies when any two or more clients consent to have their matters resolved together.[4]

The claims or defenses to be settled in an aggregate settlement or aggregated agreement may arise in the common representation of multiple parties in the same matter, for example, when damages are claimed by passengers on a bus that rolls over, or by purchasers of a fraudulently issued stock. . . . They also may arise in separate cases. For example, the rule would apply to claims for breach of warranties against a home builder brought by several home purchasers represented by the same lawyer, even though each claim is filed as a separate lawsuit and arises with respect to a different home, a different breach, and even a different subdivision.

Aggregate settlements or aggregated agreements not only arise in a variety of situations, but they also may take a variety of forms. For example, a settlement offer may consist of a sum of money offered to or demanded by multiple clients with or without specifying the amount to be paid to or by each client. Aggregate settlements or aggregated agreements can occur . . . in the civil context, for example, when a claimant makes an offer to settle a claim for damages with two or more defendants. . . .

Rule 1.8(g) deters lawyers from favoring one client over another in settlement negotiations by requiring that lawyers reveal to all clients information relevant to the proposed settlement. That information empowers each client to withhold consent and thus prevent the lawyer from subordinating the interests of the client to those of another client or to those of the lawyer.[8] Rule 1.8(g) thereby supplements the lawyer's duties under Rule 1.2(a) to defer to his clients' roles as ultimate decision-makers concerning the objectives of the representation, and to abide by his clients' decisions whether to settle a matter.[9] In acknowledgment of the heightened conflicts risks encountered when multiple clients are represented in an aggregate settlement or aggregated agreement, Rule 1.8(g) also requires that the clients' consent to the settlement or agreement be in writing, a requirement

---

[4] Rule 1.8(g) does not address obligations to other clients having such similar claims or defenses who are not included in the aggregate settlement or aggregated agreement. See Rule 1.7(a)(2).

[8] One risk posed by aggregate settlements is that the lawyer may be motivated to settle a group of many claims and reap a substantial fee without the trouble of diligent development of the clients' claims. That is likely to be a greater risk in an aggregate settlement than in the settlement of an individual claim, as the sheer number of clients may make the potential fee much greater. . . .

[9] Several courts have concluded that fee agreements that allowed for a settlement based upon a "majority vote" of the clients represented violated Rule 1.8(g). See, e.g.,*The Tax Authority, Inc. v. Jackson Hewitt, Inc.*, 873 A.2d 616, 627 (N.J. Super. Ct. App. Div. 2005), cert. granted, 878 A.2d 855 (N.J. 2005) (applying New Jersey's Rule 1.8(g) which, at the time, was practically identical to the pre–2002 ABA Model Rule); *Hayes v. Eagle–Picher Industries, Inc.*, 513 F.2d 892, 894–95 (10th Cir. 1975) (applying Kansas's version of Model Code DR 5–106). Cf.,*Abbott v. Kidder Peabody & Co.*, 42 F. Supp. 2d 1046, 1050–51 (D. Colo. 1999) (applying Colorado's Rule 1.7(b) (2) and (c)).

more strict than that imposed in the general rule on conflicts, Rule 1.7. The lawyer's duty to make disclosures under Rule 1.8(g) reinforces the lawyer's duty under Rule 1.4 to provide information reasonably necessary to permit the client to decide to engage in the proposed settlement or agreement.

In order to ensure a valid and informed consent to an aggregate settlement or aggregated agreement, Rule 1.8(g) requires a lawyer to disclose, at a minimum, the following information to the clients for whom or to whom the settlement or agreement proposal is made:

- The total amount of the aggregate settlement or the result of the aggregated agreement.

- The existence and nature of all of the claims [or] defenses . . . involved in the aggregate settlement or aggregated agreement.

- The details of every other client's participation in the aggregate settlement or aggregated agreement, whether it be their settlement contributions, their settlement receipts, . . . or any other contribution or receipt of something of value as a result of the aggregate resolution. For example, if one client is favored over the other(s) by receiving non-monetary remuneration, that fact must be disclosed to the other client(s).

- The total fees and costs to be paid to the lawyer as a result of the aggregate settlement, if the lawyer's fees and/or costs will be paid, in whole or in part, from the proceeds of the settlement or by an opposing party or parties.[13]

- The method by which costs (including costs already paid by the lawyer as well as costs to be paid out of the settlement proceeds) are to be apportioned among them.

These detailed disclosures must be made in the context of a specific offer or demand. Accordingly, the informed consent required by the rule generally cannot be obtained in advance of the formulation of such an offer or demand.

If the information to be disclosed in complying with Rule 1.8(g) is protected by Rule 1.6, the lawyer first must obtain informed consent from all his clients to share confidential information among them. The best practice would be to obtain this consent at the outset of representation if possible, or at least to alert the clients that disclosure of confidential information might be necessary in order to effectuate an aggregate settlement or aggregated agreement. If the lawyer seeks permission to share confidential information among his clients, and receives that permission, he should explain to his clients that if a dispute arises between any of the clients subsequent to his sharing their confidential information, the attorney-client privilege may not be available for assertion by any of them against the other(s) on issues of commonly given advice. Finally, in representations where the possibility of an aggregate settlement or aggregated agreement exists, clients should be advised of the risk that if the offer or demand requires the consent of all commonly-represented litigants, the failure of one or a few members of the group to consent to the settlement may result in the withdrawal of the offer or demand. . . .

---

[13] . . . When the amounts of fees and costs to be paid to the lawyer as a result of the aggregate settlement are not yet determined at the time of the settlement, the lawyer will need to disclose to each of his clients the process by which those amounts will be established and who will pay them, and the amount he will be requesting to be paid. . . .

NOTES AND QUESTIONS

1.   The Origins of the ASR. The ABA Formal Ethics Opinion states that the ASR applies to "common representation of multiple parties in the same matter" and to common representation of multiple parties "in separate cases." This is seemingly a fair reading of the rule text. At the 2008 American Law Institute annual meeting, however, Professor Charles Silver recounted a conversation with Professor John Sutton, the reporter for the committee that drafted the rule. According to Sutton, the paradigm situation contemplated by the rule drafters consisted of the representation of multiple parties in separate, unrelated cases. Specifically, the committee had focused on a practice whereby a well-known Texas plaintiffs' lawyer would represent multiple clients in separate tort cases that nonetheless happened to involve the same insurance carrier on the defense side. The lawyer would go to the insurer and offer to settle the various unrelated cases as a group, without disclosure of the grouping to the clients.

Does this history suggest that the strictures of the ASR might not fit especially well the situation of common representation of multiple parties "in the same matter"—the closest analogue to a situation potentially suitable for a class action?

2.   Why Favoritism? The ABA Formal Ethics Opinion notes that the ASR "deters lawyers from favoring one client over another in settlement negotiations." But why might a lawyer engage in such favoritism? Consider some possible explanations:

> Misallocation might . . . stem from the mixture of arrangements by which multiple claimants have come to be represented by a common lawyer. The lawyer may be obligated to pay a "forwarding fee" or "referral fee" with regard to the claimants referred to her by others but to pay no such fee as to claimants that she obtained herself. As a result, the lawyer would have an incentive, at the margin, to misallocate in favor of those claimants as to whom no fee must be paid.

> Another incentive for misallocation may arise from the lawyer's desire to enhance her credibility in the recruitment of future clients in the same area of litigation. One criticism leveled against multiple-claimant representations in asbestos litigation, for instance, is that they tend, when settled in aggregate, to overpay claimants without present-day physical impairments and to underpay claimants with severe asbestos-related disease. Such a misallocation nonetheless may enhance the credibility of the lawyer in the subsequent recruitment of additional unimpaired claimants, persons likely to be greater in absolute number than those with asbestos-related disease at a given time.

Paul H. Edelman, Richard A. Nagareda & Charles Silver, *The Allocation Problem in Multiple–Claimant Representations*, 14 S.Ct. Econ. Rev. 95, 99–100 (2006).

3.   What If Information Required by the ASR is Unavailable? The ASR requires a lawyer to tell every client who will participate in a settlement the amount that client and every other participating client will receive. This information is often unknown when a client's settlement decision must be made. For example, in the *Vioxx* MDL, the proposed global settlement contained an online calculator that claimants could use to determine the number of points the settlement administrator would assign their claims, but the dollar value of each point remained undetermined until all claims were processed. By that time, of course, the deadline for enrolling in the settlement would have long expired, so claimants had to decide whether to participate without knowing exactly how much they or anyone else would receive.

Given the impossibility of telling the clients everything the ASR required, what should a lawyer representing a group of *Vioxx* claimants have done? All of the options seem unpalatable. By advising clients to settle, a lawyer might have violated the ASR and risked being disciplined or sued. By refusing to communicate the offer on ethical grounds, however, a lawyer would have harmed clients who were better off participating in the global settlement than continuing to litigate. Those clients might have sued or filed grievances too.

4.   *Why Disclose the Total Fee?* The disclosures required by the ASR appear to be intended to enable clients to ensure that they were treated fairly relative to other members of the same litigation group. Yet, according to Formal Opinion 06–438, a lawyer must also disclose the total fee to be earned from an aggregate settlement. Does this information, which is not mentioned in the ASR, enable clients to assess the relative fairness of their proposed settlement payments? If not, does it serve any other useful purpose? Is there any possible downside to disclosing the total fee?

2.   THE WAGES OF SIN

The ASR applies in all jurisdictions of the United States, either by state adoption of the Model Rules verbatim or via a state ethical rule to the same effect. The status of the ASR as a rule of professional responsibility has one clear-cut implication: Violation of the rule carries the possibility of disciplinary action by the relevant bar against the attorney who undertook the aggregate settlement.

But might there be still other consequences? Consider the view of the Texas Supreme Court:

Burrow v. Arce

997 S.W.2d 229 (Tex. 1999)

■ JUSTICE HECHT delivered the opinion of the Court.

The principal question in this case is whether an attorney who breaches his fiduciary duty to his client may be required to forfeit all or part of his fee, irrespective of whether the breach caused the client actual damages. . . . [W]e answer in the affirmative and conclude that the amount of the fee to be forfeited is a question for the court, not a jury.

I

Explosions at a Phillips 66 chemical plant in 1989 killed twenty-three workers and injured hundreds of others, spawning a number of wrongful death and personal injury lawsuits. One suit on behalf of some 126 plaintiffs was filed by five attorneys [from the same] law firm, Umphrey, Burrow, Reaud, Williams & Bailey. The case settled for something close to $190 million, out of which the attorneys received a contingent fee of more than $60 million.

Forty-nine of these plaintiffs then filed this suit against their attorneys in the Phillips accident case alleging professional misconduct and demanding forfeiture of all fees the attorneys received. . . .

The parties paint strikingly different pictures of the events leading to this suit:

- The plaintiffs contend: In the Phillips accident suit, the defendant attorneys signed up plaintiffs *en masse* to contingent fee contracts, often contacting plaintiffs through a union steward. In many instances the contingent fee percentage in the contract was left blank and 33–1/3% was later inserted despite oral promises that a fee of only 25% would be charged. The attorneys settled all the claims in the aggregate and allocated dollar figures to the plaintiffs without regard to individual conditions and damages. No plaintiff was allowed to meet with an attorney for more than about twenty minutes, and any plaintiff who expressed reservations about the settlement was threatened by the attorney with being afforded no recovery at all.

- The defendant attorneys contend: No aggregate settlement or any other alleged wrongdoing occurred, but regardless of whether it did or not, all their clients in the Phillips accident suit received a fair settlement for their injuries, but some were disgruntled by rumors of settlements paid co-workers represented by different attorneys in other suits. After the litigation was concluded, a Kansas lawyer invited the attorneys' former clients to a meeting, where he offered to represent them in a suit against the attorneys for a fee per claim of $2,000 and one-third of any recovery. Enticed by the prospect of further recovery with minimal risk, plaintiffs agreed to join this suit, the purpose of which is merely to extort more money from their former attorneys.

These factual disputes were not resolved in the district court. Instead, the court granted summary judgment for the defendant attorneys on the grounds that the settlement of plaintiffs' claims in the Phillips accident suit was fair and reasonable, plaintiffs had therefore suffered no actual damages as a result of any misconduct by the attorneys, and absent actual damages plaintiffs were not entitled to a forfeiture of any of the attorneys' fees. In disposing of all plaintiffs' claims on these grounds, the court specifically noted that factual disputes over whether the attorneys had engaged in any misconduct remained unresolved. . . .

[In Part II of its opinion, the court concluded that a triable issue existed as to the damages, if any, suffered by the Clients as a result of the defendant attorneys' alleged violation of the ASR. The court accordingly reversed the trial judge's grant of summary judgment for the defendant attorneys on that ground.]

III

The Attorneys nevertheless argue that the Clients have not alleged grounds that would entitle them to forfeiture of any of the Attorneys' fees. Alternatively, the Attorneys contend that at most a portion of their fees is subject to forfeiture, and that that portion should be determined by the court rather than by a jury. The Clients counter that whether they sustained actual damages or not, the Attorneys, for breach of their fiduciary duty, should be required to forfeit all fees received, or alternatively, a portion of those fees as may be determined by a jury. These arguments thus raise four issues: (a) are actual damages a prerequisite to fee forfeiture? (b) is fee forfeiture automatic and entire for all misconduct? (c) if not, is the amount of fee forfeiture a question of fact for a jury or one of law for the court? and (d) would the Clients' allegations, if true, entitle them to forfeiture of any or all of the Attorneys' fees? We address each issue in turn.

A

To determine whether actual damages are a prerequisite to forfeiture of an attorney's fee, we look to the jurisprudential underpinnings of the equitable remedy of forfeiture. The parties agree that as a rule a person who renders service to another in a relationship of trust may be denied compensation for his service if he breaches that trust. Section 243 of the RESTATEMENT (SECOND) OF TRUSTS states the rule for trustees: "If the trustee commits a breach of trust, the court may in its discretion deny him all compensation or allow him a reduced compensation or allow him full compensation." Similarly, section 469 of the RESTATEMENT (SECOND) OF AGENCY provides:

> An agent is entitled to no compensation for conduct which is disobedient or which is a breach of his duty of loyalty; if such conduct constitutes a wilful and deliberate breach of his contract of service, he is not entitled to compensation even for properly performed services for which no compensation is apportioned.

. . . Though the historical origins of the remedy of forfeiture of an agent's compensation are obscure, the reasons for the remedy are apparent. The rule is founded both on principle and pragmatics. In principle, a person who agrees to perform compensable services in a relationship of trust and violates that relationship breaches the agreement, express or implied, on which the right to compensation is based. The person is not entitled to be paid when he has not provided the loyalty bargained for and promised. . . .

Pragmatically, the possibility of forfeiture of compensation discourages an agent from taking personal advantage of his position of trust in every situation no matter the circumstances, whether the principal may be injured or not. The remedy of forfeiture removes any incentive for an agent to stray from his duty of loyalty based on the possibility that the principal will be unharmed or may have difficulty proving the existence or amount of damages. . . .

To limit forfeiture of compensation to instances in which the principal sustains actual damages would conflict with both justifications for the rule. It is the agent's disloyalty, not any resulting harm, that violates the fiduciary relationship and thus impairs the basis for compensation. An agent's compensation is not only for specific results but also for loyalty. Removing the disincentive of forfeiture except when harm results would prompt an agent to attempt to calculate whether particular conduct, though disloyal to the principal, might nevertheless be harmless to the principal and profitable to the agent. The main purpose of forfeiture is not to compensate an injured principal, even though it may have that effect. Rather, the central purpose of the equitable remedy of forfeiture is to protect relationships of trust by discouraging agents' disloyalty. . . .

The Attorneys nevertheless argue that forfeiture of an attorney's fee without a showing of actual damages encourages breach-of-fiduciary claims by clients to extort a renegotiation of legal fees after representation has been concluded, allowing them to obtain a windfall. The Attorneys warn that such opportunistic claims could impair the finality desired in litigation settlements by leaving open the possibility that the parties, having resolved their differences, can then assert claims against their counsel to obtain more than they could by settlement of the initial litigation. The Attorneys urge that a bright-line rule making actual damages a prerequisite to fee forfeiture is necessary to prevent misuse of the remedy. We disagree. Fee forfeiture for attorney misconduct is not a windfall to the client. An attorney's compensation is for loyalty as well as services, and his failure to provide either impairs his right to compensation. While a client's motives may be opportunistic and his claims meritless, the better protection is not a prerequisite of actual damages but the trial court's discretion to refuse to afford claimants who are seeking to take unfair advantage of their former attorneys the equitable remedy of forfeiture. Nothing in the caselaw in Texas or elsewhere suggests that opportunistically motivated litigation to forfeit an agent's fee has ever been a serious problem. . . .

B

. . . [T]o require an agent to forfeit all compensation for every breach of fiduciary duty, or even every serious breach, would deprive the remedy of its equitable nature and would disserve its purpose of protecting relationships of trust. A helpful analogy, the parties agree, is a constructive trust. . . . Like a constructive trust, the remedy of forfeiture must fit the circumstances presented. It would be inequitable for an agent who had performed extensive services faithfully to be denied all compensation for some slight, inadvertent misconduct that left the principal unharmed, and the threat of so drastic a result would unnecessarily and perhaps detrimentally burden the agent's exercise of judgment in conducting the principal's affairs.

The proposed RESTATEMENT (THIRD) OF THE LAW GOVERNING LAWYERS rejects a rigid approach to attorney fee forfeiture. Section 49 states:

> A lawyer engaging in clear and serious violation of duty to a client may be required to forfeit some or all of the lawyer's compensation for the matter. In determining whether and to what extent forfeiture is appropriate, relevant considerations include the gravity and timing of the violation, its wilfulness, its effect on the value of the lawyer's work for the client, any other threatened or actual harm to the client, and the adequacy of other remedies.

The remedy is restricted to "clear and serious" violations of duty. Comment d to section 49 explains: "A violation is clear if a reasonable lawyer, knowing the relevant facts and law reasonably accessible to the lawyer, would have known that the conduct was wrongful." . . . Elaborating on the rule, the comments to section 49 make it clear that forfeiture of fees for clear and serious misconduct is not automatic and may be partial or complete, depending on the circumstances presented. . . .

[The] factors [listed in section 49] are to be considered in determining whether a violation is clear and serious, whether forfeiture of any fee should be required, and if so, what amount. The list is not exclusive. The several factors embrace broad considerations which must be weighed together and not mechanically applied. For example, the "wilfulness" factor requires consideration of the attorney's culpability generally; it does not simply limit forfeiture to situations in which the attorney's breach of duty was intentional. The adequacy-of-other-remedies factor does not preclude forfeiture when a client can be fully compensated by damages. Even though the main purpose of the remedy is not to compensate the client, if other remedies do not afford the client full compensation for his damages, forfeiture may be considered for that purpose.

To the factors listed in section 49 we add another that must be given great weight in applying the remedy of fee forfeiture: the public interest in maintaining the integrity of attorney-client relationships. . . .

Amici curiae, Professor Charles Silver and Professor Lynn Baker of the University of Texas School of Law, argue that section 49 of the proposed RESTATEMENT (THIRD) OF THE LAW GOVERNING LAWYERS differs from the rule applicable to other agency relationships and is bad policy. They contend that in general the remedy of forfeiture applies only when the agent is suing for payment of compensation, and for a good reason. A principal dissatisfied with an agent's conduct, they argue, should terminate the agency and withhold compensation; the principal should not be allowed to wait until after the agent has completed his service and then try to take unfair advantage by suing to recover compensation already paid. We disagree that section 49 states a different rule for attorneys. As we have already noted, section 469 of the RESTATEMENT (SECOND) OF AGENCY provides:

> An agent is entitled to no compensation for conduct which is disobedient or which is a breach of his duty of loyalty; if such conduct constitutes a wilful and deliberate breach of his contract of service, he is not entitled to compensation even for properly performed services for which no compensation is apportioned.

. . . Nor do we agree with amici that forfeiture should, as a matter of policy, be limited to the defense of an agent's claim for compensation. A client may well not know of his attorney's breach of fiduciary duty until after the relationship has terminated. An attorney who has clearly and seriously breached his fiduciary duty to his client should not be insulated from fee forfeiture by his client's ignorance of the matter. Nor should an attorney who has deliberately engaged in professional misconduct be allowed to put his client to the choice of terminating the relationship and risking that the outcome of the litigation may be adversely affected, or continuing the relationship despite the misconduct. The risk that a client will try to take unfair advantage of his former attorney does not justify restricting forfeiture to a defensive remedy when the trial court is easily able to prevent inequity in applying the remedy.

Accordingly, we conclude that whether an attorney must forfeit any or all of his fee for a breach of fiduciary duty to his client must be determined by applying the rule as stated in section 49 of the proposed RESTATEMENT (THIRD) OF THE LAW GOVERNING LAWYERS and the factors we have identified to the individual circumstances of each case.

C

. . . [W]hen forfeiture of an attorney's fee is claimed, a trial court must determine from the parties whether factual disputes exist that must be decided by a jury before the court can determine whether a clear and serious violation of duty has occurred, whether forfeiture is appropriate, and if so, whether all or only part of the attorney's fee should be forfeited. . . . Once any necessary factual disputes have been resolved, the court must determine, based on the factors we have set out, whether the attorney's conduct was a clear and serious breach of duty to his client and whether any of the attorney's compensation should be forfeited, and if so, what amount. Most importantly, in making these determinations the court must consider whether forfeiture is necessary to satisfy the public's interest in protecting the attorney-client relationship. The court's decision whether to forfeit any or all of an attorney's fee is subject to review on appeal as any other legal issue.

D

... Although the Clients make numerous allegations of misconduct against the Attorneys, the parties' arguments have tended to focus on the assertion that the Attorneys reached an aggregate settlement in violation of Rule 1.08(f) of the Texas Disciplinary Rules of Professional Conduct. The Attorneys and amici curiae argue that this rule is too vague and impractical for any violation to warrant forfeiture of an attorney's fee ... All these issues must be considered by the district court on remand.

NOTES AND QUESTIONS

1.   *The Further Story of* Burrow. According to one published report, the *Burrow* litigation settled on confidential terms prior to trial on remand. Brenda Sapino Jeffreys, *Lawyer Tries to Extend* Arce *to Defendants in Mass–Tort Litigation*, Tex. Law., Dec. 12, 2005, at 1. The same source goes on to mention additional *Burrow*-inspired litigation brought by the same lawyer who represented the clients there.

2.   *The Rise of Fee Forfeiture as a Remedy.* In portions of the *Burrow* opinion not reproduced in the text, Justice Hecht contended that Texas courts had long "held that [fee] forfeiture is appropriate without regard to whether the breach of fiduciary duty resulted in damages." *Burrow*, 997 S.W.2d at 239–40. Reviewing all the Texas cases cited in *Burrow*, Professor Silver reached the opposite conclusion. He argued that, before *Burrow*, "stunningly little authority" supported the view that Texas cases recognized the remedy of fee recoupment in the absence of harm. Charles Silver, *A Critique of* Burrow v. Arce, 26 Wm. & Mary Envtl. L. & Pol'y Rev. 323, 338 (2001). Professor Silver agreed that the RESTATEMENT (THIRD) OF THE LAW GOVERNING LAWYERS recognized the remedy, but he criticized that document on the ground that it got the prior law wrong and turned mass tort cases into minefields for lawyers. *Id.* at 342–44.

Today, the remedy of fee forfeiture in the absence of harm is well established, as shown by the next case, *Huber v. Taylor*, 469 F.3d 67 (3d Cir. 2006).

3.   *Effects on Lawyers' and Clients' Incentives.* Does the *Burrow* court underestimate the potential for fee forfeiture to be deployed to the detriment of the aggregate group rather than to its benefit? In light of the holding in *Burrow*, how would you approach the structuring of an aggregate group for purposes of settlement, were you a plaintiffs' lawyer? What do the facts of the underlying personal injury litigation in *Burrow* suggest on this score? Were the big winners in *Burrow* the clients—or someone else?

Does the ASR, coupled with the prospect of fee forfeiture, adversely affect the incentives of plaintiffs' lawyers to invest in the development of litigation involving substantial numbers of related claims? Recall here how the strictures on class certification might push plaintiffs' lawyers toward aggregate settlements as an alternative means to achieve closure for related claims, as the continuum from private contractual to public legislative devices in Chapter 1 implies.

Huber v. Taylor

469 F.3d 67 (3d Cir. 2006)

■ ROTH, CIRCUIT JUDGE

This case presents the ironic scenario of class action plaintiffs' attorneys who are being sued for breach of fiduciary duty and related counts by a putative class that the attorneys themselves formed for asbestos personal injury litigation. For the reasons stated below, we will vacate the District Court's grant of summary judgment to defendant attorneys and its denial of class certification, and remand this case for further proceedings consistent with this opinion.

I.   Background and Jurisdiction

Our case begins in Jefferson County, Mississippi, where an asbestos personal injury case, captioned *Cosey v. E.D. Bullard Co.,* No. 95–00069 (Miss. Cir. Ct. Jefferson Cty.), was commenced in 1995. Mississippi law does not provide for class actions, but it has liberal joinder rules and a reputation as a plaintiff-friendly jurisdiction. Accordingly, over the next four years, several thousand asbestos personal injury plaintiffs were joined in *Cosey,* along with more than two hundred defendants. In 1998, a trial was conducted in *Cosey* for the cases of twelve plaintiffs with malignant asbestos-related diseases. Those twelve *Cosey* plaintiffs were awarded approximately $48.5 million in damages. The sole attorneys of record for all the *Cosey* plaintiffs were Robert A. Pritchard and Christopher Fitzgerald.

At the time the *Cosey* verdict was delivered, there were more than 2,000 other asbestos cases pending in Jefferson County. The large award in *Cosey* prompted many companies with potential asbestos liability to explore settlements. In May 1999, before any settlements were reached, Pritchard brought a second asbestos personal injury mass action . . ., *Rankin v. A–Bex Corp.,* in which the Plaintiffs in this suit were joined.

The Plaintiffs, Roland L. Huber, William J. Airgood, Anthony Defabbo, John Dinio, Ernest Gishnock, John Bidlencsik, Hilma Mullins, and William Deem, are former steelworkers from Pennsylvania, Ohio, and Indiana. All eight Plaintiffs were exposed to asbestos at some point in their careers. None have developed malignant asbestos-related disease. All the Plaintiffs except Huber are or were smokers. Plaintiffs, along with 2,637 other asbestos-exposed individuals from Pennsylvania, Ohio, and Indiana (collectively the Northerners) retained counsel in their home states (Local Counsel) to prosecute their asbestos claims for a 40% retainer fee.

Local Counsel had previously entered into co-counsel agreements with Robert G. Taylor II, a Texas attorney involved in *Cosey.* Taylor had his own client base in Texas but was looking to expand his asbestos client "inventory." Taylor contracted with Local Counsel to serve as co-counsel for any future asbestos plaintiffs that Local Counsel would represent in exchange for Taylor receiving between 95% and 97.5% of Local Counsel's fees if suit were brought outside of Local Counsel's home state, and a smaller amount if suit were brought in the home state. The agreements between Taylor and Local Counsel provided that, if the asbestos suits were filed in a state other than Local Counsel's home state, Texas law would govern the contingent fee contract.

Taylor's fee arrangement is key for understanding Plaintiffs' case. First, it meant that employment as Local Counsel could only be profitable as volume, rote work because Local Counsel would keep only one to two percent of any client's recovery. Local Counsel had little incentive to focus on any particular case. Since many recoveries were in the range of a few thousand dollars, Local Counsel collected very little from any particular representation. Second, the fee arrangement meant that, all things being equal, co-counsel representations were less profitable to Taylor than representations of direct clients because of the fee-splitting involved. Third, the arrangement meant that the one to two percent Local Counsel cut, when aggregated among all Local Counsel, as it was from Taylor's perspective, represented a sizeable amount given the hundreds of millions of dollars of recoveries.

Taylor himself had entered into upstream co-counsel agreements with Fitzgerald and Pritchard, who in turn entered into an upstream co-counsel agreement with Joseph B. Cox, Jr., to negotiate settlements, for which Cox would receive four percent of all gross settlements. Plaintiffs allege that they were never informed of the various co-counsel arrangements.

Cox negotiated settlements with asbestos defendants W.R. Grace, Owens Corning, Fiberboard, and the Center for Claims Resolution (CCR), an organization created by 19 asbestos defendants to settle asbestos claims. Under the terms of all the settlements, the payout varied both by level of injury and by the home state of the claimants. In all the settlements negotiated by Cox, Northerners received payouts that were between 2.5 and 18 times lower than those received by plaintiffs from Mississippi and Texas (Southerners). Northerners, who joined in the Mississippi actions nonetheless received a larger settlement than similar asbestos plaintiffs from Pennsylvania, Ohio, and Indiana usually receive in their home state courts.[5]

Defendants, in settling these cases for Southerners, did not have to share their fees with Local Counsel, as they had to do with Northerners. Plaintiffs allege that the difference in the settlement payouts to Northerners is attributable to this incentive of Defendants to allocate a greater percentage of aggregate settlements to Southerners in order to minimize Local Counsel's percentages. This marginal percentage difference becomes significant in light of the scale of the settlements. The record contains the approximate or maximum values of eleven of the nineteen settlement agreements negotiated by Defendants. We calculate these eleven settlement agreements to total some $400 million. Therefore, on just this portion of the total settlements, Defendants stood to gain up to $10 million (2.5% of $400 million) at the expense of Northerners (and Local Counsel), depending on how the settlements were allocated between Northerners and Southerners.

Defendants reply to this allegation by asserting that the settlements were not aggregate settlements that they then allocated as they saw fit. Instead, Defendants claim that the plaintiffs in the settled cases were presented with offers that varied for different individuals based on factors such as the type of injury or asbestos exposure, lifestyle habits like smoking, and geographic origin. Defendants claim that geographic origin is an appropriate factor in determining settlement value because jury verdicts in northern states are traditionally lower than in southern states and because, in southern courts, jury verdicts for Northerners are typically lower

---

[5] We note, however, that there was an incentive for Defendants not to bring suit in Pennsylvania, Ohio, and Indiana. If suit was brought in the home state of a Local Counsel, Defendants received a smaller percentage of Local Counsels' fees, 90% for Pennsylvania and 80% for Ohio and Indiana, as opposed to 97.5% for Pennsylvania and 95% for Ohio and Indiana if suit were brought outside of Local Counsels' home state.

than for Southerners in their home state. For the purposes of this appeal, we need not resolve whether these settlements were aggregated, but we note that there is language in some of the settlement agreements that strongly supports the contention that they were aggregate settlements. Moreover, the very documents Defendants cite in their brief refer to the settlements as aggregate.

After each of the settlement agreements was negotiated, the Northerners received various disclosures. These disclosures were made by Local Counsel and by Parapro Enterprises, Inc., a paralegal service associated with Taylor. The Northerners were presented with a release, a check, and a disbursement sheet. The release was explained orally to Northerners by Parapro paralegals. The disclosures did not reveal the settlements' material terms or the nature of Defendants' involvement in the cases. The written disclosures stated that further information about the settlements was available on request. The record does not state whether any of the Plaintiffs sought to avail themselves of this information. Plaintiffs have introduced evidence that neither the Parapro paralegals nor Local Counsel were themselves aware of the full terms of the settlements or even had access to the complete settlement agreements.

The Plaintiffs brought suit in the Western District of Pennsylvania on behalf of a putative class of Northerners. Plaintiffs have not sued their Local Counsel or Parapro. Plaintiffs alleged several counts, including breach of fiduciary duty, aiding and abetting breach of fiduciary duty, and conspiracy to breach fiduciary duty. Specifically, Plaintiffs have alleged that Defendants breached their fiduciary duties of undivided loyalty and candor. Plaintiffs allege that Defendants owed them a fiduciary duty as their counsel; that Defendants engaged in an undisclosed, multiple representation; that Defendants had a conflict of interest regarding their multiple representation because of the fee arrangements that gave Defendants a larger percentage of Southerners' recoveries than of Northerners' and that this created an incentive for Defendants to negotiate settlements that paid more for Southerners' claims than for Northerners'; and that Defendants never gave proper disclosure of this conflict of interest or of the full terms of the settlement offers.

The District Court denied Plaintiffs' class certification motion . . .

The parties cross-moved for summary judgment. The District Court denied Plaintiffs' motion and granted Defendants' motion because it found that Plaintiffs had failed to present evidence of actual harm or evidence that Defendants' nondisclosures were the proximate cause of their harm, both required elements in all of Plaintiffs' claims. The District Court defined the actual harm requirement as a showing of any evidence that " 'but for' defendant attorneys' conduct, [Plaintiffs] could or would have received more favorable offers." The District Court noted that there was record evidence from representatives of the asbestos defendants that "even though Pennsylvania, Ohio, and Indiana plaintiffs undoubtedly received less money than the Mississippi plaintiffs, they still received higher settlement offers than those normally paid to asbestos claimants from those states because of the leverage these northern claimants gained from being joined with the Mississippi claimants in a Mississippi court." The District Court also noted that Plaintiffs' claims that they would have received higher settlements were only speculation, as "Plaintiffs have adduced no evidence that they would have obtained more favorable offers from any of the other asbestos defendants with whom they settled their claims." Finally, the District Court found that plaintiffs have failed to present evidence from which a reasonable person could conclude that defendants['] alleged non-disclosures proximately caused any plaintiff to accept settlements they would not have otherwise accepted. Rather, the evidence shows that plaintiffs either were given or had direct access to such information but chose to remain unaware, and at best did not recall basic facts surrounding when, where and if they read the documentation presented to them explaining the settlement.

Plaintiffs have appealed both the denial of class certification and summary judgment in respect to three claims: breach of fiduciary duty, aiding and abetting a breach of fiduciary duty, and civil conspiracy to breach of fiduciary duty. . .

II. Discussion

A. Choice of Law

The lynchpin of the District Court's decisions on class certification and summary judgment was its determination that all of Plaintiffs' causes of action required a showing of causation and actual injury. The District Court noted that the putative class had individualized injuries, which impeded class certification, while the individual Plaintiffs had not shown any personal injury, thereby defeating their action. We agree with the District Court that, if Plaintiffs must show causation and actual injury, they lose on both parts of their appeal. We disagree with the District Court, however, as to whether the relevant law requires a showing of causation and actual injury. . . .

Plaintiffs are currently seeking "disgorgement of Defendants' legal fees collected with respect to the *Cosey* and *Raken* actions, as well as compensatory and punitive damages."[15]

[W]e conclude that Texas law would apply[, and that] . . . no showing of actual harm is required to maintain an action for disgorgement for breach of fiduciary duty. . . .

B. Defendants Owed Plaintiffs A Fiduciary Duty.

Defendants have argued that the choice of law issue is superfluous because they do not owe the Plaintiffs a fiduciary duty. We find such a suggestion preposterous. Defendants acted as counsel for all the Northerners, including the Plaintiffs: they held themselves out as the Northerners' attorneys, they entered into agreements regarding representation of the Northerners, they signed and filed pleadings on the Northerners' behalf, negotiated settlements for the Northerners' claims, and collected attorneys' fees from the Northerners. Clearly, the Defendants were acting as the Plaintiffs' attorneys.

It is well-settled law, regardless of jurisdiction, that attorneys owe their clients a fiduciary duty. *Akron Bar Ass'n v. Williams*, 104 Ohio St.3d 317, 320, 819 N.E.2d 677 (Ohio 2004) ("The attorney stands in a fiduciary relationship with the client and should exercise professional judgment solely for the benefit of the client and free of compromising influences and loyalties."); *In re Tsoutsouris*, 748 N.E.2d 856, 859 (Ind. 2001); *Office of Disciplinary Counsel v. Monsour*, 549 Pa. 482, 486, 701 A.2d 556 (Pa. 1997)

---

[15] In this case, disgorgement would likely result in a larger recovery for Plaintiffs than compensatory damages. Disgorgement could entail up to 39% of their total recovery (Taylor's 97.5% of the 40% contingent fee to Local Counsel), whereas compensatory damages could be *de minimis*.

("This public trust that an attorney owes his client is in the nature of a fiduciary relationship involving the highest standards of professional conduct."); *Arce v. Burrow,* 958 S.W.2d 239, 246 (Tex. Ct. App. 1997), *rev'd on other grounds,* 997 S.W.2d 229 (Tex. 1999). The duty includes undivided loyalty, candor, and provision of material information. *Willis v. Maverick,* 760 S.W.2d 642, 645 (Tex. 1988) (provision of information material to the representation).

Defendants argue that "the fiduciary duties of disclosure at issue in this case were properly assumed and performed by each plaintiff's individually retained local counsel in Pennsylvania, Ohio, or Indiana." The performance of the duty is a question of fact for the jury, although some acts, as a matter of law, cannot constitute performance. If Local Counsel did not perform their fiduciary duty, it does not matter that they assumed the duty because the fiduciary duty of co-counsel is a joint obligation.[18] Even if the duty of disclosure is itself delegable, the duty of loyalty is inherently not, and in this case disclosure was necessary to fulfill the duty of loyalty. Thus, Local Counsel's alleged failure to fulfill the fiduciary duty of disclosure could hardly excuse the Defendants.

The fiduciary duty that an attorney owes clients is not a matter to be taken lightly. The duty may not be dispensed with or modified simply for the conveniences and economies of class actions. As then Judge Cardozo observed in *In the Matter of Rouss,* "[m]embership in the bar is a privilege burdened with conditions." 221 N.Y. 81, 84, 116 N.E. 782 (1917) (Cardozo, J.). Among those conditions are the ethical obligations of giving clients full and meaningful disclosure of conflicts of interest so that the client may decide if the representation is in his or her best interest and of the terms of proposed settlement agreements, as it is the client's, not the attorney's, decision whether to settle a case. TEX. DISCIPLINARY R. PROF'L CONDUCT1.03 (duty to keep client informed); 1.04(f) (fee division); 1.08(f) (disclosure of aggregate settlements). Even when clients are viewed as mere "inventory", they are still owed the renowned "punctilio of an honor the most sensitive." *Meinhard v. Salmon,* 249 N.Y. 458, 464, 164 N.E. 545 (1928) (Cardozo, J.). As the Texas Disciplinary Rules of Professional Conduct state the "obligation of lawyers is to maintain the highest standards of ethical conduct." Preamble.

This is the cost of doing business as an attorney at law, and we will not countenance shortcuts. Disclosures to clients must be meaningful, by which we mean something beyond form disclosures, as clients must understand a conflict to give their informed consent to an intelligible waiver. Indeed, we are embarrassed to have to explain a matter so elementary to the legal profession that it speaks for itself: all attorneys in a co-counsel relationship individually owe each and every client the duty of loyalty. For it to be otherwise is inconceivable. There is no question that defendant attorneys owed Plaintiffs fiduciary duties. . . .

C. Class Certification

The District Court's choice of law error does not affect the legal standard used to determine class certification. Class certification is a matter of federal statutory law, even when a federal court sits in diversity. Neverthe-

---

[18] We note that neither Texas' Disciplinary Rules of Professional Conduct nor the Model Rules of Professional Conduct directly address the question of allocation of professional duties in a co-counsel relationship, but in the case of duty of loyalty, its non-delegability is so patent as to be axiomatic.

less, a proper focus on fiduciary duty in this case changes our view of typicality, adequacy, predominance, superiority, and inconsistent standards of care as these elements present themselves in our consideration of class certification. Although class certification is a matter of federal statutory law (even when a federal court sits in diversity), a proper focus on fiduciary duty in this case may affect the District Court's view of typicality, adequacy, predominance, superiority, and inconsistent standards of care as these elements present themselves in its consideration of class certification. Thus, we will vacate the District Court's denial of class certification and we will direct the District Court to reconsider whether to certify the class in light of the application of Texas law.

III. Conclusion

The District Court erred in its choice of law analysis, which led it to require that Plaintiffs demonstrate actual harm in a claim of breach of fiduciary duty when the remedy sought is disgorgement. We will vacate the District Court's grant of summary judgment to the Defendants and we will vacate the denial of class certification and we will remand the case for adjudication in light of applicable Texas law.

NOTES AND QUESTIONS

1. *Why is the Third Circuit Upset?* The Third Circuit's opinion contains a strong moralistic tone. Lawyers are fiduciaries; the fiduciary duty must be taken seriously; lawyers may not delegate the duty or ignore it for the sake of convenience; etc. Is the court's tone warranted given the evidence, which it seems to accept, that the Northerners received larger settlement payments than other asbestos victims who reside in their states? Considering only the Northerners' recoveries, didn't the lawyers who negotiated the settlements do a terrific job for the claimants from the Northern states? Should the Northerners have thanked the lawyers instead of suing them?

One could quarrel with the focus on money by pointing out that clients often care about other things. They may want to participate in the litigation process, to learn why they were injured, or to obtain apologies from their injurers. See, e.g., Tamara Relis, *"It's Not About the Money!" A Theory on Misconceptions of Plaintiffs' Litigation Aims*, 68 U. Pitt. L. Rev 701, 721 (2007); Deborah R. Hensler, *Resolving Mass Toxic Torts: Myths and Realities*, 1989 U. Ill. L. Rev. 89, 99; Gerald B. Hickson et al., *Factors that Prompted Families to File Medical Malpractice Claims Following Perinatal Injuries*, 267 JAMA 1359, 1361 (1992); E. Allan Lind et al., *In the Eye of the Beholder: Tort Litigants' Evaluations of their Experiences in the Civil Justice System*, 24 Law & Soc'y Rev. 953, 965–67 (1990); Sally Engle Merry & Susan S. Silbey, *What Do Plaintiffs Want? Reexamining the Concept of Dispute*, 9 Just. Sys. J. 151, 153 (1984).

In *Huber v. Taylor*, did the Third Circuit express the concern that the Northerners' non-monetary interests were wrongly infringed? Is fee forfeiture an appropriate remedy when lawyers fail to serve clients' non-monetary interests as well as they should? Alternatively, can the Third Circuit's moralistic tone be justified on public interest grounds? Although the Northerners sued only for themselves, private tort lawsuits protect the public from harm by deterring harmful activities. Could the Third Circuit have been concerned that undisclosed interest conflicts weaken the public-protecting function of litigation, and punished the lawyers as a result?

2.   *Why not Sue the Lawyers, Regardless of the Quality of the Result?* The lawsuit against the attorneys was filed after the settlements with the asbestos defendants were reached. At this point, the Northerners no longer required the lawyers' services. The Northerners could benefit, however, by recouping the fees the attorneys received. If a malpractice lawyer offered to represent them on contingency, would they have had any reason not to file a malpractice/breach-of-fiduciary duty suit? From their perspective, isn't the lawsuit against their former attorneys all upside?

3.   *The Class Action Gambit.* Judge Roth mischaracterized matters when he pointed out the irony of "class action plaintiffs' attorneys" being sued "by a putative class that [they] themselves formed for asbestos personal injury litigation." The lawsuits against the asbestos defendants were mass actions, not class actions. In fact, had they been class actions, the follow-on breach of duty action might well have failed because the settlement involving the Northerners would have been reviewed and approved by a judge. (See the discussion of post-settlement suits by class members against class counsel for legal malpractice in Chapter 4.E.2.)

The breach of duty case was a class action, however. Given the difficulty or even the impossibility of suing an asbestos defendant on behalf of a class of injured claimants, why should the very same claimants be able to sue their common attorneys as a class for breach of fiduciary duty? Mustn't mass tort lawyers treat all their clients individually? For example, mustn't they give each client the advice best suited for that person, and might not that advice differ from the advice other clients receive?

In fact, mass tort litigation is possible only because plaintiffs' attorneys achieve economies of scale by creating large inventories of clients with related claims and treating all clients similarly. The innovations that enable lawyers to press mass tort claims successfully also make the lawyers easy targets for post-settlement class action misconduct suits.

4.   *How Strong was the Incentive to Misallocate Settlement Proceeds?* In *Taylor*, the Third Circuit seemed to attach some importance to the plaintiffs' allegation that the lawyers never told the Northerners about the incentives created by the varying co-counsel agreements. State bar rules governing fee-sharing arrangements do not require such disclosures. Under these rules, lawyers must tell Client 1 about the fee-sharing arrangement that will be used in Client 1's case. But there is no requirement to tell Client 1 about the arrangement used in Client 2's case. Nor has any other case held that a conflict of interest arises when fee-sharing arrangements differ in mass tort representations.

What if contingent fee percentages vary? Must that be disclosed too? For example, a lawyer may represent one client for a 40 percent contingent fee and another with a related case for 33 percent because the latter, but not the former, agreed to reimburse the lawyer for costs as incurred. Must this difference also be disclosed, if the cases are to be litigated or settled together?

The Third Circuit reported that the lawyers stood to "gain up to $10 million (2.5% of $400 million) at the expense of Northerners (and Local Counsel), depending on how the settlements were allocated between Northerners and Southerners." To gain the entire $10 million, wouldn't the lawyers have had to allocate the entire $400 million to the Southerners? Was it even remotely possible that they might have done that? Wouldn't the local lawyers who referred the Northerners' cases have protested? More generally, wouldn't the Northerners' local attorneys have challenged any allocation they thought was unfair? And didn't the lawyers who negotiated the settlement have an interest in keeping the local lawyers happy? Referral arrangements work because lawyers who depend on referrals have strong incentives to treat referring attorneys well.

By comparison with most referral percentages, those paid to the lawyers who signed up the Northerners as clients were small. An empirical study of New York cases found that referral fees of 25 percent or more were commonly employed. See Stephen J. Spurr, *Referral Practices among Lawyers: A Theoretical and Empirical Analysis*, 13 Law. & Soc. Inquiry 87 (1988). Presumably, the allocation conflict in *Huber* would have been even more serious had the referral percentages been larger.

3. THE PROHIBITION AGAINST EX ANTE AGREEMENTS FOR NON–UNANIMOUS CONSENT

Given the potential for bar disciplinary action and for loss of legal fees as a result of a violation of the ASR, might lawyers wish to work out in advance the decisional rules that shall govern their simultaneous representation of related claimants? For that matter, might the clients themselves regard such advance planning as desirable, at least in some situations? As reflected in the decision that follows, ex ante agreements to follow particular decisional rules short of unanimous consent are impermissible under current law:

The Tax Authority, Inc. v. Jackson Hewitt, Inc.

898 A.2d 512 (N.J. 2006)

■ JUSTICE WALLACE, JR. delivered the opinion of the Court.

The issue presented is whether our Rule of Professional Conduct (RPC) 1.8(g) prohibits an attorney who represents more than one client from entering into an aggregate settlement of the clients' claims without each client consenting to the settlement after its terms are known. In the present case, an attorney agreed to represent 154 individual franchisee-plaintiffs in their claims against franchisor-defendant Jackson Hewitt, Inc. Each plaintiff entered into an identical retainer agreement that provided for settlement of the matter if a weighted majority of plaintiffs approved the settlement. A Steering Committee of four plaintiffs was established to represent the interests of all 154 individual plaintiffs. After the Steering Committee negotiated a settlement in principle, a weighted majority of plaintiffs approved it, but eighteen others did not. Defendant sought to enforce the settlement against all plaintiffs, and the motion court granted that application. The Appellate Division held that the fee agreement violated *RPC* 1.8(g) because it required advance consent to abide by the majority's decision and reversed. We hold that RPC 1.8(g) forbids an attorney from obtaining advance consent from his clients to abide by the majority's decision about the merits of an aggregate settlement. However, for the reasons expressed in section IV of this opinion, we apply this decision prospectively. We reverse and remand.

I.

Defendant Jackson Hewitt is a nationwide tax preparation service with its principal place of business in Parsippany, New Jersey. It has franchises throughout the United States. Plaintiff The Tax Authority, Inc. is a franchisee of Jackson Hewitt with its principal place of business in Maple Shade, New Jersey.

As part of their business operation, franchisees make Refund Anticipation Loans (RAL) to individual taxpayers in anticipation of the taxpayers receiving refunds from the Internal Revenue Service. The loans are repaid when the refunds are received. Prior to the 2000 tax season, Jackson Hewitt distributed monetary rebates called "Performance Incentive Rebates" arising out of those loans to its eligible franchisees. Beginning in the 2000 tax season, Jackson Hewitt discontinued issuing those rebates.

The individual franchisees believed that Jackson Hewitt breached the franchise agreement by failing to issue rebates. Because the franchise agreement prohibited the franchisees from filing a class action lawsuit against Jackson Hewitt or its affiliates, the franchisees collectively retained attorney Eric H. Karp (Karp) of Witmer, Karp, Warner & Thuotte LLP in Boston to represent the group in a mass lawsuit. As part of that representation, each of the 154 plaintiffs entered into an identical attorney-client retainer agreement with Karp. Plaintiffs agreed that the matter would be pursued on a collective basis with fees being shared by each plaintiff on a per-RAL basis. Each retainer agreement provided that

> [t]he Client agrees that the Matter may be resolved by settlement as to any portion or all of the Matter upon a vote of a weighted majority of the Client and all of the Co–Plaintiffs. Each Plaintiff shall have one vote for each funded RAL for the 2002 Tax Season. The Client will be eligible to vote only if current in all payments required under this agreement. . . . A quorum for such vote shall be sixty percent (60%) of the votes eligible to be cast.

In addition to the majority-rules provision, the agreement provided that a four person Steering Committee would make the decisions regarding "all strategic and similar procedural matters other than the decision to settle the matter." The members of the Steering Committee were Robert Phillips, Robert Schiesel, George Alberici, and Kenneth Leese. Leese is the owner and president of the sole plaintiff herein, The Tax Authority.

The retainer agreement also specified that settlement proceeds would be apportioned according to each plaintiff's proportionate share of the RAL reserve. Specifically, the agreement provided that "[t]he Client will share in the net proceeds in the same ratio as its contribution to the RAL reserve for the 2002 Tax Season bears to the total contribution to the RAL reserve of all Co–Plaintiffs for the 2002 Tax Season." Formulas to calculate net proceeds, client contributions, and other necessary figures were also included. Prior to signing the retainer agreement, each plaintiff had an opportunity to consult with outside counsel. . . .

In August 2002, Karp filed a single complaint against Jackson Hewitt, naming each of the 154 franchisees as individual plaintiffs. Thereafter, the parties agreed to mediate their dispute. During mediation, Jackson Hewitt and the three member Steering Committee represented by Karp negotiated a settlement in principle that was reduced to a two-page document titled "JAMS Settlement Agreement" (JAMS Settlement). . . .

Ultimately, a weighted majority of plaintiffs approved the JAMS Settlement.. . . .

Jackson Hewitt filed a motion to enforce the settlement agreement against all plaintiffs. . . .

III

. . . In 1984, New Jersey adopted the ABA's Model Rules of Professional Conduct(1983) (Model Rules) [including RPC1.8(g) popularly known as the aggregate settlement rule]. . . .

The precursor to that rule was DR5–106. It is necessary to review the evolution of DR 5–106 and the case law interpreting it to better understand the meaning of RPC 1.8(g). . . .

The seminal case interpreting *DR 5–106* is *Hayes v. Eagle–Picher Industries, Inc.*, 513 F.2d 892 (10th Cir. 1975). There, the eighteen plaintiffs retained a single lawyer to file an action against the defendant. On the eve of trial, the parties reached a settlement agreement, which thirteen of the eighteen plaintiffs approved. The following day, in open court, the trial court inquired whether any of the plaintiffs were opposed to the settlement. After receiving no objections, the court entered a judgment of settlement. Thereafter, two members of the plaintiff group claimed they did not hear the court's question and challenged the settlement. After initially vacating the judgment, the trial court reconsidered and reinstated the settlement.

The Tenth Circuit reversed, finding that an agreement that authorized settlement of a case "contrary to the wishes of the client and without his approving the terms of the settlement is opposed to the basic fundamentals of the attorney-client relationship." *Id.* at 894. The court was troubled by the majority-rules provision, stating that

> [i]t is difficult to see how this could be binding on non-consenting plaintiffs as of the time of the proposed settlement and in the light of the terms agreed on. In other words, it would seem that plaintiffs would have the right to agree or refuse to agree *once the terms of the settlement were made known to them.*

[*Id.* at 894 (emphasis added).]

. . . The court reasoned that "it was untenable for the lawyer to seek to represent both the clients who favored the settlement and those who opposed it." *Ibid.* As a result, the court concluded that "in a non-class action case such as the present one," an arrangement that allows a majority to control the rights of the minority "is violative of the basic tenets of the attorney-client relationship in that it delegates to the attorney powers which allow him to act not only contrary to the wishes of his client, but to act in a manner disloyal to his client and to his client's interests." *Id.* at 894–95.

More than ten years later, the Appellate Court of Illinois reached a similar result. In *Knisley v. City of Jacksonville*, 497 N.E.2d 883 ([Ill. App. Ct.]1986), also decided under *DR 5–106*, the court invalidated a settlement agreement that had been approved by a majority of the plaintiffs. . . .

The [Illinois appellate] court [in *Knisley*] then discussed the "sharp distinction" between class action lawsuits and simple joinder actions. *Id.* at 887. The court noted that unlike class action lawsuits, which require a court to determine the reasonableness of a settlement, "[i]n a joinder action there is no judicial review of the settlement and a party should not be bound unless he has specifically agreed to it." *Id.* at 887–88. The court found that "[f]undamental fairness is violated when a settlement is allowed to bind parties who object and no safeguards have been added to protect their interests." *Id.* at 888. . . .

We conclude that RPC1.8(g) forbids an attorney from obtaining consent in advance from multiple clients that each will abide by a majority decision in respect of an aggregate settlement. Before a client may be bound by a settlement, he or she must have knowledge of the terms of the settlement and agree to them.

IV..

. . . The general rule is that judicial decisions will be applied retroactively. *Velez v. City of Jersey City*, 850 A.2d 1238 ([N.J.] 2004). Even so, "[o]ur tradition is to confine a decision to prospective application when fairness and justice require." *Montells v. Haynes*, 627 A.2d 654 ([N.J.] 1993). . . .

Such is the case here. This is the first opportunity for this Court to interpret RPC 1.8(g). Plaintiffs' counsel represented plaintiffs that were from many different states and successfully sought to have all plaintiffs agree in advance to be bound by a weighted majority. That effort was a plausible, although incorrect, interpretation of RPC1.8(g). In addition, defendant was led to believe that plaintiffs had agreed among themselves to be bound by a weighted majority vote and relied on that in reaching the settlement. . . .

On balance, we conclude that prospective application of our holding, and thus enforcement of the settlement against The Tax Authority, is the appropriate and equitable disposition of this matter.

V.

Lastly, we recognize that some commentators have proposed that RPC1.8(g) be changed to accommodate mass lawsuits. Professors Charles Silver and Lynn Baker suggest the rule should be amended to permit litigants to agree to abide by majority rule. [Charles Silver & Lynn A. Baker, *Mass Lawsuits and the Aggregate Settlement Rule*, 32 Wake Forest L. Rev. 733, 769–70 (1997).] They agree that "[b]ecause the stakes are so large and the issues so complex, settlement is both more urgent and more difficult in mass lawsuits than in other litigation, and the aggregate settlement rule is a complication that often gets in the way." *Id.* at 735–36. The complications they refer to include generating expense and delay, preventing defendants from obtaining finality, invading plaintiffs' privacy, and allowing a single claimant to hold out or block an entire settlement. *Id.* at 755–56.

In light of those and other concerns advanced in favor of permitting less than unanimous agreement in multi-plaintiff mass litigation, we refer this issue to the Commission on Ethics Reform for its review and recommendation to the Court.

NOTES AND QUESTIONS

1.The American Law Institute's Proposal. As the *Tax Authority* court notes, considerable controversy has emerged in the scholarly literature over whether the ASR should be revised to permit ex ante agreements to abide by non-unanimous consent. What dangers would such waivers pose, if permitted? For a proposal along these lines, see PRINCIPLES OF THE LAW OF AGGREGATE LITIGATION § 3.17(b) (Prelim. Draft No. 5, 2008) (permitting ex ante agreement to abide by "the collective decisionmaking of a substantial majority of the claimants represented by one lawyer or group of lawyers who are covered by the proposed settlement").

The Comments accompanying this section of the ALI draft explain:

This Section modifies the current approach by adding an alternative: a waiver of individual approval may be valid and binding provided that it is knowingly and voluntarily made, is in writing, is signed by the claimant after full disclosure, and vests decisionmaking power in the claimants either collectively or through some voting structure. Waivers of important rights are valid in a variety of areas, including the most cherished of constitutional rights. Thus, this Section rejects the view that individual decisionmaking over the settlement of a claim is so uniquely important that it cannot be subject to a contractual waiver in favor of group decisionmaking, provided there is a requirement of approval by a substantial majority of claimants.

Current law prohibits waiving individual-claimant settlement decisionmaking, thereby empowering individual claimants to exercise unfair control over a proposed settlement and to demand premiums in exchange for approval. Moreover, in many instances, multiple claimants derive substantial benefits from joint representation by one lawyer or law firm, particularly one with expertise and stature in the particular area of law in which the claimant's claims arise. To the extent that reasonable aggregate settlements—achieved after good-faith, arm's-length negotiations—cannot go forward because one claimant (or a small number of claimants) objects, the other claimants lose the benefit of the collective representation. Indeed, there are numerous reported cases invalidating collective settlements for non-compliance with the aggregate-settlement rule. This Section takes the view that giving veto power to individual claimants (as opposed to collectively) is not necessary to ensure the fairness of aggregate settlements. Further, even the threat of such a hold-out may cause the defendant to withhold the premium associated with complete peace, thereby inuring to the detriment of all the represented claimants.

For the waiver to be effective, counsel must in good faith inform the claimant of the specific information that should be set out in any implementing legislation or ethical rule. Such information should include:

(1) The claimant agrees that he or she has retained the lawyer because of the lawyer's expertise and reputation in the particular area of law that the representation involves;

(2) The claimant is receiving the benefit of the lawyer's ability to represent the claimant more effectively as a result of the lawyer's representation of other individuals with similar claims;

(3) In the course of representation (whether or not proceedings have been commenced), a defendant and counsel for the claimants might find it mutually beneficial for all parties to settle all the claims of the same type that the claimants' lawyer or group of lawyers is handling at the same time; and

(4) In the event of such a proposed settlement, the claimant agrees to be bound by the collective decisionmaking of a substantial majority of the claimants represented by one lawyer or

group of lawyers who are covered by the proposed settlement, under the following conditions:

> (A) The claimant is informed of the total amount of the settlement offer, the total amount to be charged as costs, and the total amount of fees that the lawyer or group of lawyers representing all of the affected claimants will receive;

> (B) The claimant is informed of the manner in which the settlement will be divided among all claimants jointly represented in the matter by one lawyer or group of lawyers, regardless of whether the division will be achieved through a negotiated allocation across categories of claims or will be left to subsequent distribution through an internal claims-resolution procedure;

> (C) The claimant is informed of the category into which such claimant has been placed, if that determination has been made prior to the time the proposed settlement has been presented to all claimants for consideration and possible approval;

> (D) The claimant is informed of the existence of any other related or unrelated claims held by other claimants represented by the same lawyer or group of lawyers against the same defendant that will not be covered by the terms of the proposed settlement;

> (E) If a proposed settlement distinguishes significantly among different categories of claimants, each category of similarly situated claimants must approve the proposed settlement by a vote of a substantial majority of claimants in that category; and

> (F) The claimant is informed that waivers are permissible only in cases exceeding a specified size and dollar amount as set out in the applicable legislation or rule.

In some instances, informed consent may require advising the client (or prospective client) to seek the advice of other counsel before executing a waiver.

This Section recognizes that, under prevailing ethics rules, a lawyer may not obtain a nonrevocable assignment of the client's individual authority to decide whether to settle a case and for what amount. Consequently, under this Section, the authority to settle without complying with the aggregate settlement rule is *not* given to counsel but, instead, remains with the collective claimants, who may act to accept a settlement pursuant to a waiver only upon agreement of a substantial majority of the claimants who are covered by the proposed settlement (or a substantial majority of the claimants in each significant settlement category). This Section does not define "substantial majority" but leaves that issue to legislative drafting. One possible model for legislatures or rule-making bodies is Section 524(g) of the Bankruptcy Code, which requires a supermajority of 75 percent of "the class or classes" of asbestos creditors (typically asbestos claim-ants) to approve a plan of reorganization in an asbestos bankruptcy.

Id. § 3.17 cmt. a, at 278–82. Does the ALI draft put forward a convincing case for change? Or would such an approach only further advantage large, well-capitalized plaintiffs' law firms in mass litigation?

2.   *Would Plaintiffs Game Majority Voting Rules?* Is the risk of strategic gamesmanship by individual clients overstated? Consider the following critique of the ALI proposal:

> Under the aggregate settlement rule, it is unethical for a common attorney to seek advance approval from clients of settlement terms agreed to either by the lawyer alone or by a portion of the group. As a result, defendants should be satisfied with a "walk-away provision [that] gives the defendant the right to abandon the settlement if more than a certain percentage of plaintiffs decline their offers." According to one plaintiffs' lawyer, an acceptance rate of 90% is often used. Defendants do not typically expect 100% of class members in an opt-out class action to agree to a proposed settlement; therefore, they should not be expected to require unanimity in the typical non-class mass lawsuit. If the facts are otherwise, there ought to be some way to demonstrate how often this occurs.

> Even when unanimity is required, an individual plaintiff's ability to act strategically may be limited. For example, a common attorney can reduce the possibility of holdouts by clarifying at the outset that the individual offers are "take it or leave it" and that no one will receive a premium in exchange for approving the settlement. Once it is clear that no premium is available, individual plaintiffs will reject the offer only when they believe that they can do better by continuing with the litigation. When this happens, the defendant can still come back with an offer to settle the remainder of the attorney's cases, leaving the holdout plaintiff isolated and forced to continue her case at her own expense.

Nancy J. Moore, *The American Law Institute's Proposal to Bypass the Aggregate Settlement Rule: Do Mass Tort Clients Need (or Want) Group Decision Making?*, 57 DePaul L. Rev. 395, 403–04 (2008). Does the prospect of "walk-away" provisions adequately guard against strategic gamesmanship by individual clients?

3.   *Walk–Away Provisions Versus Voting Rules.* A walk-away provision entitles a defendant to kill a deal unless plaintiffs' participation surpasses an identified threshold. These provisions can be simple or complicated. In asbestos settlements, defendants often vary participation requirements by disease categories. They may require 100 percent of claimants with mesothelioma to accept a settlement but only 90 percent of claimants with other illnesses. Aggregate participation requirements may exist too. For example, a defendant may insist that claimants accounting for 95 percent of the total dollars offered in settlement sign on.

Participation requirements protect defendants by preventing plaintiffs' attorneys from cherry-picking cases. But for these requirements, rational plaintiffs' lawyers might encourage clients with weak claims to settle while advising those with strong claims to keep suing. The result would be a settlement in which a defendant paid top-dollar to settle weak claims.

Litig.], 611 F.Supp.[1296,] 1304–05 [(E.D.N.Y. 1985)]; *In re Joint Eastern and Southern District Asbestos Litig.*, 129 B.R. 710, 784 (E.D.N.Y. 1991); Class Action Fairness Act of 2005, 28 U.S.C. § 1332(d)(11)(A) (permitting removal of "mass" actions to the federal courts). The large number of plaintiffs subject to the same settlement matrix approved by the court; the utilization of special masters appointed by the court to control discovery and to assist in reaching and administering a settlement; the court's order for a huge escrow fund; and other interventions by the court, reflect a degree of court control supporting its imposition of fiduciary standards to ensure fair treatment to all parties and counsel regarding fees and expenses.

No one except the trial judge, assisted by special masters, can exercise this ethical control of fees effectively. Many of the individual plaintiffs are both mentally and physically ill and are largely without power or knowledge to negotiate fair fees; plaintiffs' counsel have a built-in conflict of interest; and the defendant is buying peace and is generally disinterested in how the fund is divided so long as it does not jeopardize the settlement.

B.   General Ethical Supervision

1.   Law

The judiciary has well-established authority to exercise ethical supervision of the bar in both individual and mass actions. See, e.g., *Ex parte Burr*, 22 U.S. (9 Wheat.) 529, 530 (1824) ("[I]t is extremely desirable that the respectability of the bar should be maintained, and that its harmony with the bench should be preserved. For these objects, some controlling power, some discretion ought to reside in the Court"). See also Charles W. Wolfram, *Modern Legal Ethics* 22–27 (1986). This authority includes the power to review contingency fee contracts for fairness. See *Taylor v. Bemiss*, 110 U.S. 42,45–46 (1884) ("This . . . does not remove the suspicion which naturally attaches to such [contingency] contracts, and where it can be shown that they are obtained . . . by any undue influence of the attorney over the client, or by any fraud or imposition, or that the compensation is clearly excessive, so as to amount to extortion, the court will in a proper case protect the party aggrieved").

A federal court may exercise its supervisory power to ensure that fees are in conformance with codes of ethics and professional responsibility even when a party has not challenged the validity of the fee contract. *Rosquist v. Soo Line R.R.*, 692 F.2d 1107, 1111 (7th Cir. 1982). Supervision includes the power to determine that the fee contract was not obtained through undue influence or fraud and that the amount of the fee is not unfair or excessive under the circumstances of the case. See, e.g., *Rosquist*, 692 F.2d at 1111.

The explication of the reasons for reviewing contingency contracts in *Farmington Dowel* is persuasive. This was an antitrust suit filed under the Clayton Act. After plaintiff Farmington Dowel Company prevailed on its claims, the district court determined that $85,000 was a reasonable attorney's fee pursuant to section 4 of the Act. Upon examining the existing fee contract between Farmington Dowel and its attorneys, however, the district court refrained from awarding counsel any additional fee, in spite of the award required by section 4. It believed any increase in fee beyond that agreed upon in the contract would be unethical. *Farmington Dowel Prod. Co. v. Forster Mfg. Co.*, 297 F. Supp. 924, 925–930 (D. Me. 1969).

On appeal, the Court of Appeals concluded that the Clayton Act's fee award was statutorily mandated. Nonetheless, the court noted that the

American Bar Association Canons of Professional Ethics place ethical limitations on attorney's fees; it recognized the district judge's authority to determine the maximum fee that would be appropriate within those limits. *Farmington Dowel Prod. Co. v. Forster Mfg. Co.*, 421 F.2d 61, 87, 90 (1st Cir. 1969). Accordingly, the court remanded the issue, instructing the district court to award the statutorily mandated "reasonable fees," while using its discretion to restructure the terms of the original agreement so that the total fee would be in accordance with the Canons of Ethics. *Id.* at 90–91.

The *Farmington Dowel* court explained that a client's willingness to abide by his original fee contract "is relevant but not controlling, for the object of the court's concern is not only a particular party but the conformance of the legal profession to its own high standards of fairness." *Id.* at 90 n.62. Excessive fees would adversely reflect on the courts and the bar, providing judges with strong reason to ensure that any fee contract meets reasonable standards. See also, *e.g., Jacobs v. Mancuso*, 825 F.2d 559, 564 (1st Cir. 1987) (the final determination as to the reasonableness of the attorney's fees is firmly entrusted to the discretion of the court); Charles Kocoras, *Commentary: Contingent Fees—A Judge's Perch*, 47 DePaul L. Rev. 421, 422 (1998) ("It is sometimes a difficult enough job to bring about a just result in the substantive disputes between parties. The idea of getting enmeshed in determining how much a client should pay his lawyer is distasteful and unappetizing. Lawyers' fee issues, whether arising as part of a contingent fee contract or by virtue of statutory or other types of considerations, do not rank high on a judge's menu of things he or she cannot wait to address. But trial judges were not afforded the vote to oversee these matters—we have that responsibility and obligation by virtue of our office.").

Those courts that have considered the matter agree that their supervisory power does not imply a duty to examine every attorney's fee contract. The Court of Appeals for the Seventh Circuit, for example, advocates a case-by-case determination of the need for review. *See Rosquist*, 692 F.2d at 1111 (while "[a]n agreement between two freely consenting, competent adults will most often be controlling. . . . in the circumstances of this case, the district court was right to be wary not to become an unwitting accessory to an excessive fee"). In *Farmington Dowel*, the Court of Appeals for the First Circuit explained that a court's exercising of its supervisory power— an "ethical judgment" requiring the court "to arrive at a figure which it considers the outer limit of reasonableness"—must be "reserved for exceptional circumstances." *Farmington Dowel*, 421 F.2d at 90.

2.   Application of Law to Facts

While the plaintiffs' attorneys in the present case are highly skilled and have achieved an exceptional result for their clients, there is a danger that adherence to any previously negotiated contingency fee contracts might result in excessive fees. The total settlement amount held in escrow is large, and the over 8,000 individual plaintiffs involved in the settlement are represented by only a handful of firms, all of whom can be expected to gain substantial fees from their numerous clients' combined recoveries. Yet these firms all benefitted from the effectiveness of coordinated discovery carried out in conjunction with the plaintiffs' steering committee and from other economies of scale, suggesting a need for reconsideration of fee arrangements that may have been fair when the individual litigations were commenced.

The risk of excessive fees is a matter of special concern here because of the mass nature of the case. As the *Farmington Dowel* court recognized, excessive fees can create a sense of overcompensation and reflect poorly on the court and its bar. *Farmington Dowel*, 421 F.2d at 90 n.62. See also *Rosquist*, 692 F.2d at 1111 ("Courts have a stake in attorney's fees contracts; the fairness of the terms reflects directly on the court and its bar."). Public understanding of the fairness of the judicial process in handling mass torts—and particularly those involving pharmaceuticals with potential widespread health consequences—is a significant aspect of complex national litigations involving thousands of parties. These considerations are enhanced where, as here, the Judicial Panel on Multidistrict Litigation has assembled all related federal cases "for coordinated or consolidated pretrial proceedings . . . [to] *promote the just and efficient conduct of such actions.*" 28 U.S.C. § 1407 (emphasis added). Litigations like the present one are an important tool for the protection of consumers in our modern corporate society, and they must be conducted so that they will not be viewed as abusive by the public; they are in fact highly beneficial to the public when adequately controlled. Cf. generally Lester Brickman, *Lawyers' Ethics and Fiduciary Obligation in the Brave New World of Aggregative Litigation*, 26 Wm. & Mary Envtl. L. & Pol'y Rev. 243 (describing the financial incentives for lawyers bringing aggregate cases as risking both procedural and substantive fairness in some of these cases); Monograph [by Jack B. Weinstein], Individual Justice in Mass Tort Litigation 79–83 (1995) (describing ethical concerns regarding fees in mass actions).

V.   Parallel State Law

Since this is a series of diversity jurisdiction cases, it is particularly useful to examine state law on fees. . . .

The trend in the states is to limit contingent fees in substantial cases to 33 1/3% or less of net recovery where fees are large. [Lengthy citation to state authorities omitted.]

Because the court recognizes the exceptional and complicated nature of this important case, the skilled work of the able attorneys involved in it, and the exceptional result achieved, fees in the present case have not been capped at 33 1/3%—almost a national norm—but rather at 35%, with the power in the special masters to depart upwards to a maximum of 37.5% and downwards to a minimum of 30% on the basis of special circumstances in individual cases.

It should be emphasized that the applicable fee under many state laws is less than the maximum fixed by this order. Nevertheless, the imposed cap is considerably less than the 40% or more insisted upon plaintiffs' attorneys in their discussion with the special masters. This order is likely to save tens of millions of dollars for the clients.

VI.   Conclusion

Fees in all settling actions in this multidistrict litigation shall be determined as follows: (1) all legal fees for "Track A" claims ($5,000) shall be capped at no more than 20%, with a maximum of $500 for costs and expenses to come off the top before computation of fees; (2) all other legal fees shall be capped at 35% of the client's recovery, regardless of whether the underlying retainer agreement or state law permits for a higher fee; (3) the special masters shall have discretionary authority to conduct case-by-case evaluations and to order reductions or increases of maximum fees down to 30% or up to 37.5% on the basis of special circumstances in individual cases; (4) the special masters shall have authority to ensure that costs and disbursements charged to individual plaintiffs are restricted to those reasonably allocated to the individual case and that they come off the top of the recovery before fee computation; (5) the costs, disbursements and fees of the plaintiffs' steering committee shall be paid out of the general settlement fund rather than by individual plaintiffs and the amount of this payment shall be approved by the special settlement masters; (6) the special settlement masters are only to act as a group and not individually; and (7) clients and attorneys may appeal to the court from any decision of the special settlement masters. Should state law or the private fee arrangement between client and counsel provide for a lesser fee than that provided under this order, the least fee shall be the one enforced.

NOTES AND QUESTIONS

1. *Identifying "Quasi–Class Actions."* Is the notion of a "quasi-class action" conceptually coherent? How is a court supposed to know one when it sees it? Are all MDL consolidations "quasi-class actions" under the reasoning in *Zyprexa*?

Does judicial recognition of the "quasi-class action" category amount simply to recognition of the continuum sketched in Chapter 1, which ranges from conventional, one-on-one litigation to class actions—and, further on, to public legislation? Understood in light of that continuum, does the analysis in *Zyprexa* risk allocating the gray area between individual settlements and class settlements entirely to the regulatory framework for fees—third-party, judicial oversight—associated with the latter? If an accurate description of aggregate settlements along the lines of *Zyprexa* would place them midway between individual settlements and class settlements, then should the right judicial response with respect to fees actually be more of a *mixture* of contractual notions and third-party regulation? Why didn't the plaintiffs' lawyers with consolidated cases in *Zyprexa* work out fee allocation questions themselves?

Functionally, and considering only certain ideal types, class actions and multidistrict litigations may seem to be polar opposites. One ideal-typical class action, which aggregates claims too small to justify conventional lawsuits, remedies a litigation drought by making collective litigation feasible and profitable for an attorney to pursue. On the other hand, an ideal-typical MDL helps judges handle a flood of conventional cases, each of which is viable individually, by channeling them into a single federal district court for coordinated pretrial processing. Given this structural difference between the two procedures, does it make sense for judges to import class action procedures into MDLs? For a negative answer, see Charles Silver and Geoffrey P. Miller, *The Quasi–Class Action Method of Managing Multi–District Litigations: Problems and a Proposal*, 63 Vand. L. Rev. 107 (2010).

2. *An Emerging Category?* The assertion of judicial authority in *Zyprexa* to override the fee arrangements in individual lawyer-client retention agreements is by no means anomalous. Other district courts subsequently have relied on Judge Weinstein's *Zyprexa* opinion to support the exercise of similar authority in consolidated federal litigation over the prescription drug Vioxx and over Guidant implantable defibrillators, respectively. *In re Vioxx Prods. Liab. Litig.*, 574 F. Supp. 2d 606 (E.D. La. 2008); *In re Guidant Corp. Implantable Defibrillators Prods. Liab. Litig.*, 2008 WL 682174 (D. Minn. 2008). In the words of the *Vioxx* court:

[T]here are substantial similarities between the global settlement currently before the Court and the global settlement at issue in *Zyprexa*. First, the court in *Zyprexa* found that the case could be treated as a quasi-class action in part because of "[t]he large number of plaintiffs subject to the same settlement matrix approved by the court." *In re Zyprexa*, 424 F. Supp. 2d at 491. Similarly, there are approximately 50,000 eligible claimants currently enrolled in the Vioxx Settlement Program, all of whom are subject to the same settlement matrix for awarding points and valuating claims. Second, like the court in *Zyprexa*, which utilized special masters "to control discovery and to assist in reaching and administering a settlement," this Court has benefited from the efforts of special masters throughout the course of the MDL proceedings and the settlement administration. Moreover, the $4.85 billion settlement fund in the instant case is similar to the large settlement fund held in escrow in *Zyprexa*. In light of these factors, the Court finds that the Vioxx global settlement may properly be analyzed as occurring in a quasi-class action, giving the Court equitable authority to review contingent fee contracts for reasonableness.

Vioxx Prods. Liab. Litig., 574 F. Supp. 2d 606, 611–612. Do these decisions amount to a significant expansion of judicial authority under the MDL statute? A necessary elaboration of what is already there? An unwarranted expansion?

Do approaches along the foregoing lines risk overcompensating the lawyers on the plaintiffs' steering committee for the MDL-consolidated proceedings for work of common benefit to claimants? How might courts account for the preexisting incentives of all lawyers with cases in the consolidated group to do work of common benefit outside the context of MDL consolidation—not to benefit others but, rather, to benefit their own clients?

More fundamentally, should the lawyers on the plaintiffs' steering committee for the consolidated proceedings be the same ones who actually do legal work of common benefit? Or should they instead be in a position to choose who, as among their plaintiffs'-side colleagues, should be retained to do common benefit work? What if the transferee court were to prefer as lead counsel for all plaintiffs—at least as a presumptive first-cut—the lawyer with the largest percentage of consolidated claims, along the lines of the PSLRA model? Or would such an approach just encourage plaintiffs' lawyers, in the run-up to MDL consolidation, to recruit and to get on file in the federal system the most marginal or dubious sorts of claims, simply as a means to increase their body count? On that score, consider the difficulties presented by the voting process for confirmation of reorganization plans under Chapter 11 of the Bankruptcy Code—specifically, § 524(g) therein for asbestos-related reorganizations—a subject taken up later in this Chapter.

3. *Problems Associated with Control of Fees and Other Aspects of MDL Governance.* Ordinarily, lawyers work for the clients who retain them, and the duty to represent those clients zealously is reinforced by, among other things, the clients' control of fees. In most plaintiff representations, lawyers' incentives to represent clients well are strengthened by the use of contingent percentage fees, which link lawyers' payments to the amounts clients recover.

Ordinary incentive arrangements break down in MDLs, for several reasons. First, judges give control of MDLs to certain preferred attorneys whom they appoint to lead positions. As a practical matter, the lead lawyers control the litigation, to the exclusion of other lawyers who are relegated to inferior positions. The criteria governing lead counsel appointments are so abstract and vague that MDL judges can appoint whatever lawyers they want. Even lawyers with no cases in an MDL have held lead counsel positions. In *Zyprexa*, Judge Weinstein appointed Melvyn I. Weiss, a seasoned securities lawyer, to chair the Plaintiffs' Steering Committee, even though Weiss' law firm had no clients who were injured by the drug.

Second, when MDLs generate settlements, judges award lead attorneys common benefit fees, which they typically generate by reducing the fees non-lead attorneys can collect from their clients. In the *Vioxx* MDL, Judge Eldon Fallon transferred about $315 million in fees. The lead attorneys divided this fund among themselves on an impressionistic basis that included hours expended and other considerations that do not normally figure in contingent percentage fee arrangements.

Third, MDL judges tend to cap lawyers' fees below the amounts set in lawyers' contracts with their clients. A non-lead lawyer with a contractual right to a 40 percent contingent fee might wind up collecting 25 percent or less. Presumably, these fee reductions greatly reduce non-lead lawyers' incentives to work hard for their clients.

Given the extent to which judges control fees in MDLs, one might reasonably ask whether lawyers involved in MDLs work for their clients or someone else, the obvious alternative being the judges who control their fates and fortunes. The possibility that the lawyers work for the judges is strengthened by the tendency of some MDL judges to threaten or punish lawyers who question their authority. For example, in the *Vioxx* MDL, Judge Fallon entered *sua sponte* orders escrowing the fees of lawyers who challenged his prior order cutting their fees. At the same time, however, he allowed lawyers who accepted his fee cut order to receive their fees without delay.

It is also important to know how participation in an MDL changes lawyers' professional responsibilities. Do lead attorneys become fiduciaries for all claimants with cases in an MDL, including those who are not their signed clients but who depend on them for high-quality representation? Must lead attorneys continue to follow orders given by their signed clients post-appointment? Do lead attorneys become fiduciaries for other lawyers with cases in an MDL who are denied lead counsel positions?

Unfortunately, few matters relating to the governance structures used on the plaintiffs' side in MDLs have been litigated or discussed in published opinions, and the body of authority from appellate courts is thin. Even basic matters, such as whether district court judges may appoint attorneys with few or no clients to lead counsel positions in MDLs, remain unaddressed. Academic commentary on these subjects is also limited. For recent discussions, see Lynn A. Baker and Charles Silver, *Fiduciaries and Fees: Preliminary Thoughts*, 79 Fordham L. Rev. 1833 (2011); and Charles Silver, *The Responsibilities of Lead Lawyers and Judges in Multidistrict Litigations*, 79 Fordham L. Rev. (2011).

5. SAMPLING

Class action settlements and aggregate settlements to resolve substantial numbers of related claims characteristically do not arise out of the blue.

In order to reach an agreement on settlement terms—e.g., which sorts of claims warrant payment, how much, and what the criteria for eligibility should be—the settling lawyers need some base of information. In *Amchem*, that information came from lengthy experience by both class and defense counsel with asbestos litigation. Recall the importance of historical settlement averages for the various types of asbestos-related diseases and their use by the *Amchem* class settlement negotiators.

However, one need not wait for years, even decades, of litigation and settlement in order to develop a base of information about related claims. The Zyprexa litigation illustrates one alternative: relying on special masters to evaluate the various claims and inform the settlement negotiations. Another, and increasingly common alternative, takes a very familiar form: plain, old, ordinary individual trials. As introduced briefly in Chapter 1, courts, lawyers, and commentators encapsulate this idea with the term "bellwether" trials. The judge draws a sample of cases from the aggregation and then tries the sampled cases. Sometimes the resulting decisions of common issues can be given preclusive effect. More commonly, the method is used to facilitate settlement. When the sample is representative of the aggregation, attorneys can use the verdicts in the sampled cases to extrapolate settlement values for the rest of the aggregation. Moreover, valuations on both sides are likely to converge given the common base of sample verdicts, and convergent valuations facilitate settlement.

The bellwether trial method is one example of the use of statistical sampling techniques to resolve related cases in an aggregation. Statistical sampling, however, need not be limited to facilitating settlement or enabling issue preclusion, at least in theory. Instead, a judge might try the cases in the sample, extrapolate from the sample verdicts to outcomes for all other cases, and impose those outcomes as final judgments without regard to settlement. One way to extrapolate outcomes is to use an average of the sample verdicts. Another, more complex, way is to construct a regression equation and use it to generate case outcomes more finely tailored to case-specific factors. Either way, most plaintiffs in the aggregation receive an amount that averages to some extent over all the claims. Thus, depending on the degree of heterogeneity in the group of aggregated cases and the error rate of individual trials, plaintiffs with high-value cases can receive less than they would from an individual trial and plaintiffs with low-value cases can receive more. For most large aggregations, however, the defendant ends up paying a total amount that is very close to the total amount generated by the sum of individual trial verdicts (because errors on the high and low ends tend to cancel out with a large enough sample). See Robert G. Bone, *Statistical Adjudication: Rights, Justice, and Utility in a World of Process Scarcity*, 46 Vand. L. Rev. 561 (1993).

The following discussion first considers the bellwether trial procedure, and then briefly examines the more ambitious use of sampling to generate binding outcomes. As we shall see, courts frequently use bellwether trials for settlement purposes in MDL and other types of aggregations. However, they employ statistical sampling techniques to generate binding outcomes very rarely. Indeed, there is reason to doubt whether courts—and especially federal courts—have the power to use sampling in this more ambitious way, even if it might be desirable as a policy matter.

a.   BELLWETHER TRIALS

Bear in mind that there are at least two sorts of functions that bell-wether trials can serve. One function—what one might dub a relatively hard-edged version of bellwether trials—is for the judgment in such trials to have some preclusive effect vis-a-vis the much larger number of untried, individual cases. Another function—a softer-edged version—is for the bell-wether trials to exert no formal preclusive effect but for the results therein to influence in a more rough-hewn and informal way the design of settle-ment terms for the remaining untried cases. In this softer-edged version, one might say, one can get valuable information from bellwether trials in a manner that nonetheless stops short of full-fledged preclusion. Cf. Eldon E. Fallon, Jeremy T. Grabill & Robert Pitard Wynne, *Bellwether Trials in Multidistrict Litigation*, 82 Tul. L. Rev. 2323, 2331–32 (2008) (distinguish-ing between a "binding" approach and an "informational" approach to bell-wether trials).

Consider the following case, involving a consolidation of individual suits, which conveys the tradeoffs between hard-edged and soft-edged ver-sions of bellwether trials:

In re Chevron U.S.A., Inc.

109 F.3d 1016 (5th Cir. 1997)

■ ROBERT M. PARKER, CIRCUIT JUDGE:

Chevron U.S.A., Inc. ("Chevron") petitions this Court for a Writ of Mandamus seeking relief from an order of the district court . . . containing a trial plan for this litigation. We DENY the petition as it relates to the scheduled trial of the thirty selected plaintiffs referenced in the district court's order, but GRANT the petition as it relates to utilization of the re-sults of such trial for the purpose of issue or claim preclusion.

UNDERLYING FACTS AND PROCEDURAL HISTORY

This controversy arose out of the alleged injuries suffered by over 3,000 plaintiffs and intervenors ("Plaintiffs"), who claim damages for per-sonal injuries, wrongful death, and property contamination allegedly caused by Chevron's acts and omissions. The Plaintiffs and their allegedly contaminated property are located in the Kennedy Heights section of Hou-ston, Texas. The Plaintiffs contend that their subdivision was constructed on land used in the 1920s by Chevron for a crude oil storage waste pit. Ac-cording to the Plaintiffs, when Chevron ceased using the property as a tank farm, it failed to take appropriate measures to secure the site, thereby al-lowing other waste to be deposited on the land. Later, Chevron sold the property for residential development knowing that the land was contami-nated. Various developers filled these waste pits without remediating the land. Plaintiffs assert that the hazardous substances which were stored in the waste pits have migrated into the environment, including the drinking water supply for the Kennedy Heights section. As a result, Plaintiffs claim personal injuries and property damage.

The [district court adopted a] trial plan [that] provided for a unitary trial on the issues of "general liability or causation" on behalf of the re-maining plaintiffs, as well as the individual causation and damage issues of the selected plaintiffs, and ordered the selection of a bellwether group of thirty (30) claimants, fifteen (15) to be chosen by the plaintiffs and fifteen

(15) to be chosen by Chevron. Chevron contends that the goal of the "unitary trial" was to determine its liability, or lack thereof, in a single trial and to establish bellwether verdicts to which the remaining claims could be matched for settlement purposes. It is this selection process which Chevron argues will not result in a representative group of bellwether plaintiffs.

Chevron filed with the district court the affidavit of Ronald G. Frankiewicz, Ph.D. which evaluated the district court's trial plan for selecting the thirty plaintiffs, concluding that such a plan was "not representative." Instead, Frankiewicz detailed the "stratified selection process" which should be used by the district court in selecting the bellwether group which would result in a representative group of plaintiffs. The district court however struck Frankiewicz's affidavit as untimely filed and redundant in substance. . . . [T]he district court denied Chevron's request to certify an interlocutory appeal. This Petition for Writ of Mandamus ensued.

DISCUSSION

1.   Standard of Review

Our review of a trial court's plan for proceeding in a complex case is a deferential one that recognizes the fact that the trial judge is in a much better position than an appellate court to formulate an appropriate methodology for a trial. We have consistently noted that a writ of mandamus is an extraordinary remedy and is available in only limited circumstances.

Our traditional reluctance to meddle in the formulation of a district court's trial plan is tempered by the demands placed upon judicial resources and the extraordinary expense to litigants that typically accompanies mass tort litigation. We, therefore, as we proceed, do so mindful of the admonition contained in Rule 1—that what we do should serve the compelling interests of justice, speed, and cost-containment. . . .

2.   The Plan

The trial court has in our view quite properly categorized this litigation as complex. The mere fact that there are potentially some 3,000 claimants in and of itself complicates traditional dispute resolution. Additionally, when large numbers of claimants assert both property damage claims and claims for personal injury as well as claims for injunctive relief, it removes any question that may linger regarding the complexity of the task visited upon the lawyers and the trial court.

This case is a classic example of a non-elastic mass tort, that is, the universe of potential claimants are either known or are capable of ascertainment and the event or course of conduct alleged to constitute the tort involved occurred over a known time period and is traceable to an identified entity or entities. When compared to an elastic mass tort where the universe of potential plaintiffs is unknown and many times is seemingly unlimited and the number of potential tortfeasors is equally obtuse, the task of managing the non-elastic mass tort is infinitely less complex. In the non-elastic context, the necessity for the obtainment of maturity as reflected by a series of verdicts over time is not required in order to test the viability of plaintiffs' claims or the defendant's defenses.

The district court, after designating the case as complex, then articulated the goals of its trial plan as seeking to achieve the greatest efficiency and expedition in the resolution of *all* issues involved in the case. Pursuant to those goals, it structured the trial as follows:

1.   Composed of thirty (30) plaintiffs, fifteen (15) chosen by the plaintiffs and fifteen (15) chosen by the defendants. The thirty (30) plaintiffs chosen shall come from the lists submitted by the parties. . . . However, each side is permitted to substitute or replace not more than five (5) plaintiffs, within its discretion. . . .

4.   The trial shall focus on the individual claims of each of the selected plaintiffs and on the issue of the existence or nonexistence of liability on the part of Chevron for the pollutants that, allegedly, give rise to all of the plaintiffs' claims.

Thus, a unitary trial on the issues of general liability or causation as well as the individual causation and damage issues of the selected plaintiff shall occur. . . .

Initially, we note the obvious. The trial plan, while clearly designed to resolve the issue of liability on the part of Chevron to *all the plaintiffs* by referring to a unitary trial on the issues of general liability or causation, does not identify any common issues or explain how the verdicts in the thirty (30) selected cases are supposed to resolve liability for the remaining 2970 plaintiffs. It is impossible to discern from the district court's order what variables may exist that will impact on both the property and personal injury claims in this litigation. Similar litigation typically contains property issue variables that are related to time, proximity, and contamination levels of exposure to any pollutants that may be present, and personal injury claims that contain a mix of alleged exposure related maladies that also may be affected by time, proximity, and exposure levels. We, however, may not speculate on the homogeneity of the mix of claims, the uniformity of any exposure that may have existed and what diseases, if any, may be related to that exposure. Instead our review is restricted to the record and to an examination of the district court's order.

3.   A Bellwether Trial

The term bellwether is derived from the ancient practice of belling a wether (a male sheep) selected to lead his flock. The ultimate success of the wether selected to wear the bell was determined by whether the flock had confidence that the wether would not lead them astray, and so it is in the mass tort context.

The notion that the trial of some members of a large group of claimants may provide a basis for enhancing prospects of settlement or for resolving common issues or claims is a sound one that has achieved general acceptance by both bench and bar. References to bellwether trials have long been included in the MANUAL FOR COMPLEX LITIGATION. . . § 33.27–.28 (3d ed. 1995). The reasons for acceptance by bench and bar are apparent. If a representative group of claimants are tried to verdict, the results of such trials can be beneficial for litigants who desire to settle such claims by providing information on the value of the cases as reflected by the jury verdicts. Common issues or even general liability may also be resolved in a bellwether context in appropriate cases.

Whatever may be said about the trial contemplated by the district court's . . . order, one thing is clear. It is not a bellwether trial. It is simply a trial of fifteen (15) of the "best" and fifteen (15) of the "worst" cases contained in the universe of claims involved in this litigation. There is no pretense that the thirty (30) cases selected are representative of the 3,000 member group of plaintiffs.

A bellwether trial designed to achieve its value ascertainment function for settlement purposes or to answer troubling causation or liability issues common to the universe of claimants has as a core element representativeness—that is, the sample must be a randomly selected one of sufficient size so as to achieve statistical significance to the desired level of confidence in the result obtained. Such samples are selected by the application of the science of inferential statistics. The essence of the science of inferential statistics is that one may confidently draw inferences about the whole from a representative sample of the whole. The applicability of inferential statistics ha[s] long been recognized by the courts. See, e.g., *Castaneda v. Partida*, 430 U.S. 482 (1977) (using statistical data to prove discrimination in jury selection); *Capaci v. Katz & Besthoff, Inc.*, 711 F.2d 647, 653–57 (5th Cir. 1983) (using census data in gender discrimination case); *Exxon Corp. v. Texas Motor Exchange, Inc.*, 628 F.2d 500 (5th Cir. 1980) (using statistical sampling in trademark infringement suit); *Ageloff v. Delta Airlines, Inc.*, 860 F.2d 379 (11th Cir. 1988) (using evidence of life-expectancy tables to determine damages); *G.M. Brod & Co. v. U.S. Home Corp.*, 759 F.2d 1526, 1538–40 (11th Cir. 1985) (using expert testimony as to profit projections based on industry norms); *United States v. 449 Cases Containing Tomato Paste*, 212 F.2d 567 (2d Cir. 1954) (approving inspector's testing of samples, rather than requiring the opening of all cases).

The selected thirty (30) cases included in the district court's "unitary trial" are not cases calculated to represent the group of 3,000 claimants. Thus, the results that would be obtained from a trial of these thirty (30) cases lack the requisite level of representativeness so that the results could permit a court to draw sufficiently reliable inferences about the whole that could, in turn, form the basis for a judgment affecting cases other than the selected thirty. While this particular sample of thirty cases is lacking in representativeness, statistical sampling with an appropriate level of representativeness has been utilized and approved. As recognized by the Ninth Circuit, "[i]nferential statistics with random sampling produces an acceptable due process solution to the troublesome area of mass tort litigation." *In re Estate of Marcos Human Rights Litigation*, 910 F. Supp. 1460, 1467 (D. Haw. 1995), aff'd. sub. nom. *Hilao v. Estate of Marcos*, 103 F.3d 767 (9th Cir. 1996) (holding that the random sampling procedures used by the district court do not violate due process).

We, therefore, hold that before a trial court may utilize results from a bellwether trial for a purpose that extends beyond the individual cases tried, it must, prior to any extrapolation, find that the cases tried are representative of the larger group of cases or claims from which they are selected. Typically, such a finding must be based on competent, scientific, statistical evidence that identifies the variables involved and that provides a sample of sufficient size so as to permit a finding that there is a sufficient level of confidence that the results obtained reflect results that would be obtained from trials of the whole. It is such findings that provide the foundation for any inferences that may be drawn from the trial of sample cases. Without a sufficient level of confidence in the sample results, no inferences may be drawn from such results that would form the basis for applying such results to cases or claims that have not been actually tried.

We recognize that in appropriate cases common issues impacting upon general liability or causation may be tried standing alone. However, when such a common issue trial is presented through or along with selected individuals' cases, concerns arise that are founded upon considerations of due process. Specifically, our procedural due process concerns focus on the fact that the procedure embodied in the district court's trial plan is devoid of safeguards designed to ensure that the claims against Chevron of the non-represented plaintiffs as they relate to liability or causation are determined in a proceeding that is reasonably calculated to reflect the results that would be obtained if those claims were actually tried. Conversely, the procedure subjects Chevron to potential liability to 3,000 plaintiffs by a procedure that is completely lacking in the minimal level of reliability necessary for the imposition of such liability.

Our substantive due process concerns are based on the lack of fundamental fairness contained in a system that permits the extinguishment of claims or the imposition of liability in nearly 3,000 cases based upon results of a trial of a non-representative sample of plaintiffs. Such a procedure is inherently unfair when the substantive rights of both plaintiffs and the defendant are resolved in a manner that lacks the requisite level of confidence in the reliability of its result.

We recognize that our due process concerns seem to blur distinctions between procedural and substantive due process. However, our difficulty in compartmentalization does not detract from the validity of our concern that is ultimately based on fundamental fairness.

The elements of basic fairness contained in our historical understanding of both procedural and substantive due process therefore dictate that when a unitary trial is conducted where common issues, issues of general liability, or issues of causation are coupled with a sample of individual claims or cases, the sample must be one that is a randomly selected, statistically significant sample. See *Hilao*, 103 F.3d at 782–84, 786.

We express no opinion on whether the mix of claims that collectively make up the consolidated case lend themselves to the sampling techniques required to conduct a bellwether trial or whether this is an appropriate case for a stand-alone, common-issue trial.

We are sympathetic to the efforts of the district court to control its docket and to move this case along. We also are not without appreciation for the concerns a district court might have when it concludes that some of the issues raised may be motivated by delay tactics. However, our sympathies and our appreciation for the efforts of the district court in this case do not outweigh our due process concerns.

CONCLUSION

The petition, therefore, for mandamus as it relates to the trial of the thirty (30) selected cases is DENIED. Whether the district court wishes to proceed with that trial, to secure thirty (30) individual judgments, is a matter within the discretion of the trial court. Likewise, whether the trial judge wishes to attempt to structure a common-issues trial or conduct a bellwether trial based on a properly selected sample are matters also within the discretion of the district court. The results of any such trials and appropriateness of the requisite findings necessary to so proceed will then be matters for another panel to consider in the event those decisions are subject to appellate review.

The petition for mandamus is GRANTED insofar as it relates to utilization of the results obtained from the trial of the thirty (30) selected cases for any purpose affecting issues or claims of, or defenses to, the remaining untried cases.

■ EDITH H. JONES, CIRCUIT JUDGE, specially concurring:

I agree with Judge Parker's conclusions that mandamus must be granted in this case, that the district judge's method of selecting "bellwether" cases is fatally flawed, and that the most expeditious remedy is, without interfering with the setting of these cases, to deprive them of preclusive consequences. . . . [But] I also have serious doubts about the major premise of Judge Parker's opinion, *i.e.*, his confidence that a bellwether trial of representative cases is permissible to extrapolate findings relevant to and somehow preclusive upon a larger group of cases. . . .

[T]his is an "immature" mass tort action, in which the defendant's liability has not even been tested, much yet firmly established. The use of innovative judicial techniques particularly to resolve immature mass tort actions has been disfavored. For instance, this Court in *Castano v. American Tobacco Company*, 84 F.3d 734 (5th Cir. 1996), refused to certify an immature tort class action brought on behalf of tobacco users. Likewise, in *Matter of Rhone–Poulenc Rorer, Inc.*, the Seventh Circuit granted mandamus to vacate the class certification of hemophiliacs who had contracted the AIDS virus through contaminated blood transfusions. Both opinions note the potentially devastating impact of a class certification decision and its tendency to force defendants to settle even when they might have meritorious defenses. Conducting an imperfect bellwether trial in this case threatens a similar effect. An imperfectly designed bellwether group cannot yield a statistically reliable set of verdicts. Nevertheless, once in place, the verdicts would create enormous momentum for settlement. There would then be nothing to review on appeal and no realistic opportunity for Chevron to appeal.

The lack of correlation here between the bellwether plaintiffs selected and the need for a representative verdict suggests why the court's order represents a usurpation of power. Even if a bellwether trial is an appropriate vehicle for the resolution of mass tort cases, a point I question below, the results cannot serve their function of guaranteeing reliability unless the cases selected are statistically representative of the group of 3,000 plaintiffs. . . .

Mandamus relief would also and more emphatically be compelled if the federal courts are not authorized to permit binding verdicts to be rendered against non-parties to bellwether trials or against a defendant with respect to plaintiffs whose cases were not tried in the bellwether group. Although Judge Parker need not have reached this larger question, he appears to have done so, asserting that the notion of a bellwether trial "is a sound one that has achieved general acceptance by both bench and bar." He further asserts that common issues or even general liability may be resolved in a bellwether context in appropriate cases. I have serious doubts about the procedure even where, as here, Chevron *agreed* to use of a statistically sound bellwether trial process.

The only case cited in the MANUAL FOR COMPLEX LITIGATION concerning a bellwether strategy was tried by Judge Parker when he sat on the district court. *Cimino v. Raymark*, 751 F. Supp. 649, 653, 664–65 (E.D.[ ]Tex.[ ]1990), cited in MANUAL FOR COMPLEX LITIGATION § 33.27–.28 (3d Ed. 1995). One other recent case, affirmed in a split verdict of the Ninth Circuit, also used a bellwether technique. *Hilao v. Estate of Marcos*, 103 F.3d 767 (9th Cir.1996). These are not necessarily the only examples of bellwether trials, but they appear to be most unusual.

The use of statistical sampling as a means to identify and resolve common issues in tort litigation has, however, been severely criticized. See *In re Fibreboard Corp.* [893 F.2d 706 (5th Cir. 1990)]; *Hilao, supra* at 787–88 (Rymer, Judge, concurring in part and dissenting in part). Among other things, the technique may deprive nonparties of their Seventh Amendment jury trial right. In *Matter of Rhone–Poulenc Rorer Inc.*, Judge Posner observed that bifurcating liability and causation questions may require the same issue to be reexamined by different juries. That is, even if the bellwether jury found liability on the part of Chevron, later juries could be called upon to reassess that decision when faced with questions of comparative causation or comparative negligence. That all the plaintiffs are here represented by a single set of attorneys does not, in my view, alleviate Seventh Amendment concerns; to the contrary, it compounds them with potential ethical problems. Additionally, as Judge Higginbotham cautioned in *In re Fibreboard Corp.*, there is a fine line between deriving results from trials based on statistical sampling and pure legislation. Judges must be sensitive to stay within our proper bounds of adjudicating individual disputes. We are not authorized by the Constitution or statutes to legislate solutions to cases in pursuit of efficiency and expeditiousness. Essential to due process for litigants, including both the plaintiffs and Chevron in this non-class action context, is their right to the opportunity for an individual assessment of liability and damages in each case. Nowhere did the district court explain how it was authorized to make the results of this bellwether trial *unitary* for any purposes concerning the 2,970 other plaintiffs' cases pending before him. In sum, I simply do not share Judge Parker's confidence that bellwether trials can be used to resolve mass tort controversies.

On the narrow basis that the court's adoption of non-bellwether methods for conducting a bellwether trial is uniquely harmful and unauthorized, I concur with the majority's award of mandamus relief.

NOTES AND QUESTIONS

1.   *Relationship to* Cimino. As Judge Jones notes in her concurrence, the author of the panel opinion in *Chevron*—former U.S. District Judge Robert Parker, who was a member of the Fifth Circuit at the time of the *Chevron* decision—had substantial experience with bellwether trials and statistical sampling by way of his oversight of the *Cimino* asbestos litigation. Recall from the notes after *Amchem* in Chapter 2, that Judge Parker's experiment with hard-edged statistical sampling in asbestos litigation met with reversal by the Fifth Circuit—e.g., in the *Fibreboard* opinion that Judge Jones mentions. Does this perhaps shed light on why the opinion in *Chevron* emphasizes the lack of proper statistical sampling as the basis for reversal of the trial plan, while explicitly leaving open the possibility—questioned by Judge Jones—that bellwether trials in a representative sampling of cases might validly yield preclusive effect as to common issues?

Would such a hard-edged use of bellwether trials to yield preclusive effect be permissible? Does the due process problem, if any, consist primarily of the abridgement of the defendant's rights or the claimants' rights in the non-sampled, untried cases—or both the defendant's and the claimant's rights?

Would the trial plan in *Chevron*—even if it had involved a representative sample of cases—have recreated the problems discussed in Chapter 1 concerning the limits of preclusion as a way to resolve related civil claims? Recall the analysis of issue preclusion in *Parklane Hosiery Co. v. Shore*, from Chapter 1. What if common issues concerning the alleged contamination in *Chevron* were actually litigated and determined against the defendant Chevron in sampled case #1? Does it actually complicate the *Parklane* analysis that there might be sampled cases #2–10, in which the same common issues might be determined differently? Which case yields issue-preclusive effect on a *Parklane*-type analysis?

Now consider what happens if Chevron prevails on the merits of the common issues in sampled case #1. What does the Supreme Court's post-*Chevron* decision in *Taylor v. Sturgell*—again, recall Chapter 1—suggest about the prospects for preclusive effect as to non-sampled cases? Again, what if the determinations on the common issues are mixed across the run of sampled cases #1–10?

2.   *Hard-versus Soft–Edged Bellwether Trials*. Does the interchange between Judge Parker and Judge Jones ultimately suggest that a better use of bellwether trials would take not a hard-edged form (so as to generate some manner of preclusion) but, rather a soft-edged form (simply to generate information to guide the terms of settlement for untried cases, short of formal preclusion)? Can one, in short, get much of the informational benefit from bellwether trials without the preclusion baggage? Or would such a distinction be too formalistic? Note that, in everyday individual litigation, lawyers routinely counsel clients as to the advisability of settlement based on rough and often impressionistic notions of the settlements that other, broadly similar cases have garnered. Does this observed reality in ordinary litigation buttress the case for soft-edged bellwether trials over hard-edged ones?

In practical terms, does the insistence upon a representative sample of cases effectively *dictate* that they not be used in a hard-edged, preclusion-generating way but, instead, in a soft-edged, information-generating way? Doesn't a representative sample inherently present the possibility—indeed, arguably, celebrate the possibility—of different outcomes on common issues across the sampled cases?

3.   *Representative Sampling*. Judge Parker focuses on the need for a representative sample and objects to the trial judge's procedure because it is likely to generate a sample consisting of the 15 strongest and the 15 weakest cases. For an argument that sampling from the extremes of the distribution in this way does not necessarily undermine the extrapolation benefits of sampling, see Edward K. Cheng, *When 10 Trials Are Better Than 1000: An Evidentiary Perspective on Trial Sampling*, 160 U. Pa. L. Rev. 955, 963–64 (2012).

4.   *Bellwether Trials and Democracy*. Aside from considerations of accuracy and fair process for the parties involved, are there larger, systemic benefits from the use of bellwether trials, even soft-edged ones? Consider the view of one commentator:

> Bellwether trials . . . promote democratic decisionmaking by providing a procedure for citizens to be involved in the process of determining the outcome of mass tort cases instead of abdicating this role to lawyers with minimal judicial oversight. The inclusion of democratic decisionmaking is especially important in mass tort cases. Because of their scale, mass tort cases require the courts to adopt a regulatory function, which has usually involved jettisoning the jury trial. Involv-

ing the jury legitimizes court resolution of mass tort cases because it inserts an element of democratic participation.

Alexandra D. Lahav, *Bellwether Trials*, 76 Geo. Wash. L. Rev. 576, 594 (2008).

5. *Significance for Class Certification.* Rule 23(b)(3) calls for a judicial determination that certification of an opt-out class action would be "superior to other available methods for fairly and efficiently adjudicating the controversy." One might use bellwether trials in a class action by sampling cases from the class. Could such a use be invoked to counter manageability problems and thus shore up a (b)(3) superiority finding? Consider this question again after you read *Hilao* below. On the other hand, does the prospect of bellwether trials in a non-class aggregation make the required (b)(3) finding of superiority less likely? In practical terms, would the possibility of bellwether trials arise only in some areas of class action litigation but not others?

Now consider the class certification question, were it to arise *after* the conduct of bellwether trials. What if, based on the results of such trials, the lawyers (or, perhaps, only some of them) craft a proposed class settlement agreement and then seek certification of a settlement-only class for implementation purposes? When would implementation of the settlement "grid" by way of a class settlement be thought necessary, as compared to implementation via aggregate settlements? Recall here the distinction mentioned in *Chevron* between "elastic" and "non-elastic" mass torts.

6. *Relationship to MDL Consolidation.* Although *Chevron* involved an ordinary Rule 42 consolidation of individual suits, bellwether trials have been used quite often in MDL litigation. If there is reason to think that soft-edged bellwether trials might advance the resolution of related civil claims, then what effect should that recognition have on the selection of the transferee court for MDL-consolidated litigation? If bellwether trials are to be conducted, then which cases does such a transferee court have authority to try? Does the answer to that question shed light on *which* federal district court the MDL Panel should select as the transferee court? What attributes should the MDL Panel seek?

Judge Eldon Fallon of the United States District Court for the Eastern District of Louisiana, the transferee judge in MDL-consolidated product liability litigation over the prescription pain reliever Vioxx, notes the use of bellwether trials in that setting:

> One of this Court's first priorities was to assist the parties in selecting and preparing certain test cases to proceed as bellwether trials. In total, this Court conducted six Vioxx bellwether trials. . . . Only one of the trials resulted in a verdict for the plaintiff. Of the five remaining trials, one resulted in a hung jury and four resulted in verdicts for the defendant. During the same period that this Court conducted its six bellwether trials, approximately thirteen additional Vioxx-related cases were tried before juries in the state courts of Texas, New Jersey, California, Alabama, Illinois, and Florida. With the benefit of experience from these bellwether trials, as well as the encouragement of the several coordinated courts, the parties soon began settlement discussions in earnest.

In re Vioxx Prods. Liab. Litig., 574 F. Supp. 2d 606, 608 (E.D. La. 2008). In subsequent academic writing, Judge Fallon and two co-authors elaborate in more general terms:

> A typical bellwether case often begins as no more than an individual lawsuit that proceeds through pretrial discovery and on to trial in the usual binary fashion: one plaintiff versus one defendant. Such a case may take on "bellwether" qualities, however, when it is selected for trial because it involves facts, claims, or defenses that are similar to the facts, claims, and defenses presented in a wider group of related cases. . . . [T]he results of bellwether trials need not be binding upon consolidated parties with related claims or defenses in order to be beneficial to the MDL process. Instead, by injecting juries and fact-finding into multidistrict litigation, bellwether trials assist in the maturation of disputes by providing an opportunity for coordinating counsel to *organize* the products of pretrial common discovery, *evaluate* the strengths and weaknesses of their arguments and evidence, and *understand* the risks and costs associated with the litigation. At a minimum, the bellwether process should lead to the creation of "trial packages" that can be utilized by local counsel upon the dissolution of MDLs, a valuable by-product in its own right that supplies at least a partial justification for the traditional delay associated with MDL practice. But perhaps more importantly, the knowledge and experience gained during the bellwether process can precipitate global settlement negotiations and ensure that such negotiations do not occur in a vacuum, but rather in light of real-world evaluations of the litigation by multiple juries.

Fallon et al., 82 Tul. L. Rev. at 2325.

Even if bellwether trials are desirable as a policy matter, does an MDL judge have the power to order even a soft-edged bellwether procedure, given the statutory limitation of MDL transfer and consolidation to pre-trial matters?

    7.   *Informing the Design of Aggregate Settlements.* One way to make use of the information generated by soft-edged bellwether trials is by way of conventional aggregate settlements of the sort addressed previously in this Chapter. But, now, consider a somewhat different path: embodiment of the settlement grid in contractual agreements between the settling defendant and the major plaintiffs' law firms involved—i.e., firms that represent substantial numbers of claimants in the untried cases. As discussed later in this Chapter, these sorts of contracts were used in the Vioxx litigation after the completion of bellwether trials.

b.   STATISTICAL ADJUDICATION

    The most ambitious hard-edged use of bellwether trials involves sampling cases and extrapolating from sample results to impose *binding* outcomes on all cases. To illustrate with a simple example, suppose that 1000 cases are aggregated in a single proceeding through an MDL, class action, or other aggregation device. Suppose that liability is established in a collective manner and only damages remain to be determined. Suppose that there are 250 cases in the aggregation with low damages ($100,000), 500 cases with medium damages ($500,000), and 250 cases with high damages ($1 million). Neither the court nor the lawyers know this distribution in advance of sampling, nor do they know which particular cases fit into which categories. Concerned that 1000 trials would be too costly and generate unacceptable delays, the judge decides to draw a 10% random sample (i.e., 100 cases), try the sample cases, and give all the cases in the aggregation the average of the sample verdicts.

Since it is randomly selected, the sample should reflect roughly the same distribution as the underlying population. It follows that 25 of the sampled cases should have low damages, 50 medium damages, and 25 high damages. Therefore, if all the sampled cases are tried with perfect accuracy, the results should be: 25 verdicts of $100,000, 50 verdicts of $500,000, and 25 verdicts of $1 million. Following her trial plan, the judge then gives the cases in the aggregation the average of the sample verdicts, which is $525,000.

Notice that the defendant's total liability with the sampling procedure is exactly the same as it would have been if all the cases had been tried individually (once again, assuming perfectly accurate trials). With the sampling procedure, the defendant is liable for $525,000 × 1000 cases = $525 million. With individual trials, the defendant would be liable for 250×100,000 + 500×500,000 + 250×1,000,000 = $525 million. However, some plaintiffs are adversely affected. Those plaintiffs with high damages end up receiving just a little over half of their entitlement ($525,000 instead of $1 million) and those with low damages receive considerably more than their entitlement ($525,000 instead of $100,000). Of course, all plaintiffs save litigation costs.

One might initially balk at the use of statistics to adjudicate cases in this way. Most plaintiffs in the aggregation are denied an opportunity to litigate their own suits, which raises potential Seventh Amendment and Due Process problems. Recall Chapter 1's discussion of *Taylor v. Sturgell* and the strict limits placed upon nonparty preclusion in the name of protecting the individual right to a day in court. Furthermore, as we saw in our simple example, the averaging effect of sampling is likely to produce outcomes for some high-value plaintiffs that are less than their entitlements and less than they would receive from individual trials (unless the aggregation is unusually homogenous). This result raises fairness concerns, as well as concerns about modifying the substantive law. And some might question the legitimacy of a statistical procedure that seems so foreign to the individualist ethos of traditional adversarial litigation.

Before rushing to judgment, however, consider the following. First, much of the law depends upon statistical generalizations, and statistics are used in a variety of ways to resolve cases. For example, the tort doctrines of *res ipsa loquitor* and market share impose liability on the basis of statistical characteristics of cases. The likelihood of confusion test in trademark law makes liability turn on a probabilistic measure of likely confusion rather than on actual confusion. In fact, general rules usually are based on statistical features of cases.

In addition, statistics are used in a variety of ways to aid in adjudication. For example, parties are sometimes allowed to use a sample of records to support inferences about liability when there are so many records that it is impractical to consider each individually. So too, statistical models are used to estimate damages in complex cases when losses must be measured relative to a counterfactual baseline (such as estimating prices in a competitive market free of the defendant's illegal monopolization).

Finally, as we saw in the previous discussion, bellwether trials produce results that reflect statistical averages, which, in turn, can be used as a basis for settlement. Of course, the use of bellwether trials to facilitate settlement presupposes consent to any settlements that are reached. But how real is party consent in a large-scale MDL or other case aggregation controlled by lead counsel and a plaintiffs' steering committee? Recall the Vioxx settlement discussed earlier in this Chapter. Furthermore, what if injured parties are not likely to sue individually, or individual trials are not practically feasible, so some form of statistical adjudication is necessary for an adjudicative resolution? Indeed, it is possible that statistical adjudication might suffer less from the sort of agency problems that plague collective settlements.

Consider these questions when you read the following case, *Hilao v. Estate of Marcos*. *Hilao* is probably the most well-known application of statistical adjudication. While *Hilao* was a class action, the use of sampling to impose binding outcomes is not necessarily confined to the class setting. In theory at least, it can be used in an MDL proceeding, ordinary consolidation, or any other type of large-scale case aggregation.

Hilao v. Estate of Marcos

103 F.3d 767 (9th Cir. 1996)

■ FLETCHER, CIRCUIT JUDGE:

The Estate of Ferdinand E. Marcos appeals from a final judgment entered against it in a class-action suit after a trifurcated jury trial on the damage claims brought by a class of Philippine nationals (hereinafter collectively referred to as "Hilao") who were victims of torture, "disappearance," or summary execution under the regime of Ferdinand E. Marcos. . . . [W]e affirm.

FACTUAL BACKGROUND

This case arises from human-rights abuses—specifically, torture, summary execution, and "disappearance"—committed by the Philippine military and paramilitary forces under the command of Ferdinand E. Marcos during his nearly 14–year rule of the Philippines. . . .

PROCEDURAL HISTORY

Shortly after Marcos arrived in the United States in 1986 after fleeing the Philippines, he was served with complaints by a number of parties seeking damages for human-rights abuses committed against them or their decedents. . . .

In 1991, the district court certified the Hilao case as a class action, defining the class as all civilian citizens of the Philippines who, between 1972 and 1986, were tortured, summarily executed, or "disappeared" by Philippine military or paramilitary groups; the class also included the survivors of deceased class members. Certain plaintiffs opted out of the class and continued, alongside the class action, to pursue their cases directly. . . .

Marcos died during the pendency of the actions, and his wife Imelda Marcos and son Ferdinand R. Marcos, as his legal representatives, were substituted as defendants. . . .

The district court ordered issues of liability and damages tried separately. In September 1992, a jury trial was held on liability; after three days of deliberation, the jury reached verdicts against the Estate and for the class and for 22 direct plaintiffs and a verdict for the Estate and against one direct plaintiff. . . .

The district court then ordered the damage trial bifurcated into one trial on exemplary damages and one on compensatory damages. The court ordered that notice be given to the class members that they must file a proof-of-claim form in order to opt into the class. Notice was provided by mail to known claimants and by publication in the Philippines and the U.S.; over 10,000 forms were filed.

In February 1994, the same jury that had heard the liability phase of the trial considered whether to award exemplary damages. After two days of evidence and deliberations, the jury returned a verdict against the Estate in the amount of $1.2 billion.

The court appointed a special master to supervise proceedings related to the compensatory-damage phase of the trial in connection with the class. In January 1995, the jury reconvened a third time to consider compensatory damages. The compensatory-damage phase of the trial is explained in greater detail below. After seven days of trial and deliberation, the jury returned a compensatory-damage award for the class of over $766 million; after two further days of trial and deliberation, the jury returned compensatory-damage awards in favor of the direct plaintiffs.

On February 3, 1995, the district court entered final judgment in the class action suit. The Estate appeals from this judgment. . . .

DISCUSSION

. . .

IX.   Methodology of Determining Compensatory Damages

[Among other objections,] [t]he Estate challenges the method used by the district court in awarding compensatory damages to the class members.

A.   District Court Methodology

The district court allowed the use of a statistical sample of the class claims in determining compensatory damages. In all, 10,059 claims were received. The district court ruled 518 of these claims to be facially invalid, leaving 9,541 claims. From these, a list of 137 claims was randomly selected by computer. This number of randomly selected claims was chosen on the basis of the testimony of James Dannemiller, an expert on statistics, who testified that the examination of a random sample of 137 claims would achieve "a 95 percent statistical probability that the same percentage determined to be valid among the examined claims would be applicable to the totality of claims filed." Of the claims selected, 67 were for torture, 52 were for summary execution, and 18 were for "disappearance."

1.   Special Master's Recommendations

The district court then appointed Sol Schreiber as a special master (and a court-appointed expert under Rule 706 of the Federal Rules of Evidence). Schreiber supervised the taking of depositions in the Philippines of the 137 randomly selected claimants (and their witnesses) in October and November 1994. These depositions were noticed and conducted in accordance with the Federal Rules of Civil Procedure; the Estate chose not to participate and did not appear at any of the depositions. (The Estate also did not depose any of the remaining class members.)

Schreiber then reviewed the claim forms (which had been completed under penalty of perjury) and depositions of the class members in the sample. On the instructions of the district court, he evaluated

> (1) whether the abuse claimed came within one of the definitions, with which the Court charged the jury at the trial . . . of torture, summary execution, or disappearance; (2) whether the Philippine military or paramilitary was . . . involved in such abuse; and (3) whether the abuse occurred during the period September 1972 through February 1986.

He recommended that 6 claims of the 137 in the sample be found not valid.[8]

Schreiber then recommended the amount of damages to be awarded to the 131 claimants. . . . [H]e applied Philippine, international, and American law on damages. In the cases of torture victims, Schreiber considered:

> (1) physical torture, including what methods were used and/or abuses were suffered; (2) mental abuse, including fright and anguish; (3) amount of time torture lasted; (4) length of detention, if any; (5) physical and/or mental injuries; (6) victim's age; and (7) actual losses, including medical bills.

In the cases of summary execution and "disappearance", the master considered

> (1) [the presence or absence of] torture prior to death or disappearance; (2) the actual killing or disappearance; . . . (3) the victim's family's mental anguish[;] and (4) lost earnings [computed according to a formula established by the Philippine Supreme Court and converted into U.S. dollars].

The recommended damages for the 131 valid claims in the random sample totalled $3,310,000 for the 64 torture claims (an average of $51,719), $6,425,767 for the 50 summary-execution claims (an average of $128,515), and $1,833,515 for the 17 "disappearance" claims (an average of $107,853).

Schreiber then made recommendations on damage awards to the remaining class members. Based on his recommendation that 6 of the 137 claims in the random sample (4.37%) be rejected as invalid, he recommended the application of a five-per-cent invalidity rate to the remaining claims. . . .

He recommended that the award to the class be determined by multiplying the number of valid remaining claims in each subclass by the average award recommended for the randomly sampled claims in that subclass. . . .

By adding the recommended awards in the randomly sampled cases, Schreiber arrived at a recommendation for a total compensatory damage award in each subclass [and] a total compensatory damage award [for the class as a whole] of $767,491,493.

2.   Jury Proceedings

A jury trial on compensatory damages was held in January 1995. Dannemiller testified that the selection of the random sample met the standards of inferential statistics, that the successful efforts to locate and

---

[8] Three torture claims and one summary-execution claim were recommended as invalid because the claimants presented insufficient proof that the abuses were committed by military or paramilitary forces. One summary-execution claim and one "disappearance" claim were recommended as invalid for insufficient evidence.

obtain testimony from the claimants in the random sample "were of the highest standards" in his profession, that the procedures followed conformed to the standards of inferential statistics, and that the injuries of the random-sample claimants were representative of the class as a whole. Testimony from the 137 random-sample claimants and their witnesses was introduced. Schreiber testified as to his recommendations, and his report was supplied to the jury. The jury was instructed that it could accept, modify or reject Schreiber's recommendations and that it could independently, on the basis of the evidence of the random-sample claimants, reach its own judgment as to the actual damages of those claimants and of the aggregate damages suffered by the class as a whole.

The jury deliberated for five days before reaching a verdict. Contrary to the master's recommendations, the jury found against only two of the 137 claimants in the random sample. As to the sample claims, the jury generally adopted the master's recommendations, although it did not follow his recommendations in 46 instances. As to the claims of the remaining class members, the jury adopted the awards recommended by the master. The district court subsequently entered judgment for 135 of the 137 claimants in the sample in the amounts awarded by the jury, and for the remaining plaintiffs in each of the three subclasses in the amounts awarded by the jury, to be divided pro rata.[10]

B. Estate's Challenge

The Estate's challenge to the procedure used by the district court is very narrow. It challenges specifically only "the method by which [the district court] allowed the validity of the class claims to be determined": the master's use of a representative sample to determine what percentage of the total claims were invalid. . . .

The Estate . . . argues that the method was "inappropriate" because the class consists of various members with numerous subsets of claims based on whether the plaintiff or his or her decedent was subjected to torture, "disappearance," or summary execution. The district court's methodology, however, took account of those differences by grouping the class members' claims into three subclasses.

Finally, the Estate appears to assert that the method violated its rights to due process because "individual questions apply to each subset of claims, *i.e.*, whether the action was justified, the degree of injury, proximate cause, etc." It does not, however, provide any argument or case citation to explain how the methodology violated its due-process rights. Indeed, the "individual questions" it identifies—justification, degree of injury, proximate cause—are irrelevant to the challenge it makes: the method of determining the validity of the class members' claims.[12] The jury had already determined that Philippine military or paramilitary forces on Marcos' orders—or with his conspiracy or assistance or with his knowledge and failure to act—had tortured, summarily executed, or "disappeared" untold

---

[10] Although never expressly explained by the district court, the mechanics of this division, as represented by Hilao, are as follows: The 135 random-sample claimants whose claims were found to be valid would receive the actual amount awarded by the jury; the two sample claimants whose claims were held invalid would receive nothing. All remaining 9,404 claimants with facially valid claims would be eligible to participate in the aggregate award, even though the aggregate award was calculated based on a 5% invalidity rate of those claims.

[12] The degree of injury would, of course, be relevant to the computation of damages for each claim, but, as noted above, the Estate has waived any challenge to the computation of damages.

numbers of victims and that the Estate was liable to them or their survivors. The only questions involved in determining the validity of the class members' claims were whether or not the human-rights abuses they claim to have suffered were proven by sufficient evidence.

Although poorly presented, the Estate's due-process claim does raise serious questions. Indeed, at least one circuit court has expressed "profound disquiet" in somewhat similar circumstances. *In re Fibreboard Corp.*, 893 F.2d 706, 710 (5th Cir. 1990). The *Fibreboard* court was reviewing a petition for a writ of mandamus to vacate trial procedures ordered in over 3,000 asbestos cases. The district court had consolidated the cases for certain purposes and certified a class for the issue of actual damages. The district court ordered a trial first on liability and punitive damages, and then a trial (Phase II) on actual damages. In the Phase II trial, the jury was "to determine actual damages in a lump sum for each [of 5] disease categor[ies] for all plaintiffs in the class" on the basis of "a full trial of liability and damages for 11 class representatives and such evidence as the parties wish to offer from 30 illustrative plaintiffs" (half chosen by each side), as well as "opinions of experts . . . regarding the total damage award." 893 F.2d at 708–09. The Fifth Circuit noted that the parties agreed that "there will inevitably be individual class members whose recovery will be greater or lesser than it would have been if tried alone" and that "persons who would have had their claims rejected may recover." *Id.* at 709. The court said that

> [t]he inescapable fact is that the individual claims of 2,990 persons will not be presented. Rather, the claim of a unit of 2,990 persons will be presented. Given the unevenness of the individual claims, this Phase II process inevitably restates the dimensions of tort liability. Under the proposed procedure, manufacturers and suppliers are exposed to liability not only in 41 cases actually tried with success to the jury, but in 2,990 additional cases whose claims are indexed to those tried.

Id. at 711. The court granted the petitions for mandamus and vacated the trial court's order, but it did so not on due process grounds but because the proposed procedure worked a change in the parties' substantive rights under Texas law that was barred by the *Erie* doctrine.

On the other hand, the time and judicial resources required to try the nearly 10,000 claims in this case would alone make resolution of Hilao's claims impossible. The similarity in the injuries suffered by many of the class members would make such an effort, even if it could be undertaken, especially wasteful, as would the fact that the district court found early on that the damages suffered by the class members likely exceed the total known assets of the Estate.

While the district court's methodology in determining valid claims is unorthodox, it can be justified by the extraordinarily unusual nature of this case. " 'Due process,' unlike some legal rules, is not a technical conception with a fixed content unrelated to time, place and circumstances." *Cafeteria and Restaurant Workers Union, Local 473 v. McElroy*, 367 U.S. 886, 895 (1961). In *Connecticut v. Doehr*, 501 U.S. 1 (1991), a case involving prejudgment attachment, the Supreme Court set forth a test, based on the test of *Mathews v. Eldridge*, 424 U.S. 319 (1976), for determining whether a procedure by which a private party invokes state power to deprive another person of property satisfies due process:

> [F]irst, consideration of the private interest that will be affected by the [procedure]; second, an examination of the risk of erroneous deprivation through the procedures under attack and the probable value of additional or alternative safeguards; and third, . . . principal attention to the interest of the party seeking the [procedure], with, nonetheless, due regard for any ancillary interest the government may have in providing the procedure or forgoing the added burden of providing greater protections.

501 U.S. at 11. The interest of the Estate that is affected is at best an interest in not paying damages for any invalid claims. If the Estate had a legitimate concern in the identities of those receiving damage awards, the district court's procedure could affect this interest. In fact, however, the Estate's interest is only in the total amount of damages for which it will be liable: if damages were awarded for invalid claims, the Estate would have to pay more. The statistical method used by the district court obviously presents a somewhat greater risk of error in comparison to an adversarial adjudication of each claim, since the former method requires a probabilistic *prediction* (albeit an extremely accurate one) of how many of the total claims are invalid. The risk in this case was reduced, though, by the fact that the proof-of-claim form that the district court required each class member to submit in order to opt into the class required the claimant to certify under penalty of perjury that the information provided was true and correct. Hilao's interest in the use of the statistical method, on the other hand, is enormous, since adversarial resolution of each class member's claim would pose insurmountable practical hurdles. The "ancillary" interest of the judiciary in the procedure is obviously also substantial, since 9,541 individual adversarial determinations of claim validity would clog the docket of the district court for years. Under the balancing test set forth in *Mathews* and *Doehr*, the procedure used by the district court did not violate due process. . . .

■ RYMER, CIRCUIT JUDGE, concurring in part and dissenting in part:

Because I believe that determining causation as well as damages by inferential statistics instead of individualized proof raises more than "serious questions" of due process, I must dissent from Part IX of the majority opinion. Otherwise, I concur. . . .

[C]ausation and $766 million compensatory damages for nearly 10,000 claimants rested on the opinion of a statistical expert that the selection method in determining valid claims was fair to the Estate and more accurate than individual testimony; Hilao's counsel's contact with the randomly selected victims until they got 137 to be deposed; and the Special Master's review of transcripts and finding that the selected victims had been tortured, summarily executed or disappeared, that the Philippine military was "involved," that the abuse occurred during the relevant period, and that moral damages occurred as a proximate result of the Estate's wrongful acts.

This leaves me "with a profound disquiet," as Judge Higginbotham put it in *In re Fibreboard Corp.*, 893 F.2d 706, 710 (5th Cir. 1990). Although I cannot point to any authority that says so, I cannot believe that a summary review of transcripts of a selected sample of victims who were able to be deposed for the purpose of inferring the type of abuse, by whom it was inflicted, and the amount of damages proximately caused thereby, comports with fundamental notions of due process.

Even in the context of a class action, individual causation and individual damages must still be proved individually. As my colleagues on the Sixth Circuit explained in contrasting generic causation—that the defendant was responsible for a tort which had the capacity to cause the harm alleged—with individual proximate cause and individual damage:

> Although such generic causation and individual causation may appear to be inextricably intertwined, the procedural device of the class action permitted the court initially to assess the defendant's potential liability for its conduct without regard to the individual components of each plaintiff's injuries. However, from this point forward, it became the responsibility of each individual plaintiff to show that his or her specific injuries or damages were proximately caused by [the defendant's conduct]. We cannot emphasize this point strongly enough because generalized proofs will not suffice to prove individual damages. The main problem on review stems from a failure to differentiate between the general and the particular. This is an understandably easy trap to fall into in mass tort litigation. Although many common issues of fact and law will be capable of resolution on a group basis, individual particularized damages still must be proved on an individual basis.

Sterling v. Velsicol Chem. Corp., 855 F.2d 1188, 1200 (6th Cir. 1988).

There is little question that Marcos caused tremendous harm to many people, but the question is which people, and how much. That, I think, is a question on which the defendant has a right to due process. If due process in the form of a real prove-up of causation and damages cannot be accomplished because the class is too big or to do so would take too long, then (as the Estate contends) the class is unmanageable and should not have been certified in the first place. . . .

NOTES AND QUESTIONS

1. *The Procedure in* Hilao. The district judge in *Hilao* used a rather complicated procedure. Rather than trying the 137 sample cases and calculating total damages based on the average of the sample verdicts, the judge instead appointed a special master, who estimated damages based on discovery and proof-of-claim forms in the sample cases. The special master calculated average damages separately for torture victims, victims of summary executions, and disappeared victims, and then calculated a total damages figure for each group and a total for the class as a whole. The special master also submitted his recommendations to a jury, which reviewed and adjusted the amounts. Why such an elaborate procedure? Does the jury's involvement in checking aggregate damages adequately address potential Seventh Amendment objections?

Note, too, that the sampling procedure was used to adjudicate more than just the amount of compensatory damages. As Judge Rymer's separate opinion makes clear, the district judge used the procedure to adjudicate aspects of each individual's entitlement to damages. Judge Rymer notes in particular that the special master determined that "the selected victims had been tortured, summarily executed or disappeared, that the Philippine military was 'involved' that the abuse occurred during the relevant period, and that moral damages occurred as a proximate result of the Estate's wrongful acts." Moreover, the special master reduced total damages by 5% based on his finding that 6 of the 137 claims in the random sample were invalid, and his invalidity finding reflected evidentiary and other problems with proving entitlement. Is the use of sampling to calculate the amount of damages more appropriate than its use to determine both amount and entitlement? See Laurens Walker & John Monahan, *Sampling Liability*, 85 Va. L. Rev. 329 (1999).

2. *Federal versus State Law.* Many of the cases in large-scale aggregations involve mass torts or mass accidents that implicate state tort claims which are in federal court under diversity jurisdiction. This was true for *In Re Chevron* and also for *Cimino v. Raymark Industries, Inc.*, 751 F. Supp. 649 (E.D. Tex. 1990), discussed in Chapter 2, in which Judge Parker (then on the federal district court) used sampling to adjudicate damages for 2,298 asbestos cases. When state claims are involved, there is always a risk that sampling might alter state substantive law in violation of *Erie*'s dictates. Indeed, this was one of the reasons why the Fifth Circuit reversed Judge Parker's sampling procedure in *Cimino*. *Cimino v. Raymark Industries, Inc.*, 151 F.3d 297 (5th Cir. 1998).

The *Hilao* litigation, however, proceeded in federal court based upon a jurisdictional grant in the Alien Tort Statute (ATS), 28 U.S.C § 1350. In its present form, modified only slightly since its adoption in 1789, the ATS provides simply that: "The [federal] district courts shall have original jurisdiction of any civil action by an alien for a tort only, committed in violation of the law of nations or a treaty of the United States." Section 1350 authorizes federal subject-matter jurisdiction over civil actions that seek a federal common law remedy for violations of certain norms of customary international law. *Sosa v. Alvarez–Machain*, 542 U.S. 692 (2004).

Should the source of substantive law make a difference to the court's authority to use sampling?

3. *The Effect of* Wal–Mart Stores, Inc. v. Dukes*?* In the context of addressing the effect of monetary recovery on certification under 23(b)(2), the Supreme Court in *Wal-Mart Stores, Inc. v. Dukes*, 131 S. Ct. 2541 (2013), opined on the use of statistical sampling to adjudicate Title VII backpay awards. The issue arose because the plaintiffs sought to certify a (b)(2) class action for backpay as well as injunctive and declaratory relief. Title VII provides that when an employer has been found prima facie liable for discrimination, it cannot be held liable for backpay if "the employer can show that it took an adverse employment action against an employee for any reason other than discrimination." *Id.* at 2560–61. Wal–Mart argued that the availability of this affirmative defense meant that the backpay portion of the suit was not manageable in class form and therefore could not be included in a class action certified under (b)(2). The Ninth Circuit rejected this argument and, relying on *Hilao*, suggested that the district judge might consider using a statistical sampling procedure to adjudicate backpay awards. See *Dukes v. Wal–Mart Stores, Inc.*, 603 F.3d 571, 625–28 (9th Cir. 2010). The Supreme Court categorically rejected this option:

> The Court of Appeals believed that it was possible to replace [individual] proceedings with Trial by Formula. A sample set of the class members would be selected, as to whom liability for sex discrimination and the backpay owing as a result would be determined in depositions supervised by a master. The percentage of claims determined to be valid would then be applied to the entire remaining class, and the number of (presumptively) valid claims thus derived would be multiplied by the average backpay award in the sample set to arrive

at the entire class recovery—without further individualized proceedings. We disapprove that novel project. Because the Rules Enabling Act forbids interpreting Rule 23 to "abridge, enlarge or modify any substantive right," 28 U.S.C. § 2072(b); see *Ortiz*, 527 U.S., at 845, a class cannot be certified on the premise that Wal–Mart will not be entitled to litigate its statutory defenses to individual claims. And because the necessity of that litigation will prevent backpay from being "incidental" to the classwide injunction, respondents' class could not be certified even assuming, *arguendo*, that "incidental" monetary relief can be awarded to a 23(b)(2) class.

Wal-Mart Stores, Inc. v. Dukes, 131 S. Ct. at 2561.

Recall that even the dissenters in *Wal-Mart* agreed that claims for backpay should not have been certified under (b)(2). Whether their agreement with the result extends to all of the majority's reasoning, including the quoted passage, is surely debatable. Nevertheless, the passage was endorsed by a majority of the Court.

What are the implications of this passage for the use of statistical adjudication more generally? Certainly the pejorative label, "Trial by Formula", signals disapproval. But does the passage foreclose the specific use of sampling in *Hilao*? Note that *Wal-Mart*, like *Hilao*, involves a federal and not a state claim. The quoted passage focuses on the way that sampling adversely affects Wal–Mart's entitlement to litigate its affirmative defenses under Title VII. Does this mean that *Wal-Mart* restricts the use of sampling to adjudicate liability elements but not necessarily to determine damage amounts?

The Court relies on the Rules Enabling Act, and not the Due Process Clause or some other constitutional provision. What is the Rules Enabling Act objection exactly? A well-designed sampling procedure should produce an extremely good estimate of defendant's total liability (and at a lower litigation cost for the defendant). As the *Hilao* court recognized, the defendant has a legitimate interest in this total amount and not in how the total is distributed among the different claimants: "the Estate's interest is only in the total amount of damages for which it will be liable." Thus, it is difficult to see how the defendant's right to pay only what the substantive law requires is "abridged, enlarged, or modified" in the aggregate. The Supreme Court suggests that the Rules Enabling Act protects Wal–Mart's right to "litigate its statutory defenses to individual claims." Does this make sense? In thinking about this question, keep in mind that the limitations on the rulemaking power in the Act were intended by the Act's drafters to distinguish between matters that are properly delegated to the Supreme Court as procedural rulemaker from those that are best left to the legislative process or common law adjudication. See Stephen Burbank, *The Rules Enabling Act of 1934*, 130 U. Pa. L. Rev. 1015 (1982).

Do you think Wal–Mart actually wants to litigate its affirmative defenses to each plaintiff's backpay claim individually? If not, why is Wal–Mart insisting on individual litigation? If Wal–Mart isn't really harmed by a sampling procedure and if sampling offers the best hope for plaintiffs to recover backpay awards, what is the Court so concerned about? Is it actually concerned about the constitutional legitimacy of a sampling procedure? If so, why doesn't the Court rely on the Constitution directly? One advantage of relying on the Rules Enabling Act is that it leaves room for Congress, if it wishes, to authorize a sampling procedure in appropriate cases.

4.   Due Process Objections. The *Hilao* court addresses the Estate's due process objections by relying on the balancing test from *Connecticut v. Doehr* and *Mathews v. Eldridge.* This test, developed originally for administrative hearings in *Mathews,* and then applied to judicial prejudgment attachment proceedings in *Doehr*, balances three factors: the private interest adversely affected by the challenged procedure, the risk of error with the challenged procedure and the probable value of additional procedures, and the interest of those adversely affected by the additional procedures as well as the government interest at stake. The *Hilao* court finds that the sampling procedure used in the case minimized the risk of error and did not seriously affect the Estate's interest in an accurate determination of its aggregate liability and that "Hilao's interest in the use of the statistical method . . . is enormous, since adversarial resolution of each class member's claim would pose insurmountable practical hurdles, [and] [t]he "ancillary" interest of the judiciary in the procedure is obviously also substantial, since 9,541 individual adversarial determinations of claim validity would clog the docket of the district court for years." Is this an adequate response to the due process concerns? What if a class member preferred to litigate her claims individually and objected to the sampling procedure on due process grounds? Recall from Chapter 1 the Supreme Court's strong endorsement in *Taylor v. Sturgell* of the due process right to a personal day in court. Can you square the result in *Taylor* with the *Doehr/Mathews* balancing test? Should the latitude for statistical sampling be greater when the court exercises a lawmaking role in the elaboration of underlying substantive doctrine?

5.   Is Statistical Adjudication Justified as a Policy Matter? Consider a mass tort involving tens of thousands of injured parties. Assume that if all the plaintiffs sue individually, there would be such a huge backlog of cases that those plaintiffs who manifest injury later, or for some other reason must sue later, would face huge delay costs. Indeed, the present value of any future recovery for these plaintiffs would be so greatly reduced by the delay that they would likely settle for only a small fraction of their entitlement. Also, suppose that even if the common questions could be litigated in a collective manner, there would be such a large number of individual questions left to litigate that backlog and delay costs would still be very serious. Can one justify statistical adjudication under these circumstances?

First, consider the effects of statistical adjudication on outcomes. The defendant cannot seriously complain about its total liability since a well-designed sampling procedure gives a very good estimate in the aggregate. Plaintiffs with high-value claims who file early enough might complain that sampling would give them less than an individual trial. But are those complaints legitimate if it is purely arbitrary where a plaintiff ends up in the litigation queue? One might consider outcome effects from a different perspective. What is the likely impact of sampling on the defendant's and the plaintiffs' incentives to invest in litigating the sample cases? If the plaintiffs are likely to invest less than the defendant, for example, the sample cases could produce verdicts skewed in the defendant's favor. Any evaluation, however, must be comparative, and differential litigation investments can also produce skewed outcomes in individual suits. Moreover, since virtually all aggregations settle, an important question is how the sampling procedure affects settlements. Indeed, the prospect of sampling can affect the parties' incentives to settle even before the sampling procedure is implemented. Effects on investment and settlement incentives are complex. For a discussion, see Robert G. Bone, *Statistical Adjudication: Rights, Justice, and*

Utility in a World of Process Scarcity, 46 Vand. L. Rev. 561 (1993); Robert G. Bone, *A Normative Evaluation of Actuarial Litigation*, 18 Conn. Ins. L. J. 227 (2011).

Second, consider effects on day-in-court participation values. The defendant might complain that it is denied its day in court by not having an opportunity to litigate all the individual issues in each case separately. But how strong an argument is this when the defendant can litigate the issues in the sample cases that determine the results for all other cases? Those plaintiffs in the cases that were not chosen for the sample might complain about being denied their day in court. But how much weight should be given to this argument when providing them with a day in court would generate delays that significantly impair the recovery of other plaintiffs? Should it matter if all plaintiffs would have agreed to the sampling procedure had they been able to contract in advance of being injured—or contract in a hypothetical bargaining situation in which they do not know their relative positions in the litigation queue?

Third, consider possible effects on institutional legitimacy. Does the use of sampling in narrowly drawn situations impair the legitimacy of adjudication? Is it likely to have an adverse effect on public perceptions? Is it inconsistent with fundamental features of adjudication that are essential to its normative legitimacy? For a discussion of these issues, see Bone, *A Normative Evaluation of Actuarial Litigation*, 18 Conn. Ins. L. J. at 259-65.

6. *A Postscript to* Hilao. Since the decision in *Hilao*, the class has been trying to collect on the judgment it won. One such effort produced a Rule 19 opinion from the Supreme Court in 2008: *Republic of the Philippines* v. *Pimentel*, 553 U.S. 851 (2008). The *Hilao* class—or as the Supreme Court refers to it, the *Pimentel* class—sought to recover assets that the Marcos government had placed with Merrill Lynch in New York. Unfortunately for the class, the same assets were also claimed by the Philippine Presidential Commission on Good Government, a commission created by the Philippine government to recover all property that Marcos wrongfully took from the Philippines.

Uncertain about who should receive the assets, Merrill Lynch filed a statutory interpleader action under 28 U.S.C. § 1335, naming as defendants the *Hilao* class, the Presidential Commission, the Republic of the Philippines, and some others. The Commission and the Republic asserted sovereign immunity and moved to dismiss the action under Rule 19 of the Federal Rules of Civil Procedure. The district court held that the Commission and the Republic were persons required to be joined if feasible under Rule 19(a)(1)(B)(i) because of their competing claims to the same assets, and it also held that the assertions of sovereign immunity made it impossible to join them. The court nevertheless decided that it could proceed under Rule 19(b) without the Commission or the Republic. The Court of Appeals affirmed.

The Supreme Court reversed. It held that the lower courts had given insufficient weight in the 19(b) balance to the sovereign immunity interest at stake. "[W]here sovereign immunity is asserted, and the claims of the sovereign are not frivolous," the Court held, "dismissal of the action must be ordered where there is a potential for injury to the interests of the absent sovereign." *Id.* at 867. And as the Court noted, "[t]his leaves the . . . class, which has waited for years now to be compensated for grievous wrongs, with no immediate way to recover on its judgment against Marcos." *Id.* at 872.

For additional background on the *Hilao* litigation and on efforts by the class to collect on the judgment, see UN Human Rights Committee, Communication No. 1320/2004, available at http://www.unhchr.ch/tbs/doc.nsf/(Symbol)/2b64d3c0499e38fdc12572ce0049fb3b?Opendocument. In a March 1, 2011 article, the New York Times reported that 7,526 class members will finally receive some money as a result of a $10 million settlement with the family of a Marcos associate. The total represents only a small fraction of the $2 billion judgment, and each person will receive only a small amount ($1000). See Seth Mydans, *First Payments Are Made to Victims of Marcos Rule,* available at http://www.nytimes.com/2011/03/02/world/asia/02philippines.html?_r=1&ref=global-homesome.

6.   AGGREGATE SETTLEMENT VIA CONTRACTS WITH PLAINTIFFS' LAW FIRMS

Individual lawsuits that happen to be consolidated before a single federal district court can be settled, of course, just like other individual lawsuits, by way of contracts between the settling defendant and each individual plaintiff. But is that the only option available when similar lawsuits are consolidated in large numbers? *Should* it be the only option, particularly given the difficulty of using a settlement class action post-*Amchem*?

Consider the alternative approach taken in the Vioxx litigation, as described in a press release from the defendant manufacturer Merck:

Merck & Co., Inc. today announced that it has entered into an agreement with the law firms that comprise the executive committee of the Plaintiffs' Steering Committee of the federal multidistrict VIOXX litigation as well as representatives of plaintiffs' counsel in state coordinated proceedings to resolve state and federal myocardial infarction (MI) and ischemic stroke claims already filed against the Company in the United States. The agreement, which also applies to tolled claims, was signed by the parties this morning after they met with three of the four judges overseeing the coordination of more than 95 percent of the current claims in the VIOXX litigation.

If certain conditions under the agreement are met, the Company will pay a fixed amount of $4.85 billion into a settlement fund for qualifying claims that enter into the resolution process. This is not a class-action settlement. Claims will be evaluated on an individual basis. . . .

The conditions in the agreement, which is open only to those cases filed or tolled on or before Nov. 8, 2007, include:

- To qualify, claimants will have to pass three gates: an injury gate requiring objective, medical proof of MI or ischemic stroke (as defined in the agreement), a duration gate based on documented receipt of at least 30 VIOXX pills, and a proximity gate requiring receipt of pills in sufficient number and proximity to the event to support a presumption of ingestion of VIOXX within 14 days before the claimed injury;

- Individual cases will be examined by administrators of the resolution process to determine qualification based on objective, documented facts provided by claimants, including records sufficient for a scientific evaluation of independent risk factors;

- The agreement provides that Merck does not admit causation or fault;

- Neither stroke claims that are hemorrhagic in nature nor transient ischemic attacks will qualify;

- Law firms on the federal and state Plaintiffs' Steering Committees and firms that have tried cases in the coordinated proceedings must recommend enrollment in the program to 100 percent of their clients who allege either MI or ischemic stroke;

- The parties agree to seek court orders from the four coordination judges requiring plaintiffs' attorneys to promptly register all of their VIOXX claims, whether filed or tolled, and to identify the alleged injury—in order to establish the universe of all existing claims in the United States;

- Participation conditions: payment obligations under the agreement will be triggered only if, by March 1, 2008 (subject to extension by Merck), plaintiffs enroll in the settlement process: (a) 85 percent or more of all currently pending and tolled MI claims, (b) 85 percent or more of all currently pending and tolled ischemic stroke claims; (c) 85 percent or more of all eligible claims involving a death; and (d) 85 percent or more of all eligible claims alleging more than 12 months of use; and

- This agreement applies only to U.S. legal residents and those who allege that their MI or ischemic stroke occurred in the United States.

Under the agreement, separate funds will be created by the Company in the amount of $4 billion for MI claims and $850 million for ischemic stroke claims. Once triggered, Merck's total payment for both funds of $4.85 billion is a fixed amount to be allocated among qualifying claimants based on their individual evaluation. While at this time the exact number of claimants covered by this agreement is unknown, the total dollar amount is fixed. Payments to individual qualifying claimants could begin as early as August 2008 and then will be paid over a period of time. Merck retains its right to terminate this process without any payment to any claimant, and to defend each claim individually at trial if any of the participation conditions in the agreement are not met.

The Company expects to record a fourth-quarter 2007 pre-tax charge in the amount of $4.85 billion to cover the cost of the agreement.

"This agreement is the product of our defense strategy in the United States during the past three years and is consistent with our commitment to defend each claim individually through rigorous scientific scrutiny. Under the agreement, there will be an orderly, documented and objective process to examine individual claims to determine if they qualify for payment," said Bruce N. Kuhlik, senior vice president and general counsel of Merck. "This agreement also makes sense for the Company because since 2004, we have reserved approximately $1.9 billion for defending VIOXX litigation and, absent this agreement, could anticipate that the litigation might stretch on for years."

"Creating a process to look at individual claims is the fairest way to efficiently and quickly provide payment to qualified claimants," said Russ Herman, Liaison Counsel in the federal multidistrict VIOXX litigation and Chair of the Plaintiffs' Negotiating Committee. "Specific causation has been a very difficult issue. This is an opportunity to end a long and difficult litigation that has stretched on for more than three years. A fair resolution is in everybody's best interest. This agreement would only apply to claims already filed or tolled."

"This is the right time for an agreement," said Mr. Kuhlik. "Recent court rulings confirmed that the window has closed for filing suits in a number of states, consistent with our view that statutes of limitations have expired in almost every state. Additionally, three of the coordination judges have issued orders that require non-eligible and non-participating plaintiffs to provide documentation of the factual basis for their claims early in the litigation process. Merck reserves the right under this agreement to terminate our involvement unless the vast majority of eligible claimants elect to participate."

Forty-two states, Puerto Rico and the District of Columbia have statutes of limitations of three years or less. Already, New Jersey Superior Court Judge Carol Higbee and Federal District Court Judge Eldon Fallon have issued orders in cases from New Jersey and eight other jurisdictions ruling that the statutory period for making VIOXX personal injury claims has passed. Merck voluntarily withdrew VIOXX from the marketplace on Sept. 30, 2004.

The discussions between Merck and the plaintiffs were originally requested by Judge Fallon, Judge Higbee, California Superior Court Judge Victoria Chaney, and Texas County Court Judge Randy Wilson. Judges Fallon, Higbee and Chaney, who met with the parties prior to the agreement being signed, issued case management orders that will require plaintiffs seeking to pursue VIOXX claims outside this resolution process to provide in a timely fashion certified copies of their medical and pharmacy records, as well as expert causation opinions.

Merck has submitted a similar order to Judge Wilson.

The Company will continue to defend all claims that are not included in the resolution process. . . .

Juries have now decided in favor of the Company 12 times and in plaintiffs' favor five times. One Merck verdict was set aside by the court and has not been retried. Another Merck verdict was set aside and retried, leading to one of the five plaintiff verdicts. There have been two unresolved mistrials.

As of Oct. 9, 2007, in the United States, the Company had been served or was aware that it had been named as a defendant in approximately 26,600 lawsuits, filed on or before Sept. 30, 2007, which include approximately 47,000 plaintiff groups, alleging personal injuries resulting from the use of VIOXX, and in approximately 264 putative class actions alleging personal injuries and/or economic loss.

Merck has entered into a tolling agreement with the multi-district litigation Plaintiffs' Steering Committee that establishes a procedure to halt the running of the statute of limitations for certain categories of claims allegedly arising from the use of VIOXX by non-New Jersey citizens. The Tolling Agreement requires any tolled claims to be filed in federal court. As of Sept. 30, 2007, approximately 14,100 claimants had entered into Tolling Agreements. The parties agreed that April 9, 2007, was the deadline for filing Tolling Agreements and no additional Tolling Agreements are being accepted.

The claims of over 5,550 plaintiff groups had been dismissed as of Sept. 30, 2007. In addition, about 20 cases scheduled for trial were either dismissed or withdrawn from the trial calendar by plaintiffs before a jury could be selected.

News Release, Merck Agreement to Resolve U.S. VIOXX® Product Liability Lawsuits (Nov. 9, 2007), available at http://www.aei.org/files/2008/01/07/ 20080109_MerckPressRelease.pdf. In fact, the 85–percent cutoff for claimant participation specified in the Vioxx settlement agreement was met by a comfortable margin.

Note that the contracting parties here consist of Merck and the plaintiffs' lawyers on the steering committee for the MDL-consolidated Vioxx litigation, *not* Merck and the actual plaintiffs in those lawsuits. What complications arise from this type of arrangement, as distinct from that in *Zyprexa*? Consider this passage from the Vioxx settlement agreement:

1.2.8.　　　While nothing in this Agreement is intended to operate as a "restriction" on the right of any Claimant's counsel to practice law within the meaning of the equivalent to Rule 5.6(b) of the ABA Model Rules of Professional Conduct in any jurisdiction in which Claimant's Counsel practices or whose rules may otherwise apply, it is agreed that (except to the extent waived by Merck in its sole discretion in any instance):

1.2.8.1.　　By submitting an Enrollment Form, the Enrolling Counsel affirms that he has recommended, or . . . will recommend by no later than the earlier of the date of service of the Certification of Final Enrollment and February 28, 2008, to 100% of the Eligible Claimants represented by such Enrolling Counsel that such Eligible Claimants enroll in the [settlement] Program.

1.2.8.2.　　If any such Eligible Claimant disregards such recommendation, or for any other reason fails (or has failed) to submit a non-deficient and non-defective Enrollment Form on or before the earlier of the date of service of the Certification of Final Enrollment and June 30, 2008, such Enrolling Counsel shall, on or before the earlier of June 30, 2008 and the 30th day after the date of service of the Certification of Final Enrollment . . . , to the extent permitted by the equivalents to Rules 1.16 and 5.6 of the ABA Model Rules of Professional Conduct in the relevant jurisdiction(s), (i) take (or have taken, as the case may be) all necessary steps to disengage and withdraw from the representation of such Eligible Claimant and to forego any Interest in such Eligible

Claimant and (ii) cause (or have caused, as the case may be) each other Enrolling Counsel, and each other counsel with an Interest in any Enrolled Program Claimant, which has an Interest in such Eligible Claimant to do the same.

Settlement Agreement Between Merck, Inc. and the Counsel Listed on the Signature Pages Hereto, Dated as of November 9, 2007, available at http://www.officialvioxxsettlement.com/documents/Master%20Settlement%20Agreement%20-%20new.pdf. As Merck's press release emphasizes, this deal is not a class action settlement. So, what is doing the "cramdown" work here to enforce the deal?

On the use of broadly similar arrangements outside the Vioxx litigation, see Nathan Koppel & Heather Won Tesoriero, *Pfizer Settles Lawsuits over Two Painkillers*, Wall St. J., May 3, 2008, at A3 (discussing settlements between Pfizer Inc. and plaintiffs' law firms representing "200 out of the thousands of people" who sued over the prescription pain medications Celebrex and Bextra).

B. REORGANIZATIONS IN BANKRUPTCY

To put the point mildly, bankruptcy law is a complex subject appropriately suited for coverage in a full-scale course in its own right. The treatment of bankruptcy here cannot possibly do justice to the richness of the subject. The materials that follow focus on one corner of the bankruptcy world that highlights the position of reorganizations in proximity to class settlements as a means of achieving closure with respect to related civil claims for damages. Developments like the decision in the Zyprexa litigation suggest that, in the post-*Amchem* period, there has been experimentation with aggregate settlements that effectively operate, in Judge Weinstein's apt phrasing, as a "quasi-class action." In effect, this involves a movement from class actions to the left within our continuum of aggregate litigation from Chapter 1—in the direction of private contract. Now, consider a significant additional development that moves to right along the continuum—in the direction of public legislation.

1. INTRODUCTION TO ASBESTOS–RELATED REORGANIZATIONS UNDER § 524 OF THE BANKRUPTCY CODE*

In 1982, the leading firm in the asbestos industry, Johns–Manville Corporation, filed for protection under Chapter 11 of the Bankruptcy Code. Six years later, Manville garnered final judicial approval for a reorganization plan that would create a separate legal entity—a trust fund—to handle asbestos claims against the firm. *Kane v. Johns–Manville Corp.*, 843 F.2d 636 (2d Cir. 1988). The Manville trust proved to be a perilous institution, however, with large numbers of claims quickly overwhelming its initial capitalization. This, in turn, precipitated dramatic markdowns in the payout levels originally described in the reorganization plan and repeated judicial interventions to prop up the finances of the trust.

The Manville proceedings took place under Chapter 11 of the Bankruptcy Code, 11 U.S.C. §§ 1101–74, which provides for reorganization of the

---

* This note and the one following it are adapted from a more extensive treatment in Richard A. Nagareda, MASS TORTS IN A WORLD OF SETTLEMENT ch. 9 (2007).

debtor corporation rather than liquidation under Chapter 7. The basic idea behind Chapter 11 is that creditors sometimes will be better off with the debtor able to continue in business rather than having its assets sold off in pieces. This justification for Chapter 11 has long been contested in the bankruptcy literature, with some scholars arguing that the case for reorganizations over liquidations is overstated. Douglas G. Baird, *The Uneasy Case for Corporate Reorganizations*, 15 J. Legal Stud. 127 (1986); Michael Bradley & Michael Rosenzweig, *The Untenable Case for Chapter 11*, 101 Yale L.J. 1043 (1992). Chapter 11 nonetheless remains a well-entrenched part of bankruptcy law.

The potential for the reorganization process to enhance the resources available for distribution to creditors helps to explain why the law does not insist upon a showing of insolvency as a precondition to the invocation of Chapter 11. Nor does use of Chapter 11 depend upon the kind of showing regarding the debtor's assets and liabilities that the *Ortiz* Court required for certification of a mandatory, limited-fund class action. The idea, instead, is that the debtor corporation may seek protection in bankruptcy at times before its situation has become so dire as to undermine the potential for substantial gains through reorganization. The relative strictness of the *Ortiz* opinion actually has the effect of protecting the terrain of Chapter 11 and the procedural strictures specified therein from intrusion by the class action device.

The major innovation of the Manville reorganization lay in measures designed, at least in theory, to enable asbestos claimants to benefit from the improvement that the reorganization itself would bring for Manville's business prospects. The centerpiece of the reorganization plan was its creation of a trust fund separate in the eyes of the law from Manville Corporation. A "channeling injunction" issued under the general equitable powers of the bankruptcy court under § 105(a) of the Code was supposed to confine both present and future asbestos claimants to seek compensation exclusively from the trust, thereby removing the cloud of mass tort liability from the reorganized Manville. The consequent improvement in Manville's business prospects, in turn, would enable the firm to continue as a "going concern" and thus provide an "evergreen" source of funding for future claimants. In addition to Manville's insurance proceeds, the principal sources of funding for the trust consisted of stock in the reorganized corporation and a right to receive up to 20 percent of its profits for as long as needed to compensate asbestos claimants. In effect, the funding package for the trust would make asbestos claimants the largest block of shareholders in the reorganized corporation.

The viability of the Manville trust turned crucially upon the willingness of financial markets to back the business ventures of the reorganized Manville Corporation. Open questions remained, however, concerning the legal basis for each of the matters central to the reorganization. That uncertainty stemmed, at bottom, from the design of the Bankruptcy Code with conventional business creditors in mind. Mass tort claimants, by contrast, stand to make demands upon the debtor that are likely to extend years into the future and, at the same time, that may be less readily amenable to valuation in the manner of conventional business debts.

The credibility of the Manville reorganization depended upon the existence of authority to confine future asbestos claimants to the resources in the trust. Yet, as the bankruptcy court itself acknowledged, considerable uncertainty remained over whether the category of "claims" dischargeable under the Bankruptcy Code encompasses future demands for compensation in tort. In the Manville proceedings, the bankruptcy court sought to finesse this issue, asserting that future tort claims were not actually being discharged but simply would be subject to the court's channeling injunction that would prevent them from suing the reorganized Manville. *In the Matter of Johns–Manville Corp.*, 68 B.R. 618, 628–29 (Bankr. S.D.N.Y. 1986). The scope of the channeling injunction itself—designed to shield not only the reorganized corporation but also those doing business with it—represented an expansive reading of the general equitable powers provided to the bankruptcy court by § 105(a).

The process for confirmation of the Manville reorganization plan also was unusual. By its terms, Chapter 11 provides for the confirmation of a reorganization plan in the face of objection from particular creditors "if such plan has been accepted by creditors . . . that hold at least two-thirds in amount and more than one-half in number of the allowed claims" within each creditor class impaired by the plan. 11 U.S.C. § 1126(c). The bankruptcy court for Manville, nonetheless, sought to avoid the need to value each pending asbestos claim as a prelude to reorganization. For purposes of voting, the court simply fixed at one dollar the value of each pending asbestos claim against Manville and deemed acceptance by those claimants to consist of an affirmative vote by two-thirds in number. *Johns–Manville*, 68 B.R. at 631. On appeal, the Second Circuit sidestepped the validity of this procedure, holding that any alleged violation of the Code specifications constituted harmless error. *Kane v. Johns–Manville Corp.*, 843 F.2d 636, 646–48 (2d Cir. 1988). The specifics of the voting process aside, the hard negotiations that produced the reorganization plan took place at the behest of a creditors' committee that included plaintiffs' lawyers representing the largest blocks of pending claims against Manville. To add to the innovations of the proceeding, the court also had appointed a separate representative for future asbestos claimants—commonly dubbed a "futures representative"—who did not himself have an inventory of pending claims.

The lingering uncertainty over each of the foregoing features—the treatment of future claims, the channeling injunction under § 105(a), the voting procedure, and the appointment of a futures representative—made for considerable drag on the ability of the Manville to garner the backing of investors after its reorganization. In the meantime, a second asbestos defendant, UNR Industries, had pursued a similar reorganization plan. Responding to pleas to set the legality of these reorganizations on a more secure footing, Congress added § 524(g) to the Bankruptcy Code in 1994. In substance, § 524(g) blessed retrospectively the major features of the Manville reorganization and, more importantly, set them as a model for future asbestos-related reorganizations.

Even § 524(g) does not lump future asbestos claims within the general category of "claims" dischargeable in bankruptcy. Congress instead created a separate category of "demands" that are not dischargeable claims at the time of the reorganization but that nonetheless arise "out of the same or similar conduct or events" that give rise to the reorganization. 11 U.S.C. § 524(g)(5). Section 524(g) goes on to authorize the use of a trust, separate from the reorganized debtor, to pay both present claims and future "demands." In turn, the trust must treat those demands "in substantially the same manner," insofar as they are "similar" in nature, apart from their timing. *Id.* § 524(g)(2)(B)(ii)(V). As a precondition for confirmation of such a trust arrangement, the bankruptcy court must appoint a separate futures representative, *id.* § 524(g)(4)(B)(i)—the counterpart in § 524(g) to what *Amchem* later would prescribe for representation in mass tort class actions.

Most significantly, § 524(g) also specifies the voting procedure for confirmation of an asbestos-related reorganization plan and the scope of the channeling injunction that gives it force. Confirmation of a reorganization plan under § 524(g) calls for satisfaction of the normal voting specifications under Chapter 11 plus—as a condition for the further protection of a channeling injunction—a favorable vote by at least 75 percent of "the claimants whose claims are to be addressed" by the trust to which the injunction channels claims. *Id.* § 524(g)(2)(B)(ii)(IV)(bb). Having carved out future claimants into the separate category of "demands," § 524(g) thus effectively affords bargaining power in its voting process to present claimants—a move in keeping with the goal of writing the Manville negotiations into law. As to the channeling injunction, § 524(g) sweeps broadly, authorizing the injunction to encompass not only the debtor corporation itself but also many kinds of third parties that form financial relationships with the debtor—through loans, insurance, or ownership of a financial interest, for example—as well as any "past or present affiliate" corporation. *Id.* § 524(g)(4)(A)(ii)–(iii).

For present purposes, the specifics of § 524(g) are less significant than the overarching premise behind them. In writing the Manville example into law, Congress proceeded from a fundamentally static conception of the reorganization process. Section 524(g) enshrines a process that had evolved, ad hoc, from negotiations concerning a debtor already in bankruptcy. The Manville bankruptcy petition had taken asbestos plaintiffs' lawyers by surprise, at which point all of the key players—Manville, its business creditors, asbestos plaintiffs' lawyers, and the bankruptcy court—faced the task of working out a reorganization plan. At the time of § 524(g), no one seems to have foreseen its effect upon the dynamics of peacemaking in the asbestos litigation. Section 524(g) would become not so much a framework for years of negotiation in bankruptcy—as in the Manville example—but, instead, a blueprint for how private negotiations might largely bypass the conventional reorganization process. The story of this transformation of bankruptcy is the story of pre-packaged reorganization plans for asbestos defendants in the aftermath of *Amchem*.

2. THE INTERSECTION OF § 524 REORGANIZATIONS AND CLASS SETTLEMENTS

It is far from unusual in the business world for creditors to work out their competing demands upon the resources of a debtor wholly outside of bankruptcy. In fact, when a corporation borrows heavily to finance the acquisition of another firm through a "leveraged buyout," creditors routinely put into place, in advance, financial arrangements designed to smooth the path for reorganization of the corporation in the event that it later encounters financial distress. Michael C. Jensen, A THEORY OF THE FIRM: GOVERNANCE, RESIDUAL CLAIMS, AND ORGANIZATIONAL FORMS 74–77 (2000). In many business settings, bankruptcy law stands simply as an off-the-rack set of procedures when the relevant players have not contracted in advance for some other arrangement.

Pre-packaged reorganization plans stand as an intermediate solution by comparison to arrangements that aspire to bypass bankruptcy entirely. Outside the mass tort context, conventional business creditors have used pre-packaged reorganizations since the mid–1980s. New Generation Research, Inc., THE 2004 BANKRUPTCY YEARBOOK& *Almanac* 163 (Christopher M. McHugh & Thomas A. Sawyer eds., 14th ed. 2004). Pre-packs entail invocation of the Bankruptcy Code, but they hold out the promise of a quicker, easier trip through its rigors based upon the working out in advance of a reorganization plan. Invocation of the Bankruptcy Code nonetheless remains essential, for it is what makes binding upon mass tort claimants the terms of the plan.

The bankruptcy of Manville and several other leading players in the asbestos industry added to the financial strain on the remaining asbestos defendants. The effect was to shift liability to the remaining solvent defendants in such a way as to increase the chances that those firms, too, eventually would seek protection in bankruptcy. Anup Malani & Charles Mullin, *Assessing the Merits of Reallocation under Joint and Several Liability, with an Application to Asbestos Litigation* (Dec. 21, 2004), *available at* http://www.law.virginia.edu/home2002/pdf/malani/asbestos.pdf.

Of the 73 asbestos-related bankruptcy filings from 1976 to 2004, more than half occurred after 1997—that is, in the period since *Amchem*. Stephen J. Carroll et al., *Asbestos Litigation* (2005). By the mid–2000s, pre-packaged reorganization plans under § 524(g) emerged as the most innovative technique for the resolution of asbestos claims in bankruptcy. Ronald Barliant et al., *From Free–Fall to Free-for-All: The Rise of Pre–Packaged Asbestos Bankruptcies*, 12 Am. Bankr. Inst. L. Rev. 441, 446 (2004). As pre-packaged reorganizations under § 524(g) proceeded forward, however, both the scholarly literature and the business press began to question the bargaining process behind them. Mark D. Plevin et al., *Pre–Packaged Asbestos Bankruptcies: A Flawed Solution*, 44 S. Tex. L. Rev. 883 (2003); Roger Parloff, *Tort Lawyers: There They Go Again!*, Fortune, Sept. 6, 2004, at 186; Alex Berenson, *A Caldron of Ethics and Asbestos*, N.Y. Times, Mar. 12, 2003, at C1, C22. These voices of criticism ultimately garnered support in a pathbreaking opinion from the Third Circuit concerning one of the most ambitious of the § 524(g) pre-packs. The excerpts that follow include much of the business background to the pre-pack so as to convey the transactional nature of the arrangement:

In re Combustion Engineering

391 F.3d 190 (3d Cir. 2004)

■ SCIRICA, CHIEF JUDGE.

This case involves twelve consolidated appeals from the District Court's order approving Combustion Engineering's bankruptcy Plan of Reorganization under 11 U.S.C. § 1101*et seq.* We will vacate and remand.

I.   Overview

For decades, the state and federal judicial systems have struggled with an avalanche of asbestos lawsuits. For reasons well known to observers, a just and efficient resolution of these claims has often eluded our standard legal process—where an injured person with a legitimate claim (where liability and injury can be proven) obtains appropriate compensation without undue cost and undue delay. See Fed. R. Civ. P. 1 (goal "to secure the just, speedy and inexpensive determination of every action"). . . .

Efforts to resolve the asbestos problem through global settlement class actions under Fed. R. Civ. P. 23(b)(3) and 23(b)(1)(B) have so far been unsuccessful. See *Amchem Prods. v. Windsor*, 521 U.S. 591 (1997) (affirming denial of class certification of nationwide settlement class of asbestos claimants); *Ortiz v. Fibreboard Corp.*, 527 U.S. 815 (1999) (reversing grant of class certification in limited fund class action under Fed. R. Civ. P. 23(b)(1)(B)). More than once, the Supreme Court has called on Congress to enact legislation creating a "national asbestos dispute-resolution scheme," but Congress has yet to act. *Amchem*, 521 U.S. at 598; *Ortiz*, 527 U.S. at 822.

For some time now, mounting asbestos liabilities have pushed otherwise viable companies into bankruptcy. The current appeal represents a major effort to extricate a debtor and two non-debtor affiliates from asbestos liability through a prepackaged Chapter 11 bankruptcy reorganization that includes 11 U.S.C. §§ 524(g) and 105(a) "channeling injunctions" and a post-confirmation trust fund for asbestos claimants. The Plan has been presented as a pre-packaged Chapter 11 reorganization plan, but it more closely resembles, in form and in substance, a liquidation of the debtor with a post-confirmation trust funded in part by non-debtors. Although pre-packaged bankruptcy may yet provide debtors and claimants with a vehicle for the general resolution of asbestos liability, we find the Combustion Engineering Plan defective for the reasons set forth.

A.   Combustion Engineering's Asbestos–Induced Bankruptcy

Combustion Engineering defended asbestos-related litigation for nearly four decades until mounting personal injury liabilities eventually brought the company to the brink of insolvency. In the fall of 2002, Combustion Engineering and its parent company, Asea Brown Boveri, Inc. ("U.S. ABB"), attempted to resolve Combustion Engineering's asbestos problems, as well as those of two U.S. ABB affiliates, ABB Lummus Global, Inc. and Basic, Inc., through a pre-packaged Chapter 11 bankruptcy reorganization.[4]

To this end, Combustion Engineering contributed half of its assets to a pre-petition trust (the "CE Settlement Trust") to pay asbestos claimants with pending lawsuits for part, but not the entire amount, of their claims. The remaining, unpaid portion of these claims, known as "stub claims," provided prepetition trust participants with creditor status under the Bankruptcy Code. Combustion Engineering then filed a prepackaged bankruptcy Plan of Reorganization under Chapter 11. The centerpiece of the Plan is an injunction in favor of Combustion Engineering that channels all of its asbestos claims to a post-confirmation trust (the "Asbestos PI Trust") created under § 524(g) of the Bankruptcy Code. The Plan also extends this asbestos liability shield to the non-debtor affiliates Basic and Lummus. Millions of dollars in cash and other assets have been offered to the post-confirmation trust by Combustion Engineering, Basic and Lummus, as well as their respective parent companies, U.S. ABB and ABB Limited, to compensate asbestos claimants and to cleanse the companies of asbestos liability.

---

[4] A pre-packaged (or "pre-pack") bankruptcy allows a debtor to obtain votes of its creditors on a plan of reorganization before actually filing a petition for Chapter 11 relief. At the time the debtor files for relief, it presents the bankruptcy court with a plan of reorganization and a tally of creditors' votes approving the plan. To gain approval, the plan must receive (1) a majority of votes by number by class and (2) two-thirds of votes weighted by the amount of allowed claims for that class. 11 U.S.C. § 1126(c). In addition, if, as here, the plan contains a § 524(g) channeling injunction, it must be approved by 75% of the debtor's current asbestos claimants by number. See 11 U.S.C. § 524(g)(2)(B)(ii)(IV)(bb).

After considerable negotiation, the Plan won approval from the majority of the asbestos claimants over the objections of several insurers and certain persons suffering from asbestos-related injuries. The Bankruptcy Court recommended confirmation of the Plan, but made two significant modifications. First, it added a "super-preemptory" provision to protect the pre-petition rights of certain insurers. Second, it reconfigured the § 524(g) injunction in favor of Basic and Lummus as an equitable injunction under § 105(a).

The District Court adopted the Bankruptcy Court's findings of fact and conclusions of law and confirmed the Plan with two changes. The District Court modified the language of the "super-preemptory" provision and added a "neutrality" provision purporting to protect the debtor's and insurers' prepetition rights under certain insurance policies.

B.   Issues Presented on Appeal

Although several difficult issues are presented on appeal, three are paramount. First, on the facts of this case, does the Bankruptcy Court have "related to" jurisdiction over the derivative and non-derivative claims against the non-debtors Basic and Lummus? Second, can a non-debtor that contributes assets to a post-confirmation trust take advantage of § 105 of the Bankruptcy Code to cleanse itself of non-derivative asbestos liability? Third, did the two-trust structure and use of "stub claims" in the voting process—which allowed certain asbestos claimants who were paid as much as 95% of their claims prepetition to vote to confirm a Plan under which they appear to receive a larger recovery than other asbestos claimants— comply with the Bankruptcy Code? Also implicated are issues involving appellate standing and the propriety of the voting process.

We summarize our holding. On the appellate standing issues, we conclude the Objecting Insurers and London Market Insurers have limited standing—that is, they only have standing to challenge the District Court's modification of the super-preemptory provision. On that issue, we will vacate the District Court's modification of the super-preemptory provision, and reinstate paragraph 17 of the Plan as initially drafted by the Bankruptcy Court. The Certain Cancer Claimants have standing to challenge Plan confirmation, including the propriety of the voting process, entry of the § 105(a) injunction in favor of Lummus (but not Basic), and issues relating to the validity of the two-trust structure.

Based in part on the lack of factual findings in support of "related to" subject matter jurisdiction, we will vacate the § 105(a) injunction in favor of non-debtors Basic and Lummus. As the Plan's proponents contend, and both the Bankruptcy Court and District Court found, extending the injunction to Basic and Lummus was essential to the Plan. As a practical matter, therefore, vacating the § 105(a) injunction defeats the proposed Plan of Reorganization. While we would normally remand for additional fact finding on the issue of subject matter jurisdiction, none is required here because the § 105(a) injunction must be rejected on substantive grounds as well. On the facts of this case, we hold the Bankruptcy Code precludes the use of § 105(a) to extend a channeling injunction to non-derivative third-party actions against a non-debtor.

With regard to the two-trust structure, we believe the pre-petition payments to the CE Settlement Trust participants and the use of stub claims to secure confirmation votes may violate the Bankruptcy Code and the "equality among creditors" principle that underlies it, requiring a remand to the District Court for further development and review in considering any revised reorganization proposal.

II. Background

A. Combustion Engineering

The story of Combustion Engineering sounds a familiar refrain in the asbestos world. From the 1930s through the 1960s, Combustion Engineering manufactured steam boilers containing asbestos insulation. The company was first named as a defendant in an asbestos-related lawsuit in the 1960s, and its asbestos liability increased steadily over the next thirty years. By the mid–1970s, Combustion Engineering was receiving a few hundred asbestos-related claims per year. That number grew to 19,000 annual cases by 1990, and jumped again to over 79,000 cases by 2002.

Declining insurance reimbursements over the same period exacerbated the financial strain on the company. Prior to the mid–1990s, two-thirds of Combustion Engineering's asbestos liability was covered by insurance. By 2002, some of the company's insurers took the position that only one-third of Combustion Engineering's asbestos liabilities were reimbursable. As a result, between 1990 and 2002 Combustion Engineering received only $517 million in insurance reimbursements for $950 million in asbestos-related liabilities. These factors left Combustion Engineering unable to meet its asbestos obligations without significant capital infusions from its parent corporation, U.S. ABB.

U.S. ABB acquired Combustion Engineering in 1990 in a leveraged buyout for $1.6 billion as part of a global acquisition of power technology companies by its parent company, ABB Limited, a diversified holding company of over 2,000 corporate entities based in Zurich, Switzerland. Between May 2000 and March 2002, U.S. ABB contributed $900 million in cash and other assets toward Combustion Engineering's asbestos obligations. By late 2002, Combustion Engineering's asbestos liability began to threaten ABB Limited's financial viability as well. ABB Limited had borrowed heavily to finance an aggressive global expansion during the 1990s. As these acquisition costs came due, ABB Limited faced a $1.5 billion debt repayment obligation in December 2002, followed by another $2.1 billion repayment obligation in 2003. At the same time, ABB Limited experienced falling demand in its core businesses and a debt downgrade that reduced the conglomerate's historical sources of liquidity. Significant debt obligations and Combustion Engineering's rising asbestos liabilities threatened ABB Limited's survival. With the conglomerate facing insolvency, ABB Limited's lenders demanded immediate action and insisted that ABB take steps to resolve Combustion Engineering's asbestos liabilities before extending additional credit. Some creditors threatened to institute an involuntary bankruptcy against U.S. ABB.

ABB Limited devised a divestment and restructuring program to resolve this financial crisis. ABB Limited's lenders determined that certain businesses should be sold as part of the restructuring program, including Lummus and the rest of the oil, gas and petrochemical division of ABB, of which Lummus was part. ABB's lenders purportedly determined these units could not be sold so long as Lummus carried asbestos liabilities. Therefore, ABB attempted to cleanse Lummus of asbestos-related liabilities before putting the company up for sale. In October 2002, Combustion Engineering and ABB began to formulate a voluntary Chapter 11 pre-packaged bankruptcy reorganization to cleanse not only Combustion Engineering, but also Basic and Lummus, of asbestos liability once and for all.

Combustion Engineering and ABB Limited communicated with several key players in the world of asbestos litigation to facilitate the design and implementation of a pre-pack plan, including an attorney to serve as advisor on the interests of current claimants, and the general counsel of the Johns–Manville trust and president of the Claims Resolution Management Corporation (which manages claims processing for the Johns–Manville trust) to represent the interests of future claimants.[8]

By late October 2002, the parties had negotiated the basic structure of a pre-packaged plan of reorganization. Combustion Engineering would place half its assets into a pre-petition settlement trust (the "CE Settlement Trust") to pay Combustion Engineering asbestos claimants who had claims in the legal system. Subsequently, Combustion Engineering, ABB Limited and several non-debtor subsidiaries of ABB Limited would contribute assets to a post-confirmation bankruptcy trust (the "Asbestos PI Trust") created under § 524(g) of the Bankruptcy Code. The pre-pack plan would release certain parties from asbestos liability, including Combustion Engineering, Basic and Lummus, by channeling asbestos claims against those entities to the post-confirmation bankruptcy trust.

B. The Master Settlement Agreement

The parties funded and implemented the pre-petition CE Settlement Trust through a Master Settlement Agreement on November 22, 2002. To fund the trust, Combustion Engineering contributed $5 million in cash, a promissory note in the principal amount of approximately $100 million, and a $402 million loan agreement between U.S. ABB as borrower and Combustion Engineering as lender payable on demand. ABB Limited guaranteed both the note and the loan. These contributions comprised approximately half of Combustion Engineering's total assets.

The District Court found that participation in the CE Settlement Trust was offered to all pre-petition claimants with claims pending against Combustion Engineering as of November 14, 2002. Participation was not expressly conditioned upon a vote in favor of the pre-pack Plan, although the Master Settlement Agreement provided that counsel for participating claimants would recommend, consistent with their ethical obligations, that each participating claimant accept the pre-pack Plan of Reorganization. Non-participating Combustion Engineering claimants were left to recover in the bankruptcy proceeding.

The Master Settlement Agreement initially provided for three categories of distribution from the CE Settlement Trust to current Combustion Engineering asbestos personal injury claimants, depending upon the status of their respective claims. Category One included claimants who had reached a final enforceable settlement with Combustion Engineering to be paid prior to November 15, 2002. Given the advanced stage of their respective settlement agreements, the Plan's proponents allegedly believed this group of claimants might force Combustion Engineering into involuntary bankruptcy if not paid immediately. Category One claimants were to receive 95% of their settled claim value. Category Two included claimants who also had satisfied all conditions and requirements for settlement with Combustion Engineering, but had settlement payments due after Novem-

---

[8] Mr. David Austern was appointed to act as future claims representative for Combustion Engineering under 11 U.S.C. § 524(g)(4)(B)(i). . . .

ber 14, 2002 and prior to March 1, 2003. Category Two claimants were to receive 85% of their settled claim value. Category Three provided a catch-all category for all otherwise eligible Combustion Engineering personal injury claimants who did not satisfy the requirements of Categories One or Two. Category Three claimants were to receive an initial payment of 37.5% of their settled claim value upon submission of certain required information, followed by a second payment not to exceed an additional 37.5% (for a maximum recovery of 75%) taken pro-rata from the CE Settlement Trust after all Category One and Two claims had been paid at the applicable rates.

Late in the pre-pack negotiations, 25,000–30,000 additional claimants qualifying for payment under the Master Settlement Agreement appeared. These claimants were concentrated in jurisdictions with historically high asbestos claims payment averages. Once these additional Combustion Engineering claimants were factored in, it became clear the existing pre-petition trust assets were insufficient to pay participating claims under the original payment terms. ABB Limited, therefore, agreed to contribute an additional $30 million in cash to the CE Settlement Trust to pay these newly identified claimants—designated as Category Four claimants—under the terms of a separate settlement agreement. The Category Four claimants agreed to accept less than 37.5% payment on their liquidated claim value, and to subordinate their right to any second payment to the other settling claimants.

In exchange for these payments, CE Settlement Trust participants agreed to forbear the prosecution of claims against Combustion Engineering outside of bankruptcy, but reserved the right to pursue the remainder of their claims in bankruptcy. These "stub claims" provided CE Settlement Trust participants with creditor status in bankruptcy, which allowed them to vote on the pre-pack Plan and share proportionally in the post-confirmation trust.

C.   The Pre–Pack Plan

Concurrent with the CE Settlement Trust negotiations, the claimants' representatives undertook a due diligence review of Combustion Engineering and its affiliates. This included an assessment of ABB Limited's financial condition and an examination of certain transactions between ABB entities and Combustion Engineering for evidence, among other things, of possible fraudulent transfers. In addition, the Combustion Engineering future claimants' representative, Mr. Austern, retained several advisors to determine the value of available insurance assets, the financial condition of ABB Limited, and its ability to contribute to the Asbestos PI Trust. Following this review, Mr. Austern insisted that ABB Limited augment its financial contributions to the Plan. The Official Committee of Unsecured Creditors likewise demanded several modifications to the trust distribution procedures. The parties settled on the final terms in January 2003.

The centerpiece of the pre-pack Plan involved an injunction in favor of debtor Combustion Engineering and non-debtors Basic and Lummus, channeling all asbestos-related claims against those companies to a single asbestos trust (the "Asbestos PI Trust") created under 11 U.S.C. § 524(g) and prohibiting claims other than against the Asbestos PI Trust (the "channeling injunction"). The parties agreed the post-confirmation trust would be funded by contributions from Combustion Engineering, ABB Limited, U.S. ABB, Lummus and Basic. The Bankruptcy Court found that under the Plan Combustion Engineering would contribute its rights to proceeds under certain insurance policies and settlement agreements with a face amount exceeding $320 million. It would also contribute $51 million in cash, future excess cash flows and a $20 million secured note convertible into 80% of the equity of the restructured entity. ABB Limited would contribute 30,298,913 shares of its common stock (with an estimated value of $82 million), $250 million in cash from 2004 to 2006, and an additional $100 million between 2006 and 2011, contingent in part on its future financial performance. This commitment was guaranteed by various ABB Limited affiliates. ABB Limited also agreed to release all claims and interests in insurance policies covering Combustion Engineering's asbestos personal injury claims. U.S. ABB agreed to indemnify all of Combustion Engineering's environmental liabilities (estimated at the time at more than $100 million), to release its indemnification rights against Combustion Engineering for asbestos claims asserted after June 30, 1999, and to contribute a $5 million Limited Carrier Indemnity. Contingent upon the sale of Lummus within eighteen months of the effective date of the Plan, U.S. ABB would make additional payments of $5 million to the Asbestos PI Trust and $5 million to the pre-petition CE Settlement Trust. In addition, U.S. ABB agreed to contribute almost $38 million, deposited into a segregated account, to pay asbestos claims attributed solely to Basic and Lummus. Basic and Lummus agreed to release and assign to the Asbestos PI Trust all of their rights to proceeds under insurance policies covering asbestos personal injury claims.

Distributions from the Asbestos PI Trust were governed by trust distribution procedures similar to those historically used by the Connecticut Valley Claims Service Company ("CVCSC") in servicing Combustion Engineering's asbestos claims. Combustion Engineering and the Asbestos PI Trust were given the exclusive right to determine whether to allow asbestos claims under the trust distribution procedures. Under the pre-pack Plan, participating insurers were therefore excluded from the Asbestos PI Trust's claims determination process.

D. Plan Voting and Approval

Solicitation for the pre-pack Plan began on or around January 22, 2003, when documents including a Disclosure Statement, the proposed Plan of Reorganization, a ballot, and letters from the current creditors' representative and futures' representative were sent to approximately 350 asbestos plaintiffs' counsel. These solicitations, seeking approval of the Plan, were extended to any firms representing plaintiffs with claims against Combustion Engineering, Basic or Lummus. The packages included both master and individual ballots. Master ballots for multiple claim holders required the agent casting the ballot to include a valid power of attorney, proxy, or other written evidence of agency for every Asbestos PI Trust claim holder identified on the ballot. CVCSC, Combustion Engineering's claims processing organization, or Trumbull Associates, Combustion Engineering's balloting agent, would communicate with any law firm that submitted a master ballot without a valid power of attorney.

Approximately 232,000 ballots were cast by the February 19, 2003 voting deadline, with 186,000 votes in favor of the Plan and 46,000 votes against. More than 107,908 of these ballots were not counted or were invalidated by Combustion Engineering's balloting agent because they were not accompanied by a valid power of attorney. An additional 8,432 ballots were invalidated for other reasons. Of the resulting 115,787 valid ballots, 111,986 Combustion Engineering claimants voted in favor of the Plan (approximately 97% of total remaining claimants) while 3,594 voted against. Of the 8,017 pending Lummus personal injury claims, 1,846 voted in favor of the Plan, and two voted against. Of the 3,715 pending Basic personal injury claims, 206 Basic claimants voted in favor of the Plan, and fourteen voted against. An estimated 99,000 of the tabulated votes appear to have been "stub claim" votes cast by CE Settlement Trust participants.

E. The Bankruptcy Court Proceedings

On February 17, 2003, Combustion Engineering filed a voluntary petition for bankruptcy relief under Chapter 11 of the Bankruptcy Code, along with a proposed Disclosure Statement and Plan of Reorganization, in the United States Bankruptcy Court for the District of Delaware. On March 31, 2003, this Court issued an order designating Judge Alfred M. Wolin as the district court judge and providing that the parties "will have an opportunity to be heard as to which aspects of the matter Judge Wolin will hear in the District Court and which matters will remain with . . . the Bankruptcy Court."

On May 9, 2003, Judge Wolin entered an order referring the case to the Bankruptcy Court. The order designated all matters to be adjudicated as part of Plan confirmation, including matters arising under 11 U.S.C. §§ 524(g) and 502(c), as non-core matters subject to de novo review and final order by the District Court.

The Bankruptcy Court conducted hearings on the Disclosure Statement and the Plan between April and June of 2003. Various parties objected to the Disclosure Statement, the Plan and the pre-pack solicitation procedures. Certain insurance companies argued that Plan provisions assigning policy proceeds to the Asbestos PI Trust violated existing policies and/or settlement agreements with Combustion Engineering. Other insurers who had negotiated pre-petition settlements with Combustion Engineering (the "Indemnified Insurers") objected to the Plan on the ground that it impermissibly channeled indemnities under the settlements to the post-confirmation trust without providing sufficient funding to pay those indemnities. As a result, the Indemnified Insurers argued they were entitled to vote on Plan confirmation. The Certain Cancer Claimants argued the Plan impaired their substantive rights to recover through the tort system.[15] The Bankruptcy Court allowed discovery on these objections, which resulted in several modifications to the proposed Plan and Disclosure Statement.

On June 23, 2003, the Bankruptcy Court entered findings of fact and conclusions of law regarding core matters, and proposed findings of fact and conclusions of law as to non-core matters. *In re Combustion Eng'g*, 295 B.R. 459 (Bankr. D. Del.2003). The Bankruptcy Court overruled all objections raised by the insurers and Certain Cancer Claimants as to core matters, and recommended the District Court overrule all remaining objections as to non-core matters. *Id.* at 462. The Bankruptcy Court found the trust distribution procedures provided the same protocol as the CVCSC previously used to adjudicate and pay asbestos claims, and therefore did "not change

---

[15] The Certain Cancer Claimants are 291 persons, or their legal representatives if deceased, suffering from cancers caused by exposure to asbestos contained in Combustion Engineering's products. All of the Certain Cancer Claimants are creditors of Combustion Engineering under § 101(10) of the Bankruptcy Code and are identified in a Bankruptcy Rule 2019 statement. In addition, some of the Certain Cancer Claimants hold independent claims against Lummus. Others still hold claims against both Combustion Engineering and Lummus. There is no indication in the record or the briefs of the parties that any of the Certain Cancer Claimants hold independent claims against Basic.

whatever rights the insurers had pre-petition regarding the payment of claims." *Id.* at 473. "Although the [trust distribution procedures] do not provide for insurers to have a say in what claims are paid . . . the insurers did not have such input pre-petition." *Id.* But recognizing the Plan should not modify the contractual rights of insurers, the court added a provision to make clear the Plan did not alter the contractual rights of insurers under any insurance policy or settlement agreement. The super-preemptory provision provided:

> [N]otwithstanding anything to the contrary in this Order, the Plan or any of the Plan Documents, nothing in this Order, the Plan or any of the Plan documents (including any other provision that purports to be preemptory or supervening), shall in anyway [sic] operate to, or have the effect of, impairing the insurers' legal, equitable or contractual rights, if any, in any respect. The rights of insurers shall be determined under the Subject Insurance Policies or Subject Insurance Settlement Agreements as applicable.

Id. at 494. The Bankruptcy Court explained, "the Plan has been modified to make clear that *nothing* impairs [the insurers'] rights." *Id.* at 474 (emphasis in original). As a result, the Bankruptcy Court concluded the Objecting Insurers did not have a right to vote on Plan confirmation because the Plan expressly stated that "the rights of insurers shall be determined under the subject insurance policies or subject insurance agreements as applicable and nothing in the Plan is to affect that." *Id.* The court also found there was "no litigation pending that would implicate the indemnities." *Id.* at 475.

The Bankruptcy Court further determined the Plan satisfied the confirmation requirements set forth in §§ 1129(a) and 524(g) of the Bankruptcy Code. The Bankruptcy Court noted that, as a practical matter, the Plan offered the only feasible mechanism for ensuring Combustion Engineering's creditors would receive any recovery. Moreover, the court found the purpose of negotiating the Master Settlement Agreement and CE Settlement Trust was to "buy immediate peace from thousands of asbestos lawsuits (pending and potential) against Combustion Engineering so that Combustion Engineering could file a prepackaged bankruptcy plan rather than face a freefall bankruptcy." *Id.* at 466. Contrary to the objections of the Certain Cancer Claimants, the Bankruptcy Court found that "[p]articipation in the [Master Settlement Agreement] was offered to all pre-petition claimants," and participation "was not conditioned upon a favorable vote on the proposed plan." *Id.* at 468.

With respect to the Asbestos PI Trust, the Bankruptcy Court concluded § 524(g)(4)(A)(ii) of the Code did not permit the inclusion of independent claims against non-debtors Basic and Lummus in the channeling injunction. But the Bankruptcy Court granted precisely the same relief—that is, channeling asbestos-related claims against Basic and Lummus to the Asbestos PI Trust—under § 105(a). Analyzing the factors announced in *In re Dow Corning Corp.*, 280 F.3d 648, 658 (6th Cir. 2002) ("*Dow Corning II*"), the Bankruptcy Court determined it was appropriate to enjoin the independent, non-derivative claims against Basic and Lummus under § 105(a).

In *Dow Corning II*, the Court of Appeals for the Sixth Circuit held that a bankruptcy court may permanently enjoin third-party claims against a non-debtor if seven factors are met:

> (1) there is an identity of interests between the debtor and the third party, usually an indemnity relationship, such that a suit

against the nondebtor is, in essence, a suit against the debtor or will deplete the assets of the estate;

(2) the nondebtor has contributed substantial assets to the reorganization;

(3) the injunction is essential to the reorganization, namely, the reorganization hinges on the debtor being free from indirect suits against parties who would have indemnity or contribution claims against the debtor;

(4) the impacted class, or classes, has overwhelmingly voted to accept the plan;

(5) the plan provides a mechanism to pay all, or substantially all, of the class or classes affected by the injunction;

(6) the plan provides an opportunity for those claimants who choose not to settle to recover in full[;] and . . .

(7) the bankruptcy court made a record of specific factual findings that support its conclusions.

In re Combustion Eng'g, 295 B.R. at 483 (citing *Dow Corning II*, 280 F.3d at 658).

The Bankruptcy Court concluded the injunction satisfied *Dow Corning II* factors one, two, three, six and seven. On the first factor, the court found Combustion Engineering shared an "identity of interest" with non-debtors Basic and Lummus because "ABB's need to sell Lummus . . . instigated ABB's willingness to contribute to Combustion Engineering's plan funding." *Id.* at 484. On factor two, the court found that Basic and Lummus contributed to the Asbestos PI Trust their rights to certain shared insurance policies. The court determined the injunction satisfied factor three because it allowed ABB to restructure its debt and contribute substantial assets to the post-confirmation trust. The court found the injunction satisfied factor six because the $38 million in assets segregated to pay Basic's and Lummus' asbestos liabilities was "sufficient to provide the opportunity to pay any non-accepting creditor." *Id.*

But the Bankruptcy Court initially held the Plan did not satisfy *Dow Corning II* factors four and five. The court concluded it was unclear from the record "what, if any, effort was made to identify, notify and solicit votes from creditors with claims only against Lummus and only against Basic; i.e., not shared with Combustion Engineering." *Id.* Likewise, the court did not believe the Plan provided the requisite funding and distribution processes to pay the direct creditors of Lummus and Basic. Therefore, despite its approval of the Disclosure Statement and Plan, as modified through June 4, 2003, the Bankruptcy Court recommended the District Court withhold confirmation for ten days to allow the Plan's proponents to provide additional information concerning the Basic and Lummus claimants. Specifically, the Bankruptcy Court ordered the Plan proponents to submit supplemental documentation showing that Basic and Lummus creditors were provided sufficient notification of the injunction, as well as establishing the process by which these creditors would be paid and identifying the source of funds.

On July 10, 2003, the Bankruptcy Court entered a Supplemental and Amendatory Order Making Additional Findings and Recommending Confirmation of the Plan of Reorganization. In its supplemental order, the Bankruptcy Court found, *inter alia*: the notice given to Lummus and Basic creditors comported with due process "under the unique circumstances of the case"; Basic claimants would receive more than they would receive without the Plan and Lummus claimants would receive at least as much as they would receive without the Plan; and the trust distribution procedures establish a sufficient method of paying Basic and Lummus claimants.

F.   District Court Proceedings and Plan Confirmation

In reviewing the Bankruptcy Court's proposed Findings of Fact and Conclusions of Law, the District Court acknowledged the proposed Plan of Reorganization was not without defect: "Today we consider for confirmation a pre-packaged bankruptcy plan. The plan is not perfect, but then we operate in an imperfect system and will substitute fairness and the greatest good for the greatest number for perfection." The District Court recognized the Plan was "fragile," and had to be confirmed "promptly to preserve ABB's economic viability." The District Court further explained that "[w]ere ABB to become insolvent, the possibility that Combustion Engineering could emerge as a reorganized debtor would be remote," as would the "prospect of a viable trust to pay persons suffering from exposure to Combustion Engineering's asbestos."

In an unpublished oral opinion, the District Court rejected or overruled objections to Plan confirmation. The District Court concluded the insurers lacked standing to object to Plan confirmation because their pecuniary interests were not "directly and adversely affected" by the order of the Bankruptcy Court. The court explained the super-preemptory provision added by the Bankruptcy Court made clear the insurers' pre-petition rights would not be altered by the Plan:

> [T]he plan specifically provides that payment of claims is subject to the rights of insurers under their policies or other agreements. Should the insurers claim that this provision [i.e., the super-preemptory provision] has been violated in the course of the administration of the personal injury trust, that will be the time to determine the rights of insurers in an appropriate proceeding.

Nonetheless, on the motion of the Future Claimants Representative and the Official Committee of Unsecured Creditors, the District Court modified the super-preemptory provision to state:

> Notwithstanding anything to the contrary in this Order, the Plan or any of the Plan Documents, nothing in this Order, the Plan or any of the Plan documents (including any other provision that purports to be preemptory or supervening), shall in any way operate to, or have the effect of, impairing the insurers' legal, equitable or contractual rights, if any, *in respect of any claims (as defined in Section 101(5) of the Bankruptcy Code).* The rights of insurers shall be determined under the Subject Insurance Policies or Subject Insurance Settlement Agreements, as applicable, *and under applicable law.*

(emphasis added to indicate changes). In addition, the District Court supplemented the super-preemptory provision with the following "neutrality provision":

> Nothing in the Plan or in the Confirmation Order shall preclude any Entity from asserting in any proceeding any and all claims, defenses, rights or causes of action that it has or may have under or in connection with any Subject Insurance Policy or any Subject Insurance Settlement Agreement. Nothing in the Plan or the Con-

firmation Order shall be deemed to waive any claims, defenses, rights or causes of action that any Entity has or may have under the provisions, terms, conditions, defenses and/or exclusions contained in the Subject Insurance Policies and the Subject Insurance Settlement Agreements, including, but not limited to, any and all such claims, defenses, rights or causes of action based upon or arising out of Asbestos PI Trust Claims that are liquidated, resolved, discharged, channeled, or paid in connection with the Plan.

The District Court provided no rationale for these modifications.

Proceeding to the substantive objections, the District Court found the pre-petition trust payments did not induce CE Settlement Trust participants to vote in favor of the Plan, and rejected the argument that the pre-petition payments and creation of the stub claims were intended to manufacture a confirming vote. Instead, the District Court concluded that Combustion Engineering created the stub claims because it had "insufficient funds to pay the settlement trust claimants 100 percent of their claims," and that the purpose of such payments was to provide Combustion Engineering "a little time, a breathing space, while the pre-packaged plan was negotiated." Moreover, the court found the votes of the stub claims were not invalid as a result of a Master Settlement Agreement provision prohibiting CE Settlement Trust participants from pursuing their stub claims outside of bankruptcy.

The District Court found the Plan satisfied all requirements of 11 U.S.C. § 1129. Specifically, the District Court found the Plan provided between two and three times more assets than would a Chapter 7 liquidation, satisfying the § 1129(a)(7) "best interests of the creditors" test. In so holding, the District Court rejected the argument that the pre-petition transfer of assets to the CE Settlement Trust constituted a voidable preference under § 547 of the Bankruptcy Code, reasoning that this argument was "simply a restatement of the argument already dispensed with by comparing the liquidation value of the company with the value paid to claimants under the plan." The District Court also found the Plan had been proposed in good faith under § 1129(a)(3).

The District Court rejected all challenges to the § 524(g) channeling injunction. The District Court found the contention that the Plan violated § 524(g) by treating present and future claimants differently was not supported by the record. Specifically, it found that all present claimants were free to participate in the Plan, and that the Asbestos PI Trust (from which future claimants would be paid) and the CE Settlement Trust employed substantially the same claims handling procedures. The court recognized that pre-petition settlement participants might receive more for their claims than non-participants, but reasoned this did not violate § 524(g) because these persons "simply were not similarly situated." The District Court also found the reorganized Combustion Engineering satisfied the "going concern" requirement of § 524(g) because it would own and operate a real estate business after emerging from bankruptcy. The court rejected the argument that § 524(g)(2)(B)(i)(II) required Combustion Engineering to pay dividends, instead concluding § 524(g) merely required any dividends the company in fact paid be included in future payments to the Asbestos PI Trust. The court found the fact that the Bankruptcy Court did not estimate the total value of all asbestos claims did not defeat Plan confirmation, noting the Plan did not prevent estimation of claims in the future, if feasible.

The District Court concluded the Bankruptcy Court correctly analyzed the application of § 105(a) under *Dow Corning II* and properly extended the channeling injunction to non-debtors Basic and Lummus. In support of this conclusion, the District Court found the non-debtors' asbestos liability was, in many cases, derivative of Combustion Engineering's asbestos liability, and the channeling injunction was integral to the Plan.

On the issue of jurisdiction over claimants with independent claims against the non-debtors, the District Court found the analysis of the § 105(a) injunction and the "related to" jurisdiction inquiry "substantially overlap." The court described a "unity of interest" between Combustion Engineering and the non-debtors that provided a basis for exercising "related to" jurisdiction over the independent claims against the non-debtors:

> Here we have corporate affiliates, shared insurance, even joint operations at single sites leading to the asbestos personal injury claims at issue. The premises on which the plan is based establish the extensive financial interdependence between the entities.

Having dismissed all appeals and overruled all objections to the Plan, the District Court affirmed and adopted the Bankruptcy Court's proposed findings of fact and conclusions of law, and confirmed Combustion Engineering's Plan of Reorganization.

G.   The Consolidated Appeals

Primary and excess insurers of Combustion Engineering, Lummus and Basic filed thirteen separate appeals challenging aspects of the District Court's confirmation order. The Certain Cancer Claimants filed a separate appeal. . . . The parties entered a stipulated "standstill agreement" to halt implementation of the Plan pending appeal before we could rule on those motions. . . .

III. Standing

. . . There are four groups of appellants in this case whose claims must be examined for purposes of appellate standing. The first group consists of the Objecting Insurers—those providing primary and excess insurance coverage to Combustion Engineering. The second group consists of the London Market Insurers—the insurers providing primary and excess insurance coverage for non-debtors Basic and Lummus. The third group is the Indemnified Insurers—insurance companies that entered pre-petition settlement agreements with Combustion Engineering to resolve contested coverage issues. Finally, the Certain Cancer Claimants consist of 291 individuals (or, if deceased, their legal representatives) who suffer from asbestos-related injuries. . . .

In sum, the Objecting Insurers and London Market Insurers have limited appellate standing to challenge the operation of the super-preemptory provision as modified by the District Court. The London Market Insurers also have standing to challenge those aspects of the Bankruptcy Court's order that purport to violate anti-assignment provisions in the primary and excess insurance policies of Basic and Lummus. The remaining issues raised by the Objecting Insurers and London Market Insurers do not directly and pecuniarily affect their rights under the insurance policies and settlements. Therefore we will dismiss the remaining challenges to Plan confirmation raised by the Objecting Insurers and London Market Insurers for lack of appellate standing. . . .

V. Section 105(a) Equitable Injunction

The Bankruptcy Court entered a channeling injunction under § 524(g) in favor of Combustion Engineering and also in favor of Basic and Lummus for their derivative asbestos-related claims. The court correctly found that § 524(g) did not authorize a channeling injunction over the independent, non-derivative third-party actions against non-debtors Basic and Lummus. To extend the channeling injunction to include the non-derivative claims against the non-debtors, the Bankruptcy Court relied upon its equitable powers under § 105(a).

Based on the facts here, we do not believe that § 105(a) can be employed to extend a channeling injunction to non-debtors in an asbestos case where the requirements of § 524(g) are not otherwise met. Because the injunctive action on independent non-derivative claims against non-debtor third parties in this case would violate § 524(g)(4)(A), would improperly extend bankruptcy relief to non-debtors, and would jeopardize the interests of future Basic and Lummus claimants, we will vacate the § 105(a) injunction.

A. The Requirements of Section 524(g)(4)(A)

Section 524(g) provides a special form of supplemental injunctive relief for an insolvent debtor facing the unique problems and complexities associated with asbestos liability. Channeling asbestos-related claims to a personal injury trust relieves the debtor of the uncertainty of future asbestos liabilities. This helps achieve the purpose of Chapter 11 by facilitating the reorganization and rehabilitation of the debtor as an economically viable entity. At the same time, the rehabilitation process served by the channeling injunction supports the equitable resolution of asbestos-related claims. In theory, a debtor emerging from a Chapter 11 reorganization as a going-concern cleansed of asbestos liability will provide the asbestos personal injury trust with an "evergreen" source of funding to pay future claims. This unique funding mechanism makes it possible for future asbestos claimants to obtain substantially similar recoveries as current claimants in a manner consistent with due process. To achieve this relief, a debtor must satisfy the prerequisites set forth in § 524(g) in addition to the standard plan confirmation requirements.

Importantly for this case, § 524(g) limits the situations where a channeling injunction may enjoin actions against third parties to those where a third party has derivative liability for the claims against the debtor:

> Notwithstanding the provisions of section 524(e), such an injunction may bar any action directed against a third party who is identifiable from the terms of such injunction (by name or as part of an identifiable group) and is alleged to be directly or indirectly liable for the conduct of, claims against, or demands on the debtor[.]

11 U.S.C. § 524(g)(4)(A)(ii). More specifically, the statute identifies the four circumstances under which such third-party liability will arise: "the third party's ownership of a financial interest in the debtor, a past or present affiliate of the debtor, or a predecessor in interest of the debtor," 11 U.S.C. § 524(g)(4)(A)(ii)(I); "the third party's involvement in the management of the debtor or a predecessor in interest of the debtor, or service as an officer, director or employee of the debtor or a related party," 11 U.S.C. § 524(g)(4)(A)(ii)(II); "the third party's provision of insurance to the debtor or a related party," 11 U.S.C. § 524(g)(4)(A)(ii)(III); or "the third party's in-

volvement in a transaction changing the corporate structure, or in a loan or other financial transaction affecting the financial condition, of the debtor or a related party." 11 U.S.C. § 524(g)(4)(A)(ii)(IV).

The Plan proponents do not contend that Basic and Lummus are "liable for the conduct of, claims against, or demands on" Combustion Engineering, as required by § 524(g)(4)(A)(ii). As the Bankruptcy Court correctly noted, "[t]he Debtor owned [Basic and Lummus]; they did not own Debtor." *In re Combustion Eng'g*, 295 B.R. at 482 n.41. Certain claims against Basic and Lummus allege independent liability, wholly separate from any liability involving Combustion Engineering. As the plain language of the statute makes clear, § 524(g)(4)(A) does not permit the extension of a channeling injunction to include these non-derivative third-party actions.

B.   Section 105(a)

Recognizing the limitations imposed by § 524(g), the Bankruptcy Court instead relied upon its equitable powers under § 105(a) to expand the scope of the channeling injunction. . . .

Section 105(a) of the Bankruptcy Code expressly provides bankruptcy courts the equitable power to "issue any order, process, or judgment that is necessary or appropriate to carry out the provisions of this title." 11 U.S.C. § 105(a). This section has been construed to give a bankruptcy court "broad authority" to provide equitable relief appropriate to assure the orderly conduct of reorganization proceedings. [*United States v. Energy Res. Co.*, 495 U.S. 545, 549 (1990)] ("[Section 105(a) is] consistent with the traditional understanding that bankruptcy courts, as courts of equity, have broad authority to modify creditor-debtor relationships.").

Nevertheless, the equitable powers authorized by § 105(a) are not without limitation, and courts have cautioned that this section "does not 'authorize the bankruptcy courts to create substantive rights that are otherwise unavailable under applicable law, or constitute a roving commission to do equity.'" [*Schwartz v.*] *Aquatic Dev. Group, Inc.*, 352 F.3d [671,] 680–81 [(2d Cir. 2003)] (citation omitted). Importantly for this case, § 105(a) does not "'give the court the power to create substantive rights that would otherwise be unavailable under the Code.'" *United States v. Pepperman*, 976 F.2d 123, 131 (3d Cir. 1992).

The general grant of equitable power contained in § 105(a) cannot trump specific provisions of the Bankruptcy Code, and must be exercised within the parameters of the Code itself. See generally *Norwest Bank Worthington v. Ahlers*, 485 U.S. 197, 206 (1988) ("Whatever equitable powers remain in the bankruptcy courts must and can only be exercised within the confines of the Bankruptcy Code."). When the Bankruptcy Code provides a specified means for a debtor to obtain a specific form of equitable relief, those standards and procedures must be observed. See *In re Fesco Plastics Corp.*, 996 F.2d 152, 154 (7th Cir. 1993) ("[W]hen a specific Code section addresses an issue, a court may not employ its equitable powers to achieve a result not contemplated by the Code."); *Resorts Int'l v. Lowenschuss (In re Lowenschuss)*, 67 F.3d 1394, 1402 (9th Cir. 1995) ("Section 105 does not authorize relief inconsistent with more specific law"); *In re Zale Corp.*, 62 F.3d [746,] 760 (5th Cir. 1995) ("A § 105 injunction cannot alter another provision of the [C]ode.").

Here, the Bankruptcy Court relied upon § 105(a) to achieve a result inconsistent with § 524(g)(4)(A). Although the Bankruptcy Court has broad equitable authority to craft remedies necessary to facilitate the reorganization of a debtor, this power is cabined by the Code. *Ahlers*, 485 U.S. at 206. As both the plain language of the statute and its legislative history make clear, § 524(g) provides no specific authority to extend a channeling injunction to include third-party actions against non-debtors where the liability alleged is not derivative of the debtor. Because § 524(g) expressly contemplates the inclusion of third parties' liability within the scope of a channeling injunction—and sets out the specific requirements that must be met in order to permit inclusion—the general powers of § 105(a) cannot be used to achieve a result not contemplated by the more specific provisions of § 524(g).

It also bears noting that the practical effect of the § 105(a) injunction here is to extend bankruptcy relief to two non-debtor companies outside of bankruptcy. While the § 105(a) injunction may facilitate Combustion Engineering's reorganization by permitting significant contributions by ABB Limited and its affiliates to the Asbestos PI Trust, it also allows Basic and Lummus to cleanse themselves of non-derivative asbestos liability without enduring the rigors of bankruptcy. Despite their own asbestos-related liabilities, there is no evidence that either Basic or Lummus need to reorganize under Chapter 11. If they do, as U.S. companies facing asbestos liabilities both Basic and Lummus could conceivably petition for Chapter 11 reorganization and injunctive relief from those liabilities under § 524(g). Although some asbestos claimants here may benefit from an augmented fund, equity does not permit non-debtor affiliated entities to secure the benefits of Chapter 11 in contravention of the plain language of § 524(g).

In addition, the use of § 105(a) to enjoin and channel the claims of future Basic and Lummus asbestos claimants may jeopardize the rights of those claimants. The several prerequisites set forth in § 524(g) are designed to protect the interests of future claimants whose claims are permanently enjoined. Among these, the plan must be approved by a super-majority of current claimants, and must provide substantially similar treatment to present and future claimants. Furthermore, the court must appoint a futures representative to act as fiduciary for the interests of future claimants. See 11 U.S.C. §§ 524(g)(2)(B)(ii)(IV)(bb), 524(g)(4)(B)(I), 524(g)(2)(B)(i)(V).

Neither court here made explicit findings whether the § 524(g) requirements were satisfied with respect to the channeling injunction as applied to the independent, non-derivative claims against Basic and Lummus. Nor did the Bankruptcy Court formally appoint a separate representative to act on behalf of future asbestos claimants asserting non-derivative claims against Basic and Lummus. There is some evidence in the record that Mr. Austern agreed to act in this capacity while also serving as the Combustion Engineering futures representative. But the interests of the future Basic and Lummus asbestos claimants are not necessarily aligned with those of future Combustion Engineering asbestos claimants. The future asbestos claimants of the non-debtors might prefer having recourse against solvent entities rather than being limited to proceeding against the Asbestos PI Trust, a limited fund subject to depletion by current and future Combustion Engineering asbestos claimants. As such, the channeling injunction against these future asbestos claimants may not have accorded them the requisite protections. We will vacate the Basic and Lummus channeling injunction because § 105(a) under these facts cannot be used to circumvent the more specific requirements of § 524(g).

VI. Two–Trust Structure

Eighty-seven days before filing its pre-pack bankruptcy, Combustion Engineering transferred more than $400 million in assets to the CE Settlement Trust to partially pay personal injury claims of participating Combustion Engineering asbestos claimants. At the time, the Plan proponents allegedly feared that claimants with settlements pending or awaiting payment would force Combustion Engineering into involuntary bankruptcy and stymie its reorganization effort. See *In re Combustion Eng'g*, 295 B.R. at 467 n.9. Accordingly, payments from the CE Settlement Trust were based upon the length of time a claimant's case had been pending. Claimants who had settled with Combustion Engineering and were awaiting payment received the greatest compensation (95% of the full liquidated value of their claim); claimants who had agreed to settlement or a dispute resolution process, and whose payment was due at a future date, received less (85%); a third, catch-all category of claimants received an initial payment of 37.5%, with the possibility, if sufficient funds remained, of later recovering up to 75%; and a fourth group of claimants, who came into the process late in the negotiations, agreed to a lesser sum. None of the participating Combustion Engineering claimants received full payment, and the remaining, unpaid portion of each claim was treated as surviving for purposes of bankruptcy creditor status. The surviving "stub claims" enabled CE Settlement Trust participants to vote on the reorganization Plan.

The Bankruptcy Court determined that payments from the CE Settlement Trust were designed "to compensate people who already had claims in the tort system or on file with [Combustion Engineering] and to provide [Combustion Engineering] with a reprieve from litigation." The District Court likewise determined the purpose of the CE Settlement Trust was to provide Combustion Engineering "a little time, a breathing space, while the pre-packaged plan was negotiated." The court reasoned the CE Settlement Trust only partially paid claims because "there were simply insufficient funds to pay the settlement trust claimants 100 percent of their claims," and not because the settling parties sought to "gerrymander" the vote. The District Court concluded that payments from the CE Settlement Trust did not induce participants to vote in favor of the Plan or otherwise manipulate the voting process.

The Certain Cancer Claimants lodge two primary objections to the two-trust structure. First, they contend it violates the Bankruptcy Code's "equality among creditors" principle because the CE Settlement Trust participants effectively receive greater compensation for their asbestos claims than similarly situated non-participants. Second, the Certain Cancer Claimants argue the funding of the CE Settlement Trust and creation of the stub claims violate the Code by "artificially impairing" the claims of participants in order to effect an impermissible manipulation of the voting process.

A. Discriminatory Treatment of Claims

"Equality of distribution among creditors is a central policy of the Bankruptcy Code." *Begier v. IRS*, 496 U.S. 53, 58 (1990). The Certain Cancer Claimants contend the Plan violates this principle, as well as the specific requirements of §§ 524(g)(2)(B)(ii)(V) and 547(b), because the two-trust structure provides the CE Settlement Trust participants with preferential treatment over non-participant asbestos personal injury claimants. The Plan proponents maintain this framework complies with the literal terms of the Code. Nonetheless, we believe the Combustion Engineering bankruptcy Plan may impermissibly discriminate against certain asbestos personal injury claimants. Because the record is inadequate to resolve the issue, we will remand for additional fact-finding.

The Bankruptcy Code furthers the policy of "equality of distribution among creditors" by requiring that a plan of reorganization provide similar treatment to similarly situated claims. Several sections of the Code are designed to ensure equality of distribution from the time the bankruptcy petition is filed. Section 1122(a) provides that only "substantially similar" claims may be classified together under a plan of reorganization. Section 1123(a)(4) requires that a plan of reorganization "provide the same treatment for each claim or interest of a particular class." And § 524(g) states that "present claims and future demands that involve similar claims" must be paid "in substantially the same manner."

To complement these provisions, which address the treatment of claims post-petition, § 547 operates to ensure that equality among creditors is not undermined by transfers to creditors in contemplation of bankruptcy. Section 547(b) provides that a bankruptcy trustee may avoid any transfer by the debtor:

> (1) to or for the benefit of a creditor;
>
> (2) for or on account of an antecedent debt owed by the debtor before such transfer was made;
>
> (3) made while the debtor was insolvent;
>
> (4) made—
>
>> (A) on or within 90 days before the date of the filing of the petition; . . . and
>
> (5) that enables such creditor to receive more than such creditor would receive if—
>
> (A) the case were a case under chapter 7 of this title; [and]
>
> (B) the transfer had not been made . . .

11 U.S.C. § 547(b).

Section 547(b) furthers equality of distribution among creditors by preventing the debtor from favoring one creditor or group of creditors over others by transferring property shortly before filing for bankruptcy. The Supreme Court has noted the preference avoidance rule contained in § 547 serves an important purpose in managing the debtor-creditor relationship:

> A preference is a transfer that enables a creditor to receive payment of a greater percentage of his claim against the debtor than he would have received if the transfer had not been made and he had participated in the distribution of the assets of the bankrupt estate. . . . [T]he preference provisions facilitate the prime bankruptcy policy of equality of distribution among creditors of the debtor. Any creditor that received a greater payment than others of his class is required to disgorge so that all may share equally.

Union Bank v. Wolas, 502 U.S. 151, 160–61 (1991) (citing H.R. Rep. No. 95–595 at 177–78 (1977)).

Based on the record, we believe the pre-petition payments to the CE Settlement Trust may constitute voidable preferences. Eighty-seven days before filing for bankruptcy, while the company was insolvent, Combustion Engineering transferred payment for outstanding asbestos liability to a group of CE Settlement Trust participants who received up to 95% of their claim value—far more than they would have received in a Chapter 7 liquidation had no transfer been made. This suggests that the payments to the settlement trust satisfy at least four of the five criteria under § 547(b).

Prior to filing for bankruptcy, Combustion Engineering transferred over $400 million, or approximately half of its assets, to the CE Settlement Trust for the benefit of participating asbestos claimants, who were then creditors of Combustion Engineering. 11 U.S.C. § 547(b)(1). As such, partial payments from the CE Settlement Trust constituted payments for antecedent debts owed by the debtor. 11 U.S.C. § 547(b)(2). Moreover, Combustion Engineering was insolvent when it funded the pre-petition trust on November 22, 2002, and its petition for voluntary Chapter 11 bankruptcy was filed on February 17, 2003—eighty-seven days after funding the CE Settlement Trust. 11 U.S.C. § 547(b)(3) and 11 U.S.C. § 547(b)(4).

The only remaining issue is whether the assets transferred to the CE Settlement Trust entitled participants in that Trust to receive more than they otherwise would have received in a Chapter 7 liquidation. 11 U.S.C. § 547(b)(5). Crediting the liquidation analysis conducted by Pamela Zilly, senior managing director of the Blackstone Group, and testimony by Mr. Austern, the Bankruptcy Court concluded the Plan would pay more to future claimants than would be paid under a Chapter 7 bankruptcy or no bankruptcy at all. See *In re Combustion Eng'g*, 295 B.R. at 488. Specifically, the Bankruptcy Court found the assets available to Combustion Engineering in Chapter 7 would be between $210 and $250 million, while assets available under the Plan would be between $640 and $789 million as a result of the additional contributions by ABB Limited and other non-debtors. *Id.* at 485–86. The District Court likewise dismissed the argument that the pre-petition transfer constituted a voidable preference:

> [T]he allegation that the establishment of the settlement trust was a voidable preference is simply a restatement of the argument already dispensed with by comparing the liquidation value of the company with the value paid to claimants under the plan. Without the settlement trust, there would be no plan. It has already been established that future claimants will fare better with the plan than without it.

This analysis was incorrect as a matter of law because a comparison of the funds available for future claimants is not the proper inquiry. Section 547(b)(5) refers to transfers for the "benefit of a creditor" that "enables such creditor to receive more than such creditor would receive if (A) the case were a case under chapter 7 of this title; (B) the transfer had not been made; and (C) such creditor received payment of such debt to the extent provided by the provisions of this title." 11 U.S.C. § 547(b)(5). As this provision specifies, the relevant question is whether the CE Settlement Trust participants—not the future claimants—received more or less than they would have received under Chapter 7 if the pre-petition payments had not been made.

The record suggests that pre-petition settlement participants received more for their asbestos claims than they would have received in a Chapter 7 liquidation. The CE Settlement Trust paid participants up to 95% of their claim value, and, according to the Certain Cancer Claimants' expert, provided an average payout to participants of 59%. A Chapter 7 liquidation, in contrast, may have yielded an average payout to asbestos claimants of significantly less, perhaps 28% of their claim value.[54] Were this disparity established as a matter of fact, the CE Settlement Trust preferences would be voidable under § 547(b).

The pre-petition transfer in this case also implicates the fundamental bankruptcy policy of "equality of distribution among creditors." In this regard, we consider the bankruptcy scheme as an integrated whole in order to evaluate whether Plan confirmation is warranted. Viewing the Combustion Engineering pre-pack bankruptcy as a whole, the record reveals that it may lack the requisite equality of distribution among creditors. The Plan, as it relates to asbestos claimants, consists of two elements: the pre-petition CE Settlement Trust and the post-petition Asbestos PI Trust.[56] Under this interdependent, two-trust framework, the Certain Cancer Claimants, the future asbestos claimants, and other non-parties to the pre-petition settlement appear to receive a demonstrably unequal share of the limited Combustion Engineering fund. The Certain Cancer Claimants' expert testified that while CE Settlement Trust participants recover, on average, 59% of the liquidated value of their claims, future claimants would recover 18% of the liquidated value of their claims under the Asbestos PI Trust. This disparity, if in fact it exists, is even more striking when considering that Category One claimants in the CE Settlement Trust received 95% of the liquidated value of their claims. But neither the District Court nor the Bankruptcy Court made findings with respect to the recovery of CE Settlement Trust participants relative to non-participating asbestos claimants.

Additionally, there are two considerations here that are absent in the ordinary commercial bankruptcy: the Plan's treatment of current asbestos claimants relative to future asbestos claimants, and its treatment of malignant asbestos claimants relative to non-malignant asbestos claimants.[57] The Certain Cancer Claimants challenge the disparate treatment of current and future asbestos claimants under the two-trust structure, and also whether the most seriously injured asbestos claimants received fair treatment under the Plan. Again, the record is insufficient to rule on these contentions. Neither the Bankruptcy Court nor the District Court evaluated the CE Settlement Trust's treatment of current, future, malignant and non-malignant asbestos claimants, or evaluated the overall Plan from the perspective of settlement participants versus non-participants and malignant versus non-malignant asbestos claimants. Even absent the Plan's other de-

---

[54] Combustion Engineering's assets were between $800 million and $1 billion prior to the pre-petition settlement. With respect to Combustion Engineering's outstanding asbestos liability, the Certain Cancer Claimants' expert, Dr. Timothy Wyant, estimated it to be approximately $3.6 billion. The Plan proponents contest the methodology employed by Dr. Wyant in arriving at this figure, and the Bankruptcy Court did not credit his testimony. But neither the Bankruptcy Court nor the District Court adopted contrary findings. Assuming Dr. Wyant's estimate is correct, asbestos claimants would have recovered, at most, an average of 28% ($1 billion in assets divided by $3.6 billion in liability) of their claim value in a Chapter 7 liquidation.

[56] The record establishes that the CE Settlement Trust was a necessary element of the overall reorganization Plan. The parties entering the pre-petition settlement expressly contemplated the subsequent reorganization; the settlement itself provided that participating counsel "recommend to each Participating Claimant the acceptance of a CE Plan of Reorganization"; and the "stub claims" represent a direct link between the pre-petition trust and the reorganization vote.

[57] See generally *Ortiz*, 527 U.S. at 854–55 (emphasizing that a limited-fund asbestos settlement must provide for "equity among members of the class" and "fairness of the distribution of the fund among class members"). Though *Ortiz* was decided under Fed. R. Civ. P. 23(b)(1)(B), the Court's requirement of fair treatment for all claimants—a principle at the core of equity—also applies in the context of this case.

fects, the two-trust structure requires a remand for further findings on these issues.

B.   Creation of the "Stub Claims"

The Certain Cancer Claimants contend the CE Settlement Trust "artificially impaired" or contrived the stub claims in order to garner sufficient votes in favor of confirmation. As a condition of plan confirmation, the court must find "at least one class of claims that is impaired under the plan has accepted the plan, determined without including any acceptance of the plan by any insider." 11 U.S.C. § 1129(a)(10). A claim is not impaired if the plan "leaves unaltered the legal, equitable, and contractual rights to which such claim or interest entitles the holder of such claim or interest" or if the plan cures or compensates for past default. 11 U.S.C. § 1124(1). "Artificial" impairment occurs when a plan imposes an insignificant or de minimis impairment on a class of claims to qualify those claims as impaired under § 1124. The chief concern with such conduct is that it potentially allows a debtor to manipulate the Chapter 11 confirmation process by engineering literal compliance with the Code while avoiding opposition to reorganization by truly impaired creditors. While there is nothing in either §§ 1129(a)(10) or 1124 expressly prohibiting a debtor from "artificially impairing" the claims of creditors, courts have found this practice troubling.

In the context of this asbestos-related bankruptcy, so do we. Unlike the ordinary commercial bankruptcy, where stub claims may be used to facilitate a workout plan in the overall best interests of creditors, the use of stub claims in this case may constitute "artificial impairment" under § 1129(a)(10).

"The purpose of [§ 1129(a)(10)] is 'to provide some indicia of support [for a plan of reorganization] by affected creditors and prevent confirmation where such support is lacking.'" *In re Windsor on the River Assocs.*, 7 F.3d [127,] 131 [(8th Cir. 1993)]. As such, § 1129(a)(10) requires that a plan of reorganization pass muster in the opinion of creditors whose rights to repayment from the debtor are implicated by the reorganization. By providing impaired creditors the right to vote on confirmation, the Bankruptcy Code ensures the terms of the reorganization are monitored by those who have a financial stake in its outcome. Bankruptcy provides a framework for the consensual and cooperative reorganization of an insolvent debtor, and "stub claims" negotiated pre-petition may play a role in this process.

But in this case, Combustion Engineering made a pre-petition side arrangement with a privileged group of asbestos claimants, who as a consequence represented a voting majority despite holding, in many cases, only slightly impaired "stub claims." On the facts here, the monitoring function of § 1129(a)(10) may have been significantly weakened. *See generally John Hancock Mut. Life Ins. Co. v. Route 37 Bus. Park Assocs.*, 987 F.2d 154, 158 (3d Cir. 1993) (stating § 1129(a)(10) "would be seriously undermined if a debtor could gerrymander classes"). This type of manipulation is especially problematic in the asbestos context, where a voting majority can be made to consist of non-malignant claimants whose interests may be adverse to those of claimants with more severe injuries. *See* Stephen J. Carroll, et al., Asbestos Litigation Costs and Compensation: An Interim Report 46 (RAND 2002) (reporting that non-malignant claimants typically represent 80% to 90% of outstanding asbestos claims); S. Elizabeth Gibson, *Symposium– Mass Torts: A Response to Professor Resnick: Will This Vehicle Pass Inspection?*, 148 U. Pa. L.Rev. 2095, 2112 (2000) ("A distinct minority—for example, those tort claimants with especially serious injuries and strong cases—

might get outvoted by a large number of holders of small claims who favor a quick pay-out of relatively small amounts with little proof required.").[62]

Here, Combustion Engineering made pre-petition payments to current asbestos claimants that exceeded any recovery obtainable by other current asbestos claimants (such as the Certain Cancer Claimants) in bankruptcy. As a result, the CE Settlement Trust participants, many of whom received as much as 95% of the full liquidated value of their claims pre-petition, had little incentive to scrutinize the terms of the proposed Plan. Rather, their incentive appears to have been otherwise, given that the favorable pre-petition settlements were conditioned, at least implicitly, on a subsequent vote in favor of the Plan.

Furthermore, the Plan initially provided a release for all avoidance and/or preference actions against participants in the CE Settlement Trust. Although the release was subsequently removed from the Plan, this did not occur until after the solicitation and voting process was completed. Thus, when participants in the pre-petition CE Settlement Trust voted on the Plan, they possessed a significant financial incentive directly opposed to nonparticipants, whose only recourse was to the post-petition Asbestos PI Trust. This conflict was not considered by either the Bankruptcy Court or the District Court. In these circumstances, Combustion Engineering's use of stub claims may constitute "artificial impairment" in violation of § 1129(a)(10).

The Combustion Engineering stub claims also implicate due process. In the resolution of future asbestos liability, under bankruptcy or otherwise, future claimants must be adequately represented throughout the process. *Amchem*, 521 U.S. at 625–28; *Ortiz*, 527 U.S. at 856; 11 U.S.C. § 524(g)(4)(B)(i). Here, the first phase of the integrated, global settlement—the establishment of the CE Settlement Trust—included neither representation nor funding for future and other non-participating claimants.

Had the future and other non-participating asbestos claimants been adequately represented throughout the reorganization process, including the CE Settlement Trust negotiations, then perhaps the corresponding stub claims would demonstrate the "indicia of support by affected creditors" required under § 1129(a)(10). But they were not. Instead, as discussed, a disfavored group of asbestos claimants, including the future claimants and the Certain Cancer Claimants, were not involved in the first phase of this integrated settlement. The result was a Plan ratified by a majority of "stub votes" cast by the very claimants who obtained preferential treatment from the debtor. As noted, an estimated 99,000 of the approximately 115,000 "valid" confirmation votes appear to have been stub claim votes. Given this structural inadequacy, *see Ortiz*, 527 U.S. at 855–57, the Plan may have lacked the requisite "indicia of support" among creditors. We recognize that stub claims are often used in ordinary commercial bankruptcies without generating the problems described here. But in this case, their use is problematic. We will remand for further consideration of "artificial impairment" under § 1129(a)(10).

Additionally, the Certain Cancer Claimants contend that the use of stub claims within a two-trust framework violates the good faith require-

---

[62] There is evidence in the record that Combustion Engineering's asbestos liability profile mirrors nationwide trends, and that a majority of Combustion Engineering claimants suffer from non-malignant injuries. But the record does not establish the precise breakdown, by disease category, of either Combustion Engineering claimants as a whole or CE Settlement Trust participants.

ment of the Bankruptcy Code. As a condition of plan confirmation, a debtor must propose a plan of reorganization "in good faith and not by any means forbidden by law."[67]11 U.S.C. § 1129(a)(3). Courts and commentators have recognized the good faith requirement provides an additional check on a debtor's intentional impairment of claims. See *In re Greate Bay Hotel & Casino, Inc.*, 251 B.R.[213,]240 [(Bankr. D.N.J. 2000)] ("Of course, the classification and treatment of classes of claims is always subject to the good faith requirements under § 1129(a)(3)."); see also 7 Collier on Bankruptcy ¶ 1129.03[10], at 1129–62 (15th ed. rev.2000) ("Because the test of [§ 1129(a)(10)] is somewhat mechanical on its face, and thus would not under a plain meaning analysis permit of an inquiry into motive, courts have indicated that attempts to manufacture artificially, or to gerrymander, classes to obtain an accepting impaired non-insider class raise questions of good faith."). Although the Code does not define "good faith" in the context of § 1129(a)(3), we have stated that "[f]or purposes of determining good faith under section 1129(a)(3) . . . the important point of inquiry is the plan itself and whether such a plan will fairly achieve a result consistent with the objectives and purposes of the Bankruptcy Code." *In re PWS Holding Corp.*, 228 F.3d [224,] 242 [(3d Cir. 2000)] (citing *In re Abbotts Dairies of Pa., Inc.*, 788 F.2d 143, 150 n. 5 (3d Cir. 1986)).

Both the Bankruptcy Court and District Court found the Plan satisfied the good faith requirement of § 1129(a)(3). In rejecting the proposition the Plan had been proposed in bad faith, the District Court concluded "it cannot be seriously argued that the good faith requirements of section 1129 would bar a plan intended to pay victims and resolve crippling and uncertain tort liabilities." The District Court found Combustion Engineering created the stub claims merely to purchase "a little time, a breathing space," and because "there were simply insufficient funds to pay the settlement trust claimants 100 percent of their claims."

The District Court also found the purported goal of the Plan in paying asbestos claimants and definitively resolving the asbestos liabilities of the debtor was consistent with the objectives of the Bankruptcy Code. The Certain Cancer Claimants contend the purpose of the two-trust framework was to secure improperly the required confirmation votes from a privileged group of claimants at the expense of the future and other non-participating claimants. We will remand for further consideration of good faith in light of the issues we have identified with the two-trust structure.

NOTES AND QUESTIONS

1.   *The Aftermath of* Combustion Engineering. In 2005, Combustion Engineering negotiated a modified reorganization plan with those who had successfully challenged the original plan. The centerpiece of the modified plan consisted of an additional infusion of $204 million from the ABB Group to fund the § 524(g) trust for future claimants. *In re Combustion Engineering*, No. 03–10495–JKF, at 17 (Bank. D. Del. Dec. 19, 2005), *aff'd* Misc. No. 06–21(JEI) (D. Del. Mar. 1, 2006).

The availability of these additional resources was itself a product of the time that the ABB Group effectively had bought with the original reorganiza-

---

[67] There are numerous "good faith" requirements associated with the bankruptcy reorganization process. In addition to § 1129(a)(3), a court may "designate" (i.e., disqualify from voting) the ballot of "any entity whose acceptance or rejection" of the plan "was not in good faith, or was not solicited or procured in good faith." 11 U.S.C § 1126(e). . . .

tion plan and the period of wrangling over its validity. By 2005, the ABB Group stood "in a far more financially secure position in comparison to its status in 2003," having staved off the distress that had precipitated the Combustion Engineering pre-pack in the first place. *Id.* at 28.

The $204 million infusion from the ABB Group enabled plan proponents to persuade the bankruptcy court that future claimants and pending ones would be treated equitably under the modified plan, with each group of claims now expected to be paid 45–48 percent of their value. *Id.* at 4, 33. The modified plan included modestly beefed-up medical criteria, providing that "all diagnoses must be based upon a physical examination of the claimant by the physician providing the diagnosis" and imposing specifications for the professional qualifications of physicians diagnosing asbestos-related disease. *Id.* at 19. For cancer claimants, the modified plan adjusted its payment ratios so that those claimants would receive a dramatically higher percentage of their value than non-malignant cases. *Id.*

Still, the central structural problem of the original plan—the two-trust format—remained. The modified plan deemed the settlement trust to be the sole source of compensation for pending claimants with stubs, such that they now would be ineligible for additional payment from the § 524(g) trust. In effect, the modified plan wiped out the value of the stubs. But that move, in itself, "change[d] the expectations" of claimants who had participated in the settlement trust, thereby "entitling them to vote"—just like before—on the confirmation of the modified reorganization plan for future claimants. *Id.* at 22. That vote, like the first, went overwhelmingly in favor of the modified plan. The bankruptcy court and district court that had confirmed the original reorganization plan not surprisingly confirmed the modified one. And, this time, no one appealed.

Would the revised reorganization plan have passed muster under the Third Circuit's reasoning? Does the ultimate confirmation of the modified plan mean that the Third Circuit's earlier decision was largely ineffectual?

2. The Futures Representative. Does the Third Circuit's decision suggest that the problem with the § 524(g) reorganization process lies with the futures representative? David Austern, who served in that capacity in *Combustion Engineering*, was neither a neophyte nor a shill. Quite to the contrary, he was widely regarded as a person of considerable integrity and expertise in the asbestos litigation, having served as the administrator of the Manville Trust. But by the time Austern came on the scene, what was there left for him to do on behalf of future claimants?

Eight of the eleven pre-packs initiated through 2005 involved futures representatives who previously served, or would serve, in the same capacity in other asbestos-related reorganizations—in several instances, other pre-packs. Nagareda, *Mass Torts in a World of Settlement*, 178. Why would there be such prevalent use of "repeat players" in this regard? Recall Justice Breyer's dissent in *Ortiz*, in which he questioned where exactly one would find experienced lawyers on the plaintiffs' side of the asbestos litigation who somehow did not have vast inventories of present-day clients.

Does the reasoning in *Combustion Engineering* shed doubt on the core prescription offered by *Amchem* and *Ortiz*—namely, separate representation of future mass tort claimants?

3. *The Further Adventures of* Amchem *Class Counsel.* To whom did the ABB Group turn when seeking to craft a reorganization plan that would make for a quick trip in and out of bankruptcy under § 524(g)? None other than Joe Rice, one of the asbestos plaintiffs' lawyers who earlier had served as class counsel in *Amchem.* For his efforts in the design of the Combustion Engineering pre-pack, Rice stood to gain a "success fee" in the same amount—$20 million—as Sulzer had offered Richard "Dickie" Scruggs to garner support for the hip implant class settlement discussed in Chapter 4.

Is there anything problematic about Rice's retention to design the Combustion Engineering pre-pack? One asbestos claimant whose rights stood to be governed by the plan went so far as to sue Rice for breach of fiduciary duty. A federal district court dismissed the lawsuit, however. *Pope v. Rice*, 2005 WL 613085 (S.D.N.Y. 2005). The court concluded that Rice owed no fiduciary duty to claimants, like the plaintiff Pope, who had not retained him as their lawyer and who remained represented by other members of the asbestos plaintiffs' bar. Why didn't Rice's own clients sue him? Does the answer to that question shed light on the alleged breach of fiduciary duty in *Pope?*

4. *Final Injunctive Order Barring Direct Claims against Non–Debtor Third Party Immune from Collateral Attack.* In 2009, the U.S. Supreme Court addressed litigation relating to the anti-suit injunction issued by the Manville bankruptcy court in 1986. *Travelers Indemnity Co. v. Bailey*, 557 U.S. 137 (2009). The occasion for it to do so arose when asbestos victims sued Travelers, arguing that it was directly liable to them for misconduct it committed when defending Manville in asbestos cases. Travelers sought an injunction from the bankruptcy court on the ground that the 1986 anti-suit injunction barred direct lawsuits against it as well as actions asserting derivative liability for Manville's misconduct. Following mediation, in which Travelers agreed to pony up $400 million, the bankruptcy court issued a clarifying order explaining that the 1986 order did bar the direct claims. On appeal, the Supreme Court held that the 1986 order was final. Therefore, the bankruptcy court's jurisdiction to issue that order could no longer be challenged, either directly or in collateral actions. The majority then held that the 1986 order barred direct actions against Travelers, even though it was a non-debtor third party, and that the clarifying order was both correct and within the bankruptcy court's continuing jurisdiction to enforce the 1986 order.

C. GOVERNMENT AS PLAINTIFF

Recall the suggestion in Chapter 1 that procedures for aggregating civil claims can be understood, at least in part, as responses to the need for mass governance of related claimants. The principal responses of class action law consist of governance first by class counsel (in rare instances, with help from the class representative) and, second, through third-party regulation in the form of judicial review (principally, at the class certification and class settlement approval stages). Insofar as these governance mechanisms may be vulnerable precisely because of their one-shot, this-litigation-only nature, then why not rely on an ongoing regime for governance in the aggregate—namely, government itself? Or does the notion of the government litigating alleged wrongdoing, in some fashion, on the behalf of many of its citizens replicate the problems seen in private, aggregate litigation? Is the government a more adequate representative than an experienced, well-capitalized plaintiffs' law firm? What happens when the citizenry is of different minds about the harm and the remedy?

One government role along the foregoing lines is fairly easy to discern. The government might sue to enforce the terms of regulatory requirements promulgated by public administrative agencies. These enforcement actions and the framework for challenges to them on the part of regulated persons or entities form the stuff of courses on administrative law and the major subject areas of the modern administrative state (food and drug law, securities law, employment discrimination law, antitrust law, and the like). As we have seen already, private class action lawsuits in these subject areas sometimes follow upon public enforcement proceedings. Recall, for example, the class action to challenge price fixing among high-end auction houses.

Public enforcement actions might result in a monetary recovery—e.g., some manner of civil penalty for violating regulatory requirements. But they generally do not encompass recovering damages that then are distributed to the public "victims." For example, if the Environmental Protection Agency brings an enforcement action against a factory owner, that action does not typically recover damages that go to persons who breathed the excessive levels of air pollutants emitted.

This Section focuses on two situations that differ from conventional administrative enforcement actions. Neither, to be sure, involves literally obtaining and distributing damages to some group of injured persons, but they do involve the government suing on the basis of an underlying mass wrong.

The first situation consists of litigation by the government to obtain reimbursement of expenditures made under a public benefit program (like Medicaid) as a result of misconduct by the defendant vis-à-vis some group of citizens. Here, the government sues in its capacity as a proprietor, alleging an economic loss to the public fisc. The landmark $516 billion settlement reached between the attorneys general of the vast majority of states and the tobacco industry arose from precisely this context. A major aspect of the states' claims against the tobacco industry concerned reimbursement of the health care expenditures made by state governments pursuant to the federal Medicaid program as a result of smoking-related illnesses wrongfully caused in citizens—the states alleged—by the tobacco industry. One can understand a government lawsuit for reimbursement of such expenditures as a kind of aggregation, for the money sought consists of the aggregate loss to the public fisc over the aggregate unit of the private citizens covered by the relevant public benefit program.

The second situation consists of litigation by government on a theory of "public nuisance"—a doctrine with a substantial history in tort law. Litigation by the state of Rhode Island against the manufacturers of lead-based paint in light of the well-documented risks posed by that product to children who ingest it—e.g., from paint chips in older housing stock— illustrates this second approach. The Rhode Island lead paint litigation also provides a convenient occasion to explore an additional question in both public nuisance and government reimbursement litigation: whether the government should be permitted (and, if so, under what limitations, if any) to retain private law firms within the plaintiffs' bar to litigate on the state's behalf on a contingency-fee basis.

Before turning to these two traditional governmental roles, consider a larger question: should the government (through a state or the U.S. attorney general) play a greater enforcement role in the wake of recent Supreme Court decisions such as *Wal–Mart Stores, Inc. v. Dukes*, which strengthened the commonality standard, and *AT & T Mobility v. Concepcion*, which forces many would-be class actions into private arbitration? Both decisions made traditional class-action litigation more difficult either to certify or to litigate in federal courts at all. Yet, historically, the modern class action was developed in part to address a concern about relying solely on government enforcement, which might be subject to budgetary constraints or agency capture. See Harry Kalven Jr. & Maurice Rosenfield, *The Contemporary Function of the Class Suit*, 8 U. Chi. L. Rev. 684 (1941). Nevertheless, at least two commentators contend that states' attorneys general should fill the role previously occupied by "private attorneys general"—i.e., plaintiffs' attorneys. As you read an excerpt of their argument, think about some of the hurdles that these actions might present: what are the limits to a state's *parens patriae* power, when should the state's action preclude subsequent litigation by private citizens, and is the state attorney general always an adequate representative?

Myriam Gilles & Gary Friedman, *After Class: Aggregate Litigation in the Wake of AT & T Mobility v. Concepcion*

79 U. Chi. L. Rev. 623, 660–62, 664–66 (2012).

In our view, state attorneys general—alone among public enforcers—have the ability to fill the void left by class actions, primarily through expanded use of the parens patriae powers that are currently on the books in most states. Parens patriae suits are not subject to Rule 23 or contractual waiver provisions, and so avoid the majority of impediments to contemporary class actions. And while states may lack the resources and expertise to step into the enforcement gap, they have broad latitude to leverage the substantial resources and expertise of the private bar—and do so in a fashion that ameliorates the most criticized features of class action practice. Whether state AGs will in fact use these tools and seize the mantle of aggregate litigation is another question.

1.   Parens patriae authority

In parens patriae cases, the state AG is generally acting on behalf of citizens of the state, seeking injunctive relief or damages. In the typical formulation, parens patriae standing is said to exist where the state is not merely a "nominal party" acting on behalf of a private interest, but is rather asserting its "quasi sovereign interest in the health and well being—both physical and economic—of its residents in general." Where the state asserts parens patriae authority as a matter of the common law, courts have wrestled with this "quasi-sovereign interest" requirement. But as Professor Margaret Lemos has explained, "private interests can rise to the level of a quasi-sovereign state interest when sufficiently aggregated" and, as a consequence, "the operative question is whether the injury in question affects a 'sufficiently substantial segment of the state's population.'" In any event, most assertions of parens patriae authority nowadays are grounded not in the common law, but in statutes that "explicitly authorize the attorney general to sue on behalf of the state's citizens to redress particular wrongs." And here, where there is express statutory authorization, standing concerns evaporate.

In broad strokes, then, state AGs will generally have standing to step into cases that could otherwise be prosecuted as class actions, unless there is some statutory impediment. In state common law cases, standing should generally lie; after all, if Rule 23(a)(1) numerosity would be satisfied, the "substantial segment of the population" test is likely met. Likewise, the state remedial statutes that are most prominent in class action practice—including deceptive trade, antitrust and wage-and-hour laws—are generally covered by broad legislative grants of parens patriae authority.

* * *

2.   Parens patriae and the challenges to class actions.

As enforceable class action waivers proliferate, we think it is only a matter of time until a defendant makes the argument that a state AG's parens patriae action is barred by the uniform terms of the contracts between the defendant and the AG's constituent consumers and workers. Facing parens patriae claims that might otherwise have been brought by persons that are bound by arbitration clauses and class action waivers, defendants will argue that agency principles apply, under which an agent is deemed bound by the arbitration agreements of the principal.

But the centuries-old doctrinal underpinnings of parens patriae are incompatible with any notion of agency. The whole idea behind parens patriae suits is that the state has its own interest at stake in the litigation. The state's "quasi-sovereign" interest supporting the claim is not derived from an agency relationship with third-party constituents. Instead, the state's *own* interest kicks in once a sufficient number of its constituents have suffered injury. Moreover, the sine qua non of agency is control; there is no agency relationship absent an "understanding of the parties that the principal is to be in control of the undertaking." In a parens patriae case—as in a criminal prosecution, and quite unlike an ordinary private lawsuit—the injured party is simply not "in control of the undertaking." And indeed, this precept finds support in *EEOC v Waffle House, Inc*, where the Supreme Court held that an employee's arbitration clause did not bar the EEOC from seeking victim-specific damages. So class waivers are unlikely to affect parens patriae suits.

Absent a radical expansion of current doctrine, parens patriae suits are likewise impervious to the increasingly restrictive rules governing class certification, including the ascertainability requirement. It is hard to see why it should matter if an AG has a knowable list of persons affected by an unfair trade practice or environmental nuisance, so long as the AG can ascertain the amount of aggregate damages suffered by his citizenry. A court in a class action may feel obliged to ensure that any relief will ultimately be distributed to the injured parties, and it may conclude that problems identifying those parties render the class device unmanageable within the meaning of Rule 23(b)(3). But state AGs have no obligation to distribute damages at all—much less are they obligated to do so with any precision. Liberal use of *cy pres*, escheatment to the public fisc, and the application of rough justice principles in distributing awards are unquestioned hallmarks of parens patriae litigation. And while the defendant surely has a due process interest in ensuring that it does not incur liability greater than the aggregate damages it inflicted upon affected state residents, it surely has no interest in the AG's subsequent disposition of those damages.

A more complicated problem is presented by the potential application, in parens patriae cases, of the heightened proof standards demanded by *In re Initial Public Offerings Securities Litigation* and *In re Hydrogen Peroxide Antitrust Litigation* for the certification of damages classes, and by *Dukes* for injunctive cases. As AG-initiated suits come to take the place of private class actions, we expect a push from defendants to subject parens patriae cases to a sort of shadow Rule 23 standard, arguing for threshold determinations that mirror commonality and predominance inquiries. Indeed, we have already seen defendants argue that parens patriae cases should be removable under CAFA because they resemble class actions; that is, that parens patriae cases are often "class actions in disguise" and, when they are, they should be regulated like class actions. And while this view has been rejected by most courts, it was accepted by the Fifth Circuit in *Louisiana v Allstate Ins. Co*, and has found predictable traction in conservative circles—which implies it could well receive a favorable reception in the Roberts Court.

If the "class actions in disguise" argument takes hold, why stop at removability under CAFA? Why not subject parens patriae actions to something like commonality and predominance inquiries? It is not difficult to imagine courts conducting an early-stage hearing into parens patriae standing, and demanding the AG make a showing that the injuries to his constituents are capable of cohesive common proof that predominates over individual inquiries, as a prerequisite to finding that the state's quasi-sovereign interests are implicated. The numerosity requirement is already baked into the standing inquiry, and courts arguably have inherent power to police manageability in any case, even without Rule 23. Presumably, courts would borrow from class action case law the requirement that the AG make these showings by a preponderance standard.

One place where AGs *do* have to make a Rule 23 showing is where the parties wish to endow their settlement with the res judicata reach of a class action settlement. This may not be easy: the Texas Supreme Court, for one, has held a state AG is not a "typical" class representative within the meaning of Rule 23, or Texas's analogue. However, post-*Concepcion*, obtaining a class-wide global release will often be less consequential, given the reduced risk of additional litigation by nonreleased parties.

Whatever the merits of grafting Rule 23-like requirements onto parens patriae cases, this approach is certainly attuned to the legal zeitgeist and, in our view, represents a plausible outcome. But the effect will be limited and will not reach class action waivers. No matter how heavily the parens patriae standing inquiry borrows from Rule 23, it is clear that the state itself has an interest in redressing widely distributed harms to its citizens and, as a consequence, remains beyond the reach of contractual arbitration clauses. Likewise, there is nothing here to alter the analysis of the ascertainability requirement. The state's ability to make even a rigorous showing of cohesiveness (or numerosity, or commonality) simply will not depend on "proof of purchase" evidence or known lists of injured persons.

NOTES AND QUESTIONS

1. *Problems with Parens Patriae Authority.* What problems exist in relation to greater enforcement through *parens patriae*? Although the government is often not subject to rigorous class certification standards, not subjecting these actions to stringent certification standards means that there is no check on adequate representation as there would be in a class action. This, in turn,

means that the preclusive scope of the judgment is uncertain at best, particularly when an attorney general sues for both indivisible and divisible remedies.

    2. Scope of the Parens Patriae Authority. When should the state be permitted to pursue rights that its citizens might prefer to litigate on their own? Some cases are easy in that they involve aggregate rights where the state sues to vindicate its citizens' public (as opposed to private) interest. For example, when a state sues another state for the right to divert and use water, the resulting judgment binds both the state and its citizens. See *Wyoming v. Colorado*, 286 U.S. 494, 506–07, 509 (1932). The same result should be true when a state sues to establish public transit system fares, implement federal wildlife-management statutes, or determine whether a cellular company can build its towers. See *Barman v. Denver Tramway Corp.*, 197 F.2d 946, 951 (10th Cir. 1952) (public transit system fares); *Alaska Legislative Council v. Babbitt*, 15 F. Supp. 2d 19, 23 (D.D.C. 1998), *aff'd* 181 F.3d 1333 (D.C. Cir. 1999) (federal wildlife statute); *Lucas v. Planning Bd. of LaGrange*, 7 F. Supp. 2d 310, 328–29 (S.D.N.Y. 1998) (cell phone towers).

    But what about the harder cases where the character of the underlying action involves both public questions and private rights? The Supreme Court has been enigmatic in this area. Currently, as parens patriae, the state can seek compensation for sovereign or quasi-sovereign claims, but it must have an interest that is distinct from individual citizens' interests. See *Alfred L. Snapp & Son, Inc. v. Puerto Rico*, 458 U.S. 592, 600 (1982). The Supreme Court has not defined "quasi-sovereign" interests, but "it is clear that a state may sue to protect its citizens against 'the pollution of the air over its territory or of interstate waters in which the state has rights.'" *Satsky v. Paramount Communications, Inc.*, 7 F.3d 1464, 1469 (10th Cir. 1993) (internal citations omitted). Yet, states cannot "sue to assert the rights of private individuals." *Id.* Nevertheless, as we will see, states do not always limit their authority to well-traveled "quasi-sovereign" interests like environmental and antitrust enforcement. Moreover, even though questions about standing and adequacy are not new, they are far from resolved.

1. REIMBURSEMENT OF GOVERNMENT EXPENDITURES

Robert L. Rabin, *The Tobacco Litigation: A Tentative Assessment*

51 DePaul L. Rev. 331, 337–40 (2001)

    The pioneering venture in the state health care reimbursement litigation, the Mississippi case, was filed less than two months after *Castano* [*v. American Tobacco Co.*, an unsuccessful attempt at certification of a nationwide class action in tort against the tobacco industry.] In some ways, the two efforts to recover for aggregated claims shared an affinity beyond near-simultaneous filing. Both were undertaken by attorneys experienced in mass tort litigation who were convinced that the unfolding revelations of the tobacco industry's indifference to public health concerns could be translated into mass industry liability, as in asbestos litigation. But the health care reimbursement claim, which would soon be replicated in one state after another across the nation, rested on a very different premise from *Castano*. Although the reimbursement claim was based on precisely the same tort-type conduct, the state's theory of recovery was, in fact, not based on products liability law because the state was not a "direct" victim suffering from a tobacco-related disease. Instead, Mississippi and the states that were to follow its lead argued for relief on equitable grounds such as unjust enrichment.

In essence, the states' legal theories, which later came to include statutorily based claims, such as violation of consumer protection laws, asserted that the industry's deceptive and misleading conduct constituted a wrong against the public, as well as against individual smokers. In arguing unjust enrichment, the claim was for restitution of public tax funds that were allocated to treating impecunious smokers whose health problems were allegedly the industry's responsibility. A similar theory, wrongfully profiting at the expense of the public, undergirded claims of conspiracy and consumer fraud, particularly those targeted against industry tactics aimed at making smoking attractive to underage youths.

In reality, these theories were largely untested, and the claim that the state's interest was independent of and distinct from the individual smoker's generally rested on a shaky foundation. Untested or not, the theories of recovery multiplied to include deceptive advertising, antitrust violations, federal Racketeer Influenced Corrupt Organizations (RICO) claims, unfair competition, a variety of fraud allegations, and in at least two states, Florida and Massachusetts, statutory claims based on the enactment of specific health care cost recovery legislation. The number of states bringing suit also multiplied. By the summer 1997, the roster had grown to forty states. Blue Cross and labor union insurers were devising parallel lawsuits, and, in California, cities and counties had joined in the fray.

Then, after months of rumors, in June 1997, the states and the major tobacco companies reached a "global settlement"—in reality, a detailed legislative proposal that was presented to Congress as an effort to virtually extinguish the tobacco wars. The tobacco industry, which for more than forty years had proudly proclaimed its invincibility from product liability, was now prepared to underwrite the largest civil settlement ever by paying $368.5 billion over twenty-five years to reach closure on this front.

Beyond doubt, the June 1997 agreement was a testament to the awesome threat posed by the litigation strategy. What the industry was willing to buy, at a very considerable price, was relief from litigation uncertainty. This latter point is underscored by the quid pro quo concessions offered by the anti-tobacco forces in the proposal. Under the plan, the state health care reimbursement suits would have been settled, and the industry would have been granted immunity from all other forms of class action. Thus, in one fell swoop, the industry would have eliminated its greatest nightmare—the prospect of catastrophic loss from a cluster of state recoupments, certified classes of tort claimants, or third-party sources, such as Blue Cross or union health plans, successfully convincing juries that the industry's past course of conduct warranted potential multibillion dollar recoveries in compensatory and punitive damages for the legions of injury victims represented in the particular cases. Moreover, under another provision in the settlement plan, there would have been no punitive damages allowed in individual cases for industry conduct prior to the enactment by Congress of the legislation. Once again, this provision directly targeted a massive source of uncertainty—the prospect of a breakthrough in individual cases with one jury after another reacting with vehemence against the narrative of industry deceit. A third provision would have capped the total annual liability for awards on future individual claims at five billion dollars, which is a considerable sum, but nonetheless a fixed cap that would contribute from yet another perspective to the predictability that the industry sought.

There were other restrictions on litigation as well, but the point is clear. The state health care cases may have rested on dubious theoretical premises, but a realistic assessment of the threat presented by potential catastrophic loss litigation requires more than just finely honed theoretical analysis. By mid–1997, the industry faced the prospect of being sued by virtually every state in the country, represented on a retainer basis by a cadre of the most experienced and skilled tobacco lawyers, pressing a variety of common law and statutory claims. Other third-party claims lurked in the background. The documents told a tale of industry deceit and indifference to public health considerations. Could trial court judges in every, or virtually all, state health care recovery cases be counted on to enter summary judgment, or would the industry be at the mercy of juries exposed to the tale of industry wrongdoing?

What the negotiating parties failed to recognize was that once their "settlement" reached the halls of Congress, it would take on a life of its own. Almost immediately, as the wave of anti-industry public sentiment crested, a far more draconian legislative proposal emerged. The [bill as amended and popularly known as "the McCain bill" after its Senate sponsor] would have obligated the industry to pay $516 billion over twenty-five years, and, even more strikingly, the bill incorporated virtually all of the earlier-negotiated public health provisions. Moreover as amended, the bill would have eliminated the industry's hard-fought quid pro quo, which was the litigation immunity provisions. Perhaps inevitably, a reversal of the legislative tide occurred. It was bolstered by an urgent industry advertising blitz and the backing of industry congressional supporters. In the end, no federal legislation was enacted.

As the congressional battle waxed and waned, the industry—perhaps as a strategy to promote a new image in timely fashion—settled individually with the four states that were closest to trial, and that, with one exception (Texas), perhaps presented the greatest threat of a litigation setback: Mississippi, Florida, Texas, and Minnesota. In the absence of these settlements, one might well have concluded, as the congressional deliberations collapsed in June 1998, that the . . . aggregation strategy had yielded precious little beyond massive additional documentation of industry wrongdoing.

But the four individual state settlements did amount to some forty billion dollars, to be paid out over twenty-five years. And within a year, in November 1998, the industry and the forty-six remaining states had negotiated a $206 billion settlement of all outstanding state health care reimbursement claims, which was considerably less in industry payout than the failed June 1997 agreement. On the other hand, the new agreement contained none of the immunity provisions from class action litigation and punitive damages included in that earlier package.

Hanoch Dagan & James J. White, *Governments, Citizens, and Injurious Industries*

75 N.Y.U. L. Rev. 354, 373–382 (2000)

By their separate agreements with four states and the Settlement with the remaining forty-six, the tobacco manufacturers have made agreements that will cause them to pay more than $240 billion to the fifty states by the year 2025. We believe that the states had only one meritorious claim against the tobacco manufacturers, namely subrogation to the claims of their citizens against the tobacco manufacturers in tort. . . . Since in subrogation actions the manufacturers could raise all defenses that they could have raised against the subrogors (assumption of risk, causation, and the like)—given the [previous] record of individual suits—it is likely that less than half of the state suits would have been successful.

Even if the states could have won on behalf of every injured smoker, the settlement would still greatly exceed the expended costs. Because the states pay no part of Medicare and approximately one-half of Medicaid costs, and because private insurance companies and the smokers themselves pay most health care costs associated with smoking, the part of the total cost actually borne by the states is small. A state's additional medical expenses attributable to a decedent's smoking are approximately $557. Multiplying the number of deaths from smoking by the $557 figure produces an annual cost to all of the states of approximately $223 million. . . .

In agreeing to the Settlement, the tobacco companies have thus probably agreed to pay the states a much larger amount than the states could have expected to recover had every case gone to judgment (even if we assume some additional, unidentified costs attributed to legitimately subrogated preventative and ameliorative costs). Yet, the tobacco companies have received no direct protection from bankruptcy. . . .

Why would an industry agree to pay far more than the present value of its probable liability and agree to a settlement that does not give it what it most needs—protection from bankruptcy? We see several reasons, some plain, some subtle and speculative. First, the tobacco manufacturers did gain important indirect protections from bankruptcy. Second, the tobacco manufacturers achieved explicit provisions that minimize competition from new tobacco manufacturers who did not sign the Settlement.

1.   Safety from Bankruptcy

We believe the holy grail for the tobacco manufacturers is federal protection from bankruptcy.

The financial stakes in the state suits were particularly great because the tobacco manufacturers faced a queue of state plaintiffs thirty or forty deep, each of whom could observe earlier trials and learn from the mistakes of each prior plaintiff by bringing their suits in seriatim fashion. Since any judgment would be due and owing in full on the exhaustion of the defendants' appeals, the amount of the judgment would have to be booked as a liquidated liability and, absent an agreement with the plaintiff, would have to be paid at once, not over twenty-five years out of future earnings.

Tobacco manufacturers would have faced financial dangers from any large jury verdict even if the companies were eventually successful on appeal. The prospect of obtaining a bond to cover such a judgment, which might include punitive damages and treble damages, posed a formidable threat. The cost of a bond would be enormous, and bonding companies might no longer be willing to write such bonds for defendants facing thirty or forty more suits. . . .

Although the Settlement did not provide the kind of explicit protections from bankruptcy that the [original multistate agreement that culminated in failed federal legislation] would have, it staved off threats of insolvency in two important ways. First, insofar as states' claims are concerned, the Settlement completely forestalled the possibility of a lucky hit that would have knocked all of the companies into bankruptcy. It enabled the tobacco companies to pay over many years, to book the liability piecemeal, and, perhaps, even to reduce the discounted cost of the total stream of payments.

Second, the Settlement will enlist the states and beneficiaries of the payments to the states as new lobbying allies of the tobacco companies in Congress in favor of liability-limiting bills. If the tobacco companies filed a petition in Chapter 11, their payments under the Settlement would be indefinitely postponed. Since the payments have been negotiated and characterized as payments by a tortfeasor to the states (as the injured party or as a subrogee to the injured party) and not as taxes, the states would not enjoy the benefits that the Bankruptcy Code confers on some state tax claims. It seems likely that the states' claims would be treated as mine-run unsecured claims, requiring the states to compete with individual smokers. No state would relish a fight with victims suffering debilitating and deadly diseases over limited funds.

Bankruptcy would thus threaten the fortunes of many powerful beneficiaries in the states, beneficiaries who are likely to come from all parts of the political spectrum: from teachers unions on the left (who benefit from use of the tobacco money for education), to municipalities in the middle, to businesses and individuals on the right (who will face increased taxes if the tobacco money dries up). When a manufacturer suffers the first threatening judgment and turns to the states, municipalities, unions, and others requesting they use their influence with Congress, we predict the various beneficiaries will spring to action—just as any well paid lobbyist should.

2.   Protection Against Competition

To meet its payments under the Settlement, the tobacco companies would have to raise the price per pack of cigarettes. At some point new manufacturers (who, by hypothesis, have committed no torts) might be able to enter the market and undersell the existing manufacturers. The agreement with the states contains a diabolically clever set of provisions to insulate the cigarette manufacturers from such competition.

Section IX(d), titled "nonparticipating manufacturer adjustment," adjusts the principal payments (particularly the "base amount" which rises from $5 billion in 2001 to $9 billion in the year 2018 and thereafter) downward if "nonparticipating manufacturers"—new tobacco manufacturers—take market share from the participating manufacturers. A particular state's share of the payments is not merely reduced dollar for dollar for the loss of share; it is reduced by a multiple of the sales lost to the new entrants. If, for example, the participating tobacco manufacturers lose 10% of their market share to new entrants, they will have a right under subsection (d) to reduce their payments to the states by as much as 24%.

Any state that passes the Settlement's model statute is freed from any adjustment. The model statute imposes a tax on new tobacco entrants equal to approximately twenty cents per package in the year 2000, rising to thirty-six cents in the year 2007. If new entrants make inroads on the signing manufacturers' market share, the nonparticipating adjustment attributable to those inroads is spread among states who have not adopted a similar tax. For example, if California adopts the model tax on new entrants but half of the states do not, and a new entrant takes 10% of the signers' market share in California, California will receive its regular base payment while the states who have not adopted a similar tax will suffer a reduction in their base payment (amounting to as much as 24% of California's share). So a failure to tax new entrants can cost a state not only an exponential reduction of payments that it would otherwise have received, but also an additional reduction for inroads by new entrants in states that did adopt a tax.

If, as we suspect, the new entrant tax and nonparticipating manufacturers' reduction will effectively exclude new entrants, the only loss that will be suffered by the manufacturers' shareholders will come from the reduction in demand caused by increased price. How elastic cigarette demand is remains to be seen. If it is completely inelastic and if new competition does not erupt among the existing manufacturers, the entire cost of the deal is thrown on the backs of future smokers. . . .

NOTES AND QUESTIONS

1.   *Relationship to Tort Litigation.* Note the ingenuity behind the states' reimbursement theory. It had the strategic virtue of deflecting attention from individual smokers (whom the defendant industry could attempt to characterize as blameworthy, in whole or in part, for their own smoking-related disease) to "innocent" taxpayers (the general public said to bear the additional increment of cost to public programs for medical care attributable to the tortious misconduct of the industry). But does the reimbursement theory really overcome the barriers to certifying a conventional class action for personal injury in tort? Insofar as *Castano* is rightly decided on the class certification question, why should reimbursement actions brought by the states fare any better? Does the presence of a governmental body—an ongoing agent for the aggregate mass of taxpayers, one might say, rather than a temporary, this-case-only kind of agent in the form of class counsel—make all the difference?

2.   *Relationship to Legislation.* What do you make of the original multistate settlement agreement, designed to be implemented through federal legislation? Does it reinforce the institutional proximity of aggregate settlements to full-fledged public legislation? Recall the continuum of settlement arrangements from Chapter 1.

3.   *Settlement Pressure Revisited.* Does the tobacco industry's willingness ultimately to settle the state reimbursement litigation attest, once again, to aggregate litigation's power (albeit in various forms) to exert considerable settlement pressure? Or does the concern over "a lucky hit," summarized by Professors Dagan and White, present a different sort of concern? If anything, did the defendant tobacco industry learn the settlement-pressure lesson all too well, opting to obtain by settlement what it had not garnered via legislative lobbying within the various states? Who, if anyone, got taken to the cleaners here—the defendants or the states? The taxpayers on whose behalf the states supposedly sued? Future smokers?

4.   *Government as Adequate Representative.* Were the state attorneys general adequate representatives of the taxpaying public? Does it matter that the attorneys general were politically accountable, or does that feature only worsen their adequacy as representatives?

Precious little of the payments made by the tobacco industry to the states pursuant to the MSA have gone toward health care measures related to smoking. American Heart Association, et al., A Broken Promise to Our Children: The

1998 State Tobacco Settlement Six Years Later (2004). Is this problematic from the standpoint of the adequate representation of public taxpayers? Insofar as the additional increment of health care expenditures occasioned by tobacco industry misconduct resulted in additional expenditures from the general public fisc, is it actually appropriate that any funds recovered should go back there, without any manner of earmarking for tobacco-related programs?

Recall the concern in *Amchem* over the potential for class counsel there to make detrimental tradeoffs within the all-encompassing plaintiff class—specifically, between class members with present-day asbestos-related disease and those at risk of disease in the future. Does the content of the MSA suggest that there existed a potential for detrimental tradeoffs to be made by the state attorney general—indeed, a potential that was ultimately realized in the deal they embraced? Tradeoffs between whom? Past smokers and future smokers? Who is, in effect, being taxed to benefit the broader populace?

A common observation holds that modern government serves many different functions. Among other things, government acts as a regulator. In addition, government itself has a considerable role as a proprietor, chiefly through the provision of social welfare programs—Medicare, Medicaid, and the like in the area of medical care—funded primarily by general taxation. For further discussion of these roles, see William B. Rubenstein, *On What a "Private Attorney General" Is—and Why It Matters*, 57 Vand. L. Rev. 2129, 2140–41 (2004). The taxpaying public, of course, cares about both sound regulatory policy and sound management of the propriety side of government. Does the MSA reflect detrimental tradeoffs between the regulatory and propriety roles of government? Does the positioning of government as plaintiff represent an improvement as compared to conventional class action litigation? Or does it actually recreate the adequate representation problems seen there?

Note that the involvement of the states *as states* is crucial to immunize from antitrust scrutiny collaboration by the firms within the tobacco industry to inhibit competition pursuant to the terms of the MSA. As one court vividly remarked: "Had the executives of the major tobacco companies entered into such an arrangement without the involvement of the States and their attorneys general, those executives would long ago have had depressing conversations with their attorneys about the United States Sentencing Guidelines." *Freedom Holdings, Inc. v. Spitzer*, 357 F.3d 205, 226 (2d Cir. 2004). Does the capacity of the state attorneys general to serve as antitrust immunizers raise doubt about their representational adequacy?

    5.   *Monetary Recovery and Res Judicata.* The government sued to recover its own expenditures in the tobacco litigation, but had it sought to collect damages on behalf of individual smokers, should citizens have been entitled to notice and the right to exclude themselves from the lawsuit? The Hart–Scott–Rodino Antitrust Improvements Act, which allows states (as opposed to just the individuals harmed by the anticompetitive activity) to sue companies for violating antitrust laws in federal court, requires state attorney general actions to publish notice of the action, but does not require individual notice. It likewise gives citizens the right to opt out and affords a res judicata effect to those who do not. Some state statutes granting *parens patriae* authority also include notice and opt-out procedures for individuals because these suits are explicitly binding on individuals who do not opt out. See *West Virginia ex rel. McGraw v. Comcast Corp.*, 705 F. Supp. 441, 453–54 (E.D. Pa. 2010). This means that, as

Gilles and Friedman argue, parens patriae actions can perform similar functions as the class action. But government suits avoid the hurdles presented by Rule 23. Does this suggest that courts should subject *parens patriae* actions for individual damages to the same requirements as Rule 23 or at least have some supervisory authority over the settlement? Or would this pose a separation-of-powers concern? Should a *parens patriae* action preclude individual citizens from vindicating the same public interest? What if the government relies on a different theory of the case than a private citizen would?

Consider the availability of punitive damages. The MSA contained a broad release that covered claims by states acting as *parens patriae*, private attorney generals, and taxpayers who were seeking relief on behalf of the general public. So, when private parties later sued for punitive damages, the tobacco companies claimed that those damages remedied a public harm and were thus barred by res judicata. A number of courts agreed: punitive damages, they reasoned, punished misbehavior for the public good and deterred wrongful conduct. Thus, individuals retained no private interest in punitive damages. See *Brown & Williamson Tobacco Corp. v. Gault*, 627 S.E.2d 549, 553–54 (Ga. 2006); *Fabiano v. Phillip Morris, Inc.*, 54 A.D. 3d 146 (N.Y. App. 2008). On the other hand, one California court reached the opposite conclusion based on the "primary rights" test, which requires courts to examine the harm suffered and to bar subsequent actions only when they arise out of "the same injury to the same right." *Bullock v. Phillip Morris USA, Inc.*, 131 Cal. Rptr. 3d 382, 392 (Cal. Ct. App. 2011). Because an individual's punitive damage claim arises out of her own personal and emotional injuries, not the economic harms and anticompetitive activities that the attorney general pursued as *parens patriae*, the MSA had no preclusive effect on punitive damages. What does this suggest about a defendant's ability to achieve closure through *parens patriae* actions?

6. Regulatory Policy. Does the MSA reflect desirable regulatory policy with regard to tobacco? The tobacco industry could have funded its obligations under the MSA with a cigarette price increase of roughly 19 cents per pack. In fact, the industry actually implemented a 45–cents–per–pack increase at the time of their initial compliance with the MSA, an increase that eventually would rise to a total of 76 cents per pack by the mid–2000s. *A.D. Bedell Wholesale Co. v. Philip Morris, Inc.*, 263 F.3d 239, 246 (3d Cir. 2001). But is such a price hike a bad thing?

One review of the empirical literature suggests that a 10 percent increase in cigarette prices reduces overall cigarette consumption by 2.5 to 5 percent. Frank J. Chaloupka et al., *Taxing Tobacco: The Impact of Tobacco Taxes on Cigarette Smoking and Other Tobacco Use*, in Regulating the Tobacco Industry 53 (Robert L. Rabin & Stephen D. Sugarman eds. 2001). Smoking by high school students, in particular, rose by an estimated 33 percent from 1991 to 1997—the year prior to the MSA—but subsequently dropped by nearly 40 percent as of 2003. Centers for Disease Control, *Cigarette Use among High School Students—United States, 1991–2003*, 53 Morbidity & Mortality Wkly. Rep. 499, 499 (2004). The causal role, if any, of the MSA nonetheless remains quite difficult to pinpoint, given that smoking in the United States generally had been in a "sustained decline" even before the MSA. Centers for Disease Control, *Cigarette Smoking among Adults—United States, 2003*, 54 Morbidity & Mortality Wkly. Rep. 509, 510 (2005).

Apart from the possible effects of MSA-related price hikes on present-day smoking rates, is the MSA undesirable regulatory policy for a different reason—its inhibitory effect on additional regulatory moves in the future that might undercut the business prospects of the tobacco industry and, thus, its capacity to pay the states pursuant to the MSA?

2. Public Nuisance

State v. Lead Industries Association, Inc.

951 A.2d 428 (R.I. 2008)

In this landmark lawsuit, filed in 1999, the then Attorney General, on behalf of the State of Rhode Island (the state), filed suit against various former lead pigment manufacturers and the Lead Industries Association (LIA), a national trade association of lead producers formed in 1928.

[The] trial, spanning four months, became the longest civil jury trial in the state's history. This monumental lawsuit marked the first time in the United States that a trial resulted in a verdict that imposed liability on lead pigment manufacturers for creating a public nuisance.

After a four-month trial, . . . a jury found defendant manufacturers, NL Industries, Inc. (formerly National Lead Co.) (NL), The Sherwin–Williams Co. (Sherwin–Williams), and Millennium Holdings LLC (Millennium) (collectively defendants), liable under a public nuisance theory. . . . The defendants filed an appeal from the judgment entered against them.

[Due to the considerable number of legal issues presented on appeal, different members of the court authored different portions—designated as "Tracks"—of the unanimous opinion. The portions reproduced here concern, respectively, the public nuisance theory on the merits and the Attorney General's retention on a contingency-fee basis of the prominent plaintiffs' law firm of Motley Rice—the same lawyers who should by now be familiar from such other matters as *Amchem*, the tobacco MSA, and *Combustion Engineering*.]

Track 1

Liability

■ Chief Justice Williams, for the Court.

[D]efendants . . . argue that the trial justice erred by: (1) misapplying the law of public nuisance; (2) finding a causal connection between defendants' actions and lead poisoning in Rhode Island; and (3) failing to hold that this action is barred by the constitutional provision concerning separation of powers. . . . For the reasons set forth herein, we reverse the judgment of the Superior Court as to the liability of defendants . . . because we conclude that the trial justice erred by denying defendants' motion to dismiss. More specifically, we conclude that the state has not and cannot allege any set of facts to support its public nuisance claim that would establish that defendants interfered with a public right or that defendants were in control of the lead pigment they, or their predecessors, manufactured *at the time* it caused harm to Rhode Island children.

In reaching this conclusion, we do not mean to minimize the severity of the harm that thousands of children in Rhode Island have suffered as a result of lead poisoning. Our hearts go out to those children whose lives forever have been changed by the poisonous presence of lead. But, however grave the problem of lead poisoning is in Rhode Island, public nuisance law simply does not provide a remedy for this harm. The state has not and cannot allege facts that would fall within the parameters of what would constitute public nuisance under Rhode Island law. As set forth more thoroughly herein, defendants were not in control of any lead pigment at the time the lead caused harm to children in Rhode Island, making defendants unable to abate the alleged nuisance, the standard remedy in a public nuisance action. Furthermore, the General Assembly has recognized defendants' lack of control and inability to abate the alleged nuisance because it has placed the burden on landlords and property owners to make their properties lead-safe. . . .

I

Facts . . .

It is undisputed that lead poisoning constitutes a public health crisis that has plagued and continues to plague this country, particularly its children. The General Assembly has declared that although "[c]hildhood lead poisoning is completely preventable," G.L. 1956 § 23–24.6–2(3), it is "the most severe environmental health problem in Rhode Island." Indeed, Providence has received the unfavorable nickname "the leadpaint capital" because of its disproportionately large number of children with elevated blood-lead levels.

A

Dangers of Lead Poisoning

Lead is a toxic chemical that contributes to the "most common environmental disease of young children." Office of Lead–Based Paint Abatement and Poisoning Prevention, 61 Fed.Reg. 29170 (June 7, 1996) (quoting Strategic Plan for the Elimination of Lead Poisoning, Centers for Disease Control (CDC), U.S. Department of Health and Human Services, Atlanta, Georgia (1991)). . . . Contact with low levels of lead may lead to "permanent learning disabilities, reduced concentration and attentiveness and behavior problems, problems which may persist and adversely affect the child's chances for success in school and life." . . . Children exposed to elevated levels of lead can suffer from comas, convulsions, and even death.

Lead was widely used in residential paints in the United States until the mid–1970s. There is no doubt that lead-based paint is the primary source of childhood lead exposure. . . .

C

Legislative Responses

In 1971, Congress recognized the prevalence of childhood lead poisonings and enacted chapter 63 of title 42 of the United States Code, the Lead–Based Paint Poisoning Prevention Act (LPPPA), a law aimed at studying the effects of childhood lead exposure and eliminating lead-based paint from federally owned or federally financed housing. Finally, in 1978, the Consumer Product Safety Commission banned the sale of residential paint containing more than 0.06 percent lead.

Rhode Island, with a housing stock of older homes, also has recognized the depth of this problem. . . .

[I]n 1991, the General Assembly enacted the Lead Poisoning Prevention Act (LPPA), chapter 24.6 of title 23, which required RIDOH to implement various programs, including statewide blood-screening programs, lead-poisoning prevention programs, and educational programs. The LPPA's stated purpose was to establish "a comprehensive program to reduce exposure to environmental lead and prevent childhood lead poisoning, the most severe environmental health problem in Rhode Island."

To supplement this initiative, in 2002, the General Assembly later enacted the Lead Hazard Mitigation Act (LHMA). . . . The LHMA imposed, *inter alia*, several duties on the owners of rental dwellings that were constructed prior to 1978, which included correcting lead hazards on their premises. . . .

The General Assembly's approach to Rhode Island's leadpaint problem and [a state agency's] promulgation of regulations aimed at reducing lead hazards have proven effective and, as a result, the entire state—including its "core cities"—has experienced substantial declines in lead poisoning.

D

Attorney General's Lawsuit

On October 12, 1999, the Attorney General, on behalf of the state filed a ten-count complaint against eight former lead pigment manufacturers, John Doe corporations, and the LIA. . . .

The state alleged that the manufacturers or their predecessors-in-interest had manufactured, promoted, distributed, and sold lead pigment for use in residential paint, despite that they knew or should have known, since the early 1900s, that lead is hazardous to human health. The state also contended that the LIA was, in essence, a coconspirator or aider and abettor of one or more of the manufacturers from at least 1928 to the present. The state asserted that defendants failed to warn Rhode Islanders of the hazardous nature of lead and failed to adequately test lead pigment. In addition, the state maintained that defendants concealed these hazards from the public or misrepresented that they were safe. The state further alleged that defendants' actions caused it to incur substantial damages. . . . The state also requested equitable relief to protect children in Rhode Island.[15] The state sought compensatory and punitive damages, in addition to an order requiring defendants to (1) abate lead pigment in all Rhode Island buildings accessible to children and (2) fund educational and lead-poisoning prevention programs. . . .

[Upon denial of numerous pre-trial motions by the defendants, the case proceeded to trial.] The jury . . . found that the "cumulative presence of lead pigment in paints and coatings on buildings throughout the State of Rhode Island" constituted a public nuisance. The jury further found that defendants, Millennium, NL, and Sherwin–Williams, were liable for causing or substantially contributing to the creation of the public nuisance. Lastly, the jury concluded that those three defendants "should be ordered to abate the public nuisance." The jury found that a fourth defendant, ARCO, was not liable.

II

Analysis

. . .

---

[15] The state eliminated that count of its original complaint seeking equitable relief to protect children when it filed its second-amended complaint.

B
Public Nuisance

1
History of Public Nuisance

... Today, public nuisance and private nuisance are separate and distinct causes of action, but both torts are inextricably linked by their joint origin as a common writ, dating to twelfth-century English common law. See Richard O. Faulk, John S. Gray, *Alchemy in the Courtroom? The Transmutation of Public Nuisance Litigation*, 2007 Mich. St. L. Rev. 941, 951 (2007) (citing C.H.S. Fifoot, *History and Sources of the Common Law: Tort and Contract* 3–5 (1949); Donald G. Gifford, *Public Nuisance as a Mass Products Liability Tort*, 71 U. Cin. L. Rev. 741, 790–91, 794 (2003). In its earliest form, nuisance was a criminal writ used to prosecute individuals or require abatement of activities considered to "be *'nocumentum iniuriousum propter communem et publicam utiliatem'*—a nuisance by reason of the common and public welfare." Gifford, 71 U. Cin. L. Rev. at 793–94 (citing Henry de Bracton, 3 BRACTON ON THE LAWS AND CUSTOMS OF ENGLAND 191, f. 232b (Samuel E. Thorne ed., 1977)). Public nuisance, or common nuisance as it originally was called, was "an infringement of the rights of the Crown." 4 RESTATEMENT (SECOND) TORTS § 821B, cmt. a at 87 (1979). Although the earliest cases involved encroachments on the royal domain, public nuisance law evolved to include "the invasion of the rights of the public." *Id.*

By the fourteenth century, courts began to apply public nuisance principles to protect rights common to the public, including "roadway safety, air and water pollution, disorderly conduct, and public health . . . ." Faulk & Gray, 2007 Mich. St. L. Rev. at 951. Nuisance became a "flexible judicial remedy" that allowed courts to address conflicts between land use and social welfare at a time when government regulations had not yet made their debut. *Id.*

It was not until the sixteenth century that the crime of public nuisance largely was transformed into the tort that is familiar in our courts today. Faulk & Gray, 2007 Mich. St. L. Rev. at 952. However, additional parameters were necessary to limit the reach of the new tort. A private party seeking to bring a public nuisance claim was required to demonstrate that he or she had "suffered a 'particular' or 'special' injury that was not common to the public." *Id.*

Ultimately, "[a]t common law public nuisance came to cover a large, miscellaneous and diversified group of minor offenses . . . ." 4 RESTATEMENT (SECOND) TORTS § 821B, cmt. b at 40. Notably, all these offenses involved an "interference with the interests of the community at large-interests that were recognized as rights of the general public entitled to protection." *Id.*

Public nuisance as it existed in English common law made its way to Colonial America without change. Faulk & Gray, 2007 Mich. St. L. Rev. at 953. In time, public nuisance became better known as a tort, and its criminal counterpart began to fade away in American jurisprudence. As state legislatures started enacting statutes prohibiting particular conduct and setting forth criminal penalties there was little need for the broad, vague, and anachronistic crime of nuisance. 4 RESTATEMENT (SECOND) TORTS § 821B, cmt. c, at 88. . . .

2

Public Nuisance in Rhode Island

... In Rhode Island, actions to abate public nuisances originally were brought in the form of an indictment. Today, the state Attorney General is empowered to bring actions to abate public nuisances. ...

This Court recognizes three principal elements that are essential to establish public nuisance: (1) an unreasonable interference; (2) with a right common to the general public; (3) by a person or people with control over the instrumentality alleged to have created the nuisance when the damage occurred. After establishing the presence of the three elements of public nuisance, one must then determine whether the defendant caused the public nuisance. We will address each element in turn.

i

Unreasonable Interference

Whether an interference with a public right is unreasonable will depend upon the activity in question and the magnitude of the interference it creates. Activities carried out in violation of state laws or local ordinances generally have been considered unreasonable if they interfere with a public right. See, e.g., *Pucci v. Algiere*, 261 A.2d 1, 10 ([R.I.] 1970) (dilapidated structure in violation of local ordinance); *Aldrich v. Howard*, 7 R.I. 213–14 (wooden building in violation of state statute). Activities that do not violate the law but that nonetheless create a substantial and continuing interference with a public right also generally have been considered unreasonable. See, e.g., *Wood v. Picillo*, 443 A.2d 1244, 1245–48 (R.I.[ ]1982) (chemical dump that emitted noxious odors and eventually caught fire, causing multiple explosions and groundwater contamination); *Lapre v. Kane*, 36 A.2d 92, 94–95 ([R.I.] 1944) (swine operation that emitted noxious odors and required that large quantities of "swill" be transported and dumped onto property); *Braun v. Iannotti*, 175 A. 656, 657 ([R.I.] 1934) (greenhouse that continually emitted smoke); *Blomen v. N. Barstow Co.*, 85 A. 924, 924–25 ([R.I.] 1913) ("drop or hammer" that caused noise and vibration that could be felt at some distance). The plaintiff bears the burden of showing that a legal activity is unreasonable. ...

ii

Public Right

... This Court also has emphasized the requirement that "the nuisance must affect an interest common to the general public, rather than peculiar to one individual, or several." *Iafrate*, 190 A.2d 476 (quoting Prosser, TORTS, ch. 14, § 72 at 402). This is not to say that public nuisance only is actionable if it occurs on public property. Rather, public nuisance is actionable even when the nuisance itself is present on private property, so long as the alleged nuisance *affects* the rights of the general public. ...

The RESTATEMENT (SECOND) provides further assistance in defining a public right.

> "A public right is *one common to all members of the general public*. It is collective in nature and not like the individual right that everyone has not to be assaulted or defamed or defrauded or negligently injured. Thus the pollution of a stream that merely deprives fifty or a hundred lower riparian owners of the use of the water for purposes connected with their land does not for that reason alone become a public nuisance. If, however, the pollution

prevents the use of a public bathing beach or kills the fish in a navigable stream and so deprives all members of the community of the right to fish, it becomes a public nuisance." 4 RESTATEMENT (SECOND) TORTS § 821B, cmt. g at 92 (emphasis added).

. . . As the RESTATEMENT (SECOND) makes clear, a public right is more than an aggregate of private rights by a large number of injured people. Rather, a public right is the right to a public good, such as "an indivisible resource shared by the public at large, like air, water, or public rights of way." *City of Chicago v. American Cyanamid Co.*, 823 N.E.2d 131. Unlike an interference with a public resource,

> "[t]he manufacture and distribution of products rarely, if ever, causes a violation of a public right as that term has been understood in the law of public nuisance. Products generally are purchased and used by individual consumers, and any harm they cause—even if the use of the product is widespread and the manufacturer's or distributor's conduct is unreasonable—is not an actionable violation of a public right. * * * The sheer number of violations does not transform the harm from individual injury to communal injury." Gifford, 71 U. Cin. L. Rev. at 817. . . .

iii

Control

As an additional prerequisite to the imposition of liability for public nuisance, a defendant must have *control* over the instrumentality causing the alleged nuisance *at the time the damage occurs.* . . .

Indeed, control at the time the damage occurs is critical in public nuisance cases, especially because the principal remedy for the harm caused by the nuisance is abatement.

iv

Causation

. . . Although it is true that public nuisance is characterized by an unreasonable interference with a public right, basic fairness dictates that a defendant must have caused the interference to be held liable for its abatement. See *Citizens for Preservation of Waterman Lake v. Davis*, 420 A.2d 60 (holding that the defendant was not liable when "there [was] virtually no evidence establishing that such odors were caused by any actions on the part of [the] defendant").

In addition to proving that a defendant is the cause-in-fact of an injury, a plaintiff must demonstrate proximate causation. . . .

3

Whether the Presence of Lead Paint Constitutes a Public Nuisance

After thoroughly reviewing the complaint filed by the state in this case, we are of the opinion that the trial justice erred in denying defendants' motion to dismiss. . . .

Even considering the allegations of fact as set forth in the complaint, we cannot ascertain allegations in the complaint that support each of these elements. The state's complaint alleges simply that "[d]efendants created an environmental hazard that continues and will continue to unreasonably interfere with the health, safety, peace, comfort or convenience of the residents of the [s]tate, thereby constituting a public nuisance." Absent from the state's complaint is any allegation that defendants have interfered with a public right as that term long has been understood in the law of public nuisance. Equally problematic is the absence of any allegation that defendants had control over the lead pigment at the time it caused harm to children. . . .

A necessary element of public nuisance is an interference with a public right—those indivisible resources shared by the public at large, such as air, water, or public rights of way. The interference must deprive all members of the community of a right to some resource to which they otherwise are entitled. See 4 RESTATEMENT (SECOND) TORTS § 821B, cmt. g at 92. The RESTATEMENT (SECOND) provides much guidance in ascertaining the fine distinction between a public right and an aggregation of private rights. "Conduct does not become a public nuisance merely because it interferes with the use and enjoyment of land by a large number of persons." *Id.*

Although the state asserts that the public's right to be free from the hazards of unabated lead had been infringed, this contention falls far short of alleging an interference with a public right as that term traditionally has been understood in the law of public nuisance. The state's allegation that defendants have interfered with the "health, safety, peace, comfort or convenience of the residents of the [s]tate" standing alone does not constitute an allegation of interference with a public right. See *Beretta U.S.A. Corp.*, 821 N.E.2d 1114. The term public right is reserved more appropriately for those indivisible resources shared by the public at large, such as air, water, or public rights of way. Expanding the definition of public right based on the allegations in the complaint would be antithetical to the common law and would lead to a widespread expansion of public nuisance law that never was intended. . . .

The right of an individual child not to be poisoned by lead paint is strikingly similar to other examples of nonpublic rights cited by courts, the RESTATEMENT (SECOND), and several leading commentators. See *Beretta U.S.A. Corp.*, 821 N.E.2d at 1114 (concluding that there is no public right to be "free from unreasonable jeopardy to health, welfare, and safety, and from unreasonable threats of danger to person and property, caused by the presence of illegal weapons in the city of Chicago"); 4 RESTATEMENT (SECOND) TORTS § 821B, cmt. g at 92 (the individual right that everyone has not to be assaulted or defamed or defrauded or negligently injured is not a public right); Gifford, 71 U. Cin. L. Rev. at 815 (there is no common law public right to a certain standard of living, to a certain standard of medical care, or to a certain standard of housing). . . .

The Illinois Supreme Court recently hypothesized on the effect of a broader recognition of public right. In *Beretta*, the Illinois Supreme Court considered whether there was a public right to be "free from unreasonable jeopardy to health, welfare, and safety, and from unreasonable threats of danger to person and property, caused by the presence of illegal weapons in the city of Chicago." *Beretta U.S.A. Corp.*, 821 N.E.2d at 1114. In concluding that there was not, the court acknowledged the far-reaching effects of a decision otherwise. *Id.* at 1116. The court speculated that

> "[i]f there is public right to be free from the threat that others may use a lawful product to break the law, that right would include the right to drive upon the highways, free from the risk of injury posed by drunk drivers. This public right to safe passage on the highways would provide the basis for public nuisance claims against brewers and distillers, distributing companies, and pro-

prietors of bars, taverns, liquor stores, and restaurants with liquor licenses, all of whom could be said to contribute to an interference with the public right." *Id.*

In taking the analogy a step further, the court considered the effect of other product misuse, stating:

"Similarly, cell phones, DVD players, and other lawful products may be misused by drivers, creating a risk of harm to others. In an increasing number of jurisdictions, state legislatures have acted to ban the use of these otherwise legal products while driving. A public right to be free from the threat that other drivers may defy these laws would permit nuisance liability to be imposed on an endless list of manufacturers, distributors, and retailers of manufactured products that are intended to be, or are likely to be, used by drivers, distracting them and causing injury to others." *Id.. . . .*

The state filed suit against defendants in their capacity "either as the manufacturer of . . . lead pigment . . . or as the successors in interest to such manufacturers" for "the cumulative presence of lead pigment in paints and coatings in or on buildings throughout the [s]tate of Rhode Island." For the alleged public nuisance to be actionable, the state would have had to assert that defendants not only manufactured the lead pigment but also controlled that pigment at the time it caused injury to children in Rhode Island—and there is no allegation of such control. . . .

[O]ur decision that defendants' conduct does not constitute a public nuisance as that term has for centuries been understood in Anglo–American law does not leave Rhode Islanders without a remedy. For example, an injunction requiring abatement may be sought against landlords who allow lead paint on their property to decay. In addition, [state law] provides for penalties and fines against those property owners who violate its rules or procedures. [Another provision of state law] further authorizes a private cause of action to be brought on behalf of households with at-risk occupants to seek injunctive relief to compel property owners to comply with the act.

Apart from these actions, the proper means of commencing a lawsuit against a manufacturer of lead pigments for the sale of an unsafe product is a products liability action. The law of public nuisance never before has been applied to products, however harmful. Courts in other states consistently have rejected product-based public nuisance suits against lead pigment manufacturers, expressing a concern that allowing such a lawsuit would circumvent the basic requirements of products liability law. . . .

A product-based public nuisance cause of action bears a close resemblance to a products liability action, yet it is not limited by the strict requirements that surround a products liability action. Courts presented with product-based public nuisance claims have expressed their concern over the ease with which a plaintiff could bring what properly would be characterized as a products liability suit under the guise of product-based public nuisance. . . .

. . . Addressing this distinction and the danger of a product-based public nuisance suit against gun manufacturers, wholesalers, and retailers, a New York appellate court explained that

"giving a green light to a common-law public nuisance cause of action today will . . . likely open the courthouse doors to a flood of limitless, similar theories of public nuisance, not only against these defendants, but also against a wide and varied array of other commercial and manufacturing enterprises and activities." *People v. Sturm, Ruger & Co.*, 761 N.Y.S.2d 192, 196 (N.Y. App. Div. 2003).

"All a creative mind would need to do is construct a scenario describing a known or perceived harm of a sort that can somehow be said to relate back to the way a company or an industry makes, markets and/or sells its non-defective, lawful product or service, and a public nuisance claim would be conceived and a lawsuit born." *Id.*

The Rhode Island General Assembly has recognized that lead paint has created a public health hazard and, pursuant to its power to legislate, has adopted several statutory schemes to address this problem. Collectively, [existing statutes] reflect the General Assembly's chosen means of responding to the state's childhood lead poisoning problem. The legislative body made clear policy decisions about how to reduce lead hazards in Rhode Island homes, buildings, and other dwellings and who should be responsible. Importantly, the General Assembly has recognized that landlords, who are in control of the lead pigment at the time it becomes hazardous, are responsible for maintaining their premises and ensuring that the premises are lead-safe. Quite tellingly, the General Assembly's chosen means of remedying childhood lead poisoning in Rhode Island did not include an authorization of an action for public nuisance against the manufacturers of lead pigments, despite the fact that this action seeking to impose liability on various lead pigment manufacturers was well under way at the time the [legislation] was enacted. . . .

Conclusion

For the foregoing reasons, we conclude that the trial justice erred in denying defendants' motion to dismiss. . . .

Track V

The Contingent Fee Issue

■ JUSTICE ROBINSON for the Court.

Although this Court has today held that the legal construct known as public nuisance does not constitute an appropriate cause of action in a case involving facts such as those presented by this case, thus technically rendering moot the issue of whether or not the execution of a contingent fee agreement between the Attorney General and certain private law firms was appropriate, we have nevertheless decided to address the legal issues surrounding the permissibility *vel non* of such an arrangement.

I

Facts . . .

The public health issues surrounding the use of lead paint in Rhode Island prompted the immediately previous Attorney General to commence a civil action against defendants in the Superior Court on October 12, 1999. Prior to commencing that civil action, cognizant of the fact that there were not adequate resources to finance such a demanding and substantial civil case, that same Attorney General had executed a contingent fee agreement with the law firms of Ness, Motley, Loadholt, Richardson & Poole (now known as Motley Rice LLP) and Decof & Grimm (now known as Decof & Decof). That agreement provided that, in return for their legal representation on behalf of the state in the lead paint litigation, Contingent Fee Counsel would be entitled to a fee reflecting 16 2/3 percent of any monies recovered.

During the course of this litigation, defendants sought a ruling by the Superior Court that the contingent fee agreement was unenforceable and void because, in defendants' view, said agreement (1) constituted an unlawful delegation of the Attorney General's authority and (2) was violative of public policy. . . .

[The court then recognized that its holding on the merits of the public nuisance claim mooted the dispute over the retention of Contingent Fee Counsel. The court nonetheless exercised its discretion to speak to the latter issue on the ground that it is capable of repetition in the future but would evade review.]

IV

The Propriety of Contingent Fee Arrangements

Although we are keenly aware of the gravity of the issue and of the fact that thoughtful and potent policy-based arguments have been made on both sides of the issue, in the end we have concluded that, in principle, there is nothing unconstitutional or illegal or inappropriate in a contractual relationship whereby the Attorney General hires outside attorneys on a contingent fee basis to assist in the litigation of certain *non-criminal* matters. Indeed, it is our view that the ability of the Attorney General to enter into such contractual relationships may well, in some circumstances, lead to results that will be beneficial to society-results which otherwise might not have been attainable. However, due to the special duty of attorneys general to "seek justice" and their wide discretion with respect to same, such contractual relationships must be accompanied by exacting limitations. In short, it is our view that the Attorney General is not precluded from engaging private counsel pursuant to a contingent fee agreement in order to assist in certain civil litigation, so long as the Office of Attorney General retains **absolute and total control over all critical decision-making** in any case in which such agreements have been entered into. In our view, it is imperative that the case-management authority of the Attorney General, where a contingent fee agreement is involved, be "final, sole and unreviewable." *Philip Morris Inc. v. Glendening*, 709 A.2d 1230, 1243 (Md. 1998).

[A]ttorneys general are charged with the special duty to seek justice— a duty which is quite different from the responsibilities of the usual advocate. In accordance with that principle, we wholeheartedly agree with Chief Judge Mikva of the United States Court of Appeals for the District of Columbia when he wrote in almost perfervid language:

> "Government lawyers . . . should also refrain from continuing litigation that is obviously pointless, that could easily be resolved, and that wastes Court time and taxpayer money. . . . [A] government lawyer has obligations that might sometimes trump the desire to pound an opponent into submission." *Freeport–McMoRan Oil & Gas Co.*, 962 F.2d 47, 48.

The usual advocate, on the other hand, is not held to quite such an abnegatory and demanding standard. Accordingly, in order to ensure that a contingent fee agreement is not adverse to the standards that an attorney representing the government must meet, it is vital that the Office of the

Attorney General have absolute control over the course of any litigation originating in that office. . . .

In order to ensure that meaningful decision-making power remains in the hands of the Attorney General, it is our view that, at a bare minimum, the following limitations should be expressly set forth in any contingent fee agreement between that office and private counsel: (1) that the Office of the Attorney General will retain complete control over the course and conduct of the case; (2) that, in a similar vein, the Office of the Attorney General retains a veto power over any decisions made by outside counsel; and (3) that a senior member of the Attorney General's staff must be personally involved in all stages of the litigation. . . .

Conclusion

We conclude our discussion of the contingent fee issue by emphasizing our awareness that this issue involves competing values—each of which deserves respect. Attorneys who choose to litigate under contingent fee agreements understandably often have motives that, in whole or in part, are monetary in nature. Such motivation is qualitatively different from the more pristine considerations that should guide the Attorney General's decision-making. While we do not look upon contingent fee agreements with a jaundiced eye due to the fact that they inherently implicate personal profit-making as a motivation, it is precisely because of the possibility of that motivating factor having an influence on decisions made by contingent fee counsel that it is utterly imperative that absolute primacy be accorded at all times to the decision-making role of the Attorney General when he or she has entered into an agreement with contingent fee counsel. Such absolute primacy is necessary in order to ensure that the profit-making motivation is always subordinated to the Attorney General's "common law duty to represent the public interest." *Newport Realty, Inc.*, 878 A.2d 1032 (internal quotation marks omitted). . . .

NOTES AND QUESTIONS

1. Negligent Marketing of Guns as a Public Nuisance. As the Rhode Island Supreme Court's citations reflect, the other major context in which governments—specifically, local governments rather that states—have sought to invoke the public nuisance theory in recent years is in litigation against the firearms industry. The main contention there is that the industry negligently markets guns—i.e., does not reasonably oversee gun retailers, designs and markets guns to appeal to persons on the basis of their usefulness for criminal activities, and "saturates" markets with less restrictive gun control laws (largely, in the South) such that many of the guns sold there are likely to find their way illegally into other jurisdictions (the plaintiff localities, mostly in the North) that have comparatively strict gun laws. The localities sought various forms of relief, not only injunctive remedies to change industry marketing practices but also, in some instances, recovery of the additional increment of expenditures from the public fisc in connection with gun-related violent crime (e.g., for responsive police or emergency medical services) said to result from the defendant industry's negligence.

In legal terms, the results of the public nuisance lawsuits against the firearms industry were decidedly mixed, at best. For a helpful roadmap, see Timothy D. Lytton, *Introduction: An Overview of Lawsuits against the Gun Industry*, in SUING THE GUN INDUSTRY 10–14 (Timothy D. Lytton ed. 2005). In any event, before public nuisance litigation in the gun context could fully run its course, Congress stepped in, generally barring civil lawsuits—including those pending at the time—against firearms manufacturers, dealers, or trade associations for any form of relief resulting from the "criminal or unlawful misuse" of a firearm by a third party. 15 U.S.C. §§ 7901–03 (2006).

2.   *The Limits of the Public Nuisance Concept.* Does the crux of the Rhode Island Supreme Court's rationale consist of the assertion: "We shouldn't extend the public nuisance concept into the domain of conventional product liability, because that simply would give rise to too much liability"? Is this a proper justification for the court's disinclination to extend the concept? Does the commonlaw character of the concept in Rhode Island make such a justification more or less persuasive than in, say, a case involving the interpretation of a state statute authorizing the Attorney General to sue on public nuisance grounds?

In emphasizing the element of control, does the court effectively gut the use of public nuisance liability as a means to position the government to sue on account of widely dispersed harms? What difficulties would a traditional product liability action against the lead paint industry have encountered? Can you imagine a realistic scenario in which public nuisance liability would work as a way, in effect, to get something like a class action but with the government as plaintiff?

Should it make a difference to the scope of the public nuisance doctrine whether the available remedies are limited to injunctive relief, as distinct from damages? Note that even the requested injunctive relief in the Rhode Island litigation—abatement of the nuisance—would have been quite costly.

3.   *Retention of Contingency–Fee Counsel.* At the federal level today, a government agency generally may not retain private counsel to litigate on behalf of the United States on a contingency-fee basis. An Executive Order issued in 2007 by President George W. Bush provides that "no agency shall enter into a contingency fee arrangement for legal or expert witness services . . . unless the Attorney General has determined that the agency's entry into the agreement is required by law." Order No. 13433, § 2(b), 72 Fed. Reg. 28.441 (May 16, 2007).

A future President, of course, might rescind this Executive Order. But a future President, acting alone, could not repeal the Antideficiency Act, a longstanding federal statute that provides:

An officer or employee of the United States Government . . . may not—

> (A) make or authorize an expenditure or obligation exceeding an amount available in an appropriation or fund for the expenditure or obligation;

> (B) involve [the] government in a contract or obligation for the payment of money before an appropriation is made unless authorized by law. . . .

31 U.S.C. § 1341(a)(1). As described by the U.S. General Accountability Office:

> The Antideficiency Act is one of the major laws through which Congress exercises its constitutional control of the public purse. . . . The fiscal principles underlying the Antideficiency Act are really quite

simple. Government officials may not make payments or commit the United States to make payments at some future time for goods or services unless there is enough money in the "bank" to cover the cost in full. The "bank," of course, is the available appropriation.

http://www.gao.gov/ada/antideficiency.htm. Does this mean that, strictly as a legal matter, the Bush Executive Order was unnecessary? Or is the matter more complicated than that? To the extent that the government has authority to seek damages, why shouldn't a contingency fee be viewed as an enforcement cost? In other words, does an agency actually need explicit legislative authority with respect to fees, or is the authorization to seek damages sufficient?

As the Rhode Island lead paint decision reflects, the permissibility of contingency-fee retention of counsel may present an open question in a given state. Does the Rhode Island court's conception of the Attorney General as a public official obliged to "seek justice" fully capture the concerns about contingency-fee retentions? Why should the state be uniquely disabled to enter into a retention agreement for legal services that a private citizen would be permitted to use?

Is there a separation-of-powers problem here, given that such retention sidesteps legislative oversight of the nature and level of law enforcement by the Executive via the ordinary budgetary process? As the court notes, the main financial reason for retention of contingency-fee counsel by Rhode Island consisted of the lack of budgetary resources in the Attorney General's office to pursue the lead paint litigation through more conventional means—e.g., assignment of attorneys within that office to pursue such a lawsuit, with the attendant opportunity cost to conventional civil enforcement actions that the Attorney General otherwise might bring.

If, as the court suggests, the public nuisance litigation in Rhode Island was so discordant with the policy choice of the legislature to focus legal remedies on property owners, rather than the lead paint industry, then why didn't the legislature step in to disallow the contingency-fee retention? As a matter of political economy, does the legislature actually have an incentive to be complicit with contingency-fee litigation at odds with its earlier actions, at least when the litigation holds the prospect of expanding the scope of liability? *Could* the legislature have disallowed the retention agreements of the Attorney General after those agreements had been signed? If not, then is the separation-of-power problem just exacerbated? Or is it enough that the legislature might pass a law barring such retentions in the future? Enough that the legislature might pass a law forbidding the expenditure of appropriated funds by the Attorney General to supervise a specific preexisting retention, such that the Attorney General could no longer satisfy the control requirement articulated by the court?

Should it matter that the Attorney General of a given state is an elected official and, as such, might receive campaign contributions from prominent plaintiffs' law firms who might wish to be retained by the state on a contingency-fee basis? Or is this concern just the flip side of the usual one that a state official might receive campaign contributions from a significant regulated industry within the jurisdiction or one that might be positioned to compete for state business? Would the retention in the lead paint litigation have been less problematic if the Attorney General had undertaken a competitive bidding process to select contingency-fee counsel? Or does that just replicate the difficulties seen in auction-based approaches for the selection of class counsel? For that matter, did the state actually get a fairly good deal in its retention agreement with contingency-fee counsel, insofar as they agreed to work for a contingent percentage of just over 16 percent—much less than the standard 33 percent or thereabouts prevalent in ordinary, individual litigation?

CHAPTER 6

AGGREGATION MEETS ARBITRATION

This Chapter presents a brief introduction to a topic that has garnered significant attention in recent years even though it does not directly involve litigation in court. In a wide variety of contexts, contractual agreements include clauses that empower either side to compel the other to arbitrate any dispute under the contract rather than to file a conventional civil lawsuit in court. The rise of arbitration clauses in consumer and employment contracts, to take two common contexts, is part of the larger move toward alternative dispute resolution in the civil justice system generally. That larger topic extends well beyond the field of aggregate litigation.

Section A of this Chapter presents a brief overview of the rise of arbitration and the major contexts in which arbitration clauses are used. Section B then turns to a pressing issue at the intersection of arbitration and class-action law: Can arbitration clauses be used in contracts of adhesion not only to force arbitration, but also to ban class arbitration and thus force individual arbitration. Suppose, for example, that a company selling cell phone and wireless services inserts an arbitration clause in its consumer contracts and also includes a clause banning class-wide arbitration. If the company can enforce these clauses—and the Supreme Court made it easier to do so with its decision in *AT & T Mobility, LLC v. Concepcion*, 131 S. Ct. 1740 (2011), which you will read later—then it can force consumers to resolve their claims in *individual* arbitration proceedings even when it is costly for them to proceed individually. As will become apparent, the debate over class-wide arbitration replays many of the themes encountered in previous Chapters: e.g., the relationship between aggregate procedure and underlying substantive law, and the relationship between notions of "private" contract and "public" legislation.

A. THE EXPANSION OF ARBITRATION

Since the 1980s, the Supreme Court has greatly expanded the availability of arbitration, and it has done so primarily through broad interpretations of the Federal Arbitration Act (FAA), 9 U.S.C. §§ 1–16. Congress adopted the FAA in 1925 to counter judicial hostility to arbitration. During the late nineteenth and early twentieth centuries, judges applied the so-called "ouster doctrine" to refuse specific enforcement of pre-dispute arbitration agreements. The ouster doctrine held that a private agreement could not prevent a court from exercising jurisdiction it otherwise possessed. When one of two contracting parties sued in court and the other tried to dismiss the suit in reliance on an arbitration agreement entered into before the dispute arose, a judge applying the ouster doctrine would refuse to dismiss and go ahead and try the case. By 1925, Congress had become convinced of the value of arbitration, especially for commercial disputes, and it adopted the FAA to counter this hostility. See Ian R. Macneil, AMERICAN ARBITRATION LAW 15–24 (1992) (describing judicial attitudes toward arbitration agreements before the FAA).

The following two article excerpts provide a nice overview of the history of the FAA, the Supreme Court's efforts to broaden its reach, and the responses to those efforts. The first excerpt is from an article by Professor Aaron–Andrew Bruhl. He describes how the Supreme Court, through a series of decisions starting roughly in the 1980s, expanded the reach of the FAA and turned it into an instrument promoting very broad enforcement of arbitration clauses. The second excerpt is from an article by Professor Jean Sternlight. She focuses on an extremely controversial use of arbitration, what she calls "mandatory arbitration." Mandatory arbitration, in the sense she uses the term, arises when a more powerful party enters into a take-it-or-leave-it contract of adhesion with a less powerful party and the contract includes an arbitration clause. For example, a consumer who purchases cell phone services is unlikely to read the detailed sales agreement and even notice that it has an arbitration clause (and likely also a ban on class arbitration). Moreover, even if she does read it, she is not likely to appreciate the significance of the arbitration clause unless she has legal training. And even if she appreciates its significance, she can't bargain for different terms because the agreement is a standard contract of adhesion. The upshot is that the consumer *must* arbitrate future disputes rather than sue in court, and she is forced to do so without giving informed and truly voluntary consent. Or so the critics of mandatory arbitration claim. Professor Sternlight is one of the most vocal of these critics and the excerpt included here paints a rather gloomy picture.

Aaron–Andrew P. Bruhl, *The Unconscionability Game: Strategic Judging and the Evolution of Federal Arbitration Law*

83 N.Y.U. L. Rev. 1420, 1426–32 (2008)

The FAA was enacted in 1925 to bolster the enforceability of agreements to arbitrate future disputes. Its key provision, section 2, states:

> A written provision in . . . a contract evidencing a transaction involving commerce to settle by arbitration a controversy thereafter arising out of such contract . . . shall be valid, irrevocable, and enforceable, save upon such grounds as exist at law or in equity for the revocation of any contract.

In other words, an arbitration agreement involving commerce—whether a freestanding agreement or a clause within a larger contract—stands on equal footing with other agreements. Like all contracts, it is susceptible to familiar defenses such as fraud, duress, or lack of consideration (i.e., "grounds as exist at law or in equity for the revocation of any contract"), but it cannot be invalidated merely because it is an agreement to settle a dispute outside the judicial system.

The short passage quoted above holds within it the seeds of several major interpretive debates. Is the FAA merely a procedural rule operative only in federal courts or instead a substantive national policy that state courts must apply to the exclusion of their own law? To which types of contracts does it extend (or, in other words, what is a "contract evidencing a transaction involving commerce")? And what types of causes of action can be sent to arbitration—only common law actions or statutory claims as well? . . .

To begin, for many years the FAA was generally thought not to apply in state courts. Indeed, as late as 1967 the Supreme Court had not even definitively established that the FAA applied in *federal* courts in diversity cases to override state policies. To be sure, during the course of the twentieth century most states adopted their own statutes or judicial policies recognizing or bolstering the enforceability of arbitration agreements, but these state policies were often less favorable to arbitration than was the FAA.

Moreover, even in a court in which it applied, the FAA was initially limited in scope to a fairly confined set of transactions. As we have seen, the FAA requires enforcement of arbitration provisions in a "contract evidencing a transaction involving commerce." The section defining "commerce" states that it means interstate or international commerce. To a modern reader, this definition may evoke the vast sweep of current Commerce Clause power, which reaches almost all economic activity. But at the time of the FAA's enactment, in 1925, the scope of federal regulatory power was, of course, much narrower. And although federal authority substantially expanded through the course of the New Deal and then World War II, the Supreme Court did not expand the scope of the FAA to match the full reach of that expanded constitutional power. Moreover, the FAA's definition of "commerce" expressly excluded (at least certain types of) employment contracts that would otherwise fall within the statute, which further tended to restrict the statute's reach.

Finally, the FAA was limited in the types of causes of action to which it applied. The Supreme Court held in 1953 in *Wilko v. Swan* that actions under the Securities Act of 1933 were not arbitrable, concluding that arbitration was contrary to the language and intent of the statute. Later decisions applied that holding to various other statutory schemes.

As a result of all the above limitations—of forums in which the statute applied, of the types of transactions subject to regulation, and of the kinds of claims that were arbitrable—the FAA's reach was for decades quite restrained. Arbitration under the FAA was during this time largely a tool for resolving commercial disputes between businesspeople, not a phenomenon that pervaded virtually every corner of the daily economy.

That constrained, somewhat timid FAA is no more. With the Supreme Court's encouragement, it has grown into the broadly sweeping, muscular statute we know today. The metamorphosis was not instantaneous, but it is fair to say that the major stages of growth occurred in the 1980s. The causes for this change are uncertain. Likely playing a role was the Court's view that litigation had become excessive and needed to be curtailed. In 1976, Chief Justice Burger promoted and spoke at the Pound Conference on the Causes of Popular Dissatisfaction with the Administration of Justice, the chief message of which was that the "litigation explosion would have to be controlled." The Pound Conference took place against a background of the business community's growing dissatisfaction with the legal system. Yet enthusiasm for arbitration can hardly be attributed only to conservative Justices who let pro-business views overcome their professed solicitude for federalism; early rulings strengthening the FAA found support from left-leaning nationalist Justices as well.

Chief Justice Burger would soon become the author of the important 1984 decision in *Southland Corp. v. Keating*, in which the Court held that the FAA is preemptive federal substantive law that applies in both state and federal courts to the exclusion of any conflicting state law. The Court therefore invalidated the California Franchise Investment Law, which the

California Supreme Court had interpreted as barring arbitration of franchise disputes. Several Justices dissented, and the decision has remained the object of sustained criticism. Nonetheless, it has since been reaffirmed and extended several times.[38]

Also overrun was the restrictive reading of "contract[s] evidencing a transaction involving commerce" to mean only commerce that was foreign or interstate in a narrow sense (as opposed to the broad sense of those terms represented by modern constitutional doctrine). Under the old regime, states with arbitration-restricting policies could decline to apply the FAA to local transactions. Alabama was one such state, and its courts routinely applied a state statute invalidating pre-dispute arbitration clauses, reasoning that the FAA applied only to transactions in which the parties actively contemplated substantial interstate activity. In the mid–1990s, the Supreme Court granted certiorari in a case involving a pest-control contract between an Alabama homeowner and a local Terminix franchisee. Rejecting the state court's narrow reading of the FAA, the Supreme Court held that the FAA applied to the full reach of the modern Commerce Clause power.[41] And that is, of course, a broad reach indeed; it easily encompassed the pest-control contract because some of the treatment and repair materials moved in interstate commerce and because Terminix (though not its local franchise) is a multistate business. When the Alabama Supreme Court later fashioned another narrow reading of the FAA's scope, the Supreme Court summarily reversed the state court and reiterated that the FAA applies broadly to economic activity that affects interstate commerce in the aggregate, whether or not the *particular* contract at issue itself substantially affects interstate commerce.

There at least remained the fact that section 1 of the FAA excluded from the statute's reach "contracts of employment of seamen, railroad employees, or any other class of workers engaged in foreign or interstate commerce." Just as the Supreme Court had now begun to read section 2's reference to contracts "involving commerce" broadly to reach the edge of the Commerce Clause, presumably the exclusion in section 1 for workers "engaged in foreign or interstate commerce" could be read with parallel breadth to exempt almost all employment disputes from the FAA's grasp. The Ninth Circuit thought so, but the Supreme Court interred that reading in 2001.[45] The Court held that the phrase "any other class of workers engaged in foreign or interstate commerce" had to be read in light of the same provision's earlier reference to seamen and railroad workers, such that the entire exemption applied only to "transportation workers." In other words, despite reference to "commerce" in both sections, the scope of the FAA sweeps broadly in section 2, but the employment exception in section 1 is narrow.

Finally, the modern FAA has also been held to apply to statutory causes of action. The Court began by distinguishing *Wilko* and ruling that the duty to arbitrate reached claims under the 1934 Securities Exchange Act and the Racketeer Influenced and Corrupt Organizations Act (RICO).[47] Soon, the Court expressly overruled *Wilko*'s holding that claims under the

---

[38] *E.g., Preston v. Ferrer*, 128 S. Ct. 978, 983 n.2 (2008) (refusing invitation to overrule *Southland*); *Allied–Bruce Terminix Cos. v. Dobson*, 513 U.S. 265, 272 (1995) (same).

[41] [Citing *Allied–Bruce Terminix Cos. v. Dobson*, 513 U.S. 265, 268 (1995)].

[45] *Circuit City Stores, Inc. v. Adams*, 532 U.S. 105, 109 (2001).

[47] *Shearson/Am. Express, Inc. v. McMahon*, 482 U.S. 220, 227–42 (1987).

1933 Securities Act were not arbitrable.[48] Perhaps most importantly of all, the Court held in 1991 that statutory age discrimination claims could be arbitrated, a dramatic expansion of arbitration into the workplace.[49] Following that decision, all circuits now hold that employment discrimination claims under Title VII—among the most frequently invoked federal statutory protections—can be subject to arbitration.

Jean R. Sternlight, *Creeping Mandatory Arbitration: Is it Just?*

57 Stan. L. Rev. 1631, 1635–42(2005)

The emergence of "mandatory" arbitration occurred during the last fifteen to twenty years. Its rise is linked to the Supreme Court's issuance of a series of decisions that permitted businesses to use arbitration in situations they had never previously thought permissible. . . .

While the earliest cases marking this shift involved arbitration between two business entities, by 1989 the Court had applied these precedents to . . . require courts to enforce arbitration clauses imposed by securities brokerage houses on their investors. In *Moses H. Cone Memorial Hospital v. Mercury Construction Corp.*,[27] the Court enunciated, for the first time, the idea that federal policy favors arbitration of commercial disputes.[28] Then, in 1991, in *Gilmer v. Interstate/Johnson Lane Corp.*,[29] the Court held that a securities broker could be compelled to arbitrate his federal age discrimination claim against his employer. This decision shocked many employers and employees, who had previously assumed that public policy concerns would prevent courts from compelling employees to resolve employment discrimination claims through binding arbitration.

Once the Supreme Court began to issue decisions stating that commercial arbitration was "favored" and that arbitration of employment claims could be permitted, businesses jumped on the opportunity to compel arbitration in contexts where they previously thought arbitration agreements would not be enforced. In an era when they feared aspects of litigation including publicity, jury awards, punitive damages, extensive discovery, and class actions, companies saw arbitration as potentially protecting them from all of these "evils." Thus, companies in a wide array of areas soon followed the lead of the securities industry and began to use form agreements to require their customers to agree to resolve all future disputes through arbitration rather than litigation. By reading the decisions in reported cases, one can see that arbitration soon began to be mandated by a broad range of industries, including financial institutions (as to personal accounts, house and car loans, payday loans, and credit cards), service providers (termite exterminators, gymnasiums, telephone companies, and tax preparers), and sellers of goods (mobile homes, computers, and eBay). Arbitration has even been mandated in connection with games spon-

---

[48] *Rodriguez de Quijas v. Shearson/Am. Express, Inc.*, 490 U.S. 477, 479–85 (1989).

[49] *Gilmer v. Interstate/Johnson Lane Corp.*, 500 U.S. 20, 35 (1991).

[27] 460 U.S. 1 (1983).

[28] Id. at 24–25 (explaining that because questions of arbitrability "must be addressed with a healthy regard for the federal policy favoring arbitration," "any doubts concerning the scope of arbitrable issues should be resolved in favor of arbitration, whether the problem at hand is the construction of the contract language itself or an allegation of waiver, delay, or a like defense to arbitrability").

[29] 500 U.S. 20 (1991).

sored by the McDonald's hamburger chain and with respect to a mail-in on a Cheerios cereal box. In this new millennium, consumer arbitration has quickly expanded as well to health care (hospitals and health maintenance organizations), nursing homes, and educational institutions. Also, some companies are now using arbitration offensively, to obtain speedy default judgments against consumers who allegedly owe them money.

It is difficult to assess how common mandatory arbitration clauses have become, but they certainly seem ubiquitous. Readers can each do their own empirical study on this question by taking note of how often they come across mandatory arbitration clauses in their own life. I have seen arbitration mandated by my bank, my broker, my cell phone provider, various credit cards, and my mortgage lender. One recent study of the "average Joe" in Los Angeles showed that approximately one-third of the consumer transactions in his life were covered by arbitration clauses.[41] With respect to employment, while the percentage of employees required to arbitrate future disputes is probably lower than one-third, it is rising.

The new consumer and employment arbitration has a few features that were not present even in the securities arbitration upon which it was based. First, whereas the arbitration clauses prepared by brokerage houses were typically included in documents required to be signed by investors, companies soon realized that an actual signature was not required in order for an arbitration agreement to be enforced by many U.S. courts. The FAA requires that arbitration agreements be written, but does not mandate they be signed, in order to be enforceable. Thus, companies often impose arbitration on their consumers by including an arbitration agreement in a document that is received by the consumer but not necessarily read and certainly not signed. Specifically, it is now common to include arbitration clauses in small print notices, envelope stuffers, or warranties contained in boxes or sent to consumers in the mail. Some arbitration clauses are contained in Web sites, and some arbitration clauses have even been e-mailed to customers.

Second, whereas the arbitration imposed by securities brokers was typically required at the beginning of the business relationship—that is, at the time that the customer opened the account—companies now commonly impose arbitration after the relationship has already commenced. Credit card companies, for example, often send their customers small print notices stating that all future disputes will be governed by arbitration. Sometimes companies even attempt to use such clauses to replace ongoing litigation with arbitration. For example, a clause issued by Banana Republic in June 2004 states that "[t]he New Arbitration Provision applies to Claims previously asserted in lawsuits filed before the effective date of any previous arbitration provision."

Third, the broad expansion of consumer arbitration has likely meant that a less educated cadre of persons is now covered by arbitration clauses. Though not all securities investors are well educated, it seems reasonable to assume that such investors are better educated than the general public. In contrast, virtually all consumers have phones and credit cards, purchase

---

[41] Linda J. Demaine & Deborah R. Hensler, *"Volunteering" to Arbitrate Through Predispute Arbitration Clauses: The Average Consumer's Experience*, Law & Contemp. Probs., Winter/Spring 2004, at 55 (focusing on industries that provided what the authors term "important purchases"—transactions that were expensive (e.g., automobile purchases), ongoing (e.g., long distance telephone service), or that had a potentially large impact (e.g., purchase of health care services)).

termite extermination services, and so on. Thus, courts have had to face situations in which consumers to whom arbitration notices were provided denied that they were aware of the clause, understood the clause, were literate, or could see.

A fourth important feature of the new consumer arbitration is that companies are increasingly using their arbitration clause not only to require arbitration but also to further limit consumers' procedural and even substantive rights. For example, some companies have included clauses in their arbitration agreements that shorten statutes of limitations, limit or eliminate discovery, require a claimant to file in a distant forum, prevent consumers from joining together in a class action, or bar consumers from recovering particular forms of relief (injunctive relief, compensatory damages, punitive damages, or attorney fees).

B. ADDITIONAL BACKGROUND ON ARBITRATION

Arbitration is a complex field and the FAA has generated a complex body of case law. The previous excerpts discuss the reach of section 2 of the FAA, which requires judicial enforcement of valid arbitration clauses except on "such grounds as exist at law or in equity for the revocation of any contract." Section 2, for example, would preempt a state law that expressly bars enforcement of arbitration clauses in consumer contracts without affecting any other contract terms or types of contracts. Any such law would not be a "grounds . . . for revocation of any contract" within the meaning of section 2.

While it is not possible to do justice to the subject here, a few additional points about arbitration and the FAA will be useful to understanding what follows. First, it is critical to bear in mind that arbitration is almost exclusively a creature of contract. The parties must agree to resolve their disputes through arbitration and can specify which disputes they wish to arbitrate. Moreover, they can design their own arbitration procedures (subject to very few limitations). It's quite common, however, for an arbitration agreement to incorporate standard procedural templates created by private arbitration associations, such as the American Arbitration Association or JAMS, or by industry-specific groups. These arbitration procedures tend to be more limited than procedures in court, especially regarding discovery.

Second, the FAA also provides a mechanism for enforcing arbitration agreements. Section 3 requires a federal court to stay its proceeding in favor of arbitration if a party requests it, and Section 4 allows a party to obtain an order from a federal court compelling arbitration. Before a court enforces an arbitration agreement, however, it must be sure the agreement is valid. This generates one of the more complicated questions in arbitration law: Which issues arguably pertaining to validity are for the court to decide and which are for the arbitrator?

Third, the parties choose and pay for their own arbitrators. Arbitrations are frequently conducted by a single arbitrator, but they can also be handled by a panel of three arbitrators. In the latter case, known as tripartite arbitration, the parties usually choose two arbitrators and those two then choose a third. One concern about arbitration, especially between companies and consumers or companies and employees, is that arbitrators might be biased in favor of the company if it is a repeat player in arbitration because arbitrators are interested in being selected for future arbitrations. See Lisa B. Bingham, *Employment Arbitration: The Repeat Player*

Effect, 1 Emp. Rts. & Emp. Pol'y J. 189 (1997). However, the available empirical evidence does not clearly support the existence or absence of a serious repeat-player bias problem, so the best we can say is that the matter is uncertain. See Theodore Eisenberg et al., *Arbitration's Summer Soldiers: An Empirical Study of Arbitration Clauses in Consumer and Nonconsumer Contracts*, 41 U. Mich. J. L. Reform 871, 872–73 (2008) (summarizing arguments pro and con mandatory arbitration, including claims of biased outcomes compared to litigation); David Sherwyn et al., *Assessing the Case for Employment Arbitration: A New Path for Empirical Research*, 57 Stan. L. Rev. 1557, 1570–72 (2005).

Fourth, the grounds for appeal of an arbitration award are very limited, much more limited than for appeal of a court judgment. Section 10 of the FAA limits the grounds mainly to procedural defects. In particular, an award cannot be vacated on the usual ground of error as to law or fact. Moreover, parties cannot expand the scope of appellate review by contract (this is an exception to the general principle that arbitration is a creature of contract). See *Hall Street Associates, L.L.C. v. Mattel, Inc.*, 552 U.S. 576 (2008).

C. CLASS–WIDE ARBITRATION

One of the most important questions surrounding arbitration clauses today concerns their relationship with aggregate procedures. May a corporation in a consumer contract, for example, not only require the arbitration of any claims against it—something that such a corporation plainly may do under the line of decisions summarized by Professors Bruhl and Sternlight—but also forbid any such arbitration proceedings from going forward on a class-wide basis?

In upholding arbitration clauses generally under the FAA, the Supreme Court repeatedly has stated that

> [b]y agreeing to arbitrate a statutory claim, a party does not forego the substantive rights afforded by the statute; it only submits to their resolution in an arbitral, rather than a judicial, forum. It trades the procedures and opportunity for review of the courtroom for the simplicity, informality, and expedition of arbitration.

Mitsubishi Motors Corp. v. Soler Chrysler–Plymouth, Inc., 473 U.S. 614, 628 (1985). If anything, the repetition of this language in the Court's FAA case law has turned the foregoing passage into something of a mantra. See, e.g., *EEOC v. Waffle House, Inc.*, 534 U.S. 279, 295 n.10 (2002); *Circuit City Stores, Inc. v. Adams*, 532 U.S. 105, 123 (2001); *Gilmer v. Interstate/Johnson Lane Corp.*, 500 U.S. 20, 26 (1991); *Rodriguez de Quijas v. Shearson/Am. Express, Inc.*, 490 U.S. 477, 481 (1989); *Shearson/Am. Express, Inc. v. McMahon*, 482 U.S. 220, 229–30 (1987). For the Court, arbitration clauses in private contracts are, "in effect, a specialized kind of forum selection clause." *Scherk v. Alberto–Culver Co.*, 417 U.S. 506, 519 (1974). But does an arbitration clause with a further waiver of class-wide arbitration do something more in a way that should affect its permissibility under this line of Supreme Court decisions?

Class arbitration got a boost from a 2003 Supreme Court decision, *Green Tree Financial Corp. v. Bazzle*, 539 U.S. 444 (2003). A plurality of the *Bazzle* Court held that whether arbitration can proceed as class arbitration is for the arbitrators and not the court to decide, unless the parties specify otherwise. At least as important, however, was the implied support for class arbitration. Inspired in part by the *Bazzle* decision, the American Arbitration Association promulgated supplementary rules for class arbitration, rules that closely parallel the rules for class actions in court. The use of class arbitration increased, and arbitrators sometimes decided that a case was suitable for class arbitration even when the parties' agreement did not clearly say so.

Then in 2010, the Supreme Court decided *Stolt–Nielsen S.A. v. AnimalFeeds Int'l Corp.*, 559 U.S. 662, 130 S.Ct. 1758 (2010). A majority of the Court held that arbitrators could not impose class arbitration without a basis for it in the parties' agreement. AnimalFeeds entered into a charter agreement with Stolt–Nielsen, a maritime shipping company, to ship its products worldwide. The shipping agreement included an arbitration clause covering "any dispute arising from the making, performance or termination of [the charter agreement]." After a Department of Justice investigation revealed that Stolt–Nielsen and several other companies had engaged in illegal price-fixing, AnimalFeeds filed a class action lawsuit in federal district court alleging antitrust claims against these parties. Other shippers filed parallel suits, and all of these lawsuits were consolidated by the Judicial Panel on Multidistrict Litigation. Stolt–Nielsen eventually succeeded in compelling arbitration, and AnimalFeeds (and some other plaintiffs) then served Stolt–Nielsen with a demand for class arbitration.

Relying on *Bazzle*, the parties submitted to the arbitrators the question whether their arbitration agreement permitted class arbitration. The contract was silent on the matter, and—this is crucial—the parties stipulated that this meant that they had reached no agreement one way or the other. 130 S.Ct. at 1766. The arbitration panel ordered class arbitration. The arbitrators relied on the fact that the arbitration clause did not forbid class arbitration and that arbitrators after *Bazzle* had construed a wide range of arbitration agreements to permit class arbitration. *Id.* at 1767–68.

In a 5–to–3 decision, the Supreme Court vacated the panel decision. (Newly appointed Justice Sotomayor did not participate.) The Court held that parties must agree to authorize class arbitration before arbitrators can require it. It is not enough that the arbitration agreement is silent on the subject and the arbitrators believe that class arbitration is a good idea. Emphasizing that arbitrators derive their authority from the parties' contract and that their powers are limited by that contract, *id.* at 1773–75, the Court concluded that the arbitration panel in the case had exceeded the scope of its powers by relying on policy in the way a common law court might do rather than by asking whether the parties agreed to class arbitration according to contract interpretation rules:[*]

> a party may not be compelled under the [Federal Arbitration Act] to submit to class arbitration unless there is a contractual basis for concluding that the party *agreed* to do so. In this case, however, the arbitration panel imposed class arbitration even though the parties concurred that they had reached "no agreement" on that issue.

Id. at 1775 (emphasis in original).

---

[*] According to the majority, "what the arbitration panel did was simply to impose its own view of sound policy regarding class arbitration," much as a common law court would, rather than search the applicable law for guidance. The dissent disagreed with this characterization of the panel's approach, noting references in the panel's decision to the parties' agreement, New York law, and federal maritime law. *Id.* at 1780–82.

The Court acknowledged the general principle that "parties that enter into an arbitration agreement implicitly authorize the arbitrator to adopt such procedures as are necessary to give effect to the parties' agreement." *Id.* But the Court held that this principle did not extend to class arbitration because "class-action arbitration changes the nature of arbitration to such a degree that it cannot be presumed the parties consented to it by simply agreeing to submit their disputes to an arbitrator." The Court elaborated:

> Consider just some of the fundamental changes brought about by the shift from bilateral arbitration to class-action arbitration. An arbitrator chosen according to an agreed-upon procedure, . . . no longer resolves a single dispute between the parties to a single agreement, but instead resolves many disputes between hundreds or perhaps even thousands of parties. . . . Under the Class Rules [of the American Arbitration Association], "the presumption of privacy and confidentiality" that applies in many bilateral arbitrations "shall not apply in class arbitrations," . . . thus potentially frustrating the parties' assumptions when they agreed to arbitrate. The arbitrator's award no longer purports to bind just the parties to a single arbitration agreement, but adjudicates the rights of absent parties as well. . . . And the commercial stakes of class-action arbitration are comparable to those of class-action litigation, . . . even though the scope of judicial review is much more limited. . . . We think that the differences between bilateral and class-action arbitration are too great for arbitrators to presume, consistent with their limited powers under the FAA, that the parties' mere silence on the issue of class-action arbitration constitutes consent to resolve their disputes in class proceedings. . . . Contrary to the dissent, but consistent with our precedents emphasizing the consensual basis of arbitration, we see the question as being whether the parties *agreed to authorize* class arbitration. Here, where the parties stipulated that there was "no agreement" on this question, it follows that the parties cannot be compelled to submit their dispute to class arbitration.

Id. at 1776.

As this quotation from *Stolt–Nielsen* makes clear, whether an arbitration proceeding may take place on a class-wide basis can have significant consequences. One way to guarantee that there will be no class arbitration is to include a waiver of class arbitration in the agreement. In fact, one empirical study conducted before the Supreme Court decided *AT & T Mobility L.L.C. v. Concepcion*, the opinion you will read next, found that companies routinely combine class waivers—indeed, waivers of aggregation in general—with arbitration clauses in consumer contracts. Theodore Eisenberg et al., *Arbitration's Summer Soldiers: An Empirical Study of Arbitration Clauses in Consumer and Nonconsumer Contracts*, 41 U. Mich. J.L. Reform 871 (2008). The authors of the study compared consumer contracts with contracts between firms and found that arbitration clauses were much more common in the consumer contracts. They concluded that companies used arbitration in consumer contracts mainly to avoid aggregate dispute resolution. *Id.* at 882–85, 888.

There is a serious problem, however, especially for those cases where lawsuits will only be brought if they can be aggregated. Consider the following analysis and prediction:

In recent years, there have been hundreds of academic articles and scores of books written about class action litigation. The law reviews abound with doctrinal critiques, letters to Congress, moralist manifestos, and economists' prescriptions for optimized class action rules. Reading it all, one would certainly think that abusive class action litigation is running amok in the United States. . . .

It is, I think, overly dramatic to say that all of this scholarship misses the point. And yet, almost universally, the staggering heap of academic reform proposals ignores a fundamental and transformative point: in the ongoing and ever-mutating battle between plaintiffs' lawyers and the protectors of corporate interests, the corporate guys are winning. And they are winning because they have developed a new set of tools powerful enough to imperil the very viability of class actions in many—actually, most—areas of the law. In fact, I believe it is likely that, with a handful of exceptions, class actions will soon be virtually extinct.

Two factors guide this prediction: the demise of mass tort class actions and the rise of contractual class action waivers. First, as recently as ten years ago, a significant percentage of all class actions were tort cases; by most accounts, almost twenty percent. Since that time, the mass tort class action has met a fate similar to that of the Dodo bird. The latter was last seen on the island of Mauritius in 1680; the former has rarely been glimpsed since the issuance of broad class decertification opinions by federal appellate courts in asbestos, tobacco, and product liability cases in the 1980s and 1990s.

Second, and more significantly, the vast majority of the remaining class actions are based on some sort of contractual relationship. Virtually all consumer class actions, for example, arise out of some form of contract (adhesive or otherwise), just as employment discrimination class actions arise out of employment contracts. Federal antitrust class actions necessarily grow out of contracts (indeed, standing rules require as much), and the same is true for class actions relating to insurance benefits, ERISA plans, mutual funds, franchise agreements, and an endless variety of other matters.

All of these contract-based class actions are, I believe, on their way to Mauritius. Corporate caretakers have concocted an antigen, in the form of the class action waiver provision, that travels through contractual relationships and dooms the class action device. Where class actions are based on some sort of contractual relationship, this toxin is quite lethal. Developed in the late 1990s by marketers for one of the arbitral bodies, among others, the waiver works in tandem with standard arbitration provisions to ensure that any claim against the corporate defendant may be asserted only in a one-on-one, nonaggregated arbitral proceeding. More virulent strains of the clause force the would-be plaintiff to waive even her right to be represented as a passive, or absent, class member in the event some other injured person manages to commence a class proceeding. . . .

[If these sorts of contractual provisions] emerge[] more or less unscathed from the current round of judicial challenges, [then] it is only a matter of time before these waivers metastasize throughout the body of corporate America and bar the majority of class actions as we know them.

Myriam Gilles, *Opting Out of Liability: The Forthcoming, Near–Total Demise of the Modern Class Action*, 104 Mich. L. Rev. 373, 373–77 (2005).* Consider this analysis as you read the following important Supreme Court opinion dealing with enforceability of class action waivers:

AT & T Mobility LLC v. Concepcion

131 S.Ct. 1740 (2011)

■ JUSTICE SCALIA delivered the opinion of the Court.

Section 2 of the Federal Arbitration Act (FAA) makes agreements to arbitrate "valid, irrevocable, and enforceable, save upon such grounds as exist at law or in equity for the revocation of any contract." 9 U.S.C. § 2. We consider whether the FAA prohibits States from conditioning the enforceability of certain arbitration agreements on the availability of classwide arbitration procedures.

I

In February 2002, Vincent and Liza Concepcion entered into an agreement for the sale and servicing of cellular telephones with AT & T Mobility LCC (AT & T).[1] The contract provided for arbitration of all disputes between the parties, but required that claims be brought in the parties' "individual capacity, and not as a plaintiff or class member in any purported class or representative proceeding."[2] The agreement authorized AT & T to make unilateral amendments, which it did to the arbitration provision on several occasions. The version at issue in this case reflects revisions made in December 2006, which the parties agree are controlling.

The revised agreement provides that customers may initiate dispute proceedings by completing a one-page Notice of Dispute form available on AT & T's Web site. AT & T may then offer to settle the claim; if it does not, or if the dispute is not resolved within 30 days, the customer may invoke arbitration by filing a separate Demand for Arbitration, also available on AT & T's Web site. In the event the parties proceed to arbitration, the agreement specifies that AT & T must pay all costs for nonfrivolous claims; that arbitration must take place in the county in which the customer is billed; that, for claims of $10,000 or less, the customer may choose whether the arbitration proceeds in person, by telephone, or based only on submissions; that either party may bring a claim in small claims court in lieu of arbitration; and that the arbitrator may award any form of individual relief, including injunctions and presumably punitive damages. The agreement, moreover, denies AT & T any ability to seek reimbursement of its attorney's fees, and, in the event that a customer receives an arbitration award greater than AT & T's last written settlement offer, requires AT & T

---

* Reprinted from MICHIGAN LAW REVIEW, December 2005, Vol. 104, No. 3. Copyright 2005 by The Michigan Law Review Association.

[1] The Conceptions' original contract was with Cingular Wireless. AT & T acquired Cingular in 2005 and renamed the company AT & T Mobility in 2007.

[2] That provision further states that "the arbitrator may not consolidate more than one person's claims, and may not otherwise preside over any form of a representative or class proceeding."

to pay a $7,500 minimum recovery and twice the amount of the claimant's attorney's fees.[3]

The Concepcions purchased AT & T service, which was advertised as including the provision of free phones; they were not charged for the phones, but they were charged $30.22 in sales tax based on the phones' retail value. In March 2006, the Concepcions filed a complaint against AT & T in the United States District Court for the Southern District of California. The complaint was later consolidated with a putative class action alleging, among other things, that AT & T had engaged in false advertising and fraud by charging sales tax on phones it advertised as free.

In March 2008, AT & T moved to compel arbitration under the terms of its contract with the Concepcions. The Concepcions opposed the motion, contending that the arbitration agreement was unconscionable and unlawfully exculpatory under California law because it disallowed classwide procedures. The District Court denied AT & T's motion. It described AT & T's arbitration agreement favorably, noting, for example, that the informal dispute-resolution process was "quick, easy to use" and likely to "promp[t] full or . . . even excess payment to the customer *without* the need to arbitrate or litigate"; that the $7,500 premium functioned as "a substantial inducement for the consumer to pursue the claim in arbitration" if a dispute was not resolved informally; and that consumers who were members of a class would likely be worse off. Nevertheless, relying on the California Supreme Court's decision in *Discover Bank v. Superior Court*, 36 Cal. 4th 148 (2005), the court found that the arbitration provision was unconscionable because AT & T had not shown that bilateral arbitration adequately substituted for the deterrent effects of class actions.

The Ninth Circuit affirmed, also finding the provision unconscionable under California law as announced in *Discover Bank*. It also held that the *Discover Bank* rule was not preempted by the FAA because that rule was simply "a refinement of the unconscionability analysis applicable to contracts generally in California." In response to AT & T's argument that the Concepcions' interpretation of California law discriminated against arbitration, the Ninth Circuit rejected the contention that " 'class proceedings will reduce the efficiency and expeditiousness of arbitration' " and noted that " '*Discover Bank* placed arbitration agreements with class action waivers on the *exact same footing* as contracts that bar class action litigation outside the context of arbitration.' "

We granted certiorari.

II

The FAA was enacted in 1925 in response to widespread judicial hostility to arbitration agreements. See *Hall Street Associates, L. L. C. v. Mattel, Inc.*, 552 U.S. 576, 581 (2008). Section 2 the "primary substantive provision of the Act," . . . provides, in relevant part, as follows:

> "A written provision in any maritime transaction or a contract evidencing a transaction involving commerce to settle by arbitration a controversy thereafter arising out of such contract or transaction . . . shall be valid, irrevocable, and enforceable, save upon such grounds as exist at law or in equity for the revocation of any contract." 9 U.S.C. § 2.

---

[3] The guaranteed minimum recovery was increased in 2009 to $10,000.

We have described this provision as reflecting both a "liberal federal policy favoring arbitration," . . . and the "fundamental principle that arbitration is a matter of contract. . . ." In line with these principles, courts must place arbitration agreements on an equal footing with other contracts, . . . and enforce them according to their terms. . . .

The final phrase of § 2, however, permits arbitration agreements to be declared unenforceable "upon such grounds as exist at law or in equity for the revocation of any contract." This saving clause permits agreements to arbitrate to be invalidated by "generally applicable contract defenses, such as fraud, duress, or unconscionability," but not by defenses that apply only to arbitration or that derive their meaning from the fact that an agreement to arbitrate is at issue. *Doctor's Associates, Inc. v. Casarotto*, 517 U.S. 681, 687 (1996); see also *Perry v. Thomas*, 482 U.S. 483, 492–493, n.9 (1987). The question in this case is whether § 2 preempts California's rule classifying most collective-arbitration waivers in consumer contracts as unconscionable. We refer to this rule as the *Discover Bank* rule.

Under California law, courts may refuse to enforce any contract found "to have been unconscionable at the time it was made," or may "limit the application of any unconscionable clause." Cal. Civ. Code Ann. § 1670.5(a) (West 1985). A finding of unconscionability requires "a 'procedural' and a 'substantive' element, the former focusing on 'oppression' or 'surprise' due to unequal bargaining power, the latter on 'overly harsh' or 'one-sided' results. . . ."

In *Discover Bank*, the California Supreme Court applied this framework to class-action waivers in arbitration agreements and held as follows:

> "[W]hen the waiver is found in a consumer contract of adhesion in a setting in which disputes between the contracting parties predictably involve small amounts of damages, and when it is alleged that the party with the superior bargaining power has carried out a scheme to deliberately cheat large numbers of consumers out of individually small sums of money, then . . . the waiver becomes in practice the exemption of the party 'from responsibility for [its] own fraud, or willful injury to the person or property of another.' Under these circumstances, such waivers are unconscionable under California law and should not be enforced." *Id.*, at 162 (quoting Cal. Civ. Code Ann. § 1668).

California courts have frequently applied this rule to find arbitration agreements unconscionable. . . .

III

A

The Concepcions argue that the *Discover Bank* rule, given its origins in California's unconscionability doctrine and California's policy against exculpation, is a ground that "exist[s] at law or in equity for the revocation of any contract" under FAA § 2. Moreover, they argue that even if we construe the *Discover Bank* rule as a prohibition on collective-action waivers rather than simply an application of unconscionability, the rule would still be applicable to all dispute-resolution contracts, since California prohibits waivers of class litigation as well. See *America Online, Inc. v. Superior Ct.*, 90 Cal. App. 4th 1, 17–18 (2001).

When state law prohibits outright the arbitration of a particular type of claim, the analysis is straightforward: The conflicting rule is displaced by the FAA. But the inquiry becomes more complex when a doctrine normally thought to be generally applicable, such as duress or, as relevant here, unconscionability, is alleged to have been applied in a fashion that disfavors arbitration. In *Perry v. Thomas*, 482 U.S. 483 (1987), for example, we noted that the FAA's preemptive effect might extend even to grounds traditionally thought to exist " 'at law or in equity for the revocation of any contract.' " *Id.*, at 492, n.9 (emphasis deleted). We said that a court may not "rely on the uniqueness of an agreement to arbitrate as a basis for a state-law holding that enforcement would be unconscionable, for this would enable the court to effect what . . . the state legislature cannot." *Id.*, at 493, n.9.

An obvious illustration of this point would be a case finding unconscionable or unenforceable as against public policy consumer arbitration agreements that fail to provide for judicially monitored discovery. The rationalizations for such a holding are neither difficult to imagine nor different in kind from those articulated in *Discover Bank*. A court might reason that no consumer would knowingly waive his right to full discovery, as this would enable companies to hide their wrongdoing. Or the court might simply say that such agreements are exculpatory—restricting discovery would be of greater benefit to the company than the consumer, since the former is more likely to be sued than to sue. See *Discover Bank*, [36 Cal. 4th], at 161 (arguing that class waivers are similarly one-sided). And, the reasoning would continue, because such a rule applies the general principle of unconscionability or public-policy disapproval of exculpatory agreements, it is applicable to "any" contract and thus preserved by § 2 of the FAA. In practice, of course, the rule would have a disproportionate impact on arbitration agreements; but it would presumably apply to contracts purporting to restrict discovery in litigation as well.

Other examples are easy to imagine. The same argument might apply to a rule classifying as unconscionable arbitration agreements that fail to abide by the Federal Rules of Evidence, or that disallow an ultimate disposition by a jury (perhaps termed "a panel of twelve lay arbitrators" to help avoid preemption). Such examples are not fanciful, since the judicial hostility towards arbitration that prompted the FAA had manifested itself in "a great variety" of "devices and formulas" declaring arbitration against public policy. And although these statistics are not definitive, it is worth noting that California's courts have been more likely to hold contracts to arbitrate unconscionable than other contracts. . . .

The Concepcions suggest that all this is just a parade of horribles, and no genuine worry. "Rules aimed at destroying arbitration" or "demanding procedures incompatible with arbitration," they concede, "would be preempted by the FAA because they cannot sensibly be reconciled with Section 2." The "grounds" available under § 2's saving clause, they admit, "should not be construed to include a State's mere preference for procedures that are incompatible with arbitration and 'would wholly eviscerate arbitration agreements.' "[4]

We largely agree. Although § 2's saving clause preserves generally applicable contract defenses, nothing in it suggests an intent to preserve state-law rules that stand as an obstacle to the accomplishment of the

---

[4] The dissent seeks to fight off even this eminently reasonable concession. It says that to its knowledge "we have not . . . applied the Act to strike down a state statute that treats arbitrations on par with judicial and administrative proceedings," (opinion of BREYER, J.), and that "we should think more than twice before invalidating a state law that . . . puts agreements to arbitrate and agreements to litigate 'upon the same footing.' "

FAA's objectives. . . . As we have said, a federal statute's saving clause " 'cannot in reason be construed as [allowing] a common law right, the continued existence of which would be absolutely inconsistent with the provisions of the act. In other words, the act cannot be held to destroy itself.' " *American Telephone & Telegraph Co. v. Central Office Telephone, Inc.*, 524 U.S. 214, 227–228 (1998) (quoting *Texas & Pacific R. Co. v. Abilene Cotton Oil Co.*, 204 U.S. 426, 446 (1907)).

We differ with the Concepcions only in the application of this analysis to the matter before us. We do not agree that rules requiring judicially monitored discovery or adherence to the Federal Rules of Evidence are "a far cry from this case." The overarching purpose of the FAA, evident in the text of §§ 2, 3, and 4, is to ensure the enforcement of arbitration agreements according to their terms so as to facilitate streamlined proceedings. Requiring the availability of classwide arbitration interferes with fundamental attributes of arbitration and thus creates a scheme inconsistent with the FAA.

B

The "principal purpose" of the FAA is to "ensur[e] that private arbitration agreements are enforced according to their terms. . . ." This purpose is readily apparent from the FAA's text. Section 2 makes arbitration agreements "valid, irrevocable, and enforceable" as written (subject, of course, to the saving clause); § 3 requires courts to stay litigation of arbitral claims pending arbitration of those claims "in accordance with the terms of the agreement"; and § 4 requires courts to compel arbitration "in accordance with the terms of the agreement" upon the motion of either party to the agreement (assuming that the "making of the arbitration agreement or the failure . . . to perform the same" is not at issue). In light of these provisions, we have held that parties may agree to limit the issues subject to arbitration, . . . to arbitrate according to specific rules, . . . and to limit *with whom* a party will arbitrate its disputes. . . .

The point of affording parties discretion in designing arbitration processes is to allow for efficient, streamlined procedures tailored to the type of dispute. It can be specified, for example, that the decisionmaker be a specialist in the relevant field, or that proceedings be kept confidential to protect trade secrets. And the informality of arbitral proceedings is itself desirable, reducing the cost and increasing the speed of dispute resolution. . . .

Contrary to the dissent's view, our cases place it beyond dispute that the FAA was designed to promote arbitration. They have repeatedly described the Act as "embod[ying] [a] national policy favoring arbitration," and "a liberal federal policy favoring arbitration agreements, notwithstanding any state substantive or procedural policies to the contrary." Thus, in *Preston v. Ferrer*, holding preempted a state-law rule requiring exhaustion of administrative remedies before arbitration, we said: "A prime objective of an agreement to arbitrate is to achieve 'streamlined proceedings and expeditious results,' " which objective would be "frustrated" by requiring a dispute to be heard by an agency first. 552 U.S. [346,] 357–358. That rule, we said, would "at the least, hinder speedy resolution of the controversy." *Id.*, at 358.[5]

---

[5] Relying upon nothing more indicative of congressional understanding than statements of witnesses in committee hearings and a press release of Secretary of Commerce Herbert Hoover, the dissent suggests that Congress "thought that arbitration would be used primarily where merchants sought to resolve disputes of fact . . . [and] possessed roughly equivalent

California's *Discover Bank* rule similarly interferes with arbitration. Although the rule does not *require* classwide arbitration, it allows any party to a consumer contract to demand it *ex post*. The rule is limited to adhesion contracts, *Discover Bank*, 36 Cal. 4th, at 162–163, but the times in which consumer contracts were anything other than adhesive are long past.[6] . . . The rule also requires that damages be predictably small, and that the consumer allege a scheme to cheat consumers. *Discover Bank, supra*, at 162–163. The former requirement, however, is toothless and malleable (the Ninth Circuit has held that damages of $4,000 are sufficiently small . . .), and the latter has no limiting effect, as all that is required is an allegation. Consumers remain free to bring and resolve their disputes on a bilateral basis under *Discover Bank*, and some may well do so; but there is little incentive for lawyers to arbitrate on behalf of individuals when they may do so for a class and reap far higher fees in the process. And faced with inevitable class arbitration, companies would have less incentive to continue resolving potentially duplicative claims on an individual basis.

Although we have had little occasion to examine classwide arbitration, our decision in *Stolt–Nielsen* is instructive. In that case we held that an arbitration panel exceeded its power under § 10(a)(4) of the FAA by imposing class procedures based on policy judgments rather than the arbitration agreement itself or some background principle of contract law that would affect its interpretation. We then held that the agreement at issue, which was silent on the question of class procedures, could not be interpreted to allow them because the "changes brought about by the shift from bilateral arbitration to class-action arbitration" are "fundamental." This is obvious as a structural matter: Classwide arbitration includes absent parties, necessitating additional and different procedures and involving higher stakes. Confidentiality becomes more difficult. And while it is theoretically possible to select an arbitrator with some expertise relevant to the class-certification question, arbitrators are not generally knowledgeable in the often-dominant procedural aspects of certification, such as the protection of absent parties. The conclusion follows that class arbitration, to the extent it is manufactured by *Discover Bank* rather than consensual, is inconsistent with the FAA.

First, the switch from bilateral to class arbitration sacrifices the principal advantage of arbitration—its informality—and makes the process slower, more costly, and more likely to generate procedural morass than final judgment. "In bilateral arbitration, parties forgo the procedural rigor and appellate review of the courts in order to realize the benefits of private dispute resolution: lower costs, greater efficiency and speed, and the ability

---

bargaining power." Such a limitation appears nowhere in the text of the FAA and has been explicitly rejected by our cases. "Relationships between securities dealers and investors, for example, may involve unequal bargaining power, but we [have] nevertheless held . . . that agreements to arbitrate in that context are enforceable." *Gilmer v. Interstate/Johnson Lane Corp.*, 500 U.S. 20, 33 (1991); see also *id.*, at 32–33 (allowing arbitration of claims arising under the Age Discrimination in Employment Act of 1967 despite allegations of unequal bargaining power between employers and employees). Of course the dissent's disquisition on legislative history fails to note that it contains nothing—not even the testimony of a stray witness in committee hearings—that contemplates the existence of class arbitration.

[6] Of course States remain free to take steps addressing the concerns that attend contracts of adhesion—for example, requiring class-action-waiver provisions in adhesive arbitration agreements to be highlighted. Such steps cannot, however, conflict with the FAA or frustrate its purpose to ensure that private arbitration agreements are enforced according to their terms.

to choose expert adjudicators to resolve specialized disputes." 559 U.S., at
___, 130 S. Ct. 1758. But before an arbitrator may decide the merits of a
claim in classwide procedures, he must first decide, for example, whether
the class itself may be certified, whether the named parties are sufficiently
representative and typical, and how discovery for the class should be conducted. A cursory comparison of bilateral and class arbitration illustrates
the difference. According to the American Arbitration Association (AAA),
the average consumer arbitration between January and August 2007 resulted in a disposition on the merits in six months, four months if the arbitration was conducted by documents only. AAA, Analysis of the AAA's Consumer Arbitration Caseload, online at http://www.adr.org/si.asp?id=5027
(all Internet materials as visited Apr. 25, 2011, and available in Clerk of
Court's case file). As of September 2009, the AAA had opened 283 class arbitrations. Of those, 121 remained active, and 162 had been settled, withdrawn, or dismissed. Not a single one, however, had resulted in a final
award on the merits. Brief for AAA as *Amicus Curiae* in *Stolt–Nielsen*, O.
T. 2009, No. 08–1198, pp. 22–24. For those cases that were no longer active,
the median time from filing to settlement, withdrawal, or dismissal—not
judgment on the merits—was 583 days, and the mean was 630 days. *Id.*, at
24.[7]

Second, class arbitration *requires* procedural formality. The AAA's
rules governing class arbitrations mimic the Federal Rules of Civil Procedure for class litigation. Compare AAA, Supplementary Rules for Class Arbitrations (effective Oct. 8, 2003), online at http://www.adr.org/
sp.asp?id=21936, with Fed. Rule Civ. Proc. 23. And while parties can alter
those procedures by contract, an alternative is not obvious. If procedures
are too informal, absent class members would not be bound by the arbitration. For a class-action money judgment to bind absentees in litigation,
class representatives must at all times adequately represent absent class
members, and absent members must be afforded notice, an opportunity to
be heard, and a right to opt out of the class. *Phillips Petroleum Co. v.
Shutts*, 472 U.S. 797, 811–12 (1985). At least this amount of process would
presumably be required for absent parties to be bound by the results of arbitration.

We find it unlikely that in passing the FAA Congress meant to leave
the disposition of these procedural requirements to an arbitrator. Indeed,
class arbitration was not even envisioned by Congress when it passed the
FAA in 1925; as the California Supreme Court admitted in *Discover Bank*,
class arbitration is a "relatively recent development." And it is at the very
least odd to think that an arbitrator would be entrusted with ensuring that
third parties' due process rights are satisfied.

Third, class arbitration greatly increases risks to defendants. Informal
procedures do of course have a cost: The absence of multilayered review
makes it more likely that errors will go uncorrected. Defendants are willing
to accept the costs of these errors in arbitration, since their impact is limited to the size of individual disputes, and presumably outweighed by savings from avoiding the courts. But when damages allegedly owed to tens of
thousands of potential claimants are aggregated and decided at once, the
risk of an error will often become unacceptable. Faced with even a small

---

[7] The dissent claims that class arbitration should be compared to class litigation, not bilateral arbitration. Whether arbitrating a class is more desirable than litigating one, however,
is not relevant. A State cannot defend a rule requiring arbitration-by-jury by saying that parties will still prefer it to trial-by-jury.

chance of a devastating loss, defendants will be pressured into settling questionable claims. Other courts have noted the risk of "in terrorem" settlements that class actions entail, and class arbitration would be no different.

Arbitration is poorly suited to the higher stakes of class litigation. In litigation, a defendant may appeal a certification decision on an interlocutory basis and, if unsuccessful, may appeal from a final judgment as well. Questions of law are reviewed *de novo* and questions of fact for clear error. In contrast, 9 U.S.C. § 10 allows a court to vacate an arbitral award *only* where the award "was procured by corruption, fraud, or undue means"; "there was evident partiality or corruption in the arbitrators"; "the arbitrators were guilty of misconduct in refusing to postpone the hearing . . . or in refusing to hear evidence pertinent and material to the controversy[,] or of any other misbehavior by which the rights of any party have been prejudiced"; or if the "arbitrators exceeded their powers, or so imperfectly executed them that a mutual, final, and definite award . . . was not made." The AAA rules do authorize judicial review of certification decisions, but this review is unlikely to have much effect given these limitations; review under § 10 focuses on misconduct rather than mistake. And parties may not contractually expand the grounds or nature of judicial review. *Hall Street Assocs.*, 552 U.S., at 578. We find it hard to believe that defendants would bet the company with no effective means of review, and even harder to believe that Congress would have intended to allow state courts to force such a decision.[8]

The Concepcions contend that because parties may and sometimes do agree to aggregation, class procedures are not necessarily incompatible with arbitration. But the same could be said about procedures that the Concepcions admit States may not superimpose on arbitration: Parties *could* agree to arbitrate pursuant to the Federal Rules of Civil Procedure, or pursuant to a discovery process rivaling that in litigation. Arbitration is a matter of contract, and the FAA requires courts to honor parties' expectations. . . . But what the parties in the aforementioned examples would have agreed to is not arbitration as envisioned by the FAA, lacks its benefits, and therefore may not be required by state law.

The dissent claims that class proceedings are necessary to prosecute small-dollar claims that might otherwise slip through the legal system. But States cannot require a procedure that is inconsistent with the FAA, even if it is desirable for unrelated reasons. Moreover, the claim here was most unlikely to go unresolved. As noted earlier, the arbitration agreement provides that AT & T will pay claimants a minimum of $7,500 and twice their attorney's fees if they obtain an arbitration award greater than AT & T's last settlement offer. The District Court found this scheme sufficient to provide incentive for the individual prosecution of meritorious claims that are not immediately settled, and the Ninth Circuit admitted that aggrieved customers who filed claims would be "essentially guarantee[d]" to be made

---

[8] The dissent cites three large arbitration awards (none of which stems from classwide arbitration) as evidence that parties are willing to submit large claims before an arbitrator. Those examples might be in point if it could be established that the size of the arbitral dispute was predictable when the arbitration agreement was entered. Otherwise, all the cases prove is that arbitrators can give huge awards—which we have never doubted. The point is that in class-action arbitration huge awards (with limited judicial review) will be entirely predictable, thus rendering arbitration unattractive. It is not reasonably deniable that requiring consumer disputes to be arbitrated on a classwide basis will have a substantial deterrent effect on incentives to arbitrate.

whole. Indeed, the District Court concluded that the Concepcions were *better off* under their arbitration agreement with AT & T than they would have been as participants in a class action, which "could take months, if not years, and which may merely yield an opportunity to submit a claim for recovery of a small percentage of a few dollars."

* * *

Because it "stands as an obstacle to the accomplishment and execution of the full purposes and objectives of Congress," *Hines v. Davidowitz*, 312 U.S. 52, 67 (1941), California's *Discover Bank* rule is preempted by the FAA. The judgment of the Ninth Circuit is reversed, and the case is remanded for further proceedings consistent with this opinion.

It is so ordered.

JUSTICE BREYER, with whom JUSTICE GINSBURG, JUSTICE SOTOMAYOR, and JUSTICE KAGAN, join, dissenting.

The Federal Arbitration Act says that an arbitration agreement "shall be valid, irrevocable, and enforceable, *save upon such grounds as exist at law or in equity for the revocation of any contract.*" 9 U.S.C. § 2 (emphasis added). California law sets forth certain circumstances in which "class action waivers" in *any* contract are unenforceable. In my view, this rule of state law is consistent with the federal Act's language and primary objective. It does not "stan[d] as an obstacle" to the Act's "accomplishment and execution. . . ." And the Court is wrong to hold that the federal Act preempts the rule of state law.

I

The California law in question consists of an authoritative state-court interpretation of two provisions of the California Civil Code. The first provision makes unlawful all contracts "which have for their object, directly or in-directly, to exempt anyone from responsibility for his own . . . violation of law." Cal. Civ. Code Ann. § 1668 (West 1985). The second provision authorizes courts to "limit the application of any unconscionable clause" in a contract so "as to avoid any unconscionable result." § 1670.5(a).

The specific rule of state law in question consists of the California Supreme Court's application of these principles to hold that "some" (but not "all") "class action waivers" in consumer contracts are exculpatory and unconscionable under California "law." In particular, in *Discover Bank*, 36 Cal. 4th 148, 160 (2005), the California Supreme Court stated that, when a class-action waiver

> "is found in a consumer contract of adhesion in a setting in which disputes between the contracting parties predictably involve small amounts of damages, and when it is alleged that the party with the superior bargaining power has carried out a scheme to deliberately cheat large numbers of consumers out of individually small sums of money, then . . . the waiver becomes in practice the exemption of the party 'from responsibility for [its] own fraud, or willful injury to the person or property of another.'"
> *Id.*, at 162–63.

In such a circumstance, the "waivers are unconscionable under California law and should not be enforced."

The *Discover Bank* rule does not create a "blanket policy in California against class action waivers in the consumer context." . . . Instead, it represents the "application of a more general [unconscionability] principle. . . ." Courts applying California law have enforced class-action waivers where they satisfy general unconscionability standards. . . . And even when they fail, the parties remain free to devise other dispute mechanisms, including informal mechanisms, that, in context, will not prove unconscionable. . . .

II

A

The *Discover Bank* rule is consistent with the federal Act's language. It "applies equally to class action litigation waivers in contracts without arbitration agreements as it does to class arbitration waivers in contracts with such agreements." 36 Cal. 4th, at 165–166. Linguistically speaking, it falls directly within the scope of the Act's exception permitting courts to refuse to enforce arbitration agreements on grounds that exist "for the revocation of *any* contract." 9 U.S.C. § 2 (emphasis added). The majority agrees.

B

The *Discover Bank* rule is also consistent with the basic "purpose behind" the Act. We have described that purpose as one of "ensur[ing] judicial enforcement" of arbitration agreements. . . . As is well known, prior to the federal Act, many courts expressed hostility to arbitration, for example by refusing to order specific performance of agreements to arbitrate. . . . The Act sought to eliminate that hostility by placing agreements to arbitrate "'upon the same footing as other contracts.'" *Scherk v. Alberto–Culver Co.*, 417 U.S. 506, 511 (1974) (quoting H. R. Rep. No. 96, at 2; emphasis added).

Congress was fully aware that arbitration could provide procedural and cost advantages. The House Report emphasized the "appropriate[ness]" of making arbitration agreements enforceable "at this time when there is so much agitation against the costliness and delays of litigation." And this Court has acknowledged that parties may enter into arbitration agreements in order to expedite the resolution of disputes. . . .

But we have also cautioned against thinking that Congress' primary objective was to guarantee these particular procedural advantages. Rather, that primary objective was to secure the "enforcement" of agreements to arbitrate. . . .

Thus, insofar as we seek to implement Congress' intent, we should think more than twice before invalidating a state law that does just what § 2 requires, namely, puts agreements to arbitrate and agreements to litigate "upon the same footing."

III

The majority's contrary view (that *Discover Bank* stands as an "obstacle" to the accomplishment of the federal law's objective) rests primarily upon its claims that the *Discover Bank* rule increases the complexity of arbitration procedures, thereby discouraging parties from entering into arbitration agreements, and to that extent discriminating in practice against arbitration. These claims are not well founded.

For one thing, a state rule of law that would sometimes set aside as unconscionable a contract term that forbids class arbitration is not (as the majority claims) like a rule that would require "ultimate disposition by a jury" or "judicially monitored discovery" or use of "the Federal Rules of Evidence." Unlike the majority's examples, class arbitration is consistent with the use of arbitration. It is a form of arbitration that is well known in California and followed elsewhere. . . . Indeed, the AAA has told us that it has found class arbitration to be "a fair, balanced, and efficient means of resolving class disputes." Brief for AAA as *Amicus Curiae* in *Stolt–Nielsen S. A. v. AnimalFeeds Int'l Corp.*, O. T. 2009, No. 08–1198, p. 25. And unlike the majority's examples, the *Discover Bank* rule imposes equivalent limitations on litigation; hence it cannot fairly be characterized as a targeted attack on arbitration.

Where does the majority get its contrary idea—that individual, rather than class, arbitration is a "fundamental attribut[e]" of arbitration? The majority does not explain. And it is unlikely to be able to trace its present view to the history of the arbitration statute itself.

When Congress enacted the Act, arbitration procedures had not yet been fully developed. Insofar as Congress considered detailed forms of arbitration at all, it may well have thought that arbitration would be used primarily where merchants sought to resolve disputes of fact, not law, under the customs of their industries, where the parties possessed roughly equivalent bargaining power. . . . This last mentioned feature of the history—roughly equivalent bargaining power—suggests, if anything, that California's statute is consistent with, and indeed may help to further, the objectives that Congress had in mind.

Regardless, if neither the history nor present practice suggests that class arbitration is fundamentally incompatible with arbitration itself, then on what basis can the majority hold California's law pre-empted?

For another thing, the majority's argument that the *Discover Bank* rule will discourage arbitration rests critically upon the wrong comparison. The majority compares the complexity of class arbitration with that of bilateral arbitration. And it finds the former more complex. But, if incentives are at issue, the *relevant* comparison is not "arbitration with arbitration" but a comparison between class arbitration and judicial class actions. After all, in respect to the relevant set of contracts, the *Discover Bank* rule similarly and equally sets aside clauses that forbid class procedures—whether arbitration procedures or ordinary judicial procedures are at issue.

Why would a typical defendant (say, a business) prefer a judicial class action to class arbitration? AAA statistics "suggest that class arbitration proceedings take more time than the average commercial arbitration, but may take *less time* than the average class action in court. . . ." Data from California courts confirm that class arbitrations can take considerably less time than in-court proceedings in which class certification is sought. . . . And a single class proceeding is surely more efficient than thousands of separate proceedings for identical claims. Thus, if speedy resolution of disputes were all that mattered, then the *Discover Bank* rule would reinforce, not obstruct, that objective of the Act.

The majority's related claim that the *Discover Bank* rule will discourage the use of arbitration because "[a]rbitration is poorly suited to . . . higher stakes" lacks empirical support. Indeed, the majority provides no convincing reason to believe that parties are unwilling to submit high-stake disputes to arbitration. And there are numerous counterexamples. Loftus, Rivals Resolve Dispute Over Drug, Wall Street Journal, Apr. 16, 2011, p. B2 (discussing $500 million settlement in dispute submitted to arbitration); Ziobro, Kraft Seeks Arbitration In Fight With Starbucks Over Distribution, Wall Street Journal, Nov. 30, 2010, p. B10 (describing initiation of an arbitration in which the payout "could be higher" than $1.5 billion); Markoff, Software Arbitration Ruling Gives I.B.M. $833 Million From Fujitsu, N. Y.

Times, Nov. 30, 1988, p. A1 (describing both companies as "pleased with the ruling" resolving a licensing dispute).

Further, even though contract defenses, *e.g.*, duress and unconscionability, slow down the dispute resolution process, federal arbitration law normally leaves such matters to the States. . . . A provision in a contract of adhesion (for example, requiring a consumer to decide very quickly whether to pursue a claim) might increase the speed and efficiency of arbitrating a dispute, but the State can forbid it. . . . The *Discover Bank* rule amounts to a variation on this theme. California is free to define unconscionability as it sees fit, and its common law is of no federal concern so long as the State does not adopt a special rule that disfavors arbitration. . . .

Because California applies the same legal principles to address the unconscionability of class arbitration waivers as it does to address the unconscionability of any other contractual provision, the merits of class proceedings should not factor into our decision. If California had applied its law of duress to void an arbitration agreement, would it matter if the procedures in the coerced agreement were efficient?

Regardless, the majority highlights the disadvantages of class arbitrations, as it sees them. But class proceedings have countervailing advantages. In general agreements that forbid the consolidation of claims can lead small-dollar claimants to abandon their claims rather than to litigate. I suspect that it is true even here, for as the Court of Appeals recognized, AT & T can avoid the $7,500 payout (the payout that supposedly makes the Concepcions' arbitration worthwhile) simply by paying the claim's face value, such that "the maximum gain to a customer for the hassle of arbitrating a $30.22 dispute is still just $30.22. . . ."

What rational lawyer would have signed on to represent the Concepcions in litigation for the possibility of fees stemming from a $30.22 claim? See, e.g., *Carnegie v. Household Int'l, Inc.*, 376 F.3d 656, 661 (.7th Cir. 2004) ("The *realistic* alternative to a class action is not 17 million individual suits, but zero individual suits, as only a lunatic or a fanatic sues for $30"). In California's perfectly rational view, nonclass arbitration over such sums will also sometimes have the effect of depriving claimants of their claims (say, for example, where claiming the $30.22 were to involve filling out many forms that require technical legal knowledge or waiting at great length while a call is placed on hold). *Discover Bank* sets forth circumstances in which the California courts believe that the terms of consumer contracts can be manipulated to insulate an agreement's author from liability for its own frauds by "deliberately cheat[ing] large numbers of consumers out of individually small sums of money." 36 Cal. 4th, at 162–163. Why is this kind of decision—weighing the pros and cons of all class proceedings alike—not California's to make?

Finally, the majority can find no meaningful support for its views in this Court's precedent. The federal Act has been in force for nearly a century. We have decided dozens of cases about its requirements. We have reached results that authorize complex arbitration procedures. . . . We have upheld nondiscriminatory state laws that slow down arbitration proceedings. . . . But we have not, to my knowledge, applied the Act to strike down a state statute that treats arbitrations on par with judicial and administrative proceedings. . . .

At the same time, we have repeatedly referred to the Act's basic objective as assuring that courts treat arbitration agreements "like all other contracts. . . ." And we have recognized that "[t]o immunize an arbitration agreement from judicial challenge" on grounds applicable to all other contracts "would be to elevate it over other forms of contract. . . ."

These cases do not concern the merits and demerits of class actions; they concern equal treatment of arbitration contracts and other contracts. Since it is the latter question that is at issue here, I am not surprised that the majority can find no meaningful precedent supporting its decision.

IV

By using the words "save upon such grounds as exist at law or in equity for the revocation of any contract," Congress retained for the States an important role incident to agreements to arbitrate. 9 U.S.C. § 2. Through those words Congress reiterated a basic federal idea that has long informed the nature of this Nation's laws. We have often expressed this idea in opinions that set forth presumptions. See, e.g., *Medtronic, Inc. v. Lohr*, 518 U.S. 470, 485 (1996) ("[B]ecause the States are independent sovereigns in our federal system, we have long presumed that Congress does not cavalierly pre-empt state-law causes of action"). But federalism is as much a question of deeds as words. It often takes the form of a concrete decision by this Court that respects the legitimacy of a State's action in an individual case. Here, recognition of that federalist ideal, embodied in specific language in this particular statute, should lead us to uphold California's law, not to strike it down. We do not honor federalist principles in their breach.

With respect, I dissent.

[The concurring opinion of Justice Thomas is omitted.]

NOTES AND QUESTIONS

1. *Who is Actually Harmed?* Suppose that consumers are not able to aggregate their claims and as a result cannot bring suit. They cannot aggregate in court because of arbitration clauses and they cannot aggregate in arbitration because of class and aggregation waiver clauses. Who is harmed? One's first response might be that the consumers are harmed. But is this necessarily so? Is there any way that consumers can benefit from the enforceability of class-action waivers? If arbitration in a non-class setting is less costly than adjudication, the company saves litigation costs. Under what circumstances might the company pass some of those savings on to consumers? Moreover, are consumers likely to care very much about the small recoveries in these actions? If not, how should we think about the harms that *Concepcion* threatens?

2. *The Impact of* Concepcion. Several commentators predicted in the wake of *Concepcion* that the decision would spell virtually the end of consumer class actions in court and class proceedings in arbitration—and thus the end of robust private enforcement of the substantive law. See, e.g., David S. Schwartz, *Claim–Suppressing Arbitration: The New Rules*, 87 Ind. L. J. 239, 266–70 (2012); Jean R. Sternlight, *Tsunami*: AT & T Mobility v. Concepcion *Impedes Access to Justice*, 90 Or. L. Rev. 703 (2012); Myriam Gilles & Gary Friedman, *After Class: Aggregate Litigation in the Wake of* AT & T Mobility v. Concepcion, 79 U. Chi. L. Rev. 623 (2012). Do you agree? Are there ways to distinguish *Concepcion*?

3. *Unconscionability Analysis.* On its face, the language of section 2 of the Federal Arbitration Act appears to direct challenges to waivers of class-wide arbitration toward general contractual defenses, such as unconscionabil-

ity. Section 2 declares arbitration clauses to be enforceable, "save upon such grounds as exist at law or in equity for the revocation of any contract." 9 U.S.C. § 2. Is there any room left after *Concepcion* for striking down a class-action waiver clause, and perhaps the entire arbitration agreement that has such a clause, on grounds of unconscionability? What would the plaintiff have to show? See *Lau v. Mercedes–Benz USA, LLC*, 2012 U.S. Dist. LEXIS 11358 *19 (N.D. Cal. 2012) (finding an arbitration clause prohibiting classwide arbitration unconscionable and construing *Concepcion* to permit a "traditional" fact-specific unconscionability analysis)); *Sanchez v. Valencia Holding Co., LLC*, 201 Cal. App. 4th 74, 87–89 (2011) (holding that an arbitration clause with a class action waiver in a consumer contract is unconscionable because it is too one-sided, and distinguishing *Concepcion* on the ground that it dealt with the *Discover Bank* rule rather than fact-specific unconscionability analysis); *Mayers v. Volt Management Corp.*, 203 Cal. App. 4th 1194, 1203–04 (2012) (construing *Concepcion* to allow the invalidation of an arbitration clause with a class action waiver on unconscionability grounds). However, it is important to note that, as of the time of writing this note, the California Supreme Court had granted review in *Sanchez* and *Mayers*. See *Mayers*, 278 P.3d 1167 (2012); *Sanchez*, 272 P.3d 976 (2012).

4.   *The Effect of* Stolt–Nielsen. Was it really necessary for AT & T Mobility LLC to include a class-action waiver clause in the arbitration agreement in order to avoid class arbitration? If the agreement had said nothing about class arbitration, could the arbitrators have ordered it? Recall that the Supreme Court in *Stolt–Nielsen* held that the parties must agree to authorize class arbitration before arbitrators can require it, and that an arbitrator cannot derive such an agreement simply from an agreement to arbitrate, standing alone, when the arbitration agreement is otherwise silent on the matter. Suppose that the Court had affirmed the invalidity of the class-action waiver clause in *Concepcion*. Could an arbitrator in that case then have ordered class arbitration?

The answer to this question depends, in part, on how much latitude arbitrators have to use contract interpretation principles to find an *implicit* agreement to class arbitration when the arbitration clause says nothing expressly about the matter (and the parties have not entered into any stipulation, as in *Stolt–Nielsen*). On December 7, 2012, the United States Supreme Court granted certiorari in a case that should shed some light on this issue. See *Sutter v. Oxford Health Plans LLC*, 675 F.3d 215 (3d Cir. 2012) cert. granted *Oxford Health Plans LLC v. Sutter*, 133 S. Ct. 786 (2012) (holding that an arbitrator did not exceed his powers by construing a broad arbitration clause to authorize class arbitration when he "articulat[ed] a contractual basis" for his conclusion). For an excellent discussion of the relationship between *Conception* and *Stolt–Nielsen*, see Alan Scott Rau, *Arbitral Power and the Limits of Contract: The New Trilogy*, 22 Am. Rev. Int'l Arb. 435 (2011).

5.   *Current United States Supreme Court Developments*. We may know much more about the scope of *Concepcion*'s holding and the future of small claim class actions after the Supreme Court renders its decision in *Italian Colors Rest. v. American Express Travel Related Svc. Co.* (In Re *American Express Merchants' Litig.*), 667 F.3d 204 (2d Cir. 2012), cert. granted, 133 S. Ct. 94 (2012). In this case, the Second Circuit created an exception to the enforcement of class-action waiver clauses under circumstances where individual actions are "financially impossible" and class proceedings are needed to vindicate federal

statutory rights through private enforcement. The court distinguished *Concepcion* in the following way:

> It is tempting to give both *Concepcion* and *Stolt–Nielsen*. . . a facile reading, and find that the cases render class action arbitration waivers per se enforceable. But a careful reading of the cases demonstrates that neither one addresses the issue presented here: whether a class-action arbitration waiver clause is enforceable even if the plaintiffs are able to demonstrate that the practical effect of enforcement would be to preclude their ability to vindicate their federal statutory rights. . . .
>
> . . . [W]e are persuaded by the record before us that if plaintiffs cannot pursue their allegations of antitrust law violations as a class, it is financially impossible for the plaintiffs to seek to vindicate their federal statutory rights. Since the plaintiffs cannot pursue these claims as class arbitration, either they can pursue them as judicial class action or not at all. If they are not permitted to proceed in a judicial class action, then, they will have been effectively deprived of the protection of the federal antitrust law. The defendant will thus have immunized itself against all such antitrust liability by the expedient of including in its contracts of adhesion an arbitration clause that does not permit class arbitration, irrespective of whether or not the provision explicitly prohibits class arbitration . . . Therefore, in light of the fact that the arbitration provision at issue here does not allow for class arbitration, under *Stolt–Nielsen* and by its terms, if the provision were enforced it would strip the plaintiffs of rights accorded them by statute. We conclude that this arbitration clause is unenforceable. We remand to the district court with the instruction to deny the defendant's motion to compel arbitration.

Id. at 212, 218.

Not all the courts agree with the Second Circuit's approach. See *Cruz v. Cingular Wireless LLC*, 648 F.3d 1205, 1213 (11th Cir. 2011) (rejecting a factually supported challenge to the AT & T Mobility class action waiver clause based on the argument that the waiver would prevent the vindication of rights under Florida law in violation of Florida public policy because the claims involve small amounts and might "go unprosecuted unless they may be brought as a class"); Coneff v. AT & T Corp., 673 F.3d 1155, 1158–59 (2012) (relying on *Concepcion* and FAA preemption to reject a challenge to a class action waiver clause in an arbitration agreement like the one in *Concepcion* and *Cruz* based on a substantive unconscionability argument that the class waiver "preclude[s] effective vindication of state and federal rights").

INDEX

References are to Pages